Networks of Influence and Power

During the nineteenth century, Liverpool became the heart of an international maritime network. As the 'second city' of Empire, its merchants and shipowners operated within a transnational commercial and financial system, while its trading connections stimulated the development of new markets and their integration within an increasingly global economy. This ground-breaking volume brings together ten original contributions that reflect upon the development of the city's business community from the early-nineteenth century to the outbreak of the First World War with an emphasis on the period from 1851 to 1912.

It offers the first detailed analysis of Liverpool's merchant community within a conceptual and historiographical framework which focuses on the economic, social, and cultural role of business elites in the nineteenth century. It explores the extent to which business success was predicated on the maintenance of networks of trust; analyses the importance of business culture in structuring commercial operations; and discusses the role of ethics, trust, and reputation within the changing framework of the business environment. Particular attention is paid to the role of women and the important contribution of the family to commercial success and the maintenance of social networks.

Changes in business practice and social networks are also examined within a spatial context in order to assess the impact of the development of a distinct commercial centre and the clustering of commercial activity on interaction, reputation, and trust, while particular attention is paid to the effect of suburbanization on existing associational networks, the social cohesiveness of business culture, and the cultural identity of the merchant community as a whole.

Robert Lee was the Chaddock Professor of Economic and Social History at the University of Liverpool where he is now an emeritus and research professor. He has written widely on European demographic, economic, and social history, particularly on the nineteenth century and specifically on nineteenth-century Germany.

Routledge Studies in Modern British History

Respectability, Bankruptcy and Bigamy in Late Nineteenth and Early Twentieth-Century Britain
John Benson

The Beveridge Report
Blueprint for the Welfare State
Derek Fraser

The Modern British Data State, 1945–2000
Kevin Manton

Labour's Ballistic Missile Defence Policy 1997–2010
A Strategic-Relational Analysis
James Simpkin

Legacies of an Imperial City
The Museum of London 1976–2007
Samuel Aylett

Politics, Propaganda and the Press
International Reactions to the Falklands/Malvinas Conflict
Louise A. Clare

Oil for Britain
The United Kingdom and the Remaking of the International Oil Industry, 1957–1988
Jonathan R. Kuiken

GPs, Politics and Medical Professional Protest in Britain, 1880–1948
Chris Locke

Entryism and the Revolutionary Socialist Left in Britain
Nicolas Sigoillot

Networks of Influence and Power
Business, Culture, and Identity in Liverpool's Merchant Community, c.1800 to 1914
Edited by Robert Lee

For more information about this series, please visit: www.routledge.com/history/series/RSMBH

Networks of Influence and Power

Business, Culture, and Identity in Liverpool's
Merchant Community, c.1800 to 1914

Edited by Robert Lee

 Routledge
Taylor & Francis Group

LONDON AND NEW YORK

First published 2024
by Routledge
4 Park Square, Milton Park, Abingdon, Oxon OX14 4RN

and by Routledge
605 Third Avenue, New York, NY 10158

Routledge is an imprint of the Taylor & Francis Group, an informa business

British Library Cataloguing-in-Publication Data
A catalogue record for this book is available from the British Library

Library of Congress Cataloging-in-Publication Data
Names: Lee, W. Robert, editor.
Title: Networks of influence and power : business, culture and identity in Liverpool's
    merchant community, c.1800 to 1914 / edited by Robert Lee.
Description: Abingdon, Oxon ; New York, NY : Routledge, 2024. | Series: Routledge
    studies in modern British history | Includes bibliographical references and index.
Identifiers: LCCN 2023033854 (print) | LCCN 2023033855 (ebook) | ISBN
    9781409406082 (hardback) | ISBN 9781032309521 (paperback) | ISBN 9781315597836
    (ebook)
Classification: LCC HF3520.L5 N48 2024 (print) | LCC HF3520.L5 (ebook) |
    DDC 381.09427/5—dc23/eng/20230906
LC record available at https://lccn.loc.gov/2023033854
LC ebook record available at https://lccn.loc.gov/2023033855

ISBN: 978-1-409-40608-2 (hbk)
ISBN: 978-1-032-30952-1 (pbk)
ISBN: 978-1-3155-9783-6 (ebk)

DOI: 10.4324/9781315597836

Typeset in Times New Roman
by Apex CoVantage, LLC

In Memory

of all those friends and colleagues who enriched our understanding of the port and maritime history of Merseyside, contributed to the success of the Mercantile Liverpool Project, or provided invaluable support:

John Armstrong, Peter Davies, Sam Davies,
Skip Fisher, Bernard Foley, John Harris, Francis Hyde,
Gordon Jackson, Sheila Marriner, Mike Power,
Eric Taplin, Arthur Thomas, Edward Paget-Tomlinson, Mike Stammers, and
David Williams.

Dedication

To my amazing family:

Kicki, Jenny, Susanna, Malena, and Oskar—to whom I will always owe so much.

Contents

Lists of figures   xi
List of tables   xiv
List of contributors   xvi
Acknowledgements   xviii
List of Abbreviations   xx

1 **Networks of Influence and Power: The Forging of Liverpool's Merchant Community**   1

ROBERT LEE

2 **The Mercantile Liverpool Project Database: Sources and Findings**   25

RANDOLPH COCK, JOHN DAVIES, ROBERT LEE, AND SARI MÄENPÄÄ

3 **The Business Environment**   75

GRAEME MILNE

4 **Ethics, Trust and Reputation**   92

GRAEME MILNE

5 **'The Visible Embodiment of Modern Commerce': The Development of Liverpool's Commercial Centre**   109

JOSEPH SHARPLES

6 **Kinship, Friendship and Partnership: The Social Networks of the Liverpool Merchant Community**   141

SARI MÄENPÄÄ

7 **Intersecting Worlds: Women, the Family, and Merchant Culture**   165

ROBERT LEE AND SARI MÄENPÄÄ

8 **'The Mark of Opulence, Taste and Skill': Liverpool Merchants' Houses, c.1750-c.1900**   210

JOSEPH SHARPLES

9   'To Purer Air and Brighter Skies': Escaping from the City   237
    JOSEPH SHARPLES AND ADRIAN JARVIS

10 Suburbanisation, Community Building, and the Fragmentation of
    Business Culture: The Impact on Liverpool of Residential Development
    on the Wirral   270
    ROBERT LEE

11 Deconstructing Liverpool's Merchant Networks: Transience, Religion,
    Politics, and Business Interests   324
    ROBERT LEE

12 Associational Culture, Social Influence, and the Cultural Embeddedness
    of Merchant Networks: A Reassessment   393
    ROBERT LEE

13 Postscript   466
    ROBERT LEE

    Index   479

Figures

1.1	Plan of the Town and Borough of Liverpool with Birkenhead, c.1865	4
2.1	Number of merchants, by trade	33
2.2	Number of firms recorded in the database in sample years, 1851–1912	34
2.3	Explicit father and son partnerships, 1851–1912	35
2.4	Relative growth and decline in type of business organisation, all trades	36
2.5	The rise of partnerships: General Brokers, 1851–1912	37
2.6	The rise of limited companies: Shipowners, 1851–1912	38
2.7	The persistence of business structures: coal merchants in Liverpool, 1851–1912	38
2.8a	The number of merchants registered as resident in Liverpool, on the Wirral, and elsewhere, by decade, 1851–1912	44
2.8b	The locational residence of merchants in Liverpool, on the Wirral, and further afield (in per cent), 1851–1912	45
2.9	Merchants moving as a percentage of total merchant population, 1851–1901	47
2.10a	Changes of address: moves within and between Liverpool and the Wirral	48
2.10b	Moves within Liverpool/Wirral (in per cent), 1851–1901	48
2.11a	Moves into and out of Liverpool/Wirral, 1851–1901	49
2.11b	Moves into and out of Liverpool/Wirral (in per cent)	50
2.12a	Average number of servants (shipping and finance) as a percentage of all trades, 1851–1901	57
2.12b	Average number of servants by trade category (foodstuffs, fuel, manufactures, and raw materials) as percentage of all trades, 1851–1901	58
2.13	Country of birth of merchants born overseas, 1851–1901	59
3.1	The Cotton Market, Liverpool (1874)	79
4.1	The Liverpool Cotton Corner, *The Graphic*, 8 October 1881	103
5.1	'Water Street', by William Herdman, 1860 (with kind permission of the Liverpool Record Office)	110
5.2	The Exchange and Nelson's Monument, Liverpool (by William Westall, A.R.A., 1781–1850)	113
5.3	The newsroom in the new Exchange Buildings of 1863–70	117
5.4	Elevantion of Batavia Buildings, Hackins Hey, 1862 by William Culshaw for Arnold de Beer Baruchsen (by kind permission of Lancashire Record Office)	119
5.5	Brown's Building (J. A. Picton, architect)	120
5.6	First-floor plan of Berey's Buildings, 1864, by William Culshaw for the Trustees of Samuel Berey (by permission of the Lancashire Record Office)	123
5.7	Elevation of Berey's Buildings, George Street, 1864, by William Culshaw for the Trustees of Samuel Berey	124

5.8	Elevation of the Albany	127
5.9	Elevation of Knowsley Buildings, Bixteth Street, 1864, by William Culshaw for William Farrer (by permission of the Lancashire Record Office)	128
6.1	The Wellington Rooms, Mount Pleasant (1830), in S. Austin et al., *Lancashire illustrated from original drawings* (London, 1831), facing p. 16	145
6.2	The Royal Mersey Yacht Club Regatta, 1910, the *Keewaydin* and *Comrade*	147
6.3	Royal Liverpool Golf Club Pavilion, Hoylake (undated postcard, pre-1914)	147
6.4	The Liverpool Athenaeum (by courtesy of The Liverpool Athenaeum)	148
6.5	The Liverpool Philomathic's Centenary Dinner, 16 February 1926 (courtesy of Liverpool University Special Collections and Archives)	150
7.1	The Liverpool Female Orphan Institution, c. 1900 (contemporary postcard)	185
7.2	The Birkenhead Borough Hospital, c. 1900 (contemporary postcard)	186
7.3	Philip Henry Rathbone and his daughter Elfreda (courtesy of the Williamson Art Gallery and Museum)	193
7.4	*Home: A Family Group* by Phil. R. Morris, ARA	194
7.5	The Unitarian Chapel in Paradise Street (engraved by J. Smith after a picture by G. & C. Payne)	194
7.6	*The New Governess*, c. 1910 (contemporary postcard)	196
8.1	Drawing of John Colquitt's eighteenth-century house and warehouse (with permission of the Liverpool Record Office)	212
8.2	Abercrombie Square (1829). To the Residents Of Which This Plate Is Respectfully Inscribed, drawn by G. & C Pyne, engraved by J. Starling, in S. Austin, J. Harwood and G. & C. Pyne (eds.), Lancashire Illustrated (London, 1829)	217
8.3	Thingwall Hall, Broad Green (contemporary postcard, c. 1950)	221
8.4	The dining room at 34 Alexandra Drive, photographed by H. Bedford Lemere (1896)	224
8.5	Upton Manor, Upton (Wirral) with two of the housemaids	224
8.6	The picture room, Dawpool, Thurstaston, 1896 (with permission of Historic England Archive)	226
8.7	The library at Seaforth Hall with bookcases of 1840 by W. J. Roberts for James Muspratt (with permission of the Liverpool Record Office)	227
8.8	Broughton Hall, Yew Tree Lane, West Derby (designed by Walter Scott for G. C. Schwabe)	228
9.1	'Liverpool From Toxteth Park' drawn by George Pickering (1784–1857) and engraved by James Sands (1793–1882)	239
9.2	The Entrance to Rock Park, Rock Ferry (pre-1914 postcard)	242
9.3	Princes Park, Liverpool (1842–43) (pre-1914 postcard)	243
9.4	'Rustic Bridge, Birkenhead Park and Zoological Institution' (engraved by Newman and Co, *Pinkney's Birkenhead Views*, No. 7 (Birkenhead, c. 1847))	243
9.5	Hardwick Grange, Shropshire (drawn and published by John Preston Neale, 1818–1829)	246
9.6	A railway and road map of Liverpool and its immediate hinterlands (c.1908) (from G. W. Bacon, 'Liverpool and Its Environs', plate 15, London, c. 1908)	249
9.7	Pier Entrance, Seacombe (pre-1902 postcard)	251
9.8a	Horse-drawn tram of the Liverpool Tramways Co. manufactured at the Birkenhead factory of George Starbuck & Co. (c.1870s)	256
9.8b	A Liverpool horse-drawn tram, No. 178 (Kirkdale, Scotland Road, Lime Street), 1898 (pre-1914 postcard)	257

9.9   'Tunnel under the Mersey at Liverpool', *National Encyclopaedia: A History of Universal Knowledge by writers of Eminence in Literature* (London, 1886)   260

9.10 Birkenhead Park Station (pre-1914 postcard)   261

9.11 'Opening of the Liverpool Docks Overhead Electric Railway, The Pier Head Station', *The Illustrated London News*, 11 February 1893, p. 168   262

10.1 Map of the Hundred of Wirral, c.1847 from W. W. Mortimer, A History of the Hundred of Wirral (London, 1847) (courtesy of Wirral Archives Service)   272

10.2 Heswall Golf Club (1904 postcard)   277

10.3 1844 Plan of New Park by Joseph Paxton (courtesy of the Williamson Art Gallery and Museum, Birkenhead)   279

10.4 Birkenhead School (photograph, c. 1880)   288

10.5 Wirral Hospital and Dispensary for Sick Children (1909 postcard)   292

10.6 The New Church at Upton (1905 postcard)   296

10.7 'The Greys' Trooping the Colours, Birkenhead Park (pre-1914 postcard)   298

10.8 Mr. John Laird MP, 'Statesman, No. 144, "He built the 'Alabama' and the 'Captain'"   299

10.9 'St Aidan's Theological College, Birkenhead', *The Illustrated London News*, 10 October 1863   300

10.10 Mariners' Park, Wallasey (undated postcard, c. 1910)   307

11.1 Leighton Hall, Welshpool, Montgomeryshire (undated postcard)   333

11.2 Osmaston Manor, Derbyshire (undated postcard, c. 1895)   336

11.3 Mostyn House School, Parkgate: Cheshire (The Beagle Kennels) (undated postcard, c. 1910)   340

11.4 Chester, A Meet at Eaton Hall (undated postcard, c. 1910)   341

11.5 Gustaf Adolfs Kyrka (Scandinavian Seamen's Church), Liverpool (photograph by Jan Wallin)   342

11.6 Interior of St. Anne's Church, Birkenhead (pre-1914 postcard)   344

11.7 'The New Conservative Club-House, Liverpool', *The Illustrated London News*, 22 April 1882   354

12.1 'The Mayor of Liverpool's Treat for the Poor', *The Illustrated London News*, 31 January 1874   396

12.2 The Seamen's Orphanage, Liverpool opened by the Duke of Edinburgh, *The Graphic*, 6 January 1872   400

12.3 'New Branch Sailors' Home, Liverpool', *The Illustrated London News*, 9 December 1876, p. 564   401

12.4 The Hahnemann Homeopathic Hospital, Liverpool (late-nineteenth century photograph)   408

12.5 'Sir Andrew Barclay Walker', *Vanity Fair*, 'Men of the Day', No. 471 (1890)   412

12.6 'Cliff House', Mariners' Park, Wallasey (pre-1914 postcard)   421

12.7 'The Gordon Working Lads' Institute, Stanley Road, Liverpool', *The Graphic*, 18 December 1886, p. 652   421

13.1 'View of Lewis's Good House of Business in Ranelagh Street, Liverpool, Where The Public Are Provided With The Very Best Articles, All At Fair Prices', *Illustrated London News*, 3 February 1883   470

13.2a The Liverpool Cotton Exchange designed by Matear & Simon, 1905–06: the grand trading floor with its highly polished columns made of Larvikite rock, opened in 1906 (contemporary photograph)   474

13.2b The real world: workers in Old Hall Street outside Liverpool's new Cotton Exchange (photograph, c. 1910) (Cavendish Archive)   475

Tables

1.1	The age distribution of male merchants and agents on Merseyside, 1901 (by age group, in per cent)	12
2.1	Merchants recorded in the database (from all sources), by decade	32
2.2	The longevity of Liverpool merchant businesses (all firms, partnerships, and sole traders), 1851–1902	39
2.3	The longevity of Liverpool merchant businesses first recorded between 1870 and 1872	41
2.4	The number of merchant residents in Merseyside postcode districts by decade, 1851–1911	45
2.5	Liverpool's mercantile community (members of the Wellington Club): median probate wealth by decade, 1860–1950 (in 2019 prices)	51
2.6	Median probate wealth by occupation, 1860–1918, for members of the Wellington Club (in 2019 prices)	52
2.7	The average number of servants per merchant household in Liverpool and on the Wirral, 1851–1901	54
2.8	Average number of servants by trade of merchant head of household, 1851–1901	56
2.9	The average number of servants by place of birth of head of household	61
2.10	The origins of merchants who became naturalised British subjects (by region)	62
2.11	Merchants born overseas as a percentage of all merchants resident in modern postcode areas	63
3.1	B. G. Orchard's classification of cotton firms, 1892	82
5.1	Office buildings near the Liverpool Exchange, c.1830–c. 1870s (including banks and insurance companies with lettable accommodation)	131
6.1	Members of selected Liverpool clubs by occupation (in per cent), 1850–1900	151
6.2	The geographic distribution of Liverpool club membership by place of residence (in per cent), 1850–1900	152
7.1	Occupational intermarriage within the Liverpool merchant community	168
7.2	The pattern of female co-residence in merchant families on Merseyside	180
7.3	The marital status of Liverpool cotton brokers, 1851–1901	181
7.4	The household structure of Liverpool cotton brokers, 1851–1901	181
7.5	Women's involvement in cultural associations and societies	183
7.6	The extent of family-based participation in institutional charities on Merseyside, 1870–1912	190

8.1   The amount paid in window duty in the 12 largest provincial towns,
      1850 (in £)   216
10.1 Average rates of population growth in Wirral townships and parishes,
      1831–1911 (per cent, per annum)   273
10.2 The associational infrastructure of Hoylake and West Kirby, 1897–1906   283
10.3 The spatial pattern of local involvement in associational culture on the
      Wirral (by type, in per cent)   284
10.4 Localism and associational involvement on the Wirral by category
      (societies, sports clubs, schools, churches, and hospitals), 1851–1913 286
10.5 The spatial distribution of members of the Royal Liverpool Golf Club
      (RLGC) and the Royal Mersey Yacht Club (RMYC) (in per cent)   287
10.6 The associational involvement of Wirral merchants by category (societies,
      sports clubs, schools, churches, and hospitals), 1851–1913   295
10.7 Wirral subscribers to Liverpool charities (hospitals, seamen's welfare, and
      welfare), 1850–1912 (in per cent)   308
11.1 Place of birth: Liverpool shipowners and timber merchants   330
11.2 The confessional affiliation of Liverpool merchants, c.1900 (in per cent) 343
11.3 The political representation of the merchant community in Liverpool and
      Birkenhead (commissioners, councillors, and aldermen)   356
11.4 Merchant political involvement by occupational classification, 1893–1911
      (number, per cent)   359
11.5 Membership of the Liverpool Chamber of Commerce as a proportion of
      active merchants, 1851–1891   368
11.6 Liverpool merchants: distribution of interlocking directorships in 1893
      and 1911   370
12.1 The extent of merchant committee representation on Liverpool charities 398
12.2 Merchant representation on the committees of Liverpool's maritime
      charities, 1869–1912 (in per cent)   399
12.3 Median probate wealth of members of the Wellington Club by occupation,
      1860–1918 (in 2019 prices)   419
12.4 Entrepreneurial benefactions as a proportion of total probate wealth
      (in 2019 prices)   424
12.5 University College, Liverpool (Liverpool University): endowment of chairs,
      1880–1919   428
12.6 University College/Liverpool University: private benefactions for capital
      developments, 1882–1910 (in £)   431
12.7 University College/Liverpool University: sources of income, 1894–1914
      (in per cent)   433
12.8 Merchant involvement in learned societies in Liverpool and Birkenhead
      (founded between 1804 and 1906 and including regional associations for
      Lancashire and Cheshire)   436
12.9 Female membership of learned societies on Merseyside, 1880–1909 (by
      decade, in per cent)   445
12.10 The Liverpool Philomathic Society: attendance data, 1847–48 to 1901–02 446

Contributors

Randolph Cock was a Research Fellow in the School of History at Liverpool University, taking over responsibility for the development and analysis of the Maritime Liverpool Project database from Sari Mäenpää. Now Prize Papers Record Specialist at the National Archives of the UK, he is co-author, with Nicholas Rodger, of *A Guide to the Naval Records in the National Archives of the UK*, and has published articles on aspects of naval, maritime, social, economic and legal history, and archives. He will never make a 'proper' historian, because he tends to prefer a good story to a good theory.

John Davies, having obtained his MSc and PhD, he undertook in his early career post- doctoral research in acoustics at The University of Liverpool. This work developed his skills in computer programming and the use of microcomputers in research. He moved into computer services in an academic setting and supported research across a variety of academic Departments and Faculties. One focus of support was the use of databases in research, with publications across an eclectic mix of disciplines including history, clinical psychology, veterinary science and the investigation of the causes of accidents.

Adrian Jarvis, having studied history at Liverpool University, was employed for the whole of his working life by Liverpool City Museums (from 1988 National Museums Liverpool), firstly as Trainee and as Assistant Keeper in Shipping, then as Keeper of Social and Industrial History (1977–88), and from 1988 to his retirement in 2005 as the Curator of Port History. In addition, he held the following honorary posts at the University of Liverpool: Honorary Fellow in History (from 1991); Honorary Lecturer in Civil Engineering (1995–98), and Co-Director, Centre for Port and Maritime History (1996–2005). In 2001 he was awarded a PhD by published work by Leeds Metropolitan University.

His published research monographs include *Liverpool Central Docks* (1991), *The Liverpool Dock Engineers* (1996), *Samuel Smiles and the Construction of Victorian Values* (1997), *In Troubled Times: the Port of Liverpool 1905–1938* (2003), *Liverpool, a history of "The Great Port"* (2014). He also contributed around 40 research papers to refereed journals including the *International Journal of Maritime History, The Northern Mariner, Transactions of the Newcomen Society, ICE Proceedings: Forensic Engineering*, and the *Journal of Transport History*, as well as to *Festschriften* and other collections. He was a member of the Editorial Boards for the *International Journal of Maritime History* and *The Northern Mariner/Le Marin du Nord*, and Area Editor for the *Oxford Encyclopaedia of Maritime History*.

Robert Lee was the Chaddock Professor of Economic and Social History at the University of Liverpool, where he is now an Emeritus and Honorary Professor. He was the Co-Director of the Centre for Port and Maritime History from its foundation in 1996 until 2011. He has been the author, editor or co-editor of 21 books with a focus on the demographic, economic, maritime and social history of Germany and Europe in the modern period. He is currently working on the political economy of urban greenspace provision and the cultural and social history of public parks, particularly Birkenhead Park, Britain's first municipally funded park.

Graeme Milne is a Senior Lecturer in Modern History at the University of Liverpool. His publications include 'Collecting the sea shanty: British maritime identity and Atlantic musical cultures in the early twentieth century', *International Journal of Maritime History,* 29, 2 (2017); *People, place and power on the nineteenth-century waterfront: Sailortown* (Palgrave Macmillan, 2016); *North East England, 1850–1914: The dynamics of a maritime-industrial region* (Boydell, 2006); and *Trade and traders in mid-Victorian Liverpool: Mercantile business and the making of a world port* (Liverpool University Press, 2000).

Sari Mäenpää (PhD, University of Liverpool) is working on an article for a book about the transformation of maritime professions in European shipping between 1850 and 2000. She has recently published articles about human-animal relations in maritime history and a book on the development of cruise vessel design. Her main research interest has been in the history of maritime labour, as well as gender issues within seafaring. She works as the curator of collections at Maritime Centre Forum Marinum in Turku, Finland.

Joseph Sharples From 1990 to 2001 Joseph Sharples was the curator of Liverpool's Walker Art Gallery. His long-standing interest in architecture and the need to conserve our Victorian urban heritage led to some major contributions to Pevsner's Architectural guides. He was the author of the *Pevsner Guide to Liverpool* (New Haven and London, 2004); provided an important contribution to R. Pollard and N. Pevsner, *Lancashire: Liverpool and the South-West* (New Haven and London, 2006); and he has also researched and written on the architecture of Aberdeen. His involvement with the Historic Environment of Liverpool Project and research for the Mercantile Liverpool Project reinforced his reputation as one of the leading architectural historians of the city and its region. Important publications include *Merchant Palaces Liverpool and Wirral Mansions Photographed by Bedford Lemere & Co.* (Liverpool, 2007) and *Built on Commerce Liverpool's central business district* (with John Stonard) (Swindon, 2008), together with contributions to several books and journals, including a comparison of the relationship between commerce and culture in Liverpool and Glasgow in 1900, secular Gothic revival architecture in mid-nineteenth century Liverpool, merchants' houses in Victorian Liverpool, and the residential development of Sefton Park between 1872 and the end of the century. He is currently Curator of Mackintosh Collections and Applied Arts at the Hunterian, University of Glasgow, with a recent article in *Architectural History* on the workers who built the University between 1867 and 1871.

Acknowledgements

It is unusual to start with an apology. In this case, however, it is necessary. The Mercantile Liverpool Project was one of the largest externally funded research projects undertaken by staff at Liverpool's School of History. It had an exciting interdisciplinary agenda; employed a methodology that offered an unprecedented level of nominal and institutional linkage; and provided a unique insight into the role of the merchant community by locating commercial operations within their wider cultural, familial, political, and social context. The completion of a 'final' manuscript incorporating all the major findings from the project, quite naturally, was the priority after my retirement. Unfortunately, as we all know, the best laid plans seldom run smoothly. A diagnosis of prostate cancer, followed by robotic surgery, hormone treatment, and radiotherapy, radically affected my plans. None of the interventions were successful and both research and writing became casualties of severe depression. The first cycle of chemotherapy had a positive impact, but the failure of a third cycle is ominous. Without the NHS, in particular the skills of my urologist (Mr Kumar), and the wonderful staff at the Clatterbridge Cancer Centre, in particular my oncologist (Amir Montazeri), psychiatrist (Jane Younger) and therapist (Anne-Marie Orford), this volume might never have been completed. My family has been an immense and constant support, full of helpful ideas to improve my health and wellbeing.

In addition, friends and colleagues have provided a form of social therapy. Perhaps because of the cohesiveness of the former Department of Economic and Social History, the meetings of ESHGOM (the association of Economic and Social History Grumpy Old Men) remain very so enjoyable with the participation of Will Ashworth, Henry Finch, Rory Miller, Nigel Swain, Mike Tadman, and on special occasions, Pat Hudson and Eve Rosenhaft. We still mourn the loss of Peter Davies, Bernard Foley and Arthur Thomas. In a similar context, the meetings of a group of friends from Birkenhead School from a time when it was a Direct Grant Grammar School have been important and I am grateful for the support of Keith Housley, Adrian Jarvis, and Paul Williams, in particular.

I never gave up the intention of completing this book, primarily because of my debt towards everyone who was involved in the project. Together with my co-director, Adrian Jarvis, we were able to assemble an excellent team of researchers with a range of interdisciplinary skills (Randolph Cock, Graeme Milne, Sari Mäenpää, and Joseph Sharples). Colleagues from computer services, John Davies and Brenda Lowndes, provided essential technical advice, while an immensely hard-working data-entry team (including Jennifer Doty, Kati Nurmi, John Siddell, and Fred West, assisted initially by Sari Mäenpää) was instrumental in creating a unique database which provided detailed information on the changing size and composition of Merseyside's merchant community, its business and social networks and the changing commercial and cultural environment in which individual actors operated.

Such a large-scale research project would not have been feasible without significant funding support, specifically from the Leverhulme Trust, English Heritage, the Philip Holt Trust, and Liverpool City Council's World Heritage Site, for which I remain immensely grateful. The critical role of a wide range of archives has been acknowledged in individual chapters, but particular thanks are due to the staff at the Liverpool Record Office (Helena Smart), the Maritime Archives and Library collections, National Museums Liverpool (Sarah Starkey), the Special Collections and Archives, University of Liverpool (Robyn Orr), and the Wirral Archives Service (Will Meredith and his staff). At a time when the funding of public library services within the Liverpool City Region is under threat as a result of government austerity measures, it is important to emphasise again their continuing contribution to academic research and the wider understanding of processes of historic change, whether locally or internationally. Particular thanks are due to the librarians and staff at the Bebington, Birkenhead and Wallasey Reference Libraries, and the Local Archives and History Service at Crosby Library.

Other scholars and friends have contributed significantly to the project. Colum Giles (then of English Heritage) played a major role in ensuring that the built environment, both commercial and residential, became an important research focus, thereby highlighting the significant benefits of partnership working. Right from the start an international advisory panel was established to offer advice and guidance on the project's management. Until its merger in 2019 with the Board of the Centre for Port and Maritime History, it included many distinguished and well-known scholars, including the late John Armstrong, Peter Davies, Skip Fisher, Gordon Jackson, and Mike Stammers. Despite the irreplaceable loss of senior maritime historians over the last decade or so, I remain grateful for the individual and collective contributions of Di Ascott, Janet Dugdale, Di Frost, Adrian Jarvis, Paul Jones, Margarette Lincoln, Rachel Mulhearn, Nancy Ritchie-Noakes, Sarah Palmer, Suzanne Schwarz, Tony Tibbles, and Tony Webster.

Sheryllynne Haggerty and Will Ashworth offered helpful advice on three of the book's chapters (1, 11, and 12 respectively); Oskar Eriksson-Lee helped to improve the quality of some of the figures; and Dr. Peter Buckles proved to be indispensable in providing assistance in preparing the final manuscript and in creating an excellent index. The MS Access database that was created to provide a unique insight into the lives of Merseyside merchants is currently being converted for web application to enable a wider audience to make use of this resource for research purposes. I am grateful to Andrew Douglas, as well as Maureen and Simon Davies, for funding to take this forward.

If anyone has been omitted from what is an extensive list of acknowledgements, I hope they will forgive me. The book is dedicated to those friends and scholars who have contributed significantly to the history of the port of Liverpool, including its workers, and the Merseyside mercantile community, in particular the original members of what is known as the Liverpool School of Maritime Business History (Francis Hyde, Sheila Marriner, and Peter Davies). I hope very much that they would have welcomed the contributions of the Mercantile Liverpool Project to both the national and international historiography of port and maritime history and endorsed our attempts to re-assess some of the deeply embedded and questionable assumptions about the wider role of Merseyside's mercantile community in the nineteenth century.

Finally, a word of praise for the outstanding staff at Routledge who have shared a long journey with the manuscript. Rob Langham and his editorial assistants, Dana Moss and Julie Fitzsimmons, have been an immense source of support, well beyond the normal call of duty. They have always demonstrated a clear belief that the book would be finished, despite my health issues. I hope they will be delighted with the final product.

Robert Lee
Birkenhead
January 2023

Abbreviations

BBH Birkenhead Borough Hospital
BCA Birkenhead & Cheshire Advertiser
BCA&WR Birkenhead & Cheshire Advertiser & Wirral Reporter
BCL Birkenhead Central Library
BH Business History
BHR Business History Review
BICR&IC Birkenhead Improvement Commission, Road and Improvement Committee
BLA&MI Billinge's Liverpool Advertiser; and Marine Intelligencer
BRL Birkenhead Reference Library
BPP British Parliamentary Papers
BSA Birkenhead School Archives
EcHR Economic History Review
IJMH International Journal of Maritime History
JEH Journal of Economic History
LaRO Lancashire Record Office
LES Liverpool Engineering Society
LM Liverpool Mercury
LNFC Liverpool Naturalist's Field Club
LPS Liverpool Philomathic Society
LRO Liverpool Record Office
LUSL&A Liverpool University Special Collections and Archives
MMMMAL Merseyside Maritime Museum, Maritime Archives and Library
PHSL&C Proceedings of the Historic Society of Lancashire and Cheshire
PLBotS Proceedings of the Liverpool Botany Society
PLBS Proceedings of the Liverpool Biological Society
PLNFC Proceedings of the Liverpool Naturalist's Field Club
PL&PS Proceedings of the Literary and Philosophical Society
PLPhS Proceedings of the Liverpool Physical Society
PLPS Proceeding of the Liverpool Philomathic Society
PTLBS Proceedings and Transactions of the Liverpool Biological Society
RLSOP Reports of the Liverpool Seamen's Orphan Institution
TCUHB The Cambridge Urban History of Britain (1750–1950)
WAS Wirral Archives Service
THSL&C Transactions of the Historic Society of Lancashire and Cheshire

TL&CAS Transactions of the Lancashire and Cheshire Antiquarian Society
SH Social History
UH Urban History
WHR Women's History Review
WKLS West Kirby Literary Society

1 Networks of Influence and Power

The Forging of Liverpool's Merchant Community

Robert Lee

Introduction

The role of social networks in sustaining business activity and in reinforcing the viability of family firms has been widely debated in recent years. Some historians have questioned the general applicability of the Chandlerian paradigm with its emphasis on managerial initiative as a primary agent of economic change and its criticism of Britain's 'personal capitalism' and small firm mentality as an inferior variant to the competitive or cooperative managerial models of the United States and Japan.[1] Research on the role of business networks over the last two decades or so has reinforced this critique. Despite competing definitions, it is generally accepted that networks played a vital role in supplying information on entrepreneurial opportunities, in reducing transaction costs, and in facilitating information monitoring. They also fostered trust in an economic environment in the nineteenth century still characterised by volatility and serious market imperfections.[2] Entrepreneurial opportunities were constituted through 'dense material networks' with a diverse array of 'actants'; networks were 'an integral part of economic activity'; both reputation and regard were constructed primarily through networking activities; while businessmen operated within a framework of both strong and weak ties.[3]

Drawing on general theories of social capital and social exchange, considerable progress has been made in defining the operational mechanisms which underpinned the formation, operation and benefits of networks, whether based on family and kin, confessional affiliation, or ethnicity, although as Granovetter noted their effectiveness was often predicated on the relative homogeneity of the business community and its ability to enforce sanctions.[4] Membership of clubs and associations became an important element in the process by which business networks were constructed as they helped to extend the radius of trust within the circle of merchants and other businessmen among whom cooperative norms were increasingly operative. Social clubs, as well as collective involvement in charitable or philanthropic activities, became sites where social elites encountered each other in a context in which personal relations could be cultivated under informal circumstances. Voluntary associations have been ascribed a fundamental role in the formation of social capital: they provided a 'social glue' for business enterprises and civic society by fostering and strengthening individual friendships, while affiliated members enjoyed a higher social capital than non-members.[5]

The proliferation of clubs and societies in cities and towns during the nineteenth century facilitated an intensification of capitalist relationships and extended the transactional radius of middle-class networks. The gradual development of a distinct 'clubland' as a tangible expression of the 'art of association' reinforced the formation of social capital. But it had a wider significance in overcoming divisions within the middle class; in reinforcing the economic and political power of local business elites; and in providing an 'ideal medium' for exercising civic

DOI: 10.4324/9781315597836-1

leadership unaffected by partisan tensions generated by political and religious differences.[6] It also underpinned the growth of a common business culture by offering members and subscribers regular opportunities for interaction, the sharing of experience, and the strengthening of mutual trust. Within this context, non-economic institutions were 'useful instruments' for creating bonds of mutual obligation, for promoting honesty among potential business partners, and for inculcating the cultural attributes which enabled business networks to operate effectively by overcoming traditional barriers to diversification.[7]

It is generally accepted that the creation of a common business culture based primarily on personal relations, shared attitudes, and mutual trust provided a solution to problems of agency and asymmetric information, while business networks facilitated risk-spreading, reduced market uncertainties, and offered the possibility of efficiency gains.[8] This was specifically the case in port-cities dominated by commerce and trade where firms were frequently confronted by an inflated degree of risk because of losses at sea, warehouse fires, imperfect information flows, and market volatility. If individual merchants had a good chance of acquiring significant wealth, they were also more likely to suffer bankruptcy than other occupational groups. Many merchant firms and partnerships had only a limited life-span and there was a considerable degree of turnover within the trading community.[9] Moreover, the creation and maintenance of effective business networks was more problematic in a port-city because of the higher risk of entrepreneurial failure, the disproportionate role of in-migrant merchants drawn from more distant, overseas locations, and the difficulty of maintaining reliable connections at local, regional, national, and international levels at a time when the expansion of international trade was associated with increased transaction costs.[10]

The business environment of major ports in the nineteenth century provides valuable material for research into these issues. Firstly, trading firms frequently operated at both local and global levels by exploiting extensive information systems of varying reliability, confidentiality, and symmetry, as well as by exploiting new communications technology, such as the telegraph system and telephones.[11] Secondly, mercantile firms were subject to greater external scrutiny than those operating in other sectors of the economy because their activities brought them to the attention of the customs authorities. Thirdly, firms of specialist brokers, whether dealing in commodities, finance, information, or ships, maintained records of customer networks, while banks and insurance companies in commercial ports attempted to maintain a closer scrutiny of their clients because of the inflated risk of bankruptcy and failure. Finally, trade specialisation, technological change, and the development of large-scale steamship companies provide a framework for assessing the extent to which business networks continued to influence economic performance, while governance efficiency was itself a result of the interaction between markets, firms, entrepreneurial networks, and business culture.[12]

Liverpool's merchant community offers fruitful ground for such an analysis. During the nineteenth century Liverpool became the heart of an international maritime network. As the 'second city' of the Empire, its merchants and shipowners operated within a transnational commercial and financial system, while its trading connections stimulated the development of new markets and their integration within an increasingly global economy. The merchant community played a key role in the rapid expansion of Liverpool's overseas trade. Successful shipowners and merchants were members of an elite group which exercised considerable political authority and leadership. They often held political office, invested conspicuously in the built environment, and were important benefactors of charitable and cultural institutions. But the merchant community, which was essentially responsible for the port-city's commercial success between the mid-nineteenth century and the outbreak of the First World War, has never attracted any in-depth analysis, particularly in terms of its cultural embeddedness, ethnicity, or institutional framework, while broader debates relating to the significance of business networks for the creation of social capital and mutual trust have seldom utilised Liverpool data, despite important research on earlier periods.[13] The following sections will set out a brief historiographical framework for this study and then summarise its research objectives.

The Expansion of Liverpool's Trading Role

The authors of contemporary guidebooks and handbooks were aware of the significance of Liverpool's dock infrastructure which underpinned its status as one of the most important centres for international commerce and trade. The docks, in terms of their number, magnitude, and importance, were 'entitled to priority of notice'; they were 'the finest in the world'; and the foundation of Liverpool's greatness.[14] Travel-writers, although more inclined to comment on prominent buildings such as the Town Hall and the Exchange as well as the 'all-pervading smoke' of the city, were also aware that the 'grandeur of the town' was most apparent in the commercial quarter, where business was transacted in 'sumptuous offices' and 'great mercantile houses'.[15]

The relative importance of trade for the prosperity of Liverpool was well understood, even if earlier attempts to quantify its precise contribution to the local economy were undermined by imprecise occupational data. According to Baines, the 1851 census confirmed the extent to which the people of Liverpool were 'completely' dependent on commerce, shipping, and the trades connected with those pursuits, but if almost 50 per cent of all males above 20 years of age were engaged in this sector it must be noted that the figures also included those employed in domestic service.[16] Muir may well have been correct in concluding that there was probably no other British city of comparable size 'in which so small a proportion of the population is maintained by permanent and stable industrial work', but local industries such as sugar refining, tobacco manufacturing, and milling, were 'more numerous than is supposed', even if the processing of raw material imports was itself a consequence of Liverpool's trading profile.[17]

When the 22-year-old Johan Peter Bager, the son of a successful Malmö merchant, travelled to Liverpool in 1840 as part of a wider tour of Britain, he was impressed, like many other visitors, not only by the extent and scale of the dock infrastructure, but also by the volume of trade, particularly in cotton, and the size of the merchant fleet. In fact, he had arrived in what was 'correctly' called 'Little London', a reflection of the extent to which Liverpool already rivalled the capital as the hub of an international trading and financial network which more than justified its status as the second port of the Empire.[18] Even at the very start of the nineteenth century Liverpool was recognised as the most important provincial port in the realm. It had achieved 'supremacy' in the slave trade, having overtaken Bristol as the leading port. Its importance within the British-Atlantic trading economy was based not only on the products of largely slave-based economies, such as sugar and tobacco, but on an 'extremely diverse' range of trades, while its wider role, whether within an international or regional context, was underpinned by the development of an important entrepôt function.[19] Liverpool's position was further reinforced in the following decades by the rise of bulk cargo trades with an increasing degree of diversification in terms of product range and trading zone.[20]

If Bager had returned to Merseyside less than two decades later, he would have been astounded at the pace of dock construction, a process that underpinned Liverpool's ascendancy in international trade. Despite the economic instability of the 1840s and early 1850s, and the international depression which followed from the collapse of the speculative railway mania, this was a time of unprecedented infrastructural development both on the Liverpool and, to a

Figure 1.1 Plan of the Town and Borough of Liverpool with Birkenhead, c.1865

lesser extent, on the Birkenhead side of the Mersey. A parliamentary act in 1841 had authorised the construction of the Albert Dock (opened in 1846 at a cost of £884,000), but this was simply the start of a large programme of works between 1844 and 1852 that included six new docks and the Wapping Basin at a combined cost of £2.4 million (all borrowed on the bond market). The plans to develop a dock system in Birkenhead were inaugurated by the opening of Morpeth Dock on 5 April 1847 (the same day as Birkenhead Park, the first public park in the world to be funded by a local authority). But it had a complex history and, as a result of fraudulent practices, overlapping interests, and incompetence, progress was halted by bankruptcy. The Birkenhead Docks Act of 1855 finally transferred ownership to the Liverpool Dock trustees, who gradually were able to develop their potential as part of an integrated dock system without parallel in the modern world.[21]

According to Baines, the 'pre-eminent prosperity' of Liverpool in the mid-nineteenth century was due to the fact that the 'greater part' of Britain's foreign and colonial trade passed through the port 'first in the form of raw materials imported, and then of manufactured goods exported'.[22] Indeed, Liverpool accounted for approximately 45 per cent of the country's export trade and handled one third of its imports: 'King Cotton reigned supreme', with 76 per cent of raw cotton imports arriving in Liverpool. It was acknowledged as 'the greatest shipping port for Iron of any in the world'. Indeed, its merchant community was involved in an extremely wide range of trades, including timber, corn, coal, salt, sugar, tea and coffee, wine and spirits, tobacco, hemp, oil, and tallow, each of which contributed in its own way to the growing prosperity of the port.[23] In the eyes of some contemporaries, Liverpool had become 'the queen of British

ports' and the maritime metropolis of the world as a result of 'the enormity of its shipping operations' which lay at the heart of the port-city's 'greatness'.[24]

Many aspects of Liverpool's trade between the mid-nineteenth century and the outbreak of
the First World War have already been established. The period between 1855 and 1875 was
characterised by short-term fluctuations, together with increased specialisation and functional
demarcations. Some traditional trades continued to expand, while new ones became more important, including palm oil from Africa, tanning materials and hides from South America, refrig-
erated meat, and petroleum.[25] In addition, between 1876 and the early twentieth century there
was a significant growth in live animal imports, in particular of cattle, sheep, and pigs.[26] Even
if the West Indian trade had become 'traditional and stereotyped', the cotton trade remained
predominant and Liverpool was effectively the national centre for the grain, provision, and
timber trades.[27]

However, the emigrant trade, which had helped to underpin the dominance of Liverpool shipping companies in transatlantic trade from the 1830s onwards, was already in decline by 1900,
primarily as a result of shifts in market structure and increased international competition, and
several passenger lines went out of business.[28] Throughout the latter decades of the nineteenth
century Liverpool retained its role as the second most important port in Europe after London, at
least in terms of tonnage handled, which increased three-fold between 1870 and 1905, while the
net registered tonnage of shipping using the port rose by 34.9 per cent between 1900 and 1910.
But by the beginning of the twentieth century there were ominous signs that Liverpool's pre-
eminence as a focal point for international trade and commerce was increasingly under threat
and it had already suffered a noticeable decline in its relative position, having been overtaken by
continental European ports including Hamburg, Antwerp, and Rotterdam.[29]

The Development of Liverpool's Merchant Community in the Eighteenth and Early Nineteenth Century

Recent research on the eighteenth and early nineteenth centuries has explored key issues of
direct relevance to the current study, while providing a benchmark for analysing the subsequent
growth and function of the merchant community. If a small group of 'great merchants' had
emerged by the 1680s, a century later commerce and trade was to a large degree controlled by
approximately 330 'men of substance' with extensive overseas connections at a time when the
trading community as a whole accounted for between 2.5 and 3.5 per cent of the total population.[30] Its estimated size in the early nineteenth century stood at around 3,000, of whom fewer
than 50 per cent were merchants. By the late 1830s the number of registered agents, brokers, and
merchants had risen to approximately 2,000. However, by 1845, a time of buoyant economic
conditions, it has been claimed that 8,000 'businessmen' were involved in commercial activities in Liverpool.[31] But this rise was only in line with the overall growth rate of the borough's
population; merchants were simply a subset of the business community as a whole; and the
number of active merchants in the early 1850s was considerably lower than some historians
have imagined.[32] The growth in Liverpool's trade in the first half of the nineteenth century
had been impressive, but it had not been matched by an equivalent increase in the size of its
merchant community as a smaller number of firms accounted increasingly for a larger share of
trade, particularly in cotton and timber.[33]

Several points need to be emphasised. Firstly, despite a noticeable diversity in terms of trading activity, wealth, religion, and place of birth, it is often argued that Liverpool's merchants
demonstrated a significant degree of cohesion. The new council after 1695 was characterised by
a 'unity of purpose and friendship' at a time when the port's small size encouraged a significant

degree of homogeneity amongst its mercantile elite. Its increasing commercial success in the second half of the eighteenth century was due, in part, to 'a relatively homogenous, commonly understood and conformed-to business culture'. The establishment of a new Chamber of Commerce in February 1850 has been interpreted as evidence for the willingness of 'gentlemen' with different commercial interests and political opinions to act for 'a common object' in a context in which there was 'no fundamental fracture in the mercantile elite'.[34] In a commercially competitive environment, cohesion within the merchant community may well have been reinforced by overlapping trading interests, the development of relatively large open-ended networks and investment groups, and the persistence of multi-functional roles. But the extent to which these factors continued to operate throughout the second half of the nineteenth century remains open to doubt.[35]

Secondly, increased specialisation was already evident well before the mid-nineteenth century. If general merchants had traditionally performed a range of functions and acted 'so to speak (as) their own brokers or salesmen', increased functional differentiation was reflected in the growing number of brokers, as well as shipping, forwarding, and commission agents; a trend away from doing mixed business in favour of operating on their own account; and a tendency towards specialisation within specific trades, including cotton. The re-distribution of operational roles between firms depended on their level of capitalisation and their relative position within the local hierarchy, as the 'old intertwined system of close personal connections' between general merchants slowly withered away.[36]

Thirdly, there were significant changes in the institutional framework of merchant activity. The first Chamber of Commerce had operated with some success from 1774 until the mid-1790s and had given expression to a 'balanced local unity of views' despite evidence of a considerable diversity of opinion. But the establishment of individual trade associations designed in each case for 'the protection and enhancement of commercial interests' was symptomatic of wider changes within the merchant community and the emergence of specific interest groups.[37] Both the Committee of the Africa Merchants Trading from Liverpool and the West India Merchants' Association had been created in the second half of the eighteenth century and they were followed by the foundation of the American Chamber of Commerce (1801), the Liverpool Underwriters' Association (1802), the Liverpool Shipowners' Association (1810), and the General Brokers' Association (1838). Indeed, the proliferation of factional trade institutions became more marked as the nineteenth century progressed and when the initial meeting of the (second) Chamber of Commerce was held in 1850 it included deputies who represented 11 of the most important trade associations in the community.

Fourthly, the embeddedness of the merchant community, in terms of its dominant network structures and their cultural, social, and political framework, was well established by the late eighteenth century, if not earlier.[38] The significance of business networks, whether within a local, regional, or international context, has been widely acknowledged, even if a disproportionate increase in size led to reduced efficiency and opaque network contacts were sometimes exploited for ulterior purposes.[39] In the case of Liverpool, it has been argued that merchants in the early eighteenth century were bound together 'by trade, family ties and friendship', with local networks reinforced by sharing the same ships.[40] The impact of most networks was 'inherently beneficial' because they were 'receptive' or 'open' to in-migrants. Slave trading and privateering were both regarded as high-risk activities, but voyages were managed by relatively large investment groups, thereby providing access to necessary resources, expert knowledge, and practical skills in a manner that strengthened network cohesion. Indeed, this was reinforced by the port's increasing dependency on the slave trade. The Common Council, essentially a self-perpetuating body, was dominated by African and West Indian traders, while 100 Liverpool merchants paid the entrance fee of £2 to become members of the Company of Merchants trading to Africa (commonly known as the African Company), founded in 1750, and attended meetings of its Liverpool Committee. Five out of the six insurance offices in 1752 had been established by 'African merchants'.[41] Network viability over time was strengthened by iterative business activity, but it was underpinned by family ties and kinship, ethnicity, denominational affinity, and socially constructed interpersonal relationships.[42] But it is sometimes difficult to identify key players and to disentangle the complex processes of relations generated by simultaneous membership of a number of different networks, particularly when merchants were dependent on both 'strong' and 'weak' ties.[43] The longevity of a firm might be dependent on the quality and utility of the initial relationships established within a network framework, but an overriding sense of long-term obligation, under certain circumstances, could also act as a constraint on business performance and threaten survival.[44] However, network cohesion was strengthened by a 'remarkable' growth in clubs and societies from 1780 onwards. In 1825 all six of the founder members of the Liverpool Philomathic Society had been drawn from the business community and the merchant elite dominated the intellectual life of the port-city.[45] Cultural institutions, as well as philanthropy, were not simply solvents for resolving differences within the merchant community or for generating a 'new esprit de corps'. They also facilitated the identification of common attributes, such as probity and respectability, and extended the radius of trust, which was a critical factor in sustaining commercial activity.[46]

Liverpool's Merchant Community from the Mid-Nineteenth Century to 1914

In contrast to the excellent work on Liverpool's business networks in the late eighteenth and early nineteenth century, relatively little research has been undertaken on their significance in the Victorian period, particularly from the 1860s to 1914 at the height of its maritime trading ascendency. Between the late 1950s and the early 1980s what is now known as the Liverpool School of Maritime History made very significant contributions to the development of business history. Detailed studies of some of the port's most successful shipping companies, including Blue Funnel, Harrisons, Cunard, and Elder Dempster, set a benchmark for the analysis of managerial performance far removed from the traditional form of 'descriptive house history', while further studies by Hyde and Marriner demonstrated the central importance of research on commerce and trade for understanding the long-run development of the port and the history of Merseyside as a whole.[47]

However, the primary focus was on analysing the determinants of company performance in terms of the marginal efficiency of capital, the profitable use of available resources, and the financial return on investment. It was generally understood that most members of Liverpool's ship-owning elite 'undertook many social and charitable activities', but the selective absence of diaries and personal correspondence justified the failure to explore the extent to which entrepreneurial performance was socially embedded or culturally conditioned.[48] Moreover, the research consistently focused on successful, large-scale shipping companies, apart from a few innovative studies on other aspects of Liverpool's mercantile operation, including the commission merchants Rathbone Bros. & Co. (with its increasingly diversified portfolio of business interests), ship-broking, marine insurance, and the development of banking and financial networks.[49] It was only recognised belatedly that decision-making processes in commercial firms could never be explained entirely on the basis of rational choice or economic analysis because of the importance in certain cases of 'personal idiosyncrasies' and the role of chance.[50]

Subsequently, individual studies of shipping companies began to explore the wider social context of entrepreneurial activity, but no attempt was made to analyse the relevance of factors such as educational background and denominational affiliation in moulding business networks or the significance of philanthropic commitment in consolidating the local merchant hierarchy. All too often the importance of family links and other social factors are mentioned in passing, but seldom explored in detail. The marriage in 1829 of Anna Booth and Philip Holt represented a union of two leading non-conformist families which was 'characteristic of the religious and social background of Liverpool', but no evidence is offered to substantiate this claim. The 'stately locomotion' by carriages and pairs of leading Unitarians to and from the Renshaw Street Chapel signalled the importance of denominational identity for many prominent merchants, but the wider relevance of religious affiliation for business connections remains unexplored.[51] In 1838, Alfred Holt was sent to a Knutsford school run by a Unitarian minister where he was never taught any subject 'systematically', but there were other pupils from like-minded Liverpool families at the same institution, some of whom played an important role in his later career. However, no attempt is made to establish whether this was a common practice within the merchant community or to assess whether a shared school background was of general significance for subsequent business collaboration. At the same time, George Holt, his father, was strengthening his position as one of Liverpool's leading merchants with an increasingly diverse range of business interests, including cotton trading, banking, and commercial property development. But while it is acknowledged that his public standing was reinforced by a keen interest in providing non-sectarian schools for poor children and developing educational facilities for girls, the importance of these activities for business networking has never been examined.[52] Indeed, an overriding focus on explaining the behaviour of businessmen solely in terms of profit maximisation and rational expectation inevitably precluded any serious analysis of the wider determinants of entrepreneurial performance.

The legacy of the Liverpool School of Maritime History has been very considerable, but subsequent publications on shipping companies, including Blue Funnel, the Bibby Line, the Liverpool and North Wales Steamship Company, and Yeoward & Company, consistently failed to locate either their development or performance within the wider framework of Liverpool's merchant community.[53] However, they do provide occasional insights into the private lives of some of its leading members. Some merchants developed an overt preference for country life and leisure maximisation. Frederick James Harrison had a 'fascination for rural affairs' and was a keen member of the local hunt; Thomas Henry Ismay and his wife 'loved the quiet of a country life' which they enjoyed during weekends at Dawpool, their house in Thurstaston, with its magnificent views over the Dee and the Welsh Hills; and William Cunard acquired a succession of 'beautiful country houses near London'. From 1880 onwards Alfred Holt spent a great deal of time during the summer months sailing his private yacht, *Argo*, far removed from Liverpool's business environment, and he was not alone in enjoying this form of relaxation.[54] It is also clear that civic responsibility sometimes had its costs. The success of Rathbones may well have reflected the continued importance of established ties of family, trade, and religion, but at times the firm's viability was seriously undermined by the prioritisation of philanthropic interests. In other cases, family life was visibly dysfunctional. The relationship between members of the Bibby family in the mid-nineteenth century was far from harmonious, with acrimonious disputes over wills, blackmail, bankruptcies, libel actions, and quarrels.[55]

It was not until the publication of Milne's important study of Liverpool's trading community in the mid-Victorian period that the focus of research finally shifted away from large liner companies to the multitude of small firms which were far more representative of the port-city's commercial environment.[56] By providing a broad, cross-sectional analysis of the operation the trading community as a whole during the 1850s and 1860s, Milne was able to highlight a number of key issues, including the continued importance of small firms, often undercapitalised and

over-extended, and their pivotal role in complex information networks; the significant demarca-
tion lines between different kinds of trading functions; and the accelerated degree of specialisation in most trades which gave Liverpool a greater degree of flexibility in withstanding periodic
crises. Both operational and structural changes within the trading community during the third
quarter of the nineteenth century were influenced by the extension of the telegraph system and
the increased rapidity of communication, while business practices were also affected by the
greater access to published commercial information which in some cases encouraged existing
businesses to make pragmatic use of new financial possibilities.[57] Indeed, by seeking to focus on
the 'widespread characteristics' of Liverpool's business community Milne touched upon some
of the key issues which will be explored in greater depth in the current volume, including the
transience of many Liverpool trading firms; the persistence of a distinct merchant hierarchy;
and the extent to which suburbanisation increased the 'residential detachment' of the local business elite. But equally relevant is the role of 'clubbable affability', reinforced by both private
and professional interaction, in underpinning the cohesiveness of the business community; the
profile of individual merchants and shipowners as active art collectors and patrons of shared
cultural activities; and the importance of wives and daughters in binding together the port-city's
mercantile elite. Archival material relating to Liverpool's merchant community in the nineteenth century has been used primarily within the framework of wider studies on the development of multinational trading firms and the growth of large-scale enterprises in British shipping.
These, in turn, have emphasised the importance of overlapping business, political and religious
connections in Liverpool and other ports; the significance of knowledge complementarities and
network-based communication; the hazardous nature of trade; and the importance of extended
family ties and personal status. It is also clear that there was a high turnover of Liverpool firms
even at the end of the nineteenth century and foreign merchant houses (particularly those established by German merchants) played an important role in facilitating the long-run expansion of
overseas trade, in particular cotton re-exports to continental Europe.[58]

More detailed research has helped to illuminate aspects of Liverpool's trading community of
direct relevance to the agenda of the current study. Firstly, increased functional specialisation
and the emergence of cotton brokers as 'a new group of middlemen' underpinned the port-city's
preeminent role in the cotton trade. But a number of other factors were also important, including
the establishment of an effective associational framework (specifically after the foundation in
1841 of the Liverpool Cotton Brokers Association); a significant increase in market information
through the publication of daily circulars and weekly market reports; improved access to capital; and the development of a futures market from the 1860s onwards. Even within this sector,
however, there were noticeable differences in specialisation, capitalisation, and the involvement
of foreign-born partners.[59]

Secondly, research by Jarvis on the background of elected members of the Mersey Docks &
Harbour Board, the majority of whom were shipowners, merchants, or brokers, has emphasised
the institutional divide between Liverpool's trading and municipal interests. Council representation on the board was consistently rejected because of the fear that it might generate party
rivalry, although several of its members had clearly defined political interests. However, cohesion within the business community was reinforced in some cases by interlocking directorships,
secondary interests in business and finance, and membership of trade associations. As might be
expected, most Board members were involved in some form of charitable work, but a preference
for 'pocket country estates' was not reflected in an active interest in sporting activities and only
a few were directly involved in the actual management of clubs or associational societies.[60] By
contrast, as Stammers demonstrated, merchants, shipowners, and bankers dominated and ran
the Royal Mersey Yacht Club. Two of the early commodores, Thomas Littledale (1848–61) and

Samuel Graves (1861–73), were elected because of their status within the port-city's merchant community and were clearly expected to maintain a close interest in the club, while in the late 1890s the shipowners Frank Bibby and Harold MacIver owned steam-yachts of over 200 tons and made regular use of them.[61]

A prosobiographical methodology has been utilised to analyse the business elites of other English cities in the late nineteenth and early twentieth century and some studies have explored the political representation of 'large businessmen' in local authorities, but no equivalent research has been undertaken on Liverpool.[62] Despite a number of contemporary compilations of detailed biographical data covering prominent Liverpool merchants, including publications on specific trades such as the members of the Cotton Exchange, the primary focus of research has been on 'uncovering the lives of the rich and powerful' amongst the 'Old Families' in terms of their political influence, philanthropy, outward display, and 'autocratic tendencies'. Despite its merits, it cannot provide a suitable basis for analysing the dynamics of structural change within the trading community in general.[63]

Other studies have demonstrated the vulnerability of established firms in the face of increased competition, specifically in the case of the African trade from the mid-nineteenth century onwards. Despite a background of active involvement in local politics, both the Horsfall and Tobin families ultimately failed to capitalise on their earlier achievements, irrespective of whether they adopted a joint stock company framework and merged with the Company of African Merchants or simply tried to remain a family business. The fact that James Tobin's judgements were often 'faulty' in comparison with those of his father and uncle had inevitable consequences, while the survival of the firm was not helped by his acquisition of a large and extravagant establishment on the south coast.[64]

Generational issues, albeit of a different type, were evident in the case of the Bates family. The shipowner Edward Bates was 'a hard-driven entrepreneur': he remained outside the cooperative ethos of the dominant shipping networks; took no part in local matters; showed no interest in any local benevolent enterprise; and 'never attempted to become intimately known' in Liverpool. By contrast, his son, Edward Percy Bates, enjoyed an insider status within local business circles. In some cases, a public school education and astute marriage strategies reinforced the integration of third-generation family members within the contemporary cultural framework at a time when 'trustworthiness' and perceived competence underpinned the operation of international maritime business.[65] Trust relations within the merchant community were also reinforced through cooperation in trade associations and the Chamber of Commerce. For example, by the late 1850s the East India and China Association represented the second most important branch of commerce in the port. But its lobbyist function was strengthened by close collaboration with the Chamber of Commerce which often simply endorsed the recommendations of its East India and China trade section.[66]

The Mercantile Liverpool Project and Its Objects

This study analyses the development of Liverpool's merchant community from the early nineteenth century to the outbreak of the First World War with a specific emphasis on the period from 1851 to 1912. It offers a detailed analysis of its changing composition and structure within a conceptual framework that focuses not only on its economic role, but also on its social and cultural embeddedness. It explores the extent to which commercial success was predicated on the maintenance of networks of trust; analyses the importance of business culture in structuring commercial operations; and discusses the role of ethics, trust, and reputation within the changing framework of the business environment. Particular attention is paid to the role of women and the important contribution of the family to commercial success and the maintenance of social networks. Changes in business practice and social networks are also examined within a spatial context in order to assess the impact of the development of a distinct commercial centre and the clustering of commercial activity on interaction, reputation, and trust, while particular attention is paid to the effect of suburbanisation on existing associational networks, the social cohesiveness of business culture, and the cultural identity of the merchant community as a whole.

The following paragraphs provide an outline of the five main sections of the book, following a brief historiographical review of recent research on Liverpool merchants and their firms. These focus, in turn, on the creation and utilisation of the Mercantile Liverpool Project database, business practices and business structures, the role of social networks in structuring business relations, the impact of increasing suburbanisation on Liverpool's business culture, and the persistent complexity of networks of power and influence.

(i) Reconstructing Liverpool's Merchant Community: The Mercantile Liverpool Project Database

The construction of a database with detailed information on the size and composition of the merchant community was a prerequisite for pursuing some of the issues highlighted by recent research and for locating the operation of individual firms and business networks within a cultural, familial, and social framework. Chapter 2 discusses the range of source materials utilised in constructing the MLP database; the type of information obtained from each of the sources; and its specification and design. The technical manipulation of the database provided a framework for analysing the merchant community in terms of particular trades, or groups of trades, business diversification, partnerships and directorships, the geographical origins and nationality of merchants, and their changing spatial patterns in terms of both business and residential location.[67]

An outline of the merchant community's development from 1861 onwards was obtained from the published decennial census returns. By 1871 membership of the 'commercial class' was defined on the basis that a merchant bought, transported, and sold commodities without effecting any change in their nature. But there was lack of consistency in classification; a failure to distinguish between merchants, agents, and general dealers; and a preference by 1901 to list the two former categories with accountants who did not necessarily fulfil a mercantile role. An analysis of long-term trends was further complicated by boundary changes to registration districts and sub-districts, the selective absence of disaggregated data for other areas of Merseyside, such as Wallasey, and the failure to adopt a consistent age-group classification.

Despite these deficiencies the census data reveal that the merchant community was never a significant component of Liverpool's population. Although the number of male 'mercantile persons' (including general dealers registered as merchants) in the Borough of Liverpool increased from 2,096 in 1861 to 4,057 in 1901, the latter figure included a significant (but unspecified) number of accountants, and by 1911 it had fallen to only 2,101.[68] Moreover, their share in overall male employment, whether in Liverpool or Birkenhead, declined consistently from the 1850s onwards. Although the census returns disguise the full extent of their contribution, women were also part of the mercantile community, but their role remained limited until the end of the nineteenth century when there was a significant increase in the number of female commercial clerks. In 1861, only 79 women in Liverpool Borough were registered as engaged 'in mercantile pursuits', but by 1901 there were 100 female merchants and agents, a figure which had risen further by 1911 to 230 when they accounted for 9.8 per cent of the merchant class.[69] Miss Margaret Ward ran her small-scale business as a coal merchant in New Brighton between 1902 and 1912,

Table 1.1 The age distribution of male merchants and agents on Merseyside, 1901 (by age group, in per cent)

Borough	10–14	15–24	25–44	45–64	65+
Birkenhead	–	14.1	44.4	36.4	4.9
Wallasey	–	13.2	54.4	28.2	3.9
Liverpool	0.02	13.1	51.0	32.0	3.8
Bootle	–	19.5	47.5	27.2	5.5

Note: The occupational classification used in the 1901 census also included accountants.

Source: Census data for 1901.

but other women operated at a higher level within the merchant community, including the cotton broker Margaret Bagshaw (1870) and the licensed broker Ellen Francis (1902), although such cases remained very much an exception.[70]

The census data also suggest that responsibility for Liverpool's commercial success at the end of the nineteenth century rested in the hands of relatively young men aged between 25 and 44 (Table 1.1). In 1901, 44 per cent of male merchants and agents in Birkenhead were from this age group, but a higher percentage was registered in other parts of Merseyside, including Bootle (47.8), Liverpool (51.0), and Wallasey (54.4). Traditionally in established merchant houses career progression was predicated on serving an apprenticeship and completing a clerkship, although there were few, if any, legal constraints particularly in trades with low entry costs to prevent newcomers from establishing their own business at a young age. In comparison with other occupations, however, there were comparatively few merchants under the age of 24, but more significantly there was a noticeable decline in the number of merchants actively involved in trade after the age of 44, with relatively few continuing to pursue a commercial career after 65.

All too often, historians and social scientists in seeking to explore the merchant communities of port-cities have focussed on a small number of leading families, whether in Barcelona, Bremen, or Fremantle, and this has been very much the case as far as Liverpool is concerned.[71] By contrast, the present study is based on an extensive database that provides a means of analysing Liverpool's business community in a systematic manner. It utilises nominative data from the household enumerator returns for the decennial censuses between 1851 and 1901, together with the alphabetical and trade sections of Gore's Street Directories for overlapping years (1851, 1862, 1872, 1882, 1892, 1902, and 1912), to create an extensive database of merchants, agents, brokers, and shipowners. The census returns provided a range of information on the family and household members of merchants by age, gender, occupation, place of birth, and marital status, while data on both primary and secondary trades, as well as business and residential location, were extracted from the Street Directories. To examine short run, rather than decadal or long-term changes in the merchant community, information was entered from the Street Directories for 1870, 1871, and 1872, a time of buoyant market conditions prior to the onset of the 'Great Depression'.

In addition, a wide range of other archival sources was used to improve the usefulness of the database for analysing the social and cultural networks of individual merchants, including membership records of clubs, societies, freemasonry lodges, charitable institutions, chapels, and churches. Address books and other records of local schools patronised by members of the merchant community, together with detailed biographical material from contemporary publications and printed obituaries, were also utilised. The database consists of approximately 350,000 records of which 170,000 derive directly from different sources, while the remainder represent relationships between different records. It covers almost 27,000 members of Liverpool's business community who traded in 15,883 firms, partnerships, or companies and generated information on its changing size and composition in terms of the development of specific trades. It provides invaluable information on the spatial origins, associational profile, residential location, denominational affiliation, family and household composition, and relative wealth of Merseyside's mercantile community.

Both the overall size of the merchant community, as reconstituted in the database, as well as its development over time, were generally in line with information extracted from the published census returns. More importantly, the database offers a means of examining in detail processes of compositional and structural change within Liverpool's merchant community. Chapter 2 analyses the merchant community in terms of specific trades, or groups of trades, overlapping partnerships and directorships, and business diversification. It explores the geographical origins and nationality of merchants, their changing spatial patterns in terms of both business and residential location; and provides an insight into the dynamics of the merchant community over time with evidence of increasing specialisation, despite the continued importance of small-scale, family-based firms and structural changes in the different types of business organisations.

(ii)   Business Practices and Business Structures

The external parameters of trading activity in nineteenth century Liverpool had a significant impact on its merchant community. This was particularly the case as a result of the transition from sail to steam, globalisation (including the boom in Atlantic migration and population mobility), advances in communications, and the development of faster business processes, specifically the adoption of futures trading. Accelerated trading practices and faster communications radically altered some aspects of Liverpool's business environment in this era, while leaving others apparently untouched. Chapter 3 focusses on the changing business environment. It identifies areas of change and continuity as Liverpool business evolved from a time when railways and steamships were relatively new inventions, to one in which commodity traders had begun to rely on instant telecommunications. It examines developments in markets, communications, and the transport infrastructure; assesses the business implications of these changes; and pays specific attention to the impact on business life of new information systems, including the effect of telecommunications on the prevailing face-to-face business culture. It also addresses the increasing formalisation of institutional and associational procedures, as exchanges, trade associations, shipping conferences, and official regulators codified trading practices. Most of this environment remained voluntary, however, enabling the trading community to self-regulate and maintain its individualistic business culture.[72]

Change and growth in Liverpool's business community also required new processes for monitoring trust and credit worthiness and for assessing the respectability of firms and individuals. Chapter 4 examines issues relating to business ethics, trust, and reputation. It begins with an examination of Liverpool's attitudes to the variety of corporate forms available in this era. In particular, the growing popularity of joint-stock structures in shipping is contrasted with distrust of that form in most mercantile and brokering sectors. Large ship-owners, however, maintained a public commitment to the higher ethics supposedly associated with a culture of personal capitalism at a time when the sector was undergoing significant structural change. The central themes are those of power and responsibility, because traders worked to retain the respectability and authority of partners in private firms while reducing the risks and liability inherent in that traditional form of business activity. As trade speeded up and Liverpool's trading community grew, traditional forms of monitoring were stretched. This chapter considers the role of credit and trade-protection agencies, which grew rapidly in this era, and the continuing work of more traditional 'reputation-brokers' (banks and major firms). It also assesses the role of associations in promoting the reputation of trade in general and of specific regional and commodity trades in particular. Liverpool's overall reputation as a mercantile city in regional, national, and international business networks was a matter of some debate at the time. These issues are analysed in detail by focusing on specific crisis periods, including the American Civil War, the promotion of the Manchester Ship Canal, and growing fears of a European war in the early twentieth century with its potential impact on the security of Britain's food and raw material supplies.[73]

Chapter 5 highlights the wider significance of business landscapes for the development of Merseyside's trading environment and commercial success. In the course of the nineteenth century, the demands of the mercantile economy transformed central Liverpool into a dedicated business district, as residential buildings and warehouses were largely replaced with purpose-built office blocks, banks, exchanges, and other buildings providing ancillary services. This chapter traces the origins of these developments in the late eighteenth century when the workplaces and dwellings of successful merchants first began to be physically separated. It analyses in detail the rise of speculative office buildings which began in Liverpool at an exceptionally early date and considers the role of merchants as property developers. It assesses the extent to which specialist zones provided a focus for particular trades, with the location of key buildings reflecting a web of shared interests which bound together elements of the business community. The chapter also explores how the architectural treatment of exteriors and grand public places constituted a form of advertising, while the internal planning of the workplace reflected operational requirements and a substantial growth in the size of the workforce. This, in turn, throws new light on the way in which day-to-day business activity was done and the importance of the physical environment in supporting business efficiency. In Liverpool's progressive, self-confident environment, technology was also harnessed to meet specific practical needs, notably a requirement to improve fireproofing, natural lighting, and vertical circulation.

(iii)   Social Networks and Business Culture

Shared values and beliefs were important factors in structuring business relations particularly at a time when merchants operated within a fluid web of information, contact, and credit which was embedded in an extended network of favour and obligation. This section of the book analyses the extent to which the creation of a cohesive business community in nineteenth-century Liverpool was predicated on the establishment of a common business culture based on shared aspirations, kinship ties, social networks, and confessional affiliation. The development of a specific business culture was a key ingredient in determining the operational framework of individual Liverpool firms. Chapter 6 analyses the changing pattern and role of social networking within Liverpool's merchant community, focusing on a range of associations, clubs, and charitable organisations (both denominational and non-denominational) in order to assess the extent to which it was bound together by family ties and friendship, with business networks dependent on the identification and maintenance of common social attributes. From a business perspective, social networks helped to reduce transaction costs and reinforced a belief in the importance of shared values within the business community. This chapter also examines the role of clubs and societies in reinforcing social exclusivity and defining urban culture, and analyses the extent to which they provided a mechanism for inter-generational succession and a framework for integrating in-migrant members of the merchant community (whether from elsewhere in the United Kingdom or from overseas).[74]

Chapter 7 focuses on the existence of intersecting worlds, namely the role of women and the family in moulding and sustaining merchant culture. It explores the role of families and households in supporting business activity by examining the nature and importance of women's networks and the extent to which they helped to consolidate business enterprise. The charitable and philanthropic work of women involved overlapping networks which reinforced the inter-connectedness between the public and private spheres of merchant activity. In most cases, married women played a very active role in their husbands' careers by managing the household and participating in social networks, and through direct involvement in business ventures. The chapter explores the changing function of the merchant family and household; assesses the nature and significance of domestic entertainment, including dinner parties; and analyses the role of female visitors in cementing family and business connections. It evaluates the extent to which the wives and daughters of merchants participated in Liverpool's associational culture, as well as in charitable and philanthropic work, thereby creating complementary networks which reinforced trust and reputation within the business community. It also discusses the importance of the domestic environment for businessmen. The pursuit of business interests and the fulfilment of family responsibilities were seldom mutually exclusive: although the home remained a site for social networking, family friendships were often embedded within a well-defined domestic and household context.[75]

The extent to which domestic architecture and decoration reflected the self-image, aspirations, and lives of members of the merchant community are examined in Chapter 8. It charts the increasing size and styles of houses, the different accommodation offered by the urban terraced property and the suburban villa, developments in internal planning for greater comfort and privacy, and improvements in servicing and servant accommodation. Houses and their contents were powerful expressions of status in a society characterised by flux and instability, and while the affluent sought seclusion from the unpleasant aspects of urban life, they also indulged in conspicuous display directed at their peers. This chapter examines how houses were used for receiving and entertaining visitors, often as an adjunct to business life, and explores the development of dining rooms, billiard rooms, music rooms, conservatories, and picture galleries, as well as circulation spaces such as halls and staircases. Some of the mercantile class imitated the respectability of 'old money', but others opted for the ostentation associated with newly acquired wealth and this chapter focuses on architecture, furnishings, and the collection and display of art as evidence of changing patterns in mercantile taste.[76]

(iv)   Suburbanisation and Business Culture

The nineteenth century witnessed the increasing withdrawal of the mercantile elite to new residential areas in the suburbs and beyond. Chapter 9, in examining the long-term process of suburban development, surveys the situation in the late eighteenth and early nineteenth centuries, when it began with the development of Duke Street, Rodney Street, and Mosslake Fields. This was followed by private, out-of-town park estates in the 1830s and 1840s (Rock Park, on the Birkenhead side of the Mersey, and Fulwood Park in Liverpool) and the construction of elite housing as a means of financing the provision of urban parks, beginning with Princes Park (1842–44) and Birkenhead Park (1843–47). The spread of suburban housing was often dependent on transport improvements and the chapter discusses the significance of private carriage use and public transport facilities, such as ferries, canal boats, omnibuses, and railways, in facilitating the development of new areas for residential housing. A constant theme was the quest for cleaner, greener, quieter locations, with greater privacy and seclusion, and yet still within easy reach of the business centre. The chapter analyses the role of individual merchants as suburban property developers and assesses the extent to which high rates of residential mobility were due to fluc-tuating prosperity, changes in fashion, family ties, and the need to fulfil a role in public life.[77]

Particularly from the mid-nineteenth century onwards there was an increasing tendency for merchants and other members of Liverpool's middle class to move away from the urban core and to take up residence in the developing suburbs, particularly on the Wirral. Chapter 10 explores the rate of out-migration from the inner urban areas and charts the increasing diversity in the social geography of the merchant community. It assesses the impact of increasing subur-banisation and residential mobility on existing network structures as a result of the development of alternative, suburban-based clubs, associations, and charitable institutions, and examines the extent to which out-migration and residential relocation involved a fragmentation of Liverpool's business culture with a reduced involvement in the city's public affairs and associational activ-ity. The relationship between cities and their suburbs has often been neglected by historians, but this chapter suggests the creation of alternative associational networks on the Wirral had a wider effect on the business culture of Liverpool as suburbanisation contributed to a series of dynamic changes in established social networking patterns along clearly defined spatial lines.[78]

(v)   Networks of Influence and Power

The final section (Chapters 11 and 12) offers both a synthesis of some of the project's key themes and a more detailed analysis of the political and social influence of Liverpool's mer-cantile community. As one of the world's leading port cities during the nineteenth century, mer-chants and other elements of its business community have attracted considerable attention from historians in recent decades. But most studies have focused on a relatively small group of elite merchant families. By exploiting the extensive information contained in the MLP database, these two chapters will re-evaluate the historiography of the mercantile community and reassess the validity of a number of hypotheses which have become deeply embedded in recent literature. Such an approach also provides a means of assessing the extent to which merchant networks, whether based on commercial and trading interests, associational membership, philanthropic commitment, or political engagement, provided a sufficiently robust basis for the exercise of influence and power, as well as continued business success.

Despite claims to the contrary, the merchant community in Liverpool was never an entirely homogenous construct, although networks based on trust and reputation remained important for facilitating commercial transactions and generating wealth. It was characterised by a high degree of transience and volatility, an underlying tension between established firms and aspir-ing entrepreneurs, and structural fragmentation in terms of denominational affiliation, political allegiance, and, increasingly, residential location. Chapter 11 provides a critical re-assessment of the way in which Merseyside's merchant networks operated. It explores the impact of a number of variables, including politics, religion, and spatial transience, on the articulation and effectiveness of business networks in providing social capital, and in consolidating influence and power. It challenges some of the normative assumptions in network theory by deconstruct-ing Liverpool's business networks and analysing the extent to which they were mediated or moulded by other variables such as confessional affiliation, political allegiance, and spatial mobility. It explores the impact of institutional change on the merchant community, in particular the increasing role of trade associations, the Chamber of Commerce, the growing importance of limited liability companies, and a greater reliance on interlocking directorships. Chapter 12 assesses the significance of associational culture, charitable work and philanthropy for business networking, and their role in delivering the social cohesiveness that was increasingly seen as the hallmark of middle-class culture. It provides a framework for evaluating their contribution to the formation of civic society and suggests that the existing historiography in this field needs to be reassessed. It emphasises the need for caution in interpreting the available data; the dangers inherent in basing embedded theories on limited evidence; and the importance of deconstructing Merseyside's merchant community at a time when business networking was affected by the persistence of structural factors, including ethnic, political, and religious and socio-economic diversity.[79]

(v)   Postscript

The postscript (Chapter 13) offers an overview of the project's achievements and discusses some of its shortcomings. The creation of the MLP database was a tremendous asset in examining Merseyside's mercantile community from the mid-nineteenth century to the outbreak of the First World War. It provided a detailed insight into the world of merchants and other businessmen, entrepreneurs, and manufacturers involved directly in Liverpool's maritime trading economy. Because the underlying objective was to analyse and deconstruct the mercantile community as a whole, for the first time we were able to escape some of the operational constraints that restricted the approach of previous studies. Without wishing to underplay the contribution of merchants who belonged to the so-called 'directing class', the database revealed the underlying complexity of the mercantile community, in terms of its changing occupational structure, its internal divisions, whether based on ethnicity, politics or religion, and high rates of transience in comparison with urban manufacturing centres. Both in a business and cultural sense, technological change, scientific progress, and institutional specialisation affected the dynamics of networking, while the wider influence of merchants was undermined by their increasing withdrawal from the local political scene, a trend that was aggravated in the latter decades of the nineteenth century by high rates of out-migration to rural areas and suburban settlement outside the boundaries of the City of Liverpool.

In creating a comprehensive database of all Merseyside's merchants (with over 12,000 separate individuals over a period of some 60 years of business activity), it became clear that their historic record, as reflected in the available archives and secondary material, is highly uneven. We still know comparatively little about small-scale traders, their sector-specific business links, and their relative success (or failure) in consolidating and extending their commercial operations. The postscript highlights other sections of Liverpool's business and professional community that ideally should have been integrated into the project, including solicitors, but a more inclusive approach was precluded by financial considerations. It also raises methodological issues relating to the reliability of network analysis. Despite an extensive research agenda, various forms of networking which involved members of the mercantile community, including the Volunteer Movement and Freemasonry, were either omitted, or only partly included in the analysis. Nor was there an opportunity to analyse the wider cultural environment of Merseyside, the growing opportunities for public interaction, or the gender-specific construction of urban space, partly because of the continuing absence of research on the growing market for cultural events or the impact of structural changes in retailing on more informal social networking. Indeed, all too often network analysis is limited both temporally and spatially: it can seldom capture the inherent complexity of interpersonal relationships in either a business or social context.

Chapter 13 also highlights the means by which future research in this field might benefit from methodological improvements and theoretical insights. The operational scale is always important if only to avoid questionable results that are dependent on limited data. In addition, historians should be encouraged to adopt a stronger interdisciplinary approach through the collation and analysis of a wider range of data than has previously been the case. The Mercantile

Liverpool Project was multi-disciplinary, drawing on the expertise of scholars with different, but complementary, skills. In contrast to maritime business historians who have sometimes been criticised, perhaps unfairly, for focussing on the performance of individual shipping firms with only limited concern for the socio-political context of commercial operations, our approach incorporated a range of factors, all of which impinged to a varying extent on the network connectivity of Merseyside merchants, in particular the role of their families and households, the design and utility of their commercial offices, and the impact of suburbanisation on civic and cultural associations.

From a historiographical perspective, this volume in intended to fill a major gap in research by providing an in-depth analysis of Liverpool's merchant community within its wider context. Many years ago, Sheila Marriner and Peter Davies drew up a proposal for a book on *Business and Society: Liverpool 1880–1940* with the intention of examining the business community's involvement in politics, philanthropy, religion, and education, as well as its social and leisure activities. The intention was to reveal 'the scale, extent and depth' of the role of merchants and other members of the business community in every aspect of Liverpool's life. Regretfully, the book was never finished. Its descriptive approach was dependent to a large extent on published sources and its focus on the 'leading commercial families' who acquired their fortunes in the nineteenth century would have limited its analytical utility. But its pioneering agenda reflected many of the issues that are addressed in the current volume. It is thanks to the insights of an earlier generation that we set out to provide a better framework for understanding the embeddedness of the merchant community within contemporary society and the extent to which commercial success was dependent on a range of cultural and social factors, including the exploitation of networks of power and influence. I hope very much that they would both have been pleased with the results of this research.

Notes

1   Alfred D. Chandler, *The Visible Hand: The Managerial Revolution in American Business* (Cambridge, MA, 1997); William Lazonick and David J. Teece (eds.), *Management Innovation: Essays in Honour of Alfred D. Chandler, Jr.* (Oxford, 2012); Francesca Carnevali, 'Social Capital and Trade Associations in America, c.1860–1914: A Microhistory Approach', *EcHR*, 64, 3 (2011), pp. 905–28; J. F. Wilson, *British Business History, 1720–1994* (London, 1995), p. 22.

2   Stanley Wasserman and Katherine Faust, *Social Network Analysis: Methods and Applications* (Cambridge, 1994), p. 20; Joel M. Podolny and Karen L. Page, 'Network Forms of Organization', *Annual Review of Sociology*, 24 (1998), p. 59; James E. Rauch, 'Business and Social Networks in International Trade', *Journal of Economic Literature*, 39 (2001), p. 1178. For a more detailed discussion of this issue, see Sheryllynne Haggerty, *'Merely for Money?' Business Culture in the British Atlantic, 1750–1815* (Liverpool, 2011), pp. 162–4.

3   Philip Roscoe, Allan Discua Cruz and Carole Howorth, 'How Does an Old Firm Learn New Tricks? A Material Account of Entrepreneurial Opportunity', *BH*, 55, 1 (2013), pp. 53–72; Robin Pearson and David Richardson, 'Business Networking in the Industrial Revolution', *EcHR*, 54, 4 (2001), p. 659; Jon Stobart, 'Information, Trust and Reputation', *Scandinavian Journal of History*, 30, 3 (2005), p. 299; S. Jack, 'The Role, Use and Activation of Strong and Weak Network Ties: A Qualitative Analysis', *Journal of Management Studies*, 42, 6 (2005), pp. 1233–59.

4   Mark S. Granovetter, 'The Strength of Weak Ties', *The American Journal of Sociology*, 78, 6 (1973), pp. 1360–80; 'Business Groups and Social Organization', in Neil J. Smelser and Richard Swedberg (eds.), *The Handbook of Economic Society* (New York and Oxford, 2005), pp. 429–50; James S. Coleman, 'Social Capital in the Creation of American Capital', *American Journal of Sociology, Supplement*, 94 (1988), pp. S95–S120; Lyn Spillman and Michael Strand, 'Interest-Oriented Action', *American Review of Sociology*, 39 (2013), pp. 85–104; L. Molm, M. Whitham and D. Melamed, 'Forms of Exchange and Integrative Bonds: Effects of History and Embeddedness', *American Sociological Review*, 77 (2012), pp. 141–65; Mark Casson, 'Culture as an Economic Asset', in Andrew Godley and Oliver Westall (eds.),

Business History and Business Culture (Manchester, 1996), pp. 48–76. For a review of recent research in this field, see Robert Lee, 'Commerce and Culture: A Critical Assessment of the Role of Cultural Factors in Commerce and Trade from c.1750 to the Early Twentieth Century', in Robert Lee (ed.), *Commerce and Culture Nineteenth-Century Business Elites* (Farnham, 2011), pp. 4–23.

5 Gergei M. Farkar, 'Service Club Membership and Forms of Social Capital among Swedish Community Elites', *Journal of Civil Society*, 8, 1 (2012), pp. 63–90; Dag Wollebaek and Per Selle, 'Participation and Social Capital Formation: Norway in a Comparative Perspective', *Scandinavian Political Studies*, 26, 1 (2003), pp. 67–8; Jouko Nurmiainen, 'Northern European Elites in Historical Perspective', *Scandinavian Journal of History*, 30, 3 (2005), pp. 216–24.

6 Simon Gunn, *The Public Culture of the Victorian Middle Class Ritual and Authority and the English Industrial City 1840–1914* (Manchester, 2000), pp. 84–101; R. J. Morris, *Class, Sect and Party: The Making of the British Middle Class, Leeds 1820–1850* (Manchester, 1990), pp. 161–203; 'Structure, Culture and Society in British Towns', in Martin Daunton (ed.), *TCUHB, vol. 3: 1840–1950* (Cambridge, 2000), p. 399; 'Introduction: Civil Society, Associations and Urban Places: Class, Nation and Culture in Nineteenth-Century Europe', in Graeme Morton, Boudien de Vries and R. J. Morris (eds.), *Civil Society, Associations and Urban Places Class Nation and Culture in Nineteenth-Century Europe* (Aldershot, 2006), pp. 1–16.

7 Margrit Schulte Beerbühl, 'The Commercial Culture of Spiritual Kinship amongst German Immigrant Merchants in London, c.1750–1830', in Lee, *Commerce and Culture*, p. 225; R. Lloyd-Jones and M. J. Lewis, 'Business Networks, Social Habits and the Evolution of a Regional Industrial Cluster: Coventry, 1880s–1930s', in J. F. Wilson and A. Popp (eds.), *Industrial Clusters and Regional Business Networks in England, 1750–1970* (Aldershot, 2003), p. 230.

8 Casson, 'Culture as an Economic Asset', pp. 48–76; Mark Casson and Mary B. Rose, 'Institutions and the Evolution of Modern Business: Introduction', *BH*, 39, 4 (1997), pp. 1–8; Mary B. Rose, 'Family Firm, Community and Business': A Comparative Perspective on the British and American Cotton Industries', in Godley and Westall, *Business History and Business Culture*, pp. 162–88; S. R. H. Jones, 'Transaction Costs and the Theory of the Firm: The Scope and Limitations of the New Institutional Approach', *BH*, 39, 4 (1997), pp. 9–26; Gordon Boyce, *Information, Mediation and Institutional Development: The Rise of Large-Scale Enterprise in British Shipping, 1870–1919* (Manchester and New York, 1995), p. 3; Pamela Walker Laird, 'Introduction: Putting Social Capital to Work', *BH*, 50, 6 (2008), p. 687.

9 Julian Hoppit, *Risk and Failure in English Business, 1700–1800* (Cambridge, 1987).

10 Robert Lee, 'The Socio-Economic and Demographic Characteristics of Port Cities: A Typology for Comparative Analysis?', *UH*, 25, 2 (1998), pp. 147–72; Pearson and Richardson, 'Business Networking', pp. 657–99.

11 G. H. Boyce and L. Leper, 'Assessing Information Quality Theories: The USSCo: Joint Venture with William Holyman & Sons and Huddart Parker Ltd., 1904–35', *BH*, 44, 4 (2002), pp. 85–120; G. J. Milne, 'Knowledge, Communications, and the Information Order in Nineteenth-Century Liverpool', *IJMH*, 14, 1 (2002), pp. 209–24; idem., 'British Business and the Telephone, 1878–1911', *BH*, 49, 2 (2007), pp. 163–85.

12 M. Granovetter, 'Economic Action and Social Structure: A Theory of Embeddedness', *American Journal of Sociology*, 91 (1985), pp. 481–510; Y. Kaukiainen, 'Shrinking the World: Improvements in the Speed of Information Transmission c.1820–1870', *European Review of Economic History*, 5, 1 (2001), pp. 1–28; Seija-Riitta Laakso, *Across the Oceans Development of Overseas Business Information Transmission 1815–1875* (Studia Fennica Historica 13) (Tampere, 2007).

13 See, for example, Diana E. Ascott, Fiona Lewis and Michael Power, *Liverpool 1660–1750: People, Prosperity and Power* (Liverpool, 2006); Sheryllynne Haggerty, *'Merely for Money'? Business Culture in the British Atlantic, 1750–1815* (Liverpool, 2011).

14 *The Stranger in Liverpool; or: An Historical and Descriptive View of the Town of Liverpool and Its Environs* (2nd ed., Liverpool, 1829), p. 54; H. S. Hele-Shaw and H. Percy Boulnois, 'Docks and Other Engineering Works', in W. A. Herdman (ed.), *Handbook to Liverpool and the Neighbourhood* (Liverpool, 1896), p. 102; *The Foundations of Liverpool's Greatness Docks and Shipping published in Celebration of the Opening of the Gladstone Dock System by His Majesty the King 19th July 1927* (supplement to *Liverpool Daily Post*, 18 July 1927).

15 Nathaniel Hawthorne, *Our Old House: A Series of English Sketches* (London, 1863); Walter H. Rideing, 'England's Great Sea-Port', *Harper's New Monthly Magazine*, 344, 58 (January, 1879), pp. 161–75: both cited by David Seed, *American Travellers in Liverpool* (Liverpool, 2008), pp. 118, 280.

16 Thomas Baines, *Liverpool in 1859: The Port and Town of Liverpool and the Harbour, Docks, and Commerce of the Mersey in 1859* (London, 1859), p. 4. The data relate to the Liverpool Union and not to the parliamentary borough.

17 Ramsay Muir, *A History of Liverpool* (Liverpool, 1907), p. 306; Helen Dandy Bosanquet, *Social Conditions in Provincial Towns* (London, 1912), pp. 39–40; David Williams, 'Bulk Trades and the Development of the Port of Liverpool in the First Half of the Nineteenth Century', in Valerie Burton (ed.), *Liverpool Shipping, Trade and Industry: Essays on the Maritime History of Merseyside 1780–1860* (Liverpool, 1989), pp. 19–22.

18 J. P. Bager, *Impressions of London from the Late Summer of 1840 the Thoughts and Experiences of a Swedish Gentleman* (London and Whitby, 2001), pp. 136–44; Tony Lane, *Liverpool: Gateway of Empire* (London, 1987), p. 22.

19 David Richardson, Suzanne Schwarz and Anthony Tibbles (eds.), *Liverpool and Transatlantic Slavery* (Liverpool, 2007); Sheryllynne Haggerty, 'Risk and Risk Management in the Liverpool Slave Trade', *BH*, 51, 6 (2009), pp. 817–34; J. Langton, 'Liverpool and Its Hinterland in the Late Eighteenth Century', in B. Anderson and P. Stoney (eds.), *Commerce, Industry and Transport* (Liverpool, 1983), pp. 1–20.

20 George Chandler, *Liverpool* (London, 1957), p. 305; Williams, 'Bulk Trades', p. 9.

21 Adrian Jarvis, *Liverpool a History of 'the Great Port'* (Liverpool, 2014), pp. 72–3, 85–97; Philip Sulley, *History of Ancient and Modern Birkenhead* (Liverpool, 1907), pp. 154–213; Robert Lee, *Birkenhead Park: The First Municipally Funded Park, The People's Garden, and an English Masterpiece* (Liverpool, 2024), Chapter 4 (in the press).

22 Thomas Baines, *History of the Commerce and Town of Liverpool and of the Rise of Manufacturing Industry in the Adjoining Counties* (London and Liverpool, 1852), p. 749.

23 Francis E. Hyde, *Liverpool and the Mersey: An Economic History of a Port 1700–1970* (Newton Abbot, 1971), p. 98; Braithwaite Poole, *Statistics of British Commerce: Being a Compendium of the Productions, Manufactures, Imports, and Exports of the United Kingdom, in Agriculture, Minerals, Merchandise, etc. etc. etc.* (London, 1852), p. 110; *The Commerce of Liverpool* (Liverpool and London, 1854), p. 51.

24 Anon., *Liverpool of Today: The Maritime Metropolis of the World an Epitome of Results* (London, c.1886), p. 33; *The Foundation of Liverpool's Greatness Docks and Shipping* (Liverpool, 1927) (supplement to the *Liverpool Daily Post*, 18 July 1926).

25 Sheila Marriner, *The Economic and Social Development of Merseyside* (London, 1982), p. 92.

26 Ken McCarron, *Meat at Woodside: The Birkenhead Livestock Trade 1878–1981* (Birkenhead, 1991).

27 Francis E. Hyde (with assistance from J. R. Harris), *Blue Funnel a History of Alfred Holt and Company of Liverpool from 1865 to 1914* (Liverpool, 1956), p. 18; Sir William B. Forwood, 'Trade and Commerce of Liverpool', in W. A. Herdman (ed.), *Handbook to Liverpool and the Neighbourhood* (Liverpool, 1896), p. 134.

28 Graeme J. Milne, *Trade and Traders in Mid-Victorian Liverpool: Mercantile Business and the Making of a World Port* (Liverpool, 2000); Marriner, *The Economic and Social Development of Merseyside*, p. 93; Martin Lynn, 'Trade and Politics in 19th Century Liverpool: The Tobin and Horsfall Families and the Liverpool-African Trade', *THSL&C*, 142 (1992), p. 101.

29 Muir, *A History of Liverpool*; Hyde, *Liverpool and the Mersey*, p. 96; A. Durand, *La politique française a l'égard des ports maritimes sous la troisième république* (Paris, 1904), pp. 287–9. By 1900, Liverpool had already been overtaken by Hamburg, Antwerp, and Rotterdam.

30 Ascott, *Lewis and Power, Liverpool 1660–1750*, p. 18; Sheryllynne Haggerty, 'The Structure of the Trading Community in Liverpool 1760–1810', *THSL&C*, 151 (2002), pp. 105–6; Haggerty, *'Merely for Money'?*, p. 6.

31 *Gore's Directory of Liverpool and Its Environs* (Liverpool, 1839); the figure excludes those who were primarily involved with the retail trade, including cigar dealers, quill and feather dealers, flour dealers and bakers, grocers and tea dealers, curriers and leather dealers, and marine store dealers. There was no separate entry for shipowners.

32 John Belchem and Nick Hardy, 'Second Metropolis: The Middle Class in Early Victorian Liverpool', in A. Kidd and D. Nicholls (eds.), *The Making of the British Middle Class? Studies of Regional and Cultural Diversity since the Eighteenth Century* (Thrupp, 1998), p. 60; Richard Lawton, 'The Components of Demographic Change in a Rapidly Growing Port-City: The Case of Liverpool in the Nineteenth Century', in Richard Lawton and Robert Lee (eds.), *Population and Society in Western European Port Cities c.1650–1939* (Liverpool, 2002), pp. 102–3; William Farrer and J. Brownbill (eds.), *A History of*

the County of Lancaster (Victoria County History) (London, 1911), vol. 4, pp. 37–8; MLP database, see Randolph Cock, John Davies, Robert Lee, and Sari Mäenpää, Chapter 2. If the population recorded in 1841 in the registration sub-districts of Toxteth Park and West Derby is included, the business community in the 1840s (as derived from *Gore's Directories*) only represented 2.1 per cent of the total.

33 D. M. Williams, 'Merchants in the First Half of the Nineteenth Century: The Liverpool Timber Trade', *BH*, 8 (1966), p. 91; 'Liverpool Merchants and the Cotton Trade, 1820–50', in J. R. Harris (ed.), *Liverpool and Merseyside: Essays in the Economic and Cultural History of the Port and Its Hinterland* (Liverpool, 1969), p. 189.

34 Michael Power, 'Creating a Port: Liverpool 1695–1715', *THSL&C*, 149 (2000), p. 65; Ascott, *Lewis and Power, Liverpool 1650–1750*, p. 178; Haggerty, *'Merely for Money'?*, p. 26; W. A. Gibson Martin, *A Century of Liverpool's Commerce* (Liverpool, 1950), p. 9; Belchem and Hardy, 'Second Metropolis', p. 61.

35 Power, 'Creating a Port', p. 63; Katie McDade, 'Liverpool Slave Merchant Entrepreneurial Networks, 1725–1807', *BH*, 53, 7 (2011), pp. 1092–109.

36 James Boardman, *Liverpool Table Talk a Hundred Years Ago; or: A History of Gore's Directory with Anecdotes Illustrative of the Period of Its First Publication in 1766* (Liverpool, 1871), p. 37; Marriner, *The Economic and Social Development of Merseyside*, p. 41; Haggerty, 'The Structure of the Trading Community', pp. 112–13; Williams, 'Liverpool; Merchants and the Cotton Trade', p. 195; John R. Killick, 'Risk, Specialisation and Profit in the Mercantile Sector of the Nineteenth Century Cotton Trade: Alex Brown & Sons, 1820–80', *BH*, 16, 1 (1974), p. 13; 'Bolton Ogden & Co.: A Case Study in Anglo-American Trade, 1790–1850', *Business History Review*, 48, 4 (1974), p. 502.

37 Robert J. Bennett, *The Voice of Liverpool Business: The First Chamber of Commerce and the Atlantic Economic 1774–c.1796* (Liverpool, 2010), p. 2; Bennett, *Local Business Voice: The History of Chambers of Commerce in Britain, Ireland, and Revolutionary America* (Oxford, 2011), pp. 682–6.

38 For a discussion of the view that economic relations between firms or individuals are embedded in actual social networks, see Mark Granovetter, 'Economic Action and Social Structure: The Problem of Embeddedness', *American Journal of Sociology*, 19 (1985), pp. 481–510.

39 Mark Casson and Howard Cox, 'International Business Networks: Theory and History', *Business and Economic History*, 22, 1 (1993), pp. 42–53; John F. Wilson and Andrew Popp, 'Business Networks in the Industrial Revolution: Some Comments', *EcHR*, 56, 2 (2003), pp. 355–61; Haggerty, *'Merely for Money?'*, pp. 162–4; John Haggerty and Sheryllynne Haggerty, 'The Life Cycle of a Metropolitan Business Network: Liverpool 1750–1810', *Explorations in Economic History*, 48, 2 (2011), pp. 189–206; Tim E. Crumplin, 'Opaque Networks: Business and Community in the Isle of Man, 1840–1900', *BH*, 49, 6 (2007), pp. 780–801.

40 Power, 'Creating a Port', p. 71; Ascott, Lewis and Power, *Liverpool 1660–1750*, p. 184.

41 Nicholas James Radburn, 'William Davenport, the Slave Trade, and Merchant Enterprise in Eighteenth-Century Liverpool', unpublished MA thesis, Victoria University of Wellington (2009), pp. 72–106; Sheryllynne Haggerty, 'Risk and Management in the Liverpool Slave Trade', *BH*, 51 (2009), pp. 817–34; McDade, 'Liverpool Slave Merchant Entrepreneurial Networks, 1725–1807', pp. 1092–109; Sheryllynne Haggerty, 'Risk, Networks and Privateering in Liverpool during the Seven Years War, 1756–1763', *IJMH*, 30, 1 (2018), pp. 30–51; John Haggerty and Sheryllynne Haggerty, 'Networking within a Network: The Liverpool African Committee 1750–1810', *Enterprise and Society*, 18, 3 (2017), pp. 687–721; Jane Longmore, '"Cemented by the Blood of a Negro?" The Impact of the Slave Trade on Eighteenth Century Liverpool', in David Richardson, Suzanne Schwarz and Anthony Tibbles (eds.), *Liverpool and Transatlantic Slavery* (Liverpool, 2007), p. 236; Jessica Moody, 'The Memory of Slavery in Liverpool Public Discourse from the Nineteenth Century to the Present Day', unpublished PhD, University of York (2014), p. 44.

42 Apart from prominent Unitarian merchants (sometimes referred to as a Liverpool mafia), several Quaker families, including the Binns and the Rathbones (although they became Unitarians in 1805), were 'highly respected in business', in part because of their associational and philanthropic roles. See Eveline B. Saxton, 'The Binns Family of Liverpool and the Binns Collection in the Liverpool Public Library', *THSL&C*, 111 (1959), pp. 167–80; Nottingham, *Rathbones Brothers*; Anne Holt, *Walking Together: A Study in Liverpool Nonconformity* (Liverpool, 1938); Edward H. Milligan, *British Quakers in Commerce and Industry 1775–1920* (York, 2007).

43 John Haggerty and Sheryllynne Haggerty, 'Visual Analytics of an Eighteenth-Century Business Network', *Enterprise and Society*, 11, 1 (2010), pp. 1–25; Francesca Carnevali, 'Social Capital and Trade Associations in America, c.1860–1914: A Microhistory Approach', *EcHR*, 64, 3 (2011), pp. 905–28; Haggerty and Haggerty, 'The Life Cycle of a Metropolitan Business Network', pp. 189–206.

44 McDade, 'Liverpool Slave Merchant Entrepreneurial Networks', pp. 1092–109; Emily Buchnea, 'Strategies for Longevity: The Success and Failings of Merchant Partnerships in the Liverpool-New York Trading Community, 1763–1833'.

45 Arline Wilson, 'Custom and Commerce: Liverpool's Merchant Elite c.1790–1850', unpublished PhD., University of Liverpool (1997); Wilson, 'The Cultural Identity of Liverpool, 1790–1850: The Early Learned Societies', *THSL&C*, 147 (1998), pp. 55–80; Edmund Morris, 'The Formation of the Gallery of Art in the Liverpool Royal Institution, 1816–1819', *THSL&C*, 142 (1992), pp. 87–98.

46 Chandler, *Liverpool*, p. 456; Pearson and Richardson, 'Business Networking in the Industrial Revolution', p. 673; Francis Fukuyama, 'Social Capital and Civil Society', *International Monetary Fund*, 1 October 1991, www.imf.org/external/pubs/ft/seminar/1999/reforms/fukuyama.htm.

47 Hyde (with assistance from Harris), *Blue Funnel a History of Alfred Holt & Company of Liverpool from 1865 to 1914*; Francis E. Hyde (with contributions from J. R. Harris and A. M. Bourne), *Shipping Enterprise and Management 1830–1939 Harrisons of Liverpool* (Liverpool, 1967); Francis E. Hyde, *Cunard and the North Atlantic 1840–1973 a History of Shipping and Financial Management* (London, 1975); Peter N. Davies, *The Trade Makers: Elder Dempster in West Africa, 1852–1972* (London, 1973); Hyde, *Liverpool and the Mersey*; Marriner, *The Economic and Social Development of Merseyside*. For an excellent piece of maritime history research on the late eighteenth century, albeit on Bristol, see Peter Buckles, 'Merchants and Crisis in the Bristol-West India Sugar Trade, 1783–1802', unpublished PhD thesis, University of Liverpool (2021).

48 Peter N. Davies, 'The Liverpool School of Maritime History', *IJMH*, 17, 2 (2005), p. 251; Hyde, *Shipping Enterprise and Management*, pp. vii, 65.

49 Sheila Marriner, 'Rathbone's Trading Activities in the Middle of the Nineteenth Century', *THSL&C*, 108 (1956), pp. 105–27; *Rathbones of Liverpool 1845–1873* (Liverpool, 1961); P. N. Davies, *Henry Tyrer: A Liverpool Ship Agent and His Enterprise* (London, 1979); B. L. Anderson, 'Institutional Investment before the First World War: The Union Marine Insurance Company 1897–1915', in Sheila Marriner (ed.), *Business and Businessmen Studies in Business, Economic and Accounting History* (Liverpool, 1978), pp. 37–80; B. L. Anderson and P. L. Cottrell, 'Another Victorian Capital Market: A Study of Banking and Bank Investors on Merseyside', *EcHR*, 28, 4 (1975), pp. 600–15.

50 Peter N. Davies, 'Business Success and the Role of Chance: The Extraordinary Philipps Brothers', *BH*, 23, 2 (1981), pp. 208–32.

51 A. H. John, *Merchant House Being the History of Alfred Booth and Company 1863–1958* (London, 1959), pp. 19–20; L. P. Jacks, *The Confession of an Octogenarian* (New York, 1942), p. 138. Alfred and Charles Booth established Alfred Booth & Co. in 1863, while Philip Holt was the founder of the Ocean Steamship Company. The prominent Unitarian families who attended the Renshaw Street Chapel on a regular basis included the Holts, Jevons, Gaskells, Brunners, Tates, Jones, Thorneleys, Mellys, Hollands, and Gairs. For a wider discussion of the influence of Unitarians, see Ruth Watts, *Gender, Power and the Unitarians in England, 1760–1860* (Harlow, 1998).

52 Hyde, *Blue Funnel*, pp. 8–9. His fellow pupils included Samuel Gaskell, George Fairburn, Charles and Edward Thorneley, John Barrett, and Philip Rathbone.

53 Malcolm Falkus, *The Blue Funnel Legend a History of the Ocean Steam Ship Company, 1865–1973* (Basingstoke, 1990); Edward W. Paget-Tomlinson, *Bibby Line: 175 Years of Achievement* (Liverpool, 1982); Oswald Jones, Ally Ghobadian, Nicholas O'Regan and Valerie Antcliff, 'Dynamic Capabilities in a Sixth-Generation Family Firm: Entrepreneurship and the Bibby Line', *BH*, 55, 6 (2013), pp. 910–41; John Shepherd, *The Liverpool and North Wales Steamship Company* (Cleckheaton, 2006); Theodore W. S. Barry, *Sunward by Yeoward: The Story of Yeoward of Liverpool: The First 100 Years* (Cambridge, 1994).

54 Graeme Cubbin, 'Portrait of a Liverpool Shipowner Frederick James Harrison', in Antony J. Barratt (ed.), *Merseyside Maritime Research* (Liverpool, 2007), p. 57; Wilton J. Oldham, *The Ismay Line: The White Star Line, and the Ismay Family Story* (Liverpool and London, 1961), p. 65; Kay Grant, *Samuel Cunard Pioneer of the Atlantic Steamship Company* (New York and Toronto, 1967), pp. 185–6; Ian Collard, *Blue Funnel Line: An Illustrated History* (Stroud, 2010), p. 11. In 1893, for example, *Argo* left Liverpool on 19 June, but did not return until 9 August. However, as Adrian Jarvis has pointed out, it was not always a pleasure craft, but was also used for scientific research.

55 Lucie Nottingham, *Rathbone Brothers from Merchant to Banker 1742–1992* (Oxford, 1992), pp. 41, 69; Nigel Watson, *The Bibby Line 1807–1990: A Story of Wars, Booms and Slump* (Liverpool, 1990), p. 14.

56 Milne, *Trade and Traders in Mid-Victorian Liverpool*; 'Knowledge, Communications and the Information Order', pp. 209–14.

57 Milne, 'Knowledge, Communications, and the Information Order in Nineteenth-Century Liverpool', pp. 209–24.

58 Boyce, *Information, Mediation and Institutional Development*; 'Networks, Knowledge and Network Routines: Negotiating Activities between Shipowners and Shipbuilders', *BH*, 45, 2 (2003), pp. 52–76; Stanley Chapman, *Merchant Enterprise in Britain from the Industrial Revolution to World War I* (Cambridge, 1992); *The Rise of Merchant Banks* (London, 1984). For a more detailed discussion of these contributions, see Graeme Milne, Chapter 3.

59 Nigel Hall, 'The Cotton Brokers and the Development of the Liverpool Cotton Market c.1800 to 1914', unpublished D.Phil., Oxford (1999); 'The Emergence of the Liverpool Raw Cotton Market, 1800–1850', *Northern History*, 38, 1 (2001), pp. 65–81; 'The Business Interests of Liverpool's Cotton Brokers, c.1800–1914', *Northern History*, 41, 2 (2004), pp. 339–55. See also, John R. Killick, 'Risk, Specialisation and Profit in the Mercantile Sector of the Nineteenth Century Cotton Trade: Alexander Brown & Sons, 1820–80', *BH*, 16, 1 (1974), pp. 1–16.

60 Adrian Jarvis, 'The Members of the Mersey Docks & Harbour Board and Their Way of Doing Business, 1858–1905', *IJMH*, 6, 1 (1994), pp. 122–39; idem., 'The Members of the Mersey Docks & Harbour Board Re-Visited: 1895–1936', in Margrit Schulte Beerbühl and Jörg Vögele (eds.), *Spinning the Commercial Web International Trade, Merchants, and Commercial Cities, c.1640–1939* (Frankfurt am Main, Berlin, Bern, Brussels, New York, Oxford, Vienna, 2004), pp. 175–90; 'Daggers Drawn: Relations between the Mersey Docks & Harbour Board and Outside Bodies from Central Government Downwards', *The Mariner's Mirror*, 93, 2 (2007), pp. 180–95; *In Troubled Times: The Port of Liverpool, 1905–1938* (Research in Maritime History, 26) (St. John's Newfoundland, 2003), pp. 12–14; 'Maintaining the Trust: The Mersey Docks & Harbour Board, 1858–1972', *The Mariner's Mirror*, 94, 4 (2008), p. 434.

61 Michael Stammers, 'The Royal Mersey Yacht Club: A Social History, 1844–1944', *THSL&C*, 159 (2010), pp. 99–121. For an earlier review of the Club's development, see J. D. Hayward, *A Short History of the Royal Mersey Yacht Club 1844–1907* (Liverpool, 1907).

62 Hartmut Berghoff, *Englische Unternehmer 1870–1914 Eine Kollektivbiographie führender Wirtschaftsbürger in Birmingham, Bristol und Manchester* (Bürgertum Beiträge zur europäischen Gesellschaftsgeschichte, 2) (Göttingen, 1991); idem., 'Regional Variations in Provincial Business Biography: The Case of Birmingham, Bristol and Manchester, 1870–1914', *BH*, 37, 1 (1995), pp. 64–85; Hartmut Berhoff and Roland Müller, 'Wirtschaftsbürger in Bremen und Bristol 1870–1914', in H-J. Puhle (ed.), *Bürger in der Gesellschaft der Neuzeit* (Göttingen, 1991), pp. 156–77; idem., 'Tired Pioneers and Dynamic Newcomers? A Comparative Essay on English and German Entrepreneurial History, 1870–1914', *English Historical Review*, 2nd series, 47, 2 (1994), pp. 262–87; E. P. Hennock, *Fit and Proper Persons Ideal and Reality in Nineteenth-Century Urban Government* (Studies in Urban History, 2) (London, 1973); John Garrard, *Leadership and Power in Victorian Industrial Towns 1830–80* (Manchester, 1983).

63 B. Guinness Orchard, *A Liverpool Exchange Portrait Gallery-First Series: Being Twenty Literary Portraits of Business Men: Sketched from Memory* (Liverpool, 1884); idem., *Liverpool's Legion of Honour* (Birkenhead, 1893); William Thomas Pike (ed.), *Liverpool and Birkenhead in the Twentieth Century: Contemporary Biographies* (Brighton, 1911); Robert Head, *Cheshire at the Opening of the Twentieth Century: Contemporary Biographies* (edited by W. T. Pike, Pike's New Century Series, 11) (Brighton, 1904); J. Naylor (ed.), *Lancashire Biographies Rolls of Honour* (London, 1917); J. Wallace Coop and Seymour Taylor, *Bulls and Bears: Cartoons of Members and Ring Traders of Liverpool; Cotton Exchange* (reprinted from the Liverpool 'Courier') (Liverpool, 1908); *Our Shipping Highlights a Collection of Biographical Sketches with Photographs Reprinted from "the Syren and Shipping Illustrated"* (London, 1900); George Thompson, *Liverpool's Scroll of Fame: A Memorial of Liverpool Soldiers and Sailors Who Gave Their Lives for This Country in the Great War Part I Commissioned Officers* (Liverpool, 1920); Lane, *Liverpool Gateway of Empire*, pp. 53–84; John Lansley, 'The Involvement of the Liverpool Business Elite in the Voluntary Sector 1920–90', in J. C. Martín de la Cruz and R. Román Alcalá (eds.), *Las Cuidades Históricas Patrimonio y Sociabilidad* (Córdoba, 2000), pp. 499–500.

64 Lynn, 'Trade and Politics in 19th Century Liverpool', pp. 99–120.

65 Gordon Boyce, 'Language and Culture in a Liverpool Merchant Family Firm, 1870–1950', *BHR*, 84, 1 (2010), pp. 1–26; Orchard, *Liverpool's Legion of Honour*, p. 151.

66 Baines, *Liverpool in 1859*, p. 126; Anthony Webster, 'Liverpool's Asian Networks 1800–1914: Some Insights into a Provincial British Commercial Network', in Sheryllynne Haggerty, Anthony Webster and Nicholas J. White (eds.), *The Empire in One City: Liverpool's Inconvenient Imperial Past*

(Manchester, 2008), pp. 35–54; J. Davies, 'The Liverpool Chamber of Commerce and the Burma-China Railway', *THSL&C*, 139 (1989), pp. 113–36. For a discussion of the port's China trade in general, see Christina Baird, *Liverpool China Traders* (Oxford, 2007).

67 See Randolph Cock, John Davies, Robert Lee, and Sari Mäenpää, Chapter 2.

68 In addition, 1,554 'mercantile' individuals, as listed under Clause III, Commercial, were registered in 1861 in West Derby (excluding all general dealers). In 1902, the number of accountants in business in Liverpool was approximately 410, including officers and members of the Liverpool Society of Chartered Accountants and members of the Liverpool and District Society of Incorporated Accountants: see *Gore's Directory of Liverpool and Its Environs* (London and Liverpool, 1902), pp. 1605–7.

69 The lower and upper bands for female merchants in the database were 0.5 and 1.7 per cent respectively, assuming the same surname or any entry as an individual. A far larger number of women played a role in marketing and distribution networks, as retail dealers, hucksters, costermongers, hawkers, and pedlars.

70 MLP database.

71 Gary Wray McDonogh, *Good Families of Barcelona: A Social History of Power in the Industrial Era* (Princeton, 1986); Patricia M. Brown, *The Merchant Princes of Fremantle: The Rise and Decline of a Colonial Elite 1870–1900* (Perth, 1996); Nicola Wurthmann, *Senatoren, Freunde und Familie Herrschaftsstrukturen und Selbstverständnis der Bremer Elite zwischen Tradition und Moderne 1813–1848* (Bremen, 2009); Lane, *Liverpool*, pp. 53–84; see Randolph Cock, John Davies, Robert Lee, and Sari Mäenpää, Chapter 2.

72 See Graeme Milne, Chapter 3.

73 See Graeme Milne, Chapter 4.

74 See Sari Mäenpää, Chapter 5.

75 See Robert Lee and Sari Mäenpää, Chapter 6.

76 See Joseph Sharples, Chapter 8.

77 See Joseph Sharples and Adrian Jarvis, Chapter 9.

78 See Robert Lee, Chapter 10.

79 See Robert Lee, Chapter 11.

2 The Mercantile Liverpool Project Database

Sources and Findings

Randolph Cock, John Davies, Robert Lee,
and Sari Mäenpää

Introduction

One of the main aims of the Mercantile Liverpool Project was to use a range of historical sources in order to reconstruct the Liverpool merchant community in the period between the mid-nineteenth century and 1914 as a means of addressing a series of issues relating to the business community, its composition, trading patterns, and forms of business organisation. The analysis was also intended to explore the development and significance of commercial, religious, and recreational networks, as well as the working environment of merchants within a developing central business district and their residential distribution at a time of increasing suburbanisation. To address these issues, information was collected from trade directories, census records and a range of other sources, which was collated in a relational database. This provided, in turn, detailed information on the composition and structure of Liverpool's merchant community during a period of considerable trade expansion, commodity specialisation, and technological change. The individual merchants denoted by records from the various sources were identified and entries in the database were linked in order to represent these relationships of identity. Although the findings must be qualified by constraints imposed by the limitations of the sources and the record-linking process, they shed new light on the Liverpool merchant community in the period under examination.

This chapter sets out the methodology used to construct the relational database and discusses the range of sources involved as well as their relative robustness. In presenting the main findings of the analysis, it focuses on the size and changing composition of Liverpool's merchant community in terms of the number and structure of companies, the type of business organisation, and the longevity of firms. By using data on the residential and business addresses of merchants, it examines in depth the complex pattern of urban mobility, including in- and out-migration and residential relocation within Liverpool and the Wirral based on current postcodes. The chapter also assesses the wealth of merchants using the number of servants per household as a proxy indicator and explores the changing nationality of the mercantile community by country of birth and naturalisation. As such, the database provides an unrivalled opportunity to analyse key aspects of Liverpool's merchants and to explore issues which have never been explored in depth.

Methodology

The process of reconstructing Liverpool's merchant community involved the extraction of nominative data from Gore's street directories at ten-year intervals (1872, 1882, etc.) and from the decennial census returns between 1851 and 1901. In order to test the methodology, a pilot project was carried out using Gore's Directory of 1871. This confirmed that the closest linkage

DOI: 10.4324/9781315597836-2

in terms of information coverage was obtained by selecting directories which were published in the year after the decennial census. Earlier studies had not been able to trace the exact publication date of the directories, but evidence from the Maritime Archives and Library at the Merseyside Maritime Museum revealed that they were received from the distributors in late December.[1] Since it must have taken some time to compile the directories, a directory published in, say, 1872, must have been compiled some months earlier. Since publishers aimed to distribute their directories by the beginning of each calendar year, the information in the 1872 directory would have been compiled within a few months of the 1871 census, early in April.[2]

As a first step, both companies and individuals connected with shipping and trade, such as merchants, brokers, ship-owners, underwriters, and average adjusters, were identified by using the classified list of trades in the Liverpool directories. In order to extract this information from the directory, the research team had first to identify the relevant companies and then, using the name of the company as a starting point, to locate the individual merchants from the alphabetical list of inhabitants elsewhere in the directory. The connection between individuals and firms was most easily resolved for partnerships, since the names of most firms of this type incorporated the names of the merchants, as was the case, for example, with the steam packet agents, Allan Brothers & Co., listed in the 1871 directory. The trade section reveals that Allan Brothers had two offices, one in James Street and another in Regent Road, both in Liverpool. The alphabetical list, in turn, provides us with two men with the surname Allan, namely Alexander Allan and Bryce Allan, with the company name included in the entry in brackets. The 'personal' entries reveal their home addresses and some additional information regarding their other trading activities: they both lived in Holly Road in East Liverpool and they were also steamship owners. But even for partnerships it was not always possible to link a specific name with either companies or individuals.

Nineteenth-century directories are invaluable for confirming the address of an individual. This also provides a means of locating him in the census which, in turn, allows access to the demographic, familial, and social background of merchants. Indeed, trade directories are most useful when used in conjunction with other primary sources, while the linking of the directories with census data provided some check on the accuracy with which the residential addresses of merchants had been recorded.

The Database

There have been previous attempts to compile a database of information from trade directories.[3] Several projects have digitised trade directories, but these are simply digital reproductions of the original publications which only allow users to browse and view the images.[4] The Mercantile Liverpool Project database is a relational database incorporating information collected from a range of sources.[5] The principal source was Gore's Trade Directories, from which was compiled a list of individuals who, for the purposes of this study, were taken to constitute the Liverpool merchant community. Using the addresses of these individuals (obtained from the directories) as the means of reference, they were identified in the census records, from which additional personal and professional information was obtained. These records were supplemented with information from biographical dictionaries, obituaries, and the membership records of various clubs, societies, and associations.[6]

It was implicit in the nature of the sources and indeed *necessary* for our purposes, that there would be duplication within and between sources—that is, that multiple records from one source and records from other sources would all relate to the same individual. The most fundamental problem in using these sources as a means of collecting information about individuals was to resolve these duplications and to group together information which related to specific merchants or other members of the business community. Given the size of the database (170,000 principal records drawn from five classes of source material), this would have been an impossible task to have attempted manually.[7] It was therefore reduced to a largely automated process, once all the data had been entered from all the sources, involving the matching of data both *within* and *between* sources, based on certain criteria of similarity in key fields such as name, address, occupation, year and place of birth, spouse's name and place of birth, etc.[8] Thresholds were set representing a degree of similarity between records which indicated beyond reasonable doubt that they referred to the same individual. A degree of flexibility was built into the matching process. For example, 'fuzzy matching' of surnames was implemented in an attempt to overcome the problem of names being misspelled or rendered differently in different sources, which was not uncommon, particularly with Scottish names beginning 'Mac', 'Mc', or 'M'', and names of foreign origin.

But this kind of operation can never be an exact science aspiring to comprehensiveness or complete accuracy. It can only find a match between two records when the original sources supply information of sufficient similarity: where the sources differ significantly—whether as a result of omission or inconsistency in the original records, or because they were originally compiled for different purposes, or because, for example, they relate to different years—then the degree of agreement may be insufficient to justify confidence in a posited match. The guiding principle was always to err on the side of caution and where evidence was less than convincing, to reject a putative match rather than to create an erroneous one. For these reasons, as anticipated from the beginning, the matching process was able to identify all the records in the database relating to only a proportion of individuals and only a proportion of the records relating to others. Nevertheless, in excess of 50,000 matches were made and the resultant database provides reasonably comprehensive information from the range of sources for a significant number of individuals who were active in Liverpool's commercial and trading community.[9]

The Sources

(i)   *Trade Directories*

Trade directories are a source widely used for local and family history. Although, as with any historical source, they should be used with a keen appreciation of their limitations, especially regarding their reliability and comprehensiveness, they provide better coverage of the elite business communities which were the subject of this study, than of small traders or those in working-class occupations. Trade directories were born out of the need to enable buyers and sellers to meet each other: therefore, members of the business community, especially those operating at the higher end of the distribution chain, had a strong incentive to appear in their pages.[10]

Recent research has highlighted the significance of shared values and a common culture in determining economic performance. Within this context, the project had a number of wider objectives beyond investigating what information on local companies and individual merchants could be extracted from the trade directories.[11] Firstly, it was intended to test the extent to which trade directories used in conjunction with other sources can provide evidence of inter-linkages within the business community, as well as other aspects of contemporary business operations, including risk-taking and risk-spreading. Secondly, it was designed to assess the way in which companies were influenced by new forms of business organisation (primarily the development of joint-stock companies) and technological change, such as the diffusion of steam power, especially in the shipping sector.

Information drawn from the trade directories was the foundation of the database, since the Liverpool business community was defined initially by listing all the merchants and brokers identified in the directories. Liverpool was an excellent subject for this case study: it has an almost continuous sequence of directories covering the nineteenth and early twentieth centuries; it was a major port-city whose economic success was largely determined by the activities of its merchant community; and commercial success contributed to a rapid expansion of its middle-class population. In 1851, by one measure, 6.5 per cent of Liverpool's occupied males were involved in middle-class occupations, but this figure had risen to 10.5 per cent in 1891 and to 12–13 per cent by 1911.[12]

The availability of British directories grew extensively in the late nineteenth century. Whereas 55 directories were published in the 1870s, 130 appeared during the 1880s.[13] In part, this was a reflection of urban growth and the expansion of trading activities in many urban communities, including Liverpool, whose population increased by 38 per cent from 395,000 in 1851 to 625,000 in 1881.[14] In addition, improvements in the transport and communication networks, together with increased competition and a further growth in the size of the urban population, reinforced the value of trade and street directories as a source of information, especially in large cities. The method of compiling trade directories varied: it is important to be aware of these differences because they have an impact on the reliability of directories as a source for business and urban history. As earlier studies have emphasised, the compilation of a directory was a private undertaking, so it should not be surprising that errors did occur, especially in the early nineteenth century when private surveys were far from accurate.[15] Directories produced in a regular series would have been more reliable than single compilations, since the updating of existing information would have been relatively straightforward and less time-consuming compared with the problems of starting from scratch. Many larger regional and national firms involved in publishing trade directories employed professional agents to collect the information, although another common method of collecting names and addresses was to send out circulars to be filled in and returned to the publisher. A majority of local directories, however, were published by non-specialists, which increased the possibility of errors and the likelihood of dishonesty or plagiarism.[16] Practice varied from town to town, but some directories charged for inclusion and agents were sometimes hired on commission based on how many addresses they could bring in.[17] There is some evidence that pressure was put on people to buy directories by implying that if they declined they would not be included in the next edition.[18]

The first Liverpool directory was published in 1766: by the second half of the nineteenth century Gore's Directory had become an annual publication consisting of three main elements: a list of private inhabitants, a list of streets, and a classified list of trades.[19] Significant improvements had also been made in the numerical listing of houses and the recording of people's names.[20] By that time, many directories had grown in size to such an extent that their complete transcription into a database for systematic analysis would be both excessively time-consuming and prohibitively expensive. Whereas the first directory included about 1,134 names of which 188 were described as merchants, by 1874 the number of registered names had risen to approximately 92,380.[21] However, the nineteenth-century directories can be used effectively to reconstruct particular groups of inhabitants and to study changes in their living arrangements and business patterns. Directories are especially useful for analysing spatial mobility within urban areas: they can help to trace the movements of individual families and businesses and are invaluable in providing a precise address in larger towns where a search through the census returns would be impracticable and, in the case of business locations, often impossible. Furthermore, directories often contain other interesting information that can be utilised for this purpose. Gore's directories, for example, contain the 'Annals' of Liverpool (from 1813 onwards), one-page advertisements, maps, lists of representatives and the locations of local churches, clubs, and associations, as well as economic data on dock charges and the routes of shipping lines. This additional information can be useful for examining the business culture of the trading community, particularly in terms of charitable, political, and religious activities and more informal networking in local clubs and societies.

Trade directories were designed in a world where business transactions between strangers were often associated with an inflated degree of risk and locating prospective customers and suppliers was a complex process. They were published in order to provide information for those searching primarily for business contacts. Small traders and tavern keepers were under-represented in directories since they had little incentive to advertise themselves, especially if the business operation did not require any official sanction. By contrast, wholesale traders and members of the business elite, as economically significant elements within urban communities, were well represented since they sought to exploit the opportunities provided by the increasing availability and distribution of published directories.[22] But trade directories are not unproblematic as a source for studying companies and their owners. One complication in using trade directories is that a single merchant may be recorded under several headings in the list of classified trades, while additional commercial activities are advertised in the alphabetical section of the directory under his home address. Multiple entries of this nature are an intrinsic feature of directories.[23] In the case of the 1871 Liverpool directory there were 475 duplicate entries from a list of 3,394 companies (or 14 per cent of the total). Since a merchant could be involved in several partnerships of varying duration and might well have had more than one business address, identifying which entries related to specific individuals was not an uncomplicated task.

Directories, along with other sources, also suffer from serious inconsistencies in the recording of addresses. Some entries list the name of a building, others the street name and number instead. It is not uncommon for an address to consist of a house name either alone or in combination with a general indication of the area or district. Neither were areas or districts denoted consistently or unambiguously: some entries record the Liverpool postal districts (N, S, E, W), or districts beyond Liverpool's city centre, such as Mossley Hill, Sefton Park, Bootle, or Oxton and Claughton on the Wirral side of the Mersey. In other instances, however, such information was omitted, creating ambiguity in a significant number of cases in the second half of the nineteenth century when streets of the same name occurred in several places within the area covered by the directory. Other classified entries provided only the name of the business premises on the assumption that the reader would have known the actual address. Locating private residences and business premises on contemporary maps was therefore not a trivial task, especially given the scale of the analysis undertaken by this project. The problem was exacerbated by the fact that it was sometimes impossible to locate the home address of a merchant in the list of inhabitants, indicating that he did not live locally or operated through an agent or a manager who represented his firm's interests in Liverpool. Sometimes the home address of a manager was provided instead.

Names alone, of course, do not provide adequate evidence that two entries relate to the same person. And even when two entries give the same name, address, and trade, this cannot be taken as conclusive proof because it was common in this period for the eldest son to be named after his father, to enter the family business, and (until married) to reside at the family home. Even when 'junior' or 'senior' was specified in the source, such terms were not, of course, invariable over time. Certain surnames such as Davies were very common in Liverpool, then as now, further complicating the search. As a result of these methodological difficulties which were encountered in the pilot project, the scope of the final project was restricted. The initial objective had been to include in the database *all* individuals connected with trade and shipping (including ship-builders, rope-makers, and sugar refiners) and manufacturing (engineers, foundry-owners, etc.), as well as the service sector (bankers and insurers). The difficulties encountered in linking individual entries in the alphabetical and trades sections of the 1871 directory meant that the final project had to be limited to the merchant community, simply because of time constraints and attendant inputting costs.

Another shortcoming of trade directories, which affected our figures in some cases, is that trade classifications were not entirely consistent across the years, which presents problems when trying to track merchants involved in specific trades over time. For example, although Gore's directory for 1851 included a separate classified heading for Cotton Merchants, as did those published from 1892 onwards, there was no such category in the intervening years when cotton merchants were simply listed among cotton brokers and general merchants. Data on individual trades derived solely from the directories, therefore, must be viewed with some care, and in certain cases, their long-term development can only be analysed by the incorporation of other evidence derived from census returns and associational records.

Related to the problem of inconsistent classification is the evolution of trade categories, which can be illustrated by reference to shipowning. Until fairly recent times merchant ships were owned mainly by merchants, often for the purpose of transporting goods in which they were trading, a relationship which was complicated, but not negated, by the risk-spreading practice of owning shares, or sixty-fourths, in a number of ships, instead of the riskier practice of owning one ship outright.[24] Shipowning only seems to have emerged as a distinct occupation after the Napoleonic Wars. The Liverpool Shipowners Association was founded in 1810, followed by the Liverpool Steamship Owners Association in 1858, but it was not until the second half of the nineteenth century that shipowning became widespread as a service industry, independent of the merchants whom it served.[25] This development is reflected in the trade directories: before the 1870s, there was no classification of shipowner (sailing ships) or steamship owner, because such enterprises continued to be regarded as subsidiary interests of merchants who were engaged primarily in trade. It was only with the rise of mainly passenger-carrying shipping companies, such as the Inman Line, that their owners finally saw themselves as primarily involved in the business of shipowning.[26] However, long before this date, there were individuals within these companies who *were* primarily concerned with the shipping side and this was reflected in the registration of a significant number of shipowners in the censuses and trade directories of the 1850s and 1860s.[27]

(ii)   The Census

Although census information cannot of course be regarded as completely reliable, of all the sources used in the project it remains, in general, the one least likely to be subject to substantial errors or omissions. The fuzzy-matching of surnames, as described earlier, helped to reduce the incidence of an inappropriate rejection of matches between records due to accidental or insignificant variation in the recording of names, such as may occur, for example, through mis-reading the handwritten enumerators' books. Inconsistencies in the ages of individuals as recorded in successive censuses, which seemed to be a fairly common source of error, were allowed for by basing all comparisons on an approximate year of birth calculated from the age given in the census with a margin of plus or minus two years, which several studies of census data suggest would have covered perhaps 94–96 per cent of all cases. Even with this allowance, the incorrect recording of age could have been sufficient to cause a match between two records to be rejected erroneously in a small number of cases. There were also identifiable variations and inconsistencies in other fields such as place of birth, partly due to the location being recorded in a more specific manner in one census than in another.[28] For example, a birthplace of Blundellsands in one census might become Crosby in another, or Salford might be recorded as Manchester or simply as Lancashire.

A potential match between two records was rejected outright if the surnames did not match (according to fuzzy criteria), or if the approximate years of birth differed by more than two years. Candidate matches were then assigned a numerical score representing the degree of similarity they exhibited in a number of other fields. Thus, for example, if place of birth differed, a match was not automatically rejected if the match was sufficiently close in other fields. The fundamental constraint on the accuracy and comprehensiveness of the record-matching process was, of course, the nature and accuracy of the data. Links between records could only be established, whether automatically or manually, based on the information contained in the sources. In a significant number of cases, the sources simply supplied insufficient information to decide whether two records related to the same individual or to two different ones. But given these constraints, a process was devised which satisfactorily exploited the information that was available.

Even such apparent constants as addresses were far from fixed in the second half of the nineteenth century and two apparently different addresses might not infrequently refer to the same dwelling. For example, in 1856 the streets of Liverpool were systematically re-numbered (a process which involved some 40,538 house numbers) and further partial re-numberings of specific streets were not unknown. It was not considered practicable to take account of these changes, but street numbers in any case contributed only a proportion of a good match score and probably few, if any, matches were rejected simply because of a disparity between pre- and post-1856 addresses. A further complication with addresses, not unique to Liverpool, was that many dwellings were denoted by a number within a 'building' or 'terrace' in a named street and might itself have been assigned a number in that street. Especially in the period under consideration, all the elements of such an address would seldom be specified.[29] As a result, a particular dwelling might be identified by various combinations of selective elements at different times and according to various sources, making it difficult (but generally not impossible) to compare such addresses.

Occupations as given in the census returns were recorded in the database, but they proved too idiosyncratic to be used as a basis for analysing business activity. Although merchants were listed consistently as a separate occupational category between 1861 and 1891, they were subsequently returned together with agents in 1901 and with agents and accountants in 1911. Moreover, merchants were also returned with dealers in the case of specific trades, such as, in 1881 for example, coal, corn, hardware, hops, timber, and silk. But the listing of trades was seldom consistent and the criteria for occupational differentiation remain unclear. The original Census Office clerks faced a similar task in producing abstracts of the occupational data, but they were provided with carefully constructed occupational dictionaries to facilitate the task.[30] These dictionaries were judged unsuitable for our purposes, however, and it would have been impracticable to have constructed a separate one ourselves. More reliable and more manageable for that purpose were the trade categories in the classified sections of the trade directories and it was in terms of these 250 or so categories that the occupational data was analysed.

(iii)   Other Sources

The project also included a wide range of nominative data relating to individual merchants involved in local associations, clubs, societies, schools, and religious communities, with the intention of identifying evidence of social networks among the merchant community. The entire membership lists of a number of these associations, such as the Liverpool Athenaeum, the

Wellington Club, the YZ Club, the Royal Liverpool Golf Club, the Royal Mersey Yacht Club, the Historic Society for Lancashire and Cheshire, and the Liverpool Philomathic Society, were entered into the database.[31] The same matching process was used to identify records relating to merchants who had already been identified from the trade directories and/or the census in order to make the appropriate links between records. This was successful in a significant number of cases, but again it was dependent on the extent and quality of the information obtainable from the available sources. Where club records gave the name, address, and occupation of a member, there was a sound basis for identifying that individual in the database, but where clubs recorded more limited information the evidence was sometimes insufficient to justify a correct linkage. A similar approach was adopted in relation to Freemasons, where it could be established that at least 25 per cent of the membership of specific lodges was composed of men who were listed as merchants, as was the case with the Merchants' Lodge.[32] Further information, mostly about the more notable individuals represented in the database, was obtained from obituaries and from local contemporary biographical dictionaries, in particular Orchard's *Liverpool's Legion of Honour* and Pike's volume on *Liverpool and Birkenhead in the Twentieth Century*, although it should be noted that the range and quality of the material was dependent, to a large extent, on what was submitted with 'many persons' demonstrating a degree of reticence while some declined to participate.[33]

Findings

(i)   The Size and Composition of the Merchant Community

The database contains information concerning 12,182 individuals engaged in mercantile activities, but the database covers a period of some 60 years of business activity so that the actual size of Liverpool's merchant community at any one time was never more than under 5,000 (Table 2.1).

The overall trend reveals a marked increase in the size of the merchant community over time until it reached a peak in the 1890s, while the dip in the 1880s probably reflected a temporary contraction as a result of the economic slump of the early 1870s. The marked contraction in the size of the community in the early years of the twentieth century can be explained partly as an artefact of the project's methodology, since there were fewer sources available in the absence of the 1911 census returns. But this would not have had a major impact on the figures, however, since they are based largely on the merchants listed in the trade directories. It therefore seems fair to conclude that the trend reflected a real change in the size and composition of the merchant community as modern forms of business organisation, specifically the growth of

Table 2.1 Merchants recorded in the database (from all sources), by decade

Decade	Number of Merchants
1850s	1821
1860s	2513
1870s	3851
1880s	3646
1890s	4435
1900s	3837
1910s	1873

Source: Mercantile Liverpool Project (MLP) database

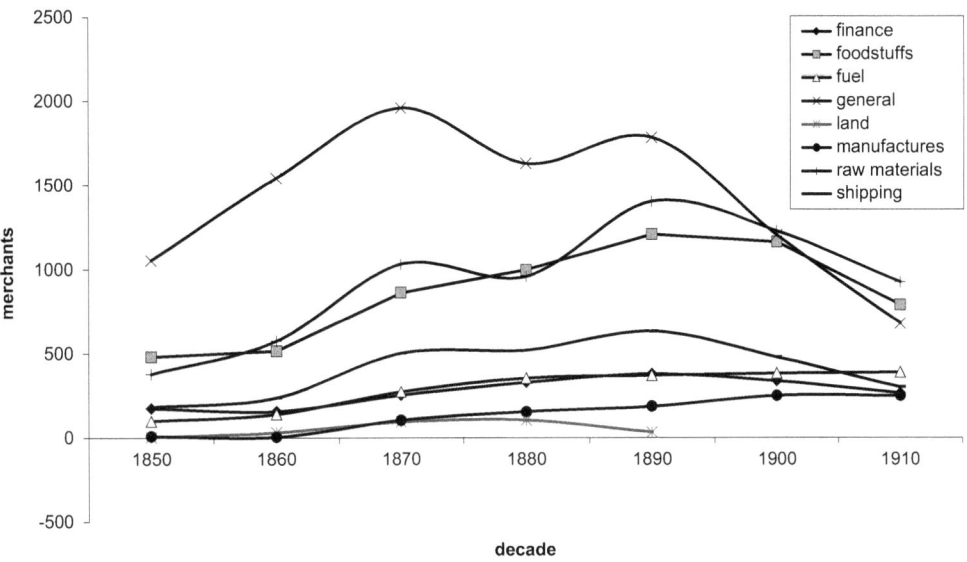

Figure 2.1 Number of merchants, by trade

limited companies, replaced more traditional partnerships and sole traders. These new companies employed professional managers and appointed boards of directors who were less likely to be listed in trade directories since they were not in business on their own account. A similar trend is apparent in Figure 2.1 which shows the number of individual merchants grouped into broad trade classifications.

It is also possible that this reflected wider changes in Liverpool's commercial and trading environment. Although there was a continuing growth in the number of agents listed in the directories, particularly between 1892 and 1912 (from just over 1,200 to over 2,000), this was more than counterbalanced by a decline in brokerage activity and merchanting. The overall number of brokers fell by over 40 per cent (from approximately 1,270 to 740), while the total number of merchants registered a reduction of almost 60 per cent (from 4,435 to 1,873).[34] To some extent, this may have reflected a shift within the business community away from merchanting and brokerage, as agents assumed responsibility for an increasing range of products and services during the early twentieth century. But it also represented the start of a longer-trend in Liverpool's commercial community characterised by the gradual decline in the role of merchants as a whole, whose traditional function in some sectors, such as oil-refining, was displaced increasingly by a growth in the number of registered companies.

At the same time, the classification of trades in the street directories provides evidence of a trend towards increased specialisation within Liverpool's business community, or at least a demand for a more differentiated reporting of commercial activities. In the late 1850s only six categories of agents were listed (with a clear majority simply recorded as miscellaneous), while the seven categories of brokers included a considerable number specialising in ships (166) and cotton (159), but there were also 151 general brokers and 138 miscellaneous brokers.[35] By 1912, however, both occupations encompassed a far wider range of trades with 31 different types of brokers and 77 types of agents listed. It is difficult to assess the extent to which changes in reporting practices affected the listing of individual trades, but the proliferation of distinct commercial activities prior to the outbreak of the First World War suggests that Liverpool's business community had witnessed a far greater degree of specialisation than had been the case in the mid-nineteenth century.[36]

(ii)   The Size of the Merchant Community: Numbers of Companies

The number of records in the database relating to uniquely named companies is 15,883, somewhat greater than the number of individual merchants. This reflected the fact that some merchants were involved in more than one business, either simultaneously or over time. However, it must also be borne in mind that the final figure represents an over-estimate of the number of companies operating in Liverpool because of the presence of a few unresolvable duplicates, since it was not possible in every case to determine whether two companies with similar names were in reality the same company or to always identify businesses which traded under several names or which changed their names over time (for example, by adding or dropping the names of individual partners or as a result of incorporation). The actual number of businesses in terms of distinct units of business activity (from sole trader to limited company) represented in the database must therefore be somewhat below this figure. The number of businesses in merchant trades for the sample years is shown in Figure 2.2: it reveals a similar trajectory to the number of Liverpool-based merchants, with evidence of a noticeable decline from a peak in the early 1890s to 1912.

In order to identify those firms which were most obviously family concerns, the database was queried for partnerships of a father and son (or sons). The absolute numbers are represented in Figure 2.3. What is interesting to note in comparison with Figure 2.2 is that the proportion of all businesses represented by family concerns remained remarkably constant from 1851 to 1912, with a marginal increase between the early 1870s and 1880s. Contrary to expectation, there was no significant decrease in the relative importance of family firms in comparison with other forms of business organisation.

The primary business of owners of family firms often represented only one aspect of their wide array of activities, and by examining the alphabetical section of the directories it was

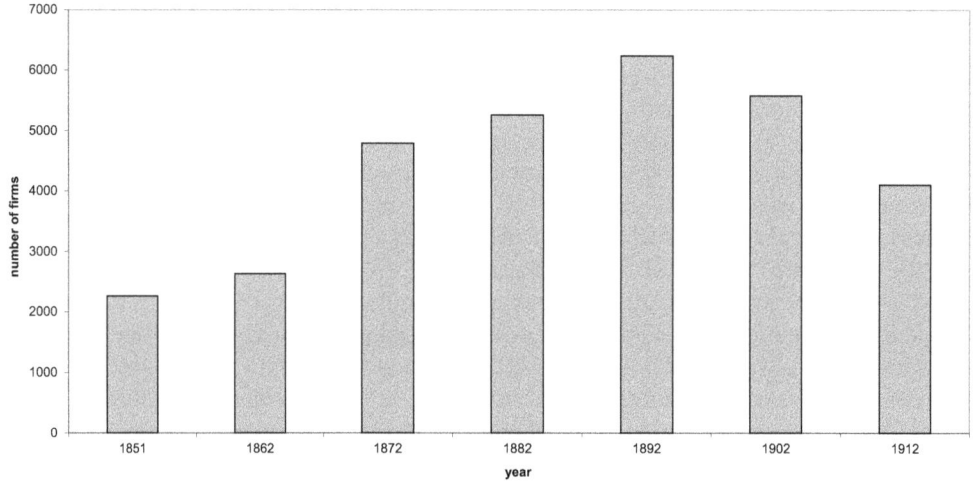

Figure 2.2 Number of firms recorded in the database in sample years, 1851–1912

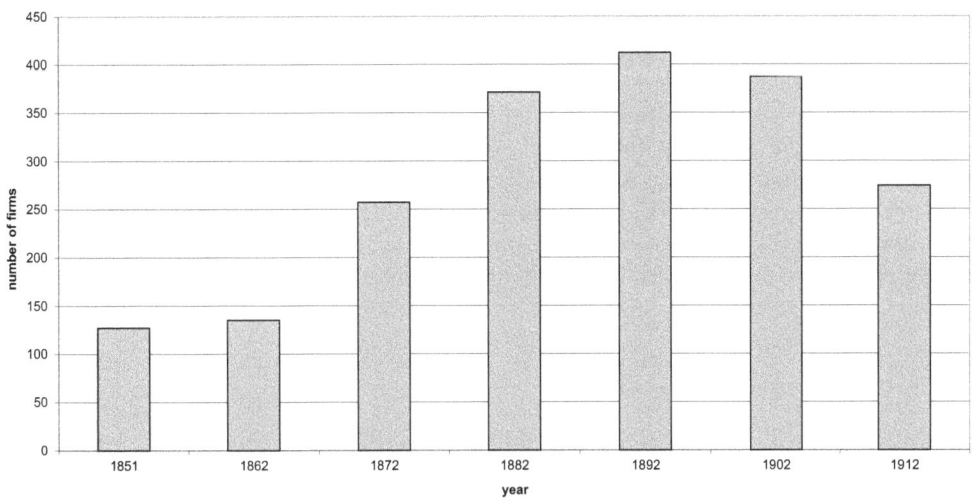

Figure 2.3 Explicit father and son partnerships, 1851–1912

possible to obtain a much fuller account of individual merchants' business operations.[37] The alphabetical list contains additional information on other trades in which individual merchants were involved, including relatively minor operations which were included mainly for advertising purposes. Many merchants, traders, and businessmen who were involved in individual companies were also in business on their own account and the alphabetical section of the directory provides more details of their commercial activities than the list of trades. An analysis of these 'secondary' trades (other trading activities that were not listed in the trade section of the directory) reveals that there were over 560 distinct types of specialist merchants in Liverpool. As Grindon noted:

> Liverpool is a city of agents. Its function is not to make, but to transfer. Nearly every bale or box of merchandise that enter the town is purely en route. Hence it comes that Liverpool gathers up coin even when times are 'bad'. Whether the owner of the merchandise eventually loses or gains, Liverpool has to be paid the expenses of the passing through.[38]

Many merchants were also involved in agenting, broking, and manufacturing as part of their business enterprise, illustrating the extreme fluidity with which individual traders operated in the distribution chain. Agenting and broking were the most common 'secondary activities' of merchants, which is not initially apparent from only studying the list of trades. For example, the company Robert Jones & Sons was listed as a bullion merchant in the list of trades, but the alphabetical section of the directory revealed that Robert Jones also acted as a goldsmith, jeweller, and watchmaker, as well as a dealer in bullion and precious stones.

The project also studied the commodity specialisation of merchants. One third of the companies had one or more 'secondary trades', with general and commission merchanting representing the most common combination. General merchants, in particular, were a very fluid category with many individuals also advertising themselves as East India merchants or as traders in various types of textiles, such as canvas, sack, jute, and hemp, or tobacco and cigar merchants. The extent of merchant involvement in agenting was considerable. Very often, a merchant would be trading in his own name, with a company or a partnership of his own, while at the same time acting as an agent for several other companies.[39] Merchants were reasonably advanced in commodity specialisation: most often the products or services were closely inter-connected and companies had several 'complementaries' available simultaneously. However, general trading spread risks but raised costs, while specialisation reduced costs but also limited the degree of flexibility.[40] Builders' merchant John Powell, for example, traded in slate, nails, stone, tiles, timber, encaustic tiles, and paint. Merchants were very flexible: they not only operated at different stages of the retailing chain, but also in several related trades at the same trading stage. A good example of this kind of pattern was George W. Rutter, a merchant who was listed in 1871 as being involved in timber, stone, cement, drainpipes, encaustic tiles, nails, slate, and tiles. He was also involved in agenting.

(iii)   Types of Business Organisations

Trade directories also proved a good starting point for analysing business culture and the survival strategies of merchants. For example, the study confirmed that the family firm was still the most common type of business formation in Liverpool at the beginning of the 1870s. Although limited liability was introduced in 1862, it did not become widespread in England before the 1880s.[41] This was certainly the case in Liverpool: according to the trade directories, only two per cent of companies in the early 1870s were limited companies, and the family firm and the private partnership were still predominant (Figure 2.4).

Being involved with more than one partnership at a time was not unusual: over ten per cent of merchants were involved in more than one partnership and a company on average would have two partners at any one time. However, shipowning and iron and coal businesses were exceptions to this rule, because limited liability was already relatively common in these trades. The high cost of building steamships and increased competition between different steam-liner services made the concentration of resources in this sector a necessity. Early ocean-going liner companies such as the Cunard Line and the Collins Line operated in this fashion: despite being publicly known as competitors, they used the same sources of investment and ended up forming the first international steamship cartel in 1850.[42]

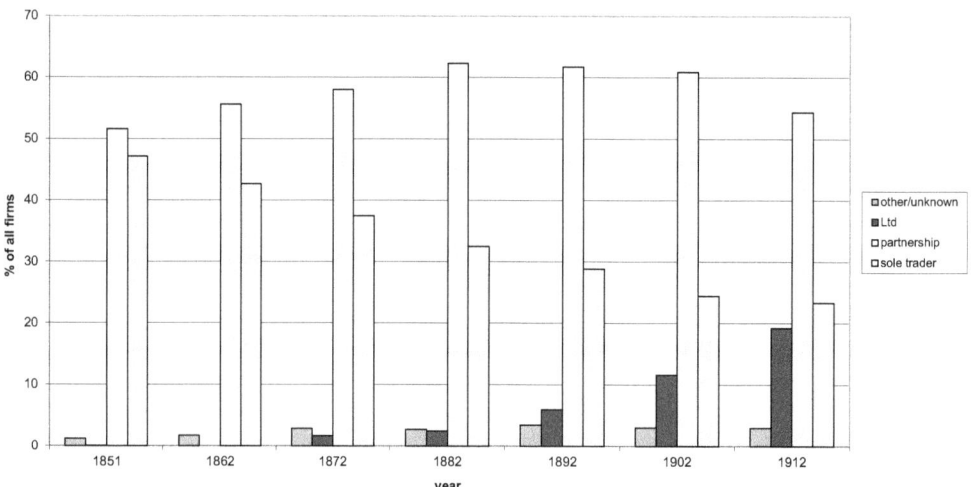

Figure 2.4 Relative growth and decline in type of business organisation, all trades

Figure 2.4 demonstrates the continued prevalence of partnership as a form of business organisation throughout this period, but it also indicates the continuous decline of sole trader-ships from the mid-nineteenth century onwards, as well as the rise from the 1870s of limited liability companies. The evidence suggests that there was a tendency for sole traders to go into partnership as trade increased, but this is an aggregate picture which lumps together all the registered trades.

By considering trades individually, different trends in business organisation can be identi-fied, specifically by focussing on three groups of trades. Firstly, some trades were characterised by a rise in partnerships at the expense of sole traders, since the latter sought to spread risk and raise additional capital through partnership agreements. This was the typical pattern for general brokers, as well as brokers specializing in stocks and shares, cotton, and corn, but it was also evident in the case of general, commission, and provision merchants, as well as merchants trad-ing in oil and colour, cotton, and corn.

In 1851 general brokers were split equally between sole traders and partnerships (Figure 2.5), but by 1902 only 26 per cent were sole traders whereas a clear majority (74 per cent) operated as partnerships. The same trend was visible in the case of stock and share brokers in which the ratio between sole traders and partnerships went from 72:28 in 1851 to 47:52 by 1912.

A second group of trades (Figure 2.6) illustrates the rise of limited liability companies, mainly as a result of conversions from existing partnerships and, in some cases, sole traders. An improved access to capital which limited liability provided, together with greater security for personal wealth, made it an attractive form of business organisation initially in capital-intensive and traditionally risky enterprises, such as shipowning (especially in the case of steamships).[43]

The proportion of shipowning businesses with limited company status rose from 3 to 37 per cent between 1872 and 1912 (Figure 2.6), but in the case of steamship firms 46 per cent were limited companies prior to the outbreak of the First World War, reflecting the need to raise higher levels of capital for the construction and operation of their vessels. From the mid-1860s onwards, the growth in steamship construction and ownership on Merseyside was accompa-nied by a high degree of capital accumulation and concentration, particularly on the part of

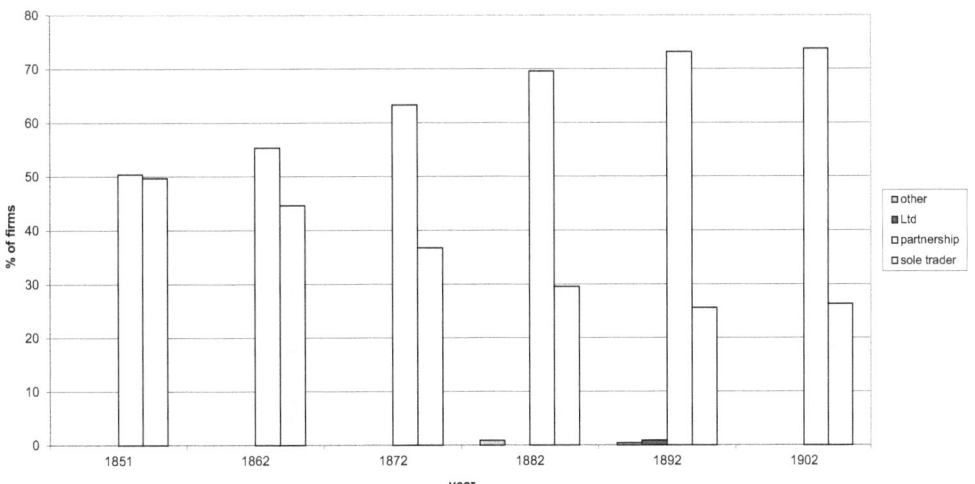

Figure 2.5 The rise of partnerships: General Brokers, 1851–1912

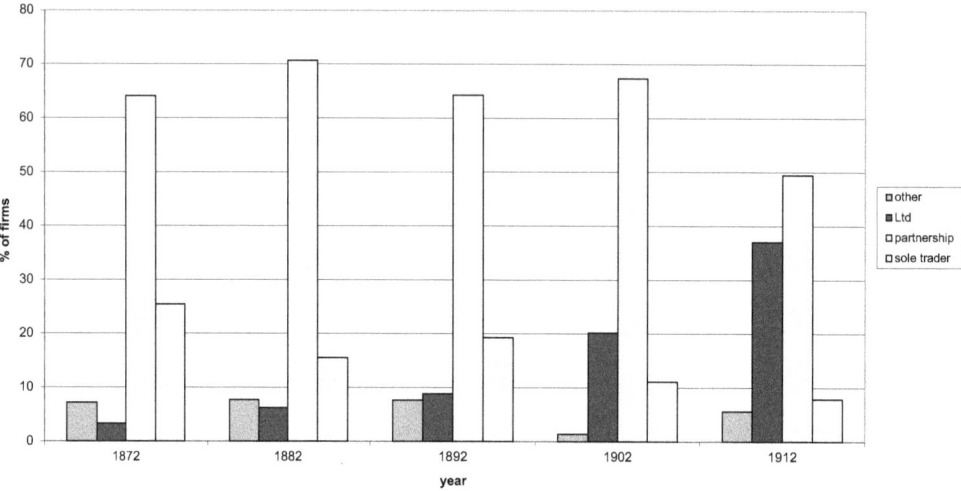

Figure 2.6 The rise of limited companies: Shipowners, 1851–1912

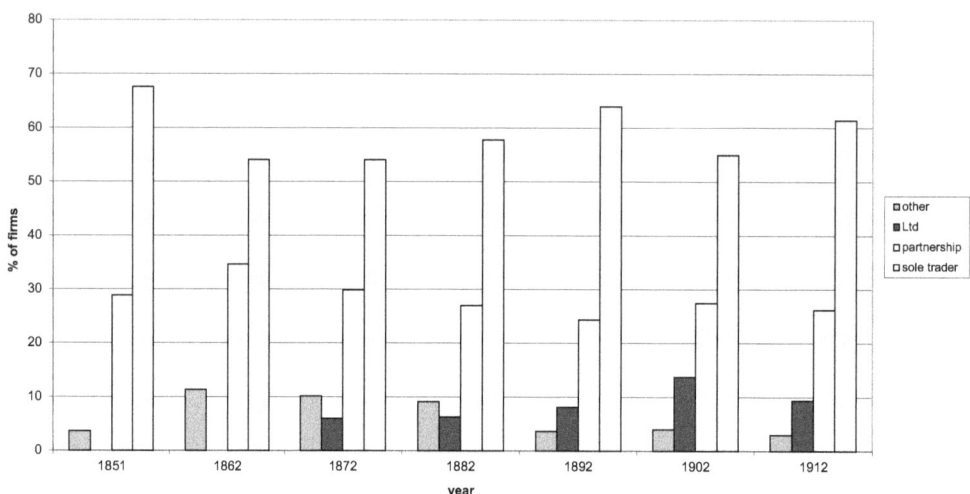

Figure 2.7 The persistence of business structures: coal merchants in Liverpool, 1851–1912

the principal shipping lines, which reinforced the increasing preference for limited company status.[44] However, this trend was even more marked in the case of copper merchants: in 1872 no copper merchants operated as limited companies, but by 1902 half the businesses were formally incorporated as limited companies.

By contrast, a final group of trades, including fruit and coal merchants, continued to operate with the framework of traditional organisational forms. For example, the coal merchant business remained dominated by sole traders who represented 68 per cent of all businesses in 1851 and 62 per cent in 1912 (Figure 2.7), while 59 per cent of fruit merchants were involved in partnerships both in 1862 and 1902, although the period prior to the outbreak of the First World War was characterised by an increasing preference for limited company status. In the case of coal merchants, a trend towards more sophisticated forms of business organisation was probably obscured by the highly differentiated structure of trading enterprising: at the one extreme, large-scale suppliers to steamship lines which were most likely to embrace incorporation and, at the other, a significant number of small-scale domestic retailers. Indeed, except for ship-owning most port-related businesses remained small-scale even at the end of the period under consideration.[45]

(iv)   The Longevity of Firms

Another characteristic of late nineteenth-century firms in Liverpool was the relative unimportance of professional management, particularly in the case of family enterprises. In the 1872 directory, for example, a specialist manager was only listed in 28 cases out of a total of almost 3,400 (less than one per cent of the sample). In almost every case, therefore, managerial control and ownership were still combined, which indicates that most companies were still comparatively small and family membership was still an important criterion for trustworthiness. The fact that most merchants can be located in the directory on the basis of a company's name (because the company often carried the name of its owner) indicates that many late nineteenth-century businesses were still very much a product of their creator. It might therefore be expected that they would have relatively short lifespans, given the underlying vulnerability of the merchant community, the uncertainty of trading operations, and the continued risk of failure.[46] To a large extent, this is borne out by the available data (Table 2.2).

Table 2.2 The longevity of Liverpool merchant businesses (all firms, partnerships, and sole traders), 1851–1902

First Recorded			All Firms			
			Still Recorded			
			%			
	1862	1872	1882	1892	1902	1912
1851	41	29	17	13	10	7
1862		43	21	14	9	6
1872			22	13	9	5
1882				34	20	12
1892					34	17
1902						33

First Recorded			Partnerships			
			Still Recorded			
			%			
	1862	1872	1882	1892	1902	1912
1851	40	28	18	13	10	7
1862		42	21	15	10	7
1872			25	14	9	6
1882				35	22	13
1892					42	23
1902						37

(Continued)

Table 2.2 (Continued)

First Recorded		Sole Traders				
		Still Recorded				
		%				
	1862	1872	1882	1892	1902	1912
1851	32	21	9	6	4	2
1862		40	17	9	5	3
1872			17	7	5	2
1882				27	12	5
1892					20	7
1902						24

Source: MLP database

The table provides an indication of the relative longevity of Liverpool businesses in general, particularly partnerships and sole traderships. Since only decennial samples were taken from the directories (except for the early 1870s), and none before 1851, the year in which a firm was first recorded cannot be taken as the year of its formation. Similarly, a firm last recorded in 1912, the last year sampled, could have continued in existence indefinitely beyond that year. The 'All Firms' data include businesses, such as steamship lines, iron works, etc, which were not obviously (based on their name) either partnerships or sole traders, as well as limited liability companies. Businesses which started as sole traders, partnerships, or 'companies', and later became limited companies, are treated in the longevity tables as single entities under their original type of business organisation.

In the case of partnerships, the data show that 60 per cent of the businesses recorded in 1851 had already disappeared from the trade directories by 1862, while a further 12 per cent which survived from 1851 to 1862 had also ceased to trade by 1872, and so on. In fact, only 7 per cent of the partnerships recorded in 1851 were still in existence 61 years later, while throughout the six decades under review a clear majority of partnerships (around 60 per cent) lasted less than ten years. As far as sole traders were concerned, the risk of failure was consistently greater than for partnerships or other types of business and long-term survival was comparatively rare. For example, 83 per cent of sole traders recorded in 1872 were not heard of again, whereas the comparable figure for partnerships was 75 per cent. Of those sole traders first recorded in 1892, 80 per cent appear to have met a similar fate, compared with 59 per cent of registered partnerships and 66 per cent of other companies. This may be attributed in part to the greater vulnerability of the sole trader as compared with the risk-spreading and greater capital reserves of larger firms. Although the figures reflect the fact that some merchants, after an initial period of trading on their own, joined partnerships or formed limited companies, while others decided to pursue different activities, there can be no doubt that the ranks of Liverpool's business community were subject to a high level of turnover in a trading environment wherein long-term success was difficult to achieve.

The three contiguous years from 1870 to 1872 were sampled in order to analyse the question of longevity in greater detail.

The British economy underwent substantial growth during the early years of the 1870s with noticeable peaks in 1872 and 1873. Although there were perceptible shifts in the structure of British foreign trade, including a decline in the proportion of exports to Latin America after 1872, this was a period which witnessed a further expansion in the size of the merchant navy

Table 2.3 The longevity of Liverpool merchant businesses first recorded between 1870 and 1872

First Recorded			All Firms			
			Still Recorded			
			%			
	1871	1872	1882	1892	1902	1912
1870	78	66	33	20	13	8
1871		52	17	8	5	4
1872			22	13	9	5

First Recorded			Partnerships			
			Still Recorded			
			%			
	1871	1872	1882	1892	1902	1912
1870	80	67	35	21	14	9
1871		53	18	10	7	5
1872			25	14	9	6

First Recorded			Sole Traders			
			Still Recorded			
			%			
	1871	1872	1882	1892	1902	1912
1870	73	61	24	11	5	2
1871		55	17	7	3	1
1872			17	7	5	2

Source: MLP database

and annual increases in the tonnage handled by Liverpool docks.[47] Despite buoyant trading conditions, over 20 per cent of all firms first recorded in 1870 failed to survive longer than 12 months, while almost half of the businesses first registered in 1871 were not included in the 1872 directory. Liverpool's shipping had been characterised by volatility throughout the 1860s, but rapid economic growth in the early 1870s was associated with an accelerated level of failure, since many firms established by speculative new entrants only enjoyed a short lifespan. After a peak in 1871, there was a gradual decline in the growth rate of tonnage handled by the Liverpool docks until the onset of the 'Great (or 'Long') Depression' heralded the beginning of adverse trading conditions. The evidence suggests that new businesses, whether partnerships or sole traders, established in the later phases of the trade cycle, were more likely to disappear from the record (often as a result of failure) than those already in existence. For example, of those partnerships first recorded in 1871, only 18 per cent were still registered in 1882, compared with 35 per cent of those first recorded the year before. Although a number of these firms had been founded in 1870, the majority had been established in the decade since 1861. A similar pattern is evident in the case of sole traders and registered companies.

But the overall longevity of Liverpool firms remained restricted: of all businesses registered in 1870 only 8 per cent survived until 1912, with only 2 per cent of the sole traders still in operation prior to the outbreak of the First World War. In such a context, most firms only enjoyed a limited lifespan. Firms were dissolved and new co-partnerships were formed on a regular basis, while bankruptcy remained a problem even for honest traders. Between 1835 and 1859, of those British and Continental European firms that provided steamship services across the Atlantic (excluding, as outliers, Cunard and Nord Deutscher Lloyd), average longevity was no more than 4.1 years, irrespective of their technological profile. Although the situation at the end of the century had improved markedly for shipping companies, it is salutary to note that many sole traders and partnerships in Liverpool's mercantile community continued to face a similarly high level of risk and commercial failure.[48]

It must be noted, however, that the methodology used to generate these figures is not entirely robust because of a tendency to underestimate the actual longevity of individual firms. If the name of a firm changed significantly (which was a particularly common occurrence in the case of partnerships, as individual partners were added or removed), or if it moved from Liverpool or ceased to appear in the trade directory for any other reason, it would appear in these figures as if it had ceased to exist. For example, the cotton brokers Rogers & Calder had been operating in Liverpool for over 80 years at the time of the death of its senior partner, Fletcher Rogers, in 1891, but it had been founded as Bourne & Lathom and had become successively Lathom & Rogers, and Rogers, Bourne & Rogers, in line with partnership changes. Deeds would often be drawn up on the dissolution of partnerships and on the agreement of new co-partnerships, but in many cases the core business of the firm remained the same.[49] It cannot be inferred, therefore, that just because there was a sharp fall in the estimated longevity of partnerships in the 1870s that they were simply going out of business. In fact, some firms may have taken on more part-ners (thus disguising their identity to our automated data-processing methods), because their business was flourishing.

(v)   *The Residential and Business Addresses of Liverpool Merchants*

The database supplies information on the organisation of urban space, the development of the built environment, and the changing status of different districts. In the early 1870s, most busi-nesses were still concentrated in a relatively small area in central Liverpool, centred in and around Dale Street, with a particular focus on the Exchange where 'a large portion of the busi-ness of Liverpool' was 'commenced and completed'.[50] The central business district also included the Stock Exchange on the opposite side of Exchange Buildings, the Cotton Exchange Build-ing (1808) adjacent to Exchange Flags, and the Corn Exchange (1809) in Brunswick Street, while the fruit and produce trades (including butter, cheese, cured meats, and tinned fish) were concentrated in and around Victoria Street. Before the adoption of the telephone (from 1879 onwards), face-to-face contact and physical proximity were essential for doing business and this reinforced the development of a highly concentrated business district.[51] Almost 30 per cent of the business premises of the entire Liverpool merchant community were to be found in this area, with a high proportion of businesses concentrated in only 15 streets. The town centre was predominantly given over to industries servicing shipping and trade, while the older industries of shipbuilding and pottery had already been pushed out from the inner areas of the city.[52]

The limitations of the original sources, as well as the nature of nineteenth-century business practices, meant it was not practicable to make a consistent distinction between the home and business addresses of merchants.[53] However, the complete database contains enough informa-tion to locate individual merchants within fairly well-defined districts of Liverpool and the Wirral. It therefore provides a basis for analysing changes in the spatial location of the trading community as well as the mobility and migration pattern of merchants during the period covered by this study.

The database includes information from a number of sources which detail merchants at particular locations on specific dates (a specific night at ten-yearly intervals in the case of census data, to within a year or so in the case of data derived from trade directories and other sources). The starting point for this analysis was normalised data where individuals had been identified within the database. Four tables were constructed:

people   (unique individuals),
streets   (in a standardised form),
areas   (locations specified in source document)
person-location-date

Ordnance Survey data, sourced from Edina,[54] was used to generate modern road names for Liverpool and Wirral with corresponding postcodes. Road names from the OS data were converted to the standardised form used in the database. However, this data was not sufficient by itself to uniquely identify the locations where merchants lived, since road names were subject to duplication over the area of the study. For example, to an even greater extent in nineteenth-century Liverpool than today, each district such as Bootle, Crosby, and Birkenhead tended to have its own Church Street or High Street, etc. Supplementary information was therefore required to uniquely identify a location, whether a road or street in a particular area specified in the database. Additional tables were then created to link the areas defined in the database with modern postcode districts (for example, Birkenhead was linked with the postcodes CH41, CH42, and CH43, which cover its current area). Not all area descriptions specified in the database could be translated into postcodes. Four distinct groups were identified: *c* and *l* for Cheshire (Wirral) and Liverpool; *x* for areas which were external to Merseyside; and *u* for areas where it was impossible to specify a postcode because of the use of a generic designations (for example Liverpool or the South). Some streets in areas classified as *u* were unique to Merseyside and were still useful for placing individual merchants within specific postcode districts, although *u*-rated streets with several postcode districts were not included in the analysis.

Two techniques were employed to refine the postcode information. Some instances of addresses of individuals were recorded with insufficient data to specify postcodes, but the same address (street name) could have a postcode allocated from other records. Where roads were not matched with modern road names, or road names were not known, the description of the location was sufficient to allocate a postcode district.

In the database there were 85,833 records of merchants at locations at specific times: 66,725 (78 per cent) were resolved with a postcode or were identified as external to Liverpool. With these tables in place, individuals could be assigned to modern postcode districts at known dates. By combining the data tables from the MLP database, OS postcode data and area/postcode districts, the following information was generated:

personId
street
postCodeDistrict
year

Some streets span several postcode districts. To avoid double counting in such cases, the aforementioned data was reduced to the first (alphabetically sorted) postcode district. For example, Borough Road stretches through postcode districts CH41, CH42, and CH44, so all references to Borough Road (Birkenhead) were assigned to the single postcode district CH41.

The data was further reduced to the first instance when an individual merchant was identi-fied in a postcode district within a decade. If the individual moved to a new postcode district within a specific decade, then two entries would be made. Individuals could be at several loca-tions in a given decade, but only one combination of person and postcode district per decade was recorded. This method caters for cases in which merchants in the study moved house or individuals owned multiple properties, but one of its limitations, which was judged acceptable for our purposes, was that those moving to another house within the same present-day postcode district would not be counted as having moved at all. In general, the robustness of this analysis is dependent on the comprehensiveness with which the database represents the population of merchants, whether resident in Liverpool or on the Wirral, and the accuracy of the linkages between the historical data and modern postcodes. Nevertheless, some interesting and plausible trends emerge.

Figures 2.8a and 2.8b present a comparison of the numbers of merchants living in Liverpool and on the Wirral, but it is when these large regions are disaggregated into individual present-day postcodes that significant trends become apparent. Table 2.4 gives the raw figures for the number of merchants (recorded in the database) residing in each present-day postcode district in each decade of the study. There had already been a tendency both in the late eighteenth century and in the early decades of the nineteenth century for some merchants to move out of Liverpool and take up residence elsewhere.[55]

In the period covered by this study there was a significant movement of merchants out of the Liverpool city centre (postcodes L1, L2, and L3) as members of the business community were 'repelled by the congestion and squalor of the mean streets and alleys of lower Liverpool' and new office blocks replaced old warehouses and merchants' houses.[56] This trend was initially visible in the centre itself (L1), where the number of resident merchants peaked in the early 1860s, whilst a similar process of net out-migration by merchants from L2 and L3 only occurred about ten years later. The merchant Edward Falkner, for example, left Old Hall Street in the city

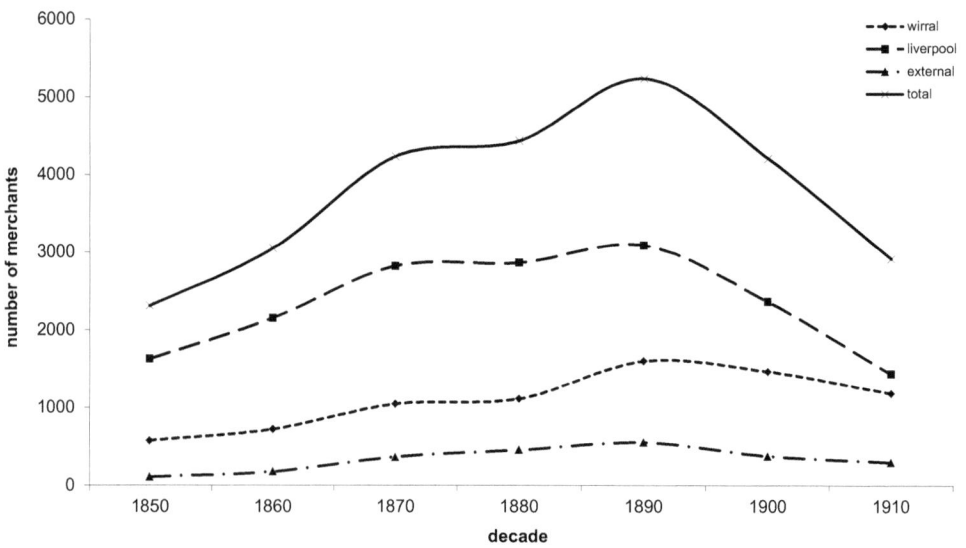

Figure 2.8a The number of merchants registered as resident in Liverpool, on the Wirral, and elsewhere, by decade, 1851–1912

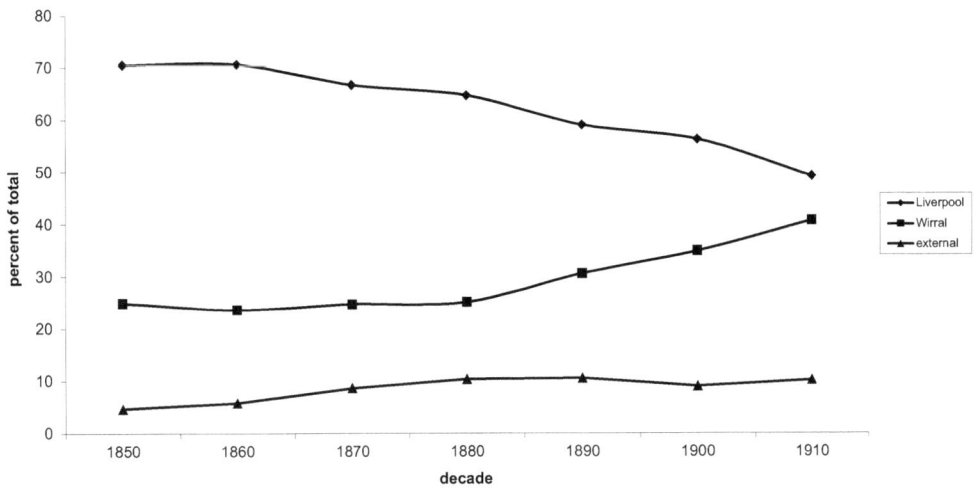

Figure 2.8b The locational residence of merchants in Liverpool, on the Wirral, and further afield (in per cent), 1851–1912

Table 2.4 The number of merchant residents in Merseyside postcode districts by decade, 1851–1911

Post Code	1851	1861	1871	1881	1891	1901	1911
CH41	180	133	248	103	125	71	51
CH42	173	144	385	288	349	262	133
CH43	110	225	501	384	587	443	318
CH44	170	161	332	214	303	217	125
CH45	34	52	158	102	203	310	276
CH46	1	1	9	6	23	19	23
CH47		1	22	22	87	103	84
CH48		2	8	6	27	41	41
CH49					2	1	
CH60			3	8	3	5	8
CH61	1			2	3		
CH62	19	37	86	58	112	72	46
CH63	5	71	102	107	108	62	25
CH64	4	12	25	20	40	42	34
CH66	3	10	28	22	39	28	17
L1	219	236	116	50	41	39	29
L10		3	7	6	11	3	2
L11			1	1		1	
L12	10	10	59	23	15	6	6
L13	140	251	380	271	252	183	98
L14	8	13	16	4	3	3	3
L15	96	120	265	98	139	111	55
L16		1	2	2	3	2	4
L17	112	96	219	161	232	151	91
L18	7	39	57	67	124	92	60
L19	15	62	89	70	163	124	74
L2	1	19	41	42	3	9	25
L20	71	76	205	145	178	130	94
L21	55	89	177	136	110	65	33

(Continued)

Table 2.4 (Continued)

Post Code	1851	1861	1871	1881	1891	1901	1911
L22	19	57	210	151	244	218	118
L23	1	49	158	199	247	222	174
L24			1	3	5	1	1
L25	19	44	85	45	100	74	38
L26		2	2	6	2		
L29				3			
L3	97	49	89	44	17	28	21
L30		1	1		1	1	
L31	2	8	25	29	10	16	12
L32		1	5	3	8	7	7
L34	2	3	7	2	3	1	3
L35	3	16	27	21	19	8	1
L36	20	47	165	107	112	77	43
L37		5	16	46	63	57	58
L38		1	1				12
L39		6	12	5	9	11	16
L4	137	177	276	231	129	98	52
L5	91	121	168	90	50	30	29
L6	126	79	229	149	152	137	47
L69	98	109	161	60	53	29	11
L7	209	259	363	205	220	119	51
L8	283	306	856	764	892	578	182
L9	29	47	118	47	96	72	56
x	55	132	465	376	515	467	358

Source: MLP database

centre when it 'lost its fashionable character' and subsequently resided in Fairfield Hall, but such a move was typical of many merchant families who sought to exploit the social and health benefits of suburban life.[57] L3, one of the original suburbs immediately to the north and east of the city centre and well within walking distance of the commercial district, registered a steady exodus from 144 resident merchants in the 1850s to only 17 in 1912, despite the presence of the formerly fashionable residential area of Mount Pleasant.

By contrast, the leafy middle-class suburbs of Sefton Park, Mossley Hill, and Aigburth (broadly equating with the present-day postcodes L17, L18, and L19 respectively) saw a corresponding rise to a peak around 1891, assisted perhaps by the extension of horse-tramways to these areas in the 1880s.[58] It is tempting to interpret these twin trends as representing the relocation of merchants' residences from their traditional sites in the city centre, where they served a dual purpose catering for both domestic and business needs, to increasingly fashionable suburbs, with dedicated offices retained in the central business districts.[59] However, the picture may be more complicated, since Figure 2.8a does not trace the actual movements of individuals, but only aggregate changes. These findings are certainly consistent with the pursuit of 'rural fantasies' among elements of the middle class in reaction to the spread of industrialisation. As Wiener noted, it was the comparatively well-off, such as merchants, who formed the vanguard of suburbanisation and 'exurbanisation', the movement from the urban core towards the peripheral areas of the city where high-class residential villas were built often around private residential parks.[60]

The figures for L8 need to be treated with some caution, since the modern postcode includes not only the stylish Georgian townhouses around Upper Parliament Street, Canning Street, Falkner Street, and Falkner Square, which were very popular as a merchant neighbourhood, but also the much larger mixed industrial and working-class district of Toxteth. Nevertheless, the figures clearly indicate a very marked rise in the merchant population of L8 in the late 1860s and early 1870s, corresponding to the exodus from the central districts. Indeed, L8 was the last recorded postcode of 25 per cent of the merchants who are known to have moved out of Liverpool and the Wirral between 1851 and 1901. Another factor was that the area around Falkner Square was built as a speculative investment specifically to attract the wealthy commercial elite or 'carriage folk' escaping from the city centre, but it was not well populated until the trams reached it in the latter years of the century because the steep hill from the city centre tended to restrict the use of carriages. This area, which includes the neighbouring streets around Abercromby Square, Bedford Street, and Mount Pleasant located today in the modern postcode areas of L7 and L3, sustained over 1,000 merchant residences throughout the last three or four decades of the nineteenth century and easily represented the greatest concentration of merchant residences in the city. The figures also show a rapid decline in the popularity of L8 with elite merchants (from a peak of 617 households in the 1890s) as the area took on an increasingly working-class character prior to the outbreak of the First World War.

From 1817 onwards a regular steam ferry service between Liverpool and Birkenhead increased the popularity of the Wirral (corresponding to the CH postcodes) as a site for leisure activities and residential relocation, but further improvements to the transport infrastructure and improved links across the Mersey in the second half of the nineteenth century meant that more distant locations, such as Hoylake (CH47), became viable places of residence for merchants and members of the business community beyond the immediate coastal areas of settlement including Birkenhead (CH41–43), Seacombe (CH44), and New Ferry (CH62). As a result of the improvements made to ferry services in the 1860s and 1870s, and the opening of the railway tunnel under the Mersey in 1886 which linked the Wirral directly to Liverpool city centre, there was a further increase in the propensity of merchants to locate their residences on the other side of the river.[61] North of Liverpool, Waterloo, Crosby, Blundellsands, and Southport also became increasingly popular amongst wealthy merchants as a result of improvements in the transport infrastructure, to the extent that by 1911 Southport had a substantial middle-class suburban population of 15.9 per cent.[62]

The database provided the means to track the movements of all individual merchants. Figure 2.9 gives an indication of just how mobile the merchant community was: during the 1860s,

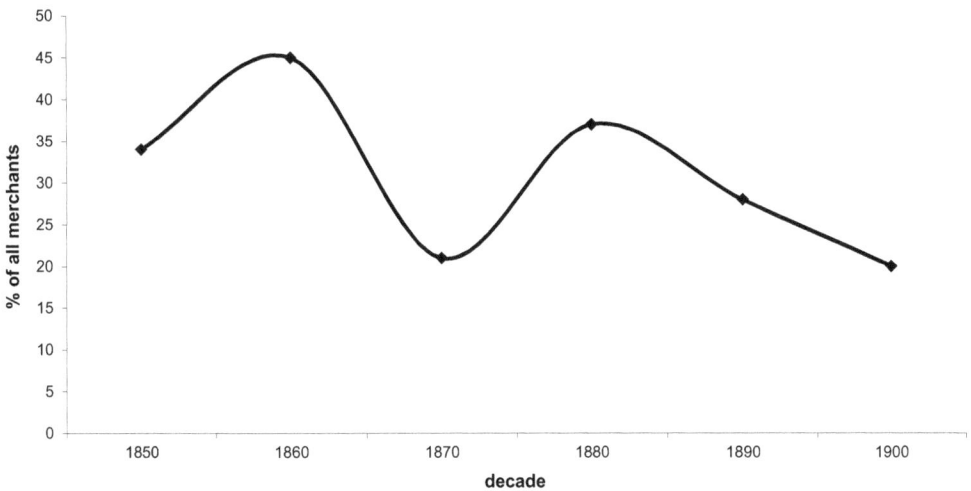

Figure 2.9 Merchants moving as a percentage of total merchant population, 1851–1901

for example, 45 per cent moved house to a different postcode.[63] The sharp dip in residential relocation in the 1870s may be attributed to the economic downturn of those years associated with the Great (or Long) Depression, but overall there seems to have been a trend towards decreasing mobility as the century progressed, perhaps reflecting an increasing propensity to buy property in preference to renting.[64]

The changing popularity of Liverpool as a site for residential location by members of the merchant community is evident in Figures 2.10a and 2.10b. In the 1860s, 60 per cent of the

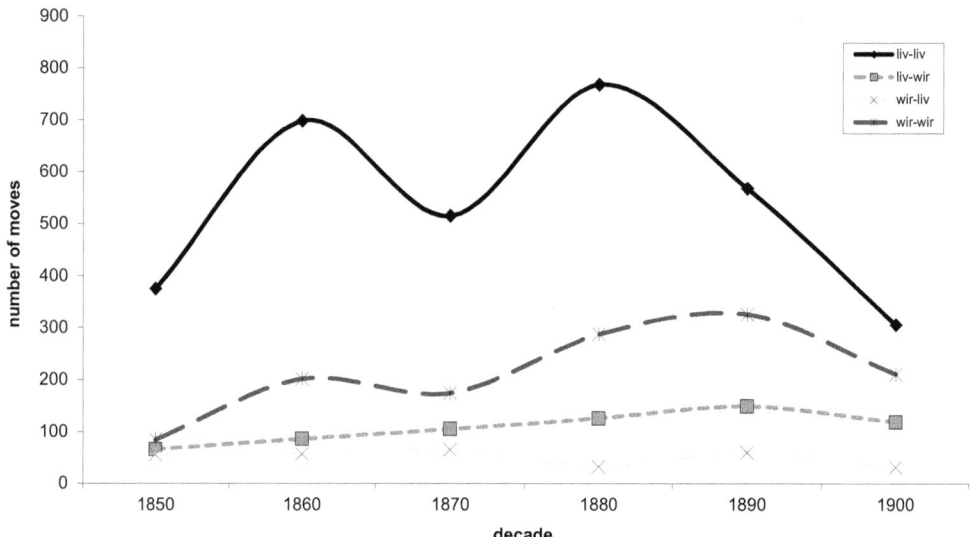

Figure 2.10a Changes of address: moves within and between Liverpool and the Wirral

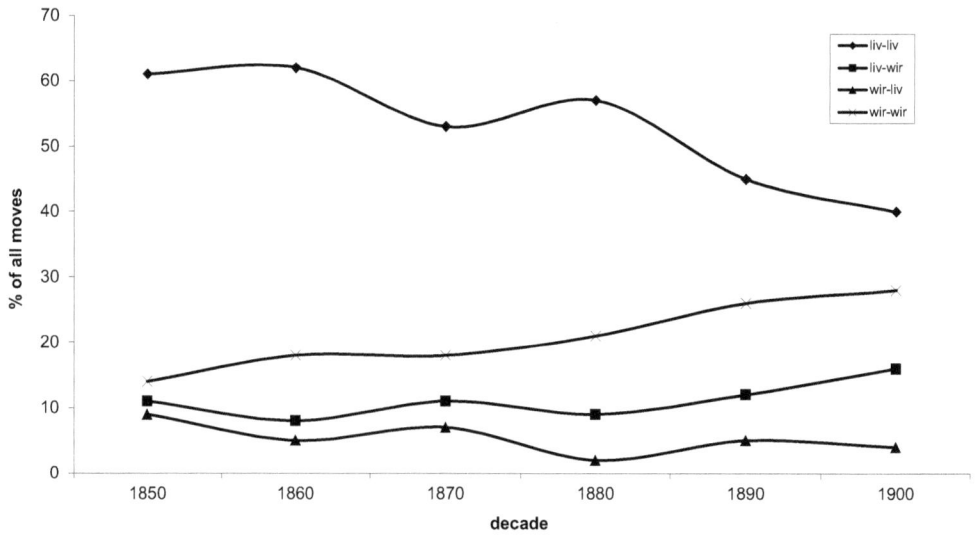

Figure 2.10b Moves within Liverpool/Wirral (in per cent), 1851–1901

merchants resident in Liverpool who moved house during the decade moved to a new residence within the city (i.e., the modern-day L-postcodes), whereas by the end of the century, 60 per cent moved elsewhere, a significant proportion to the Wirral, facilitated by improvements to the transport infrastructure and a growing preference for the health and leisure benefits of suburban life. The trend towards residence on the Wirral was reinforced by a corresponding decrease in movements in the opposite direction and a tendency for those once there to stay on that side of the Mersey.

The data can also be used to analyse the migration of merchants from farther afield into the Merseyside area (focusing on Liverpool and the Wirral together), as well as movements in the opposite direction. In general, the merchant community appears to have been relatively well established with a high degree of persistence. Although there was a great deal of movement within the Merseyside area, as a whole, the extent of both in- and out-migration remained limited. Figures 2.11a and 2.11b show that whilst out-migration from the Wirral (other than to Liverpool) was generally balanced by the inward movement of merchants, except for the final decade under consideration, the situation in relation to Liverpool was markedly different. Even in the mid-nineteenth century, Liverpool registered a net out-migration of members of the merchant community and throughout the period the proportion of those moving out of Liverpool (L-postcodes) was around double that of those moving in. It is generally assumed that both success and failure contributed to the propensity of individual merchants to leave Liverpool: whereas the former sought to realise their assets by purchasing landed property in Cheshire, North Wales, and the Lake District or by relocating to London and the South East, the latter were anxious to avoid their creditors by establishing a new career elsewhere.[65] But the cumulative trend represented a gradual dilution of the merchant presence in the city itself.

The foregoing analysis does not cover all aspects of residential mobility because it only measures movements from one modern postcode district to another. In fact, there was considerable mobility within individual postcodes, since people moved from one house to another in the same general location (sometimes on the same or an adjacent street). This was a common

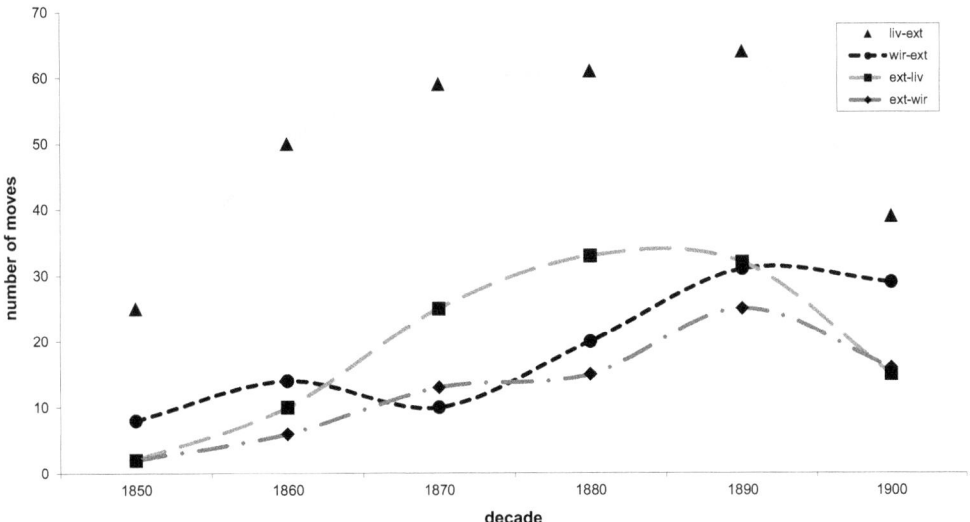

Figure 2.11a Moves into and out of Liverpool/Wirral, 1851–1901

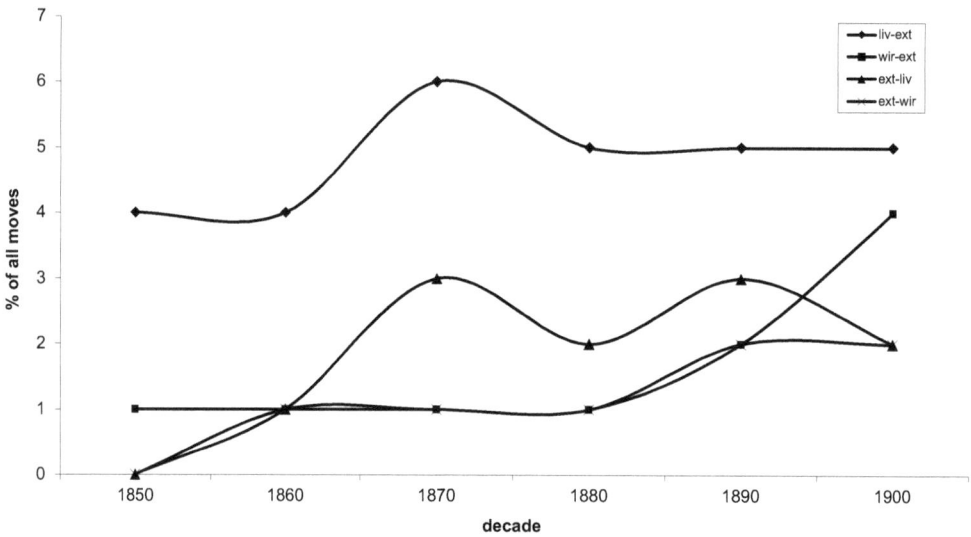

Figure 2.11b Moves into and out of Liverpool/Wirral (in per cent)

practice in the nineteenth century, especially at a time when many properties were rented and moving house was a relatively simple affair, at least for middle-class families. To investigate the extent of short-distance mobility, moves within one postcode district were analysed in detail with Birkenhead (CH41) chosen as a sample area. It was found that only one in eight merchants was resident in Birkenhead for two or more successive censuses. However, it cannot be concluded from this that an overwhelming majority moved away from Birkenhead each decade, because a significant proportion of those identified at a particular date as merchants in one or other of the main sources used to construct the database were not found in subsequent years. This methodological problem is therefore likely to account for what appears to be an extremely high turnover of residents. But of those who were identified as remaining in Birkenhead (CH41) for two or more decades, 46 per cent were registered during these years as moving to another residence within the same postcode district. Despite methodological reservations which reflect the nature of the source material used in this study, if the mobility rate within Birkenhead is compared with the movement between postcodes (Figure 2.8a), it seems reasonable to conclude that it was slightly more common for merchants to move within a locality than to migrate between districts.[66]

(vi)   The Wealth of the Merchant Community

According to the poet Walter Allingham, writing in 1873 under the pseudonym of Patricius Walker, the 'comfortable and luxurious villas' which could be found in the countryside for miles around Liverpool were simply a reflection of the ability of 'ship-owners, ship-insurers, corn merchants, cotton brokers, emigrant agents, etc., etc.' to make money.[67] But although Liverpool's growth in the decades prior to the outbreak of the First World War reflected the success of its shipowners, merchants, and bankers, detailed information on the accumulation and distribution of wealth within the business community is limited and little is known about the lives of the 'rich and powerful'.[68] The slave trade, despite its high risks, had generated considerable wealth for a significant number of Liverpool merchants as well as other members of the business community, while 40 local firms benefited directly from substantial compensation payments to slave-holders in the 1830s.[69] Contemporary commentators were well aware of the extent of wealth, at least in specific cases: the cotton broker, E. E. Edwards, was able to retire after a few years in business 'with a handsome fortune'; George Holt, who played a prominent role in the cotton trade, 'became exceedingly wealthy'; while the merchant John Marke Wood, who was also a director of the Bank of Liverpool, the Mersey Forge Company, and the Sea Insurance Company, was reputed to be in 'very comfortable circumstances'.[70]

At a national level, probate and tax data, despite their limitations, reflect Liverpool's status as the 'greatest of northern commercial cities'. Income tax data for 1800–01 suggest that 3 per cent of the total population controlled 56 per cent of the town's total income, with the top four taxpayers registering an average income of £17,000. Indeed, it was not uncommon for 40 to 50 per cent of total income in towns and cities during the early nineteenth century to be held by the top 5 per cent of households. In 1850, 11,343 houses were subject to the Window Tax Assessment in comparison with only 7,754 in Manchester; it accounted for almost 15 per cent of all declared millionaires, including some who belonged to Britain's most wealthy families; and the number of residents subject to Schedule D in income tax assessment was noticeably higher than in Manchester, Glasgow, Edinburgh, or Dublin.[71]

In order to cast some light on overall trends in wealth-holding and the relative distribution of wealth within the different elements of the mercantile community, the probate records of 218 members of the Wellington Club were examined. The Wellington Club was very much an elite establishment where 'naval and military officers, distinguished foreigners, aristocrats, and others important enough' were taken 'to make acquaintance with our most brilliant social section in its most dazzling phase' and, to this extent, the probate valuations of its members are not strictly representative of the business community as a whole.[72] Nevertheless, a significant proportion of the sample who died between 1860 and 1918 were involved in general merchanting or brokerage (35.1 per cent), in the trade in raw materials or foodstuffs (30.3 and 8.9 per cent respectively), or in shipping (13.1 per cent). Some of Liverpool's most prominent citizens were elected to the Club's council, including J. Hartley Bibby (copper-smelter), Charles H. Brancker (general broker), and Heywood Bright (general merchant), while the Graves brothers, who were well known in commercial circles, were equally 'prominent and popular' in 'that social sphere of which the Wellington Club is the central point'.[73]

The general trend in wealth-holding is instructive (Table 2.5), although it must be borne in mind that probate valuations, at least in several cases, included fortunes acquired, in part, through family inheritance rather than commercial acumen. They reflected the accumulation of assets over the life cycle of individual members of the merchant community, as well as the negative

Table 2.5 Liverpool's mercantile community (members of the Wellington Club): median probate wealth by decade, 1860–1950 (in 2019 prices)

Decade	Wealth £	Sample Size	Decade	Wealth £	Sample Size
1860	10,740,000	2	1910	5,129,000	36
1870	4,169,000	20	1920	5,591,000	23
1880	13,590,000	13	1930	6,546,000	28
1890	7,340,000	39	1940	2,531,000	14
1900	3,602,000	37	1950	1,809,000	6

Source: MLP database; probate records; membership data of the Wellington Club

Table 2.6 Median probate wealth by occupation, 1860–1918, for members of the Wellington Club (in 2019 prices)

Occupation	Wealth £	No.	Occupation	Wealth £	No.
General broker	22,090,000	15	Finance broker	15,420,000	4
Cotton broker	19,890,000	23	Shipowner	14,700,000	17
Raw materials broker	17,890,000	4	Merchant	5,700,000	70

Source: MLP database; probate records; membership data of the Wellington Club

impact in some cases of premature death. More importantly, they only recorded the value of the personal effects of the deceased, excluding landed property, investments in stocks and shares, and bequests that had already been made. If the onset of the 'Great (or Long) Depression' in the 1870s, with its adverse impact on Liverpool's trade, was reflected by a decline in median probate wealth, the recovery in wealth-holding by the following decade was very substantial. However, this trend was not maintained: there was a cumulative fall in the relative wealth of elite merchants during the 1890s and 1900s. There was a modest recovery between 1910 and the end of the inter-war period, but the significant collapse by the 1950s reflected a long-term deterioration in Liverpool's position as a major international port.[74]

Within the merchant community, there was a significant degree of variation in the level of wealth-holding by main occupation (Table 2.6).[75] In general, brokers, irrespective of their specific role, were able to accumulate a higher level of wealth than shipowners, while merchants were far less likely to enjoy the apparent benefits of extreme riches. But their collective wealth-holding profile was overshadowed by members of the Wellington Club who were engaged primarily in industry, whose median probate valuation exceeded £30 million. This group included the brewer and colliery owner Sir Andrew Barclay Walker whose personal effects were valued on his death at Gateacre Grange in 1893 at £303,700,000 (at 2019 prices). It represented 'an amount very rarely equalled in Liverpool' and was one of the largest fortunes registered in Britain in the nineteenth century, although it excluded extensive freehold property, in particular Osmaston Manor in Derbyshire, which had been purchased in 1884 for £250,000.[76] Nine members of the Wellington Club directly involved with the business community had a personal wealth at death in excess of £50 million, but four of them, including Walker, had made their fortunes in other sectors of the local or regional economy and not primarily in commerce and trade. The sugar refiner Sir Henry Tate had accumulated £132m, despite his extensive philanthropy; the ship-builder (and later shipowner) Sir Thomas Royden, whose shipyard was the only one still in operation on the east side of the Mersey at the end of the nineteenth century, bequeathed £66.2m to his successors; while the soap manufacturer Thomas Sutton Timmis, who had been one of the managers of William Gossage & Sons at the Soapery in Widnes, as well as a director of the Royal Insurance Co. Ltd, left £62.1m.[77]

However, the profitability of shipowning was reflected in the wealth-holding of four individuals. James Jenkinson Bibby inherited a 'substantial shipping business' from his father; he played a key role in the creation of the Liverpool & Mediterranean Screw Steam Shipping Co. in 1850; and became the first chairman of the Liverpool Steamship Owners' Association in 1858. He was a 'hugely wealthy' man and left a substantial fortune which was valued at £165,100,000.[78] Sir Edward Bates was regarded as one of Liverpool's 'principal shipowners' who enjoyed 'astonishing success in securing opulence' and grew 'richer and richer as years passed', primarily as a result of expanding his fleet by reinvesting earnings and by exploiting the insurance value of so-called 'coffin ships'. On his death in October 1896 his personal wealth was valued at £87.5m, but this did not include Gryn Castle near Holywell in Flintshire with its 367-acre estate which he had purchased in 1853, or a country house and two further landed estates.[79] The firm of T. & J. Brocklebank Ltd. played a critical role in the development of the Peruvian guano trade; it accounted for a significant proportion of Liverpool's trade with India; and by the early 1840s it owned at least 50 vessels. Sir Thomas Brocklebank had been born in 1814, the only son of Wilson and Anne Fisher, but he had assumed the Brocklebank family name in 1845 under the terms of the will of his late uncle, Thomas. The firm, with its extensive fleet of sailing ships, became one of the largest shipowners and merchants in Liverpool and by the end of the nineteenth century it 'remained unsurpassed' as a private company. Thomas had only been made a partner in the firm in 1843, but five years later, he was able to purchase Storeton Village on the Wirral, with 1,171 acres and numerous cottages and houses, and his personal estate in 1906 was valued at over £66 million.[80] Finally, George Holt of Lamport & Holt also deserves to be classified as one of the elite shipowners. Although he was associated with many beneficent institutions in the city, including University College, his personal estate on death amounted to £64 million. The firm had been founded in 1845, trading initially with North and South America, as well as South Africa and India, and it enjoyed the 'highest reputation' on account of the extent of its operations and the way in which business was conducted. Its success also enabled the partners to enjoy significant wealth.[81]

The evidence on wealth-holding amongst the elite members of the Wellington Club is instructive. Firstly, shipowners and industrialists dominated the select pantheon whose private estates exceeded £50 million. Commerce lay at the heart of the local economy and some of the very wealthy shipowners continued to operate as merchants, yet its only representative was the general merchant Hans Gaspard Schintz who had been born in Switzerland and died at Childwall Hall in July 1912 with a fortune valued at £87.2 million.[82] Secondly, although the median probate wealth of brokers, in general, exceeded that of shipowners, the further expansion of Liverpool's international trading role during the second half of the nineteenth century meant that shipowning offered unparalleled opportunities for a small group of individuals. Apart from those who were members of the Wellington Club, other shipowners left a substantial personal estate at death, including Frederick Leyland (1832–1892), Robert Rankin (1830–1898), Thomas Henry Ismay (1837–1899), and Alexander Elder (1834–1915), whose effects were valued (in 2019 prices) at £73.7m, £40.4m, £56.3m, and £22.9m respectively. But some prominent families, such as the Rathbones and the Muspratts were arguably 'never all that wealthy' and the dividing line between the multi-millionaires and those who were simply rich was very marked.[83] Indeed, membership of the Wellington Club was no guarantee of ultimate success, whether commercially or socially. Pierre Mussabini had been born in Smyrna in 1818: he became a successful cotton broker and was the Ottoman Consul in Liverpool. But his business with his co-partner Emmanuel Pantoleon Draco was liquidated in 1875 under the terms of the Bankruptcy Act of 1869, although at the time of his death in 1898 his estate was valued at £156,700.[84] Other members of the merchant community suffered far more dramatically from the consequences of business failure: for example, the personal effects of the broker George Edwin Taunton who died in 1894 were only valued at £105.60.

For many contemporaries the size of a household's domestic establishment was a reliable indicator of its social status and a direct reflection of the master's wealth, although the number of servants retained by households reflected a range of factors, including the size and composition of individual families, the civil status and age of their members, the cost of retaining an appropriate establishment, and the residual wealth of the household head.[85] In the absence of comprehensive data on the income and wealth of the merchant community as a whole, the number of servants employed in individual households in the second half of the nineteenth century can be taken as proxy indicator of the relative wealth and standing of the occupants. Table 2.7 gives the average number of servants in Liverpool merchant households per decade, broken down by modern postcode areas.

Table 2.7 The average number of servants per merchant household in Liverpool and on the Wirral, 1851–1901

Postcode	1851	1861	1871	1881	1891	1901
ALL	2.5	2.4	2.3	2.1	2.0	1.9
CH41	2.1	2.0	1.9	1.7	1.3	1.3
CH42	2.0	2.3	1.6	1.3	1.3	1.2
CH43	2.2	2.5	2.4	2.7	2.6	2.7
CH44	1.6	1.8	1.6	1.9	0.7	0.6
CH45	2.8	2.7	2.5	1.9	1.4	1.3
CH46					0	1.5
CH47	3.0		2.4	1.6	2.0	2.4
CH48	2.7	2.2	3.3	3.6	2.6	4.0
CH49	2.0		4.0	4.0	3.9	3.6
CH60	4.0		4.0	2.9	3.4	2.0
CH61				4.0	1.7	
CH62	2.0	4.7	2.7	2.9	3.0	4.2
CH63	1.0	1.9	1.9	2.2	3.2	2.0
CH64	2.5	4.3	3.2	4.4	3.4	2.8
CH66	1.0		3.0	3.0	2.7	1.5
L1	2.2	2.4	2.1	2.0	2.9	1.4
L11			2.0	0	2.3	
L12	4.2	3.8	4.6	4.7	4.3	3.3
L13	3.3	2.8	2.7	1.7	1.6	1.5
L14	4.2	2.0	3.5	3.0	1.3	1.2
L15	3.5	2.7	3.4	2.5	2.1	1.9
L16		5.0			0	
L17	3.8	3.5	3.7	3.1	3.3	3.2
L18	6.9	6.5	5.1	4.4	4.7	3.8
L19	2.6	3.7	3.0	2.9	2.6	2.4
L2		4.0	1.0		0	2.0
L20	2.3	1.8	1.6	1.2	1.2	1.1
L21	2.7	2.3	2.4	2.2	1.6	1.6
L22	2.4	2.2	2.5	2.2	1.7	1.5
L23	2.0	1.8	2.8	2.3	2.2	2.2
L24	2.0			1.5	2.8	
L25	5.5	4.3	3.6	4.7	4.9	5.3
L26	3.0					
L27					10.0	
L28			5.0			
L29				2.3		
L3	1.8	1.8	1.4	1.4	0.8	0.6
L31	2.0			1.9		
L34			4.0	2.0	1.5	
L35	2.5			2.4	2.6	2.0
L36	4.9	3.9	3.0	2.9	3.0	2.4
L4	2.5	1.6	1.8	0.9	0.7	0.6
L5	2.2	1.7	1.2	0.8	0.7	0.4
L6	2.1	2.0	1.6	1.2	1.1	1.0
L69	3.1	2.6	3.7	2.2	2.3	2.2
L7	2.3	2.0	2.2	1.6	1.2	1.3
L8	2.2	2.3	2.4	2.3	2.1	1.9
L9	3.6	2.2	2.1	1.7	1.9	1.5
X	1.0	3.0	3.9	2.5	1.8	3.2

Source: MLP database

Taking all Liverpool and Wirral postcodes together, there was a remarkably steady, slow, downward trend in the servant count over the entire period, for which there could be various explanations. From the early nineteenth century there had been an increase in the absolute number of domestic servants in Liverpool which reflected an expansion in trade, the growth of the middle classes, and an apparent reduction in the amount of household work undertaken by wives and daughters because of an 'excessive demand' for female servants.[86] A major port, such as Liverpool, offered an increasing range of employment opportunities for general servants, chambermaids, cooks, housekeepers, ladies' maids, nurses, pantry maids, sewing maids, and tea maids, in addition to laundresses and washerwomen. Although the number of female domestic servants increased by approximately 23 per cent between 1871 and 1901, their relative importance within the female population gradually declined and their share of the female work force fell from 43.6 per cent (1861) to 34.1 per cent (1911), while even in locations dominated by elite families, such as Abercromby Square, the servant ratio (the number of servants per 100 households) reached its peak by 1901.[87]

Various explanations have been put forward to explain a trend that was evident increasingly in many towns and cities. On the supply side, most servants, particularly maids, had seen little improvement in their wages prior to 1860; the wage premium for age or experience was small; and opportunities for promotion were rare. But in the absence of alternative employment options, life-cycle service continued to represent a well-established, rational choice. Increased urbanisation, fuelled by high rates of in-migration by younger age cohorts, accelerated the relative decline in rural population, while the further growth of a consumer society, with the development of large-scale retailing outlets, provided an alternative to domestic service where employees could be dismissed instantly for defying 'proper orders' and some women were undoubtedly subject to abuse, ill-treatment, and condescending or denigrating attitudes (although their scale is difficult to determine). For most women, domestic employment was seldom pleasurable and there was a high turnover in personnel. From the 1850s onwards Liverpool's profile as a retailing centre was reinforced by the establishment of a series of large-scale retailing stores, including George Henry Lee (1853), Lewis's (1856), Compton House in Church Street (1867), Owen Owen (1868), Blackler's (1909), Woolworth's first British store (1909), and T. J. Hughes (1912). Bold Street acquired an enviable reputation as the 'Bond Street of the North' with a range of dining facilities to cater for those who needed to recuperate from shopping expeditions, including the 'Grand Salon' at the Yamen Café.[88] The department stores, sometimes known as 'universal providers', together with an expanding service, provided employment opportunities for large numbers of young women. In addition to fixed hours of work, some of them offered a half day off each week and a trust fund for retired members of staff. It is not surprising, therefore, that there were increasing complaints in the late nineteenth century at the shortage of domestic servants as wider changes in consumption patterns took place. Moreover, it was a problem which could not be resolved by exploiting the potential of continental European countries, such as Norway and Sweden, which still had an extensive rural population and where young women were believed to be hard-working and obedient.[89]

In terms of the changing demand pattern for servants, by the 1890s domestic labour was gradually being substituted by household machinery, including electrically powered upright vacuum cleaners, wringer washers, and gas cookers, the purchase of which was offset by savings in servant wages and the cost of board and lodging. As a publication from 1913 emphasised, the 'rich-householder, the striving working mistress, the solitary, the helpless, the thriftless and the shiftless' would remain dependent on servants, but 'all other people might possibly be happier, healthier and wealthier if servantless'. They might also escape coping with the high turnover of servants and the unavoidable problems of sharing their house with strangers. Even high-quality, semi-detached villas built in the mid-nineteenth century often failed to incorporate a back stair-case, so that the master and mistress of the house, together with their children, could not avoid close physical contact with servants whose prime site of production was in the basement, but whose sleeping quarters were in the attic. Once domestic service became *declassé*, it lost its traditional function and became stigmatised, particularly amongst professional women.[90]

It is difficult to determine whether the gradual, downward trend in the average number of servants retained by members of the merchant community was a result of a decline in relative wealth or, more likely, a reflection of a tendency for the wealthy to move elsewhere in a search of residential exclusiveness and their replacement by a less prosperous class of tradesman. Certainly, within specific postcodes very clear trends emerge which can be related directly to the changing fortunes of the area. For example, the average servant count of merchant households in Bootle (L20) fell from 2.3 to 1.1 (1851–1901) as the area changed its character. The decline was even more marked in L4 and L5, covering Walton and Everton and Vauxhall, where the servant count dropped from 2.5 to 0.6, and from 2.2 to 0.4 respectively, reflecting the fact that by the end of the nineteenth century both areas had ceased to be popular as a residential location for even moderately wealthy merchants.[91] By contrast, other areas were consistently popular, such as Sefton Park (L17) with a servant count of around 3.5, which reflected not only the avail-ability of quality housing but also the increasing provision of urban parks, including Princes Park (1842), Sefton Park (1872), and Greenbank Park (1897).[92] For example, the area surround-ing Sefton Park in the early twentieth century remained 'fairly costly and responsible'.[93] On the Wirral, Wallasey and New Brighton (CH44 and CH45) were districts where the relative wealth of resident merchants appears to have declined as the construction of 'cheap lodging houses' and the increasing popularity of New Brighton as a 'resort of the tripper', prompted families which had been attracted in earlier days by 'villas and excellent residences' to relocate elsewhere.[94] The reverse was true in others areas such as Prenton (CH43) with its bowling, cricket, and golf clubs and the pleasant seaside district of West Kirby (CH48) where the rail-link to Liverpool via Birkenhead (opened in 1878) made commuting a practical reality.[95]

Within specific occupation groups, however, the size of the domestic establishment varied greatly. For the purposes of comparative analysis, the 250 trades of Liverpool merchants listed in the trade directories have been grouped under eight broad headings according to the nature of the commodity traded. Thus, cotton brokers and cotton merchants were classified together under 'raw materials', ship brokers, shipping agents, and shipowners under 'shipping', and banking and insurance trades under 'finance'. In Table 2.8, the average number of servants per merchant household within each of these categories is compared for each decade of the study.

Table 2.8 Average number of servants by trade of merchant head of household, 1851–1901

Commodity	1851	1861	1871	1881	1891	1901
ALL	2.5	2.4	2.3	2.1	2.0	1.9
Finance	2.6	2.3	2.0	2.0	2.2	2.5
Foodstuffs	2.1	2.2	2.1	1.9	1.8	1.7
Fuel	1.9	1.8	1.4	1.4	1.1	1.3
General	2.7	2.5	2.5	2.5	2.5	2.5
Land		0	1.2	1.2	0.9	1.3
Manufactures	2.4	2.6	2.0	2.1	1.7	1.6
Raw Materials	2.4	2.4	2.4	2.2	2.1	2.1
Shipping	2.2	2.2	2.5	2.5	2.8	2.9

Source: MLP database

Figure 2.12a charts the increase in wealth (as represented by the number of servants) of merchants engaged in shipping and finance, relative to the norm for all trades considered together (with 100 on the scale reflecting the average number of servants for the merchant population as a whole).

On aggregate, merchants engaged in shipping enjoyed significant rise in relative prosperity. From a position in the 1850s when they were generally rather less wealthy than the norm (88 per cent of the average), by the beginning of the twentieth century they were 50 per cent above the overall average. There was a consistent increase from the mid-nineteenth century in the net registered tonnage of shipping using the port of Liverpool, which also benefited from the general expansion of world trade from the 1880s onwards. Many of the port-city's leading shipowning families, such as the Holts, Harrisons, and MacIvers, played a critical role in expanding the global operation of their business enterprises, and the growth in capital accumulation in the ten principal shipping lines was particularly marked.[96] Their relative wealth was very substantial indeed. By the early twentieth century, Sudley, the Holt family home, had one of the highest rateable assessments within the West Derby Union, excluding separate valuations for a lodge, a cottage, piggeries, parkland, and a plantation, while the capital book value of J. Bruce Ismay's estate in June 1917 was over £1.4 million (excluding investments and cash held in the name of his wife).[97]

Despite the growth of banking and the development of financial institutions in Liverpool between the early 1770s and 1825, many of the private banks remained small businesses with continued links with commerce and trade.[98] Following the crisis of 1825 northern textile firms became increasingly dependent on Liverpool banking houses whose individual partners increasingly enjoyed considerable wealth.[99] In 1839, J. H. Schröder opened in Liverpool and in the same year Frederick Huth & Co. established a local branch, thereby strengthening links with Anglo-German banks in London.[100] It is not surprising, therefore, that financiers started from a slightly higher position in terms of relative wealth, but by the 1860s they had already been overtaken by shipping entrepreneurs. Although they enjoyed a similar and probably not unrelated rise throughout the rest of the century, they always remained about ten percentage points below the estimated wealth of shipping magnates.

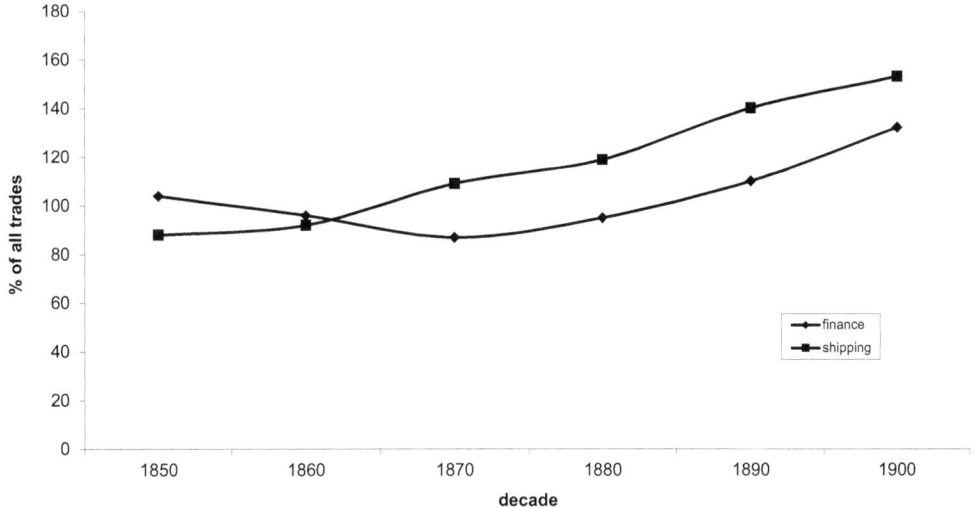

Figure 2.12a Average number of servants (shipping and finance) as a percentage of all trades, 1851–1901

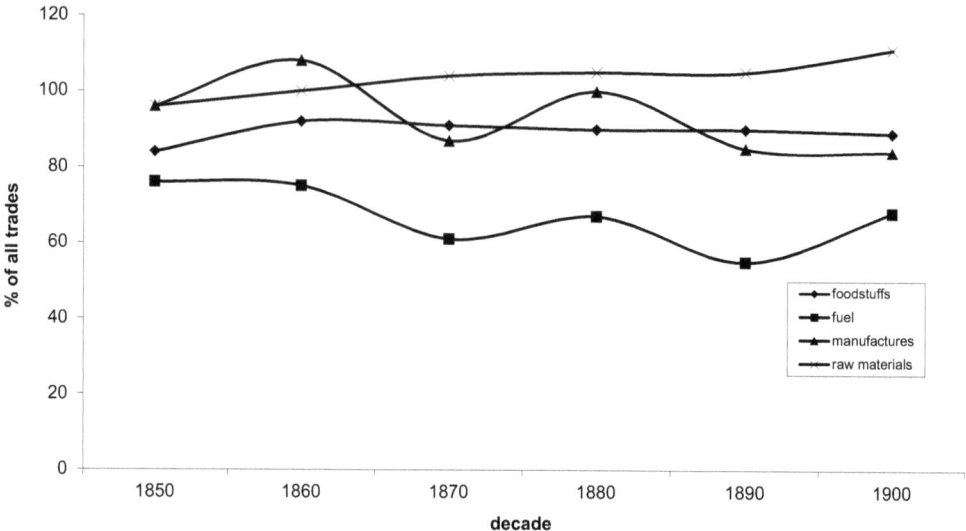

Figure 2.12b Average number of servants by trade category (foodstuffs, fuel, manufactures, and raw materials) as percentage of all trades, 1851–1901

As far as other trades were concerned (Figure 2.12b), they were relatively less prosperous, tracking the general trend in the average number of servants per household. Thus, fuel merchants (principally those involved in the coal trade) had between 60 and 80 per cent of the average number of servants in the merchant community in general, whereas manufacturers registered a slight decline from 5 to 10 per cent above the average to a similar margin below. The servant count of those dealing in raw materials including cotton climbed steadily, but at a slower rate than finance and shipping from slightly below the average in the 1850s to about 10 per cent above by the end of the century. All these cases suffer to some extent from the amalgamation in these categories of wealthy and less prosperous elements, but plausible trends are still discernible.

In fact, the size of the domestic establishment within specific occupation groups varied greatly, as a comparison between the households of cotton brokers and coal merchants reveals (see Table 2.7). By the mid-nineteenth century, Liverpool had become the world's leading cotton market and local cotton brokers exercised considerable power and influence, but the coal trade, despite its increasing importance, had lower entry costs and it was less well organised.[101] Despite these differences, the maximum number of servants in both cases seldom exceeded ten or eleven, although the households of cotton merchants retained on average a higher number of domestic servants in line with their greater wealth. However, there were households with family dependents in both occupational groups which did not employ any resident domestic servants, revealing substantial income variations within the business community. Individual Liverpool households sometimes employed a large number of domestic servants and in a minority of cases the size of the servant establishment was a clear reflection of considerable wealth, bearing in mind Mrs. Beeton's recommendation that a family with around £1,000 per annum would be expected to retain a cook, an upper- and undermaid, and a manservant.[102] Twelve households were registered as employing 30 servants each and a similar number had domestic establishments of 22 or 23. In the early 1860s, Emma Holt, the daughter of the prominent cotton broker and shipowner George Holt, regularly gave Christmas presents to 15 servants, including a pocket handkerchief in 1862 to Jarvis who had been 'only a week' in employment.[103] In 1901, the household of a foreign import merchant, Stewart H. Brown (who was also a retired banker), contained nine female servants, a butler, and a footman, with two coachmen, a groom, and a gardener, together with their families, accommodated in cottages in the grounds.

By contrast, almost 5,000 households within the merchant community had no servants, while 11,431 had only one, even when family circumstances would have justified a larger establishment. The German cotton merchant Julius Alexander Prior and his Liverpool-born wife Edith only retained a single domestic servant in 1901, despite living in a solidly middle-class area close to Sefton Park.[104] The contrast within a specific occupational group was particularly visible amongst coal merchants. In 1851, John Grant Morris, who lived in Grassendale Abbey, Aigburth, employed eight servants, including six women and a male groom in the house, together with a gardener (with his family) in a separate lodge. The coal merchant, William Minshall, however, lived in a predominantly working-class area of Birkenhead (at 35 Mallaby Street): although he operated in 1912 out of a coal-yard in neighbouring Brassey Street, the family income was clearly inadequate for supporting a domestic servant, even if there had been sufficient space in the family home.[105]

(vii) Nationality and Country of Birth

A clear majority of Liverpool merchants were native to the UK, with 7,425 born in England, 993 Scots, 682 Irish, and 370 Welsh. But the merchant community included a significant proportion born overseas, whose presence was celebrated each year by the holding of the Foreigners' Ball in honour of the 'numerous foreigners' who had settled in Liverpool.[106] Figure 2.13 shows the composition of this part of the community over the period of the study.

It is immediately clear that by far the biggest group were continental Europeans (excluding the 44 individuals born in Greece who were included in the Near East category, along with 29 Turks, 7 Egyptians, and 8 Syrians). Among the continental Europeans, Germans formed the largest group with a total of 224 individuals over the half-century covered by the data.[107] The

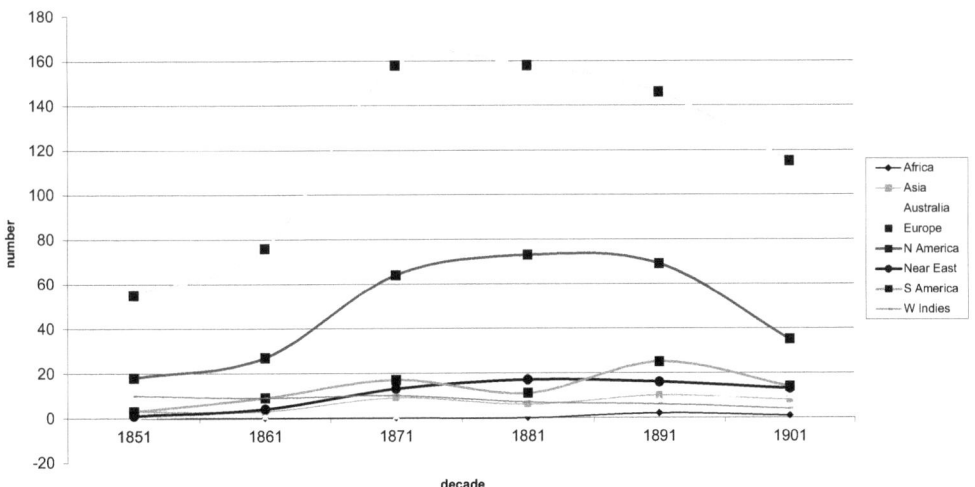

Figure 2.13 Country of birth of merchants born overseas, 1851–1901

only other sizeable group were the North Americans (USA and Canada) who generally numbered about one third of the Europeans: 95 had been born in the USA and 92 were Canadians. In addition, there were a small number of merchants trading in Liverpool from most other parts of the globe.

However, it is instructive to note that the largest foreign-born group came from continental Europe, a region which accounted for the greatest share (38 per cent) of British overseas trade in the period 1854–56, while the second most important in-migrant group came from North America which was the country's next biggest trading partner (responsible for 23 per cent of overseas trade).[108] As far as Liverpool's trade in the mid-nineteenth century was concerned, North America (in particular the United States) remained the premier trading region, despite the growth of new business opportunities in the Far East and Latin America, but the second most important trade was with continental Europe which registered a consistent increase in total value between 1854 and 1875.[109] If Liverpool's trade with North America attracted a considerable number of in-migrant merchants, whether from the United States or Canada, the disproportionate presence of traders from continental Europe reflected Liverpool's role as an important trading intermediary re-exporting produce from America and the colonies, with cotton re-exports reaching their peak in the 1870s and 1880s.[110] Significantly, the following decades witnessed a reduction in the number of overseas merchants from both continental Europe and North America, although the representation of other international regions was unaffected by changes in the pattern of Liverpool's overseas trade.

In general, foreign-born merchants were economic migrants who sought to exploit the new opportunities offered by Liverpool's increasing role in international trade.[111] For example, William Brown, who had been born in Baltimore, quickly established a reputation for 'unquestionable security' as a merchant banker, having started his business career in Liverpool in 1810 as an importer of American produce, while in-migrants from a number of countries not only profited individually from the port's increasing pre-eminence in trade and shipping, but also extended and reinforced the international networks which underpinned its overall growth throughout the nineteenth century. If Stephen Barker Guion, who had been born in New York in 1820, effectively exploited the growing demand in the emigrant trade for steerage accommodation, initially by founding the Black Star Line, the shipping company established in 1864 by Ramon de Larrinaga (and two other Spanish nationals) subsequently extended its services to the Far East and the Caribbean.[112] German merchant houses played a 'crucial role' in sustaining the growth of the British textile industry, by facilitating trade with continental Europe; Norwegian shipowners quickly recognised the port's significance as a gateway into new trades and successfully developed an important and highly specialised role in the North Atlantic timber trade; and Greek-born merchants, described by Orchard as 'shrewd and prosperous', utilised their extensive trading contacts in the Eastern Mediterranean and the Levant to consolidate Liverpool's role as a major importer of cotton, raisins, and wheat while opening up new markets for textile exports in a region where the British mercantile presence remained weak.[113] Indeed, by the late 1860s the Greek (Chiot) presence was already substantial: Ralli Brothers had established a sizeable branch in Liverpool and P. Schilizzi & Co. (shipowners) was classified as a 'good' (if second-rate) firm.[114] However, the extent to which in-migrants were able to benefit from the expansion of trade and commerce varied considerably depending on a range of factors, including the profitability of trade with their country or region of origin, the extent and effectiveness of their networking within Liverpool's business community, the success of marriage strategies in consolidating business links, and the relative attractiveness of assimilation in comparison with the retention of ethnic identity or overseas status.

Table 2.9 The average number of servants by place of birth of head of household

Place of Birth	1851	1861	1871	1881	1891	1901
ALL	2.5	2.4	2.3	2.1	2.0	1.9
Africa					1.5	1
Asia	2.0	2.0	3.4	2.0	3.6	2.5
Australia		2.0	1.0	2.0	1.6	3.3
Continental Europe	2.2	2.2	2.6	2.4	2.2	2.3
N America	2.5	2.1	2.5	2.7	2.9	3.3
Near East	3.0	3.5	3.3	2.2	2.4	2.8
S America	3.0	3.0	3.4	3.7	3.6	4.0
UK	2.4	2.3	2.2	2.0	2.0	2.0
W Indies	3.5	3.2	3.2	2.6	3.0	3.8

Source: MLP database

Something of the wealth and standing of merchants from overseas may be gleaned from Table 2.9, which shows the average number of servants retained by merchants who had been born in various parts of the world.

In some cases the figures are based on a small sample size, but in-migrant merchants (particularly those from Asia, continental Europe, and North and South America) were not affected to the same extent as the business community as a whole by the relative decline in the average number of domestic servants between 1851 and 1901.[115] In fact, in five cases (Asia, Australia, continental Europe, and North and South America), the size of the domestic establishment was actually greater in 1901 than it had been in the mid-nineteenth century. Indeed, the evidence suggests that merchants born in South and North America and Australia, together with in-migrants from the Near East, were disproportionately successful in accumulating and retaining wealth as reflected in this size of their domestic establishment.

However, even within specific in-migrant groups there were wide variations in their relative wealth as measured by the size and composition of their household establishments. This was certainly the case as far as German-born merchants were concerned. In 1901 the commission merchant Theodor von Heyder (of Blessing, Braun & Co.) employed ten servants, including seven females and one male groom, at his residence, Stone House, Yewtree Road, Allerton, together with a coachman and a gardener who lived separately with their own families in the grounds of the property. But there were other in-migrants who failed to maintain any domestic staff, despite the presence in some cases of young children. The family home of the wine agent, John Kind, in 1901 contained five children, but no domestic staff. His 21-year-old son, John, worked as a clerk in the family firm and some of the co-resident daughters may well have helped with domestic tasks, but the family's income was apparently insufficient to justify the employment of a resident servant.[116] To this extent, in-migration did not necessarily lead to commercial success and ethnic communities remained highly fragmented in terms of wealth and social status.

The willingness of in-migrant merchants to acquire British citizenship can also be used as indicator for their acculturation and integration within the Liverpool business community. In most cases, naturalisation was sought for economic reasons, primarily to access credit or to acquire landed property, since British nationality was often a requirement for opening a bank account. It also enabled merchants who had been born overseas to play a political role within the local community or to stand for office with potential commercial benefits.[117] Naturalisation implied a long-term commitment to settling in Britain, if not the city of Liverpool, but it was

Table 2.10 The origins of merchants who became naturalised British subjects (by region)

Origin	Number of Merchants
Continental Europe	133
N America	6
Near East	11
S America	4
W Indies	1

Source: MLP database

much more prevalent among continental Europeans than the second largest group of foreign-born merchants from North America (Table 2.10).

Almost two-thirds (65.5 per cent) of the foreign-born merchants who successfully sought British nationality were from Germany and its constituent federal states.[118] In contrast to the eighteenth century when only 15 naturalised German merchants are known to have settled in Liverpool, the simplification of naturalisation procedures after 1844 encouraged a significant proportion of German-born merchants to become British citizens during the second half of the nineteenth century, despite the fact that migrants from Prussia and other German states were entitled to a ten-year period of uninterrupted residence abroad without automatically losing their citizenship.[119] The absence of personal papers makes it difficult to infer the reasons behind individual naturalisation decisions, but their propensity to seek British citizenship was probably influenced by long-standing trading links with Germany, in particular with the Hanseatic city states of Bremen and Hamburg, as well as their important role as trading intermediaries between Britain and the continent specifically in cotton and other colonial goods.[120]

In some cases, naturalisation reflected ethnic or religious considerations, since Jewish merchants from Frankfurt, Hamburg, and other German cities sought a commercial environment which was not restricted by political considerations or discrimination. In Liverpool, they found a ready market for their skills and the 'opulence' of the local community was visible in the 'new and elegant' synagogue which was opened in 1808.[121] More importantly, the decision to obtain naturalisation was affected by the choice of a local bride, whether from Liverpool or Merseyside. Over one third of the German merchants who obtained naturalisation had married locally and such a decision was reinforced by the presence of children, particularly when they had been born in Liverpool or elsewhere in Great Britain. To this extent, a high rate of intermarriage, which can be viewed as an important element of business networking within the merchant community, was a critical factor in accounting for the predominance of German-born merchants amongst the list of naturalised British subjects. But it was also affected by wider political considerations: some of the most successful German merchants had applied for naturalisation in the late 1840s, whereas the rise of German nationalism in the late nineteenth century had been accompanied by a marked decline in the propensity to seek British citizenship.[122]

By contrast, very few of the other European or overseas in-migrant merchants ever applied for naturalisation. Although ten Greek, nine Dutch, and eight Turkish merchants sought British citizenship, the combined total for all other nationalities was still below the figure for German in-migrants alone. Although there were numerous visitors to Liverpool from the United States of America, the resident business community was 'constantly changing': Nathaniel Hawthorne quickly established himself in 1853 as his country's consul in Liverpool, but his period in office was relatively brief; very few of his co-patriots remained in the city for longer than a decade; and the majority were simply transients who regarded themselves primarily as 'citizens of the world'.[123] At times, a merchant's ties to his country of birth remained extremely strong. Even after the restructuring in 1885 of the shipping line founded over 20 years earlier by Ramon de Larrinaga and Jose Antonio de Olano, the ships continued to be registered in Bilbao, reflecting the Basque origins of its principal founder. In other cases, the deliberate emphasis on the need to retain close kinship links meant that in-migrant merchants sometimes 'lived in a world of their own'. A petition forwarded to the King of Sweden in 1883 designed to secure funds for the construction of a Scandinavian church in Liverpool was signed by 53 individuals, including a number of merchants, ship brokers, and agents, who were regarded as 'new English', but it was intended to sustain Lutheranism, as well as the language and culture of the constituent Nordic countries, while Nicholas G. Paspati, 'the best known local representative of the great Greek firm, Ralli Brothers', like many of his fellow countrymen, 'lived much apart from the native social circles', in a community dedicated to the preservation of Greek language and the Orthodox religion.[124] Indeed, on those rare occasions when membership was sought in elite clubs and associations it was sometimes undertaken as collective community strategy, as was the case in 1863 when 16 Greek cotton merchants became members of the Royal Mersey Yacht Club.[125]

In terms of their residential location, Table 2.11 indicates that foreign-born merchants were unevenly spread throughout the city, but they tended to be concentrated in certain areas. In the

Table 2.11 Merchants born overseas as a percentage of all merchants resident in modern postcode areas*

Postcode Area	1850	1880	1900
L1	5	17	11
L3	3	–	26
L5	5	3	6
L6	8	4	7
L69	7	–	*
L7	8	11	3
L8	9	20	13
L12	*	23	12
L13	–	8	3
L15	6	13	5
L17	5	17	18
L18	–	24	11
L19	10	9	4
L21	9	8	3
L22	*	6	8
L23	–	7	6
L25	–	16	14
CH41	8	7	5
CH42	5	5	2
CH43	4	9	6
CH44	8	12	–
CH45	4	3	6
CH47	*	7	5
CH48	–	–	4
CH62	–	–	7
CH63	–	9	3

* Denotes a small sample indicating figures that cannot be relied upon to be representative. The exact number of overseas-born merchants was as follows: L69 14 (1900); L12 5 (1850); L22 9 (1850); and CH47 1 (1850).

Source: MLP database

1880s, for example, those born overseas made up 20 per cent of the merchant community in modern-day L8, corresponding to Toxteth, and a remarkable 24 per cent in the high-class Mossley Hill district of L18 (which Table 2.6 shows had an average of 4.4 servants per household, compared with the overall average among Liverpool merchants at that time of 2.1). West Derby, in particular Sandfield Park, was also an important enclave for successful German-born merchants: John A. Bencke (who had been born in Danzig in 1814) built 'Oliva' in Sandfield Park in 1855, while other residents included the general merchants Emil Springmann and Francis C. Braun, as well as Gustavus C. Schwabe who was the first resident of Broughton Hall (designed by Walter Scott and completed around 1858–59).[126] Hayman's Green in West Derby attracted a number of wealthy German in-migrants, including the general merchant Augustus Tappenbeck, the cotton merchant Gustav Busch, and the cotton broker Edward P. Busch. By contrast, many of the Greek merchants, including Michael A. Ralli, together with 'most of the other foreigners of a similar class', tended to congregate around Princes Park and Sefton Park which had a lower proportion of 'best known families'. Some foreign-born merchants were related, with close family connections confirmed by newspaper accounts of their funerals.[127]

Despite the fact that a small number of wealthy overseas merchants became pillars of Liverpool society with a high level of integration, residential concentration was particularly marked in the early 1880s but less evident at the beginning of the twentieth century when a number of districts (including L7, L8, and CH44) witnessed a marked decline in the presence of overseas merchants. A higher degree of concentration at an earlier stage in Liverpool's development reflected changes over time in the overall scale of in-migration with new entrants in the business community arguably seeking informal support from existing residents, whereas their reduced presence in Toxteth (L8) and Seacombe (CH44) reflected a general decline in the popularity of these districts as locations for merchant settlement. By contrast, L3 (one of the original suburbs close to the city centre) registered a considerable increase in the presence of overseas merchants, but these were largely new or temporary migrants who were able to occupy premises vacated by more established members of the business community.

Conclusion

The Mercantile Liverpool Project set out to study the nature and composition of a community of merchants in a thriving port in the half century or so before the First World War. Some of the key features of this community were identified by collecting both commercial and personal information relating to Liverpool merchants from a variety of sources which was then collated in a relational database in order to establish individual-level linkages from the different sources.

The picture which emerged was of a community of around 3,000 to 4,000 individuals. The overall number of merchants active in Liverpool increased markedly from the 1850s to reach a peak of 4,435 by the early 1890s, but this was followed by a relatively rapid decline to a level just above the level for the mid-nineteenth century. The bulk of the merchants were engaged in trading a range of commodities and there was relatively little specialisation, although an exclusive concentration on a particular trade was certainly not unknown. As the century progressed, many sole traders and partnerships were replaced or transformed into joint-stock companies with boards of directors employing professional managers. This was especially so in capital-intensive businesses, pre-eminently for Liverpool in shipping, whereas 'pure trading' businesses, such as brokers, continued to operate for the most part as partnerships.

In common with Liverpool's middle-class population in general, merchants moved their residence frequently, renting or purchasing better quality housing as their fortunes rose, or relocating to less expensive areas of the city if their business enterprises failed to thrive. Our analysis showed that they frequently moved just a short distance to another house in the same street or just around the corner. But there was a similar level of mobility between different city districts or within the Merseyside region as a whole. The most marked and easily explained internal migration was from the crowded streets of the Liverpool central business district to the more attractive residential communities of Birkenhead and the Wirral in general, a move which was facilitated by improved rail and ferry links across the Mersey. But merchants who prospered as a result of the business opportunities which Liverpool offered sometimes failed to retain any loyalty to the city and emigrated elsewhere, often acquiring landed property in the North West or in London, while businessmen faced with bankruptcy or the collapse of their commercial operations also favoured out-migration as a means of avoiding their creditors.

The community of merchants was highly fragmented in terms of relative wealth (as measured by the number of domestic servants), ranging from humble retail coal merchants who supplied domestic households in a few local streets, to extremely wealthy shipping magnates such as T. H. Ismay, the MacIvers, and the Holts. Such people naturally chose to live in different and discreet neighbourhoods. Although out-migration from the urban core was already evident in the late eighteenth century, the period after 1850 witnessed a significant movement of merchants out of the city centre as part of wider process of suburbanisation which increasingly favoured more rural or relatively undeveloped locations, such as Blundellsands and Cressington Park, as well as Heswall and West Kirby on the Wirral which were now more accessible as a result of improvements in the local transport infrastructure.[128] Conversely, inner-urban areas (such as L3 and L8) which had previously provided suitable accommodation for a significant number of merchants lost their popularity, while areas of initial settlement on the Wirral, including Birkenhead, Seacombe, and New Ferry, also witnessed a further out-migration of members of the business community.

The choice of trade also had a direct bearing on future wealth, although port-city business communities in general continued to confront an inflated degree of risk because of market volatility, losses at sea, warehouse fires, and imperfect information flows. But perhaps predictably, the fortunes of different trades (as measured by the size of the domestic establishment of individual traders) followed a differentiated trajectory, with financiers and those engaged in shipping registering a perceptible rise in estimated wealth in comparison with the *relative* impoverishment of traders in manufactures, foodstuffs, and fuel. Given that Liverpool's local economy was founded primarily on shipping-related activities and commercial distribution, it is not surprising that the data confirm the extent to which the port's prosperity had a visible effect on wealth accumulation by specific types of traders. And whilst Englishmen, by a wide margin, made up the majority of the merchant community—many of them drawn from the immediate hinterlands in Lancashire and Cheshire—there was a significant minority of traders from all continents and many countries, often reflecting the volume of trade conducted with their homelands, as befitted Liverpool's standing and *raison d'être* as a major international port.

In comparison with earlier studies of the mercantile community, whether resident in Liverpool or on the Wirral, this is the first attempt to analyse in detail its changing composition and structure between the mid-nineteenth century and the pre-1914 period. The MLP database served as a basis for exploring a range of themes, which are pursued in subsequent chapters. Because of funding and time constraints, as well as the loss over time of archival sources, membership details in several societies could not be inputted. In some cases, areas of merchant interaction, including membership of Freemason lodges, was only partially included in the database; there was no opportunity to include extensive data collated on their involvement in learned societies and clubs (whether political, social, or sporting); and other roles, such as their contribution to school management or the Volunteer Movement, have not been captured, although primary and secondary material have been utilised in the analysis.[129] Despite these limitations, the database provided a unique opportunity to reconstruct Merseyside's mercantile community in detail at a time when Liverpool continued to consolidate its role as one of the dominant ports in the world, even if signs of relative decline were already visible by the end of the nineteenth century. As such, it offers significant methodological benefits for analysing merchant communities in general, rather than depending on a limited sample of elite merchants; for assessing their wider contribution to civic development; and the extent to which the disproportionate importance of commerce and trade enabled them to exercise political influence.

Notes

1   The Gore's Directories in the Maritime Archives and Library were deposited by the Liverpool Underwriters' Association. A note of when each volume was received by the Association was written on the flyleaf.

2   The census dates in the late nineteenth century were 30 March 1851, 7 April 1861, 2 April 1871, 3 April 1881, 5 April 1891, and 31 March 1901. See Edward Higgs, *Making Sense of the Census Revisited: Census Records for England and Wales, 1801–1901* (London, 2005), p. 167.

3   A recent attempt is described in Sheryllynne Haggerty's study of the trading communities of Liverpool and Philadelphia in the late eighteenth century, *The British-Atlantic Trading Community 1760– 1810: Men, Women, and the Distribution of Goods* (Leiden, 2006).

4   An urban history project at Leicester University digitally reproduced various directories from the 1850s to the 1920s and its website has an excellent search engine. However, it is not a database but, more accurately, a provider of raw data like the original trade directories. The Digital Library of Historical Directories is available online at www.historicaldirectories.org.

5   Other databases focussing on shipping activities or maritime communities have adopted a similar approach, albeit using different software applications. See, for example, Jean-Pierre Dedieu, Silvia Marzagalli, Pierrick Pourchasse, and Werner Scheltjens, 'Navigocorpus: A Database for Shipping Information: A Methodological and Technical Introduction', *IJMH*, 23, 2 (2011), pp. 241–62; Silvia Marzagalli, 'Clio and the Machine: New Database Projects in Maritime History', *IJMH*, 24, 1 (2012), pp. 253–6; Stephen D. Behrendt, Carl W. Blackman, Linda R. Gray, and Robert A. Hurley, 'Designing a Multi-Source Relational Database: Liverpool as a Trading Port, 1700–1850', *IJMH*, 24, 1 (2012), pp. 265–300. The database was developed using Microsoft Access. Currently, it remains in this format, but steps are currently underway to transform it into a website hosted by the University of Liverpool to encourage further research on the available material. We are very grateful for funding support for making this possible, specifically from Mrs. Maureen Davies, Simon Davies and his wife Blanca, and from Andrew Douglas, a former student from the Department of Economic and Social History whose thesis was supervised by the late Peter Davies, as well as from an anonymous donor.

6   Bernard Guinness Orchard, *Liverpool's Legion of Honour* (Birkenhead, 1893); William Thomas Pike, *Liverpool and Birkenhead in the Twentieth Century: Contemporary Biographies* (Brighton, 1911).

7   By 'principal' records is meant those records deriving directly from the historical sources; when the records are added in that represent relationships between those records, the total is in the order of 350,000.

8   Other types of historical records have also been analysed using primarily automated processes, although with varying success. See, for example, Roger Schofield, 'Automatic Family Reconstitution: The Cambridge Experience', *Historical Methods*, 25, 2 (1992), pp. 75–9; Jeremy Atack and Fred Bateman, 'Matchmaker, Matchmaker, Make Me a Match', *Historical Methods*, 25, 2 (1992), pp. 67–74; Steven Ruggles, 'Linking Historical Censuses: A New Approach', *History and Computing*, 14, 1–2 (2003), pp. 213–24.

9   For literature on record linking for historical projects, see E. A. Wrigley (ed.), *Identifying People in the Past* (London, 1973), R. J. Morris, 'In Search of the Urban Middle Class: Record Linkage and Methodology: Leeds, 1832', in *Urban History Yearbook* (Leicester, 1976); *History and Computing: Special Issue on Record Linkage*, I (1992), II (1994); C. Harvey, E. Green and P. Corfield, 'Record Linkage Theory and Practice: An Experiment in the Application of Multiple Pass Linkage Algorithms', *History and Computing*, 8 (1996), pp. 78–89.

10 Jane E. Norton, *Guide to the National and Provincial Directories of England and Wales, Excluding London, Published before 1856* (Royal Historical Society. Guides and Handbooks No. 5) (London, 1950), p. 1.

11 A. Godley and O. M. Westall, 'Business History and Business Culture: An Introduction' and M. Casson, 'Culture as an Economic Asset', in A. Godley and O. M. Westall (eds.), *Business History and Business Culture* (Manchester, 1996), pp. 1, 48 respectively.

12 Richard Trainor, 'The Middle Class', in Martin Daunton (ed.), *TCUHB* (Cambridge, 2000), vol. 3, pp. 678–9.

13 Gareth Shaw, 'Directories as Sources in Urban History: A Review of British and Canadian Material', in *Urban History Yearbook* (Leicester, 1984), pp. 36–44.

14 Geoffrey Best, *Mid: Victorian Britain 1851–75* (London, 1971), p. 29. For detailed information on the population development of Liverpool in the nineteenth century, see Richard Lawton, 'The Components of Demographic Change in a Rapidly Growing Port-City: The Case of Liverpool in the Nineteenth Century', in Richard Lawton and Robert Lee (eds.), *Population and Society in Western European Port-Cities c.1650–1939* (Liverpool, 2002), pp. 91–123.

15 W. K. D. Davies, J. A. Giggs, and D. T. Herbert, 'Directories, Rate Books and the Commercial Structure of Towns', *Geography*, 238, 53, Part 1 (1968), p. 42.

16 Gareth Shaw, 'The Content and Reliability of Nineteenth-Century Trade Directories', *The Local Historian*, 13, 4 (1978), pp. 205–6; Norton, *Guide to the National and Provincial Directories*, p. 17; Mills, *Rural Community History*, p. 14.

17 Norton, *Guide to the National and Provincial Directories*, p. 18.

18 Mills, *Rural Community History*, p. 14.

19 However, no directory was published in 1852, 1854, 1861, and 1863: see James Boardman, *Liverpool Table Talk a Hundred Years Ago; or: A History of Gore's Directory with Anecdotes Illustrative of the Period of Its First Publication in 1766* (Liverpool, 1871), p. 53.

20 George T. Shaw, *The Liverpool Homes of Mrs. Hemans* (Liverpool, 1897), p. 10. The compilers of earlier directories had been 'careless' about the spelling of names and improvements in the numbering of houses had been adopted in 1839, 1856, and 1859.

21 J. A. Picton, 'History and Curiosities of the Liverpool Directory', *THSL&C*, 29 (1876–77), p. 12.

22 Shaw, 'Directories as Sources in Urban History', pp. 36–44; Penelope Corfield, 'Giving Directions to the Town: The Early Town Directories', in *Urban History Yearbook* (Leicester, 1984), p. 22; Adrian Jarvis, 'An Historical Backwater: The Fishing and Fish Trading of Liverpool', in *Northern Seas Yearbook* (Association for the History of the Northern Seas, Esbjerg, 1995), p. 53.

23 J. Benson, A. Alexander, D. Hodson, J. Jones, and G. Shaw, 'Sources for the Study of Urban Retailing, 1800–1950, with Particular Reference to Wolverhampton', *The Local Historian*, 29, 3 (1999), p. 172; Davies, Giggs and Herbert, 'Directories, Rate Books and the Commercial Structure of Towns', p. 42.

24 David J. Clarke, *Report on Liverpool Shipowners: 1820–1914*, unpublished PhD, Memorial University, Newfoundland (2005), pp. 7–8. The practice of dividing vessels into sixty-fourths did not become law until 1854, although it was a well-established tradition in shipowning.

25 Clarke, *Report on Liverpool Shipowners*, pp. 150, 156. See also Sarah R. Palmer, 'Investors in London Shipping, 1820–50', *Maritime History*, II (1972), pp. 46–68; S. Jones, 'Shipowning in Boston, Lincolnshire, 1836–1848', *Mariner's Mirror*, 65 (1979), pp. 339–49; Stephanie K. Jones, 'A Maritime History of the Port of Whitby, 1700–1914', unpublished PhD thesis, University of London (1982); Helen Doe, *Enterprise, Women and Shipping in the Nineteenth Century* (Woodbridge, 2009).

26 Graeme J. Milne, *Trade and Traders in Mid-Victorian Liverpool: Mercantile Business and the Making of a World Port* (Liverpool, 2000), pp. 137–8.

27 In 1861, for example, 175 men over the age of 20 were registered on Merseyside as shipowners (Birkenhead—42; Liverpool—59; West Derby—74). By 1881, however, shipowners appear to have been included in a wider occupational category (13) which covered 'Persons working and dealing in ships and boats', as opposed to ship, boat, or barge builders.

28 Higgs, *Making Sense of the Census Revisited*, pp. 24, 88–92.

29 Higgs, *Making Sense of the Census Revisited*, pp. 66–7. Richard Lawton, 'Census Data for Urban Areas', in Richard Lawton (ed.), *The Census and Social Structure: An Interpretative Guide to Nineteenth Century Censuses for England and Wales* (Abingdon, 1978), Chapter 3, pp. 82–145 (2012 reprint).

30 Higgs, *Making Sense of the Census Revisited*, pp. 136–7, 153–64, 204–5.

31 See Sari Mäenpää, Chapter 6. In addition, membership records were transcribed by hand from 22 societies, 9 hospitals or medical associations, 7 maritime charities, and 7 other charitable bodies in Liverpool.

32 John Macnab, *History of the Merchants' Lodge of Freemasons No. 241 Liverpool 1780–1907* (Liverpool, 1907).

33 Orchard, *Liverpool's Legion of Honour*, pp. 569, 707; Pike, *Liverpool and Birkenhead*. Use was also made of Pike's companion volume for Cheshire, *Cheshire at the Opening of the Twentieth Century: Contemporary Biographies* (Pike's New Century Series, 11) (Brighton, 1904) and other collective biographies, including *Our Shipping Highlights: A Collection of Biographical Sketches with Photographs . . . Reprinted from "the Syren & Shipping" . . ., Illustrated* (London, 1900) and J. Wallace Coop and Seymour Taylor, *Bulls and Bears: Cartoons of Members and Ring Traders of Liverpool Cotton Exchange* (reprinted from 'The Liverpool Courier') (Liverpool, 1908).

34 Although the number of cotton and corn brokers fell by 31.8 and 37.3 per cent respectively, there was a greater reduction in the number of listed ship brokers (47.3 per cent) and general brokers (68.1 per cent).

35 *Gore's Street Directory for Liverpool and Its Environs for 1859* (Liverpool, 1860).

36 MLP database. By 1912, the general and miscellaneous categories had been deleted from the Directory in the case of brokers, although 575 general agents were still listed (replacing the earlier designation of miscellaneous.

37 Mary B. Rose, 'The Family Firm in British Business, 1780–1914', in Maurice W. Kirby and Mary B. Rose (eds.), *Business Enterprise in Modern Britain* (London and New York, 1994), p. 79.

38 Leo H. Grindon, *Lancashire: Brief Historical and Descriptive Notes* (London, 1892), pp. 54–5.

39 For example, William Lockhart was a partner in the firm of Lockhart, Tozer & Co., listed as iron merchants. They also acted in 1871 as agents for at least six other companies selling iron, tin, and tinplate: see MLP database.

40 Milne, *Trade and Traders*, p. 97.

41 Rose, 'The Family Firm', p. 68.

42 Edward W. Sloan, 'The First (and Very Secret) International Steamship Cartel, 1850–1856', in David J. Starkey and Gelina Harlaftis (eds.), *Global Markets: The Internationalization of the Sea Transport Industries Since 1850* (Research in Maritime History, 14) (St John's Newfoundland, 1998), p. 39.

43 For the development of limited liability, see B. C. Hunt, *The Development of the Business Corporation in England, 1800–1867* (Cambridge, MA, 1936); John Saville, 'Sleeping Partnerships and Limited Liability, 1850–1856', *EcHR*, 8 (1956), pp. 418–33; Kevin F. Forbes, 'Limited Liability and the Development of the Business Corporation', *The Journal of Law, Economics and Organization*, 2, 1 (1988), pp. 163–77; J. R. Edwards, *A History of Financial Accounting* (London, 1989), chapter 9.

44 Francis E. Hyde, *Liverpool and the Mersey an Economic History of a Port 1700–1970* (Newton Abbot, 1971), pp. 63–4. The capital employed by the ten principal shipping lines increased between 1870 and 1880 from £3.5 million to £5.6 million.

45 Milne, *Trade and Traders*, p. 292.

46 Milne, *Trade and Traders*, p. 149; Robert Lee, 'Configuring the City: In-Migration, Labour Supply and Port Development in Nineteenth-Century Europe', *IJMH*, 17, 1 (2005), p. 104; Stana Nedadic, 'The Small Family Firm in Victorian Britain', *Business History*, 35 (1993), p. 93; Roy Church, 'Ossified or Dynamic? Structure, Markets and the Competitive Process in the British Business System of the Nineteenth Century', *BH*, 42, 1 (2000), pp. 1–20, specifically p. 14.

47 Derek H. Aldcroft and Harvey W. Richardson, *The British Economy 1870–1939* (London, 1969), p. 25; R. A. Church, *The Great Victorian Boom 1850–1873* (London and Basingstoke, 1975), p. 77; Franz von Juraschek, *Uebersichten der Weltwirtschaft, Band VI, 1885–1889* (Berlin and Bern, 1896), p. 705; Milne, *Trade and Traders*, p. 149.

48 Milne, *Trade and Traders*, pp. 149–50; James Boyd, 'Mechanising Migration: Transnational Relationships, Business Structure and Diffusing Steam on the Atlantic', *IJMH*, 32, 1 (2020), p. 19. Based on evidence from the Bills of Entry, only 21.3 per cent of the firms registered in 1855 were still operating 15 years later.

49 See the obituary for Fletcher Rogers in the *Liverpool Mercury*, 21 December 1891.

50 Thomas Baines, *Liverpool in 1859: The Port and Town of Liverpool and the Harbour, Docks and Commerce of the Mersey in 1859* (London, 1859), p. 119.

51 See Joseph Sharples, Chapter 5; Joseph Sharples and John Stonard, *Built on Commerce Liverpool's Central Business District* (Swindon, 2008), pp. 10, 19. Most of the cotton trade was conducted on

Exchange Flags until 1896 when the trade moved indoors to converted premises in neighbouring Brown's Building, prior to the construction of a new Cotton Exchange in 1905–6 in Old Hall Street. In fine weather the business of the corn trade was also transacted in Brunswick Street itself, but in 'stormy weather' it was conducted in offices and in the Corn Exchange.

52 Richard Lawton, 'From the Rural Port of Liverpool to the Conurbation of Merseyside', in William T. S. Gould and Alan G. Hodgkiss (eds.), *The Resources of Merseyside* (Liverpool, 1982), p. 3.

53 See, Joseph Sharples and Adrian Jarvis, Chapter 9.

54 http://edina.ac.uk/digimap/.

55 See, Joseph Sharples and Adrian Jarvis, Chapter 9; Robert Lee, Chapter 10.

56 William Enfield, *An Essay Towards the History of Liverpool* (Liverpool, 1773), p. 114; J. E. Allison, *Sidelights on Tranmere* (Tranmere, 1976), p. 67; see Joseph Sharples, Chapter 5.

57 James Hoult, *West Derby, Old Swan and Wavertree* (Liverpool, 1913), p. 153.

58 See, Joseph Sharples and Adrian Jarvis, Chapter 9.

59 See, Joseph Sharples, Chapter 8.

60 Martin J. Wiener, *English Culture and the Decline of the Industrial Spirit, 1850–1980* (Cambridge, 1981), p. 49; Lawton, 'The Components of Demographic Change', pp. 111–15.

61 For a more detailed discussion of the timing and motives behind the settlement of merchants on the Wirral, see Robert Lee, Chapter 10; for a wider discussion of the impact of transport improvements on residential mobility, see Joseph Sharples and Adrian Jarvis, Chapter 9.

62 Trainor, 'The Middle Class', p. 679. The equivalent figure for Birkenhead on the Wirral was 12.1 per cent. See Joseph Sharples and Adrian Jarvis, Chapter 9 and Robert Lee, Chapter 10.

63 Our methodology will have underestimated the actual number of times an individual moved house, since we counted as a move only moves from one postcode to another. A move to another house in the same postcode (a more common practice in the nineteenth century than nowadays) would not have been counted.

64 Colin G. Pooley, 'Patterns on the Ground: Urban Form, Residential Structure and the Social Construction of Space', in Daunton, *TCUHB, vol. 3: 1840–1950*, p. 445.

65 Some merchants effectively 'immured themselves in the fastness of North Wales'. See Hyde, *Liverpool and the Mersey*, p. 66.

66 In some cases, death also involved mobility so that the coffins of deceased merchants could be interred in family graves some distance from their last place of residence. For example, Thomas Bold's last residence was at 14 Hamilton Square, Birkenhead. He was a prominent member of the local Conservative party and 'at one time well known on the Liverpool Stock Exchange'. On his death in October 1883, he was buried in 'a massive oak coffin' in the family grave at St. James's Cemetery in Liverpool. The chief mourners were met by three coaches at the landing stage, having crossed the river Mersey by ferryboat. See 'The Late Mr. Thomas Bold', *LM*, 29 October 1883.

67 William Allingham, *Rambles* (by Patricius Walker) (London, 1873), p. 209.

68 Lane, *Liverpool Gateway of Empire*, p. 54.

69 J. E. Inikori, 'Market Structure and the Profits of the British African Trade in the Late Eighteenth Century', *Journal of Economic History*, 41, 4 (1981), pp. 745–76; Lynn Martin, 'Trade and Politics in 19th Century Liverpool: The Tobin and Horsfall Families and Liverpool's African Trade', *THSL&C*, 142 (1992), p. 105; Nicholas Draper, *The Price of Emancipation: Slave Ownership, Compensation and British Society at the End of Slavery* (Cambridge, 2009); Legacies of British Slave-Ownership database, www.ucl.ac.uk/lbs.

70 Orchard, *Liverpool's Legion of Honour*, pp. 641, 396, 730.

71 T. V. Jackson, 'British Incomes Circa 1800', *EcHR*, Ns, 52, 2 (1999), p. 280; J. G. Williamson, 'British Inequality during the Industrial Revolution: Accounting for the Kuznets Curve', in Y. S. Brenner, H. Kaeble and M. Thomas (eds.), *Income Distribution in Historical Perspective* (Cambridge, 1991), pp. 57–75; *Builder*, 20 April 1850, p. 189; W. D. Rubinstein, 'The Victorian Middle Classes: Wealth, Occupation and Geography', *EcHR*, 30, 4 (1977), pp. 602–23; 'British Millionaires, 1809–1949', *Bulletin of the Institute of Historical Research*, 116 (1974), pp. 202–23; *Men of Property: The Very Wealthy in Britain Since the Industrial Revolution* (London, 1981); Hartmut Berghoff, 'A Reply to W. D. Rubinstein's Response', *BH*, 34, 2 (1992), pp. 82–5. Until 1898 probate valuations excluded the value of unsettled land and it was only in 1926 that settled land was included; they did not reflect the transfer of assets prior to death; and the extent of tax avoidance is difficult to estimate, particularly after the increase in death duties in 1894.

72 Orchard, *Liverpool's Legion of Honour*, p. 53; see Sari Mäenpää, Chapter 6; Robert Lee, Chapter 11.

73   Orchard, *Liverpool's Legion of Honour*, pp. 174, 199, 202, 336–7. Heywood Bright was a director of the Lancashire & Yorkshire Railway Company, but no longer actively in business by the early 1890s.

74   For a more detailed discussion of probate data, see Robert Lee, Chapter 11.

75   It is important to note, however, that despite an increasing degree of specialisation, many members of the merchant community were still engaged in a range of interrelated commercial activities.

76   Orchard, *Liverpool's Legion of Honour*, pp. 690–1; Rubinstein, 'British Millionaires', p. 210; James Moore, 'The Art of Philanthropy? The Formation and Development of the Walker Art Gallery in Liverpool', *Museum and Society*, 2, 2 (2004), p. 72; Derbyshire Record Office, D1849/16/2/1–9, Wills, codicils and related papers of Andrew Barclay Walker 1865–1890. By the early 1870s, Walker had acquired extensive chains of public houses. Brewing, a key industry in the food, drink, and tobacco sector, inevitably involved substantial commercial activities. For the purpose of this analysis, however, it has been grouped with a small number of other industrial activities on Merseyside. See, also, Robert Lee, Chapter 12.

77   For further information, see Tom Jones, *Henry Tate 1819–1899 a Biographical Sketch* (Liverpool, 1960); J. A. Watson, *A Hundred Years of Sugar Refining the Story of Love Lane Refinery 1872–1972* (Liverpool, 1973); W. Heaton Wakefield, *A Brief History of Thomas Royden & Sons Liverpool 1808–1930* (Liverpool, 1931); Sir Ernest B. Royden, *Thomas Royden & Sons Shipbuilders Liverpool 1818–1893* (privately published, 1953); W. T. Pike, *Lancashire at Opening of XX Century Contemporary Biographies* (Brighton, 1903), p. 400; D. W. F. Hardie, *A History of the Chemical Industry of Widnes* (Birmingham, 1950), pp. 79, 125; Orchard, *Liverpool's Legion of Honour*, pp. 602–3, 662–3, 676. In November 1892, Sutton's partnership with Frederick H. Gossage was dissolved 'by mutual consent': see *The London Gazette*, 9 November 1894, 6296. See, also, Robert Lee, Chapter 12.

78   Milne, *Trade and Traders*, p. 138; Edward William Paget-Tomlinson, *Bibby Line: 175 Years of Achievement* (Liverpool, 1982), p. 6; Nigel Watson, *The Bibby Line 1807–1990: A Story of Wars, Booms and Slumps* (Liverpool, 1990), p. 24.

79   William Bower Forwood, *Recollections of a Busy Life: Being the Reminiscences of a Liverpool Merchant, 1840–1910* (Liverpool, 1910), p. 50; Milne, *Trade and Traders*, p. 134; Orchard, *Liverpool's Legion of Honour*, pp. 152–6.

80   John Frederic Gibson, *Brocklebanks, 1770–1950* (Liverpool, 1953); John Clarkson, *Anchor and Brocklebank Lines* (Preston, 1994); Dave Hollett, *More Precious Than Gold: The Story of the Peruvian Guano Trade* (Cranbury, NJ, 2008), p. 271; Forwood, *Recollections of a Busy Life*, p. 50; Orchard, *Liverpool's Legion of Honour*, pp. 205–6; MAL, B/BROC/12/1–19, History notes and documents.

81   Hyde, *Liverpool & the Mersey*, p. 53; Orchard, *Liverpool's Legion of Honour*, p. 397; Lamport & Holt, *The Lamport & Holt Line History 1845–1936* (Liverpool, 1936).

82   In the 1861 census Schintz, who had been born in Zurich in 1812, was enumerated as a general merchant residing at 16 Upper Canning Street. The only known biographical reference related to his wife Dora Cecilia, who was on the committee of the Refuge for Female Incurables. See Orchard, *Liverpool's Legion of Honour*, p. 621.

83   David Cannadine, 'Fred Freeman Annual Lecture on Philanthropy', University of Liverpool, 12 November 2013.

84   The liquidation of the cotton-broking firm that traded under the Mussabini name was initially announced in the *London Gazette* (14 April 1874). Mussabini was issued with his naturalisation certificate in October 1852, although he was registered in the 1851 as a British citizen resident at 22 Hamilton Square, Birkenhead.

85   Theresa McBride, *The Domestic Revolution: The Modernisation of Household Services in England and France 1820–1920* (London, 1976), p. 35; Robert Lee, 'Domestic Service and Female Domestic Servants: A Port-City Comparison of Bremen and Liverpool, 1850–1914', *History of the Family*, 10 (2005), p. 447.

86   *Census of England and Wales, 1871* (London, 1873), vol. 4, p. xlii; James Walvin, *English Urban Life 1776–1851* (London, 1984), p. 53.

87   Lee, 'Domestic Service and Female Domestic Servants', pp. 440–1; Adrian R. Allan, *The Building of Abercromby Square* (Liverpool, 1986).

88   See Robert Lee, Chapter 13.

89   Jacob F. Field, 'Domestic Service, Gender and Wages in Rural England, c.1700–1860', *EcHR*, 66, 1 (2013), pp. 249–72; Selina Todd, 'Domestic Service and Class Relations in Britain, 1900–1950', *Past and Present*, 203, 1 (2009), pp. 181–204; Eric W. Sager, 'The Transformation of the Canadian Domestic Servant, 1871–1931', *Social Science History*, 31, 4 (2007), pp. 509–30; Edward Higgs,

Domestic Servants and Households in Rochdale: 1851–1871 (London, 1986), Chapters 6 and 7; Witold Rybczynski, *Home a Short History of an Idea* (London, 1988), p. 155; Jon Stobart, 'The Shopping Streets of Provincial England, 1650–1840', in Jan Hein Furnée and Clé Lesger (eds.), *The Landscape of Consumption Shipping Streets and Cultures in Western Europe* (London, 2014), pp. 16–36; Jon Stobart, 'Cathedrals of Consumption? Provincial Department Stores in England, c.1880–1930', *Enterprise and Society*, 18, 4 (2017), pp. 810–45; Ian Mitchell, *Tradition and Innovation in English Retailing, 1700–1850: Narratives of Consumption* (Farnham, 2014), pp. 174–8. For an overview of the development of retailing, see D. Alexander, *Retailing in England during the Industrial Revolution* (London, 1970). For merchants and other businessmen the city centre offered grander dining facilities, such as the Baronial Dining Hall at the Crocodile Restaurant in Cable Street, 'The Only First-Class Continental Restaurant and Rendezvous for Connoisseurs in Town'.

90 Quentin Outram, 'The Demand for Residential Domestic Service in the London of 1901', *EcHR*, 70, 3 (2016), pp. 893–918; Mrs J. G. Frazer, *First Aid to the Servantless* (London, 1913) (reprinted as *The Servantless Household How to Cope: Some Polite Advice* (East Grinstead, nd.); Sheila McIsaac Cooper, 'Service to Servitude? The Decline and Demise of Life-Cycle Service in England', *The History of the Family*, 10, 4 (2005), pp. 367–86; Alison Mackinnon, *Love and Freedom: Professional Women and the Reshaping of Personal Life* (Cambridge, 1997); Pamela Horn, *The Rise and Fall of the Victorian Servant* (New York, 1975).

91 Joseph Leigh, 'One of the Most Pushing and Rich of Our Enterprising Merchants' who had been a resident of Everton subsequently moved to Belmont, 'a splendid place in Cheshire'. See James Aspinall, *Liverpool a Few Years Since by an Old Stager* (Liverpool, 1885), p. 56.

92 C.-F. Brown, 'Growth and Change: Princes Park and Sefton Park 1840–1961', unpublished Special Study, Liverpool University School of Architecture (1966); Katy Layton-Jones and Robert Lee, *Places of Health and Amusement Liverpool's Historic Parks and Gardens* (Swindon, 2008), pp. 15–21, 36–44; The Sefton Park Civic Society, *Sefton Park* (Liverpool, 1984).

93 *Liverpool Painted by J. Hamilton Hay Described by Dixon Scott* (London, 1907), p. 132.

94 George Livesey, 'Wallasey', in Alfred Holt (ed.), *Merseyside a Handbook to Liverpool District Prepared on the Occasion of the Meeting of the British Association for the Advancement of Science in Liverpool, September 1923* (Liverpool, 1923), p. 96; Antony M. Miller, *The Inviting Shore a Social History of New Brighton Part One 1830–1939* (Birkenhead, 1996); E. Cuthbert Woods and P. Calverwell Brown, *The Rise and Progress of Wallasey a History of the Borough* (Wallasey, 1929), p. 151.

95 John M. Birtwhistle, 'Old Prenton Remembered: The Growth of Prenton Golf Club and Woodchurch Road', *Wirral Champion Journal,* 13, 2 (2006), pp. 33–6; W. H. Heaps, *The History of the Parish of Prenton the Churches of St. Stephen and St. Alban* (Prenton, 1995), p. 5; John Brownbill, *West Kirby and Hilbre a Parochial History* (Liverpool, 1928), pp. 80–1; John W. Graham, *Steel Wheels to Deeside the Wirral Railway Past and Present* (Rock Ferry, 1983); The population of Hoylake and West Kirby increased from 3,722 (1881) to 14,009 (1911). See Robert Lee, Chapter 10.

96 Francis E. Hyde, 'The Growth of Liverpool's Trade 1700–1950', in W. Smith (ed.), *A Scientific Study of Merseyside* (Liverpool, 1953), pp. 148–63; *Liverpool and the Mersey: An Economic History of a Port 1700–1970* (Newton Abbott, 1971), pp. 96–100; Francis E. Hyde, with contributions from J. R. Harris and A. M. Bourn, *Shipping Enterprise and Management 1830–1939 Harrisons of Liverpool* (Liverpool, 1967); Tony Lane, *Liverpool Gateway of Empire* (London, 1987), p. 5; H. MacIver, *Clan Iver* (Liverpool, 1912); Malcolm Falkus, *The Blue Funnel Legend a History of the Ocean Steam Ship Company, 1865–1973* (Basingstoke, 1990). Between 1865 and 1875, for example, the capital employed in the ten principal shipping lines increased from £3.5 to £5.6 million: see Hyde, *Liverpool and the Mersey*, p. 64.

97 MMM, MAL, DX/504/1/1–15, Papers relating to J. Bruce Ismay's House, Sandheys, Mossley Hill Road; DX/504/6/1–12, Papers relating to the will of J. Bruce Ismay (1912–17).

98 Hyde, *Liverpool and the Mersey*, p. 19; Sheila Marriner, *The Economic and Social Development of Merseyside* (London and Canberra, 1982), p. 41; M. Collins and P. Hudson, 'Provincial Bank Lending: Yorkshire and Merseyside, 1826–60', *Bulletin of Economic Research*, 31 (1979), pp. 69–79; Michael Collins, *Banks and Industrial Finance in Britain 1800–1939* (Houndmills, 1991), p. 24; Stanley Chapman, *Merchant Enterprise in Britain from the Industrial Revolution to World War I* (Cambridge, 1992), pp. 147–8; B. L. Anderson and P. L. Cottrell, 'Another Victorian Capital Market: A Study of Banking and Bank Investors on Merseyside', *EcHR*, 28 (1975), pp. 598–61; W. A. Thomas, *The Provincial Stock Exchanges* (London, 1973).

99 For a discussion of the relative wealth of bankers in Victorian Britain, see W. D. Rubinstein, 'The Victorian Middle Classes: Wealth, Occupation and Geography', *EcHR*, 30 (1976), pp. 602–23; José Harris and Pat Thane, 'British and European Bankers, 1880–1914: An "Aristocratic" Bourgeoisie', in Pat Thane, Geoffrey Crossick, and Roderick Floud (eds.), *The Power of the Past: Essays for Eric Hobsbawm* (Cambridge, 1984), pp. 215–34; Yossef Cassis, 'Bankers in English Society in the Late Nineteenth Century', *EHR*, 38 (1985), pp. 201–29.

100 J. H. Schröder & Co., which was managed initially by Nikolaus Mahs and Charles W. H. Pickering, was established to exploit the potential for increased cotton shipments from the southern states of America, while the Liverpool branch of Huth & Co. was intended to take over all the agency services which had previously been undertaken by local firms. See Richard Roberts, *Schroders, Merchants & Bankers* (London, 1992); Manuel Llorca-Jaña, 'The Economic Activities of a Global Merchant-Banker in Chile: Huth & Co. of London, 1820s–1850s', *Historia* (Santiago), 45, 2 (2012); Wolfgang Sartor, *Das Haus Mahs Eine internationale Unternehmerfamilie im Russischen Reich 1750–1918* (St Petersburg, 2009), p. 31.

101 David Williams, 'Liverpool Merchants and the Cotton Trade, 1820–1850', in J. R. Harris (ed.), *Liverpool and Merseyside: Essays in the Economic and Social History of the Port and Its Hinterland* (London, 1969), pp. 182–211; Nigel Hall, 'The Liverpool Cotton Market: Britain's First Futures Marker', *THSL&C*, 149 (2000), pp. 99–118; Sari Mäenpää, 'Combining Business and Pleasure? Cotton Brokers in the Liverpool Business Community in the Late Nineteenth Century', in Adrian Jarvis and Robert Lee (eds.), *Trade, Migration and Urban Networks in Port Cities c.1640–1940* (Research in Maritime History, No. 38) (St. John's Newfoundland, 2008), pp. 149–67.

102 I. M. Beeton, *The Book of Household Management* (London, 1861); Molly Harrison, *The Kitchen in History* (Reading, 1972), p. 106.

103 LRO, 920 DUR 3/29/5, Emma Holt (1802–71), Correspondence and papers. See also Sari Mäenpää, Chapter 7.

104 MLP database.

105 MLP database. William Minshall subsequently lived at 334 Park Road North: he was Robert Lee's maternal grandfather.

106 In 1892, the committee for the Foreigners' Ball consisted of 214 members, many of whom were drawn from the in-migrant merchant community, including the cotton merchant Demetrius A. Galetti (D. A. Galetti & Co.), Constantine C. M. Ralli (Ralli Bros), and Edward C. Sanxay, an oil importer and the sole agent for E. H. Kellogg & Co., who had been born in New York in 1849, together with a number of prominent representatives from the German community. Although some members of the committee, such as the American cotton importer Andrew Fachivi, were only active in Liverpool for a limited period, a significant number were second generation residents: see Orchard, *Liverpool's Legion of Honour*, pp. 37–8, 363–4. The annual ball was initiated by the Liverpool Society of Friends of Foreigners in Distress and its committee was congratulated in 1882 on the 'success and eclat' of the event which was held at the Philharmonic Hall in Hope Street: see *Liverpool Journal*, 14 January 1882.

107 Robert Lee, 'Divided Loyalties? In-Migration, Ethnicity and Identity: The Integration of German Merchants in Nineteenth-Century Liverpool', *BH*, 54, 2 (2012), pp. 117–54. In addition, there were a few German-speaking Austrians in the mercantile community, while even before the 'Compromise' of 1867 and the formal endorsement of the Dual Monarchies of Austria and Hungary, Hungarian-born residents in Liverpool were registered as Hungarian. In most cases, they were craftsmen (including tailors and upholsterers), while merchants tended to be transient and were listed in the census returns as lodgers or boarders. The Hungarian community in Liverpool included some Jewish families. For an insight into the Hungarian presence on Merseyside, we are grateful to Nigel Swain. See also John Pinfold, 'A Burden Upon the Public or Fighters for Liberty? The Reception of Hungarian and Polish Refugees in Liverpool in 1851, Part 1', *Liverpool History Journal*, 17 (2018).

108 These figures on British overseas trade relate to the period 1854–56 and are taken from Simon Ville, 'The Growth of Specialization in English Shipowning, 1750–1850', *EcHR*, 46 (1993), pp. 702–22, specifically p. 710.

109 Milne, *Trade and Traders*, pp. 55–7, Figure 3.1.

110 Stanley Chapman, *The Rise of Merchant Banking* (London, 1984), p. 5.

111 This had certainly been the case in relation to German in-migrants in the late eighteenth century. See Margrit Schulte Beerbühl, 'German Migrants in Eighteenth-Century Liverpool', unpublished paper, International Urban History Congress, Stockholm (2006).

112 Aytoun Ellis, *Heir of Adventure the Story of Brown, Shipley & Co. Merchant Bankers* (London, 1960), p. iv; Milne, *Trade and Traders*, pp. 142–4; R. W. Jordan, 'Larrinagas of Liverpool', *Sea Breezes*, 48 (January 1974), pp. 81–94.

113 Chandler, *The Rise of Merchant Banking*, p. 145; Eivind Merok and Espen Ekberg, 'Norwegian Shipping in the Port of Liverpool, 1855–1895: Niche Specialization and the Anglo-Norwegian Networks', *IJMH*, 21, 2 (2009), pp. 221–40; Orchard, *Liverpool's Legion of Honour*, p. 71; Maria Christina Chatziioannou, 'Greek Merchants in Victorian England', in Dimitris Tziovas (ed.), *Greek Diaspora and Migration since 1700: Society, Politics and Culture* (Farnham, 2009), pp. 45–60; Geoffrey Jones, *Merchants to Multinationals: British Trading Companies in the Nineteenth and Twentieth Centuries* (Oxford, 2000), p. 25; Ioanna Pepelasis Minoglou and Helen Louri, 'Diaspora Entrepreneurial Networks in the Black Sea and Greece, 1870–1915', *Journal of European Economic History*, 26 (1997), pp. 69–104.

114 London Metropolitan Archives, CLC/B/186/MS23822, Ralli Bros. Ltd., correspondence 1868–72.

115 For an overview of contemporary trends, see Pamela Horn, *The Rise and Fall of the Victorian Servant* (Thrupp, 1990). In fact, the total number of female domestic servants in Liverpool increased by approximately 23 per cent between 1871 and 1901, based on the adjusted figure for 1871 and including those under 20 years of age, although their relative importance within the female workforce declined. See Lee, 'Domestic Service and Female Domestic Servants', p. 440.

116 MLP database; Lee, 'Divided Loyalties?', pp. 117–53.

117 Margrit Schulte Beerbühl, 'Naturalization and Economic Integration: The German Merchant Community in 18th-Century London', in Randolph Vigne and Charles Littleton (eds.), *From Strangers to Citizens: The Integration of Immigrant Communities in Britain, Ireland and Colonial America, 1550–1750* (Brighton, 2001), pp. 511–18; Chapman, *Merchant Enterprise in Britain*, p. 132.

118 Those naming pre-unification birthplaces such as Prussia, Bavaria, etc., have all been included in the category 'Germans'.

119 Margrit Schulte Beerbühl, 'German Migrants in Eighteenth-Century Liverpool', unpublished paper presented at an International Workshop on German Migrants and European Development: In-Migration, Acculturation and Identity from the Eighteenth Century to the Present Day, Centre for Port and Maritime History, University of Liverpool, 5–6 September 2008; Andreas Fahrmeier, 'Nineteenth Century Citizenships: A Reconsideration', *Historical Journal*, 40, 3 (1997), pp. 721–55; Howard Sargent, 'Diasporic Citizens: Germans Abroad in the Framing of German Citizenship Laws', in Krista O'Donnell, Renate Bridenthal, and Nancy Reagin (eds.), *The Heimat Abroad the Boundaries of Germanness* (Ann Arbor, 2005), pp. 18–30.

120 Chapman, *The Rise of Merchant Banking*, p. 5; Nigel Hall, 'The Emergence of the Liverpool Raw Cotton Market, 1800–1850', *Northern History*, 38, 1 (2001), pp. 65–81.

121 David Cesarani, 'The Jews of Bristol and Liverpool, 1750–1850: Port Jewish Communities in the Shadow of Slavery', in David Cesarani and Gemma Roman (eds.), *Jews and Port Cities 1590–1990 Commerce, Community and Cosmopolitanism* (Edgware and Portland, 2006), p. 152; *The Stranger in Liverpool, or, an Historical and Descriptive View of the Town of Liverpool and Its Environs* (2nd ed., Liverpool, 1810), p. 99.

122 On the basis of 88 German naturalisation papers held in the National Archives, the decadal distribution was as follows (percentage figures in brackets): 1840s—8 (9.0); 1850s—7 (7.9); 1860s—30 (34.0); 1870s—19 (21.5); 1880s—17 (19.3); 1890s—7 (7.9); 1900s—0 (0).

123 David Seed (ed.), *American Travellers in Liverpool* (Liverpool, 2008); Chapman, *Merchant Enterprise*, pp. 150–1; Bill Ellis (ed.), *Nathanial Hawthorne the Consular Letters 1853–1855* (Ohio, 1988), p. 13; 'Americans in Liverpool', *The Liverpool Critic* (January 13, 1877), vol. 2, p. 22; LRO, Hq 050 LIV.

124 Robert Lee, *From Scandinavia to Liverpool: A History of Merseyside's Nordic Community* (Liverpool, 2008), p. 4; Orchard, *Liverpool's Legion of Honour*, p. 539; Chatziioannou, 'Greek Merchants in Victorian England', p. 57; Maria-Christina Chatziioannu and Gelina Harlaftis, 'From the Levant to the City of London: Mercantile Credit in the Greek International Commercial Network of the Eighteenth and Nineteenth Centuries', in Philip L. Cottrell, Even Lange and Ulf Olsson et al. (eds.), *Centres and Peripheries in Banking: The Historic Development of Financial Markets* (Aldershot, 2007), pp. 14–40. For information on the Greek Orthodox Church of St Nicholas which opened in 1870, see Sarah Brown and Peter de Figueiredo, *Religion and Place Liverpool's Historic Places of Worship* (Swindon, 2008), p. 27.

125 Mike Stammers, 'The Royal Mersey Yacht Club: A Social History, 1844–1944', *THSL&C*, 159 (2010), p. 110; MLP database.

126 J. G. Cooper and A. D. Power, *A History of West Derby* (Ormskirk, 1982), pp. 162, 236, 250; Joseph Sharples, *Merchant Palaces Liverpool and Wirral Mansions Photographed by Bedford Lemere & Co.* (Liverpool, 2007), pp. 16–18. The idea for the creation of the Oceanic Steam Navigation Company, subsequently known as the White Star Line, was apparently suggested by Schwabe to Thomas Henry Ismay during a game of billiards at Broughton Hall.

127 Orchard, *Liverpool's Legion of Honour*, p. 71; Stephen Guy, 'A History of Lowlands', *Liverpool History Journal*, 12 (2013), p. 4; Joseph Sharples, 'The Residential Development of Sefton Park, Liverpool c.1872–c.1900', *THSL&C*, 165 (2016), pp. 57–78. For example, the brothers Constantine Constantine Ralli and George Constantine Ralli were virtual neighbours in Linnet Lane, while the first four park-side villas approved by the Toxteth Urban District Council in August 1872 were built for Greek merchants.

128 See Joseph Sharples and Adrian Jarvis, Chapter 9, and Robert Lee, Chapter 10.

129 See Robert Lee, Chapter 12.

3   The Business Environment

Graeme Milne

Business historians have done a great deal of work on Liverpool. Indeed, the 1950s and 1960s saw the emergence of a distinct Liverpool School of maritime-business history, so called because most of its members had posts at Liverpool University and its main focus was on Liverpool firms and archives—this continues to be cited as a key influence on the development of company history, especially in the maritime sector.[1] The Liverpool School is best known for its close forensic accounting of corporate finance and management, but it also raised a number of questions, less fashionable at the time, which re-emerged in the new business history of the 1990s and 2000s. For example, Davies's work on Henry Tyrer, a shipbroker, demonstrated the importance of small, specialist intermediary firms in shipping and commerce. Anderson raised issues surrounding networks of information and finance, which have recently become central to the wider discipline, while Marriner's research into the Rathbone family assessed the roles of religion and kinship and helped to demonstrate that trading firms, and not just major steamship companies, could be studied profitably.[2]

The latest generation of maritime-business historians has made rather less use of Liverpool evidence. To cite just two examples, Boyce's work is widely seen as the core text of a new focus on information, networks and institutional structures in the maritime sector and offers a major alternative perspective to internal managerial histories of firms in the Chandler tradition, while Chapman focuses on issues of reputation and knowledge in the growth of multinational trading firms.[3] Both use some evidence from Liverpool companies, but they are less concerned with the question of whether particular places were unusually conducive to business formation and development.

Bringing questions of locality and environment together with a better grasp of business processes and practices is therefore an evident way forward. Here, the recent historiography mainly focuses on the manufacturing sector and its tendency to cluster into 'industrial districts', often tracing its interpretive roots back to the work of Alfred Marshall and his quest to define the industrial 'atmosphere' that characterised such places.[4] Maritime and commercial cities like Liverpool add another dimension to this kind of work, given that interactions between firms were even more important in urban centres with large numbers of small firms, many of which worked in brokering roles. Just as it provided crucial evidence for an earlier school of business history, therefore, Liverpool's trading community can again serve as an important case study.

Trade, Shipping and Victorian Globalisation

During the second half of the nineteenth century, British manufacturing and commercial capitalism accelerated to world dominance in many fields, building a maritime-industrial complex of unprecedented scale and scope. Other countries industrialised in turn, and others still became

DOI: 10.4324/9781315597836-3

producers of foodstuffs and raw materials to supply the needs of the urbanising northern hemisphere. People moved in unprecedented numbers during a long boom in migration from the 1840s to the beginning of the twentieth century, creating an increasingly integrated world system of producers, traders and consumers.[5] These patterns are important in their own right, but their particular significance here is in the opportunities they created for business and the nature of business responses. Victorian globalisation was, at root, managed by the trading communities of a few major port cities, and ultimately by individual merchants, brokers, shipowners, their clerks and other employees. Many inter-related dynamics were at work, but three have special prominence in Liverpool's development: the transition from sail to steam, the boom in Atlantic migration and mobility, and the increasing globalisation of trade in raw and partly processed commodities.

The transition from sail to steam increased the locational concentration of the shipping industry into a relatively small number of ports, both in ownership and operation, because of the high capital demands of the ships themselves and the infrastructure surrounding them. Only ports with large and growing traffic in general cargo could justify the fullest development of docks, quays, landing-stages, railway connections, warehouses and all their associated built environments, which in turn encouraged further investment in larger ships. Even in the middle decades of the nineteenth century, ports like Liverpool were working on a considerable scale, and entrepreneurs seeking to work in the major steam routes had little prospect of doing so from lesser ports. Liverpool therefore became a well-known magnet for aspiring businessmen.[6]

Liverpool's shift from sail to steam was also a transition from external to local ship-owning. Up to the 1850s, Liverpool was largely a sailing-ship port, dominated by American shipowners on the Atlantic routes; thereafter, the accelerating trend was toward steam services operated by Liverpool owners. Liverpool steam entrepreneurs also created new capacity and regularity in the Mediterranean and West African trades, and shortly afterward on the Far East routes. The diversity and interconnectivity of trades and services allowed individuals to develop their technical and managerial skills and raise capital, becoming better equipped to take advantage of engineering advances and economic opportunity. Luck was also important: the American Civil War effectively closed down the operations of the US shipping industry; by the end of the 1860s the north Atlantic routes were dominated by large steam fleets owned in Liverpool.

One of the most important drivers of steamship development was the boom in Atlantic passenger and emigrant traffic, which encouraged entrepreneurs to create the high-profile shipping lines that cemented Liverpool's image as a major port city.[7] The Atlantic passenger trade also developed a complicated local web of ancillary businesses and networks as firms struggled for market share. This created opportunities for small businesses in brokering, agency and intermediary roles, but also for innovation in systems and processes. The White Star Line was reportedly the first to organise through-booking with US and Canadian railway companies, so that travellers could leave Liverpool already armed with tickets for their final destinations anywhere in North America.[8] Protecting emigrants from exploitation became a priority after scandals in the 1840s and passenger shipping firms began to place great weight on their reputations for safety and honesty: they also learned to work closely with government in an increasingly regulated sector.[9]

Liverpool's outward passenger and emigrant traffic was an important balance to its inward raw material trades and made Atlantic shipping an attractive market for aspiring liner operators. Patterns of ocean trade were inevitably asymmetrical, with individual ports having extremely diverse ratios of inward to outward cargo. Commodity trades expanded along with passenger traffic in the later decades of the nineteenth century, encouraged by increasing demand for food and raw materials in the industrial districts, and by rising production in the areas of the new world being colonised by European settlers. By the mid-nineteenth century, the supply of cotton to Lancashire's textile industry had become Liverpool's most prominent single activity, but cotton never dominated Liverpool to the extent that bulk trades like coal and iron took over the economies of South Wales or North East England. Specialised ports in those districts found it difficult to diversify and both their physical infrastructure and business environments were closely focussed. Liverpool's diversity, by contrast, created synergies that encouraged further innovation.

In this era too, a broad liberalisation of trading regimes broke down old assumptions about national food supplies, although market forces had already been expanding international trade in foodstuffs since the later eighteenth century.[10] Falling transport costs and increasing logistical capabilities were also crucial, since the steamship, along with refrigeration and canning technologies, made it possible to carry perishable cargoes over long distances. Some of the shifts in British trade and consumption patterns were dramatic: foreign-grown wheat rose from around 10 per cent to around 80 per cent of British consumption between 1850 and 1914.[11] Liverpool captured some of these trades, becoming the major import centre for the frozen meat traffic from the River Plate, for example, although London remained dominant in the Australian branch of the same commodity.[12] Birkenhead developed major capacity for livestock imports in the last quarter of the century.[13] By the 1880s, Liverpool was claiming to be Britain's largest import fruit market, handling 40,000 barrels of grapes and 30,000 barrels of apples a week at the peak of the season. Although rapid transport of fruit had been an important motivation for introducing steam services from the Mediterranean, fruit was also a growing cargo for Atlantic steamers as the century progressed.[14]

Liverpool entrepreneurs were able to establish their port as a key hub in the new food trades because northern England had become an industrialised, urbanised hinterland for the Mersey. Much of this relationship had its roots in cotton, Liverpool's long-standing signature commodity, but also in the wider engineering and manufacturing complex that surrounded and complemented textiles. Although threatened by a resurgent Manchester from the 1890s, Liverpool retained its role as the dominant market in raw cotton into the mid-twentieth century and it was also important as a market centre for a range of foodstuffs and other raw materials. That developing market power, perhaps even more than the physical movement and handling of goods and passengers, drove change in business and trading practices in the later decades of the century, and further solidified Liverpool's financial and commercial strength. It is within this environment that the activities of the town's business community need to be examined.

Communications, Processes and Practices

The pace of business accelerated in the Victorian era, with far-reaching consequences for the lives of business people and for the infrastructural base of the cities in which they lived. Although steamships and telecommunications have had the most attention from historians, the international business world was already shrinking in the half-century before those innovations became widely adopted.[15] Systematic mail services carried by packet ships allowed information to travel faster than the goods carried on normal cargo ships. In many ways, this was a fundamental philosophical shift at the heart of business practice and culture. Even the briefest advance knowledge of commodity shipments encouraged merchants to start trading before the goods had actually arrived, while subsequent communications improvements speeded transactions further, widening the gap between 'spot' trading with the goods present, and more abstract dealing in prices and predictions. The implications of those latter forms are considered in more detail later in this chapter and in Chapter 4.[16]

Alongside their well-known advantages, Victorian communications improvements posed extensive problems for business. The first use of steamships to carry transatlantic mails in the 1840s made Liverpool's contacts with important markets more regular and predictable, but business sometimes struggled to obey rigid rules of carriage and strict timetables. The same was true of the telegraph, which cut message times over international distances from weeks to hours in the 1860s, but it was not immediately reliable, and required a new language of codes and abbreviations. Business exploited these new capacities, although take-up varied from sector to sector, and the formal business letter continued to dominate communications between firms.[17]

Difficulties arose from trying to coordinate the timetables of different elements of business practice. In the 1860s, for example, traders compiled weekly returns of activity on the northern markets each Friday. They therefore wanted mail steamers to leave Liverpool and London late on Friday or early on Saturday in order to carry this information to their overseas branches and agents and this continued to be important even after long-distance cables were installed.[18] Such an apparently straightforward process depended on the reliability of inland telegraphs, mail trains and local postal deliveries, and a minor change in any of those elements had businessmen scrambling for alternative routes. Losing an hour between Liverpool and London could miss a mail-steamer and therefore cost a week between London and Bombay. Firms needed information flows that were not just fast, but also predictable, reliable and capable of integration with existing processes.

Indeed, the last great communications advance of the nineteenth century, the telephone, was predominantly local in its business impact. The early exchange networks focussed on linking firms within compact business districts rather than providing long-distance services. Broking firms dramatically increased their productivity, compared to their existing practice of visiting the offices of shipowners and merchants or sending numerous messengers in pursuit of charters. Reliability continued to be a problem, however, and the telephone service emerged as a major issue of business grievance in the 1890s, for all its world-shrinking potential.[19]

Communications, information and commodity flows were important in themselves and for their broader economic impact, but their immediate significance here is in their effect on business practices. The evolution of Liverpool's cotton trade is a useful example of the interaction between these wider environmental changes and the working of the business community. The first great structural change, in the 1840s, was the rise of the buying broker, whose primary task was to buy cotton on behalf of spinners. Previously, the trade had been dominated by selling brokers or dealers, who worked on behalf of the importing merchants. Although this seems like a rather minor distinction, the effects were considerable. The new brokers gathered samples in their own offices instead of touring the merchants' offices with their spinner clients. This was not only convenient for spinners, but it made the market more competitive because spinners could compare various samples in one place. The improving railway network also enabled spinners to visit their Liverpool brokers more easily, concentrating market power there rather than in Manchester.[20] Importers and selling brokers objected, of course, and passed a motion banning the practice at the Cotton Brokers' Association in 1845, but they were unable to enforce this because of the rising power of the new type of broker.[21] This was an early example of the limited authority of Liverpool's trade associations, which could often only follow rather than lead their members.

The cotton trade, which played such an important role in Liverpool's commercial life (Figure 3.1), was also dealing with an increasingly standardised and classified product by mid-century, enabling more reliable sales by sample and the creation of trading rules based on generic grades of cotton. As a direct consequence, auctions became less common and an increasing volume of trade was conducted without need for the goods to be physically examined. This was

Figure 3.1 The Cotton Market, Liverpool (1874)

important to the development of futures trading which was probably the most striking innovation of the later nineteenth century on a number of Liverpool exchanges, most notably cotton and grain.[22] Even between 1840 and 1849, the amount of cotton reported as bought 'on speculation' in Liverpool had increased by over three-fold and a fully functioning futures market was operating by the 1860s.[23] Widely misunderstood at the time, this attracted huge opprobrium. Futures trading allowed firms to buy and sell cotton for delivery at a future date, but without ever intending to take delivery of it: contracts were cancelled when the futures were sold on again, and the market effectively dealt in price fluctuations, not in solid goods. Critics who argued that it was mere gambling were not entirely wrong.

For most of those involved, however, it was quite the opposite: it reduced their level of risk. Futures became vital to the operational security of the trading complex.[24] In short, futures enabled everyone in the market to be a buyer and a seller at the same time, thereby averaging out both positions and reducing losses caused by price fluctuations. Most futures trading worked in close conjunction with trading in real goods. A spinner, for example, buying real cotton for delivery to his mill in two months' time, had to pay the price that applied on the day of purchase. He therefore faced losing business if the price of cotton fell, because competitors who bought their cotton later would be able to produce cheaper yarn and undercut him. However, if he also sold some cotton futures of an equivalent value to his real cotton, he would gain enough in that transaction to balance the loss on the other. Equally, the Liverpool merchant who sold the real cotton could simultaneously buy equivalent futures to cover any possible losses.

Promoters of the system argued that the markets could never have handled the volume of cotton they did were it not for the insurance element created by futures. It was therefore a step-change in business practice, bringing modern communications and information technology to bear on the previously dangerous fluctuations of market prices. By the late 1870s, the Liverpool cotton market had adopted the new system comprehensively and it was becoming impossible to trade in any other way. Barings told one of its New Orleans contacts that it recognised that some firms remained willing to accept their own liability

> as in the old days, for any want of judgement and carelessness . . . but as you are well aware the modern system of business has changed all this and both buyer and seller are now compelled to base all transactions in 'futures' or Liverpool arbitration.[25]

This had by then become, in the telling phrase embedded in many trading agreements, the 'ordinary terms current in the Trade'. As futures trading became vital to commodity flows, however, the practice also attracted criticism, both within Liverpool business and, crucially, in colouring external perceptions of Liverpool as a trading centre (these aspects will be considered in more detail in Chapter 4).[26]

Faster, more abstract trading processes required increasingly elaborate financial systems for the movement of funds. One commentator claimed in the 1890s that cotton traders sent their financial transactions through banks, and no longer drew bills of exchange directly on each other. Banks were only willing to do this, though, because they knew that such deals were supported by futures: they would not accept the account of anyone trading without futures, because such an individual would be 'carrying on his business as a sheer speculation'.[27]

Faster business processes often created weaknesses and loopholes elsewhere in the system, which were tolerated until a specific event forced a formalisation. For example, the volume and speed of Liverpool's live cattle trade from North America outstripped the existing financial safety measures in the 1880s. Steamship firms delivered cattle to slaughterhouses under indemnities from their bankers so that the meat could be distributed nationwide within 24 hours and they did not wait to ensure that all the intermediary firms working in the cattle trade paid their bills on arrival. This allowed one cattle dealer to bounce a cheque on Barings in 1888: he had already received his consignment of cows and paid up within three days following receipt of a writ, but Barings noted that the system was 'somewhat lax', and that they would in future 'stop' cattle at the docks until bills were paid.[28] Whether Barings were in fact able to do this is unclear, but unlikely—traders usually had to adapt to accelerating processes by taking out insurances or modifying their payment systems, and were rarely able to slow them down again.

Trading firms engaged with their banks in a mixture of routine and *ad hoc* transactions. Overdrafts were often established over long periods, with regular renewals and confirmations of amounts, often fortnightly or monthly. This financing was common in shipping and trading alike, judging by the broad range of firms named in banks' loan registers in this era.[29] In addition, individual deals were put forward to bankers for support, as and when they presented themselves; in many cases, banks seem to have been happy to back customers when they spotted an opportunity. One major cotton broking firm told the Liverpool Union Bank in 1907 that it had 'an important straddle operation on with New York', and might need to overdraw its account to £50,000 for a time. The firm offered securities, but the bank extended the overdraft limit without them, noting that the firm's profits in the previous year had been £20,000.[30] Some transactions were extremely unusual, but they reflected bankers' confidence in their select customers. In 1880, for example, the North & South Wales Bank stood £1,000 bail for a leading shipowner facing charges following a collision at sea.[31]

Liverpool's experience was similar to that of many financial and trading centres in the late nineteenth century with increasing reliance on firms and institutions that facilitated the movement of financial instruments alongside those handling goods and people. It also developed institutional mechanisms through trade associations for overseeing faster trading systems with more complex rules. Methodologically, this opens valuable avenues for historians, in that financial institutions and trade associations began to record business practice and activity in greater detail, thereby reducing our reliance on the fragile archives of firms themselves. For contemporaries, it had widespread implications for the place of the individual businessman in an increasingly structured commercial landscape.

From Individual to Collective: Firms and Associations

Most of Liverpool's maritime-related business sectors were dominated by small firms working in competition with many others, and often in intermediary trades. As *Porcupine* put it in 1877, 'We are a town of brokers. Liverpool lives on commission'.[32] Even in areas where relatively few firms worked, as for example in Atlantic passenger liner shipping, it was rare for any of them to dominate the market. Entry thresholds in steam shipping certainly rose in the later decades of the nineteenth century as capital requirements grew, but new firms continued to be created. In addition, the inherent mobility of the industry meant that established shipowners from other ports could start services from Liverpool in competition with the 'home' fleet if opportunities emerged. In commodity trades, there were usually a few very large operators, but also many small and sometimes short-lived businesses; entry and exit thresholds alike were low. By the end of the nineteenth century, however, these open and competitive dynamics were being counter-balanced by associations and networks which aimed to present the port's customers and competitors with a more monolithic face. These ranged from trade associations which imposed rules on those seeking to work in a specific sector, to cartels of firms which sought monopoly power in their fields. This section considers questions of scale in Liverpool business and then addresses the tension between increasing associational development and the long-standing culture of business individualism.

The sheer variety and number of firms operating in Liverpool's trading sectors has been demonstrated in the previous chapter, but assessing the scale of a firm's activities is much harder.[33] After all, the smallest shipbroker and the largest steamship-owner each had only one entry in a trade directory, but their contributions to Liverpool's business environment were radically different. Quantifying the scale of Victorian business operations has posed great challenges for historians, and contemporaries often found it no easier. Some successful recent work has benefited from sources—local authority rate books, for example—that either do not exist in Liverpool, or which have limited value in office districts, as opposed to industrial areas.[34]

Orchard's 1893 survey of Liverpool business biography included an attempt to classify leading cotton firms and his results are summarised in Table 3.1. This is revealing, as much for the difficulty Orchard encountered in devising his analysis as for his results. Orchard struggled to find a single scale which would be meaningful, even in the cotton trade; his descriptive classification tried to balance capital against turnover, and range of connections against sheer volume of business. The first four categories were not exclusive, with 25 firms appearing in both '3' and '4', for example. Categories '5' and '6' were exclusive and indicated the very top ranks of the cotton trade. The high degree of diversity within the cotton sector was also reflected in a list from 1900 of 43 Liverpool cotton brokers with accounts at the Bank of England: whereas Reynolds & Gibson had a capital of £300,000, twelve firms had less than £1,000 and some of these were described as 'very weak', 'very small' or 'poor'.[35]

By the end of the 1830s, 89 per cent of British cotton supplies were imported through Liverpool and there is some evidence that scale of operation in cotton-importing increased in the

Table 3.1 B. G. Orchard's classification of cotton firms, 1892

	Classification	No. of firms
1	Large capital	13
2	Large operations	14
3	Good connections. The firm may be small or large, with sufficient capital, yet scarcely if ever incurring risks on its own account, such being undertaken for respectable clients	33
4	Long standing, highly respectable. May be rich, with extensive transactions, or small with little or no capital, doing moderate business. In such firms, *some* of the partners may be well-off and independent. To this section belong several small spinner brokers, who regularly make modest incomes, never run risks of magnitude, and transact comparatively limited business	47
5	Large or fairly large capital, very large turnover, first-class connections or clients, highly respectable, and long established	32
6	An immense turnover and unlimited capital for whatever they may attempt in cotton. Those take the very front place as regards operations and resources	3
7	Not very conspicuous, but likely to become so	7

Source: B. Guinness Orchard, *Liverpool's Legion of Honour* (Birkenhead, 1893). Total number of firms: 103 (some categories not exclusive).

middle decades of the century, since it became concentrated in the hands of a relatively small number of houses.[36] By the 1850s, only wealthy firms could risk buying large quantities of cotton, given fluctuations in the quantity and quality of the crop in any given year, although the insurance effect of the futures market later reduced the need for importers to amass great capital reserves.[37] In addition, cotton brokers were much more dependent on credit than on capital, so they had always occupied a broader spectrum from large, solid firms to much more transient operators, often referred to as 'men of straw'. *Porcupine* argued that there were two very distinct classes of brokers on the Liverpool Exchange—the 'big brokers' were perfectly capable of looking after themselves and each other, but the 'little brokers' had 'just enough credit to ruin others, just enough capital to ruin themselves'.[38]

This pattern of a minority at the very top followed by a much larger number of small firms is borne out in other sources. Banks devised league tables of creditworthiness, and always had a few firms for whom this was unquantifiable. Such companies were simply trusted for whatever they were undertaking. By the end of the nineteenth century, around half a dozen Liverpool cotton firms typically appeared in this category on lists circulated by bankers, along with three corn merchants, and one or two from the other major mercantile trades. In cotton, another 20 or so firms were trusted for up to £20,000, but only with the security of trading documents relating to the cargoes in question; the corn trade had about 15 firms in the equivalent category.[39] Below that, firms would be subject to closer individual scrutiny when they applied for credit.

The implications of these rankings for issues of reputation and ethics will be discussed more fully in the following chapter.[40] Here, the important point is that the scale and number of firms working in a wide range of trades raised questions about individual and collective attitudes. Mercantile business conveyed a strong individualistic image, with an ideal of personal capitalism which gave both the partners and owners of private businesses great social cachet. Merchants expected to work on their own or in a small partnership with one or two others who were often related by birth or marriage. They would start out learning the trade, usually having secured an apprenticeship through the recommendation of a relative. They would then start trading on their own account, either establishing a new partnership or in some cases being taken into partnership by the firm in which they had served their training. Over time, partnerships were reformed and renewed with the transition from one generation to another, sometimes with a continuing family involvement. Having become a partner in a trading business, an individual had a high degree of autonomy and independence.

Not everyone could succeed in such aspirations. One tobacco broker who had moved from Glasgow to Liverpool early in the twentieth century did well enough for several years, but then wiped out most of his capital—only £500 in any case—in a single ill-chosen deal in 1910. Although willing to try again, he told his bankers that he was also exploring the option of going to work for the Imperial Tobacco Company.[41] Sometimes a move into trading turned out not to be successful, but partners were able to regroup and find an alternative approach. One cotton-broking partnership was dissolved after 18 months in 1905, the partners having decided that they were both a little rash and therefore did not suit each other; both found positions in other firms, however, and seem to have been respected for their candour.[42] Others were desperate or pragmatic enough to endure what must have been a humiliating development, selling out to new owners and being kept on as salaried managers of their former firms.[43] One American commentator praised the amalgamation and agglomeration movement in some parts of US business precisely on those grounds. It created large numbers of posts for men who would otherwise have to start their own firms and, in most cases, struggle for a living, although he conceded that they had to give up the 'greater independence and the dignity of proprietorship'.[44]

Many sectors, both in Britain and in the United States, were slower to adopt this managerial corporate model. As is well known, the rise of the joint-stock company was very uneven across the British economy with some sectors continuing to be dominated by small partnerships far into the twentieth century. After the radical changes in company law in the 1850s and 1860s, which permitted limited liability, extensive debates continued for decades over the impact of the new forms on commercial morality. In addition, joint-stock firms did not work in a vacuum, but had to grow out of, and continue to interact with, the existing business environment.

Even the largest Liverpool joint-stock firms of the late nineteenth century, mainly shipping companies, were still steeped in the culture of personal capitalism. In many cases, men who already had their own small shipowning or shipbroking partnerships set up limited shipping companies to run specific services; the existing firms continued in being, pursuing their routine business while their partners also served as directors of the new joint-stock ventures. In addition, many investors in joint-stock firms were themselves leading businessmen with firms of their own. Correspondence between George Melly and George Holt in 1891, for example, reveals close interest in the personalities and policies of the Ocean Steamship Co.[45] At about the same time, John Holt, a prominent West Africa trader, wrote forceful letters to the British & African Steam Navigation Co., accusing its directors of neglecting their firm and, by extension, the interests of their shareholders.[46] Only gradually, and well into the twentieth century, did it become common for a managing director to be committed wholly to a single firm and to be a more recognisably 'corporate man' rather than an individual, self-determining merchant or shipowner.

The other challenge to the autonomous man of business came from associational and organisational institutions. These were created to help business, of course, as fragmented and fluid clusters gradually moved toward more formal structures in order to achieve some security and certainty in their proceedings. In Liverpool, different trades took different paths to formalisation. Cotton brokers met weekly in each other's offices in the early decades of the nineteenth century, working on a simple rota; this was of course in addition to their daily encounters on the Exchange Flags.[47] The weekly meetings were to discuss policy—an associational function—whereas the Exchange was the venue for daily deal-making and involved meeting traders other than cotton brokers. In 1841, they formed the Liverpool Cotton Brokers' Association and began to formulate rules for the market. Then, in the 1860s, the crisis of the American Civil War, the advent of the Atlantic telegraph and greatly increasing steamship capacity on the cotton routes all encouraged the development of more structured trading systems, with the motive of making a volatile trade more predictable. As was often the case, such institutionalisation created outsiders as well as insiders and the early 1880s saw a dispute between cotton brokers and importing merchants; this was resolved with another structural shift in 1882 and the creation of the Liverpool Cotton Association.[48]

Corn traders also institutionalised their procedures, forming an association in 1853, which was eventually incorporated as the Liverpool Corn Trade Association in 1886.[49] Liverpool's Corn Exchange had emerged as a separate entity in 1808. These bodies developed ever more detailed rules for grading and classifying their commodities. Committees dealt with commodity standards and membership rules, aiming to improve the reliability of trade and traders alike.[50] The Corn Exchange continued to have a strong Irish dimension; a group of traders gathered there sent a congratulatory telegram to William Gladstone on his eighty-fourth birthday in 1893 referring to themselves as 'Liverpool Irishmen'.[51] Ireland was also important to the produce and provision traders, but so increasingly were their links with North America. The Liverpool Provision Trades Association, formed in 1874, opened a newsroom in 1886 and then established an exchange of its own in Victoria Street in 1902, reflecting the rising importance and complexity of the trade in foodstuffs. In fact, it had converted itself into a joint-stock company to facilitate that last step.[52]

The conventional wisdom was that these associations should become the guardians of business standards. One newspaper listed 14 Liverpool associations specialising in particular trades or functions in 1887, concluding that 'with such organisations in operation, there is no fear of anything creeping in . . . to the prejudice of commerce in general, and to that of Liverpool in particular'.[53] There was always, however, a thin line between working for the benefit of trade and seeking to control it. Trade associations and similar organisations naturally encouraged loyalty within their specific sector rather than across the community as a whole, and members came to expect their misfortunes to be kept secret. The press complained that members of Liverpool's stock exchange, for example, managed to 'wash their dirty linen so very privately'.[54]

Trade associations sometimes struggled to enforce their rules, especially when they threatened the autonomy of individual firms and businessmen, or when they attempted to take a firm line where there was no consensus. The activities of clerks—especially the more ambitious— exposed weaknesses in many of Liverpool's trading systems. Clerks trading on their own account posed a common problem: this was banned by most of the trade and exchange associations, but such prohibitions seem to have been sporadically enforced. This is an important example because it captures the tensions between the ability of individual businessmen to manage their affairs as they saw fit and the wider interest and reputation of the trading community. It was complicated by seeming to be a victimless process in many cases, raising concerns that associations tended to create unnecessary rules and forget that they were supposed to be serving their members, and not vice versa.

The Cotton Association tried to address trading by clerks on a several occasions, but clearly stretched its internal cohesion in the process. The 1889 case of John Jackson became public when Jackson's bankruptcy hearing was read a list of distinguished cotton broking firms, all of whom, it was claimed, had happily traded with him in his own name while knowing that he was just an employee. At the subsequent (internal) inquiry, the Association heard a range of excuses, mostly to the effect that firms had started trading with Jackson because they knew others already were, and felt they 'might as well have the brokerage as other people'; other brokers blamed their salesmen. The Association decided that the actions of the brokers had been 'reprehensible' and vowed to pass rules banning the practice outright.[55] Revealingly, though, after the publicity had died down, a series of meetings rejected such decisive action. In the end, the cotton traders would go no further than a statement that members were 'cautioned against' such activity.[56]

Little had evidently been learned from earlier cases. In 1877, for example, a clerk with Allan Bros, a steamship line, was dismissed after rumours that he had been trading in petroleum and corn, but the scale of his operations only subsequently came to light. He had embezzled just over £900 to pay for his trading activities and several major firms had been happy to broker for him without checking whether he was entitled to be trading at all. His prosecutor thought that those firms had behaved 'deplorably' and that 'common prudence' would have saved a young man from ruin and his employer from embarrassment.[57] Much to the incredulity of prosecutors, firms continued to claim in successive cases running over decades that they had dealt with clerks in good faith and had never had cause to question whether they were merchants in their own right.[58]

There was an important dilemma here for the business classes. Many clerks knew the business well enough to operate on their own account, and firms often benefited from their knowledge. Indeed, in specialist trades, businessmen who wanted to break into a new trade tried to identify and recruit such experts from existing firms. Potential customers were reassured by the demonstrable competence of the clerks, as well as by the reputation of the partners, and recruiting the right people might create a virtuous snowball effect. When the Tyneside shipowner James Knott was trying to find a way into Liverpool's West Africa trades, for example, he was advised to poach the chief clerk and the cashier from Elder Dempster; if he had managed that, they would probably have brought the best shipping masters in the African trade with them.[59] Allowing such men to trade on their own account, despite the rules, was therefore an important unofficial element in the apprenticeship process, and many senior businessmen had doubtless done it themselves early in their careers. When associations tried to tame this individualism too zealously, their members would resist. Research elsewhere has demonstrated that opportunities for clerks to make the transition to the merchant classes became more limited at the turn of the century, but some aspects of the business environment continued to work in their favour, albeit by encouraging particularly risky activities.[60]

Collaborating against the public interest was always a criticism of business associations as well as less formal networks. T. H. Ismay's thoughts on competition in the ocean liner trades are indicative of the producer-lobby mentality that coloured relations between the major shipping companies and their customers and also between them and government in the growing debates over protectionism and economic nationalism around the turn of the century. Ismay claimed to have offered to put up half the capital required to save the struggling Inman Line in 1886 if a fellow tycoon would match him; this was rejected, and the assets were instead purchased by the International Navigation Co., a US firm that already had substantial shipping interests. This, argued Ismay, simply brought a powerful competitor into the Liverpool market, with millions of dollars of capital behind it and the right to use an established Liverpool trading name: 'Would it not have been better to have kept that weak line going?'[61]

Whether ordinary customers, passengers and the taxpayers who funded shipowners' mail subsidies would have benefited from propping up the status quo in Atlantic shipping was not Ismay's concern, although to be fair the Atlantic passenger market was more open to competition than many of the world's goods routes. In Africa and the Far East, the whole culture of large-scale shipowning was isolated from the concerns of customers by the development of shipping conferences. Liverpool shipping firms were instrumental in establishing the conference concept, by which merchants were offered rebates for using conference services, but only after they had stayed loyal to the conference for at least six months. Using outside shipping firms in the meantime would cost them their rebate.

The conference system has in general had a good press, despite vehement criticism at the time.[62] It is claimed that conferences encouraged collaboration among shipowners as well as between shipowners and merchants, thereby avoiding the booms and busts of relentless competition. Merchants almost certainly paid higher freight rates than they would have faced in a system of free competition, but they avoided a range of other costs. Negotiating each shipment separately would have been expensive and having a reasonably secure guarantee of delivery dates saved them storage costs and litigation by their customers. In any case, the relative openness of the industry was seen as insurance against extortion, since merchants who found their conference partners intolerable could always seek independent shipping firms to carry their goods.[63] It is also evident that shipowners remained competitive with one another and jockeyed for position in advance of the periodic re-negotiations that characterised the conference system.[64]

At any given point, all this is true. The problem with restrictive business practices and the cultivation of favoured insiders is, however, the gradual erosion of competitiveness over time. Major merchants increasingly admitted that they did not mind what they paid, so long as they all paid the same. Rather than striking the best possible deals between themselves, shipping conferences working from the major British ports and their local merchant houses passed on their costs to inland manufacturers and overseas buyers.[65] In most cases, disorganised overseas customers lacked good information and were often unaware of the rebate system, which suggests that merchants did not pass the rebate on to their customers. A new mercantile association was formed in 1897, for example, by traders who felt excluded from the existing South African Merchants Committee, because that Committee allegedly had a close relationship with the shipping conferences and with the major colonial institutions. The association hoped that by publicising these connections it would help to open up the trade and encourage customers to ask awkward questions.[66]

Securing better deals from shipowners required unanimity among merchants, which proved elusive. John Holt told a Hamburg merchant in 1901 that 'the only way to speak with authority to any of these shipowners is to be in a position to act if they do not agree'; ultimately, he argued, it might only be by running their own ships that merchants would truly be able to negotiate from a position of strength.[67] Taking on the shipowners often required firms to give up some short-term advantage and it was difficult to persuade them to do so. Holt concluded that 'much as the advantages might ultimately be it is difficult to get ordinary minds to comprehend them, and besides there are so many conflicting interests to arrange that the task becomes very difficult'.[68] Individualism remained a powerful force, driving entrepreneurial success but also limiting capacity for collective action where that might have been desirable.

Building alliances and collective negotiating strength within a sector was also difficult when the largest operators could rely on personal access to those in positions of power and influence. The most important example is probably the relationship between major steamship companies and the British government over subsidies. Here, the directors of individual firms dealt directly with senior officials and ministers, with no need for mediating and representative bodies. Such negotiations looked particularly cosy in 1887, when T. H. Ismay (White Star) and John Burns (Cunard) had to send their latest subvention terms to the Secretary to the Admiralty, who happened to be Arthur Forwood MP, former managing director of Liverpool's West India & Pacific Steam Navigation Co.[69] While there was no guarantee that any three Liverpool shipowners would be disposed to help one another, the total number of individuals working at the top level of business was small enough that coincidences of this sort were almost inevitable. Government work was important to Liverpool and acquiring official contracts (and subsidies) for mail- and troop-carrying had been a valuable source of income for early steamship ventures in the 1850s. Long memories and an awareness of political connections running over decades enabled some businessmen to make approaches to senior officials and ministers. In 1880, for example, William Rathbone sent a long letter to George Melly, setting out in some detail how Melly should apply to Lord Hartington, Secretary of State for India, for the government's East Indies agency. Rathbone told Melly to emphasise his connections with the Rathbones (who were giving up the agency) and with W. E. Gladstone (an old political ally of Melly); then, in a carefully choreographed sequence of letters, Gladstone and Rathbone would in turn support Melly's application. A few days later, Rathbone saw Hartington personally and discussed the matter.[70]

Only a small proportion of the trading elite had that sort of access to power and decision-making, or the capacity to bid for major contracts. For most merchants and shipowners, their contact with government consisted of trying to influence the content of industrial and commercial regulation, an increasing volume of which was introduced in the later decades of the nineteenth century. In addition, business was able to self-regulate to some extent, achieving national and international agreements over trading rules and practices. Here, individual businesses relied on associations to employ the officers and negotiators capable of overcoming bureaucratic and informational hurdles. The international trading environment of the turn of the century made external contacts and communications important to trading associations, as well as increasing their significance for individual firms.

Marine insurance is a useful example and one which is relatively neglected in the historical literature. Insurers found that their information-handling role became appreciably more complex with the rise of the steamship, of telecommunications and of organised insurance markets in various parts of the world. Coordinating strategies for marine insurance became multilateral and decisions had to be taken ever more quickly. London was the long-standing hub of the marine insurance industry and the Secretary of the Liverpool Underwriters Association received a constant flow of letters from his London counterpart asking for information. Local knowledge, but also local contacts and personal approaches were valued. For example, when the ship *Cyclops* ran aground near Jeddah in 1910, a dispute broke out involving some Australian underwriters interested in some of the cargo; London's underwriters asked Liverpool's if they could personally talk to the ship's owners, the Ocean Steamship Co., and try to 'remove the deadlock'.[71]

At other times, the relationship with London revealed tensions in Liverpool's national and international role. In 1883, the chairman of the new Liverpool Average Adjusters Association claimed that Liverpool had no difficulty following London, providing London would actually lead; his association had been created in large part because Liverpool business was dissatisfied with the services on offer from the metropolis. The problem was that the scale and rapidity of Liverpool's growth in shipping was creating the need for local structures and for a body which could resolve policy issues as they arose, rather than waiting for the infrequent meetings of a more distant organisation.[72] The following year, the Association helped convene a general conference of shipowners and merchants, which became a forum for the mercantile business community to discuss legal and insurance-related questions.[73] In marine insurance, as in other maritime business sectors, Liverpool's representative trade associations sometimes struggled to maintain difficult balances between the local interests of their members, the collective needs of the port's business as a whole, and the opportunity to play a major international role in evolving policy debates.

Other Liverpool trade associations had to confront the reality of increasing government power and authority in parts of the world where they had previously enjoyed a lengthy period of relative autonomy. This was nowhere more obvious than in West Africa, because imperial expansion created tensions between colonial administrators and Liverpool merchants and ship-owners. Attempts to resolve these included the creation of the Joint West Africa Committee, which brought delegates of the Liverpool, Manchester and London Chambers of Commerce together with officials from the Colonial Office.[74] From the first meetings in 1905 onward, there were disagreements about the status of the committee, with the traders complaining that they were not consulted about events in West Africa, while the officials argued that the delegates could hardly expect to make policy in detail. Particularly traders objected to expenditure on infrastructure such as railways (which was paid for by taxing their businesses) and to the fact that they only met with officials, and not with ministers. The Colonial Office did concede in 1906 that the committee could meet the Under-Secretary more regularly, but traders failed to gain any more influence. Liverpool's leading delegate—Alfred Jones—often took a concilia-tory line in these discussions, persuading his fellow traders that they were fortunate to have the committee and could not expect government to surrender its authority to them. Jones, of course, had multifarious connections with government and administration in West Africa which were probably far more lucrative than any concessions he was likely to win through a consultative committee.[75]

Jones's role on the West Africa Committee personified many of the tensions that emerged between individual and collective attitudes and actions in this era, therefore, but which nonethe-less produced a business environment that offered support to traders while rarely threatening their autonomy. A clear hierarchy is also evident in most trades, with a minority of large firms and particularly influential businessmen being able to establish far-reaching connections, while also playing key roles in the direction and administration of Liverpool's internal affairs. Below them, a much larger group of traders maintained solid but unspectacular positions, dependent on the leadership of the elite in their trade associations, and also, as will be seen in a later chapter, reliant on their approval for credit and support in times of commercial crisis.[76]

Conclusion

Liverpool's business environment developed several important and sometimes seemingly con-tradictory characteristics in the second half of the nineteenth century. The port rose to global prominence thanks to its steamship fleets and commodity markets, while becoming more self-sufficient and autonomous in its business decision-making. Liverpool-based merchants and shipowners dominated the port from the 1860s through to the 1890s, eclipsing the earlier role of American shipowners, but ultimately in their turn giving some ground to London-based mul-tinational firms, markets and trade associations. While large joint-stock companies came to dominate Liverpool's liner shipping, small firms were the norm in mercantile business, and the independent, autonomous gentleman on 'Change remained the key figure in the town's eco-nomic elite. However, these men increasingly found that they were working in a more structured institutional environment, as trading systems accelerated and financial mechanisms required the intervention of specialists in banking and insurance. Many branches of the mercantile sector also expanded their associational connections in this era, both to give them greater collective weight when lobbying government, and to establish systems for self-regulation. The specific implications of this business environment for Liverpool's sense of commercial ethics will be discussed in the following chapter, but it also, more generally, underpins the wider social and cultural landscapes assessed throughout the rest of the book.[77]

Notes

1 Peter N. Davies, 'The Liverpool School of Maritime History', *IJMH*, 17, 2 (2005), pp. 249–60.

2 Peter N. Davies, *Henry Tyrer: A Liverpool Shipping Agent and His Enterprise, 1879–1979* (London, 1979); B. L. Anderson, 'The Lancashire Bill System and Its Liverpool Practitioners: The Case of a Slave Merchant', in W. H. Chaloner and Barrie M. Ratcliffe (eds.), *Trade and Transport: Essays in Economic History in Honour of T. S. Willan* (Manchester, 1977), pp. 59–96; B. L. Anderson, 'Institutional Investment before the First World War: The Union Marine Insurance Company', in S. Marriner (ed.), *Business and Businessmen: Studies in Business Economic and Accounting History* (Liverpool, 1978), pp. 169–97; B. L. Anderson and P. L. Cottrell, 'Another Victorian Capital Market: A Study of Banking and Bank Investors on Merseyside', *EcHR*, 28, 1975, pp. 598–615; Sheila Marriner, *Rathbones of Liverpool, 1845–73* (Liverpool, 1961).

3 Gordon H. Boyce, *Information, Mediation and Institutional Development: The Rise of Large-Scale Enterprise in British Shipping, 1870–1919* (Manchester, 1995); Stanley Chapman, *Merchant Enterprise in Britain: From the Industrial Revolution to World War I* (Cambridge, 1992).

4 John F. Wilson and Andrew Popp (eds.), *Industrial Clusters and Regional Business Networks in England, 1750–1970* (Aldershot, 2003); Andrew Popp, *Business Structure, Business Culture and the Industrial District: The Potteries, c.1850–1914* (Aldershot, 2001); Alfred Marshall, *Industry and Trade* (London, 1919).

5 A. G. Kenwood and A. L. Lougheed, *The Growth of the International Economy, 1820–2000* (4th ed., London, 1999).

6 F. E. Hyde, *Liverpool and the Mersey* (Newton Abbot, 1971).

7 Drew Keeling, 'The Transportation Revolution and Transatlantic Migration, 1850–1914', *Research in Economic History*, 19 (1999), pp. 39–74.

8 *Fairplay*, 6 November 1891, p. 1019.

9 Oliver Macdonagh, *A Pattern of Government Growth 1800–60: The Passenger Acts and Their Enforcement* (London, 1961); Graeme J. Milne, 'Maritime Liverpool', in John Belchem (ed.), *Liverpool 800 Culture, Character & History* (Liverpool, 2006), pp. 287–90.

10 Morton Rothstein, 'Centralising Firms and Spreading Markets: The World of International Grain Traders, 1846–1914', *Business and Economic History*, 17 (1988), pp. 103–13; R. C. Michie, 'The International Trade in Food and the City of London since 1850', *Journal of European Economic History*, 25 (1996), pp. 369–406.

11 Richard Perren, 'Structural Change and Market Growth in the Food Industry: Flour Milling in Britain, Europe and America, 1850–1914', *EcHR*, 43 (1990), pp. 420–37.

12 W. Weddell & Co., *Review of the Frozen Meat Trade* (1899), LSE library.

13 Ken McCarron, *Meat at Woodside* (Birkenhead, 1991).

14 *Liverpool Review*, 27 November 1886, p. 10.

15 Yrjö Kaukiainen, 'Shrinking the World: Improvements in the Speed of Information Transmission, c.1820–1870', *European Review of Economic History*, 5 (2001), pp. 1–28; Seija-Riita Laakso, 'Managing the Distance: Business Information Transmission between Britain and Guiana, 1840', *IJMH*, 16, 2 (2004), pp. 221–46.

16 Graeme Milne, see Chapter 4.

17 L. R. Fischer and H. Nordvik, 'Economic Theory, Information and Management in Shipbroking: Freanley and Eger as a Case Study, 1869–1972', in Simon Ville and D. M. Williams (eds.), *Management, Finance an Industrial Relations in Maritime Industries* (St John's, 1994), pp. 1–29.

18 British Parliamentary Papers (BPP), Select Committee on the practical working of the present system of telegraphs . . . East Indies, 1866 vol. 9 428, qq. 1,032.

19 Graeme J. Milne, 'British Business and the Telephone, 1878–1911', *BH* 49, 2 (2007), pp. 163–85; 'Business Districts, Office Culture and the First Generation of Telephone Use in Britain', *International Journal for the History of Engineering & Technology*, 80, 2 (2010), pp. 199–213.

20 Nigel Hall, 'The Business Interests of Liverpool Cotton Brokers, c 1800–1914', *Northern History* 41, 1 (2004), pp. 339–55.

21 Obituaries of James Wrigley, *Daily Post*, 31 January 1884; 4 February 1884.

22 Graham L. Rees, *Britain's Commodity Markets* (London, 1972), pp. 88–9, 129–40.

23 Braithwaite Poole, S*tatistics of British Commerce: Being a Compendium of the Productions, Manufacturers, Imports and Exports of the United Kingdom in Agriculture, Minerals, Merchandise etc.* (London, 1852), p. 109; Hall, 'The Business Interests of Liverpool Cotton Brokers', p. 342. Between 1841 and 1849, the number of bales of cotton bought 'on speculation' rose from 192,210 to 791,820.

24 Charles Stewart, *Cotton Futures: What They Are, and How They Work in Practice* (Liverpool, 1926), LSE Library.
25 Baring Archive, 102141, 4 May 1878.
26 Milne, see Chapter 4.
27 Stewart, *Cotton Futures*.
28 Baring Archive, 102134, 5 July 1888.
29 HSBC Group Archives, North & South Wales Bank, Loans register, M97.
30 Lloyds TSB Archives, Liverpool Union Bank, B/817/a/7, 'N', January 1907.
31 HSBC Group Archives, N&S Wales Bank, Board minutes, M19, 6 April 1880.
32 *Porcupine*, 8 December 1877.
33 See Randolph Cock, John Davies, Robert Lee, and Sari Mäenpää, Chapter 2.
34 Popp, *Business Structure, Business Culture and the Industrial District*.
35 Hall, 'The Business Interests of Liverpool's Cotton Brokers', Appendix, p. 355.
36 Nigel Hall, 'The Emergence of the Liverpool Raw Cotton Market, 1800–1850', *Northern History*, 38, 1 (2001), p. 69; David M. Williams, 'Liverpool Merchants and the Cotton Trade, 1820–1850', in *Liverpool and Merseyside: Essays in the Economic and Social History of the Port and Its Hinterland* (Liverpool, 1969), pp. 182–211.
37 Stewart, *Cotton Futures*.
38 *Porcupine*, 23 February 1878.
39 For example, listing in Baring Archive, 102136, 30 August 1900.
40 See Graeme Milne, Chapter 4.
41 Lloyds TSB Archives, Liverpool Union Bank, B/817/a/17, 'C', May 1910.
42 Lloyds TSB Archives, Liverpool Union Bank, B/817/a/17, 'M', July 1905.
43 Lloyds TSB Archives, Liverpool Union Bank, B/817/a/17, 'D', October 1904.
44 Henry Wood, *Natural Law in the Business World* (Boston, 1887), pp. 166–7.
45 LRO, 920 MEL/33, Holt to Melly, 5 May 1891.
46 LRO, 380 HOL I 4/5, Holt to Sir William McOnie, 25 October 1889.
47 *Liverpool Mercury*, 24 November 1892.
48 Thomas Ellison, *The Cotton Trade of Great Britain, Including a History of the Liverpool Cotton Market* (London, 1886).
49 *The Liverpool Corn Trade Association, 1853–1953* (Liverpool, 1953).
50 For example, MMM, MAL, B/LCTA/13/1 (Grading Committee); B/LCTA/15/1 (New Members Committee).
51 *The Times*, 30 December 1893, p. 7.
52 Liverpool Provision Trades Association, *Liverpool New Produce Exchange* (Liverpool, 1902).
53 *Liverpool Review*, 4 June 1887, p. 11.
54 *Liverpool Citizen*, 5 November 1890, p. 12.
55 LRO, 380 COT 5/2, minutes of 19 June 1889.
56 LRO, 380 COT 6/3, minutes of 15 July, 30 September 1889.
57 *Liverpool Mercury*, 23 January 1878, p. 8; Embezzlement was occasionally a serious problem and caused serious losses to firms. George Wilson, McQuie's principal clerk, was suspended in October 1868 suspected of embezzlement. He was subsequently found guilty and sentenced to five years penal servitude. It also emerged that the late clerk, John McLean, had been 'the confederate' of the thief. See MMM, MAL, DX/641/6/2, Records of a Family History continued, commencing AD.1867, Peter R. McQuie, Thornton Lodge, Bootle, 9 October, 29 October 1868.
58 *Liverpool Courier*, 5 July 1912, p. 10.
59 LRO, 380 HOL I 4/5, Holt to Knott, 30 November 1891.
60 R. Guerriero Wilson, 'Office Workers, Business Elites and the Disappearance of the "Ladder of Success" in Edwardian Glasgow', *Scottish Economic and Social History*, 19 (1999), pp. 55–75.
61 *Fairplay*, 30 November 1899, p. 914.
62 Francis E. Hyde, *Blue Funnel: A History of Alfred Holt and Company of Liverpool from 1865 to 1914* (Liverpool, 1956), p. xvi.
63 Boyce, *Information, Mediation and Institutional Development*, pp. 160–74.
64 Frank Broeze, 'Albert Ballin, the Hamburg-Bremen Rivalry and the Dynamics of the Conference System', *IJMH*, 3, 1 (1991), pp. 1–32.
65 BPP, Royal Commission on Shipping Rings, 1909, vol. 47, Cd. 4670, qq. 3,624.
66 Chamber of Commerce, *Monthly Record* (1897), p. 270.

67 LRO, 380 HOL I 4/8, Holt to Glaiser, 18 November 1901.

68 LRO, 380 HOL I 4/8, Holt to Weber and Schaer, 7 January 1902.

69 BPP, Correspondence respecting subvention of merchant steamers, 1887, vol. 52, C. 5006.

70 LRO, 920 MEL/26, Rathbone to Melly, 19 May 1880; Rathbone to Melly, 31 May 1880.

71 Guildhall Library, 31878, vol. 1, 27 April 1910.

72 MMM, MAL, Average Adjusters Association, DX41/8/3.

73 MMM, MAL, Average Adjusters Association, DX41/8/1, 3 April 1884.

74 The following evidence comes from the committee's minutes in Guildhall Library, 16507, vols. 1–2.

75 For Jones, see Peter N. Davies, *The Trade Makers: Elder Dempster in West Africa, 1852–1972, 1973–1989* (2nd ed., St. John's, Newfoundland, 2000).

76 See Graeme Milne, Chapter 4.

77 See Graeme Milne, Chapter 4.

4   Ethics, Trust and Reputation

Graeme Milne

Several generations of change in the business environment brought with them shifting attitudes to business ethics. Liverpool commentators in the late nineteenth century often focussed on questions of reputation and morality in trade and commerce, and a clear chronology emerges from such writing. In particular, the American Civil War seems to have been a watershed in perceptions of appropriate behaviour among Liverpool traders, although that conflict may just have been the most memorable in a series of related patterns working to change business practice and attitudes in the 1860s. Joint-stock company law and the rise of unsubsidised steam shipping were also relevant, alongside the major upheaval in the cotton trade caused by the Civil War. As the century went on the periods before and after the war increasingly solidified as different eras in Liverpool's commercial morality and the oldest of Liverpool's businessmen were hailed as survivors from that pre-war era. When Thomas Brandon died in 1895, for example, his career was recounted as a 'link with the old shipping days', explicitly the time 'before the war'.[1] J. A. Tinne (1808–84), a West Indies trader, was said to be one of the few left who had worked in the time when 'the British merchant's word was his bond'.[2] Ralph Brocklebank (1803–92), was 'another of the few remaining links connecting the commercial Liverpool of the past with that of today'; one of the 'old school of commercial princes'.[3] Some thought that standards overall had been higher before the war and pointed to the increasing extravagance of the business classes in the 1870s; it had once been 'considered very un-businesslike' for merchants to take carriages to the Exchange, for example.[4]

All that said, there was little outright nostalgia for earlier eras of business, and antiquity was considered more quaint than actually desirable. This created a slight tension, with older firms citing their longevity as a measure of stability and trustworthiness, while also making it clear that they were up to date in their connections and energy. The firm of Thomas Whalley, seed merchants, was founded as far back as 1773, but 'at the present time, the stability and standing which result to a business house from long and honourable existence, are joined to the ample resources and systematic improvements of the most modern establishments'.[5] New firms, on the other hand, could not just stress their novelty, but tried to acquire some heritage by association. Indeed, commentators on the business classes demonstrated a keen sense of family connections and background, maintaining an almost genealogical concern for the career paths of senior businessmen, tracing the firms in which they were apprenticed, the various junior posts held, and then the sometimes lengthy series of partnership changes that marked a mercantile career. Jolly & Gaskell, general brokers, acknowledged that they had only been in business for two years, but were careful to cite their business genealogy. Jolly had spent 16 years in the employ of 'the large and well-known oil firm of Messrs Meade, King & Robinson', with Gaskell recently 'graduating' from Bigland Sons & Jeffreys.[6]

DOI: 10.4324/9781315597836-4

Weaving the past into contemporary business life was not just a tool for positive image-makers. Sometimes, the radical press drew historical evidence into current affairs, quite willing to invoke much older and unsavoury trading practices and condemn a perceived lack of change. In 1884, when the issue of employers' liability was causing controversy, the *Liverpool Review* alleged that the Atlantic slave trade, unquestionably the largest skeleton in Liverpool's closet, lived on in the attitudes of shipowners to their seamen. Eighteenth-century merchants and nineteenth-century shipowners had alike been regarded as 'humane and honourable men' in their day, while paying little attention to human costs: 'Liverpool's slave trade is yet a long way off extinction'.[7]

By the end of the nineteenth century, then, closely connected questions of reputation and heritage were important elements in the image and self-image of the Liverpool business elite, increasingly reinforced by profiles and obituaries in the local press, and, as will be discussed, by press reaction to scandals and crises. Underlying this public discourse, however, were a number of layers of private monitoring and scrutiny, designed both to assess the trustworthiness of individuals in trading situations, and to encourage a higher level of morality and ethics in business dealings more generally. The main task of this chapter is to assess this heavily nuanced and uncertain information environment.

Structures and Individuals

As was noted in the previous chapter, joint-stock companies remained relatively uncommon in Liverpool outside the liner shipping sector, but the wider political debates over the morality and ethics of the new corporate forms were as familiar to Liverpudlians as they were in any other major business centre.[8] Contemporaries took sharply polarised positions, crediting joint-stock liberalisation with mobilising capital and enterprise, or condemning its separation of ownership from management, and the alleged recklessness and commercial immorality that followed. The idea of limited liability in particular was the subject of continuing suspicion and unease.[9] Even firms that did not convert into joint-stocks had to work in a business landscape and ethical framework altered by the activities and perceptions of those that did.

The financial upheavals of the 1860s put many joint-stock firms in a bad light, even when their joint-stock status was only marginally relevant to their difficulties. Much of the early opprobrium was aimed at joint-stock banks, rather than at firms more generally. Liverpool had its share of these, although in the most notorious case, Barned's Bank did not convert to joint-stock status until after it was in deep financial trouble. It failed in 1865, less than a year after conversion, and it continued to be vilified in the Liverpool press from time to time, such as when one of its founders died in the 1880s.[10] In 1879, when the North & South Wales Bank was considering joint-stock status—encouraged by the conversion of the National & Provincial Bank of England—its staff consulted its customers to ascertain their views. The manager of the central Liverpool branch reported that he would not expect a material withdrawal of deposits if the bank converted, provided a sufficient reserve of capital was seen to be set aside. His view was important, because he handled most of the large mercantile accounts, while the bank's other branches in Liverpool mainly catered for small tradesmen, builders and the like. Only one of the chief shareholders in Liverpool was against conversion and the board decided to recommend joint-stock status to the next full meeting of proprietors.[11]

Shipping was an active sector for joint-stock promotions, many of which never became working services, and the trade press was often sceptical. *Fairplay*, despite its mission to support even the most intransigent shipowners during industrial disputes, often condemned questionable business ventures. In 1891, for example, the paper was derisory about the reputations of the younger generation of Liverpool's MacIver family, rejecting their grandiose scheme to start a new steam service to Australia. This seemed to be no more than 'a plan to transfer to the public the ownership of some old vessels and the contracts for [the building of] new ones', being hatched by men with no record in this particular trade. When the promotion was withdrawn soon after, *Fairplay* remained puzzled that the MacIvers had demonstrated 'such a total misconception of their own standing in the shipping trade'.[12]

Shipping companies in the passenger sector inevitably attracted more public attention than those that only handled cargo. Questions of reliability, safety and trustworthiness became part of the corporate image of many firms, most famously Cunard, which worked hard to avoid risk in its high-profile services.[13] Cunard, notably, was less concerned with other reputation-related issues such as quality of personal service, leaving other lines like White Star to exploit those aspects.[14] Liverpool was also home to shipowners of more dubious public standing, however. In the early 1880s, Liverpool became notorious for its adoption of the single-ship company, widely perceived as a way of using joint-stock company law to reduce a shipowners' responsibility for his vessels to dangerously low levels. Respectable shipowners argued that they used it not to avoid liability for sinkings but to guard against their entire fleets being arrested in foreign ports when one vessel fell foul of some local regulation.[15] Suspicions remained, however. Frederick Leyland had pioneered the single-ship company in Liverpool and the manipulation of corporate form by Leyland's empire's continued to be controversial even after his death. In 1897, a reorganisation of Frederick Leyland & Co., which effectively put any new ships out of reach of the firm's existing creditors, was considered 'a disgrace' by one financial journal.[16]

Conversions to joint-stock status remained much rarer in merchanting and brokering than in shipping, but they continued to attract unease. Barings lowered the credit it was willing to give to one Liverpool meat and produce importer in 1891 following its conversion, much to the firm's dissatisfaction. Although not doubting its current solvency, Barings was wary of the firm being 'no longer under one responsible head', and argued that 'there is scarcely an instance in which the attempt to turn good private business of this nature into public companies has been successful'.[17]

Recruiting suitable directors for a joint-stock company could be problematic. The reputations and contacts of directors were important to maintaining the image and position of the firm within the business community, but also *vice versa*, and this made businessmen cautious: one commentator testified that 'the more desirable he is as a director, as a rule, the more reluctant he is to become one'.[18] A Liverpool banker noted that an ordinary director ought to be 'a good business man who would not interfere too much but could communicate information'.[19] Being a 'good business man' was often hard to define and there was always the quandary that the best businessmen might have been good precisely because they devoted their full attention to their own firms and refused to join boards and committees. Some internationally known firms adopted this as a policy—it was claimed in 1902 that the Ralli Bros partners never accepted external directorships, rather 'reserving all their energies for their own business'.[20]

The corn merchant Joseph Hubback is an illuminating example. Hubback was a director of the British & American Mortgage Co., the Liverpool, London & Globe Insurance, the British & Irish Telephone & Electric Works, the English Electric Light Co. and the London & Provincial Street Lighting Co. He was also a member of the Mersey Docks and Harbour Board (1857–76), and a Liverpool Corporation Alderman (1862–80). However, his obituarist noted that he was not elected Chair of the Dock Board because it was feared that his own business dealings were shaky and that the Board might suffer the embarrassment of having its Chairman resign in finan-cial difficulty. Hubback's 'evil genius throughout life', argued that commentator, was that he could direct other firms much more effectively than he could manage his own corn merchant's business.[21]

As well as having difficulty recruiting suitable directors, reputable firms also had the prob-lem of turning away unsuitable applicants. Being a director of a well-known firm brought with it respectability and influence and for those who lacked either or both, it could be worth trying to exploit even tenuous connections. In 1889, the General Manager of the North & South Wales Bank wrote a long letter to one such applicant explaining that his bank always demanded lengthy experience in business and financial affairs from its directors, as well as local knowledge of the bank's areas of operation. The manager had once known the appli-cant's father, which explained both the application and the politeness of the response; he was much brisker in response to a second letter from the same individual, who had failed to take the hint.[22]

Some individuals, firms and families became exemplars in the eyes of the press and were held up not only as models for other traders but as having a powerful influence on the market as a whole. The *Shipping World's* profile of William Rathbone VI in 1883 is a useful case in point:

> The presence on 'Change of men like the Rathbones has a wholesome influence. It serves to clear the atmosphere of the mist which dims the conscience of traders: it sets a premium on commercial morality, and indicates the reward thereof.

That expectation of leadership by example on the part of senior merchants ties in with Liver-pool's broader search for 'old families' and the continued need for a tone-setting urban elite. Commentators often noted in the later years of the nineteenth century that wealth and power seemed transient in Liverpool and that the city lacked some of the long-standing heritage of established families and social landmarks.[23]

As well as setting the general atmosphere and ethical tone, members of the business elite were expected to wield direct power in specific circumstances and getting on the wrong side of one of these key players could have important consequences. One very respectable London firm took on a new partner only to discover that he was 'a man for whom the Bank [of England] have such a thorough contempt that they would consider it a slur on the character of any firm to have any connection with him'; the partnership was, perhaps inevitably, soon terminated.[24] The problem, of course, was that such systems gave extraordinary power to a few individuals, for good or ill. The views of a long-serving bank manager, for example, could outweigh the normal information-gathering processes of that institution and thereby make it, in turn, a weak link in the community's intelligence web. Brown Shipley welcomed the retirement of one Liverpool banker in 1868 on the grounds that 'the Directors [of the bank] are to be consulted on matters in which they are likely to be informed, such as the standing of people opening and holding accounts, more than has lately been the case'.[25]

There was clearly a balance to be struck between the role of individuals and of broader systems in assessing reputational questions. In addition, business morality had to be held to dif-ferent standards depending on whether there was a risk to third parties. Much of the furore over joint-stock companies and passenger shipping lines stemmed from the danger to the innocent public as shareholders and customers, whereas the trading community expected that business-men would be better able to look after themselves in their own, internal dealings. Inevitably, assessing those latter, much more secretive, information environments poses greater problems of evidence.

Monitoring Systems

Business historians began to pay much more attention to information during the 1990s. They recognised that in many sectors of the economy, the ability of firms and individuals to gather and use information can be as important as better-known aspects of business activity, such as the management of capital, plant, workforces and materials. As with all of those elements, information is not free, and information costs can be a significant, although often hard to quantify, part of business calculations. The need for information was manifest in two major ways in late nineteenth century Liverpool, and Casson's distinction between factual and moral information offers a useful framework.[26] The fluidity and rapid turnover of the business community, accompanied by accelerated communications and business routines, made it ever more vital to have a quick and reliable measure of the trustworthiness of firms. At the same time, of course, those very characteristics of the commercial environment made it harder to gather such information, because transactions had to be concluded more quickly, and the increasing size of business communities made it difficult for traders to know each other personally.

In the later decades of the nineteenth century, businesses made a series of attempts to institutionalise the sort of reputation-monitoring which had long been done informally through individual conversations, gossip and rumour. Some of the new structures, such as the rules and sanctions of trade associations, were intended to prevent firms straying from accepted practices in the first place; others were aimed to monitor firms at work. Obviously, the simple existence of monitoring systems was also supposed to encourage good behaviour. Lawrence Dicksee, an early management academic, identified four broad types of report that could be sought by firms seeking to identify trustworthy clients and customers, and these, with some variation, characterise the information environment more generally. Such information could come from banks, from other firms, from individuals with personal knowledge of those involved, and from the increasing number of credit reference agencies. All types were subject to conflicts of interest and raised tensions between opposing loyalties.[27]

Businessmen have always used personal and informal information-gathering methods, and this did not change in the nineteenth century. Indeed, given the increased ease of long-distance communication and business travel, as well as higher levels of migration and mobility, direct connections remained a valuable way of learning about the trustworthiness of potential collaborators, suppliers and customers. Firms with branches in more than one place, as well as those which simply had been in business longer than average, were able to benefit from the development of far-reaching networks of contacts. However, locality remained crucial, with most firms and individuals working hard to develop a solid grounding with a local business community so that there would always be those willing to testify in their favour. Personal reputation was crucial to individual private traders and directors of joint-stock companies alike, with a businessman getting credit 'far beyond his means' if his standing was good.[28] Reputation was explicitly equated with capital: new firms which had yet to build their reputations needed more capital in order to do the same level of trade.[29]

Firms used their networks to gather information and corroborate their impressions. This was not always easy, especially in periods of business uncertainty when businesses might fail with little warning after years of real or apparent strength in the market. At such times, the accuracy and currency of reputation-related information became more important than usual, and the risk of misjudgement was also elevated. Firms which had been proved wrong in their assessment of failed businesses became reluctant to pass judgement next time, lest there seem to be a reflection on them. Antony Gibbs & Son's London office reported to Liverpool in 1900 that 'after recent disclosures concerning firms of supposed good repute, there is more hesitation than formerly in expressing opinions'.[30]

Asking too many questions about a firm could damage the firm's reputation, and there was an element of self-restraint within the community. Brown Shipley heard that a cotton-broking firm seemed unlikely to have the resources to import goods on its own account, but found it difficult to learn more: 'We did not press Mr Smith [a banker] to say more because we saw that he did not at all wish to do so, and we cannot investigate the matter further because their credit out of doors is still unshaken'.[31] In other words, while private enquiries to banks and a select few leading firms were considered acceptable in such circumstances, seeking opinions from a wider range of firms was not. At the same time, however, firms generally known to be in difficulty were openly talked about, although the firms themselves seem not to have been confronted with this directly. This enabled businesses that were struggling, but which had not actually failed, to maintain the public face 'that their embarrassments are not known, whilst everybody is at the same time discussing them'.[32] Such convenient fictions were presumably not maintained for very long, but they evidently allowed some firms the breathing space to try to recover their positions.

A number of different triggers aroused suspicion and firms tried to anticipate trouble. Traders who started working outside their usual boundaries were watched closely. In 1868, for example, Brown Shipley noted that Maclean Maris &Co. seemed to be doing well, but it was now certain that they had moved away from their established commission business and were trading heavily in cotton on their own account.[33] Kleinworts responded to a query about a firm in the copper trade with the thought that 'some people think they combine too many businesses in one'.[34] Even major internationally known firms took risks with their reputations in this way. Brown Shipley reported that Antony Gibbs & Son had fallen somewhat in the community's estimation since they started getting involved in financing rather than trading; the Moscow Gas Works had 'turned out very badly', it seemed, and there was another 'bad big thing' looming.[35] Getting involved in banking was seen as especially dangerous in the turbulent international economy of the 1860s, which created a particular problem for Greek trading firms. Barings kept a list of such businesses, with such comments as 'has mixed himself up with banking business, therefore caution'; 'have large means but are altogether in finance'; and 'a banker merely'.[36] Part of the problem with firms which diversified their activities was that they undermined one of the standard elements in character referencing. Assessments of firms very often included stock phrases to the effect that they were to be trusted 'in the regular ordinary course of their business', or that they were 'good for what they do'.[37] Character books listed the normal business of firms and referees often urged that any deviation from these existing specialisms should be discouraged.[38]

Generational changes also provoked concern and the firms tried to ascertain the extent to which established companies were likely to survive succession. Although the fecklessness of youth was a common complaint, some cases also involved the older generation letting family obligation interfere with normal business sense. The Liverpool & Manchester District Bank reported in 1868 that one of its directors, no less, was insisting on setting his son up in business despite the latter being 'quite unfit in the opinion of everyone but his father to carry it on if left to himself'. The son had become 'very fast and extravagant, keeping a woman in a very ostentatious and expensive style', but no-one had the courage to tell the father. Importantly, though, the bank's officials clearly had no qualms about informing leading firms which made enquiries of the need for caution in dealing with the new venture.[39] In other cases, the absence of family succession was the problem. William Lowe, a Liverpool grain merchant, maintained an extensive system for monitoring his various Irish contacts in the trade. One such enquiry focussed on a firm in which the senior partner was highly respectable but well into his seventies, while the son had already emigrated to Australia for his health. That, unfortunately, left an unrelated active partner 'of a very different standing' from the others.[40]

More routine succession questions also caused uncertainty. A key issue was establishing the 'responsible capital' of a firm.[41] This was the capital actually available to the directors, as opposed to the total sums nominally associated with the firm. The latter included personal assets of the older generation and various guarantee arrangements which might not prove enforceable. Although retiring partners often left capital in a firm, it was rarely clear what their executors would do when they died, and apparently wealthy companies could suddenly look rather thin. Even the well-established Rathbone Bros was thought to have much reduced capital by the early twentieth century as older members of the family died and their capital was divided and channelled out of the business.[42]

Establishing responsible capital was part of the wider problem of separating personal from business assets in family firms and partnerships where such distinctions were unclear. Individuals sometimes used the same bank account for a variety of investing, trading and personal purposes, so even their banks were not sure where the boundaries were—and given the importance of banks in the wider information environment, that contributed to a wider frustration among those managing credit agencies.[43] Shares in railway companies were widely used as securities for bank loans and overdrafts, and became a kind of parallel currency underpinning many of the business community's processes. Some bankers' loan register books from the 1880s had tables of railway dividend summaries for recent years pasted inside the front cover, presumably so that clerks recording a new or renewed loan could immediately assess the value of the security being offered.[44] However, in most cases, these shares belonged to the partners, rather than to the firm, and this was likely to be problematic in a sudden crisis when ownership of assets and liabilities became disputed. On the other hand, some traders deliberately kept their firm's affairs separate from their own, in an effort to keep information from their bankers. One Liverpool shipowner had a personal account with the North & South Wales Bank and a business account with the Bank of Liverpool in the 1880s. His bankruptcy hearing was told that this had been arranged deliberately so that the stock speculations which he ran from the former might not damage his credit with the latter.[45]

Certain firms and institutions became particularly important elements in these information flows, to the point that they effectively became certifiers of reputations, although it seems unlikely that they welcomed that role. The names of bankers, and of the leading two or three firms in any given trade, repeatedly appear in the correspondence and character books of firms as having been approached for their opinions. Sometimes a chain of information was involved, including at some point the authoritative voice of one of these figures. Examples are numerous, often along the lines of 'Arthur Heywood [a banker] knows from a trustworthy source . . .', or in letters from a major local firm passing on information from 'friends' elsewhere; in those circumstances, the information coming from the often un-named 'friends' was implicitly attested by the reputation of the Liverpool firm.[46]

The mobility of firms and their multi-branch operations stretched the monitoring capacity of the business community. One firm working in the Liverpool timber trade was well respected, but most of its finances were reportedly arranged through Canadian banks, which make it difficult to assess its capital; this was more worrying than usual in 1900, when the firm lost a large stock in an Ottawa fire, and its level of insurance was unclear.[47] Such emergencies exposed weaknesses in information gathering. Another transatlantic firm presented a slightly different problem, in that the capital associated with its Liverpool branch was well known but seemed inadequate to cover its large business. Only after extensive enquires in Boston and New York, and an effort to unpick the complicated partnership structures of various branches, were the firm's activities revealed to be solid enough.[48] Even firms working closer to home could attract attention in this way, and some of these information horizons were very local. Antony Gibbs & Son highlighted a firm of merchants who 'appear to have no banking account in Liverpool', and while it emerged that they had bankers in Manchester, this evidently put them beyond the everyday information-gathering circles of Liverpool business.[49]

The currency of information was a major concern. As Orchard noted in his discussion of Liverpool's leading businesses, 'A firm that had £100,000 capital when this book went to the printer may have lost every penny before it was published'.[50] The credit reference agencies were well aware of this problem and maintained continuously updated files in addition to publishing their annual commercial lists. Subscribers were sent the annual volume but could then approach the agency for its most recent opinion on a particular firm at any point in the year. When Antony Gibbs & Son sought the views of R. G. Dun's London office on a San Francisco firm, they were told that the most recent volume credited the firm with a capital of $1m, but that they would provide a 'full report' soon.[51] Seyd & Co., publishers of the *Commercial List* which ranked firms on a scale from one to four, provided information which was apparently more detailed and qualitative when asked, although many of the stock phrases which lay behind the classification also appear in these reports. Businessmen reading the key to the numerical rating would gain as much information as being told explicitly that a certain firm had 'excellent standing and reputation' or was 'possessed of large resources', so the importance of the special individual report was its currency, not that it was likely to offer more detail.[52]

Mercantile reference agencies became very busy toward the end of the nineteenth century. The British Mercantile Agency, for example, which was not one of the better-known firms, handled 7,223 enquiries in 1890, rising to 35,455 by 1911; assuming a five-and-a-half day week, that was more than 120 queries a day by the latter date.[53] Stubbs Mercantile Offices, probably the biggest British firm, claimed to make more than half a million company investigations a year by 1900.[54] Although there is little evidence of the attitudes of British business toward credit agencies, at least one American campaigner doubted whether agencies could really be doing the work they claimed to do. Thomas Meagher's 1876 analysis of what he called the 'secret inquisition' alleged that agencies would have needed three times the staff just to gather information, let alone process and distribute it; he also argued that much of the apparently scientific rating process was influenced by religious bias, conflicts of interest and a general lack of accountability. Agency reports, thought Meagher, consisted of 'Delphic doubtfulness and wary inconsequence' dressed up in codes and numbers.[55]

Information associated with the reputations, capital and creditworthiness of firms was obviously valuable in a financial as well as an operational sense, and confidentiality was important. Character books, for example, were often maintained with numerical codes and a separate index, so that it was impossible to tell at a glance which firm was the subject of which reference. This practice seems to have declined over time, with later examples being organised by simple alphabetical listings.[56] The sheer volume of work undoubtedly made it more efficient to restrict access to the books in the first place. Reference agencies insisted that their rating books be kept under lock and key and only used by subscribers personally, although of course they had no way of policing that. When they sent reports through the post, Seyd & Co. referred to their subjects by initials, and other examples exist of firms being referred to only as 'the firm in question', presumably relying on a given business not making so many simultaneous enquiries that confusion would result.[57]

Such individual enquiries were naturally expensive and firms devised rough rules of thumb to reduce the costs of gathering information in particular situations. When the cotton industry was struggling in the early 1880s, for example, Barings advised that bills from spinners could be accepted with some caution, but that there was not much risk on 100 to 200 bales from anyone—beyond that, 'we think it will be prudent to call for a special report'.[58] Later, Barings recommended that bills from manufacturers in Oldham be avoided, but that those from Bolton and Manchester men were likely to be sound in moderate quantities. Such generalisations clearly grouped together firms of varying reliability, but in the troubled circumstances of that season's trading, the costs of a minor loss presumably outweighed the costs of investigating every firm individually.[59]

Although information flows sometimes appear very free and far-reaching, there were clearly some limits. Firms could insist that their bankers not reveal certain aspects of their activities more widely, placing an additional weight on the bankers' own standing—the bank was in effect asking enquirers not only to trust the firm in question, but also the bank's judgement as to the importance of the information being concealed. One firm, for example, told its bank not to divulge the identity of a sleeping partner who had taken an interest in the company; the bank respected this wish and continued to tell any enquirers that the firm was very respectable, but it did not reveal the existence (let alone the identity) of the sleeping partner.[60]

In other cases, business worked behind the scenes to manage bad news. Failures in a particular trade often drove widespread speculation about whether other firms would be dragged down, and banks were especially susceptible to such gossip. The North & South Wales Bank reported in 1876 that rumours were circulating in Ulster about its exposure to various Liverpool corn-trading firms recently bankrupted. The bank wrote to one senior figure 'as an old friend' reassuring him that it held ample securities and would lose no money; if he heard such rumours, it hoped that he would 'not simply out of friendship for me, but in the interests of truth, give them a prompt and unqualified contradiction'. As for the cause of the rumours, 'I suppose our great success inspires some people with a spite against us'.[61]

Some battles over reputation were fought in public, as firms and individuals pursued their critics in the courts or through the newspapers. The entire business complex was infused with this fear of allowing negative publicity to stand unchallenged, even in apparently trivial matters. In 1890, the *Daily Post* had to carry a correction to its report that a cotton broker had collapsed and died at the Angel Hotel in Dale Street. The tragedy had in fact occurred in 'an adjoining restaurant having no connection with that establishment'—and none of the numerous eateries serving the office district wanted to be known as a place where businessmen dropped dead.[62] Shipowners became sensitive to allegations that they were reckless with their ships and crews, and won libel cases when such stories were published. The press tried to disguise their targets but were sometimes not very sophisticated. William Price, owner of the Liverpool ship *Mow Hill*, took £500 in damages from the *Wide World Magazine* when it printed allegations about a ship called *Mole Hill* operated by 'William Cost'.[63]

Famous firms had reason to fear that their names would be abused in other ways. In 1894, a London shipbroker trading under the name T. & R. Brockelbank (sic) tried to charter a ship from one J. W. Link, implying that he ran the London office of Liverpool's well-known Brocklebank & Co.; this was almost enough to persuade Link to trust him, but subsequent checks exposed the broker as having no connection with the Liverpool firm and no prospect of paying for the charter either. Importantly, though, Brockelbank was careful never to claim the Liverpool connection in writing, and it would have been hard to convict him of any criminal charges. His activities only came to light when he foolishly sued Link for backing out of the charter and lost.[64]

The end result of this complicated web of monitoring and classification often seems rather mundane, with Liverpool's greatest firms reinforcing each other's reputations and accepting each other's credit in a virtuous circle. It probably made much more of a difference to the operations of lesser firms, both for those which were spared dealing with unreliable traders, and for those drummed out of business by having poor reports circulated about them. In addition, there is evidence that lesser firms and tradesmen used information networks in a different way from larger operators. In 1898, a House of Lords committee expressed some scepticism that people below the ranks of the elite would feel able to ask a large firm for references or guarantees before doing business; rather, they would be much more dependent on seeking the advice of their bankers.[65] This raises important questions about the extent to which information was limited not only by cost but by some combination of social deference and exclusive membership of elite circles; most of the evidence used in this study includes at least one element of elite involvement. It would be intriguing, but very difficult, to reconstruct the information environment within which lesser traders, retailers and tradesmen dealt with one another, evidently separate in large part from the elite systems under consideration here.

Fraud, Failure and Responsibility

The dark side of business practice clearly occupies a wide spectrum of behaviour and opinion, from universally recognised criminality to actions of more debatable legitimacy. Liverpool's business community had to address the full range over time. Many people were arrested, charged and convicted of fraud and other crimes relating to their business activities, and evidence for these events is available, even if crime has long been an area of particular methodological difficulty for historians. Non-criminal business failures are well recorded when they led to bankruptcy; many publications carried lists of so-called 'mercantile embarrassments', and historians have also made extensive use of central government records in this area.[66] Evidence becomes much more elusive when assessing behaviour that did not fall into those categories, but which nonetheless breached the norms and standards of the business community. Indeed, close reading of criminal and bankruptcy proceedings often reveals a range of other activities of concern to business elites that usually did not get so far.

Some cases relate to wider concerns about changes in the business environment as outlined earlier in this chapter, and in particular to the supposedly loose rules surrounding the management and finance of joint-stock companies. William Tapscott, for example, informed the bankruptcy court in 1897 that his shipowning and fleet-managing business had liabilities of more than £30,000 and no assets, while the accounts of six separate steamship firms under his management were found to be in deficit by more than £40,000.[67] Tapscott was no fly-by-night. His firm had been established by his father in 1847 and it had traded successfully in shipbroking and managing the emigrant trade until 1877. Then, the firm failed to make its payments and reached a private arrangement to pay its creditors 10s on the pound. This was common enough and 10s was appreciably higher than many such settlements, so the broader opinion in the community was probably favourable. Before a second bankruptcy hearing could be convened, however, Tapscott was arrested on the orders of the Treasury in London and charged with 37 counts of deceiving shareholders and otherwise violating the various Companies Acts; he was ultimately convicted and sentenced to three years in prison. However, the Liverpool jury only convicted him on some counts, not all, and the magistrate even reduced the level of bail demanded. Such nuances may reflect a sense within the city that Tapscott was not a serious offender and that the Treasury's prosecution of the company law violations was an intrusion into Liverpool's affairs.

A similar ambivalence is evident in many cases. Decisions over bankruptcy could be fraught, especially if creditors had conflicting interests. It was common for the largest creditors in a given case to favour private arrangements rather than go through the bankruptcy procedure, but smaller creditors might be less able to absorb losses and more inclined to pursue debtors as far as possible. One commentator claimed that creditors who were not in the same line of business, or who had limited dealings with the debtor over time, were less likely to support private arrangements.[68] Whether a failed firm went bankrupt probably owed a good deal to how diverse its creditors were—the smaller and better-known its circle, the less likely it would be forced through the courts.

The extent to which bankruptcy could be administered by the business community itself remained controversial, and successive legal reforms brought varying degrees of official involvement and oversight. The new law in 1883 was intended to stop creditors taking too lenient a view, but some commentators felt that it had swung too far the other way. Sometimes there were utilitarian reasons for keeping a failed merchant engaged in the process: one international trader dealt in such a complex variety of 'weights and carriages, languages and customs', that his creditors paid him a salary to help the accountants wind up the business in an orderly manner.[69] More usually, creditors agreed to accept small repayments in the case of 'an honourable failure', such as losses incurred by an overseas agent when the local firm had always acted in good faith. This might be overruled by a judge insisting on more severe punishment, but surely, complained the otherwise-supportive *Liverpool Review* in one such instance, 'creditors, who are businessmen, know better about such matters than a judge'.[70]

More radical voices saw the same patterns as a question of collective guilt, especially when there was a measure of fraud involved. Small shopkeepers and tradesmen seemed more likely than major merchants to be taken to court. Perhaps the large firms were just more ethical, or maybe the affairs of victims and perpetrators were so closely entwined that no one could risk speaking out: 'In the present *rouge et noir* system of business, men who are creditors often find themselves so involved in other business relations with their debtors that they deem it in their interest to be quiescent'.[71]

How firms—and more importantly, individuals—behaved in adversity was a crucial element in the ongoing definition of their standing in the community. An appropriate humility was appreciated, as was a certain degree of stoicism. A contemporary opinion of the cotton trader Charles Prioleau captures the flavour of many such comments, not least because in this case the writer was sympathetic to his subject and wanted to see him get back into business:

> I candidly own I should have thought better of him if he had gone into a small house. People are becoming very sore, especially the old steady going people in reference to failed firms' style of living etc etc. Prioleau keeps his Brougham and to all appearances lives better than a good many folks [who] have paid their debts and some plain truths are now pretty generally spoken in reference to such things.[72]

The reckless trader, it was alleged by the 1880s, had become easy to spot, living comfortably on other people's money and usually having his property in his wife's name: this barely coded equation of business immorality with a lack of manly responsibility appears frequently in the sources.[73] On the other hand, a degree of *chutzpah* was secretly admired in many quarters and businessmen knew that they had to be seen to hold their nerve. *Porcupine* recounted the story in 1870 of one trader who cut short a meeting of his creditors discussing whether to bankrupt him, insisting that he had to appear on 'Change at his usual time.[74]

There was a consensus that businessmen who behaved fraudulently deserved punishment, but decisions about what form of sanction was appropriate tended to involve a good deal of pragmatism. When a leading corn merchant failed in 1890, the Liverpool Union Bank considered bringing a prosecution, but its chairman thought that 'unless we are *quite* clear we should get a conviction and ample punishment, I don't think it is advisable to go into court, and recent incidents don't encourage us much'. It might be better, perhaps, just to threaten to prosecute and thereby encourage one or both of the partners to leave Liverpool: the chairman even suggested a possible intermediary to deliver such a message to the guilty party.[75]

The highest profile failures of the 1880s and 1890s were the cotton-cornerers Morris Ranger and William Steenstrand. Ranger had been born in Prussia in 1835 and lived at 31 Catherine Street, both before and after his bankruptcy. He was known by *The Illustrated London News* as the so-called 'Big Operator' (Figure 4.1) and had successfully cornered the Liverpool cotton market in both 1879 and 1881. Despite the shock and suffering caused by his bankruptcy, he was remembered for philanthropy toward poorer members of the Jewish community, softening criticism of his trading practices.[76] William Steenstrand was 'a German Jew', by birth: he was known as the 'Cotton King' and was 'a strongly built man'. He began to corner the market in March 1890 and failed in July. Although he had reputation as a 'shrewd judge of the cotton market', at one point he apparently lost $1m in an hour. Irrespective of the widespread losses which caused his fall, he 'evoked much sympathy among men on 'Change, among whom he is best known'.[77] In both cases, fellow traders were supportive, despite the extensive damage inflicted on other firms. Neither man did anything criminal, but their attempts to corner the cotton market brought down many firms and caused much distress in the cotton-manufacturing districts. Cotton corners were not just a matter of internal dispute in Liverpool business and they need to be seen in the context of broader social attitudes toward commercial practice and morality. Liverpool was itself divided over the appropriate use of the new futures trading practices and there was a sense that some firms were likely to stray when offered the temptation of more speculative trading. Firms were said to 'take a view of the market'—this code appears in many character references and referred to cotton-brokers especially who engaged in trend-spotting and speculative buying or selling.[78] Whitaker, Whitehead & Co., Liverpool cotton brokers, condemned the

1. Surrounding the Big Operator.—2. A Spinner.—3. The End of the Corner.—4. The Big Operator.—5. " Futures."—6. A Young Broker.—7. An Old Broker.—8. On 'Change : Announcement of Sales by the Secretary.

THE LIVERPOOL COTTON CORNER

Figure 4.1 The Liverpool Cotton Corner, *The Graphic*, 8 October 1881

cornering and speculating that had 'become a curse to their trade and what, in our opinion, is a disgrace to the Cotton Exchange of Liverpool'.[79]

Whitakers were right to be concerned about Liverpool's image. The Manchester Chamber of Commerce considered it 'incredible' that Morris Ranger had been widely forgiven in Liverpool and condemned the 'gambling in cotton', which seemed characteristic of the city's market.[80] The issue of gambling in futures turned many commentators against the seemingly impenetrable activities of traders in the 1880s and 1890s. Charles W. Smith, an author of various polemics on the issue, drew most of his evidence from the Liverpool markets, and argued that 'there could be no justice in permitting the depreciation and ultimate ruin of our agriculture, trade and commerce in order to enrich a few thousands of speculative operators'.[81]

The practiced of futures trading in corn was even more emotive, because critics claimed that Liverpool's merchants were gambling with the nation's food supplies. The Liverpool corn market began working in futures in 1883 and London subsequently adopted the practice.[82] A new generation of landowners and farmers revived issues assumed to have been laid to rest with the abolition of the Corn Laws in the 1840s. In 1894, the Central and Associated Chambers of Agriculture passed a motion that 'the system of gambling in wheat and other produce, known as 'options' and 'futures' paralyses legitimate trading and injures producers'.[83] Similar resolutions can be found in the minutes of many agricultural interest groups in this era. American agrarians were also concerned about the increasing influence of the Liverpool market on grain prices. Even if traders pursued ethical methods, the ability of a single market to set prices was unnerving, and American producers urged their government to promote trade with other parts of the world and to encourage the establishment of competing markets that would reduce Liverpool's power and influence.[84]

Throughout the 1890s and into the first decade of the twentieth century, protectionists increasingly challenged the free trade orthodoxy of the previous decades and used alleged commercial immorality to attack the international trading system. Legislation in some parts of the United States and Europe severely limited futures trading and such developments were closely watched by both sides in Britain. Like its counterpart in Liverpool, the New York Cotton Exchange became a focus for a wide range of critics.[85] The Berlin Produce Exchange dissolved itself briefly in 1897 rather than abide by a law banning futures trading in agricultural produce—traders argued that the measure simply gave the big American markets more business.[86] Several bills were promoted in the British Parliament aiming to ban such trading, although none succeeded; under one example from 1909, any cotton broker handling a futures transaction would have had his office defined as a 'common gaming-house' and made subject to gambling legislation.[87]

Research into a number of markets in the US and Britain has concluded that commodity exchanges rarely took robust steps against market manipulation in this era. Their administrative priority was, rather, to enforce contracts between their members.[88] It is hardly surprising, then, that Liverpool's markets attracted criticism from outside. In addition, Victorian fears about gambling more generally became entangled with concerns about financial speculation, although most research into these matters has focused on stock markets rather than commodity exchanges.[89]

Some firms tried to assuage bad publicity through education, explaining futures trading and its value. Weld & Co., a major cotton broking firm with houses in Liverpool, Boston, Philadelphia, New York, Houston and Bremen, even published a pamphlet in 1905 for distribution to spinners and other inland manufacturing interests. Weld & Co. carefully crafted the document to reassure doubters, arguing that 'a futures contract is, to the trade in natural cotton, what currency is to the general commerce of the world'. Importantly, Weld & Co. stressed the institutional and contractual apparatus of futures trading, reprinting various contract forms and listings of trading rules to emphasise the weight of regulation and formality involved. In addition, the Liverpool Cotton Contract had been repeatedly accepted in the courts as 'a genuine trade contract, and not a gambling or speculative medium'.[90]

Monitoring reputation and reliability was part of a wider business culture which placed heavy reliance on self-regulation. This was perceived to have long roots, with frequent allusions to the alleged activities of medieval guilds. Looking back from the early twentieth century, however, C. F. Birdseye, a New York lawyer (and father of the frozen food pioneer), argued that modern arbitration and self-regulation developed in 1860s Liverpool. Disputes over cotton after the American Civil War drove a movement in associational governance of business communities which rapidly became the norm in British business with remarkably few cases ever reaching the courts. Only after the financial crisis of 1907 did the New York Chamber of Commerce seek to formalise its arbitration procedures, having first sent requests 'to England for all possible literature upon the subject'.[91]

Birdseye recognised that self-governance worked better in some trading environments than in others and he set out a revealing list of criteria likely to facilitate the process. An association seeking to manage the activities of its members should have a close and definite focus, dealing with homogeneous goods and services; it should also establish clear rules, standardise its contracts, and appoint arbitrators of unimpeachable reputation. In such circumstances, disputes would be relatively rare anyway. When a tribunal did hear a case, though, it should bear in mind 'the larger ethical and business interests of the organisation and its members as affected by the particular dispute'.[92] This balance between collective and individual interests was at the heart of mercantile self-regulation, and required some sacrifice of the latter in the short term.

Liverpool associations claimed much success in these terms. The chairman of the Stock Exchange testified in 1878 that 'we settle all our disputes by arbitration before the committee' and that actions in law were 'very infrequent'. The Stock Exchange also banned failed members who opted for formal bankruptcy when they could have come to an arrangement with their fellow brokers. Such an approach naturally encouraged settlements to be kept within the association's ranks.[93] Associations were good at self-regulation, but many business transactions, of course, crossed associational boundaries—members of the Cotton Association did business with members of the Steamship Owners Association, for example, and neither body had jurisdiction over those deals. There was therefore some agitation in this era for a more general system of commercial tribunals capable of extending self-regulation by individual trades to business communities as a whole. These would be particularly valuable, one lawyer argued, in the 'first class maritime towns, in Liverpool, in Bristol and in Hull', where complex trading systems operated.[94]

Some of the wider implications of a self-regulation culture need further exploration. For example, Liverpool's bankruptcy rate in relation to total employment in the late nineteenth century was appreciably lower than that of most major English cities, with the exception of Manchester, and this is usually assumed to have been the result of having fewer small tradesmen of the sort who were statistically most likely to suffer bankruptcy. In addition, Liverpool suffered far less violent swings in bankruptcy rates from year to year than most cities. On the other hand, the bankruptcy system itself was widely accepted to have failed during the 1870s when creditors (that is, local business communities) had control of the system, and is regarded as improving only when central government scrutiny was re-introduced after 1883.[95] Given the considerable local variation in these patterns, however, the role of self-regulation and business culture in individual towns, cities and economic sectors needs a more detailed assessment.

Conclusion

Liverpool's business elite became increasingly conscious of its image in the later nineteenth century, and, in particular, of the ways in which its routine commercial practices coloured perceptions of its ethical standing. That consciousness, however, did not alter Liverpool's determination to set its own standards without paying too much attention to metropolitan opinion. Closer to home, disputes with Manchester and the textile manufacturing interests in the late nineteenth century helped, if anything, to solidify the sense that Liverpool business represented a high level of free-trading commercial integrity, in contrast to the perceived protectionist and regulatory inclinations of the hinterland. It is also evident that new institutions and mechanisms were superimposed on existing structures, rather than replacing them. Credit reference agencies are widely considered to have been an important innovation in the later nineteenth century, for example, the upper levels of mercantile business made use of their services without abandoning personal, local networks. While occasionally embarrassed by business failures and scandals, Liverpool's elite retained great faith in their systems for gathering information and monitoring reputations, while their general success and prosperity enabled them to resist suggestions that traders and markets should be subject to closer official scrutiny.

Notes

1 *Daily Post*, 16 November 1895.
2 *Courier*, 21 January 1884.
3 *Courier*, 3 February 1892; *Mercury*, 3 February 1892.
4 *Porcupine*, 1 May 1875.
5 *The Century's Progress: Lancashire* (London, 1892), p. 219.
6 *The Century's Progress*, p. 214.
7 *Liverpool Review*, 5 April 1884, p. 10.
8 See Graeme Milne, Chapter 3.
9 Mary B. Rose, 'The Family Firm in British Business, 1780–1914', in Maurice W. Kirby and Mary B. Rose (eds.), *Business Enterprise in Modern Britain* (London, 1994), pp. 61–87.
10 LRO, Liverpool Worthies, reel 1, *Daily Albion*, 27 May 1881, Charles Mozley.
11 HSBC Group Archives, North & South Wales Bank, Board minutes, M19, 6 January 1880.
12 *Fairplay*, 17 July 1891, p. 139; 7 August 1891, p. 287.
13 Crosbie Smith, Ian Higginson and Phillip Wolstenholme, '"Imitations of God's Own Works": Making Trustworthy the Ocean Steamship', *History of Science* 41 (2003), pp. 379–426; Crosbie Smith, '"A Most Terrific Passage": Putting Faith into Atlantic Steam Navigation', in Robert Lee (ed.), *Commerce and Culture Nineteenth-Century Business Elites* (Farnham, 2011), pp. 285–316.
14 Robin Bastin, 'Cunard and the Liverpool Emigrant Traffic, 1860–1900', unpublished MA thesis, University of Liverpool (1971), pp. 59–61.
15 British Parliamentary Papers (BPP), Royal Commission on Loss of Life at Sea, 1887, vol. 43, C.5227-II, qq. 16,695.
16 *Investors' Review*, X (1897), p. 168.
17 Baring Archive, 102134, 17 January 1891.
18 BPP, Select Committee on the Companies Bill, 1897, vol. 10, 384, qq. 452.
19 Lloyds TSB Archives, Liverpool Union Bank, A/35/6/20, 6 January 1876.
20 *Fairplay*, 10 April 1902, p. 567.
21 *Liverpool Courier*, 7 September 1883.
22 HSBC Group Archives, N&S Wales Bank, Letter Book, M116, 2 April 1889, 11 April 1889.
23 B. Guinness Orchard, *Liverpool's Legion of Honour* (Birkenhead, 1893).
24 Guildhall Library, Antony Gibbs & Son papers, 11038C, 20 December 1883.
25 Guildhall Library, Brown Shipley papers, 20108/1, 18 January 1868.
26 Mark Casson, *Information and Organisation: A New Perspective on the Theory of the Firm* (Oxford, 1997), chapter 6.

27   Lawrence R. Dicksee, *Business Organisation* (London, 1910), pp. 176–81.
28   BPP, Select Committee on the Companies Bill, 1896, vol. 9, 342, qq. 1,991–2.
29   Dicksee, *Business Organisation*, p. 2.
30   Guildhall Library, Antony Gibbs & Son papers, 11069C, 20 July 1900.
31   Guildhall Library, Brown Shipley papers, 20108/1, 4 January 1868.
32   Guildhall Library, Brown Shipley papers, 20108/1, 13 February 1868.
33   Guildhall Library, Brown Shipley papers, 20108/1, 22 April 1868.
34   Guildhall Library, Kleinwort Sons & Co. information books, 22030, vol. 1, James Lewis and Woodgate Anderson & Co. (1887).
35   Guildhall Library, Brown Shipley papers, 20108/1, 11 November 1868.
36   Baring Archive, HC16.19, listing of 17 December 1860.
37   Guildhall Library, Kleinwort Sons & Co. information books, 22033, vol. 1, Edward Challoner (1900); Duncan Ewing (1901).
38   MMM, MAL, William Lowe character book, DX190 2/11, Bostock & Co., 30 May 1889.
39   Guildhall Library, Brown Shipley papers, 20108/1, 25 June 1868.
40   MMM, MAL, William Lowe character book, DX190 2/11, Richard Perrin & Sons, 23 November 1888.
41   Guildhall Library, Kleinwort Sons & Co. information books, 22033, vol. 1, Straus & Co. (1911).
42   Guildhall Library, Kleinwort Sons & Co. information books, 22033, vol. 1, Rathbone Bros (1903).
43   BPP, Select Committee on the Registration of Firms Bill, 1900, vol. 8, 281, qq. 18.
44   HSBC Group Archives, N&S Wales Bank, Loans register, M97.
45   *Liverpool Mercury*, 28 August 1885, p. 6.
46   Guildhall Library, Antony Gibbs & Son papers, 11038C, September 1882 (Haywood); 11069C, 10 Sept. 1883 ('friends').
47   Baring Archive, 102136, 9 May 1900.
48   Baring Archive, 102136, 1 May 1903.
49   Guildhall Library, Antony Gibbs & Son papers, 11069C, 7 March 1901.
50   Orchard, *Liverpool's Legion of Honour*, p. 80.
51   Guildhall Library, Antony Gibbs & Son papers, 11069C, 26 June 1903.
52   For example, Guildhall Library, Antony Gibbs & Son papers, 11069C, 10 September 1902.
53   Calculated from Guildhall Library, 28881.
54   BPP, Select Committee on the Registration of Firms Bill, 1900, vol. 8, 281, qq. 1–7.
55   Thomas Meagher, *The Commercial Agency 'System' of the United States and Canada Exposed: Is the Secret Inquisition a Curse or a Benefit?* (New York, 1876), pp. 12–19.
56   For example, the early coded books and later alphabetical books of Barings in the HC16 sequence; the late-century alphabetical books of Antony Gibbs & Son, Guildhall Library, 11038C, 11069C.
57   Guildhall Library, Antony Gibbs & Son papers, 11069C, 10 September 1902.
58   Baring Archive, 102134, 10 September 1883.
59   Baring Archive, 102134, 9 October 1891.
60   Guildhall Library, Antony Gibbs & Son papers, 11069C, Jas Thompson & Son (1889).
61   HSBC Group Archives, N&S Wales Bank, Letter book M116, 29 April 1876.
62   *Daily Post*, 30 August 1890, 2 September 1890.
63   *Fairplay*, 8 December 1898, p. 950.
64   *The Times*, 2 February 1894, p. 3.
65   BPP, Select Committee on the Companies Bill, 1898, vol. 9, 392, qq. 45, 84.
66   V. Markham Lester, *Victorian Insolvency: Bankruptcy, Imprisonment for Debt, and Company Winding-Up in Nineteenth-Century England* (Oxford, 1995).
67   This and the following evidence is taken from *Fairplay*, 24 June 1897, p. 1,051, 8 July 1897, p. 53, 27 July 1897, p. 183, 9 September 1897, p. 453; *The Times*, 6 September 1897, p. 4, 29 September 1897, p. 7, 13 December 1897, p. 10.
68   Dicksee, *Business Organisation*, pp. 189–94.
69   *Liverpool Review*, 7 January 1888, p. 11.
70   *Liverpool Review*, 31 May 1884, p. 11.
71   *Porcupine*, 2 April 1870, p. 6.
72   Guildhall Library, Brown Shipley papers, 20108/1, 30 January 1868.
73   *Liverpool Review*, 27 September 1884, p. 10.
74   *Porcupine*, 9 July 1870, p. 141.
75   Lloyds TSB Archives, Liverpool Union Bank, A/35/6/20, 9 December 1890.

76 Ranger had been born in Prussia in 1835, but by 1871 he was living at 31 Catherine Street, Liverpool, with his American wife, Isabelle, together with their three-year-old son who had also been born in the USA. His first attempt to corner the cotton market took place in 1878 and he was successful in 1879 and 1881. To all intents and purposes, he was bankrupt well before it was officially declared in 1884 leaving debts estimated at £400,000 (£42m in 2019 prices) and causing the collapse of numerous firms and cotton mills. The manipulation of the cotton market by 'cliques' continued to be condemned for its impact on 'disorganising this great branch of commerce'. See 'The Liverpool Cotton Corner', *The New York Times*, 22 September 1881, p. 5; *The London Gazette*, January 1884, p. 311; *The Daily News*, 4 September 1888. Nigel Hall, 'Morris Ranger: The Rise and Fall of Liverpool Cotton's Market's Greatest Speculator, 1835 to 1884', *THSL&C*, 180, 1, pp. 69–92. For an overview of the development of the Liverpool futures market, see Nigel Hall, 'The Liverpool Cotton Market: Britain's First Futures Market', *THSL&C*, 149, pp. 99–117; A Bryce Muir, *Cotton Futures: A Collection of Articles on a Technical Subject* (Liverpool, 1936); MLD.

77 *The Times*, 3 September 1890, p. 8. Among other cotton brokers which were bankrupted by Steenstrand's failure in the previous year to corner the Liverpool market was Holliashead, Tetley & Co., with liabilities of approximately £130,000. His failure received worldwide coverage and cartoons were published featuring the 'Corner Men': see 'The Liverpool Cotton Corner', *Wanganui Herald*, XXVIII, issue 6964, 22 November 1889, p. 2.

78 For example, Guildhall Library, Kleinwort Sons & Co. information books, 22033, vol. 2, Minoprio Forgan (1911).

79 *The Times*, 2 October 1889, p. 12.

80 *Liverpool Daily Post*, 6 November 1883, p. 4.

81 *The Times*, 12 May 1894, p. 13.

82 Anon., *The Liverpool Corn Trade Association, 1853–1953* (Liverpool, 1953), p. 13.

83 *The Times*, 7 February 1894, p. 7.

84 Morton Rothstein, 'America in the International Rivalry of the British Wheat Market, 1860–1914', *Mississippi Valley Historical Review*, 47 (1960), pp. 401–18.

85 Cedric B. Cowing, 'Market Speculation in the Muckraker Era: The Popular Reaction', *Business History Review*, 31 (1957), pp. 403–13; Kenneth J. Lipartito, 'The New York Cotton Exchange and the Development of the Cotton Futures Market', *Business History Review* 57 (1983), pp. 50–72.

86 BPP, Options and futures in foodstuffs, 1903, vol. 68, Cd 1756.

87 BPP, Bill to prohibit gambling in futures and options, 1909, vol. 2, 195.

88 Stephen Craig Pirrong, 'The Self-Regulation of Commodity Exchanges: The Case of Market Manipulation', *Journal of Law and Economics* 38 (1995), pp. 141–205.

89 J. Jeffrey Franklin, 'The Victorian Discourse of Gambling: Speculations on *Middlemarch* and *The Dukes Children*', *English Literary History*, 61 (1994), pp. 899–921; David C. Itzkowitz, 'Fair Enterprise or Extravagant Speculation: Investment, Speculation and Gambling in Victorian England', *Victorian Studies*, 45 (2002), pp. 121–47.

90 Weld & Co., *Cotton Futures: Their Use and Method of Working* (Liverpool, 1905) (copy in British Library).

91 Clarence F. Birdseye, *Arbitration and Business Ethics: A Study of the History and Philosophy of the Various Types of Arbitration and Their Relations to Business Ethics* (New York, 1926), pp. 69, 94.

92 Birdseye, *Arbitration and Business Ethics*, pp. 3–5.

93 BPP, Royal Commission on the London Stock Exchange, 1878, vol. 19, 265, qq. 7,833, 7, 947–9.

94 BPP, Select Committee on the expediency of establishing tribunals of commerce, 1873, vol. 9, 36, qq. 1,182.

95 Lester, *Victorian Insolvency*, pp. 263–4, 282–4.

5 'The Visible Embodiment of Modern Commerce'[1]

The Development of Liverpool's Commercial Centre

Joseph Sharples

Introduction

In the course of the nineteenth century, the rapid growth of a mercantile economy transformed central Liverpool into a dedicated business district, as residential buildings and warehouses were replaced increasingly with purpose-built office blocks, banks, exchanges and other ancillary buildings which reflected the needs of merchants and traders, as the watercolour, 'Water Street' from 1860, by William Herdman clearly illustrates (Figure 5.1). Liverpool, like other port-cities with a significant commercial sector, witnessed the development of a well-defined central business district, despite the absence of any conscious commitment to a formal zone system.[2] Although this was part of a wider process of spatial segregation, its significance in terms of operations management and business efficiency has seldom been explored, while the symbolic significance of commercial, as opposed to public buildings, in ordering social relationships and in structuring class-specific hierarchies has often been ignored.[3] The origins of a central business district can be found in the late eighteenth century and the development of speculative office buildings took place at a relatively early date. This chapter will analyse the role of merchants in configuring the business district and assess the extent to which specific zones provided a focal point for specific trades. It will also explore the changing design of office buildings as a response to the practical needs of merchants for fireproofing, natural lighting and vertical circulation, and examine the wider symbolism of office design and construction.

The Origins of a Central Business District

Writing in 1873, the local architect and historian J. A. Picton (1805–89) vividly described the revolution that had transformed the appearance of central Liverpool since the beginning of the century. Once an area where dwellings and business premises were combined, it had become an office district, populated almost entirely by commuters:

> The town is a sphere to do business in, to make money or—to lose it; but that done, the omnibus, the steamboat, the railway, whirl off their thousands to purer air and brighter skies, until the dawn of another day recalls the busy crowds to another struggle in the battle of life. Far different was the case at the commencement of the century. The merchant or broker lived in the town and was of it. If the head of the firm resided in Bold Street, his office was in Wood Street immediately behind. If in Duke Street, his counting-house and warehouse would be in [parallel] Parr Street or Henry Street.[4]

DOI: 10.4324/9781315597836-5

Figure 5.1 'Water Street', by William Herdman, 1860 (with kind permission of the Liverpool Record Office)

Changes similar to those described by Picton affected all large British towns as nineteenth-century industrialization proceeded. In Liverpool, however, with its mercantile economy of shipowning, commodity trading, banking and insurance, the demand for office accommodation was exceptionally high. It led at a comparatively early date to the formation of a concentrated and coherent business district, to which hundreds of merchants and thousands of record-keeping clerks travelled to work each day. To this extent, what Picton termed 'the insatiable want of commerce' proved to be a key determinant in creating a central business district which reflected the needs of the merchant community as a whole.[5]

From the Middle Ages onwards, the combined Exchange and Town Hall was the 'official' centre of Liverpool's mercantile life. When the Old Dock opened in 1715, a second focus was created, five hundred metres to the south. Although both these hubs were important, and commercial activity was spread between and around them, it was the Exchange which predominated. As rebuilt by the corporation in 1749–54, to the designs of John Wood of Bath, it was a powerful architectural statement of Liverpool's wealth and mercantile prowess. Rich external sculpture celebrated the town's overseas trading links, while the inner courtyard had arcaded walks modelled on London's Royal Exchange. However, this court was dark and confined, and the merchants preferred to transact business outside in the surrounding streets. By the middle of the eighteenth century there were several coffee houses in these streets, where traders could meet to discuss their affairs, and where public sales were held. But there were also coffee houses near the Old Dock, serving much the same purpose. When, at the end of the century, a number of newsrooms were established (including the Athenaeum in Church Street, the Lyceum in Bold

Street, the Union News Room in Duke Street and the hotel at the corner of Whitechapel and Lord Street), they were somewhat removed from both the Old Dock and the Exchange.[6] In other words, the eighteenth-century town was too small and compact to have separate zones for different activities, there was as yet no distinct and exclusive business district, and commercial and residential uses were completely interwoven.

Nevertheless, the separation of workplace and dwelling, and the first intimations of what would grow into the central business district, had already begun by the 1780s. New areas outside the historic centre were being developed for purely residential use, notably Rodney Street from 1783, while somewhat further out Everton was becoming a district of grand suburban villas. Those who moved out of the centre but continued to do business there needed to maintain a base near their fellow merchants, close to the docks, warehouses, banks and Exchange. No doubt former houses were adapted to meet this requirement, but at least one purpose-designed office development was built at this early date by the corporation, explicitly for rent to brokers.

In 1786 the corporation obtained an Improvement Act and embarked on an ambitious programme of street-widening and rebuilding.[7] As part of this programme, the Select Improvement Committee demolished some broker's offices and houses in Exchange Alley—a narrow court on the south side of Water Street—and rebuilt them on a new site, facing the Exchange's newly-exposed west flank.[8] They seem to have been ready for occupation by July 1788, when rents were agreed with the tenants.[9] Named Exchange Alley after its predecessor, the development consisted of a pair of two-storey ranges of offices with vaults underneath, facing each other across a court eight yards wide, with a well and pump in the centre. It could be entered only at the east end, and only by pedestrians.[10]

Gore's directory for 1790 lists a total of nine offices in the Alley. Of those tenants whose residential addresses are also given, only one lived in the pre-eighteenth-century town centre, in Old Hall Street, while the rest had houses east of Whitechapel, an area which had already witnessed significant expansion. Notable among them was the merchant and future mayor George Dunbar, who lived at 12 Martindale's Hill (now 68 Mount Pleasant) on the very edge of the built-up area, in a newly developing street of large houses with extensive gardens. Dunbar's substantial detached house survives, built on a plot that he leased from the corporation in July 1788, having previously lived in Dale Street, right by the Exchange.[11] His new house, in other words, was exactly contemporary with Exchange Alley. Dunbar had probably already split his office from his residence before this date—he had been a tenant of the old Exchange Alley—but the building of the new, improved Alley must have facilitated his removal to Mount Pleasant, thereby making it possible for him to maintain a business presence in the very heart of the town, while enjoying domestic life in the quiet, spacious, green surroundings which were only available on its fringes.

It is not clear if other property owners immediately followed this example and built speculative offices. However, it seems that the corporation expected imitators and was anxious to protect its investment, for within a few weeks of starting to build, the Select Improvement Committee ordered that in all conveyances of property near the Exchange a covenant be inserted 'on the part of purchasers not to let or suffer to be occupied any part of their buildings as brokers' offices for the space of three years from the date of each respective conveyance'.[12]

Meeting the Demands of the Merchant Community: The New Exchange

However, the needs of the growing merchant community could not be checked by the corporation's restrictions: the earlier Exchange was no longer adequate to cope with the increasing volume of business transactions; and Exchange Alley was eclipsed within 20 years by an incomparably grander building consisting largely of lettable commercial premises: the new Exchange.[13] In 1793, when John Wood's Town Hall-cum-Exchange was being extended northwards to the designs of James Wyatt, the merchants petitioned the Council to be allowed to use the ground floor of the new addition as an indoor extension to the Exchange courtyard, but without success.[14] The situation changed dramatically in 1795, when the interior of Wood's building was completely destroyed by fire, and a 25-year campaign of rebuilding began within the old walls. At first it was proposed to rebuild the west side of the ground floor as a coffee room and offices for the 'convenience' of the merchants and for 'transacting the public business of the town', but in 1801 the more ambitious idea of providing an entirely separate building to accommodate the town's mercantile life was conceived.[15] An Act of Parliament was obtained in 1802; construction began the following year to the designs of John Foster Senior (probably with the involvement of James Wyatt); and the new Exchange opened in stages from 1808 onwards.[16]

The Foster-Wyatt Exchange was a U-shaped block with arcaded walks at ground level, situated immediately behind John Wood's old Exchange (the latter, henceforward called the Town Hall, remained the seat of municipal government and the venue for civic entertainments). However, just as important as the new building was the *piazza* which it enclosed, which was known as the Exchange Flags. Here merchants could transact business in the open air as they traditionally preferred, while the arcaded walks provided shelter in bad weather. The east wing was occupied by the Newsroom—originally called the Coffee Room—where subscribers had access to the newspapers which were their chief source of commercial information, and above this was the underwriters' room. The matching west wing and the linking north wing—approximately two thirds of the building—consisted almost entirely of offices and counting houses for rent, with warehousing above.[17] Overall, it offered 'dignity and repose' and it was generally agreed that the combination of commercial and municipal buildings had 'never been surpassed'.[18] It was twice the size of the London exchange 'and perhaps the most splendid structure ever raised in modern times for purposes purely commercial' (Figure 5.2).[19]

Despite its great size covering two acres and its impact on what today would be called the public realm, the new Exchange was not a municipal project. Although it had the Corporation's blessing, and 9 of its 23 leading promoters were members of the Common Council, it was in fact an entirely commercial undertaking by 'a spirited body of proprietors' all of whom 'united' in a company specifically for this purpose.[20] The estimated cost of £80,000 was raised by the sale of 800 shares at £100 each and the income from rents on the offices and warehouses, as well as from subscriptions to the newsroom, was intended to provide shareholders with an annual dividend. The cost of construction was higher than expected—£110,848—and it was some years before dividends were forthcoming, but between 1818 and 1840 shareholders received annual payments varying from 3.5 per cent to 4.5 per cent.[21] As might be expected from a building promoted by the cultural luminary William Roscoe, the Exchange was intended to rationalize and beautify Liverpool's cramped and irregular centre, and in the words of a brochure issued in 1801, 'greatly contribute to the convenience, improvement and ornament of the town'.[22] At the same time, it was a hard-headed speculative development by men who recognised that there was money to be made from supplying office and warehouse space for rent. Although no individual was allowed to hold more than ten shares, the subscription list was filled in less than two hours.[23]

The construction of the new building, and the creation of the Flags, enormously enhanced the role of the Exchange as the focus of the town's commercial life. It became 'the great resort of the merchants and brokers of Liverpool'; it had extended hours of opening (from eight in the morning until eight in the evening); and quickly became 'the principal place of business'.[24] Its

Figure 5.2 The Exchange and Nelson's Monument, Liverpool (by William Westall, A.R.A., 1781–1850)

importance as the key location within the emerging central business district was reinforced by the choice of Brunswick Street as 'the chosen seat of the corn trade' and the construction of the Corn Exchange in 1807–08, again financed as a private development with the capital of £10,000 raised on the basis of 100 shares sold at £100 each.[25] It was 'a handsome structure of plain Grecian architecture', and, despite initial objections from members of the business community 'wedded to ancient systems, established customs', it enabled merchants to avoid 'the enormous expense of travelling' and proved to be 'an excellent expedient'.[26] Merchants wanted to be based as close as possible to the business centre, particularly to the New Exchange, which drove up property prices and stimulated private speculative office developments. The precise history of these developments before the 1840s is difficult to trace, but a few examples can be cited and it would be surprising if they did not represent a wider trend. In 1805, while the new Exchange was still being built, a hatter named James Hargraves erected Hargraves Building directly opposite the future newsroom, conducting his hat-making business in part and letting the rest as offices. Then in the 1820s came the construction of Exchange Court in Exchange Street East and Exchange Alley North in the angle of Old Hall Street and Chapel Street.[27] To judge from maps, these resembled the Exchange Alley of the 1780s, consisting of offices grouped around inner courtyards, isolated from the bustle of the streets.

In 1826, the Bank of England was preparing to open a Liverpool branch, and the records of its search for suitable accommodation are interesting for the light they shed on the town's evolving business centre.[28] A house in Church Street, previously used as a bank, was rejected as being too old and insubstantially built. A property in Castle Street, also old, was surrounded by tall warehouses which made it too dark and confined. Premises at the corner of Lord Street and Whitechapel, and at number 4 Lord Street, were both considered, but the Surveyor to the Bank,

John Soane, advised that the latter would be a good location only when the current widening and rebuilding of the street was complete. In the end, the Bank settled on the former house of Thomas Seel in Hanover Street, '7 minutes walk from the Exchange & Town Hall, a short distance from the Custom House, and from the site on which the New Custom House &c is about to be erected, near the Post Office and immediately contiguous to the Excise Office'. The buildings considered by the Bank were spread over quite a wide area, indicating that commercial activity was still fairly diffuse, but the magnetic pull of the Exchange is clear from the huge difference in price between two of the sites: the Hanover Street property was offered at £3,000, or about £4 4s per square yard, while the asking price for the Castle Street premises—old and gloomy, but just a stone's throw from the Flags—was £4,725, or about £13 10s per square yard.

The rebuilding of Lord Street to which Soane referred was carried out under the Improvement Act of 1826, which also provided for the creation of St. George's Crescent and the widening of North and South John Streets and South Castle Street. Under the supervision of the corporation surveyor, John Foster Junior (c.1787–1846), the new frontages were built to a consistent height, classically detailed, and faced with stucco. A record of these largely vanished streets exists among the engraved plates of *Lancashire Illustrated*, which show how Foster oversaw the transformation of Liverpool into a provincial echo of John Nash's London.[29] Harrington Chambers in North John Street survives, along with an adjoining block at the corner of Cook Street. The latter was built by the attorney and notary Thomas Avison and is dated 1828, while Harrington Chambers was built by the accountant Harmood Banner on a site acquired in 1830.[30] It has ground-floor shops, but trade directories show that in the 1830s it was largely occupied by the offices of attorneys and merchants, as well as Banner's own premises. The original plan cannot now be reconstructed, but on the ground floor at the south end is a brick-vaulted strong room with a cast-iron door manufactured by Messrs Foster & Griffin. This has every appearance of being contemporary with the original building, and if it is, it is an early example of the kind of fire-proof 'bookcase' for storing ledgers that became typical of mid-century Liverpool offices.

Thomas Ellison (1833–1904), a historian of the Liverpool cotton trade who gathered information directly from merchants active in the early nineteenth century, described the typical mercantile establishment of this period as 'partly counting-house and partly warehouse'.[31] It was a convenient arrangement, which meant a potential buyer could thoroughly inspect the goods before making a purchase. According to J. A. Picton, many such office-warehouse buildings were put up after the opening of the Prince's Dock in 1821, but the type goes back at least to the Foster-Wyatt Exchange of 1803–8, in which there were rooms for cotton storage above the ground-floor offices, with vertical rows of taking-in doors at the rear.[32] A building in Chapel Street, apparently combining these functions, was drawn by G. and C. Pyne and published in 1831, and a very late example survives in Tempest Hey, designed by William Culshaw in 1849 for the brokers Messrs Rowlinson.[33] By this date, however, changes in the way business was conducted had made such buildings outmoded as far as the cotton trade was concerned. During the first half of the century, improvements in the sorting and packing of raw cotton by American growers meant that bales became more consistent in quality and volume, which in turn meant that dealers and spinners could decide whether to make a purchase by examining a small sample of cotton, without having to inspect each bale individually.[34] The result was that by the 1850s, in Picton's words, 'the immediate connexion of offices and warehouses was no longer necessary'.[35] At the same time, the desire on the part of merchants to be based near the Exchange increased the demand for offices in this narrowly defined area, driving out less profitable uses such as warehousing, which concentrated instead in the streets near the docks.

Merchant Capital and the Profitability of Office Construction

The date at which offices first began to seem more profitable than warehouses is marked by the construction of India Buildings, erected between 1833 and 1834 by the cotton broker George Holt (1790–1861). The site fronted Water Street, the principal thoroughfare leading from the Exchange to the docks, and extended back between two narrower side streets, Fenwick Street and Chorley Street. Holt's original intention was to have offices facing Water Street, and warehouses with taking-in doors along Fenwick Street. The Corporation wanted him to make the warehouse doors open onto an inner court, where carts could load and unload without blocking the street, and they offered £500 to compensate him for the consequent loss of warehouse space. In July 1833, however, Holt wrote to the Chairman of the Finance committee that he was having second thoughts about building warehouses at all: 'Subsequently we have taken into consideration the desirableness of building offices only, and are now making comparative estimates with a view to a decision upon that point, the strong feeling of my mind being to offices alone'.[36] In the end, Holt did decide in favour of offices and India Buildings became Liverpool's first large-scale, privately funded, speculative office block. As the *Liverpool Mercury* said of it on completion, 'As regards extent, style of architecture, and general convenience, it far exceeds any private undertaking for a similar object in the town': it was without doubt 'the first great office-pile built in Liverpool' and 'one of the most extensive and magnificent'.[37]

Holt was a Unitarian, a member of Liverpool's Nonconformist mercantile elite, and, as a man of business, he was 'energetic, shrewd, and successful': he had also 'acquired large property in the town'.[38] For him, success in business was not merely about the accumulation and enjoyment of private wealth; it also entailed responsibilities to the wider community. Responding to the Corporation's offer of compensation, he wrote:

> I shall consider myself under obligation to expend every farthing of the amount on an improved elevation along the whole fronts of both Fenwick and Water Streets, to the satisfaction of your surveyor, or according to plans now in my possession & ready for your inspection. At the same time, let it be understood that I do not contemplate any thing further, than erecting most substantial & handsome buildings, capable of standing perhaps for hundreds of years.[39]

As with the Unitarian Roscoe and his promotion of the Exchange scheme 30 years earlier, Holt aimed to combine the pursuit of profit with the architectural enhancement of the town.

The author of an 1861 memoir of Holt wrote that his plan for India Buildings was at first regarded with scepticism, but 'from the time when these buildings were completed . . . to the present day, they have always been fully occupied, justifying thereby their owner's sagacity, and inducing him, and many others, to build new piles of offices'.[40] The success of India Buildings does appear to have attracted a steady stream of imitators. Canton Buildings and Commercial Buildings were erected c.1837 on neighbouring sites in Water Street. Both have been demolished, but Royal Bank Buildings in Dale Street, completed in 1838, survives. All three blocks, as well as India Buildings itself, were shaped by the Corporation's street improvement strategy, and they were set back to conform with a new, regular building line for the main cross-town route to the river. Barned's Buildings in Sweeting Street followed c.1840, then Brunswick Buildings in Brunswick Street c.1842, and in 1843–46 Holt added two new blocks onto India Buildings, called Fenwick Chambers and Fenwick Court.

By this date the profitability of speculative office developments was demonstrable. In 1841, the receipts from India Buildings already amounted to over £40,000 and by the early 1850s they exceeded in some years the trading profits of George Holt & Co.[41] In the 1840s, acknowledging the commercial primacy of the area round the Exchange, the Bank of England finally moved from Hanover Street to Castle Street, and as its majestic new building which combined 'strength with refinement' was nearing completion, its architect C. R. Cockerell prepared plans for an office block to be developed by the Bank on the adjacent site in Cook Street. Writing to the Committee for Building, he described the proposed offices as appropriate 'to the wants and conveniences of Brokers, Merchants, and Solicitors. . . . The East side is suited to cotton and sugar brokers, and the vicinity of the Exchange renders them all highly desirable'.[42] Cockerell was able to cite a comparable development already successfully undertaken by a near neighbour, pointing out that his designs were 'framed upon . . . examples of similar offices erected on the opposite side of Cook Street by the Commercial Bank, all of which are let.' He calculated the cost of the site for the proposed building to be £7,400 and the cost of the building itself £10,000, which at interest rates of 3 and 5 per cent respectively meant annual outgoings of £722. The rental income of the offices he estimated at £1,250, 'so that a very handsome interest will be secured.'

Cockerell's letter is exceptional, because firm evidence about the economics of office-building in nineteenth-century Liverpool is generally hard to come by. Reports of new buildings in the architectural press sometimes note the cost of land and of bricks and mortar, and occasionally the rents of individual office suites, but such reports are few in relation to the total number of new offices built, and the figures do not permit meaningful comparisons. What is clear, however, is that in the middle of the century Liverpool's business core experienced a remarkable property boom. The *Liverpool Albion* described the situation in 1856 and the story was picked up by *The Builder*: 'In obedience to the spirit of centralisation, the merchants and brokers of Liverpool are crowding to the neighbourhood of the Exchange, in the vicinity of which splendid piles, chiefly in the Italian style of architecture, are rising in every direction. The natural result is an increase in rents to fabulous prices.'[43]

With no comprehensive data about rent levels, information on individual cases is difficult to interpret, but the London-based architectural press considered Liverpool rents high enough to be newsworthy. In 1857, for instance, *The Builder* noted that the Cunard Company had agreed to pay £1,000 a year for the ground floor of the brand new Middleton Buildings and was impressed the following year when it learned that for a set of offices in the Liverpool & London Insurance Co.'s new building, 'as much as 750*l* a year is paid'.[44] George Holt recorded in 1854 that he was 'gradually raising the rents of the Counting House property [i.e. India Buildings]', having just upped the sum paid by one of his tenants from £300 to £400 a year—and three years later observed complacently that 'with every change of Tenants the Rents of this to us important Property, [are] gradually & most materially increasing'.[45]

In this climate it is not surprising that owners of old warehouses were ready to replace them with more remunerative office blocks, if they could afford to do so. Between 1846 and 1856, the South Wales ironmaster Sir Joseph Bailey demolished his warehouses at the foot of Water Street and built Tower Buildings on the site, while the merchant banker William Brown did the same in Chapel Street, and erected Hargreaves Buildings and Richmond Buildings. Describing this undertaking, Brown said that 'he had pulled down two old buildings . . . which were valuable, and . . . rebuilt them, the result being that they now brought in nearly double the return that they did before.'[46] But Bailey and Brown were among the richest men of their day,[47] and not all owners of warehouses had the means to follow their example. In 1852, Messrs McGregor adopted a less radical—and less costly—approach when they commissioned William Culshaw to convert a six-storey warehouse in Brunswick Street, transforming the lower three floors into offices with a fancy Italianate façade, while retaining warehouse use on the upper three.[48] Lack of capital, rather than a lack of vision, must have constrained other property owners too: Rev. T. D. Anderson only replaced his Covent Garden Building (an old-style office-warehouse block in Water Street) when it was destroyed by fire in 1863, though the £4,000 insurance money alone would not have been enough to pay for its successor, the technologically progressive Oriel Chambers.[49]

Brown's comments on the profitability of his Chapel Street buildings were made at an 1862 meeting of the proprietors of the Exchange, called to consider the proposed demolition and replacement of the old Foster-Wyatt building. By 1850 the dividend on shares had risen to 8.5 per cent—almost double what it had been in 1840[50]—but the structure had many practical short-comings, and with warehousing on its upper stories and arcades taking up a good deal of the ground floor, the site was seriously underdeveloped. In Ellison's words, 'The increased demand for offices, to meet the growing business requirements of the port, suggested the reconstruction of the buildings for office and saleroom purposes only'.[51] A new company was incorporated in 1859, which bought the existing buildings and land for £317,000, equivalent to just over £70 a square yard, and an architectural competition was announced at the end of 1862.[52] Review-ing the entries, *The Builder* informed its readers bluntly that the new buildings were to be 'a purely commercial undertaking, with the object of realizing a remunerative rate of interest on the capital invested'.[53] Nevertheless, the winning design by T. H. Wyatt was extremely showy with square-domed towers and much sculpture on maritime and commercial themes. As it rose, *The Builder* adopted a more reverent tone, admitting that 'Commerce is justified in her children in the extent and magnificence of the fanes they have reared in her service' (Figure 5.3).[54]

However, there was one branch of Liverpool commerce in which office accommodation and warehousing continued under the same roof, long after the arrangement had been abandoned by the cotton merchants. In the fruit and provision trade, where dealers handled relatively small quantities of perishable goods, not too bulky and with a fairly rapid turnover, combined office-warehouses continued to be built. The trade was tightly concentrated in and around Victoria Street and Stanley Street, where many blocks were built in the 1860s-80s for dealers in cheese, bacon, butter and fresh and dried fruit. Usually, the taking-in doors of these buildings were out of sight at the back, with the more dignified office accommodation fronting the street, so that the warehouse element was not immediately obvious.

Figure 5.3 The newsroom in the new Exchange Buildings of 1863–70

The Primacy of Commerce and the Supply of Office Accommodation

Because of the almost complete absence of contemporary building control records, and the transformation of the business district by later waves of redevelopment, it is impossible to define precisely the extent of rebuilding in the mid-nineteenth century, although local architects, such as Lewis Hornblower, were only too willing to speculate on the location of future building sites.[55] However, from maps and trade directories, reports in the architectural press, and the surviving records of the prolific office-designing firm of Culshaw & Sumners, a fairly detailed picture can be pieced together. It is possible to compile a list (see Table 5.1) of over 70 buildings, wholly—or in a few cases partly—used as speculative offices, erected between the late 1820s and the late 1860s; and there were almost certainly more.

That there was a risk of over-supply was recognised at the time. Already in 1858 *The Builder* acknowledged that this was a problem, but pointed out that 'those who believe that the commerce of Liverpool, great as it is, is not yet fully developed, and they are not a few, will say there is room for many additional buildings of this sort'.[56] A decade later, the local magazine *Porcupine* wrote that 'offices have been overdone in Liverpool,' observing how 'in every direction in the neighbourhood of the Exchange the eye rests upon piles of costly offices, with the inevitable "To Be Let" staring from the windows. The loss of money arising from the idleness of property must be something enormous'.[57] Un-let offices, however, did not necessarily make a building unprofitable, and the Exchange Company was able to declare a dividend of 5 per cent in 1871, despite many rooms on the upper floors being untenanted.[58] The true extent of such under-occupation is impossible to measure, but even if it were as widespread as the *Porcupine* suggested, it did not put a stop to further office-building, and if redevelopment slowed in the 1870s, it certainly did not cease.

The advantage conferred by proximity to the Exchange continued into the second half of the century. In 1857, *The Building News* observed that 'the value of property increases or diminishes in an enormous ratio in proportion to its distance from this centre'.[59] The following year, *The Builder* reported that land for the Liverpool & London Insurance Co.'s new building, a uniquely advantageous island site between Dale Street and the Exchange Flags, had cost £50 a square yard, while the site of the new Queen Insurance building at 11 Dale Street, just a 125 feet further from the Flags, had cost a little under £16 a square yard.[60] Prestige was no doubt part of the allure of sites near the Exchange. However, in an age when deals were transacted face to face, and vital commercial information had to be gathered by conversation on the Exchange Flags or by reading in the Exchange Newsroom, there were sound business reasons for wanting to be as near as possible to this focus of activity. Newspaper advertisements for offices to let speak constantly of their closeness to the Exchange, either in terms of distance ('25 yards'; '200 yards from the entrance to the Underwriters' rooms') or time ('five minutes walk'; 'within one minute's walk of 'Change'). For those whose offices were only slightly removed, the permeability of the intervening streets and buildings was most important. When in the mid-1860s the merchant Arnold de Beer Baruchson sold the site in Exchange Street East on which Mason's Building was subsequently erected, he stipulated it should incorporate a ground-floor passage to give easy access between the Flags and his own Batavia Buildings in Hackins Hey (the decorative doors at each end of this passage survive to this day); and when Peters Buildings was erected at about the same time between Covent Garden and Rumford Street, the owners of Tower Buildings tried unsuccessfully to preserve a through-route across its site, by purchasing the right of way for an annual rent.[61] Significantly, the terms of the 1862–63 competition for the new Exchange stipulated that the three existing passages giving pedestrian access to the Flags from the surrounding streets must be preserved, even though they took up extremely valuable ground that could have been used for rent-yielding offices.[62]

Merchants as Property Developers

Due to a lack of source material such as rate books, land tax assessments and building control records, it is surprisingly difficult to identify the property developers behind Liverpool's nine-teenth-century office boom. Again, reports in the architectural press are useful in this respect, as are the Culshaw & Sumners drawings, many of which are inscribed with clients' names. The minutes of the Council's Finance Committee offer occasional insights, as do publications by Picton and Ellison. Even when identification is possible, however, biographical details are often hard to uncover. Of those private developers who have been identified so far, about half belonged to Liverpool's merchant class or were intimately involved in the town's commercial life. Cotton merchants were to the fore, including John Stock (builder of Exchange Court in Exchange Street East), William Farrer (Grosvenor Building, Tithebarn Street and Knowsley Buildings, Bixteth Street), Thomas Joynson (Manchester Buildings, Tithebarn Street) and of course George Holt. There was the iron merchant Samuel Stitt (Seaton Buildings and Commercial Court, Drury Lane) and the general merchant Arnold de Beer Baruchson (Batavia Buildings, Hackins Hey) (Figure 5.4); the banker R. C. Naylor (The Albany, Old Hall Street); and J. C. Ewart, a former broker and a director of various companies including the Liverpool & London Insurance Co. and the Peninsular & Oriental Steam Navigation Co. (Brunswick Buildings, Brunswick Street). Most prolific, and best represented by surviving buildings, was the merchant and banker William Brown, who was responsible for Brown's Buildings in Exchange Street West (Figure 5.5) and the Temple in Dale Street, as well as Hargreaves and Richmond Buildings.

Not only did such men know the practical requirements of the tenants they hoped to attract, but they also brought to the business of office-building the attributes on which a successful mercantile career depended: a network of contacts, a keen sense of supply and demand and a willingness to speculate. B. G. Orchard, a contemporary biographer of Liverpool's business

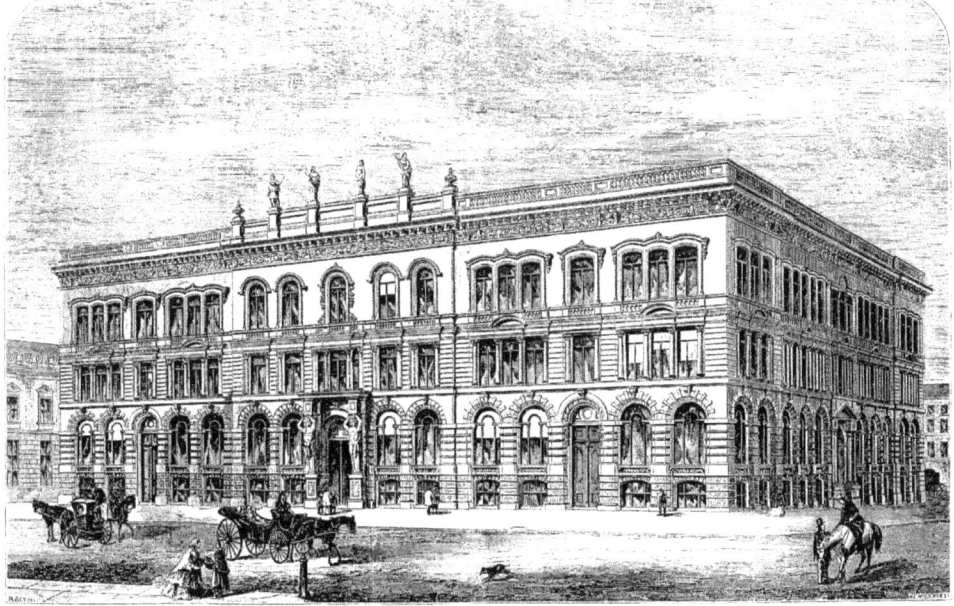

STREET ARCHITECTURE OF LIVERPOOL: BROWN'S BUILDINGS.——MR. J. A. PICTON, ARCHITECT.

Figure 5.4 Elevation of Batavia Buildings, Hackins Hey, 1862 by William Culshaw for Arnold de Beer Baruchsen (by kind permission of Lancashire Record Office)

Figure 5.5 Brown's Building (J. A. Picton, architect)

elite, recognised that office-building could be an important area of mercantile enterprise, when he described the foresight that enabled William Brown

> to perceive, long ere other men had begun even to consider the subject, the true value of new projects or novel financing arrangements. . . . It was thus that he reared pile after pile of

stately offices at a moderate cost, and left them, a noble inheritance, to some of his heirs; his acuteness leading to this years before possible competitors for the land had discovered how soon such investments would become valuable.[63]

Buying at the bottom of the market and waiting until prices rose could be just as profitable with land as with cotton. As well as assembling the site of his own speculative office development in Silkhouse Court, the cotton broker William Farrer paid £7,000 for a long, thin strip on the east side of Exchange Street East. It was too narrow to erect a substantial building on, but Farrer 'had an eye to the constantly increasing value of land in the neighbourhood of the Exchange', and his astuteness eventually paid off.[64] He did not live to profit by it himself, but after he died in 1886, the land was sold in 1898 for £45,000 for an extension to the Liverpool Stock Exchange next door.[65]

As well as individual merchants, there were also corporate developers of office buildings. In London, Edward l'Anson observed that the Limited Liability Act of 1855 led to an increased demand for building sites in the City by 'large public companies and insurance offices', and Summerson has shown how the Victorian rebuilding of the City was started by insurance offices, which proliferated following the 1844 Joint Stock Companies Act.[66] The office-building activities of financial institutions in Liverpool began at much the same time, with the construction of Royal Bank Chambers in Dale Street, c.1837–38, and, as in London, the boom years were from the 1840s to the 1860s. The Liverpool Commercial Bank, established in 1831, and a branch of the Bank of England, as already mentioned, built office blocks in quick succession around 1848, and in the same year the Royal Insurance Co., founded in Liverpool in 1845, built grand headquarters in North John Street. Designed by William Grellier, one of the architects premiated in the competition for the new Royal Exchange in London, this palatial stone building cost between £17,000 and £18,000, in addition to about £10,000 for the site, and consisted largely of lettable offices.[67] In the late 1850s, the Liverpool & London Insurance Co. built speculative blocks in connection with its new headquarters designed by C. R. Cockerell, while the Queen Insurance Co. built premises that included extensive lettable space. Banks erected in the 1860s followed the same pattern, with the Adelphi (before 1864), Mercantile & Exchange (1864), North-Western (before 1868) and Alliance (1868) all providing offices for rent as well as accommodation for themselves. Among other corporate property developers, at least two firms of cotton brokers built imposing blocks housing their own premises as well as office suites for rent: Waterhouse's Building (1842), for Nicholas Waterhouse & Sons, stood at the corner of Chapel Street and Old Hall Street; and Apsley Buildings (1854), for Messrs Myers, occupied a site directly opposite.[68]

The Design and Planning of Liverpool's Victorian Office Blocks

Photographs and architects' drawings of demolished buildings, together with the evidence of those that survive, give a very clear picture of the typical early-Victorian Liverpool office block. Until the last two decades of the nineteenth century, these buildings were usually of three principal storeys, with an attic above and a day-lit semi-basement below. Under the semi-basement there would often be one or two levels of bonded vaults, which could be rented out for the storage of high-value merchandise such as wines and spirits, exploiting to the full the income-generating potential of the site. The semi-basement, reached by a short flight of steps from the pavement, was sometimes used for offices, or might be occupied by shops or a restaurant, since it was just as accessible as the ground floor. The three main floors would all have suites of offices and perhaps associated sample rooms. The attic had the great advantage of being well lit by skylights, but the disadvantage of being at the top of three sets of stairs, and as the least valuable part of the building it was generally given over to toilets, water cisterns and the care-taker's flat. Architects' drawings sometimes show sample rooms on the attic floor, but whether they were actually used as such is uncertain. To help ventilate stairs and corridors, the street entrance was often closed with an iron gate, rather than a solid door.

With regard to overall height, *The Building News* pointed out in 1857 that the architect designing a Liverpool office block had to rein in his natural desire to impress and take account of the primary need to make the building pay: 'The storeys cannot be made very lofty, as the value of the upper floors would be thereby lessened'.[69] It was not until the increasing use of pas-senger lifts from the late 1880s onwards, followed by the introduction of steel-framed construc-tion in the 1890s, that it became both practicable and profitable to build higher.[70] It was at this date that Liverpool's mid-century office buildings first started to be replaced with taller ones. William Grellier's four-storey Royal Insurance headquarters of 1848 was replaced in 1896 by J. Francis Doyle's mighty six-storey building for the same company, steel-framed and served by two electric lifts; and J. A. Picton's original Tower Buildings of the 1840s–50s was replaced in 1906 with an eleven-storey steel-framed structure of the same name, designed by W. Aubrey Thomas.[71] It is sometimes argued that British architects were slow to take up innovations in con-struction techniques for commercial buildings, but this was not the case in Liverpool, where the redevelopment of the central business district at the turn of the century was characterised by a rapid assimilation of contemporary American developments. Many Liverpool businessmen and shipowners had a fascination with American technology and its local application was a result of strong trading links with New York and Chicago where the development of skyscrapers was most apparent. When the construction of the Liver Building for the Royal Liver Friendly Soci-ety was completed in 1911, it not only incorporated relatively new building techniques but was the tallest office building in Britain.[72] In the 1920s the original India Buildings, together with the neighbouring Canton and Commercial Buildings, were all subsumed into the giant new nine-storey India Buildings, and Brown's Buildings and Walmer Buildings gave way to the towering ten-storey Martins Bank.

Internal planning varied according to the nature of the site. A central court, admitting light and air and serving as a circulation space, was a common feature in larger blocks, and can be seen already in prototype in the late eighteenth-century Exchange Alley. At Brunswick Build-ings, c.1842, the court had a roof of glass and iron with tiers of cast-iron galleries giving access to the office suites, and a similar arrangement was adopted by Cockerell at Liverpool & Lon-don Chambers in 1856–58, which was reputed to be 'one of the purest classic buildings in the country'.[73] Such glass-roofed courts became widespread, a good surviving example being that at Imperial Chambers in Dale Street, of the early 1870s. Where sites were irregular or narrow in proportion to their depth, a central court was not possible, and it took considerable ingenuity to devise a plan that would let in enough light. As the *Porcupine* noted, 'In not a few instances the architects have had many and serious difficulties to contend with in adopting the structure to the locality in which it is placed, so as to secure an economical occupation of the land—generally of very great value—and at the same time to obtain an advantageous distribution of light suited to the display of samples of produce, by means of which a large portion of the commercial busi-ness of the community is carried on'.[74] A typical office suite consisted of two interconnected rooms: an outer 'general office' for the clerks, and an inner 'private room' for the proprietor or partners. Usually there would also be a strong room or walk-in safe for the storage of ledgers, and a sample room for the examination of merchandise, if the business required it. Larger busi-nesses might occupy more rooms, or an entire floor of the building. Spaces were highly flexible and could be subdivided with timber and glass partitions in order to suit the needs of specific tenants (Figures 5.6 and 5.7).

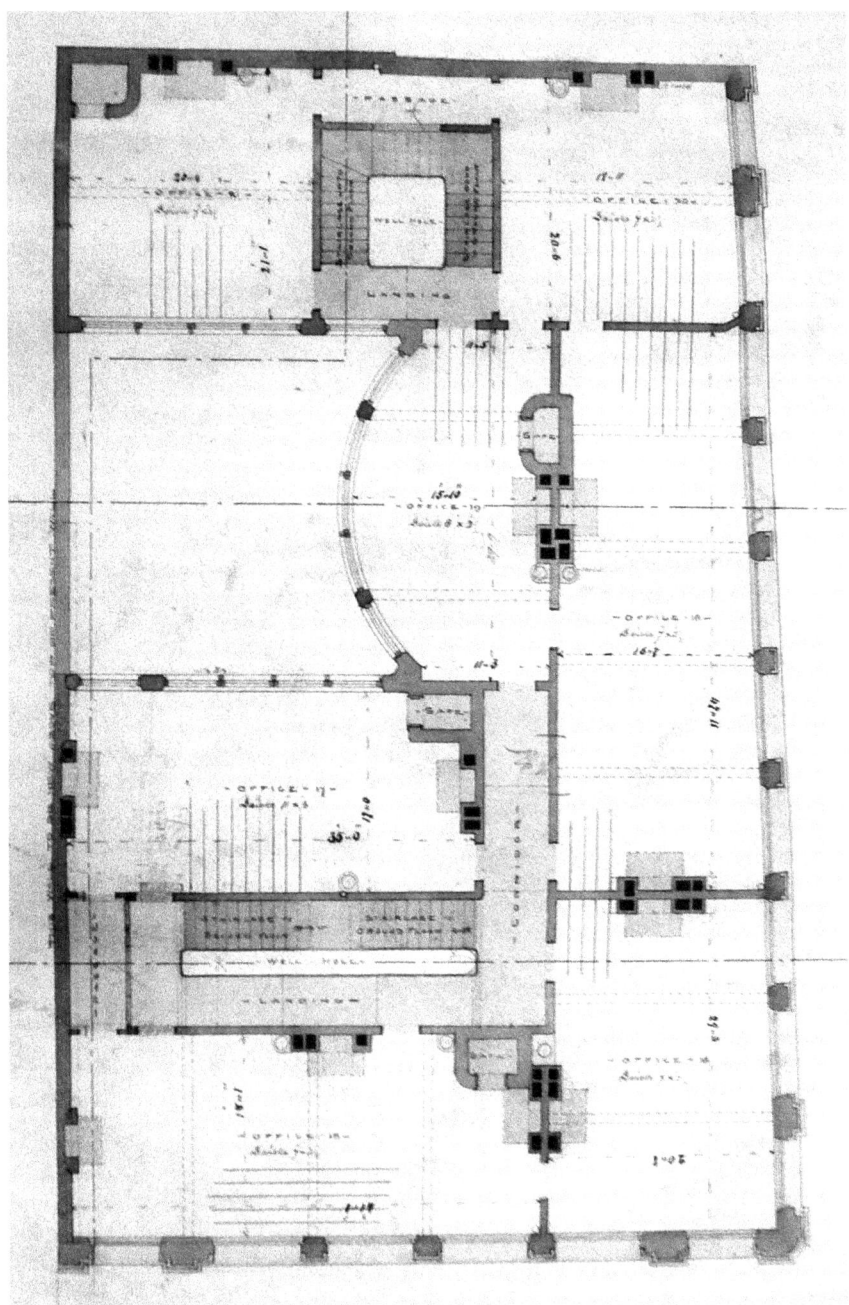

Figure 5.6 First-floor plan of Berey's Buildings, 1864, by William Culshaw for the Trustees of Samuel Berey (by permission of the Lancashire Record Office)

Figure 5.7 Elevation of Berey's Buildings, George Street, 1864, by William Culshaw for the Trustees of Samuel Berey

When H. E. Stripe worked for the iron merchants Messrs. Bibby in the 1830s, the office was shabby, with a haphazard assortment of furniture.[75] According to Stripe, it was typical of merchants' offices at that time. Gradually, greater ostentation became the rule and by the time speculative commercial building was at its height in the 1860s the *Porcupine* noted with a touch of sarcasm that 'offices are designed by high-art architects at high-art prices, and are furnished by high-art upholsterers and cabinet-makers in a style of "princely magnificence"'.[76] In 1870, F. R. Leyland moved Messrs. Bibby's to Pacific Buildings, James Street, where he remodelled the offices to his own taste, fitting them with costly mahogany, which he had personally selected in Paris.[77] Whereas in the middle of the century, 'anything in the shape of ornamentation, or in the least degree artistic, raised grave doubts as to the business qualifications of those who indulged in such fripperies',[78] by the 1870s a merchant's private office was often used to display his refinement and sophisticated tastes. The French corn merchant Jules Bourgeoise (of Cornelius & Bourgeoise) filled his with 'artistic furniture and good pictures' and clearly treated it as his *salon*; James Lord Bowes, a wool broker and a collector of Japanese art, indulged in William Morris wallpaper; while at Pacific Buildings, Leyland surrounded himself with old masters from Italy, Spain and the Netherlands.[79] Union Buildings in Cook Street, where the solicitor Alfred Billson had his offices, showed 'just a slight touch of the aesthetic mania', with rooms that resembled 'a well-appointed library in the house of a country gentleman who possesses excellent taste and has an eye to his own personal comfort'.[80] Indeed, one of the most extraordinary Liverpool interiors of the late nineteenth century must have been the board room of the Lancashire Finance Association in Castle Street, decorated with Art Nouveau mermaids and seashells by the sculptor W. R. Colton.[81]

There were still those, such as Robertson Gladstone, who liked plain, old-fashioned premises.[82] It was a preference which may have delivered commercial advantages. In the Liverpool office of the fictional Mr. Winmore, 'nothing appeared to be new'; clients therefore concluded that 'the counting-house, its furniture, and its occupants must all have been in their present positions for considerably more than a century, [and] became impressed with a feeling of entire confidence in Winmore & Co'.[83] Alfred Holt took the view that 'showy offices at high rents don't make business, and only encourage habits of extravagance in those about you', while in his brother Robert's office in Fenwick Street there was 'no attempt at ornate ornamentation', so that to the *Liberal Review* it seemed 'a place which is kept for business purposes, and where much business is transacted'.[84]

Illuminating and Securing the World of Commerce

For some merchants and brokers the quality of the artificial light provided by candles and gas had obvious disadvantages when conducting business transactions and before the adoption of electric lighting in the 1890s, the single most important consideration facing the designer of an office block was how to admit as much daylight as possible to each desk. Windows could be made broader in proportion to their height, or several could be grouped together to fill more of the wall surface, but traditionalist architectural critics lamented the consequent loss of 'dignified repose' in the facade.[85] Older buildings could be upgraded by substituting big new windows with cast-iron lintels and mullions for the old timber sashes, while architects deliberately designed offices around light wells faced with reflective white-glazed tiles or light-coloured brick in order to 'obtain an advantageous distribution of light suited to the display of samples of produce'.[86]

The quest for better lighting led Peter Ellis to use projecting windows at Oriel Chambers (1864) and enormous expanses of glazing at 16 Cook Street (complete by 1868). According to a later commentator, 'It is on the courtyard elevations that we see the most remarkable use of this daylighting system where, stripped of all decoration, long bands of glass project from the structural system interrupted only by the stone cross-walls at each third bay'.[87] But his work was condemned in the architectural press for its eccentricity. Projecting windows with sloping glazing at the top were not invented by Ellis—they were being employed in Liverpool at least as early as 1846,[88] and had become common by the 1860s—but they were generally confined to rear or courtyard elevations. The scientific argument in their favour was set out by James Boult in 1880: the sun's rays strike a conventional window obliquely and consequently much light is reflected back; but the angle at which they strike sloping glazing is closer to the vertical, so more light penetrates to the interior of the building.[89] Desks or counters positioned under such windows were particularly well lit.[90]

It was perhaps Ellis that *The Builder* had in mind when it remarked in a review of the new Exchange that 'the problem how to make an architecturally successful building, and yet give the amount of light which cotton salesmen seem to expect, is a task almost beyond the ingenuity of any architect'.[91] Cotton sample rooms in particular needed abundant daylight for examining the cotton fibres and were therefore provided with very large windows directly over the desks. Northern light was preferred, being free from glare and varying little during the course of the day, and advertisements for offices to let would make a point of saying if the accommodation was north-facing with 'excellent north light' or had 'cotton lights'.[92] In fact, the increasing adoption of electricity from the 1890s onwards did not lead to a reduction in the demand for natural light, especially in the cotton trade, and these design characteristics reached their fullest development in 1905–06 in the north façade of Matear & Simon's Cotton Exchange. The classically detailed cast-iron panels which incorporated very large windows were designed expressly to illuminate counters where cotton samples were displayed.[93]

Fireproof construction, consisting of brick-vaulted floors carried on cast-iron columns, was used from the 1840s in certain Liverpool warehouses, in part as a response to a significant increase in insurance premiums as a result of the frequency of dockland fires, but it is not clear when the technology was first applied to office buildings.[94] Some, such as Liverpool & London Chambers and Oriel Chambers, used it throughout, but in most cases the added expense was probably regarded as unjustifiable and usually it seems to have been reserved for basement vaults where flammable materials, such as spirits, might be stored. The parts of the building in office use generally had timber floors, with thin cast-iron columns providing intermediate support, though the safe or strong room belonging to each suite would be fireproof. For structural reasons, these small but very solidly constructed rooms would be positioned one above the other on each floor, rising through the building like a chimney stack.

By the 1860s other methods of fireproof construction were in use.[95] T. H. Wyatt's new Exchange Buildings of 1863–70 had concrete floors of the type devised by Messrs. Fox & Barrett, but still they were confined to the ground floor and basement, used as bonded stores for flammable goods. In 1865 *The Builder* observed that 'fire-proof flooring is much in esteem in Liverpool. It comes, perhaps, of a community of merchants that chances should be calculated to a nicety, and that all risk should be reduced to the minimum as far as expenditure can insure that desirability. In the court of the block of offices called the Temple . . . there are huge piles of offices in course of erection in white and red bricks, with iron girders to carry the floors and iron mullions to the window openings'.[96] What *The Builder* described at the Temple was probably not true fireproof construction, but simply the use of iron for certain components that would traditionally have been made of combustible timber. Peter Ellis employed cast iron instead of wood for the spiral staircase of 16 Cook Street in the mid-1860s and by the 1880s cast-iron staircases were widely used.[97]

The Style and Symbolic Significance of Liverpool's Office Blocks

As for style, most mid-nineteenth-century Liverpool office buildings were Classical, and many took the form of Italian Renaissance palaces. The *palazzo* style became dominant in Liverpool's central business district throughout the redevelopment period of the 1840s and 1850s, with the construction of Brunswick Buildings in c.1842 heralding the start of a new era. The *palazzo* had been adopted by Charles Barry in the 1830s as a suitable model for gentlemen's clubs and the novelty of using it for commercial buildings immediately caught the attention of critics. One wrote of Brunswick Buildings that 'placed in Pall Mall [it] would be taken for an aristocratic Club-house', and as late as 1858 *The Builder* was still making the same comparison, observing that 'in Liverpool there appears to be a passion for building blocks of offices under one roof, with a club-house aspect'.[98] Hargreaves Buildings, completed c.1860, was built in the style of a Venetian *palazzo*, with the carved heads of explorers such as Cortez and Columbus located in a row above the ground-floor windows.[99] The Gothic Revival made an occasional appearance, but contemporaries were struck by the almost universal preference for Classicism. When the competition for the new Exchange was held in 1863, *The Builder* remarked that only three of the 44 designs submitted were Gothic, showing how 'the influence of the style of the present and surrounding buildings has been too strong even for Medieval talent to overcome' (Figures 5.8 and 5.9).[100]

While it seems likely that Liverpool's Victorian businessmen would have enjoyed the connotations of the Renaissance *palazzo*, there is unfortunately very little written evidence for their architectural tastes. When commissioning buildings, William Brown seems to have been chiefly concerned with keeping costs down, arguing against holding an architectural competition for the new Exchange because it might result in 'a very florid scheme and an expensive one', whereas his own wish was for 'good, substantial buildings, without extraneous ornaments'.[101] With regard to style he apparently had no particular view and he gave his architect J. A. Picton *carte blanche* in designing Brown's Buildings.[102]

But whatever the views of the merchants, visitors were encouraged to see Liverpool as the architectural heir of the great trading cities of Renaissance Italy. 'Venice,' wrote the author of an

Figure 5.8 Elevation of the Albany

Figure 5.9 Elevation of Knowsley Buildings, Bixteth Street, 1864, by William Culshaw for William
Farrer (by permission of the Lancashire Record Office)

1861 guidebook, 'whose merchants were princes, possesses the . . . vast, massive, ducal palace,
the Pregadi, or Senate Hall, the fine painting gallery, the great library of San Marco, and the
grand palace of the doges. Florence contains . . . the palaces of the Pitti, Ricardi, Strozzi, Corsini
Borghese, and many others. Genoa has its palaces and churches, rising amphitheatrically round
her fleet, whose princes also were merchants. It is not extraordinary, then, that the like causes
produce the same results in modern times; accordingly we find that the wealth which peace-
ful commerce pours into the lap of Liverpool has been partly expended in adorning the town
with magnificent architectural structures'.[103] Venice and Genoa, the seats of maritime trading
empires, were obvious sources of inspiration for Liverpool architects and Picton looked forward
to the day when the restrained Georgian terraces of Castle Street would be rebuilt as a succession of splendid financial palaces, making it Liverpool's answer to Genoa's Via Nuova.[104] This
is very much what came to pass in the last quarter of the nineteenth century, when W. D. Caroe,
Richard Norman Shaw and especially the local architects Grayson & Ould transformed Castle
Street with a collection of sumptuous buildings in costly and colourful materials.[105]

It is striking how Liverpool office buildings of the 1840s-60s did not usually show the sort of
assertive individualism that might be expected from rival commercial premises, and in at least
two cases different owners co-operated so that unified façades could extend across their properties. Brown's Buildings was linked in this way with the offices of the Phoenix Fire Co. next door,
and Carlton Buildings, as rebuilt by the executors of Ralph Peters, matched the neighbouring

Borough Buildings, belonging to H. B. H. Blundell.[106] The first new office building in a street would stand out from its earlier neighbours in scale and materials, like the block described disparagingly by William Wilson in his novel *The Melvilles*, set in the Liverpool of 1847:

> Mr Wardrop's office is in a dingy street near the Exchange—a street of a mixed character, with rude shops for sailors. . . . The stone building would be handsome if it could—that it is stone is undeniable, and in a region of brick, this is something; besides that, it has windows with which some heavy gambols have been played, by way of making them ornamental; but the attempt has not succeeded. On the other side, those begrimed brick erections are low, and give all possible advantage to their opposite neighbour.[107]

As more properties were rebuilt, however, the street would assume a new character in which individual differences were less important than overall harmony. Commenting on the half-built new Exchange in 1868, the critic Samuel Huggins noted that although it differed in style from the old Exchange and the Town Hall—a kind of French or Flemish Renaissance instead of Neoclassical—it had 'become one with the chief buildings round it, uniting several hitherto dissevered blocks of commercial buildings into one continuous series . . . till there would, when it was finished, be a complete district of fine commercial buildings, all in perfect accord, and unmistakably commercial in character, that he believed the metropolis only could parallel in this country'.[108] With the tendency to build higher from the 1880s, this unity began to break down, to be replaced by a variety of styles and materials and an overt competitiveness. It was a tendency that reached its climax at the start of the twentieth century, with the construction of the three enormous and wildly diverse office buildings at the Pier Head.[109]

Conclusion

Speculative offices became the defining buildings of Liverpool's commercial centre in the middle decades of the nineteenth century. Public buildings for civic administration were also a significant presence and there were clubs and hotels to service the business community, but office blocks unquestionably dominated. They were given coherence by the all-important focus of the Exchange Flags and by the surrounding grid of streets, systematically broadened and straightened from the 1780s onwards. Within this strong framework, subsidiary centres emerged in the immediate vicinity.[110] Other specialised exchanges attracted their own clusters of offices—corn in Brunswick Street, fruit and produce in Victoria Street, stocks in Dale Street and, later, cotton in Old Hall Street. Shipowners gravitated to office blocks in Water Street and James' Street, close to the river; lawyers and accountants to Cook Street and North John Street, near the Law Association's premises; and insurers to the financial centre of Castle Street, near the Bank of England. All, however, were contained in a compact area less than half a mile wide. Numerous comments in the contemporary architectural press show that the rebuilding of the streets round the Exchange attracted national attention, but the transformation was perhaps best summed up by J. A. Picton, writing from a local perspective. In a lavish 1864 volume of lithographs entitled *Views in Modern Liverpool*, he emphasised the symbolic role of these new office blocks—several of which he had designed—as the unambiguous expression of Liverpool's commercial importance: 'The group of buildings, of which the Town Hall forms the centre and nucleus, are the visible embodiment of modern commerce; and, whatever criticism may be passed upon them, they are certainly not amenable to the charge of pettiness and poverty. Their dimensions are noble, their aspect is stately; and, on the whole, they worthily represent the vast commercial transactions which daily take place within their walls'.[111]

In a wider context, the development of a well-defined central business district from the late eighteenth century onwards demonstrated the primacy of commerce and the political influence of merchants in securing radical changes to the urban landscape in response to their changing operational needs. If the construction of the new Exchange in the early years of the nineteenth century heralded 'the first impulse to concentration', it was quickly recognised that 'to be outside the charmed circle narrowly drawn round the Exchange is almost equivalent to being ostracised from business'.[112] The increasing degree of market specialisation, whether in cotton or corn, heralded an end to the 'primitive arrangement' whereby merchants' offices had been widely dispersed and considerable time was lost in visiting different warehouses for buying and selling.[113] Merchants were active as speculative investors in the construction of purpose-built office accommodation, fully aware of the prospect of rising rental income, while the Town Council was more than willing to accommodate the demands from the merchant community for the widening of roads or the clearing of older properties, irrespective of their architectural merit or historic significance, in areas adjacent to the central business district. In the course of the nineteenth century commercial practices were transformed by faster communication and the adoption of new business structures, but Liverpool's merchants and traders were also able to strengthen their comparative position as a result of the construction of a physical trading environment which fostered functional specialization, a more efficient utilization of available resources, and the availability of purpose-built office accommodation in line with contemporary needs.[114]

Table 5.1

Office buildings near the Liverpool Exchange,
c.1830–c.1870 (including banks and insurance
companies with lettable accommodation)

	Date	Building (d = demolished)	Owner	Architect	References
1	1828	18 North John Street	Thomas Avison	John Foster Jun.?	Liverpool Record Office (LRO), 352 MIN/IMP II 1/3, Improvement Committee minutes, 23 June 1828.
2	c.1829	Exchange Alley North, Old Hall Street (d)			T. Ellison, *Gleanings and Reminiscences* (Liverpool, 1905), pp. 222–23.
3	c.1830	Harrington Chambers, North John Street	Harmood Banner		LRO, 352 CLE/CON 5/22, Charles Okill's street index to registers of leases, vol. B, f. 146.
4	1832	Bretherton's Buildings, North John Street (d)	Bartholomew Bretherton	Mr. Hadfield	J. A. Picton, *Memorials of Liverpool*, 2 vols (London and Liverpool, 1875), II, p. 107; 'Coaching King's Masterpiece', *Liverpool Post & Mercury*, 4 May 1929, p. 7.
5	1833–34	India Buildings, Water Street (d)	George Holt	Joseph Franklin	*A Brief Memoir of George Holt, Esquire, of Liverpool* (Liverpool, 1861), pp.70–72; LRO, Hf 942.7213 IND, *Holt's India Building, Water Street.*
6	Before 1836	Rumford Court, Rumford Place	Mr. Graham	William Culshaw	M. A. Gage, *Trigonometrical Plan of the Town and Port of Liverpool* (1836); Preston, Lancashire Record Office (LaRO), DDX 162/64/12.
7	1836–39	Royal Bank Buildings, Dale Street	Royal Bank	Samuel Rowland	Picton, *Memorials*, II, p. 106; 'The Royal Bank Buildings', *Albion* [Liverpool], 7 January 1839, p. 3.

(Continued)

	Date	Building (d = demolished)	Owner	Architect	References
8	c.1837	Canton Buildings, Water Street (d)	Thomas Birkett		LRO, 352 MIN/IMP II 1/4, Improvement Committee minutes, 15 February 1836 and 30 May 1836; *Gore's Directory*, 1839.
9	c.1837	Commercial Buildings, Water Street (d)	James Stitt		LRO, 352 CLE/CON 2/22; *Gore's Directory*, 1839.
10	1839–40	Barned's Buildings, Sweeting Street	Israel Barned		*Gore's Directory*, 1841.
11	c.1842	Brunswick Buildings, Brunswick Street (d)	Joseph C. Ewart	A. & G. Williams	'Improvements in Liverpool – Advance of Architecture', *Civil Engineer and Architect's Journal*, 5 (1842), p. 278.
12	1842	Waterhouse's Building, Chapel Street (d)	Messrs Waterhouse	William Culshaw	LaR0, DDX 162/14/31–DDX 162/14/38 and DDX 162/14/42–DDX 162/14/48; 'Improvements in Liverpool – Advance of Architecture', *Civil Engineer and Architect's Journal*, 5 (1842), p. 278.
13	1842	Adelaide Buildings, Chapel Street (d)	Messrs Waterhouse	'Mr C. S. Rowland', probably Samuel Rowland	*LM*, 25 November 1842.
14	1843–46	Fenwick Chambers and Fenwick Court, Fenwick Street (d)	George Holt	J. A. Picton	LRO, 920 DUR 1/1 and 920 DUR 1/2.
15	1846	Tower Buildings (north part), Water Street (d)	Joseph Bailey	J. A. Picton	'Local Intelligence', *Liverpool Mercury and Lancashire General Advertiser*, 11 December 1846, Supplement, p. 592.
16	1846	20 Chapel Street (d)	A. & H. Graham	William Culshaw	LaRO, DDX 162/44/40, DDX 162/44/45 – DDX 162/44/46 and DDX 162/44/48–DDX 162/44/49.
17	Before 1848	Commercial Bank Buildings, Cook Street (d)	Commercial Bank	John Cunningham	London, Bank of England archives, PRE/B565/6, Committee for Building minutes, 30 August 1848.
18	c.1848	Bank Chambers, Cook Street (d)	Bank of England	C. R. Cockerell	London, Bank of England archives, PRE/B565/6, Committee for Building minutes, 30 August 1848.

	Date	Building (d – demolished)	Owner	Architect	References
19	1848	Royal Insurance Buildings, North John Street (d)	Royal Insurance Co.	William Grellier	Editorial, *Builder*, 6 (1848), pp. 613–14.
20	1850s	Victoria Buildings, Hackins Hey (d)	W. Higgins	William Culshaw	LaRO, DDX 162/02/29– DDX 162/02/44, DDX/162/75/23 and DDX/162/75/24.
21	1851	Corn Exchange, Brunswick Street (d)	Corn Exchange	J. A. Picton	Picton, *Memorials*, II, p. 99.
22	1851	9 Rumford Street (d)	Mr. Peters	William Culshaw	LaRO, DDX 162/83/01 and DDX 162/83/05–DDX 162/83/09.
23	1852	Macrae's offices, Hackins Hey (d)	J. H. Macrae	William Culshaw	LaRO, DDX 162/29/16– DDX 162/29/20.
24	1853	Walmer Buildings, Water Street (d)	Messrs. Myers	William Culshaw	LaRO, DDX 162/24/6– DDX 162/24/16 and DDX 162/24/19–DDX 162/24/22.
25	1853	Melbourne Buildings, North John Street		J. A. Picton	*Civil Engineer and Architect's Journal*, 16 (1853), p. 460.
26	1853–56	Drury Buildings, Water Street (d)	T. Bouch, T. France Bennett, W. Furness, A. Waterhouse, R. Waterhouse, W. Balleny		LRO, 352 CLE/CON 3/9, lease dated 22 January 1853.
27	1854	Argyll/Clarendon Buildings, Hackins Hey (d)	John Campbell	William Culshaw	LaRO, DDX 162/84/1 – DDX 162/84/9 and box DDX 162/75/1.
28	1854	Apsley Buildings, Old Hall Street (d)	Messrs. Myers	William Culshaw	LaRO, DDX 162/14/39– DDX 162/14/41; DDX 162/14/49; DDX 162/24/17– DDX 162/24/18; DDX 162/24/23 and DDX 162/24/25–DDX 162/24/37.
29	1854	4 Water Street (d)	Royal Exchange Assurance	William Culshaw	LaRO, DDX 162/80/69– DDX 162/80/71.
30	1854	New Hall, Old Hall Street (d)	J. Briscoe	William Culshaw	LaRO, DDX 162/9/22– DDX 162/9/47.
31	1854–63	Borough Buildings, Water Street (d)	Executors of R. B. B. H. Blundell; H. B. H. Blundell	William Culshaw	LRO, 720 KIR 2839.
32	1855	Weaver Buildings, Brunswick Street (d)	P. Marrow	William Culshaw	LaRO, DDX 162/75/05– DDX 162/75/13; DDX 162/60/10.
33	1856–57	Manchester Buildings, Tithebarn Street (d)	Thomas Joynson	J. D. Jee	LRO, Acc. 2961, drawings by J. D. Jee.

(*Continued*)

	Date	Building (d = demolished)	Owner	Architect	References
34	1856–58	Liverpool & London Chambers, Dale Street	Liverpool & London Insurance Co.	C. R. Cockerell	'The Social Science Association and Liverpool', *Builder*, 16 (1858), p. 705.
35	1856–58	Albany Building, Old Hall Street	R. C. Naylor	J. K. Colling	'The Albany, Old Hall Street, Liverpool', *Building News*, 4 (1858), pp. 576–77.
36	Before 1857	York Buildings, Dale Street (d)		J. A. Picton	'York Buildings, Liverpool', *Building News*, 3 (1857), pp. 582–83.
37	1857	Tower Buildings (south part), Water Street (d)	Joseph Bailey	J. A. Picton	Picton, *Memorials*, vol. 2, p. 83.
38	1857	Middleton Buildings, Water Street (d)		J. A. Picton	Editorial, *Builder*, 15 (1857), p. 301.
39	1857	Leith Offices, Moorfields (d)			'To Be Let – Business Premises', *LM*, 24 August 1857, p. 1.
40	*c.*1858	Hargreaves Building, Chapel Street	William Brown	J. A. Picton	'The Social Science Association and Liverpool', *Builder*, 16 (1858), p. 705.
41	*c.*1858	Richmond Building, Chapel Street (d)	William Brown	J. A. Picton	'The Social Science Association and Liverpool', *Builder*, 16 (1858), p. 705.
42	*c.*1859	Pekin Buildings, Harrington Street			*Gore's Directory*, 1860.
43	1859	Queen Insurance, 11 Dale Street	Queen Insurance Co.	J. A. Picton	'Building Progress in Liverpool', *Building News*, 5 (1859), p. 463.
44	1860–64	Knowsley Buildings, Bixteth Street (d)	William Farrer	William Culshaw	LaRO, DDX 162/52/22–DDX 162/52/46.
45	1861–63	Brown's Buildings & Phoenix Fire Co, Exchange Street West (d)	William Brown	J. A. Picton	'Liverpool Architecture: Brown's Buildings', *Builder*, 19 (1861), pp. 178–79; 'Liverpool Architecture: Brown's Buildings', *Builder*, 21 (1863), p. 35.
46	1861–69	Grosvenor Buildings, Tithebarn Street (d)	William Farrer	William Culshaw	LaRO, DDX 162/52/22–DDX 162/52/46.
47	1862	Batavia Buildings, Hackins Hey (d)	Arnold Baruchson	William Culshaw	LaRO, DDX 162/25/30–DDX 162/25/45.
48	1862–64	Law Association Buildings, Cook Street and Harrington Street (d)	Liverpool Law Association Ltd	William Culshaw	LaRO, DDX 162/80/19-DDX 162/80/37; *Liverpool Mercury*, 31 December 1864.

	Date	Building (d = demolished)	Owner	Architect	References
49	1863	Carlton Buildings, Rumford Street (d)	Executors of Ralph Peters	William Culshaw	LaRO, DDX 162/83/02, DDX 162/83/12–DDX 162/83/14 and DDX 162/83/24–DDX 162/83/25.
50	1863	National Bank of Liverpool, 14 Cook Street	National Bank of Liverpool	William Culshaw	LaRO, included in DDX 162/80/19-DDX 162/80/37.
51	1863	The Temple, Dale Street	William Brown	J. A. Picton	*Whitty's Guide to Liverpool* (Liverpool, 1871), p. 40.
52	1863–70	Exchange Buildings (d)	Liverpool Exchange Co.	T. H. Wyatt	'Liverpool Exchange Buildings Competition', *Builder*, 21 (1863), pp. 381–82; 'The Exchange Buildings, Liverpool', *Builder*, 28 (1870), pp. 119–20.
53	1864	Berey's Buildings, George Street	Trustees of Samuel Berey	William Culshaw	LaRO, DDX 162/88/95–DDX 162/88/102 and DDX 162/88/104–DDX 162/88/107.
54	1864	Parana Buildings, Tithebarn Street (d)	Robinson & Hadwen	William Culshaw	LaRO, DDX 162/52/73–DDX 162/52/80.
55	1864	Windsor Buildings, George Street	William Higgins	William Culshaw	LaRO, DDX 162/29/11–DDX 162/29/12 and DDX 162/29/35–DDX 162/29/39.
56	1864	Exchange Court, Exchange Street East (d)	John Stock	William Culshaw	LaRO, DDX 162/52/03–DDX 162/52/13.
57	1864	Alexandra Buildings, Ormond Street (d)	William Higgins	William Culshaw	LaRO, DDX 162/48/78–DDX 162/48/90.
58	1864	Oriel Chambers, Water Street	Thomas Anderson	Peter Ellis	'A Lounge in Liverpool', *Builder*, 23 (1865), p. 776.
59	1864	Peters Buildings, Rumford Street (d)	Executors of Ralph Peters	William Culshaw	LaRO, DDX 162/83/10, DDX 162/83/11, DDX 162/83/15, DDX 162/83/17, DDX 162/83/22 and DDX 162/83/26–DDX 162/83/33.
60	1864	Mercantile & Exchange Bank, Castle Street		J. A. Picton	*LM*, 7 November 1864.
61	Before 1866	Northern Insurance Buildings, Tithebarn Street (d)		J. A. Picton	Ellison, *Gleanings*, p. 272.
62	1866	Dod's Buildings, Chapel Street (d)		Joseph Boult	'New Buildings in Liverpool', *Building News*, 15 (1868), p. 90.
63	1866	Liver Chambers, Tithebarn Street (d)		Culshaw & Sumners	LaRO, DDX 162/7/17–DDX 162/7/19.

(Continued)

Date	Building (d = demolished)	Owner	Architect	References
64 *c.*1866	Mason's Building, Exchange Street East	William Mason	John Cunningham	'New Buildings in Liverpool', *Building News*, 15 (1868), p. 90; Ellison, *Gleanings*, p. 202.
65 1866–67	Seaton Buildings and Commercial Court, Drury Lane (d)	Samuel Stitt	Culshaw & Sumners	LaRO, DDX 162/80/01–DDX 162/80/18.
66 1866–69	Fowlers Buildings, Victoria Street	Fowler Brothers	J. A. Picton & Son	*Builder*, 23 (1865), p. 179, p. 180.
67 Before 1868	Mellor's Buildings, Exchange Street East (d)		Picton, Bradley, & Chambers	*Building News*, 15 (1868), p. 90.
68 Before 1868	North Western Bank, Dale Street (d)	North Western Bank	Picton & Co	'New Buildings in Liverpool', *Building News*, 15 (1868), pp. 105–6.
69 *c.*1868	16 Cook Street		Peter Ellis	'To Be Let', *Liverpool Journal*, 30 May 1868, p. 10.
70 *c.*1868	Irwell Chambers East, Union Street			'To Be Let: Offices', *LM*, 9 April 1868, p. 2.
71 1868–69	Alliance Bank, Castle Street	Alliance Bank	Lucy & Littler	'The Alliance Bank, Liverpool', *Builder*, 27 (1869), pp. 306–7.
72 *c.*1869	Lombard Chambers, Bixteth Street	T. P. Jones		'To Be Let: Offices', *Liverpool Mercury*, 12 July 1869, p. 2.
73 1869	Lancaster Buildings, Tithebarn Street (d)		Picton, Chambers, & Bradley	*Architect*, 1 (1869), p. 60.
74 1869	Additions to Rumford Court, Rumford Place	Alfred and Henry Graham	Culshaw & Sumners	LaRO, DDX 162/76/01–DDX 162/76/08, DDX 162/76/11–DDX 162/76/12 and DDX 162/76/14–DDX 162/76/15.

Notes

1 William Herdman and James Orr Marples, *Views in Modern Liverpool* (Liverpool, 1864), p. 33. This chapter appeared originally in a slightly different form in *Architectural History*, 61 (2018), pp. 131–73. Table 5.1 provides details on most, if not all, the commercial properties constructed near the Liverpool Exchange between c. 1830 and c. 1870.

2 C. A. Oakley, *The Second City* (London and Glasgow, 1946), p. 70; Spencer Jordan, Peter Wardley and Matthew Woollard, 'Emerging Modernity in an Urban Setting: Nineteenth-Century Bristol Revealed by Property Surveys', *UH*, 26, 2 (1999), pp. 190–210; Frederic C. Howe, *European Cities at Work* (London and Leipsic, 1913), pp. 101–3.

3 Colin G. Pooley, 'Patterns in the Ground: Urban Form, Residential Structure and the Social Construction of Space', in Martin Daunton (ed.), *TCUHB, Vol. 3: 1840–1950* (Cambridge, 2000), p. 436; J. Wilson, 'An Historical Perspective on Operations Management', *Production and Inventory Management Journal*, 35, 3 (1995), pp. 60–6; Niall Piercy, 'Business History and Operations Management',

BH, 54, 2 (2012), pp. 154–87; Paul Jones, 'Putting Architecture in Its Social Place: A Cultural Political Economy of Architecture', *Urban Studies*, 6, 12 (2009), pp. 2519–36; *The Sociology of Architecture Constructing Identities* (Liverpool, 2011), pp. 53–4.

4   James Allanson Picton, *Memorials of Liverpool Historical and Topographical Including a History of the Dock Estate* (2 vols, London, 1873), vol. 2, pp. 269–70.

5   Picton, *Memorials of Liverpool*, vol. 2, p. 27.

6   For coffee houses, see Thomas Ellison, *Gleanings and Reminiscences about Old Cotton Brokers and Their Offshoots* (Liverpool, 1905), pp. 52 ff.; Arthur Henry Arkle, 'The Early Coffee Houses of Liverpool', *THSL&C*, 64 (1912), pp. 1–16.

7   LRO, 352 MIN/IMP I 1/1, pp. 13–55.

8   LRO, 352 MIN/IMP I 1/1, 13 April and 24 June 1786.

9   LRO, 352 MIN/IMP I 1/1, 8 July 1788.

10 LRO, Herdman Collection, 127 and 368B. A photograph of a lost watercolour by Herdman records its appearance in 1859, showing a freestanding cylindrical structure that must have housed the well and pump, and a railed-off stairwell that presumably led to the vaults. Another watercolour by Herdman, of the same date, shows that there was a dignified façade to the street, taller and with a pediment right across.

11 LRO, 352 CLE/CON 3/4, Register of Leases C, entry 13 under letter D. Gore's directory, 1787, gives Dunbar's address as 'Dale-street, near the Exchange'.

12 LRO, 352 MIN/IMP I 1/1, 27 June 1786.

13 E. W. Beaumont, G. F. Horsfall Christofides and T. E. Hall, 'An Historical Survey of the Area between the Exchange Flags and Custom House', unpublished manuscript, School of Architecture, University of Liverpool (1936).

14 James Touzeau, *The Rise and Progress of Liverpool from 1551–1835* (Liverpool, 1910), p. 643.

15 *Gore's Liverpool General Advertiser*, 19 March 1795; William Moss, *The Liverpool Guide: Including a Sketch of the Environs: With a Map of the Town* (Liverpool, 1796), p. 76; LRO, Binns Collection, vol. 30, p. 165; *BLA&MI*, 4 May 1801.

16 Ellison, *Gleanings and Reminiscences*, p. 57: H. M. Addey, *The Picturesque Hand-Book of Liverpool a Manual for Resident and Visitor: With a Day at Birkenhead and a Series of Pleasure Excursions in the Environs* (5th ed., Liverpool, 1846), p. 66.

17 *Builder*, 23 (1865), p. 193; Herdman and Marples, *Views*, pp. 31–2; *Whitty's Guide to Liverpool* (Liverpool, 1871), p. 30.

18 Picton, *Memorials of Liverpool Historical*, vol. 2, p. 35.

19 Anon., *The Stranger in Liverpool; or: An Historical and Descriptive View of the Town of Liverpool and Its Environs* (2nd ed., Liverpool, 1824), pp. 69–73.

20 Thomas Baines, *Liverpool in 1859: The Port and Town of Liverpool and the Harbour, Docks, and Commerce of the Mersey in 1859* (London, 1859), p. 120.

21 A cutting from *BLA&MI* of 24 March 1817, in the Liverpool Record Office's extra-illustrated copy of Thomas Troughton, *The History of Liverpool* (Liverpool, 1810), gives the building costs. Annually from 1829, in the last week of January or first week of February, the *Liverpool Times and Bilinge's Advertiser* published the dividend payable on shares. A receipt book for dividends paid in 1815 is in the Liverpool Record Office, 380 MD 32. By the late 1850s, the dividend amounted to £9 9s per share: see Thomas Baines, *Liverpool in 1859: The Port and Town of Liverpool and the Harbour, Docks, and Commerce of the Mersey in 1859* (London, 1859), p. 121.

22 LRO, Binns Collection, vol. 30, p. 165.

23 *Times*, 13 October 1802.

24 Baines, *Liverpool in 1859*, pp. 119–20.

25 Henry Lacey (publisher), *Pictorial Liverpool: Its Annals; Commerce; Shipping; Institutions; Public Buildings; Sights; Excursions; etc., etc.: A New and Complete Hand-Book for Residents, Visitors and Tourists* (2nd ed., Liverpool, 1844), p. 159.

26 Picton, *Memorials of Liverpool*, II, p. 109; Anon., *The Stranger in Liverpool*, p. 75.

27 Ellison, *Gleanings and Reminiscences*, pp. 193–5, 199–200 and 222–3.

28 Sir John Soane's Museum, MBi/67 set LXVII, memo dated 12 December 1826.

29 *Lancashire Illustrated, from Original Drawings, by S. Austin, J. Harwood and G. & C. Pyne, with Descriptions* (London, 1831).

30 LRO, 352 CLE/CON 5/22, Charles Okill's street index to registers of leases, vol. B, f. 146.

31 Ellison, *Gleanings and Reminiscences*, p. 208.

32 LRO, *Liverpool's Three Exchanges*, Hf 942.7213 EXC, p. 11.

33 *Lancashire Illustrated*, facing p. 38. LaRO, Culshaw & Sumners papers, DDX 162/23/38 and DDX 162/23/44-DDX 162/23/48.

34 Ellison, *Gleanings and Reminisces*, pp. 63–5.

35 Herdman and Marples, *Views*, pp. 31–2.

36 LRO, 920 DUR 2/16/7, 20 July 1833.

37 *LM*, 28 November 1834; *Pen-and-Ink Sketches of Liverpool Town Councillors by a Local Artist Reprinted from the "Liverpool Mercury" 1857* (Liverpool, 1866), p. 22; Benjamin Guiness Orchard, *Liverpool's Legion of Honour* (Birkenhead, 1893), p. 396.

38 Picton, *Memorials of Liverpool*, vol. 2, p. 291; *Pen-and-Ink Sketches*, p. 22.

39 LRO, 920 DUR 2/16/7, 20 July 1833.

40 *A Brief Memoir of George Holt, Esquire, of Liverpool* (Liverpool, 1861), pp. 71–2.

41 LRO, 920 DUR 2/20/1–31, Household accounts and profits and loss accounts, 1823–1859, 1864, George Holt, 1841, 1853.

42 Bank of England archives: Committee for Building minutes, PRE/B565/6, 30 August 1848; Reilly, *Some Liverpool Streets*, p. 36. In 1844, Cockerell had been commissioned to prepare plans for Bank of England offices in Liverpool, Manchester and Bath. For further details of his professional career and interests, see D. Watkin, *The Life and Work of C. R. Cockerell* (London, 1974); A. Bordelau, 'Charles Robert Cockerell, Architecture and the Language of Ornaments', *Journal of Architecture*, 14, 4 (2009), pp. 465–91; Lynda Mulvin, 'Charles Robert Cockerell's Encounter with Ireland: Drawings, Observations & Buildings', *Irish Architectural and Decorative Studies Journal of the Georgian Society*, 12 (2009), pp. 133–55.

43 *Albion* (supplement), 4 August 1856; *Builder*, 14 (1856), p. 437.

44 *Builder*, 15 (1857), p. 301 and 16 (1858), p. 705.

45 LRO, 920 DUR 1/3, Holt family diary, 3 September 1854 and 5 April 1857.

46 *Liverpool Courier*, 19 November 1862.

47 Joseph Mordaunt Crook, *The Rise of the Nouveaux Riches* (London, 2000), pp. 213–14, states that Bailey left £600,000 on his death in 1858. Brown left £900,000 in 1864, as well as real estate valued at almost £300,000 (National Archives, IR26/2359, fol. 505).

48 LaRO, Culshaw & Sumners papers, DDX 162/56/20-DDX 162/56/24.

49 *Daily Post*, 4 July 1863; John Gore, *An Everyday History of Liverpool* (2 vols., Liverpool, no date), not paginated.

50 *Liverpool Times and Billinge's Advertiser*, 28 January 1840; *Liverpool Times*, 31 January 1850.

51 Ellison, *Gleanings and Reminiscences*, pp. 297–8.

52 *Builder*, 23 (1865), p. 193.

53 *Builder*, 21 (1863), pp. 381–2.

54 *Builder*, 23 (1865), p. 776. William Allingham ('Patricius Walker') took a different view, describing the new Exchange as 'pretentiously mean—true cork-cutter's Renaissance' in *Fraser's Magazine*, new series, 2 (1870), pp. 735–53.

55 Lewis Hornblower, 'A Peep into Futurity; or, the Future Building Sites of Liverpool', *Proceedings of the Liverpool Architectural and Archaeological Society*, 13th session (1860–61), pp. 167–8. By contrast, there is substantial data on house construction during this period: see LRO 352 BUI/8/1, General information, folio 119, 'General Statistics for Fifty Years 1836 to 1886. Houses erected, Assessments, Police Strength etc.; P. Laxton, 'The Built-Up Area, 1800–1913', in J. Patmore and A. Hodgkiss (eds.), *Merseyside in Maps* (London, 1970), p. 17; Colin Pooley, 'Living in Liverpool: The Modern City', in John Belchem (ed.), *Liverpool 800 Culture, Character & History* (Liverpool, 2006), p. 210.

56 *Builder*, 16 (1858), p. 705.

57 *Porcupine*, 10 (1868), p. 60.

58 *Architect*, 5 (1871), p. 118.

59 *Building News*, 3 (1857), p. 582.

60 *Builder*, 16 (1858), p. 705.

61 Ellison, *Gleanings and Reminiscences*, pp. 202, 237.

62 *Builder*, 21 (1863), pp. 381–2. For a discussion of the development of architectural competitions, see Roger H. Harper, *Victorian Architectural Competitions an Index to British and Irish Competitions in the Builder 1843–1900* (London, 1983).

63 Orchard, *Liverpool's Legion of Honour*, p. 214.

64 Ellison, *Gleanings and Reminiscences*, p. 200.

65 *The Centenary Book of the Liverpool Stock Exchange 1836–1936* (Liverpool, 1936), p. 35.

66 Edward l'Anson, 'Some Notice of Office Buildings in the City of London', in *Papers Read at the Royal Institute of British Architects, Session 1864–5* (London, 1865), pp. 25–36; John Summerson, *The Unromantic Castle* (London, 1990), pp. 196–202.

67 *Builder*, 6 (1848), pp. 613–14; *Whitty's Guide to Liverpool* (1871), p. 38.

68 LaRO, Culshaw & Sumners papers, DDX 162/14/31-DDX 162/14/49, DDX 162/24/17-DDX 162/24/18, DDX 162/24/23 and DDX 162/24/25-DDX 162/24/37.

69 *Building News*, 3 (1857), p. 582.

70 Hydraulic passenger lifts were in use in Liverpool by the 1860s—there was one in the rebuilt Exchange in 1866—and by the early 1880s several office blocks such as Commercial Saleroom Buildings in Victoria Street and Central Buildings in North John Street had them. They became more efficient and more widespread from 1888, after the Liverpool Hydraulic Power Co. introduced a system of high-pressure water mains. Electricity was an alternative source of power, and after Liverpool Corporation took over the supply in 1896 its use for passenger lifts seems gradually to have supplanted hydraulic power. See Sharples and Stonard, *Built on Commerce*, p. 61.

71 Peter Pugh, *Absolute Integrity the Story of Royal Insurance 1845–1995* (Cambridge, 1995), pp. 81–2.

72 Sidney Pollard, 'Britain's *Prime and Britain's Decline the British Economy 1870–1914* (London, New York, Melbourne and Auckland, 1990), p. 47; Peter De Figueiredo, 'Symbols of Empire: The Buildings of Liverpool Waterfront', *Architectural History*, 46 (2003), pp. 237–9; Leslie Thomas, 'Built Like Bridges: Iron, Steel and Rivets in the Nineteenth-Century Skyscraper', *Journal of the Society of Architectural Historians*, 69, 2 (2010), pp. 234–61; Gail Fenske, 'The Beaux Arts Architect and the Skyscraper', in Roberta Moundry (ed.), *The American Skyscraper, Cultural Histories* (Cambridge and New York, 2005), pp. 19–37.

73 *Civil Engineer and Architect's Journal*, 5 (1842), p. 278; *Builder*, 16 (1858), p. 705; J. F. Smith, Gordon Hemm and Alderman A. Ernest Shennan, *Liverpool Past: Present-Future* (Liverpool, 1948), pp. 21–3.

74 *Porcupine*, 10 (1868), p. 349.

75 MMM, MAL, DX/1477, transcript of 'Sketch of the Commercial Life of H.E. Stripe'.

76 *Porcupine*, 10 (1868), p. 60.

77 MMM, MAL, DX/1477, transcript of 'Sketch of the Commercial Life of H.E. Stripe'.

78 Ellison, *Gleanings and Reminiscences*, p. 300.

79 George James Short Broomhall and John H. Hubback, *Corn Trade Memories, Recent and Remote* (Liverpool, 1930), p. 233; LRO, 920 KUR 1/15, diary of A.G. Kurtz, 6 December 1875; *Athenaeum*, 30 September 1882, p. 438. James Lord Bowes became the first overseas consul to be appointed by Japan: see MLP database; Orchard, *Liverpool's Legion of Honour*, pp. 192–4.

80 'Interviews with Great Men (imaginary): Alfred Billson', *Liberal Review*, 4 June 1881.

81 *Studio*, 16 (1899): pp. 272 ff.

82 Orchard, *Liverpool's Legion of Honour*, p. 329.

83 *Winmore & Co, a Tale of the Great Bank Failure* (London, 1881), p. 35.

84 LRO, H 920 HOL, Fragmentary Autobiography of Alfred Holt, written at various dates, printed 1911, p. 22. 'Interviews with Great Men (Imaginary): Mr. R.D. Holt', *Liberal Review*, 12 March 1881.

85 *Porcupine*, 7 (1866), p. 380; *Liverpool Courier*, 7 January 1863; *Building News*, 3 (1857), p. 582.

86 For example, Adelaide Buildings in Chapel Street and Canton Buildings in Water Street, altered by William Culshaw in 1862 and 1863 (LaRO, Culshaw & Sumners papers, DDX 162/39/36-DDX 162/39/41, and DDX 162/10/20-DDX 162/10/21); *Porcupine*, 10, (1868), 'Improvements in Liverpool: Architectural', p. 349.

87 Quentin Hughes, *Seaport Architecture & Townscape in Liverpool* (London, 1969), p. 60.

88 This feature can be seen in William Culshaw's drawings for A. and H. Graham's offices in Chapel Street, on the west side of Rumford Place, in LaRO, Culshaw & Sumners papers, DDX 162/44/40, DDX 162/44/45-DDX 162/44/46, and DDX 162/44/48-DDX 162/44/49.

89 Joseph Boult, 'The Economy of Daylight', Proceedings of the Liverpool Architectural Society, fifth meeting, 7 January 1880. Boult had been president of the Liverpool Architectural and Archaeological Society in 1862–64.

90 An outstanding example of this type of glazing, recently demolished, was at the back of Windsor Buildings. Drawings for it are in LaRO, Culshaw & Sumners papers, DDX 162/29/11-DDX 162/29/12 and DDX 162/29/35-DDX 162/29/39.

91 *Builder*, 28 (1870), p. 119.

92 *LM*, 15 November 1871 (classified advertisements for offices to let): offices at Dod's building, Chapel Street and Tempest-hey, the latter 'communicating with the Exchange'.

93 Joseph Sharples and John Stonard, *Built on Commerce Liverpool's Central Business District* (Swindon, 2008), p. 59.

94 Colum Giles and Bob Hawkins, *Storehouses of Empire Liverpool's Historic Warehouses* (London, 2004), p. 3; Robin Pearson, *Insuring the Industrial Revolution: Fire Insurance in Great Britain 1700–1850* (Aldershot, 2004), p. 214. In 1842, there is evidence of collusion between the insurance companies when they raised premiums by 83 per cent in response to heavy losses incurred as a result of serious fires in preceding years.

95 For a general discussion of developments in this field, see S. Wermiel, 'The Development of Fireproof Construction in Great Britain and the United States in the Nineteenth Century', *Construction History*, ix (1993), pp. 3–26.

96 *Builder*, 23 (1865), p. 776.

97 There are particularly impressive—and ornamental—examples at 14 Castle Street, Mersey Chambers in Old Church Yard and Union House, Victoria Street.

98 *Companion to the Almanac* (1843), pp. 254–6; *Builder*, 16 (1858), p. 705.

99 Kay Parrot, *Pictorial Liverpool the Art of WG & William Herdman* (Liverpool, 2005), p. 46.

100 *Builder*, 21 (1863), pp. 381–2.

101 *Liverpool Courier*, 19 November 1862.

102 *Liverpool Courier*, 7 January 1863.

103 *Fraser's Guide to Liverpool*, 1861, pp. 211–12.

104 Picton, *Memorials*, vol. 2, p. 28.

105 Joseph Sharples, *Liverpool* (Pevsner Architectural Guides) (New Haven and London, 2004), p. 139.

106 *Builder*, 19 (1861), p. 178; LRO, Edmund Kirby papers, 720 KIR 2839; LaRO, Culshaw and Sumners papers, DDX 162/83/2.

107 William Wilson, *The Melvilles* (London, 1852), p. 34.

108 *Builder*, 26 (1868), p. 296. This unity of effect was not to everyone's taste. The Liverpool architect T. Mellard Reade, writing in the *Porcupine*, 7 (1866), p. 416, saw a lack of imagination in the streets around the Exchange: 'First, Mr. A. puts up a building with a handsome stone front. Then, Mr. B.'s clients, not to be outdone, put up another handsome building, with another handsome stone front, alongside, and the process is repeated from street to street, from year to year, in the most unvarying manner. . . . There is no life—no break—no skyline—no roof to be seen; nothing but a dull, level uniformity'.

109 De Figueiredo, 'Symbols of Empire', pp. 229–54.

110 D. K. Stenhouse, 'Liverpool's Office District, 1875–1905', *THSL&C*, 133 (1984), pp. 71–87; Sharples and Stonard, *Built on Commerce*, pp. 19–31.

111 Herdman and Marples, *Views*, p. vii.

112 Picton, *Memorials of Liverpool*, vol. 2, p. 160.

113 Picton, *Memorials of Liverpool*, vol. 2, pp. 109, 160.

114 Graeme Milne, 'Knowledge, Communications, and the Information Order in Nineteenth-Century Liverpool', *IJMH*, 14, 1 (2002), pp. 209–24.

6 Kinship, Friendship and Partnership

The Social Networks of the Liverpool Merchant Community

Sari Mäenpää

Introduction

Liverpool became the second largest port in Britain in the late nineteenth century and its trading community played a central role in its economic growth. Merchanting and ship owning were especially dominant in a global port city which was dependent primarily on commerce and shipping, unlike many other northern towns and cities where manufacturing was a much more important activity. During the course of the nineteenth century, Liverpool witnessed the consolidation and further expansion of a commercial elite which included some extremely wealthy members who, in turn, often dominated the city's municipal affairs, cultural life and philanthropy.[1] At the same time, the proliferation of clubs and societies, as a key component of a nascent 'subscriber democracy', helped to generate a transactional density which enabled the elite to fashion its relationship with other elements of urban society and strengthen class cohesion.[2] Local associations, societies and private clubs were used increasingly by the merchant community for a variety of purposes, but they became an important part of business culture and formed an integral component of the social networks of local merchants. These networks were essential for commercial activities since trust, which remained the most vital aspect in business relations, was fostered essentially through individual bonding. Indeed, recent research has emphasised the extent to which trust was just as important as competition in shaping business culture because it facilitated effective co-operation between individual entrepreneurs.[3] According to Davidoff and Hall, the interchange between kinship, friendship and partnership contributed to the survival of the middle class in an uncertain economic and demographic environment in the period before the 1850s.[4] Morris, in his analysis of voluntary societies in the early nineteenth century, has argued that the nature of middle-class associational culture was both elitist and defensive, while Simon Gunn has described the nineteenth-century gentlemen's clubs as 'the most exclusive' and 'impervious to change'.[5]

The importance of religious and political sectarianism in the historiography of Liverpool has been studied extensively, but the significance of cross-sectional networks in strengthening reputational status and facilitating business transactions has often been overlooked.[6] Social or cross-sectional associations were promoted partly out of the desire to extend the bonds of loyalty and obligation beyond political and religious boundaries, but they provided a framework not only for consolidating business networks but also for defining the nature of civil society. This chapter will explore the significance of cross-sectional merchant networks, in contrast to other areas of civic life, including political representation and charitable work, which continued to be characterised by sectarian attitudes, although it should be noted that the boundaries between different types of associational activity were often flexible and sometimes overlapping. At one level, cross-sectional associations were based on fraternalism in the sense that they

DOI: 10.4324/9781315597836-6

were designed to create or to sustain bonds of loyalty beyond the family and they therefore had a wider occupational and social membership as compared to extended families and religious networks.[7] As a result, these clubs and societies offered access to a range of business information; an opportunity for 'image-making'; and the possibility of gaining social prestige outside a merchant's immediate denominational affiliation or political allegiance.

This chapter will consider the number and role of merchants involved in voluntary associations, learned societies and sports clubs, drawing from an extensive range of primary source material, and discuss whether they helped to increase trust within the business community and if so, in what ways. If this was not the case, did they have some other function? Did the social networks of Liverpool's merchant community act as information channels for business purposes or did club membership have a more exclusionary function, which was simply to improve or defend the existing *social* status of merchants? It will describe the mechanisms of selection to these social networks and the importance of reputation and trust in this process, while the membership of these clubs and associations will be explored in terms of its occupational and residential composition. In analysing the exclusionary practises of individual clubs and associations, the chapter will also assess the importance of kinship and fraternity in maintaining privilege and in exploiting informal information systems.

Clubs were places where their members were able to relax and engage in activities they enjoyed and were interested in. However, merchants and brokers might also have developed their associational culture for more opportunistic reasons. In order to discuss the usefulness of a common business culture for merchants, use will be made of the membership records of a selective sample of Liverpool private clubs and associations. These clubs had some common characteristics and features which distinguished them from other societies and forms of associational culture. Since the dominant cultural values of the late nineteenth century also moulded the experience of the merchant community, the general characteristics of these clubs can be interpreted as representative expressions of Liverpool's contemporary business culture.[8]

Network Analysis

Merchants had a considerable influence on Liverpool's politics, as well as on its built environment, social life, educational institutions and charitable organisations. In a wider context, merchants' culture is an essential element in studying their business activities.[9] Previous studies have highlighted the inadequacy of strictly economic explanations in interpreting economic phenomena or entrepreneurial performance and have emphasised the extent to which economic and cultural values are intertwined, while the application of social network analysis has played a key role in recent research in exploring the dynamics of business communities and assessing the performance of individual firms, whether in a contemporary or historical context.[10] Members of a network were dependent on a range of resources, whether material goods or information, which were controlled by its participants. Although an individual's relative position within a network could vary, the underlying principle was the assumption by all participants that co-operation would produce mutual benefits for individual actors as well as for the wider economy.[11]

The maintenance of good business networks, which could perform a range of positive functions, was especially important in port cities where firms were confronted by an inflated degree of risk because of slow and imperfect communications by sea.[12] Indeed, the continued viability of merchant enterprises depended on a wide range of business networks which helped to reduce market uncertainties, facilitated risk-spreading, enhanced communication, reduced transaction costs and delivered important efficiency gains.[13] Long-standing networks were particularly well suited for transmitting information in cases when high reliability was at a premium and they were often sustained by intermarriage as well as by common values which played a critical role both in maintaining existing business contacts and in creating new ones.[14]

Reputation often dictated the decisions which merchants took in public life. A good reputation was crucial for merchants because it guaranteed better access to information, which was, in turn, critical for success. Indeed, information was often the key motive behind networking activities, because access to up-to-date information remained vitally important for reducing risk. Networks served as channels for the transmission of up-to-date business information which helped to reduce uncertainty and information costs, but they also helped to increase trust within the merchant community. If the cross-sectional social clubs were indeed important for business networks, they should have included mechanisms which were designed to secure the reliability and reputation of newcomers. This chapter will seek to identify the techniques which were employed to achieve this objective; discuss the operative principles of inclusion and exclusion; and assess the extent to which they reflected the economic and cultural values of Liverpool in the late nineteenth century at a time when it was the second most important port city in Britain and a dominant force in the development of international trade.

The Mercantile Liverpool Project identified three basic types of informal networks amongst Liverpool merchants based on extended family connections, philanthropic activities and cross-sectional or inter-denominational affiliations. Despite overlapping elements, each type of informal network can be regarded for the purpose of this analysis as a distinct entity, including networks designed to provide philanthropy. In contrast to the late eighteenth century when the author of a guidebook claimed that the town's charitable contributions failed to match the income of one major merchant, there was a great upsurge of charitable effort during the latter decades of the nineteenth century.[15] Although it was motivated by both religious and humanistic considerations, a great deal of welfare provision continued to be delivered within a denominational framework which was reinforced by the development of charitable institutions for specific in-migrant groups, including the Irish, Scots and Welsh, as well as Lutherans from northern Germany and Scandinavia.[16] Informal, family-based business networks were equally important in controlling information flows. In fact, an 'extended family', created through intermarriage and often consisting of members with the same religious affiliation, could form very effective networks.[17] For example, the Unitarians in Liverpool were notably successful in business due primarily to their extremely efficient 'extended family' networks.[18]

However, membership in many clubs and associations was not confined to specific political or religious group or dominated by members of family-based networks. These cross-sectional or inter-denominational clubs, which are the main concern of this chapter, frequently offered excellent opportunities for networking across religious and political boundaries. Merchants and brokers bonded in these associations in order to establish and maintain personal relations, control information flows and improve their reputation within the wider community. Indeed, they were often played a very influential role in this type of information network, since more than a half of the members of the associations and societies included in this study consisted of merchants, brokers and ship owners.

The Development of Social Networks in Liverpool

The social network role of cross-sectional clubs and associations in the second half of the nineteenth century was based on earlier traditions which became increasingly embedded within the merchant community. Liverpool's growing importance in the Atlantic economy during the second half of the eighteenth century, specifically in relation to the slave trade, was underpinned by the development of large business networks based on general reputation and trust. Merchants were dependent on 'strong' and 'weak' ties; their networks were both 'receptive' and 'open'; but detailed information on the extent and significance of informal associations is seldom available.[19] Initially, coffee houses and taverns provided opportunities for both informal interaction and the exchange of business information, but the establishment of social clubs in the mid-eighteenth century, primarily, if not exclusively, for prominent members of the merchant community, reinforced the sense of cohesion which was a 'vital factor' in Liverpool's commercial success.[20] The gradual establishment of clubs was accompanied by the foundation of benevolent institutions, including the first Liverpool Infirmary (1749) and the Hospital for Decayed Seamen (1751), some of which were dependent on subscriptions from a wide range of residents irrespective of their denominational affiliation and benefited from the business skills of merchants willing to serve on their management committees.[21] More importantly, the potential transactional density within the merchant community was reinforced in the late eighteenth and early nineteenth centuries by the flowering of intellectual pursuits and the emergence of learned societies dominated by the merchant elite. The growth of societies from the 1780s onwards was 'remarkable': 22 new benevolent institutions were founded between 1800 and 1824; there was a steady growth in the number of learned societies particularly in the second half of the nineteenth century; and an increasing willingness to establish select clubs which catered for the specific interests of their members.[22] The Liverpool Library had been founded in 1758 and was one of the first subscription libraries in Europe, but the Amicable Book Society (1812) whose 20 members were elected by ballot ('as harmony in one') arguably provided a more meaningful framework for social networking since the meetings to discuss such books as Mungo Park's *Travels* and Clarkson's *History of the Abolition of the Slave Trade* were held 'in each other's houses'.[23]

Sources and Methodology

This chapter draws its core source materials from the Mercantile Liverpool Project database which contains information on Liverpool merchants and brokers derived from census returns, trade directories and the membership lists of various clubs and associations.[24] The membership lists of seven very different clubs or associations with specific rules and regulations have been used in this analysis, together with other primary and secondary source materials, such as committee minutes and contemporary biographical collections. Over 300 obituaries of members of the local elite were incorporated into the database and analysed to cast further light on the business and social activities of prominent Liverpool merchants during the second half of the nineteenth century when the port-city had a considerable number of middle-class cross-sectional clubs and associations.[25] The seven clubs analysed in this study were chosen according to specific criteria, including the availability and quality of the extant source material. Newspaper reports and other contemporary secondary sources were used to establish the wider framework of associational culture during this period, but the sample of cross-sectional clubs was selected to illustrate the variety of options available to elite members of local society—ranging from ballroom dancing, debating and dining, to golf, history and yachting. Membership data was keyed into the database as discrete spheres of cultural, social and sporting activity.

(i) Social Clubs

The Wellington Club (Figure 6.1) was the oldest of the clubs surveyed. It was founded in 1814 'for the purpose of having balls and other entertainments': it existed primarily for social purposes, even if it had a much more important function.[26] It became one of the main social institutions for

Figure 6.1 G. & C. Pine. The Wellington Rooms, Mount Pleasant (1830), in S. Austin et al., *Lancashire illustrated from original drawings* (London, 1831), facing p. 16

members of the town's elite whether involved in trade and commerce or one of the professions. According to Orchard, it was the 'sanctum sanctorum' of Liverpool's most exclusive families and consistently maintained its prestigious standing. Its regular balls, of which there were five or six in each season, attracted a large number of patrons; they were attended by ladies 'dressed with gorgeousness such as befits the wives and daughters of the wealthiest men in Great Britain's greatest seaport'; and the dancing which commenced at 9.30 p.m. ceased 'precisely' at 1.30 a.m.[27] The balls held at the Club, in particular the triennial bachelors' ball, were important events in the social calendar when introductions were arranged between suitable future marital partners and where young ladies and gentlemen formed friendships 'not only for a dance but for life's long journey'.[28] Indeed, at one level managing families and firms had many common characteristics. For prominent families within the merchant community, arranging appropriate marriages required a conscious and deliberate strategy, since a successful marriage was one of the central mechanisms of securing the family firm's future.

The YZ Club was purely an elite social and literary club founded in 1870. Originally, it had only 5 members, but its membership was subsequently raised to 12 and then, in May 1876, to 18. No new members were to be admitted without the unanimous assent of existing members. Its founding members included leading Liverpool merchants and academics from different political and religious backgrounds, such as Sir James Picton, Christian D. Ginsbury (who was appointed in 1870 as the first member of a committee to revise the English version of the Old Testament), and Dr. Campbell Brown (the City Analyst). The members met once a month over dinner when they discussed topical issues such as the education of women, Darwinism, trade unions, the 'immorality of the Port', drunkenness, atheism and the problem of succession in family firms.[29] The meetings were held at either the Royal or the Alexandra Hotel when members could also introduce a limited number of visitors and the proceedings consisted of an early dinner, 'accompanied by a restricted allowance of wine', followed by 'conversation of the most varied character' accompanied by the 'introduction of coffee and cigars'.[30]

(ii) Sporting Clubs

The Royal Mersey Yacht Club (RMYC) was a sporting club founded on 26 July 1844 at a meeting attended by 20 local businessmen and gentlemen convened at the Mersey Hotel, Old Church Yard, Liverpool. The Royal Warrant was received on 24 September in the same year.[31] Its first premises were in Dale Street, but already by 1846 it had established a Marine Station for the summer season at the Birkenhead Hotel. The Club later built its own facilities across the River Mersey at Bedford Road East, Rock Ferry, which included a clubhouse and a gridiron on which vessels could be dried out for hull maintenance. The club followed both military and patriotic ideals with considerable emphasis on honouring the flag and maintaining appropriate etiquette, while the overall importance of yachting skills for a maritime empire was highlighted in contemporary newspaper accounts of its foundation. It was a club designed for bigger yachts where it was expected that members would sail reasonably long distances, compete in open regattas and make use of them for leisure and entertaining purposes. In 1856, Thomas Wilkinson Tetley (1824–1903) won the Club's Grand Challenge Cup in the 'celebrated cutter' *Surprise* (of 20 tons)' and a number of members had sufficient time and wealth to embark on a 12-month world tour (including Thomas Hughes Jackson of the Manor House, Claughton). For that reason, it was relatively common for members to retain membership of several yacht clubs simultaneously and, more importantly, to seek membership of the Royal Yacht Squadron. There was a good market in luxury second-hand yachts, particularly if they had been previously owned by members of the aristocracy, and to seek membership of the Royal Yacht Squadron. For example, the industrialist and M.P. for Wigan (1868–74) John Lancaster bought the yacht *Deerhound* in 1857 and joined the RMYC. It had been built originally at the Laird shipyard in Birkenhead for the Duke of Leeds and was sold again at auction in 1868, by which time Lancaster had already been a member of Royal Yacht Squadron for four years. The RMYC offered accommodation and dining facilities at its premises, as well as a place to store yachts. The club had approximately 400 members by the end of the nineteenth century, some of whom owned steam-yachts, but only smaller yachts competed in the Club's local regattas (Figure 6.2).[32]

The Royal Liverpool Golf Club (RLGC) was established at Hoylake on the Wirral in 1869 at a meeting which included several leading Liverpool merchants, including Alexander Balfour, J. Muir Dowie and John T. Forman. Dowie, a Scottish merchant, ship broker and shipowner, became its first captain. Hoylake was a considerable distance from Liverpool, but some of the founding members were already resident on the Wirral and other Liverpool-based players subsequently moved to the peninsula as the process of suburbanisation created new residential locations for wealthy members of Liverpool's merchant community.[33] A considerable number of additional, prestigious golf clubs were also founded on the Wirral. However, the Royal Liverpool Golf Club was the first to introduce the Scots' national game to Merseyside (Figure 6.3).[34] Subsequently, four more golf clubs were founded in an area north of Liverpool in the late nineteenth century and the rate of expansion on the Wirral was also very extensive. These clubs had interlocking membership especially among merchants with a Scottish background who featured prominently in Liverpool's business circles.[35] Easy access to almost all these country clubs was

Figure 6.2 The Royal Mersey Yacht Club Regatta, 1910, the *Keewaydin* and *Comrade*

Figure 6.3 Royal Liverpool Golf Club Pavilion, Hoylake (undated postcard, pre-1914)

facilitated by the building of railway lines and, in the case of Hoylake, by improved ferry facilities across the Mersey. It gained royal status in 1871 when Prince Arthur agreed to be one of the patrons of the club and its membership had increased from 50 to almost 600 by 1899.[36]

(iii)   Cultural Clubs

The Liverpool Athenaeum was founded in 1797 at a time when there was a concerted attempt to establish institutions which offered both conviviality and intellectual stimulation (Figure 6.4).[37] The Athenaeum was initially established on a site in Church Street made available by the mayor and council: the building was completed and opened in 1799. The club was re-located a few times, but it was always situated near the business district: according to Washington Irving it was 'one of the first places to which a stranger is taken in Liverpool'.[38] The most important facilities of the club were the newsroom and the reference library, which had over 18,000 volumes by the mid-1840s.[39] In the early period, access to London newspapers was an important reason to join but later it provided a convenient meeting place in the town centre where merchants, doctors and lawyers could take lunch and consult a wide range of newspapers and journals. According to Picton, the Athenaeum had traditionally been 'the resort of what may be called the "upper crust" of Liverpool mercantile society'.[40]

   The Historic Society for Lancashire and Cheshire was established in 1848 with 180 members in order to bring 'the non-scientific subjects into greater prominence'. It was argued that there would be a 'manifest advantage' in offering 'a diversity of subjects', and 'sectional members' of council were elected in 1854 to cover archaeology, literature and science.[41] The most famous of the founders was the antiquarian and clergyman Abraham Hume, who took an active part in many of the town's public, scientific, educational and ecclesiastical movements. The society's activities included regular meetings where papers were read relating to the region's history, antiquities or any of the other topics which were included in the original prospectus.[42] A library and museum were established where 'collected valuable or rare books, manuscripts, coins, antiquities, specimens of natural history, manufactures or curiosities' were stored.[43] Shortly after its foundation the Historic Society had 251 members, a figure which had increased by the early

Figure 6.4 The Liverpool Athenaeum (by courtesy of The Liverpool Athenaeum)

1860s to 389, but by the beginning of the twentieth century it had only 241 individual and insti-tutional members, together with three associate and five honorary members.

The Liverpool Philomathic Society was founded in 1825 as a debating society for members of Liverpool's business community with the specific objective of promoting 'the attainment of knowledge' through offering facilities for debate and discussion on a wide range of top-ics.[44] Like the Literary and Philosophical Society, which had been established in 1812, it was designed to reflect the cultural profile of Liverpool and to demonstrate the inherent compatibil-ity of commerce and culture.[45] Of the 14 meetings in each season, 2 were taken up by addresses by the president and one of the vice-presidents; 'two are usually given up to reading of essays by members, which also call forth all the writer's mental powers'; while the Christmas dinner and the summer excursion were 'always largely attended'.[46] Although the surviving records do not include a continuous register of the Society's membership, they do contain a useful range of documents which reflect in detail the operational framework of a debating society dominated by merchants and businessmen. It had 6 founding members, but by 1846 its membership had grown to 60 with a further significant increase to 377 by 1884. It celebrated its centenary in 1912 with a special dinner at the Adelphi Hotel (16 February 1926) when the principal speaker was Sir Arthur Quiller Couch (Figure 6.5).[47]

Membership Composition

The evidence from membership data and obituaries suggests that merchants were extremely active in social and public affairs. As far as middle-class clubs and associations were concerned, they frequently played a dominant role. Their active attendance and overall support for these types of informal networking will be analysed in detail to determine the extent to which they were the driving force behind the visible pattern of extensive socialisation, entertaining and intellectual stimulation. Liverpool merchants were engaged in various types of social associa-tions at a time when 'scientific' topics, together with sports, languages, literature and music, were very much in fashion. To be seen publicly as 'civilized' in contrast to the 'vulgar' rep-resentatives of the working class remained an important consideration for many businessmen during the second half of the nineteenth century. Although some merchants were committed to alleviating the problems caused by destitution and poverty, social contacts with the working class were generally avoided. In fact, the working class often had parallel social institutions, whether in the political arena or in sports, while businessmen tended to idealise the life-style of the landed gentry and 'old families' with aristocratic roots.[48]

Some prominent Liverpool families appear on the membership lists of many of the inter-denominational associations included in the sample, which suggests that these clubs deliber-ately sought to enhance their prestige by attracting people of superior social status. Individual clubs often offered concessions to certain members of local society who were deemed to be desirable and whose presence as members was expected to improve the club's profile. These families were permitted to join without balloting; quota restrictions were not applied; or they were simply admitted without paying the full membership fees. The Athenaeum, the Wellington Club and the Royal Liverpool Golf Club showed a preference for members from old families, as well as from the navy, the army and the volunteer movement, whereas the Historic Society sought to recruit 'learned scientific and literary foreigners not residing within Lancashire or Cheshire', as well as 'any persons who shall have rendered special service to the society'. At a meeting on 14 December 1854, it was decided that the privilege of joining the Historic Society without a formal election or the payment of an entrance fee could be offered to gentlemen 'likely to become full members', a group which included 'eight mayors of boroughs, 18 clergymen, 21

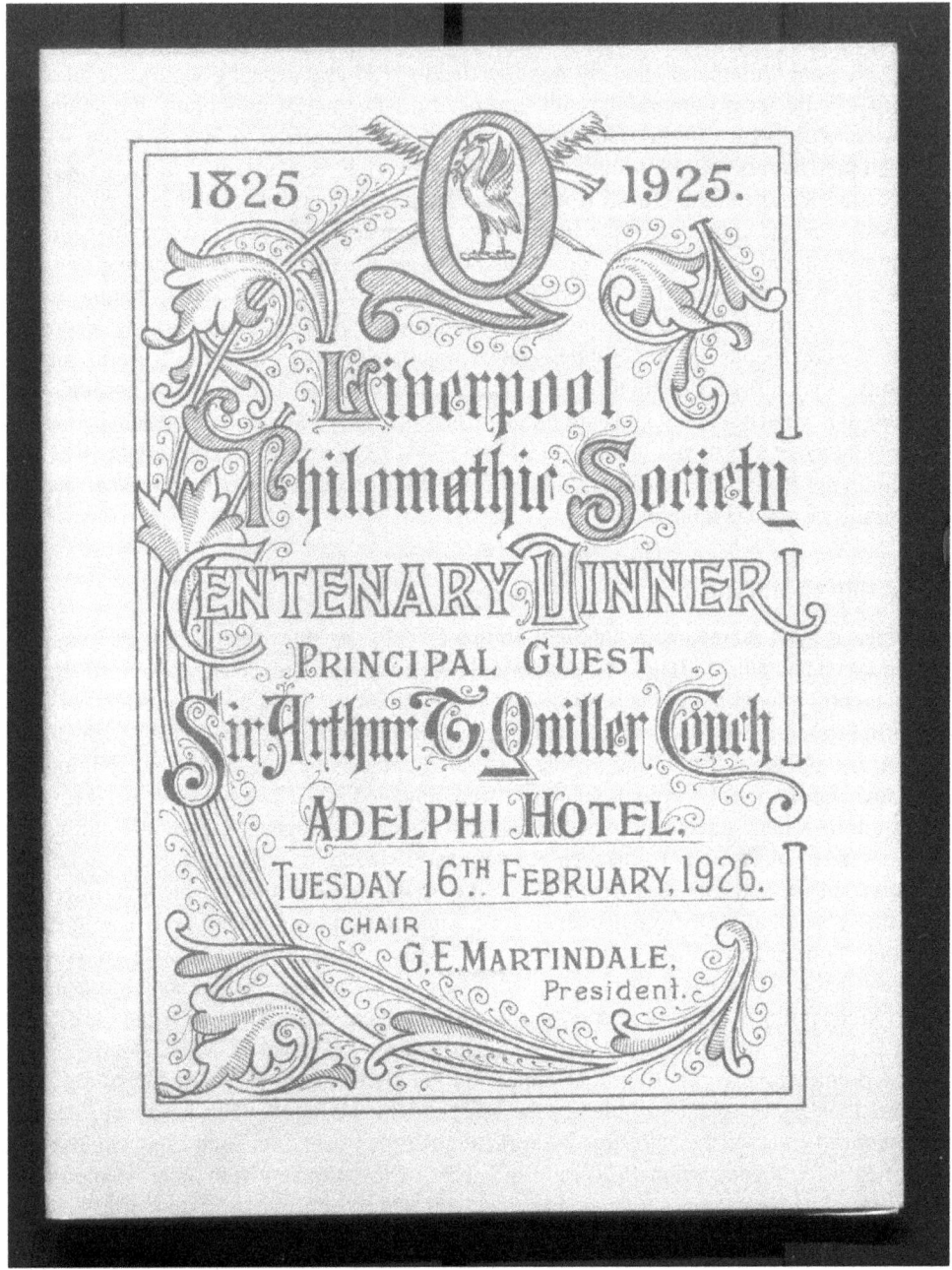

Figure 6.5 The Liverpool Philomathic's Centenary Dinner, 16 February 1926 (courtesy of Liverpool University Special Collections and Archives)

graduates, three participants of public institutions and eleven fellows or members of metropolitan societies'. Over two thirds of these gentlemen (67 per cent) were classified as 'resident'.[49] In general, clergymen from the Church of England were regarded as desirable members, as well as elected mayors, the Earl of Derby and many of the old-established Liverpool families, such as the Earles, the Forwoods and the Langtons. These three families were also prominent members of the Wellington Club, but they were represented in every social club surveyed, except the YZ Club. By contrast, salaried employees, shopkeepers or individuals from Liverpool's Irish community formed only a tiny minority of the overall membership.[50] In fact, in the case of the Wellington Club, servants and housekeepers were explicitly excluded from membership in its rules and regulations.[51] In some cases, local societies deliberately restricted their membership by social class. For example, the Liverpool Philomathic Society in its original rules confined membership exclusively to gentlemen who were in business on their own account. Somewhat later this requirement was relaxed, but only to a limited extent, and in 1928 it was stated that the society consisted of 'individuals who follow the busy vocations of life, whose time is devoted to commercial, and the more active professional, pursuits'.[52] By contrast, the Historic Society was only willing to offer the privilege of membership to 'such gentlemen as may be thought desirable'.[53]

The cross-sectional character of the clubs and societies was often emphasised in the rules or at one of the initial meetings and it was generally regarded as an important principle. The first meeting of the YZ club concluded that 'every phase of politics and religion has been represented: Liberals, Conservatives, Liberal Unionists, Radicals, Churchmen, Non-Conformists, Catholics, Hebrews, and Unitarians'; the Mersey Royal Yacht Club established a rule that no political subject should be discussed at a club meeting; and the Philomathic Society stipulated that 'no questions on controversial theology' should ever be debated at its meetings.[54] The cross-sectional principles imposed by these clubs implied a shared acceptance of the need for a cohesive elite with a distinct middle-class identity underpinned by co-operation across political and religious boundaries.

In general, a clear majority of members of cross-sectional clubs and societies were businessmen, specifically merchants, brokers and shipowners, where they mingled with representatives of the local gentry as well as professionals, including solicitors, architects, engineers and professors. In the sample of Liverpool clubs and societies businessmen and shipowners formed 63.7 per cent of the membership and exercised a considerable influence on their activities and general operation. Other influential groups included solicitors and 'gentlemen', who represented 8.0 and 6.8 per cent respectively of the total membership, although the latter category included individuals who had previously been active within the merchant community but had subsequently retired from business (Table 6.1). The Athenaeum attracted the highest number of clergymen from the Church of England, but other denominations, especially Presbyterians and Unitarians, appear in most membership lists. The fact that the clubs were inter-denominational made them important venues for local businessmen. As George Shaw, the librarian in the Athenaeum between 1889 and 1909, wrote: 'It [the Athenaeum] is, and must continue to be, the only neutral ground on which influential men engaged in all forms of religious, political and social work in the city can meet'.[55]

Table 6.1 Members of selected Liverpool clubs by occupation (in per cent), 1850–1900

Occupation	%	Occupation	%
merchant	39.8	solicitor	8.0
broker	12.5	gentleman	6.8
shipowner	11.4	manufacturer	3.2
engineer	4.1	other	14.3

Sources: MLP database, membership records of the selected clubs

The data suggest that merchants were remarkably active in cross-sectional social networks, but there were noticeable variations between individual clubs. At one extreme, in the Royal Mersey Yacht Club, 27 per cent of the early members (c.1870–1900) were merchants, 12.4 per cent were brokers and 8.5 per cent were shipowners, so that the commercial élite formed 48 per cent of the total membership. Other prominent groups included engineers (11.2 per cent), as well as solicitors and manufacturers (7 per cent). Other clubs were not dominated in quite the same way by the mercantile community.

Important inferences relating to the nature and function of these networks can be drawn by looking at the geographical distribution of members in the second half of the nineteenth century. In particular, the number of non-residential members, as compared to Liverpool residents, is especially interesting. Membership of the clubs included in the sample extended beyond the boundaries of Liverpool, across the Mersey to the Wirral and further afield to Cheshire and Lancashire, or beyond (Figure 6.1). Indeed, the objective of the Historic Society was to attract members from throughout Lancashire and Cheshire: shortly after its foundation almost 70 per cent is its members were resident in Liverpool or on Merseyside, but by the end of the 1860s only 112 of its 256 members (43.7 per cent) were 'resident'.[56]

Some of the clubs and societies therefore attracted a regional rather than purely local membership, which suggests that they underpinned the operation of regionally dispersed social networks. In fact, only approximately half of the members of the seven clubs and societies in the sample were Liverpool residents (53 per cent): almost 20 per cent lived on the Wirral and 7 per cent were located in Lancashire, while a significant group (14 per cent) lived in London. However, it was still customary for members to register their business address, even if their domestic residence was no longer within the designated boundaries of Liverpool, with the result that the proportion of Liverpool residents may have been exaggerated, particularly as an increasing number of merchants during the second half of the nineteenth century demonstrated a preference for a suburban residence, whether on the Wirral or elsewhere.[57]

Members of the business community increasingly commuted by carriage, ferryboat or train to work, although commuting by horseback was no longer a viable option by 1900. The importance of local train connections and improved accessibility was especially evident in the case of prestigious golf clubs which were founded following the opening of the Northern Railway Line, together with railway improvements on the Wirral, particularly after the opening in 1886 of the Mersey Railway Tunnel and subsequent electrification in 1903. Improved public transport also facilitated the attendance of non-residential members at club activities. For example, members of the Royal Liverpool Golf Club were able to arrive by train at Hoylake, particularly after the late 1880s when the Wirral Railway Company operated 22 trains in each direction between West Kirby and Birkenhead Park where passengers could change from the trains

Table 6.2 The geographic distribution of Liverpool club membership by place of residence (in per cent), 1850–1900

Area	%	Area	%
Liverpool and environs	53	Manchester	3
other	14	Lancashire (other)	7
The Wirral	12	London	5
Cheshire (other)	3	overseas	2
		Wales	1

Sources: MLP database; membership records of the selected Liverpool clubs

operated by the Mersey Railway, but a considerable number of members almost certainly used private transport.[58]

Liverpool clubs had frequent contacts both with each other and with other clubs nationally. The Royal Liverpool Golf Club held regular tournaments with other golf clubs in England and Scotland, as well as with local canoe and beagle clubs. The Historic Society had a wide regional membership base and maintained close contacts with the Historic Society of New York. The Philomathic Society had an interlocking membership with both the Liverpool and Southport Literary and Philosophical Societies, but it also kept in regular contact with other Philomathic Societies regionally.[59] Networking opportunities within a regional framework were reinforced by the fact that prominent businessmen were often members of different clubs and societies simultaneously. Golf players, in particular, were frequently members of a number of different golf clubs and a similar phenomenon was evident in the case of leading members of the Royal Mersey Yacht Club.[60] Frequent contacts were reinforced through sponsoring each other's cups and by organising joint events, while in the case of the Historic Society it was admitted in the early 1850s that many members 'embraced' other cultural societies in Liverpool, in some cases even reading the same paper at different venues.[61]

Civic pride was often an important reason for establishing a club and the inaugural minutes of several Liverpool clubs and societies emphasised the desirability of following the example of London or other provincial cities, and the organisational model which they adopted, together with the rules and regulations, were frequently copied from an existing club. For example, the Royal Liverpool Golf Club adopted its rules and organisation from St. Andrews Golf Club. In many cases there was a national network of societies which provided an operational model which Liverpool residents were able to follow: the Athenaeum was modelled on the Newcastle Literary and Philosophical Society, while the Royal Mersey Yacht Club adopted a similar set of rules to those already operated by prestigious yacht clubs such as the Royal Cork Yacht Club and the Royal Thames Yacht Club founded in 1720 and 1775 respectively.[62]

In fact, interlocking membership was essential for the merchant community in order to provide reciprocal hospitality and maintain a regional and national framework for the operation of social networks. For many social institutions, such as the Wellington Club, it was essential to allow strangers and visitors temporary access to their activities, including balls and other forms of entertainment, primarily as a means of introducing new candidates for matrimony. For in-migrant merchants, irrespective of their country of origin, an invitation to attend as a guest represented an opportunity to establish their suitability as full-time members, while in the case of the YZ Club no one could become a paid-up member without having previously enjoyed guest status. To this extent, the clubs and societies operated according to highly selective membership criteria which emphasised the importance of common values.

Membership and Wealth

All the clubs in the sample accepted membership applications from suitable candidates from a variety of political and religious backgrounds, but there were other factors, such as balloting and the cost of membership, which restricted access. These mechanisms ensured that the clubs and societies retained their exclusivity; helped to guarantee that their members were of a sound economic and social standing; and designed to ensure that anyone who was admitted shared the social and cultural values of existing members. In order to establish respectability and suitability, agreed criteria were used to assess eligibility. All the clubs, except the YZ Club, operated a complicated system of graded membership. Firstly, new members would normally pay a joining fee (as in the case of the Royal Liverpool Golf Club) or buy a share as a proprietor (as laid down in the rules of the Wellington Club and the Athenaeum), or both. In addition, an annual subscription was payable. Life membership was also available, while non-residential members or strangers were often granted a reduced membership fee. Residency was determined by business location, not the address of a member's private residence, which reflected the continued importance of commerce and trade both for personal identity and for social networking. If a person had business interests in Liverpool, regardless of where he lived, he was automatically regarded as resident and liable for a higher fee and regular membership was only available on this basis. Both the Athenaeum and the Royal Liverpool Golf Club were very precise in determining a member's residential status, as measured by the spatial distance in miles from Liverpool.[63] However, the maximum distance for qualifying as a residential member changed over time, in line with Liverpool's urban expansion and the wider process of suburbanisation. The Athenaeum originally defined a resident as somebody who lived within 8 miles of Liverpool, but the radial distance was increased to 15 miles in 1855 and finally to 25 miles by 1880. Indeed, it became increasingly difficult for clubs and societies to insist on a residential status within the boundaries of Liverpool (despite five extensions prior to 1913). Merchants and other members of the business community gradually moved further and further away from the urban core and many of the most important sports clubs, such as the Royal Liverpool Golf Club and the Royal Mersey Yacht Club, were located on the Wirral.

The ability to bring along guests was an important feature of all the clubs and societies included in the sample, although this facility was strictly regulated. In 1852 the laws of the Historic Society were amended to allow each member 'to introduce two gentlemen, not one, at any of the ordinary meetings', as a means of boosting membership.[64] In general, the clubs and societies provided elaborate and congenial surroundings ideal for impressing a client or for carrying out business negotiations. Two factors reinforced the important role of clubs and societies for business networking: the general requirement that all prospective members enjoyed a sound economic status; and the facility to introduce guests. Clubs with a high social standing were important places to be seen at, but they also offered relatively safe locations for developing and consolidating new business contacts. The Wellington Club had a very snobbish reputation. *The Porcupine* reported: 'Yes, here you behold the very upperest crust of the Liverpudlian social strata, the top-sawyers of the maritime capital, the concentration of all the refinement, and elegance, and wealth, and influence, and enterprise, and (this is a whisper!) utter vulgarity and complete snobbishness in the city of the Liver!'[65]

A system of graded membership provided a means of highlighting differences in the financial and residential status of individual members. According to Morris, before the mid-nineteenth century graded membership was a key feature of middle-class voluntary associations which served to emphasise hierarchical distinctions and this continued to be the case in respect to the sample of Liverpool clubs and societies prior to 1914.[66] Those who could afford to purchase a share, to pay the specified joining fee or to take out a life membership were guaranteed permanent access to the clubs, provided their financial position did not deteriorate significantly.

The membership fee was very high at some clubs, particularly those with a social or sporting function, intent on maintaining social exclusivity. The entrance fee for the Royal Liverpool Golf Club in 1900 was £15 15s, while the annual subscription amounted to 3 guineas. A single share in the Wellington Club in 1897 was worth £3 10s, but the annual subscription was 3 guineas and a member's double ticket cost 5 guineas.[67] Some of the members were critical of the high fee levels and frequently complained that they were simply out of reach of their sons who wished to join in their own right.[68] By contrast, learned societies, such as the Historical Society of Lancashire and Cheshire, had more reasonable membership fees: its annual subscription in

1851 was 10s, 6d in addition to a joining fee of £1, while the equivalent rates for the Literary and Philosophical Society were 1 guinea and 10s 6d respectively.[69]

In fact, there is evidence that sometimes members had difficulties in paying their membership fees, but any financial problems were hidden to avoid damaging gossip. The case of Mr. Brattan is a good example of the self-regulating function of local social networks. In 1881, he had difficulties in paying his membership of the Royal Liverpool Golf Club and his cheque paid to the treasurer bounced. When it appeared that he had no money in his account to cover the fee, he offered a series of explanations to the committee based on the claim that he had separate accounts in two different banks. His clerk had paid a cheque by mistake into the wrong account which had meant that he had no money in the other account to cover his membership payment: as a result, the cheque had bounced. The Club went to great efforts to find out whether he was lying or not. They interviewed the bank manager, who gave them very detailed information about the balance of Brattan's accounts and told them that the cashier remembered the case and confirmed that it was Brattan himself, not the clerk, who paid the money into the account. He had obviously been lying. He had no funds in his own account, while the other account was his father's. Instead of immediate expulsion, the committee gave him an opportunity to resign which was refused as several appeals were sent to the council stating: 'I trust as this is a mistake which is serious to business relationship you will reconsider your intention of publishing what was a very unfortunate clerical error'.[70] But the original decision was upheld. In fact, all the clubs and societies had a very strict policy in relation to membership fees, the payment of which was carefully monitored, and the way in which annual payments were scrutinised could also be interpreted as a monitoring mechanism on creditworthiness. For example, the rules of the Royal Liverpool Golf Club stated that 'if a member be adjudicated bankrupt or be declared a defaulter on the stock or any other exchange . . . he shall *ipso facto* cease to be a member of the club'.[71]

Balloting and Reputation

Balloting was another mechanism for restricting entry and most Merseyside clubs adopted this practice ensure new members could be trusted and shared common values. The Wellington Club's first rule made explicit the importance of maintaining an exclusive membership: 'The object of the Wellington Club is to secure for a society of ladies and gentlemen, all connected with each other by a common bond of social and personal acquaintance, a convenient and agreeable place of meeting for the holding of Balls during the Winter and Spring months'.[72] As far as the balloting process was concerned, a key selection criterion was the reputation of candidates and how this had been earned in business circles. Most clubs required the proposer and seconder to write a letter of recommendation to the committee or council. Normally the proposer would know the candidate personally, unlike the seconder who might have supported the application at the proposer's request. These letters of recommendation, which occasionally survive in the records, are an important source for studying how reputation and trust were established and articulated within Liverpool's merchant community in the second half of the nineteenth century.

In order to become a member, clubs required all candidates to demonstrate that they enjoyed an appropriate economic and social status. Indeed, the letters of recommendation reveal that a sound economic and social reputation was the main prerequisite for membership. The Candidates File from the Royal Mersey Yacht Club includes many letters which were typical for the period. Mr. Bland, for example, held 'a responsible position in the London & City and Midland Bank, Blackpool and has been with them since leaving school': another applicant was reported to be 'in a good position with the Manchester & Liverpool Bank', although his proposer added that 'I am inclined to understand that he has private means.' These letters of recommendation sometimes contained very detailed information on the financial position of applicants and acted as important information channels in club-based business networks. In the case of one candidate, his proposer wrote that 'I understand that he is in receipt of a pension from the Admiralty, also has an independent income of some £200/300 a year which he supplements by acting as assistant master at Mr. Stewart Edward's school'. Another proposer testified that 'since his father's death his means have become such as to admit of his taking things easily'.[73]

Letters of recommendation were especially important if a candidate was a new arrival and hence not yet engaged in business in Liverpool. Finding a suitable contact was essential in order to guarantee access to business networks. Then again, personal associations were invaluable. There are several letters of this type in the archives of the Royal Mersey Yacht Club in which the existing member introduced a candidate from another city or from abroad. In the case of an application by a Manchester businessman, the proposer revealed that he had already taken informal soundings with local 'friends' to confirm his suitability:

> He is senior partner in a firm in Manchester. . . . He is a member of the Reform Club, Manchester, the Manchester Motor Club & C. . . . I have only known Mr Cunliffe from the commencement of the present season. He is a typical Manchester man, attentive to his business, of a genial and happy disposition, married and from my observation a good family man. I have spoken to one or two Manchester friends regarding him, and their opinion was very favourable.[74]

A standard printed letter which was sent out to all members of the Royal Mersey Yacht Club willing to act as proposers suggests that the length of acquaintanceship was the most important factor in letters of recommendation. In fact, this information was recorded in every single letter of recommendation submitted to the Club. The importance placed on the length of time the proposer had known the applicant suggests that trust was a very important factor in constructing social networks. However, the two following letters of recommendation demonstrate the importance of 'gentlemanly appearance', drinking and smoking habits and appropriate social skills in determining eligibility. The proposer of Mr. Jones confirmed he was a 'personal friend of mine and I have known him for over 20 years'; he enclosed 'photographs of Mr. Jones playing golf etc. Which I hope you will put in the club album'; and added, as a postscript, 'I think the committee will see by the photographs that he has the makings of an excellent member'. In another case, a proposer provided some personal details relating to the candidate and went out of his way to emphasise his inherent clubability:

> He is of kindly disposition, honest, generous to a fault, has lost one back tooth, prefers cigarettes to cigars, walks with a slight stoop. About 6 feet in height, weight 11 stones 10 bs and carries not one ounce of superfluous flesh, usually wears light under vest and woollen drawers. Always temperate in his habits and prefers beer to whiskey, very willing to put his hand down and it is always a pleasure to meet him.[75]

While the proposer needed to trust the newcomer, equally the new arrival must have *earned* the trust of his proposer. By acting as a proposer, an existing club member was extending a clear token of trust to the candidate, especially since the former was often responsible for the latter's joining fee and his first year's subscription.[76] Furthermore, recommending somebody for club membership could entail a considerable social risk, since the proposer's reputation might be at stake if the candidate misbehaved or failed to conform to the club's rules and regulations. Indeed, it is noticeable that proposers were often assumed to be of a better economic standing than the candidates they were willing to support. In that sense, both the future status of a new member and his standing within club-based business networks depended, to some extent, on the standing of his proposer who was willing to effect introductions within local business circles.

In some cases, clubs specified that membership candidates needed to demonstrate a range of specific skills or expertise. The Royal Liverpool Golf Club naturally required new members to be skilled at golf, although the Royal Mersey Yacht Club specified that they should have an interest in sports in general. But a candidate's economic and social standing generally remained the most important criterion. Unsurprisingly, the Royal Mersey Yacht Club was supported by men with a genuine interest in yachting, although a certain level of wealth and social standing were always required in order to become a member. Another factor which reinforced a candidate's application was an existing membership in another prestigious club. Club membership and the way in which clubs and societies operated provide an important insight into the nature of business culture and the social and economic standing of individual merchants. Membership *itself* was proof of a certain economic status and a passport which enabled merchants to mingle with the wealthy, even if the official minutes of a club seldom reveal a great deal about business dealings. This interpretation of the role of clubs and societies is reinforced by evidence from the Rules and Regulations of the Royal Liverpool Golf Club which stipulated that bankruptcy automatically led to the immediate termination of membership. The Royal Liverpool Golf Club's bankruptcy clause is a good example of this. Regardless of the exact nature of the business dealings transacted inside the Club's premises, membership alone was an important signifier of an individual's economic standing and evidence of trustworthiness. In the case of the Royal Mersey Yacht Club members often emphasised the significance of the trust factor by stating whether candidates had previously been reliable sailing partners.[77] Therefore, the activities pursued in these clubs not only served to promote trust, but also provided a framework for collaboration in business circles, whether in Liverpool, on Merseyside or further afield. By contrast, the bankruptcy of members often had profound economic consequences, but the automatic termination of club membership, with its exclusion from its range of activities, also had social implications.

Kinship

It is clear from almost all the inter-denominational associations included in the sample that they also offered a means of obtaining an explicit advantage for male kin, which remained an important feature of elite social clubs in general. The overriding purpose was to privilege the existing members and to make it more difficult for outsiders to gain entrance. This form of nepotism often discriminated against women, but sometimes they benefited from these practices, for example, when clubs granted concessions to unmarried or economically dependent daughters still resident within the family.

In this sense, patterns of social networking illustrate how closely the 'public' and 'private' spheres were interconnected in the lives of Victorian businessmen. On the one hand, good reputation, for which being a fine husband and father were vital prerequisites, helped to provide access to these networks. More importantly, many network-based activities were directed towards ensuring a successful career for the sons of individual members which would help, in turn, to secure the succession of the family firm. All the associations analysed in this chapter provided opportunities for existing members to grant male kin important social and, by implication, economic advantages, which would help to secure longer-term family interests. An overriding majority (85 per cent) of the membership was middle or upper-middle class, and merchants, brokers and solicitors were predominant. Within such a context, the clubs and societies provided a framework for 'horizontal networking'. This enabled established members to create and to consolidate a level of mutual trust which continued to be important for social and business purposes, including establishing marital alliances.

A prominent feature of British business culture throughout the nineteenth century was the continued reliance on the family firm as the most common form of business where kinship connections were critically important in its successful operation.[78] The effective integration of sons into family business ventures was regarded as crucial for the survival of individual firms. Indeed, as Mary Rose has argued, the future prosperity of a family firm invariably rested on securing a suitable succession: without this its survival could not be guaranteed.[79] Even if it were well known that succession based on nepotism might damage family firms, it was still widely practised. According to Owens, family-driven inheritance priorities guaranteed the survival of the firm, although for many merchants the overriding objective was to ensure the future of their families and not their firms.[80]

A letter from John J. Stitt to Samuel Stitt illustrates a father's concern over the family succession. In the early 1860s, Stitt Brothers (later Vance, Stitt & Co.) was involved in the cotton trade in Liverpool, first as merchants and, from the late 1870s onwards, as brokers. In 1862 Samuel was intent on retiring and wanted his son James to become a partner in the firm. Despite James's ill health and his 'expressed' dislike of the mercantile profession, Samuel almost begged his fellow partner John to take him on as a partner. In his letter to Samuel, John was more than willing to accede to the request:

> I consider it to be not unnatural that as a Father you should desire a position in Water Street to be kept open to your eldest son in the hope that Residence may bless the means being used to restore his health, and enable him at some future day to resume business pursuits. . . . I also am a Father and have a family dependent upon men and their claims. . . . I cannot overlook in such arrangement as that now before us.

Not only 'as a question of business, but also as a question of feeling', John agreed on the condition that James Stitt was prepared to invest an appropriate amount of capital and would accept one eighth of the firm's profits for three years.[81]

In Liverpool business circles, male kin were effectively drawn into existing social networks in a manner which reflected a key aspect of British business culture. Nationally, 57 per cent of business leaders between 1870 and 1889 were themselves the sons of businessmen and the way in which club membership was handled in Liverpool suggests that the port-city's business élite operated in a similarly efficient manner. Family firms were almost invariably directed by men and business networks were essentially fraternal in nature. Clubs and societies played a critical role in underpinning contemporary business culture because they provided a context in which male kin were able to practise important skills in a well-defined social arena, establish business contacts in their own right, and consolidate their reputation for trust and reliability.

There were several ways in which the male kin of existing members were favoured by Liverpool's clubs and societies. The rules of the Royal Liverpool Golf Club contained clauses which offered various concessions to the sons of existing members. In most cases, membership in élite clubs was restricted numerically. However, at the RLGC the sons of members could join from a supernumerary list and if they were under 18, they could join for a significantly reduced fee (10s a year). In 1900 a further concession was granted: the sons of members, provided they were under 21, were to be placed at the top of the list when they applied for membership. The minimum age of joining was only 15 if the father was a member, but otherwise it was 18.

Other elite clubs and societies offered similar concessions for the male kin of existing members. The rules of the Historic Society stipulated that 'each member shall have the privilege of nominating any young man, under 21, being one of his blood relation, to read in the library and have access to the museum'.[82] The Athenaeum guaranteed the use of its library for young men under 21 years old (an age limit which was later increased to 26), while in the case of the Wellington Club a lower transfer fee was to be paid when shares were transferred within a family, either from fathers to sons, from brothers to brothers, or when the transferee lived at the same address as the father.[83]

Conclusion

Social networks formed an integral part of the business culture of merchants. Due to the gate-keeping role of élite clubs, membership itself could be a crucial factor in determining a merchant's success. Firstly, being a member of an association or a club was often proof of a good economic standing which encouraged trust on the part of other members of the informal network. Secondly, membership in these clubs enabled individuals to negotiate business matters in an environment where a certain social standing could be assumed. In addition, access to information and the maintenance of a good reputation was critically important for a merchant and therefore membership in appropriate clubs and associations was vital for those engaged in commerce. The linkages which they facilitated served as channels for information dissemination and the consolidation of affection in a manner which both constrained and facilitated commercial activity. Kinship, friendship and partnership served as guarantees of trust and were essential components of contemporary commercial activity in a community where loyalty and credit worthiness were difficult to assess without personal knowledge of potential business partners. To maintain these connections, cross-sectional networks were vital. The clubs and societies with their well-defined regulations and relatively extensive membership offered a tangible guarantee of a member's sound economic standing, while high annual membership fees automatically served to exclude individuals who did not enjoy sufficient trust or failed to demonstrate a satisfactory business reputation.

The available evidence confirms that 'public' business culture in Liverpool and on Merseyside was dominated by 'private' concerns and many of the leading institutions reflected an overriding concern to facilitate the inclusion of male kin into existing business circles. Although individual clubs and societies had well-defined objects, in terms of specific sports or intellectual pursuits, they served as social networks which helped to consolidate the local business community and to ensure the survival of the family firm. In a sense, they underpinned a set of values which reflected the defensive and elitist nature of contemporary social networks in general. The clubs and societies played an active role in defending the social position of the commercial élite at a time when business was still a very personal affair. Success in business depended largely on 'personal favours' and access to extended credit from trusted members of a well-defined social circle. The ability to create friendships, or at least alliances, was a decisive factor in an environment where social status was both an important prerequisite for commercial success and the ultimate ambition of individual members of the merchant community.

Social skills and a good range of existing connections were clearly useful for someone who was looking for membership in these associations and, to this extent, wealth was not the only factor which guaranteed or facilitated inclusion. The universal custom that the proposer was responsible for an applicant confirms the importance of reputation and trust in the operation of informal, club-based networks. Indeed, both fraternalism and masculinity were key principles which characterised the associational culture of merchants. As opposed to inter-denominational networks, which often involved women and other family members, cross-sectional networks were almost exclusively male. In such a context, the absence of women strengthened their importance as focal points for the informal discussion of business affairs. Wealth and reputation together were the main selection criteria for Liverpool's clubs and societies: they represented the core values of the local business community and constituted an integral element of contemporary risk-minimisation strategies in a society in which access to information still greatly depended on personal contacts. To this extent, élite clubs and societies played a key role in consolidating and maintaining social networks because they continued to act as effective monitors of business success or failure.

Notes

1 B. Guinness Orchard, *Liverpool's Legion of Honour* (Birkenhead, 1893), pp. 77–96; Tony Lane, *Liverpool: Gateway of Empire* (London, 1987), pp. 53–84. Of the 296 firms listed by Orchard as Liverpool's 'grandest', as 'the most prominent and honoured in the eyes of the mercantile community', over 88 per cent were from the trading or shipping-related sectors.
2 R. J. Morris, 'Voluntary Societies and British Urban Elites, 1780–1850: An Analysis', *The Historical Journal*, 26, 1 (1983), p. 96; 'Structure, Culture and Society in British Towns', in Martin Daunton (ed.), *TCUHB, vol. 3: 1840–1950* (Cambridge, 2001), p. 399; 'Introduction: Civil Society, Associations and Urban Places: Class, Nation and Culture in Nineteenth-Century Europe', in Graeme Norton, Boudien de Vries and R. J. Morris (eds.), *Civil Associations and Urban Places Class, Nation and Culture in Nineteenth-Century Europe* (Aldershot, 2006), p. 8.
3 Mark Casson, 'Entrepreneurship and Business Culture' in Jonathan Brown and Mary B. Rose (eds.), *Entrepreneurship, Networks and Modern Business* (Manchester, 1993), p. 30.
4 Leonore Davidoff and Catherine Hall, *Family Fortunes: Men and Women of the English Middle Class, 1780–1850* (London, 1987), p. 225.
5 Morris, 'Voluntary Societies and British Urban Elites', p. 96; Simon Gunn, *The Public Culture of the Victorian Middle Class: Ritual and Authority in the English Industrial City 1840–1914* (Manchester, 2000), p. 84.
6 Joan Smith, 'Class, Skill and Sectarianism in Glasgow and Liverpool, 1890–1914', in R. J. Morris (ed.), *Class, Power and Social Structure in British 19th Century Towns* (Leicester, 1986), p. 198; John Belchem, 'Introduction', in idem, *Popular Politics, Riot and Labour: Essays in Liverpool History 1790–1940* (Liverpool, 1992), p. 11.
7 Roger Burt, 'Freemasonry and Business Networking during the Victorian Period', *EcHR*, 56, 4 (2003), p. 658. For an analysis of political and sectarian divisions within the mercantile community, see Robert Lee, Chapter 11.
8 For the importance of culture in determining business performance, see Mary B. Rose, 'Beyond Buddenbrooks: The Family Firm and the Management of Succession in Nineteenth-Century Britain', in Jonathan Brown and Mary B. Rose (eds.), *Entrepreneurship, Networks and Modern Business* (Manchester, 1993), p. 132.
9 See, for example, individual contributions in Robert Lee (ed.), *Commerce and Culture Nineteenth-Century Business Elites* (Farnham, 2011).
10 Martin J. Wiener, *English Culture and the Decline of the Industrial Spirit, 1850–1980* (Cambridge, 1981), p. 4; M. Casson, 'Entrepreneurship and Business Culture', in Jonathan Brown and Mary B. Rose (eds.), *Entrepreneurship, Networks and Modern Business* (Manchester, 1993), p. 30; G. H. Boyce, *Information, Mediation and Institutional Development* (Manchester, 1995), p. 4; Margrit Schulte Beerbühl and Jörg Vögele (eds.), *Spinning the Commercial Web: International Trade, Merchants, and Commercial Cities, c.1640–1939* (Frankfurt-am-Main, 2004); Paloma Fernández Pérez, 'Small Firms and Networks in Capital Intensive Industries: The Case of Spanish Steel Wire Manufacturing', *BH*, 49, 5 (2007), pp. 616–36.
11 John Haggerty and Sheryllynne Haggerty, 'Visual Analysis of an Eighteenth-Century Business Network', *Enterprise and Society*, 11, 1 (2010), pp. 1–25.
12 Mary B. Rose, 'The Family Firm in British Business, 1780–1914', in Maurice W. Kirby and Mary B. Rose (eds.), *Business Enterprise in Modern Britain* (London, 1994), p. 66; Simon Ville, *Shipbuilding in the United Kingdom in the Nineteenth Century: A Regional Approach* (St. John's, 1993), p. 713; Jari Ojala, 'The Problem of Information in Late Eighteenth- and Early Nineteenth-Century Shipping: A Finnish Case', *IJMH*, 14, 1 (2002), p. 195; John Haggerty and Sheryllynne Haggerty, 'The Life Cycle of a Metropolitan Business Network: Liverpool 1750–1810', *Explorations in Economic History*, 48, 2 (2011), pp. 189–206.

13 Gordon Boyce, 'Network Knowledge and Network Routines: Negotiating Activities between Ship-owners and Shipbuilders', *BH*, 45, 2 (2003), pp. 52–76; Pamela Walker Laird, 'Introduction: Putting Social Capital to Work', *BH*, 50, 6 (2008), p. 687.

14 Mika Kallioinen, *Verkostoitu tieto. Informaatio ja ulkomaiset markkinat Dahlströmin kauppahuoneen liiketoiminnassa 1800-luvulla* (Helsinki, 2002), pp. 113–14.

15 Jane Longmore, 'Civic Liverpool: 1680–1800', in Belchem, *Liverpool 800*, p. 149; Margaret Simey, *Charitable Effort in Liverpool in the Nineteenth Century* (Liverpool, 1951); reissued as *Charity Redis-covered: A Study of Philanthropic Effort in Nineteenth-Century Liverpool* (Liverpool, 1992); J. Calvert, 'The Means of Cleanliness: The Provision of Baths and Wash-Houses in Early Victorian Liverpool', *THSL&C*, 137 (1987), pp. 117–36.

16 Robert Lee, 'Configuring the City: In-Migration, Labour Supply and Port Development in Nineteenth-Century Europe', *IJMH*, 17, 1 (2005), pp. 118–19; *From Scandinavia to Liverpool: A History of Mer-seyside's Nordic Community* (Liverpool, 2008), pp. 4–11; John Belchem and Donald M. MacRaild, 'Cosmopolitan Liverpool', in Belchem, *Liverpool 800*, pp. 332, 354–5, 362, 364; John Belchem, *Irish, Catholic and Scouse: The History of the Liverpool Irish, 1800–1939* (Liverpool, 2007), specifically chapter 4 'Faith and Fatherland: Ethno-Sectarial Collective Mutuality', pp. 95–120.

17 Eleanor Gordon and Gwyneth Nair, *Public Lives: Women, Family and Society in Victorian Britain* (New Haven and London, 2003), p. 52.

18 See especially M. Kirby, 'Quakerism, Entrepreneurship and the Family Firm in North-East England', in Jonathan Brown and Mary B. Rose (eds.), *Entrepreneurship, Networks and Modern Business*, pp. 105–26; A. H. John, *A Liverpool Merchant House Being a History of Alfred Booth & Co. 1863–1958* (Liverpool, 1959).

19 Katie McDade, 'Liverpool Slave Merchant Entrepreneurial Networks 1725–1807', *BH*, 53, 7 (2011), pp. 1092–109; Haggerty and Haggerty, 'The Life Cycle of a Metropolitan Business Network', pp. 189–206.

20 A. H. Arkle, 'The Early Coffee Houses of Liverpool', *THSL&C*, 64 (1912), pp. 1–16; William Moss, *The Liverpool Guide: Including a Sketch of the Environs: With a Map of the Town* (Liverpool, 1796), p. 91; Longmore, 'Civic Liverpool', p. 166. The informal social clubs included the Ugly Face Club (1743), the Unanimous Club (1753), the Noble Order of the Bucks (1756), the Mock Corporation of Sephton (1764), the Conversation Club (1768) and the Debating Society (1795): see Edward Howell, *Ye Ugly Face Clubb, Leverpoole, 1743–1753* (Liverpool, 1912); LRO, 367 UGL: Engelbert Horley, 'The Mock Corporation of Sephton, Part I', *THSL&C*, 33 (1881), pp. 223–46; Michael W. Royden, *Pioneers and Perseverance a History of the Royal School of the Blind, Liverpool 1791–1991: A Bicen-tennial Celebration* (Rock Ferry, 1991), p. 23.

21 George McLoughlin, *A Short History of the First Liverpool Infirmary 1749–1824* (London and Chich-ester, 1978), pp. 43–6. Almost all voluntary hospitals were run on a very limited budget with income dependent on subscriptions, although some were recipients of adequate funds. For example, the School for the Blind (1791) 'met a most liberal patronage': see, Henry Smithers, *Liverpool, Its Commerce, Statistics and Institutions with a History of the Cotton Trade* (Liverpool, 1825), p. 240.

22 Arline Wilson, 'The Cultural Identity of Liverpool, 1790–1850: The Early Learned Societies', *THSL&C*, 147 (1997), pp. 55–80; Arline Wilson, 'The Florence of the North? The Civic Culture of Liverpool in the Early Nineteenth Century William Roscoe and the Cultural Identity of Liverpool', in Alan Kidd and David Nicholls (eds.), *Gender, Civic Culture and Consumerism: Middle-Class Identity in Britain, 1800–1940* (Manchester, 1999), pp. 34–46; Smithers, *Liverpool*, Table X. Whereas the first half of the nineteenth century had witnessed the establishment of six new learned societies, that num-ber had more than doubled between 1850 and 1899, although some of them clearly catered for more professional interests. See Chapter 11.

23 LRO, 374 AMI, 1 Amicable Book Society, Minute Book, 1812–1829.

24 See Randolph Cock, John Davies, Robert Lee and Sari Mäenpää, Chapter 2.

25 Gore's directories are a good source for establishing Liverpool's range of clubs during the Victorian period because they listed most of the associations on an annual basis.

26 LRO, 367 WTN 6, Wellington Club, Annual Reports with rules, resolutions and lists of members 1814–1913.

27 Orchard, *Liverpool's Legion of Honour*, pp. 51, 53.

28 LRO, 920 DUR1/4, Family Diaries maintained by Emma Holt, later by Anne Holt, 30 January 1863; Orchard, *Liverpool's Legion of Honour*, p. 53.

29 Other clubs, such as the 30 Club, adopted a similar membership strategy. Its first meeting was held at the Exchequer Hotel, Tithebarn Street on 2 December 1895. Membership was restricted to 30 and

although 'conversation shall be free and unlimited', the subject material was expected 'to incline towards Art and Literature'. See, LRO 367 THI 1/1, 30 Club, 1895–1900.

30 LRO, 367 YZ/1. Other topics of conversation included Jewish people, the Manchester Ship Canal, 'Do Niggers Have Souls?', University College, the Mersey Tunnel (January 1884), the Education Bill, and the arrival of the telephone. Following the discussion on the issue of succession in family firms, it was concluded that 'talents and mental gifts scarcely ever remain in the family for three generations.'

31 By 1851 there were 17 yacht clubs in the United Kingdom (ten English, four Irish, two Scotch and one Welsh), with 521 registered yachts. By 1914 there were over 200. See Braithwaite Poole, *Statistics of Commerce being a Compendium of the Productions, Manufactures, Imports and Exports of the United Kingdom, in Agriculture, Minerals, Merchandise etc.* (London, 1852), p. 324; Roger Ryan, 'The Emergence of Middle-Class Yachting in the North-West of England from the Later Nineteenth Century', in Stephen Fisher (ed.), *Recreation and the Sea* (Exeter Maritime Studies) (Exeter, 1997), pp. 150–81.

32 Michael Stammers, 'The Royal Mersey Yacht Club: A Social History, 1844–1944', *THSL&C*, 159 (2010), pp. 99–121; M. J. Omelock (ed. and arranger), *Thomas Hughes Jackson Voyage 1855 a British Gentleman's Extraordinary Adventures Abroad* (Ailemo Books, 2009).

33 Guy B. Farrar, *The Royal Liverpool Golf Club a History 1869–1932* (Birkenhead, 1933), p. 18; John Behrend and John Graham, *Golf at Hoylake: A Royal Liverpool Golf Club Anthology* (Worcestershire, 1900); Joe Pinnington, (photography by Guy Woodland), *Mighty Winds . . . Mighty Champions: The Official History of the Royal Liverpool Golf Club* (Lydney, 2006), particularly Chapter 7, 'The Course and the Clubhouse', pp. 116–46. For a detailed analysis of the process of suburbanisation on the Wirral, see Robert Lee, Chapter 10.

34 There was at least one golf club in Northram, Devonshire, which predated the founding of the RLGC. *Liverpool Courier*, 7 June 1869.

35 Harry Foster: *Links Along the Line: The Story of the Development of Golf between Liverpool and Southport* (Southport, 1996), pp. 9, 15–16.

36 RLGC, Minute Book 1869–1899, July 1871; Minute Book 1869–1899, Annual General Meeting 1 February 1899; see Chapter 10 (Robert Lee).

37 Longmore, 'Civic Liverpool: 1680–1800', p. 142; J. McCreery (printer), *Laws and Regulations of the Athenaeum in Liverpool* (Liverpool, 1799); George T. Shaw (revised by W. Forshaw Wilson), *History of the Athenaeum, Liverpool 1798–1898, and Proceedings of the Centenary of the Athenaeum, Liverpool* (Liverpool, 1898–99); Robert W. Mackenna, *The Athenaeum, Liverpool* (Liverpool, 1928); Mark R. M. Towsey and David Brazendale, 'The First Minute Book of the Liverpool Athenaeum, 1797–1809', *The Record Society of Lancashire and Cheshire*, 5, 157 (2020). This period also witnessed the establishment of the Lyceum (1802), the Botanic Gardens (1802) and the Royal Liverpool Institution (1814). See also Jon Stobart, 'Culture versus Commerce: Societies and Spaces for Elites in Eighteenth-Century Liverpool', *Journal of Historical Geography*, 28, 4 (2002), pp. 471–85; John Whale, 'The Making of a City of Culture: William Roscoe's Liverpool', *Eighteenth-Century Life*, 29, 2 (2005), pp. 91–107; Guy Kitteringham, 'Science in Provincial Society: The Case of Liverpool in the Early-Nineteenth Century', *Annals of Science*, 39, 4 (1982), pp. 329–48. For information on the Liverpool Royal Institution, see H. A. Ormerod, *The Royal Liverpool Institution* (Liverpool, 1953).

38 George Chandler, *Liverpool* (London, 1957), p. 204; Henry Lacey (publisher), *Pictorial Liverpool: Its Annals; Commerce; Shipping; Institutions; Public Buildings; Sights; Excursions; etc., etc.: A New and Complete Handbook for Residents, Visitors, and Tourists* (2nd ed., Liverpool, 1844), p. 168.

39 Frederick G. Blair, *The Athenaeum Library, Liverpool: The Substance of Four Talks to the Proprietors on the 9th January, 6th March, 3rd April and 15th May, 1946* (Liverpool, 1946); F. Harlan Taylor, *Liverpool and the Athenaeum* (Liverpool, 1965).

40 J. A. Picton, *Memorials of Liverpool Historical and Topographical* (London, 1873), vol. 2, p. 184.

41 Rev. A. Hume, 'The Inaugural Address', *PHSL&C*, 1, 1, 1848–49 (Liverpool, 1849), pp. 5–10; 'Proceedings, Seventh Session, 1854–55, Annual General Meeting, 18 October 1854', *THSL&C for the Session 1854–55* (Liverpool, 1855), p. iv; see also Robert Lee, Chapter 12. The decision to adopt the three designated subject areas, or 'heads', stemmed from an abortive attempt to merge with the Literary and Philosophical Society in order to form a larger and more influential association.

42 Rev. A. Hume, 'Concluding Address', *Proceedings and Papers of the HSL&C, Session III, 1850–51* (Liverpool, 1851), pp. 134–5.

43 'Laws of the Society', printed in *THSL&C*, IV, 1851–1852 (Liverpool, 1852).

44 Michael D. Stephens and Gordon W. Roderick, 'Middle-Class Non-Vocational Lecture and Debating Subjects in 19th Century England', *British Journal of Educational Studies*, 2, 2 (1973), pp. 192–201.

45 Apart from the Royal Institution with its specific objective of promoting literature, sciences and the arts, a number of other associations had been established by the 1850s to perform this function including the Literary and Philosophical Society (1812), the Polytechnic Society (1838), the Architectural and Archaeological Society (1848), and the Liverpool Geological Society (1859). See *Gore's Directory for Liverpool and Its Environs* (Liverpool, 1855), pp. 116–17; W. Hewitt, *The Liverpool Geological Society, Established December 13 1859: A Retrospect of Fifty Years Existence and Work* (Liverpool, 1909). For an overview of national trends, see Philippa Levine, *The Amateur and the Professional: Antiquarians, Historians and Archaeologists in Victorian England* (Cambridge, 1986). The membership of the Architectural and Archaeological Society consisted primarily, but not exclusively, of men who were active in their profession: see Christopher Crouch, *Design Culture in Liverpool 1880–1914* (Liverpool, 2002), p. 76 and Chapter 10 (Robert Lee).

46 Orchard, *Liverpool's Legion of Honour*, p. 54.

47 ULSC&A, LPS, 'A Philomathic Retrospect: Inaugural Address Delivered at the Opening of the Seventy-Fifth (Diamond) Session of the Liverpool Philomathic Society, 27 September 1899', delivered by James Kidman (Liverpool, c.1899), p. 16.

48 Wiener, *English Culture*, p. 49.

49 The Historic Society of Lancashire and Cheshire, Minutes Book 1854–1860, Society meeting—Literary section, 14 December 1854. This decision to admit new members without demanding an entrance fee was made following the failure of the proposed merger with the Literary and Philosophical Society.

50 *The Porcupine* wrote of the Wellington Club: 'Take my word for it, no one is admitted within the sacred portals *who is known* to have traded, except by wholesale and in a superior sort of way' (17 May 1878).

51 LRO, 376 WTN/6, The Wellington Club, Rules and Regulations 1814. In practice, they would never have been able to afford the high cost of membership.

52 ULSC&A, LPS 2/4. Address delivered by the President, September 1828.

53 'Proceedings, Seventh Session, 1854–55', p. 213.

54 LRO, YZ Club, Minutes 1870–1886; RMYC, Minutes, First monthly meeting of the Club, 6 August 1844.

55 George T. Shaw, 'The Athenaeum and Its Place in Liverpool History II', *Liverpool Review*, III, 6 (June 1928), p. 23. Shaw went on to become the chief librarian of the Liverpool Public Libraries between 1909 and 1929.

56 'List of Members: Session 1848–9', *PSL&C*, 1/1, 1848–9 (Liverpool, 1849), pp. vii–xiii; 'List of Members Session XXII', *THSL&C*, N.S.XI, Session 1870–71 (Liverpool, 1871), pp. vii–xviii; 'Report for the Year 1910 Presented 19th January 1911', *THSL&C for the Year 1910*, LXII, N.S. XXVI (Liverpool, 1911), pp. 182–3. Immediately prior to the First World War, however, less than one fifth of the membership was non-resident, despite an increase in institutional members, particularly from free public libraries in other Lancashire towns, as well as libraries overseas.

57 See Chapter 2 (Randolph Cock, John Davies, Robert Lee and Sari Mäenpää); Chapters 9 (Joseph Sharples and Adrian Jarvis) and 10 (Robert Lee).

58 John W. Gahan, *Steel Wheels to Deeside the Wirral Railway Past and Present* (Rock Ferry, 1983), pp. 16, 73; Foster, *Links Along the Line*, p. 4. See also Robert Lee, Chapter 10.

59 ULSC&A, LPS 1/1/1, Incoming Correspondence; 1/1/8, Contacts with Southport Lit. and Phil.

60 Foster, *Links Along the Line*, pp. 26–7.

61 Hume, 'Concluding Address', p. 135.

62 The Royal Cork Yacht Club traced its origins to the Water Club of the Cork Harbour, founded in 1720. For further information on the Royal Thames Yacht Club, see Bob Ward, *The Chronicles of the Royal Thames Yacht Club* (Arundel, 2000).

63 The Athenaeum, Rules and Regulations, 1868; RLGC, Rules and Regulations, 1898.

64 'Special General Meeting', *Proceedings and Papers of the HSL&C*, VII for the Session 1854–55 (Liverpool, 1855), Law XXII, p. 208.

65 *The Porcupine*, 17 May 1878, p. 101.

66 Morris, 'Voluntary Societies and British Urban Elites', p. 102.

67 Orchard, *Liverpool's Legion of Honour*, p. 53. The real cost of the RLGC entrance fee would have been £1,710 in purchasing power at 2019 prices, while the equivalent cost of a single share and an annual subscription to the Wellington Club would have been £394.10 and £360 respectively. These sums were calculated by multiplying the percentage increase in the RPI between 1897/1900 and 2019: see Lawrence H. Officer, 'Purchasing Power of British Pounds from 1264 to Present', http://measuringworth.com/calculators/ppoweruk/index.php.

68 RLGC, Minutes of Meetings, Annual general meeting 27 January 1890.
69 'Treasurer's Accounts, 1878–79', *PL&PS of Liverpool during the Sixty-Eighth Session, 1878–79*, XXXIII (London and Liverpool, 1879), p. xli. The equivalent cost of the annual subscription and joining fee in 2019 prices would have been £110.30 and £57.91 in the case of the Historic Society and £102.70 and £51.33 in the case of the Literary and Philosophical Society respectively.
70 RLGC, Minutes of Captain and Council 1875–1888, 8 June 1881.
71 RLGC, 'Rules of the Royal Liverpool Golf Club, 1900, Rule VIII. f.
72 LRO, 367 WTN, The Wellington Club, Rules and Regulations, 1902.
73 RMYC, Candidates file 1908–1911.
74 RMYC, Candidates file 1908–1911.
75 RMYC, Candidates file 1908–1911.
76 RLGC, Rules and Regulation; RMYC, Rules and Regulations.
77 RMYC, Candidates file 1908–1911.
78 See Randolph Cock, John Davies, Robert Lee and Sari Mäenpää, Chapter 2.
79 Rose, 'Beyond Buddenbrooks:', p. 133.
80 Alastair Owens, 'Inheritance and the Life-Cycle of Family Firms in the Early Industrial Revolution', *BH,* 44, 1 (2002), pp. 29–30, 37.
81 MMM, MAL, D/B/115/B1/1/1. Stitt Firm and Family Papers, Letter from John J. Stitt to Samuel Stitt, 15 November 1862.
82 'Laws of the Society, 1851'.
83 LRO, 376 WTN, The Wellington Club, Minutes 9 November 1882.

7 Intersecting Worlds

Women, the Family, and Merchant Culture

Robert Lee and Sari Mäenpää

Introduction

As far as recent scholarship on the nineteenth century is concerned the categories 'public' and 'private' remain problematic, especially in the context of the continuing debate on the paradigm of separate spheres.[1] It is frequently argued that industrialization created the separation of home and work, restricted women's occupational choices, and confined them to a narrowly defined domestic sphere of responsibility.[2] However, the concept of separate spheres has often only been applied in discussing the position of women in Victorian society and comparatively little research has been undertaken on areas of domestic management and family support where gender interests and responsibilities either intersected or overlapped. It is increasingly recognized that associational networks played an important role in constructing and validating middle class values, such as solidity, respectability, and probity, which underpinned mercantile enterprise, but social network analysis has seldom analysed the role of women and other female family members in cementing interpersonal links, strengthening knowledge complementarities, or facilitating business agency.[3] As Gordon and Nair have suggested, the concept of separate spheres only provides a limited insight into the lives of nineteenth-century men and women, since gender roles were far more complex and interconnected than suggested by the basic dichotomy between 'public' (man) and 'private' (woman).[4] This chapter seeks to widen the debate over the relationship between the 'public' and 'private' lives of middle-class men and women by examining the role of merchant households in Liverpool in constructing public identities and supporting business activities. Married women played a very active role in their husbands' careers through managing the household, hosting dinner parties, and participating directly in various business ventures. The analysis will focus on the changing size and structure of the merchant household, the extent and significance of domestic entertainment, the importance of female-based friendship circles for the career progression and business success of merchants, and the wider implications of the involvement of wives and daughters in overlapping associational networks and charitable work. As Tosh has noted, any attempt to explore the history of men within a family context is predicated on an understanding of the family as an interactive group, instead of 'a zone cordoned off for women and children'. By placing men within the household context, the gulf between the public lives of merchants and their emotional and domestic existence can be broken down.[5]

Several business historians have portrayed the Victorian family in a negative light.[6] This chapter takes a different viewpoint and explores the family home as a central source of support in maintaining business contacts and in creating new ones. The importance of household and family connections for commercial networking and business culture is of paramount interest in such a context, but the analysis will also focus on the extent to which Liverpool businessmen participated in domestic life. Social acceptance and reputation were of the utmost importance

DOI: 10.4324/9781315597836-7

in commercial life, since information transmission greatly depended on personal access to business networks. But success in business and the accumulation of wealth were often vital in determining marriage prospects, while social acceptance and the maintenance of a firm's business reputation were predicated on the choice of an appropriate marriage partner and the satisfactory handling of both company succession and family inheritance. Commercial transactions were not simply confined to the world of offices and boardrooms even in the late nineteenth century when the home continued to play a central part in business life. For many merchants and their families, public and private spheres were intertwined. The home was not necessarily synonymous with 'private' or 'domestic' activities and a place for 'pleasure': it was an integral element in the world of business. Conversely, merchant involvement in clubs and association was not simply for business purposes.[7] Although associational membership enabled merchants to socialize within their peer group and enhance their reputation, it also served a family-specific function. Membership of clubs and societies, reinforced by regular attendance at meetings and social events, also enabled sons and other male kin to gain access to prestigious business networks and thereby provided a mechanism for securing the long-term survival of individual families within Liverpool's elite circles.

By the end of the nineteenth century, Liverpool merchants had acquired a distinct occupational identity and a self-image developed primarily through co-operation and collaboration.[8] Despite a proliferation of vested interests between the 1850s and 1914, a growing number of voluntary associations helped to legitimize merchant interests, provided a mechanism for bridging religious and political differences, and facilitated the assimilation of in-migrants by establishing their 'honour' and reliability.[9] But other forms of co-operation, located primarily within the domestic sphere outside the more formal venues of business and commerce, were equally important in promoting occupational identity and reducing transaction costs.[10] For many merchants, particularly those who belonged to the dominant group of Liverpool businessmen, a culture of co-operation became strongly embedded as a result of family connections, intermarriage, and religious affiliation, as well as through formal trade associations and membership of socially exclusive clubs and societies. This was reinforced by home visiting, the hosting of dinner parties and other social events, the strengthening of kin and family links as a result of marriage strategies, and the sharing of common moral values among different denominational groups. In this context, the domestic sphere played an important role in facilitating socialisation and reinforcing business culture.

In order to assess the extent to which public and private spheres overlapped, use will be made of material from the project's relational database and qualitative evidence obtained from the letters and diaries of individual families, including the sailing ship owner Edward Wrake Turner, the cotton merchant George Melly, the ship owner Peter R. McQuie, the ship-builder (and explorer) Macgregor Laird, and the cotton broker and shipowner George Holt.[11] By definition, the available material is selective, but it provides an insight into the role of the family and household in constructing contemporary business culture. The Holts, for example, were a highly respected merchant and shipowning family especially prominent in the cotton trade. George Holt and his family belonged to an elite circle of Unitarians who, economically and politically, constituted one of the most powerful networks in Liverpool. Indeed, they were at the very centre of this network. Their house acted as a regular meeting place for the local Unitarian community which was famous for its close-knit ties in both business and marriage, and the diaries of George Holt and his sister, Anne, contain minute details of the daily routines of a large merchant household, including house visits, dinner parties, household expenses, church-going, and trips abroad. The analysis also draws on other evidence, ranging from marriage settlements and wills, the involvement of merchants' wives and daughters in local charities and societies, and their role in church communities and religious affairs. It will therefore offer a useful corrective to previous historical research on Liverpool's business community which has mainly concentrated on commerce and trade, rather than the domestic arrangements and family environment of merchants.[12] Relatively little is known of the marriage patterns, household composition, and family circumstances of members of Liverpool's merchant community, yet the family context of merchants had important implications for social relations, business culture, and even the economic performance of firms.

Marriage Strategies and Business Interests

Throughout the Victorian period, women played an important role within middle-class households, whether as wives, daughters, mothers, or servants. Although there was increasing recognition that a companionate marriage could provide significant emotional benefits, it was also accepted that the choice of the right partner was essential for maintaining a good reputation in business circles. From a financial perspective, a successful marriage was of the utmost importance for many businessmen because it involved both economic and social capital. Wives often brought capital into a family business, either as a dowry or through the terms of a marriage settlement; they helped to establish or cement network connections, whether in a business, familial, or social context; and they contributed to the successful management of the household economy which was an important factor in constructing and maintaining the public image of merchants and traders.[13] According to Dickinson, the household was a fundamental economic relationship, at the heart of which lay the marriage partnership, the so-called marital economy.[14] Not only were wives expected to be proficient at running a household, but at a time when the survival of a family firm could be jeopardised by the premature death of its head or senior partner, the management competence of a widow might be of critical importance. The choice of a marriage partner was not simply an expression of personal preference: it reflected parental, family, and business considerations.

Throughout most of the nineteenth century, the family firm remained the most common form of business, although there was a progressive decline in the number of sole traders and a concomitant rise in the frequency of partnerships within Liverpool's business community.[15] Given the constraints on capital availability outside existing family networks, at least until the 1860s, the choice of a suitable marriage partner was often of critical importance in sustaining the medium-term viability of family firms. Marriage provided access to additional capital, reinforced the firm's credit standing and extended the operational and spatial range of trust-based networks. External marriages strengthened business networks by incorporating new contacts and skills, whereas intermarriage between families with existing business interests consolidated capital, reinforced trust, and intensified the density of relationships.[16] Despite the growing emphasis on companionate marriages and changing views on the purpose of marriage itself, for many merchant families the choice of a suitable marriage partner for both sons and daughters continued to reflect parental concerns and an underlying need to safeguard and strengthen the family's business interests.[17] But marriage was not simply an opportunity to cement business contacts: it represented new obligations and responsibilities which could affect the future development of commercial enterprise.

Amongst the more prominent members of Liverpool's merchant community, as portrayed by Pike in the early years of the twentieth century, there was a high degree of occupational endogamy with merchants selecting brides from families with a similar background in commerce and trade (Table 7.1). A small number of brides came from families with a legal, military, manufacturing, or religious background, but the overwhelming majority (76.8 per cent)

Table 7.1 Occupational intermarriage within the Liverpool merchant community

Bridegroom's Occupation	Occupation of Bride's Father		
	Same	*Related*	*Other*
Merchant	12	8	12
Shipowner	3	10	1
Broker (stockbroker)	3	14	4
Other (average adjuster, sugar refiner, underwriter)	–	5	–
Total	33	37	21
%	36.2	40.6	23.0

Source: William Thomas Pike, *Liverpool and Birkenhead in the Twentieth Century: Contemporary Biographies* (Brighton, 1911): sample size 91

had well-established links within mercantile society. Over one third of the merchants married wives who had been brought up in merchant households, while only one shipowner selected a bride from outside the merchant community. In 1895, the German-born cotton merchant Hans Kern took as his bride the *Freiin* Irmgard von Keyserlingk (the youngest daughter of the German General von Keyserlingk), but he was an exception: as far as can be ascertained no other merchant married into the aristocracy (whether British or continental European). In the latter decades of the nineteenth century some of their sons and daughters were more than willing to seek upward social mobility by this means, even if their parents were sceptical of such a move. For example, the shipowner Thomas Henry Ismay did not approve of the marriage in 1892 of his favourite son, James, to Lady Margaret Seymour, the eldest daughter of the Marquis of Hertford.[18]

A similar emphasis on strategic alliances within the merchant community can be deduced from church marriage registers. At the Unitarian Chapel on Hope Street, almost two thirds of the marriages solemnized between 1880 and 1900 involved partners from different sectors of the merchant community. In 1887, for example, James Frame, a 41-year-old corn dealer from 371 Oxford Street, married Mary Jane Finlay, the 32-year-old daughter of the master mariner, Henry Finlay (deceased), of 15 Pine Street, Liverpool.[19] At Fairfield English Presbyterian Church (1873–98) the rate of occupational endogamy for grooms (including merchants, brokers, and coal exporters) was over 80 per cent.[20] Many churches, particularly those established in the expanding suburban districts, were socially selective, which reinforced the tendency to choose marriage partners from similar socio-economic backgrounds. Wavertree, for example, had developed as a fashionable Liverpool suburb and the Congregational Chapel was attended increasingly by 'people of wealth and importance' so that 'during the hours of worship the carriages of its well-to-do-members stretched right down the lane'.[21] Given the prominent role of the merchant community in the congregation, such a degree of exclusivity encouraged endogamous marriages and underpinned group cohesion.

The social impact of occupational endogamy was strengthened by the fact that many grooms tended to choose a local bride. In 146 cases drawn from Pike's biographical collection, the place of birth of both the bride and groom could be traced using census information included in the database. In-migrants were an important component of the urban elite in most European port-cities in the nineteenth century and in this respect Liverpool was no exception, while merchants were highly mobile, because of the need to acquire commercial skills, establish business contacts, or monitor the reliability of overseas partners. Nevertheless, there was a persistent tendency for members of the merchant community to select a marital partner from the local community. Over one third of the marriages (35.6 per cent) involved partners who had both been born on Merseyside. A similar propensity to select Liverpool brides was evident in the case of overseas in-migrants: 34 per cent of the German-born merchants resident in Liverpool who obtained naturalisation were married to local women, whether from the port-city itself or from the Wirral.[22] Only in a minority of cases (8.9 per cent) did in-migrant merchants choose a bride with the same place of birth. This practice was more common amongst Scottish merchants than other ethnic groupings, but it may simply have represented a higher incidence of family migration.[23]

A significant proportion of both Liverpool-born and in-migrant merchants chose their brides from the local marriage market, perhaps as a means of strengthening business connections or as a deliberate strategy to secure integration within the business community. Liverpool's social calendar offered young people from elite groups a number of opportunities for interaction, whether at the Wellington Rooms where there was often 'a very full Ball' and the triennial Bachelors' Ball required the acceptance of a strict dress code, the Croxteth Hunt Ball, at private events for 'young Ladies and Gentlemen' when the presentation of a drama might be followed by dancing, or at the Grand Ball for Ladies hosted by Arthur Earle in January 1891.[24] By comparison, more distant venues for meeting prospective brides, such as the elegant hotels of Harrogate with their 'match-making mamas', 'fierce looking papas', and daughters 'who want to be married, of course, without a penny', involved a higher degree of risk and uncertainty.[25]

In the absence of personal diaries, it is difficult to establish the precise motives behind a successful proposal of marriage, but in a number of cases it is possible to infer a direct link between the choice of a bride and business interests, particularly if overseas trading commitments provided an opportunity to combine business with pleasure. John Ernest Tinne, of Sandbach, Parker, and Company, had first been sent out to Demerara in 1873: in the following year he married the eldest daughter of the mayor of Port-of-Spain, while the general American merchant, Maxwell Hyslop Maxwell, chose as his bride Jessie Bulloch, the daughter of the representative of the Confederate States in Great Britain during the American Civil War.[26] In 1901, the wholesale fruit merchant, John Meek, a partner in the firm of Bellis and Meek with extensive interests in the Caribbean, married Isabel Moffat from Port-au-Prince, Haiti.

In other cases, partners were selected from well-known families, bound by friendship, religion, or business interests. In 1790, William Rathbone IV established the partnership Rathbone and Benson, having selected Robert Benson, the husband of his sister Sarah, from a staunch Quaker family in Kendal, 'to share the workload'.[27] At the end of December 1857, James B. McQuie, the third son of the shipowner and merchant Peter Robinson McQuie, married Ellen Broadribb, the second daughter of 'our old friends' Mr. and Mrs. Broadribb.[28] Both the eldest and the second son of the 'prosperous Liverpool merchant' James Cropper married sisters from the same Quaker family, the Wakefields of Kendal, while after the death of his first wife, Mary, the oil refiner James Bibby married her sister Margaret who was the fifth daughter of the yeoman, John Pye, from Quernmore, Lancashire.[29] Indeed, religious affiliation or membership of a particular congregation was sometimes an important factor in determining the choice of marriage partner at a time when correct religious alliances remained mandatory for some denominations.[30] New churches were often established to serve the needs of specific in-migrant groups, or as a result of doctrinal differences, schism, or evangelism, and marriage partnerships were frequently formed within a clearly defined denominational framework.[31] As far as the Quakers were concerned, when disownment could be instigated for a number of reasons, including drinking to excess, commercial dishonesty, and habitual absence, marriage to a non-Friend in England and Wales was not legally possible until 1860 because it was 'a religious ordinance and not a mere civil compact'.[32] The membership lists for the Hardshaw West monthly meetings, which included most areas of Liverpool, illustrate how religious affiliation determined the choice of marriage partner: Sarah and Ann, the two daughters of the broker Amos Bigland of Brougham Terrace, Everton, dutifully married husbands who were members of other Quaker meetings.[33]

In terms of the internal dynamics of Liverpool's merchant community intermarriage between some of the leading families was arguably of greater strategic importance. In 1857, two of the leading shipowning and merchant dynasties, the Booths and the Holts, were linked through intermarriage, when Philip Holt and Anna Booth (the eldest daughter of Charles Booth) were married. The family connections within the Unitarian business community were further reinforced in 1887 when Hugh M. Melly, the second son of the shipowner George Melly, married Cecily Holt, the second daughter of William Holt, at the Ancient Chapel of Toxteth.[34] In fact, dynastic alliances amongst leading Liverpool families were not exceptional. The merchant, shipowner, and agent Samuel R. Graves MP became connected through the subsequent marriages of his children to the families of the merchant John Bibby (30 April 1873), the shipowner Charles McIver (19 August 1874), and the coal merchant Robert Neilson (19 July 1882), while in 1881 the eldest daughter of the general merchant, Kenneth McKenzie Dowie (of 12 Fulwood Park), married Charles McIver's fourth son, Henry. The marriage at Christ Church, Bootle, on 5 June 1872 between Charles Clement Bowring and Violet Camilla Ball established a family connection between two prominent shipping companies, just as the wedding on 7 August 1876 between Ernest Harrison Forwood and Isabel Muspratt brought together two other leading families from Liverpool's business community, although with somewhat different interests.[35] The exact place of residence of the bride and groom could only be established in 22 of the cases contained in the Wakefield collection of marriages in leading Liverpool families, but 12 (54.5 per cent) involved partners who came from either Liverpool or the Wirral, thereby reinforcing the role of close-knit family links within a well-defined spatial area. The tendency for children from leading merchant families to seek local marital partners may simply reflect the dominant pattern of socialisation for young people in the latter decades of the nineteenth century, which continued to revolve around family relations, church events, and exclusive social occasions. But the practice of intermarriage strengthened social cohesion and reinforced economic ties. Marriage was less a vehicle for achieving social mobility than an opportunity to reaffirm status and consolidate trust-based business networks.

Women and the World of Business

Contrary to the assumption that middle-class family life was characterized by clearly defined separate spheres with a growing emphasis on suburban domesticity, the family diaries written by women reveal how much they were involved with businesses affairs. The Holt family diaries list the latest imports and exports of cotton, new captains on Alfred Holt's steamers, and the leading political topics of the week.[36] The wives of merchants were involved in keeping track of their husbands' social commitments and arranging dinner parties for business associates, but they often acquired a knowledge of commercial affairs through wider social connections, particularly extended family networks, an involvement in philanthropic and charitable work, and the widespread practice of social visiting. Unmarried daughters were also exposed to information flows from the world of commerce and business. Anne Holt was a keen participant in the social life of Liverpool and actively involved in charitable work, but she was also very aware of the business interests of her father and brothers. She regularly bought newspapers and journals which provided information on investment opportunities and utilised financial advice both from male members of the family and a certain Mr. Smith.[37] The Holt family took up residence in its new house in Sefton Park around 1877–78, which immediately became a very public place where male and female interests intersected with little evidence of the existence of separate spheres, although occasionally there was a tacit acceptance that female family members should reserve themselves 'for objects that are more suitable for a lady to take an interest in'.[38]

In fact, the wives and daughters of merchants participated directly in business ventures, often in support of the family firm. The mother of the shipowner E.W. Turner lent his father 'a sum which was less than £1,000' to enable the business to continue and was 'a constant supporter' of the family's commercial interests, while kin helped to bail out firms under threat.[39] Daughters sometimes received a fixed income from the family firm and benefited from the creation of separate trusts of both shares and income prior to their marriage. For example, Anne Holt received a monthly payment of £5 'from office', as well as allowances from her mother and father for her daily private expenses, while the American bride of the shipowner J. Bruce Ismay relied on substantial income from three separate estates and private investments.[40] In some cases, women were able to develop a portfolio of shares which provided a regular source of income. Anne Holt was given her first shares in the Bank of Liverpool from her father, but her main investments were in railway companies, including the London and North West Railway Company and the Lancashire and Yorkshire Railway. She also purchased shares in ships, a practice which was relatively common amongst spinsters and widows. In 1870, for example, approximately 3 per cent of the shareholders of Liverpool-registered ships were women, although the level of investment in any particular vessel was limited.[41] The fact that a daughter's initial capital endowment generally came from her parents implied an element of reciprocity and an expectation that accumulated income should be used to support family business interests. Anne Holt invested £10,000 in her brother's firm, the Ocean Steam Ship Company, and this represented her largest capital holding, while diary evidence confirms the extent to which business was regarded as a family affair.[42]

In the period before the Married Women's Property Acts of 1870 and 1882, married women were not allowed to own property or to make contracts in their own name under common law. However, data from three Yorkshire towns (Beverley, Halifax, and Scarborough) provide evidence of female-owned property portfolios in the mid-nineteenth century and middle-class marriage settlements were already common practice amongst the well-to-do middle class.[43] In fact, the Acts of 1870 and 1882 gave married women the right to own property, provided the entitlement was clearly specified, while trusts were used to enable women to enjoy limited property rights. For example, prior to the marriage in 1877 of the cotton broker, Robert Hinshaw, to the widow Elizabeth Stockley, a trust valued at £23,000 was created which would continue after his death 'for her sole and separate use'.[44] When the shipowner J. Bruce Ismay was drawing up his will, he was advised to make arrangements as 'you think best': after his death, his widow would be entitled to £10,000 per annum even 'if she marries again'.[45] Although recourse to the Court of Chancery was expensive and marriage settlements were only worth undertaking if the property were large enough, a significant number of both upper- and middle-class women entered marriage with a protected and independent income, even before the introduction of parliamentary legislation.[46] Apart from providing a woman with some private property of her own, a marriage settlement could be advantageous for the husband's business. A settlement from both parties was essential for setting up a household and the amount available as a dowry portion was vital in selecting a suitable partner. In a letter to his son, George Holt discussed the marriage of Charlotte Hope to George Denman: her family was 'proud of the new connection'; the husband was 'a nice young fellow enough'; and her settlement 'is convenient and necessary'.[47]

Indeed, a married woman's private property, especially if secured by a formal marriage settlement, was sometimes a crucial factor in a family's survival, particularly in cases in which the husband's business subsequently ran into to difficulties or became bankrupt. Evidence from the parliamentary papers suggests that marriage settlements were almost universal amongst businessmen because they ensured that some property was left to a family member in a case of bankruptcy. Since creditors could not touch the property assigned in the wife's name, a marriage settlement provided businessmen with a comfortable safety net at a time when the trading environment remained volatile and the consequences of unlimited personal liability were considerable.[48] In 1868 the White Star Line, founded by Henry Threlfall Wilson, was declared bankrupt and the flag together with goodwill was sold to Thomas Henry Ismay. However, a significant proportion of Wilson's wealth was protected by the terms of his marriage settlement and investments taken out in the name of his wife and children: on 31 December 1868 they were owed a total of £19,655 18s 7.[49] When the cotton broker William Winter Raffles went bankrupt in May 1878 due to 'outrageous' speculations and excessive borrowing, the manufacturer A. G. Kurz noted in his diaries: 'I don't think it will make much difference to his mode of living as his wife is reported to have a large private income.'[50] The need to protect business interests, therefore, overrode the dominant ideology of separate, gender-specific spheres and enabled the wives of merchants together with their children to enjoy a significant degree of financial independence.

The financial wealth of female members of merchant households was sometimes considerable. Most married men made provision in their wills for their wives, even if the subsequent use of the estate was hedged in by various restrictions, limited to a life interest, or nullified on remarriage, but their legal position was strengthened by the appointment as administrators, executors, or trustees.[51] The estate left to the widow of the merchant James Drinkwater included property in Liverpool and the Isle of Man, together with a share in the Royal Institution (Colquitt Street) and seats in three separate churches; the wine merchant William Lapell of Woolton who died in January 1851 left his entire estate ('a moderate fortune') to his widow, apart from charitable bequests of £5,000; while Anne Holt was bequeathed by her parents an estate valued at £35,000.[52] Where single merchants continued to reside in the family home or sought accommodation elsewhere, the widowed mother invariably had 'private means' or the female head of household was registered as a 'house owner' in her own right.[53] In practice, many women were able to own property which represented a valuable and secure asset, in addition to investments in stocks and shares. But their financial wealth, whether as widows, wives, or spinsters, was seldom enjoyed in isolation from wider family considerations. Particularly in Liverpool where family firms or partnerships remained predominant, there was a general expectation that accumulated wealth and inherited assets would be used, if required, to secure reputation, sustain new business interests, and make effective provision for the maintenance of family control in subsequent generations.

In selecting a suitable marital partner, it is unlikely that Liverpool merchants paid very much attention to the business competence of their future brides, given the contemporary emphasis on domesticity and the apparent exclusion of women from the market economy. Less than 0.5 per cent of the merchants found in the Liverpool trade directories between 1851 and 1912 were women. But this only indicates that women seldom acted as heads of businesses or at least did not advertise themselves as such, whereas other evidence has confirmed the importance of female enterprise and entrepreneurship during the Industrial Revolution.[54] In fact, there were a considerable number of cases in which men were listed in the trade directories as owners of companies or as partners in business enterprises, although they were not registered in the census as resident at their home address or were known to be deceased. Conversely, women traded on their own account but were not listed in the trade directories: they were either widowed or single and enumerated as heads of household often trading in the names of their deceased husbands or brothers. For example, Ellison Frodsham was classified in the 1851 trade directory as a general merchant but was not found at his listed home address. Instead, a 48-year-old widow, Harriett

Frodsham, was registered as head of household as a 'forwarding agent'. In 1871 and 1882 Archibald Gilfillan was recorded in the trade directories as a coal merchant of 6 Spellow Lane, but there was no trace of him at this address in the census returns. However, a single woman, Margaret Gilfillan (aged 28), was enumerated as a coal merchant and head of the household: she had no children but lived with six sisters at the same premises and was listed as a coal merchant under her own name both in 1892 and 1912. Occasionally, both the husband and wife were enumerated as having separate occupations: in 1881, Jane Blackwell of Liscard was listed as a mineral broker, while her husband, George, was a manganese merchant: Mary Dovey, also from Liscard, was recorded as a 'professional vocalist' in 1891, although her husband, Henry, was a ship-broker.[55] In other cases women were enumerated as 'annuitants' or 'householders', regardless of their status as *de facto* traders, while other sources confirm their independent trading status.[56] For example, the Quaker membership lists for the Hardshaw West Monthly Meeting recorded the presence of a female merchant and four female tea dealers, some of whom were professionally active for a number of decades.[57]

   For some women, business competence was a prerequisite for securing family survival following their husbands' premature death. Despite benefiting from a continuing class-specific differential and a gradual increase in life expectancy, business careers were still suddenly curtailed by premature death. Many of the male friends and acquaintances of the shipowner Peter Robinson McQuie lived to an old age, but there were notable exceptions: Samuel Smart died in 1850 at the age of 32 and George Canning Hinson did not survive beyond the age of 48. Thomas Littledale, a highly successful merchant and Commodore of the Mersey Yacht Club, died in 1861 at the age of 42, and left behind a widow, three daughters, and two sons, while the merchant Alexander Balfour was buried in 1885 leaving 'a young family'.[58] The merchant and ship-broker John Taylor Crook died aged 50 'by his own act' hanging in his bedchamber at his lodgings having suffered deteriorating health for some time. There was still a risk of premature death in the early twentieth century. The shipowner Robert Sutherland Johnston died in 1909 at the age of 38 having been diagnosed with 'heart strain' a year earlier, while the cotton merchant William Henry Minoprio died of a heart attack in 1918 when he was only 42 years old.[59] The final disposition of business interests in such cases often reflected both commercial and family considerations, but evidence suggests that widows sometimes assumed full responsibility. William B. Forwood recalled how his grandmother became a successful businesswoman when she was still quite young following the death of her husband, William Bower. For seven years she went to the office every day making her business 'one of the largest and most prosperous on the Cotton Exchange'.[60] Previous studies have confirmed that widows often took care of a family business in the case of their husband's death, but the extent of their contribution remained invisible primarily because they were not accepted as independent economic agents and their role was often masked by the manner in which the census returns were compiled.[61]

The Importance of the Domestic Sphere in Supporting Business Culture

Formally, women from Liverpool's merchant community were not expected to be involved in business affairs, but wives often played a dynamic role in middle-class households because the domestic sphere was expected to support or complement contemporary business culture. As far as activities in the public sphere were concerned, the emphasis was on the role of a wife in helping her husband or a mother in assisting a son. For example, the mother of the sailing ship owner Edward Wrake Turner was a 'constant supporter' of the family's business enterprise, while George Melly's mother regretted that she could not talk to him 'by the fireside as of old while you smoke'.[62] Anne Holt's mother, Emma, played a critical role in ensuring that their household in Rake Lane became a central meeting point for both business and social events:

> I never knew any entertainment in Rake Lane, which for some years were very numerous, from the small friendly tea-party and the more formal dinner party to dances and balls, or breakfasts and soirees of an almost public nature in connection with institutions in which our father took interest, that were not successful, well managed and pleasant both at the time and in our own recollections and that did not I am confident, make an agreeable impression on the quests.

Within the domestic world of a prominent member of Liverpool's merchant community, a wife was expected to fulfil a multi-faceted role which also required an ability to effectively manage the household economy:

> Our mother was not only a good wife, a true help mate to our father . . . but also a good mother, a true friend, but also a good mistress, as the general order and comfort of her household proved and as the sorrowful 'There was never any one like Missis' of her surviving servants testify.[63]

Historically, the household represented the most fundamental of economic relationships, at the heart of which lay a marriage partnership which underpinned the operation of a 'marital economy'.[64] Running a household or two (as was the case with a number of successful Liverpool merchants) was a business venture like any other because expenses were often considerable and represented a not insignificant proportion of business profits. The cotton broker George Holt gave his wife around £4,000 a year for household expenses during the 1850s which amounted to approximately 10 per cent of his annual turnover, while Sandheys, the house of J. Bruce Ismay, had 39 separate rooms, excluding cellars and lavatories.[65] Managing a household in an appropriate and professional manner was just as important from a reputational perspective as the location, size, and architectural style of the house, as well as the number, range, and reliability of domestic servants and gardening staff. All these factors helped to determine or confirm the implicit trustworthiness of a businessman. The following section will focus on the role of women in supporting business culture through a range of activities, including arranging dinner parties, effecting introductions, maintaining social networks through visiting, and managing the household economy.

Married women played an active role in supporting their husbands' careers and enhancing the family's reputation by hosting successful dinner parties. For leading members of Liverpool's merchant community the effective propagation of class identity depended partly on the 'preservation of an impressive and refined domestic environment' which served simultaneously as a symbol of business success and a reflection of good taste.[66] It was important that guests recognised that the family home was 'pleasing and tastefully adorned', particularly when visitors required overnight accommodation.[67] The cotton broker Charles P. Melly was 'very fond of society': he 'went out a good deal and entertained his friends at Riversley during the earlier years of his married life', while the Holts regularly threw large parties for Liverpool society at their house in Rake Lane or later in Ullet Road.[68] On 3 May 1879 they held a musical party to which 100 people were invited and in September, early in the following season, they hosted an evening party for 115, mainly Unitarians. In November there was a political dinner for 21 guests and in February 1882, 140 people were invited to a dance party where refreshments and supper were served. In August 1883, a party of 150 people 'among them all the elite of Liverpool who are in town' was organized in honour of the High Sheriff. Later in October the Prime Minister, William Gladstone, had lunch in their house with 35 other people, at a time when Robert Durning Holt, one of George Holt's sons, was a member of parliament for the Liberal party.

The Holt women had a very professional approach to hosting dinner parties. The family records include account books which provide details of dinner parties given or attended, and the names of those who were invited or unable to attend.[69] They provide a unique insight into the importance of household entertaining amongst the elite of Liverpool's merchant community, although the frequency of party engagements was affected by residence outside the city, particularly during the summer period, and lengthy overseas visits. In the mid-nineteenth century the Holts attended an average of 24 parties in any given year, although less than one third of these events were held at home. By contrast, in 1881 the family invited guests to their house on 23 separate occasions, although they were in France between 23 March and 26 April.[70] Entertaining reached a peak in the winter season between November and February; there was a high degree of reciprocity with a limited number of other families; and evidence of overlapping business and social circles, with George Holt encountering the same individuals at dinner parties hosted by other acquaintances who had been entertained at the Holt family home. Both religious and family links remained important: 'pleasant little parties' were held for visiting relations, while visitors who were repeatedly invited to parties were invariably relatives, fellow Unitarians, or close business partners.[71] But dinner parties were held not only to strengthen but also to initiate social links within local communities dominated by merchants and businessmen, particularly when 'several new people' took up residence in the neighbourhood.[72]

Merchants' wives were expected to supervise arrangements for a wide range of social engagements, from small family parties to large-scale dances, often constrained by social etiquette which required an appropriate gender balance.[73] The shipowner Peter McQuie attended a dance with 'a large party of Friends', but also dined with his son and his wife in their new residence at Sunnyside, Blundellsands, whereas the cotton broker George A. Brown preferred to dine at home with a small number of friends or business associates.[74] At times, arrangements had to be made for entertaining 'national' visitors. For example, in 1855, Mrs. Harriet Beecher Stowe stayed at Dingle Bank, the house of John and Anne Cropper where Mathew Arnold was also a frequent guest.[75] Although luncheon engagements were largely held at clubs and restaurants in the city centre, guests were also invited to private houses where the mistress of the household would be called upon to make appropriate arrangements.[76] The success of such events, whether a formal dance for many guests or an intimate supper to welcome visiting friends or relatives, often required careful planning and preparation, but the ability of married women to exercise these skills remained an important factor in maintaining the family's reputation in social circles and within the business community. A positive outcome was important, with a great deal of emphasis placed on whether parties were 'a decided success', 'very enjoyable', 'varied and cheerful', or 'not so successful'.[77]

Moreover, the social role of married women became more demanding during the second half of the nineteenth century with both a greater emphasis on household management and the rising influence of the women's movement. Elite women were expected to compensate for the lack of the vote by exercising personal and political influence within the family.[78] Increasingly, some women from highly successful merchant families needed to manage several households, including a summerhouse, which might involve a different pattern of entertaining and complementary lists of possible guests and visitors. As early as 1789, the Staniforth family, with considerable interests in the African trade (including slaves), Greenland fisheries, and banking, had purchased a cottage in Broad Green which was enlarged into a 'country retreat', while the cotton broker André Melly purchased a 'very excellent and comfortable country place in Lodge

Lane' in 1835 with 40 acres of grass and arable land, in addition to his existing town residence.[79] The shipowner James Cropper, whose partnership with Richard Benson was generating an estimated daily income of £1,600 in the early nineteenth century, resided at Dingle Bank, but spent an increasing amount of time at Fearnhead, his 'farm colony' near Bickerstaff, where food and employment were offered 'to all and sundry' if they were willing to work.[80]

By the 1850s it was increasingly fashionable for successful Liverpool merchants to acquire rural property, in part because of potential health benefits, but also as a result of an explicit interest in country pursuits, including grouse shooting. In 1851, the shipowner Charles Lamport provided a 'pleasing account of recently purchased Estates', while members of the Holt family began to spend considerable time at their cottage at Ambleside, where they frequently entertained visitors.[81] The precise extent to which Liverpool's merchants acquired rural properties is difficult to assess, but by the early twentieth century Grasmere and Windermere were still popular locations for second homes, although for some members of the mercantile community the attraction of the Lake District had been superseded by Welsh locations. The grain merchant Robert Montgomery acquired Bayridge, Criccieth, while the cotton broker Arthur Washington Willmer made extensive use of his rural retreat 'Islawrdef' in Dolgellau.[82] However, the acquisition of a country estate or a rural 'cottage' inevitably meant an additional range of responsibilities for their wives, whether in terms of practical household management or arranging entertainment and hospitality for both family and business visitors.[83]

A merchant's wife was primarily responsible for managing the household, particularly domestic servants, and for maintaining a complex web of credit relations. Moreover, the tendency for staff size to increase during the Victorian period because of greater prosperity, a growing disinclination for wives and daughters to undertake household work, and functional specialisation meant that domestic management sometimes became a heavy burden.[84] The servant ratio (the number of servants per 100 households) reached a peak in 1901 in many English towns and cities, as was the case amongst elite families resident in Abercromby Square, including many merchants, where it rose from 95.1 (1881) to 100.0 (1901), a figure considerably higher even than that of Hampstead (81.4), despite its high social standing among London's boroughs.[85] In the early 1860s the Holt family retained 15 servants; in 1901 the merchant and seed-crusher Arthur Earle employed 17 servants; and the shipowner James H. Ismay had a domestic establishment of 19 (including nine female and four male servants, two laundresses in a laundry cottage, and four gardeners accommodated in separate cottages with their families).[86] A large staff, by definition, implied a significant degree of specialisation: in 1881, for example, the household of the shipowner and general merchant Ralph Brocklebank included a cook, a maid, a nurse, a housemaid, an under-housemaid, a kitchen maid, an under-kitchen maid, and a professional nurse.[87] Occasionally, a housekeeper would assume responsibility for personnel management, but in most cases a merchant's wife would supervise all domestic servants. This was equally the case in households where the servant ratio was low. It is often assumed that the size of the domestic establishment was a reflection of social class, but the wide variation in the average number of female domestic servants in the households of cotton brokers and coal merchants was not solely a result of significant wealth differentials.[88] At the end of the nineteenth century, elite families from Liverpool's merchant community employed, on average, 3.5 domestic servants, but the households of the oil refiner and seed crusher James Bibby and the fruit merchant Walter J. Bellis only contained a single servant, despite the presence in the latter case of five children.[89]

The skills required to manage a domestic establishment were considerable, particularly at a time when there was an increasing shortage in the supply of domestic servants. The proliferation of guidebooks on managing domestic staff was indication of the importance of this issue, both for an efficient running of the household and external perceptions of social standing. Nursery maids were required to keep infants 'extremely clean'; a servant's dress had to be suited to her work; while 'good taste' was only to be exercised 'in the choice of suitable and becoming colours'.[90] Although they were seldom poorly paid, at least in elite merchant families, there was often a high turnover. Three servants gave notice to Emma Holt on the same day; Atkinson, a new man servant, left in December 1861 after 'some weeks' and returned to his last place of employment without stating a reason; and other staff suffered a premature death—Hannah the cook was 'run over' and the servant Margaret Deekin was 'found drowned' in a well.[91] In other cases, household retainers left service 'in a not nice or considerate way', were obliged to quit because of parental pressure, or were prosecuted for theft.[92] For example, in September John Swindle, the servant of Joseph Finney, a flour dealer in New Ferry, appeared before the Birkenhead magistrate charged with having embezzled from his master 'certain monies' and with taking 'certain books and accounts' which had been discovered in Swindle's dwellinghouse.[93]

Moreover, the process of recruiting appropriate domestic staff was seldom straightforward, particularly if upper middle-class families were unwilling to advertise directly in the local press or utilize the services of a growing number of employment agencies. As a response to the increasing shortage of reliable domestic staff it became increasingly common to them from other European countries, but it was always the wife of the head of household who wrote directly to the Scandinavian Seamen's Church seeking 'a good Norwegian maid' or 'a nice steady Swedish young woman as General'.[94] The recruitment of domestic servants, which involved interviewing candidates, reviewing references, and assessing their suitability, remained a major responsibility for the wives of many merchants. Not only did the successful running of a household directly reflect the family's social standing, but the mistress was also expected to play a wider educational role in training young housemaids and supervising their performance.

This was particularly important when the husband was away on business or pleasure. Many middle-class families enjoyed a mobile lifestyle: both men and women travelled a lot, but merchants were frequently away on business, sometimes for prolonged periods of time, or at country houses enjoying rural sports. The shipowner and merchant William Earle was 'often much away from home', while George Melly was 'exceedingly fond of short and pleasant tours', although he received regular reports on household events from his wife.[95] McGregor Laird spent a great deal of time in the 1840s and 1850s developing his business interests on Merseyside, but his wife and family remained in Blackheath, despite his fear that domestic concerns might become too onerous.[96] In such circumstances, overall responsibility for managing the domestic economy, including the family's servants, fell to women members of the household. Anne Holt not only assumed responsibility for catering arrangements and staff management in the absence of her parents, she took care of outstanding business matters, even if she usually stayed away from the office. She settled domestic affairs, dealt with the monthly household books, and sometimes authorised the payment of half-yearly bills which meant that she 'was occupied rather longer than usual about such things'.

But managing the household with its web of credit relations was not necessarily a simple task and some women found domestic management both demanding and time-consuming.[97] There was certainly real affection for long-serving members of the household, in particular old nurses who occasionally acquired quasi-familial status; servants were sometimes included in women's wills; and servants who had stayed with the same family for some time were occasionally presented with special gifts. For example, in September 1861, a copy of a published memoir on George Holt was given to Elizabeth Power by Mrs. Holt and her family 'as a mark of their regard for her long and faithful service.[98] However, the relationship between family members and domestic staff remained problematic simply because it reflected insuperable class distinctions. In 1862 Emma Holt noted that the family had been forced to make further changes among its servants than ever before, but 'increased acquaintance does not increase our respect for them, either men or women, as a class'.[99]

Women, Information Flows, and the Maintenance of Social Networks

Entry into nineteenth-century business circles and the development of commercial interests often depended on appropriate letters of introduction or the willingness of more established members of the merchant community to promote the interests of a friend.[100] But women played a role in introducing strangers into local business networks. The way in which Andrew Melly achieved entry into prominent business circles in Liverpool illustrates the importance of knowing the right women. Melly was a son of a Genevan merchant: after finishing his apprenticeship he used his existing web of friendships and acquaintances to gain access to Manchester's business circles, specifically the Conversational Club, where he received invitations to various social events. He was introduced through a Miss Ward (a family friend) to Mrs. Carr, who later invited him to live at her home in Liverpool and helped to establish him as an agent to Mr. Grabau, a London-based merchant importing and selling Egyptian cotton. He got to know the Rathbones as early as 1824, a family which was already 'quite established in Liverpool and on very friendly and intimate terms with several families' and became a frequent visitor at their home at Greenbank. His exploitation of female contacts meant that 'within a year he had established himself'.[101] His wife described his position to their son, Charles, who became a member of the Unitarian community in Liverpool and a close friend of the Holts:

> Though a foreigner, and so recently a stranger, he had won a high social position, receiving both foreigners of distinction, and the best society, literary and scientific, in town; intimate with many, and within the prospect of a nearer union with one of the best families of his acquaintance.[102]

The role of female visitors in structuring and maintaining social networks, whether family- or friendship-based, was even more important. If the concept of mutuality within Quaker communities laid the basis for developing close links with other members, improvements to the transport infrastructure in the course of the nineteenth century and an increasing emphasis on personal autonomy for middle-class women reinforced the scale and frequency of visiting.[103] They developed an energetic visiting culture embracing a wide circle of friends which often overlapped with the business, political, and religious networks of their male counterparts and rigid distinctions were seldom made between family friends and business partners. Single women from elite families were frequently at the centre of extensive family networks both as active visitors and prolific letter writers, while visiting by unmarried women played a crucial role in reinforcing family links.[104] On some occasions, special events were organised to welcome female visitors: on Friday 24 December 1852, for example, a small evening party with approximately 40 guests was held to meet 'young Miss Crompton now staying with Charles Booth'.[105] In fact, at least among families characterised by 'intense sociability', it was unusual not to have a steady stream of female visitors, as the following entry from the Holt family diary reveals:

> Mrs Barfield remained with us nearly three weeks and was joined by Miss Booth, who stayed ten days and was succeeded by Mary Smith. After she left us we were alone for a few days and then came Miss Egerton Smith, Mr and Mrs Thorn and Anna in the afternoon, Mr Barclay joining our party by day but sleeping at the hotel.[106]

Census evidence confirms the extent to which visitors were a frequent feature of middle-class families across a wide range of occupations. As late as 1901, almost 10 per cent of Liverpool's merchant households had visitors, a figure which had probably declined from the 1850s.[107] Occasionally, visitors stayed for lengthy periods or had travelled some distance: in July 1852, Mrs. Ribbeck returned to Germany having spent a month in the Holt household, while in 1891 Elizabeth Zeritzmeyer from Prussia was listed as a visitor in the household of the shipowner Alfred Booth.[108] However, female visitors with an overseas connection were unusual: the majority were British nationals and many had been born locally, either on Merseyside or in Lancashire and Cheshire.[109] On other occasions, visits were of a limited duration, but household guests could still arrive with extensive luggage and their own domestic servants.[110] In 1901, women accounted for 60 per cent of all adult visitors. Although some were married (and accompanied by their husbands and children) or widowed, the majority (68 per cent) were single and the average age of all female visitors was 34.4 years.[111] Visitor status was occasionally accorded to women who were almost certainly employed in the household, including a private governess, a lady's companion, a teacher-governess, and a commercial book-keeper, but in most cases the presence of female visitors reflected their continuing contribution to the maintenance of social networks, often, but not exclusively, kinship-based.

The practice of visiting relatives, friends, and acquaintances was deeply embedded in contemporary society. For example, the diary of 21-year-old Agnes Sarah Tinley reveals a daily pattern of visiting, except on days such as 6 February 1847 which were 'so rainy and miserable', while invitations to call upon new acquaintances were formerly approved by her mother, Mary, whose 'opinion is everything'.[112] Visiting by middle-class women (and men), whether married or single, organised or casual, was not only important for cementing networks, it was part of a gift economy based on the mutual exchange or resources and services and a mechanism for providing information which helped consolidate the social standing of individual families.[113] Women transmitted information on the quality of household management and the internal décor of family homes which affected a merchant's general reputation, while the maintenance of a well-managed and fashionable residence was a factor in determining a businessman's reputation. On 9 April 1861 Anne Holt returned from a six-day visit to Mrs. Thomas Ashton. It was duly noted that 'her household and family of nine little children give great evidence of active and sensible management'.[114] The drawing room of Rice House, owned by R. C. Lowndes, had a novel appearance, with 'five small transparencies of stained glass lighted in the evening by gas'; Brombrough Hall, the residence of the commission merchant William B. Forwood, was described as 'old style and decidedly attractive'; and the grain merchant Charlie Williamson's home near Bishop Eaton was 'a rather nice house'.[115] To this extent, the custom of visiting helped to reinforce merchant culture by maintaining both family and business networks, but it also validated the wider social acceptability of members of the business community.

Female Co-Residence and the Domestic Arrangements of Liverpool Merchants

The available evidence suggests that there was a higher frequency of extended families amongst the Victorian middle class than within the British population as a whole: female kin from the same generation were particularly prominent. Occasionally, other relatives were permanent or semi-permanent co-residents, since it was relatively common for households to contain individuals who were not members of the immediate nuclear family. Single sisters were important figures, particularly within relatively prosperous households; nieces took care of unmarried siblings, childless aunts, or widowed parents; while the role of maiden aunts was informally legitimized through family service.[116] In Glasgow, sisters and sisters-in-law accounted for over

45 per cent of non-nuclear kin in a sample of middle-class families, although they were often to be found in households headed by women.[117] The situation in Liverpool was not dissimilar where siblings, including cousins, aunts, and nieces, played an important role in wider kinship networks within the merchant community (Table 7.2).[118]

Female co-residents were present in approximately 30 per cent of all merchant households, but sisters, sisters-in-law, and nieces were predominant, accounting for over 60 per cent of the sample. By comparison, other female residents, whether drawn from older or younger generations of the nuclear family or from the extended family circle, were relatively insignificant. Although the precise role of female co-residents within merchant households was seldom specified, in many cases they were formally enumerated as living 'on their own means'. The overwhelming majority were spinsters, but relatively few were of marriageable age. In 1901, for example, the household of the cotton broker William Biggs contained an unmarried sister, aged 63, who had been born in Leicester and was living on her own means, while the provision merchant Robert Broadbent provided accommodation for three single sisters, Mary, Emily, and Margaret, aged 48, 44, and 37 respectively, all of whom had been born in Liverpool. The household of the merchant Phillip Blessig included a widowed sister-in-law, aged 75, while an unmarried niece of the cotton broker George H. Brown of 'The Nunnery', St. Michael's in the Hamlet, was enumerated as a co-resident. Louisa was 39 years of age: she had been born in Liverpool and was listed as a school mistress.[119]

George H. Brown, however, was single and expected to live with a female relative. Young bachelors would rarely live independently and almost without exception they resided with their mothers or unmarried sisters who sometimes acted as unpaid housekeepers. Most Liverpool merchants were married, but in the case of cotton brokers there was a steady increase in the proportion of single businessmen between 1851 and 1901 (Table 7.3).

This trend can be explained by several factors, including higher entry costs to the cotton-broking profession and the growing expense of setting up a separate household, which might have had a negative effect on average age at first marriage. It might also have been due to a reduction in the attractiveness of marriage as a result of an apparent decline in domesticity, particularly after the 1870s, when changes in the position of women and the waning

Table 7.2 The pattern of female co-residence in merchant families on Merseyside

Female Co-Residents	Orchard/Pike		Liscard	
	No.	*%*	*No.*	*%*
mother	11	11.8	8	13.5
sister	20	21.5	16	27.1
sister-in-law	14	15.0	12	20.3
niece	30	32.2	9	15.2
mother-in-law	4	4.3	7	11.8
aunt	5	5.3	2	3.8
cousin	1	1.0	2	3.8
grandmother	1	1.0	0	0.0
granddaughter	5	5.3	3	5.0
(not specified)	2	2.1	0	0.0
Total	93		59	

Note: Orchard and Pike, all names beginning with B (sample size 300); Liscard, all surnames beginning A-G (sample size 246)

Source: MLP database

Table 7.3 The marital status of Liverpool cotton brokers, 1851–1901

	1851	%	1881	%	1901	%
Married	54	72.0	269	76.4	188	69.9
Unmarried	11	14.7	66	18.8	65	24.2
Widowed	10	13.3	17	4.8	15	5.9

Source: MLP database, sample size 611

Table 7.4 The household structure of Liverpool cotton brokers, 1851–1901

	1851		1881		1901	
	No.	%	No.	%	No.	%
Head	64	85.3	262	85.9	188	79.7
Son	6	8.0	20	6.6	27	11.4
Visitor	1	1.3	1	0.3	1	0.4
Brother-in-law	1	1.3	1	0.3	0	–
Brother	0	–	6	2.0	4	1.7
Lodger	0	–	2	0.7	2	0.8
Nephew	0	–	1	0.3	2	0.8
Son-in-law	0	–	1	0.3	0	–
Boarder	0	–	0	–	4	1.7
Unknown	3	4.0	11	3.6	8	3.4
Total	75		305		236	

Source: MLP database

domestic authority of men undermined the merits of marriage for some middle-class men who preferred to postpone marriage or remain single.[120] However, it was extremely rare for a businessman to live without any female companion. In about 80 per cent of the cases unmarried cotton brokers lived with a female relative, either with a mother or an unmarried sister, although young businessmen who worked for the family firm often continued to reside with their parents. Between 1881 and 1901, the proportion of cotton brokers registered as sons within their fathers' households rose from 6.6 to 11.4 per cent respectively (Table 7.4), perhaps reflecting a growing tendency for merchants' children (male and female) to leave home at a relatively later age.

Most single cotton brokers, particularly if they were not enumerated as head of household, depended on unmarried female relatives for their domestic arrangements, while the growing pro-portion of unmarried merchants by 1900 created a greater demand for co-resident female family members. It was very unusual for unmarried cotton brokers to live alone: only in three cases (out of a sample of 611) were they registered as living completely without any female compan-ion. The wealthier members of the community lived in households with a considerable number of servants. John Ryder, a bachelor of 36 years and a partner in the Liverpool firm of Mason & Ryder, lived alone with six servants, including a 19-year-old footman, a male cook in his thirties, a housekeeper, and three maids, while widowed businessmen entered into a variety of arrangements in order to discharge their domestic responsibilities: if there were children in the house, a governess was invariably employed to live on the premises to look after their needs. Depending on their circumstances, widowed cotton brokers relied heavily on servants. For example, in 1881 the 57-year-old cotton broker Fletcher Roger lived in a household with 18 residents, including 10 children and 7 servants.

In fact, spinsters, whether unmarried daughters or female co-residents drawn from more extended family circles, were expected to play a major role in supporting merchant families, both in a social and business context. There was a deep-rooted assumption that unmarried daughters should stay at home and devote their lives to caring for their aged parents. In many Victorian families one spinster in each generation usually remained at home to take care of their parents and this was generally accepted as their principal duty, particularly in those cases in which three generations of the same family lived in a single household and a trusted female relative was needed to care for an elderly mother or father.[121] Margaret, the unmarried daughter of James Cropper, kept house for her father for 32 years following the death of his wife in 1868, while Anne Holt (1821–1885), who remained single throughout her life, is a good example of the importance of spinsters in structuring and reinforcing the domestic arrangements of the merchant class.[122] She was the only daughter of six children born to George Holt and his wife and the only one who remained unmarried. Because the provision of emotional and physical support for ageing parents was regarded as an unmarried woman's task, Anne became an indispensable help in managing the household, caring for her parents, siblings, and the new-born, as well as investing money for the family business. According to the family diaries, she received at least one marriage proposal, but this was refused.[123] Indeed, it is possible to infer from a reference in her personal diary that spinsterhood was regarded as her destiny, one that she did not choose but had to accept, perhaps because of an unspoken understanding that she would remain at home to care for her parents in their old age.[124] Other elite women, however, remained unmarried as a result of a strategy to keep the family assets in the hands of male siblings. In Anne Holt's case there were enough brothers to secure the family succession and provide managerial expertise in order to maintain and expand the family's business interests, but the same pattern of allocating domestic responsibilities along gender lines occurred in the next generation when Emma Holt (1862–1944), the only daughter of George Holt (Anne's brother), remained unmarried.

Society Membership, Charitable Work, and Women's Networks

The ideology of the Victorian middle class required a public role for women because this was a key feature in constituting class identity. As a result of their involvement in charitable and philanthropic work, as well as their membership of musical and cultural societies, women created their own partially overlapping networks. These acted as additional channels for information and contact for male members of the family and enabled middle-class women to monitor the reputation, social standing, and credit worthiness of other members of the merchant community. The involvement of married women in social events and public life consolidated and extended existing family networks: it also provided opportunities to reflect their husbands' good taste, position, and wealth. In general, the public role of women was based on shared tastes and cultural interests, while social cohesion within the merchant community was reinforced by 'philanthropic zeal' and an increasing emphasis on 'good work'. The wife of the shipowner Alfred Booth played a major role in 'helping forward all good work': she had been instrumental in developing the Union of Workers among Women and Girls and had been president of both the Ladies' Liberal Association and the Ladies' Sanitary Association. The philanthropic work of Edith Bright, the wife of the steamship owner Allan H. Bright, had opened her eyes 'to many of the unfair laws which exist' and the need for greater work by women 'in cleansing our slums and bettering the lives of the people'.[125] Public perception of a wife's respectability and the social standing of her family were enhanced by a demonstrable devotion to charity and religion. On the death of Lawrencina Holt, the wife of the shipowner Robert Holt, her obituary praised her participation in her husband's social work, her abilities as a hostess (particularly during his period of office as mayor), and her support for various charities. However, her continued loyalty towards her husband was singled out for the highest praise, since it was 'generally known that Mrs. Holt was a strong supporter of her husband in his political life, although she always declined to take any active interest in politics'.[126]

In fact, relatively little is known of women's public culture in Liverpool, or the extent to which involvement in charitable and philanthropic work helped to cement informal networking within the merchant community. High status clubs and societies made little or no provision for female participation: membership of the Amicable Book Society (1812) was limited to 20 and the summer meetings between July and August were held 'at the homes of such gentlemen as possess gardens', while the 30 Club, established in 1895 in order to promote free and 'unlimited' conversations particularly on art and literature, catered for a numerically restricted male membership.[127] Debating associations or political clubs, such as the Chatham Society and the parliamentary debating societies in Birkenhead, Hoylake and West Kirby, and Woolton, retained a selective gender-based membership in the same spirit as the Canning Club (1812) which was established by a group of Liverpool gentlemen to 'promote the principles of the late Right Honourable William Pitt', and later became a focal point for anti-radical political discussions.[128] The establishment of the Athenaeum (1799) and the Lyceum (1802), together with the Royal Institution (1814), represented a deliberate attempt to reinforce the importance of intellectual pursuits, but women were not considered for membership and they remained excluded from other learned and scientific societies founded in subsequent decades, including the Birkenhead Literary and Scientific Society and the Philalethians.[129] In the early 1850s there was only one female subscriber to the Liverpool Sacred Harmonic Society and even at the beginning of the twentieth century women made up fewer than 5 per cent of the membership of the Historic Society of Lancashire and Cheshire.[130] The Royal Liverpool Yacht Club only had two female members, one of whom was Miss Duarte, the daughter of the merchant Ricardo T. Duarte, while women only represented 3.6 per cent of the membership of the Wellington Club between 1860 and 1914.[131]

But increasingly, middle-class women began to play a major role in choral, literary, and musical societies, particularly from the 1860s onwards (Table 7.5). The origins of the Liverpool Library can be traced back to the late 1750s when it was founded as an exclusively male conversation club, but the annual transfer of share ownership to women almost doubled between

Table 7.5 Women's involvement in cultural associations and societies

Society	Year	Membership %	Committee %	Merchants %
Liverpool Sacred Harmonic Society	1852–55	1.2	0	66.6+
Liverpool Library*	1862	11.7	0	
	1902	20.5		
Amicable Musical Union	1868–69	55.5	0	67.2
	1879–80	65.3	0	
Birkenhead Shakspere Literary Society	1879–80	47.0		26.2
Birkenhead Ruskin Society	1881–82	56.1		65.3
Liverpool Philharmonic Choral Society	1883		0	
Museum of Japanese Art	1890–91		54.1	42.8
West Kirby Literary Society	1900–01	58.3	0	33.3+
Italian Literary Society	1908	61.6	55.5	

Note: * shareowners; + committee members

Source: MLP database; membership records of individual associations and societies

1862 and 1902 from 11.7 to 20.5 per cent.[132] In 1868–69 sopranos and contraltos accounted for almost 70 per cent of the Amateur Musical Union's membership; women enjoyed equal representation with their male counterparts in both the Birkenhead Ruskin Society and the Birkenhead Shakspere Literary Society; and they constituted almost two thirds of the Italian Literary Society's membership.[133] The establishment of cultural societies in areas of suburban development was accompanied by a significant degree of female involvement. The West Kirby Literary Society offered a range of activities, including 'dramatic entertainment' (such as a performance in December 1895 of *Our Boys*, a comedy in three acts with orchestral support), formal talks, Liverpool University extension lectures, as well as social evenings. By the turn of the century it had attracted 644 members, of whom 58.3 per cent were women who were elected on a regular basis (at the first meeting of the Society's ninth session, for example, seven women became members).[134]

The growing level of participation by middle-class women in literary and musical associations had a wider significance in terms of family roles and the creation of overlapping networks within the merchant community. Firstly, it strengthened their role in public culture, particularly in those cases in which women were elected committee members or were appointed officers of a society (as was the case with both the French and Italian Literary Societies).[135] To this extent, it reflected contemporary trends in society as a whole, including the demand for improved access to higher education and for political rights. Secondly, the extended representation of middle-class women from merchant households in societies such as the Amateur Musical Union or the West Kirby Literary Society evolved within a well-defined familial framework. In many cases, the increased public profile of women was part of a wider family-based engagement with music, literature, amateur theatricals, and general educational. The Amateur Musical Union was dominated by family groups: the merchant Julius Servais was listed as a 'basse', while his wife was one of the sopranos; John Bridson, a general cotton broker, was accompanied by his brother, Edward (a merchant) and his two nieces. In fact, almost two thirds (61.8 per cent) of the society's membership attended rehearsals and performances with other family members.[136] Family-based membership was less pronounced in the case of the Italian Literary Society (20 per cent) which met in the Royal Institution, but it accounted in 1900 for almost three quarters of the registered members of the West Kirby Literary Society, reflecting its disproportionate importance in a suburban setting.[137] In a different context, the idea for establishing a museum of Japanese art (based on a collection amassed by the wool broker James Lord Bowes) came from his wife. Women constituted over half of the General Committee which opened the museum in 1890 and held a Japanese Fancy Fair in 1891 which attracted 20,000 visitors, thereby raising £6,000 for charity, but in most cases their husbands were also members.[138]

The growing public profile of women in cultural associations in the late nineteenth and early twentieth centuries reinforced the social role of the family, rather than undermining its legitimacy. Moreover, membership of many of these cultural societies was dominated by Liverpool's merchant community, particularly in the case of the Museum of Japanese Art and the Amicable Musical Union (Table 7.5). The combination of high levels of family-based participation with a disproportionate representation of members from the merchant community created an additional web of social contacts which underpinned business culture. Among the 78 members of the Birkenhead Ruskin Society there were 19 merchants and 10 cotton brokers, together with their wives and daughters; the cotton merchant Theodor Stahlknecht was the treasurer of the Italian Literary Society, but his wife was also its secretary.[139] The increased level of female participation in cultural societies therefore strengthened existing social networks within the merchant community where they were based on shared interests and family interaction.

The role of middle-class women was particularly strong in religious and philanthropic work, including local hospitals, residential institutions, and voluntary associations, reflecting a trend which had been evident from the early nineteenth century onwards.[140] Public space, however, remained divided along gender lines. Many philanthropic associations were officially male led, although in practice women played an important role in their administration and governance. The Ladies' Charity, established in 1796 to provide relief for 'poor married women in childbed at their own home', had a Lady Patroness: both the President and Vice-President were men, but women made up half of the elected Committee. However, women were playing an increasingly active role in the administration of charitable institutions, sometimes out of necessity. The Liverpool Female Penitentiary (1809), was initially managed by men of suitable rank and standing, but it was quickly understood that the successful running of a reformatory for prostitutes would depend on the willingness of female benefactors and subscribers to elect their own committee in order to determine the qualifications of the penitents for full admission, superintend their diet and dress, and examine their work through daily visits of each ward.[141] The Ladies' Benevolent Society (1810) was intended to provide food and clothing to the poor operated on a similar basis: its honorary officers were all women.[142]

In many cases, however, a more traditional allocation of gender roles was visible in the structure and operation of charitable and medical institutions established throughout the nineteenth century. The Charitable Society which sought to visit and relieve the 'Sick and Distressed Poor' had a separate Ladies' Committee, while a number of evangelical Bible societies created a separate Ladies' Branch in order to achieve their objectives. The Liverpool Magdalen Institution, as a Church of England charity founded in 1855 to rescue 'fallen women', had a male-only committee (with the Lord Bishop of Liverpool as President), but also a parallel Ladies' Committee with its own President, Vice-President, and Secretary. Each year, the General Committee appointed the Ladies' Committee which met weekly in order to interview 'candidates', administer the home, and manage the laundry.[143] Upper middle-class women saw it as their duty to improve 'the moral and religious training of the inmates' in order to equip them for employment in an

Figure 7.1 The Liverpool Female Orphan Institution, c. 1900 (contemporary postcard)

occupation 'such as may fit them for a life of future usefulness': in reality it became an employment agency which provided servants to wealthy households after two years of 'training'.

Moreover, their involvement in the work of the charity was overshadowed by notions of moral superiority, as the objective of rescuing working-class women was also 'to teach control of temper, as to wean from habits of lazy thriftlessness to habits of industry and conscientiousness, above all, to eradicate the love of strong drink'.[144] Similarly, the Ladies Committee of the Liverpool Female Orphan Asylum was expected 'to attend to and to direct those minutiae of domestic arrangements which none but females can understand' and 'to regulate the education and employment of the Children' in order to assess their competence as apprentices or domestic servants in respectable families. The second annual report of the Liverpool Society for the Prevention of Cruelty to Children emphasised the extent to which the Ladies Committee had 'attended to the domestic arrangements of the shelter with much care and success'; the rules and regulations of the Liverpool Seamen's Orphan Institution stipulated that the five members of the Ladies Committee should 'assist in regulating its domestic concerns'; and the male committee members of the Seamen and Boatmen's Friend Society depended on the gendered contributions in kind of the Ladies Knitting Guild (with its 47 members) and the support of the Ladies' Auxiliary Committee headed by Lady Petrie.[145]

Medical institutions, such as the Liverpool Royal Infirmary (1749), the Liverpool Homoeopathic Dispensary (1841), the Southern and Toxteth Hospital (1842), and Saint Paul's Eye and Ear Hospital (1871), initially made no provision for the establishment of a Ladies Committee, although by the 1880s and 1890s lady visitors had been elected. Other hospitals, however, depended on the contribution of female visiting committees which reflected an increase in the philanthropic role of middle-class women in the management and implementation of

Figure 7.2 The Birkenhead Borough Hospital, c. 1900 (contemporary postcard)

medical provision, a role that extended their social knowledge of the urban environment.[146] The Wirral Hospital and Dispensary for Sick Children (1869) originally had a gender-based governance structure, but by 1903 a unified board of 20 members had been created composed equally of men and women, five of whom were elected to the Hospital's Acting Committee and by 1913 the Birkenhead Borough Hospital was also managed by a mixed-sex committee (Figure 7.2).[147]

In other areas of charitable, philanthropic, and medical work women took the initiative. From the early nineteenth century, women had directed several local charitable institutions, including the Ladies' Benevolent Society (1810), the Ladies' Branch Society (1817), and the Liverpool Dorcas and Spinning Society (1817). This tradition was continued throughout the nineteenth century: Mrs. Aikin, the wife of the merchant and shipowner James Aikin, was instrumental in establishing the Female Orphan Asylum in 1840, while the Home for Incurables was founded by Josephine Butler in 1869. Its management was subsequently entrusted to a 'Committee of Ladies', but even when a 'Gentlemen's Committee' was formed in 1875 'to bring the Charity more prominently before the public', the Executive Committee continued to consist solely of women.[148] The Princes Park Hospital, as it was originally called, continued to be run by women, with the Executive Committee responsible for approving admissions, organizing collections, and dealing with administrative correspondence.[149] The Liverpool House of Help was opened in July 1890 as a temporary shelter for girls and women who had 'fallen into sin' or were 'hovering on the brink of ruin': voluntary support was supplied by a large number of 'influential ladies and gentlemen', but both the Committee and the House Committee were composed entirely of women.[150] Similarly, in 1909 the Hostel of Hope was founded by 'well-known philanthropists', Mrs. Boult and her husband Cedric (an agent and JP), Miss Constance Whishaw, and Miss Ella Karck, and within a year 177 cases had been admitted; the Liverpool Ladies Association was active in proposing the establishment of new charities to meet specific needs, including a proposal to fund a horticulture school in Knotty Ash for the physical and mental development of 'feeble-minded girls'; and the Liverpool branch of the National Vigilance Society was chaired by Lydia A. Booth (the wife of the shipowner Alfred Booth), with the Saving Girl Life week setting 'an example to other cities' in the country. Women from the Liverpool Ladies' Sanitary Association visited annually over 8,000 mothers with small babies and the Liverpool Self-Help Society for Girls depended on the 'loyal support' of 'ladies in the city'.[151] The Leasowe Open Air Hospital for Sick Children, established in July 1914 by the Liverpool Children's Association, was known locally as the Margaret Beavan Hospital after its chairman, reflecting her considerable influence in its foundation and management.[152]

Although the increasing scale and complexity of charitable provision, particularly hospital-based, may have been used as an argument to restrict women's involvement at a management level, philanthropic zeal and a general awareness that 'doing good' was increasingly 'fashionable' strengthened their role prior to the First World War at a time when a sense of class responsibility was reinforced by evangelical commitment. The overwhelming majority of visitors to the poor or sick were women; by the early 1890s there were many women working as 'paid officials' in philanthropic activities; and it was widely accepted that they were better placed than men in traversing both the private and public realms.[153] Indeed, some institutional charities, such as the Wirral Hospital and Dispensary for Sick Children, relied on lady collectors to raise money from local residents: in 1892, 37 women (7 wives and 30 spinsters, largely the daughters of merchants and middle-class professionals) were assigned their own collection areas and raised almost £600.[154] By the early twentieth century, the Liverpool Female Penitentiary also depended on 'Lady Canvassers' to follow up appeals for additional funding and the honorary treasurer was invariably a woman.[155] Indeed, some local charities, such as the Traveller's Aid

Society established 'to guard young women, irrespective of class or creed' when travelling alone, involved the active cooperation of a range of other female-led societies in a manner which required regular contact and active cooperation.[156]

The role of women in funding and supporting charitable work was also considerable. Significant charitable bequests were reported in the national press. In 1878, Mrs. Susan Higgin, the wife of a prominent American merchant, left £5,000 in her own name to the Liverpool Seamen's Orphan Institution and a further sum of £2,000 to the Liverpool Royal Infirmary; in 1902 the *Times* recorded the will of Miss Olivia Atherton of Everton, who had left £20,250 to various Liverpool charities, while Mrs. H. G. Schintz, the widow of a general merchant, bequeathed £2,000 to the Liverpool Royal Infirmary in 1912 in memory of her late husband and £1,000 to the Liverpool Seamen's Orphan Institution. Lady Margaret Ismay, the wife of the steamship owner, made provision on her death for a legacy of £1,000 in favour of the Wirral Hospital and Dispensary for Sick Children and by 1902 Mrs. Charles Turner had made two separate donations to the Home for Incurables totalling £800.[157] When a special fund was launched for the rebuilding of the Royal Infirmary in the early 1880s, six women contributed £1,000 each, while Mrs. Charles Turner had promised £2,000. Jane Ellen Yates actively canvassed all her friends to persuade them to double their subscriptions to the school founded by her father, so that an institution which had 'done so much good should continue after I am gone'.[158] As far as most medical charities were concerned, only a minority of trustees were women, but in the case of the Home for Incurables, which only catered for female inmates, they represented one third of the Trustees for Life and almost 50 per cent of the regular subscribers.[159]

The extent of financial support for specific medical or institutional charities provides further evidence of the independent financial role of middle-class women, but their contribution to charitable enterprises also reflected a high degree of commitment and a willingness to provide a wide range of assistance. The exertions of Mrs. Aikin, the founder of the Liverpool Female Orphan Asylum, were 'zealous and unremitting'. When Mrs. Gale stood down as president of the Home for Incurables in 1892, she had held the position continuously for 17 years and the success of the charity was generally attributed to the 'regularity and punctuality with which she has attended to every detail'. Mrs. Phillip Holt served as Honorary Secretary between 1880 and her death in March 1898. She regularly attended the weekly meetings of the Executive Committee and her 'constant and untiring services' provided a 'high example of devotion in the cause of suffering humanity'. When Miss Isabella Gregson died in 1908, she had been involved with the Ladies Visiting Committee of the Liverpool Infirmary for Children for no fewer than 50 years. But other female subscribers offered support in ways which suggest the absence of a strict divide between the private and public realms: Mrs. Sephton provided accommodation for two nurses from the Home for Incurables 'during the spring cleaning'; in 1862 Mrs. Benson Rathbone donated 'a large bundle of Children's Clothes, Toys' to the Liverpool Infirmary for Children; and in 1902 Mrs. J. H. Ismay presented the Wirral Hospital and Dispensary for Sick Children with 14 braces of pheasants.[160]

As in other urban centres, the development of female involvement in charitable enterprises was frequently church-based. Many of the major Liverpool charities had been founded on a non-denominational basis, but religious affiliation remained potentially divisive, particularly in a city where denominational culture was a basis both for sociability and the organization of charitable activities, including the holding of bazaars for fundraising purposes. Almost every religious denomination developed its own charitable infrastructure which often involved the creation of distinct women's committees. For example, the Trinity Presbyterian Church in Claughton, Birkenhead, had its separate Women's Missionary Association and Ladies' District Society, while the Domestic Committee of the Birkenhead Society of Friends was composed solely of female members.[161] By the early twentieth century the Liverpool Wesleyan Mission (founded in 1876) had become one of the 'most active religious and social organisations in the city', with a significant degree of female participation and Unitarian women from the merchant community were very active in promoting charitable work within the framework of the church's Domestic Mission and the Unitarian Institute (1889) where they accounted for over 25 per cent of the trustees.[162] In the early 1860s, for example, Anne Holt subscribed annually to 15 charities. Although she supported non-Unitarian institutions, such as the Liverpool Royal Infirmary (1745), the Lancashire Female Refuge (1823), and the School for the Deaf and Dumb (1825), Unitarian charities, including Charles Melly's Ragged Schools, the Liverpool Domestic Mission, and the Training School for Nurses received her main attention.[163] The closely knit Unitarian clan of the Booths, Holts, and Rathbones dominated these societies. William Rathbone had initiated the district-nursing system in England and established the first school for nurses in Liverpool; and Unitarian women, such as Anne and Frances Holt, were heavily involved in establishing nursing districts and serving as lady superintendents.[164] Later in the century, Eleanor Rathbone, the daughter of William Rathbone, became critical of the work of the Domestic Mission Society and collaborated instead with another active member of the Unitarian network, Florence Melly, in developing the North Toxteth Committee of the Mission, which became one of the most successful charitable reformatories in Liverpool.[165]

It is difficult to estimate the overall scale of women's involvement in charitable enterprise, but evidence suggests that the second half of the nineteenth century witnessed an increase in their public role. Various charities were founded and led by women, such as the Liverpool Female Orphan Asylum and the Princes Park Hospital, while many of the larger medical charities began to establish separate Ladies Visiting Committees or incorporated women members into existing management committees. As the level of institutional provision was extended in response to growing need and the professionalization of medical practice, the public role of women was reinforced. In the case of the Liverpool Infirmary for Children, for example, the number of members on the Ladies Visiting Committee rose from 7 (1861–62) to 19 (1911–12). But the public profile of women in supporting and managing charitable institutions also reinforced and extended existing network structures within the business community. In 1850, the Committee of the Liverpool Female Orphan Asylum had 33 women members, two thirds of whom were from merchant families, while the business community provided over 80 per cent of the female committee members at the Home for Incurables in 1878 and 11 of the 21 members of the Committee of the Liverpool Rescue Society and House of Help in 1902.[166] Active participation in institutional charitable work, therefore, provided an additional mechanism for interaction within a relatively select group of merchant families.

Moreover, in many cases merchants played a dominant role in the management of Liverpool's charitable institutions, but and the public involvement of women from the same family background strengthened class cohesion by reinforcing the importance of social networks and collective support for worthy causes.[167] Some women were strongly committed to charitable work for its own sake and not because of status considerations. Apart from an overriding concern for sick children, girls 'who have fallen into sin' or were 'hovering on the brink of ruin', and respectable women who suffered from 'chronic complaints of an incurable nature', there was widespread concern over the precarious economic position of middle-class spinsters. Anne Holt, for example, instructed her brother to give the remainder of her income, after meeting her immediate needs for 'comfort', to 'private charities among poor unmarried ladies who often have none to care for them', while the Liverpool Merchant's Guild, founded in 1868 to manage a fund of £10,000 bequeathed by Miss Catherine Wright, offered support for those members of the 'upper and middle classes of society' who had been unable to make adequate provision for their declining years'.[168] Although the Guild was designed to assist 'distressed' gentry and merchants, the intersection of gender and class was apparent in its commitment to provide assistance to governesses.

The development of charitable engagement by women drawn from local merchant families was embedded within wider family networks. In the early 1890s, the Tate family, with its extensive business interests in processing and selling cane sugar, was actively involved in supporting the Liverpool Hahnemann Hospital: Henry Tate was its President and Henry Tate Junior was the Deputy Chairman of the Hospital Committee. But his wife served on the Ladies Visiting Committee, which also included Miss Tate, a daughter of the President.[169] In 1881, both Mrs. Calder and her daughter were members of the Ladies Visiting Committee at the Liverpool Infirmary for Children and it was not unusual for husbands and wives to subscribe separately to the same charity.[170] In the case of charities founded by women, such as the Liverpool Female Orphan Asylum and the Home for Incurables (the Princes Park Hospital), the extent of family participation was considerable: these charities were run by committees composed of women, but supported by Gentlemen's Committees which frequently included their husbands. In 1851, for example, one third of the Gentlemen's Committee at the Liverpool Female Orphan Asylum were married to wives who had been elected to the General Committee in their own right.[171] Philanthropy, in such a context, was clearly a family concern with both partners contributing a range of complementary skills and sharing a common interest in a particular charitable enterprise. By contrast, other charities, such as the Liverpool Female Penitentiary, the Liverpool Infirmary for Children, and St. Paul's Eye Hospital, never developed a strong element of family-based support at committee level.

However, the family nexus of charitable involvement underwent a marked decline in the latter decades of the nineteenth century as the frequency of overlapping public roles diminished. Whereas almost half of the committee members in a sample of eight charities were related (mostly by marriage) in the 1870s, fewer than 20 per cent fell into this category by 1914 (Table 7.6). At the Home for Incurables, for example, a majority (5/9) of the members of the Gentlemen's Committee in the mid-1870s had wives who had been elected to the charity's main committee: by 1912 there was only a single case. Involvement in the management of institutional charities ceased to be a family-based affair and a greater number of middle-class women were increasingly undertaking public roles in a more independent manner.

Wives and daughters from merchant families clearly played an important role in supporting and managing individual charities, but the significance of such a commitment in terms of social

Table 7.6 The extent of family-based participation in institutional charities on Merseyside, 1870–1912

Decade	Extent of Family Committee Involvement		
	Family Members	Total Committee Membership	%
1870	14	30	46.6
1880	14	45	31.1
1890	12	38	31.5
1900	16	83	19.2
1910	5	29	17.2

Sources: MLP database; annual reports and committee minutes from the following charities—the Liverpool Female Orphan Asylum, the Home for Incurables, the Liverpool Seamen's Orphan Institution, the Liverpool Female Penitentiary, St. Paul's Eye Hospital, the Liverpool Infirmary for Children, and the Liverpool Society for the Protection of Children. In each case, the data relate to the involvement of husbands and wives or, more rarely, fathers and daughters on the separate committees of the individual charities.

networking and the validating of reputation is more difficult to assess. Three issues are worth emphasizing in this context. Firstly, there was a reduction in the involvement of women from the merchant community in a number of institutional charitable enterprises from the late nineteenth century onwards. At the Liverpool Female Orphan Asylum the proportion of female committee members from merchant families fell from a peak of 75.8 per cent in 1850 to 63.6 per cent by 1880. In 1892, 19 of the 21 committee members (90.4 per cent) at the Home for Incurables came from a merchant family background, but by 1912 the number had fallen to 12 (57.1 per cent).[172] To some extent, this trend may simply have reflected the impact of increased suburbanisation on the willingness of upper middle-class families to support well-established charities in the centre of Liverpool, at a time when the relative size of the merchant community was in decline and pressures were mounting for women to play a greater role in the public sphere.[173] But it does suggest that the earlier significance of individual and family-based involvement in charitable work, which had undoubtedly contributed to social networking within the merchant class, was gradually being eroded by other forms of public engagement and the prioritization of different objectives.

Secondly, charitable engagement was not necessarily conflict-free. Although the willingness of 'friends' to contribute to the pressing financial needs of individual charities is often alluded to, charitable work could also prove to be divisive, whether at a religious or personal level. Official reports seldom provide touch on conflict or dissent, but occasionally disputes threatened to undermine rather than sustain existing networks. The failure of J. W. Cropper to report the resignation of two lady visitors from a charitable hospital in 1859 led to dissension within the governing body and the asking of 'a most unpleasant question'. George Melly was invited to state what he thought of the 'Lady Visitors': in a letter to his wife he indicated that the affair 'would damn all chance of letting in certain judicious Lady visitors' and that 'these sorts of rows' would drive him 'into bigotry before long'.[174] In the case of the Liverpool Seamen's Orphan Asylum, the assumption by Mrs. Bright in 1903 that a period of non-attendance at the meetings of the Ladies Visitors by Margaret Allan was tantamount to her resignation had serious consequences. Mrs. Allan admitted 'that she had quite given up' attending the meetings, but the Charity's General Committee concluded that this did not disqualify her as a member as there was no rule 'enjoining regular attendance'. The net result was the resignation of the chairman, R. G. Allan, one of Liverpool's most prominent shipowners from 'a position he has held for many years with enormous advantage' and a recognition that the byelaws would have to be altered.[175]

Thirdly, the potential benefits of charitable involvement in cementing network connections within the merchant community, as well as the negative consequences of procedural disputes and personality conflicts, were magnified by the absence of any clear dividing line between public and private spheres. In some cases, such as the Home for Incurables, the charity was to be run 'as much as possible in the plan of a family', and many of the activities organized in support of its charitable objects took place within a domestic framework. Mrs. Maxwell organized 'a Cinematograph Entertainment' at her home to raise funds for the Liverpool Female Penitentiary, followed by a supper, while Miss Schintz entertained 'relays of patients' from the Home for Incurables at her house in Kenilworth.[176] Two women supporters of the Liverpool Rescue Society and House of Help offered their homes for 'drawing-room meetings', and the proceeds of a *Tableaux Vivants* organized by Miss Hind, Mrs. Langton, and Mrs. S. Ravenscroft were donated to the Wirral Hospital and Dispensary for Sick Children.[177] A public role supporting or managing a local charity carried out in a household context was an extension of domestic or household responsibilities, but when a family home became a place for informal business meetings and artistic and cultural entertainment designed to raise funds for specific charities, its public function was a factor in reinforcing reputation and status.

Businessmen at Home

Within Liverpool's merchant community, as elsewhere, men were not simply public beings, but active participants in family life. According to Tosh, the mid-nineteenth century was the heyday of masculine domesticity when there was an expectation that men should spend their non-working hours at home, in order 'to protect it, to provide for it, to control it, and to train its young aspirants to manhood'. Moreover, establishing a home was a crucial factor in achieving social recognition 'as an adult, fully masculine person', whose word carried much more weight than that of a bachelor.[178] In the late nineteenth century, some businessmen had their portraits painted with family members, including Philip Henry Rathbone accompanied by his daughter Elfreda, while a group portrait of the timber merchant and broker Peter Owens and his family was displayed at the Royal Academy Exhibition in 1889 (Figures 7.3 and 7.4) at a time when such portraits were seldom included in important exhibitions. Both men appear to have been more than content to have been painted at 'home', which reflected the Victorians' overriding emphasis on the importance of the family and the role of the head of household in contributing to its sense of harmony. Although this was essentially a middle-class ideal, there can be little doubt that an appropriate standing at home helped to consolidate or improve a man's position in the outside world of business and social interaction. Despite his considerable wealth, the merchant and shipowner James Cropper maintained 'a simplicity of life'; George Holt reported in his diary that he spent 'a good deal (of time) at home and at Ambleside'; while Charles P. Melly, although a 'very good equestrian', 'an excellent skater', and 'very fond of society', was praised for the fact that his tastes were 'essentially domestic'.[179]

Some businessmen enjoyed a considerable amount of free time, which was spent networking in various charitable, cultural, political, and sporting associations, while club membership, in some cases, was clearly directed at men who were either bachelors or lived like such. For example, the Hilbre Island Club, a yacht club based on the Wirral, had a reputation of being a 'bachelor's club': its members spent most weekends on the island even in winter, as well as at Christmas and New Year, and their priorities lay in socialising with male friends, rather than in spending time with their womenfolk or children.[180] Clubs of this type, however, tended to be an exception and many prominent focal points for networking and socializing, such as the Wellington Club (1815), were open to men and women. In fact, it was fairly common for merchants to spend their free time during the working week 'at home': there was increasing pressure on men to be better husbands and fathers and the recognition that more attention needed to be paid to their domestic responsibilities implied a deliberate emphasis on family-based activities.[181] But the pursuit of business interests and the fulfilment of family responsibilities were seldom mutually exclusive, because a great deal of social networking continued to occur at home. The Holts, for example, spent most of the time together as a family unit, but they frequently hosted dinner parties and seldom dined alone with immediate family members.

Indeed, 'family' membership was not necessarily restricted to its nuclear core, but often embraced an extended range of relatives and more distant kin, as well as close friends and fellow religionists, including the husbands and wives of siblings (and their children), unmarried brothers and sisters, and single or widowed kin who sometimes were resident in the household. In the case of the Holts, their most regular guests were fellow Unitarians, most of whom were prominent businessmen, and dinner parties often consisted of married couples who were mostly close friends of the family whose children went to school together and tended to marry within the same circle. Like other Liverpool merchants, they had a very close circle of friends, with a core group which consisted of perhaps three families (the Mellys, the Rathbones, and the Booths): they were present at most family occasions, frequently dined together on a reciprocal

Figure 7.3 Philip Henry Rathbone and his daughter Elfreda (courtesy of the Williamson Art Gallery and Museum)

basis, and took part in joint theatrical performances, such as a production of John Tobin's *The Honeymoon* in 1851. They attended the same Unitarian Chapel (Figure 7.5), provided collective support to several charitable organizations, maintained close connections with Freemasonry, and were members of the Liberal Party.[182] Although they constituted a powerful network, it was

Figure 7.4 Home: A Family Group by Phil. R. Morris, ARA

Figure 7.5 The Unitarian Chapel in Paradise Street (engraved by J. Smith after a picture by G. & C. Payne) in J. Harwood Austin and G. & C. Pyne (eds), *Lancashire Illustrated* (London, 1830)

based on well-established family friendships embedded within a well-defined domestic and household context.

Extant diary evidence suggests that family and friends remained a central nexus for many Liverpool merchants, with children receiving a great deal of attention. At one level, most members of the business community took an active interest in their sons' education since the choice of an appropriate school was regarded as an investment of central importance. Boys were sent out to the world to become men, but a father's standing in society also depended on whether he left behind a son who possessed manly character and was successful in his own right in stamping his mark on the world. Critical succession issues were also tied up with the successful education and training of sons, particularly in the case of family firms and partnerships. William, the second son of the merchant and shipowner Peter McQuie, was admitted as a partner in his father's business in 1853, while Edward Turner, the son of a ship agent and broker, signed a partnership agreement with his father in July 1911.[183] Direct succession within the immediate family remained the preferred option for most Liverpool merchants and to achieve this objective existing contacts were used to secure appropriate training experience with paternal advice offered on a regular basis. In 1853, Philip Holt agreed to accept a partnership in the firm of Lamport and Holt, despite a fear that such an arrangement would be jeopardized by a 'probable incompatibility of temper', but his sister Anne noted that if this arrangement had not been finalized 'papa was quite prepared to assist him to as he thought best for his own happiness'.[184] When George Holt's son, William, was about to embark on a voyage to America, his father advised him to 'take many and good introductions', while a letter from Jeremiah Todd to his son prior to his arrival in Rio de Janeiro enjoined him to 'embrace every opportunity to gain a general knowledge of the Rio business', and 'as regards women (to) seek the society of the virtuous, the good, and the accomplished'.[185] In some cases, there was a close bond between father and son— Walter A. Harrison often took the same tram as his father into his office in the town centre—but there was no guarantee that paternal support would be accepted. George Brown was 'pained re son', and Harold Littledale incurred family displeasure by being cut off from inheriting the estate of his aunt, Mrs. Bolton of Stone Abbey, because he had lost £30,000 as a young man to McNeill of Barra.[186] At the same time, fathers could have very affectionate relationships with their children and grandchildren, as a diary entry by Emma Holt reveals:

> And the outward appearance must have manifested them- what else could have made his only granddaughter [Anne] pet and play with him as she did with no-one else in the house. If he was in the room it was always to him she went. I have many a times seen her stroke and kiss his hands, take up his feet and do the same and hug his knees and if placed by him on chair or sofa, repeatedly stroke and kiss his head and hair.[187]

The death of a child also left its mark: in the case of the wine merchant William Lapell, the loss of his daughter 'threw a gloom over his views and prospects of life'.[188]

The involvement of individual merchants in family life extended to specific aspects of household management. Many men were responsible for the wine cellar, but others took a real interest in household affairs. The shipowner Henry Threlfall Wilson was responsible for paying the wages of the male domestic staff, while Robert Durning Holt was involved in managing the servants: when Tinkler, the butler, was given notice to quit, it was Robert who instructed him to carefully move and leave in order all the china and glass.[189] In fact, Robert seems to have taken an active role in household management functioning as 'a sort of universal referee about house affairs' when Mrs. Holt was away. For example, when Anne Holt was at the family cottage in Windermere, she wrote and asked him to tell their servants Hannah and Charles 'that we shall not require any more potatoes sending at present as we are beginning to gather our own'.[190]

But the relationship between businessmen and their domestic servants (whether female or male) was not straightforward, given the hierarchy of private control exercised in the family environment and the continued importance of a traditional culture of masculinity with its implicit association with violence. It has been argued that the trope of aristocratic masters who actively preyed on young servants whose work was located primarily in an intimate and relatively isolated location retained its validity in the late nineteenth century. But it was also evident in middle-class households, where the assumption that masters had sexual rights over their servants continued to cast a long shadow. The extent to which the expected rules of family life within Merseyside's mercantile community were undermined by instances of sexual assault or harassment is difficult to establish, given the ability of male heads of households to summarily dismiss domestic servants, if necessary with a financial settlement designed to ensure that such cases were never reported to the police. But it would be false to ignore this element of tension in merchant families. It reflected the persistence of class- and gender-specific inequalities in Victorian and Edwardian society which continued to affect the lives of servants.[191] The potential for sexual exploitation was publicly acknowledged (Figure 7.6). The return of a father from a day's work in his office may well have been the occasion for playful interaction with his children, but his attention is firmly focussed on the new governess.

For some merchants the importance of the domestic environment was reinforced by its role as a site for entertainment and social interaction, but also by the opportunities it provided for fashionable pastimes and pursuits. Suburbanisation was increasingly associated with the possibility of creating a rural retreat, where gardening and farming could be practised at some distance from the threat of urban pollution. Already by the end of the eighteenth century, successful Liverpool merchants had begun to acquire 'county' retreats by purchasing cottages and

Figure 7.6 The New Governess, c. 1910 (contemporary postcard)

farms in neighbouring parishes which were subsequently enlarged or redeveloped for family occupancy, while the rateable value of Sudely, George Holt's property in Mossley Hill Road, included separate valuations for a cottage, a shippon, piggeries, park land, and a plantation.[192] His son, Robert Durning Holt, developed similar interests: he cared for the animals on the farm, including dogs, brought strawberry plants into the hot house, and bought pigs. The publication in 1850 of Edward Kemp's book on garden design fuelled contemporary interest in horticultural issues and strengthened the importance of the home as a location for the realization of personal interests and for the public demonstration of good taste.[193] To this extent, increased suburbanisation during the second half of the nineteenth century served to reaffirm the link between the worlds of business and the home.

Conclusion

Recent research has stressed the importance of network-based communication in establishing mutual trust and transmitting organisational knowledge in the nineteenth century, but insufficient attention has been paid to the role of women and the family in facilitating network links or reinforcing their social embeddedness. The Victorian cult of middle-class domesticity and the widespread diffusion of the bourgeois family model, underpinned by a concept of the sexes which postulated fundamental emotional and physical distinctions, served to negate the role of women's agency in business affairs and reinforced the belief in the existence of distinct and separate spheres of influence.[194] But it is increasingly problematic to conceptualise the existence of two distinct spheres, whether 'public' and 'private', 'work' and 'home', or 'business' and 'pleasure', and this chapter has highlighted how the family and household represented sites where apparent binary opposites met. Within Liverpool's merchant community business and family interests were seldom antithetical. In the case of individual firms, partnerships, or family-owned companies, day-to-day business developments were often reported and discussed in a family context, as the available diary evidence confirms, while the household continued to play an important role within the business community as a secure setting for the informal exchange of ideas and information. If business was regarded as a personal matter, this did not preclude the involvement of the family or extended kin. In the world of business and commerce, credibility, reputation, and trust remained important in establishing dependable cooperation, but they were sustained by knowledge complementarities reinforced by the family and household context of merchant life.[195]

At one level, marriage and family life reflected a prioritization of business considerations. Intermarriage within the merchant community was relatively common and a preference for local brides suggests that family formation was viewed as a means of cementing business connections or securing more effective integration within Liverpool's dominant groups. But the role of merchants' wives and daughters was not restricted to the domestic sphere. They held private property and commercial assets in their own name even before the enactment of the Married Women's Property Acts of 1870 and 1882, and their financial wealth, particularly as widows, was sometimes considerable. A wife's ability to hold private property in her own name provided individual merchants with considerable protection against potential creditors, particularly if their business encountered difficulties or was faced with bankruptcy, but there was also a general supposition that any assets held by female family members, whether inherited or accumulated, could be used to sustain existing business interests. Other long-term household residents whether unmarried siblings or distant kin also invested money in the family firm and thereby contributed to its continued success. Indeed, far from being restricted to the domestic environment, some women ultimately played an active role in managing or directing local firms.

Following the premature death of a merchant, a widow's business competence was a prerequisite for securing the survival of the family firm and the success of some women in achieving this objective is also indicative of a prior knowledge of the world of business.

Women contributed substantially to the maintenance and development of the cultural environment which underpinned Liverpool's merchant community. By managing the household and by organizing and hosting a range of entertainment activities, married women helped to sustain their husbands' business reputation. Women facilitated social and business introductions, while the extensive pattern of social visiting, particularly in the case of spinsters, was a critical factor in maintaining information flows and strengthening social networks. The active visiting culture evident within the merchant community served to validate both the social standing of individual families and their business reputation. Female co-residents were registered in approximately 30 per cent of Liverpool's merchant households, with sisters, sisters-in-law, and nieces predominant. As a result, they played an important role in maintaining kinship and friendship networks, whether locally or within a regional and national context, which helped to sustain the continued operation of a gift economy based on mutuality. But visiting also served as an invaluable mechanism for disseminating information, whether of a personal or family nature, which underpinned the contemporary assessment of a merchant's social standing and business reputation.

For many merchants, business and family life remained intertwined. The family and household operated as a web of potential business contacts, while the social activities of merchants' wives and female relatives helped to create goodwill and trust between elite families and enhanced their reputation in the public arena. Often networks based on friendship and denominational affinity were inseparable from business networks, while intermarriage within Liverpool's business community helped to create bonds of trust between individual families by demonstrating symbolically a common set of beliefs and values. The family and household continued to function as a central nexus for members of Liverpool's business community: a great deal of social networking took place at home; suburbanisation encouraged the development of home-based hobbies and interests; individual merchants took an active role in supporting their children's education and career development; and men retained a range of private, family-based responsibilities, particularly in relation to the management of the household economy.

The household remained an important and semi-public reflection of a merchant's wealth, respectability, and taste, at a time when there was a clear expectation that business success should be predicated on a successful marriage and an appropriate fulfilment of family responsibilities. Although a woman was often expected to adopt a public role which complemented her husband's, whether in charitable, educational, or religious activities, involvement in the public sphere was generally embedded within wider family networks. It was not unusual for husbands and wives, as well as other family members, to subscribe to the same charity, while the management and direction of several local charities depended on the active engagement of both partners. A growing level of participation by middle-class women in literary and musical associations further strengthened their role in public culture, but this trend, at least initially, was often family-based, with both husbands and wives demonstrating a shared interest in music, language, and literature.

The important contribution of network analysis to debates on business performance and economic activity has been widely acknowledged, with an extended family regarded as an important network resource, but the actual role of female networks has seldom been explored.[196] Although social and economic networks were frequently 'mutually constitutive', the precise contribution of women, the family, and the household to the articulation of business culture has seldom been addressed. The available evidence for Liverpool's merchant community suggests that women played a visible role in sustaining business culture through the operation of both complementary and parallel networks. The practice of female visiting was well established by the mid-nineteenth century, and it continued to offer an ancillary mechanism for information dissemination and mutual support: in the 1901 census over 10 per cent of all merchant households had visitors, the majority of whom were women. Membership in the growing number of literary clubs and musical societies offered wives and daughters from merchant families an opportunity to extend their public role in an institutional context often dominated by members of Liverpool's business community. It also provided a framework for friendship and collaboration which had a wider significance for the maintenance of trust and the strengthening of commercial relations amongst some of the city's leading families.

The wives of Liverpool merchants were already active in founding a number of local charities in the early nineteenth century, but the monitoring and delivery of institutional care often depended on their willingness to act as 'lady visitors' or as members of a ladies' committee. The scale of women's involvement in charitable work increased significantly in the following decades, in part as a response to the gradual growth in institutional provision, but also as a reflection of their ability to traverse both public and private realms. Whereas men concentrated on horizontal networking, the creation of parallel women's networks facilitated vertical contact with other social classes, to some extent as an extension of their household responsibilities involving the management of family servants and negotiations with retailers and tradesmen. By 1914 the public role of women in charitable work had been further consolidated by the dissolution of gender-based governance structures in a several medical charities and their election to central management committees on an equal basis. To this extent, there was a significant expansion in the public role of women and a concomitant strengthening of their networking function within the city.

The family and household remained important focal points for the articulation and development of merchant culture. There was no necessary division between the public and private worlds of merchants, and associational membership and charitable work were sometimes embedded within a family framework, at least until the late nineteenth century. But the networking pattern of merchants' wives was also affected by wider social changes, in particular by suburbanisation and residential relocation. Many of the newer cultural associations established in the suburbs, such as the West Kirby Literary Society, attracted a large number of female members as out-migration from the urban core was accompanied by the development of substitute social networks, at a time when well-established Liverpool charities registered a reduction in the involvement of women from the merchant community.[197]

Female networks did not remain static but adapted to the changing spatial location of the merchant community as a whole. Nor must it be assumed that the existence of women's parallel networks necessarily sustained business culture: the fact that women were disproportionately involved in church-based charitable activities increased the risk of denominational divisiveness, while committee membership of medical charities or welfare agencies sometimes led to personal antagonism and hostility. But for most Liverpool merchants, the family and household remained integral elements in the creation and maintenance of contemporary business culture. Women and other female household members played an important role in cementing friendships, whether individual or family-based, in disseminating information, in strengthening knowledge complementarities, and in facilitating business transactions. The household and family context continued to define the reputation and trustworthiness of many Victorian merchants, while the public role of wives and their involvement in both complementary and parallel networks reinforced key aspects of business culture.

Notes

1   Robert Beathy, Beatrice Craig and Alastair Owens (eds.), *Women, Business and Finance in Nineteenth-Century Europe* (London and New York, 2006); Eleanor Gordon and Gwyneth Nair, *Public Lives: Women, Family and Society in Victorian Britain* (New Haven and London, 2003); John Tosh, *A Man's Place: Masculinity and the Middle-Class Home in Victorian England* (Yale, 1999); Leonore Davidoff and Catherine Hall, *Family Fortunes: Men and Women of the English Middle Class, 1780–1850* (London, 1987).

2   Theresa M. McBride, 'The Long Road Home: Women's Work and Industrialisation', in Renate Bridenthal and Claudia Koonz (eds.), *Becoming Visible: Women in European History* (Boston, 1977), p. 283.

3   Michael J. Power, 'Creating a Port: Liverpool 1695–1715', *THSL&C*, 149 (2000), pp. 51–72; Robin Pearson and David Richardson, 'Business Networking in the Industrial Revolution', *EcHR*, 54 (2001), pp. 657–99; Gordon Boyce, 'Network Knowledge and Network Routines: Negotiating Activities between Shipowners and Shipbuilders', *BH*, 45, 2 (2003), pp. 52–72.

4   Gordon and Nair, *Public Lives*, p. 3.

5   John Tosh, *Manliness and Masculinities in Nineteenth-Century Britain: Essays on Gender, Family and Empire* (Harlow, 2005), p. 5.

6   See the ongoing debate surrounding British 'family capitalism' as a source of industrial decline in Alastair Owens, 'Inheritance and the Life-Cycle of Family Firms in the Early Industrial Revolution' *BH*, 44, 1 (2002), pp. 21–46.

7   See Sari Mäenpää, Chapter 6.

8   See Graham Milne, Chapter 4.

9   Francis Edwin Hyde, *Liverpool and the Mersey: An Economic History of a Port, 1700–1970* (Newton Abbot, 1971), p. 132; Robert Lee, 'Configuring the City: In-Migration, Labour Supply and Port Development in Nineteenth-Century Europe', *IJMH*, 17, 1 (2005), p. 113.

10 See Francesca Carnevali, 'Crooks, Thieves, and Receivers': Transaction Costs in Nineteenth-Century Industrial Birmingham', *EcHR*, 57, 3 (2004), pp. 533–50, which looks at co-operation and trust between traders through the activity of trade associations.

11 See Randolph Cock, John Davies, Robert Lee, and Sari Mäenpää, Chapter 2; Merseyside Maritime Museum (MMM), Maritime Archives and Library (MAL), B/EWT/F34, 38, Edward Wrake Turner, family letters and papers, 1860s-1950s; Liverpool Record Office (LRO), 920 MEL, 5, 7, 23 and 40, Melly Correspondence, 1857–1892; MMM, MAL, DX/641/6/1–3, McQuie Family Papers; DX/258/2/1/1–88, letters written by Macgregor Laird; LRO, 920 DUR 1/2–1/7, 4/28/1–3, 4/30/1–13, Holt family diaries and personal papers.

12 This was specifically the case in relation to merchants involved in the cotton trade. See William Hustace Hubbard, *Cotton and the Cotton Market* (London, 1923), pp. 288–306; Thomas Ellison, *The Cotton Trade of Great Britain* (First edition, 1886), Part II; Nigel Hall, 'The Emergence of the Liverpool Raw Cotton Market, 1800–1850', *Northern History*, 38, 1 (2001), pp. 65–81; Nigel Hall, 'The Business Interests of Liverpool's Cotton Brokers, c.1800–1914', *Northern History*, 41, 2 (2004), pp. 339–55; D. M. Williams, 'Liverpool Merchants and the Cotton Trade 1820–1850' in J. R. Harris (ed.), *Liverpool and Merseyside: Essays in the Economic and Social History of the Port and Its Hinterland* (Cambridge, 1969), pp. 182–211; Francis E. Hyde, Bradbury B. Parkinson and Sheila Marriner, 'The Cotton Broker and the Rise of the Liverpool Cotton Market', *EcHR*, 8, 1 (1955), pp. 75–83.

13 Pat Jalland, *Women, Marriage and Politics, 1860–1914* (Oxford, 1986), p. 193.

14 Amy Louise Dickinson, 'The Marital Economy in Comparative Perspective', in Maria Ågren and Amy Louise Dickinson (eds.), *The Marital Economy in Scandinavia and Britain 1400–1900* (London and New York, 2005), p. 3.

15 See Randolph Cock, John Davies, Robert Lee, and Sari Mäenpää, Chapter 2.

16 Robert J. Morris, *Men, Women and Property in England, 1780–1870 a Social and Economic History of Family Strategies amongst the Leeds Middle Classes* (Cambridge, 2005), p. 265.

17 Gary Wray McDonogh, *Good Families of Barcelona: A Social History of Power in the Industrial Era* (Princeton, NJ, 1986), p. 141. Amongst the leading families of Barcelona, parental influence in the choice of marriage partners remained strong until the 1950s.

18 William Thomas Pike, *Liverpool and Birkenhead in the Twentieth Century: Contemporary Biographies* (Brighton, 1911), p. 154; Wilton J. Oldham, *The Ismay Line: The White Star Line, and the*

Ismay Family Story (Liverpool and London, 1961), p. 122. Hans Kern had been born in Germany in 1862: he was also the German Consul in Liverpool for a number of years.

19 LRO, 288 HOP/3/2, Hope Street Chapel, marriage register, 1880–1900.

20 LRO, 285 FUR, 1/1/1, Fairfield English Presbyterian Church, Marriages 1867–1919.

21 LRO, 285 WAV, 7/1, Anon., 'The Story of Wavertree Congregational Chapel Formerly Trinity Chapel, 1836–1986', p. 3.

22 See Randolph Cock, John Davies, Robert Lee, and Sari Mäenpää, Chapter 2; Robert Lee, 'Divided Loyalties? In-Migration, Ethnicity and Identity: The Integration of German Merchants in Nineteenth-Century Liverpool', *BH*, 54, 2 (2012), pp. 126–8.

23 Colin Pooley and Jean Turnbull, *Migration and Mobility in Britain since the Eighteenth Century* (London, 1998), p. 219. For an overview of migration into Liverpool, see Colin Pooley, 'Living in Liverpool: The Modern City', in John Belchem (ed.), *Liverpool, 800 Culture, Character & History* (Liverpool, 2007), pp. 171–257.

24 LRO, 920 DUR, 1/3, Family Diary maintained by George Holt, 23 February 1860, 26 February 1860: 920 DUR, 1/4, Family Diary maintained by Emma Holt, 30 January 1863. All ladies were required to appear in white or black dresses 'trimmed only with either pink or blue material'; 12 February 1871: 920 DUR, 1/6, Family Diary maintained by Robert D. Holt, 14 January 1891. The event was held in 'a large Ballroom built out and very handsomely decorated', with a dress code of white dresses for Ladies and waistcoats for Gentlemen. For a further discussion of the role of the Wellington Rooms and its membership composition, see Sari Mäenpää, Chapter 6, and Robert Lee, Chapter 12.

25 LRO, 920 MEL 7, George Melly MP, Private Correspondence, vol. 7, 628, letter from Hasso N Bright.

26 Pike, *Contemporary Biographies*, pp. 160, 183.

27 Lucie Nottingham, *Rathbone Brothers from Merchants to Bankers, 1742–1992* (Oxford, 1992), p. 21.

28 MMM, MAL, DX/641/6/1, Chronological Calendar of Events Connected with the Family of 'McQuie', 30 December 1857.

29 Frances Anne Conybeare, *Dingle Bank the Home of the Croppers: A Recollection* (Cambridge, 1925), p. 32; Pike, *Contemporary Biographies*, p. 117.

30 Yaffa Claire Draznin, *Victorian London's Middle-Class Housewife: What She Did All Day* (Westport, CT and London, 2001), p. 8.

31 For example, Canning Street Presbyterian Church, St. Andrew's Kirk, Rodney Street, and St. Paul's Presbyterian Church, Bootle, were all established by the local Scotch population. See Deacons' Court, *Jubilee Memorial of Canning Street Presbyterian Church Liverpool (1846–1896)* (Liverpool, 1896), p. 2; A. L. M. Cook, *St. Andrew's Kirk, Rodney Street* (Liverpool, 1988); Alberta J. Doodson, *The Story of St. Paul's and Trinity United Reformed Church Bootle* (Bootle, 1983). For a detailed overview of the denominational complexity of nineteenth-century Liverpool, see J. A. Kaplan, 'Geographical Aspects of Religious Change in Victorian Liverpool, 1837–1901', unpublished MA thesis, University of Liverpool (1977).

32 Edward H. Milligan and Malcolm J. Thomas, *My Ancestors Were Quakers: How Can I Find Out More about Them?* Society of Genealogists (London, 1999).

33 LRO, 289 Quaker Records, Box 7, Membership List 1837–1860. Sarah married Edward Hale in 1839, a member of Hardshaw East, while Ann married Joseph Harris in 1846 from the Padshaw meeting.

34 LRO, WAK 31/1, Marriages in Leading Liverpool Families.

35 Ibid. Forwood was from one of the most prominent merchant families in Liverpool: the Muspratts had established a substantial business in chemicals.

36 LRO, 920 DUR 1/4. The entries by Anne Holt closely followed the progress of the American Civil War, reflecting the family firm's involvement with the cotton trade.

37 LRO, 920 DUR 4/26/2.

38 LRO, 920 MEL 7, 735, 22 July 1861. Letter from Emma Holt to George Melly reiterating family disapproval of money spent at an election.

39 MMM, MAL, B/EWT, F34, p. 56; Gordon and Nair, *Public Lives*, p. 66.

40 Eleanor Gordon and Gwyneth Nair, 'The Economic Role of Middle-Class Women in Victorian Glasgow', *Women's History Review*, 9, 4 (2000), p. 802; LRO 920 DUR 4/28/1, Personal account book of Anne Holt, 1851–1859; MAL, DX/504/6/1–12: between 1878 and 1884 her average annual income

amounted to £11,839. Mrs. Ismay drew income from the capital value of two estates set up by her family in New York, the G. R. Sheffelin Estate (£4,300) and Mrs. Sheffelin Estate (£24,400), as well as from the Delaplaine Estate (£17,000).

41 LRO, 920 DUR 4/29/1, Investment book of Ann Holt. Her investments in the London and North West Railway Company amounted to £7,875 with shares purchased in 1861, 1869, and 1882, while a total of £2,600 was invested in the Lancashire and Yorkshire Railway in 1871 and 1884 respectively; MLP database, Liverpool Ship Register sample, 1871. Only in two cases were women sole owners of vessels. Hannah Singleton of Hoylake also had shares (8/64ths) in two ships. For further information on women investors in Liverpool vessels, see David Clarke, 'Liverpool Shipowners: 1820–1914', unpublished D.Phil. thesis, Memorial University of Newfoundland (2005), pp. 245–50.

42 LRO, 920 DUR 4/28.2, Investment and account book of Anne Holt, 1854.

43 Jennifer Aston, Amanda Capern and Briony McDonagh, 'More Than Bricks and Mortar: Female Property Ownership as Economic Strategy in Mid-Nineteenth Century Urban England', *Urban History*, 46, 4 (2019), pp. 695–721. The combined level of female ownership (11 per cent) suggests that urban property ownership rates were similar to those for land in rural England (10–12 per cent): see Janet Casson, 'Women's Landownership in England in the Nineteenth Century', in Mark Casson and Nigar Hashimzade (eds.), *Large Databases in Economic History: Research Methods and Case Studies* (Abingdon, 2013), pp. 200–22; Jennifer Aston, *Female Entrepreneurship in Nineteenth-Century England: Engagement in the Urban Economy* (London, 2016).

44 LRO, 920 MD 76. Indenture (Legacy and Succession Duty Office, Somerset House, London, 03.95.1898. The trust was based on £15,000 consolidated LNWR stock. On his death in 1898 it was valued at £23,000.

45 MMM, MAL, DX/504/6/3, Papers regarding the will of J. Bruce Ismay (1912–1917).

46 Morris, *Men, Women and Property*, p. 263.

47 LRO, 920 DUR 5/1/1, letter to George from George Holt, his father, 1852.

48 BPP, Select Committee Special Report with Proceedings, Minutes of Evidence 1867–68. Testimonies of John Westlake, Esq., barrister and George Woodyatt Hastings, Esq., Arthur Hobhouse, a Queen's Counsel, a charity commissioner.

49 LRO, 920 MD 283, Henry Threlfall Wilson, 1850–1869, Settled in Marriage Settlement.

50 LRO, Diaries of A.G. Kurz, 9 May 1878.

51 Alastair Owens, 'Property and the Life Course: Inheritance and Family Welfare Provision in Early Nineteenth-Century England', *SH*, 26, 3 (2001), p. 310; Morris, *Men, Women and Property*, pp. 101–5; LRO, 027 LYE 5/1, Liverpool Library, Share Transfer Book, 1861–1915. In December 1862, for example, Catharine Bickersteth was listed as the executor of her late husband, Robert Bickersteth.

52 LRO, 920 DRI, 25, 30, 33; 920 DUR 1/2, 6 January 1851; 920 DUR 4/30/1–3, The last will of Anne Holt and the probate of the will. Her estate was assessed at her death at £100,000, excluding the house, a piece of land, and several items of expensive diamond jewellery.

53 MLP database.

54 Hannah Barker, *The Business of Women: Female Enterprise and Urban Development in Northern England, 1760–1830* (Oxford, 2006); *Family and Business during the Industrial Revolution* (Oxford, 2017); Aston, *Female Entrepreneurship in Nineteenth-Century England*.

55 MLP database.

56 MLP database.

57 LRO, 289 Quaker Records, Box 7. For example, the tea dealer, Mary Wood, was registered as a member for the period between 1827 and 1857.

58 MMM, MAL, DX/641/6/1, McQuie Family Journal, 1846–66; D/SO/2/1/4, Annual Report, Liverpool Seamen's Orphan Asylum, 1885, p. 24; James Hoult, *West Derby, Old Swan & Wavertree* (Liverpool, 1913), p. 31.

59 LRO, 920 DUR 1/2, Family Diary maintained by George Holt, 2 December 1851; MLP database, obituaries. The average age at death stood at 66.8 years in the 1890s, fell to 65.8 years during the 1900s, and increased again to 68.9 years by 1910–19 (excluding merchants who were killed in action during the First World War). The sample size, per decade, was 21, 78, and 72 respectively.

60 William B. Forwood, *Recollections of a Busy Life being the Reminiscences of a Liverpool Merchant, 1840–1910* (Liverpool, 1910), p. 3.

61 See, for example, Alison C. Kay, 'Retailing, Respectability and the Independent Woman in Nineteenth-Century London', in Robert Beachy, Beatrice Craig and Alastair Owens (eds.), *Women, Business and Finance in Nineteenth-Century Europe* (Oxford, 2006), p. 152; Kathryn Gleadle, *British*

Women in the Nineteenth Century (2001), p. 57. For example, Maria Louisa Swire, the widow of the merchant and shipowner John Swire, was listed in 1850 as the executrix of her late husband's will and the owner of four shares in the 1,063 barque, *Theodor*: see, Clarke, 'Liverpool Shipowners', pp. 247–8.

62 MMM, MAL, B/EWT, F34, typewritten history of the firm E. W. Turner, p. 58; LRO, 920 MEL 23, George Melly MP, Private Correspondence, Vol. 17, 4572, letter from mother, 6 February 1872.

63 LRO, DUR 920/4/31/2, Anne Holt, 'Some Memories of our Mother 1871–1881'.

64 Dickinson, 'The Marital Economy in Comparative Perspective', p. 3.

65 LRO, MD230/8, Business Records of George Holt & Co., Day Book, 1848–1871; MMM, MAL, DX/504/1/3, Papers relating to J. Bruce Ismay's House, Sandheys, Mossley Hill Road, available accommodation, 1909–August 1910.

66 John Belchem and Nicholas Hardy, 'Second Metropolis: The Middle Class in Early Victorian Liverpool', in Alan Kidd and David Nicholls (eds.), *The Making of the British Middle Class? Studies of Regional and Cultural Diversity since the Eighteenth Century* (Thrupp, 1998), p. 67.

67 LRO, 920 DUR 1/2, 31 August 1851, George Holt's comments on the house of Richard V. Yates; DUR 1/6, 15 February 1891.

68 LRO, 920 MEL 40, *Memoirs of Charles P. Melly* (privately printed, 1889), p. 130.

69 LRO, 920 DUR 4/28/3, 'List of Parties 1867': the reasons for declining an invitation were also often cited.

70 LRO, DUR 1/2; 4/28/3: based on data from 1851–52 and for the period between 1867 and 1885.

71 LRO, DUR 4/28/3. Between 1867 and 1877, for example, the list of individuals repeatedly invited to parties hosted by the Holt family, included members of the Booth, Bright, Brocklebank, Forget, Hadwen, Melly, and Rathbone families, together with the minister of the Hope Street Chapel, the Reverend Thom. Two merchant families from the in-migrant German community, Prange and Stolterfoht, were included in this select group.

72 LRO, 920 DUR 1/6, 27 April 1892.

73 LRO, 920 DUR 4/28/3, 22 July 1874: a party was held despite the fact that Anne Holt failed to find any 'stray gentlemen'.

74 MMM, MAL, DX/641/6/1, Chronological Calendar of Events Connected with the Family of 'McQuie', 16 February 1823, 20 October 1861; LRO, 920 MD 376, Autobiographical Memoir and Diaries of George Alexander Brown, 1803–61.

75 Conybeare, *Dingle Bank*, p. 60.

76 LRO, 920 MD 283, Henry Threlfall Wilson 1850–69. On 1 February 1868, Wilson was invited to Oxton to have lunch with Mr. Jackson.

77 LRO, 920 DUR 4/28/3, List of Parties Begun 1867: 3 May 1879, 10 December 1879; 920 DUR 1/5, 18 December 1872.

78 Jalland, *Women, Marriage and Politics*, p. 189.

79 LRO, 920 STI, Staniforth family; 920 MEL 40, Memoirs of Charles P. Melly (privately published, 1889), p. 4. Thomas Staniforth, a 'man of wealth', also retained a town residence in Ranelagh Street after the construction of Broad Green Hall. See Hoult, *West Derby*, p. 84.

80 Conybeare, *Dingle Bank*, pp. 7–8; Harriet Beecher Stowe (1811–96) was a famous American author and abolitionist best known for her novel *Uncle Tom's Cabin* (1852), which portrayed the harsh living conditions of enslaved African Americans: it was taken up by abolitionists and roundly condemned by the white population of the southern states. Matthew Arnold (1822–88) was a poet and cultural critic, characterised as a 'sage writer' who instructed and chastised readers on contemporary social issues.

81 LRO, 920 DUR 1/2, Family Diary maintained by George Holt, 2 August 1852, 10 October 1852.

82 Pike, *Contemporary Biographies*, 162, 187. Only in 17 cases was the address of a second home included in the biographical entry, but the actual extent of this practice was probably under-reported.

83 See Joseph Sharples and Adrian Jarvis, Chapter 9, and Robert Lee, Chapter 11.

84 Sheila McIsaac Cooper, 'Service to Servitude: The Decline and Demise of Life-Cycle Service in England', *The History of the Family*, 10, 4 (2005), pp. 367–86; Margot Finn, *The Character of Credit: Personal Debt in English Culture, 1740–1914* (Cambridge, 2003); Draznin, *Victorian London's Middle-Class Housewife*, p. 71; Jessica Gerard, *County House Life: Family and Servants, 1815–1914* (Oxford and Cambridge, 1994), p. 143; Pamela Horn, *The Rise and Fall of the Victorian Servant* (Stroud, 1990), p. 27; James Walvin, *English Urban Life 1776–1851* (London, 1984), p. 177; Gordon and Nair, *Public Lives*, p. 149.

85 Lee, 'Domestic Service and Female Domestic Servants', p. 447; Quentin Outram, 'The Demand for Residential Domestic Service in the London of 1901', *EcHR*, 70, 3 (2016), pp. 893–918; F. M. L. Thompson, *Hampstead Building a Borough, 1650–1961* (London, 1974), p. 50.

86 LRO, 920 DUR 3/29/5; MLP database.

87 Theresa M. McBride, *The Domestic Revolution: The Modernisation of Household Service in England and France 1820–1920* (London, 1976), p. 12; MLP database.

88 Alan Armstrong, *Stability and Change in an English Country Town* (Cambridge, 1974), p. 179; Carolyn Steedman, 'The Servant's Labour: The Business of Life, England, 1760–1820', *SH*, 29, 1 (2004), p. 2. For a useful corrective to this view, see F. R. Prochaska, 'Female Philanthropy and Domestic Service in Victorian England', *Bulletin of the Institute of Historical Research*, 54 (1981), p. 84; Gerard, *County House Life*, p. 143.

89 MLP database.

90 Martha Kanya-Forstner, 'The Politics of Survival: Irish Women in Outcast Liverpool, 1850–1890', unpublished doctoral dissertation, University of Liverpool (1997), p. 118; Anon., *Introduction in Household Matters or, the Young Girl's Guide to Domestic Service Written by a Lady with an Especial View to Young Girls Intended for Service on Leaving School* (4th ed., London, n.d.), pp. 81, 95.

91 LRO, 920 DUR 1/2, 5 March 1845; 1/3, 28 October 1860; 1/4, 29 March 1861, 10 December 1861.

92 LRO, 920 DUR 1/4, 29 April 1861; MAL DX/641/6/2, 21 December 1868. Betsey Kent, a young servant girl in the McQuie household, left after several years of satisfactory employment 'at her father's unexpected request'.

93 LRO, 920 DUR 1/4, 29 April 1861; MAL DX/641/6/2, 21 December 1868. Betsey Kent, a young servant girl in the McQuie household, left after several years of satisfactory employment 'at her father's unexpected request'. WAS, B/130/11, Birkenhead Magistrates, 1847–1849, 19 September 1848.

94 Svenska Kyrkans Arkiv (SKA), Gustaf Adolfs Kyrka, Liverpool, E, Brev korrespondens, 2 December 1905, 23 June 1905, 4 September 1907. According to a letter from Mrs. D. Mackay of 65 Berkley Street, Princes Park, the employment of Norwegian girls had been recommended by articles in newspapers.

95 MMM, MAL, D/Earle/13/2, T. Algernon Earle, Earle of Allerton Tower (privately circulated, 1889), p. 41; LRO, 920 MEL 5, Melly Correspondence, 438, March 1859.

96 MMM, MAL, DX/258/1/1/1–26. In a letter from 8 April 1857 addressed to his wife at 'home' in Blackheath, Laird expressed his fear that 'you are going to knock yourself up'. See MMM, MAL, DX/258/2/1–88 for copies of the original letters written by Laird to his wife, 1848–1860.

97 Walvin, *English Urban Life*, p. 177; Finn, *The Character of Credit*.

98 Gordon and Nair, *Public Lives*, p. 45; Morris, *Men, Women and Property*, p. 243. Anne Holt's long-term servant, Jemina Ellison, witnessed her will and received an annual life-time allowance of £30. Other servants received between £10 and £20, including Alice Robinson, 'who is a decent woman and has served us a long time, tho' not a first rate laundress': see LRO, 920 DUR 4/30/1–13, probate granted 29 April 1885; 920 DUR 2/28. A memoir of George Holt had been published in *The Christian Reformer; or, Unitarian Magazine and Review* in 1861 (pp. 230–46, 257–72, 336–50). The copy presented to Elizabeth Power had been separately printed.

99 LRO, 920 DUR 1/4, 10 December 1862. In 1851, Andrew (André) Melly was listed as resident at 32 Hope Street.

100 LRO, 920 DUR 1/2, 29 August 1852; 920 MEL 5, No. 420, November 1859. George Holt advised his son, William, to 'take many and good introductions' prior to embarking on a visit to America, while George Melly received a request from a friend to provide one or two letters of introduction for his son who was leaving for Australia to take up sheep-farming.

101 LRO, 920 MEL Hq. Letters from Mrs. Melly to her son, C. P. Melly. 'Recollections of the late A. Melly, 1872'. André's Christian name was quickly anglicised as Andrew.

102 LRO, 920 MEL Hq. Letters from Mrs. Melly to her son, C. P. Melly. 'Recollections of the late A. Melly, 1872'. André's Christian name was quickly anglicised as Andrew.

103 Sandra Stanley Holton, 'Kinship and Friendship: Quaker Women's Networks and the Women's Movement', *Women's History Review*, 14, 3/4 (2005), pp. 365–84; Katherine R. Allen, *Single Women/Family Ties: Life Histories of Older Women* (London, 1989), p. 26.

104 Ruth Larsen, 'For Want of a Good Fortune: Elite Single Women's Experiences in Yorkshire, 1730–1860', *Women's History Review*, 16, 3 (2007), pp. 387–401; Morris, *Men, Women and Property*, pp. 329–35.

105 LRO, 920 DUR 1/2, Holt Family Diary, 24 December 1852. The evening party was the occasion for 'a little dancing', with carriages at 11.30.

106 Holton, 'Kinship and Friendship', p. 377; LRO 920 DUR 1/4, Holt Family Diary, 21 August 1862.

107 MLP database, 1901 census, alphabetical names beginning with A, B (sample size 418: female visitor frequency 8.1 per cent); Orchard and Pike, all names beginning with B (sample size 300: female visitor frequency 9.3 per cent). By contrast, in 1851, 28.2 per cent of the middle-class households in the Claremont and Woodside estates of Glasgow had visitors: see Gordon and Nair, *Public Lives*, p. 116.

108 LRO, 920 DUR 5/1/1; MLP database.

109 MLP database, 1901 sample.

110 On 13 November 1852, J. B. Smith, Jemima, and two little girls left the Holt family home 'after a few days', while in 1861 the household of James Butterworth, a merchant's clerk, contained a female landowner from Cambridge, together with her 12-year-old child and a nurse. LRO, 920 DUR 5/1/1; MLP database.

111 MLP database sample of 418 households from the 1901 census. By contrast, a higher proportion of male visitors were married and their average age, at 40.7 years, was higher.

112 Cavendish Archive (CA), Copy of Agnes Sarah Tinley's diary for the year 1847, 3 and 6 February 1847. Her father was the successful broker Thomas Tinley.

113 Morris, *Men, Women and Property*, p. 335.

114 LRO, 920 DUR 1/4, 9 April 1861.

115 LRO, 920 DUR 1/2, 20 October 1852; 920 DUR 1/7, 10 October 1901, 24 October 1901.

116 Gordon and Nair, *Public Lives*, p. 37; Holton, 'Kinship and Friendship', pp. 372–3; Allen, *Single Women/Family Ties*, p. 26.

117 Gordon and Nair, *Public Lives*, p. 43.

118 For a detailed discussion of this theme, see Leonora Davidoff, *Thicker Than Water: Siblings and Their Relations, 1780–1920* (Oxford, 2012).

119 MLP database. The sister of William Biggs was also enumerated in 1891 at a time when his mother was registered as head of household.

120 Tosh, *A Man's Place*, pp. 145–6.

121 Bridget Hill, *Women Alone: Spinsters in England, 1660–1850* (New Haven and London, 2001), p. 69; Patricia M. Crawford (ed.), *Exploring Women's Past: Essays in Social History* (Sydney and London, 1984), p. 130.

122 Conybeare, *Dingle Bank*, p. 42. James was the eldest son of the Liverpool merchant and shipowner James Cropper who moved to Westmoreland on his marriage in 1845.

123 LRO, 920 DUR 3/29/3, Memoranda Books etc. 1827–1884 by Emma Holt, September 1855.

124 LRO, 920 DUR 4/26/2, Personal Diaries of Anne Holt.

125 Gordon and Nair, *Public Lives*, pp. 200–1, 27; Sarah A. Tooley, *Ladies of Liverpool Magazine* (Liverpool, 1895), pp. 9–10, 169–70.

126 'Death of Mrs Robert Holt', *Daily Post & Mercury*, Friday May 25, 1905.

127 Simon Gunn, *The Public Culture of the Victorian Middle Class: Ritual and Authority in the English Industrial City 1840–1914* (Manchester, 2000), p. 93; LRO, 374 AMI, 1, Amicable Book Society, Minute Book, 1812–1829, rules and regulations 30 June 1812; 367 THI 1/1, 30 Club, first meeting, 2 December 1895.

128 LRO, 374 CHA 8/3, Chatham Society, list of members, 1858; Wirral Archives Service (WAS), YBP/1, Birkenhead Parliamentary Debating Society, minute book, Vol. 1, 2 October 1876–6 February 1895; ZWO/15/1, Hoylake and West Kirby Parliamentary Debating Society, 1909–1914, minute book 1912; LRO, 374 WOO 1, Woolton Parliamentary Debating Society, list of members, 1885; 329 CAN 1, Minute book of the Canning Club, 12 November 1812; B. Whittingham-Jones, 'Liverpool's Political Clubs, 1812–30', *THSL&C*, 111 (1959).

129 Longmore, 'Civic Liverpool: 1680–1800', p. 143; Birkenhead Central Library, BC IV 280, *The Laws and Annual Report of the Birkenhead Literary and Scientific Society from Its Formation in 1857 to the End of the Year 1900* (Birkenhead, 1900), List of Members, 1868–69; LRO, 367 PHI 1/1, Philalethians Programme Cards, c.1908; T. W. M. Lund, 'The Philathian Brotherhood', in Pike (ed.), *Contemporary Biographies*, p. 78'. See Robert Lee, Chapter 12.

130 LRO, 783 SAC 1, Liverpool Sacred Harmonic Society, Subscribers, 1852–55; *THSL&C*, LIV (1902), List of Members, corrected to November 1903, xiii–xxiii. An exclusionary policy was maintained by virtually all the local sports clubs. The Sefton Cricket Club, for example, added a separate Ladies'

Pavilion in 1908, but women had no opportunity of becoming members. See Sefton Cricket Club, *Centenary Souvenir Programme, 1860–1960* (Liverpool, 1960), p. 10.

131 MLP database. However, in 1878 the merchant T. H. Howard and his wife, Elizabeth, became separate members of the Wellington Club, and Mrs. S. Bright, of Sandheys, West Derby, joined two years before her husband, the merchant Heywood Bright. See Robert Lee, Chapter 12, Shakspere was a recognised variant of the dramatist's name during his lifetime: it was revived towards the end of the eighteenth century and used by many Victorian scholars and publishers. See David Kathman, 'The Spelling and Pronunciation of Shakespeare's Name', Shakespeareauthorship.com; Bryan H. Wildenthal, 'Early Shakespeare Authorship Doubts', Thomas Jefferson School of Law Research Paper, No. 3007393 (2019).

132 LRO, LYC 5/1, Liverpool Library, Share Transfer Book, 1861–1905; George Chandler, *Liverpool* (London, 1957), p. 455.

133 LRO, 780 AMA/1, Amateur Musical Union, list of members, season 1868–69; Birkenhead Reference Library (BRL), Birkenhead Ruskin Society, Session 1881–2, *Report of the Committee* (Birkenhead, 1882), pp. 10–11; Birkenhead Shakspere Literary Society, *Report Session 11*, 1879–80 (Birkenhead, 1880), pp. 8–11; LRO, 060 ITA, Società Letteraria Italiana di Liverpool, Settembre 1908.

134 WAS, ZWO/14/1, West Kirby Literary Society, minute book no. 3, March 1895—March 1913: 18 October 1895, 13 December 1895.

135 *Gore's Directory of Liverpool and its Environs* (London, 1904): the honorary secretary of the French Literary Society was Mademoiselle Magee.

136 LRO, 780 AMA/1, Amateur Musical Union, list of members, 1868–69.

137 LRO, 060 ITA, Società Letteraria Italiana di Liverpool, list of members, September 1908; WA, ZWO/14/1, West Kirby Literary Society, minute book no. 3, 1895–1913. The most common form of family-based membership was when a husband and wife were elected to the society, but there were numerous cases involving membership by a father, mother, and daughter.

138 LRO, 708 BOW/1, Museum of Japanese Art, General Committee, 10 January 1891.

139 BRL, Birkenhead Ruskin Society, Session 1881–2, Report of the Committee; LRO, 060 ITA, Italian Literary Society, *Comitato*, 1908–1909.

140 Davidoff and Hall, *Family Fortunes*, p. 429; Gleadle, *British Women*, p. 63.

141 LRO, 364 FEM 1, Liverpool Female Penitentiary, 1809–1921, Laws and Regulations, clause 14. The Liverpool institution reflected existing practice at similar institutions in Plymouth, Bristol, and Edinburgh.

142 In 1855, for example, Mrs. King was the treasurer and Mrs. Lister the secretary: see *Gore's Directory for Liverpool and Its Environs* (Liverpool, 1855), p. 124.

143 LRO, H 362 8 MAG, Annual Report of the Liverpool Magdalen Institution, 1905.

144 LRO, H 362 8 MAG, Annual Report of the Liverpool Magdalen Institution, 1905.

145 LRO, 362 SAL 4/1/1 (2), Liverpool Female Orphan Asylum, Annual Report, 1851, pp. 10–12; 179 CRU 13/1, 2nd Annual Report, Liverpool Society for the Protection of Cruelty to Children (Liverpool, 1885), p. 4; MMM, MAL, D/SO/2/1/1, Report of the Liverpool Seamen's Orphan Asylum for the Year Ending 31 December 1872 (Liverpool, 1873); P/CC/SF/1/3, 90th Report of the Seamen's Friend Society Formerly Known as the Seamen and Emigrant's Friend Society and Bethel Union (Liverpool, 1912), pp. 4–5.

146 LRO, 614 HAH 8/2/2, Liverpool Hahnemann Hospital, 52 Annual Report, 1893; 614 PAU 7/2, Report of Saint Paul's Eye and Ear Hospital for the Year Ending 31 August 1892, p. 3.

147 WAS, A/HH/23, Annual Report of the Wirral Hospital and Dispensary for Sick Children, 1903, p. 2; A/HH/2, Birkenhead Borough Hospital, Annual Report for 1912. In the case of the Liverpool Female Penitentiary a mixed committee was in operation by 1909, but women members were in a majority: LRO, 364 FEM 7, 99th Annual Report of the Liverpool Female Penitentiary, p. 5.

148 In the case of the Liverpool Dorcas and Spinning Society, Mrs. Raffles was the treasurer and Mrs. Bulley the secretary. See Henry Smither, *Liverpool: Its Commerce, Statistics and Institutions with a History of the Cotton Trade* (Liverpool, 1825), pp. 281, 283, 287; Alexina Forsyth, 'The Three Liverpool Orphan Asylums, 1840–1865', unpublished BA thesis, Liverpool Institute of Higher Education (1984), p. 3; LRO, 614 PRI 9/1, 6th Annual Report of the Year 1875 of the Home for Incurables, pp. 6, 9. Women from the urban elite demonstrated a 'strong social work function' in other towns and cities, including Norwich: see Barry M. Doyle, 'The Structure of Elite Power in the Early Twentieth-Century City: Norwich, 1900–35', *UH*, 24, 2 (1997), p. 192.

149 LRO, 614, PRI 1/1, General Committee Minute Book, 29.08.1877–27.12.1882.

150 LRO, 362 HOU 3/1–25, 12th Annual Report of the Liverpool Rescue Society and House of Help, p. 3.

151 LRO, 361 SOU 1/1, Liverpool Council of Social Service, local news cuttings, *Liverpool Daily Post*, 20 July 1910; *Liverpool News*, 21 October 1910; *Liverpool Courier*, 2 November 1910. The National Vigilance Society was established to prevent 'the traffic in young girl life'; *Liverpool Daily Post*, 1 December 1910; *Liverpool Courier*, 7 December 1910.

152 WAS, A/HH/273, Annual Reports of the Leasowe Hospital, 1917–1947.

153 Draznin, *Victorian London's Middle-Class*, p. 173; Robert J. Morris, 'Clubs, Societies and Associations', in F. M. L. Thompson (ed.), *The Cambridge Social History of Britain 1750–1950* (Cambridge, 1996), vol. 3, p. 430; Alan Bott and Irene Clephane (eds.), *Our Mothers: A Cavalcade in Pictures, Quotation and Description of Late Victorian Women, 1870–1900* (London, 1932); Vicinus, *Independent Women*, p. 212. The estimated total for Britain was 20,000.

154 LRO, WA, A/HH/23, Wirral Hospital and Dispensary for Sick Children, Annual Report for the Year 1892, pp. 46–7.

155 LRO, 364 FEM, 6, Liverpool Female Penitentiary, 95th Annual Report, 1905, p. 5. The Honorary Treasurer in 1905 was Mrs. Clara O'Brien.

156 SKA, Gustaf Adolfs Kyrka, Liverpool, Brev korrespondens 1898. Eight other societies were represented on the Traveller's Aid Society, including the Girls' Friendly Society (Miss Mitchell), the Ladies' Association for the Care and Protection of Young Women (Miss Grayson), the Brombro House YWCA (Mrs. Falloon), the House of Help (Miss Deakin), the Railway Mission (Mrs. Margaret Brown), the Home for Welsh Servants (Miss A. Williams), and the Jewish Association for the Protection of Girls and Women (Mrs. E. W. Yates).

157 MMM, MAL, D/SO/2/1/3, Liverpool Seamen's Orphan Institution, Annual Report, 1878, p. 73; LRO, 614 INF 5/14, Annual Report of the Liverpool Royal Infirmary, 1878; *The Times*, 24 March 1902, p. 9; LRO, 614 INF 5/27, Liverpool Royal Infirmary 164th Report, 1912, p. 11; MMM, MAL, D/SO/1/1/6, Liverpool Seamen's Orphan Asylum, Committee Minute Book, 28 October 1912; WAS, A/HH/23, 39th Annual Report of the Wirral Hospital and Dispensary for Sick Children, p. 6; LRO, 614 PRI 9/3, Home for Incurables, Annual Report 1902, p. 45.

158 LRO, 614 INF, 134th Annual Report of the Liverpool Royal Infirmary (Liverpool, 1882), List of Contributions promised to the Fund for Re-building the Royal Infirmary; 920 MEL 23, George Melly, Private Correspondence, vol. 17, no. 4530, letter from Jane Ellen Yates, 31 December 1872. Charles Turner had been chairman of the Dock Committee in the 1850s and became a Mmember of Parliament.

159 LRO, 614 PRI 9/1–12, Home for Incurables, 13th Annual Report, 1882; 23rd Annual Report, 1892.

160 LRO, 362 SAL 4/1/1 (2), Liverpool Female Orphan Asylum, Annual Report 1850, p. 7; 614 PRI 9/1–12, Annual Reports for the Home for Incurables, 1892, 1897, 1912; 614 CHI 1/2/26, Annual Report of the Liverpool Infirmary for Children for 1908 (Liverpool, 1909), p. 7; LRO, 614 CHI 1/2/4, Liverpool Infirmary for Children, Annual Report, 1862, p. 36; WAS, A/HH/23, Wirral Hospital and Dispensary for Sick Children, 34th Annual Report, 1903, p. 52. Mrs. Gale was the wife of the hide merchant John Christopher Gale of Aigburth Lodge, and Anna Holt was the wife of the steamship owner Phillip Holt.

161 LRO, 285, TRI 9/5, Trinity Presbyterian Church of England, Annual Report for 1892, pp. 8–9; WAS, YSF/25/1, Joyce Whittington, 'The History of Birkenhead Friends' Meeting', Pt. I, 1847–1892, p. 6. In general, the wives of the well-to-do were often active in philanthropic work and domestic visiting: see Gunn, *The Public Culture of the Victorian Middle Class*, p. 125.

162 LRO, 361 COU 1/1, Liverpool Council of Social Service, Local News-Cuttings, *Liverpool Courier*, 23 November 1910; 266 DOM 4/2, Liverpool Domestic Mission Society, Annual Reports 1854–1862; H 288 06 UNI, Annual Report of the Unitarian Institute, 1891.

163 LRO, DUR 4/28/1, Personal Account Book of Anne Holt 1858–1869 containing references to her subscriptions to charities for the period 1860 to 1863.

164 LRO, 920 DUR 1/4, Holt Family Diary, 1861–1862. See, for example, 29 December 1861 and 1 February 1862. Liverpool was divided into 18 separate districts. See A Member of the Committee of the Home and Training School, *Organisation of Nursing: An Account of the Liverpool Nurses' Training School, Its Foundation, Progress, and Operation in Hospital, District and Private Nursing* (Liverpool and London, 1865), p. 20.

165 Susan Pedersen, *Eleanor Rathbone and the Politics of Conscience* (Liverpool, 2004), p. 60. In 1909 Eleanor Rathbone (1872–1946) became the first woman elected to Liverpool City Council: she was elected an independent MP in 1929.

166 LRO, SAL 4/1/1 (2), Report of the Liverpool Female Orphan Asylum with the Statement of Account (Liverpool 1851), p. 5; PRI/1/1, Princess Park Hospital, General Committee Book, 29.08.1877–27.12.1882; HOU 3/1–3/25, 12th Annual Report of the Liverpool Rescue Society and House of Help (Liverpool 1902), p. 3.

167 See Sari Mäenpää, Chapter 6.

168 LRO, 362 HOU 3/1, 1st Annual Report of the Liverpool Rescue Society and House of Help, 1891; 614 PRI 1/1, Princess Park Hospital, General Committee Book, 29 August 1877; 920 DUR 4/30/5, Letter from Anne Holt to Robert Holt, 14 March 1881; The Liverpool Merchant Guild, The Charter of Incorporation, 08.04.1914. In 1861, Emma Holt had also voiced a preference for supporting 'cases of distress' particularly in the case of those 'who had been brought up in affluence, or at all events comforts, and fall into poverty in old age', rather than the 'pet scheme' put forward by William Rathbone for improving the supply of nurses: see LRO, 920 DUR 1.4, Holt family diary maintained by Emma Holt, later Anne Holt, 29 October 1861.

169 LRO, 50th Annual Report of the Liverpool Hahnemann Hospital and Home Dispensary (Liverpool, 1892). For an insight into Tate's business operations in Liverpool, see J. A. Watson, *A Hundred Years of Sugar Refining: The Story of the Love Lane Refinery 1872–1972* (Liverpool, 1973); see Robert Lee, Chapter 11.

170 LRO, 614, LHI 1/2/8, Thirty-First Annual Report of the Liverpool Infirmary for Children (Liverpool, 1882); MLP database.

171 LRO, 362 SAL 4/1/1(2), Report of the Liverpool Female Orphan Asylum with the Statement of Account (Liverpool, 1851), p. 5.

172 MLP database; see Robert Lee, Chapter 10, and Randolph Cock, John Davies, Robert Lee, and Sari Mäenpää, Chapter 2.

173 BRL, BC I, 189, Annual Report and Balance Sheet of the Birkenhead Women's Local Government Association 1909–10; see Robert Lee, Chapter 10, and Chapters 2 (Randolph Cock, John Davies, Robert Lee, and Sari Mäenpää) and 6 (Sari Mäenpää). The objective of the Association was to secure the election of 'suitable women' on local government bodies. The suffragette movement also implied a rejection of the traditional role of women as 'auxiliaries' for local charities, in favour of direct involvement in the political process. Mrs. Edith Bright was described in 1895 as one of the 'coming women' of Liverpool: she was 'an ardent women suffragist' and co-founder of the Liverpool Suffrage Society: see Tooley, *Ladies of Liverpool Magazine*, p. 169.

174 LRO, 920 MEL 5, Melly Correspondence 1857–1859, letter from J. W. Cropper, no. 419 (November 1859); letter to his wife, no. 438 (3 November 1859).

175 MMM, MAL, D/SO/7/1/45, Correspondence relating to the resignation of the Chairman, R. G. Allan and his wife; letter from William R. Forward (8 April 1903) citing information contained in Mrs. Allan's letter of 22 March 1903. Mrs. Bright, for her part, was 'deeply hurt' by a note from Mr. and Mrs. Cunningham which implied that she had acted 'in an underhand way'.

176 LRO, FEM 364/2, 95th Annual Report of the Liverpool Female Penitentiary 67 Falkner Street from January to December 1905 (Liverpool, 1906), p. 6; 614 PRI 9/1–12, Annual Report for the Home for Incurables, 1912 (Liverpool, 1913). Miss Schintz was the daughter of the general merchant H. G. Schintz who was a naturalised British subject who had been born in Switzerland.

177 LRO, 312 Liverpool House of Help, 3/2, 2nd Annual Report of the Liverpool Rescue Society and House of Help, 1892 (Liverpool, 1892), p. 10; WAS, A/HH/23, 36th Annual Report, Wirral Hospital and Dispensary for Sick Children (Birkenhead, 1905), p. 13. Miss Hind was the daughter of the merchant H. W. Hind, while Mrs. Martha Ravenscroft was married to a prominent cotton broker.

178 Tosh, *A Man's Place*, pp. 3–4.

179 Conybeare, *Dingle Bank*, p. 7; LRO, 920 DUR 1.2, Family Diary maintained by George Holt, 10 October 1852; MEL 40, *Memoirs of Charles P. Melly* (published privately, 1889), p. 130.

180 Hilbre Island Club minutes, 1881–1931 (in possession of Bryan Smith, the Wirral, whom the authors wish to thank for many useful references). Such 'bohemian' clubs also promoted excessively stylised behaviour and a self-conscious aestheticism: see Gunn, *The Public Culture of the Victorian Middle Class*, p. 97.

181 J. A. Picton, *Memorials of Liverpool Historical and Topographical*, vol. 2: *Topographical* (London, 1873, p. 238. The Wellington Rooms had been established by public subscription as a fashionable meeting place for the 'dance-loving' members of Liverpool's elite; LRO, 920 MD 283. The shipowner Henry Threlfall Wilson, for example, regularly reported in his diary that he was 'at home today' (10 January 1868; 10 March 1868, etc.).

182 LRO, 920 DUR 1/2, Family Diary maintained by George Holt, 14 January 1851. The production was held in the Rathbone home at Greenbank, and featured Alfred, Philip, and Robert Holt, Miss Booth, and other friends from Unitarian families; George Melly, Stray Leaves, 1893–94, vol. 7. The obituary for George Melly in the Liverpool Courier (28 September 1894) described him as 'a power in the ranks of Liverpool liberalism'. In 1857, he and his brother-in-law, George Holt, ('both of them young newly-married men') established a private reformatory for young boys 'just beginning a career or crime': see *The Inquirer*, November 1894.

183 MMM, MAL, DX/641/6/1, Chronological Calendar of Events Connected with the Family of 'McQuie', 19 August 1853; B/EWT/F34, typewritten history of the firm E. W. Turner, p. 58.

184 LRO, 920 DUR 4/26/2, Personal Diaries of Anne Holt, 7 July 1853.

185 LRO, 920 DUR 1/2, Family Diary maintained by George Holt, 29 August 1845; 920 MD147, Todd Naylor Papers, 3 December 1835. Jeremiah Todd also provided advice just in case his son was unable to avoid intercourse with other types of women: 'If your health is affected by any cause, lose not a moment in applying for the best professional advice', because 'many good constitutions have been ruined through neglect of what were considered slight causes'.

186 MMM, MAL, DX/258/2/1/1–88, Copies of letters written by Macgregor Laird to his wife Eleanor Hester Laird, 1848–1860, October 1848.

187 LRO, 920 DUR 1/4, Holt Family Diary, 19 July 1862.

188 LRO, 920 DUR 1/2, Family Diary maintained by George Holt, 6 January 1851. For details of charitable endowments motivated by the loss of children, see Robert Lee, Chapter 12.

189 LRO, 920 MD 283/4, Henry Threlfall Wilson, Personal Accounts, 1868; 920 DUR 4/9/1–33, letter from Robert Durning Holt to his sister Anne, nd.

190 LRO, 920 DUR 4/9/1–33, letter from Anne Holt to Robert Durning Holt, nd.

191 For a wider discussion of this issue, see Anna Clark, *Women's Silence, Men's Violence: Sexual Assault in England 1770–1845* (London, 1987); Shani D'Cruze, 'Approaching the History of Rape and Sexual Violence: Notes towards Research', *Women's History Review*, 1, 3 (1993), pp. 377–97; D. J. V. Jones, *Crime in Nineteenth-Century Wales* (Cardiff, 1992), p. 159; Jill Barber, '"Stolen Goods": The Sexual Harassment of Female Servants in West Wales during the Nineteenth Century', *Rural History*, 4, 2 (1993), pp. 123–36; Selina Todd, 'Domestic Service and Class Relations in Britain, 1900–1950', *Past & Present*, 203, 1 (2009), pp. 181–204; Edward J. Higgs, *Domestic Servants and Householders in Rochdale, 1851–1871* (London, 2016); Victoria McIntyre, '"A Sad Tale of Domestic Life": Identifying "Separate Spheres" in Violent Crime by and against Domestic Servants in Dundee, ca. 1860–1910', unpublished MA thesis, Utrecht University (2017).

192 LRO, 920 STI, Staniforth Family; MMM, MAL, DX/504/1/5, Papers relating to J. Bruce Ismay's House, Sandheys, Mossley Hill Road, Documents and newspaper clippings re the assessment of rates at Sandheys, 1910. See Chapters 8 (Joseph Sharples), 9 (Joseph Sharples and Adrian Jarvis), and 11 (Robert Lee).

193 Edward Kemp, *How to Lay Out a Small Garden* (London, 1850). Kemp, as the superintendent for Birkenhead Park, undertook commissions for local members of the merchant community, including William Laird. See WAS, B/017/3, BICR&IC, 28.07.1847, when he agreed to a proposal to reduce his salary, 'provided he be permitted to practice his profession in the neighbourhood'. The establishment of Liverpool's first Botanic Gardens in 1802 had provided an opportunity for subscribers to cultivate a better knowledge of plants, while later decades witnessed the development of middle-class groups concerned with gardening and horticulture. See Katy Layton-Jones and Robert Lee, *Places of Health and Amusement: A History of Liverpool's Parks and Open Spaces* (London, 2008), p. 14; Robert J. Morris, *Class, Sect and Party: The Making of the British Middle Class, Leeds 1820–1850* (Manchester, 1990), p. 182. On Kemp, see Robert Lee (ed.), *Edward Kemp (1817–91): Landscape Gardener* (*Garden History* 46: Suppl. 1, 2018). For a discussion of Kemp's private commissions for members of the mercantile community, see also Robert Lee, Chapter 11.

194 Boyce, 'Network Knowledge and Network Routines', pp. 52–76; Pat Hudson and W. R. Lee, 'Women's Work and the Family Economy in Historical Perspective', in idem (eds.), *Women's Work and the Family Economy in Historical Perspective* (Manchester, 1990), p. 22; Richard Trainor, 'The Middle Class', in Martin Daunton (ed.), *The Cambridge Urban History of Britain* (Cambridge, 2002), vol. 3, p. 696.

195 Boyce, *Information, Mediation and Institutional Development*, p. 39.

196 Jon Stobart, 'Personal and Commercial Networks in an English Port: Chester in the Early Eighteenth Century', *Journal of Historical Geography*, 30 (2004), pp. 277–93.

197 See Adrian Jarvis and Joseph Sharples, Chapter 9, and Robert Lee, Chapter 10.

8 'The Mark of Opulence, Taste and Skill'

Liverpool Merchants' Houses, c.1750-c.1900

Joseph Sharples

Introduction

When John W. Forney sailed up the Mersey in 1867, newly arrived from America, what first caught his attention were the merchants' houses facing the river: 'The villas of the gentry at New Brighton, one of the suburbs of Liverpool, gave me the first realisation of the residences of the English millionaires. Everything bore the mark of opulence, taste and skill'.[1] Individually, they signalled the status of their occupiers; collectively, they embodied the wealth of a great mercantile metropolis, even of a nation. It had not always been so. For much of the eighteenth century, Liverpool merchants' dwellings were combined with their offices and warehouses in the congested town centre. Here, functionality mattered more than architectural display. Towards the end of the century, new, regularly planned residential streets were laid out to the east of the old centre, and the traditional connection between workplace and dwelling was gradually abandoned. It was not until the 1840s, however, when the rapid expansion of the suburbs began, that merchants' houses started to assume the size and splendour that attracted Forney's admiration. Private comfort and luxury were only part of their purpose: they were also crucial indicators of social and commercial status. Used for business-related entertaining, the Victorian merchant's house could convey to his peers an impression of affluence and reliability, as well as subtler messages concerning taste, pedigree and respectability. Though no longer physically combined with his business premises, a merchant's house was as closely tied to his commercial life as ever.

The Eighteenth Century

The transformation of Liverpool's medieval core into a dedicated business district began as early as the 1780s. It was so comprehensive that nothing now remains of the merchants' dwellings which formerly lined Water Street, Fenwick Street, Old Hall Street and other ancient thoroughfares. The 'new built houses of brick and stone after the London fashion . . . high and even', seen by Celia Fiennes in 1698, have left no trace.[2] At the time of Fiennes's visit, the town was just beginning to expand eastwards, across the tidal inlet known as the Pool, and it was this 'New Leverpool' that Daniel Defoe described enthusiastically in the 1720s: 'They have built more than another Leverpool that way, in new streets, and fine large houses for their merchants'.[3] Here, too, commercial redevelopment has tended to obliterate the elite housing of the eighteenth century, but some traces survive in and around Hanover Street.

The development of this new street followed the opening of the Old Dock in 1715 and it became the favoured location for the largest merchants' houses. On John Chadwick's map of 1725 it is shown already partly built up, unnamed, but labelled 'To Manchester'. It had three special attractions: proximity to the Dock and direct communication with the hinterland; the

DOI: 10.4324/9781315597836-8

opportunity for self-advertisement on a busy thoroughfare; and, for residents on the south side especially, the possibility of large gardens. Although little of its early architecture survives, documentary evidence supports Picton's view that 'by the middle of the eighteenth century [Hanover Street] had become the habitat of the mercantile aristocracy of the day'.[4] The most ostentatious house was built around 1740 by Thomas Steers for the slave trader and tobacco merchant Thomas Seel, and it stood at the corner of what would later become Seel Street.[5] Stone fronted with giant Corinthian pilasters between its windows, there is no evidence of any earlier private house in the town approaching it in pretension. Next to Seel's house on the east, the Cheshire architect William Baker designed a handsome pair of houses for James Pardoe and Potter Fletcher in 1748, while to the west of it, in 1760–61, Arthur Heywood and his brother Benjamin built another pair.[6] These were all demolished following the Second World War, but on the opposite side, the refaced shell of John Colquitt's house at the corner of Peter's Lane stood until 2006, and at the corners of Wood Street and Fleet Street two much-altered houses remain, very probably of the same era.

From at least the third quarter of the eighteenth century, when the evidence of trade directories, newspapers and large-scale maps first becomes available, it is clear these grand houses were combined with their occupiers' business premises. Almost certainly this had always been the case. By 1753, Edward Forbes was operating his insurance business from his residence in Hanover Street; and when the premises of his neighbour, the merchant Thomas Hodgson, were put up for sale in 1775, they consisted of a 'Dwelling House, with Counting House, Warehouse & Stable, &c'.[7] The matching houses of the Heywood brothers formed part of an extensive complex and when Benjamin's was offered for sale in 1799, it was described as having 'two large Warehouses and Counting-house, Stables, and large Yard behind . . . affording particular convenience and security to any merchant or tradesman of extensive dealings'.[8] An 1810 survey of one of the Hanover Street houses designed by William Baker shows a range of offices extending as a wing at the rear, with a warehouse block attached, and comparison with Perry's 1769 map shows that this was probably the original plan.[9]

Alterations have made the two surviving eighteenth-century houses in Hanover Street difficult to interpret, and changes in street numbering make it hard to relate information from the earlier trade directories (pre-1840) to the buildings themselves. Nevertheless, these houses appear to show the same combination of commercial and residential uses indicated by the documentary sources. Number 62 at the corner of Fleet Street (now the Hanover Hotel) was from about 1781 occupied by the merchants T. & W. Earle. It was offered for sale in 1799, when it was described as a 'large and commodious DWELLING HOUSE, with extensive Counting-houses, Stable for five Horses, and a Coach house, together with a Warehouse measuring within the walls 14 yards by 9'.[10] The building today has a pair of long rear wings, which no doubt contained office accommodation, and a two-storey pedimented building overlooking the inner court, which was probably the stable. The warehouse in Fleet Street survives too, or it may be a later rebuild occupying the original footprint. The second surviving house is number 2 Wood Street, although its main façade looks onto Hanover Street. It is linked to two smaller, non-residential buildings, which extend along Wood Street as far as Roe Alley. By 1807 the house was occupied by the attorney George Rowe, whose office was next door, perhaps in one of these adjoining buildings.[11] Comparable to 2 Wood Street and 62 Hanover Street was the recently demolished Colquitt house, which had an attached warehouse at the rear, with a loading bay in Peter's Lane (Figure 8.1).

Beyond Hanover Street, high-class eighteenth-century Liverpool houses could contain commercial and residential space for more than one occupier. A 'new built house' in Water Street, next to the Exchange, was advertised for sale in 1794 by the assignees of the merchants Arnold

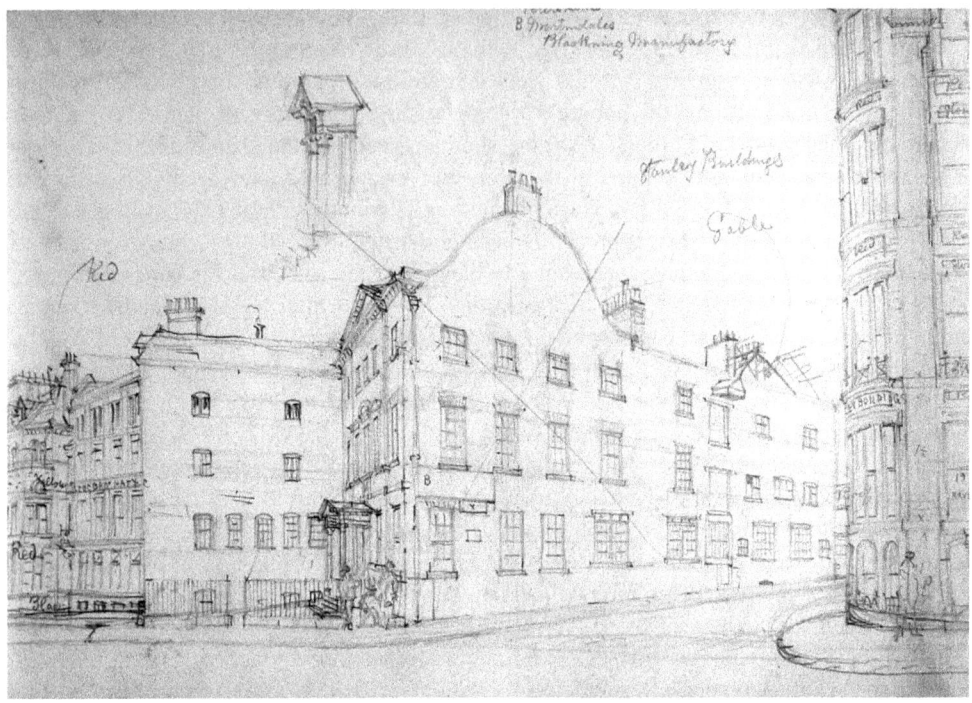

Figure 8.1 Drawing of John Colquitt's eighteenth-century house and warehouse (with permission of the Liverpool Record Office)

Meyer and Henry Wilckens, following their bankruptcy.[12] On the ground floor was a shop occupied by a sitting tenant, and a 'double office . . . very suitable for a Broker or merchant' available to rent, while above were three floors of living space. According to James Wallace, Liverpool merchants' houses were regularly provided with 'large and extensive cellaring' which was designed 'to afford warehouse room for merchandise'.[13] A combined warehouse, counting house and dwelling house in New John Street had 'two Cellars under the Warehouse and Dwelling-house, capable of containing upwards of 90 puncheons of rum, exclusive of other Cellars and Vaults sufficient for the use of the house'.[14] Such cellars might be used for warehousing goods quite independently of the dwelling above: a 'modern and elegantly finished' house in Upper Duke Street was advertised to let in 1775, 'with or without a fine set of vaults, which run part under the said premises . . . and would be completely suitable for a wine merchant'.[15] The desire of Liverpool property-owners to profit from every cubic foot of underground space would continue, and it helped shape the design of speculative office buildings throughout the nineteenth century.

A possible survival of this type of accommodation is the substantial terraced house at 14 Colquitt Street, in existence by 1796 when it was leased by the merchant Gilbert Henderson.[16] In an 1806 codicil to his will, Henderson referred to it as the 'Dwellinghouse and *premises* in Colquitt Street wherein I dwell' (my italics).[17] The rear wing (known as an outrigger in Liverpool) has been altered, but the fenestration of the corresponding wing of the neighbouring house, which has broad windows that seem to be original, suggests these outriggers may have contained office accommodation. At Henderson's house, the first floor of the outrigger is reached directly from the unusually imposing elliptical stone staircase that serves the living quarters. So, if the rear wing did contain his business premises, they must have been fully integrated into his home. Such interconnectedness of residential and commercial accommodation may not have been unusual: a 1775 advertisement for a house to let in Park Lane, with associated counting house, warehouse and stable, noted that 'these premises are very convenient for a merchant, as there is a communication between the house and every other part of them'; and according to an anonymous reminiscence of the years around 1800, published 60 years later in the *Liverpool Mercury*, lawyers and merchants 'could step from their breakfast parlours into their counting houses without going into the street'.[18] Number 14 Colquitt Street also has spacious cellars. How they were originally used is unclear, but they would have been suitable for the sort of commercial storage recorded in New John Street and Upper Duke Street.

In Hanover Street, detached and semi-detached houses of disparate design predominated, asserting the individual identity of owner or occupier. This contrasts with nearby Williamson Square and Clayton Square, where houses were built in terraces. The few that survive in Williamson Square—in existence by 1769—are extremely simple in design. On the other hand, in Clayton Square (now demolished) the houses were combined in unified compositions with pedimented centres. Modest enough in comparison with the pioneering Queen Square in Bath, of 1728–36, Clayton Square was nevertheless an important achievement on the part of its ambitious developer, the colliery owner Sarah Clayton, and when James Wallace reviewed Liverpool's 'best streets' in 1795, he noted that 'none but Clayton-square exhibits an architectural uniformity'.[19] Yet here too, warehousing was built in direct connection with high-class dwellings. To encourage the take up of plots, Mrs. Clayton acquired additional land in 1766 and laid out back streets which would be 'convenient for warehouses to the houses in the square'.[20] Richard Horwood's map of 1803, which helpfully uses different patterns of shading to distinguish between residential and commercial buildings, shows that some of the larger Clayton Square houses were indeed provided with what were almost certainly warehouses at the rear.

Big, detached houses with extensive gardens (such as Thomas Seel's in Hanover Street) were only possible on the very fringes of the built-up area, and as denser terraced housing spread from the centre in the course of the eighteenth century, suitable sites were pushed further out. In 1768, Richard Kent built a five-bay detached house with a frontage of 94 feet at the top of Duke Street, between Kent Street and Cornwallis Street. Following his death in 1790, it was occupied by the West India merchant Moses Benson and described as a 'noble palace mansion'.[21] It had 'a spacious vestibule, a capital staircase, drawing room, eating room, parlours, servants hall, kitchens,' as well as 'fourteen bed rooms, exclusive of dressing rooms and servants' apartments'; it also had 'large and convenient compting-houses to the front of Kent-street'.[22] As late as 1797–99, the iron merchant and slave trader Thomas Parr built a similarly ambitious house in nearby Colquitt Street. As in a Palladian country house, the central residential block is flanked by lower service wings, one of which was Parr's counting house, with his five-storey pedimented warehouse directly behind. It is by far the most impressive surviving example of the combined dwelling and business premises of an eighteenth-century Liverpool merchant and was described by Picton as 'one of the best examples extant of the establishment of a first-class Liverpool merchant of the period'.[23] But in size and architectural quality, houses such as Parr's and Kent's were always exceptional. Both had large gardens—Kent's behind the house, Parr's on the opposite side of Colquitt Street—but both were emphatically urban, built right up to the street, and not suburban retreats absorbed by the expanding town.

Evidence for the interior fixtures and fittings of eighteenth-century elite houses close to the Old Dock is extremely scanty. Of the few that remain, adaptation to commercial uses has obscured their internal plans and obliterated their decoration. More evidence of their polite origins was visible in the early twentieth century, when Charles Reilly visited some of the once-grand Duke Street houses that had been reduced to warehouses and described, for instance, 'a magnificent dining-room with enriched coved ceiling and a fine apse at one end' at number 78.[24] Interior details of this former house, then known as York Buildings, were drawn by Harold Chalton Bradshaw in 1911.[25] They include Neoclassical woodwork and plasterwork, and an Adam-style chimneypiece with figures of dancing maidens. Such features may have been typical—Arthur Heywood's accounts for the now-demolished house he built in Hanover Street in 1760–1 include sums of £39 1s 2d for 'Chimney pieces &c' and £29 18s 10d for 'stuco work'—but the few examples of plasterwork and woodwork that survive elsewhere are comparatively simple.[26] Is the rather crude staircase ceiling at 139 Dale Street, the c.1788 house of the distiller John Houghton, representative of contemporary Liverpool design and workmanship? Or is a more typical work the fine chimneypiece and overmantel from Finch House, the West Derby mansion built by the Gildart family of merchants c.1775, which is now installed at Knowsley Hall?[27]

Finch House survived into the early twentieth century before it was demolished and its fittings removed. In the constantly evolving commercial core of Liverpool, however, the process of stripping out such houses as they sank to humbler uses had begun a century before. In 1826, John Soane surveyed Thomas Seel's former house in Hanover Street, noting that although 'originally of a substantial and ornamental description', it was 'now generally in a dilapidated state'. Inside, wrote Soane, 'the joiners' work, with the exception of that of the staircase, is of a common description and of a heavy character, as are likewise the ceilings of the principal apartments. . . . The several rooms having of late been let out for offices and various other uses, some have undergone considerable alteration'.[28] A source of 1900 says that residents moving from the old centre to the suburbs took their valuable mahogany doors with them, and there is some contemporary evidence that this was so: when Gilbert Henderson drew up a new will in 1841, a house he owned in Duke Street was being used as a barracks, and he recorded that its mahogany doors had been removed and put into storage.[29] In the early twentieth century, the internal doors from St Domingo House, Everton, were moved to St Edward's College, Sandfield Park, where they survive to show the high quality of materials and joinery in one of the very best Liverpool houses of the late eighteenth century.

Contemporary accounts offer only the most fleeting glimpses inside the houses of Duke Street when it was still 'the favourite residence of the higher class of merchants'.[30] It was presumably in a house of suitable scale that the mayor, Henry Clay, received the Prince of Wales and the Duke of Clarence during their visit to Knowsley in 1806, when he served them 'a most elegant cold collation' in his residence at the upper end of the street.[31] When John Dalton called on Mrs. Anna Case at 149 Duke Street in 1797, he described her as living 'in high style', and owning a 'grand pianoforte' that had cost 70 guineas.[32] She was the widow of the West India merchant and Jamaican plantation owner Thomas Case.[33] Her house was re-fronted and transformed into a warehouse in the early twentieth century, but it probably resembled the neighbouring numbers 151–155 which survive, five bays wide and three storeys high. By the time John James Audubon visited Richard Rathbone's house in 1826, Duke Street was already in decline, but in describing the first-floor 'setting room', the ground-floor dining room and the walls hung with paintings, Audubon gives a hint of the street in its heyday.[34]

No doubt widespread demolition has left us with a very incomplete knowledge of Liverpool's eighteenth-century domestic architecture, and in the historic centre it may be that a disproportionate number of the better houses have been lost. However, we should not be surprised by the generally unsophisticated character of what survives. Liverpool was a town which had grown from obscurity in a relatively short time and it had neither an indigenous architectural tradition nor a well-established visual culture. Matthew Gregson, writing in 1791 about Liverpool architecture before the middle of the century, detected 'no great Signs of Genius Vysible', and summed up the houses of the period as 'sparingly finished, convenient but not costly'.[35] James Wallace echoed this, describing Liverpool merchants' dwellings as 'built under their own direction and designed more for internal convenience than external elegance'.[36]

There is a sense already in the eighteenth century that for many of its mercantile elite, Liverpool was a place of temporary residence. They endured its noise and dirt while making their fortunes, before withdrawing to a villa on the outskirts or a country house in Cheshire or Shropshire, and they may have taken the view that architectural refinement could wait until retirement.[37] Sarah Clayton's building exploits in the 1750s and 60s, and the laying out of Rodney Street by William Roscoe and others in 1783–84, described in the following, are isolated examples of the pursuit of a rational, ordered urban architecture, which took place against a general background of piecemeal, uncoordinated growth. The only eighteenth-century Liverpool merchant known to have employed an architect of national reputation on his private house is Nicholas Ashton, for whom Robert Adam remodelled Woolton Hall in the 1770s.[38] For major public works, the corporation brought in the talents of outsiders such as John Wood and James Wyatt. Its lack of confidence in local ability is suggested by the fact that, following the Improvement Act of 1786, the surveyor John Foster Senior was ordered to write to the London architect Thomas Whetton 'for different Ground Plans of houses for the inspection of any persons who may purchase ground for the intended improvements'.[39] In *Bailey's Liverpool Directory* for 1787 only two architects, William Everard and John Hope, are named as such.

Separating Home and Work: The Residential House, 1780–1840

The crucial shift in the function of a Liverpool merchant's house—the separation of dwelling from business premises—began at least as early as the 1780s. The case of (Sir) George Dunbar, described in chapter five, clearly illustrates the change.[40] In 1787 he was living in 'Dale Street, near the Exchange'. In 1788–89, when the Corporation finished building a block of speculative offices nearby called Exchange Alley, Dunbar became one of its first tenants; and at exactly the same time he built himself a splendid new house with a large garden on the edge of town, now number 68 Mount Pleasant. A carving of cherubs with a globe and compasses over the door alludes to his mercantile calling, but there is no attached warehouse and no counting house. Number 68 Mount Pleasant was unequivocally Dunbar's residence, just as his business address was in Exchange Alley.

Rodney Street laid out a few years earlier, but built up slowly over the next 35 years, embodies this new distinction between domestic and business life. Restrictive covenants prevented lessees from building business premises in connection with their houses,[41] and instead of yards for the loading and unloading of merchandise, they had gardens at the rear. Among those who moved here from the historic centre was the merchant John Gladstone.[42] On arrival in Liverpool in 1787, he had lived close to his firm's counting house in George's Dock Gates. Later he moved to Bold Street, which was at that date a residential street with counting houses in parallel Wood Street. Then, in 1792, he married, and began building himself a grand house in Rodney Street, now number 62. Thomas Booth, Gladstone's principal rival in the corn trade, was another early resident. An in-migrant from Cheshire in the 1760s, he lived first in Clayton Square, then King Street, then Union Street, all in the heart of the eighteenth-century town, before building a new residence in Rodney Street around 1789.[43] The provision merchant Peter Leicester moved to Rodney Street from Seel Street a little earlier, while Pudsey Dawson, possibly the first to settle in the new street in 1787, had lived previously in Park Lane, close to the Old Dock. And

Rodney Street was only part of a more general move outwards from the congested centre. The West India merchant Thomas Fletcher, born in Castle Street, finished his apprenticeship in 1789 while living with his mother in Lydia Ann Street, close to the Old Dock. After marrying in 1795, he lived at a succession of addresses in the developing residential fringe, in St. Ann Street, Ranelagh Place, Great George Street, Alfred Street and finally a brand new house in Huskisson Street, before bankruptcy in 1833 banished him to a cottage at Gateacre.[44]

Rodney Street established the pattern for Liverpool's mercantile and professional housing in the first half of the nineteenth century. It is a pattern which came to characterise the whole of the Mosslake Fields area centred on Abercromby Square, which was planned by John Foster Senior in 1800 and built up from 1816 onwards.[45] It also extended further south, beginning with Great George Square in 1800 and finishing with Falkner Square in the 1840s; and further north, where disconnected fragments of this type of housing survive in Clarence Street, Russell Street, Islington, St. Anne Street and Shaw Street.[46] It is a familiar enough pattern: main streets fronted by three-storey terraced houses with semi-basements, of more or less uniform elevation, often with narrow gardens at the back (and in the prestigious squares access to a large communal garden); and secondary service streets at the rear giving access to stables and coach houses. Probably there was more of this type of housing in Liverpool than in any other provincial English town. The 1850 assessment for the window tax, payable on all houses with more than eight windows, offers a rough guide to the extent of middle-class housing in these towns at mid-century. By a very wide margin, Liverpool had the highest number of houses charged (11,342) and the highest amount assessed (£32,461), and it also accounted for the highest net amount received (£28,856). By comparison, Manchester had 3,588 fewer properties liable for the window tax, and the net receipts from both Manchester and Bath were considerably lower than in the case of Liverpool (Table 8.1).[47]

Within this broadly consistent architectural framework, standards of accommodation could vary widely. At one extreme stand the first few palatial houses in Gambier Terrace with their magnificent interiors, which justified its reputation as Liverpool's 'proudest piece of architecture'.[48] However, the consistent Neoclassical façade of this development hides the fact that the houses became smaller as construction progressed, until building stopped altogether in the early 1840s. Development throughout the area took place in a piecemeal way, with intending

Table 8.1 The amount paid in window duty in the 12 largest provincial towns, 1850 (in £)

Town	Amount Assessed	Net Tax Received	%	Houses Assessed	Average per House (£)
Bath	21,893	21,278	97.1	3,722	5.7
Birmingham	16,161	14,986	92.7	3,432	4.3
Brighton	18,025	17,572	97.4	3,613	4.8
Bristol	14,675	13,280	90.4	4,350	3.1
Cheltenham	6,998	6,767	96.6	1,407	4.8
Clifton	9,429	8,896	94.3	1,373	6.4
Leeds	7,978	7,598	95.2	2,479	3.0
Liverpool	32,461	28,856	88.8	11,342	2.5
Manchester	21,925	20,586	93.8	7,754	2.6
Norwich	6,627	6,465	97.5	1,871	3.4
Newcastle on Tyne	8,320	7,822	94.0	2,854	2.7
Plymouth	12,207	11,929	97.7	4,527	2.6

Source: 'Amount of The Liverpool Window Duty etc.', *The Builder*, vol. 8 (1850), p. 189

Figure 8.2 Abercrombie Square (1829). To the Residents Of Which This Plate Is Respectfully Inscribed, drawn by G. & C Pyne, engraved by J. Starling, in S. Austin, J. Harwood and G. & C. Pyne (eds.), Lancashire Illustrated (London, 1829)

occupiers or speculators erecting single houses or short runs. Even prestigious Abercromby Square, with its houses which were 'built after a very elegant style', was only gradually built up, as the vertical joints in the brickwork make clear, and the unified terrace facades designed by John Foster Senior (to which the lessees of individual plots were required to conform) conceal some marked differences (Figure 8.2). Number 10, for instance, has a columned entrance hall, broad staircase, and more generously proportioned rooms than the earlier number 3.[49] In Rodney Street, where there was no such overall governing design, the variety of house types is clear from the outside, ranging from relatively modest houses in the long terrace at numbers 51a-75, to four-and five-bay mansions, although the overall arrangement, according to Reilly, was 'just right'.[50]

Probably representative of the smaller Rodney Street houses is number 59, the early nine-teenth-century internal arrangement of which is known in detail from a set of sketch plans made by a one-time resident, Margaret Caroline Backhouse.[51] The house belonged to her father, Thomas Hazlehurst, a painter of miniatures, but similar houses in the terrace were occupied by merchant families. It had a frontage of seven yards. On the ground floor there was a front parlour overlooking the street, with a dining room behind, and a kitchen and pantry in the projecting wing at the rear. On the first floor, the drawing room was at the front, occupying the full width of the house, with the best bedroom behind, and a small bedroom and sitting room in the rear wing. On the second floor, a nursery equal in size to the drawing room was at the front, containing three children's beds. Behind this was Mrs. Hazlehurst's bedroom, and in the rear wing a small bedroom for Margaret's brother, plus a china closet and a storeroom. There are no sketches of the cellar and attic, which presumably accommodated servants and storage. No bathroom is shown. Although the house had a small garden, this could only be reached by passing through the kitchen yard, from which it was separated by a shrubbery. A closet—presumably an earth closet—was in the yard.

Larger Rodney Street houses offered much more spacious accommodation. The one occupied in 1829 by the general merchant and Netherlands consul Daniel Willink (probably number 31) contained 'on the ground floor, a dining room, 16 feet 9 by 25 feet 8, two parlours, library, butler's pantry, servants' hall, kitchen, store rooms, &c; on the first floor, a drawing room, 16 feet 9 by 25 feet 8, four bed rooms, two dressing rooms, &c; on the second floor, five bedrooms and two dressing rooms; and on the third floor two rooms for servants'.[52] Number 34, on the opposite side, is a slightly smaller five-bay house, apparently built speculatively by Thomas Booth in 1806, and first occupied by the merchant Alexander MacGregor. What were originally the servants' garrets survived until 2004. Unheated and lit by a single, small skylight, they were only high enough to stand upright under the apex of the roof and were reached by a tortuous stair barely wide enough for an adult. By contrast, the living accommodation for the families in residence was generally deemed to be 'in good taste', with interiors characterised by a 'refined, delicate reserve' which applied equally to the plaster cornices, the staircases, handrails and balusters.[53]

Forty years later, towards the end of the development of Mosslake Fields, the broker Richard Rowlinson built himself a house in fashionable Falkner Square. The original drawings of 1845 by William Culshaw survive, as does the house itself, number 29.[54] At 26 feet wide, it was slightly smaller than earlier houses in nearby Canning Street, but it can probably be taken as representative of the better type of terraced house built in the area at this date. Kitchen, laundry, and related service areas occupied the basement. A drawing room and dining room were the main ground floor rooms, with a butler's pantry and 'back sitting room' in the rear wing. On the first floor there was an 'upper drawing room'—18 by 24 feet, plus the depth of the bay window—a retiring room, bedroom and closet, and in the rear wing a nursery with its own scullery. The second floor and attic contained a further seven bedrooms, plus closets; on the second floor there was also a bathroom with a bath tub and shower, and the only WC in the house (although there was also a privy in the back yard). By the time of the 1851 census, this accommodation was occupied by Mr. and Mrs. Rowlinson, their seven children, and three servants, including a governess.

As expectations of domestic comfort rose during the course of the nineteenth century, alterations and additions to these houses reveal what later occupiers saw as their deficiencies.[55] Accommodating a growing family could be a challenge, since by their nature terraced houses with unified facades are not easily enlarged. The end house in a row, however, had scope for a well-lit return elevation to the adjoining street, and in this way number 90 Chatham Street, at the corner of Abercromby Square, was extended in 1862 for the MP and former merchant George Melly, to provide a nursery above a library.[56] The tobacco and general merchant Maxwell Hyslop's house in Canning Street, at the corner of Falkner Square, was similarly enlarged in 1865–66 to provide a nursery, and again in 1874 when the small conservatory was sacrificed for a second kitchen.[57] The hide merchant Isaac Hadwen implemented two phases of improvement at number 3 Huskisson Street, at the corner of Catharine Street. The house had been built in 1839 by the Reverend John Jones. In 1853 the young Hadwen transformed it into what would shortly become a family home. He added a new main staircase with a combined bathroom and WC at the top, a ground-floor cloak-room with WC, a further WC for servants in the basement, a bath within a first-floor dressing room, a wine cellar, and an enclosed porch to the front door; and in 1861 he provided a butler's pantry with a bedroom over.[58] The spacious stairs were

necessary to accommodate changes in female fashion, but also to provide guests with a dignified route between the first-floor drawing room and the ground-floor dining room. As Nathaniel
Hawthorne wrote during his stay in Liverpool as American consul at exactly this time: 'I have
grown woefully aristocratic, in my tastes, I fear, since coming to England; at all events, I am
conscious of a certain disgust at going to dine in a house with a small entrance-hall, and narrow
staircase . . . and all other arrangements on a similar scale'.[59]

But the main shortcoming of houses of this type which had been built in the Rodney
Street-Mosslake Fields area was their lack of privacy, both in front, where passers-by could
see into the ground-floor rooms, and at the rear, where gardens were cramped and overlooked. John Gladstone's Rodney Street residence, now part of a continuous terrace, was
originally a detached house in its own grounds, and so was the villa in nearby Hope Street
occupied c.1801–c.1811 by his partner Edgar Corrie, which today forms part of Blackburne
House. But these were exceptions, and in general the terraced houses in the Mosslake Fields
area lacked the seclusion provided by extensive grounds. A few, such as Blackburne Terrace in the 1820s and Gambier Terrace in the early 1830s, were set back from the pavement
behind a communal carriage drive and shrubbery. Some surviving houses shown on Michael
Alexander Gage's 1836 map—in Bedford Street South and at the south end of Hope Street,
for instance—were provided with individual front gardens, but not until the north and south
sides of Falkner Square were built up in the mid-1840s was this done consistently. Around
this date, however, the rich began a new exodus in search of greener, cleaner, and more
spacious surroundings, well beyond the terraced streets of Mosslake Fields, to what are
still recognised as suburbs today.[60] The lure of the suburbs, rather than a general collapse in
the housing market, was perhaps the main reason for abandoning the construction of Gambier Terrace in the early 1840s. Some high-class terraced housing continued to be built in
the centre—numbers 45–55 Canning Street, for instance, and Alexandra Terrace in Princes
Road, both from the 1850s, and Charles Kuhn Prioleau's very grand house in Abercromby
Square of 1862–63—but these are exceptional. It was not until the 1870s that Gambier Terrace was completed, along with the terraces that line the boulevard between Upper Parliament Street and Princes Park.

Opulent Privacy: Status and Elite Society, 1840–1900

Where and how one lived was a crucial indicator of status and this was of special importance
in a community of merchants, since commercial success depended on persuading clients and
business partners of one's sound financial standing. In the 1881 Liverpool-set morality story,
Winmore & Co.—A Tale of the Great Bank Failure, the merchant Mr. Winmore lived 'in a
large house in a square which was composed solely of large houses—where indeed a house of
even moderate dimensions would have been an intolerable anomaly'.[61] His status was further
buttressed by having equally prosperous neighbours of unimpeachable reputation: 'Most . . .
were men like Mr Winmore—men of substance, men of business—while the rest included three
doctors of lucrative practice, and two solicitors, heads of firms of undoubted respectability and
antiquity'.

Mr. Winmore, whose address sounds very much like Abercromby Square rather than one
of the new, upstart suburbs such as Sefton Park or Blundellsands, 'nourished an intense hatred
to all that could possibly be thought mushroom-like'.[62] The inappropriate flaunting of rapidly
acquired riches was often described as a trait of Liverpool merchants, for instance by Nathaniel
Hawthorne in relation to John Bramley-Moore, a prosperous merchant returned from Brazil.[63]
It was a characteristic represented in fiction, too, and in the moralising of the local Liberal

press: 'Of barbarous wealth their houses are the abode; Their carnal tables Capuan luxuries load . . .' sneered the satirical magazine *Porcupine* in 1867, in a trenchant poem entitled *Nouveaux Riches*, before going on to describe the residence of a representative 'Knight of Cotton':

> His house, in which he's like a stranded fish,
> Has all within—without—that heart could wish,
> That is, a heart that takes a dear delight
> In nice upholsterer's knick-knacks, new and bright,
> And heaps of fripperies, not one year old . . .
> And varnished shams and glitter, paint and gold.[64]

But visible signs of wealth alone were no guarantee of financial reliability, and 'shams and glitter' could serve as a warning that wealth rapidly acquired might be just as rapidly lost. According to the *Porcupine*, hordes of spectators attending sales of the possessions of ruined merchants were not uncommon in the 'Vanity Fair' of mid-Victorian Liverpool.[65] The chemical manufacturer A. G. Kurtz, finding his morning train to St. Helens unusually crowded with sightseers one day, discovered they were going to the auction preview of the contents of Huyton Hall, former home of the bankrupt general merchant and shipowner Frederick Chapple. Newspaper advertisements for the sale (which included marble busts, bronzes, oriental ceramics, and not one, but two 'self-acting organs in rich rosewood and walnut cases of Gothic design . . . purchased in London at a very great cost') did not name Chapple, but they euphemistically described him as 'a gentleman who is changing his residence'.[66]

On the other hand, business failure did not always result in reduced circumstances. Despite bankruptcy in 1878, the cotton broker W. Winter Raffles remained at his fashionable house in Sunnyside, Princes Park, allegedly supported by his wife's independent income.[67] And spectacular commercial success, however fleeting and insubstantial, could be achieved without an outward show of personal wealth: the voracious cotton speculator Morris Ranger managed to dupe his fellow merchants, even though—or possibly because—he lived in a modest house in Catharine Street, 'in a very unpretending manner'.[68] In other words, a merchant's house could be a rather uncertain guide to his financial standing, and, viewed historically, such architectural evidence has to be interpreted in the light of other, documentary, sources.

The fictional Mr. Winmore had been 'established' in his commodious house for ten years, an outward sign of continuity—and therefore reliability—in a society characterised by volatile change. Previously, however, 'although he would on no account have mentioned so degrading a circumstance, he, with his wife and daughter, had occupied a much smaller house in a street in which there were actually grocers' and other "un-genteel" shops, and which besides was very near the centre of the city'; and in due course, after the wreck of his business, he was obliged to remove to a humble cottage.[69] Residential mobility was a marked feature of Liverpool's business elite, mirroring their fluctuating fortunes. Steadily increasing prosperity generally entailed removal from a terraced house near the centre to a detached villa in a respectable suburb, and then, sometimes, to a grander mansion further out. Representative of this pattern are the Thompsons, partners in Messrs. Heywood's bank.[70] Between his marriage in 1801 and his death in 1836, Samuel Thompson progressed from Slater Street to Rodney Street to Abercromby Square. His son, the banker Samuel Henry Thompson, married in 1837 and moved from Abercromby Square to Dingle Cottage, which was not in fact a cottage, but a substantial, detached house near his father-in-law's residence, West Dingle. Ten years later he bought Thingwall Hall at Broad Green, with about 300 acres of parkland, and remained there until his death in 1892, when he left over £1 million (Figure 8.3).[71] The cotton broker Joseph Leather was not so lucky. He made

Figure 8.3 Thingwall Hall, Broad Green (contemporary postcard, c. 1950)

a similar progression from a big, terraced house in Shaw Street in 1851, via a villa in salubrious Fairfield, to a magnificent Gothic Revival mansion, Cleveley, in aristocratic Allerton, designed for him by George Gilbert Scott in the 1860s. But over-speculation in cotton obliged him to move again: by the time of the 1891 census, he was living modestly at 106 Thomas Lane, Broad Green, with his unmarried son and daughter and one servant, and he ended up in a smallish town house in the comparative anonymity of Blackburne Place.[72]

Extensive suburban building in the second half of the nineteenth century, notably around Sefton Park, meant there were ever-increasing opportunities for the well-off to move house whether in search of more generous accommodation, a more attractive location, or more congenial neighbours. In 1841, the cotton broker Michael Belcher was living in Church Street, Everton; between 1843 and 1853 he was at Jordan Villa, Fulwood, Toxteth Park (and at two further addresses in the same area, which may however have been the same house); from 1859 to 1865 he occupied Springcroft, Aigburth Hall Road; by 1867 he had moved to Holmestead, Mossley Hill; by 1879 he was at the Towers, Ullet Road; and in 1881 he retired to Swindon Hall, Cheltenham. This sort of mobility was facilitated by a tendency to rent rather than buy, even among the very wealthy: Belcher died in 1888 with a personal estate worth just under £160,000 and was regarded by some contemporaries as both 'opulent and prosperous'.[73]

In the continual flux and uncertainty of commercial life, established ideas about the meaning of architecture in relation to social status became blurred. After seeing 'palatial' Woolton Hall occupied by the retail draper J. R. Jeffery, Kurtz commented tartly in his diary: 'vy. different to the places J. once inhabited. See the results of—spec!'[74] And some years later, hearing that the St. Helens chemical manufacturer David Gamble had taken on a new secretary, a Mr. Sinclair, he wrote: 'Strange to say he has gone to live at Haresfinch House, once thought a mansion for a JP, now Sinclair as *Sec[retar]y.* lives there'.[75] In the meantime, social change had even over-taken the respectable house in Stanhope Street where Kurtz himself grew up: 'It is now a Gin Palace, the dining room a tap! To such base uses may we come'.[76]

This atmosphere of perpetual and unpredictable change made it desirable to have a pedigree. In a commercial community whose elite were an 'aristocracy . . . not based on blood so much as on bank balances',[77] architectural symbols traditionally associated with the nobility were adopted as badges of respectability. Coats of arms, carved in stone or displayed in stained glass, were often resorted to. Heraldry features prominently at Quarry Bank in Allerton, a Gothic mansion built by the timber merchant James Bland in 1866–7 and designed by Henry Sumners; at Kiln Hey in Sandfield Park, home of the West Africa merchant E. H. Cookson; and at Enmore, the house of the nitrate merchant Richard R. Lockett in Alexandra Drive.[78] Moreover, the style of interior decoration adopted at modern houses such as Kiln Hey and Enmore seems to mimic the appearance of an ancestral country seat, with rooms decorated in different historical styles suggesting a centuries-long evolution.[79]

Among the early nineteenth-century terraces of Mosslake Fields, the prestige attached to certain streets and squares offered one way in which distinctions of status and wealth could be expressed. When Mary Leslie, wife of one of T. H. Ismay's business partners, was house-hunting with Margaret Ismay in 1883, her goal was a move up the social ladder from Falkner Street to Falkner Square, although the first house the two women inspected there had 'nothing to recommend it except situation'.[80] As well as the cachet attached to certain addresses, scale of accommodation and architectural quality mattered too. No one could fail to recognise the superior character of Gambier Terrace, 'a range of mansions . . . amongst the most spacious and elegant in the town'[81]; or the Greek Doric porch added by the architect Edmund Aikin to 29 Rodney Street in 1817, a fashionable and suitably erudite feature for the home of Benjamin Arthur Heywood, banker and president of the Liverpool Royal Institution. Inside such houses there might be differences in the quality of fitting out—mahogany doors here, painted pine there, and Neoclassical plasterwork in different degrees of elaboration—but the generally consistent architectural character of the area was more striking than its variety. According to the critic Samuel Huggins, the houses of Shaw Street were 'as if cast in one mould . . . from end to end facsimiles of each other'[82]; and the same could be said of long stretches of Canning and Huskisson streets.

In the suburbs, on the other hand, gradations in status could be more easily expressed, not only through residential location, but also through the overall size of the house, the provision of rooms for special purposes, the extent and character of gardens and grounds, and—in an age of eclecticism—the choice of architectural style. 'In the 'sixties,' wrote the Liverpool merchant W. B. Forwood, 'people of wealth and position surrounded themselves with certain attributes of power and wealth, which gave to the populace some indication of their rank and their social status. . . . Their homes were in the country or in the fashionable suburbs of the city, and their importance was measured by the extent of their broad acres'.[83] Of course, this expression of status through property and possessions did not begin in the 1860s, but it burgeoned with the growth of Liverpool's trade and the parallel expansion of the suburbs from the middle of the century onwards. In a mercantile society characterised by financial instability, houses were tangible expressions of prosperity. They were used for receiving and entertaining visitors, very often as an adjunct to business life, and while the affluent sought seclusion from the unpleasant aspects of urban life by withdrawing to the suburbs, they also indulged in a conspicuous display of wealth, directed at their peers.[84]

Symbols of Merchant Wealth: Dining Rooms, Galleries, Libraries, and Billiard Rooms

Nowhere was this quasi-public role of the merchant's house clearer than in the dining room. There is much evidence from contemporary diaries, as well as from biographical and literary sources, that the domestic dinner party offered a way for the Liverpool merchant to display his wealth to his business associates. Sophia Hawthorne was awed by the silver that graced William Brown's table in place of ordinary china, and by the liveried servants in Samuel Bright's dining room at Sandheys, while Robert Durning Holt took pleasure in the sumptuous hospitality offered by his neighbour, the general merchant Pandia A. Ralli: 'a most magnificent dinner, fit to set before a king'.[85] Others were less enthusiastic: 'An awful dinner party is hanging over us at the Wm. Holts,' the wife of the shipowner Albert Crompton confided to a friend in 1873; 'How we shall hate it. Their riches and luxury are quite suffocating'.[86] Such displays of wealth were intimately connected with business, since formal dinners were an important means of cultivating and cementing commercial relationships and exchanging information. Albert Crompton, for example, was associated with the Holt family as manager of the Ocean Steamship Company, and Pandia A. Ralli's office was in Fenwick Chambers, which make him a tenant of the Holts. At the very top of the social scale, T. H. Ismay would regularly entertain the directors of the Oceanic Steam Navigation Company on the occasion of their annual meeting at Dawpool.[87]

The days of combined dwellings and counting-houses may have been long gone, but in late nineteenth-century Liverpool the overlap between domestic and commercial life remained strong. Indeed, E. K. Muspratt's description of suburban Seaforth could perhaps have been applied to the city in general: 'The only social functions were formal dinner parties, and most of the people one met had few tastes outside the business in which they were engaged'.[88] The architecture and decoration of dining rooms reflected their importance as indicators of status. Photographs of John Grant Morris's at Allerton Priory, and James Muspratt's at Seaforth House, show how choice pictures and imposing furniture were used to create an atmosphere of opulence, while the dining room of the merchant and shipowner Richard R. Lockett at 34 Alexandra Drive was modelled on that of an Elizabethan manor house in an attempt to appropriate the architectural trappings of the landed gentry in order to dignify the social life of a Liverpool guano importer (Figure 8.4).[89] However, the best surviving example is perhaps Charles K. Prioleau's dining room at 19 Abercromby Square, with its elaborate *trompe l'oeil* painted ceiling incorporating the monograms of family members.

According to B. G. Orchard, few Liverpool dining rooms seated more than 30—'probably not five per cent. of the whole tenanted by men with £2000 a year'.[90] However, dances, musical performances, and other events often brought together much larger gatherings, and in older houses this could lead to overcrowding. For example, A. G. Kurtz attended 'private theatricals' at 41 Rodney Street, where he sweltered with over a hundred others 'crowded into an ordinary drawing room'.[91] Bigger suburban houses, on the other hand, could offer much more spacious accommodation. The Ismays had 160 guests to a ball at Dawpool, while a hundred or so were easily accommodated in R. D. Holt's new drawing room at 54 Ullet Road to hear a piano recital by Charles Halle.[92] Upton Manor, the shipowner William Inman's Italianate mansion on the outskirts of Birkenhead, was extended at some time between 1857 and 1875 with a dining room and a drawing room on the grandest scale, clearly intended for lavish entertaining (Figure 8.5). However, there could still be problems with overheating and poor ventilation: the stockbroker Henry Rensburg had a substantial music room in his house at 2 Grove Park—'a large eccentric place . . . well enough calculated for social purposes', according to Kurtz—but its low ceiling made it uncomfortable.[93]

As well as bigger rooms, such houses could be provided with very generous circulation spaces. Number 7 Beach Lawn, built in 1876 for the childless sugar refiner James Barrow and his wife, must have been designed with large-scale entertaining in mind: the hall with its splendid Gothic fireplace occupies about a quarter of the footprint of the whole house, from which a magnificent cantilevered staircase rises visibly through three storeys, to an allegorically painted ceiling and stained-glass skylight. Mossley House, designed for the general broker Lloyd Rayner by Alfred Waterhouse, has a similarly imposing double-height entrance hall and

Figure 8.4 The dining room at 34 Alexandra Drive, photographed by H. Bedford Lemere (1896)

Figure 8.5 Upton Manor, Upton (Wirral) with two of the housemaids

grand staircase, and when Kurtz inspected it during construction he considered it was 'laid out for parade, not home'.[94] Indeed, a disadvantage of houses designed for entertaining on this scale was that they could appear intimidatingly large for everyday domestic use. Having attended a number of musical soirées at The Towers in Ullet Road, Kurtz returned for a private meeting with the owner, the millionaire shipowner and general merchant James Marke Wood: 'What an "Institution" his house looks in the day time!' he remarked in his diary; 'The corridor—so splendid when lighted up & filled with company—looks a desert by daylight'.[95]

In a satirical article purporting to be an interview with Sir Andrew Barclay Walker, the prosperous brewer and founder of the municipal gallery was reported as saying: 'I am fond of art. I like to have plenty of good pictures that people will talk about'.[96] Picture collecting was certainly an important status symbol among Liverpool's business elite. Large suburban mansions like Walker's Gateacre Grange could accommodate big canvases; 30 were displayed in the hall and on the stairs at Frederick Chapple's Huyton Hall, 'including some of gallery size'; and smaller houses could also be very densely hung.[97] Private owners regularly loaned works to public exhibitions, where their wealth and taste were the subject of comment in the local press, and on important civic occasions they sometimes enjoyed the reflected glory that came from lending pictures to the Town Hall.[98] Other members of the merchant community, including Walter C. Clark (stock and share broker), Alfred Booth (shipowner), and John Rankin (shipowner and merchant), were important donors to the municipal art collection.[99] In fact, a number of highly discriminating British art collectors and patrons of the late nineteenth century were Liverpool merchants: George Holt was an active purchaser of contemporary British paintings in the 1870s and 1880s which were added to the existing collection of oils and watercolours by Landseer, Bonnington, Constable, and Turner; Philip Rathbone had considerable contacts with the London art market, contributed to contemporary debates about the future of art, and dominated the Liverpool Autumn Exhibitions and the Walker Art Gallery where they were held; the shipowner Frederick Richards Leyland was an important patron of D. G. Rossetti and J. M. Whistler; while the cotton broker Benson Rathbone was 'almost bohemian by nature, and was quite at home in the artist world'. Indeed, Frederic Leighton's *Psamathe* (1879–80) was painted 'for an old and much valued friend B. Rathbone'.[100] The art collection of the copper merchant John Bibby included nine Rossettis and other Pre-Raphaelites, together with works from the Aesthetic movement. His paintings by earlier British artists were exhibited at the Liverpool Art Club, where the cotton merchant Charles Minoprio also displayed some of his recent acquisitions.[101]

Some members of the business community, such as Holbrook Gaskell the foundry owner and chemical manufacturer of Woolton Wood, built dedicated galleries or museum rooms at their homes.[102] The shipowner Alfred Booth was an enthusiast for paintings of the modern Dutch school and built an extension to 46 Ullet Road to accommodate his collection.[103] Kurtz's top-lit music room at Grove House, completed in 1865, doubled as a picture gallery and was apparently decorated by the Audsley brothers, while the cotton broker William Holt created a 'china museum' at Whinmoor, his house in Sandfield Park, and had it ornamented with stained glass by Shrigley & Hunt of Lancaster.[104] Private collections such as Kurtz's could be visited by arrangement, but the museum of Japanese art attached to James Lord Bowes's Streatlam Tower in Prince's Road was conceived as a public venue and had regular opening hours. When inaugurated in 1890, it measured 98 feet by 36, and it was enlarged by half as much again the following year, when Bowes added a picture gallery. It was heralded as 'an unrivalled museum of Japanese Art' and the Japanese Fancy Fair of 1891, which was opened by the mayor, attracted 20,000 visitors and raised £6,000 for charity.[105]

The gallery at Elm House, Seaforth—50 feet long and 20 feet high—was built in 1868 for the African merchant and shipowner Peter Stuart to a design influenced by the artist Edwin Long. It inspired two imitations, one of which was erected in the early 1870s for Stuart's business partner, the shipowner Peter Douglas, at his house in Grosvenor Road, Claughton.[106] Probably no other surviving room gives such a strong sense of the princely scale of art collecting in nineteenth-century Liverpool. In an altogether different league from this, however, were T. H. Ismay's double-height picture gallery at Dawpool—by far the largest and richest room in the entire house (Figure 8.6)—and the 300-foot colonnaded sculpture gallery at Hooton Hall, designed for the banker R. C. Naylor in 1854 by J. K. Colling, the architect responsible for Naylor's Albany Building in Old Hall Street. Both Hooton and Dawpool were demolished in the early twentieth century.

There were libraries in the homes of many Liverpool businessmen, although, as with music rooms and picture galleries, some may have been status symbols rather than evidence of genuine cultural interests. The sport of mocking uneducated merchants for their literary pretensions and blunders dates back at least to the beginning of the nineteenth century, and it was still going strong towards its close: 'I like to have a good library in my house,' said Andrew Barclay Walker in the 'imaginary interview' cited earlier, 'but I do not read much'.[107] Walker's library at Gateacre Grange, as fitted out by Sir Ernest George & Peto in 1882–84 with half-height, glass-fronted bookcases, was fairly typical of the kind of library installed in many large suburban Liverpool houses towards the end of the nineteenth century. Other surviving examples are George Holt's at Sudley, Richard R. Lockett's at 34 Alexandra Drive, and Robert Brocklehurst's at St. Clare, Sandfield Park, all dating from the early 1880s.[108] More unusual was the library of the timber merchant, James Bland, at Quarry Bank of 1866–67, a polygonal room with Gothic bookcases.

Figure 8.6 The picture room, Dawpool, Thurstaston, 1896 (with permission of Historic England Archive)

There was also an older tradition of domestic libraries among the cultural luminaries of Liverpool's business elite. William Roscoe's at Allerton Hall occupied a grand room with Ionic columns, which still survives; and the literary cotton broker Francis Haywood, translator of Kant and friend of Antonio Panizzi, had a library at Edge Lane Hall that filled two or three rooms when Nathaniel Hawthorne saw it in 1857.[109] At Seaforth Hall, where Dickens and Von Liebig stayed as guests, James Muspratt's library had fine Elizabethan-style bookcases by the Liverpool cabinetmaker W. J. Roberts, somewhat at odds with the severe Greek Revival character of the rest of the house (Figure 8.7).[110] By contrast, the library of the bibliophile timber merchant Hugh Frederick Hornby at Sandown Lodge was extremely plain, although densely packed with the valuable collection he later bequeathed to the city.[111] Libraries might be furnished with a desk, but there is little firm evidence that Liverpool merchants used them to conduct business from home, even though the spread of the domestic telephone from the 1880s made this increasingly possible. In 1881, however, the Town Clerk, Joseph Rayner, was said to have a room at his house in Blundellsands which served as 'a combination of a library, a study and an office; and the aspect of it conveys the idea that the owner does a good deal of work at home'.[112]

Billiard rooms were perhaps the most widespread 'specialized' rooms in Liverpool merchants' houses in the second half of the nineteenth century, as the game became increasingly established not only in country houses, but also in upper middle-class households and merchants'

Figure 8.7 The library at Seaforth Hall with bookcases of 1840 by W. J. Roberts for James Muspratt (with permission of the Liverpool Record Office)

clubs.[113] At the exceptionally large house of the general merchant Charles Kuhn Prioleau at 19 Abercromby Square, the purpose-designed billiard room was in the basement, and at 88 Rodney Street, the end-of-terrace location made a billiard room extension possible.[114] But, generally speaking, billiard rooms were not easy to accommodate in the relatively confined space of a terraced house in the centre of town. In the case of suburban houses, however, they could be treated as virtually independent pavilions, not only securing good natural light, but also allowing scope for architectural display. Michael Belcher's billiard room at Holmestead and Henry Cookson's at Runnymede, Sandfield Park, showed contrasting Gothic and Classical treatments, while the cotton broker John Swainson (1814–79) purchased a billiard table 'in medieval style' from the 1862 International Exhibition for use at Elmswood, a house originally built by Thomas Sand.[115] More spectacular than either was Edmund Kirby's 1884 design for a billiard room extension at Ramle, the house of the shipbuilder G. R. Clover in Manor Hill, Claughton.[116] Elsewhere, as children grew up, nurseries were sometimes converted to serve as billiard rooms. This happened at the Holts' house in Rake Lane in 1861, and later at William Higgins's in Park Road West, Birkenhead.[117] The game was not an entirely male preserve—a painting of the billiard room at Speke Hall during Frederick Leyland's tenancy shows a mixed party—but generally, the billiard room was part of what Girouard has called the 'male domain', and therefore an important location for business-related socialising.[118] Famously, the founding of the White Star Line is said to have originated in a conversation over a game of billiards at Broughton Hall, the home of the commission and general merchant Gustavus C. Schwabe and one of Liverpool's most imposing Gothic residences, designed by Walter Scott (Figure 8.8).[119]

Figure 8.8 Broughton Hall, Yew Tree Lane, West Derby (designed by Walter Scott for G. C. Schwabe)

The Social Significance of Towers and Suburban Gardens

Towers were also popular, both as conspicuous symbols of social status and as vantage points, which gave the occupier of the house an almost proprietorial relationship with its wider setting. As early as 1813, John Nash provided Bamber Gascoyne's Childwall Hall with a tower which commanded a view over the 'populous and well cultivated plain', impressing the observer 'with the cheerful emotions that naturally arise on contemplating the results of successful industry'.[120] Later examples took advantage of river views. Important survivors are at Woolton Tower, a house that was built c.1856 for the cotton broker Matthew Wilson Armour, and Hartfield at Allerton, an 1840s house where the tower may have been added for the shipowner John Banks Walmsley in the 1880s. There seems to be no contemporary evidence for the popular belief that such towers were intended to give the expectant merchant a view of his returning ships, though as W. B. Forwood recalled, the general prospect of shipping was certainly part of the attraction of seaside locations such as Waterloo and Blundellsands.[121] Ultimately, a tower was an expendable luxury, and the very high, Osborne-inspired one designed by William Culshaw in 1860 for the general merchant Francis Braun at Holly Lodge, West Derby, was built only on a much reduced scale, presumably as an economy.[122]

From what he observed in the affluent suburbs of Manchester and Liverpool in the 1860s, Hippolyte Taine concluded that 'the townsman does everything in his power to cease being a townsman, and tries to fit a country-house and a bit of country into a corner of the town. He feels the need to be in his own home, to be alone, king of his family and servants, and to have about him a bit of park or garden in which he can relax after his artificial business life'.[123] In polluted, congested mid nineteenth-century Liverpool, however, a suburban garden was of more than merely symbolic or psychological value. In 1851, an American visitor to Wyncote, the Allerton home of the merchant Joseph Shipley, looked back towards Liverpool and saw that 'the thick smoke had so accumulated over the city and extended to such a height that it looked like a *heavy thunder cloud*'; and 30 years later the *Liberal Review* asserted that the majority of Liverpool's leading men chose to keep a carriage, and live 'out of town, far away from the noise, the bustle, and the dirt of the teeming masses'.[124] It was increasingly recognised that gardening was a 'delightful pastime' and away from the town centre, merchants and other members of the business community were able to enjoy their gardens which provided 'pleasure to the several occupants' and enabled them to benefit from the 'humanising and elevating influence' of everything that was beautiful, 'whether in Art or Nature'.[125]

As well as more beautiful surroundings, the grounds of a suburban residence offered greater scope for recreation and socialising than the narrow garden strip behind the typical town house. In the family garden at Rake Lane, R. D. Holt could enjoy the 'new game of croquet [*sic*]'; at Samuel Bright's Sandheys, a pair of crested cranes strutted across the lawn; and in the grounds of Elmsleigh, the Princes Park villa of the merchant Charles Tricks Bowring, lawn tennis was played.[126] Here, in contrast to the Hazlehursts' house at 59 Rodney Street, it was possible to hide such necessary but unsightly features as the kitchen yard and privy, so that they did not impinge on areas used for leisure. Above all, the suburban garden offered privacy. Already in the 1850s, Hawthorne had noted the preference of Liverpool merchants for 'locating their dwellings far within private grounds, with secure gateways and porters lodges'.[127] Such complete seclusion was the privilege only of the wealthiest, but smaller suburban properties, too, could be insulated by their gardens: Wyncote, which became the home of C. W. Neumann (apparently a retired cotton broker), was 'planted round with evergreens so as scarcely to be visible from the high-road'.[128] The smaller villas around Princes Park and Sefton Park, fronting onto public roads and backing onto public parks, were less protected from the intrusive gaze of strangers—according to Picton, the passer-by might catch 'peeps within of ormolu tables, walls lined with pictures, well-furnished sideboards, and damask curtains'[129]—but even here, maturing shrubbery made an increasingly effective barrier.

Large suburban houses would have a kitchen garden as a matter of course, but more extensive grounds could be run productively like small country estates, and a number of contemporary guides were published to provide specialist advice for such a purpose.[130] When the contents of Norris Green were sold in 1894, there were over 1,800 strawberry plants in its celebrated glass-houses, a figure that suggests the garden did more than merely supply the owner's table.[131] Taine described a wealthy Liverpool businessman who took an interest in pig breeding to escape from the stress of his work, but such rustic pursuits could also be an expression of the same attitudes that motivated a merchant's professional life.[132] George Holt was influenced by Unitarian ideas of productivity, the avoidance of waste, and a desire to utilise resources to the full, ideas that underlay his office-building projects in the town centre, and equally shaped his stewardship of the grounds surrounding his house in Rake Lane. His diary records in great detail the rearing of poultry, the construction of greenhouses and the cultivation of fruit and vegetables for domestic use, activities in which he was directly and practically involved.[133]

Alongside these essentially private purposes, gardens, like houses, presented opportunities for displaying the owner's wealth and taste to his peers. Visiting each other's gardens was not uncommon among Liverpool's merchant class, when the self-evident cost of maintaining large grounds bore eloquent witness to the owner's prosperity. When A. G. Kurtz visited Calderstones in 1874, just before the shipowner Charles McIver moved in, he estimated that 20 gardeners would be needed to keep it in order.[134] He may not have been far wrong: at Norris Green, the banker John Pemberton Heywood employed a head gardener and 13 men.[135] Following a tour of Thomas Sutton Timmis's glasshouse at Cleveley, Allerton Road, Kurtz described it as having been 'reared regardless of expense. In fact,' he went on, 'there is a recklessness of expenditure there that denoted overwhelming success'.[136] Erecting and maintaining heated glasshouses was particularly costly. As part of his enlargement of Gateacre Grange in 1883–84, Andrew Barclay Walker spent over £2,000 on hot houses and their heating apparatus.[137] Of the numerous, extensive glasshouses like Walker's recorded on Ordnance Survey maps of the 1890s and early 1900s, a rare survivor is at Crofton in North Sudley Road, home of the steamship owner Alfred Holt. Elsewhere, a few ornamental conservatories attached to houses remain. Filled with rare and exotic plants, these were often linked with rooms used for entertaining—Benson Rathbone's opened directly out of his dining room, and Richard Vaughan Yates's out of his drawing room—and thus made a significant contribution to the luxurious experience of guests.[138] The most ambitious surviving examples are those at Broughton Hall, West Derby, and Holmestead, Mossley Hill, both of which are additions to earlier houses. Thomas Avison's bow-fronted conservatory at Park Lea in Fulwood Park is much smaller, but it formed part of the original 1840s house and is therefore completely integrated into the design of the garden front.

Conclusion

The typical merchant's home had changed utterly since the late eighteenth century. Then, there had been no separation between dwelling and business premises. House, warehouse, and counting house were generally a single unit, and even the cellar below the living rooms could be used for storing goods. By the late nineteenth century, town houses and suburban villas were completely free from such commercial uses and could be devoted to the display and enjoyment of wealth that was generated elsewhere. The *Porcupine* mocked these changes, depicting merchants of the 1860s as jumped-up tradesmen who had once lived humbly 'over the shop', but who now lived out of town in 'their villers, an' their cottage hornees, as they call 'em . . .

[where] . . . you don't hear nothin' of kitchings an' parlours. Bless you, no. It's domestick hoffices an' reception rooms'.[139] And yet with their libraries and conservatories, their billiard rooms and music rooms, such houses still played a vital role in business life. They allowed the merchant to entertain his peers and impress them with signs of his prosperity and social position, qualities essential to success in a hard-headed commercial city like Liverpool. Nineteenth-century observers often spoke of Liverpool's modernity, its rapid rise from insignificance, and the correspondingly rootless, parvenu character of its mercantile aristocracy. 'Rough, busy, dirty, wealthy',[140] its daily life was dominated to an extraordinary degree by trade and the pursuit of profit. It was volatile and unpredictable, a place where men from humble backgrounds could acquire spectacular riches, while the affluent could suddenly lose everything. It was also cosmopolitan, and its business circles included individuals of uncertain origin and doubtful honesty, whose trustworthiness had to be judged partly by appearances. In this brash and materialistic culture, houses were deeply significant indicators of status.

Notes

1 John Weiss Forney, *Letters from Europe* (Philadelphia, 1867), p. 32.
2 C. Morris (ed.), *The Illustrated Journeys of Celia Fiennes 1685–c.1712* (London, 1982), pp. 160–1.
3 Daniel Defoe, *A Tour through the Whole Island of Great Britain*, edited by P. Rogers (London, 1971), p. 391.
4 James Allanson Picton, *Memorials of Liverpool Historical and Topographical Including a History of the Dock Estate* (2 vols, London, 1873), vol. 2, p. 171.
5 Henry Peet, 'Thomas Steers, the Engineer of Liverpool's First Dock, a Memoir', *THSL&C*, 82 (1932), pp. 163–242.
6 Picton, *Memorials*, vol. 2, p. 171; Richard Morrice, 'The Payment Book of William Baker of Audlem (1705–71)', in John Bold and Edward Chaney (eds.), *English Architecture Public and Private, Essays for Kerry Downes* (London, 1993), pp. 231–46; LRO, Herdman Collection, 772A; Barclay's Group Archives, Wythenshawe, Heywood's Bank records, 199/64, private ledger.
7 *The Liverpool Memorandum-Book . . . for the Year MDCCLIII*, [1752]; *General Advertiser, Liverpool*, 24 February 1775.
8 *BLA&MI*, 21 January 1799.
9 LRO, Edmund Kirby papers, 720 KIR 2421.
10 *BLA&MI*, 21 January 1799. The house was probably built between 7 September 1757, when the property was first leased to the attorney James Clegg, and 17 June 1780, when Clegg was granted a new lease with a revised description of the buildings.
11 *Gore's Directory*, 1807; *Liverpool Mercury*, 11 January 1866.
12 *BLA&MI*, 14 April 1794; the bankruptcy of Meyer and Wilckens was announced in the *Times*, 15 April 1793.
13 James Wallace, *A General and Descriptive History of the Antient and Present State of the Town of Liverpool* (Liverpool, 1797), p. 81.
14 *BLA&MI*, 13 April 1795.
15 *General Advertiser, Liverpool*, 14 April 1775.
16 LRO, 352 CLE/CON 3/5, Lease Register D, entry for 21 July 1796.
17 LRO, 920 MD 42.
18 *General Advertiser, Liverpool*, 17 March 1775; *Liverpool Mercury*, 11 January 1866.
19 Wallace, *General and Descriptive History*, pp. 280–1.
20 *Liverpool General Advertiser, or the Commercial Register*, 3 January 1766; Jane Longmore, 'Civic Liverpool: 1680–1800', in John Belchem (ed.), *Liverpool 800 Culture, Character & History* (Liverpool, 2006), pp. 163–4. Sarah Clayton's investments included property and collieries in St. Helens, as well as several houses in Liverpool.
21 J. Aspinall, *Liverpool a Few Years Since* (London, 1852), p. 37. A watercolour by Brierley is in the Athenaeum library, Liverpool Buildings box 2, no. 63.
22 *BLA&MI*, 14 April 1794.
23 Longmore, 'Civic Liverpool', pp. 155–6.

24 Charles Herbert Reilly, *Some Liverpool Streets and Buildings in 1921* (Liverpool, 1921), p. 74.

25 University of Liverpool art collections, 3385, 3387.1 and 3387.2.

26 Barclay's Group Archives, Wythenshawe, Heywood's Bank records, 199/64, private ledger.

27 LRO, James A. Waite, *Historic Houses, Churches and Other Architectural Antiquities*, vol. 3; R. D. Radcliffe, *Notes on the Township of West Derby* (Liverpool, 1918), p. 15.

28 Sir John Soane's Museum, MBi/67 set lxvii.

29 M. Honan, 'Doors and Doorways', *Builders' Journal & Architectural Record*, 7 February 1900, pp. 3–5; LRO, 920 MD 44, copy of the will of Gilbert Henderson, 17 September 1841.

30 Picton, *Memorials*, vol. 2, p. 304.

31 *Liverpool Chronicle*, 24 September 1806.

32 Emily A. Rathbone (ed.), *Records of the Rathbone Family* (Edinburgh, 1913), pp. 113–14.

33 T. C. Barker and J. R. Harris, *A Merseyside Town in the Industrial Revolution: St Helens 1750–1900* (London, 1959), pp. 50–1.

34 Alice Ford (ed.), *The 1826 Journal of John James Audubon* (New York, 1987), p. 96.

35 LRO, 942 HOL 19, Holt and Gregson papers, pp. 257–60.

36 Wallace, *General and Descriptive History*, p. 81.

37 Aspinall, *Liverpool*, p. 57. See Cock, Davis, Lee, and Mäenpää, Chapter 2; Sharples and Jarvis, Chapter 9; Lee, Chapters 10 and 11.

38 Nicholas Ashton (1742–1833) was a highly successful salt merchant who succeeded to his father's business at the age of 17: by employing Adam for the remodelling of Woolton Hall he was clearly making a statement about his wealth, social standing, and ambition. Following his marriage to Mary Philpot (1740–77), he acquired Hefferston Grange, Weaverham, Cheshire, a seven-bay brick house similar in design to Daresbury Hall, which had been built in 1741. S. A. Harris, 'Robert Adam (1728–92), Architect and Woolton Hall', *THSL&C*, 102 (1950), pp. 161–81.

39 LRO, 352 MIN/IMP I 1/1, 13 April and 31 October 1786.

40 Joseph Sharples, '"The Visible Embodiment of Modern Commerce": Speculative Office Building in Liverpool, c.1780–1870', *Architectural History*, 61 (2018), pp. 131–73; see Chapter 5. Dunbar's wealth came principally from his extensive business as a cotton broker, but he was also a major wine importer. He was Mmayor of Liverpool in 1796. J. A. Picton, *Memorials of Liverpool Historical and Topographical, vol. 2: Topographical* (Liverpool, 1873), p. 236; Alexey Krichtal, 'Liverpool and the Raw Cotton Trade: A Study of the Port and Its Merchant Community, 1770–1815', MA dissertation, Victoria University of Wellington (2013).

41 Jane Longmore, *The Development of the Liverpool Corporation Estate 1760–1835*, unpublished PhD thesis, University of Reading (1982), vol. 1, pp. 108–9.

42 S. G. Checkland, *The Gladstones: A Family Biography* (Cambridge, 1971), pp. 16–33.

43 Harriet Anna Whitting, *Alfred Booth, Some Memories, Letters and Other Family Records* (Liverpool, 1917), pp. 6–9. The house was demolished c.1807 for the widening of Leece Street and is not the present number 34, incorrectly identified by a plaque as the birthplace of Henry Booth.

44 Thomas Fletcher, *Autobiographical Memoirs of Thomas Fletcher of Liverpool (obiit 1850) Written in the Year 1843* (Liverpool, 1893).

45 Peter Mathias, *The Liverpool Corporate Estate: A Study of the Development of Housing in the Moss Lake Fields of Liverpool 1800–1875*, unpublished MA thesis, University of Liverpool (1957); A. R. Allan, *The Building of Abercromby Square* (Liverpool, 1986).

46 Falkner Square was initially laid out from 1835 onwards by the speculative property developer Edward Falkner when it was situated in almost open countryside: see David Lewis, *Walks Through History Liverpool* (Derby, 2004), p. 59.

47 *Builder*, 8 (1850), p. 189.

48 C. H. Reilly, *Some Liverpool Streets and Buildings in 1921* (Liverpool, 1921), p. 57.

49 H. M. Addey, *The Picturesque Hand-Book of Liverpool a Manual for Resident and Visitor: With a Day at Birkenhead and a Series of Pleasure Excursions in the Environs* (5th ed., Liverpool, 1846), p. 96.

50 Reilly, *Some Liverpool Streets*, p. 53.

51 LRO, M 920 HAZ/1/2. See Joseph Sharples, '"My Dear Father's House . . .": The Liverpool Home of Thomas Hazlehurst, Miniature Painter', *Furniture History*, 53 (2017), pp. 243–62.

52 *Gore's General Advertiser*, 29 October 1829; MLP database. Willink had been born in Amsterdam: by 1851 he was acting as the Vice-Consul for the Hanseatic towns.

53 Reilly, *Some Liverpool Streets*, p. 53.

54 LaRO, Culshaw & Sumners papers, DDX 162/23/49-DDX 162/23/53.

55 For a discussion of the increasing importance attached to comfort within a domestic context, see John Cornforth, *English Interiors, 1790–1848: The Quest for Comfort* (London, 1978); John Gloag, *Victorian Comfort: A Social History of Design, 1830–1900* (New York, 1973).

56 LaRO, Culshaw & Sumners papers, DDX 162/46/34-DDX 162/46/35. Melly was the senior in the firm of George Melly & Co., commission and general merchants, a firm which was responsible for the importation of the first bale of Egyptian cotton to Liverpool: see Orchard, *Liverpool's Legion of Honour*, p. 500.

57 LaRO, Culshaw & Sumners papers, DDX 162/79/58-DDX 162/79/71.

58 LaRO, Culshaw & Sumners papers, DDX 162/28/03-DDX 162/28/8; MLP database. Between 1861 and 1871 the number of resident servants at 3 Huskisson Street increased from four to five.

59 Nathaniel Hawthorne, *The English Notebooks*, ed. R. Stewart (New York, 1941), p. 269.

60 See Chapter 9.

61 *Winmore & Co, a Tale of the Great Bank Failure* (London, 1881), pp. 11–12.

62 *Winmore & Co*, p. 35.

63 Hawthorne, *English Notebooks*, p. 56.

64 *Porcupine*, 9 (1867), p. 364.

65 *Porcupine*, 19 (1877), p. 72.

66 LRO, 920 KUR 1/7, Diary of Andrew George Kurtz, 18 February 1867; *Liverpool Mercury*, 1 February 1867.

67 LRO, 920 KUR 1/18, 9 May 1878; MLP database. In 1871, his household at Sunnyside contained 16 individuals, including eight children and six servants.

68 *Liverpool Courier*, 19 April 1887. For a discussion of the activities of the cotton speculator Morris Ranger, see Graeme Milne, Chapter 4.

69 *Winmore & Co*, pp. 12 and 92 et seq.

70 John Hughes, *Liverpool Banks and Bankers 1760–1837* (Liverpool, 1906), pp. 99, 101 and 103; Calendar of Probate, 1893.

71 MLP database; Orchard, *Liverpool's Legion of Honour*, p. 672. Thompson was also a director of the Liverpool Gas Company and a board member of both the Leeds and Liverpool Canal and the London and North Western Railway.

72 LRO, 920 KUR 1/22, 3 November 1882; MLP database. The choice of Scott was symptomatic of a preference to select nationally known architects for the design of Gothic houses for Liverpool's business community. See Joseph Sharples, 'Secular Gothic Revival Architecture in Mid-Nineteenth-Century Liverpool', in Marios Costambeys, Andrew Hamer and Martin Heale (eds.), *The Making of the Middle Ages Liverpool Essays* (Liverpool, 2007), p. 219. Scott was the leading exponent of the Gothic Revival style: see George Gilbert Scott, *Remarks on Secular & Domestic Architecture, Present & Future* (2nd ed., London, 1858).

73 MLP database; William Bower Forwood, *Recollections of a Busy Life* (London, 1910), p. 44. In 1851, Belcher was listed as resident at Three Sixes, Aigburth Road and his social standing was reflected ten years later when his household contained eight domestic servants, including a stable keeper (groom), two nurses, a cook, a scullery maid, and two house-maids.

74 LRO, 920 KUR 1/6, 1 September 1866.

75 LRO, 920 KUR 1/15, 12 February 1875.

76 LRO, 920 KUR 1/10, 30 December 1870.

77 Walter Lewin, *Clarke Aspinall: A Biography* (London, 1893), pp. 20–1.

78 Sharples, 'Secular Gothic Revival Architecture', p. 219.

79 National Monuments Record, Swindon, photographs by H. Bedford Lemere, BL8931–8, BL11221–9 and BL13771–6; Joseph Sharples, 'Merchants' Houses in Victorian Liverpool', in John Dunne and Paul Janssens (eds.), *Living in the City: Elites and Their Residences, 1500–1900* (Turnhout, 2008), pp. 193–216; idem., *Merchant Palaces: Liverpool and Wirral Mansions Photographed by Bedford Lemere (Photographers of Liverpool)* (Liverpool, 2007).

80 National Maritime Museum, Greenwich, London, diary of Margaret Ismay, ISM/11, 28 May 1883.

81 *Liverpool Mercury*, 31 December 1830.

82 *Builder*, 7 (1849), p. 314.

83 Forwood, *Recollections of a Busy Life*, p. 60.

84 For a discussion of entertaining at home by Liverpool merchants, see Chapter 6.

85 Rose Hawthorne Lathrop, *Memories of Hawthorne* (London, 1897), pp. 328–9; LRO, 920 DUR 10/16/3, Diary of Robert Durning Holt, 5 June 1862.

86 Family papers in possession of Jonathan Rathbone, vol. 3, p. 321.

87 National Maritime Museum, Greenwich, London, Diary of Margaret Ismay, ISM/14, 28 April 1886; ISM/15, 13 April 1887; ISM/16, 2 May 1888; etc.

88 Edmund Knowles Muspratt, *My Life and Work* (London, 1917), pp. 118–19. According to Stana Nenadic, 'The Victorian Middle Classes', in W. Hamish Fraser and Irene Maver (eds.), *Glasgow, vol. 2: 1830–1912* (Manchester, 1996), p. 289, in Glasgow 'home-based dining among the business elite was largely undertaken on the basis of business networks'.

89 Laura Microulis, 'Gillow and Company's Furniture for a Liverpool Maecenas: John Grant Morris of Allerton Priory', *Furniture History*, 41 (2005), pp. 189–216; LRO, Hq 942 7230 SEA; National Monuments Record, Swindon, photograph by H. Bedford Lemere, BL13773.

90 Benjamin Guinness Orchard, *Liverpool's Legion of Honour* (Birkenhead, 1893), p. 72.

91 LRO, 920/KUR/1/28, 17 April 1888.

92 National Maritime Museum, Greenwich, London, Diary of Margaret Ismay, ISM/15, 4 January 1887; LRO, 920 DUR 1/5, Holt family diary, 4 May 1879.

93 LRO, 920/KUR/1/28, 20 January 1888.

94 LRO, 920/KUR/1/9, 16 October 1869.

95 LRO, 920/KUR/1/22, 24 December 1882.

96 'Interviews with Great Men (imaginary): Sir A.B. Walker,' *Liberal Review*, 14 May 1881. For a wider discussion of Walker's motives in endowing the gallery, see James Moore, 'The art of philanthropy? The formation and development of the Walker Art Gallery in Liverpool', *Museum & Society*, 2, 2 (2004), pp. 68–83.

97 *Liverpool Mercury*, 1 February 1867; 'Interviews with Great Men (Imaginary): Alderman Samuelson, JP', *Liberal Review*, 1 October 1881; LRO, 920/KUR/1/28, Diary of A. G. Kurtz, 7 February 1888.

98 Hawthorne, *English Notebooks*, p. 88; LRO, 920 DUR 10/16/1, diary of Robert Durning Holt, 19 October 1860.

99 Richard Foster and Julian Treuherz, 'Foreword', in *The Board of Trustees of the National Museums and Galleries on Merseyside: The Walker Art Gallery* (London, 1994), p. 7; Edward Morris, *Victorian & Edwardian Paintings in the Walker Art Gallery and at Sudley House* (London, 1996).

100 See LRO, 920 DUR 10/18 for the receipts for works of art in Holt's collection; 'Philip Henry Rathbone and the Purchase of Contemporary Foreign Paintings for the Walker Art Gallery', *Annual Report and Bulletin of the Walker Art Gallery*, 6 (Liverpool, 1975–6), pp. 59–81; P. H. Rathbone, *Realism, Idealism and the Grotesque in Art: Their Limits and Functions* (Liverpool, 1877); Forwood, *Recollections of a Busy Life*, pp. 117–19; Alison Smith, *The Victorian Nude: Sexuality, Morality, and Art* (Manchester, 1996), pp. 216–39. For a detailed study of the Rathbones, see Sheila Marriner, *Rathbones of Liverpool 1845–73* (Liverpool, 1961).

101 Liverpool Art Club, *Catalogue of a Loan Collection of Oil Paintings by British Artists born before 1801* (Liverpool, 1881).

102 Dianne Sachko Macleod, *Art and the Victorian Middle Class* (Cambridge, 1996); LRO, 352 BUI/3/1, plan 181; Pat Starkey (ed.), *Riches into Art: Liverpool Collectors, 1770–1880: Essays in Honour of Margaret T. Gibson* (Liverpool, 1993). Gaskell had a fine collection of paintings, including works by Constable and Turner, but he also became a renowned collector of orchids; he made significant endowments to University College, Liverpool, including a chair in botany and funds for chemistry laboratories; and on his death in 1909 he left just under £500,000 (approximately £52.5m. in 2019 prices).

103 Whiting, *Alfred Booth*, pp. 122–3.

104 'The Private Collections of England, No. LXXX, Mr Kurtz's, Wavertree, Liverpool', *Athenaeum*, 12 September 1885, pp. 341–2; LRO, 920/KUR/1/5, 31 May 1865; LaRO, DDSr/3/1, Shrigley & Hunt Register of Designs, 1021.

105 *Liverpool Mercury*, 16 June 1890; *Daily Post*, 28 October 1899; LRO, 708 BOW 1. Bowes was a successful wool broker, of J. C. Bowes & Brothers, and became the Japanese Consul in Liverpool and the Vice-President of the Liverpool Art Club.

106 Mazzini Stuart, *The Life of Peter Stuart, the 'Ditton Doctor'* (London, 1920), pp. 48–9. Edwin Long (1829–91) was an orientalist who specialised in painting Biblical and Middle Eastern subjects.

107 *Liberal Review*, 14 May 1881. For illiterate early nineteenth-century merchants, see [J. Aspinall], *Liverpool*, pp. 54–5.

108 Richard R. Lockett was a general merchant specialising in the wine trade where he was an agent for several firms, including J. & F. Martell & Co. He was also a shipowner and became a managing

director of the British Sugar Co. Ltd. Robert Brocklehurst was a South American merchant with significant interests in Brazil. See MLP database; Orchard, *Liverpool's Legion of Honour*, p. 207.

109 Hawthorne, *English Notebooks*, p. 561. For a description of 12 private libraries in Glasgow, see Thomas D. Morison, *Public and Private Libraries of Glasgow* (Glasgow, 1885).

110 LRO, Hq 942 7230 SEA. Roberts's designs were shown at the Liverpool Academy, 1840, cat. 527.

111 Henry E. Curran and Charles Robertson, *Catalogue of the Art Library Bequeathed by Hugh Frederick Hornby, Esq. of Liverpool to the Free Public Library of the City of Liverpool* (Liverpool, 1906). A photograph is in the Athenaeum Library, Liverpool Buildings box 4; the bequest also included £10,000 for a suitable building to store his library collection.

112 'Interviews with Great Men (Imaginary): Mr Joseph Rayner,' *Liberal Review*, 16 April 1881.

113 Clive Everton, *The Story of Billiards and Snooker* (Haywards Health, 1979); Kevin C. Murphy, *The American Experience in Nineteenth Century Japan* (London, 2003); Carol E. Harrison, *The Bourgeois Citizen in Nineteenth-Century France Gender, Sociability, and the Uses of Emulation* (Oxford, 1999), p. 90. The English Billiards Association had been founded in 1885.

114 Prioleau was a senior partner in Fraser, Trenholm & Co., cotton merchants and bankers, with important connections to many of the leading Confederates during the American Civil War. After the defeat of the South he established his own firm in London (Prioleau & Co., 1867–77): see NML, MMM, MAL, B/FT/8/1.

115 Sharples, 'Secular Gothic Revival Architecture', p. 221. Belcher was a highly successful cotton broker. He retired from business in 1881 after over half a century and was reported as 'enjoying the happy and comfortable repose' that he deserved. See Thomas Ellison, *The Cotton Trade of Great Britain Including a History of the Liverpool Cotton Market and of the Liverpool Cotton Brokers' Association* (London, 1886), p. 250.

116 LRO, Edmund Kirby papers, 720 KIR 671.

117 LRO, 920 DUR 10/16/2, Diary of Robert Durning Holt, 2 and 15 October 1861; 920 DUR 1/4, Holt Family diary, 15 November 1861; LaRO, Culshaw & Sumners papers, DDX 162/13/33-DDX 162/13/40.

118 Morris, *Victorian & Edwardian Paintings*, pp. 50–1; Mark Girouard, *The Victorian Country House* (New Haven and London, 1979), pp. 34 ff. The steamship owner and merchant Frederick Leyland began renting Speke Hall in September 1867 and soon afterwards converted an old kitchen into a billiard room: see MPL database.

119 William Bower Forwood, *Reminiscences of a Liverpool Shipowner* (Liverpool, 1920), pp. 40–1; Sharples, *Merchant Palaces*, p. 16; Robert Lee, 'Divided Loyalties? In-Migration, Ethnicity and Identity: The Integration of German Merchants in Nineteenth-Century Liverpool', *BH*, 54, 2 (2012), p. 126. Schwabe had been born in Hamburg in 1814: see MLP database.

120 *Lancashire Illustrated, from Original Drawings, by S. Austin, J. Harwood and G. & C. Pyne, with Descriptions* (London, 1831), p. 43.

121 Forwood, *Recollections*, pp. 165–6.

122 LaRO, Culshaw & Sumners papers, DDX 162/10/23-DDX 162/10/30. Braun had been born in Bavaria: in 1851 he was employed by Zwilchenbart, Blessig & Co., but by the early 1860s he was a partner in Blessig, Braun & Co. See MPL database.

123 Hippolyte Taine, *Notes on England*, translated by Edward Hyams (London, 1957), p. 220.

124 Liverpool University Special Collections and Archives D.823/2, photocopy of a letter from Edward Binghurst, 26 February 1851; 'Interviews with Great Men (imaginary): Mr James Allanson Picton', *Liberal Review*, 30 April 1881. For a more detailed discussion of this theme, see Chapter 9).

125 Forwood, *Recollections of a Busy Life*, p. 259; Edward Kemp, *How to Lay Out a Garden: Intended as a General Guide in Choosing, Forming, or Improving an Estate (From a Quarter of an Acre to a Hundred Acres in Extent)* (London, 1858), p. viii. Kemp, who was the first superintendent of Birkenhead Park, carried out a number of private contacts for leading families on Merseyside and further afield: see Elizabeth Davey, '"A Complete and Constant Superintendence" the Cheshire Parks and Gardens of Edward Kemp (1817–1891)', *Cheshire History*, 50 (2010–11), p. 99. His signed, but undated, plan of the garden at Thomas Arthur Hope's residence at Stanton Hall, Spital, can be found in the LaRO, Culshaw & Sumners papers, DDX 162/22/18.

126 LRO, 920 DUR 10/16/1, Diary of Robert Durning Holt, 25 June 1860; Lathrop, *Memories*, p. 228; LRO, 920/KUR/1/18, 3 July 1878.

127 Hawthorne, *English Notebooks*, p. 103.

128 LRO, 920/KUR/1/15, 3 May 1875.

129   Picton, *Memorials*, vol. 2, p. 565.

130   See, for example, J. C. Loudon (edited by Mrs. Loudon), *The Villa Gardener: Comprising the Choice of a Suburban Villa Residence: The Laying Out, Planting, and Culture of the Garden and Grounds; and the Management of the Villa Farm Including the Dairy and Poultry Yard* (London, 1850).

131   *Catalogue of the valuable appointments . . . which will be sold by auction by Messrs. Branch and Leete [3–10 April 1894] . . . at the mansion "Norris Green," West Derby, near Liverpool.*

132   Taine, *Notes*, pp. 224–5.

133   LRO, 920 DUR 1/1 and 920 DUR 1/2, Holt Family diary.

134   LRO, 920/KUR/1/14, 20 April 1874.

135   *Journal of Horticulture, Cottage Gardener, and Country Gentleman*, new series, 29 (1875): pp. 511–13.

136   LRO, 920/KUR/1/26, 7 March 1886.

137   LRO, M 350PWK/1/1/9 and M 350PWK/1/1/10, cash books of Andrew Barclay Walker. The remodelling and extension of Gateacre Grange by George & Peto cost c.£14,000, excluding interior decoration.

138   LRO, 920/KUR/1/19, 28 February 1879; 920 DUR 1/2, Holt Family diary, 31 August 1851.

139   *Porcupine*, 10 (1868), p. 225.

140   William Allingham ['Patricius Walker'], *Rambles* (London, 1873), pp. 214–15.

9 'To Purer Air and Brighter Skies'

Escaping from the City[1]

Joseph Sharples and Adrian Jarvis

Introduction

Since the early work of Dyos and Thompson, a considerable amount of research has been undertaken on the process of suburbanisation in Britain focusing on the experience of individual towns and cities, the extent of spatial differentiation, and its wider impact in terms of political fragmentation, class identity and cultural significance.[2] From the 1750s onwards, many provincial towns registered an increased rate of suburbanisation which became particularly pronounced in the early decades of the nineteenth century as urban elites sought to escape the 'sordid lanes and foetid airs' by seeking residences well removed from the environmental nuisances which early industrialisation and rapid population growth had invariably generated.[3] The search for fresh air was already apparent in Manchester by the beginning of the nineteenth century and the 'upper bourgeoisie', as in other expanding provincial towns, developed an increasing preference for 'remoter villas with gardens' where they could enjoy 'free, wholesome county air'.[4]

A similar process was evident in Liverpool where there was evidence of a well-defined social geography by 1801 with higher-status families occupying areas on the edge of the city centre, particularly if they were located on higher ground.[5] There are useful studies on the creation of park estates and the journey to work, together with general surveys of Liverpool's suburban development and detailed research on the components of demographic change by registration sub-district. But there has been relatively little research on the nineteenth-century suburbanisation process itself, its key determinants or the social composition of the new suburbanites. By contrast, considerable work has been undertaken on the relocation of lower-middle and working-class residents during the interwar period when a house-building boom led to the breaking up of pocket country estates which the plutocracy no longer wanted, conspicuously in Allerton, Childwall, parts of Knotty Ash and Mossley Hill.[6] The following chapter will discuss the main factors which contributed to suburbanisation; assess the role of the merchant community within Liverpool's suburbanisation process; and analyse the significance of improvements in the urban transport infrastructure as a potential causative factor in suburban development.

The Determinants of Suburbanisation

With its narrow medieval streets providing the only way to and from the river and docks, eighteenth-century Liverpool was an oppressive place in which to live. Before 1786, Castle Street was just eight yards wide and Joshua Dixon, who worked there in the 1760s for the apothecary and merchant Edward Parr, complained of 'the troublesome noise of the crowded street perpetually hurried with innumerable disturbances'.[7] Thirty years later, the guidebook-writer William Moss praised the sea breezes and the 'natural purity of the air', but also noted

DOI: 10.4324/9781315597836-9

the heaps of ordure in the streets and the noxious smell of the oil works by the Queen's Dock.[8] By the first half of the nineteenth century, Liverpool may not have had the clattering mills that characterised Manchester, but the continual din of heavy traffic was enough to make conversation difficult. Windmills dominated the skyline more than factory chimneys, but polluting industries were scattered throughout the town. Although it was high summer when the artist J. J. Audubon arrived in 1826, he found he could hardly breathe among 'the thousands of columns of dark smoke'.[9]

For members of the merchant class there were compelling commercial reasons for living in the heart of this noisy, congested dirty place. It was important to be as close as possible to the river and its shipping, the custom house, the exchange and the company of other merchants. For those who could afford it, however, the attractions of a permanent or temporary dwelling outside the centre were obvious and increasingly irresistible. From Joshua Dixon's time onwards, the story of Liverpool's elite housing is almost entirely one of centrifugal flight.

Moving from the Centre

In the late eighteenth and early nineteenth centuries the margin between the built-up centre and the agricultural hinterland was very fluid. In 1796 Moss described how Cleveland Square, a once-fashionable residential address near the Old Dock, had declined until it had become the site of a general market. The square and its like had been superseded by elegant Duke Street, 'the first attempt at embellished extension the town received . . . an airy retreat from the more busy and confined parts'.[10] Duke Street was still in the process of building when Moss wrote, but already it had been leapfrogged by Rodney Street laid out in 1783. Beyond Rodney Street, Hope Street at the start of the nineteenth century 'was country altogether . . . far removed from the smoke and bustle of the town'; and the house of Mr. Thomas—one of only two in the street—was described as 'possessing all the advantages of Town and Country Residence'.[11] Over the next 25 years, however, Hope Street was completely absorbed into the planned suburb of Mosslake Fields centred on Abercromby Square.

The speed of Liverpool's growth meant that high-class developments on the fringes were far from certain to succeed. Plans for Harrington, an ambitious residential suburb immediately south of Parliament Street, intended 'for gentlemen not obliged by business to reside in the centre and bustle of the town', were put forward by Cuthbert Bisbrown in 1771, but the scheme failed, and in the early 1800s his regular grid of streets was built up with inferior court housing.[12] The site, which had originally been too far from the town centre for the convenience of the well-to-do, was now too close to the southward-spreading docks for middle-class comfort.

Another project, initially more successful, was Great George Square. In 1799–1800, the corporation determined to lay out this square as the centrepiece of a grid of high-class streets to the south of Duke Street. It was a plan from which they believed 'much public Convenience, and considerable Grandeur and Ornament' would result: they were so committed to it that they were prepared to pay one of the existing lessees the considerable sum of £7,000.[13] Designs for imposing terraces were prepared in 1804, building began, and merchants, bankers, lawyers and other professional men came to live there (William Brown was an early resident).[14] Despite its initial attraction, the scheme faltered.[15] The southern half of the square's east side was only completed in the 1830s with houses of a much smaller footprint than the earlier ones and the same happened on the west side. The change of scale is clearly visible on M. A. Gage's map of 1836, as is the reason for it: those who could afford large houses no longer wanted to live in the square, now that the view from its back windows included timber yards, a foundry, a brewery and a mortar mill, particularly since houses of comparable size had become available in Mosslake Fields where industry was rigorously excluded.

Rodney Street and Mosslake Fields were within easy walking distance of the centre, but from the third quarter of the eighteenth century, prosperous Liverpool merchants aspired to a residence further from town, accessible by horse or carriage. William Enfield in 1773 noted that 'Everton, Wavertree, and Toxteth-Park, are pleasant villages, which have of late years been much improved by country houses, which several of the principal inhabitants of Leverpool have built for their summer-retreat', while by the end of the century 'several Villas, chiefly the residences of the Liverpool merchants' had been built each side of the turnpike leading to Derby village.[16] Everton, together with Mount Pleasant, because of their elevated height, offered 'the most healthful situations in the town', and James Atherton, a successful merchant, who had been embellishing and improving his own residence, was also 'forming villa after villa in his immediate neighbourhood in an elegant style'.[17] Toxteth Park became a favourite residential location for merchants and traders in the early nineteenth century (Figure 9.1) and although most of properties have been demolished, a few still survive, including May Place at Broad Green, built for William Williamson before 1768, and Olive Mount, Wavertree, built for James Swan before 1796.[18] In 1798 Thomas Earle purchased 88 acres in Smethan (Smithdown) Lane, where he subsequently built Spekelands, 'a large house' which was separated from the estates of other merchants (the Gascoignes, the Durning family and John Shaw Leigh) by the Toxteth Brook.[19]

In the first quarter of the nineteenth century, suburban houses became more numerous. James Sherriff's map of 1823 shows the countryside peppered with small estates for five or six miles

Figure 9.1 'Liverpool From Toxteth Park' drawn by George Pickering (1784–1857) and engraved by James Sands (1793–1882)

around the densely built-up town, many of them bearing the names of Liverpool merchants, and Jonathan Bennison's map of 1835 presents a similar picture.[20] Even if a merchant maintained a business address in the town centre, there was a growing preference for a suburban location for the family residence. By the early 1830s, for example, the firm of Jeremiah Todd Naylor was still based in King Street, but the family resided at Kensington House, Kensington.[21] Overseas visitors, such as Benjamin Silliman, Audubon and Dr. Spiker, the King of Prussia's librarian, were impressed by this distinctive suburban landscape which they saw as evidence of commercial dynamism.[22] John Britton summed up its appearance in 1807:

> [H]andsome modern seats, and old halls, ornament the country south of Liverpool, and, on the high grounds east of the town, are numerous pleasant, and some elegant villas, belonging to the wealthy merchants of that prosperous sea-port. Indeed the environs of Liverpool, like those of London . . . clearly indicate to the passing traveller and foreigner, that domestic comforts and luxuries are the ultimate rewards of English industry and active talent.[23]

For those with a house in town and another in the suburbs, it is difficult to determine the primary residence. Audubon's account of his 1826 visit to Liverpool suggests that the brothers William and Richard Rathbone moved quite often between their town houses in Bedford Street and Duke Street, and their suburban villas Greenbank and Woodcroft. The picture is not much clarified by street directories where extra-urban houses are not listed consistently. The directories of 1825 and 1827, for example, give the merchant Adam Hodgson's address as Slater Street, but Audubon describes visiting Hodgson at his Gothic 'cottage' outside Liverpool, from which the latter drove to his counting house in town.[24] It was clearly a substantial property—Hodgson was living there with his family and servants—but the directory does not record its existence. Hodgson's 'cottage' may have resembled the one proposed by Robert Lugar for P. B. Ainslie and probably intended to be built near Woolton, designs for which were published in 1828. As well as the usual family rooms, it included a school room and accommodation for a live-in teacher, and was described by Lugar as 'a proper summer retreat for a gentleman, [which] must be supposed to be in the neighbourhood of a large town'.[25]

It is not always clear if a suburban house took the place of a town-centre residence or was complementary to it. Before the slave-trader Thomas Earle built himself the mansion called Spekelands in Toxteth Park, c.1804–05, he put his Hanover Street house up for sale; but when the Hollishead Blundells moved from Leeds Street to West Derby ten years later, we are told they maintained their old house as a *pied à terre* until the 1830s.[26] Some suburban houses, such as John Sparling's St. Domingo in Everton, were built with retirement in mind. Though daily commuting was not a necessity for the retired merchant, ongoing business interests might require journeys into town and Everton was close enough for such visits to be reasonably convenient. Other quite distant houses, however, were the principal residences of active merchants who needed to be in constant communication with the commercial centre. The salt proprietor Nicholas Ashton, for instance, whose Woolton Hall was six miles out, was described by John Dalton in 1797 as a 'gentleman of great fortune, who comes to town every morning in a splendid coach'.[27]

The pattern of centrifugal movement established in the late eighteenth century continued throughout the nineteenth. A prosperous merchant who had left the crowded centre for the spacious streets of Mosslake Fields would move again to a suburban villa in Mossley Hill or Aigburth. The wealthiest might move further out still to a mansion in extensive grounds at West Derby, Gateacre, Woolton or Allerton. Even before the mid-nineteenth century, 'fine residences, scattered through the neighbouring parishes' could be found in the county districts around Liverpool and by 1881, according to the *Liberal Review*, most of the leading men in Liverpool society lived 'out of town, far away from the noise, the bustle, and the dirt of the teeming masses.'[28] B. G. Orchard, describing the residential patterns of the elite towards the end of the century, confirmed their tendency to live ever further from the centre, but at the same time noted the preference of 'old' families for 'the classic and peculiar district which lies between Canning Street and Grassendale, where they are within easy reach of the many whom they value because of relationship and inherited friendships'.[29] Within this large area, movement was not invariably away from the centre. A merchant who had made his fortune might move out from Mosslake Fields to a suburban villa, but his newly married children might move back, to live in a town house which was smaller and cheaper to run, and where a carriage was not absolutely necessary. Thomas Booth, for example, moved out from Rodney Street around 1807 to a villa he had built in Lodge Lane. His son, Charles, married in 1829 and moved back to Bedford Street, but in 1844–45 he built a villa of his own in Croxteth Road and moved out again.[30]

The south end of Liverpool described by Orchard was emphatically the fashionable side of town and remained so into the early twentieth century. When Charles Reilly arrived as professor of architecture at the university in 1904, he found 'great areas like Mossley Hill and Aigburth where there were hardly any small houses and where one fine estate joined another'. By the 1930s, most had been divided up and built over. The Rathbones' Greenbank alone retained its character and gave a sense of the impulse that had originally led to the building of such suburban retreats. There, according to Reilly, one could still 'walk in a walled garden lined with flowers and trimmed fruit trees or on the terrace at the back of the house and look across the artificial lake in the foreground over rolling lawns to the trees of Sefton Park and, though as near the centre of the town as the Dingle was, see nothing of it'.[31]

Park Estates

Between the terraced town house, on the one hand, and the secluded suburban mansion on the other, stand the private park estates of the mid-nineteenth century. Here, affluent residents could live on quiet, picturesquely curving streets, isolated from the busy highway. Lodges and gates gave these clusters the security normally reserved for single, much larger dwellings, while strict controls on the kind of houses that could be built ensured consistent architectural standards.[32] What may be the earliest of these estates is Rock Park, laid out in 1836–37 on the Mersey shore, southeast of Birkenhead (Figure 9.2). The attractions of its highly controlled environment were vividly described by Nathaniel Hawthorne, a resident in the 1850s:

> Rock Park . . . is private property, and is now nearly covered with residences for professional people, merchants, and others of the upper middling class; the houses being mostly built, I suppose, on speculation, and let to those who occupy them. It is the quietest place imaginable; there being a police station at the entrance; and the officer on duty admits no ragged or ill looking person to pass. There being a toll, it precludes all unnecessary passage of carriages; and never were there more noiseless streets than those that give access to these pretty residences. On either side, there is thick shrubbery, with glimpses through it at the ornamented portals, or into the trim gardens, with smooth shaven lawns, of no large extent, but still affording reasonable breathing space.[33]

The appeal of such a leafy refuge from the stresses of urban life is attested by the rash of park estates that followed. Fulwood Park, Clifton Park, Grassendale Park, Cressington Park, Sandown Park and Sandfield Park were all begun in the 1840s. Other contemporary developments such as

Figure 9.2 The Entrance to Rock Park, Rock Ferry (pre-1914 postcard)

Grove Park, Olive (later Victoria) Park and Fairfield Crescent adopted the picturesque layout of curving roads or took the form of quiet cul-de-sacs, but they dispensed with the security measure of lodges and gates. Similar estates continued to be formed later in the century: Waterloo Park and Oakhill Park date from the mid-1860s, Litherland Park is perhaps a little earlier, while Moor Park at Great Crosby seems to have been begun as late as the 1890s. The most exclusive were Sandfield Park and Fulwood Park. They had the largest houses, set in the most spacious grounds, and were home to some of Liverpool's leading families. Both retained their status throughout the nineteenth century, so that Orchard, writing in 1893, could say of Fulwood Park that 'to live . . . even in its smallest house, has long been suggestive of ultra social importance'.[34]

The picturesque combination of well-to-do housing and man-made landscape was not confined to private estates. At exactly the time Fulwood Park, Sandfield Park and the rest were being laid out, the philanthropic iron merchant Richard Vaughan Yates created Princes Park, a public park with associated housing, modelled on London's Regents Park (Figure 9.3).

The prospectus set out the thinking behind Yates's plan:

> The want of a park for the recreation of the inhabitants of Liverpool, as well as for a healthful place of residence, has long been felt, especially of late years, when almost every pleasant Suburb of the Town has been encroached upon by mean buildings and narrow and confined streets.[35]

The park, designed by Joseph Paxton, would provide an attractive outlook for the perimeter housing, while the gardens of the houses would add to the apparent extent of the park. The income from the housing was intended to offset the cost of making and maintaining the park. Princes Park was quickly followed by the much larger Birkenhead Park, laid out by Paxton in 1843–47, where once again the perimeter plots were designated for housing (Figure 9.4). The same principle was adopted for the three parks created by Liverpool Corporation in the 1860s, Stanley Park, Newsham Park and above all Sefton Park.[36]

Figure 9.3 Princes Park, Liverpool (1842–43) (pre-1914 postcard)

Figure 9.4 'Rustic Bridge, Birkenhead Park and Zoological Institution' (engraved by Newman and Co, *Pinkney's Birkenhead Views*, No. 7 (Birkenhead, c. 1847))

Blundellsands, six miles north of the centre, has features in common both with these house-fringed public parks and with the earlier private estates, and it is probably Liverpool's best example of a planned villa suburb. It was developed by the local landowner William Blundell of Crosby Hall from the 1850s, but the greater part was laid out from 1865 with a network of curving roads lined mostly with large villas. In the centre is a small park, but the real focus is the seafront. Far from being sequestered, the houses were visible from the sands and from the roads, as well as from the railway that made the suburb viable in the first place. A journalist from the *Porcupine*, who visited Blundellsands early in its development, described in unflattering detail the houses of several anonymous but easily identifiable merchants.[37] Whereas retirement and seclusion had once been the aim of suburban living, here there was arguably an element of parade.

Holiday Homes and Country Houses

Those who could not afford to own a suburban villa could always rent one: Thomas Fletcher took lodgings for his family in Woolton in the autumn of 1798 (from which he rode to town each day) and in 1818 he rented a seaside cottage near the new Waterloo Hotel at Crosby.[38] By the 1830s, the development of seaside terraces at Waterloo was specifically targeted at commuting merchants, as the prospectus for Adelaide Crescent made clear when it extolled the convenient proximity of canal packet boats and omnibuses timed to connect with the Liverpool and Manchester Railway.[39] By the same date New Brighton was being laid out, catering for a higher class of resident or visitor. Houses there were 'let to private families by the week or month, well furnished,' and the sea views offered refreshment to the 'fatigued and exhausted merchant emerging from his counting-house prison'.[40] The Holts were among those who took houses at New Brighton during the summer months.[41]

The suburban or seaside cottage continued to be a refuge from the overheated town throughout the nineteenth century. In 1865, shortly after C. K. Prioleau built his palatial house at 19 Abercromby Square, he commissioned the same architects to design a well-appointed cottage at Halewood. It had a drawing room, dining room, sewing room, four bedrooms, bath room, WC and dressing room, as well as accommodation for a servant.[42] Waterloo remained a popular retreat and the cotton and general broker John H. Turner of Abercromby Square was among those who had summer residences there in the 1860s.[43] As late as 1882, the shipowner Albert Crompton employed A. H. Mackmurdo to design a pair of cottages further north among the Formby sand dunes. By this date, however, the spread of the railways meant the weekend cottage no longer had to be on the fringes of the town. Windermere had become accessible by train in 1847 and in 1850 George Holt considered renting a cottage at nearby Ambleside. He still doubted the practicality of such a move—'the distance from Liverpool is great, inconveniently so for a person engaged in business, not only as to time, the most serious consideration, but as to expense also'—but he took the cottage from May to October the following year and found he was able to visit regularly for weekends or longer stays.[44] The chemical manufacturer A. G. Kurtz's summer home was at Penmaenmawr near Conway, where the regular rail connection with Liverpool meant that he occasionally returned for the day, if business required it.

No doubt with an eye to possible employment, the Liverpool architect Lewis Hornblower pointed out the new opportunities opened up by train travel: 'Two hours' journey suffice to place the weary merchant or trader on the Vale of Clwyd, in the centre of Cheshire, Shropshire and Staffordshire, or on the borders of Yorkshire or Cumberland, where he may rest his excited frame, and, freed from the cares of discounts and bank interest, indulge his prurient fancy in the beauties of nature'.[45] Not only cottages, but large country houses were thus brought within easier reach. The banker John Pemberton Heywood maintained his West Derby house, Norris Green, but also built the grand mansion called Cloverley in Shropshire. The brothers T. B. Horsfall and G. H. Horsfall lived respectively at Mill Bank House, West Derby, and Larkfield, Aigburth, but also acquired and extended the mansions of Bellamour Hall, Staffordshire, and Kilhendre Hall, Shropshire. Heywood employed Eden Nesfield for his country house, but the Horsfalls used a Liverpool practice—Culshaw & Sumners[46]—and there were other Liverpool clients who did the same. Ellel Grange, near Lancaster, was designed by William Weightman in 1857 for the merchant William Preston, while the banker John Naylor employed W. H. Gee at Leighton Hall near Welshpool. For some, such as the wine and spirit merchant R. C. Gardner, the acquisition of a country house allowed them to re-establish their roots. Gardner came to Liverpool in his youth from the Fylde coast, near Pilling. He lived for a time at Newsham House, then from the 1860s at Beechcroft in Croxteth Road, but he meanwhile built a mansion at Pilling, extending his estates in the area and making agricultural improvements.[47]

The wealthiest of Liverpool's business elite were willing to travel considerably further than rural Lancashire to escape. When he was not at Calderstones, the shipowner Charles McIver spent much of his time at his Maltese home, the Palazzo Sliema, while the coal proprietor John Grant Morris, whose suburban mansion Allerton Priory had been designed by Alfred Water-house, employed the same architect for his Villa Allerton at Cannes.[48] Its grounds were probably laid out by Edouard André, the Parisian landscape gardener responsible (with Lewis Horn-blower) for Sefton Park.[49] Among Morris's neighbours in the south of France were the Liverpool merchants James Bland at Villa Champfleuri and Bernard Hall at Villa Mariposa.[50] For a few men of this class a private steam yacht could serve as a kind of mobile holiday home. Cruising round the west coast of Scotland on board the *Vanadis* in 1883, the shipowner T. H. Ismay and his wife met the brewer Sir Andrew Barclay Walker and dined with him on board his famous *Cuhona*. Furnished with antiques and insured for £18,500, Margaret Ismay had viewed it earlier in the year and pronounced it 'magnificently fitted up'.[51] The Holts meanwhile holidayed on board the *Argo*, built to the designs of Alfred Holt in 1875, which took them to the Mediter-ranean, Iceland and Norway.

Distinct from summer or weekend homes were houses at a distance from Liverpool, which served as the merchant's principal residence. Since the eighteenth century, it had been common for those who made fortunes in Liverpool to retire to an estate in Cheshire or Shropshire and live the life of a country gentleman. James Aspinall recalled how, at the beginning of the nineteenth century, the Cheshire gentry feared the influx of Liverpool merchants, believing they would 'buy the acres of all the wiseacres in the county, and so exterminate the original squirearchy'. Joseph Leigh, for example, 'one of the most pushing and rich of our enterprising merchants' had subsequently moved to Belmont, 'a splendid place in Cheshire'.[52] The slave trader Thomas Parr, who gave up his newly built house in Colquitt Street before 1805 and removed to Lythwood Hall in Shropshire, was typical of many successful Liverpool merchants.[53] Although Orchard claimed in 1893 that Liverpool's 'old' families liked to remain close to the source of their wealth and to the social milieu in which their status was acknowledged, the perception of the Liver-pool merchant as a bird of passage was still strong at the end of the century. The Rev. T. W. M. Lund complained that it was 'largely the fashion for men to regard this great commercial centre merely as a happy hunting ground, in which to make a fortune; then to carry it away to sunnier climes and spend it there'.[54]

In the middle of the century, Cheshire and Shropshire, along with North Wales, Lanca-shire, Cumberland and Westmoreland, were still the favourite destinations for these men. A good example is James Jenkinson Bibby, founder of the Bibby Line, who bought the estate of Hardwicke Grange, Shropshire, in 1868, when he retired from business (Figure 9.5).[55]

Figure 9.5 Hardwick Grange, Shropshire (drawn and published by John Preston Neale, 1818–1829)

For others, such as the cotton and general broker John Higson, ongoing business connections made it desirable to remain in the orbit of Liverpool. Oakmere Hall, near Sandiway in Cheshire, was designed for Higson by John Douglas in 1867, and he died there in 1893, at the age of 76, having remained actively involved in the city's commercial life almost to the end.[56] In the last quarter of the century the lure of the Home Counties became stronger and the shipowning uncle and nephew James Harrison and Thomas Fenwick Harrison ended up respectively at Dornden near Tunbridge Wells and at King's Walden Bury in Hertfordshire.[57] Contrary to Lund's complaint, the millionaire T. F. Harrison continued to support charitable causes in Liverpool long after he left the city in 1889. He paid for new schools at St Anne's, Stanley and for the chapel of the new Blue Coat School, and he was an important donor to the Cathedral and University.

According to Orchard, London did not hold much attraction for Liverpool society. However, several Merseyside-based plutocrats did keep town houses in fashionable parts of the West End. J. Pemberton Heywood's was in Connaught Place, J. J. Bibby's in Hill Street, John Grant Morris's in Grosvenor Place and Sir John Brunner's in Ennismore Gardens. Gustavus C. Schwabe left Broughton Hall in West Derby for number 19 Kensington Palace Gardens and F. R. Leyland's celebrated house in Prince's Gate, with its Peacock Room decorated by Whistler, became the shipowner's principal residence in succession to Woolton Hall. T. H. Ismay, though often in London for business and pleasure, seems to have used hotels or stayed with friends. His principal residence was the magnificent Dawpool just eight miles from Liverpool on the Dee estuary, designed for him by Richard Norman Shaw and completed in 1886 at a cost of £53,000.[58] The site was an isolated one, but within 18 months the house had a convenient rail link with the capital via the Birkenhead Railway from Thurstaston to Hooton.

Suburban Tensions

Like John Britton at the beginning of the nineteenth century, William Allingham in 1873 was impressed by the great swathe of affluent suburban housing around Liverpool:

> the crowds of comfortable and luxurious villas that besprinkle the country for miles . . . inhabited by ship-owners, ship-insurers, corn merchants, cotton brokers, *emigrant agents, &c., &c., men with 'one* foot on sea, and one on shore,' yet to one thing constant ever— namely, money-making.' But he also noted the contrast between these dwellings of the élite and 'the thick fringe of humbler houses in the immediate suburbs wherein their clerks abide.[59]

Allingham's description presents a static picture of immutable segregation, but of course the affluent suburbs were constantly retreating before the spreading tide of mass housing. Liverpool's population rose from 286,487 in 1841 to 493,346 in 1871 and during those 30 years an average of 1,527 new houses was built annually.[60] Some wealthy enclaves were engulfed and obliterated; others became islands, cut off by the sea of courts and terraces. J. R. Isaac's aerial view of Liverpool from the south, painted in 1858, vividly shows the interface between the trim, early nineteenth-century villas of Toxteth in their neat gardens, and the inexorably advancing streets and courts.[61] Just visible in the corner is the green oasis of Princes Park. In 1877 it was described as 'more or less a village of merchant-princes' houses',[62] but by this date the 'village' was surrounded on the northwest and southwest by tightly packed terraced streets. The boulevard of Prince's Road and Prince's Avenue linked the park with the Mosslake Fields area and the commercial centre, but it was no more than a narrow causeway of affluence. Immediately behind its substantial terraces of the 1870s and 80s and its imposing places of worship, there were rows and rows of much simpler workers' houses. Nowhere is the contrast clearer than in South Street, where very small houses stand literally in the shadow of the grand ones facing the Park, a startling juxtaposition.

A. G. Kurtz, born in Liverpool in 1825, lived through this period of change. An inveterate walker, he saw the process of erosion and transformation daily as it happened and recorded it in his diary. By the time he was in his late fifties, the Liverpool of his youth seemed to be vanishing before his eyes. Lodge Lane, where he went to school (and where William Roscoe and Thomas Booth had once lived in suburban tranquillity) had become unrecognisable: 'This once pretty road is now a street of shops, & not high-class shops either'. Everton appalled him: 'What were once aristocratic & delightful suburban mansions with stately gardens are now squalid dwellings & miserable rows of houses & courts'. Kensington, where he had lived in his twenties, was just as bad—'All gone! The pretty gardens are now covered with shops & the surroundings become ugly & sordid'—and always there were further unwelcome changes in prospect: 'We returned home through the new streets they are cutting between W[aver]tree Road & Smithdown Rd & that once delightful space will shortly become covered with poor property'.[63]

Some suburban estates, more removed from the centre, proved suitable for laying out with high-class housing rather than terraces. When he died in 1854, the ironmaster Charles Tayleur bequeathed the Parkfield estate between Ullet Road and Aigburth Road to be used by his heirs for building.[64] It was ideally situated next to the villa district around Princes Park, where a critical mass of high-class housing already existed. When Sefton Park was laid out immediately to the north-east in 1867–72, the location became even more advantageous and very large houses were built along the newly formed Alexandra Drive between the mid-1860s and the early 1870s. Further north, in the vicinity of Edge Lane, redevelopment of the Fairfield Hall estate had begun under E. D. Falkner before 1833. After the estate was acquired by William Lockerby in 1847, further streets were formed and villas built, soon to be followed by fashionable churches, so that Fairfield became a very select suburb indeed by the 1860s.[65]

Lockerby was one of several Liverpool merchants who encouraged villa development on sites adjoining their own houses. It meant a loss of privacy and seclusion but made it possible to control the social and architectural character of the area and at the same time turn a profit. An outstanding developer of this kind was the iron merchant John Gibbons of Mossley Hill. Between 1869 and 1883 he built numerous large houses on land he owned in Elmsley Road and Palmerston Road adjoining his own house in Mossley Hill Road. The area was nicknamed 'Gibbonsville' by Kurtz, who marvelled at the number of villas squeezed into such a limited space.[66] Gibbons's land was crossed by the new line of the LNWR, opened in 1862, and the railway station on Rose Lane made the villas attractive to commuting merchants. However, the line cut off one small corner of the property, adjacent to Bridge Road, and this Gibbons developed with very humble terraced cottages exploiting the railway as a sort of *cordon sanitaire*.[67]

More typical must have been the experience of the Holt family. They had once been comfortably distant from the town, but by the 1860s they felt themselves under siege. On his marriage to Emma Durning in 1820, the cotton merchant George Holt established himself in Rake Lane (now Durning Road), almost two miles from the Exchange, and acquired a considerable extent of land around the house. By the time of his death in 1861, the amenity of the estate was already threatened by the encroachment of mean, ugly buildings and the corporation wanted to build a road across the property to improve north-south communications. When George's daughter Anne returned from a continental holiday in 1863, she found that a large public house had been built nearby and 'new streets of small property laid out on the adjoining desolate land'. The following year, the threat drew closer when a neighbouring mansion was demolished: 'Its grounds are to be thickly covered over with rows of small houses, which must no doubt effect a considerable change for the worse about us', wrote Anne;

> And what much more affects the inside pleasantness of our house, the green slope of Mr Leigh's park, which has always been so pretty an object from our drawing and dining room windows, is being cut up for bricks & the kiln was first lighted on Monday night. The change is melancholy enough to us, but nothing more than the vast increase of the town necessitates.[68]

In 1871 Emma Holt died, and later that year William, the eldest son, moved to a house in Sandfield Park, West Derby. He proceeded to sell off the Rake Lane estate to speculative builders, who at once began covering it with a dense grid of terraced streets for 'the artisan or clerk class'.[69] Of his four brothers, George had already moved to Sandfield Park in 1861, and Alfred to Holly Road, Fairfield, in 1865, while Philip and Robert bought sites for new houses in Sefton Park in 1872.

Transport Developments and the Journey to Work

Suburbanisation was affected by a range of factors, including social class (specifically the income of prospective residents), technological developments, geographical location, aesthetic considerations and both political and planning constraints.[70] But its spatial configuration was determined primarily by improvements in the transport infrastructure, in particular the provision of horse-drawn omnibuses, the construction of railway and tram lines and the expansion of the

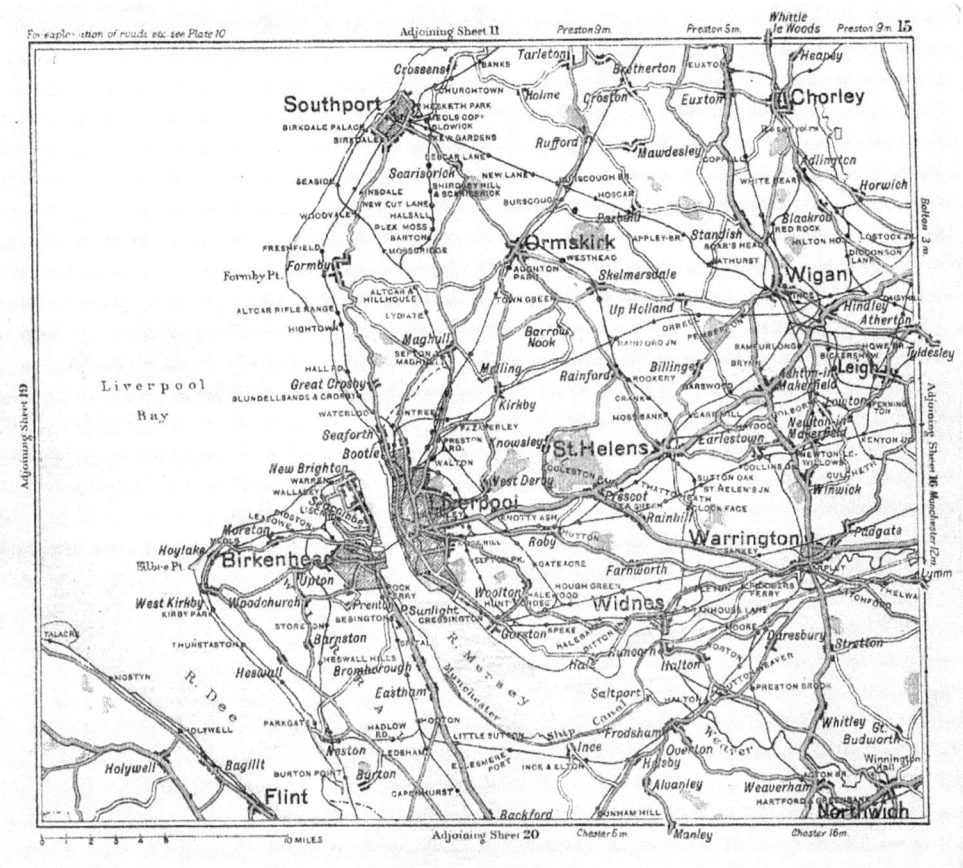

Figure 9.6 A railway and road map of Liverpool and its immediate hinterlands (c.1908) (from G. W. Bacon, 'Liverpool and Its Environs', plate 15, London, c. 1908)

existing road system (Figure 9.6) which reflected the needs of a rising number of commuters from Liverpool's business and professional community. The map is from the early twentieth century and demonstrates the extent to which Liverpool was closely bound to its Lancashire suburbs, the Wirral and more distant hinterlands, including East Cheshire, the industrial towns of Leigh, Wigan and Chorley, and North Wales.[71]

People could and did walk long distances, creating gendered space as they did: Mosslake Fields was about as far as the average merchant would wish to walk to work on a daily basis, whether rain or shine, particularly because of the uphill journey on his return home, although in February 1887 (when the 'mini ice age' was at its coldest) the shipowner Thomas Ismay, having alighted from a ferry boat, walked some eight miles to his home at Dawpool.[72] However, it was the next stage of centrifugal development characterised by the suburban villa which really created the 'journey to work' problem. Liverpool's commerce could only expand if a growing number of merchants and businessmen worked in the town centre. This created pressure on the supply of suitable residential housing, which necessitated the development of up-market residences further away from Liverpool's urban core. As a result, the distances people had to travel to work were bound to increase. Changes in taste and concerns over public health issues exaggerated this trend, as successful men increasingly sought suburban villas with gardens and later 'pocket stately homes' with plots of several acres. This simply could not happen with the level of passenger transport, public or private, which existed before 1830. Aggregate data on the local and regional mobility of merchants has already been presented in Chapter 2: this section will analyse the factors which influenced personal decisions on residential relocation. During the second half of the nineteenth century there was a continued expansion in the size of the merchant community and its members were active agents in the suburbanisation process. But to what extent did new modes of transport contribute to its spatial fragmentation?

At a meeting of the 30 Club in 1897 on the occasion of a discussion on 'Liverpool in the older days', it was noted that changing conditions had brought about 'the removal of the wealthy classes to districts lying farther away'.[73] In Liverpool, as in other large provincial cities, there was a close and observable link between the move to the suburbs and improvements in public passenger transport, especially the building of suburban railways, but the question of cause and effect remains a vexed one which will be re-examined utilising information contained in the MLP database and further evidence from street directories and OS maps.

Carriage Folk

Some merchants rode to work on horseback during our period, but with the growth of other modes of transport they were a minority. Those who lived beyond walking distance and were not riding were either driving or being driven to work in private carriages or using horse-drawn public transport (either omnibuses or trams), at least until the arrival of the first suburban railway stations. It is clear from surviving buildings and map evidence that a fair number of the elite used private carriages, probably to get to work as well as for social display, for the grounds of their houses often included a stable yard or coach house. But this was an expensive business.[74] The 'entry level' running cost for a small single brougham which might have been owned by a small-scale merchant was about 10 per cent of an assumed annual income of £500,[75] although for a young man just starting out in business it was possible to buy a little gig or curricle, complete with a suitable pony, for as little as £50 in all. Above the 'entry level', however, suppliers of both goods and services would happily relieve you of any amount of money you liked. James Evans, one of Liverpool's most successful coach builders, undertook to build to order 'carriages of every description' according to the customer's preference.[76] However, there was no direct correlation between wealth and carriage ownership. In 1851, Robert Wynne (a shipowner and merchant living in Allerton) had just two servants, of whom one was a coachman, while Thomas Earle had a coachman and four grooms out of a servant establishment of ten. Conversely, there were servant establishments of 12 or more without a coachman and in 1901 Sir Alfred Jones, who was certainly not short of money, had no resident 'equine' staff at all.

There was also the possibility of using cabs regularly. There is plentiful anecdotal evidence that our merchants used them, but no quantitative data as to how many or how often. Even in the early twentieth century, cabmen queued for customers disembarking from the Liverpool ferry boats at the Pier Entrance in Seacombe before the construction of the tram lines (Figure 9.7), but early omnibuses were regarded as superior to cabs in comfort and cleanliness. This might suggest that cabs of the day were of a decidedly low standard, but for commuting purposed, whether for business or pleasure, they still served a useful purpose. Nor were they cheap: fares started at 1s for the first mile and racked up with a gloomy inevitability for each half mile thereafter. They were not well suited to either the punctilious or the thrifty.

An alternative for merchants needing private transport, with quite large properties, a spacious drive and turning circle but no stable yard, was to rent space in a purpose-built neighbourhood mews, but their overall availability remained restricted. By engaging the services of a jobmaster

Figure 9.7 Pier Entrance, Seacombe (pre-1902 postcard)

many problems could be resolved in a cost-effective manner. He could store the customer's carriage or rent him one; supply a horse or horses and, if desired, a driver. If a groom or horse went sick, which was not uncommon, it was his problem, not the customer's. In town, the need to find a repository for the horse and vehicle, typically located a little outside the city centre (because of land price considerations) was obviated, although for shorter distances it might have been cheaper for the servant to drive the carriage home and return later to pick up his master. By 1900, at least in some of the more extravagant families, the master could telephone home with instructions as to when he needed his carriage. A 'full service' (driver and horses) could be provided to households which had their own carriage but no stables, using the turning circle in front of the house. The decline in carriage use for commuting purposes is reflected by the fact that by the end of the nineteenth century only five jobmasters were listed in Liverpool, although some of the 24 livery stable keepers offered useful facilities to aspiring carriage folk.[77]

At least on the Wirral merchants and professionals using the ferry boats to commute into Liverpool could use facilities offered by hotels to accommodate their carriages, horses and grooms, despite the additional costs involved. The Royal Rock Hotel, Rock Ferry, had a yard of c.120 ft by 60 ft surrounded by extensive stabling and coach houses, two well-separated grades of accommodation for masters and servants and a basic alehouse for staff left there while their masters were in Liverpool. Similar facilities existed at the New Ferry Hotel, at the recently demolished Woodside Hotel and the nearby Pier Hotel, of which only the servants' bar survives. Jesse Hartley had earlier solved the problem by building a coach house and stable in the Dock Yard for his personal use, but no equivalent mercantile example of a predecessor to the Directors' Car Park could be found.

It was considered distinctly *nouveau riche* among 'old' merchant families to use a formal carriage, such as a town chariot on wet days or a barouche on sunny ones, but there were those who used larger but comparatively informal vehicles like double broughams.[78] Thomas Hornby was mildly satirised in the *Liberal Review* for 19 March 1881 for the smartness of the carriage and horses which took him to his office. There is evidence that he was a less-than-brilliant chairman of the Mersey Docks & Harbour Board, but he was undoubtedly aware that maintaining the dignity of his office affected the respect in which the Board was held, which was but a short step from the question of its credit-rating and the key to its medium-term success.

This step up in carriage prestige did not just increase the feeding bill by 100 per cent. A small horse suitable for a light phaeton or small brougham might be bought for under £50, as could a tram horse, but a fine matched pair of large bays suitable for a formal vehicle for moderately grand occasions would cost up to £1,000. Spending anywhere near one's limit of affordability was foolhardy, for a minor fall might scar a horse's knees or break its tail (depending on which way it fell) which would cut a couple of hundred pounds from its value, as well as another couple of hundred from its partner's, unless one had the wonderful good fortune to find another one that matched perfectly.

Few accounts of actual 'running costs' for horses exist, but Horne and Maund's estimate that tram horses cost 9s 11½d per head per week to feed. Tram horses were about the same size and weight as good carriage horses, but they were much harder worked and therefore ate more. Stable wages and expenses added 3s 6d per horse per week. These costs would be substantially higher for carriage horses, for which some cost for exercise needed to be added, before allowing for economies of scale in a large establishment.[79]

A rough idea of the cost of hiring 'horses only' for a merchant's own carriage may be gained from the corporation's 'Mayoral Carriage Account'.[80] In 1851–52, the corporation was paying £98 15s per quarter for horse hire to J. R. Gorst & Co. and this gradually climbed to £525 per annum by 1871–72. The Lord Mayor's dress coach (1818) was drawn by two horses for low-key trips and four for grand occasions, possibly even six for a royal visit. There were other vehicles from time to time, but only ever one coachman. This might seem a lot of money for the hire of a capital asset which could be purchased outright for about four or five years' hire, but hiring eliminated several other costs, such as depreciation, paying a groom, keeping the horses in good health, well exercised when not working, well shod and, much the largest item, well fed. The incoming mayor was allowed £2,000 for his civic expenses during his year of office but paid £700 back to meet the cost of keeping the carriages. By sometimes charging items to the general rate rather than the Carriage Account the 'bottom line' always ended up close to £700 which represented a consensus on the sort of cost which councillors thought reasonable. Coaching provision had to be dignified and effective without being open to accusations of ostentation or extravagance, which is exactly what the more substantial merchant carriage-owners wanted for themselves. Of course, few elite merchants sought to emulate corporation policy since hiring carriage horses was clearly not inexpensive.

It is impossible to estimate the overall cost of carriage ownership because so many options were available, depending on the owner's means and the importance attached to his carriage(s).[81] At the top end of the market, a reasonable dress coach cost at least £500, if not considerably more, but a matched set of four really fine horses to draw it would attract a premium over two pairs of up to £1,000 per pair and it was possible to spend as much on dress harness and elaborate liveries as on the coach itself. However, attending a ball at the Town Hall was an important networking function and it is reasonable to assume that some merchants used formal vehicles, sometimes decorated with pseudo-heraldic devices on the door panels or elsewhere, particularly in the case of merchants who were not armigerous. Was that, like some of the apparent leisure activities considered in Chapter 5, a 'journey to work' as well?

It is easy to find houses which would apparently not have been built for, sold or rented to elite merchants if they were not willing to make extensive use of private carriages. In Oxton there was a cluster of very substantial houses in Wexford Road, Noctorum Road and others nearby, of which a handful survives as monuments to Edwardian plutocracy. They were poorly located for getting to work any other way than by carriage, for enabling the lady of the house to undertaken shopping or other outings and for giving or attending dinner parties.[82] In 1904–05, W. R. Henderson, a partner in the famous merchant house of Balfour Williamson, decided to add a coach house and stable block to his new house, Menlo, on the corner of Wexford Road and Budworth Road. After work had started, he asked for some alterations to allow space for a 'motor house'. It only had two stalls and one loose box, but measured c.80 ft by 40 ft, a footprint for a new house of which many professional men would have been proud. The final bill was £2,250 which would have bought a very decent house.[83] Yet the main house had a frontage of only about 110 ft and the plot was 4.6 acres, by no means the largest in the immediate vicinity. At Chenotrie, on nearby Noctorum Road, the stables and coach houses were arranged around a 50 ft square yard.[84]

But Oxton residents also made use of alternative arrangements by using cab companies: not far away from the homes of the really wealthy there were some very large 'semis' on Bidston Road, each with frontages of about 70 ft placing them well into merchant territory, which had carriage drives with turn-rounds but no outbuildings. This sudden investment in an area providing high quality housing relatively close to Liverpool was probably influenced by 'journey to work' considerations and the availability of firms able to respond to the residents' transport needs. Unfortunately, the absence of directory headings for specific occupations or businesses such as 'jobmaster' or livery stables and the inclusion of just about everything to do with horses under 'Coach and Car Proprietors' make it difficult to assess the changing level of supply. But the expensive areas were served by a small cluster of firms in Claughton Village, including the Oxton Carriage Co. with branches in Beresford Road and Wellington Road, handy for local merchant and professional residents. In Liverpool the number of 'Coach and Car Proprietors' rose from c.150 in 1876 to over 300 in 1892, before dwindling to about 200 in 1911. Some of these were undertakings of considerable size: White's Carriage Co., which advertised 'horses jobbed by the week, month or year' had twelve branches, mostly in the south end of the city.

Another way of quantifying the upper echelons of carriage users would by a simple count of 'live-in' coachmen. But this too turns out to be far from simple: of the small, wealthy cluster of Oxton residents cited previously only John Dempster, steamship agent, of Tynron, appears to have employed one.[85] However, in 1901, 23 merchants in Noctorum employed collectively nine coachmen or grooms, with the South American merchant Joseph Beausire maintaining not only a coachman and his family in a separate lodge, but also two grooms with accommodation over the stables.[86] But this relatively high ratio was not matched by other pockets of mercantile wealth, such as Highfield South where there were only two resident coachmen for 37 merchants. The fashionable part of Allerton was both remote from the town centre and ill-provided with public transport, but a total of 151 merchants provided employment for only 20 live-in coachmen and 9 grooms. The merchants of Noctorum were far more dependent on the use of private carriages than their Allerton counterparts, while the business community in Highfield South clearly relied on other forms of transport to manage the journey to work.

Carriage use was widespread: in 1900, 60 'Coach and Carriage Builders' were listed in the directory, some of them obviously large undertakings, including William Furnival's firm with seven branches and Joseph Atkinson's business with an extensive Liverpool branch (93–97 Silvester Street, Scotland Road), one in Bootle (22 Derby Road), and a head office in Leeds.[87]

Even if gentlemen travelled some distance to commission a new or second-hand carriage, the city could scarcely have supported so many firms unless there was a high level of demand for a good deal of repair and maintenance work, with the majority of firms in places like St. Anne Street, just outside the city centre. Carriages were straightforward and durable devices, so a high level of maintenance indicated a high level of use. But horses also required regular attention and the number of veterinary surgeons registered in Liverpool and its surrounding areas might offer a further means of assessing the relative use of private carriages by the business community and its impact on residential location.

The docks and associated industries on both sides of the Mersey depended heavily on horse-drawn transport, but the number of veterinary surgeons registered in the directories declined steadily over our period. However, this is not a reliable indicator of the actual number of vets practising their trade, because of an on-going process of firm amalgamations and the opening of multiple branches by established practitioners. By 1900, veterinary medicine was still not effectively professionalised and it was not until 1904 that the first veterinary school was incorporated into a British university as Liverpool sought to extend its coverage of medical sciences.[88] In the early 1880s, for example, veterinary surgeons were more likely to be located in the city centre (in Cheapside or Duke Street) or close to the docks, than in middle-class suburbs favoured by elite merchants; they were sometimes retained by livery stables; and the occasional dependency on secondary employment (as a milk dealer) or the earnings of a charwoman wife emphasises the inherent difficulty in utilising the changing distribution of veterinary surgeons as an indicator of carriage ownership.[89] More seriously, it is impossible to distinguish between the proportion of practitioners employed by commercial firms rather than the private sector.

There seems little chance of estimating accurately trends in carriage ownership among members of the merchant community, but the phenomenon of the 'public funeral' provides an indication of contemporary practice. At funerals attended by the mayor in his dress coach and full regalia, sometimes with police outriders, the hearse was normally followed by six or eight mourning carriages, but they were seldom drawn by four horses. When this occurred at the funeral of Sir William Brown it was remarked that all of the 36 horses (four each for the hearse and the eight mourning carriages) were 'fairly matched'.[90] The ability of the local jobmaster, W. & D. Busby, to respond to the undertaker's requirements indicates the considerable scale of his business operation.[91] It was customary for private carriages to follow the formal cortège and 'apologies for absence' might take the form of sending one's empty carriage. It was also commonplace to have a couple of dozen private carriages following the hearse, although in an extreme case in May 1876 for the funeral of Lt. Colonel Thomson 'about two hundred' private carriages were involved. This, be it noted, was at a funeral regarded as 'unostentatious' in the sense that the principal mourners rode in their own carriages (and only four of them), rather than in hired mourning vehicles, despite the fact that special trains for those attending were run to Broad Green Station.[92] It was an atypical occasion, however, since Thomson was one of the very few mayors to die in office, which required 'a representative gathering' with top merchants attending not only as individuals, but also as members of the Corporation (Rathbone, Holt, Forwood), as members of MD&HB (Brancker, Hubback) and as Magistrates (Langton, Stitt), accompanied by literally hundreds of other mourners on a list with over six pages of names. William Langton, a general merchant and chairman of both the Pacific Steam Ship Co. and the Bank of Liverpool, is said to have been well known for his disapproval of funerary excesses, but this did not save him from having 15 carriages follow his hearse, with a couple of hundred named mourners travelling directly to the cemetery. The funeral of S. R. Graves MP was a simple 'semi-public' affair with only seven mourning coaches, but it turned into a public spectacle with a cortège stretching over a mile, including 24 out of 27 of his MD&HB colleagues and an estimated 20,000 onlookers.

Horse-Drawn Public Transport and Electric Tramcars

Commuting by carriage was an expensive business and for many it was prohibitively so. By contrast, public transport was intended to meet the commuting needs of the wider middle class. When building plots at relatively up-market Cressington Park were first offered for sale one of their claimed advantages was proximity to the 'Omnibus station'.[93] Gentlemen using that service were doing so from choice, perhaps considering the daily use of a carriage as an extravagance: a few of the larger houses in the park had separate coach houses and stables, but they may have been more for 'social' carriage use than for commuting.

The first British omnibuses were probably those put into service in Manchester in 1824 but the vehicles only seated about ten: the first Liverpool buses (1830) were about the same size. Later horse buses seated anything up to 21 passengers and were drawn by three or occasionally four horses. While it was somewhat basic by carriage standards, it was a great improvement on any previous form of urban public transport. Horse-drawn omnibuses may not have been tailored for the crème-de-la-crème, but we find complaints of gentlemen riding on the platform rather than inside in order to enjoy a cigar along the way. Ironically, 'outside' seats were substantially cheaper than 'inside' ones and gentlemen could have travelled more cheaply, smoked their cigars and had a seat as well, but presumably that would have been insufficiently rakish. The 'omnibus' was not really 'for everybody' for fares were high: c.1840 the Old Swan & Knotty Ash omnibus cost 6d outside and 10d inside. It is said that the latter amount included (by prior arrangement only) driving the 'bus to a gentleman's door to pick him up, but it must be remembered that in 1840, Knotty Ash was an extremely prosperous area, as was much of the property along the route from the town centre to Old Swan. This was not a service for the lower orders. So far into town as Kensington there were still 'semis' to be found with 70 ft frontages and the appurtenances of carriage use. Other early routes went out to the new developments in Toxteth and on to Aigburth, a rapidly expanding élite area of which more shortly. By 1870 there were some 31 horse omnibus routes, the great majority of which served predominantly genteel destinations and fares were by then rather lower. Horne & Maund have identified 54 different operators: many were small and/or short-lived; services ran with a frequency of only a few minutes; and competition drove down prices. But the fares placed them beyond the reach of most citizens.[94]

The horse tram took matters a stage further. Its lower rolling resistance allowed higher speed, better hill-climbing using fewer horses (depending on the route), and larger seating capacities— between 32 and 48—than on omnibuses. In 1860 pretty well all existing operators merged into the Liverpool Road and Rail Omnibus Company Ltd., a sizeable operation then owning nearly 1,000 horses.[95] In short, we must not assume that the horse 'bus' was just a primitive antecedent of the tramcar or that it suffered the social stigma of the post-World War Two motor bus. It was a serious contender for the business of even major merchants in the process of suburban relocation. Particularly on minor routes some buses remained competitive right down to the municipalisation of the tram services.

The horse-drawn tramway has a fascinating story all its own, both in company ownership and (briefly) after 'municipalisation'. It began with a tram service which ran on the MD&HB's 'Line of Docks Railway' from 1859, but it was a service for business travel, not commuting. Politics now intervened and there were a couple of other failed attempts before real progress was made in 1869, when a new Liverpool Tramways Company began to construct a route to Dingle which was part of a more ambitious scheme of building an 'inner city loop' with lines radiating to the suburbs. By 1871, they had powers to build in potential commuter heartlands, including Aigburth, Wavertree, Old Swan, West Derby, Walton, Bootle and Seaforth. But the company was unsound, as were its trackbeds, and there was no commuter revolution until 1876 when the two main players merged to form a monopoly provider—or so they hoped. However, sundry pirate omnibus operators soon appeared on the scene (Figures 9.8a and 9.8b).

Horse trams extended the network, but they also made it easier to get around town rather than just in or out. In one sense, they were the harbinger of the municipal electric tramways using converted or newly built carriages in a paroxysm of investment between 1898 and 1903 after which activity slowed somewhat. These new routes and the corporation's penny fares transformed mobility: almost at a stroke they made longer-range commuting affordable to a much larger proportion of the population.

In 1908, the Corporation tried a *douceur* to the middle-class user by introducing a first-class service, with plush inside seating and a very smart and distinctive new livery. At first these cars were all first-class, but seldom operated at full capacity: the upper deck seating had not been upgraded, so they soon ran with first class inside and ordinary class on top. While they were not a huge success, the first class eventually spread to nine routes, employing a maximum of 67 cars. Some of these routes differed according to the time of day, running via Dale Street (for the businessmen) at rush hour and via Church Street at times when their wives might wish to lunch out or go shopping.[97]

The impact of the tram system on the residential location of merchants can be analysed by comparing the OS maps of 1888–89 and 1908. Aigburth Road, from Dingle to Grassendale Park, had grand houses standing in at least a couple of acres virtually all the way along the west side and most of the east. But by the later date the majority of these properties had gone, largely

Figure 9.8a Horse-drawn tram of the Liverpool Tramways Co. manufactured at the Birkenhead factory of George Starbuck & Co. (c.1870s) [note to figure[96]]

Figure 9.8b A Liverpool horse-drawn tram, No. 178 (Kirkdale, Scotland Road, Lime Street), 1898 (pre-1914 postcard)

replaced by a form of development visible on other major tram routes of short blocks of six or eight shops, with two-storey maisonettes above, almost all in Welsh pressed red brick and often with terracotta ornamentation (including the odd date plaque). Between these blocks were long side streets of high-quality terraces aimed at the man earning perhaps £150 per year. Some of the 'grand' houses, such as Roseland (with seven acres) still stood but their market value had fallen considerably. Heathfield (on Heathfield Road) suffered a similar fate: by 1908 there were terraced houses along nearly all its western boundary and almost half its southern one. The merchants had embraced improved transport as a means of escaping from the pollution and overcrowding of the city centre. They had not anticipated the impact of cheap electric tram services, which began tentatively in 1898 but had achieved a modicum of technological maturity as early as 1905 by which time the number of passenger journeys had trebled. Perhaps more important was the fact that the average fare per journey in 1902 was a mere 1s 1d. Improved technology backed by corporation policy was enabling the working class to pursue the merchants, driving them further out of town. According to Forwood:

Few towns had more attractive suburbs . . . now the tramways have encouraged the building of small property in every direction and suburban Liverpool is almost destroyed. The area available for residences has always been limited to the east and south owing to the proximity of St Helens, Wigan, Widnes and Garston. It would have been a wise policy if our city fathers had set apart a sanctuary for better-class houses, from which tramways were excluded, and thus avoid driving so many large ratepayers to the Cheshire side to find a home.[98]

The settlement of Liverpool merchants on the Wirral was already evident by the 1830s, but its popularity increased considerably over time, while relocation to the north of Liverpool was facilitated by railway routes (for there were then two) towards Southport.[99] This takes us back to the great debate about the suburbanisation process. Did railways or other transport under-takings lead development, or vice versa? This issue is complicated by the lack of adequate source material. The railway industry kept a lot of statistics for its own use; the government collected and kept a lot more; and a string of Parliamentary enquiries into railway rates and charges produced more again. None of them exhibits the slightest interest in the question of railway commuting, except on the emotive issue of workmen's cheap tickets. The key prob-lem is the absence of disaggregated data on passenger/miles that reflects the individual usage of railway lines for commuting purposes, without which it is impossible to analyse changes in commuting practice.[100]

As a result, the causative relationship between transport improvements and suburban devel-opment has only ever been addressed on a local scale. The evidence for Liverpool and its sur-rounding districts is complex, because even within a comparatively small area the relationship varied from place to place. Cressington Park was an initial failure as a development from its beginnings in the late 1840s although the situation began to improve when the railway arrived in 1866. But the original plan for the railway had no station at Cressington and there were no bridges over the railway, which meant that the (few) residents would have suffered from the annoyance of two level crossings, as well as noise and smoke, without any tangible benefits in terms of a reduction in their journey-to-work time. In 1861, ten years after building plots first became available, there were only eight households in the park. In 1871, after the opening of the station, there were 29. In this case, suburban development led the railway, as it had with the Liverpool & Manchester, although the situation was subsequently reversed. Edge Hill Station (1836) was the first 'proper' intermediate station between the two termini, built of stone with a purpose-built booking office and platforms shielded by an overall roof. Yet there was little high-grade housing close by and only the ongoing development at Fairfield offered a natural market. It was equipped with spacious road vehicle approaches on each side of the track, suggesting that it may have been intended as an 'interchange' for horse bus services and to save carriage horses negotiating the fairly severe gradient down to the town centre and back. If it was built as a devel-opment leader, it was not a huge success, for the immediate vicinity remained comparatively sparsely built up until it was engulfed by hundreds of ten-foot terrace houses in the 1860s and 1870s, built on land sold by, among others, the Holt and Earle families.[101]

Other places, like Formby, gained considerably by virtue of a railway passing through them bound for somewhere else (Southport), which brought development opportunities. But the rail-way's target was the growing traffic of Southport: Formby was a bonus. But what later became the Lancashire & Yorkshire Railway (L&YR) route from Liverpool to Southport was subject to pressures not observed elsewhere. Its route had been determined by a small predecessor company, the Liverpool, Crosby & Southport, over which two major local landowners had con-siderable influence: they gave the land for much of the route *gratis* because they expected a high dividend from the impact of development potential on their remaining land. In engineering terms, it was a very easy route and the Blundells and the Weld-Blundells boldly decided to avail themselves of the railway crash of 1847–49 and the availability of cheap labour and materials to construct their modest railway within a few months. Some developments sold better than others, but Blundellsands and Birkdale were particularly successful because the plans were deliberately intended to attract wealthy merchants and manufacturers from Liverpool and further afield.[102] There is a story that one Joseph Gardener, having asked the L&YR for an extra station to serve his immediate vicinity, was told that another five houses would need to be built to make it worth the company's while, so he built them. In this case, railway construction led the process of sub-urban development, but it was atypical: it was small, cheap and effectively controlled by two different branches of the same family who both stood to profit mightily from it.[103]

However, the available information is sometimes difficult to interpret. Rock Ferry Station was built close to the grand houses of Rock Park and the surrounding area, reaching down to the pocket estates of Highfield South. But proof of a causal connection in either direction is elusive. Rock Lane Station, about half-way between Rock Ferry and Bebington Stations, was ideally located to serve this little pocket of wealth, but it was an 1846 afterthought (the Chester to Birkenhead Railway had opened in 1840 with a single line operation) and closed in 1862, long before the area began to decline. The answer can be found again from the 1895 Ordnance Survey (25":1-mile sheet) which confirms that the population density was tiny. The smallest houses on the cheap side of Highfield South, for example, were 'semis' on 60 ft wide plots, representing about four households per acre. On the posh side were just three houses, each standing in over an acre of gardens, with carriage rides etc. and screened by over ten acres of wood and parkland. They backed onto the grounds of just two even bigger houses, giving a population density of about five acres to the household. Really wealthy areas were not necessarily a desirable target market, for although they might produce first class customers, there were simply not enough inhabitants within convenient reach of a station. The substantial terraced houses of Rock Lane were a much more likely source of plentiful custom.

Railway timetables offer a little help. The 1910 'Bradshaw's', for example, shows an incidence of short workings between Birkenhead and (for example) Hooton at commuting times with a marked shift of emphasis between freight and passenger traffic.[104] These could be facilitated by the quadrupling of track over short distances near the terminus: the Chester to Birkenhead route was partially quadrupled in an extensive rebuilding programme between Ledsham and Birkenhead, completed in 1904. Local L&YR traffic into Liverpool's Exchange Station exhibited a high density of one train around every five minutes in the morning rush hour, about half that at mid-day and then a similar frequency out of town in the late afternoon. The L&YR also ran a service jointly with the LNWR from Edge Hill which called at the right sort of places (including Waterloo, Blundellsands and Hightown), but there were only two trains each way which did not run at obvious commuter times. The Cheshire Lines' service from Southport to Liverpool was worse than half-hourly in the morning, but that was probably because they concentrated on the southern route into Liverpool via Gateacre, which passed through areas which might confidently be expected to provide first class custom and where there was less railway competition.

However, there was one railway—the Mersey Railway—which played a more clear-cut role in facilitating the development of commuting and suburban development. Like the L&MR, the Mersey was originally proposed as a goods link to Liverpool docks, but in reality it never had an affordable scheme for burrowing up to the surface in or even close to the docks: there simply was not land available for the purpose at a price that a grossly under-capitalised, small-scale railway could afford. Whatever the prospectus of 1866 may have said, it would stand or fall as a purely commuter line. It was only in 1879 that work began on the railway tunnel between Birkenhead and Liverpool and it was officially opened in 1886 (Figure 9.9). Even in this case, however, we do not have exact figures on the extent or frequency of commuting because many merchants and other members of Liverpool's business community had season tickets, but no information is available on how often they used them.[105]

The Mersey was in any case a highly unusual railway: after the completion of the Mersey Tunnel and the initiation of a regular service, its initial appeal soon wore off after and passenger receipts continued to decline until electrification in 1903. As a result, the interaction between railway provision and suburban development was late in starting. Nevertheless, the rapid growth of up-market housing in Edwardian Wirral was stimulated by the huge improvement in the Mersey Railway's services. The company took the opportunity offered by electrification

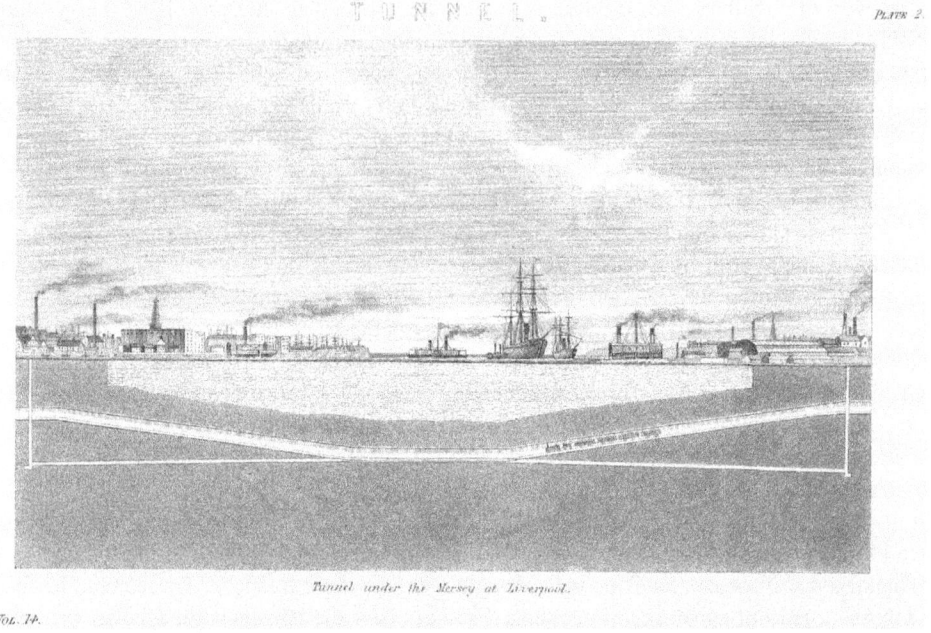

Figure 9.9 'Tunnel under the Mersey at Liverpool', *National Encyclopaedia: A History of Universal Knowledge by writers of Eminence in Literature* (London, 1886)

to give passengers not just cleaner air, but also increased train frequencies.[106] The variation in demand at different times of day was met by varying the train make-up (between two and five cars) rather than the frequency, and almost half of the total stock was first class. Even in the third class, the provision of seats in relation to standing space was generous.[107] If we analyse the percentage population growth in different parts of Wirral between 1881 and 1911, Birkenhead grew by just over 50 per cent, while the population of Wallasey trebled and that of West Kirby and Hoylake more than quadrupled.[108] The latter were served by the formerly under-used Wirral Railway which in 1888 connected with the Mersey Railway at Birkenhead Park (Figure 9.10). Both railways were well established and hence led rather than followed suburban development, but it is well to remember that both suffered extremely troubled early days with a slow growth in traffic. The Mersey Railway did not pay a dividend on its common stock until 1927 (and then only half a percentage point), while only following Mersey Railway's electrification were Wirral Railway's tracks were doubled (1894–96), by which time there were 22 scheduled trains each way on weekdays, with two to five cars extra capacity during the rush hour: by 1910 there were about 40 running each way.[109]

An analysis of the impact of transport improvements on Wallasey is problematic: it represented several widely differing districts, including New Brighton, which had a dual function, making it difficult to interpret population data. Like many seaside resorts, it began with the firmest intentions of serving a high-class demand for fresh air and sea water and early building was confined to expensive commuting properties for the merchant classes with a ferry service (from 1833) and up-market hotels. The process which followed is familiar: the same boats that conveyed George Holt and his peers to Liverpool for business or, in the reverse direction, for a summer break also brought hundreds of short-stay visitors and day-trippers turning 'tourism' into the main prop of the local economy. The proportion of heads of household from mercantile

Birkenhead.   Park Station.

The Wrench Series, No. 7578

Figure 9.10 Birkenhead Park Station (pre-1914 postcard)

or professional classes declined from 45.5 per cent in 1841 to 24.5 per cent in 1851, while the total population more than trebled by 1871.[110] This was, of course, before any railway arrived there. Nor did the major surge in Wallasey's population occur following the implementation of transport improvements (c.1905–1910), encouraged by the electrification of the Wallasey tramways (1902) and the Mersey Railway (1903). Population growth of about 50 per cent was registered between 1901 and 1911, but that rate had been achieved in each decade since 1871. Wallasey was unlike any of the other major commuter areas in that its railway connection was circuitous, but it had three ferry terminals. A likelier stimulus to growth, therefore, was the municipalisation of the Wallasey Ferries in 1862 followed by the provision of a pier and a floating stage at New Brighton in 1864. From 1879 horse trams provided enhanced access to the ferries. The local board also purchased three new boats in 1862 and a fourth in 1863, each of them larger than all but one of the old ones. The total number of passengers carried by the ferries increased from 5.5 million (1876) to 17.9 million (1906): scarcely an indication of damage from railway competition.

The improvement in usage resulting from electrification of the Mersey Railway seems very clear: in the first half of 1908 ticket sales were 5,719,572 as compared with 3,728,292 in the first half of 1901 and season ticket sales had increased from 2,028 to 5,882, representing an estimated 1,148,262 journeys in 1908, a rise in total of over 2.6 million. However, the Woodside Ferry peaked at 10,147,321 in 1903 and by 1908 was down to 7,570,316. Data for estimating the effect of seasonality are absent, but approximately half the 'new' traffic won by electrification was in fact stolen from the Birkenhead Ferries.[111]

A somewhat happier story is provided by the Liverpool Overhead Railway (LOR), opened in 1893 (Figure 9.11). Originally, its target market was people needing to get around the Dock Estate for business purposes, while its Southern Extension (1896) was aimed at commuting traffic, specifically for workers from the 'Aristocracy of Labour'. The Northern extensions (1894, 1895) served a still-prosperous Seaforth with customers able to use first class accommodation from 1895. In 1900 the LOR company opened a short (2½ mile) electric tramway to Great Crosby, which provided a useful boost to passenger figures: by 1914 the railway was carrying approximately 10 million passengers per year and the tramway 4 million.[112] These figures were linked to the rapid spread of medium-sized red-brick houses in Crosby, but the direction of the linkage is difficult to establish. It is important to note that the LOR was a small and under-capitalised company, with limited capacity to engage sensibly in speculative attempts to generate new traffic, whether in the medium or long term. The 1908 OS map shows quite promising territory for locating customers, with plenty of 40 ft 'semis' in and around Church Road, rather grander 40 ft detached residences on Crosby Road South and some larger detached houses in College Avenue. There was also plenty of land awaiting development; several streets were marked out and named, while yet unbuilt; and there was a great deal of vacant space north of Myers Road. However, the 1894 map reveals that a great deal of the better housing evident in 1908 had already been built supported by a horse bus service. The LOR directors had done well in choosing an up-and-coming area which already had an established trade, albeit small, on which they could build by providing a superior, and very frequent, service. The fast electric-train services on the Liverpool—Southport line (started in 1904) were perhaps less of a threat than might be expected because their Crosby and Blundellsands station was rather cut off from much of Crosby by the shortage of over-bridges crossing its own route. Crosby, with its fresh air and access to the sea was, and remained, an attractive place to move out to, but it would have been less attractive without ease of access.

From 1897, the Liverpool Corporation expanded and electrified its tramways at an astonishing speed. The underlying objective was the need to reduce the city centre's population density

Figure 9.11 'Opening of the Liverpool Docks Overhead Electric Railway, The Pier Head Station', *The Illustrated London News*, 11 February 1893, p. 168

because of public health concerns, but the 'Circumferential Boulevard' (Queen's Drive) and the improved radial roads and tramways out to it were avowedly built to encourage housing development.[113] The City Engineer did not, of course, have shareholders to answer to. In one sense the corporation succeeded, for they provided the incentive for private investors to build thousands of high-quality small houses away from the city centre and they built a lot more themselves whose location was in part chosen for reasons of ease of travel to work. In another sense they failed, for, by accident or design, they upset the residential pattern of the wealthy, many of whom responded by taking their considerable rateable value, servant payroll and retail spending power somewhere else, usually well outside the city boundary. The spread of middle-class suburbia was well underway by 1914 and after the war ended the pocket country estates of the wealthy were variously turned into public parks or schools or broken up to provide sites for endless small 'semis.'[114]

The experience of Liverpool and Merseyside highlights the complexity of the changing relationship between suburbanisation and transport improvements. In some locations improvements in transport provision led suburban development, whereas in other places the reverse was the case. What can be firmly established is that there was a necessary and ongoing interaction between the two, which was only broken by the arrival of mass ownership of motor cars.

That phase, at least among some sections of the merchant community, had begun well before the onset of the First World War. Local architects, such as Edmund Kirby, were commissioned to design 'motor houses' on the grounds of successful businessmen. In 1906 *Gore's* listed 5 motor engineers and 19 manufacturers, but the latter figure is misleading because many of them were either coach- or bicycle-builders.[115] The plutocrats of Noctorum, along with the aristocracy, were willing to pay around £1,200 for a Rolls Royce Silver Ghost, as introduced in 1907. In so doing, they changed the perception of the motorcar: it was no longer an expensive toy, but a fast and reliable means of transport, which enabled businessmen to drive themselves to work, although in some cases a chauffeur was retained either for social display or as insurance against the possibility of a puncture. During the second half of Edward VII's reign there began one of the greatest changes in recent urban history and the crème de la crème of Liverpool merchants led the way. Well into the 1960s, Watson's garage, adjoining Hamilton Square Station, was not only a Rolls Royce agent but also the provider (at a price) of extensive secure indoor garaging for those travelling to Liverpool. But that sort of journey to that sort of work was dwindling fast.

The Early Twentieth Century and the Fragmentation of the Suburban Hinterland

From the middle of the nineteenth century onwards, the rapid increase of Liverpool's population saw the suburban hinterland carved up between rich and poor. The elite withdrew to private park estates, insulated from the disagreeable realities of urban life; to the fringes of the new public parks, where development was strictly controlled to achieve an attractive environment; or to ever more distant locations, accessible only by relatively costly private or public transport. The 'artisan or clerk class' colonised the spaces between, in streets of terraced houses run up by speculative builders, often on the sites of former mansions and villas. By the turn of the century these developments spread ever further from the centre. Large houses in extensive grounds continued to dominate much of south Liverpool into the twentieth century—from Princes Park and Sefton Park, via Aigburth and Mossley Hill, out to Allerton, Gateacre and Woolton—but after the First World War, a radical transformation set in. As the city's economic importance declined and wealthy families moved away, the sites of more and more of these houses were sold off for building land, their places taken by comparatively modest middle-class homes. Others were acquired by the corporation, their grounds turned into public parks or built over with public housing. Others again passed into institutional use—sometimes private, sometimes public—and were converted to serve variously as schools, hospitals, convents, orphanages and university offices and residences.

The fate of Norris Green, J. Pemberton Heywood's former home at West Derby, vividly sums up the changed world of early twentieth-century suburban Liverpool. Although situated about three and a half miles from the city centre, the expanding tram system made it a suitable location for working-class housing. The corporation acquired the mansion, gardens and adjoining agricultural land and proceeded to lay out a giant housing estate for former inner-city dwellers. Building commenced in 1926, and within two years, 5,351 houses had been erected on the site.[116] It was a turn of events that would have satisfied Nathaniel Hawthorne's egalitarian instincts. He called at Norris Green in February 1856, following a visit to the Brownlow Hill workhouse in the company of Mrs. Heywood. 'Oh, these English homes,' he declared, after viewing the Heywoods' famously beautiful grounds, 'what delightful places they are! I wonder how many people live and die in the workhouse, having no other home, because other people have a great deal more home than enough!'[117]

Notes

1 J. A. Picton, *Memorials of Liverpool Historical and Topographical Including a History of the Dock Estate* (2 vols, London, 1873), vol. 2, p. 308.

2 H. J. Dyos, *Victorian Suburb: A Study of the Growth of Camberwell* (Leicester, 1961); F. M. L. Thompson, *Hampstead: Building a Borough, 1650–1964* (London, 1974); Stana Nenadic, 'The Victorian Middle Classes', in W. H. Fraser and I. Maver (eds.), *Glasgow, vol. 2: 1830 to 1912* (Manchester, 1996), pp. 265–99; P. O. Pam, *History of Enfield: 1837–1914: A Victorian Suburb* (Enfield, 1992), vol. 2; Tony Benton and Albert Parish, *Upminster: The Story of a Suburb* (Amberley, 2009); Barry M. Doyle, 'The Structure of Elite Power in the Early Twentieth-Century City: Norwich 1900–1935', *Urban History*, 24, 2 (1997), pp. 179–99; Simon Gunn, 'Class, Identity and the Urban: The Middle Class in England, c.1790–1950', *UH*, 31, 1 (2004), pp. 36–7; David Cannadine, 'Residential Differentiation in Nineteenth-Century Towns: From Shapes on the Ground to Shapes in Society', in James H. Johnson and Colin G. Pooley (eds.), *The Structure of Nineteenth-Century Cities* (London, 1982); Lynne Hapgood, 'The Literature of the Suburbs: Versions of Repression in the Novels of George Gissing, Arthur Conan Doyle and William Pett Ridge, 1890–1899', *Journal of Victorian Culture*, 5, 2 (2000), pp. 287–310. It should be remembered that Liverpool had five boundary extensions between 1835 and 1913.

3 Robert J. Morris, 'Structure, Culture and Society in British Towns', in Martin J. Daunton (ed.), *TCUHB, vol. 3: 1840–1950* (Cambridge, 2000); Robert Murray Smith, *The History of Greenock* (Greenock, 1921), p. 111; Ruth McManus and Philip J. Ethington, 'Suburbs in Transition: New Approaches to Suburban History', *UH*, 34, 2 (2007), pp. 317–27.

4 H. B. Rodgers, 'The Suburban Growth of Victorian Manchester', *Journal of the Manchester Geographical Society* (1962), p. 3; F. Engels, 'The Great Towns', in R. T. LeGates and F. Stout (eds.), *The City Reader* (London, 1996), p. 49.

5 Paul Laxton, 'Liverpool in 1801: A Manuscript Return for the First National Census of Population', *THSL&C*, 130 (1981), pp. 88–91.

6 Susan George, *Liverpool Park Estates: Their Legal Basis, Creation and Early Management* (Liverpool, 2000); Colin Pooley and Jean Turnbull, 'Modal Choice and Modal Change: The Journey to Work in Britain since 1890', *Journal of Transport Geography*, 8 (2000), pp. 11–24; Madeline McKenna, 'The Suburbanization of the Working-Class Population of Liverpool between the Wars', *Social History*, 16, 2 (1991), pp. 173–89; Charlotte Wildman, 'Urban Transformation in Liverpool and Manchester, 1918–1939', *The Historical Journal*, 55, 1 (2012), pp. 119–43 and *Urban Redevelopment and Modernity in Liverpool and Manchester, 1918–39* (London, 2016); Adam Menuge, *Ordinary Landscapes Special Places: Anfield, Breckfield and the Growth of Liverpool's Suburbs* (Swindon, 2008); David Lewis, *The Illustrated History of Liverpool's Suburbs* (Breedon, 2010);

Richard Lawton, 'The Components of Demographic Change in a Rapidly Growing Port-City: The Case of Liverpool in the Nineteenth Century', in Richard Lawton and Robert Lee (eds.), *Population and Society in Western European Port-Cities c.1650–1939* (Liverpool, 2002), pp. 105–19. For other aspects, see Lynne Hapgood, 'The New Suburbanites and Contested Class Identities in the London Suburbs, 1880–1900', in Roger Webster (ed.), *Expanding: Reviewing Suburban Narratives* (New York, 2000), pp. 31–49; Christopher French, 'Who Lived in Suburbia? Surbiton in the Second Half of the 19th Century', *Family and Community History*, 10 (2007), pp. 93–109.

7 Wellcome Library, MS.2196, letter book of Joshua Dixon, 1764–5, p. 13.

8 William Moss, *The Liverpool Guide: Including a Sketch of the Environs: With a Map of the Town* (Liverpool, 1796; facsimile reprint 1974), pp. 25, 105, 115.

9 Alice Ford (ed.), *The 1826 Journal of John James Audubon* (New York, 1987), pp. 81 and 84.

10 Moss, *The Liverpool Guide*, pp. 17, 19.

11 James Aspinall, *Liverpool a Few Years Since By an Old Stager* (London and Liverpool, 1852), pp. 10–11; *BLAMI*, 25 March 1799 (not paginated).

12 C. W. Chalklin, *The Provincial Towns of Georgian England: A Study of the Building Process, 1740–1820* (London, 1974), pp. 110–11.

13 LRO, 352 MIN/IMP I 1/1, Select Improvement Committee minutes, 20 December 1799 and 24 January 1800; 252 MIN/COU I, Council minutes, 8 March 1800.

14 David Lewis, *Walks Through History Liverpool* (Derby, 2004), p. 42.

15 Eveline B. Saxton, *More Rhymes of Old Liverpool*, illustrated by John Pride (Liverpool, 1937), p. 26: 'Mr Septimus Jones must be rich I declare,/For its rumoured he's moving to Great George Square'.

16 William Enfield, *An Essay towards the History of Leverpool* (Warrington, 1773), p. 114; Moss, *The Liverpool Guide*, p. 129.

17 Moss, *The Liverpool Guide*, pp. 110–11; Robert Syers, *The History of Everton Including Familiar Dissertations on the People and Descriptive Delineation of the Several and Separate Properties of the Township* (Liverpool, 1830), p. 281. The construction of high-quality housing in Everton was reflected in a poem by Eveline Saxton: 'Tier upon tier towards the sky/Imposing mansions met the eye'. See *More Rhymes of Old Liverpool*, p. 8.

18 Sheila Marriner, *The Economic and Social Development of Merseyside* (London and Canberra, 1982), p. 76.

19 LRO, D/Earle/13/2, T. Algernon Earle, Earle of Allerton Tower (1899) (for private circulation). John Shaw Leigh was reputed to have been 'probably the wealthiest, commoner in England': see Aspinall, *Liverpool a Few Years Since*, p. 177.

20 See also R. D. Radcliffe, *Notes on the Township of West Derby* (Old Swan, 1918).

21 LRO, 920 MD 147, Todd Naylor papers.

22 Benjamin Silliman, *A Journal of Travels in England, Holland, and Scotland . . . in the Years 1805 and 1806* (2 vols, Boston, 1812), vol. 1, p. 60; Ford, *The 1826 Journal*, p. 187; 'Description of Liverpool, by a Foreigner', cutting from *Liverpool Courier*, 13 December 1820, in LRO, Holt and Gregson papers, 942 HOL 5, p. 212.

23 John Britton, *The Beauties of England and Wales* (18 vols, London, 1801–15), vol. 9, p. 216.

24 Ford (ed.), *The 1826 Journal*, pp. 112–14 and 119.

25 Robert Lugar, *Villa Architecture: A Collection of Views, with Plans, of Buildings Executed in England, Scotland, &c* (London, 1828), plate X. What may have been a unique survival of such a cottage—the single-storey, Tudor Gothic Newstead in Beaconsfield Road, Woolton—was recently demolished.

26 T. Algernon Earle, 'Earle of Allerton Tower', *THSL&C*, 42 (1890), p. 53; Thomas Ellison, *Gleanings and Reminiscences* (Liverpool, 1905), p. 239.

27 Quoted in Emily A. Rathbone (ed.), *Records of the Rathbone Family* (Edinburgh, 1913), p. 111 et seq.

28 Cyrus Redding, *An Illustrated Itinerary of the County of Lancaster* (London, 1842), p. 132; 'Interviews with Great Men (imaginary): 'Mr James Allanson Picton', *Liberal Review*, 30 April 1881, p. 10.

29 B. Guinness Orchard, *Liverpool's Legion of Honour* (Birkenhead, 1893), p. 64.

30 Harriet Anna Whitting, *Alfred Booth, Some Memories, Letters and Other Family Records* (Liverpool, 1917).

31 Charles Reilly, *Scaffolding in the Sky* (London, 1938), p. 104.

32 George, *Liverpool Park Estates*.

33 Randall Stewart (ed.), *The English Notebooks by Nathaniel Hawthorne* (New York and London, 1941), p. 22: entry for 2 September 1853.

34 Orchard, *Liverpool's Legion of Honour*, p. 70.

35 *Liverpool Mercury*, 20 October 1843, p. 345.

36 Stanley and Newsham Parks were designed by Edward Kemp (then consulting superintendent at Birkenhead Park), while Sefton Park was the creation of Edouard André and Lewis Hornblower, a Birkenhead resident with a practice in Liverpool who had played an important role in developing Birkenhead Park. See Katy Layton-Jones and Robert Lee, *Places of Health and Amusement Liverpool's Historic Parks and Gardens* (Swindon, 2008).

37 'What "Porcupine" Saw at Great Crosby', *Porcupine*, 4 May, 11 May, and 18 May 1867, pp. 50, 59 and 68.

38 Thomas Fletcher, *Autobiographical Memoir of Thomas Fletcher of Liverpool (obiit 1850) Written in the Year 1843* (Liverpool, 1843), pp. 65, 77 and 115.

39 LRO, Binns Collection, vol. 9, p. 34.

40 Augustus Bozzi Granville, *The Spas of England and Principal Sea-Bathing Places: Midland Spas* (1841), pp. 10 et seq.

41 LRO, 920 DUR 1/2, Holt family diary, 11 March 1850.

42 LaRO, Culshaw & Sumners papers, DDX 162/89/22-DDX 162/89/23.

43 Crosby Public Library, minutes of *Waterloo with Seaforth, Sewerage and Highway and Lighting Committee of the Local Board of Health*, 17 August 1869.

44 LRO, 920 DUR 1/2, Holt Family diary, 13 November 1851. The journey from Liverpool to Ambleside took A. G. Kurtz 24 hours in 1846, mostly by water (LRO, 920 KUR 1/1, diary of A. G. Kurtz, 31 July 1846). From the early 1830s onwards, George Holt had developed an affection for the Lake District, which became increasingly popular with other members of Liverpool's business community. See John Davies, 'In Search of the Picturesque: George Holt in the English Lake District, 1832', *THSL&C*, 159 (2011), pp. 83–97; Harry Hardknott (Hugh Shimmin), *Rambles in the Lake District, July, 1857* (reprinted from *The Albion*, Liverpool) (Liverpool, 1857).

45 Lewis Hornblower, 'A Peep into Futurity; or, the Future Building Sites of Liverpool', *Proceedings of the Liverpool Architectural and Archaeological Society*, 13th Session (1860–61): pp. 167–8.

46 LaRO, Culshaw & Sumners papers, DDX 162/13/41-DDX/162/13/63, and DDX 162/40/12-DDX 162/40/19.

47 LRO, Eq 330, *Liverpool Worthies*, vol. 3, pp. 44–50.

48 LRO, Eq 330, *Liverpool Worthies*, vol. 5, p. 133; Colin Cunningham and Prudence Waterhouse, *Alfred Waterhouse, 1830–1905: Biography of a Practice* (Oxford, 1992).

49 www.culture.gouv.fr/public/mistral/merimee_fr.

50 *Liverpool Courier*, 9 April 1884, p. 5; *Liverpool Daily Post*, 22 May 1890, p. 7.

51 LRO, M 350PWK/1/1/9, cash book of Andrew Barclay Walker; National Maritime Museum, ISM 11, diary of Margaret Ismay, 29 June 1883.

52 Aspinall, *Liverpool a Few Years Since*, p. 56.

53 LUSC&A, D284/1/26/6, indenture dated 2 May 1805.

54 Thomas William May Lund, *The Ideal Citizen: An Appreciation of Philip Rathbone* (Liverpool, 1896), p. 7.

55 LRO, Eq 330, *Liverpool Worthies*, vol. 14, p. 3.

56 LRO, Eq 330, *Liverpool Worthies*, vol. 11, p. 351.

57 *Daily Post*, 8 January 1891, p. 4; *Liverpool Courier*, 30 December 1916, p. 7.

58 Wilton J. Oldham, *The Ismay Line: The White Star Line, and the Ismay Family Story* (Liverpool and London, 1961), p. 68. Ismay employed 22 indoor and 10 outdoor servants to maintain the house and to serve the needs of the family. He was also a director of the LNWR which owned the Birkenhead Railway jointly with the GWR.

59 'Patricius Walker' [William Allingham], *Rambles* (London, 1873), p. 209.

60 From statistics published by the Central Police Office, Liverpool, 17 August 1886, in LRO, 352 BUI/8/1, folio 119.

61 LRO, large framed watercolour 107.

62 *Official Guide and Album of the Cunard Steamship Company* (London, 1877), p. 115.

63 LRO, 920 KUR 1/22, 9 January 1882; 11 January 1882, 17 January 1882.

64 LRO, Acc 4118.

65 Picton, *Memorials*, vol. 2, pp. 511–12; E. I. Thurn and L. C. Wharton (eds.), *The Journal of William Lockerby, Sandalwood Trader in the Fijian Islands during the Years 1808–1809* (London, 1925), pp. xii–xiii.

66 LRO, 920 KUR 1/11, 28 November 1871; 920 KUR 1/14, 31 January 1874 and 920 KUR 1/21, 21 December 1881.

67 LRO, 352 BUI/3/7, Wavertree UDC Register of Building Plans, 1854–94.

68 LRO, 920 DUR 1/4, Holt Family diary, 13 June 1863, 29 April 1864.

69 LRO, 920 DUR 1/5, Holt family diary, 14 April 1872, 17 and 20 March 1878. See also 'Modern Overcrowding', *Porcupine*, 4 July 1874, p. 211.

70 See Paolo Capuzzo, 'Between Politics and Technology: Transport as a Factor of Mass Suburbanization in Europe, 1890–1939', in Colin Divall and Winston Bond (eds.), *Suburbanizing the Masses Public Transport and Urban Development in Historical Perspective* (London and New York, 2018), pp. 23–48.

71 G. W. Bacon & Co. was active between 1869 and 1922. The company led by George Washington Bacon had published the 1885 Plan of Liverpool with a low-detailed overview of much of Merseyside: a more comprehensive New Plan of Liverpool appeared in 1910.

72 Royal Museums Greenwich, ISM/15, 12 February 1887; ISM/14, 17 December 1886. This was a man possessed of his influence and wealth: if he had wanted a special train to pick him up and drop him off at Thurstaston, he could easily have had one, which is what he did two months earlier when he and his wife Margaret became stranded at Chester. For the wider social significance of walking, see Deborah Simonton, '"For the Gentlemen for the Town to Walk on by Way of Exchange": Gender, Space and Commerce in the Eighteenth-Century Town', in Elaine Chalus and Marjo Kaartinen (eds.), *Gendering Spaces in European Towns, 1500–1914* (Abingdon, 2019), pp. 45–74.

73 LRO, 367 THI 30 Club, 22 December 1897.

74 Some merchants living in central Liverpool had direct access to private transport: the house of Thomas Parr on Colquitt Street had two flanking pavilions which contained respectively his 'counting house' and his coach house.

75 J. Burnett (ed.), *Useful Toil* (Newton Abbot, 1975), p. 155.

76 James Evans of 46 Seel Street was the sole inventor and patentee of both the Viceroy Hansom Cab and the Alexandra Drag (well adapted for 'Ladies, Invalids, and general use'): see his advertisement in *A Local Artist, Pen-and Ink Sketches of Liverpool Town Councillors* (Liverpool, 1866), p. 2.

77 LRO, 920 DUR 10/16/1, 29 November 1844, 18 January 1852. The *Holt Diaries* include entries when the coachman was 'laid up with fever and severe cold for last few days' and the horses were sick with influenza. The *Kurtz Diaries* (19 February 1888) record that 'I begin seriously to think of getting rid of my horses as they are of so little use to me & only so much expense'. Part of a neighbourhood mews survives between Devonshire Road and South Street with a total area (coach houses and stables) of about 8,400 ft^2: the carriages and horses remained the property of local gentlemen and the staff their employees. The Sefton Mews, Princes Park, designed by John E. Reeve and built in 1884 for its 'proprietor' John Wilson, provided stall stabling for at least 43 horses, in addition to space in loose boxes: see *The Builder*, 9 February (1884). Building dimensions, unless otherwise stated, are scaled from OS maps of 25":1 mile or larger: staff data from the MLP database. Unfortunately, Gore's *Directory* did not classify jobmasters. Their horse-rental function was hidden within the heading of 'Livery Stable Proprietors', the number of which rose from 37 (1876) to 43 (1882), but then sank to just 10 in 1911. Little can be read into these figures, however, because some firms were getting larger.

78 *A fortiori* a liveried man on the box: his job was driving to functions, not to the office, while arriving by any sort of carriage to walk on 'change' was also considered somewhat crass.

79 J. B. Horne and T. B. Maund, *Liverpool Transport* (5 vols, London, 1975–87), vol. 1, pp. 80–1.

80 LRO, 352 TRE 5/2. Accounts are for the mayoral year, November to October.

81 See the foregoing examples of Robert Wynne and Thomas Earle.

82 Including, of course, her social calls and her charitable activities: see Chapter 7.

83 The 1851 Covenants governing development in Cressington Park stipulated a minimum value (house only, excluding plot, boundary walls etc.) of £400. During the period 1851–1901 construction costs rose by about 12 per cent. See B. R. Mitchell, *British Historical Statistics* (Cambridge, 1988), p. 394.

84 Adrian Jarvis, *Liverpool: A History of 'the Great Port'* (Liverpool, 2014), p. 188.

85 This was John Elder of Elder Dempster, leaders in the West Africa Trade. See Peter N. Davies, *The Trade Makers: Elder Dempster in West Africa, 1852–1972, 1973–1989* (2nd ed., St. John's Newfoundland, 2000).

86 MLP database: 'live-in' coachmen were enumerated specifically as coachmen only when they occupied a separate lodge or a cottage in the stable yard, rather than rooms in the servants' wing of the main house.

87 The number of businesses grew from 50 in 1876 to a peak of 72 by 1882: it then declined to 45 by the end of our period. Some of the later ones were in substantial multi-storey buildings following the style of an early (c.1859) example at 28 St. Anne Street. Atkinson, as a coachmaker, also produced horse-drawn vehicles, including the 'Buttler's Lurry', the 'Brewer's Float' and the 'Miller's Cart'.

88 Membership of the Royal College of Veterinary Surgeons became compulsory in 1881, but the Veterinary Surgeons Act of that year was not retrospective, so that experienced but unqualified vets could continue in practice until they retired: those who hung on may well have been mainly 'horse-doctors' or employed in inspecting imported cattle. See Richard C. Hankins, 'Liverpool and London, Development of University Veterinary Education', *Veterinary History*, 11, 2 (2008), p. 103; Alison Kraft, 'Liverpool Veterinary School: The First 100 Years', *The Veterinary Record*, 155, 12 (2004).

89 Data extracted from the 1881 census. For example, John Clayton, a veterinary surgeon at 11 Cheapside, Exchange, was also a milk dealer, who employed a 19-year-old servant as a milkman.

90 A. Bowker, *"In Memoriam" or, Funeral Records of Liverpool Celebrities* (Liverpool, 1876), p. 19. This book reprinted obituaries from local newspapers of 56 local worthies (all men) who died between 1831 and 1876, of whom 22 were merchants.

91 Busby's was a large and versatile firm which included an undertaking division, but on this occasion their role was limited to the 'provision of the mourning equipages': the overall job was by J. & W. Jefferey & Co.

92 Bowker, *"In Memoriam"*, pp. 220–32.

93 George, *Liverpool Park Estates*, p. 99. In 1871 a house in prestigious Belvidere Road was offered for sale or rent boasting that 'the omnibuses ply regularly to and from town: *Liverpool Mercury*, 15 November 1871.

94 Horne and Maund, *Liverpool*, vol. 1, p. 11, Appendix 1.

95 Horne and Maund, *Liverpool*, vol. 1, p. 79: the figure peaked at 3,162 in 1892.

96 George Starbuck established the first tramcar manufacturing business in Britain at 227 Cleveland Street, Birkenhead. It was incorporated as George Starbuck & Co. on 12 September 1871 and re-registered just over one year later (on 6 November 1872) as Starbuck Car and Wagon Company.

97 Horne and Maund, *Liverpool*, vol. 2, pp. 24–7. The first-class service was withdrawn in 1923.

98 Willam B. Forwood, *Recollections of a Busy Life* (Liverpool, 1910), p. 10. Liverpool's Lancashire hinterland had long been heavily industrialised with pollution of air and water.

99 See Randolph Cock, John Davies, Robert Lee and Sari Mäenpää, Chapter 2; Robert Lee, Chapter 10.

100 Jack Simmons, *The Railway in England and Wales 1830–1914* (Leicester, 1978); *The Railway in Town and Country, 1830–1914* (Newton Abbot, 1986); *The Victorian Railway* (London, 1991); J. R. Kellett, *The Impact of Railways on Victorian Cities* (London, 1969); Sir Juland Danvers complained about this state of affairs in 'Defects of English Railway Statistics', *Journal of the Royal Statistical Society*, 51 (1888), pp. 1–21.

101 The Earle family owned extensive lands nearby, and Hardman Earle, having initially been anti-railway, had by then joined the Board of the L&MR.

102 Marriner, *The Economic and Social Development of Merseyside*, p. 76.

103 Harry Foster, *Links Along the Line the Story of the Development of Golf between Liverpool and Southport* (Southport, 1996), p. 9 et seq.

104 The work generally cited simply as 'Bradshaw's' was an independently produced but officially informed monthly passenger timetable first published by George Bradshaw in Manchester in 1839. See Edward H. Milligan, *British Quakers in Commerce & Industry 1775–1920* (York, 2007), p. 61; Trefor Thomas, 'George Bradshaw and Bradshaw's Manchester Journal', *Manchester Region History Review*, 17, 2 (2006), p. 63.

105 The service began using steam locomotives hauling unheated wooden carriages, with four stations. The line was extended over the next six years with the addition of three stations. The Company estimated that an average of just under 100 return trips were undertaken on a season ticket per six months.

106 Between 1891 and 1902, annual train mileage varied between 238,488 and 313,595. In 1904, the first full year of electric operation, it was 827,308. M. D. Reilly, 'The Comparative Development of Urban Electric Railways in Britain and the USA, 1880–1994', unpublished PhD thesis, University of Liverpool (1985), p. 119. Trains left Liverpool Central every three minutes throughout the day.

107 In fact, a large quantity of highly detailed operational data was available: see J. Shaw, 'The Equipment and Working Results of the Mersey Railway under Steam and under Electric Traction', *Minutes of the Proceedings of the Institution of Civil Engineers*, 179 (1910), pp. 19–46, 113–229, but information on the passengers and where they were going was exceedingly scarce.

108 Myra Lea, *Birkenhead 1877–1974* (Birkenhead 1974), p. 118.

109 For a more detailed discussion of the outward migration process of members of Liverpool's merchant community, particularly in the case of the Wirral, see Chapter 2 and Chapter 10.

110 A. M. Miller, *The Inviting Shore: A Social History of New Brighton Part 1, 1830–1939* (Birkenhead, 1996), p. 59.

111 Figures for Mersey Railway from J. Shaw, 'Equipment'; those for Woodside Ferry from T. B. Maund, *Mersey Ferries* (2 vols., Glossop, 1991), vol. 1, p. 185; G. W. Parkin, *The Mersey Railway* (Liverpool, 1965).

112 Rather more passengers—about 4.25 million per year—were commuting on cheap 'workmen's tickets': see E. J. Neachell, 'Notes on the Overhead Railway, *Transactions of the LES*, 37 (1916), pp. 47–55.

113 See J. A. Brodie, 'The Development of Liverpool and its Circumferential Boulevard', *Town Planning Review* 1 (1910–11), pp. 100–10.

114 The output of private investment house building for rent in Liverpool began to rise from a long recession in 1896 and peaked at 2,358 in 1899. With some fluctuations, it remained at a high level until 1912. See J. R. Jones, *The Welsh Builder on Merseyside* (Liverpool, 1946), p. 158 (table). For a discussion of journey-to-work considerations in determining corporation housing development, see A. P. Ross, 'Urban Passenger Transport by Train', *Transactions of the LES*, 42 (1921), pp. 192–201 (see, in particular, the subsequent discussion of the paper, especially the contribution by Brodie advancing the claim of trams as against railways).

115 LRO, KIR/34–8.

116 S. Bennett, *Norris Green: A Study of Liverpool Corporation's Inter-War Suburban Housing Policy* (1989) (typescript, LRO).

117 Hawthorne, *English Notebooks*, p. 277.

10 Suburbanisation, Community Building, and the Fragmentation of Business Culture

The Impact on Liverpool of Residential Development on the Wirral

Robert Lee

Introduction

The process of suburbanisation was already under way by the mid-eighteenth century as individual merchants sought to escape from Liverpool by purchasing land or property in the port-city's hinterland. There was a noticeable acceleration of this trend in the nineteenth century, accompanied, if not caused, by the introduction and extension of significant improvements to the transport infrastructure. The broad parameters of differential demographic growth and the intra-regional redistribution of population, specifically in the case of merchants, both from the central area (the Liverpool registration district) to the suburbs and between individual suburbs have already been established, but there has been no attempt to analyse the extent to which out-migration from the urban core and class-specific suburbanisation affected the construction of localised identities or the process of community building.[1] Suburbs in the nineteenth century, whether in Europe or North America, were often seen as pastoral refuges: they maintained a functional dependency on the urban core, but an ideological connection with the countryside and what was envisaged as a 'private romantic paradise'. But they became sites of new social relations and lifestyles, with their own secular calendars of associational and sporting events, and 'intense collective political activity'. They transformed existing relationships between metropolitan space and political culture, as middle-class suburban residents forged new relationships outside the immediate orbit of the city based on residence, leisure, and community-oriented activities.[2]

In order to analyse the wider cultural and networking implications of the incremental expansion of associational networks on the Wirral the surviving records of 45 voluntary organisations will be analysed in detail. Two points deserve emphasising. Firstly, the central importance of locality in determining the allegiance and commitment of merchants to different forms of associational activity from the mid-nineteenth century to the outbreak of the First World War. Secondly, the overriding importance of residential proximity in influencing individual decisions to establish new ventures (whether sports clubs or churches) or to support their development by serving on management boards and committees. The evidence is explicit: merchants who took up residence on the Wirral became increasingly involved in a local associational framework, initially in Birkenhead and Wallasey and, subsequently, on the western side of the peninsula, such as Hoylake and West Kirby, as a result of incremental suburbanisation.

To date, many historians have failed to analyse the wider spatial context of Victorian associational culture in Liverpool because all too often the city has been treated in isolation. But what was the impact of suburbanisation, out-migration, and residential mobility on Liverpool's existing network structures? To what extent did the development of alternative suburban-based

DOI: 10.4324/9781315597836-10

associations, including charitable institutions, political and sporting clubs, schools, and church congregations on the Wirral (and elsewhere in South Lancashire) lead to a reduced involvement in associational activities in Liverpool itself? Was suburban relocation accompanied by a cumulative fragmentation of Liverpool's existing business culture with a reduced involvement in its public affairs and civic life on the part of merchants who had opted to live on the Wirral? And what effect did this have on business networking?

To explore these questions, this chapter will analyse the timing, scale, and spatial extent of suburbanisation on the Wirral from the beginning of the nineteenth century until the outbreak of the First World War. It will discuss the main factors behind the suburbanisation process and the factors that made residential settlement on the peninsula attractive to merchants and other businessmen whose commercial operations were based in Liverpool, including its transparent (or expected) health benefits, the opportunities it offered for rural sports and pleasures, the prospects for speculative investment in land and housing, together with the attraction, at least for some, of the acquisition of political influence and power. A primary focus will be on the significance of suburbanisation for the development of a new associational framework, even if it involved a replication of established models, and the extent to which a dynamic approach to the creation of cultural societies, political clubs, schools, churches, and voluntary hospitals laid the basis for social interaction and networking amongst elements of (upper-) middle class residents which reflected the primacy of suburban objectives and an explicit sense of locality. It will evaluate the role of merchants in creating and maintaining a new web of voluntary associations; their contribution to strengthening the network density of existing forms of interaction (as in the case of Freemasonry); and their adoption of new modes of collaborative activities, including the Volunteer Movement. An overriding sense of locality and a high level of merchant participation in Wirral's associational culture, however, had wider implications, and the final section will examine the extent to which suburban development undermined more traditional commitments to Liverpool-based charities, including voluntary hospitals, institutions catering for the welfare or seafarers, and other charitable bodies, including the Liverpool Female Orphanage, the Liverpool Female Penitentiary, and the Home for Incurables. The evidence is compelling. The dramatic extension of Wirral's web of associational activities as a direct response to the changing rates of in-migration and suburbanisation did not always sever the links between Wirral merchants and Liverpool charities, but it created a distinct and separate world of interaction and networking, the implications of which have been generally neglected by urban historians.

A Peninsula Transformed: The Timing and Scale of Suburban Development on the Wirral

At the beginning of the 1800s settlement density on the Wirral was low (Figure 10.1): even in the 1820s, the *Liverpool Mercury* described Woodside as a 'pleasant village', although it was 'rapidly rising into eminence'.[3] According to James Aspinall, the Wirral, indeed all of Cheshire, 'was in those days a kind of Africa, inviting and daring the young Bruces and Mungo Parks of Liverpool to explore it' as *terra incognita*.[4] However, the availability of a regular steam ferry service between Liverpool and the Wirral from 1817 onwards (initially to Tranmere and subsequently to Woodside and other locations) increased the popularity of Birkenhead and other areas of the Wirral as a site for leisure activities and residential relocation.[5] The lack of detailed research on the changing relationship between Liverpool and its hinterlands is particularly problematic in the case of the Wirral, because of a continuing neglect of 'mundane, short-distance traffic' and the assumption that the Mersey estuary was traditionally regarded as an important physical barrier.[6]

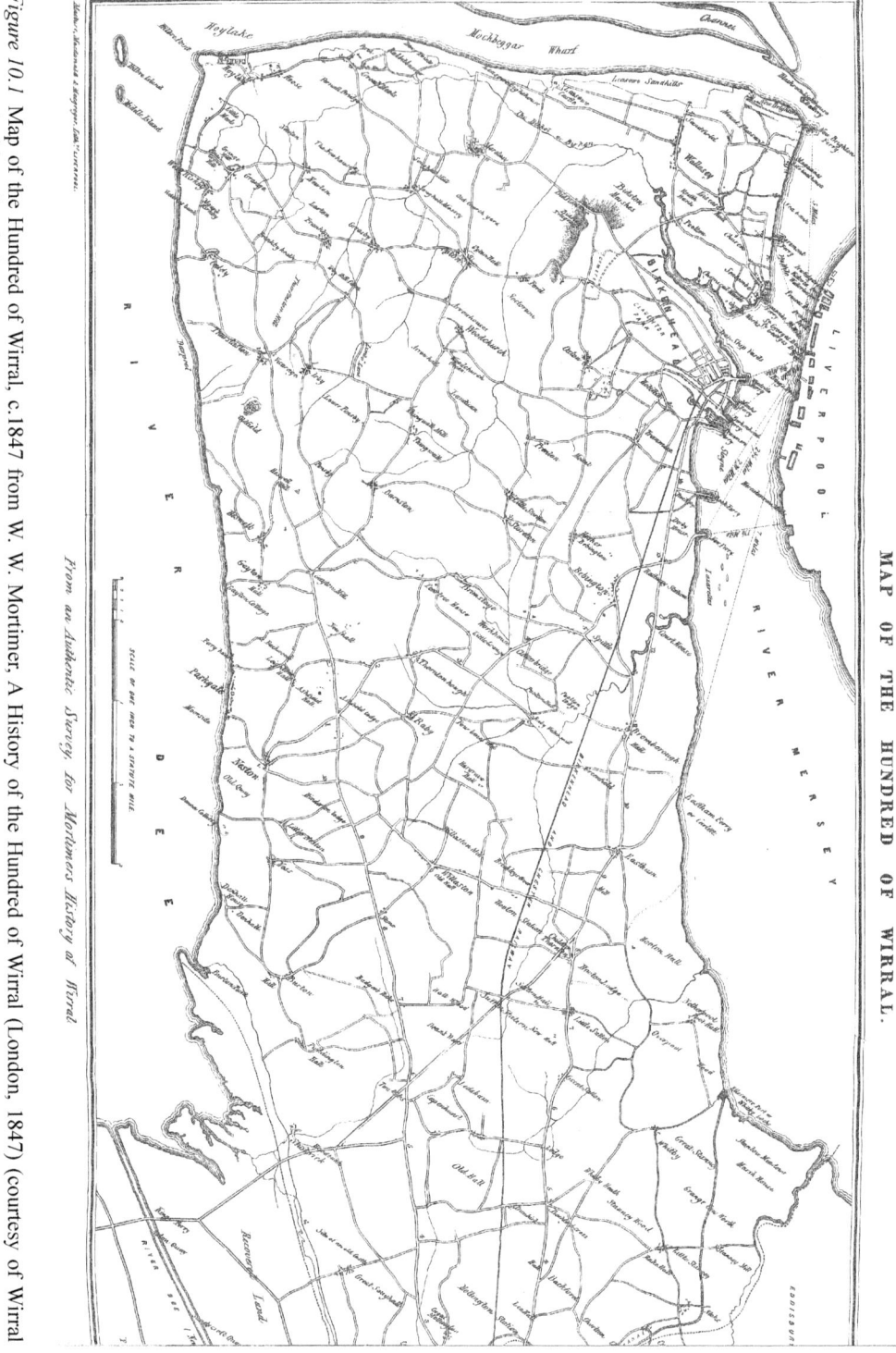

Figure 10.1 Map of the Hundred of Wirral, c.1847 from W. W. Mortimer, A History of the Hundred of Wirral (London, 1847) (courtesy of Wirral Archives Service)

Table 10.1 Average rates of population growth in Wirral townships and parishes, 1831–1911 (per cent, per annum)

Location	1831–50	1851–70	1871–90	1890–1910
Birkenhead	42.2	3.8	6.6	1.5
Wallasey	10.4	3.9	6.1	6.8
Hoylake (parish)			15.9	5.4
West Kirby		0.6	25.4	
West Kirby (parish)				5.7

Sources: census returns, secondary literature

The opening of a new steam ferry service 'opened up the prospect of urban development' on the Wirral, but it would be premature to conclude that the peninsula had been previously a 'fringe society' with only limited urban contact.[7] Parkgate was a popular holiday resort for Liverpool merchants throughout the eighteenth century with its first Assembly Building opened in 1780; Hoylake had become 'a small and rather exclusive watering place'; and horse racing, whether in Neston or Hoylake, attracted a considerable following from Liverpool merchants, some of whom were active members of Cheshire hunts.[8] However, in 1821 Birkenhead only had 19 inhabited houses and John Aspinall, who was 'devoted to horses and hunting' was one of the first Liverpool merchants to establish a permanent residence there in 1824 'in a very pretty house near the river'.[9] The pace of development from the 1820s onwards was very substantial (Table 10.1) with an unprecedented increase in the population between 1831 and 1851, despite a marked decline in the late 1840s as a result of the collapse of speculative railway investment. There was a similar, but less extensive, trend in Tranmere, with Claughton the last of the three townships to develop, primarily because of its further distance from the shore. Birkenhead's recovery from the mid-nineteenth century financial crisis was slow, in comparison with the two preceding decades. The so-called Great (or Long) Depression of the 1870s and 1880s witnessed a revival in population growth, but the years before the outbreak of the First World War saw a significant fall that symbolised the growing attraction of out-migration from Birkenhead's urban core to the quieter and more rural areas of west Wirral. Oxton capitalised on its reputation with the upper middle class as one of the healthiest residential sites on Merseyside which also offered reliable commuting opportunities to Liverpool and its population more than doubled between 1851 (2,007) and 1891 (4,429). However, the rate of population growth in most of the smaller settlements surrounding Birkenhead, including Bidston, Prenton, and Storeton, was minimal.

Liscard, Wallasey, and New Brighton also began to attract population, but their growth as dormitory suburbs, serving primarily the needs of Liverpool's labour market, was largely a phenomenon of the late nineteenth century. The highest annual rate of population growth in Wallasey (10.4 per cent) was registered between 1831 and 1850, a trend that was most visible in those areas, such as Liscard and Poulton-cum-Seacombe, that were closest to the River Mersey and to Birkenhead. This was followed by two decades of moderate expansion, but by 1911 Wallasey had a population of 78,504 as a result of a continuing rise in the supply of residential accommodation and buoyant annual rates of demographic growth (6.1 per cent and 6.8 per cent respectively between 1871–1890 and 1891–1910). But this did not alter the spatial distribution of housing which continued to be densely concentrated on the eastern side of the Borough.

The differentiated context, both spatial and temporal, of urban and population expansion was particularly visible in the case of West Wirral. Hoylake had seen a gradual growth in total population from the 1880 onwards, albeit from a low baseline, but a significant expansion of residential settlement did not occur in West Kirby until the following decade, and, more specifically in the years before 1911 by which time the parish's population had reached 14,007 (an annual increase of 5.7 per cent since 1891). The overall trend was unmistakeable. Between 1871 and 1901, some of the older settled districts on the Wirral, including central Birkenhead, began to lose population by out-migration, as suburban growth expanded to cover more peripheral townships, including Heswall, Neston, and West Kirkby.[10]

As in the case of other metropolitan areas, individual entrepreneurs, specifically Liverpool-based merchants and traders, played an important role in shaping suburban development on the Wirral.[11] The analysis of residential mobility revealed a significant rise in the number of merchants resident in Birkenhead, Prenton (including Oxton) and Bidston between 1851 and the early 1890s, followed by a noticeable decline. In Wallasey and New Brighton a similar trend was visible, but from a lower base line and with a later peak. More peripheral areas of the peninsula, such as Hoylake and West Kirby, only experienced a growth in the extent of merchant residence at the very end of the nineteenth century, contingent on further improvements in the transport infrastructure. The pattern of merchant residential location was characterised by an initial concentration in the three townships most closely adjacent to Liverpool's commercial district (Birkenhead, Claughton, and Tranmere), with an increasing and cumulative dispersion to more distant areas on the peninsula prior to 1914, at the direct cost of the older, more settled districts. The further development of shipbuilding, flour milling, and other industrial activities in Birkenhead, as well as the emergence of Wallasey and New Brighton as dormitory suburbs of Liverpool, reinforced this class-specific process of selective out-migration by merchants and other members of the upper middle class to areas of the Wirral which remained unaffected by large-scale economic change or an increase in the 'rougher' elements of society. Overall, Wirral became increasingly popular as a place of residence for members of the merchant community: between 1851 and 1881 approximately one quarter of all Merseyside merchants lived on the Wirral: by the 1890s and 1900s the proportion had risen to 32.1 per cent and 34.5 per cent respectively.[12]

Health, Sport, and a Rural Environment: Factors Behind Merchant Relocation

The process of suburban development was the result of a range of economic and social factors. For some members of the middle class in large urban centres the choice of a suburban residence represented a form of escapism from the city, with its attendant health risks, polluted environment, and congestion: it was seen as a means of avoiding Liverpool's 'squalid byways and filthy heart'.[13] But while a 'pastoral refuge' on the Wirral represented a retreat from the urban core, it offered the possibility of creating a new, aesthetically distinctive environment.[14] The choice of a Wirral residence was articulated within the framework of a contemporary discourse which prioritised the cultural and social values of a rural idyll, the enjoyment of sporting activities, and the health benefits of suburban life. Eastham was 'famed for its beauty and magnificent woods', while Claughton and Oxton were regarded as 'healthy and pleasant suburbs': even when some roads were laid out, there were still more fields than houses. In his report of 1843, Samuel Stansfield admitted that mortality in Birkenhead was 'far beyond what ought to exist', but he had no hesitation in emphasising the future benefits of suburban residence. With its 'Park, its numerous Villas', and every consideration for 'the comforts of life, and the elegancies of polished society', it offered 'peace and quiet, the beauties of scenery, and the almost unrivalled bursts of view, which are presented from so many elevated points'. Such attributes were not only conducive 'to the increase of pure intellectual pleasure', allowing those who had been crowned with success 'in the pursuits of honourable commerce', they also, by implication, provided a healthy environment for bringing up a family.[15]

Indeed, health concerns were a key factor behind out-migration from Liverpool's urban core: the large number of deaths from the typhus epidemic of 1847 convinced Dr. W. H. Duncan, Liverpool's first Medical Officer of Health, of the need to regulate and replace sub-standard accommodation in cellars and courts. Liverpool had the second highest mortality rate from cholera of all the major cities in England and Wales during the 1849 epidemic and the parish of Liverpool had the highest infant mortality rate. Infants and young children were therefore most at risk as a result of poverty, overcrowding, and insanitary housing. Most merchants were aware of the increasing risks to the family of rising mortality rates and the evidence suggests that this was an important factor in out-migration from the urban core. The iron merchant Samuel Stitt, for example, decided to relocate to Oxton because he believed that a house built on a sandstone ridge would be less vulnerable to consumption and miasmas than property constructed on clay. In the 1850s, further evidence was published on the scale of the socio-economic divide within Liverpool's population and its implications in terms of insanitary conditions and crime, while in the early 1880s the editor of the *Daily Post* felt it necessary to launch a campaign against 'Squalid Liverpool', singling out Scotland Road as a particularly unhealthy and impoverished neighbourhood 'a stone's throw from prosperous money-making Liverpool'.[16]

By the 1840s the green fields and lanes of Wallasey were becoming increasingly popular with Liverpool citizens as a desirable place of residence owing to their 'healthy position and rural character', while Poulton-cum-Seacombe was still a rural village with lanes which were 'redolent of hawthorn blossom and beautiful wild flowers'.[17] New Brighton's reputation in the 1840s as a 'favourite and fashionable watering place' encouraged Liverpool merchants, such as George Holt, to spend an increasing amount of time in the resort. At the end of May 1846 he returned to Liverpool having stayed in New Brighton for three weeks 'upon the whole pleased with our residence there', although the primary purpose of the visit had been to secure an improvement in the health of his son, Robert.[18] Such were the health benefits to be derived from the resort that various Liverpool merchants, including the tobacco broker George H. Ball, acquired a second residence there. By the late nineteenth century, Hoylake and West Kirby were renowned for their 'delightful facilities' and suitability as residential health resorts. The belief that West Kirby's climate was 'particularly suitable for pulmonary complaints' finally led to the establishment of the Convalescent Home for Children in 1881, as public benefactors belatedly recognised the potential benefits of the resort's location which had long been advocated by the suburban middle class. In 1914, the Liverpool Open Air Hospital for Children was opened on Leasowe Road, Moreton, by the Liverpool Children's Association for similar reasons.[19]

For other members of the merchant community, the opportunity of enjoying the wider benefits of rural life not too far removed from Liverpool was a reason for living on the Wirral. The Laird family often spent the summer months in a cottage along the village road in Heswall; the American writer and Consul at Liverpool Nathaniel Hawthorne valued his residence in Rock Park because it was 'the quietest place imaginable'; the merchant David Duncan of Gayton Hall, Neston, established a model farm; and the cotton broker A. K. Bulley of Neston, believed to be 'the sole representative on the Exchange of the doctrines of Agnosticism and Socialism', was 'a keen lover of Alpine plants' and well known for his interest in horticulture.[20] In some cases, a rural retreat represented a deliberate pursuit of 'a quasi-genteel', aristocratic life-style, but for others it reflected a genuine interest in rural affairs and agricultural production. Both the merchant William Barber (of Poulton Hall) and the shipowner William Lockhart (of Whetstone Lane, Tranmere) were members of the Wirral Agricultural Society's committee of management in the mid-1850s, while the annual Wirral and Birkenhead Agricultural Show was held on the model farm of the merchant Thomas Hughes Jackson attached to the Manor House, Claughton.[21]

However, there was a further factor which favoured residential relocation. Many of the Liverpool and Birkenhead merchants listed by Pike in his collection of contemporary biographies were actively involved in sporting activities: outdoor sports predominated, with golf (59 per cent), shooting (25.3 per cent), and cricket (18 per cent) registering the highest number of participants.[22] Over half of the members of the Liverpool Cotton Exchange in the early 1900s were active sportsmen: Henry Mears for example, who lived at 'Broadclyst', Hoylake, was 'fond of all outdoor sports', while George Bridge, who resided at Leighton House in Neston, was 'fond of equestrian exercise'.[23] It is not surprising, therefore, that the peninsula became an increasingly popular location for merchants because of its increasing range of sporting facilities. The Hoylake races were held on 'splendid turf; the village of Bidston had its own horse racing track; while racing at Parkgate was the occasion for 'a jolly old-fashioned picnic'.[24] The Liverpool Harriers regularly hunted on the Wirral, while the Hooton fox hounds, whose members organised an annual steeplechase at Storeton, and the Cheshire hounds provided further opportunities for field sports.[25] When the Royal Rock Beagle Hunt was established in 1845 for gentlemen 'interested in sport', over one quarter of its members were from Liverpool (or Bootle), and the Wirral Harriers, formed in 1868, continued to 'hunt the county' despite the expansion of the railway system and the extensive use of wire by farmers. The India merchant Colonel V. A. King, who resided for many years at 'Point of Ayr', Oxton, was a prominent local huntsman: at his funeral in 1882 his cortège was accompanied not only by family servants, but by a contingent of beaglers, 'the huntsmen with eight couples of hounds'.[26]

The continued availability of open land, still largely unaffected by urban development, was an important factor in the creation of sporting facilities which made Wirral an increasingly attractive option for Liverpool merchants. The popularity of bowls led to the foundation of several clubs, including the Claughton Bowling Club (1861) and the Bebington Bowling Club (1865). In the former case, the original Committee of Management consisted almost entirely of iron merchants, general brokers, and shipowners: in 1875, 84 per cent of the 44 shareholders came from the merchant community. In Bebington, a similar club was established following a meeting at which 'many gentlemen' felt it 'very desirable to have a Bowling Green and Quoit Ground in the village': over one third of those attending the meeting were merchants. A bowling green established at the King's Arms, Liscard Road, well supported by local magistrates and 'other gentlemen', was even referred to as 'The Toffs'.[27]

Other sports, by definition, required even greater space for their development, including cricket, football, golf, rugby, and tennis, although the latter could also be accommodated in the grounds of private residences. The 'original and unrivalled' Mosslake Fields Cricket Club had been established in Liverpool by 30 'gentlemen' in 1807, but its subsequent history was one of continuous relocation away from the urban core until a permanent ground was found at Aigburth (1880).[28] Not surprisingly, the other clubs which became part of the Liverpool Competition were located in the more affluent suburbs, including Bootle (1833) at a time when its surroundings were still largely rural, Huyton (1860), and Birkdale (1884). A similar process was evident on the Wirral: Birkenhead Park Cricket Club was founded in 1846, followed by other clubs in areas of the peninsula where 'beautiful residences' were being built, including New Brighton Cricket and Bowling Club (c.1860) and Wallasey Cricket Club (1864). Birkenhead Park remained an exclusive club, with a membership dominated by merchants and stockbrokers, many of whom had been educated at elite public schools, such as Charterhouse and Uppingham. On his death in May 1914, the cotton broker Joseph Henry Wild was described as an 'old member' of the club, but he had also been active in the Claughton Bowling Club 'where he won many prizes' and had been an 'ardent golfer' with both the Royal Liverpool and Wallasey Golf Clubs.[29]

Figure 10.2 Heswall Golf Club (1904 postcard)

Furthermore, Wirral was an ideal location for the siting of golf clubs: the Royal Liverpool, regarded as 'the leading pioneer of golf in England', was established at Hoylake (1869) at a meeting which included a number of leading merchants, including Alexander Balfour, J. Muir Dowie, and John T. Forman. Although some of the founding members were already resident on the Wirral, other Liverpool-based players subsequently moved to the peninsula. Prestigious golf clubs were also founded at Wallasey (1891), Leasowe (1891), Meols (1891), Heswall (1902), and Caldy (1907), often utilising marginal land close to the shoreline, while the fact that Prenton Golf Club (1905) shared facilities with the local cricket club helped boost membership. The parish of Heswall only had a population of 2,347 in 1902, but there was considerable demand for a golf course which quickly attracted approximately 200 members to its new clubhouse (Figure 10.2). Two of the original trustees, Thomas Brocklebank and Charles MacIver, were successful shipowners, and two thirds of the original council were merchants whose business experience and social status were probably invaluable in persuading railway companies to offer reduced-price return tickets for the 1903 season.[30]

Pleasure, Profit, and Politics

By the early twentieth century, Wirral possessed an extended network of sporting facilities with many clubs catering for upper-middle class demand. The creation of a range of sporting clubs provided a forum for informal exchange between members of the merchant elite, with an implicit merging of personal and business interests, while service in an honorary capacity, whether as a committee member, trustee, vice-president, or president, reinforced the social standing of individual members. But incremental suburbanisation was also a result of financial and political considerations, as individual merchants and entrepreneurs sought to realise the potential benefits generated by the development process. As was the case in London and other provincial cities, the timing of land release for suburban development on the Wirral was determined by the existing landownership pattern and the policies of individual landowners: speculative considerations were evident at a very early stage; and the local press emphasised persistently the investment potential of property accumulation.[31] According to the wine and spirit merchant Charles Grey Mott, 'Some men with very shrewd heads conceived the idea that the land at Birkenhead afforded an opportunity for the construction of a town composed almost entirely of residences to which the people of Liverpool might come'. Not only would they enjoy 'fresh air and freedom from smoke', but they would still be within easy reach of their businesses across the river Mersey.[32]

The process of suburbanisation was underpinned by a concern to maximise profits from the sale of land for residential accommodation and, to a lesser extent, industrial development. As early as 1818, James Harrison had forecast 'the probable value' of land in Birkenhead, and the ship builder William Laird was heavily involved in land speculation, purchasing land from the lord of the manor, Francis R. Price, in 1824 only to sell it three years later to Liverpool Corporation at a significant profit. In September 1826, he borrowed £6,000 from the Liverpool bankers Samuel Hope and Edward Burrell to cover some of his extensive land acquisitions in Birkenhead, although a conflict with Sir John Tobin in 1829 over two areas of land (of 54 and 156 acres respectively) in which they were 'equally interested' was only resolved after formal arbitration.[33] But Laird was only one of 'a number of Scotchmen who bought up land at a small price'. By the late 1830s and early 1840s, William Jackson, an iron monger and palm oil importer who profited from the operational legacy of the slave trade in West Africa, had invested heavily in land purchased from the Price estate (including the greater part of Claughton Manor): in March 1846 he advertised approximately 1,000 plots divided into 12 lots for residential building. Many of the promoters of dock development in Birkenhead were involved in 'extensive land speculation', with the active encouragement of the Cheshire nobility and landed gentry.[34] But the collapse of the 'railway mania' and the cataclysmic downturn of 1848 highlighted the volatility of the housing market and the implicit risks of land speculation: Jackson was unable to meet the agreed price for land on the right-hand side of the Ferry bought from Price at four guineas per square yard and subsequently sold by Price's assignees at 32s 6d 'coming upon Jackson for the difference'.[35] The collapse in business confidence was accompanied by a housing market crisis with property 'literally non-saleable', aggravated by a short-term, but significant, loss of population. Prior to these events, land in Birkenhead, 'particularly near the shore of the river', had doubled in price.

Financial considerations played an important role in the creation and development of Birkenhead Park, opened to the public on 5 April 1847 and the first park ever to be funded by a local authority (namely the Birkenhead Improvement Commissioners). The original design by Joseph Paxton of 1844 (Figure 10.3) was incorporated in the Sale Plan of September 1846 which envisaged the construction of approximately 800 houses, including 11 terraces and 54 villas.[36] Land values around the Park were expected to increase significantly following its completion, generating a return equivalent to its construction costs, but many of the lots remained unsold because of the commercial crisis and the collapse in demand for high-cost housing. Some members of the merchant community, including Laird, Jackson, and Brassey, benefited from speculative investment, but others did not: the plan by Joseph Pim and his partners to construct a residential park (modelled on Clifton Park) proved to be 'financially disastrous'.[37]

Speculative investment determined the process and pattern of suburban development elsewhere on the Wirral. Land extending from the river front at Egremont was acquired by Askew as a future 'watering place', while much of Liscard was purchased by Sir John Tobin, a highly

Figure 10.3 1844 Plan of New Park by Joseph Paxton (courtesy of the Williamson Art Gallery and Museum, Birkenhead)

successful Liverpool merchant with extensive trading interests in West Africa, primarily in the slave trade prior to its abolition. The initial development of New Brighton was due to the enterprise of James Atherton, a retired Liverpool merchant who had previously been involved in land and building speculation in Everton: 170 acres of sandhills and heathland acquired in 1830 were subsequently offered as plots for villas to wealthy businessmen 'at a price worthy of their attention'.[38] The gradual suburbanisation process, extending from the eastern areas adjacent to Liverpool to outlying townships, meant that speculative investment opportunities continued to exist throughout the nineteenth century. The purchase of the Vyner estate proved to be 'an excellent investment', while the objective of the Birkenhead Land and Building Company (1863) was to secure 'the erection of a superior class of dwelling' by making advances to future purchasers of its land on the expectation of a significant increase in value. Eight of the original eleven directors of the company were local merchants and prospective shareholders were promised 'an ample return'.[39] The local press frequently carried advertisements of land and property sales: in January 1872, for example, *The Birkenhead and Cheshire Advertiser* offered 'capitalists' the rare opportunity of acquiring Eton Grange, a 15-acre freehold farm with a 'gentleman's modern residence', while land in Egremont and Rock Ferry with 'very extensive views of the surrounding county' was offered for sale by an auctioneer and estate agent.[40]

Little is known about the development of the land market on the Wirral, but members of the merchant community were heavily involved in speculative ventures. Both the overall growth in demand for high class housing and the pace of development (with an increase of over 166 per cent in Birkenhead's housing stock between 1836 and 1842) made a diversification of business interests attractive. The construction of residential housing offered merchants a relatively secure and profitable investment opportunity: Henry Jones, a merchant of Seacombe, was recorded in the 1851 census as a 'proprietor of houses' and by the early twentieth century, Lord Brassey (the son of the railway contractor Thomas Brassey) owned 23 substantial properties in the parish of Claughton-cum-Grange alone, all of which had been acquired by his father, while the list of multiple property owners included the general merchant Stanton Eddowes (3), the produce and potato merchant Joseph Taylor (23), and the ship broker Joshua Whiting (4).[41]

But suburbs on the Wirral also became sites of collective political activity involving leading members of the community, including merchants. Space does not allow a detailed analysis of the development of political structures throughout the Wirral, but they played an important role in moulding local identity. The early growth of population on the eastern side of the peninsula led to the appointment of Commissioners for the Improvement of Birkenhead in 1833 (under the terms of the first Improvement Act): their powers were extended in 1843 through the incorpora-tion of Claughton-cum-Grange and Oxton, as a result of the third Improvement Act; and in 1877 Birkenhead finally obtained its charter following a further expansion in employment opportuni-ties, particularly in ship building, and increased residential settlement. The County Borough of Wallasey, comprising the townships of Egremont, Liscard, New Brighton, Poulton, Seacombe, and Wallasey, was not created until 1910 (having been incorporated two years earlier), while the existing parish infrastructure retained its role in many other areas of the peninsula until the crea-tion of the Hoylake and West Kirby District Council and the Ellesmere Port and Whitby UDC.[42]

The creation of new political structures with extended administrative powers was a lengthy process, but one that mirrored the pattern of incremental suburbanisation. Although the devel-oping areas of settlement, particularly on the eastern side of the peninsula, were home to an increasing variety of classes and ethnicities, with a changing balance between longer-term resi-dents and recent in-migrants, political representation was dominated by members of the mer-chant community. According to Mott, the Birkenhead Improvement Commissioners were 'able and energetic men', with the stock and share broker Maurice Mocatta, 'a gentleman of great financial ability and experience', responsible for paying off the town's debt after virtual bank-ruptcy in the late 1840s.[43] Many of the original commissioners were described as 'merchants of Liverpool' and a clear majority were involved in commerce and trade. In 1843, two thirds of the commissioners were merchants, and throughout the 1860s and early 1870s over 50 per cent were drawn from this group.[44] Initially there is some evidence of a lack of interest in serving as a commissioner, but local merchants quickly appreciated the benefits of office. Some, like the general merchant John Williamson, were regarded as 'public-spirited residents', but others were more interested in utilising their position for personal gain. For example, the oil importer William Jackson (of Hamilton, Jackson, and Co.), was first elected a commissioner in 1836: as chairman of the commissioners (from 1844 until his resignation in 1846) he was instrumental in promoting the innovative plan for Birkenhead Park, but his company also supplied the town-ship with gas at an inflated price.[45] Urban development on the Wirral created a multiplicity of opportunities for local merchants to assume a wider political role. Two thirds of Birkenhead's magistrates in 1883 were merchants; the wine merchant Christopher Bushell of Hinderton Hall, Neston, was the Chairman of Magistrates for Parkgate and Neston; while the first two MPs for Birkenhead in 1861 were the ship builder John Laird and Thomas Brassey, the son of the railway contractor, both of whom were 'large landowners in the place'.[46]

Of all the 'merchants' listed in Pike's collection of contemporary biographies, almost 30 per cent held political office at some point in their career. Although there were exceptions, most political posts were linked with residential location, particularly at the level of the town or parish council. The steamship owner Charles MacIver (of D. and C. MacIver) who resided at 'Beech-field', Heswall, played 'a prominent political role' and was chairman of the local parish council for 15 years, while the cotton broker Arthur W. Willmer of 66 Park Road West, Birkenhead, was a Liberal member of Birkenhead Town Council and served as mayor in 1910–11. Merchants chaired local parish or urban district councils, whether at Eastham (the stock and share broker R. P. Sing) or Neston and Parkgate (the marine insurance broker J. A. Pemberton).[47] They served on local boards and played a prominent role in local political associations. The Grange Conservative Club in Birkenhead was formed in 1876 by the shipowner David MacIver MP, the shipbuilder John Laird (who was chairman of the Birkenhead Conservative Association), the share broker Maurice Mocatta, and the general merchant Edmund Taylor. Although the list of its first officers included both the squire of Caldy and the licensee of the Woodside Hotel, it was dominated by members of the local mercantile community. Interest in the political process was reinforced by membership of parliamentary debating societies which served, according to Gunn, as a forum for a 'rational' exchange of views 'across a spectrum of urban opinion'. The Birkenhead Society was founded in 1876 'with many leading citizens representing different constituencies', while the initial officers of the Hoylake and West Kirby Parliamentary Debating Society (1909) included an insurance agent and a provender dealer, as well as a barrister, a solicitor, and a grocer's assistant.[48]

Suburbanisation, Locality, and the Development of an Associational Framework

Charting the development of associational culture in a suburban context is problematic, even for localities such as Birkenhead and Wallasey which acquired their own civic identity during the nineteenth century, and the topic has seldom been taken forward by urban historians. The following analysis is based on the records of 45 different clubs, societies, charities, and church congregations, but they only represent part of the associational framework which developed on the Wirral prior to 1914. Although most of the medical charities are represented, comparatively few church records or membership files from local sports clubs are in the public domain: in many cases societies often left no historical record apart from occasional announcements of forthcoming meetings in the local press or brief reports of their transactions. The Birkenhead Fair Trial and Relief Committee was active in the early 1860s, the Seacombe St. Paul's Literary and Debating Society held regular meetings in the early 1880s, while the New Brighton Amateur Operatic Society was established in 1902 to promote 'the practice and study of operatic music in Wallasey': unfortunately, like many other voluntary societies, none left any tangible evidence of their activities. The existence of the Hamilton Debating Society, the Canning Debating Society, and the Grange Road Literary Society, all based in Birkenhead, can only be established from secondary sources. Little is known about the membership of the Eclectic Society for the Furtherance of Literature, Philosophy, Science, and Art founded in Wallasey (1867), the Birkenhead Model Yacht Club (which held its first annual ball at the Monks' Ferry Hotel on 5 January 1853), or the Claughton Model Yacht Club founded by the 'artist cotton-broker' Charles H. Fox, although it was in no sense 'a toy boat affair' because one of its members was the naval architect Charles Clayton of Clover Clayton, the Birkenhead shipyard.[49]

   Despite the fragmentary nature of the archival records, it is still possible to establish a typology of local clubs, societies, and associations. According to the *Red Book* of 1902, there were only eight 'cultural' clubs or societies on the Wirral, including the Birkenhead Literary and Scientific Society, the Birkenhead Shakespeare Literary Society, the Claughton and Cleveland Club, the St. Cecilia Choral Society (Claughton), the Liscard Orchestral Society, the Rock Ferry Horticultural Society, Trinity Presbyterian Church Literary Society, and the Wirral Footpaths and Open Spaces Preservation Society.[50] This seriously underestimated the extent of associational activity in the major areas of suburban settlement on the peninsula, all of which witnessed the creation of a dense institutional network. As Morris has demonstrated, the proliferation of different types of voluntary organisation in Britain from the late eighteenth century onwards reflected the increasing complexity of civil society, with the local town invariably the focal point of activity for most subscriber associations. This was certainly the case in Liverpool and in the larger Cheshire towns, but the transposition of associational culture from the urban core to suburban areas remains, regretfully, a neglected area of research.[51]

As might be expected, separate 'cultural' societies were initially established in Birkenhead, while their subsequent diffusion pattern closely reflected the spatial extension of suburban settlement to other parts of the peninsula. At a national level, the first wave of literary and scientific societies had been founded in the 1790s, but the Birkenhead Literary Society was only founded in 1848 following the rapid expansion of the township in the early 1840s and in 1857 the Birkenhead Literary and Scientific Society was established. Despite the fact that 'many Associations of different character' already existed, there was a general need for an association 'on some more extended principle than yet existed': it was not envisaged as a competitor to the three debating societies, but would function as 'a general town society for the encouragement of literature and science, open to all parties to whatever religious denomination they might belong'.[52] Similar societies were subsequently formed elsewhere on the Wirral, often when the density of middle class residential development had created a sufficient level of demand. The Rock Ferry Athenaeum Debating Society was established in 1861 and the New Ferry Literary and Debating Society was functioning prior to 1883, but the West Kirby Literary Society was only created in 1887 and the Deeside Literary and Debating Society in 1904. A similar process was evident in the case of parliamentary debating societies designed to foster a 'rational' exchange of views across a broad spectrum of urban opinion and reinforce involvement in the political process. The first such society was established in Birkenhead in 1876; the Seacombe Parliamentary and Debating Society was holding regular debates by 1880; but the inaugural meeting of the Hoylake and West Kirby Parliamentary Debating Society did not take place until September 1909 (in the Technical Schoolroom, Hoylake) when it was agreed that seats could not be reserved.[53]

The process of suburbanisation on the Wirral was accompanied by the gradual extension of existing models of associational culture to new areas of residential settlement. If voluntary associations helped to create or reinforce a sense of middle-class urban identity in larger Victorian cities by strengthening transactional density, such a role was replicated in a suburban context. The example of the West Kirby Literary Society (1887) is instructive. By the late nineteenth century West Kirby and Hoylake were 'growing by leaps and bounds' and the society's membership fluctuated annually 'owing largely to the migratory nature of the population'. But its officers were convinced it could play a major role in the locality: there were 245 members by 1895; it was firmly believed this could be doubled 'as there are yet many in West Kirby and Hoylake who should be members of our Society'; and four years later a target of 1,000 was set as 'the smallest number' that would satisfy the committee. An active recruitment policy and an attractive programme of activities, at a time of further residential settlement in West Kirby and Hoylake, led to an increase in average attendance at the society's events from 75 (1894–95) to 206 (1897–98) and a membership figure of 659 at the very end of the century. By hosting a regular series of Liverpool University Extension lectures, talks, theatrical performances, dances, and social evenings, the society provided a public forum for social interaction. Virtually all its members were recruited from the immediate locality and over a third were merchants. Such a strong level of support, particularly by families of merchants and the professional classes, served to define the cultural parameters of the expanding residential areas of Hoylake and West Kirby.[54]

Contrary to the view that suburban relocation necessarily implied an increased emphasis on domesticity and privacy, the growth of residential communities on the Wirral was accompanied by a proliferation of new associational structures which created a dense network of informal contacts at the local level.[55] In 1891, the parishes of Hoylake and West Kirby had a population of 6,545 and 7,329 respectively: ten years later these two townships had almost 23,000 residents, but the expansion and range of local associations and societies was arguably even more impressive (Table 10.2). Although some charitable bodies, including the Hoylake Benevolent Tontine Society and the West Kirby Benevolent Fund, had been established before the rapid growth in local population, most clubs and societies were the product of residential settlement and increased middle-class demand. The pace of growth in their associational infrastructure was dramatic.

Historically, both Hoylake and West Kirby were separate townships, but the proliferation of new clubs and societies in the 1880s and 1890s contributed to community building and their

Table 10.2 The associational infrastructure of Hoylake and West Kirby, 1897–1906

1. Hoylake   Club/Society/Charity
Hoylake Ladies Golf Club
Hoylake Sailing Club (1888)
Hoylake Football and Athletic Society
Hoylake Bowling Club
Hoylake Debating Society
Hoylake Temperance Choir*
Hoylake Benevolent Tontine Society (1858)
Hoylake Relief Society (1891)
Hoylake Blue Ribbon Mission
Hoylake Teetotal Tontine Society

2. West Kirby   Club/Society/Charity
West Kirby Cycling Club
West Kirby Association Football Club (c.1888)
West Kirby Lawn Tennis Club*
West Kirby Amateur Swimming Club (1900)
West Kirby Literary Society (1887)
West Kirby Choral Society (1893)
West Kirby P.S.E. Choir
West Kirby Brass Band
West Kirby Charities (1885)
West Kirby Christian Institute (1892)
West Kirby YMCA
West Kirby Benevolent Fund (1868)
West Kirby Women's Temperance Association (1893)
West Kirby Club for Girls and Young Women*
West Kirby and District Homing Society*
West Kirby Primrose League (1885)
West Kirby Quoit Club (1904)
Deeside Literary and Debating Society, West Kirby (1904)

3. Hoylake and West Kirby Clubs, etc.
Hoylake and West Kirby District Band*
Hoylake and West Kirby Horticultural Association*
Hoylake and West Kirby Permanent Tontine Beneficial Society (1881)
West Kirby and Hoylake Social Club (1905-06)
Hoylake and West Kirby Parliamentary Debating Society (1909)

* not cited in 1897

Sources: Hoylake and West Kirby Directory, 1897 (Herald and Visitor, 1897); *Moss's Directory of Hoylake and West Kirby, 1906* (John Moss, West Kirby, 1906)

redefinition as social units. The West Kirby Choral Society (1893) quickly recruited a large membership of approximately 75 and was in 'a very vigorous condition'; the West Kirby Literary Society was 'believed to be one of the largest of its kind in the North of England', with up to 1,000 seats available in the Public Hall, Grange Road, for local residents eager to listen to a course of lectures on Russia delivered in 1905 by Mr. Pares.[56] The first 'Habitation' in Cheshire of the Primrose League, founded in 1885, was located in West Kirby: it was dominated by 'gentlemen of the neighbourhood' and was intended to contribute 'generously to the social life of the place' through holding annual balls and summer picnics. However, it was primarily a means of spreading Conservative principles and the high level of female support failed to change its 'non-committal' attitude towards women's suffrage.[57] The social evenings organised by the Deeside Literary and Debating Society in West Kirby were a 'popular feature' in its early days: it attracted an influx of new members each session and its value in fostering friendships 'should not be overlooked'. Most of the local clubs and societies, irrespective of their function, were run by members of the middle class. The provision merchant George Wall was president of the West Kirby Choral Society in 1896–97, while the shipbroker J. G. Holmes was vice-president of the Hoylake Bowling Club; and half the committee of the Hoylake and West Kirby Horticultural Society in 1906 was drawn from the merchant class. As in other areas of suburban development, the creation of clubs and societies outside the metropolitan core was an important factor in community development: it reinforced localised identities, encouraged collective action, and enabled middle-class residents to forge a distinct political culture based on residence, leisure activities, and occupational status. To this extent, the establishment of an extended associational infrastructure in suburban areas such as Hoylake and West Kirby provided a basis for social interaction and networking within an explicitly local context: some of the associations (such as the West Kirby YMCA) were branches of national organisations, but almost all their members were local residents.[58]

The central importance of locality in defining both the nature and role of associational culture was evident across the Wirral (Table 10.3). Whether in relation to cultural and political societies, sports clubs, schools, churches and associated institutes, or hospitals, a very high proportion of members (including elected honorary officers) were local. Only in the case of a few cultural societies and political clubs did the minimum level of local participation ever fall below 50 per

Table 10.3 The spatial pattern of local involvement in associational culture on the Wirral (by type, in per cent)

Type (and Number)	Local		Local+ Semi-Local*	
	Max.	Min.	Max.	Min.
Societies (16)+	96.9	33.3	98.8	55.5
Sports Clubs (8)	100.0	63.6	100.0	87.8
Schools (4)	90.0	57.1	100.0	71.4
Churches (11)	100.0	62.3	100.0	81.2
Medical Charities (6)	91.4	57.1	97.1	71.3

Notes: + Four political clubs and societies are included in this subtotal: Birkenhead Parliamentary Debating Society; Grange Road Conservative Club (Birkenhead); Hoylake Parliamentary Debating Society; Oxton Conservative Club.

* Semi-local refers to members who were from an adjacent or contiguous area to the location of a society or sports club, etc. For example, a member of a Birkenhead-based association from Oxton or Tranmere would be classified as semi-local.

Source: archival material and reports, Wirral Archives Service

cent. If semi-local members who lived in adjacent districts are included in the analysis, the overriding importance of locality is reinforced in all five categories. Indeed, it was not uncommon for all, or almost all, of committee members and subscribers to reside within the vicinity.[59] For example, a dinner in 1861 for the founders of the Claughton Bowling Club brought together a 'convivial group' of local residents and the seven members of the original management committee were drawn from an even smaller geographical area bounded by Lingdale Road (Claughton), Ashville Road (Birkenhead Park), and Cearns Road (Oxton).[60]

The Creation of New Networks of Associational Culture on the Wirral

In order to explore the dynamics of Wirral's new associational culture in the course of the nineteenth century, the following section will focus on the main categories of voluntary affiliation. It will examine the changing extent of local involvement, particularly on the part of merchants, and assess the degree to which suburbanisation rapidly created an alternative web of voluntary organisations which dominated increasingly the lives of middle-class residents, in some cases at the cost of commitments which had been made previously to established Liverpool-based bodies.

Detailed membership data for Wirral's cultural associations and political clubs have survived in a number of cases. Unsurprisingly, the majority of members between the early 1880s and 1913 lived locally. In 1882, 93.8 per cent of the members of the Birkenhead Ruskin Society were 'local' or 'semi-local' (i.e., they came from Birkenhead, Claughton, or Oxton); in 1907, 89 per cent of the membership of the Birkenhead and Literary Society were 'local', while 96.9 per cent of the West Kirby Literary Society's membership in 1900 lived in either Hoylake or West Kirby. Although presidents, vice-presidents, and trustees could be recruited, when necessary, from further afield, as was the case with the Grange Conservative Club, virtually all the societies for which membership data are available fulfilled a cultural, political, or social function within a specific locality and were both managed and supported by local residents. Only when organisations served a wider constituency, such as the Wirral Footpaths and Open Spaces Preservations Society and the Wirral Ramblers Association, was the membership profile spatially diluted, but even in the former case almost half the membership in 1888–89 lived in Birkenhead and Oxton.[61]

Most sports clubs catered primarily for local residents, but some developed a wider recruitment focus right from the beginning. Golf clubs sought to recruit 'county' members by offering reduced subscriptions for non-local players who lived within a 50-mile radius. In a limited number of cases, Wirral-based sports clubs enjoyed a regional, even national, profile, which was reflected in the spatial distribution of their membership. Both the Royal Mersey Yacht Club (RMYC) in Rock Ferry and the Royal Liverpool Golf Club (RLGC) in Hoylake were established by Merseyside merchants. They reflected the growth of sporting facilities throughout the region from the mid-nineteenth century onwards, but the choice of a location on the peninsula was determined primarily by the availability of a suitable site. The RMYC was founded in July 1844 by 20 local businessmen and gentlemen: it catered for the owners of larger yachts, offered substantial prize money, and provided both accommodation and dining facilities for its members, who included representatives of the aristocracy such as the Marquis of Anglesey and the Earl of Derby.[62] By 1870, the RLGC was firmly established having negotiated the lease of land for a nine-hole golf course and its reputation was quickly consolidated, in part because of the management skills of its honorary secretary, the merchant T. O. Potter, who had a weakness for claret and prawns.[63] In both cases, the majority of club members were from Liverpool (including its northern and southern suburbs) and the Wirral. The RLGC catered for a larger local

Table 10.4 Localism and associational involvement on the Wirral by category (societies, sports clubs, schools, churches, and hospitals), 1851–1913

1. Societies	Body	Date	Residential Location			
			Local	Semi-Local	Wirral	Other
Birkenhead Ruskin S	m	1882	93.8	4.0	2.0	1.0
Birkenhead Lit & Scientific S	m	1907	89.0	5.5	2.7	2.7
Birkenhead Shakespeare Literary	m		79.6	16.9		3.3
New Ferry Lit. & Scientific S+	m	1884	50.0	43.7	11.1	6.2
"	c	1884	33.3	22.2		22.2
West Kirby Literary S	m	1900	96.9	1.9	0.1	0.3
"	c	1896				
Grange Conservative Club	c	1887				
"	P+VP		73.9		26.0	
"	trustees				80.0	
H&WKPDS	officers	1912	62.5	12.5		
WF&OSPS WF&OSPS	c	1902				
2. Sports Clubs						
Claughton Bowling	ic	1861	85.7			
"	s	1875	75.0	25.0		
Bebington Bowling	im	1865	76.9	19.2		3.8
"	c	1867	63.6	24.2	3.0	
3. Schools						
Birkenhead School	c	1860	90.0	9.1		
"	s	1872				28.6
Birkenhead Institute	subs	1884	85.7	14.2		
"	s	1887	73.0	7.8	7.8	6.7
Caldy Grange Grammar School	c	1904	57.1	21.4		
"	c	1913	29.4	88.2		
4. Churches						
Trinity Presbyterian	founders	1863	80.0	20.0		
"	ms	1863–78	100			
" Brassey St. Mission	c	1863–78	90.3	9.6		
" "	elders	1888	100			
Birkenhead Soc. of Friends	c	1879	66.6	33.3		
Birkenhead YMCA	c	1892	76.4	23.5		
5. Hospitals						
Birkenhead Hospital & Dispensary	c	1851	85.7	14.2		
Wallasey Cottage Hospital	subs	1867	77.7	11.1		11.1
Seacombe Cottage Hospital	c	1872	100			
Birkenhead Borough Hospital	c	1901	78.2	8.6	4.3	8.6
"	subs	1903	80.9	1.7	7.5	0.2
WH&D for Sick Children	c	1870–75	91.4	5.7	2.8	
"	c	1893	72.7	18.1	9.0	
"	c	1903	80.0	10.0	10.0	
"	c	1913	60.0	24.0	16.0	
Hoylake Cottage Hospital	c	1909	70.0	10.0	10.0	10.0

Key: members = m; committee = c; President(s) and Vice-Presidents = P+VPs; initial committee = ic; shareholders = s; subscribers = subs; member sample = ms.

Abbreviations: Hoylake and West Kirby Parliamentary Debating Society (H&WKPDS); Wirral Footpaths and Open Spaces Preservation Society (WF&OSPS); Wirral Hospital and Dispensary for Sick Children (WH&D for Sick Children).

Source: Wirral Archives Service; secondary literature

Table 10.5 The spatial distribution of members of the Royal Liverpool Golf Club (RLGC) and the Royal
Mersey Yacht Club (RMYC) (in per cent)

Address for Communication	RLGC	RMYC
Liverpool and environs	57.9	38.6
Wirral (and Cheshire)	22.0	9.1
Lancashire	3.4	13.3
London and SE	5.9	3.9
Ireland	0.0	1.2
Scotland	2.7	0.6
Wales	1.4	3.3
Other GB	1.2	11.8
Overseas	1.2	2.1
Not given	3.9	16.1

Source: Club membership records; MLP database

constituency (Table 10.5), while the RMYC had a higher proportion of members from more distant locations, including ports and holiday resorts such as Fleetwood, Whitehaven, Torquay, St. Austell, and St. Ives, as well as from overseas, including Newport, USA. Both clubs were created to satisfy a rising demand for sport and leisure facilities for Merseyside as a whole, but their Wirral location reinforced the peninsula's increasing popularity as a place of residence. In the case of the RLGC, 88 of its members (20 per cent of the total membership) lived on the Wirral, of whom 32 resided in Hoylake itself.

Other sports clubs designed to appeal to a wide range of 'gentlemen on Merseyside' still recruited a significant number of local members. Over half the membership of the Royal Rock Beagle Hunt in its first season in 1845 came from Rock Ferry or New Ferry, with a further 12.2 per cent from Birkenhead and Tranmere. The Birkenhead Park Rugby Club (1871) provided convenient facilities for Liverpool club players who lived on the Cheshire side, while all the early presidents and officers of the New Brighton Football Club (1875) resided locally, whether in Liscard, New Brighton, or Wallasey. Indeed, the degree of local representation was sometimes overwhelming: for the two bowling clubs for which committee and shareholder data are available, the proportion varied between 85.7 per cent (the initial committee of the Claughton Bowling Club in 1861) and 76.9 per cent (at the time of the first meeting of the Bebington Bowling Club six years later). Once again, if 'semi-local' members are taken into consideration, the local framework for determining their operation became even more explicit. For example, all the shareholders of the Claughton Bowling Club in 1875 were either 'local' or 'semi-local'.[64]

There was an even greater degree of local involvement in the establishment and running of schools and churches. In both cases, the historic level of provision became increasingly inadequate in the face of incremental suburban development and rapid population growth. Prior to the introduction of a reliable steam-ferry service across the Mersey, Wirral only had a limited number of grammar schools, and facilities for secondary education were restricted. The earliest known reference to Wallasey Grammar School was in 1595, while the grammar schools at Calday Grange and Woodchurch had been established in 1636 and 1665 respectively. But the level of provision in the early 1800s was often poor: Wallasey Grammar School had approximately 50 pupils in 1825 and its reputation suffered from unfavourable reports, while Calday reopened in 1862 after a period of serious neglect when it had ceased to be either a 'free' or a 'grammar' school, as originally intended.[65] Increased residential development on the Wirral prompted a supply side response as individual school proprietors sought to exploit local demand. In the early 1860s, for example, Mr. Hurworth's Commercial Academy and Boarding School in New Brighton advertised itself as 'a middle class school' which guaranteed 'to impart a sound and useful English education', while Dr. Brindley's Park House in Birkenhead offered special attention to 'young and backward boys'. However, prior to the founding of Birkenhead School (1860) Wirral remained within the catchment area of established Liverpool schools, in particular the Liverpool Institute (1825) and Liverpool College (1840), and 'local' education for the sons of Wirral-based middle-class families inevitably involved a daily return journey across the Mersey.[66]

The creation of new public schools on the Wirral and the revival of existing grammar schools reflected a growing need to provide educational facilities in line with local aspirations. In every case, progress was a result of the initiative of residents and improvements in the educational infrastructure reinforced a sense of community and locality within a suburban context. Birkenhead School, established as a limited company in 1860 (Figure 10.4), was designed to 'afford to the inhabitants of Birkenhead and its neighbourhood a first-rate Education for their sons at a moderate rate and give to the town a public building worthy of its increasing wealth and importance': all seven of the original shareholders lived within half a mile of each other and the eleven committee members all resided in Birkenhead, Claughton, or Oxton; virtually all the original committee were local (or 'semi-local') residents, although by the early 1870s two of the seven shareholders resided outside Wirral.[67]

Figure 10.4 Birkenhead School (photograph, c. 1880)

The foundation of Birkenhead Institute in 1884 as a public high school offering 'a First-class Mercantile and Collegiate Education' owed a great deal to the 'unwearying energy' of George Atkin, an asphalt manufacturer and tar distiller of Egerton Park, Rock Ferry, and all the initial subscribers were local residents (from Birkenhead, Oxton, Tranmere, or Rock Ferry): by 1887 fewer than 20 per cent of the shareholders came from other parts of the Wirral or elsewhere. Support was elicited from 'many of the most influential citizens of Birkenhead' and committee members openly canvassed local tradesmen for financial contributions, 'several of whom had taken shares'.[68] This was clearly evident in the residential location of both subscribers (1884) and shareholders (1887): in the former case, all the subscribers were local or 'semi-local', whereas over 80 per cent of the shareholders belonged to these categories. To this extent, Birkenhead Institute was developed almost exclusively as a local initiative, drawing on the skills and contacts of men who lived in its immediate proximity. However, other school developments drew on a wider range of spatial support, sometimes because of legislative requirements. For example, the revival of Calday Grammar School, with financial support from Bennett's Charity, required formal approval in 1886 by the Queen in Council and the composition of the governing body of '13 competent persons duly qualified to discharge the duties of office' was set out in law. In both 1904 and 1913, the overwhelming majority of committee members were locals, well placed to attend meetings often held late on a Saturday afternoon: in 1912–13, while 15 of the governors (from a total of 17) lived either in West Kirby or Hoylake.[69] Wallasey Grammar School was re-founded in 1873 following the promulgation of the Endowed Schools Act of 1869 which served as the basis for a government-induced reform of grammar schools in general, but the improvement in its status was due to considerable support from local families. Cheshire County Council had the right to appoint a clear majority of the representative governors, but it consistently chose 'a group of well-known local men'.[70]

The development of an educational infrastructure on the Wirral reinforced localised identities. The admission and address books of prominent Liverpool schools provide evidence of their continuing ability to recruit pupils from the Wirral, but they were increasingly a minority: in 1882 there was a single pupil from Birkenhead in Liverpool Institute's High School, while T. M. Roy was the only Wirral-based student in the Upper School of Liverpool College in 1887 (from a total of 42).[71] By contrast, Wirral schools had a strong local profile in terms of recruitment. In its first year of operation, Birkenhead School had 18 boys, but by 1865 this number had risen to 85: in 1892, apart from a small number of boarders whose parents lived in Bury, Dublin, Rugby, and Manchester, almost all the intake (79.0 per cent) were from local homes. Approximately two thirds of the pupils admitted both in 1884 and 1892 were the sons of merchants or came from families involved in insurance or manufacturing. Birkenhead Institute, however, never catered for the higher echelons of the middle class. Only 14 pupils from a total of 300 admitted between 1901 and 1910 came from the merchant community, and its catchment area, as a result, was entirely local. Over two thirds of the pupils of Calday Grange Grammar School in 1911 came from West Kirby and Hoylake, while over 75 per cent of the girls attending Birkenhead High School (founded as 'a good public girls' Secondary School' in 1884) resided in Birkenhead.[72]

The creation of alumni associations strengthened further the community role of Wirral schools. The Old Girls' Association of Higher Tranmere High School for Girls (1891) had a series of branches, including field, musical, and book clubs which encouraged regular attendance by former pupils who still lived locally, although it was also open to girls who resided 'permanently or for a period at a distance'. The Old Birkonian Society, founded at a comparatively late date in 1907, developed a range of activities which underpinned its local role: a rugby football sub-committee was convened in April 1907 and in the following year the Committee 'heartily' approved the formation of an Old Birkonian Company in the 4th Battalion of the Cheshire Regiment.[73]

Churches also proved to be central institutions in creating localised identities and developing frameworks for social networking. The Act for Building New Churches of 1818 had given a stimulus to the enhanced provision of Anglican places of worship, while the continued expansion of non-conformist, dissenting, and independent congregations led to the establishment of new churches and chapels in many towns and cities. As in other suburbanising areas, church building on the Wirral followed population growth and the spatial expansion of residential settlement, although sometimes with a marked delay. But in other cases, they were viewed as 'speculative' developments, funded by the munificence of local residents and located in semi-rural areas designed to attract the settlement of new residents. In Birkenhead alone, ten new churches were opened between 1830 and 1847. The United Presbyterian Church in Grange Road West was completed in 1848 and St. Saviour's, Oxton, was consecrated in 1851. Hamilton Square Congregational Church (Birkenhead) lost a number of members when they 'moved to Hoylake' in the early 1870s, but residential relocation led directly to the establishment of a new church in the township, while the construction of a new meeting house in Park Road South for the Birkenhead Society of Friends in 1893 was largely due to the fact that many of the leading members (including the provision merchant Frederic Clibborn and his wife Henrietta) had moved to newly built properties in Oxton.[74] The relative density of church provision often reflected the denominational affiliation of new residents: Seacombe had a total population of 3,683 in 1861, but it already had five different places of worship (St. Paul's Church of England, a Welsh Calvinistic Methodist Church, a Wesleyan Church, a Welsh-speaking Wesleyan Mission Room, and a Roman Catholic Mission), even before the opening of its Presbyterian Church of England in 1862. As was the case in the outer suburbs on the other side of the Mersey, the expansion of Presbyterianism and new Methodist societies was particularly marked on the Wirral, while the existence of traditional parish boundaries restricted the development of new Anglican communities, particularly where existing churches, such as St. Oswald's, Bidston, retained a reputation for 'stylish weddings'.[75]

In almost every case, the foundation and opening of a new place of worship helped to reinforce the development of a distinct sense of locality for members of the congregation. Churches, by definition, were intended as inclusive institutions (at least within denominational and class-specific boundaries): they included women and children, household domestic servants, and unmarried or widowed members. St. Peter's Church in Rock Ferry was built in 1841–42 largely at the expense of local residents in Rock Park; 16 local 'businessmen' 'concerned about the spiritual needs of Tranmere' attended an initial meeting in August 1852 which led to the foundation of St. Paul's; and a small group of local residents, led by George Atkin, decided in March 1869 that it would be desirable 'to establish a church in Rock Ferry or its neighbourhood, in accordance with congregational doctrine'.[76]

Most churches had a predominantly local catchment area and committee members, elders, or members of management boards were invariably residents. For example, the founders of Trinity Presbyterian Church (1863) were all local or semi-local; its members (based on a sample between 1863 and 1878) were drawn entirely from the surrounding area; while in 1888 the elders of the Brassey Street Mission in 1888, established jointly with Hamilton Memorial Presbyterian Church in Park Road North, lived locally. The community-building role of churches was strengthened by a shared religious belief, often expressed in domestic mission work, and the development of wider social functions. Chapels functioned as 'social centres for the well-to-do' running clusters of societies, but in an explicit suburban context. Shortly after its opening in 1862, the Seacombe Presbyterian Church of England provided a regular Sabbath school,

Saturday evening entertainments, a mothers' meeting, a day school, adult evening classes, sewing classes, household weekly prayer meetings, Sabbath afternoon services 'for people in plain clothes', a youth's fife and drum band, and a penny savings bank. The Birkenhead Society of Friends used a series of premises for mission work, but from November 1877 onwards it ran its own literary society: all members were eligible (but election was by ballot, 'three black balls to exclude'); debates were held on a range of contemporary issues; and the social meetings were generally well attended, particularly after the society was reconstituted in 1881. Trinity Presbyterian Church, Oxton, also ran a successful literary society.[77]

Where new facilities were created, as was the case with the opening of a new building in 1891 for the Birkenhead Young Men's Christian Association (founded in 1872) and the construction of the West Kirby Christian Institute in 1892 (following a decision that 'the omission of the religious side of the work would not answer the desired end'), the local, community-based role of these institutions was reinforced by renting space to like-minded organisations. The Birkenhead Mission and the Birkenhead Choral Union were allowed to hold concerts in the new YMCA building shortly after it opened and the YMCA Camera Club, established by members in 1884 at a time when photography was still an expensive hobby, ultimately became the Birkenhead Photographic Association, while the West Kirby Christian Institute hosted meetings by the Good Templars and the literary society. By contrast, the Birkenhead Young Women's Christian Association, founded on a non-denominational basis in December 1881, utilised the dining room of Birkenhead School for its 'annual public meeting' ('by the kindness of the Headmaster') and its ambulance classes were held in the children's hospital: the net result was a strengthening of associational links both at an individual and institutional level.[78]

There has been considerable research on the development of hospital provision and its significance both for the medical profession and the survival of patients, but the extent to which medical charity was anchored within the framework of metropolitan and suburban communities has never been addressed. In fact, hospitals and dispensaries on the Wirral played an important role in the development of distinct, local identities, and provided a framework for associational affiliation and involvement. Institutional models for medical charities already existed: the establishment of a Liverpool Infirmary had been proposed in 1748 on a scale which would match provision in rival towns and a Ladies Charity had been formed in 1796: by the late nineteenth century Liverpool had 3 general hospitals, 4 dispensaries, and approximately 20 medical institutes which provided specialist treatment.[79] By contrast, the initial increase in residential settlement on the Wirral during the 1820s and 1830s did not require the creation of charitable medical institutions because most of the new residents were merchants or members of the middle class who retained their own private physicians. This situation was transformed by the expansion of employment opportunities in shipbuilding and manufacturing, particularly in Birkenhead, where it was recognised that the provision of charitable institutions remained 'at present limited', while the 'want of an Infirmary is universally admitted'.[80]

Again, the expansion of medical charities on the Wirral reflected the process of suburban settlement: new institutions were initially created in Birkenhead and Wallasey, including the Birkenhead Dispensary (1828), the Wallasey Dispensary in Liscard (1831), and the Birkenhead Ladies' Charity and Lying-in-Hospital (1845), whereas hospital provision in the outlying townships of West Kirby and Hoylake only improved from the 1880s onwards, with a particular emphasis on the creation of facilities for convalescent or chronically sick children. Except for the Heswall Children's Hospital, established by the Liverpool County Hospital for Chronic Diseases of Children, charitable foundations were created to serve the needs of specific local communities. The Seacombe Cottage Hospital and Dispensary for Children (1869) catered for the parish of Wallasey's poor, where 'the want of some Hospital accommodation in the district had been so long felt', while the Hoylake Cottage Hospital (1906), which resulted from an initiative taken by the District Nursing Committee (formed in 1899), was principally for the 'working men of the Hoylake Parish'.[81]

As was the case with other suburban (or non-metropolitan) institutions, medical charities on the Wirral depended on subscriptions and donations from residents. In 1851, all the committee members of the Birkenhead Hospital and Dispensary were local or 'semi-local'. On its foundation in 1867, it was recognised that the future development of the Wallasey Cottage Hospital would depend 'on the liberality of others', but almost all the initial subscribers were local or semi-local residents, while the funding of a new building for the Wirral Hospital and Dispensary for Sick Children in 1882 depended on the charity of 'many persons dwelling in Wirral and in neighbouring places' (Figure 10.5). Indeed, virtually in every case, the local or semi-local presence of subscribers and committee members exceeded 80 per cent, reinforcing the role and impact of voluntary provision within an explicitly defined geographical context and providing networking possibilities for local residents. In the case of the Birkenhead Borough Hospital, an explicit appeal was made in 1901 to 'those who have recently made their home in and near Birkenhead' to join the list of subscribers and there were regular complaints that 'comparatively small support' was ever received from residents in Tranmere, Rock Ferry or Bebington, let alone from those who lived in other districts 'lying in the south of the Borough'. Overall, the level of local participation in medical charities (whether as subscribers or committee members) fluctuated between 57.1 and 91.4 per cent: only rarely was the level of external involvement noticeable; and, as was the case with the committee of the Wirral Hospital and Dispensary for Sick Children between 1870 and 1913) there was hardly any change in the extent of local support for its charitable objects.[82]

Figure 10.5 Wirral Hospital and Dispensary for Sick Children (1909 postcard)

The extent to which medical charities on the Wirral functioned as focal points for community activity, particularly by members of the middle class, can be illustrated in several ways. Firstly, by drawing on the financial support from a network of local groups and associations, they reinforced a sense of community identity. Although the majority of subscriptions came from local residents, the Wallasey Dramatic Club made a donation of £28 6s 11d to the local Cottage Hospital in 1875 from two of its performances, while the Wirral Hospital and Dispensary for Sick Children benefited from the proceeds of concerts organised by the Oxton Quoit Club and the Birkenhead Dramatic Society. The management committees of individual hospitals exploited links with local churches to raise revenue: letters were regularly sent out to ministers, joint appeals were made to church congregations, and collections from churches and schools were registered in their annual reports. In 1882, for example, the Wirral Hospital and Dispensary for Sick Children reported contributions from eleven church and school collections, including £3 2s 6d from the Children's Musical and Floral Service at Trinity Presbyterian Church, Oxton.[83]

Secondly, opportunities were created for local women, often the wives or daughters of middle-class residents, to contribute to the management and resourcing of medical charities in a manner which reinforced a sense of local identity outside Liverpool's orbit as a metropolitan centre. The larger hospitals had their separate ladies committees: although women were sometimes expected to carry out subsidiary roles, such as organising concerts or dramatic entertainments 'as in former years', by the early 1900s they occupied half of the 20 seats on the Board of the Wirral Hospital and Dispensary for Sick Children, and contributed 5 members to the Acting Committee. Over 30 per cent of the subscribers to the Cottage Hospitals in both Wallasey (1881) and Hoylake (1903) were women, all but one of them contributing in their own right, but only 8.5 per cent of the Life Governors of the Birkenhead Hospital and Dispensary in 1901 were women, including six members of the Laird family.[84]

The use of lady collectors to raise funds from well-defined districts within the community further strengthened the associational framework of medical charities, specifically on a family basis. By the late nineteenth century, the Wirral Hospital and Dispensary for Sick Children had 37 lady collectors, most of whom were the daughters of local merchants and other members of the middle class: in 1892 Miss May Marquis (whose father was the broker John Marquis) had raised £57 3s 6d, while Miss M. Callender (a daughter of the stock and share broker Andrew Callender) had collected only £6 15s 6d. Almost all the collection districts were in Birkenhead itself and by the early 1900s only two outlying districts (Thornton Hough and Hoylake) had been incorporated. Moreover, the lady collectors were assigned a limited number of streets within the community: in 1895, for example, Miss Gostenhofer (daughter of the general merchant Charles Gostenhofer) was responsible for Argyle Street and Hamilton Street (with nine and six addresses respectively). Their role involved regular visits to subscriber households, which strengthen personal contacts within the community and reinforced the profile of specific medical charities. Hospitals, dispensaries, and other medical charities on the Wirral remained dependent on local funding and the continued commitment of residents, particularly members of the merchant community.[85]

Residential Location and the Network Embeddedness of Wirral Merchants

The role of merchants in Wirral's developing associational framework has already been alluded to and there can be little doubt that their collective influence was very significant. In general, they were more strongly represented on the managing committees of clubs and societies than amongst the membership; they were heavily involved in local sports clubs and private schools as shareholders or subscribers; they played an important role in many churches and associated non-denominational institutes, whether as committee members or elders, and they played an indispensable role in managing voluntary hospitals and other medical institutions. Overall, merchants accounted for over half (52.1 per cent) of all known associational involvement, but they played a more dominant role in establishing and managing local sports clubs (63.8 per cent), schools (61.7 per cent), churches (65.9 per cent), and medical charities (64.6 per cent) (Table 10.6). By contrast, they only accounted for 41.9 per cent of the overall membership of cultural associations and political clubs. They were even less prominent as committee members, whether in the case of the New Ferry Literary and Scientific Society where they only accounted for one third in 1884, the West Kirby Literary Society (29.6 per cent in 1900), or the Birkenhead Shakespeare Literary Society (26.2 per cent). The level of associational involvement in medical charities was particularly evident, with committee or board representation by members of the merchant community often accounting for two thirds of the elected membership. Indeed, the range of merchant associational activity was extensive. The fact that 39 of the 62 members of the Wirral Philharmonic Society's Provisional Committee in 1863 came from the merchant community is not surprising, given the level of contemporary support for music and the arts, but the Local (Birkenhead) Committee of the Manchester and Liverpool Agricultural Society was also dominated by merchants (21 from a total of 33), reflecting a wider interest in horticulture and farm production.[86] Moreover, there is no evidence to suggest that the level of associational involvement declined over time, irrespective of wider changes in the socio-occupational structure of local communities.

A detailed breakdown of the associational involvement of Wirral merchants (Table 10.6) highlights the range and extent of their participation. Their leading role was evident in the case of individual societies, in particular the Birkenhead Ruskin Society, elite sports clubs, such as the Claughton Bowling Club, while they accounted for more than two thirds of the committee members, shareholders, and subscribers whose support for Birkenhead School and Birkenhead Institute was critical for their future. Selectively, they played a dominant role in the foundation of individual churches, including Trinity Presbyterian, and this was almost certainly a reflection not only of the depth of their confessional commitment, but also their ability to fund the significant construction costs of new churches. But above all their role in responding to the perceived health needs of the local population was particularly prominent. With some exceptions, Wirral merchants accounted for an overwhelming majority of the subscribers and committee members who supported the work of local hospitals and dispensaries. It can be argued that this was simply a reflection of self-interest, because support for improved hospital provision reinforced their social standing and civic importance. But all these commitments took place within a spatially defined local context, while their individual contributions, whether in cash or time, were allocated in response to the apparent needs of their surrounding communities.

In several cases merchants were responsible for founding new institutions. The Claughton Bowling Club was formed by businessmen at a meeting in the Clarendon Rooms, Liverpool on 8 March 1858 and its committee was composed solely of brokers, merchants, and shipowners. A similar range of occupations was evident at a meeting on 23 May 1859, presided over by the ship builder John Laird, which led to the formation of the 1st Cheshire Rifle Volunteers, the start of a movement which 'took a great hold of Birkenhead and district'. The iron merchant W. S. Caine was responsible for erecting a building for the Seacombe Cottage Hospital in 1871 which enabled the committee 'to escape the responsibility of becoming owners' and he remitted all rental charges in its early years.[87] In other cases, an invitation to serve as president, vice-president, or trustee of a particular society was a reflection of local status and influence: the successful India merchant V. A. King served for many years as Lieutenant-Colonel of the Cheshire Rifle Volunteers until his resignation in June 1881; the Laird family was continuously involved

Table 10.6 The associational involvement of Wirral merchants by category (societies, sports clubs, schools, churches, and hospitals), 1851–1913

				Merchants	
	Body	*Date*	*no.*	*no.*	*%*
1. Societies					
Birkenhead Ruskin S	m	1882	78	51	65.3
Birkenhead Lit & Scientific S	m	1907	130	52	40.3
Birkenhead Shakespeare Literary S	m		118	31	26.2
New Ferry Lit. & Scientific S+	m	1884		4	33.3
"	c	1884	12		
West Kirby Literary S	m	1900	81	24	29.6
"	c	1896	16	6	37.5
Grange Conservative Club	c	1887	19	5	26.3
"	P+VPs		31	20	64.5
"	trustees		5	4	80.0
H&WKPDS	officers	1912	8	5	62.5
WF&OSPS	c	1902	24	14	58.3
Average			565	237	*41.9*
2. Sports Clubs					
Claughton Bowling	ic	1861	7	6	85.7
"	s	1875	44	37	84.0
Bebington Bowling	im	1865	27	10	37.0
"	c	1867	12	6	50.0
Average			83	53	*63.8*
3. Schools					
Birkenhead School	c	1860	11	7	63.6
"	s	1872	7	5	71.4
Birkenhead Institute	subs	1884	7	5	71.4
"	s	1887	65	42	64.6
Caldy Grange Grammar School	c	1904	14	6	42.8
"	c	1913	17	6	35.2
Average			128	79	*61.7*
4. Churches					
Trinity Presbyterian	founders	1863	20	17	85.0
"	ms	1863–78			
" Brassey St. Mission	c	1863–78			61.5
" "	elders	1888			77.7
Birkenhead Soc. of Friends	c	1879	6	3	50.0
Birkenhead YMCA	c	1892	17	5	29.4
Average			232	153	*65.9*
5. Hospitals					
Birkenhead Hospital & D.	c	1851	14	9	64.2
Wallasey Cottage Hospital	subs	1867	9	8	88.8
Seacombe Cottage Hospital	c	1872	13	6	46.1
Birkenhead Borough Hospital	c	1901	23	13	56.5
"	subs	1903	741		
WH&D for Sick Children	c	1870–75	35	26	74.2
	c	1871	11	8	72.7
	c	1883	23	16	69.5
	c	1893	22	16	72.7
	c	1903	20	14	70.0
	c	1913	24	17	70.8
Hoylake Cottage Hospital	c	1909	20	10	50.0
Average			252	163	*64.6*

Note: For abbreviations, see Table 10.4.

Source: Wirral Archives Service, Birkenhead Reference Library, contemporary reports, and publications

with the management of the Birkenhead Borough Hospital (a separate John Laird Memorial Fund was created in 1898 and Egerton Laird was President from 1899 until his death in 1912); while the first President of the Wallasey Yacht Club in 1903 was Sir Alfred Jones.[88]

The endowment of churches was not only an expression of religious conviction: it provided tangible evidence of wealth and status and offered opportunities for members of the merchant community to exercise local patronage. William Potter, 'a Liverpool businessman' was involved in numerous speculative developments: he purchased land in Claughton-cum-Grange and in 1840 gave permission for the building of Christ Church, although progress was delayed by his later financial difficulties and bankruptcy. The initiative to establish the Highfield Congregational Church was taken in 1869 by the tea dealer, George Atkin, and a suitable piece of land was made available (for sale) by his cousin, John Atkin, who was also in the tea trade and a partner in the same firm (Atkin & Co.).[89] The decision to build a new church at Upton in 1863 was 'almost certainly inspired' by William Inman, a partner in the Liverpool & Philadelphia Steam Ship Company, who had moved into Upton Hall in 1854 (Figure 10.6) and subsequently purchased the title and rights of Lord of the Manor, but his eldest son, Ernest, also served as churchwarden in the early 1870s. In the same year, William Inman promised to cover any additional costs for the construction of a new church at Overchurch (beyond the £1,700 already promised by other benefactors) and in 1871 he donated the west window as a gift, while the church, vicarage, and school at Moreton were built as a result of his 'munificence'.[90]

Construction costs were often considerable and support from elite members of the merchant community was critical. St. John's, Egremont, cost approximately £10,000 to build, a sum met by financial support from the merchant, landowner, and former slave trader James A. Tobin: it was designated as a proprietary church with 20 subscribers (although few, if any, expected a return on their investment). The church at Moreton (with its additional buildings) involved a

Figure 10.6 The New Church at Upton (1905 postcard)

total outlay by Inman of £8,000. It would be wrong to underestimate the religious commitment of some members of the merchant community, including R. B. Potts (Brunswick Chapel), the iron merchants Samuel Smith (Seacombe Presbyterian Church) or James Irvine and Samuel Stitt (Trinity Presbyterian Church), but the scale of their financial contributions strengthened the profile of local benefactors and reaffirmed their dominant position within existing community networks, whether as elders or churchwardens. As in other towns and cities, service in a suburban context also brought 'prominence and prestige', which enabled individual merchants on the Wirral to influence local agendas.[91]

Involvement with local clubs, societies, churches, and medical charities provided members of the merchant community with opportunities for external representation, whether at a county, regional, or national level. Some of the Wirral associations were established as branches of national organisations: the Wallasey YMCA was one of 7,000 branches set up throughout the United Kingdom after the creation in 1844 of a national organisation in London designed to provide protection to young male urban in-migrants, while the Wirral Footpaths and Open Spaces Preservation Society was affiliated to the National Footpaths Preservation Society which provided both advice and assistance. Not only were Wirral societies expected to address issues of wider significance, but elected members and officers were required to attend regional or national meetings. In 1891, for example, the general secretary of the Birkenhead YMCA was mandated to represent the northern district with colleagues from Liverpool and St. Helens. In the same year, three committee members of the West Kirby Christian Institute, including the corn miller J. A. Shone, were elected to act as delegates on a district committee of YMCA workers.[92] At a club and society level, local links were important, both on the Wirral and across Merseyside as a whole. The literary society founded by the Birkenhead Society of Friends had joint meetings with the Liverpool Institute Debating Society; the Bebington Bowling Club arranged reciprocal matches with Aigburth Bowling Club, while members of the Royal Rock Ferry Palatine Bowling Club were allowed to use the green without charge; and many Wirral cricket clubs became affiliated to the Liverpool Competition or became involved with the development of county cricket following the formation in 1891 of the Cheshire County Club. Even involvement with local churches, particularly in connection with the support of foreign missions, led to participation in a web of regional and national networks irrespective of religious denomination.[93]

The significance of institutional integration for locally established voluntary association was particularly evident in the case of Freemasonry and the Volunteer Movement. In the former case, 21 new lodges were established on the Wirral between 1840 and 1899 (of which ten were founded in the 1890s): there was a noticeable overlapping of membership and regular occasions for general meetings. The shipowner Edward Friend was one of the founder members in November 1869 of the Rock Lodge, Birkenhead, but he also became the first Master Mason of the Egerton Lodge (Birkenhead) in May 1873, while a meeting of the Provincial Grand Lodge in Birkenhead on 7 October 1846 was attended by the officers of all local lodges, together with 'a most distinguished assemblage of the elite of Birkenhead'. Although the occupational background of lodge members was often varied, three of the six original members of the West Kirby 2690 Lodge were from the merchant community, including the glass bottle merchant Edward Taylor, the corn broker James Housden, and the iron merchant John Smith; and Freemasonry had an important function in bringing together sections of the urban middle class on the Wirral, both socially and politically.[94]

Similarly, the development of the Volunteer Movement on the Wirral reinforced a sense of shared identity amongst members of the merchant community and other middle-class groups, while providing a wider framework for networking and social interaction. Eight companies were originally formed in 1859, each with a clearly designated recruitment area. The Oxton

Company was the first to be enrolled and like its Wallasey counterpart was 'composed entirely of Gentlemen', many of whom held 'responsible positions', either in the County of Cheshire or the business world of the Liverpool district, and over 40 per cent of its recruits were drawn from the merchant community. Interlinkages were considerable: all companies attended parades in Birkenhead Park (subsequently at the Birkenhead Park Rugby Football Club [Figure 10.7]), training at the Leasowe rifle range was mandatory, and an annual camp was held from 1898 onwards. A Cheshire Engineer Volunteer Corps was also established at a meeting in November 1860 with its headquarters at the Monks Ferry Hotel.[95]

Residence, locality, associational membership, and network embeddedness were mutually reinforcing in various ways. Firstly, some merchants belonged to the same range of local clubs and societies while holding other official positions. In mid-nineteenth-century Birkenhead, Laird, Jackson, King, Ledward, Ravenscroft, Segar, and Stitt were all members of the Wirral Philharmonic Society, but most of them were also involved in the Local (Birkenhead) Committee of the Manchester and Liverpool Agricultural Society or the Birkenhead Literary and Scientific Society: five held official positions (whether as magistrates or improvement commissioners); and six were shareholders in Birkenhead School. Even membership of a single association provided access to a web of other societies and their members. Of the 14 presidents of the Birkenhead Literary and Scientific Society from the merchant community, 11 were either politically active, involved in public service, or active supporters of local church congregations and charitable work. From a sample of 12 leading members of Birkenhead's merchant community from the mid-nineteenth century, most were involved in fewer than eight different associations or held office which provided a range of interconnections. But the shipbuilder John Laird (Figure 10.8) is known to have been active in ten local associations, apart from serving

Figure 10.7 'The Greys' Trooping the Colours, Birkenhead Park (pre-1914 postcard)

VANITY FAIR. May 17, 1873.

No. 237. STATESMEN, No. 144.

"He built the 'Alabama' and the 'Captain.'"

Figure 10.8 Mr. John Laird MP, 'Statesman, No. 144, "He built the 'Alabama' and the 'Captain'"

as a Birkenhead commissioner, magistrate, and MP, while the iron merchant Samuel Stitt was involved in 14, in addition to acting as the assessor (1856, 1862) and overseer of the poor (1857) for Claughton-cum-Grange, and serving as the national chairman of the Presbyterian Church of England.[96]

The shipowner David MacIver was 'a strong conservative and protectionist' and 'an active worker in its interests', a Member of Parliament for Birkenhead (1874–1886), and involved in the Volunteer Movement. The merchant C. T. Gostenhofer had twice been mayor of Birkenhead (1888–89): he was a local magistrate (1888–99); a trustee of St. Aidan's Theological College (Figure 10.9), one of the finest buildings constructed at that time in Birkenhead; a member of the first School Board of Birkenhead; a strong churchman; and 'most widely known as a philanthropist'. In Liscard, William Heap was a member of the Wallasey Local Board (1879–1900), honorary treasurer of the Wallasey Dispensary, treasurer of the Egremont Presbyterian Church, and the founder of the Primrose League in Poulton and Seacombe.[97]

A similar pattern was evident in West Kirby and Hoylake at the turn of the century, when increased residential settlement and the creation of an extended associational framework provided the basis for enhanced interpersonal links. Although the real extent of associational involvement is difficult to measure, various merchants played a significant role in public affairs, whether as magistrates, school governors, church officials, or as members or honorary officers of local clubs and associations. However, the pattern and extent of merchant associational involvement was dependent on when local associations or voluntary organisations were established. In contrast to the mid-Victorian situation in Birkenhead, an equivalent sample for Hoylake and West Kirby reveals a lower level of involvement (with an average of only three membership associations). Some merchants had a limited range of associational involvement,

Figure 10.9 'St Aidan's Theological College, Birkenhead', *The Illustrated London News*, 10 October 1863

but the provision merchant George Wall was active in eight local societies, while the merchants J. F. Ellison and Alfred Vaughan Paton had strong community profiles.[98]

Secondly, there was seldom a clear dividing line between private interest and public involvement. Birkenhead YMCA committee meetings were regularly held at the house in Noctorum of its president, the corn merchant Charles J. Procter, while the initial meeting which led to the establishment of the West Kirby Christian Institute was convened in November 1890 at the house of the shipowner John Arthur Ledward in Kirby Park. Even after his death, the committee still met at the Ledward residence, since his wife had contributed to the building fund in her own right.[99] The early meetings of the directors of Birkenhead Institute were held at the Liverpool offices of subscribers, including the cotton broker H. J. Legge and the iron merchant Samuel Stitt, while four candidates for the headship of the new school were interviewed at P. W. Atkin's office. Private schools, including Birkenhead School and Birkenhead Institute, operated as limited companies with shareholders and designated managers, while many sports clubs were established on a similar basis. Thomas Brassey had initially put up all the money to launch the Claughton Bowling Club in 1858 (with the sum to be refunded over a period of ten years), but when the committee learned of a possible sale of the land in October 1874 a limited liability company was established with a nominal capital of £2,500 divided into 250 shares 'to prevent it falling into other hands', while a limited company was formed in 1886 to acquire land and to build a pavilion for Birkenhead Park Rugby Club.[100] Knowledge of business practice was therefore an invaluable asset in developing a number of local schools and sports clubs supported by the professional experience of merchants.

Thirdly, the extent to which associational membership contributed to network embeddedness was reinforced by residential proximity and regular face-to-face contact. The coal merchant Charles Grey Mott of 4 Cavendish Road was president of the Birkenhead Literary and Scientific Society in 1863–64: his next-door neighbour the solicitor Alfred Billson (of 5 Cavendish Road) joined the society in 1865 and became, in turn, its president in 1873–74, while the cotton broker Isaac Bancroft Cooke, who held the same office in 1867–68, lived a few minutes away in Ashville Road. Twelve of its members in 1868–69 (or 10 per cent of the total) resided in Hamilton Square. The Birkenhead Ruskin Society was formed in 1881 to create a library of Ruskin's works at Birkenhead School and arrange 'Concerts or Entertainments for the poor', but most of its members came from the surrounding residential areas of Claughton and Oxton: three were resident in Park Road South and two each in Shrewsbury Road, St. Aidan's Terrace and Wellington Road. The membership distribution pattern in the case of the Birkenhead Shakespere Literary Society, founded in 1878 to promote 'the reading and critical study of Shakespere and other authors', was very similar: four members lived in Hamilton Square (Eddowes, Estil, New, and Reid), while both Beresford Road and Woodchurch Road boasted three members. Indeed, irrespective of the precise object of individual associations, the underlying emphasis on locality was underpinned by the involvement of members or subscribers who were often close neighbours. In 1860, there were only eleven initial shareholders in Birkenhead Proprietary School Ltd., but two lived in both Ashville Road and Hamilton Square. When a limited liability company was formed in 1874 to secure the future of the Claughton Bowling Club, 34 of the original 44 shareholders (or over 77 per cent) lived in a road with at least one other member, with seven subscribers resident in Devonshire Place and a further six in Devonshire Road.[101]

It might be expected that such a high degree of residential proximity amongst associational members would have occurred in the early stages of the suburbanisation process in Birkenhead, particularly since this was located around well-defined upper middle-class residential areas, but this phenomenon was still evident at the turn of the century. The Board of the Wirral Hospital and Dispensary for Sick Children consisted of 20 men and women, of whom 50 per cent were drawn from the merchant community, but 4 of them lived in Bidston Road, 2 in Ingestre Road, and 2 in Kingsmead Road South. The development of associations in the outlying townships of Hoylake and West Kirby replicated this pattern: in 1900, 12 members of the West Kirby Literary Society (from eight separate households) were resident in Prussia Road, Hoylake. Although the absence of diary evidence makes it difficult to substantiate the actual level of interaction, whether in relation to associational, business, or social matters, residential proximity facilitated individual interaction and networking and reinforced the embeddedness of local institutions.[102]

Business Priorities and the Level of Merchant Associational Involvement

In 1868 Henry Threlfall Wilson of Bidston, Wirral, was declared bankrupt. He had developed a career initially as a shipbroker, but seized the opportunities presented by the rising demand for emigrant passages by advertising the White Star Line of Boston Packets in 1849 and commencing a similar service to Australia in 1852. The failure of his business highlights the inherent risks associated with ship owning, but his personal accounts reveal a minimal involvement in associational or charitable activity. His private subscriptions only amounted to £12 9s, including membership of Underley Lodge in Kirby Lonsdale and annual contributions to St. Anne's School (Birkenhead), the Liverpool Magdalen Institute, and the Temperance Society. By contrast, Samuel Stitt (1816–1898), who arrived in Liverpool in 1820 and retired from business in 1862 at the early age of 42, demonstrated an exceptional level of involvement in associational activity, particularly in Birkenhead (see previous), reflecting a combination of extensive leisure, considerable wealth, and religious commitment. He was renowned for his 'exceptional generosity' towards Trinity Presbyterian Church, Oxton, and was 'a great benefactor' to Birkenhead Institute.[103]

Any attempt to estimate the overall level of associational involvement by members of the merchant community is complicated by the absence of membership records for a number of local clubs and societies, but data for Birkenhead (including Claughton-cum-Grange and Oxton) suggest that approximately 20 per cent were subscribers or served as committee members. In the early 1860s, 20.1 per cent of the merchants recorded as Birkenhead residents in the MLP database had an associational profile (excluding religious affiliations), while the comparative figure for the early 1880s was 18.1 per cent. Members of the merchant community played a critical role in local clubs and societies and they were instrumental in founding and supporting schools and churches, but an overwhelming majority did not engage in associational activity.

In fact, the extent to which merchants were directly involved in local associational networks was determined by a range of factors, including residential mobility, social status, and pressures of work. Middle-class society during the second half of the nineteenth century remained characterised by a considerable degree of residential mobility, a phenomenon reinforced by rapid suburbanisation, particularly on the Wirral, and the fact that many family homes were still occupied on a leasehold basis, despite a gradual growth in the extent of house ownership. In 1872, for example, the Laird family and the railway contractor Thomas Brassey owned 8 and 15 properties respectively in Hamilton Square (of which only two were used as offices), while just 4 of the 18 houses in Park Road South were owned by the actual residents.[104] In 1898, the West Kirby Literary Society attributed the loss of 149 members (24 per cent of the total) to 'the migratory nature of the population', although this was more than compensated by the enrolment of 159 new members. The inevitable result was 'a constant change in membership'. Both the Bebington Bowling Club and the West Kirby Literary Society registered the resignation of individual officers on their 'removal to Liverpool' or 'from the neighbourhood', although in the former case unpaid annual subscriptions were to be pursued by the secretary by forwarding a debit note.[105] Local churches suffered from a similar problem. In 1910, the pastor of Hoylake Congregational Church removed from the church roll 'a great many names which for some time have been doubtful' and justified such a drastic revision on the basis that a change in residence often meant that some former adherents maintained 'for a time a less than intimate connection'.[106] For some members of the merchant community, however, the recognition that any home was likely to be temporary, particularly during the earlier stages of a business career, may well have reduced their inclination to engage with local associational networks.

As far as associational involvement was concerned, there was a significant division within the merchant community. In general, the continued progress of most forms of associational activity, whether clubs and societies, private schools and church congregations, or medical charities, depended to a large degree on the commitment and support of a small group of individuals, many of whom were already well established in the local community. The asphalt manufacturer George Atkin, who had been chairman of Birkenhead Institute from its foundation in 1884 until his death in 1907, 'spent his life in the service of the School', while Egerton Laird served as president of the Birkenhead Borough Hospital for 13 years prior to his death in 1912 and Henry Thompson, who died in the same year, had been an 'old and valued supporter of the Hospital Committee since 1888' and a trustee of the John Laird Memorial Fund. The accountant John Merrett Wade resigned his post as honorary treasurer to the Wirral Hospital and Dispensary for Sick Children in 1905 after 16 years, having 'devoted an immense amount of time and trouble to the affairs of the Institution', while in 1910 the death was recorded of the sugar refiner Robert Marquis who had been a committee member for up to 20 years and 'one of its most enthusiastic and consistent supporters'. The Bebington Bowling Club reported in 1891 the 'great loss' of its past president, the accountant John Mathews, who had demonstrated 'unceasing interest' in the affairs of the club since the year after its foundation in 1865.[107]

But such a continuous level of individual commitment by members of the merchant community was the exception rather than the rule. In many cases, attendance at committee meetings was poor and the average length of service was limited. On a number of occasions in the early 1850s the Birkenhead Hospital and Dispensary Committee was inquorate and meetings were unable to proceed, while the ship builder John Laird who played an important role in its foundation was often unable to attend committee meetings being 'at present in London'. On average, only four of the nine Directors of Birkenhead Institute attended regular meetings. Only two committee members of the Wirral Hospital and Dispensary for Sick Children (from a total of 35) continued in office between 1870 and 1883, although the tobacco broker John Elliot (later appointed a JP) served continuously in this capacity before being elected president in 1903, while, on average, committee members at the Birkenhead Borough Hospital in 1902 had held office for 8.1 years, but five had attended meetings for 13, 14, 15, 17, and 20 years respectively, but a considerable number were relative novices. The vice-president of the Bebington Bowling Club, the slate merchant and forwarding agent Johnson Jenkins, was forced to resign his position in 1871 'owing to (his) inability to attend to the duties thereof'.[108]

The distinction between a relatively small core of active members and a majority with limited associational involvement was reinforced by the dominance of individual families and a significant element of inter-generational continuity. At one level, the management of the Birkenhead Borough Hospital was dominated by the Laird family: after the death of John Laird, E. K. Laird and J. M. Laird were appointed trustees in 1898 (together with eight other local dignitaries) and by 1902 twelve members of the family were registered as life governors (of whom six were still alive).[109] A few other local families from the merchant community, such as the Aspinalls and the Hinds, maintained a similar level of involvement over at least two generations. The fact that many committees were effectively self-perpetuating simply reinforced the role of families with close links to the local community. Residential persistence, therefore, enabled several families to retain a strong associational profile, while a high degree of transience amongst other members of the merchant community reduced their ability to participate in the management of suburban institutions.

The membership structure of local churches reflected the same phenomenon. Between 1840 and 1866, over half of the original congregation at the Scotch Church, Woodside, had left, in many cases having 'gone to' Scotland, Liverpool, Manchester, or Canada, or simply ceased to attend. It remained dependent on new arrivals, whether from families or individuals previously resident in Liverpool, Scotland (including Glasgow and Aberdeen), or Northern Ireland.[110] At Trinity Presbyterian Church, the average length of membership between 1863 and 1878 was 56.8 months: only a small number of communicants and their families, including the merchants Andrew Callender, William Bingham, and James A. Bryson, as well as the 'broker' and iron merchant Samuel Stitt, were still listed as members of the congregation in 1892. The membership register of the Liscard Preparative Meeting reveals an underlying element of fluidity in the receipt and forwarding of certificates to and from other destinations, while the strength of the Birkenhead Society of Friends was largely due to the continued membership of a small number of individual families, often over three generations, including the Biglands (general brokers), the Clibborns (provision merchants), and the Heatons (accountants).[111]

The long-term future of individual churches was affected by both in-, and out-migration. The Grange Road Presbyterian Church, Birkenhead, was viewed by contemporaries as the 'Mother of churches', because the subsequent migration of some of its members led to the foundation of 'the flourishing congregations of Trinity Church, Claughton, and St. Paul's, Higher Tranmere': but Trinity was established by 20 existing members 'disjoining'. The original Baptist Church in Birkenhead (1847) suffered from a similar haemorrhaging of members as a result of increased suburbanisation with 23 of its adherents leaving in 1857 in order to establish a new church in Grange Lane. At the same time, Wirral churches benefited from the relocation of Liverpool residents: for example, the tea broker Thomas Matheson had been an elder at the Canning Street Presbyterian Church between 1851 and 1861, but having moved to Rock Ferry he assumed a similar role in the local Presbyterian church.[112]

In fact, the continuing process of suburbanisation and the relocation of merchant families to outlying townships on the Wirral threatened the survival of clubs and societies, or the viability of church congregations, just as changes in contemporary fashion redirected middle-class commitment to other forms of associational activity. As New Ferry began to lose some of its initial attraction as a residential location for members of the merchant community, its literary society encountered increasing difficulties which ultimately led to its demise in April 1895. Although this was regarded as 'a serious blow to the intellectual interest of the neighbourhood', it was solely due to the 'apathy of members'. Merchants may have accounted for over 40 per cent of the members of the Birkenhead Literary and Scientific Society, but only a quarter of the 'paper givers' came from this group, and its long-term viability was always likely to be compromised by the removal of key members to other parts of the country. To this extent, the associational infrastructure of residential settlements on the Wirral was affected both by contemporary migration patterns and the suburbanisation process.[113]

Wirral and Liverpool: Local Associational Identity and Traditional Allegiances

Suburbanisation and the increasing tendency for members of the merchant community to reside on the Wirral by no means implied an immediate change in Liverpool's traditional role as a centre for business transactions, charitable provision, and cultural activities. A clear majority of

Wirral-based merchants continued to conduct their business affairs from their Liverpool offices and maintained an extensive network of professional links within the city. One advantage of living on the Wirral was that it enabled merchants to maintain their commercial interests while enjoying the benefits of a more exclusive, semi-rural environment, but the proliferation of local trade associations in the second half of the nineteenth century further reinforced Liverpool's central role as a focal point for business networking.[114] As the dominant urban centre on Merseyside, it had developed an infrastructure of charitable provision and associational culture well before the onset of suburbanisation. Nationally, there had been a proliferation of different types of voluntary organisation from the early eighteenth century onwards, whether proprietary libraries, subscriber democracies designed to fund and maintain local infirmaries, or literary and philosophical societies. Liverpool was no exception: by the 1750s it was 'plentifully endowed with clubs of all descriptions', particularly associations designed to promote sociability, while the establishment of the Athenaeum (1799), the Lyceum (1802), and the Royal Institution (1814) provided a focus for more intellectual pursuits within a well-established social framework. Prior to 1850, the city's intellectual life was dominated by the merchant elite and local associations, such as the Liverpool Philomathic Society (1825) and the Liverpool Polytechnic Society (1838), provided a basis for assimilating new entrants and reinforcing middle-class legitimacy.[115] Local branches of national organisations, such as the Liverpool Society for the Prevention of Cruelty to Children, were always more like to be established in larger urban centres than in suburban districts where societies were often a direct imitation of associations established at an earlier date elsewhere. The Liverpool Philharmonic Society, for example, had been founded in January 1840: the provisional committee for its Birkenhead counterpart was only constituted in 1861.

According to Baines, Liverpool's public charities were 'most numerous and liberal', given that they were calculated to 'meet every form of bodily distress and every form of moral evil which is capable of being mitigated by the action of benevolence'. A series of medical institutions had been established from the mid-eighteenth century onwards, but in Birkenhead and on the Wirral the provision of charitable institutions post-dated the onset of suburbanisation from the 1820s onwards. Within this context, merchants who 'removed' to the Wirral may well have retained their membership of Liverpool clubs and societies, particularly if they enjoyed considerable social status, such as the Athenaeum and the Wellington Club, while suburban relocation did not necessitate the relinquishing of official roles in charitable organisations. If improvements to the transport infrastructure facilitated residential settlement on the Wirral, even in the outlying townships of Hoylake and West Kirby, they also enabled suburban families to maintain cultural and social links with Liverpool at little opportunity cost.[116]

In fact, the emergence of alternative or competing forms of associational activity on the Wirral had a differentiated impact on Liverpool. At one level, a strong local profile, whether on the Wirral or in other suburban areas (such as Blundellsands or Southport), was often accompanied by continued participation in Liverpool's elite political clubs. In those cases where club membership was recorded by Pike, 36.5 per cent of the members of the Liverpool Conservative or Junior Conservative Clubs were from the Wirral, while the overall proportion for the Reform and Junior Reform Clubs was 48.5 per cent. Whether conservative or liberal, a significant number of Liverpool members by the early 1900s were Wirral-based. Over 20 per cent of Liverpool's Aldermen and approximately 16 per cent of its councillors and JPs were Wirral residents, while the mayor of Liverpool in 1910–11, the corn merchant and miller Samuel Mason Hutchinson, lived in Bromborough thereby demonstrating that city residence was not a prerequisite for the highest office.[117]

Some members of the merchant community resident on the Wirral played a leading role in founding and managing Liverpool charities. In 1869, the ship owner James Beazley, of 'Fern

Hill', Grosvenor Road, Claughton, proposed the establishment of a Seaman's Orphan Asylum, with an immediate commitment of £5,000 to the building fund. It was estimated that approximately 10 per cent of orphan asylum inmates were children of sailors and Beazley's initiative reflected a wider concern over 'the inefficiency of the present means to reach that needful class'. Of the twelve individuals who formally approved the creation of the Liverpool Seamen's Orphan Institution later that month, five lived on the Wirral: the attorney Clarke Aspinall (Bebington), the shipowner William Inman (Upton), the steamship owner David MacIver (Bromborough), the managing director of the African Merchants' Company J. A. Tobin (Eastham), and the ship handler Henry J. Wood (Hinderton). Beazley devoted considerable time to the charity, whether as treasurer or vice-chairman, although in December 1886 he was unable to attend the annual meeting because 'his health are not so good as one may desire': after his death his son, J. H. Beazley, of 'Oakdene', Noctorum, maintained a similar level of commitment serving for many years as chairman of the Executive Committee.[118]

Other examples could be cited. The shipowner Thomas Henry Ismay founded the Liverpool Seamen's Pension Fund in 1887 with a contribution of £20,000: although the original foundation made no provision for pensioners' widows, this omission was rectified by his wife through the creation of the Margaret Ismay Widows Fund. Prior to 1914, the average adjuster Francis Chatillon Danson, of Bidston Road, Birkenhead, was deputy chairman of the Liverpool Shipwreck and Humane Society, but he also held office in a number of professional and educational institutions in Liverpool; the steamship owner Walter L. Nickels of Noctorum served on the committee of the Northern Hospital (1888–1919); while the stock and share broker Roger Percy Sing, of 'Mill Hey', Eastham, was president of the Florence Institute for Boys and treasurer of the Liverpool Council of Education.[119]

Further evidence that suburban residence was not incompatible with an active engagement with Liverpool's associations can be derived from a detailed analysis of the charitable involvement and financial bequests of Wirral residents, as recorded in obituaries, and the charity activity profiles of merchants resident in the select suburb of Noctorum, Birkenhead. Although the obituary sample size is limited to 15 Wirral-based merchants who died between 1898 and 1915, almost 50 per cent of the charities which benefited from their individual or financial support were local, while 30 per cent had been established in Liverpool and 20 per cent operated at a national level. T. H. Ismay left a number of bequests to Liverpool-based charities, including the Seamen's Orphan Institution, the Bluecoat Hospital, and the Liverpool Seamen's Pension Fund, but provision was also made for the parish church of Thurstaston and the West Kirby Convalescent Home for Children, while significant financial support had been given to the development of Mariners' Park in Wallasey from 1887 onwards (Figure 10.10).

The charitable bequests made by the shipowner John Williamson of Claughton, Birkenhead were not atypical: he had been involved in the Liverpool Seamen's Orphan Institution, but when he died in 1915 he also left money to five local charities—the Birkenhead Borough Hospital, the Birkenhead and Wirral Children's Hospital, the Blackpool Street Mission, the Shaftesbury Boys' Club, and the Birkenhead Borough Road Mission. Elite merchants who were resident in Noctorum contributed to the operating costs of Liverpool charities, but the level of engagement was muted. In 1887, Noctorum only had 13 residents, a figure that had risen to 20 by 1902: it was one of Birkenhead's most prestigious districts where individual households owned considerable land and where rateable values increased by over 30 per cent in the late nineteenth century. Between 1871 and 1901 the number of merchants resident in Noctorum increased from three to ten, but an analysis of Liverpool charities reveals that their level of engagement was not extensive: very few served on executive committees and, although a couple were registered as life members (or trustees for life), only modest financial support was provided.[120]

Figure 10.10 Mariners' Park, Wallasey (undated postcard, c. 1910)

In fact, the development of alternative and autonomous associations in suburban areas, whether on the Wirral or elsewhere, led to a gradual disengagement by many members of the merchant community from structures which had underpinned the cultural and commercial life of Liverpool (Table 10.7). In the case of four Liverpool charities which dealt with the accommodation, educational, and medical needs of children at risk (including the Female Orphan Asylum, the Liverpool Infirmary for Children, the Liverpool Society for the Prevention of Cruelty to Children, and the Salisbury House School), just over 10 per cent of committee members during the second half of the nineteenth century were Wirral residents. At the Hahnemann Hospital there were only two Wirral-based representatives on a committee of 24 throughout the 1890s, while the General Committee of the Princes Park Hospital, established in 1869 to provide a 'House of Rest' for women suffering from incurable chronic diseases, did not have a single member from the Wirral in its complement of 15. The position in relation to Liverpool's maritime charities was somewhat better, with 28 per cent of committee members (from the Training Ship *Indefatigable*, the Liverpool Seamen's Orphan Institution, the Liverpool Sailors' Home, and the North West Seamen and Boatmen's Finance Society) drawn from Wirral residents, although this was a reflection, in part, of the tendency of wealthy shipowners (such as James Beazley, T. H. Ismay, and Thomas Royden) to build palatial residences in prestigious suburbs, such as Noctorum, or in the semi-rural townships of Frankby and Thurstaston.[121]

However, the spatial distribution of subscribers to individual charities is more indicative of the fragmentation of associational affinity. Even allowing for a limited number of corporate subscriptions from Liverpool-based firms with partners who were resident on the Wirral, the overriding picture is clear. With very few exceptions, Liverpool's medical charities could not rely on significant levels of support from families living in suburban areas on the other side of the Mersey. In 1852–53 (eleven years after its opening), the Southern Hospital had a total of 256 trustees for life (defined as 'benefactors of ten pounds and upwards at any one time and

Table 10.7 Wirral subscribers to Liverpool charities (hospitals, seamen's welfare, and welfare), 1850–1912 (in per cent)

Hospitals	Year	No.	%	Welfare	Year	No.	%
Southern	1853	9	2.3	Liverpool Female Orphanage	1862	60	6.6
				"	1861	52	6.3
Liverpool Children's Infirmary	1861		4.3	"	1870	30	4.1
"	1872		4.6	"	1881	27	4.2
"	1882	1	3.3	Liverpool Female Penitentiary	1862	7	4.8
"	1912	17	6.4	"	1881	9	6.1
" Life Governors	1862	1	5.8	"	1892	9	7.2
Liverpool Royal Infirmary	1862	22	0.8	"	1905	22	13.4
Hahnemann Homeopathic	1872	4	3.7	"	1912	26	16.0
St Paul's Eye & Ear	1872	17	3.0	" Life Trustees	1881	9	6.1
"	1892	13		"	1912	8	12.6
"	1902	12	2.9	Home for Incurables	1875	4	2.2
"	1912	20	6.3	"	1882	9	2.5
				"	1892	16	3.8
				"	1912	22	6.2
Seamen's Welfare				Liverpool Rescue Society and	1892	3	3.5
(donations of £100+)				House of Help			
Liverpool Sailors' Home	1852	3	25.0		1902	6	3.8
LSOI	1870	1	5.8		1912	31	16.1

Abbreviation: LSOI (Liverpool Seamen's Orphanage Institution)

Note: In a few cases, Wirral residents working in Liverpool may have used their business address in forwarding annual subscriptions.

Sources: membership records and annual reports, Liverpool Record Office, and the Maritime Archives and Library

ministers of religion who have preached in aid of the Hospital'), but only 9 (2.3 per cent) were from the Wirral.[122] Even if the 39 corporate benefactions are excluded, the level of individual support from the Wirral remained very modest (4.1 per cent). In general, fewer than 10 per cent of the individual subscribers to Liverpool's medical charities were Wirral-based, highlighting the extent to which the financial contributions of the middle-class were defined by a clear sense of locality. Only in the case of two charities, the Liverpool Female Penitentiary and the Liverpool Rescue Society and House of Help, did the number of Wirral-based subscribers exceed 15 per cent with an upward trend in financial support from this area in the years immediately prior to 1914. Although the preference for successful shipowners to relocate to the Wirral may explain a higher profile amongst those who donated £100 or more to the Liverpool Sailors' Home in 1852, this was not the case in relation to the Liverpool Seamen's Orphanage Institution in 1870.

Club membership is arguably a more reliable indicator of associational affiliation as it implied a significant degree of individual commitment and a wider involvement in opportunities for networking, whether on a social or business level. It helped to define social status, while clubs and societies provided a forum for business networking and represented an important component of nineteenth-century public culture. A small number of elite clubs were at the heart of Liverpool's social and cultural life. The Athenaeum (1797) provided useful facilities for its members, including a newsroom, a reference library, and an excellent restaurant, while the Wellington Club (1814) had an explicitly social function, having been founded 'for the purpose of having balls and other entertainments'. Unfortunately, residential data for members of the Athenaeum are incomplete, but in those cases where a home address can be established for members of the Wellington Club, only 32 from a total of 404 (or less than 10 per cent) lived on the Wirral. On the evening of 23 February 1860, George Holt attended 'a very full Ball' at the Wellington Club and it remained an important focus for social activities for many leading Liverpool families. Perhaps because of persistent transport difficulties in returning home late at night, despite the availability of night boats across the Mersey from 1849 onwards, relatively few middle-class Wirral residents became active members.[123]

The situation in relation to the Liverpool Library and the Lyceum was similar. The former had been founded in 1758 as the first subscription library in England with almost half of its original members (47 out of 109) drawn from the merchant community, while the Lyceum had been established in 1802 with an extensive library and newsroom. Both clubs retained their popularity throughout the nineteenth century despite a conflict which led to protracted litigation in the 1880s: the Liverpool Library consistently emphasised its 'continued prosperity' and 'satisfactory financial position', while the Lyceum had 697 shares in use by 1882 and claimed its 'prosperity' was 'fully maintained' after 1900 by further improvements in its facilities. The Liverpool Library included a number of prominent members from the merchant community amongst its shareholders, including the cotton-broker George Holt (238), the shipowner Charles Booth (368), and the sugar refiner Henry Tate (278), while the Lyceum normally held a series of popular social events, such as its 'Smoking Concert' and February ball, both of which were 'abandoned' in 1901 following the death of Queen Victoria.[124]

Wirral-based merchants were involved in both associations. The merchant Robert Galloway of Highfield Park, Rock Ferry, held his share in the Liverpool Library between 1858 and 1870, while the cotton broker Samuel M. Bulley, of Peter's Place, New Brighton, was a shareholder from September 1856 until his death in 1880. In 1901–02, the Lyceum included amongst its proprietors the patent asphalt manufacturer George Atkin of Rock Ferry (1847) and the ship broker Charles Langley of Birkenhead Road, Meols (1892), although a disproportionate number of Wirral-based members were from the professional classes or involved in manufacturing and the retail trade. But the level of Wirral-based membership in the second half of the nineteenth century was never extensive. Between 1880 and 1883 only 12.5 per cent of the Lyceum's proprietors (with names beginning with B or L) were from the Wirral, while of those registered in the share transfer book of the Liverpool Library the proportion rose gradually rose from 4.1 per cent (1862), to 7.5 per cent (1872), 10.2 per cent (1882), and 11.1 per cent (1892). This upward trend from a low base line reflected primarily improvements in the transport infrastructure, particularly the introduction in May 1890 of through workings by the Hoylake and Birkenhead Rail and Tramway Company and the Mersey Railway and the adoption of increased train frequencies following electrification in 1903. As a result, Wirral residents, even in the outlying townships of Hoylake and West Kirby, were encouraged to retain membership of elite Liverpool clubs at a time when their relative popularity (at least in the case of the Lyceum) was already in decline.[125]

In general, suburbanisation was accompanied by a reduced level of involvement in Liverpool's associational culture. Data from a sample of 14 different clubs and societies from the late 1850s to 1912 reveal that the average level of Wirral-based membership was no more than 11.2 per cent. At one extreme, the Amateur Musical Union during its 1868–69 season only had one member from the Wirral (the commercial agent and tenor Joseph Dod from Higher Tranmere), although its membership included representatives from 37 merchant households, whether as sopranos, contraltos, tenors, or basses from a total of 55, including the general broker John Brancker and his daughters together with the merchant Julius Servaes and his wife. By contrast, 25 per cent of the council members of the Financial Reform Association in 1857 were Wirral-based and when the 30 Club was founded in 1895 to encourage discussion of a wide range of subjects, with a particular inclination 'towards Art and Literature', one third of the original membership of 12 lived on the Wirral.[126] Where there was a specific focus, whether in relation to the theatre, art, or literature, Wirral members sometimes played a major role. Almost 20 per cent of the shareholders of the Theatre Royal in 1866 were from Seacombe and Oxton, while the cotton merchant J. F. Stahlknecht (Merrifield, Ziegler & Co.) of 12 Park Road, West Kirby, was the treasurer of the Liverpool Italian Literary Society between 1908 and 1912. With the Italian Consul, Dr. Londini, as one of its three presidents, the society held a series of *conversazioni* at the Royal Institution and 'any ladies or gentlemen interested in Italian' could be proposed for election. Stahlknecht's wife was also a member of the committee, while the librarian, Miss Eva Williams, was from Wallasey.[127]

Other cultural initiatives, including the Museum of Japanese Art, were developed without any significant support from Wirral residents from the merchant community, while even the Historic Society of Lancashire and Cheshire which ostensibly catered for a wider regional audience only recruited a small number of Wirral members: in 1862–63, 14.5 per cent of the total membership lived across the Mersey, but this had fallen to 11.3 per cent by 1902–03. Some Wirral residents were members of Liverpool sports clubs, such as the Liverpool Rugby Union Football Club, but they remained a small minority. To this extent, suburban residence, particularly on the Wirral, did not necessarily involve a curtailment of associational involvement in Liverpool, but it did encourage a redirection of interest towards more locally based agencies for middle class sport, entertainment, and socialisation. With very few exceptions, Wirral residents were under-represented in Liverpool's associational culture, although a few merchants played a leading role in individual clubs and societies.[128]

Conclusion

Network-based communication was undoubtedly an important factor in establishing mutual trust and reputation because business confidence depended on face-to-face meetings and 'deep interpersonal knowledge'. Social activities were 'rarely neutral in their purpose' and overlapping business, political, and religious connections played a critical role in the successful functioning of 'communicating economies'. Economic and social networks were 'mutually constitutive': they facilitated access to reliable information and helped to establish a sense of trust between individual members of the merchant community.[129] Associational culture was an invaluable, invisible resource for trade and commerce, because it helped to reduce transaction costs through the creation of common goals, shared attitudes, and mutually recognised aspirations, while clubs, societies, and other forms of subscriber democracies contributed to a new sense of urban collectivism and sociability, while providing a mechanism for consolidating middle-class identity. To this extent, associational culture was both 'a crucial domain' for the articulation of social class and a means of identifying civic space.[130]

Despite some excellent work on the composition and role of individual associations in Liverpool prior to 1850,[131] no attempt has been made to analyse the impact of suburbanisation on business culture or the process of community building. At a national level, it is often assumed that the period between 1850 and 1920 witnessed an increased integration of urban elites, facilitated, in part, by a greater density of voluntary associations. At the same time, suburbanisation, or the tendency for wealthier elements of the middle class to move to 'peripheral locations', revealed the underlying fragility of some associational structures, while a marked outflow of established merchants and manufacturers in the late nineteenth century contributed to a perceptible decline in Liverpool's middle-class culture.[132]

A detailed analysis of these issues has been constrained by two factors: the continuing failure to examine the changing relationship between urban centres and their hinterlands and the tendency for urban historians to focus on self-contained processes which operated within the boundaries of individual towns and cities. Perhaps inevitably, a recent, 'definitive' biography of Liverpool has little, if anything, to say about the interplay between the urban core and the developing suburban districts, particularly on the other side of the Mersey, despite evidence from other port-cities that the suburbanisation process after the 1850s was accompanied by increased spatial differentiation and a greater diversity in the social geography of the middle class.[133]

By the 1880s, suburbia, with its clear distinction between the home and the workplace, represented a distinctive way of life for an increasing number of middle-class families. This process was even reflected in a perceptible shift in literary location to the suburbs with their 'symbolic potential for a new kind of urban living'. The impact of suburbanisation on associational culture, however, is more difficult to disentangle, given the lack of detailed research on the formation, reinforcement and eventual disruption of middle-class urban networks. In Leeds, step-wise suburbanisation did not affect adversely the existing associational infrastructure because merchants and manufacturers retained an attachment to the pre-existing urban centre as a focal point for aesthetic and technical innovation, while greater cultural and social cohesion amongst the urban elite of Norwich after 1900 was not undermined by selective out-migration which often only involved residence at no great distance from the city centre. Indeed, in other towns, a further proliferation of voluntary associations after the 1850s may have led to a greater transactional density strengthened the integration of urban elites, despite increasing suburbanisation.[134]

In the case of Liverpool, however, suburbanisation involved residential settlement on the Wirral, on the other side of the Mersey, in parishes and townships which already had a distinct legal identity, and where both Birkenhead and Wallasey ultimately obtained their separate charters as county boroughs in 1877 and 1910 respectively. There had been a steady increase in the scale of out-migration from the urban core by members of Liverpool's merchant community from the 1820s onwards, with the provision of a regular steam ferry service and improvements in the local transport infrastructure which made it easier for the residents of Claughton, Oxton, and Rock Ferry to commute to their Liverpool offices. It is salutary to note that 25 per cent of all Liverpool merchants already lived on the Wirral by the early 1850s, but this proportion had increased to over one third by the early years of the twentieth century.[135] If residential settlement were initially concentrated in Birkenhead and other areas adjacent to Liverpool's commercial district, suburbanisation became increasingly spatially dispersed with a marked increase in population density in outlying townships, such as Hoylake, Neston, and West Kirby.

Urban life itself is increasingly viewed as 'an irreducible product of mixture' which cannot be contained within the framework of traditional typologies, but the emphasis on distanciated flows and networks is even more relevant for understanding the complex relationship between urban centres and their suburbs, particularly at a time when urban communities were characterised by a high degree of spatial mobility.[136] In order to deconstruct the impact of suburbanisation on middle-class associational culture and network-based communication, use has been made of membership data from a wide range of clubs and societies, charitable foundations, schools, and church congregations, both on the Wirral and in Liverpool itself. The available evidence confirms that the increasing preference by merchants to reside on the Wirral was accompanied by a reduced involvement in voluntary institutions in the metropolitan core and an increasing fragmentation of associational affinity. Like their counterparts on the Clyde, they placed considerable importance on the pleasures of country life, which the Wirral peninsula offered, but residential relocation often implied a significant change in existing patterns of network participation. If social policy and social service provision in the late Victorian period was dominated by 'the primacy of the local', the associational networks constructed around clubs and societies, church congregations, and schools also reflected the central importance of locality.[137] On Merseyside, suburbanisation was not synonymous with a withdrawal into the domestic sphere.

In fact, it was accompanied by the creation of a wide range of voluntary associations and local organisations which served to define new areas of residential settlement as distinct social units. As the examples of Birkenhead, Hoylake, and West Kirby illustrate, the residents of middle-class suburbs rapidly established a dense network of clubs and societies, many of which flourished despite a high level of spatial mobility and a low population baseline.

Members of the merchant community played a critical role in establishing and maintaining the associational infrastructure of suburban localities on the Wirral. Associational membership was often characterised by a significant degree of interlinkage and network embeddedness was reinforced, in some cases, by residential proximity and the likelihood of regular face-to-face contact. At the same time, there was a clear division within the merchant community. Whereas a number of families played a disproportionate role in the associational culture of residential settlements, often over two or three generations, the professional life cycle of many merchants remained subject to considerable mobility and a high degree of transience which militated against any significant engagement with local voluntary associations. Nevertheless, approximately 20 per cent of Wirral-based merchants were actively involved in clubs and societies both in the early 1860s and early 1880s, whether as committee members or subscribers. Although there is evidence of a slight reduction in the scale of their involvement during this period, the data probably underestimate the actual extent of the merchant community's engagement in local voluntary organisations, given the selective survival of archival records.

But the emphasis was consistently on the need to support and maintain structures which fulfilled a specifically local role. Although there were some notable exceptions, particularly amongst wealthy Liverpool shipowners who lived on the Wirral, suburbanisation was associated with a reduced level of involvement in metropolitan voluntary associations, including medical charities. The level of individual support from Wirral residents for Liverpool-based charities was often very low and data from various clubs and societies in the town centre reveal that the average level of Wirral-based membership from the late 1850s to 1912 was no more than 11.2 per cent. Whereas some of the leading members of the merchant community in Birkenhead in the mid-nineteenth century remained engaged with Liverpool-based institutions, their counterparts in Hoylake and West Kirby at the turn of the century failed to maintain the same degree of involvement, confirming the existence of a distinct associational distance— decay gradient.

The creation of alternative and competing associational networks in suburban areas on the Wirral had wider implications for the merchant community. Social network analysis has been used to explore the role of business networks and the significance of culture as an economic asset, but it has seldom been employed to examine the temporal clustering of interactions and connections within a suburban framework, partly because of the difficulty in mapping group dynamics in spatial areas which were primarily residential in nature and where social activities were less well recorded. But if the growth of Liverpool was accompanied by new urban collectivism, where associational networks underpinned by shared beliefs and values reduced transaction costs and improved business efficiency, the process of increased suburbanisation, particularly after the 1850s, contributed to a fragmentation of business culture.

The gradual extension of suburban settlement on the Wirral was accompanied by the creation of extensive networks of voluntary associations, whether in Birkenhead, West Kirby, or elsewhere, which helped to reinforce distinct local identities. They reflected primarily local needs and provided a framework for social interaction within a non-metropolitan context. At a time when local knowledge played an important role in national debates, the creation of Wirral-based societies provided a means of linking both developing townships and suburban areas with wider networks. But they also served a broader function. The involvement of new residents in the foundation of local churches enabled them to consolidate their influence and status, while membership of hospital boards allowed younger members of the merchant community to mix with more established figures in local society.[138] Local associational involvement had wider social ramifications as membership of debating societies or hospital committees offered other family members, including women, an opportunity for charitable work, intellectual activity, or social intercourse.

In a general sense, residence, locality, and associational membership all contributed to network embeddedness. The development on the Wirral of clubs and societies, charitable agencies, church congregations, and improved educational facilities, did not necessarily lead to a clear division between Liverpool's urban core and its suburban hinterland across the Mersey, but it did affect the operation of existing associational networks. Individual members of the merchant community resident on the Wirral retained a range of links with Liverpool: it remained the centre of business activity, while family relations and sporting activities helped to weave an intricate pattern of spatially bounded networks throughout Merseyside. Nevertheless, the extent to which suburbanisation was accompanied by a redrawing of associational allegiances cannot be denied. By the early 1900s, over one third of Liverpool's merchants were resident on the Wirral and those who were involved in voluntary associations were concerned primarily with supporting local, not Liverpool-based, activities and networks. Selective links were maintained with voluntary associations in Liverpool, but the establishment of intersecting networks on the Wirral led to the formation of new, interlinked spheres of influence which reinforced the development of separate identities of suburban place. Suburbs were not simply pastoral refuges from the city or privatized retreats from the community where the middle class were able to live out their 'strong desire' for comfort and domesticity: they often became sites of political activity in their own right, focal points for associational networking, and locations where members of the merchant community and other representatives of the middle class came together to construct new kinds of civic organisations.[139]

The relationship between cities and their suburbs has often been neglected by historians, but the evidence suggests that growing popularity of the Wirral as a residential location for successful merchants (as well as other upwardly mobile social and professional groups) affected Liverpool's long-run development from the 1830s onwards. Overall, the creation of alternative associational networks on the Wirral had a negative effect on the business culture of Liverpool. New structures for networking and interaction did not entirely replace the role of voluntary associations in the port-city's urban core, but they altered the existing framework of associational activity and encouraged members of the merchant community to develop local, Wirral-based affinities. To this extent, suburbanisation contributed to a series of dynamic changes in traditional social networking patterns and a gradual fragmentation of business culture along clearly defined spatial lines. In 1884, what was intended as an entertaining guide to the 'Great City' of Liverpool was published, praising its 'great noble families Stanley and Molyneux' and the fact that it had a 'larger fleet of merchant ships than any port in the world', but poking fun at the 'loud talking' at the Philharmonic Hall concerts which drowned out 'the base viol' and spoilt 'the high notes of the bassoon'. As far as the Wirral was concerned, Birkenhead was viewed as 'a desert county by the sea'. It had originally meant to be a town, but only some relics of its bygone prosperity remained, including a few aldermen and a member of Parliament, whereas Hoylake was overrun by the settlement of a Scottish sect called 'Golphers', 'socialist philosophers who had embraced the Darwinian theory' who spent their days 'in religious processions through the Sand-hills searching for the missing link'. Little did they imagine the extent to which associational developments on the Wirral had already undermined the cultural and social embeddedness of Liverpool's merchant community.[140]

Notes

1   See Chapters 2 (Randolph Cock, John Davies, Robert Lee, and Sari Mäenpää) and 9 (Joseph Sharples and Adrian Jarvis); Richard Lawton, 'The Components of Demographic Change in a Rapidly Growing Port-City: The Case of Liverpool in the Nineteenth Century', in Richard Lawton and Robert Lee (eds.), *Population and Society in Western European Port-Cities, c.1650–1939* (Liverpool, 2002), pp. 111–15; Colin G. Pooley, 'Living in Liverpool: The Modern City', in John Belchem (ed.), *Liverpool 800 Culture, Character and History* (Liverpool, 2006), pp. 178–81; Matthew D. Lassiter, 'The New Suburban History II: Political Culture and Metropolitan Space', *Journal of Planning History*, 4, 1 (2005), pp. 75–88; Henry C. Binford, *The First Suburbs: Residential Communities on the Boston Periphery 1815–1860* (Chicago and London, 1985), p. 1.

2   Amanda I. Seligman, 'The New Suburban History', *Journal of Planning History*, 3, 4 (2004), p. 313; Lisa McGirr, *Suburban Warriors: The Origins of the New American Right* (Princeton, 2001); R. MacManus and P. J. Ethington, 'Suburbs in Transition: New Approaches to Suburban History', *UH*, 34, 2 (2007), pp. 317–37; Richard Dennis, *Cities in Modernity: Representation and Production of Metropolitan Space, 1840–1930* (Cambridge, 2008); Dion Géorgiou, 'Leisure in London's Suburbs, 1880–1939', *The London Journal*, 39, 3 (2014), pp. 175–86.

3   Agnes L. McCulloch, *The Headland with the Birches: A History of Birkenhead* (Rock Ferry, Birkenhead, 1991), p. 19.

4   James Aspinall, *Liverpool a Few Years Since by an old Stager* (3rd ed., Liverpool, 1885), p. 29.

5   T. B. Maund, *Mersey Ferries, vol. 1: Woodside to Eastham* (Glossop, 1991), p. 13; Adrian Jarvis, 'French Spies in Liverpool: A Source Essay', in Adrian Jarvis (ed.), *Foul Berths and French Spies: Essays on the Port of Liverpool c1800–1930* (Liverpool, 2003), p. 67.

6   J. Langton, 'Liverpool and Its Hinterland in the Late Eighteenth Century', in B. Anderson and P. Stoney (eds.), *Commerce, Industry, and Transport* (Liverpool, 1983), p. 20; Robert Lee, 'Configuring the Region: Maritime Trade and Port-Hinterland Relations in Bremen, 1815–1914', *UH*, 32, 2 (2005), p. 248.

7   McCulloch, *The Headland with the Birches*, p. 17; Binford, *The First Suburbs*, p. 46.

8   Jeffrey Pearson, *Neston and Parkgate* (Rock Ferry, Birkenhead, 1985), pp. 16–20; John Pinfold, *Hoylake Race Course and the Beginnings of the Royal Liverpool Golf Club* (Prenton, 2004), pp. 3–4.

9   Graham McTear, 'Aspects of the Social and Economic Development of Birkenhead, c.1800–1877', unpublished BA dissertation, University of Leeds (1962), p. 6; Henry Kelsall Aspinall, *Birkenhead and Its Surroundings Topographical, Biographical, Autobiographical, Anecdotal, and Whimsical* (Liverpool, 1903), p. 3; Hilda Gamlin, *Twixt Mersey and Dee* (Liverpool, 1897: new edition, Broughton Gifford, 1992), p. 18.

10 Lawton, 'The Components of Demographic Change', pp. 111–12.

11 Binford, *The First Suburbs*, p. 46.

12 See Chapter 2 (Randolph Cock, John Davies, Robert Lee, and Sari Mäenpää); MLP database; Eric Hardwicke Rideout, *The Growth of Wirral* (Liverpool, 1927), p. 74.

13 LRO, TWE3, Glimpses of Liverpool Fifty Years Ago, fol.3. 7; see Chapter 9 (Joseph Sharples and Adrian Jarvis).

14 This is certainly the case in other cities: see Seligman, 'The New Suburban History', p. 321; Michael H. Ebner, *Creating Chicago's North Shore: A Suburban History* (Chicago, 1988), p. 28.

15 Sheila Marriner, *The Economic and Social Development of Merseyside* (London and Canberra, 1982), p. 74; H. B. Neilson, *"Auld-Lang-Syne": Recollections and Rural Records of Old Claughton, Birkenhead and Bidston with Other Reminiscences* (Birkenhead, 1935: reprinted Birkenhead, 1996), p. 14; W. R. S. McIntyre, *Birkenhead Yesterday and To-Day* (2nd ed., Birkenhead, 1948), p. 80; Samuel Stansfield, *Report of the Sanitary Condition of Birkenhead in the County of Chester, Together with Some Notice of the Present State, and Future Prospects of That Township; with Plans and Engineer's Report of the Intended Dock etc. Drawn Up at the Request of the Commissioners* (Liverpool, 1843). In reality, despite the deliberate gridiron design of Birkenhead as 'the city of the future', the increase in the estimated death rate between 1841 and 1846 was 'very alarming' and the housing conditions for the working class were generally inadequate, with cess pools and 'decomposing animal and vegetable matters' nullifying the natural benefits of bracing sea breezes and the 'purity of air'. See J. Hunter Robertson, M.D., *The Present Sanitory Condition of Birkenhead Dedicated by Permission to the Right Honourable Viscount Morpeth, M.P., Chief Commissioner of Woods and Forests ETC* (Birkenhead, 1847), pp. 15–16, 21, 45.

16 Romola J. Davenport, 'Urbanization and Mortality in Britain, c.1800–50', *EcHR*, 2 (2020), pp. 455–85; Hannaliis Jaadla and Alice Reid, 'The Geography of Early Childhood Mortality in England and Wales, 1881–1911', *Demographic Research*, 37, Article 58 published 12 December 2017, pp. 1861–90; Anon., *A Portrait of Trinity with Palm Grove* (Birkenhead, 1988), p. 5. Scotland Road, other parts of the City's North End and the residential neighbourhoods adjacent to the South Docks were highlighted by the Rev. Abraham Hume as sites of ill-health, poverty, and crime, while Hugh Shimmin described one area close to Scotland Road as 'Little Hell'. See Rev. Abraham Hume, *Condition of Liverpool: Religious and Social; Including Notices of the State of Education, Morals, Pauperism, and Crime* (Liverpool, 1858); *Four Maps of Liverpool, Ecclesiastical Historical, Municipal, Moral and Social* (Liverpool, 1858); Hugh Shimmin, *Liverpool Life: Its Pleasures, Practices and Pastimes* (Liverpool, 1857), p. 64; Zoë Alker, 'Street Violence in Mid-Victorian Liverpool', unpublished D.Phil., Liverpool John Moores University (2014), pp. 124–30; Neil Collins, *Politics and Elections in Nineteenth-Century Liverpool* (London, 2017 ed.).

17 Anon., *The Church of Saint John Liscard or Egremont in the Diocese of Chester, Centenary Souvenir* (Wallasey, 1933), p. 7; William McNeil and J. B. Stephen, *The Story of Seacombe Presbyterian Church of England, 1862–1939* (Wallasey, 1937), p. 11.

18 J. R. Kaighin, *Bygone Birkenhead: Sketches Round and about the Sixties* (Birkenhead, 1925), p. 270; E. Cuthbert Woods and P. Culverwell Brown, *The Rise and Progress of Wallasey: A History of the Borough* (Wallasey, 1929), p. 151; LRO, 920 DUR 1/2, 31 May 1846; see also Chapter 8 (John Sharples) of this volume. In the summer of 1878, the grocer Philip Smith spent an entire month at New Brighton; see LRO, 920 MD 425, 5 August 1878.

19 Barbara Mason, *Little Oasis: The Early History of Ashton Park, West Kirby* (Rock Ferry, Birkenhead, 1996), p. 1; *Hoylake and West Kirby Directory, 1897, Hoylake and West Kirby Urban District* (Herald Visitor, 1897), p. 5; Gamlin, *Twixt Mersey and Dee*, p. 177; WAS, A/HH/273, Leasowe Hospital, Leasowe Road, Annual Report, 1917.

20 Kaighin, *Bygone Birkenhead*, p. 270; Gamlin, *Twixt Mersey and Dee*, p. 64; John R. Stilgoe, *Borderland: Origins of the American Suburb, 1820–1939* (New Haven and London, 1988), p. 49; Charles Cowan Lundie, *The Story of the Presbyterian Church of England at Parkgate and Neston, 1858–1933* (Manchester, 1933), p. 25; J. Wallace Coop and Seymour Taylor, *Bulls and Bears: Cartoons of Members and Ring Traders of Liverpool Cotton Exchange (reprinted from 'the Liverpool Courier')* (Liverpool, 1908), No. 20; for Rock Park. To some extent, this reflected an increasing interest amongst the middle class in gardens and flower growing: see Brent Elliott, *Victorian Gardens* (London, 1986); R. J. Morris, *Class, Sect and Party" The Making of the Middle Class, Leeds 1820–1850* (Manchester, 1990), p. 182.

21 John Field, 'Wealth, Styles of Life and Social Tone amongst Portsmouth's Middle-Class, 1800–75', in R. J. Morris (ed.), *Class, Power and Social Structure in British Nineteenth-Century Towns* (Leicester, 1986), p. 99; WAS, YPX/50, Wirral Agricultural Society, 30 December 1885; Neilson, *"Auld-Lang-Syne"*, p. 59.

22 William Thomas Pike, *Liverpool and Birkenhead in the Twentieth Century: Contemporary Biographies* (Brighton, 1911).

23 Coop and Taylor, *Bulls and Bears*, No. 58 and No. 15.

24 Phil Thompson, 'An Old Racing Stable at Wallasey in Wirral', in R. D. Radcliffe (ed.), *On the Turf: The Origins of Horse-Racing in the North West* (Bebington, 1991), p. 29; Neilson, *"Auld-Lang-Syne"*, p. 94.

25 Aspinall, *Birkenhead and Its Surroundings*, pp. 3, 180; Stella M. Pincher, *From Prior to Polaris a History of Birkenhead* (Birkenhead, n.d.), p. 40.

26 Nathanial Caine, *History of the Royal Rock Beagle Hunt Issued by Subscription in the Year of Jubilee of the Hunt 1895* (Birkenhead, 1895), p. 24; Parochial Church Council of St. Saviour's Church, Oxton, Birkenhead, *Built to Serve a Growing Community: St Saviour's Church, Oxton, Birkenhead* (Birkenhead, 1891), p. 14; WAS, YPX/14/6, King, Vincent Ashfield, journals, 1841–85.

27 WAS, YSB 1/1–6, Claughton Bowling Club, 1861–1875; YBB, 1, Bebington Bowling Club, 4 December 1865; George Humphrey, *Wallasey Men's Crown Green Bowling a History* (Rock Ferry, Birkenhead, 1994), p. 43.

28 Peter N. Walker, *The Liverpool Competition a Study of the Development of Cricket on Merseyside* (Rock Ferry, 1988); Tony Onslow and John Sturgeon, *Dogs and Ladies Not Allowed: The 200 Year History of Liverpool Cricket Club* (Birkenhead, 2007).

29 Jim O'Neil, *Victorian Hoylake Recollections of Hoylake, 1865–1915* (Hoylake, 1986), p. 7; Woods and Brown, *The Rise and Progress of Wallasey*, pp. 301–11; *The Liverpool Courier*, 5 May 1914; Chris Elston, 'Birkenhead Park Cricket Club', Ms; *Birkenhead Park Cricket Club 1846–1996* (Wallasey, 1997).

30 Guy B. Farrar, *The Royal Liverpool Golf Club a History 1869–1932* (Birkenhead, 1933), p. 18; John Behrend and John Graham, *Golf at Hoylake: A Royal Liverpool Golf Club Anthology* (Worcestershire, 1990), p. 3; John M. Birtwhistle, 'Old Prenton Remembered: The Growth of Prenton Golf Club and Woodchurch Road', *Wirral Champion Journal*, 13, 2 (2006), pp. 33–6; WAS, YHGC, Heswall Golf Club, 16 June 1902; Patrick Kenney, *Heswall Golf Club, 1902–2002* (Worcestershire, 2001), p. 4.

31 Michael Jahn, 'Suburban Development in Outer West London, 1850–1900', in F. M. L. Thompson (ed.), *The Rise of Suburbia* (Leicester, 1982), p. 145; J. M. Rawcliffe, 'Bromley: Kentish Market Town to London Suburb, 1841–81', in ibid, p. 67; J. E. Allison, *Sidelights on Tranmere* (Tranmere, 1976), p. 83; O'Neil, *Victorian Hoylake*, p. 7.

32 Charles Grey Mott, *Reminiscences of Birkenhead* (Liverpool, 1900), p. 8.

33 Gamlin, *Twixt Mersey and Dee*, p. 36; *In the Matter of Arbitration between William Laird Esquire and Sir John Tobin, Award of Peter Bourne, Thomas C. Porter and William Statham Esquire*, 4 February 1829.

34 Mott, *Reminiscences*, p. 9; Gamlin, *Twixt Mersey and Dee*, p. 44; Graeme J. Milne, 'Port Politics: Interest, Faction and Port Management in Mid-Victorian Liverpool', in Lewis R. Fischer and Adrian Jarvis (eds.), *Harbours and Havens: Essays in Port History in Honour of Gordon Jackson* (St. John's, 1999), p. 53.

35 MAL, DX/258/2/1/1–88, Copies of letters written by Macgregor Laird to his wife Eleanor Hester Laird (née Nicolls), 7 September 1848.

36 William Williams Mortimer, *The History of the Hundred of Wirral with a Sketch of the City and County of Chester Compiled from the Earliest Authentic Records* (London, 1847) (Ilkley, 1983 reprint), pp. 333, 435; Aspinall, *Birkenhead and Its Surroundings*, p. 173; Jean McInniss, *Birkenhead Park* (Rock Ferry, Birkenhead, 1984), pp. 20–1; Robert Lee, 'Birkenhead Park: The First and Still the Best', *The Victorian* (March 2009), p. 10.

37 Elizabeth Davey, *Birkenhead a History* (Chichester 2009), p. 66; Gamlin, *Twixt Mersey and Dee*, p. 47; Robert Lee and Karen Tucker, '"It's My Park": Reinterpreting the History of Birkenhead Park within the Context of an Education Outreach Project', *The Public Historian*, 32, 3 (2010), p. 83.

38 Anon., *The Church of Saint John Liscard*, pp. 7, 21; Woods and Brown, *The Rise and Progress of Wallasey*, pp. 152, 181; Rideout, *The Growth of Wirral*, p. 74; Marriner, *The Economic and Social Development of Merseyside*, p. 77.

39 Gamlin, *Twixt Mersey and Dee*, p. 103; *BCA*, 25 March 1863, 29 April 1863.

40 *BCA*, 17 January 1872.

41 MLP database; WAS, B/547/26, Birkenhead Union, Parish of Birkenhead Valuation List Approved 29 April 1902. Thomas Brassey also owned the freehold of the Mostyn Arms in Parkgate from 1849 until his death in 1870, which in 1855 became Mostyn House School. The full extent of his landed holdings on the Wirral has never been researched. See Geoffrey W. Place, *150 Years of Mostyn House School: A Short History, 1854–2004* (Parkgate, 2004).

42 Kaighin, *Bygone Birkenhead*, p. 8; County Borough of Birkenhead, *Birkenhead 1877–1974* (Birkenhead, 1974), p. 5; W. Heaton Wakefield, '*Who's Who?' in the County Borough of Wallasey* (Liverpool, 1913), p. 9.

43 Mott, *Reminiscences*, p. 23.

44 John Christopher Boyle, 'A Demographic, Economic and Social Analysis of the Immigrant Irish Community in the Township of Birkenhead 1841–1877', unpublished DPhil., University of Salford (1999), p. 22; Mortimer and Harwood, *Directory of Birkenhead, 1843* (Birkenhead 1843), Commissioners of Birkenhead; William Osborne, *Osborne's Directory of Birkenhead and Its Environs* (Birkenhead, 1854), p. 2; A. Green and Company, *Directory of Liverpool and Birkenhead 1870* (London and Liverpool, 1870), Birkenhead Commissioners.

45 Philip Sulley, *History of Ancient and Modern Birkenhead* (Liverpool, 1907), pp. 129–30; Kaighin, *Bygone Birkenhead*, p. 323; Aspinall, *Birkenhead and Its Surroundings*, p. 9; Elizabeth Davey, '1805–2005 Jackson, Laird and Brassey a Celebration of Their Lives', *Birkenhead History Society Newsletter*, 101 (January 2006), p. 5.

46 *Postal Directory of the Municipal Borough of Birkenhead for 1883* (Manchester, 1883), p. 39; Jeffrey Pearson, *Neston and Parkgate* (Rock Ferry, Birkenhead, 1985), p. 35; Mott, *Reminiscences*, p. 32. Bushell showed 'great interest' in Neston, with 'generous' funding for schools and churches. Hinderton Hall, designed by the young architect Alfred Waterhouse, was built in 1855–56.

47 Pike, *Liverpool and Birkenhead*.

48 Grange Conservative Club, *Jubilee Souvenir, 1876–1926* (Birkenhead, 1926); Simon Gunn, *The Public Culture of the Victorian Middle Class: Ritual and Authority and the English Industrial City 1840–1914* (Manchester, 2000), p. 95; WAS, YBP/1, Birkenhead Parliamentary Debating Society Counsel Minute Book, vol. 1, 2 October 1876–6 February 1895; Incorporation of Birkenhead Jubilee Souvenir (Birkenhead, 1927); WAS, ZWO/15/1, Hoylake and West Kirby Parliamentary Debating Society, 14 September 1909.

49 *BCA&WR*, 25 April 1863; *BCA*, 18 February 1882; R. Sydney Marsden, *History of the Birkenhead Literary and Scientific Society 1857–1907* (Birkenhead, 1907), p. 2; Mott, *Reminiscences*, p. 35; J. Mawdsley and Sons, *Directory of the Hundred of Wirral* (Liverpool, 1861), p. lxxv; Neilson, *"Auld-Lang-Syne"*, p. 49; Wakefield, *'Who's Who?' in the County Borough of Wallasey*, pp. 31, 37.

50 Anon. (Littlebury Bros.), *The Liverpool and Birkenhead Official Red Book for 1902* (Liverpool, 1902).

51 R. J. Morris, 'Clubs, Societies and Associations', in F. M. L. Thompson (ed.), *TCSHB, vol. 3: Social Agencies and Institutions* (Cambridge, 1996), p. 395; R. J. Morris, 'Structure, Culture and Society in British Towns', in Martin Daunton (ed.), *TCUHB* (Cambridge, 2001), vol. 3, p. 409; Peter Clark, *British Clubs and Societies 1580–1800: The Origins of an Associational World* (Oxford, 2000); T. Worthington Barlow, *Cheshire: Its Historical and Literary Associations* (London, 1852).

52 Morris, 'Clubs, Societies and Associations', p. 410; Marsden, *History of the Birkenhead Literary and Scientific Society*, Reprint of 1st Annual Report, p. 2.

53 Gunn, *The Public Culture of the Victorian Middle Class*, p. 96; WAS, YBP/1, Kaighin, *Bygone Birkenhead*, p. 288; WAS, ZWO/15/1, Hoylake and West Kirby Parliamentary Debating Society, 1909–1914, fol.1.

54 Morris, 'Structure, Culture and Society', p. 399; WAS, ZWO/14/1, WKLS, Minute Book No. 3, Annual Meeting 21 April 1898, 8 February 1895, Annual Report 1898–99.

55 Simon Gunn, 'Class, Identity and the Urban: The Middle Class in England, c.1790–1950', *UH*, 31, 1 (2004), p. 38; Nick Hayes, 'The Construction and Form of Modern Cities: Exploring Identities and Community', *UH*, 29, 3 (2002), p. 419.

56 Bernard Pares was appointed to a readership in Russian History at the University of Liverpool in 1906 where he subsequently held a chair between 1908 and 1917. He was one of the most eminent Russian historians of his generation: see R. W. Seton-Watson, 'Bernard Pares', *The Slavonic and East European Review*, 28, 70 (1949), pp. 28–31.

57 See Philippe Vervaecke, 'The Primrose League and Women's Suffrage, 1883–1918', in Myriam Boussahba-Bravard (ed.), *Suffrage Outside Suffragism Women's Vote in Britain, 1884–1914* (Houndmills, 2007), pp. 180–202.

58 Binford, *The First Suburbs*, p. 6; John Moss, *Moss's Directory of Hoylake and West Kirby* (West Kirby, 1906), p. 207; Paul Mattingley, *Suburban Landscapes Culture and Politics in a New York Metropolitan Community* (Baltimore and London, 2006), p. 54; McGirr, *Suburban Warriors*; Lassiter, 'The New Suburban History', p. 76; Deeside Literary and Debating Society West Kirby (eds.), *The Story of the Society, 1904–1948* (West Kirby, 1948), p. 8.

59 The precise definition of semi-local is not straightforward as a measure of relative access to associational organisations, irrespective of their type, given boundary changes (specifically after the establishment of Birkenhead Corporation in 1877), improvements in the urban transport infrastructure, and the availability, at least to some members of the middle class, of private means of transportation (whether by carriage or, subsequently, by motor car): see Joseph Sharples and Adrian Jarvis, Chapter 9. For the purposes of this analysis, a semi-local address was one that was adjacent geographically to that of an associational organisation, so that a member of the Claughton Bowling Club who resided in Oxton would be listed in this category.

60 WAS, YSD 1/1, Claughton Bowling Club, Committee of Management, 1861; 1/5, Annual List of Members and Summary of Capital and Shares, 1875; F. May, *Claughton Bowling Club Ltd. History of the Claughton Bowling Club* (Birkenhead, c.1960), p. 3.

61 WAS, YFP/2/1, Wirral Footpaths and Open Spaces Preservation Society, Annual Report, 1888–89, pp. 12–16.

62 Michael Stammers, 'The Royal Mersey Yacht Club: A Social History, 1844–1944', *THSL&C*, 159 (2010), pp. 99–121; Chapter 5 (Joseph Sharples); Wallasey Yacht Club, *Magazines to Wallasey One Hundred Years of Wallasey Yacht Club* (Bebington, 2003), p. 3.

63 Farrar, *The Royal Liverpool Golf Club*, pp. 41, 98; Behrend and Graham, *Golf at Hoylake*, p. 3.

64 Kenney, *Heswall Golf Club*, p. 5; Caine, *History of the Royal Rock Beagle Hunt*, p. 83; Philip J. Beacall, *Birkenhead Park: The First Hundred Years: A Rugby Union Centenary* (Birkenhead, 1971), p. 1; R. D'Arcy Nesbitt, *New Brighton Football Club 1875–1925* (Liverpool, 1925), pp. 16–17.

65 Maurice Eggleshaw, *The History of Wallasey Grammar School* (Wallasey, 1976), p. 65; Woods and Brown, *The Rise and Progress of Wallasey*, pp. 274–6; Gamlin, *Twixt Mersey and Dee*, p. 187; M. J. Protheroe, *A History of Calday Grange Grammar School West Kirby 1636–1976* (Birkenhead, 1976), p. 29.

66 *BCA*, 31 January 1863; H. J. Tiffen, *History of Liverpool Institute Schools 1825–1935* (Liverpool, 1935); David Wainwright, *Liverpool Gentlemen: A History of Liverpool College, an Independent Day School from 1840* (London, 1960).

67 WAS, YSD/2/11, Birkenhead School, Memorandum and Articles, 1871; BSA, 150 SG, file no. 1 Memorandum of Association of the Birkenhead Preparatory School Ltd., 1860. For a brief history of Birkenhead School, see the Old Birkonian Society (Archives Team), *Birkenhead School a Pictorial History Part 1 1860–1960* (Barcelona, 2006); W. E. Woodhouse, *One in Heart: Reminiscences of Birkenhead School, 1860–1960* (Birkenhead, 1967). Given the small number of listed shareholders (7), any significant change in residence would have affected the locational profile of the overall group.

68 'The History of Birkenhead Institute 1889 to 1949', *The Visor* (Diamond Jubilee Number of the Birkenhead Institute School Magazine) (June 1949), pp. 5, 11; WAS, B/320/1, Birkenhead Institute Ltd., Minutes of the Directors' Meetings, Minute Book 4 May 1885.

69 Protheroe, *A History of Calday Grange Grammar School*, p. 36; WAS, ZWO/13/1, Calday Grange Grammar School, Minutes of the School Governors.

70 Eggleshaw, *The History of Wallasey Grammar School*, pp. 109, 165; Baker and Collins, 2002, p. 180.

71 LRO, 373 INS 2/2/3, Liverpool Institute High School, Roll of Admissions, 1867–1899; Liverpool College Archive, Upper School Address Book, 1887–1939.

72 BSA, Birkenhead School Admission Register I, 1884–1913; WAS, B/320/7/1, Birkenhead Institute, Admission Register, 1901–1945; Protheroe, *A History of Calday Grammar School*, p. 161; Elizabeth Davey (ed.), *Birkenhead High School a History* (Chester, 2002), p. 25.

73 WAS, YHT/1/1, Higher Tranmere High School for Girls Ltd., Preliminary Meeting, 16 February 1891; BSA, 181 OB, Old Birkonian Society.

74 Binford, *The First Suburbs*, p. 64; W. H. Heaps, *The Parish Church of Saint Catherine Higher Tranmere 1876: A History of the Parish and Present Church Building* (Tranmere, 1976), p. 3; McCulloch, *The Headland with the Birches*, pp. 35–7; Kaighin, *Bygone Birkenhead*, p. 10; WAS, YPX/67/3, A Brief History and Guide to the Building of Hoylake Congregational Church; WAS, YSF/25/1, Joyce Whittington, The History of Birkenhead Friends Meeting, Pt. I, 1847–1892 (1977).

75 McNeil and Stephen, *The Story of Seacombe Presbyterian Church of England*, p. 13; J. A. Klapas, 'Geographical Aspects of Religious Change in Victorian Liverpool, 1837–1901', unpublished MA thesis, University of Liverpool (1977), p. 79; W. H. Heaps, *The History of the Parish of Prenton the Church of St. Stephan and St. Alban* (Prenton, 1995), pp. 4–5; Gamlin, *Twixt Mersey and Dee*, p. 103.

76 LRO, 285 TRI/7/1, Trinity Presbyterian Church, Communicants roll book, 1863–c.1878; Dorothy M. Harden, *The Spire Is Rising: A History of St Paul's Church, Tranmere and its Parish* (Rock Ferry, Birkenhead, 1983); Mary Ward (ed.), *The Changing Years by Rock Ferry Local History Group* (Rock Ferry, 1991), pp. 32–3.

77 McNeil and Stephen, *The Story of Seacombe Presbyterian Church of England*, pp. 18, 23, 43; Gunn, *The Public Culture of the Victorian Middle Class*, p. 125; Morris, 'Clubs, Societies and Associations', p. 413; WAS, YSF/6, Society of Friends, Birkenhead Friends Literary Society Minutes, November 1877–May 1895; *The Liverpool and Birkenhead Official Red Book*. For a discussion of entry criteria for membership in elite societies, see Sari Mäenpää, Chapter 6.

78 WAS, YMC/1/1, YMCA (Birkenhead), General Committee Minutes, 24 February 1891; C. S. Brown, *Birkenhead Photographic Association* (Birkenhead, 1983), p. 3; WAS, ZWO/17/1, West Kirby Christian Institute Trustees, Committee Minutes, 10 June 1895; Agnes Morris, *A History of the Birkenhead YWCA: From 1883 to 1983* (Birkenhead, 1983), p. 8.

79 Roy Porter, *Disease, Medicine and Society in England, 1500–1860* (Basingstoke, 1993); T. Gelfand, 'The History of the Medical Profession', in W. F. Bynum and R. Porter (eds.), *Companion Encyclopaedia of the History of Medicine* (London, 1994), vol. 2, pp. 1119–51; Jane Longmore, 'Civic Liverpool', in Belchem, *Liverpool 800*, p. 151; Thomas H. Bickerton, *A Medical History of Liverpool from the Earliest Days to the Year 1920* (Liverpool, 1936), p. 33; Pooley, 'Living in Liverpool', p. 230.

80 Aspinall, *Birkenhead and Its Surroundings*, p. 109; Mortimer, *The History of the Hundred of Wirral*, p. 404.

81 WAS, A/H/H/201/1, Seacombe Cottage Hospital Reports 1872 to 1894, Notes of E. G. Hammond, Egremont, November 1869; A/H/H/170/1, Hoylake Cottage Hospital, Annual Report 1908, p. 1.

82 WAS, A/H/H/252/1, Report of the Wallasey Cottage Hospital for 1867, p. 4; A/H/H/23, Wirral Hospital and Dispensary for Sick Children, Annual Report, 1882, p. 9; A/H/H/2, BBH, LIXth Annual Report, 1901, p. 10 and LXth Annual Report, 1902, pp. 9–10.

83 WAS, A/H/H/252/1, Wallasey Cottage Hospital, Annual Report for 1875; A/H/H/23, Wirral Hospital and Dispensary for Sick Children, 8th Annual Report, 1877; A/H/H/1, Birkenhead Hospital and Dispensary, Committee Minutes, 14 January 1852; A/H/H/23, Wirral Hospital and Dispensary for Sick Children, Annual Report, 1875, p. 7 and Annual Report, 1882, p. 35. The proportion of local and 'semi-local' committee members at the Wirral Hospital and Dispensary for Sick Children was initially almost 100 per cent: by 1903 and 1913 the proportion had declined slightly to 90 and 84 per cent respectively, with an increase in the number of committee members resident elsewhere on the Wirral.

84 WAS, A/HH/2, BBH, LXIIth Annual Report, 1904, p. 11; A/HH/23, BBH, Office Bearers for the Year 1903, p. 2; HH/252/1, Wallasey Cottage Hospital, Report for the year ending 31 March 1881, pp. 8–11; A/HH/170/1, Hoylake Cottage Hospital, Annual Report for the year 1903, pp. 10–13; A/HH/2, BBH, Annual Report, 1901, pp. 21–2.

85 WAS, A/HH/23, Wirral Hospital and Dispensary for Sick Children, Annual Report, 1892, pp. 46–7 and Annual Report, 1895, pp. 14, 21.

86 WAS, B/104/4, Scrapbook—Birkenhead Improvements Commissioners, 1837–79, No. 95, Printed extract minute of Wirral Philharmonic, 15 October 1861; *BCA*, 10 January 1863.

87 May, *History of the Claughton Bowling Club*, p. 3; WAS, YSD/1/1, Claughton Bowling Club, Committee of Management 1861; F. W. Blood, *The Cheshire Rifle Volunteers of the Hundred of Wirral 1859 to 1906* (Birkenhead, 1941), p. 3; WAS, AHH/201/1, Seacombe Cottage Hospital, First Annual Report, 1871, p. 3.

88 WAS, YPX/14/6, King, Vincent Ashfield, journals; Blood, *The Cheshire Rifle Volunteers*, p. 14; WAS, A/HH/2, BBH, Annual Report, LX, 1902, p. 7; Wallasey Yacht Club, *Magazines to Wallasey*, p. 10. For a brief biography of Alfred Jones, see Peter N. Davies, *The Trade Makers: Elder Dempster in West Africa, 1852–1972 1973–1989* (St. John's Newfoundland, 2000), pp. 37–56.

89 Adrian Jarvis, 'Land Policies in the Port of Liverpool, 1709–1857', *IJMH*, 10 (2000), p. 81; Joan Evans, *Christ Church Birkenhead: A Glimpse of Its History* (Rock Ferry, 1994), p. 1; Ward, *The Changing Years of Rock Ferry*, pp. 32–3; MLP database.

90 Robert A. Pullan and Kenneth J. Burnley, *Set Upon a Hill: The Story of St. Mary's Church and Parish Upton, Wirral* (Wallasey, 1993), pp. 16, 27; W. H. G. Jones, 'Historical Guide Overchurch Parish and Upton Township', *THSL&C*, 111 (1959), pp. 77–92; *Hoylake and West Kirby Directory* (1897), p. 22.

91 W. A. Cook, *The Parish Church of St. John Egremont (or Liscard): A Short History and Guide* (Wallasey, 1958), p. 3; *Hoylake and West Kirby Directory* (1897), p. 22; Kaighin, *Bygone Birkenhead*, p. 155; McNeil and Stephen, *The Story of Seacombe Presbyterian Church of England*, pp. 23, 31; Arnold Herschell, *History of Trinity Presbyterian Church with Special Reference to Brassey Street Mission* (Birkenhead, 1910), p. 1; Ronald Johnston, *Clydeside Capital, 1870–1920: A Social History of Employers* (East Lothian, 2002), p. 99; Richard Trainor, 'The Middle Class', in Martin Daunton (ed.), *TCUHB* (Cambridge, 2001), vol. 3, p. 700. James Irvine (1835–1926), for example, was an elder of Trinity Church for 58 years.

92 Morris, 'Clubs, Societies and Associations', p. 421; WAS, YFP/1/1, Wirral Footpaths and Open Spaces Preservation Society, Annual General Meeting, 1888; YMC1/1, Young Men's Christian Association (Birkenhead Branch), General Committee Minutes, 12 May 1891; ZWO/17/1, West Kirby Christian Institute Trustees Committee minutes, 19 March 1891.

93 WAS, YSF/6, Society of Friends, Birkenhead Friends Literary Society minutes, 17 March 1880; YBB/1, Bebington Bowling Club, minute book, 9 May 1867 and 14 June 1867; Walker, *The Liverpool*

Competition; Elston, Birkenhead Park Cricket Club file; Jeffrey Cox, 'Were Victorian Nonconformists the Worst Imperialists of All?', *Victorian Studies*, 46, 2 (2004), pp. 243–55.

94 John Armstrong, *A History of Freemasonry in Cheshire* (London, 1901), pp. 117–19; Chapter 6, above; David Harrison, *The Transformation of Freemasonry: 'The Revolution of the World!'* (Bury St. Edmunds, 2010). See also Barry M. Doyle, 'The Structure of Elite Power in the Early Twentieth-Century City: Norwich, 1900–35', *UH*, 24, 2 (1997), p. 185.

95 Blood, The Cheshire Rifle Volunteers, pp. 5–6, 20; County Borough of Birkenhead, *Birkenhead 1877–1974*, p. 95.

96 The sample consisted of eight merchants, two brokers, one ship builder, and one shipowner. Laird was a committee member of the Birkenhead Hospital and Dispensary (1850), an active proponent for the establishment of the Volunteer Movement (1859), a shareholder in Birkenhead School (1860), the honorary secretary to the Bank for Savings (1861), a member of the Philharmonic Society (1861) and the local (Birkenhead) committee of the Manchester and Liverpool Agricultural Society (1863), the treasurer of the Birkenhead Borough Hospital (1864), an honorary member of Birkenhead Literary and Scientific Society (1868–69), a patron of the Wirral Hospital and Dispensary for Sick Children (1870), and a shareholder in the Claughton Bowling Club (1875). Stitt was active in the Volunteer Movement (1860), a member of the Philharmonic Society (1861) and the Birkenhead Literary and Scientific Society (1869–98), a subscriber to the Claughton Bowling Club (1861), a committee member and trustee of the Wirral Hospital and Dispensary for Sick Children (1871), a shareholder in Birkenhead School (1884) and Birkenhead Institute (1885), a vice-president of the Wirral Footpaths and Open Spaces Preservation Society (1888), a trustee of the Brassey Street Savings Bank (1893), and a governor for life at the Birkenhead Borough Hospital. In addition, his religious and political commitments were reflected in his role as superintendent of Trinity Presbyterian Church (1865), treasurer of the Missionary and Benevolent Society, and chairman of the Birkenhead Liberal Association.

97 Marsden, *History of the Birkenhead Literary and Scientific Society*, pp. 47–8; John Millar, *William Heap and His Company* (4th ed., Hoylake, 1994), pp. 90–1; Alistair Cooke, *A Gift from the Churchills: The Primrose League, 1883–2004* (London, 2010). One of its objectives was to fight for free enterprise.

98 By contrast, Wall was vice-president of the West Kirby Cycling Club (1897), president of the West Kirby Choral Society (1897), a governor of Calday Grammar School (1898), a leading figure in the West Kirby Charities (1906), president of the West Kirby and District Homing Society (1906), a member of the Hoylake, West Kirby, and District Horticultural Society (1906), a vice-president of the Hoylake Cottage Hospital (1909), and a member of the West Kirby Christian Institute (1912).

99 WAS, YMC/1/1–6, Young Men's Christian Association (Birkenhead Branch), General Committee minutes; ZWO/17/1, West Kirby Christian Institute, Trustees Committee minutes, 11 November 1890, 26 March 1895.

100 WAS, B/320/1, Birkenhead Institute Ltd., Minutes of Directors' Meetings, 2 February 1885, 18 September 1888, 31 October 1888; May, *History of the Claughton Bowling Club*, p. 3; WAS, YSD/1/2, Claughton Bowling Club, Committee of Management, 1 October 1874; Beacall, *Birkenhead Park*, pp. 3–4.

101 Marsden, *History of the Birkenhead Literary and Scientific Society*, pp. 19–20, 27–8, 37–8; WAS, BC IV 280, Birkenhead Literary and Scientific Society, Annual Report and List of Members, 1868–9, pp. 6–8; BCL, Birkenhead Ruskin Society, Report of the Committee for 1881–2; BCL, BC IV 270, Birkenhead Shakespere Literary Society, 2nd annual report 1880; BSA, 150 SG, File No. 1; WAS, YSD/1/5, Claughton Bowling Club, List of Members, 1875.

102 WAS, A/HH/23, Wirral Hospital and Dispensary for Sick Children, Annual Report, 1903; ZWO/14/1, WKLS, Membership Roll, 1900.

103 LRO, 920 MD 283/4, Henry Threlfall Wilson, Personal Accounts, 1868; Anon., *A Portrait of Trinity*, p. 5; The History of Birkenhead Institute, p. 26.

104 WAS, B/547/3, Birkenhead Union Assessment, Valuation List, 1872. Even in the late nineteenth century, the freehold to all the housing on the eastern side of the Square was still held by a single individual.

105 WAS, ZWO/14/1, WKLS, Annual Meeting, 21 April 1898, Annual Report, 1899–1900, and Report of Session 1902–03; YBB/1, Bebington Bowling Club, Minute Book, 22 March 1867.

106 WAS, YPX/67/11, Hoylake Congregational Church, manual of 1911.

107 The History of Birkenhead Institute, p. 30; WAS, A/HH/2, BBH, Annual Report of the Committee, LXX, p. 7; A/HH/23, Wirral Hospital and Dispensary for Sick Children, 37th Annual Report, 1906,

p. 13 and 42nd Annual Report, 1911; YBB/1/2, Bebington Bowling Club, Committee Minutes 22 May 1891.

108 WAS, B/320/1, Birkenhead Institute, Minutes of Directors' Meeting, 1884–85; A/HH/1, Birkenhead Hospital and Dispensary, General Committee, 12 February 1851, 14 July 1852; A/HH/23, Wirral Hospital and Dispensary for Sick Children, Annual Reports, 1870–83; A/HH/2, BBH, LXth Report of the Committee, 1902; YBB/1, Birkenhead Hospital and Dispensary, 30 September 1871; A/HH/1, Bebington Bowling Club, General Committee, 10 April 1850.

109 WAS, A/HH/2, BBH, List of Persons who are or have been Governors for Life by contributing £20 or upwards at one payment, pp. 21–2; Annual Report for 1903.

110 LRO, M285, PRE/11/61, Communicants' Roll Book or Names, Designations etc. of members belonging to The Scotch Church, Woodside, 1840–1866.

111 LRO, M285 PRE/11/61, Communicants' Roll Book or Names, Designation etc of Members belonging to The Scotch Church, Woodside, 1840–1866; 285 TRI/7/1, Trinity Presbyterian Church, Communicants' roll book, 1863–c.1878; WAS, YSF/12, Liscard Preparatory Meeting, Register of Members c.1891; YSFD/125/1, Joyce Whittington, The History of Birkenhead Friends Meeting, Pt.1, 1847–1892, p. 4; Bill Stallybrass, *The Biglands of Cheshire* (Caithness, 1988).

112 Grange Road Presbyterian Church, Birkenhead, Jubilee Memorial, 12 July 1896, Brief Historical Account, p. 7; *Grange Road Baptist Church Jubilee Souvenir 1858–1908* (London, 1908), p. 19; Deacons' Court, *Jubilee Memorial of Canning Street Presbyterian Church Liverpool, 1846–1896* (Liverpool, 1896), p. 11.

113 WAS, YPX/88/1, New Ferry Literary and Debating Society, Committee Minutes, 25 April 1895; BCL, BCIV 280, Birkenhead Literary and Scientific Society, List of Members, 1868–69.

114 See Graeme Milne, Chapter 3.

115 See Robert Lee, Chapter 11.

116 Morris, 'Clubs, Societies and Associations', p. 395; LRO, 942 BIC 13, T2; Longmore, 'Civic Liverpool', p. 143; Arline Wilson, 'The Cultural Identity of Liverpool, 1750–1850: The Early Learned Societies', *HSL&C*, 147 (1998), pp. 55–80; LRO, 179 CRU/13/1, Liverpool Society for the Prevention of Cruelty to Children, 1st Report, 19 April 1883; L. J. Mawdsley & Co., Gore's Directory (Liverpool, 1857), p. 72; WAS, B/104/4, Scrapbook, printed extract, minute of Wirral Philharmonic Society, 15 October 1861; Thomas Baines, *Liverpool in 1859: The Port and Town of Liverpool and the Harbour, Docks and Commerce of the Mersey in 1859* (Liverpool, 1859), p. 115; see also Chapter 8 (Joseph Sharples).

117 Pike, *Liverpool and Birkenhead*, p. 102; MLP database. In Southport, for example, the engineer Dr. James Wood continued to progress his business affairs in Liverpool, played a dominant role in the resort's politics (serving four times as mayor), and was heavily involved in the Methodist movement, relating to home and foreign missions, as well as undertaking 'evangelistic tours'. See Eliza A. Wood, *Memorials of James Wood, LL.D., J.P. of Grove House, Southport* (London, 1902).

118 MAL, D/SO/1/1/1, Liverpool Seamen's Orphan Institution, Executive Committee minute book, 17 February 1869, 27 February 1869; D/SO/2/1/4, Annual Report 31 December 1886; D/SO/1/8, Annual Reports, 1901–05.

119 MAL, DX/504/4/1/10, Correspondence and news cuttings concerning J. Bruce Ismay and the Earl of Derby, regarding the Liverpool Seamen's Pension Fund, the Mercantile Marine (widows) Fund and the Titanic Relief Fund; Pike, *Liverpool and Birkenhead*, pp. 128, 179; A. L. M. Cook, *Liverpool's Northern Hospital; 1834–1978* (Liverpool, 1981), p. 129.

120 MPL database; Wilton J. Oldham, *The Ismay Line: The White Star Line, and the Ismay Family Story* (Liverpool and London, 1961), pp. 87, 135; MAL, 414 MER/Pk, Mariners' Park Estate Centenary Booklet (n.d.); WAS, B/550/1, Birkenhead Union Parish of Noctorum, Valuation List, December 1884–September 1914.

121 LRO, 614 HAH/8/2/2, Hahnemann Hospital, Annual Reports, 1891–1901; 614 PRI/1/1, Princes Park Hospital, General Committee Minute Book, 29 August 1877–27 December 1882.

122 LRO, 614 SOU 1/1/, Report of the Southern and Toxteth Hospital with a list of Subscriptions and Donations, Liverpool 1853, pp. 13–18.

123 See Chapter 8 (Joseph Sharples); Paul Elliott, 'The Origins of the "Creative Class": Provincial Urban Society, Scientific Culture and Socio-Political Marginality in Britain in the Eighteenth and Nineteenth Centuries', *Social History*, 28, 3 (2003), p. 365; LRO, 367 WTN/6, Wellington Club, Annual Reports with rules, resolutions and lists of members, 1813–1913; MLP database; LRO 920 DUR 1/3, Family Diary maintained by George Holt, 23 February 1860. See Chapter 6 (Sari Mäenpää) and Chapter 12 (Robert Lee).

124 Longmore, 'Civic Liverpool', pp. 142–3; Chapters 5 (Joseph Sharples) and 11 (Robert Lee); LRO, 027 LYC 1/1/1-, Liverpool Library, General Committee Minute Book, Annual General Meeting 21 May 1880; 027 LYC 17/1, The Lyceum Annual Report, May 1882; 027 LYC 17/2, The Lyceum Annual Report, May 1899; 027 LYC 4/1, Liverpool Library, Share Register; 027 LYC 17/2, The Lyceum Annual Report, May 1901.

125 LRO, 027 LYC 4/1, Liverpool Library Share Register, share numbers 124, 478; LYC 17/3, The Lyceum, Report, Laws and List of the Proprietors, May 1901; John W. Graham, *Steel Wheels to Deeside: The Wirral Railway Past and Present* (Rock Ferry, 1983); Chapter 9 (Joseph Sharples and Adrian Jarvis); Gunn, *The Public Culture*, p. 86. For a wider discussion of the impact of transport development on the suburbanisation process, see Colin Divall and Winstan Bond (eds.), *Suburbanizing the Masses: Public Transport and Urban Development in Historical Perspective* (Aldershot, 2003); see Chapter 8 (Joseph Sharples).

126 LRO 780 AMA/1, Names and Addresses of the Members of the Amateur Musical Union, 1868–69; MLP database; Mawdsley & Co., *Gore's Directory for 1857*; LRO THI 30 Club, List of Members, 1895.

127 LRO, 792 ROY/4, Theatre Royal, List of Shareholders, 1866; 060 ITA, Liverpool Italian Literary Society, Committee 1911–12; MLP database.

128 LRO, 701 BOW/1, Museum of Japanese Art, General Committee, 1890; *THSL&C*, New Series III (1863), pp. vii–xix and New Series LIV (1904), pp. xiii–xxiii; LRO, 796 RUG, Liverpool Rugby Union Football Club, 3/1, List of Members, September 1911.

129 Mark Casson and Andrew Godley, 'Cultural Factors in Economic Growth', in Mark Casson and Andrew Godley (eds.), *Cultural Factors in Economic Growth* (Berlin, Heidelberg and New York, 2000), p. 6; Gordon Boyce, 'Network Knowledge and Network Routines: Negotiating Activities between Shipowners and Shipbuilders', *BH*, 45, 2 (2003), pp. 59–63; Ewen A. Cameron, 'Glasgow's Going Round and Round: Some Recent Scottish Urban History', *UH*, 30, 2 (2003), p. 283; Jon Stobart, 'Personal and Commercial Networks in an English Port: Chester in the Early Eighteenth Century', *Journal of Historical Geography*, 30 (2004), p. 290.

130 Mark Casson, 'Culture as an Economic Asset', in Andrew Godley and Oliver Westall (eds.), *Business History and Business Culture* (Manchester, 1996), pp. 48–76; Mark Casson and Mary B. Rose, 'Institutions and the Evolution of Modern Business: Introduction', *BH*, 39, 4 (1997), p. 3; Elliott, 'The Origins of the "Creative Class"', p. 365; R. J. Morris, 'Voluntary Societies and British Urban Elites, 1780–1850', *Historical Journal*, 26 (1983), pp. 95–11; 'Civil Society and the Nature of Urbanism: Britain, 1750–1850', *UH*, 25, 3 (1998), pp. 289–301; Gunn, 'Class, Identity and the Urban', pp. 29–30; Robert Gray, 'The Platform and the Pulpit: Cultural Networks and Civic Identities in Industrial Towns, c.1850–70', in Kidd and Nicholls, *The Making of the British Middle Class?*, p. 130.

131 Arline Wilson, 'Custom and Commerce: Liverpool's Merchant Elite c.1790–1850', unpublished PhD, University of Liverpool (1997); 'The Cultural Identity of Liverpool', pp. 55–80.

132 Spencer Jordan, Peter Wardley, and Matthew Woolard, 'Emerging Modernity in an Urban Setting: Nineteenth-Century Bristol Revealed in Property Surveys', *UH*, 26, 2 (1999), p. 208.

133 Lee, 'Configuring the Region', pp. 247–9; Belchem, *Liverpool 800*; Gunn, 'Class, Identity and the Urban', pp. 29–47; Timothy R. Mahoney, 'Middle-Class Experience in the United States in the Gilded Age, 1865–1900', *Journal of Urban History*, 31, 3 (2005), p. 361.

134 Lynne Hapgood, 'The Literature of the Suburb: Versions of Repression in the Novels of George Gissing, Arthur Conan Doyle and William Pett Ridge, 1890–1899', *Journal of Victorian Culture*, 5, 2 (2000), p. 288; Gunn, *The Public Culture*, p. 39.

135 MLP database.

136 Ash Amin and Nigel Thrift, *Cities Reimagining the Urban* (Oxford, 2002), pp. 3, 53; Colin Pooley and Jean Turnbull, *Migration and Mobility in Britain since the 18th Century* (London, 1998), p. 62.

137 Stena Nenadic, 'The Middle Ranks and Modernisation', in T. M. Devine and Gordon Jackson (eds.), *Glasgow, vol. 1: Beginnings to 1830* (Manchester, 1995), p. 288; Cameron, 'Glasgow's Going Round and Round', p. 283; Philip Harling, 'The Centrality of Locality: The Local State, Local Democracy, and Local Consciousness in Late-Victorian and Edwardian Britain', *Journal of Victorian Culture*, 9, 2 (2004), p. 216.

138 Robert Gray and Donna Loftus, 'Industrial Regulation, Urban Space and the Boundaries of the Workplace: Mid-Victorian Nottingham', *UH*, 26, 2 (1999), p. 218; WAS, A/HH/23, Wirral Hospital and Dispensary for Sick Children: in the early twentieth century the age of members varied between 21 and 60 years.

139 Hayes, 'The Construction and Form of Modern Cities', p. 419; Alan Kidd and David Nicholls, 'Intro-duction: The Making of the British Middle Class?', in Kidd and Nicholls, *The Making of the British Middle Class?*, p. xxviii; Robert Lewis (ed.), *Manufacturing Suburbs: Building Work and Home on the Metropolitan Fringe* (Philadelphia, 2004).
140 (By Triplets), *Ye True and Autuentique Historie of Ye Good Old Towne of Leverpoole and Ye Trade Thereof and Eke a Guide for Ye Pilgrimme and Wayfarer* (Liverpool, 1884), pp. 11, 20, 21. The publication was not without an element of racism: if the entire Mersey flotilla (including barges and coasting craft) were placed stem to stern, it was a 'negro steward' who would need 77,414 years to take a brandy and soda from the saloon of the end vessel to a passenger in the smoking room of the first vessel, 'without counting times necessary for sleep and refreshment'.

11 Deconstructing Liverpool's Merchant Networks

Transience, Religion, Politics, and Business Interests

Robert Lee

Introduction

The importance of business networks has been widely acknowledged, particularly when they were underpinned by overlapping political, religious, and social connections. Network-based communications, irrespective of their operational form, facilitated face-to-face meetings and shared agency which, in turn, were especially important at times of crisis, while social connectedness also helped to promote class-specific cohesion and stability. In general, impersonal transactions have always been mediated by personal relations based on friendship, habit, or obligation, while both business practices and commercial decisions were often culturally conditioned. Social and economic networks, particularly in the late eighteenth and early nineteenth century, were mutually constitutive: they were an integral part of economic activity; trust relations based on family, ethnic, and religious ties generated efficiency gains and maximised trading opportunities; and the information flows facilitated by network membership provided individual participants with a competitive advantage. If family- and kin-based networks offered a reliable basis for developing and managing high-risk, long-distance commercial transactions, marriage strategies were constructed to consolidate capital by cementing ties of kinship or friendship. Moreover, ethnic- or kinship-based networks were not a backward form of economic organisation, but in many cases offered a basis for sustainable long-run development. The religious background of business partners was frequently important in constructing networks of reciprocity and obligation. Religious minorities established extensive trading networks which enjoyed significant commercial success, while most trading diasporas were characterised by strong religious traditions which underpinned community cohesion, economic solidarity, and personal trust.

Despite the importance of shared experience, whether based on family, kin, ethnicity, or religion, the widespread application of network analysis and social capital theory by historians has been subject increasingly to criticism because of definitional, evidential, and theoretical problems. Firstly, it is difficult to capture the complexity of different networks, to assess their transactional density, or to measure their radius of trust with any certainty. Large network groups inevitably developed an inner hierarchy which involved both functional and status distinctions, as well as privileged access to commercial information. Increased network size was also associated with greater functional opacity and the introduction of corrupt practices, particularly in a context in which appropriate forms of corporate governance were still imperfect, while institutional diversification which was evident in most urban communities during the second half of the nineteenth century tended to undermine the effectiveness of existing networks.

Secondly, in seeking to apply a network-based concept of individual-level social capital it is important to distinguish between the brokerage role of network mechanisms and their tendency

DOI: 10.4324/9781315597836-11

towards social (and economic) closure. Network membership was often restricted to specific sections of local society and the strength of moral bonds, whether sustained by common business interests, confessional identity, or ethnicity, implied a reduced level of trust towards outsiders or in-migrants. Path dependency in such a context restricted the ability of individual merchants to draw on a wider range of connections outside the existing networks and personal ties, particularly at a time of rapid institutional change or economic crisis. Moreover, within any network there were implicit core-periphery patterns, with interpersonal relations reflecting a wide spectrum of both strong and weak ties, while in- and out-category ties were often a reflection of the relative size of the network group.

Thirdly, the 'centrality of trust' whereby the success of any commercial venture was built on well-defined social bonds developed within a network framework may well be an 'overworked concept', not simply because familial or social connections cannot in themselves ensure reliability and trustworthiness, but also because of continuing doubts over the determinants of individual behaviour. Social capital theory and network analysis are both predicated on the assumption that individuals operate primarily according to self-interest, although often in a way which has been culturally constructed. Pure self-interest remains the central explanatory principle for rational choice theory, despite Adam Smith's conclusion that its impact on the economy and society was implicitly dysfunctional. Even if it is accepted that actors are complex variables, participation in collective action, whether in the form of a network based on trading interests or a philanthropic society, is often attributed to imitative behaviour, while insufficient attention has been paid to individual heterogeneity, mental schemas, and their construction, as well as the determinants of personal inceptive capacity.[1]

Finally, too little is known about the determinants of network creation and transformation, the interface between local, regional, and national networks, the dynamic context in which networks operated, and the impact of larger processes of socio-economic change on the viability and significance of local networks based on personal contacts, kinship, and ethnicity. It is sometimes assumed that network communication amongst the urban middle class, particularly within a specific cultural or social framework, was essentially local in nature, but this ignores its spatial diversity, itself a product of high rates of population mobility, the extent to which specific types of clubs and societies were established as part of a national movement, and the evidence of increasing regional and national links through regular conferences and meetings.

This chapter challenges some of the normative assumptions in network theory by exploring the extent to which cultural, economic, religious, and social factors were instrumental in structuring network formation and persistence. The case for prioritising business networks was strong, particularly in a trading environment that was frequently uncertain and volatile. Too often it has been assumed that Liverpool's merchant community was cohesive because self-interest was the prime determinant of business behaviour. But how far did out-migration, whether as a result of the successful acquisition of landed property or commercial failure, threaten networking? To what extent were business networks mediated or determined by other variables? How important were confessional differences in determining commercial networks in a society in which religion remained a socio-economic and political construct? Was this equally evident politically in a manner which divided the merchant community and weakened their collective influence on local and national government? Did merchants continue to play a strategic role in local politics and civic government? Between the mid-nineteenth century and the First World War the operative framework for business and commerce underwent a series of institutional changes. There was a stronger emphasis on the role of trade associations and the lobbying powers of chambers of commerce; changes in company law led to the growing importance of limited liability companies; and there is evidence of a greater reliance on interlocking directorships. How did these institutional changes affect the traditional model of business networking or the ability of merchants to act as pressure groups?

Liverpool's Merchant Elites: Theory and Practice

In addressing these issues, it is helpful to set out a framework for analysing how the role of the mercantile community was affected by a range of socio-economic variables. Traditionally, it has been accepted that merchants and businessmen used their wealth to influence 'every aspect of Liverpool's life'. Local loyalties were stronger than national affiliations; many members of the mercantile community led 'very disciplined lives'; and their families were expected to be hard-working and self-denying. In general, they 'immersed' themselves in local politics as a means of influencing the city's development and ensuring the provision of local services, rather than seeking self-advancement. However, many of these assumptions are either incorrect or only applicable to a limited extent as the following sections will illustrate.[2]

But an equally important task is to locate the mercantile community within a theoretical framework. The MLP database contains information on 12,182 individuals who were involved in commerce and trade between the 1850s and 1910s, but the range of material for many small-scale merchants (such as those involved in coal distribution at a local level) is limited, whereas the census data and trade directory entries for members of the elite have been supplemented by an extensive range of archival material and secondary literature. The collective biographies of Orchard and, to a lesser extent, of Pike, provide a baseline for estimating the overall size of the mercantile elite in the late nineteenth century and in the years immediately prior to the outbreak of the First World War, even though neither can claim to have been entirely comprehensive. To this extent, the database offers a unique insight into the composition and operation of the mercantile community over six decades, but a more detailed analysis, by definition, is limited to those who were regarded as having been involved 'in a very wide range of non-business activities'.

Furthermore, most historians have been unwilling to view Liverpool's elite merchants from a theoretical perspective. Cities, such as Liverpool, offer productive possibilities for analysing the movement between different experiences of power over time and space. Descriptive accounts of elites can offer a useful framework, but, ideally, social network analysis requires information on whole populations rather than a specific sample, in order to explore the complex connections and ties between individuals, groups, and institutions, whether formal or informal. Elites, by definition, hold and exercise power, although power itself often remains a contested concept. In such a context, it is important to deconstruct the different ways in which elite power (economic, social, or cultural) is constituted and exercised; its 'discursive formation' through socialisation and community building; and its spatial location in geographies of affluence and privilege, as well as perceived elite territoriality. Family upbringing, education, marriage strategies, and cultural socialisation were undoubtedly important factors in reinforcing the cohesiveness of elite structures, but it is doubtful whether a clear sense of identity was ever fully present in formal networking activity, which invariably tended to 'drain out into other networks.'[3]

For historians, however, it is difficult to capture the extent to which different discursive regimes within elite groups operated in time and space, or the factors which influenced the varying patterns of access to elite structures as a function of both upward and downward mobility, bearing in mind the contrast between a high degree of transience and evidence of a growth in social immobility. Elite contacts and networks should not be interpreted as ascriptive results of prior conditioning, because their practical value was dependent on merchants and businessmen who were in a position to bridge diverse worlds and specialist fields, while aspects of regulatory power (as in the case of trade associations) might be counter-productive in comparison with measures designed to maximise productive responses from cooperating agents. Moreover, as several authors have indicated, social relations at the local level were not defined solely by the activities, values, and cultures of 'old-established' families, but by in-migrants who elected to belong to existing elite structures, rather than remain 'locally indifferent'. Applying these concepts to Liverpool's mercantile community between the mid-nineteenth century and 1914 is not straightforward, largely because of data problems. Even if the elite powers exercised by the 'merchant princes' were beginning to wane by 1900, successful businessmen and traders were still accorded a special role in the port-city's development. Individual firms were publicly recognised for their 'honourable and enterprising dealing' (such as the timber merchant John Gale & Co., which had been operating for over 50 years) or their senior partners were praised for their 'strict honour and probity', as was the case with the general broker Charles Page & Co., but without a wider analytical framework it is difficult to assess whether these traditional virtues were still as relevant for business success as they had been in earlier decades. By moving away from a reliance on descriptive narrative and by seeking to deploy relevant theoretical insights, where feasible, the following sections will hopefully provide a robust basis for deconstructing Liverpool's merchant networks.[4]

Business Instability and the Importance of Networks

The MLP database enabled the project team to address some important issues relating to the organisation of business activity, the role of networks, and the cultural embeddedness of the commercial world. Because of the inherent volatility of trade, networks of trust and obligation, whether based on family, shared ethnicity, confessional identity, or nationality, played a particularly important role in port-cities, such as Liverpool, by enabling firms to lower information and transaction costs and by providing access to resources and capabilities which enabled them to overcome internal constraints. Such arguments have generally been applied in relation to overseas trade in the early modern period, including the slave trade, but they remain highly relevant in the nineteenth century when periodic crises, generally induced by bank failures, resulted in global economic instability and market uncertainty.[5] Despite the investment booms of 1852–53, 1863–65, and 1871–73, the third quarter of the nineteenth century was a time of underlying uncertainty, despite considerable optimism and speculative activity. The onset in 1873 of the 'Great Depression' (now known as the 'Long Depression') was initiated by a contraction in money supply in the United States and led to the ending of the bimetallic standard and the forced adoption of the Gold Standard. It was the direct cause of widespread bank failures both in America and elsewhere and heralded the onset of adverse international trading conditions for several years.[6]

A reconstruction of the business cycle's chronology (peaks to troughs during the three decades after 1840) reveals the underlying volatility of the national economy (1840–42, 1845–47, 1848–50, 1854–55, 1856–58, 1860–62, 1866–68). The impact of economic crises on Liverpool's merchant community was substantial: trade was severely disrupted by a 'money panic' almost every tenth year (as in 1847, 1857, and 1866), in each case accompanied by high rates of bankruptcy. Even before the onset of the economic crisis in the late 1840s, the cotton broker George Holt recorded the death of a merchant who was 'a victim to Railway Speculation' following the failure of several stock and share dealers. By October 1847, the 'crisis' was attributed to the 'dearth of a common means of trade' in part due to hoarding and other causes; and Liverpool's 'trading classes' were increasingly distressed, particularly after the North and South Wales Bank suspended operations at the end of that month. But the collapse of prices in 1848 led to numerous bankruptcies and the demise of many firms. According to Macgregor Laird, the level of distress in Liverpool was 'awful'; some men 'accustomed to luxury' were forced to seek relief from their parish; and household property and land were 'literally non-saleable' in both Birkenhead and Liverpool (from Everton to Birkenhead Park). The Improvement Commissioners for Birkenhead were close to bankruptcy and it was not until the mid-1850s that the township (heralded in the mid-1840s as 'the city of the future') finally began to recover. The liquidation of the Borough Bank of Liverpool in 1857, which was attributed to 'overextended trade', had 'disastrous consequences', both economic and personal. In February 1859, there was 'a shock to the commercial world' which meant that Liverpool charities lost many of their subscribers. The outbreak of the American Civil War in 1861 was followed by the imposition of an embargo by the Union of raw cotton exports which could not be compensated by attempts to secure additional imports from Egypt and India. As early as October Liverpool charities reported a rapid increase in cases 'coming upon us', with people who had been brought up in affluence falling into poverty in old age. The Civil War was an 'unmitigated catastrophe' for the British cotton industry, business was 'difficult and dangerous', and greed and speculation exacerbated market conditions that were already confused and uncertain. The level of distress in Birkenhead in 1863 was exceptional and in the following year there were reports in the Liverpool cotton market of 'severe money pressure', 'renewed depression', and rumours of 'large failures', while the cessation of hostilities in 1865 led to a 'collapse of factitious inflation'.[7]

According to Henry Tate, the sugar refiner, writing in August 1867, the market was 'very flat and prices for our product seriously low'. He did not know what would become of the trade, but the flooding of the British market with cheap loaf sugar would only make the situation worse. The cotton trade in the late 1860s was far from prosperous: there was a high incidence of failure amongst the early steamship companies, irrespective of how well they were managed; and the 'Long Depression' (1873–96), combined with a drift towards protectionism, witnessed a collapse in raw material prices for grain, cotton, and palm oil (particularly in the late 1880s), together with a fall in profit levels and interest rates. A 'tide of South American troubles' in the late 1870s led to the retirement of William Just, a shipowner, ship insurance broker, and the first manager of the Pacific Steam Navigation Co. A 'severe trade depression' in 1880 prompted the establishment of a fund to provide relief to dock labourers and cotton porters, with the shipowner Henry MacIver as its honorary treasurer. In 1883–84, a severe commercial depression had a multiplier effect: donations to many charities, including the Liverpool School of Science, fell considerably; and educational and welfare provision were curtailed at a time when additional support was needed. Although there was no uniform trend pattern in economic performance indicators, increased production was accompanied by rising unemployment and a fall in prices, profits and interest rates. It was a worrying time for many Liverpool merchants.[8]

Liverpool's trading environment was associated with a significant rate of failure even in the case of businesses which were managed and run in an essentially honest and efficient manner.[9] Certainly, a number of family firms included in Orchard's 1893 sample had survived for three or four generations and were therefore 'generally respected'. George Morrell belonged to a family which had been in the provision trade for four generations, while the corn merchants Robert Procter & Sons had survived for a long period of time as a result of 'three generations of sagacity, probity and energy'. However, the circle of 'old families' was small and only approximately 5 per cent of the port-city's successful merchants could claim an extended, continuous lineage.[10] The cotton broking firm of Francis W. Reynolds JP had its origins in 1806: he was 'much esteemed by his fellow Roman Catholics' and he became very wealthy, but the innate fragility of business enterprise was reflected by the fact that his commercial credit remained unaffected 'by occasional severe losses'. In fact, longevity was not a 'common characteristic' even when traders ran their businesses in an honest fashion. There were too many cases of a visible 'descent from the higher platforms of connexion and wealth, stage after stage, to the lower levels of poverty and obscurity'; many 'magnates of the day' had passed away 'like a vision, and left nothing behind'; and it was generally accepted that there was a great deal of business failure, although 'no one knows how much'.[11]

The evidence from the database reveals a very high level of turnover: of all the firms first recorded in 1851, 41 per cent were still operating just over a decade later, but a mere 7 per cent survived until 1912. Almost 30 per cent of shipowners ceased to operate within five years, while the failure rate for both cotton and timber merchants was noticeably higher at 49.6 and 54.9 per cent respectively. During the later stages of the trade cycle, as was the case between 1870 and 1873, increased speculative activity resulted in an inflated short-term mortality rate for merchant enterprises as existing partnership arrangements were modified and new entrants failed to establish themselves. Severe disequilibrium created by periodic crises led to the demise of well-established enterprises. At a time of increased specialisation within the merchant community most maritime-oriented businesses remained small-scale and suffered from a low survival rate as a result of both external and internal constraints, including limited access to credit, management deficiencies, and unreliable information flows. The local economy was based primarily on an extended web of sole proprietorships and partnerships and the trading environment was inherently volatile. Within such a context, merchant networks remained important as a defensive mechanism against business failure. This continued to be an overriding concern despite the benefits of technological change, including the development of the telegraph (1866) and telephone (1876), which offered access to new methods of information gathering and more efficient forms of communication. Under these circumstances, it is not surprising that many merchants re-affirmed the importance of network interlinkages, even if they were aware of their inherent fragility.[12]

Transience and the Changing Structure of the Merchant Community

The potential significance of social networks in fostering the growth of commerce and trade was reinforced by the fact that the development of Liverpool's merchant community had been dependent to a marked degree on in-migration. Indeed, it was claimed that the port's expansion was a result of the impetus derived 'mainly from new comers.' Of the merchants listed in the database, 9.4 per cent were Scots, 6.4 per cent Irish, and 3.5 per cent Welsh, but 10.0 per cent had been born overseas (in a few cases to British parents). Although the overwhelming majority were English born (70.4 per cent), a substantial number were in-migrants, including some of the most prominent families: the Harrisons came from Garstang, near Preston, the Holts from Halifax, and the Rathbones from Rochdale. It was generally accepted that the sons of established members of the merchant community were 'more trusted than unknown men' and that a 'young shoot from an old stock' reputedly enjoyed 'special advantages', whereas in-migrants were consistently faced with problems of assimilation and integration into an essentially well-established commercial and cultural framework.[13] The fact that a considerable number of in-migrants, whether from other regions of Britain or from overseas, established themselves amongst the port-city's elite suggests that commercial success was underpinned by the establishment of effective trust relationships. But if the process of integration was facilitated by their acceptance and integration within existing social networks, it was sustained by 'intricate familial connections', a strong associational culture and favourable marriages, as was the case in relation to in-migrants from Ireland (both Catholic and Protestant), Scotland, and Wales, as well as from continental European countries such as Germany and Sweden.[14]

Table 11.1 Place of birth: Liverpool shipowners and timber merchants

Date of Birth	Shipowners	Local		In-migrant		Timber Merchants	Local		In-migrant	
	Total	Total	%	Total	%	Total	Total	%	Total	%
pre-1829	117	25	21.3	92	78.6	120	44	36.6	76	63.3
1830–49	131	50	38.1	81	61.8	127	72	56.6	55	43.3
1850–69	119	66	55.4	53	44.5	105	62	59.0	43	40.9
1870+	21	13	61.9	8	38.0	24	19	79.1	5	20.8

Note: Local represents births registered in Liverpool and on Merseyside as a whole.

Source: MLP database

The composition of the merchant community, in terms of the spatial origins of its traders, underwent a gradual change during the period under consideration. The proportion of English-born merchants increased continuously from 73.2 per cent in 1851 to 82.4 per cent in 1901 and there was a slight rise in the relative importance of Welsh-born traders from 2.6 to 3.9 per cent (1861–1901). By contrast, the first-generation Scots presence within the merchant community declined considerably between 1851 and 1901 from 15.6 to 8.4 per cent respectively, while a downward trend was noticeable amongst Irish-born merchants (from 9.2 per cent in 1861 to 5.1 per cent by 1901). The level of in-migration from overseas also fell in the case of merchants from Holland and Switzerland from 1871 onwards, while the German, Italian, and Turkish presence declined after 1881, as was the case for merchants born in Canada and the United States. The greater reliance on English-born merchants, particularly those whose families came from Merseyside, was a reflection of the growing importance of natural increase rather than in-migration as the key determinant of Liverpool's long-run population growth which was reflected in the cumulative increase in locally born shipowners and timber merchants (Table 11.1).

In both cases, in-migrants had been predominant amongst those born before 1829, but by the turn of the century an overwhelming majority had been born in Liverpool itself or elsewhere on Merseyside. The long-run development of Liverpool's merchant community was no longer dependent on extensive in-migration because its members were far more likely to have been born locally than elsewhere in Britain or overseas. This process was a result of a number of factors, including changing market conditions, the impact of new technology on business communications, and the reduced attractiveness of Liverpool as a focal point for international trade.[15] Cultural and social networks in the early nineteenth century operated in a manner which encouraged or facilitated the integration of newcomers irrespective of their origins and enabled individual families such as the Holts and Harrisons to achieve significant commercial success. By the end of the nineteenth century they served increasingly to reinforce a merchant community which was now more self-sustaining and well established than had previously been the case, but perhaps less welcoming to new arrivals seeking to start their business careers.

The transient and fluid structure of Liverpool's merchant community was aggravated by high rates of out-migration, not only to the emergent suburbs on both sides of the Mersey, but further afield. According to Orchard, 'a large section of our best people' had always been inclined to live 'a good way out of town', but from the late 1870s onwards this tendency became very pronounced.[16] The scale of out-migration, with the proportion of merchants moving out of Liverpool double that of those moving in, has already been discussed in detail, together with the impact of suburbanisation on the spatial structure of social networks, but this process has a wider significance for understanding the internal fragmentation within the merchant community. Liverpool was 'a place to make money in, not to spend it'. In this respect it fared even worse than other cities because 'in no other place does acquired wealth leave it' with such alacrity, a trend reinforced by 'retirements' and a well-established tradition of withdrawing from business in later life to enjoy income from rentier investment. Commercial success was sometimes followed by the purchase of a country house as a principal residence, a deliberate emulation of the landed gentry and a gradual separation from the world of commerce and trade.[17]

This pattern of land acquisition was already evident from the late eighteenth century onwards, if not earlier, as Jane Longmore and Joseph Sharples have demonstrated, but it was reinforced by the high net profitability of specific Liverpool-based trades. One of the most prominent slave traders, Thomas Staniforth (1735–1803), purchased a cottage and farm in Broad Green which was subsequently enlarged as a 'county retreat', while Sir George Drinkwater, one of Liverpool's most prominent merchants in the early nineteenth century, whose family had been heavily involved in the slave trade for many years, inherited or purchased extensive estates at Wood Plumpton, Preston, and the Isle of Man. Thomas Earle was the eldest son of William Earle who had dealt 'not a little in the slave trade, which was then one of the most important of foreign enterprises, and considered so small a question of humanity'. He successfully extended his trading portfolio to include iron, oil, silk, and sugar, but also purchased 88 acres on Smithdown Lane in 1798 where he built Spekelands, 'a large house': he subsequently acquired part of the Allerton Hall Estate. This was indicative of a general trend as the wealth accumulated from the slave trade was invested increasingly in rural estates, as West African merchants sought to achieve 'gentility' and acceptance into aristocratic circles.[18]

From Longmore's sample of 201 merchants, 23 acquired property in the countryside around Liverpool (within easy commuting distance of the town's business centre), while 16 invested in county homes at a greater distance from the Mersey. But only one, Moses Benson, is known to have purchased in the 1780s a large estate in Shropshire, Lutwyche Hall, near Wenlock. Liverpool merchants, however, also played an important role in developing the profitable trade in palm oil with West Africa, the proceeds of which were devoted, in part, to the purchase of landed property. For example, Liscard Hall in Wallasey (originally called Moors Hey House) was built in 1832 for Sir John Tobin; his nephew, James, acquired Eastham House; and George Henry Horsfall's estate covered 671 acres. In 1857, Thomas Horsfall, MP for Liverpool between 1853 and 1868, purchased Ballamour Hall, Colton (Staffordshire), where he demonstrated considerable concern for the estate's inhabitants by endowing and erecting a village school and a reading room, as well as presenting the village with a closed burial ground. Both the Tobin and Horsfall families were heavily involved in the slave trade and were owners of estates in the West Indies which generated significant income. Their subsequent success in the palm oil trade was largely based on network connections developed at an earlier stage in their West African business.[19]

A more comprehensive overview of the extent of out-migration resulting from the acquisition of landed property can be derived from Orchard's sample of the most prominent members of the merchant community, of whom at least 41 (or 6.8 per cent) acquired landed property not only within Liverpool's immediate hinterland of Lancashire and Cheshire, but also in predominantly rural counties such as Herefordshire, Oxfordshire, Northumberland, Shropshire, and Westmoreland, as well as in North Wales, Scotland, and Ireland. If Chester and Southport had 'quite a colony of Liverpool gentlemen', both Robertson Gladstone and Robert Durning Holt acquired estates some distance from Liverpool (in the latter case at High Borrows, Westmoreland); the provision merchant Arthur J. J. Bamford and the steamship owner R. P. Houston established themselves 'in the Birmingham direction'; while Edward Bates, one of 'our principal shipowners', purchased Manydown Park in Hampshire before acquiring Gyrn Castle, near Holywell in Flintshire in 1853.[20]

At the same time, not a few of the 'numerous' and 'prosperous' Scotchmen in Liverpool had 'nice bits of land, or perhaps only mansions, beyond the Tweed'. This trend was already evident in the early nineteenth century, specifically in the case of the Gladstone family. John Gladstone (1764–1851), the shipowner and corn and sugar merchant, bought a Scottish estate at Fasque in 1829 which later became the family home; Robert Gladstone (1773–1835), his brother, specialised in trade with India, but had 'Scotch estates sufficient to maintain the family's dignity'; while Thomas Steuart Gladstone, his eldest son, retired from the East India trade in 1851, after which he resided (until his death in 1882) 'on the beautiful estate of Capenort, Dumfriesshire, which he had purchased the year before. In the case of the general merchant, Alfred T. Parker, whose family came from Scotland, it was simply noted that he 'now has estates there', while the cotton broker James Smith (who resided at Dalmorton House, New Brighton) passed part of each year on his estate, Cragielands, Moffat, and served as a JP for Dumfriesshire. The West Africa merchant and shipowner Thomas Stanley Rogerson had been born in Liverpool in 1838, but had spent his early career in Edinburgh. He acquired a Scottish residence at Argaty, near Doune in Perthshire and, having caught a cold there, died in 1910 at the age of 72. The desire to utilise wealth accumulated through trade in order to acquire landed property in North Britain or close to their place of birth was not restricted to Scottish merchants: members of the Woodward family, which originally came from Worcestershire, had been involved in the corn trade in Liverpool since 1803, but more than one partner on retiring from the firm returned there, purchased land, 'and lived the country gentleman life which seems native to them all'.[21]

It could be argued that only a minority of the most prominent and wealthy merchants opted for a rural lifestyle. Within a national context, there is no consensus on the extent of land acquisition by successful merchants and 'captains of industry' before 1914. According to Rubinstein, relatively few wealthy entrepreneurs purchased land on a large scale (over 2,000 acres), but recent research has suggested that almost 25 per cent of elite businessmen had land with a median value exceeding £250,000 and their acquisition of landed wealth was 'considerable' and positively correlated with total wealth. In fact, the data selection methodology adopted by Orchard favoured the inclusion of large-scale residential rural residences acquired by Merseyside merchants, whereas obituary evidence suggests that the purchase of landed estates was a widespread phenomenon. Over 70 per cent of the merchants in the MLP sample had acquired properties at death beyond the borders of Merseyside, with the Lake District, North Wales, Cheshire, and Scotland the favoured destinations for those who sought rural relocation. In most cases their estates were not extensive, perhaps because, like the 'prosperous Liverpool merchant' James Cropper, whose estate at Dingle Bank was 'a field' of 30 acres, they had noted the warning in Adam Smith's *Wealth of Nations* against the 'great individual accumulation of property'. Other merchants preferred overseas locations for investment or retirement far removed from the daily practices of Liverpool's commerce and trade, including Madeira, the USA, Yokohama, and Zurich (although in the latter case, Hans Gaspard Schintz, of Schintz & Co., had been born there).[22]

A further indication of the increasing tendency of Liverpool merchants to acquire rural retreats, although seldom on a very grand scale, can be derived from the private commissions undertaken by Edward Kemp, the first 'fixed' superintendent of Birkenhead Park (who had been appointed in 1843 on the recommendation of Joseph Paxton). According to *The Gardeners' Chronicle*, the publication in 1850 of *How To Lay Out A Small Garden* would lead to 'an entire reformation in the decoration of middle class gardens and pleasure grounds': it succeeded John Claudius Loudon's *Suburban Gardener and Villa Companion* 'as the most prominent horticultural book of its time and enabled Kemp to become one of the most influential landscape designers in the North West and nationally. The book was aimed at property owners with land ranging from 'a quarter of an acre to thirty acres in extent', but by the time of the second edition in 1858 the upper limit had been extended to 100 acres. Kemp recognised that railway construction and road improvements had enabled a 'town merchant' to relocate himself up to 30 miles from town, thereby benefiting from 'country air and rural pastimes'. Although his client base was broad, including extensive landscaping work at Leighton Hall, Montgomeryshire (1855–56) for the Liverpool banker John Naylor, many of his commissions came from merchants and businessmen who had acquired enough wealth to establish a suitably impressive residence in the countryside (Figure 11.1). Unsurprisingly, a good number of them were Liverpool merchants. From a total of 50 known private commissions between 1848 and 1859, at least 17 of the clients were from the mercantile community (and a further three were members of the Historic Society of Lancashire and Cheshire). They included Alan Higgins (an iron merchant), Adam Hodgson (a cotton broker), and John Owens Johnson (a merchant). Some of the estates were extensive: in Cheshire, for example, Stanacres, which had been acquired by the timber merchant Owen Jones, included a lake covering 1.5 acres, while Norley Hall which Kemp landscaped for the wine importer Sam Woodhouse (1855–56) had large grounds and a substantial model farm. Nor was Kemp's work confined to Lancashire and Cheshire. Underscar Manor at Underskiddar, Cumbria, was developed for the Liverpool merchant William Oxley. It was designed in the Italianate style by Charles Verelst (formerly Reed) of Birkenhead and built between 1856 and 1863, but its extensive gardens were landscaped by Kemp: according to a contemporary newspaper report, it stood in 'its own grounds of many acres and from its graceful design forms a prominent landmark on the landscape.' Kemp was not the only landscape gardener practising on Merseyside at that time, but details of his commissions provide an invaluable source for reassessing the scale

Figure 11.1 Leighton Hall, Welshpool, Montgomeryshire (undated postcard)

of rural settlement. They also demonstrate that a narrow focus on large estates (of 2,000 acres or more) fails to capture the general pattern of urban-rural mobility, although some of the properties acquired by Liverpool merchants were extensive.[23]

But out-migration had wider consequences for Liverpool's economy, including a potential loss of capital investment, a reduced demand for service provision and a fracturing of existing network contacts. In some cases, the acreage of landed estates purchased by merchants and businessmen was extensive and the amount of capital investment very considerable. The banker and slave trader Thomas Leyland (c.1752–1827) failed to buy land during his lifetime, but made provision in his will for his accumulated wealth (exceeding £327,000) to be used for 'delayed-action gentrification'. The ultimate beneficiaries were the three sons of his niece, Dorothy Naylor, who proceeded to purchase large estates in line with Leyland's instructions: over 17,000 acres at Haggerston Castle in Northumberland, approximately 11,000 acres in Montgomeryshire and Shropshire (including Leighton Hall, purchased by Charles Leyland in 1845 for £85,503 12s 7p and given to John Naylor and his wife as a wedding present), and over 8,000 acres at Hooton Hall, Cheshire (for 82,000 guineas, with a further 50,000 guineas spent on extensive improvements, including a vast, ornate orangery, a racecourse, a polo field, and a heronry). Perhaps inevitably, their involvement with the world of banking and business quickly ceased. It is difficult to represent this process as a re-feudalisation of elements of the merchant community, but the transfer of capital out of Liverpool was considerable, as was the case in all other instances of purchases of large rural estates. There were differing motives behind the acquisition of a large estate or country house, a decision influenced by the desire for a 'pretty solitary place' or the need to diversify an investment portfolio, but the choice of a retirement location was an important aspect of the life cycle strategy of the Victorian middle class. What is clear, however, is that a decision to remove a family's principal residence to Cheshire or other rural areas led to a reduced presence in Liverpool. There was an increasing trend towards gentrification after the mid-nineteenth century and evidence in some cases of deliberate attempts to emulate the landed aristocracy, whether in relation to the 'aristocratic aspirations' of their residences or their preference for a lifestyle prominently displayed in contemporary publications. Even when fancy dress balls were held in aid of public charities, the choice of costume by leading merchants and their wives reflected an implicit emulation of the Court and the aristocracy. In March 1844, for example, the list of participants included the merchant and agent George G. Hornby dressed 'as a Russian noble'; the broker Harold Littledale of Liscard Hall, Wallasey, as Maurice, Elector of Saxony (c.1550); and Mrs. A. G. Kurtz as the Duchess of Devonshire in a court dress from the reign of George II.[24]

According to Orchard, a small proportion of Liverpool's 'commercial men' had always been 'welcome guests in county families' and this was notably higher than in other trading centres. Indeed, the preference for a country residence is unmistakeable. The general merchant Gustav Christian Schwabe (1813–97) had moved in the 1870s to Yewden Manor, near Henley, while about the same time the timber merchant Peter Owen acquired the Elms in Great Sutton (in the Hundred of Wirral) with its 100 acres. By the early 1890s, the merchant Charles Langton, whose family had played an important role in the development of Liverpool from the beginning of the nineteenth century, was ranked 'among the landed gentry of Great Britain'; the shipowner Sir Thomas Brocklebank of Springwood, Allerton, and Greenlands, Irton, Cumberland, had 'the tastes of a stalwart active country gentleman'; and the accountant J. S. H. Banner preferred 'the more vigorous pursuits open to a country gentleman with ample means and master of his own time'. But these cases were symptomatic of a broader trend: the dried-fruit merchant John Twigge was not interested in entering public life, because he had 'so much of the country gentleman in his blood' and preferred to spend time at Upton where his grounds contained 'some remarkably fine elms' and a pear tree, known as 'The Master's Own' which produced fruit of 'unsurpassed excellence'.[25]

The Harrison Line owned over 70 ships, but by 1914 most of the family members responsible for its management and commercial success had demonstrated a clear preference for a rural lifestyle: James Harrison retired in 1880 to live on his country estate at Dorden, Tunbridge Wells, while both Heath and Thomas Fenwick Harrison departed 'for the shires' in the 1890s. Frederick James Harrison, in particular, revealed a continuing fascination for rural affairs: by 1887 he was a substantial landowner in Lancashire; in 1889 he rented Arrowe Hall on the Wirral; and in 1892 purchased Maer Hall in Staffordshire from the pottery manufacturer George Davenport with over 3,000 acres of prime land for £90,000. Other members of Liverpool's merchant community sought to emulate the pastimes of Britain's elite. George Warren, a 'wealthy' shipowner, not only rode with the Cheshire Hunt, but shared other interests with members of the aristocracy: he was a big game hunter, a tarpon fisherman, and a competitive yachtsman. But he was not alone in his preference for out-door sports, since the sugar refiner Colonel H. J. Robinson purchased an estate at Woolton in Shropshire to 'gratify his natural disposition for hunting'. The cotton broker and shipowner George Melly MP (1830–94) celebrated shooting 'twenty or thirty brace of grouse a day'; the start of the season in 1861 was heralded as 'What a day for ye grouse'; and Rathmullan House in Donegal was regarded as the 'third best in the Kingdom' for woodcock shooting. Richard Durning Holt could always find 'a bright spot' at a time when neither business nor politics were running smoothly because 'the coming grouse season should be well above average'. Other members of Liverpool's merchant community sought to raise their social profile by acquiring landed estates: the broker George Edwin Taunton, who died at St. Mawes in Cornwall in 1894, had previously acquired Cobham Hall in Stanningfield, Sussex, and was regarded as a significant land and house owner; the timber merchant William Hollis Anthony became a 'landed proprietor' who employed ten men and two boys on his estate of 260 acres at Wynches in Hertfordshire; while the merchant and shipowner Sir James Rankin, of Rankin, Gilmour & Co., acquired 3,300 acres in Herefordshire (at Lyston Court and Bryngwyn) since his tastes and habits 'were largely those of a country gentleman'. Others, such as the shipowner Samuel G. Sinclair, were simply content with having 'many aristocratic Scotch connections.'[26]

To date, no attempt has been made to analyse the scale of selective out-migration and its significance for the operation of Liverpool's economy and its merchant community. Despite a contemporary claim that the social status of merchants was measured 'by the extent of their broad acres', it is generally assumed that the business elite favoured the acquisition of 'pocket county estates' within easy reach of the city centre. In some cases, additional purchases of land were undertaken as a defensive mechanism, for example, 'to prevent the erection of small cottages' on land adjacent to an existing estate. Very few admitted to sharing Arthur Bibby's love of hunting and racehorses, although the shipowner Edward Percy Bates could be met 'in connection with polo and every fashionable amusement' and the merchant George Curzon Dobell (who died in January 1914 at the age of 83) was 'formerly well known as the owner of famous racehorses'. In the early 1890s the family of the cotton broker and shipowner Robert Durning Holt spent most of August and September at High Borrows 'to get ready for the Twelfth' and to enjoy the shooting. Sometimes, however, the outcome of blood sports was unfortunate: the merchant S. Sandbach Parker (of Sandbach, Tinne & Co.), who had been suffering from heart disease, died suddenly in 1905 'while having a day's shooting'.[27]

A detailed analysis of merchant members of the elite Wellington Club whose probate records could be traced within the period 1860 to 1918 suggests that a preference for a rural lifestyle was not unusual. From a sample of 141 merchants and businessmen, 31 (21.9 per cent) acquired country estates far removed from Liverpool, 8 (5.6 per cent) established themselves as members of the local gentry in Lancashire or Cheshire, while 16 (11.3 per cent) relocated to other urban centres, often to prestigious addresses in London, such as Kensington and Chelsea. The rectifier and distiller Frederick Augustus Williamson had his principal residence in London, but he was still listed in Walford's *County Families* as a member of the landed gentry because he owned 2,070 acres of land in Wavertree with a yearly value of £3,960. The members of the Wellington Club undoubtedly represented the elite of Liverpool society, but it is more than likely that other, less wealthy merchants were just as interested in purchasing a rural retreat, but on a smaller scale. However, only a minority kept a residential presence in Liverpool. The shipowner Sir Thomas Brocklebank of Irton Hall, Cumberland, continued to reside at 13 Abercromby Square and the brewer, Sir Andrew Barclay Walker, retained his family home at Gateacre Grange following the purchase of Osmaston Manor in Derbyshire in 1884 at a cost of £250,000, which also included a model village, the advowson, and all the furniture, a move which entitled him to be regarded as 'a great county gentleman' (Figure 11.2).[28]

In most cases out-migration represented the severance of regular ties with Merseyside since their newly acquired estates were not within commutable distance of Liverpool. It also led to the assumption of new public responsibilities far removed from Merseyside. For example, the oil importer J. B. Adams became a parish councillor for Gresford, Denbighshire; the banker Christopher J. Leyland was a JP for Montgomeryshire (although he subsequently took up residence at Haggerston Castle, Beal, Northumberland); the shipowner John Rankin became a JP for Westmorland and was appointed High Sheriff in 1910, following in the footsteps of the Liverpool paper merchant and mill owner James Cropper, who had been appointed to the same position in 1875 and subsequently elected MP for Kendal (1880–85). Indeed, a county estate was sometimes a precondition for winning a Parliamentary seat outside Liverpool. The timber

Figure 11.2 Osmaston Manor, Derbyshire (undated postcard, c. 1895)

merchant John Roberts represented Flint Borough, but after he retired his son, John Herbert Roberts, was returned in 1892 for Denbighshire West: while trading in Liverpool, both his father and grandfather had resided for over 50 years at Bryn Gwenalla. The stock and share broker G. H. F. Robertson was a JP for Denbigh, the High Sheriff for Denbighshire and a member of the Denbighshire Standing Joint Committee. The brewer Sir Andrew Barclay Walker was not atypical in demonstrating a financial and representational commitment to his new locality: after acquiring Osmaston Manor he proved to be 'extremely generous', donating £1,000 towards the rebuilding of the Derbyshire Royal Infirmary and serving on seven local committees.[29]

The fact that some Liverpool merchants assumed important representative positions, whether as a JP, a high sheriff, or a deputy lieutenant, in the areas where their rural estates were located suggests that the primary motive for out-migration was to achieve acceptance into gentry society and to become members of what has been termed the 'aristocratic-bourgeois club'. English landed society and gentry status were closely associated with the historic importance of these positions, whose incumbents were appointed directly by the Crown. The oath of confirmation for justices of the peace required them to swear that they possessed an estate in the county or riding where they would act and the lack of remuneration (apart from reimbursement for travelling expenses) reinforced the expectation that they would be men of substance. The appointment of high sheriffs (for one year only) was regulated by an historic process of nomination and selection by the Sovereign, but they had to cover themselves the cost of ceremonial uniforms and court dress. Even after reform legislation clarified and consolidated the role of justices of the peace and some of their traditional powers were transferred to other bodies, they remained men of 'great power and influence', while high sheriffs and deputy lieutenants continued to operate as acknowledged representatives of Royal influence and the landed establishment. By acquiring rural estates and by fulfilling the responsibilities of these important positions, Liverpool merchants demonstrated clearly that their prime objective was integration within landed society, irrespective of whether they retained an interest in commerce and trade or not.[30]

The motives for purchasing rural property were undoubtedly varied and individual case studies reveal the importance of different strategies whether in relation to social acceptance, political responsibilities, social climbing, family building, or simply enjoyment (invariably in the context of rural sports, specifically shooting). But landownership retained its attractive power. It could be argued that the acquisition of a landed estate or a country house was a lifecycle phenomenon which reflected the choice of a different, but socially superior, lifestyle, after retirement from a competitive business environment or as a consequence of changes in company ownership. For example, James Jenkinson Bibby (1813–1897)—also known as 'Bybee'—had served as the Liverpool office manager for the family's shipping line for many years but opted to retire to Shrewsbury after Frederick Leyland acquired majority control in 1873. Indeed, the acquisition and refurbishment of country houses continued after the turn of the century. The shipowner and art collector Ralph Brocklebank had Haughton Hall in Cheshire rebuilt (1891–94) by the architect J. F. Boyle, while Burton Manor, the last country house on the Wirral to be reconstructed in 'the grand manner', was completed in 1904 for W. E. Gladstone's third son, the Liverpool businessman and estate manager, Henry Neville Gladstone, together with his wife, Maud, the daughter of the armaments manufacturer Lord Rendel, with the extensive gardens designed by Thomas Mawson. Even when the decision to purchase a rural residence was the result of commercial success, it accelerated the process of disengagement from the merchant community. Duncan Graham (1826–1901), the senior partner of Graham, Rowe, and Co., South American merchants, took up residence in Willaston on the Wirral in the early 1860s (having purchased the Lydiate in 1856): he endowed the church; erected a vicarage; and made 'generous subscriptions' to the Village Institute and the National School. Apparently, there was no better model of 'what every country squire should be' and on his death there was 'scarcely a cottage home where tears have not been shed to his memory'. Moreover, in terms of understanding the value system which underpinned the maintenance of commercial enterprise, the sons of merchants sometimes aspired to a way of life far removed from that of their traditional commercial upbringing. James Henry Stock, for example, whose father had 'accumulated a handsome fortune' as a cotton broker, studied law and became an army officer before being elected for the Walton Division of Liverpool in 1892, but he had 'always lived the life of a country gentleman' and was 'an ardent follower of field sports', including shooting, fishing, and foxhunting. Two of the sons of Sir Andrew Barclay Walker became highly successful horse breeders, while his eldest son, Peter C. Walker (who inherited the baronetcy and assumed management responsibility for his father's brewing empire), had little time for politics and public life, but pursued his passion for big game hunting, whether in Assam, Ceylon, Colorado, or Norway. He became a member of the Royal Yacht Squadron and, on one occasion, spent six months in the south seas aboard a 30-foot coasting schooner. But even the daughters of Liverpool merchants were encouraged to take up rural interests. Miss Susan Dora Cecilia Schintz, born in 1869 to Hans Gaspard Schintz and his wife, a merchant specialising in the extraction and marketing of Chilean nitrates, was gifted by her parents in 1906 Thickthorn Estate in Kenilworth, Warwickshire, where she established a highly successful stud for hackney horses.[31]

The wider cultural and social significance of involvement in rural sports, particularly foxhunting and grouse-shooting, is difficult to establish, whether in reshaping existing commercial networks through the acquisition of upper-class connections or in influencing the attitudes and career expectations of subsequent generations of Liverpool merchant families. Most rural sports represented a 'display of ruling class power': foxhunting was a 'ritual of social class' and a performance of symbolic significance; while the visit of Queen Victoria and Prince Albert to the Atholl Estate in 1844 helped to popularise rural sports, including grouse-shooting among the gentry, by providing an explicit Royal endorsement. Even in the mid-1880s, when the rural landscape in some areas of the country was being rapidly transformed by agricultural improvements and the straightening of fences, it was claimed that the 'votaries' for hunting continued to increase, despite the 'sneers of overburdened intellects', because 'its health giving, invigorating, and manly unselfish influences are more and more appreciated'. However, even staunch supporters had reservations about the growing practice of 'heading and badgering cubs and foxes to death', particularly if it resulted in the countryside being stained with blood. Practical guidebooks on the art of shooting proved to be very popular from the late eighteenth century onwards, while the development of doubled-barrelled, breach-loading shotguns in the 1850s led to increased levels of participation and a keener sense of competition through rigorous scorekeeping.[32]

Within a Merseyside context, assessing the importance of rural blood sports for business networking remains problematic in the absence of membership data for some of the 'country' hunts in Cheshire and South Lancashire. In the early decades of the nineteenth century the Liverpool Hunt Club was supported by 'leading gentlemen of equestrian proclivities' and certainly included prominent members of the mercantile community: it was 'famous far and wide', with 'good riders, good horses, and good days', while the squires who dominated the Cheshire Hunt were 'old-fashioned English gentlemen'. But the Royal Rock Beagle Hunt, founded in 1845, offers evidence of their wider networking role. Of the 67 initial members, 56 (83.5 per cent) came from the mercantile community; over half of them were residents of Rock Ferry (or New Ferry); and 24 travelled from Liverpool and Bootle to participate in the hunts. Annual membership was four guineas, payable in advance. When out with their hounds, members were required to wear the Hunt's uniform: green coats and white breeches. During the hunting season they were all 'brother beaglers', while 'off time' was often spent together at other sporting events, including golf, tennis, rowing, and athletic pursuits.[33]

The Royal Rock Beagle Hunt was founded by prominent Merseyside merchants, unlike more established rural sports which continued to be dominated by the aristocracy and gentry, where networking operated in a different context. As Huggins has emphasised, upper class rural sports have seldom been the focus of academic research, although important contributions have been made on the history of foxhunting, supplemented, in some cases, by narratives on local hunt clubs. Grouse-shooting has attracted even less attention, despite a plethora of contemporary guidebooks on 'gunning gear', the locating of birds (including pheasant, wood pigeon, and other game), and detailed advice to 'young shooters'. The rapid commercialisation of grouse hunting from the 1850s onward involved the laying out of extensive estates specifically for letting purposes even on the eastern side of the Island of Lewis in the Outer Hebrides, because driven grouse-shooting became a popular and fashionable sport for wealthy patrons who could exploit the expanding railway network to access distant locations. According to F. G. Afalo, it cost up to £1,200 a year to rent a grouse moor in Yorkshire, while the daily wage of 40 beaters was 4s each. The income which grouse-shooting generated was one factor in securing the survival of landed society at a time when agricultural prices were falling rapidly in the latter decades of the nineteenth century.[34]

No attempt has been made to quantify the growing popularity of either fox hunting or grouse-shooting, specifically in terms of the level of participation by Merseyside businessmen and merchants. Orchard's 'memoirs of individuals' reveal that by the early 1890s over 34 per cent of his sample were involved in rural sports, although information on recreational pursuits was not always recorded. Golf was very much the most popular sport (59 per cent), followed by shooting (25.3 per cent), cricket (18.0 per cent), and hunting (9.6 per cent).[35] Pike's collections of contemporary biographies for Liverpool and Birkenhead, together with Wirral residents included in his Cheshire volume, published almost 20 years later, contain far fewer references to recreational activities; but 63.3 per cent of those for whom data is available had rural pursuits, including agriculture, horse racing, and riding. Shooting, however, was the most popular (38.3 per cent), followed by golf (15 per cent) and hunting (11.6 per cent).[36]

The Liverpool press provided detailed coverage of the start of the grouse-shooting season, including the composition of shooting parties in North Ribbledale, the Clitheroe district, Westmorland, and North Wales, and published a satirical comment by a Frenchman on what was claimed to be a 'favourite pastime' ("What a fine day; let us go out and kill something"). In 1891, for example, 'a large contingent of Liverpool men' was departing from Merseyside for Scotland, Lancashire, and Yorkshire on the eve of the start of the season, while four years later Liverpool furnished 'a numerous contingent of sportsmen' who traversed the northern moors in search of their prey. Prominent members of Merseyside's mercantile community were clearly attracted to rural sports, specifically shooting and hunting. The India merchant Robert Gladstone was 'fond of many outdoor sports' and had 'shot grouse for many years'; the shipowner and broker Thomas Hughes Jackson was 'well-known with the Cheshire hounds'; while the shipowner and director of the British and Eastern Shipping Company, William Walter Kellock of Highfields, Audlem (Cheshire), listed hunting and shooting as his principal recreations, although he also bred short horns and shire horses. His brother, Charles Walford Kellock, the owner of the extensive Highfields Estate, had identical sporting interests and was the owner of the famous short-horn cow, 'Sarah'.[37]

Shooting played a central role in the lives of both the rich and poor across large swathes of the British countryside, while foxhunting (specifically the custom of holding an annual hunt ball) offered a framework for forging alliances, making marriages, and strengthening economic ties. Each hunt was distinctive: its area was well defined; its members wore a distinctive

No. 7.

MOSTYN HOUSE SCHOOL : PARKGATE : CHESHIRE.
(THE BEAGLE KENNELS).

Figure 11.3 Mostyn House School, Parkgate: Cheshire (The Beagle Kennels) (undated postcard, c. 1910)

uniform; and they often had an established list of hunting songs (some of which had a long-standing local significance). Membership was self-reinforcing and the network links that were established helped to strengthen social cohesiveness. The available evidence suggests that an increasing proportion of Merseyside's merchants enjoyed participating in fashionable rural sports, specifically foxhunting and grouse-shooting, and some of them sent their sons to local schools, such as Mostyn House School in Parkgate, because they had their own beagle pack (Figure 11.3). Interest that was fostered by reports by specialised sporting journalists in local and national newspapers and the publication of a range of magazines aimed at elite members of rural society, such as *The Field*, *The New Sporting Magazine* (1831), *The County Gentleman*, *Baily's Magazine of Sports and Pastimes*, *Baily's Hunting Directory*, *Sporting Pictorial*, and *The Sportsman* (some of which were published as popular anthologies). By the mid-1860s, *The Liverpool Mercury* included a regular column on 'Sporting Intelligence', which on one occasion highlighted the importance of Melton Mowbray as the 'great metropolis of foxhunting'. Moreover, this growing popularity of blood sports took place at a time when they were facing mounting opposition, whether from farmers worried about the lack of consideration for their land and crops or members of the Society for the Prevention of Cruelty to Animals. When the mayor of Birkenhead at a branch meeting of the society in April 1888 claimed that even 'the fox liked the sport' he provoked outrage amongst its members which led to letters to the press: 'I cannot believe the man exists who has not felt for one moment some shame and horror as he has gazed upon the spectacle of a poor animal struggling to get away from the savage dogs and the still more brutal animals called courtesy men', whose behaviour displayed 'not an atom of manliness'. But for some members of the mercantile community rural sports not only provided

Chester, A Meet at Eaton Hall.

Figure 11.4 Chester, A Meet at Eaton Hall (undated postcard, c. 1910)

enjoyment, they offered an opportunity to share recreational activities with the local aristocracy, including the Duke of Westminster at his regular 'meet' at Eaton Hall (Figure 11.4), Cheshire, or the prominent members of the Tarporley Hunt (founded in 1762), such as Sir Philip Egerton of Oulton Park and Thomas Cholmondeley, First Baron Delamere. Sporting magazines often carried portraits of members of the aristocracy as masters of hunts, such as the Hon. William Ernest Duncombe, M.P. (the Bedale Hunt) and the Earl of Bessborough (the Buckhounds). Grouse-shooting retained its elite profile until after the end of the First World War, when efforts were made to broaden its appeal to men of more limited means. Moreover, as active participants in rural sports Merseyside merchants were able to cultivate reciprocity by inviting friends to join them ('if you come you need only bring your gun') and to use their trophies from grouse-shooting as part of a cultural gift economy (as was the case with the cotton merchant George Melly).

The wider implications of participation in blood sports for networking, social mobility, and integration within the elite circles of rural society are difficult to assess. But for those merchants who moved away from Merseyside, in part to enjoy their country pursuits more effectively, it was another factor in the process of physical and social distancing from the commercial world where they had made their fortunes. According to the Birkenhead brewer and amateur historian H. K. Aspinall, hunting closely resembled 'the wonderful institution of freemasonry; in that it so frequently engenders a lifelong intimacy'.[38]

Confessional Fragmentation and the Religious Divide

In a context in which confessional affiliation remained a major determinant of social action, so-called 'inter-denominational' clubs and societies offered important opportunities for networking across well-defined religious and political boundaries. But the religious background of potential business partners continued to play a role in constructing networks of reciprocity and obligation while reflecting visible and persistent differences within Liverpool's merchant community in general. Like other major urban centres, Liverpool had a wide range of church denominations, including a strong non-conformist tradition and confessional affiliation remained an important reference point, particularly for in-migrant merchants seeking to establish themselves within the local business community.[39] But extensive in-migration from Ireland, Scotland, and Wales, as well as from overseas, in the nineteenth century reinforced the diversity of the port-city's denominational profile. Prior to 1914, Liverpool had at least 415 churches and separate mission halls covering all the main faiths, including the Church of England (105), Roman Catholicism (40), Wesleyan Methodism (28), Primitive Methodism (19), and Calvinistic Methodism together with Welsh Presbyterianism (20). In addition, there were 20 Congregational and 20 Baptist congregations. It also catered for a range of smaller denominations, including the (Swedenborgian) New Church, founded in 1835, and the Liverpool Lodge of the Theosophical Society which was established shortly after the Society's formation in 1875. In addition, there were churches where 'numerous foreign residents', whether from China, Germany, Greece, Sweden (Figure 11.5), or Norway, continued to celebrate their own religions, and a mosque was opened in 1889 at 8 Brougham Terrace for itinerant seamen and relatively well-to-do English converts.[40] In many cases, individual churches helped to preserve a form of community, specifically for in-migrants, and they served as focal points for the provision of charitable support and the delivery of other welfare activities.[41]

Although it is difficult to quantify, the level of involvement in religious affairs by merchants and their families was very considerable. In 1851, approximately 10 per cent of the total population in

Figure 11.5 Gustaf Adolfs Kyrka (Scandinavian Seamen's Church), Liverpool (photograph by Jan Wallin)

Table 11.2 The confessional affiliation of Liverpool merchants, c.1900 (in per cent)

	Non-conformist	*Anglican*	*Other*	*Sample Size*
Legion of Honour	65.4	21.8	12.7	55
Cotton Exchange	40.0	46.6	13.3	15
Commerce	48.0	40.0	12.0	25

Sources: B. Guinness Orchard, *Liverpool's Legion of Honour* (Birkenhead, 1893); J. Wallace Coop and Seymour Taylor, *Bulls and Bears. Cartoons of the Members and Ring Traders of Liverpool Cotton Exchange (reprinted from 'the Liverpool Courier')* (Liverpool, 1908); William Thomas Pike, *Liverpool and Birkenhead in the Twentieth Century: Contemporary Biographies* (Brighton, 1911)

England and Wales was non-conformist, but even at the turn of the century over half of the elite business community in Birmingham and Manchester belonged to dissenting congregations.[42] The biographical data for Liverpool's merchant community, despite a limited sample size, indicate that non-conformists played a similar, if not greater, role on Merseyside, although Anglicans were more prominent amongst members of the Cotton Exchange (Table 11.2).

A number of Roman Catholics were actively involved in the maritime business community in the late eighteenth century, but only three were listed amongst the ranks of elite merchants a century later despite the scale of Irish immigration.[43] In fact, almost all denominations attracted adherents from the merchant community. The Canning Street Presbyterian Church (Free Church of Scotland) was supported by 'well-to-do leading Caledonians'; by the 1870s and 1880s the Congregational Chapel in Wavertree included 'more people of wealth and importance than ever before'; while a number of prominent merchants and shipowners, including Bryce Allan and David Ramsay, were regular members of the Fairfield United Reformed Church. The Welsh Calvinistic Church in Seacombe represented a gathering of 'suburban swelldom', including many merchants and traders, while the cotton merchant Hans Kern, who had been born in Hanover in 1861, was a trustee and churchwarden of the German Lutheran Church.[44] Some of the most 'famous names' from the merchant community were Unitarians; a number of Congregational Churches were attended regularly by Merseyside's social elites, while the existence of many 'large and prosperous Presbyterian churches' was due almost entirely to the financial support of prominent Scots businessmen.[45]

Merchants played a pivotal role in the founding of new churches, particularly in the expanding suburban areas where 'new structures in this class are infinitely more numerous than those belonging to any other'. By 1846, the general merchant (and banker) William Potter owned more than 140 acres of prime building land in Birkenhead, although he continued to reside in Everton. As 'a zealous but moderate-minded Churchman', he paid, largely from his own funds, for the construction and fitting out of two impressive local churches, St. Anne's in Birkenhead and Christchurch in Oxton (Figure 11.6). But their completion was delayed by Potter's bankruptcy following the collapse of the railway mania, although it was noted in *The Liverpool Mail* following his death in 1866 that he 'retained almost to the last the sanguine elasticity of his youth'. In 1854 Charles MacIver 'warmly seconded' the foundation of a Presbyterian church in Bootle, not because he intended to become a member, but as an expression of his deep interest 'in the spiritual welfare of his servants'. The banker Pemberton Heywood was a major contributor to the construction costs of St. Mary's, West Derby, which was consecrated in 1856. Fairfield Presbyterian Church was built in 1864 at a cost of £3,200, a great deal of which was subscribed by four merchants: Bryce Allan, Alexander Balfour, John Graham, and John Reid. The cotton and iron merchant John Phillips Mather donated £8,000 towards the foundation of Christ Church, Bootle, in memory of his crippled daughter, Sophia, who had died in 1864, while

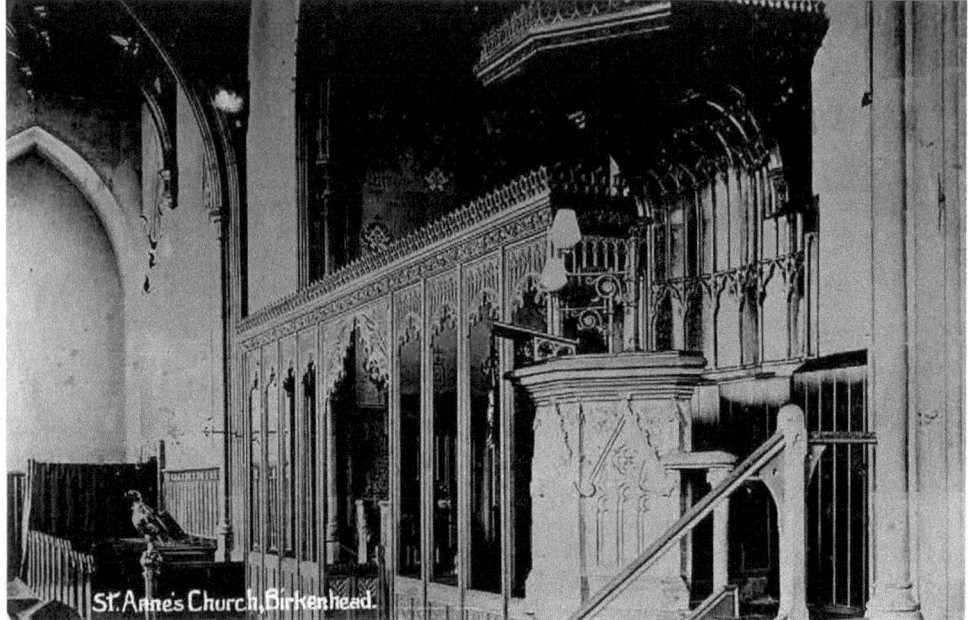

Figure 11.6 Interior of St. Anne's Church, Birkenhead (pre-1914 postcard)

the sugar refiner and wholesale grocer William Crosfield was a key figure in the development of the Edge Hill Congregational Church which opened in 1868 having obtained 'all that was required'. Five out of the six members of the committee convened in 1871 to take forward the establishment of a new parish church at Mossley Hill came from the merchant community.[46]

Some merchants in the first half of the nineteenth century are known to have purchased at considerable expense the advowson to Anglican churches, if only to strengthen their local standing and rights of patronage, but the level of collective involvement in the running and management of individual churches was extensive.[47] For example, approximately one third of the trustees of both Edge Hill Congregational Church and St. Paul's and Trinity Church in Bootle (designed for 'the Scotch population') were merchants who were 'well known in trade and industry'; 50 per cent of the deacons at the Pembroke Chapel in 1855 were from the merchant community; while 13 of the 34 subscribers to the Liverpool Unitarian Fellowship Fund in 1911 were involved in commerce and trade.[48] By leaving legacies to individual churches, members of the merchant community were able to sustain their charitable and welfare work, as was the case with the Liverpool Wesleyan Mission.[49]

It has been claimed that the early 1890s marked the 'high watermark' of church provision both on Merseyside and in Britain as a whole, since after that date attendance rates started to decline, except in the case of Roman Catholics.[50] However, throughout most of the nineteenth century, the religious commitment of individual merchants was widely known and much respected at a time when attendance at church services was the 'principal social activity' of the middle class and some merchants had an intense and personal relationship with the Bible.[51] In the early decades of the nineteenth century, the American merchant and shipowner James Cropper (1773–1841), a 'staunch Quaker until the end', always dressed in the 'quiet garb of their sect'. The wine broker Charlton Robert Hall, who had been born in New Orleans, was 'especially active in chapel building'; the commission merchant Thomas Allan Leigh was not only 'god (-) fearing' and the president of the local branch of the Evangelisation Society, but had achieved prominence 'among those gentlemen of good social position in Liverpool who are most vigorous in undenominational Christian work'. The prosperous sugar broker Edward Penbury Parry became 'the most devoted lay helper' to the Bishop of Liverpool, while the iron merchant and shipowner Samuel Stitt was 'chiefly engaged by religious and benevolent objects, mostly in connection with Presbyterianism'. The merchant J. Nicholas Stolterfoht, the son of a German in-migrant, interested himself 'in Church work'; while John Wilson, the president of the Liverpool Corn Trade Association in 1891–92, was well known as 'a stout churchman'. Philip Smith (1822–98), a provision dealer from Ireland, not only attended the Catholic Club suppers at the Adelphi Hotel, but recorded in his diary the deaths of Pope Pious IX and Cardinal Cullen of Dublin.[52]

The motives behind a strong and public commitment to religion amongst individual members of the merchant community were varied, given its wider role in Victorian and Edwardian society, its ethnic and regional affinities, and its significance in validating and sustaining social status. In some cases, however, there can be little doubt of the strength of their religious faith. Samuel Smith, who became an authority on the cotton market and was subsequently elected to Parliament, was 'an intense student of the Bible' with a strong belief in prayer, while the coal merchant Daniel Key Rea carried his Sunday religion 'through the week'. The Nonconformist merchant John Cropper, who died in 1884, lived 'a life of faith in the Son of God' and Presbyterians, in general, were regarded as 'intensely evangelistic'. Such commitment and religiosity were reinforced by local publications, whether in pamphlet or book form, which reveal the continued popularity of religious topics, including periodicals encouraging support for missionary work. But Donald Munro Drysdale, a highly successful timber and stave merchant, even resolved to become a preacher following the death of 'a dear friend': he began to distribute tracts after dusk and to address strangers on the street; in 1877 he held regular Sunday services during the winter months at Hengler's Circus; and large attendances were assured by the leafleting of over 50,000 households by an army of volunteers who also delivered hymnbooks. Yet, his firm remained 'continuously prosperous' and Drysdale's evangelism did not prevent it from becoming 'the largest business in the kingdom in his line'.[53]

Some merchants devoted a considerable amount of time to their churches. The cotton broker George Henry Brown attended the same Presbyterian church for 80 years; the sailing ship owner Edward Wrake Turner served a total of 53 years as the vicar's warden at St. Mary's Church, Garston; while the merchant Charles R. B. McGilchrist was the session clerk of Egremont Presbyterian Church for 20 years. The provision merchant Charles Pearson was a local preacher, Honorary Secretary of the Wesleyan Foreign Missionary Society for the Liverpool District and president of the Wallasey Sunday School Union, while Hartley Wilson, also a provision merchant, was a Sunday school teacher and superintendent of the Liverpool Wesleyan Mission for over 40 years.[54] Among the members and ring traders of the Liverpool Cotton Exchange prior to 1914 there were some who stood out in terms of their religious commitments: for example, Joseph Armstrong took 'a deep interest in the welfare of the Church of England'; Herbert Bickersteth was a prominent member of Trinity Presbyterian Church, Claughton, and 'ever mindful of the higher duties of life'; and John Coney had been a warden of St. James' Church, Birkdale, and was a 'staunch Churchman'.[55]

Active church membership had wider implications, not only in terms of social interaction, but also in relation to business networks. Presbyterians were regarded as being 'to the fore in every kind of business enterprise connected with the port', with a perceptively different class structure to that of the Congregationalists, while the Unitarians, 'the élite of Nonconformity', effectively controlled 'large sections of the city's economic life'.[56] Many churches offered a range of activities that were particularly attractive to in-migrants and newcomers, as well as to established residents, depending on their interests and confessional affiliation, which reinforced the importance of denominational networks for both social and business interaction.[57] Samuel Smith, who had arrived 'friendless' in Liverpool joined the Canning Street Society connected with the Presbyterian Church: it led him into 'kindly intercourse with active-minded and religious men', some of whom became successful merchants and politicians in their own right, while the first general manager of the Royal Insurance Company was recruited as a result of close connections with Rev. Dr. Baylee, the principal of St. Aidan's Theological College, Birkenhead. Indeed, for young men starting their business careers in Liverpool without capital or good friends, the best advice was to join and to become 'active, useful and respected in a large dissenting congregation'.[58]

Indeed, most churches, irrespective of their denominational affiliation, were a focal point for social interaction and networking. The Quakers founded a Liverpool Friends Institute in 1859 'for the purpose of Mutual Improvement and Social Intercourse'; the lives of many members of Trinity Princes Road Presbyterian Church of England were centred on the church which was always 'active and very full' with well-known citizens, particularly from the merchant community, worshipping there on a regular weekly basis. The Welsh Calvinistic Methodist Chapel in Chatham Street was a major social centre which offered a range of religious and educational functions throughout the week, while individual merchants are known to have joined various movements connected with church life. For example, the stock and share broker Edward Duncombe Fish was for many years a member of the Wesley Chapel in Higher Tranmere and particularly involved with the Wesley Literary Society where he read several papers on natural history.[59] In some cases, church-based network solidarity was reinforced by the fact that committee members met on a monthly basis at each other's homes. Moreover, because a great deal of welfare provision continued to be delivered along denominational lines there were regular opportunities for subscribers to assess the commitment and reliability of their fellow church members.[60]

The wide range of denominations was a potential cause of division within the merchant community with confessional affiliation a marker for visible and persistent distinctions. In Liverpool, the divide between church and dissent was like 'a wall harder than the wall of Balbus to leap over'. The separate denominations had very distinct profiles and even within the ranks of the Nonconformists there was a clear divide between the prosperous churches (such as Sefton Park Presbyterian and Ullet Road Unitarian) and other congregations. A great gulf existed between Orthodox dissenters in general and the Unitarians. Methodists, in the view of outsiders, were 'exclusive' and 'isolated', while the Unitarians from the Renshaw Street Chapel established a new Chapel Society in 1885 because of a need for 'a drawing together on all sides'. Nineteenth-century Congregationalism was characterised by 'firm cohesion', particularly in Liverpool, and Congregationalists and Baptists were 'reasonably friendly', but there was a distinct element of hostility towards the Wesleyans. The latter, however, as the largest Methodist denomination, witnessed the secession of smaller denominations between the 1790s and the 1850s, including the Methodist New Connexion, the Primitives, the Bible Christians, and the Free Methodists, while a group of younger Wesleyans, led by the 'fiery' Hugh Price Hughes, launched in 1885 a liberal newspaper (*The Methodist Times*) which challenged directly the social conservatism of the Wesleyans.[61]

Throughout the nineteenth century theological disagreements remained the cause of religious and cultural conflicts. Relations between members of the established churches, Protestant dissenters, and Roman Catholics continued to be acrimonious and even the census enumeration of religious denominations proved to be contentious. Apart from the Unitarians, at least until the 1860s, and smaller denominations, such as the New Church Swedenborgians, Nonconformity, in general, tended to sectarianism. The Independents, who had retained a firm grasp of Calvinist theology, were known for their 'rigorous evangelism', while evangelical imperatives led to the adoption by Congregationalists of a regional and national structure designed to unleash 'enthusiasm and fervour'. After 1850 Liberal Protestantism enjoyed a new lease of life with militant dissent reaching a peak in the 1870s and 1880s. In the 1860s and 1870s, the evangelical gospel of the Church of England was threatened by three new theological movements—ritualism, neologianism, and Keswick spirituality. If the Oxford Movement led to the revitalisation of Anglicanism, anti-Ritualism was regarded initially by J. C. Ryle, the first Anglican Bishop of Liverpool (1880–1900) and a 'thorough lover of Puritan theology', as part of as wider campaign to rejuvenate the established church. But it was co-opted subsequently by more militant evangelical elements. By contrast, the Catholic revival was based on the concept of the Catholic 'ghetto' as a reaction to persistent hostility and the need to articulate a separate sub-culture as a means of achieving a stronger sense of internal cohesion.[62]

There was a great deal of competition, even outright hostility, between the different denominations which was fuelled, at times, by sectarian violence, and attempts to achieve a greater degree of confessional unity often failed. It was claimed that the Sunday services connected with the Evangelistic Movement were not sectarian because preachers were drawn from all churchmen, including Independents, Presbyterians, Baptists, and Wesleyans, but it seldom achieved its objective. Similar pleas for greater unity between the various churches were made as a means of taking forward the work of the Liverpool Domestic Mission which had been established in 1859. The intention had been to secure support not from among the members of 'any one sect exclusively', but from all Christian churches. However, it failed to attract support and its success was very limited. The cotton merchant George Melly was forced to conclude that Orthodox and Unitarian 'will never pull together' and even reaching agreement on what hymns could be sung proved to be contentious and problematic, while John Hastings Ziegler, also a cotton merchant, was a consistent advocate of non-sectarian education, but progress was painfully slow at a time when denominational evangelism was increasingly dominant.[63]

At another level, relations between the Anglican Church and Liverpool's Jewish community were compromised by the extent of proselytising and antisemitism. The first synagogue in Liverpool was established in 1742, following earlier in-migration by Sephardi Jews from Spain and Portugal: by 1851 there were 159 households with 848 individuals, but a decade later the total number of residents had risen to almost 3,000. A great deal has been written about the development of Liverpool's Jewish community, but it is a narrative that focusses primarily on its institutional framework, the different places of worship, and the range of welfare, educational, and cultural associations, including the Liverpool Jewish Literary Society (1906), 'a choice and cultured circle'. The Anglo-Jewish Liverpool Hebrew Philanthropic Society had been founded in 1811, but the influx of new (largely Ashkenazi) migrants in the latter decades of the nineteenth century, many fleeing brutal pogroms in central and eastern Europe instigated by the Russian authorities, necessitated a local response, including the establishment of a Jewish Visitation Committee in 1884 and the Society for Temporarily Sheltering Poor Strangers of Jewish Faith in 1889. The growth and changing composition of the Jewish community in terms of ethnicity and religious practice led inevitably to disputes: a secession in 1838 was followed by the establishment in 1842 of the New Hebrew Congregation (as a breakaway from the Old Hebrew Congregation), a move that led to the 'utter discomfiture' of the 'nihilistic element' and a period of 'severe trial' for the parent community. But 'Hebrew pagans' remained within the fold 'only to attack Judaism the more readily'. Internal conflicts were reinforced by a growing disparity in wealth and social status between those who established successful careers in business or the professions and the majority who lived in extended families, dependent on employment in the service sector, often as tailors, butchers, and small-scale traders, or employees of other Jews. Indeed, the wealth differential within the Jewish community was aggravated significantly by the arrival on Merseyside of eastern European migrants, although the majority emigrated to the USA.[64]

The foundation in 1809 of the London Society for Promoting Christianity amongst the Jews signalled the start of a missionary commitment to convert practising Jews to Christianity. According to Scult, it was the first missionary organisation 'devoted exclusively to converting the Jews' (although with limited success). It enjoyed extensive support in high places, with Lord Shaftesbury serving as its President (1848–85) and the Archbishop of Canterbury as its sole patron. It was nothing short of a 'national project'; its average annual income in the late 1840s was approximately £28,000; and it raised funds from a considerable number of auxiliary branches. The Liverpool branch was established in 1819. Its annual meetings, whether in the Royal Amphitheatre or the Collegiate Institution, were always well attended with 'many ladies' amongst the audience, and its annual receipts amounted to around £750, although this was deemed 'small for this town' and prompted a suggestion to use missionary boxes. Most of the money was transferred to the London Society, which, in turn, covered the salary costs of missionaries. The conversion of Jews in Liverpool, as elsewhere, was taken seriously. Between 1841 and 1850 J. G. Lazarus (the appointed missionary and almost certainly a convert himself) witnessed 56 Jewish baptisms before his transfer to the society's Manchester auxiliary branch: his role was taken over temporarily by the Rev. Joseph Baylee of St. Aidan's Theological College, Birkenhead, until the appointment in 1852 of the Rev. David Jacoby Hirsch, a converted Jew and the minister of Liverpool's German Church. He had been ordained by the Bishop of Chester and then embarked on his 'good work' leading many Jews 'to a knowledge of our Lord'.[65]

Some Jewish organisations continue to condemn evangelistic missionary activities directed specifically at converting Jews to Christianity as antisemitic, while Claude J. G. Montefiore (1858–1933), the intellectual founder of Anglo-Liberal Judaism, consistently argued that antisemitism was not a problem in Britain. The views of some of the members of the Liverpool auxiliary branch are instructive in this context: the Jews were 'a peculiar people' and Liverpudlians were only doing their duty 'carrying back to the Jews the gospel we originally received from them'. Even if Liverpool stood out as a community where men had reflected 'greater credit to the Jews of England', the archetypal image of the Jew persisted as an 'old, decrepit and slouching individual with a long white beard reaching to his waist', while Christian teaching reinforced the myth of Jews as 'Jesus-killers'. Indeed, the fact that the Liverpool branch continued to receive substantial financial support, including a bequest of £1,500 in 1895 from the will of the sugar broker E. P. Parry, is indicative of a sustained commitment to convert Jews to Christianity. But such a strategy with its implicit antisemitism led by leading evangelical figures in the Church of England acted as a barrier to Anglo-Jewish initiatives: it also reinforced the hostility between the Liverpool's Jewish communities and the established church.[66]

Most other denominations adopted a similar strategy towards evangelical work as the Church of England, but without any antisemitic implications. Following the restoration of the hierarchy and the formation of the Liverpool diocese in 1850, the Catholic Church was desperate to meet the demand for priests created by the rapid increase in the Catholic, largely Irish-born, population; Methodists were enjoined to be 'Zealous for good works' and under the leadership of the Rev. Charles Garrett were committed increasingly to 'total evangelism'; while the Welsh revival at the start of the twentieth century meant that the Welsh Calvinistic Church in Princes Road was full with 'densely packed, visibly excited people'. Particularly in the expanding residential areas on both sides of the Mersey there was open competition for new adherents. The new Congregational Church in Oxton Road, Birkenhead, which was opened in 1858 (together with a school-house) had cost £5,475, but the 'hopes of sanguine pioneers' were not immediately realised: 'the field was being entered by the Baptist brethren, the United Presbyterians, and the Wesleyans, and, no doubt, their emulative activity retarded increase'.[67]

All too often, confessional fragmentation was compounded by theological tensions, serious doctrinal disputes, revivalism, and secessions, as was the case with Methodists in Liverpool and other Lancashire towns. The cohesion of the Baptist chapel in Byrom Street was disrupted by the departure of brethren who preferred 'a strict adherence to the Calvinistic system of theology'; St. Andrew's Church in Rodney Street catered primarily for Presbyterians who had migrated from Scotland to Liverpool, but persistent doctrinal disputes led to the suspension of its minister and the establishment of an alternative chapel in Bold Street; the Presbyterian Church of England suffered from deep-rooted, ecclesiastical differences culminating in the Disruption of the Church of Scotland in 1843, while Presbyterians in general were characterised by 'crippling disunity'.[68]

Between the 1830s and 1914, conflict between Protestantism and Roman Catholicism was the main religious issue in Liverpool, with the 'No Popery' campaign (1837–1844) and the riots of 1904 to 1909 'particularly vicious outbreaks of bigotry'. According to Neal, anti-Catholicism was 'endemic' in Victorian England at all levels of society and the reinstatement of the Catholic hierarchy in 1850 sparked an outburst of religious antagonism. When ratepayers in Birkenhead convened a meeting to protest about 'encroaching Romanism' on 26 November 1850 they were attacked by several thousand Irish navvies; military assistance was required to quell a further riot in 1859; and the Garibaldi riots of 1862 led to considerable property damage in central Birkenhead and numerous injuries to police constables and rioters in what became a major clash between Irish Catholic immigrants and those required to uphold law and order. At a national level, the late nineteenth century may well have witnessed the spread of 'religious doubt and secularism', but this was hardly the case in Liverpool or on Merseyside where the local press was 'instrumental' in creating and reinforcing the stereotyped perceptions of Irish Catholics. Colonel T. M. Sandys was elected M.P. for the Bootle Division in 1885, having been brought in for reasons that remained inscrutable for most electors, but his 'vehement' speeches were 'strongly Orange and Old Tory'. Indeed, the years immediately preceding the outbreak of the First World War witnessed a 'lamentable recrudescence of sectarian strife': the 'Protestant Crusade' was launched in 1901 by Pastor George Wise (1855–1917); the Orange Order (which had been revived in the 1840s) had approximately 20,000 local members by 1909 and its 'ill-judged' interference led to 'warfare' being waged on all non-Catholics at a time when collective violence was becoming increasingly common. The North End Domestic Mission Society was forced to terminate its work at its Bond Street Mission. The original building no longer met planning requirements, but the consolidation of Irish settlement in the surrounding areas had led to Protestant out-migration, while the 'recrudescence of the melancholy sectarian rowdyism which for years had been a disgraceful feature of Liverpool life' culminated in 'A Reign of Terror' in July 1909 which made it impossible to continue its work. In September 1912, approximately 250,000 Liverpool protestants, many of them members of the Orange Order, gathered in one of the city's parks to protest at the proposal for Irish Home Rule which was interpreted as a threat to their own supremacy. The demonstration may well have served a symbolic purpose, but Protestant Liverpool, according to Jackson, was 'deadly serious' and the vehemence of the crowd was unmistakeable.[69]

The extent to which doctrinal differences and confessional fragmentation affected Liverpool's merchant community and the networks which underpinned its operation is difficult to assess, but they almost certainly had a considerable impact on day-to-day operations. Individual merchants were fully aware of the significance of contemporary events: some were involved directly, as improvement commissioners, councillors, and justices of the peace, in trying to contain outbursts of religious hatred; and both Liverpool and Birkenhead were normally characterised by a 'high sectarian temperature'. In some cases, religious differences led to the termination of existing network links. For example, William Rathbone IV was 'disowned' by the Society of Friends in 1805 for heretical opinions, as was his son, William Rathbone V in 1829, who subsequently became a leading member of the Unitarian congregation at the Renshaw Street Chapel. The first son of the stock-broker Edward Bayliffe from Birkenhead was also officially disowned in 1856 for similar reasons.[70] In a city dominated by merchants and traders, a small number of Quaker and Unitarian families played a disproportionate role in commerce and politics with a high level of involvement in the voluntary sector, largely, but not exclusively, 'those of the Unitarian body to which they belong'. Their networks were based on denominational allegiance and reinforced by kinship ties and intermarriage: they also had a practical significance in terms of safeguarding and promoting business interests. But even in such cases differences of opinion on a range of issues could undermine group solidarity, as was the case in 1862 when a new headmaster, the Rev. Joshua Jones, was selected by the Board of Liverpool Institute at a meeting attended by Alfred Holt and other Unitarians (amongst others) where 'there was no small display of temper'.[71]

For some members of the merchant community confessional affiliation had a direct impact on their business activities. 'The Doctrine of Waste', as adopted by prominent Unitarians such as Alfred and Philip Holt, led to an emphasis in ship construction on economy and reliability in order to achieve the complementary goals of material and moral perfection. Some merchants regarded their religion as a private matter, others did not. The china merchant Thomas Matheson J.P. was one of Liverpool's 'gentlemen' who held 'evangelical opinions' on religious matters, but he lived 'in conformity therewith privately' and with his immediate associates. By contrast, the corn merchant and broker John Patterson J.P., reared in Ulster, 'the hotbed of uncompromising Protestantism', was a 'disputatious and unyielding' Presbyterian of extreme Christian views who apparently slept 'with a clearer conscience' than most other businessmen. William P. Lockhart, a Baptist who had taken over his father's firm involved in the Spanish trade, was so committed to Christian principles that he became an unsalaried pastor at a spacious tabernacle erected in Park Road, while the commission merchant Thomas Allen Leigh was for 22 years the honorary secretary to the Daily Noon Prayer Meeting and for 30 years was engaged in 'aggressive mission work' at New Brighton.[72]

For many Liverpool merchants, irrespective of their denomination, Christian principles were paramount: it seems reasonable, therefore, to infer that their business networks and commercial dealings reflected their deep-rooted religious beliefs. They also affected social interaction. For example, Patterson's clothes were 'ill-cut and shabby' while his sectarian prejudices 'and obstinate proclamation of extreme views made him rather unclubbable'. When Albert Crompton retired in 1901 from his position as Manager of the Ocean Steamship Company after nearly 20 years of service, Richard Durning Holt noted in his diary that he had always been 'a very kind and agreeable friend' in business, but he regretted that his 'peculiar views' (as a Positivist) in religion had prevented him from extending that friendship to social life.[73]

It would be premature to conclude that these examples were typical of the merchant community as a whole or that confessional fragmentation adversely affected the formation of network contacts across the religious divide. Despite the existence of 'strong evangelical cultures' in British shipping during the mid-Victorian period, the founding fathers of the Cunard Steamship Company operated outside the framework of their moderate evangelicalism within a business nctwork which included Low Church Anglicans, Episcopalians, and members of both the Free Kirk and the Church of Scotland.[74] Amongst the 13 members of the Mersey Docks & Harbour Board in the early 1900s whose church affiliation can be established, there were 9 non-conformists (three Congregationalists, three Presbyterians, two Unitarians, and one Methodist), two Anglicans, and one Catholic (the shipowner David Kennedy who served between 1883 and 1893).[75] Indeed, it is important to avoid exaggerating the significance of denominational identity as a determinant of business activity, particularly from the late nineteenth century onwards at a time of increasing secularisation and declining church attendance, given a tendency nationally for self-made non-conformists to convert to Anglicanism and the problems encountered by liberal-minded Catholics.[76] Only a quarter of the merchants listed in Orchard's *Legion of Honour* mentioned their religious commitment, while a mere 18 per cent of the members of the Cotton Exchange had a clear religious profile. Indeed, the proportion designated 'religious' in Pike's *Contemporary Biographies* fell continuously from 23.8 per cent for the cohort born in the 1850s to only 6.6 per cent in the case of those born in the 1870s.[77]

Even before the end of the nineteenth century, the level of spiritual and financial commitment was beginning to wane. Indeed, as early as the 1840s the Canning Street Presbyterian Church encountered difficulties in persuading elected elders to accept their responsibilities, while the cotton broker George Holt complained about poor attendance at the Renshaw Street Unitarian Chapel, particularly if the Sunday weather was poor or wet, while the number attending the afternoon service (at 3.30) had fallen off 'to practically nothing'. The position of some inner-urban churches became increasingly problematic as a result of suburbanisation, the loss of members, particularly from the merchant community, and wider patterns of socio-economic change. The Wesley Chapel in Stanhope Street was unable to retain its 'aristocratic character' after the 1890s; the Presbyterian Church in Myrtle Street was in a 'semi-state; and even the Unitarians suffered from relative decline after the turn of the century. The Wavertree Congregational Chapel had to cope with significant difficulties prior to 1914 as a result of the death or removal of members who had given long service. The death of prominent merchants, such as Samuel Stitt who 'did much for the United Presbyterian cause in and around Liverpool', had long-term consequences. But religious faith and a belief 'in the life everlasting' was threatened by scientific progress, not least by the work of Charles Darwin (1809–1882): in the opinion of Anne Holt, 'increasing scientific light seems to darken that precious hope'. In a wider context, the role of religion in determining electoral behaviour was gradually being undermined and even in the case of the Unitarians there was clear evidence of decline in the early twentieth century, particularly after the relocation of the Hope Street congregation from the centre of the city to suburban Ullet Road.[78]

Denominational allegiance was 'proverbially fluid' during this period: for example, contemporary diarists reported cases when friends or acquaintances changed churches, often because of the death of a child, financial difficulties, or for political advancement. But extensive population mobility as a result of in- and out-migration, suburbanisation, and residential relocation within specific districts had a direct impact on the membership of individual churches and reduced their importance as focal points for social and business networking. In some cases, attendance at religious services was irregular, since 'some friends came for a time and then left', but all churches registered a regular loss of members as individuals and families transferred elsewhere, migrated to other parts of the country, left for overseas destinations, or simply allowed their membership to lapse.[79] The cotton broker Samuel Smith benefited considerably from his membership of Canning Street Presbyterian Church on his arrival in Liverpool, but he was ultimately forced to sever his connections having relocated to Liscard Vale, New Brighton 'in a sweet situation embosomed in trees'. By joining the 'new Presbyterian cause formed at Egremont', however, his network links with his business friends at Canning Street became more attenuated, a process which was symptomatic of the wider impact of suburbanisation on the role of individual churches as focal points for the maintenance of network links. In other cases, out-migration from the urban core by middle-class members of church congregations, often prompted by a desire for upward social mobility or 'a more respected locality', led to chapels in the urban core being used for popular amusement with the pews 'filled with devoted worshippers at the shrine of sentimental singing, nigger dancing and gymnastics'.[80]

Political Divisions and Business Networks

Particularly in a port-city such as Liverpool religion and politics were often inseparable: according to the cotton merchant Samuel Smith, religion lay at 'the basis of the social edifice'; politics were rooted in religion; protestant prejudice affected to some degree all the non-conformist denominations; and sectarianism still remained the 'first interest' of electors in the early twentieth century.[81] Even in the context of increasing institutional pluralism at a national level, the division between Liberal Dissent and Tory Anglicanism became more structured after the 1850s at a time when rivalry between urban elites was reflected in intense inter-denominational competition and religious issues reinforced political conflicts. Both middle-class groups held a significant proportion of elite posts in local government and businessmen, in particular, demonstrated a 'high willingness' to support political parties, to stand for local election and to serve as magistrates, although there were noticeable differences between individual towns and cities. But non-conformists almost by definition tended to be politically liberal (except for prosperous middle-class Wesleyans), while Anglican 'churchmen' were generally Tory. Moreover, religious issues were at the forefront of general elections, whether in relation to disestablishment (1868 and 1885), or Irish home rule, after it was first put before Parliament in 1886 with non-conformist distrust of the Irish priesthood and deep-seated anti-Catholicism affecting electoral outcomes, as even some Unitarians turned increasingly Unionist.[82]

Merchants, as well as professional men, found it relatively easy to gain influence in local government because relevant business experience was especially valued as a useful qualification for office-holding, particularly during the second half of the nineteenth century which witnessed a noticeable increase in local government expenditure and an extension of municipal responsibilities. In some cases, businessmen consistently dominated local politics, whether in Glasgow, Salford, or Nottingham.[83] Although the mercantile class played an increasingly important role in representing civic interests during the central decades of the nineteenth century, there is evidence of a subsequent decline in their representational profile prior to 1914.[84] But a willingness to stand for local office and to play an active role in public life offered both individual and collective benefits. Individually, there were close network links between those involved in economic, political, and social leadership; a proven claim to local knowledge provided a platform for participation in national debates; and representational success at a local level could serve as a basis for a political career. Indeed, it has even been suggested that a collective dominance of local politics meant that councils sometimes acted as 'a mouthpiece' for business interests and elite groups were able to progress the construction of their concept of urban, social identity along agreed lines.[85]

A great deal has been written about the political history of Liverpool between the mid-nineteenth century and the outbreak of the First World War, but the nature and extent of merchant involvement in local administration has not been analysed in depth, nor its significance for business networking fully explored.[86] It is generally accepted that the local political arena was dominated by members of the commercial and professional classes who were 'among the wealthiest in the town'. Their precise role reflected a range of characteristics which were evident amongst elite groups not only in Liverpool, but in other major towns and cities, despite differences in the sectoral structure of their economies.[87] Perhaps, as a result of a reliance on an elite model of political representation, there has been a tendency in the case of Liverpool to underplay the significance of political tensions and to emphasise the implicit homogeneity of the merchant community, whether in the context of the early modern period or the nineteenth century. The new council appointed in 1695 demonstrated a 'unity of friendship and purpose' in a context in which political differences were not important and the port's small size encouraged the emergence of a 'homogeneous mercantile political elite'; Liverpool's commercial success in the eighteenth century was due to the presence of a 'relatively homogeneous community' and the ability to sustain 'a balanced local unity of views' in the face of a wide diversity of opinion; and most leading politicians claimed to be their own men at a time when party labels were 'not very meaningful'. Furthermore, there was no evidence of a 'fundamental fracture' in the mercantile elite during the turbulent 1840s and the establishment of a new Chamber of Commerce in February 1850 was due primarily to the existence of a 'community' of 'capitalist entrepreneurs' and a recognition that unity was 'an essential strength'.[88]

In fact, the articulation of collective concerns by the mercantile elite was often undermined by factional interests whether influenced by political, religious, or economic considerations. The old Town Council, although it consisted of some of the 'most respected men in the place', was largely self-elected, oligarchic, and dominated by Tory Anglicans. It was 'too much a family affair'; 'extreme Toryism' reflected a need to guard against the introduction of too many 'outsiders' at a time of conflicts with radical non-conformists; while the disappearance of several cultural and philanthropic institutions in the late eighteenth century was attributed to intra-elite rivalries. Local politics in the early nineteenth century remained dominated by the Tory interest, reinforced by a deliberate use of government patronage and an effective control of Parliamentary seats which contributed to Liverpool's reputation as 'one of the most corrupt constituencies' in England.[89] Even if the political atmosphere changed significantly with the election of a new council in December 1835, which heralded the start of a brief period of Liberal control, the partisan nature of municipal politics remained unchanged. Despite an emphasis on the 'personal merits' of individual candidates, party competition became more intense during the 1850s; elite rivalry was again evident after the passing of the Municipal Franchise Amendment Act of 1869; the School Board Election of 1872 was fiercely contested; and the period between 1870 and 1895 was characterised by a revival of deep-rooted political antagonism.[90]

Indeed, political satire was deployed, sometimes in a 'bitingly sarcastic' manner, to highlight the hypocritical attitude of church-going merchants involved in the slave trade; the systemic weaknesses in Liverpool's system of governance and its 'municipal pomposity'; local councillors who either paid little attention to civic affairs or sought to exploit their official position for personal gain; those who had abused their position to profit from the exercise of political power; and shipping companies that had (allegedly) been involved in insurance fraud. Building on a tradition established by William Shepherd in the early nineteenth century, the writings of Hugh Shimmin exposed the factionalism and corruption that was deeply embedded in mid-Victorian politics, while the editors of *The Liverpool Review* (1878–1883) and *The Liverpool Review of Politics, Society, Literature and Art* (1883–1904) deliberately used satire as a means of attacking and exposing the Tories who continued to control local politics.[91]

At the same time, the organisation of politics at the local level was strengthened by the establishment from the late 1870s onwards of party-political clubs, while the late Victorian period witnessed an increased centralisation of party machinery.[92] Earlier attempts to create clubs for party members had not been successful since they were never 'overcrowded', but the new institutions reinforced divisions between the two principal political parties. If the Reform Club (1879) and the Junior Reform Club functioned as the 'social hub of Liverpool Whiggery', an extensive Conservative Club House, designed in French Renaissance style, was formerly opened in Dale Street in 1883 (Figure 11.7), followed by the establishment of a new Junior Conservative Club (as a limited company) in 1893.[93] During the 1880s, largely as a reaction to conflicts over Irish Home Rule, there was a significant growth in the number of political clubs, as was the case in London and other major cities, and by the late 1890s an extensive infrastructure had been established in Liverpool, on the Wirral, and further afield in Southport. The 26 Conservative clubs listed in *Kelly's Directory* included 5 branches of the Conservative Working Men's Association; the Liberal Party had 19 separate clubs; while a solitary Socialist Club had been founded in Aubrey Street, Everton.[94] Many Liberals despaired of the Tory hold on power which was strengthened further during this period as part of a national trend. The shipowner Arthur Bower Forwood, who had first been elected a town councillor in 1871, became a dominant figure within the local Conservative Party, an active supporter of the Tory democracy movement, and an astute manager of elections on strict party lines: it was noted that he sacrificed opportunities of enriching himself to 'his political zeal'. His successor, Archibald Salvidge, proved to be a supreme party organiser: he explicitly utilised the Conservative Working Men's Association to secure his party's continued dominance and was widely regarded as

Figure 11.7 'The New Conservative Club-House, Liverpool', *The Illustrated London News*, 22 April 1882

the 'King of Liverpool' who could make or break political candidates. He was closely involved with the drink interest on Merseyside: his father had become a publican, having struggled as a mineral water manufacturer, and his wife was a publican's daughter. Having secured employment with Bents Brewery, he became its managing director and a key figure representing the drinks industry.[95]

Political divisiveness was reinforced by party infighting, particularly in the case of the Liberal Party over the issue of Irish Home Rule. This led to the formation in May 1886 of a Liverpool Liberal Unionist Committee which attracted over 100 members, including representatives of prominent 'renegade' families, although many of its supporters ultimately found that they occupied a political wilderness and were never consulted by the Conservative Party. The Conservatives, in turn, suffered from periods of discord and disruption in a context in which political parties at the local level were often broad-based and unstable coalitions.[96]

Political tensions were aggravated by sectarian issues. As Belchem has emphasised, Liverpool's Irish Catholics were 'the most sizeable and pivotal Irish formation within the Irish diaspora', to the extent that the port-city had the largest Catholic Irish political representation in Britain. The first electoral success was in the Scotland Ward in 1875, but Laurence Connolly was only the first of 48 Irish Nationalist councillors who had been elected by 1922. By 1900, Irish Nationalists had become the main opposition party on the Conservative-dominated city council while second generation Liverpool-born Irish, such as Austin Harford and his brother (owners of a highly successful retail and wholesale business trading in cloths and linen) had become the 'hegemonic political force in Edwardian Irish Liverpool'. As a counterweight, the National Protestant Electoral Federation, established with the support of the Orange Order in May 1903, also set out to challenge Conservative hegemony, but in this case to secure 'Protestant objectives over Conservative priorities'.[97]

The extent to which political divisions in Liverpool became increasingly institutionalised within a wider framework of persistent and increasing sectarianism raises important issues in relation to the cohesiveness of the merchant community and the operation of commercial networks. Although an analysis of their ramifications for business practice is complicated by the limited availability of records for many of the firms contained in the MLP database, it is clear that the predominant role of the merchant community in municipal affairs was gradually undermined between the 1850s and 1914 (Table 11.3), despite the high regard in which municipal office was held.[98]

In 1845, 29 (almost 70 per cent) of the 44 town councillors had been engaged in a 'commercial career': a decade later, on the basis of Shimmin's sketches, almost 55 per cent were either merchants or shipowners.[99] By the late 1890s, however, they accounted for less than half of the town council. Although the number of elected members from the mercantile community by 1914 was approximately the same as it had been 60 years earlier, the significant growth in the total number of councillors and aldermen to 137, largely as a result of the incorporation of suburban districts, meant that the collective role of the 'merchant aristocracy' was diminished considerably. It was increasingly difficult to persuade 'wealthy men' to stand for municipal office against the challenge from small proprietors and there were frequent complaints that those with wealth, culture, or social prestige were abandoning their moral responsibility to society and leaving municipal politics to 'inferior men'.[100] In Birkenhead, the decline in political representation by the merchant community was even more marked, from two thirds of the Birkenhead commissioners in 1842–43 to one third of the elected councillors and aldermen by 1891–92 as tradesmen, including bakers, printers, and representatives from the hotel trade, exercised an increasingly important role in municipal politics. This was part of a longer-term trend as responsibility for municipal government lay increasingly 'in the hands of the energetic men who

Table 11.3 The political representation of the merchant community in Liverpool and Birkenhead (commissioners, councillors, and aldermen)

(i). Liverpool

Year	Total	Merchants	%
1845	44	29	65.9
1857	64	35	54.6
1896–97	84	36	42.8

(ii). Birkenhead

Year	Total	Merchants	%
1842–43	21	13	66.6
1851–52	23	12	52.1
1853–54	21	11	52.3
1863–64	21	11	52.3
1869–70	21	11	52.3
1891–92	57	19	33.3

Sources: directories and MLP database; Belchem and Hardy, 'Second Metropolis: The Middle Class in early Victorian Liverpool', in A. Kidd and D. Nicholls (ed.), *The Making of the British Middle Class? Studies of Regional and Cultural Diversity since the Eighteenth Century* (Thrupp, 1998), p. 65; Hugh Shimmin, *Pen-and-Ink Sketches of Liverpool Town Councillors By a Local Artist (reprinted from the 'Liverpool Mercury', 1857)* (Liverpool, 1866)

control the large retail trades' as few of the leading shipowners and merchants entered the political arena. A similar process was evident in the case of Irish Nationalist representation on Liverpool city council. By 1900, the more prosperous Liverpool-born Irish Nationalists had been replaced by 'butchers, shopkeepers, penny-a-week insurance collectors and undertakers'.[101]

Leadership of the town council ceased to be a prerogative of representatives of the merchant community: during the 1860s, 80 per cent of Liverpool's mayors came from a mercantile background, but by the first decade of the twentieth century only 40 per cent had a career in shipping and trade.[102] Although the powers of a mayor's office did not match those of their continental counterparts, they were nevertheless expected to fulfil an important representational role and contribute to the development of civic culture. This was particularly the case in Liverpool which surrounded the office of mayor with 'greater dignity and pomp' than other provincial cities and where every incumbent was expected to maintain the city's wider reputation by carrying out social and judicial functions 'such as devolve on the chief of no other municipality'.[103] In total, 17 merchants were appointed mayor, whether in Liverpool, Birkenhead, or elsewhere on Merseyside, sometimes on more than one occasion. In Birkenhead, for example, the ship builder John Laird was elected its first mayor in 1877 because 'his large works' meant that he was able to exercise a 'dominant' influence as a Conservative: his son William subsequently held mayoral office on three separate occasions and the merchant Charles T. Gostenhofer twice became mayor of the borough.[104]

A similar trend was evident in other areas of civic representation. The Freedom of the City of Liverpool was normally granted to individuals in recognition of exceptional services, usually to the city itself, but only a third of the 18 recipients between 1886 and 1912 came from the merchant community.[105] By the 1890s, merchants continued to dominate the magistracy in Birkenhead where they accounted for three quarters of the bench, but this was not the case in Liverpool where the proportion had fallen to barely 50 per cent.

Civic office was traditionally associated with political influence, patronage, and access to power, while the position of a magistrate, although less politicised, brought with it a significant degree of prestige and local standing, particularly amongst the urban elite. Municipal administration had been transformed by the mid-1870s and in the following decades the power of political leaders increased significantly as municipal enterprise was encouraged by central government incentives. Leading businessmen, whether in Birmingham or in other major cities, were 'queuing-up' to enter the hustings motivated, in part, by the civic gospel and an increasing realisation that personal charity and philanthropy would never resolve the persistent social and welfare problems of urban communities.[106] Despite the claim that the Liverpool Corporation could be compared to 'a German principality put into commission' because of the extent of its estate, revenues, and influence, a reverse trend was evident on Merseyside. The fact that local government was increasingly 'abandoned to inferior men' while those with wealth, culture, and social prestige ignored their 'moral responsibility to society' cannot be explained by a reduction in the pool of potential candidates from the merchant community which reached a peak in the 1890s, although this was followed by a significant fall in the overall number of merchants prior to 1914.[107]

Increased international competition, the decline of the emigrant trade, and the demise of several passenger lines around the turn of the century may have necessitated a greater prioritisation of business interests and deterred some members of the merchant community from seeking elected office, while the adoption of party-political organisational strategies and the greater divisiveness of local politics may have had a similar effect.[108] Other factors contributed to the gradual disengagement of merchants from municipal politics. The Tory Party never effectively relinquished power; local brewers were its 'most lavish supporters'; and its most prominent members were the 'chief employers of labour' who were 'haughtily convinced of their own worth'. Structural changes in the local economy led to an increasing emphasis on processing and manufacturing industries both in Liverpool and its hinterland, as well as on the retail sector. Moreover, the existence of alternative institutions, such as the Mersey Docks & Harbour Board, the chamber of commerce, and an increasing number of trade associations, provided the basis for a more direct articulation of business interests by members of the merchant community. In the case of the West India trader Francis Shand, he explicitly prioritised Dock Board issues above those of the council and displayed 'more interest in Dock than in Council proceedings.'[109]

Membership of a junior political club was sometimes the initial stage in recruiting party-political sympathisers and some merchants were able to combine their business interests with an extended career in local politics stretching in some cases over a quarter of a century.[110] But there were important differences within the merchant community in the extent of participation in local politics. In some cases, merchants were 'not prominent' in political questions or were not active politicians, as was the case with the wine merchant James Smith who was 'not forward in public life', despite being 'a well-informed and hearty Nonconformist Liberal'. The flour miller Edward Hutchinson, who had built up an important business on the Corn Exchange, took little part in public affairs although he was widely recognised as a 'stout Liberal'. By contrast, a far greater number of traders and merchants were singled out for their 'active', 'ardent', or 'energetic' commitment to a party-political cause: the cotton broker Alexander Eccles was 'an ardent and prominent liberal', while the merchant and shipowner Charles Tricks Bowring was described as a 'pronounced liberal'. The shipowner Francis Henderson was 'a hearty Conservative' who found time for 'energetic' political work, while the provision merchant Thomas Jennings had been 'an active political worker' for the Conservative Party, both in Liverpool and Birkenhead. A significant number of merchants held office as councillors or aldermen or were chairmen or senior members of political clubs and party-political associations. For example, the stock and share broker John Arnitt Dear was chairman of the Junior Liberal Club; the cotton merchant P. E. J. Hemelryk was a member of the Political Committee of the Conservative Party for many years; and the shipowner Edmund Taylor was an 'indefatigable' deputy chairman of the Birkenhead Conservative Association for 25 years.[111]

Furthermore, the 'mutually jealous and politically ambitious businessmen' who dominated the local parties in the late eighteenth and early nineteenth centuries were often forced to seek Parliamentary seats elsewhere because of the port-city's limited representation. In 1868 a third Parliamentary seat was created but it was only in 1885 that the 'Second City of Empire' finally achieved a level of representation in line with its substantial increase in population and its commercial importance when the existing three seats were split into nine divisions. Liverpool Borough seats were contested with a great deal of acrimony and corrupt practices were endemic, even after the Great Reform Act of 1832. A total of 28 members of the local business community were elected members of Parliament between the 1850s and 1914. This reflected close links between politicians and firms, although older businesses were relatively unaffected by the electoral success of senior partners. But most members of the mercantile community held seats in other parts of the country well removed from Liverpool and Merseyside, including Plymouth (the shipowner Sir Edward Bates, 1872–96); Malden and Lincoln (the Brazilian merchant John Bramley-Moore, 1854–59, 1862–63); St. Andrews Burgh and the Kilmarnock Boroughs (the shipowner Stephen Williamson, 1880–85, 1886–95); and Hexham (the cotton broker Richard Durning Holt, 1907–18). The merchant and shipowner William Rathbone, having been a M.P. for Liverpool for 12 years (1868–80) declined to stand again because he had refused to vote for the Home Rule Bill, but he subsequently held the Liberal seat of Caernarvonshire (1881–95) which enabled him to enjoy his main pastimes, including riding, viewing mountain scenery, and learning Welsh. By contrast, the consolidation of local economic and political power was all too evident in Birkenhead where John Laird (Senior) became its first M.P. in December 1861: he was re-elected on three further occasions, thereby strengthening the local dominance of the Conservative Party, and continued to represent the borough until his death in 1874. For those members of Merseyside's mercantile community who either opted or felt it necessary to contest and win parliamentary seats in other parts of Britain, electoral success led to the opening of new network connections, whether at a local, regional, or national level, but it also contributed to a weakening of existing links closer to home.[112]

To what extent did party-political affiliation affect business relations and network? Its significance for network relationships was almost certainly dependent on individual ideological commitment, the extent of involvement with a specific political party, and the willingness to stand in local elections as a tangible expression of political allegiance. The three collections of biographical material around the turn of the century reveal a similar pattern of active political involvement, defined in terms of office holding (whether as a councillor or alderman), involvement with a local or regional political association, or a party-political affiliation which was deemed to have been worthy of note. From a combined sample of 902 merchants, 254 (or 28.1 per cent) were known to have been involved directly in party-political work. However, a decline in active participation was visible from a level of 30.0 per cent in the early 1890s to 20.8 per cent by 1911, while the extent of party-political affiliation amongst ring traders and other leading members of the Cotton Exchange in 1908 was 22.8 per cent. If membership of a political club is taken as evidence of a wider commitment to party-political objectives, then the overall extent of politicisation within the merchant community prior to 1914 was greater. Forty-three merchants were recorded as elected office holders in 1911, but a further 61 were listed as members of political clubs, primarily in Liverpool, but also in London.[113] Overall, however, only a minority had an active political profile.

Of the 169 merchants in Orchard's *Legion of Honour* whose political affiliation was recorded, 88 were Conservatives and 81 were Liberals. Approximately two decades later the increasing dominance of the Tory Party was reflected in a shift in allegiance within the merchant community. Of the 144 who were politically active or members of a political club, 104 (61.5 per cent) were Conservatives and only 40 (38.4 per cent) were Liberals. In terms of occupational classification, there were no noticeable differences in political allegiance towards the end of the nineteenth century, except for a tendency for the Conservative Party to recruit a greater number of bankers and businessmen from the maritime sector, including shipowners, steamship agents, and shipbrokers (Table 11.4). Traditionally, the Tory Party in Liverpool attracted widespread support from brewers and merchants involved with the drink trade, large-scale contractors, and manufacturers, specifically shipbuilders. Toryism was underpinned by 'a landlord mentality and sectarianism', but its local dominance was reinforced by close connections with the brewing industry. Arthur Barclay Walker, the 'chief of its most extensive publican business', was accused of conspiring with Conservative interests on the town council to grant a free trade in licences as a means of consolidating monopoly control; the sympathy of Conservative magistrates ensured the smooth renewal of his licences; while his political influence was strengthened by his election as a councillor in 1867 and an alderman in 1872 without having manifested 'any talent for municipal work'.[114]

By contrast, a number of sugar refiners and soap and chemical manufacturers were active or prominent members of the Liberal Party, but it failed to attract supporters from other sectors of the local economy and its leaders tended to belong to an 'exclusive set' of richer merchants, shipowners and brokers, often with a strong commitment to the temperance movement. According to the cotton broker Samuel Smith, the drink trade was 'the curse of the town' and the temperance debate remained highly polarised precisely because some Liberals were 'extreme teetotallers'. James Wood, of Henry Pooley & Son, iron founders and weighing-machine makers, 'grieved over any who were led astray by strong drink' and, like Smith, was a strong advocate of Sunday closing as a means of destroying 'the fearful and degrading habit of excessive drinking'. In individual cases the link between Liberalism and the temperance movement was explicit: for example, the coal merchant John Lea who sat on the City Council as a Liberal councillor for Abercromby Ward was 'an able advocate' of the temperance and social purity movements; for the iron merchant W. S. Caine, who was elected a Liberal Member of Parliament in 1884–85, temperance was 'the first love of his life'; and the merchant and

Table 11.4 Merchant political involvement by occupational classification, 1893–1911 (number, per cent)

Occupation	1893				1911			
	Conservative	%	Liberal	%	Conservative	%	Liberal	%
shipowner	18	20.6	13	16.0	18	28.1	9	22.5
shipbuilder	4	4.5	–		1	1.5	–	
merchant	38	43.6	36	44.4	24	37.5	20	50.0
broker	17	19.5	23	28.3	8	12.5	7	17.5
stock broker	5	5.7	2	2.4	6	9.3	4	10.0
banker	5	5.7	6	7.4	2	3.1	–	
other			1	1.2	5	7.8		
total	87		81		64		40	

Source: B. Guinness Orchard, *Liverpool's Legion of Honour* (Birkenhead, 1893); W. T. Pike (ed.), *Liverpool and Birkenhead in the Twentieth Century: Contemporary Biographies* (Brighton, 1911)

shipowner William Benjamin Bowring became President of the United Kingdom Temperance Alliance.[115]

The same party-political, occupation-specific divisions within the merchant community were visible prior to the 1914. The Conservatives attracted twice as many shipowners (and managers) than the Liberals; both parties had a similar proportion of active party members, and depended to a great extent on the continued commitment of individual merchants. In contrast to the situation in the early 1890s, the role of brokers within both political parties had declined significantly, because their commercial function had been gradually undermined by improved communications and new technology, while the gradual disappearance of ship-building on the eastern side of the Mersey (as a direct result of the continued expansion of the dock system) had curtailed the political contribution of their owners to the Conservative Party.[116] Despite concern within the merchant community over 'a dangerous growth of Socialism' which appalled the shipowner Richard Holt and most of his contemporaries, at least one member of the Liverpool Cotton Exchange, Arthur K. Bulley, was a 'pronounced Socialist' who defended its 'idealistic theorists', but he was the sole representative of 'the doctrines of Agnosticism and Socialism', just as James Galway, a marine store dealer, was the only Orangeman included in *Liverpool's Legion of Honour*, although he represented a wider trend towards a more strident support for ascendant Protestantism which culminated in the establishment of the Liverpool Protestant Party in 1903 and the religious riots of 1910.[117]

There is some evidence that partisan politics had a negative impact on business relations within the merchant community. In the 1840s, at a time when many Liberals were actively supporting free trade and the repeal of the Corn Laws, Liverpool Tories remained committed to protectionism, and their parliamentary candidates were selected from the West India trade, which was staunchly protectionist, although they did seek to remove restrictions on 'long voyage shipping'. Despite the need to avoid normative assumptions based on an implied relationship between commercial interest and party-political affiliation, there can be little doubt as to the 'depth of the ideological cleavage' in 1846, both locally and nationally.[118] The 'already riven ranks' of the merchant community were divided 'more fiercely than before' by the American Civil War. No order for a new ship was ever placed by the Holts, as prominent members of Liverpool's Unitarian and Liberal communities, with the shipyard of John Laird, the Tory M.P. for Birkenhead, who had been a notorious supplier of sloops-of-war (the Birkenhead 'rams'), including the raider *CSS Alabama*, to the Confederate States. Among the elite residents of Abercromby Square, however, a number openly expressed support for Confederacy: James Spence (No. 10, 1864–73) acted as a propagandist; his immediate predecessor, Robert Preston (1852–64), the chairman and chief engineer of the Preston & Fawcett Engineering Co., sold arms to both the Confederacy and the North; and Charles Kuhn Prioleau (No. 19, 1862–70), a highly successful financier and trader from Charleston, South Carolina, also helped to supply arms. They all belonged to what was known as the Southern Club.[119]

Although the Liberal Party under Gladstone remained committed to free trade principles, despite rising tariffs in Continental Europe from the 1870s onwards, there was increasing political pressure for Britain to adopt retaliatory measures in order to negotiate a reduction in foreign trade barriers. Political divisions over tariff policy at a national level were replicated locally within the merchant community. When the shipowner David MacIver was elected to Parliament in 1885 to represent Birkenhead he distinguished himself 'by unflinching advocacy of Protectionist principles at a time when few adherents of the old system were bold enough to declare that its restoration would be advantageous'.[120] Even on issues relating to taxation reform, or the need to improve municipal administrative efficiency, a lack of political consensus often prevented collective action, while religious differences militated against the articulation of consistent policies which would have benefited business interests as a whole.[121]

Urban politics in Liverpool, as elsewhere, continued to be dominated by conflicts within the middle class and the configuration of business networks reflected the continuing failure to establish a unitary elite structure. For some members of the merchant community a high level of political involvement reinforced network activity with like-minded individuals. Almost 60 per cent of the original members of the Liverpool Conservative Association (1832) had been either merchants or brokers, and obituaries from the 1890s of members of the Liverpool Constitutional Association, its immediate successor, regularly testified to their role as 'valued workers' and constant Party supporters suggesting a high degree of interaction amongst its membership to secure party-political objectives.[122] In Birkenhead, David MacIver, the shipbuilder John Laird, the share broker Maurice Mocatta, and the general merchant Edmund Taylor were instrumental in establishing the Grange Conservative Club in 1876 with an initial list of officers dominated by local merchants. John Laird, as the chairman of the Birkenhead Conservative Association, was effectively 'the local party manager', while his elder brother, William, was a Knight of the Primrose League, a membership he shared with a number of other local businessmen, including the sugar refiner and merchant Thomas Easton and the cement and lime merchant A. J. Pilkington. It had been established in 1883 to uphold and support 'God, Queen, and Country, and the Conservative Cause' and played an important role in propagating a 'potent political subculture' by encouraging the participation of activists, particularly in localities such as Liverpool and Birkenhead where the Party was already relatively well organised.[123]

Leading figures within the business community provided significant financial support to their respective political parties. The cotton broker George Holt placed his time and money 'freely at the service of the Liberal cause'; the alkali manufacturer E. K. Muspratt was one of 15 'gentlemen' who subscribed £1,000 each towards the erection of the Reform Club in Dale Street; the cotton broker Alexander Eccles contributed 'freely' to the funds of the Liberal Party; while Joseph Gibbons Livingstone, who 'never appeared to be in active business', was a generous financial supporter of the Conservative Party. Indeed, the latter was a resolute advocate of a close association with the 'public-house interest' and 'an uncompromising wirepuller' for his party.[124]

Increased political antagonism by the end of the nineteenth century, reinforced by ideological differences, improved party organisation, and more aggressive operational styles, aggravated the underlying divisions within the merchant community. Robert Holt, the leader of the Liberal Party for 15 years, believed that there was 'no cause to feel that politics would sully the intercourse of polite society' and continued to dine with prominent Liberal Unionists after the split over Irish Home Rule in 1886. But council meetings were held with 'an utter absence of propriety and dignity' and in February 1901 a breaking of an agreement over the election of aldermen led to a veritable 'storm'. His Conservative counterpart, A. B. Forwood, missed no opportunity of saying 'the bitterest things', while a number of Conservative Party members in Liverpool ascribed to the concept of 'pure party politicians' and endorsed the view that Liberalism had been taken over by fanatical Nonconformists as a conspiracy of 'faddists and caucusmongers'. Under these circumstances, the maintenance of business networks across the political divide was highly unlikely, even in circumstances in which there might have been a clear economic rationale.[125]

Politics, by definition, had always been a contested arena and in Liverpool conflicts were common. At one of the parliamentary elections in the period before the Great Reform Act of 1832 business was suspended for a few days: it engendered 'hatred, envy and malice' and left wounds 'in family circles' which would take years to heal. In 1851, the cotton broker George

Holt welcomed Sunday as 'a blessed day' 'after business, politics and warfare about the Docks and Water'. However, evidence from diaries and correspondence, although often subjective by nature, provides a useful means of assessing the relative intensity and volatility of political discourse. According to the *Daily Post*, 'few of our merchant princes belonging to an old Liverpool family ever made such a name in the political world' as the merchant and shipowner George Melly. At the time of his death in September 1894 after a 'lingering and painful illness', he was a director of the Liverpool Legal and General Insurance Co., the Bank of Liverpool Ltd., and the Union Marine Insurance Co., and a member of the Mersey Docks and Harbour Board. Although he had represented Stoke-on-Trent in Parliament as a Liberal for 'several years', he remained integrated within Liverpool's business and commercial community and had been 'largely and honourably engaged in mercantile affairs.' But his 'singularly happy attitude for public life' was not reciprocated by his political opponents. A letter from Hugh Bright in April 1859 made explicit the existence of local opposition to Melly's plans to secure a Parliamentary seat: 'many people, in Liverpool, who whether from jealousy or some other causes, do not quite like the idea of you becoming an MP' and some were 'dead against' him 'as a Whig and heretic'. On one occasion, his active involvement in the Volunteer Movement gave rise to an 'unintentional offence' and made him feel 'publicly slighted', even if it ultimately proved to be a misunderstanding which was quickly resolved. Military analogies were deployed in his dealings with council officials, specifically when the gates to Princes Park were unexpectedly closed on a Sunday and Melly decided to take 'the war into the enemies' camp'. A similar approach was adopted in 1872, when he advised a 'dear and impulsive Friend' not to be afraid, because Forwood 'shall be completely blown up and the thing should only be done the more thoroughly because it is not done in a brutal hurry'.[126]

Some three decades later, the diary of another scion of a long-established Unitarian family, which had played a major role in the city's development, its commercial success, and philanthropy, highlights the extent to which the cut and thrust of politics had become increasingly ruthless. Richard Durning Holt (1868–1941) had been born into a very prosperous family and at the age of 27 he became one of three new directors (or 'managers') of Alfred Holt & Company. Like his father, Robert, who had become Liverpool's first Lord Mayor in 1893, Richard was intent on pursuing a political career, in addition to retaining his involvement in shipping and commerce. But his diary provides extensive evidence of the hostile political environment which characterised Liverpool in the early years of the twentieth century. The General Election of 1900 would be 'ever remembered owing to the baseness and blackguardliness' of the Tories, who had denounced their Liberal opponents, both nationally and locally as 'traitors', while the Tory Party under Salvidge's leadership played 'a very astute Tammany game'. In 1902, Tory hostility to granting the Boers any concessions which might undermine the concept of Empire led to a violent mob attacking the Philharmonic Hall where the South Africa Conciliation League was holding its annual meeting. When he stood (unsuccessfully) in 1903 at a by-election for the West Derby Division, his opponent was William Rutherford, a 'staunch Protestant' who was very much in the Salvidge mould of Toryism and voters had been bribed by 'blatant hospitality' by the previous incumbent who had even organised day-trips to the Isle of Man. In 1909, after his father's death, he returned to the family home at 54 Ullet Road: the main motive behind this move reflected the implacable, personal hostility between the local Liberal and Tory parties because 'I should hate to part with the house my father built and loved—perhaps to a Tory'.[127]

Despite the existence of an increasing party-political divide within the merchant community, its overall significance should not be exaggerated. According to Berghoff, the business community in major provincial cities invariably demonstrated 'a high willingness' to support political parties and to stand for municipal election. Almost one third of the members of the

Mersey Docks & Harbour Board (1858–1905) had some involvement with local politics, but the evidence for Liverpool and Birkenhead reveals a declining level of active participation, particularly in the late nineteenth century, when those who had 'wealth, culture and social prestige' increasingly turned their backs on local government and public affairs. In fact, 131 of the merchants listed in Orchard's *Legion of Honour* in 1893 (21.3 per cent of the sample) were specifically referred to as non-political and an even larger number took no active part in politics, in some cases despite having a strong political affinity. If the soap manufacturer William Crosfield became involved in Liberal politics 'when little more than a youth', the underwriter Robert Norris Dale preferred to live 'a quiet life' cultivating orchids at Bromborough Hall. Although some merchants 'often met in connection with politics', others took no part in politics and avoided public life even when they possessed 'important qualifications', or they simply did not 'come much to the fore'.[128]

More significantly, business considerations often precluded any form of involvement in party politics. The energies of the general broker John Brancker were confined to business, although it was acknowledged that he possessed 'important qualifications' for politics; the shipowner Alfred Lewis Jones refused to comply with frequent requests to enter public life because of 'his intense devotion to African affairs', particularly after he obtained control of Elder Dempster in 1884; R. R. Lockett, a shipowner, merchant, and a director of several large companies, was prevented from taking part in municipal political life because of the 'responsibilities connected with these enterprises'; while the timber merchant Peter Owen was eminent in commerce 'like many others', but deliberately avoided any exertion of his 'large general powers' in other directions and rejected all opportunities to play a prominent role in local politics. In 1868, when William Rathbone was elected Member of Parliament, he relinquished all management responsibilities for the family firm, although he was probably aware that the opportunity costs of a political career could be considerable. Other prominent members of the merchant community deferred their entry into politics until commercial success had been secured, as was the case with the cotton merchant John Gladstone. Occasionally, they even waited until their formal retirement from business, although George Bahr, the senior partner of the well-established firm of Bahr, Behrend, and Ross (shipowners and ship brokers) left the realisation of his political ambitions too late: having resigned his partnership in 1880 he presented himself as the Liberal candidate for Preston, but died from cancer of the throat on the eve of the General Election.[129]

For many merchants and traders business concerns remained their priority and the potential benefits of active involvement in local politics in terms of social networking and enhanced personal status provided no compensation for the potential loss in time, money, and profitability, particularly in a context in which the risk of failure remained high. The merchant and steamship owner, Henry W. Gair, confined his attention 'mainly to his extensive business'; all the energies of the shipowner A. F. Holme were 'devoted to business'; while the corn merchant Edward Paul avoided 'every political or other engagement which might interfere with his direct commercial occupations'. In the case of the merchant and shipowner Alfred Booth, although the demands of business did not take up 'so much time that he could not undertake some of those social obligations which, as a citizen of Liverpool, he felt it his duty to fulfil', he had no inclination to take an active role in politics, even though he was a 'staunch Liberal', and publicity of any kind was 'entirely foreign to his temperament'.[130]

It has been argued that the political representation of business interests in major British cities was far greater than in Germany, but it was not uncommon for members of Liverpool's merchant community to refuse political office. The chemical merchant Edward Evans of Evans, Sons & Co. was publicly praised as 'the embodiment of the sturdiness of British Liberalism', but he did not feel justified in standing for Parliament and separating himself from his 'extensive business'; the steamship owner Thomas Henry Ismay, the founder of the Oceanic Steam Navigation Company (the White Star Line), declined several offers to stand as an M.P.; while the African merchant J. A. Tobin, whose family had owned 'vast estates' in African and the West Indies, invariably declined to stand for parliamentary office despite his prominent political role in Liverpool. The shipowner David MacIver, having been elected M.P. for Birkenhead in 1885, declined the seat in the following year 'owing to the pressure of business engagements'; and the shipowner Joseph Hoult, who reputedly had 'great energy and business tact', refused an invitation to occupy Liverpool's mayoral chair.[131] To this extent, individual merchants and traders, even if they subscribed to the policies of a particular political party and were involved in local politics, were careful to restrict their level of engagement and were unwilling to assume representational duties if they threatened the wider interests of their firms.

Even when they held elected municipal office their level of commitment was sometimes less than satisfactory, as Shimmin's sketches from the mid-nineteenth century reveal. The timber merchant John Farnworth 'had not devoted much time to his municipal duties'; the broker Thomas Littledale who had been Mayor of Liverpool in 1851–52, needed to give up more time 'to the business of the Corporation'; and the attendance at council meetings of the timber merchant James Holme was regarded as 'somewhat lax'. Indeed, the potential economic costs of political activism were sometimes significant: Thomas Littledale's mayoral role prevented him from taking a leading part in managing the family firm (T. & J. Littledale & Co.) and Samuel Smith's 20-year partnership in James Finlay & Co. (Glasgow) was terminated on his election to Parliament in 1882.[132]

The factors which influenced the choice and extent of party-political allegiance amongst individual members of the merchant community are difficult to establish with any accuracy. Family, religion, and ethnicity undoubtedly contributed to the structuring of political attitudes and behaviour, particularly during childhood, while peer group influence and business considerations played an important role. In many cases there was a close correlation between denominational identity and political affiliation: the Tory Party drew significant support from adherents of the Established Church, while Nonconformists traditionally provided many of the more active members of the local Liberal Party. James Tyrer, who was rumoured to have accumulated 'a princely fortune' through his involvement in 'corn, cotton and currency', was a high churchman and a 'spicy, unflinching Tory in his politics', and the corn merchant John Wilson was 'a stout Churchman, and an uncompromising Tory'. Samuel Greg Rathbone who was sent to China in 1843 to 'open a house in connection with Rathbone Bros.' was a Liberal and Unitarian, 'staunch in adherence to both causes', while Benjamin Bowring, apart from being a 'most energetic businessman', was a committed Unitarian, a 'fluent and cultured speaker', and a 'profound' liberal. Religion and politics, therefore, were closely interconnected. However, extreme religious beliefs made active involvement with an established political party difficult to maintain. For example, the views held by the corn merchant John Patterson meant that he was 'too thorough' to be fully accommodated within the Liberal Party. At the same time, political allegiances were not invariably pre-conditioned by family or religious pressures, nor did they remain immutable or preclude marriage alliances with local families with different beliefs. David Hodgson, who was elected Liverpool's mayor in 1845, had been a member of the Society of Quakers and a Liberal in politics until he reached the age of 60 when he became a 'furiously bigoted church man and Tory'. The merchant Robertson Gladstone was a Conservative and churchman in early life who believed in the rights of property, but under the influence of his younger brother, W. E. Gladstone, he 'veered to almost the opposite extreme' and became both a Liberal and a Unitarian. Other examples can be cited. The tobacco broker Edward Samuelson joined the Conservative Party for which he did 'valuable work', although his five brothers were all 'advanced

Liberals'. The general broker John Barnes Brancker was a man of 'liberal opinions', but he was related to the Tobins and Aspinalls who were at the heart of elite control of Liverpool politics in the mid-nineteenth century and firm advocates of the Tory interest, while the shipowner Arthur Bower Forwood, who dominated the local Conservative Party throughout the 1880s and 1890s, twice married into Liberal families.[133]

But such cases remained an exception rather than the norm. Although political allegiances were fluid and reflected changes in both the ideological appeal and organisational efficiency of individual parties, the distribution of party-political affiliation by occupational category, defined in terms of active involvement or general support for either the Tory or Liberal Party, demonstrates the extent to which the merchant elite was not cohesive. Indeed, differences were evident even in their choice of architectural designs, whether for residential property, political clubs, or denominational churches. As Sharples has revealed, the cotton broker George Holt was strongly opposed to the Gothic Revival because it was at odds with 'Nonconformity, Sobriety and Dignity', whereas Conservatives, High Church Anglicans, and the *nouveaux riches*, like the brewer Andrew Barclay Walker, the very wealthy coal proprietor John Grant Morris, and the wine and spirit merchant Christopher Bushell, had no hesitation in adopting its key architectural principles, always at great expense.[134] Despite evidence of an increasing withdrawal from local politics by members of the merchant community, political divisions became more acute and conflicted during the late nineteenth and early twentieth centuries, at a time which witnessed a revival of sectarianism.

Institutional Diversification and Business Networking

If religion and politics remained important factors in structuring the framework of network interaction and the articulation of inter-personal relations, the role, nature, and complexity of local networks were affected during the period 1850 to 1914 by institutional diversification and the further proliferation of different forms of associational culture. The development of trade associations in Liverpool had its origins in the second half of the eighteenth century: they reflected the emergence of specific interest groups and the presence of significant entrepreneurial clusters concerned primarily with the protection of well-defined trading interests. The Underwriters' Association (1802) was founded to promote the common commercial interests of brokers, merchants, shipowners, and underwriters at a time when insurance was becoming increasingly specialised, while the Brazilian Association, representing merchants and shipowners trading to Brazil, lobbied Parliament in 1833 to secure a reduction in duties levied on their products, specifically sugar. Trade associations provided a useful focal point when merchants with regional commercial interests, whether in Africa or the West Indies, sought mutual support in negotiations with the port authority. By the mid-nineteenth century there were 11 recognised 'commercial' associations: by the 1890s their number had risen to at least 17 while the Liverpool Shipping and Forwarding Agents' Association was established in 1901 'to promote and protect the interests of trade in general'. However, only 15 were formally represented in the chamber of commerce by their nominated deputies. Other associations, such as the Liverpool and London Steamship Protection Association, the Liverpool Sailing Shipowners' Mutual Protection and Indemnity Association, and the Liverpool Shipowners' Freight, Demurrage, and Defence Association, had no representation.[135]

Trade associations, by encouraging collective self-management of a specific trading sector, generally sought to control similar product markets as a subset of inter-firm competition, often as a means of reducing market instability. Their members were usually competitors who recognised the benefits of collective action for political lobbying, for controlling entry conditions, and for punishing non-compliance with rules established to regulate the conduct of members or to prevent collusion.[136] Certainly, the carrying out of a lobbying function was often a priority as 'commercial' associations were established 'to promote objects connected with those interests, which are beyond the power of individuals'. The Brazilian Association petitioned Parliament in 1851 in support of the Brazilian Government's attempt to repeal Lord Aberdeen's Act of 1845 which had introduced a costly preventive system to suppress the slave trade both inland and in its territorial waters. The Steamship Owners' Association, founded in 1858, at a time when 'a new order' was developing in Liverpool, sought to protect and advance 'the common interests of proprietors of steam ships' (Rule III) and was consistently vigilant in monitoring the charges levied by the Mersey Docks & Harbour Board. The initial objective of the American Chamber of Commerce (1801) had been to regulate payments and customs fees, and local issues remained its main concern, particularly the representation of merchants on the Dock Board and the efficient management of the Dock Estate. At times, trade associations acted collaboratively to achieve a common objective. In 1856, for example, the American Chamber of Commerce and the Cotton Brokers' Association memorialised the Chamber of Commerce of New Orleans and Mobile 'on the evils arriving from the practice of irregular packing'.[137]

But the efficient regulation of trade as a means of strengthening the comparative advantage of association members was equally important. The Cotton Brokers' Association established in 1841 a successful system of arbitration to ensure that transactions were conducted with a 'promptitude, clearness, and integrity never surpassed in the annals of commerce'; the General Brokers' Association enabled business to be conducted 'with extraordinary promptitude and regularity'; while members of the Corn Trade Association were threatened with suspension or a fine of £1,000 if they failed to comply with its general rules. But the merchant community was often disinclined to penalise reckless traders, even when the extent of financial and reputational damage was severe; and trade associations were sometimes unwilling to apply their own rules in full, despite the increasing criminalisation of fraud.[138]

Trade associations were also social organisations which were expected to generate cooperation and trust by delivering broader functions than the efficient facilitation of commercial transactions. As such, they contributed to the 'processes of relations' which underpinned the operation of business networks.[139] Individual merchants may have enhanced their social capital through membership of a trade association, but any benefits were unevenly distributed within a network framework which suffered from core-periphery issues and problems of economic closure. Strict byelaws were utilised to regulate the admission of new members and more efficient management structures were introduced in the late nineteenth century following the adoption of limited company status in order to restrict competition. In the case of the Cotton Brokers' Association, their directors exercised considerable power and influence, but they were only selected from well-established firms. All membership applicants were required to have served a proper apprenticeship and had to provide a deposit of £1,000 (only £500 in the case of the sons of current or deceased members) and a release of securities was only possible after three years of compliance with its rules and regulations. Individual associations were dominated by a 'powerful and exclusive' group of members (council members and directors) and their public status of was reinforced by their role as formal representatives of important sectional interests. For example, J. H. Hubback, who was president of the Liverpool Corn Trade Association in 1886, played 'a prominent part' in securing for Liverpool traders equal railway rates with other competitor ports, while Edward Paul was regarded by his fellow corn traders as 'their representative man'.[140]

The role of individual associations as focal points for business networking was affected by both inter- and intra-sectoral conflicts, differences in the level of organisational efficiency, and the loss of membership support. In 1877, cotton merchants expressed their concerns over the encroachment on their trade of the Cotton Brokers' Association, but failure to win concessions after a period of 'considerable friction' resulted in the establishment of a new, more inclusive institution, the Liverpool Cotton Association, in place of the original trade association. Sector-specific divisions were evident amongst shipowners: shipowning was 'very much subdivided' and the Steamship Owners' Association, which was one of the 'most powerful' in the country, did not include all steamship owners operating out of the port of Liverpool and only belatedly created coastwise and short-sea voyage sections in 1904. Nor did it represent the immediate or strategic concerns of shipowners in general, particularly those who 'clung stubbornly' to wind propulsion until the 1870s and continued to promote their own interests through the Ship-owners' Association. Some trade associations failed. The Brazilian Association was no longer 'fully organized' by the 1850s and the American Chamber of Commerce which had previously enjoyed 'a strong financial position' with long-serving officers rewarded with silver plate or substantial monetary gifts, suffered a gradual decline in membership throughout the 1890s which led to its ultimate demise in 1908.[141] Indeed the proliferation of trade associations in the second half of the nineteenth century contributed to the structural fragmentation of the merchant community as sectional interests became more entrenched and business networking operated increasingly within a well-defined, specialist framework. The 'very diversify of interests', as represented by the different trade associations, represented 'the weakness as well as the strength of Liverpool'.[142]

Liverpool's first Chamber of Commerce was founded in 1774: it was initially highly success-ful in 'sustaining a balanced local unity of views in the face of a wide diversity of opinion' and reinforced the extent to which local business interests were 'strongly interconnected'. Its demise was followed by a period when sectional commercial interests were predominant, although this did not prevent merchants and 'other commercial bodies' from seeking to secure the abolition of the salt tax and salt monopoly of the East Indian Company, securing a reduction in tea duties, or exhorting railway companies 'to contract their new works, and to abstain from enforcing calls on shareholders'.[143] However, it was not until 1849 that a new Chamber of Commerce was established 'to promote measures calculated to benefit the mercantile and trading interests of its members, and of the town and neighbourhood generally'. As such, it confirmed the existence in Liverpool of a 'community' of 'capitalist entrepreneurs' who were willing to exclude 'all ques-tions of party politics, general or local' in pursuit of shared 'commercial purposes' and helped to sustain a 'shared capitalist consciousness'.[144] Chambers of commerce placed businessmen in a stronger negotiating position in relation to both central and local government by drawing together members from a broad spectrum of local economic interests. They facilitated network interaction based on shared values, promoted a steady growth of 'capitalist unity', functioned as an effective propaganda lobby, and created a legal and institutional framework that facilitated economic expansion. Certainly, the Liverpool Chamber exercised an important lobbyist role, whether in relation to the consolidation of Customs and Excise into one department, trade duties on goods exported to Asia, fiscal policy in India, the importance of colonial trade in general for the future of the British economy, or the need for improved telegraphic facilities. However, its wider contribution to the development of shared values within the merchant community is more difficult to establish, even after its formal incorporation in 1867.[145]

In the view of the Chamber's president in 1901, Sir Alfred Lewis Jones, an 'energetic' cham-ber of commerce functioned like 'a sort of local Parliament'. If Liverpool had looked after its interests more effectively in the previous 25 years 'she would have been in a better position to-day', a statement that alluded to the fact that the Chamber had to be reconstituted in 1878 after it had acquired a bad reputation 'through becoming too political'.[146] But such a statement

Table 11.5 Membership of the Liverpool Chamber of Commerce as a proportion of active merchants, 1851–1891

Year	Chamber Members	No. of Merchants	%
1851	409	1821	22.2
1861	567	2531	22.4
1871	526	3851	13.6
1881	739	3646	20.0
1891	736	4435	16.5

Note: Over time the membership of the Chamber of Commerce included an increasing number of other businessmen and professionals, including accountants, solicitors, and individuals involved in the retail trade, although they never constituted a significant proportion of total members.

Source: Paul Cherpeau, 'A Movement Divided? Chambers of Commerce in port and manufacturing areas', unpublished paper, Centre for Port and Maritime History Annual Conference, 'The "Otherness" of Port Cities', Liverpool, 12–13 September 2013; *The Chamber of Commerce of Liverpool (Incorporated) Forty-Second Annual Report* (Liverpool, 1892); MLP database (see Chapter 2)

underlines the significance of structural weaknesses in the way the Chamber operated and its failure to support either inclusivity or business networking by avoiding economic closure on the basis of well-defined sectional interests. Firstly, the Chamber was never fully representational of the merchant community. Even in 1851, shortly after its foundation, only one fifth of local merchants were registered members and its representativeness was undermined further during periods which witnessed a marked increase in the overall size of the trading community, as in the early 1870s and 1890s, when new traders sought to establish themselves in an increasingly competitive environment (Table 11.5). Moreover, a significant number of members came from the same family or firm, highlighting the relative dominance of leading enterprises and representatives from the business elite, while providing substance to the claim that the Chamber had not always enjoyed 'the confidence of the people' of Liverpool.[147] In 1891, merchants accounted for almost half of the total membership of 736, which also included 166 brokers (22.5 per cent) and 79 shipowners (10.7 per cent). But, again, some commercial interests were more strongly represented than others: there were 29 African, 28 corn, and 25 iron merchants, but only one representative from the coal, oil, and salt trades respectively. The 47 general brokers accounted for 27.9 per cent of their occupational group, but they were outnumbered by the 65 cotton brokers (38.6 per cent), while the presence of 51 steamship owners reflected the growing dominance of this sector in Liverpool's maritime economy.

Secondly, the way in which the Chamber operated replicated existing divisions within the merchant community rather than promoting business networking across a wider range of trading sectors. By the late nineteenth century, its business was conducted through various committees and five trade sections which mirrored the structure of Liverpool's commerce as it had evolved over time. An Animal and Meat Trade section was subsequently established to reflect the growing importance of the livestock trade, specifically at Birkenhead. Responsibility for the effective conduct of its affairs rested with a council composed originally of honorary officers and 21 elected members, together with 12 deputies nominated by the most important commercial associations, but this number was subsequently increased to include a further 8 deputies who represented the interests of trade sections. The predominant role of shipping companies, as in chambers of commerce in other port-cities (such as Greenock), was all too evident. Both the Steam Ship Owners' Association and the Shipowners' Association were accorded two deputies, while all the other trade associations had only one. Far from providing a forum which would have strengthened the sectoral diversity of business networking, many merchants trading on Merseyside, particularly small-scale operators, remained excluded from the Chamber which was dominated by trade associations and sectional interests. On many policy issues it simply rubber-stamped their recommendations: it was viewed in some quarters as a 'dry-as-dust concern' whose debates only attracted merchants who were either 'treaty-mad or statistics-mad' or who were simply great talkers.[148]

Business networking was affected by changes in company law in the 1850s and 1860s, the increasing proliferation of limited liability companies, and a trend towards interlocking directorates which provided a further channel of exchange and interaction within the business community. Recent research on interlocking directorships at the beginning of the twentieth century has suggested that the British corporate elite was more interconnected than has often been assumed. At a time when the economy was at a crucial point in its transition from liberal to organised capitalism a significant proportion of the directors of the top 250 joint-stock companies held multiple directorships which facilitated knowledge transfer and promoted interdependencies. Although many directors held only one position, a considerable minority occupied multiple positions which allowed an inner circle to exploit the networking process and to 'scan' the business environment, reduce transactional uncertainty, and strengthen social cohesion.[149]

It is generally assumed that these wider processes of institutional change with their important ramifications for professional networking and social exchange were found in provincial centres, including Liverpool, where elite business families strengthened their regional links to major enterprises through extended network-based communications.[150] As Jones has demonstrated, many of the more successful trading companies in the early nineteenth century had been based on interlocked partnerships and it is not surprising, therefore, that a similar principle was adopted in appointing directors to newly incorporated banks and insurance companies particularly after the 1844 Act was passed.[151] The directors of the Liverpool Life and Fire Insurance Company (1836) included representatives of the 'best-known' local families, while the board of the Royal Insurance Company (1845) provided interlocks with the Bank of Liverpool, the Mersey Forge Co., and a number of railway companies.[152] Many Liverpool trades continued to be dominated by small-scale firms which retained a traditional organisational form and joint-stock companies were viewed in some quarters with suspicion because of their implied association with gambling and immorality, but the 1856 Act favoured large investors. Major fleet enterprises were established on a joint-stock company basis in the late 1860s and early 1870s with a significant increase in capital employed, while a series of new promotions was launched during the 1880s in line with national trends, including a major restructuring of the Harrison Line on the basis of the 1880 Companies Act. Existing firms from a range of trading sectors became limited companies, sometimes as a defensive mechanism against increasing competition, but also as a reaction to the collapse of the City of Glasgow Bank in 1878 which highlighted the underlying weaknesses of unlimited liability. Indeed, there was growing concern in the early 1890s that 'the conversion of so many private businesses into joint-stock companies' was undermining the viability of local charities, since they often either failed to recognise or simply ignored their civic obligations. In a wider context, joint-stock company formation on Merseyside, specifically in shipping, affected the institutional framework of business because it led to a greater concentration of power within the business community and aggravated existing core-periphery problems.[153]

The extent to which the formation of joint-stock companies led to the creation of interlocking directorships is reflected in data taken from the contemporary biographies compiled by Orchard and Pike (Table 11.6). Despite differences in sample size, they both reveal a significant degree of interlocking, particularly in comparison with other evidence for Britain and the US based on

Table 11.6 Liverpool merchants: distribution of interlocking directorships in 1893 and 1911

(i) By Number	1893		1911	
Directorships	No.	%	No.	%
1	48	41.3	24	43.6
2	27	23.2	10	18.1
3	18	15.5	8	14.5
4	13	11.2	8	14.5
5	1	0.8	3	5.4
6	5	4.3	2	3.6
7	1	0.8		
unknown	3	2.5		
Total	116		55	
(ii) By Occupation	1893		1911	
Occupation	No.	%	No.	%
Shipowner	24	20.6	22	40.0
Merchant	44	37.9	15	27.2
Broker	25	21.5	8	14.5
Banker	5	4.3	1	1.8
Manufacturer	5	4.3	2	3.6

Note: The unknown category in 1893 includes two cases in which merchants had either 'several' or 'numerous' directorships.

Sources: B. Guinness Orchard, *Liverpool's Legion of Honour* (Birkenhead, 1893); W. T. Pike, *Liverpool and Birkenhead in the Twentieth Century: Contemporary Biographies* (Brighton, 1911)

specific sectors or representative multinational companies wherein the proportion of company directors with more than one directorship was never greater than 17 per cent.[154] In Liverpool, the proportion of board members holding three or more directorships increased from 34.4 per cent to 38.1 per cent between 1893 and 1911, but some members of the mercantile community had already acquired an extended range of company interests. For example, the shipowner T. H. Jackson had been chairman of the Queen Insurance Co. where he gained 'great popularity with the shareholders' and following its amalgamation with the Royal Insurance Co. he became a member of its board. But he also held directorships in a further six companies with very diverse interests. Moreover, Orchard's data probably understates the extent of interlocking, since the number of reported directorships failed to reflect the overall level of merchant involvement whose experience was 'utilised on boards of various large undertakings' and by 'other important companies'.[155] Significantly, the role of shipowners within the power geometries of interlocking directorships increased over time, from 20.6 per cent to 40 per cent of the sample, while the position of both merchants and brokers declined. Bankers, however, remained peripheral, despite evidence that the promoters of new banks in Liverpool prior to 1860 invariably came from local businesses and the existence of interlocking directorships with manufacturing firms in other parts of the country. In fact the number of bankers holding directorships fell from five to one during the period under consideration.[156] At the same time, there was increasing diversification in the type of company where members of the merchant community were represented on the board: in 1893 four key sectors (insurance, banking, railways, and shipping) accounted for 73.2 per cent of the companies listed in the sample, but by 1911 they accounted for just under 60 per cent, with a countervailing increase in mining and processing firms.

Merchants were involved in companies that operated in Liverpool's immediate hinterland, whether in textiles, mining, or insurance, and some members of the trading community developed specialist profiles as directors of insurance or railway companies. But interlocking directorships were particularly prominent within the framework of Merseyside's local economy. Corn merchants became involved in supply-chain operations, as directors of the Grain Transport and Storage Co., and the United Grain Elevator Ltd. (Bootle); merchants were strongly represented on the boards of local utilities (such as the Liverpool Electric Supply Co., the Formby Gas Co., and the Wirral Waterworks Co.), as well as transport companies, including the Liverpool Overhead Railway Co.; while the Mersey Forge Co. (Toxteth) consistently recruited a number of directors with a trading background.[157] However, the extent of interlocking was most apparent in the case of banks and insurance companies which had been established in Liverpool itself. In the early 1890s the Liverpool, London, and Globe Insurance Co. had 13 board members who had been recruited from the merchant community, while board representation was also substantial at the Bank of Liverpool (11), the Royal Insurance Co. (9), and the Union Marine Insurance Co. (6).[158] In contrast to most provincial centres dominated by manufacturing industry, Liverpool merchants were represented on the boards of a wide range of overseas companies whether in India, Latin America, West Africa, or the West Indies, which reflected their well-established trading experience. The African merchant Harry Cotterell was a director of the Bank of Nigeria and a board member of three other West African companies, while the West Indian merchant John Ernest Tinne was deputy chairman of the Demerara Railway Co. 'for many years'.[159]

Interlocking directorships involving prominent members of Liverpool's merchant community provided an additional mechanism for promoting interdependencies and for fostering the development of a corporate community. Multiple board positions helped to link companies together, while individual directorships enabled some major companies to operate in a relatively compact network, particularly in the financial and shipping sectors. Some merchants were 'singularly active' as directors and their services were 'highly valued' and sought after by various companies. Limited liability had reduced the burden of individual responsibility for directors, and concerns over moral hazards tended to diminish over time. It was not uncommon for some merchants to hold significant shareholdings in the companies they represented or to be 'familiar' figures at shareholder meetings. There was an increasing concentration of merchant representation on the boards of companies which enjoyed a high reputation. None but 'very high class men' (including the shipowner and South American merchant Henry Brocklehurst) found seats on the board of the Standard Marine Insurance Co., while a number of companies had a reputation for selecting as directors only 'gentlemen of the highest reputation for business ability', including the Royal Insurance Co. and the Pacific Loan and Discount Co. Indeed, a seat on the board of the Royal Insurance Co. was seen as 'a mark of commercial standing' and 'no slight certificate of commercial repute', just as a directorship of the Bank of Liverpool was 'coveted by all except the few eccentric wealthy merchants who avoid all directorates'. It is difficult to quantify the precise impact of interlocking directorships on the performance of limited companies or to assess whether the acceptance of external responsibilities had negative consequences for the firms of individual directors. In some cases, members of the merchant community continued to act as directors after their formal retirement from business, as was the case with the East India merchant H. B. Gilmour, the brass founder Sir David Radcliffe, and the tin plate merchant Elisha Smith. Other directors, such as the sugar refiner James Barrow, were simply listed as 'not in business', but the overwhelming majority were still actively involved in Liverpool's trade and commerce. Whereas the elite associational profile of the 23 shipowners who held company directorships in the early 1890s was relatively weak, nine of them held interlocking directorships which not only offered a more extensive framework for networking, but also reinforced the trend towards greater hierarchical institutionalism within the merchant community.[160]

Conclusion

The development of Liverpool's merchant community in the nineteenth century was a complex process. The primacy of commerce and trade led to the accumulation of immense wealth which benefited merchants in general, but particularly elite members of the trading community. But to what extent was commercial success predicated on the creation and maintenance of effective networking arrangements, whether embedded within a family-based, ethnic, or social framework? Does network theory offer a sufficiently robust explanation for Liverpool's increasing dominance of British and international trade, with its wide range of forelands, whether in the USA, Continental Europe, British imperial and dominion territories, and the 'informal Empire' of Central and Latin America and China? How significant was the consolidation and expansion of Merseyside's hinterland connections in structuring local business networks in both a regional and national framework? What factors determined network functionality, whether in a business or social setting, and how far was the mercantile community, or, more accurately, its elite members, able to retain access to political power and consolidate their control over local authority policies and civic culture?

Much has been made of the traditional cohesiveness of Liverpool merchants in proposing and implementing objectives which improved the port's trading infrastructure or were intended to provide an effective forum for collective action. Such a view has become part of an established discourse often deployed to explain its growing commercial success from the 1750s until the outbreak of the First World War, a process which transformed it into a 'Great Port', despite the fact that it was never 'marked out by nature' for such a role because of its inhospitable estuary. The available evidence from the eighteenth century tends to support this hypothesis. Firstly, the decision to construct the world's first commercial wet dock (1708–1715) generated benefits for both the Corporation and individual merchants and shipowners, although its short-term impact was 'scarcely revolutionary'. Secondly, the establishment of a Chamber of Commerce in 1774 was predicated on a unity of purpose within the mercantile community and a widespread recognition that it would enable the realisation of common objectives in a more effective manner. Thirdly, despite political and social divisions, the rise of Liverpool as 'the metropolis of slavery' served as a unifying focus for the interests of many of its merchants, even those whose involvement was marginal and simply part of a wider trading portfolio. Slave trading and privateering were both regarded as high-risk activities, but individual voyages were managed by relatively large investment groups, thereby providing access to necessary resources, expert knowledge, and practical skills in a manner that strengthened network cohesion. Liverpool's population by 1801 was approximately 89,000 (including Toxteth Park and the West Derby Registration District), but the residential distribution pattern was determined by social class and occupation (with some merchants continuing to combine business premises with their family homes), with the result that face-to-face contacts with other traders were still a common occurrence.[161]

Although the range of Liverpool's trade in the late eighteenth century should not be underestimated, the contrast with the situation a hundred years later was nevertheless substantial. The port-city had been transformed by unprecedented population growth, largely a result of high rates of in-migration, substantial trade diversification with an increasing range of foreland linkages, particularly in Asia, Australasia, and the Americas. This had been reinforced by the installation of a successful transatlantic telegraph cable in 1866; the creation of one of the most extensive dock systems ever built (including additional dock facilities in Birkenhead and Garston); improved hinterland connectivity with the construction of a dense railway network; and the creation of an efficient national postal system. Its spatial presence had been expanded significantly, with extensive suburbanisation involving five boundary extensions and high rates of settlement in Birkenhead and elsewhere on the Wirral, as well as in South Lancashire. And yet, there is an implicit assumption that trading networks within the mercantile community were not radically affected by these changes. After all the establishment of a new Chamber of Commerce in 1850 was evidence of the existence of a 'community' of 'capitalist entrepreneurs': it reflected a similar unity of purpose to that of the previous century and demonstrated the absence of any 'fundamental fracture' within the mercantile élite, a situation which is assumed to have persisted in the following decades.[162]

However, such an assumption is highly questionable. As this chapter has demonstrated, Liverpool's economy, based to a large extent on commerce and trade, continued to be subject to significant cyclical instability, often aggravated by greed and speculation. In the opinion of William Allingham, its commerce was 'almost synonymous with Speculation'. The trading environment remained volatile, despite technological improvements in communication, which required managerial and entrepreneurial skills in handling both short- and medium-term trends. Liverpool's position was not unique in this context, in comparison with towns and cities with a stronger manufacturing base, but the ramifications for its working-class population, often dependent on casual and unreliable labour markets, were considerable. Furthermore, although there were several 'old firms' (of at least three generations) which had been founded between the mid-eighteenth century and the early 1800s the extent of transience within the business community throughout the period under consideration was substantial. If many of the leading merchants were themselves in-migrants, commercial success (and failure) was often followed by out-migration, in the former case often motivated by the acquisition of a county estate either because of family connections (particularly to their place birth) or the irresistible attraction of upward social mobility. This, according to Long, became more frequent in the second half of the nineteenth century. Geographical mobility within what is now the Liverpool City Region was extensive and frequent, as revealed by the analysis of residential data in the Mercantile Liverpool database, but the ownership of rural estates further afield offered access to important representational roles, whether as a M.P., JP, high sheriff, or a lord lieutenant or his deputy, as well as an opportunity to consolidate their social standing by philanthropic donations designed to address the educational and religious needs of the local population. Extensive out-migration, however, had wider implications. It signified a weakening and fragmentation of Liverpool-based networks in a commercial, cultural, and religious context by undermining the continuity of family representation in the city, while the acquisition of a different lifestyle, which often included the pursuit of rural blood sports, was in stark contrast to the day-to-day pressures of business activity. In contrast to the earlier decades of the nineteenth century, the increasing preference of elite members of the mercantile community for rural residences and county estates was not compensated, to the same extent, by the arrival of new in-migrants eager to make a career on Merseyside, as the increased proportion of locally born merchants in the MLP database confirms.[163]

Business volatility and spatial mobility were two variables which should have reinforced the value of networking within Liverpool's mercantile community at a time when bankruptcy remained an underlying fear and transience was still an extensive phenomenon. However, there were other factors of greater significance. Much has been made of Liverpool's exceptionalism in the modern period, even if a robust analytical framework based on comparative data is still lacking. Commercial networks were based historically on mutually beneficial business relations, they were strongly embedded in multiple and synergistic structures which required a set of competences (whether in relation to a knowledge of trade practices and production processes), but also an acknowledgement of obligations based on family, ethnicity, and religion. Their 'subjective collectivity' was defined by family, ethnicity, denominational affiliation, or political allegiance. However, in exploring the extent and practice of merchant networking in Liverpool between the mid-nineteenth century and 1914, business historians have tended to ignore the significance of religious and political variables in moulding the environment in which businessmen and merchants operated. Age-old theological disagreements were a cause of religious and cultural conflicts, both between different denominations and within individual churches, while the evangelical revival unleashed 'enthusiasm and fervour', revitalised the sense of religious community, and led to increased hostility between the established churches, Protestant dissenters, and Roman Catholics. Religious commitment by some members of the mercantile community might involve active preaching, extensive charity work on a clearly defined denominational basis, the maintenance of a 'high moral character', and a willingness to live in conformity with religious precepts, not only privately, but among immediate business associates. Even if most denominations, excluding Roman Catholicism, witnessed a gradual reduction in church attendance from the 1890s onwards, sectarianism continued to dominate the port-city and its surrounding areas. Neal has claimed that anti-Catholicism was evident 'at all levels of society' in Victorian England and the available data confirm the extent to which some merchants and businessmen on Merseyside had deeply entrenched and mutually antagonistic religious views. Indeed, extensive brawling and riots between Protestants and Catholics, particularly in the pre-1914 period, reflected tensions that were felt across the whole of the city, irrespective of social class.[164]

A persistent strand in the historiography of Liverpool is the belief that there was a general unity of interest within the mercantile community, irrespective of denominational or trade-specific differences. The primacy of commerce and trade, as in many other port-cities, reinforced the cohesiveness of merchant capital, even if there were clear differences of opinion on specific issues. However, this was compromised by denominational differences, while the impact of sectarianism on business relations was aggravated by its political repercussions. In general, political connectedness reflected the strength of individual contacts and the level of activism, but it was often mediated by denominational affiliation. As Marriner and Davies emphasised some time ago, political activity was dominated by denominational divisions, which became more acute as the century progressed: Anglicans tended to be Conservative in their political orientation and for most of the period under investigation the Tory Party retained control of the council, both in Liverpool and Birkenhead; while Unitarians, together with other dissenting congregations, were most likely to support the Liberal Party. Of course, both denominational belief and political affiliation was sometimes fluid, even within individual families, but this broad division reinforced underlying differences within the mercantile community. Political fragmentation became increasingly evident from the early 1870s onwards: both Tories and Liberals established a network of clubs in Liverpool and Merseyside; party business and electoral preparations were organised more efficiently with adversarial intent; and by 1900 the Irish Nationalists were the main opposition party on the city council. At the same time, political control, which had long been held by elite members of the mercantile community began to slip away. In the mid-1840s, two thirds of the elected council members had been merchants: by the late 1890s they accounted for fewer than 50 per cent. Furthermore, this weakening of political influence was replicated in other areas of civic life, whether in relation to the composition of the magistracy, the leadership of the town council, or the recipients of the Freedom of the City of Liverpool.[165]

Nor did institutional changes in business organisation provide a counterweight to contemporary trends towards increased fragmentation. The proliferation of trade associations improved transaction efficiency and reliability at a sectoral level, but they operated within a competitive, sometimes hostile environment (particularly in shipping and the cotton trade); they had an exclusionary management structure, dominated by an elite group of council members and directors; they favoured insiders (specifically the sons of existing members), rather than new entrants from elsewhere; and provided an important, but highly restricted, focal point for business networking. The Chamber of Commerce, which should have played a coordinating role by representing the general interests of the trading and business community, never succeeded in achieving its objectives. In the early 1850s, only a minority of Liverpool's merchants were members of the new Chamber; it replicated the wider fragmentation of commerce and trade; some commercial interests were never adequately represented; and its reconstitution in 1877, because of claims that it had been too political, did not lead to a more dynamic approach in responding to the collective needs of the mercantile community. An increasing frequency of interlocking directorships, with the appointment of highly-regarded merchants and shipowners to the boards of local banks and insurance companies, had obvious benefits in terms of effective networking, but some directors were no longer active in business; recent evidence reveals that these linkages made little difference to the commercial behaviour of individual actors; and they only reinforced the institutional hierarchy of the port-city's commercial world, with its attendant operational constraints. To this extent, the continued emphasis on the cohesiveness and solidarity of Liverpool's mercantile community is far from compelling: it seriously underplays the reality of business competition; even if its influence in moulding Liverpool's development cannot be doubted, the ability of merchants to exercise power became increasingly constrained.[166]

Notes

1   Pamela Walker Laird, 'Introduction Putting Social Capital to Work', *BH*, 50, 6 (2008), p. 687; Lyn Spillman and Michael Strand, 'Interest-Oriented Action', *American Review of Sociology*, 39 (2013), pp. 85–104; M. Hechter and S. Kanazawa, 'Sociological Rational Choice Theory', *American Review of Sociology*, 23 (1997), pp. 191–214; J. Whitmeyer and K. S. Cook, 'Social Structure and Social Exchange', in S. C. Chew and J. D. Knottnerus (eds.), *Structure, Culture and History: Recent Issues in Social Theory* (Lanham, 2002), pp. 271–88; Jack Barbalet, 'Self-Interest and the Theory of Action', *British Journal of Sociology*, 63, 3 (2012), pp. 412–29; Andrew Popp and Robin Holt, 'The Presence of Entrepreneurial Opportunities', *BH*, 55, 1 (2013), pp. 9–28.

2   Sheila Marriner and Peter Davies, 'Business and Society: Liverpool 1880–1940', draft book proposal, unpublished (Liverpool, c.1984).

3   Gary Bridge and Sophie Watson, 'Lest Power Be Forgotten: Networks, Division and Difference in the City', *The Sociological Review*, 50, 4 (2002), pp. 511–12, 522; Mike Savage and Karel Williams, 'Elites: Remembered in Capitalism and Forgotten by Social Sciences', *The Sociological Review*, 56, 1 (2008), pp. 1–24; John Scott, 'Modes of Power and the Re-Conceptualization of Elites', *The Sociological Review*, 56, 1 (2008), pp. 25–43; Mike Savage, 'The Politics of Elective Belonging', *Housing. Theory and Society*, 27, 2 (2010), pp. 115–35; Niall Cunningham and Mike Savage, 'The Secret Garden? Elite Metropolitan Geographies in the Contemporary UK', *The Sociological Review*, 63, 2 (2015), pp. 321–48.

4   Jane Marceau, *Class and Status in France Economic Change and Social Immobility, 1945–1975* (Oxford, 1977), p. 84; Norbert Elias and John L. Scotson, *The Established and the Outsider: A Sociological Enquiry into Community Problems* (London, 1965); Maarten Hogenstijn, Daniel Van Middlekoop and Kees Terlouw, 'The Established, the Outsiders, and Scale Strategies: Studying Local Power Conflicts', *The Sociological Review*, 56 (2007), pp. 144–61; Sharan B. Merriam, Juanita Johnson-Bailey, Ming-Yeh Lee, Youngwha Lee, Gabo Ntseane and Mazanah Muhamed, 'Power and Positionality: Negotiating Insider/Outsider Status within and across Cultures', *International Journal of Lifelong Education*, 20, 5 (2010), pp. 405–16; *Liverpool Today* (Liverpool, 1889), pp. 64, 67.

5 For an excellent study of crises on Bristol's sugar trade with the West Indies in the late eighteenth century, see Peter Buckles, 'Merchants and Crisis in the Bristol West India Sugar Trades, 1783–1802', unpublished PhD, University of Liverpool (2021).

6 Stephan D. Behrendt, 'Markets, Transaction Cycles, and Profits: Merchant Decision Making in the British Slave Trade', *The William and Mary Quarterly*, 58, 1 (2001), pp. 171–204. The instability of local banks was not a new phenomenon: as early as 1816 the bank in which William Roscoe was a senior partner, Roscoe, Clark, and Roscoe, was forced to suspend payments which led to the enforced sale of his collection of drawings and paintings. As a result of as successful subscription campaign, most of them were acquired by the Liverpool Royal Institution. See Edward Morris, 'The Formation of the Gallery of Art in the Liverpool Royal Institution', *THSL&C*, 142 (1992), p. 92.

7 Stephen Broadberry, Bruce Campbell, Alexander Klein, Mark Overton and Bas van Leeawen, *British Economic Growth, 1270–1870* (Cambridge, 2015); LRO, 1/2, Holt Family—family diaries, George Holt Senior, 26 July, 3 November 1845; 'The Crisis Continues', 'Stoppage of the North and South Wales Bank', *Liverpool Mercury*, 26 October 1847; MMM, MAL, DX/258/2/1/1–88, Copies of letters written by Macgregor Laird to his wife, Eleanor Hester Laird (née Nicolls) (1848–60), 7 September 1848; B. L. Anderson and P. L. Cottrell, 'Another Victorian Capital Market: A Study of Banking and Bank Investors on Merseyside', *EcHR*, NS, 28, 4 (1975), pp. 598–615; LRO, 362 SAL 4/1/1 (2), Liverpool Female Orphan Institution, Annual Report, 28th February 1859, p. 2; Forrest Capie, 'British Financial Crises in the Nineteenth and Twentieth Centuries' (pp. 9–23) and Marc Flandreau and Stefano Ugolini, 'The Crisis of 1866' (p. 93), in Nicholas Dimsdale and Anthony Hotson (eds.), *British Financial Crises Since 1825* (Oxford, 2014); Sir William Bower Forwood, *Recollections of a Busy Life* (Liverpool, 1910), p. 65; Aytoun Ellis, *Heir of Adventure the Story of Brown, Shipley & Co. Merchant Bankers 1810–1960* (London, 1960), p. 67; John Rankin, *A History of Our Firm: Some Account of the Firm of Pollok, Gilmour & Co. and Its Offshoots and Connections* (Liverpool, 1908), p. 255; Samuel Smith, *My Life Work* (London, 1902), p. 75; J. A. Picton, *Memorials of Liverpool Historical and Topographical Including a History of the Dock Estate* (London and Liverpool, 1875), vol. 1, p. 255; LRO, DUR, 1/4, Holt Family diaries, (by Emma Holt, later Anne Holt), 29 October 1861; Nigel Hall, 'The Liverpool Cotton Market and the American Civil War', *Northern History*, (1998), pp. 149–69; Jim Powell, 'Cotton, Liverpool and the American Civil War', unpublished D.Phil., University of Liverpool (2018), pp. 20, 27 and Chapter 3; E. J. Donnell, *Chronological and Statistical History of Cotton* (New York, 1872), p. 529. MacGregor Laird (1808–1961) was the younger son of Agnes and William Laird who migrated from Greenock to Liverpool and, subsequently, to Birkenhead, where his father founded what became the most important shipbuilding firm on Merseyside. After his return from an extensive exploration of the River Niger (1832–34) undertaken primarily for commercial purposes, he became one of the promoters of the British & American Steam Navigation Co. (1835–41). See M. L. Tanner, 'MacGregor Laird: The Five Percent Failure', unpublished M.A. dissertation, University of Western Ontario (1979); Davies, *The Trade Makers*, Chapter 1 'The Pioneers', pp. 35–51.

8 J. Watson, *A Hundred Years of Sugar Refining the Story of the Love Lane Refinery 1872–1972* (Liverpool, 1973), p. 11; Sheila Marriner, *Rathbones of Liverpool 1845–73* (Liverpool, 1961), p. 16; Francis E. Hyde, *Cunard and the North Atlantic 1840–1973* (London and Basingstoke, 1975), p. 28; Martin Lynn, 'Trade and Politics in 19th Century Liverpool: The Tobin and Horsfall Families and Liverpool's African Trade', *THSL&C*, 142 (1992), p. 111; S. B. Saul, *The Myth of the Great Depression 1873–1896* (Studies in Economic and Social History) (2nd ed., London and Basingstoke, 1985); Broadberry, Campbell, Klein, Overton and van Leeawen, *British Economic Growth*; D. J. Coppock, 'The Cause of the Great Depression, 1873–96', *Manchester School*, 29, 3 (2008), pp. 205–32; Richard James, *Economy and Society in Nineteenth Century Britain* (London, 2005), pp. 23–4; Orchard, *Liverpool's Legion of Honour*, pp. 429, 483; Gordon W. Roderick and Michael D. Stephens, 'Approaches to Technical Education in England Part II: The Liverpool School of Science', *The Vocational Aspect of Education*, 22, 53 (1970), p. 155. The human cost of periodic crises has seldom been explored, but there is no doubting its severity. For example, a trading colleague of the stockbroker George Alexander Brown was 'floored' by the panic of 1857 and had to be confined in a lunatic asylum. See LRO 920 MD 376, 3, Autobiographical Memoirs and diaries of George Alexander Brown, 1803–61, 6th June 1860.

9 Hannah Barker and Mina Ishizu, 'Inheritance and Continuity in Small Family Businesses during the Early Industrial Revolution', *BH*, 54, 2 (2012), pp. 227–44; Graeme J. Milne, *Trade and Traders in Mid-Victorian Liverpool Mercantile Business and the Making of a world port* (Liverpool, 2000), p. 149; see Randolph Cock, John Davies, Robert Lee, and Sari Mäenpää, Chapter 2.

10 B. Guinness Orchard, *Liverpool's Legion of Honour* (Birkenhead, 1893), pp. 3–28, 509, 561–2.

11 J. A. Picton, 'History and Curiosities of the Liverpool Directory', *THSL&C*, 3rd Series, 5 (1877), pp. 11–12; Orchard, *Liverpool's Legion of Honour*, pp. 73, 588–9; See Graeme Milne, Chapter 3.

12 See Randolph Cock, John Davies, Robert Lee, and Sari Mäenpää, Chapter 2; Joel Tarr, 'The City and the Telegraph: Urban Telecommunications in the Pre-Telephone Era', *Journal of Urban History*, 14, 1 (1987), pp. 38–80; Graeme Milne, 'British Business and the Telephone, 1878–1911', *BH*, 49, 2 (2007), pp. 163–85.

13 Orchard, *Liverpool's Legion of Honour*, pp. 5, 7; Robert Lee, 'Configuring the City: In-Migration, Labour Supply and Port Development in Nineteenth-Century Europe', *IJMH, History*, 17, 1 (2005), pp. 110–12.

14 See Randolph Cock, John Davies, Robert Lee, and Sari Mäenpää, Chapter 2. For an overview of Liverpool's in-migrant communities, see John Belchem and Donald M. MacRaild, 'Cosmopolitan Liverpool', in John Belchem (ed.), *Liverpool 800 Culture Character and History* (Liverpool, 2006), pp. 311–92. For a comparative study of Belfast, see Kyle Hughes, *The Scots in Victorian and Edwardian Belfast: A Study in Elite Migration* (Edinburgh, 2014).

15 Richard Lawton, 'The Components of Demographic Change in a Rapidly Growing Port-City: The Case of Liverpool in the Nineteenth Century', in Richard Lawton and Robert Lee (eds.), *Population and Society in Western European Port-Cities c.1650–1939* (Liverpool, 2002), p. 115; Colin G. Pooley, 'Living in Liverpool: The Modern City', in John Belchem (ed.), *Liverpool 800 Culture Character & History* (Liverpool, 2006), pp. 179–88. For a discussion of the significance of new developments in communication technology, see Graeme Milne, Chapter 3. See also Randolph Cock, John Davies, Robert Lee, and Sari Mäenpää, Chapter 2.

16 Orchard, *Liverpool's Legion of Honour*, p. 63; see Joseph Sharples and Adrian Jarvis, Chapter 9.

17 See Chapters 2 (Randolph Cock, John Davies, Robert Lee, and Sari Mäenpää), 9 (Joseph Sharples and Adrian Jarvis), and 10 (Robert Lee); Picton, *Memorials of Liverpool*, vol. 2, p. 269; R. J. Morris, *Men, Women and Property in England, 1780–1870: A Social and Economic History of Family Strategies amongst the Leeds Middle Classes* (Cambridge, 2005), p. 149; Barker and Ishizu, 'Inheritance and Continuity', pp. 227–44; LRO, 614 INF 5/6, *The One Hundred and Forty-Fifth Report of the Liverpool Royal Infirmary for the Year 1893* (Liverpool, 1894), p. 1; 614 INF 5/14, *Report of the Liverpool Royal Infirmary, Lunatic Asylum and Lock Hospital for the Year 1863* (Liverpool, 1864). For a discussion of these issues, see Martin J. Wiener, *English Culture and the Decline of the Industrial Spirit* (Cambridge, 1981); W. D. Rubinstein, *Capitalism, Culture, and Decline in Britain, 1750–1990* (London and New York, 1993); Hartmut Berghoff, 'A Gentrified Bourgeoisie? On the Social History of Ennobled Businessmen in Prussia and Britain, 1870–1918', *German Yearbook on Business History* (1995), pp. 9–36.

18 Jane Longmore, 'Portrait of a Slave-Trading Family the Staniforths of Liverpool', in Katie Donington, Ryan Hanley and Jessica Moody (eds.), *Britain's History and Memory of Transatlantic Slavery Local Nuances of a 'National Sin'* (Liverpool, 2017), pp. 60–82; LRO, STI, Staniforth Family; LRO, 920 DRI Drinkwater Family, 6, 23; MMM, MAL, D/Earle, 13/2, *Earle, T. Algernon, Earle of Allerton Tower* (Liverpool, 1889), pp. 31, 38.

19 Jane Longmore, 'Rural Retreats: Liverpool Slave Traders and Their Country Houses', in Madge Dresser and Andrew Hann (eds.), *Slavery and the British Country House* (Swindon, 2013), pp. 30–45; Peter Earle, *The Earles of Liverpool: A Georgian Merchant Dynasty* (Liverpool, 2015), in particular Chapter 10; Joseph Sharples and Adrian Jarvis, Chapter 9; Martin Lymm, 'The Profitability of the Early Nineteenth-Century Palm Oil Trade', *African Economic History*, 20 (1992), pp. 77–97; idem, 'Trade and Politics in 19th-Century Liverpool: The Tobin and Horsfall Families and Liverpool's African Trade', *THSL&C*, pp. 98–118, in particular p. 111, www.ucl.ac.uk/lbs/person/view/67653; 946224849.

20 Orchard, *Liverpool's Legion of Honour*, pp. 145, 151, 326–7, 399, 405.

21 Orchard, *Liverpool's Legion of Honour*, pp. 64, 326–30, 536, 637, 733; A. H. Rowson, 'Edward Bates: Shipowner', in P. E. Bates (ed.), *Bates of Bellefield, Gyrn Castle and Manydown* (n.p., 1994), pp. 226–8.

22 W. D. Rubinstein, 'Businessmen into Landowners: The Question Revisited', in N. B. Harte and R. E. Quinault (eds.), *Land and Society in Britain, 1700–1914: Essays in Honour of F.M.L. Thompson* (Manchester, 1996), pp. 90–118; F. M. L. Thompson, *Gentrification and Enterprise Culture: Britain 1780–1980* (Oxford and New York, 2001); Julia A. Smith, 'Land Ownership and Social Change in Late Nineteenth-Century Britain', *EcHR*, 53, 4 (2000), pp. 767–76; Tom Nicholas, 'Businessmen and Land Ownership in the Late Nineteenth Century Revisited', *EcHR*, 53 (2000), pp. 27–44; David

R. Green and Alastair Owens, 'Geographies of Wealth: Real Estate and Personal Property Owner-ship in England and Wales, 1870–1902', *EcHR*, 66, 3 (2013), pp. 848–72; Frances Anne Conybeare, *Dingle Bank the Home of the Croppers a Recollection* (Cambridge, 1925), pp. 1, 13; MLP database and obituaries file, no. 478. Even at the end of the nineteenth century, Dingle Bank remained 'a still untouched and almost rural home, on the bank of the Mersey': see James Cropper, *Notes and Memories: Being Selections from a Book of Notes, Together with Recollections of Men and Their Sayings* (Kendal, 1900), p. ii.

23 David Bawden, '"In This Book-Making Age": Edward Kemp as Writer and Communicator of Hor-ticultural Knowledge', in Robert Lee (ed.), *Edward Kemp (1817–91): Landscape Gardener* (*Garden History*, 46, Suppl. 1 (2018), p. 145; John Claudius Loudon, *The Suburban Garden and Villa Com-panion: Comprising the Choice of a Suburban or Villa Residence, or of Situation on Which to Form One; the Arrangement and Furnishing of the House; and the Laying Out, Planting, and General Management of the Gardens and Grounds* (London, 1838); Elizabeth Davey, 'Landscape Design for "Gentlemen of Wealth": Edward Kemp's Private Commissions', in Lee, *Edward Kemp*, pp. 120–5; *Carlisle Journal*, Friday 10 May 1861, p. 6; Davey, 'Gazetteer of Identified Commissions by Edward Kemp, 1843–87, by Historic (pre-1974) Counties', in Lee, *Edward Kemp*, pp. 205–6. Kemp also landscaped the gardens at Oxley's house in Mossley Hill, Liverpool.

24 Thompson, 'Life after Death', pp. 53–4; MMM, MAL, DX2463, will of Thomas Leyland; LRO, DUR 1/2, Holt Family—family diaries, George Holt Senior, 18 July 1852; DUR 1/5, Anne Holt, 6 June 1871; Hartmut Berghoff and Roland Müller, 'Wirtschaftsbürger in Bremen und Bristol 1870–1914', in H.-J. Puhle (ed.), *Bürger in der Gesellschaft der Neuzeit* (Göttingen, 1991), p. 172; Thomp-son, *Gentrification and the Enterprise Culture*; Morris, *Men, Women and Property*, p. 328; Gunn, *The Public Culture of the Victorian Middle Class*, p. 25; John Belchem and Nick Hardy, 'Second Metrop-olis: The Middle Class in Early Victorian Liverpool', in Alan Kidd and David Nicholls (eds.), *The Making of the British Middle Class? Studies of Regional and Cultural Diversity since the Eighteenth Century* (Thrupp, 1998), p. 65; 'Grand Fancy Dress Ball in Aid of the Public Charities', *Liverpool Mercury*, Friday 29 March 1844; Edward Morris, 'Provincial Internationalism: Contemporary For-eign Art in Nineteenth-Century Liverpool and Manchester', *THSL&C*, 147, p. 100; Rev. F. O. Mor-ris, *A Series of Picturesque Views of Seats of Noblemen and Gentlemen of Great Britain and Ireland* (Edinburgh and Dublin, c.1870), vols. 1–3; Mrs. Kurtz's husband, A. G. Kurtz, was the owner and manager of a chemical works in St. Helens, a talented musician, and a patron of British painters of the Classical Revival. See Edward Morris and Christopher Fifield, 'A. G. Kurtz: A Patron of Classical Art and Music in Victorian Liverpool', *Journal of the History of Collections*, 7, 1 (1995), pp. 103–14.

25 Orchard, *Liverpool's Legion of Honour*, pp. 31, 147, 205, 443, 533–4, 597, 632, 684–5; A. F. Petrie, *A Short History of Yewden Manor and Greenlands* (Henley Archaeological and History Group) (Hen-ley, 1979). Schwabe also purchased a London residence, 19 Kensington Palace Gardens, where he died in 1897. Thomas Brocklebank (1774–1848), a partner in Thomas and John Brocklebank, mer-chants and shipowners, had the existing hall at Irton in the Lake District extended around 1820: it came with an extensive demesne estate.

26 Graeme Cubbin, *Harrisons of Liverpool a Chronicle of Ships and Men 1830–2002* (Gravesend and Preston, 2003), pp. 30, 54; 'Portrait of a Liverpool Shipowner Frederick James Harrison', in Antony J. Barratt (ed.), *Merseyside Maritime Research* (Liverpool Nautical Research Society) (Liverpool, 2007), p. 2; Orchard, *Liverpool's Legion of Honour*, pp. 356, 577; *The London Gazette*, 3 February 1882, p. 451; George Melly, *Recollections of Sixty Years (1833–93): Political, Social and Sportive* (Coventry, 1893), p. 161; LRO, 920 MEL 7, Melly Correspondence, 784, 12 August 1861; 920 MEL 23, George Melly M. P., Private Correspondence, vol. 17, 4463, 1st September 1871; LRO 920 DUR 14/27/170, Richard Durning Holt to F. W. Hirst, cited by D. J. Dutton, 'Introduction', in David J. Dutton (ed.), *Odyssey of an Edwardian Liberal the Political Diary of Richard Durning Holt* (The Record Society of Lancashire and Cheshire, 129) (Gloucester, 1989), p. xvii; National Probate Cal-endar (Index of Wills and Administrations), 15 April 1890, 2 May 1894; Rankin, *A History of Our Firm*, p. 90. Melly's commitment to shooting was highlighted in his obituaries: according to the *Daily Post*, 29 September 1894, he had been all his life 'an ardent devotee of shooting and other out-of-door sports'; was 'constantly to be seen in the cricket or polo field'; and had shown great interest in the Liverpool Polo Club.

27 Forwood, *Recollections*, p. 60; LRO, DUR 1/2, Holt Family—family diaries, George Holt Senior, 11.11.1844–31.12.1854, 4th September 1845; *Deaths and Inquests*, 1914; PRO DUR 920, 1/6, Fam-ily Diary (maintained by Robert D. Holt), 11 August, 13 September 1891; Adrian Jarvis, 'The Port

of Liverpool and the Shipowners', *The Great Circle*, 16 (1994), p. 13; MLP database and obituaries (George Curzon Dobell, *Liverpool Mercury*, 20 January 1914; Orchard, *Liverpool's Legion of Honour*, pp. 156, 454–5, 657, 690, 714: see Randolph Cock, John Davies, Robert Lee, and Sari Mäenpää, Chapter 2 and Sari Mäenpää, Chapter 6.

28 Edward Wakefield, *The County Families of the United Kingdom* (London, 1881); Orchard, *Liverpool's Legion of Honour*, pp. 205, 687; MLP database.

29 Pike, *Contemporary Biographies*, pp. 108, 172, 174; Orchard, *Liverpool's Legion of Honour*, pp. 454, 594–5. Walker became president of the Derbyshire Royal Infirmary (1886), a committee member of the Derbyshire Agricultural Society and Derby Charity Organisation Society, vice-president of Derby County Cricket Club and the Derbyshire Natural History and Archaeology Society, a patron of Derby Burn's Club, and a director of Francis Wright's Trent College.

30 Richard Burn, *The Justice of the Peace, and Parish Officer* (15th ed., London, 1785), vol. 3, p. 21; R. H. Maudsley and J. W. Davies, 'The Justice of the Peace in England', *University of Miami Law Review*, 18, 3 (1964), pp. 525, 530. Only in the case of Ireland, where absentee landlordism was endemic, did it prove difficult to find suitable Protestant gentry to serve as justices of the peace: see Niamh Howlin, 'Nineteenth-Century Justice: Uniquely Irish or, Simply "Not English"', *The Journal of Legal History*, 30, 3 (2009), pp. 67–89. Property qualifications for the justices of the peace were not abolished until 1906.

31 W. D. Rubinstein, 'New Men of Wealth and the Purchase of Land in Nineteenth-Century Britain', *Past and Present*, 92 (1981), pp. 125–47; F. M. L. Thompson, 'Life after Death: How Successful Nineteenth-Century Businessmen Disposed of Their Fortunes', *EcHR*, 2nd ser., 43, 1 (1990), p. 58; Mark Rothery, 'The Wealth of the English Landed Gentry, 1870–1935', *Agricultural History Review*, 55, 2 (2007), p. 251; Orchard, *Liverpool's Legion of Honour*, p. 174; P. L. Cottrell, 'Liverpool Shipowners, the Mediterranean, and the Transition from Sail to Steam during the Mid-Nineteenth Century', in Lewis R. Fischer (ed.), *From Wheel to Counting House: Essays in Maritime Business History in Honour of Professor Peter Neville Davies* (Research in Maritime History, No. 2) (St. John's, Newfoundland, 1992), pp. 153–202; 'Owners and Occupiers of Ottershaw Park', www.johnathersuch.com/op_website/op_chapel_text.htm; J. M. Lee, *Social Leaders and Public Persons a Study of County Government in Cheshire since 1888* (Oxford, 1963), pp. 26, 42; R. Radcliffe Carter, *Pictures and Engravings at Haughton Hall, Tarporley, in the Possession of Ralph Brocklebank* (London, 1904); Linden Groves, *Historic Parks & Gardens of Cheshire* (Malta, 2004), p. 160; MLP database. In 1889, Graham became the first permanent chairman of Cheshire County Council: he also supplied at his own cost piped water to the cottagers of Willaston. J. J. Bibby was probably one of those members of Liverpool's mercantile community who declined to submit material for Orchard's collective biography: he was simply listed as residing 'in Shropshire'.

32 Peter Bailey, 'The Politics and Poetics of Modern British Leisure', *Rethinking History*, 3, 2 (1999), p. 150; J. Howe, 'Fox Hunting as Ritual', *American Ethnologist*, 8, 2 (1981), pp. 278–300; Garry Marvin, *The Sociological Review*, 51, 2 (2003), pp. 46–60; Caspian Richards, 'Grouse Shooting and Its Landscape the Management of Grouse Moors in Britain', *Anthropology Today*, 20, 4 (2004), p. 10; Borderer, *Hunting Notes in Shropshire and Cheshire 1884–85 with Illustrations by H. F. Mylton* (London and Shrewsbury, 1885), pp. 1, 3; Burgenland Thomas, *The Shooter's Guide: Or, Complete Sportsman's Companion: Containing Every Possible Instruction for the Juvenile Shooter* (3rd ed., London, 1811); R. Rayner and A. Ellis, *The Story of the Sporting Gun* (Newton Abbot, 1991). It was reported in 1872 that the Maharaja Duleep Singh, a deposed Sikh monarch, had bagged 440 birds in a single day on the Sottish Highland estate of Grandtully.

33 James Stonehouse, *The Streets of Liverpool* (Liverpool, 1869: 2002 ed.), p. 43; Aspinall, *Liverpool a Few Years Since*, pp. 162, 167; Nathaniel Cane, *History of the Royal Rock Beagle Hunt Issued by Subscription in the Year of Jubilee of the Hunt 1895* (Birkenhead, 1895), pp. 6, 81.

34 Mike Huggins, 'Sport and the British Upper Classes c.1500–2000: A Historiographic Overview', *Sport in History*, 28, 3 (2008), pp. 364–88; Raymond Carr, *English Foxhunting: A History* (London, 1976); David Itzkovitz, *Peculiar Privilege: A Social History of English Foxhunting 1753–1885* (London, 1977); Allyson N. May, *The Fox-Hunting Controversy, 1781–2004: Class and Cruelty* (London, 2013); Gordon Fergusson, *The Green Collars: The Tarporley Hunt Club and Cheshire Hunting History Incorporating Hunting Songs (Eleventh Edition) by Rowland Egerton Warburton* (London, 1993); Sir Ralph Payne-Gallway, *Letters to Young Shooters (Third Series) Comprising a Short Natural History of British Wildfowl and Complete Directions in Shooting Wildfowl on the Coast and Inland* (London, 1896); David S. D. Jones, *Soval: The History of a Lewis Sporting Estate* (Fovant,

2010); G. T. Teasdale, 'Shooting British Islands Generally', in Frederick G. Aflalo (ed.), *The Cost of Sport* (London, 1899), pp. 31–79; Alastair Durie, '"Unconscious Benefactors": Grouse-Shooting in Scotland, 1780–1914', *International Journal of Sport*, 15, 3 (1998), pp. 57–73; Edward Bujack, 'Sport and the Survival of Landed Society in Late Victorian Suffolk', in Richard W. Hoyle (ed.), *Our Hunting Fathers: Field Sports in England after 1850* (Lancaster, 2007), pp. 72–95.

35 Orchard, *Liverpool's Legion of Honour*, pp. xv–xvi. In 83 cases (out of a total of 259 memoirs) no information was provided, perhaps because recreational pursuits for some members of the mercantile community remained a personal matter, but some entries included up to four different activities. The relative popularity of different sports has been calculated based on the total number of listed activities.

36 Pike, *Liverpool and Birkenhead*; W. T. Pike (ed.), *Cheshire At the Opening of the Twentieth Century by Robert Head: Contemporary Biographies* (Pike's New Century Series, No. 11) (Brighton, 1904). The sample size was 60.

37 Pike, *Cheshire*, p. 181; 'The Twelfth', *LM*, 13 August 1891, p. 6; 'The Twelfth', *LM*, 13 August 1892, p. 6; 'Day to Day in Liverpool', *LM*, 13 August 1895, p. 6.

38 Cuthbert Bradley, *Fox-Hunting from Shire to Shire with Many Noted Packs: A Companion Volume to Good Sport, Seen with Some Famous Packs* (London, 1912); Cicely Fox Smith, *Lancashire Hunting Songs, and Other Modern Leys* (Bristol, 2008); R. E. Egerton Warburton, *Hunting Songs* (London, 1877); Vanessa Greatorex, *Parkgate and Neston Through Time* (Stroud, 2014); 'Sporting Intelligence', *The Liverpool Mercury*, 2 April 1864; 18 April, 20 April 1888; 'Cheshire Hunt Difficulty Farmers' Strong Protest', *Cheshire Observer*, 25 May 1907; 'The Hon. William Ernest Duncombe, M.P.', 'The Earl of Bessborough', *Baily's Magazine of Sports and Pastimes*, 6 (1863), pp. 109–10, 163–4; Richard Clapham, *Rough Shooting for the Man of Moderate Means: With Some Notes on Game Preservation and Vermin Extermination* (London, 1923) LRO, 920 MEL 7, Melly Correspondence 30 September 1861–4 May 1863, 785, 788; H. K. Aspinall, *Birkenhead and Its Surroundings* (Birkenhead, 1903), p. 222. A typical anthology drawing on articles published in *The Field* was Evan G. Mackenzie's, *Grouse Shooting and Deer-Stalking* (London, 1907). Alfred Waterhouse re-design Eaton Hall between 1870 and 1882 at a cost of £803,000: it had massive stables and huge kennels and if overnight accommodation was required for members of the Cheshire Hunt, over 150 bedrooms were available.

39 Anne Holt, *Walking Together: A Study in Liverpool Nonconformity* (Liverpool, 1938); James Murphy, 'The Old Quaker Meeting House in Hakins Hey, Liverpool', *THSL&C*, 106 (1954), pp. 79–98; David J. Jeremy, *Capitalism and Christians: Business Leaders and the Churches in Britain, 1900–1960* (Oxford, 1990), p. 18.

40 D. Caradog Jones (ed.), *The Social Survey of Merseyside* (Liverpool, 1934), vol. 3, pp. 321–42; A. L. Doodson, *The Presbyterians in Liverpool: A Social and Religious Survey Up to 1972* (Liverpool, 1972); Alfred Percy Sinnett, *Early Days of Theosophy in Europe* (Kessinger, 2003); Eduard Rosenkranz, *Geschichte der deutschen evangelischen Kirche zu Liverpool* (Stuttgart, 1921); Robert Lee, 'Divided Loyalties? In-Migration, Ethnicity and Identity: The Integration of German Merchants in Nineteenth-Century Liverpool', *BH*, 54, 2 (2011), pp. 137–40; *History and Heritage: The Scandinavian Seamen's Church in Liverpool* (Liverpool, 2008); Sarah Brown and Peter de Figueiredo, *Religion and Place Liverpool's Historic Places of Worship* (Cambridge, 2008), pp. 27, 77.

41 Alasdair Munro and Duncan Sim, *The Merseyside Scots: A Study of an Expatriate Community* (Birkenhead, 2001), p. 36; John Belchem, 'Liverpool in 1848: Image, Identity and Issues', *THSL&C*, 147 (1997), pp. 11–12; Robert Lee, *From Scandinavia to Liverpool: A History of Merseyside's Nordic Community* (Liverpool, 2008), pp. 9–11, 15.

42 Jeffrey Cox, 'Were Victorian Nonconformists the Worst Imperialists of All?', *Victorian Studies*, 46, 2 (2004), pp. 243–55; Hartmut Berghoff, 'Regional Variations in Provincial Business Biography: The Case of Birmingham, Bristol and Manchester, 1870–1914', *BH*, 37, 1 (1995), p. 79.

43 D. J. Pope, 'The Geographical Origins and Socio-Economic Backgrounds of "the Liverpool Catholic and Maritime Business Community" in the Second Half of the Eighteenth Century', *North West Catholic History*, 30 (2003), pp. 28–56.

44 Munro and Sim, *The Merseyside Scots*, p. 41; Anon., 'The Story of Wavertree Congregational Church Formerly Trinity Chapel 1836–1986', LRO, 285 WAV 7/1; LRO, 285 FUR 4/1/1, Fairfield United Reformed Church, Communion Roll Book, 1880–1905; Gwilym Hughes, *Evan Roberts, Revivalist: Story of the Liverpool Mission* (Dolgelley, 1905), p. 39; Pike, *Liverpool and Birkenhead*, p. 154.

45 J. H. Klappas, 'Geographical Aspects of Religious Change in Victorian Liverpool, 1837–1901', unpublished MA thesis, University of Liverpool (1977), pp. 28, 32; Kenneth MacLeod Black, *The Scots Churches in England* (Edinburgh and London, 1906), p. 323.

46 'Public Improvements, 2. Churches', *The British Almanac of the Society for the Diffusion of Useful Knowledge, for the Year of Our Lord 1848* (London, 1848), p. 224; Bob Knowles (Oxton Research Group), 'William Potter and Family', htpps://history.theoxtonsociety.co.uk>2020/11; Doodson, *The Story of St. Paul's and Trinity United Reformed Church*, p. 4; Anon., *Fairfield Presbyterian Church 1864–1939* (Liverpool, 1939), p. 7; LRO, 285 FUR 4/1/1, Fairfield Presbyterian United Reformed Church, Communion Roll Book, 1880–1905; J. G. Cooper and A. D. Power, *A History of West Derby* (Ormskirk, 1982), p. 113; Andrew F. Richardson, *Central Bootle a Walking Tour of the Buildings and Monuments* (West Derby, 1993), p. 5; Edge Hill Congregational Church, Marmaduke Street, Liverpool, *Jubilee Souvenir Handbook, 1878–1928* (Liverpool, 1928), p. 6; Ernest Hugh Smith, *A History of Mossley Hill Parish 1875–1975* (Liverpool, 1975), p. 2. For a wider discussion of the role of philanthropists in supporting the Church of England and the establishment of new churches, see Sarah Flew, *Philanthropy and the Funding of the Church of England, 1856–1914* (London, 2014).

47 Thomas Henry Bankier, *History of St. Luke's Church, Liverpool* (the Trustees of St. Luke's Day Schools) (Liverpool, 1900), p. 30; Henry Lacey, *Pictorial Liverpool: Its Annals, Commerce; Shipping, Institutions; Public Buildings; Sights; Excursions; etc, etc. a New and Complete Hand-Book for Residents, Visitors and Tourists* (2nd ed., Liverpool, 1842), p. 228.

48 Doodson, *The Story of St. Paul's and Trinity United Reformed Church*, p. 8; Ian Sellars, *Salute to Pembroke: The Story of the Rise, Progress, Decline and Fall of a Most Remarkable Dissenting Congregation Pembroke Chapel Liverpool 1838–1931* (Alsager, 1960), p. 46; *Report and Resolutions Passed at the Final Meeting of the Liverpool Unitarian Fellowship Fund Society June 30th 1912 together with a List of Subscribers and Statement of Accounts* (Liverpool, 1912); MLP database.

49 LRO, 287 LMM Minute Book, Liverpool Wesleyan Mission. Record of Legacies.

50 Klappas, 'Geographical Aspects of Religious Change', p. 104; R. J. Morris, 'Clubs, Societies and Associations', in F. M. L. Thompson (ed.), *TCSHB, 1750–1950. Vol. 3: Social Agencies and Institutions* (Cambridge, 1996), p. 420; Jones, *The Social Survey of Merseyside*, p. 341 (Table II). There is a continuing debate on the causes, timing, and extent of secularisation: see, for example, Jeremy Morris, 'The Strange Death of Christian Britain: Another Look at the Secularization Debate', *The Historical Journal*, 46, 4 (2003), pp. 963–76; Callum G. Brown, *The Death of Christian Britain: Understanding Secularisation, 1800–2000* (London, 2007); Dominic Erdozain, 'The Secularisation of Sin in the Nineteenth Century', *Journal of Ecclesiastical History*, 62, 1 (2011), pp. 59–88.

51 John Smith, 'Urban Elites c.1830–1930 and Urban History, *UH*, 27, 2 (2000), p. 268; Timothy Larsen, *A People of One Book: The Bibles and the Victorians* (Oxford, 2011).

52 Conybeare, *Dingle Bank*, p. 1; Orchard, *Liverpool's Legion of Honour*, pp. 347–8, 450–1, 538, 656, 658, p. 723; Pike, *Liverpool and Birkenhead*, p. 155; LRO MD 425, Diaries of Philip Smith, 7 February, 14 October 1878.

53 Orchard, *Liverpool's Legion of Honour*, p. 639; Smith, *My Life-Work*, p. 40; Klappas, 'Geographical Aspects of Religious Change', p. 78; LRO 942 WAK, Wakefield MSS, 7 (9–11), Biographies of Liverpool Men, Box 10, Rea family, pp. 76–92; *"In Memoriam" or, Funeral Records of Liverpool Celebrities, Containing many Interesting Reminiscences of Local Men* (Liverpool, 1876), p. 55; Albert J. Mott, 'Books Published in Liverpool', *THSL&C*, New Series 1, 1860–61 (1861), pp. 103–66; Thomas Dawson, 'The Pamphlet Literature of Liverpool', *THSL&C*, New Series, 5 1864–65 (Liverpool, 1865), pp. 73–138; Felicity Jensz and Hanna Acke, 'Forum: The Form and Function of Nineteenth-Century Periodicals: Introduction', *Church History*, 82, 2 (2013), pp. 368–73' Orchard, *Liverpool's Legion of Honour*, pp. 281–3. For example, the religious publications in 1849–50 included works by David Thom, D. D., *On the Scotch Kirks and Congregations of Liverpool; being a Brief Sketch of their Rise and Progress* (Liverpool 1850) and Rev. J. Martineau, 'A Discourse on the Watch-night Lamp' (Liverpool, 1849).

54 Pike, *Liverpool and Birkenhead*, pp. 121, 158, 169, 188; MMM, MA&L, B/EWT, F34, Typewritten history of firm E. W. Turner (by son, Edward H. E. Turner), p. 58.

55 J. Coop Wallace and Seymour Taylor, *Bulls and Bears: Cartoons of the Members and Ring Traders of Liverpool Cotton Exchange (reprinted from 'the Liverpool Courier')* (Liverpool, 1908).

56 Ian Sellers, 'Congregationalists and Presbyterians in Nineteenth Century Liverpool', *Transactions of the Congregational Historical Society*, 20, 2 (1965), p. 81; David W. Bebbington, *Victorian Nonconformity* (Eugene, Oregon, 2011), p. 4.

57 Simon Gunn, *The Public Culture of the Victorian Middle Class Ritual and Authority and the English Industrial City 1840–1914* (Manchester, 2000), p. 109.

58 Smith, *My Life-Work*, p. 15; Peter Pugh, *Absolute Integrity: The Story of Royal Insurance 1845–1995* (Cambridge, 1995), p. 35; Orchard, *Liverpool's Legion of Honour*, p. 42. In the early 1890s, St. Peter's Church, for example, offered its members 14 different activities, including a literary society and a branch of the National Protestant League. See *'The Sunlight'* (St. Peter's Magazine), IV/5 (1893).

59 M. M. Shearer, *Quakers in Liverpool* (Liverpool, 1882), p. 19; R.W. Forster, *Trinity Princes Road, Presbyterian Church of England, Liverpool: Souvenir Brochure* (Liverpool, 1964), p. 8; Arthur Thomas, *Chatham Street Chatham Building* (Liverpool, 2003), p. 5; D. Fish, *The Genealogy and Descendants of Luke Fish in Chronological Order from 1760 to 1904* (Philadelphia, 1904), pp. 55–6; MLP database. Fish was also a member of the Birkenhead Literary and Scientific Society and of the Liverpool Field Naturalists' Society, vice-president of the Liverpool Entomological Society (1884), and a frequent lecturer on post control methods to farmers in South Lancashire.

60 George Eyre Evans, *A History of Renshaw Street Chapel and Its Institutions with Some Account of the Former Chapels in Castle Hey and Benn's Garden, Liverpool* (London, 1887), p. 19; D. W. Bebbington, 'Nonconformity and Electoral Strategy', *The Historical Journal*, 27, 3 (1984), p. 637; Maldwyn Edwards, *Methodism and England: A Study of Methodism in Its Social and Political Aspects during the Period 1850–1932* (London, 1943), p. 168.

61 Augustine Birrell, *Some Early Recollections of Liverpool in a Letter Addressed to the Lord Mayor of That City* (Liverpool, 1924), p. 7; *Things Past Redress* (Liverpool, 1937), p. 13; J. H. S. Kent, 'The Role of Religion in the Cultural Structure of the Later Victorian City', *Transactions of the Royal Historical Society*, 23 (5th series) (1973), pp. 153–71; Klappas, 'Geographical Aspects of Religious Change', p. 38; LRO ULL 288, 3/12/6, Renshaw Street Chapel Society, Visitors Book, 22 October 1885; Sellars, 'Congregationalists and Presbyterians', p. 75; Waller, *Democracy and Sectarianism*, p. 15.

62 Kathrin Levitan, *A Cultural History of the British Census: Envisioning the Multitude in the Nine-teenth Century* (Basingstoke, 2011); Christopher Harvie, 'Gladstonianism, the Provinces, and Popular Political Culture', in Richard Bellamy (ed.), *Victorian Liberalism Nineteenth-Century Political thought and Practice* (London and New York, 1990), p. 158; Bebbington, *Victorian Nonconformity*, p. 7; Robert William Dale, *History of English Congregationalism* (London, 1907); Richard J. Helm-stadter, 'Orthodox Nonconformity', in Denis G. Paz (ed.), *Nineteenth-Century English Religious Tra-ditions: Retrospect and Prospect* (Westport, 1995), p. 61; Anthony J. Steinhoff, 'Protestantism', in Stefan Berger (ed.), *A Companion to Nineteenth-Century Europe 1789–1914* (Oxford, 2006), p. 250; David Bundy, *Keswick: A Bibliographic Introduction to the Higher Life Movement* (Westmore, Ken-tucky, 2012); Ben Rogers, 'Ryle and Evangelical Identity', *Foundations an International Journal of Evangelical Theology*, 70 (2016), pp. 94–111; J. C. Ryle, *Facts and Men: Being Pages from English Church History between 1553 and 1683* (London, 1882), p. 196; Gareth Jenkins, 'Nationalism and Sectarian Violence in Liverpool and Belfast, 1880s–1910s', *International Labor and Working Class History*, 78 (2010), pp. 164–80; Neil Collins, *Politics and Elections in Nineteenth-Century Liver-pool* (Aldershot, 1994), p. 116; Michael Wheeler, *The Old Enemies: Catholics and Protestants in Nineteenth-Century English Culture* (Cambridge, 2006); Oded Heilbronner, 'The Age of the Catholic Revival', in Berger, *A Companion to Nineteenth-Century Europe*, pp. 242–3; H. McLeod, 'Building the "Catholic Ghetto": Catholic Organizations 1870–1914', in W. J. Sheils and Diana Wood (eds.), *Studies in Church History: Voluntary Religion* (Oxford, 1986); Eric G. Tenbus, *English Catholics and the Education of the Poor, 1847–1902* (London, 2010).

63 C. A. Piper, *A Century of Service the Story of the Liverpool North End Domestic Mission Society's First Hundred Years 1859–1959* (Liverpool, 1959), p. 8; LRO, 920 Melly, 5, Melly Correspondence, 1857–59, letter to Hugh Bright, 6 April 1859; 'The Evangelistic Movement in Liverpool. Extraordi-nary Incident', *The Public Ledger*, 16 May 1879; Timothy George (ed.), *Mr. Moody and the Evangeli-cal Tradition* (London and New York, 2005), Appendix, p. 160; Anne Holt, *A Ministry to the Poor being the History of the Liverpool Domestic Mission Society, 1836–1936* (Liverpool, 1936), p. 85; Frank Neal, *The Liverpool Experience, 1819–1914: An Aspect of Anglo-Irish History* (Manchester, 1988); Orchard, *Liverpool's Legion of Honour*, p. 738.

64 Mervyn Goodman, 'The Jewish Community of Liverpool', *The Jewish Journal of Sociology*, 38, 2 (1996), p. 103; Anon., 'The History of the Liverpool Jewish Community', *Jewish World*, August 1877; Alysa Levene, 'Jewish Households and Religious Identity in Mid-Nineteenth-Century Britain', *Journal of Family History*, 43, 3 (2018). pp. 281–301; Petra Laidlaw, 'Jews in the British Isles in

1851', *Jewish Journal of Sociology*, 56, 1/2 (2013), p. 115; B. L. Benas, 'Records of the Jews in Liverpool', *THSL&C*, 51 (1899), pp. 45–84; Bertram B. Benas, 'Later Records of the Jews in Liverpool', *THSL&C*, 80 (1928), pp. 150–202; idem., 'A Survey of the Jewish Institutional History of Liverpool and District', *THSL&C*, 17 (1951–52), pp. 23–37; Belchem and MacRaild, 'Cosmopolitan Liverpool', pp. 361–4; Nicholas Kokosalakis, *Ethnic Identity and Religion: Tradition and Change in Liverpool Jewry* (Washington, 1982). Both the 1848 revolutions in continental Europe and the Crimean War gave rise to increase rates of Jewish immigration to Liverpool. For comparative material on the Jewish presence in Britain, see Bill Williams, *The Making of Manchester Jewry, 1740–1875* (Manchester, 1976); W. D. Rubinstein, *A History of Jews in the English-Speaking World: Great Britain* (Basingstoke, 1996), pp. 7–21.

65　William Thomas Gidney, *The History of the London Society for Promoting Christianity amongst the Jews from 1809 to 1908* (London, 1908), p. 282; Mel Scult, 'English Missions to the Jews: Conversion in the Age of Emancipation', *Jewish Social Studies*, 35, 1 (1973), pp. 3–17; Agnieszk Jagodzińska, '"For Zion's Sake I Will Not Rest": The London Society for Promoting Christianity among the Jews and its Nineteenth-Century Missionary Periodicals', *Church History*, 82, 2 (2010), pp. 381–7; 'Society for Promoting Christianity amongst the Jews', *LM*, 21 October, 1842, p. 3; 'London Society for Promoting Christianity amongst the Jews', *LM*, 23 May 1848, p. 5; 'Society for Promoting Christianity amongst the Jews', *LM*, 23 October 1860, p. 3.

66　William Nicholls, *Christian Antisemitism: A History of Hate* (Lanham, Boulder, New York, Toronto and Oxford, 1993); Claude G. Montefiore, 'Anti-Semitism in England' (1881), reprinted in *Anti-Semitism and Jewish Nationalism* (Virginia Beach, 1981); 'Society for Promoting Christianity amongst the Jews', *LM*, 23 October 1860, p. 3; 'Society for Promoting Christianity amongst the Jews', *LM*, 23 June 1875, p. 6; Anon., 'The History of the Liverpool Jewish Community'; 'Will of E. P. Parry', *LM*, 10 June 1895, p. 6; 'Wills and Bequests', *LM*, 4 June 1897, p. 6. Aristocratic support for the London Society at the end of the nineteenth century was evident in a bequest of £1,000 from Lady Victoria Catherine Mary Nole Tylney Long Wellesley in 1897: her gross estate was valued at £333,754 12s 9d.

67　Peter Doyle, *Mitres & Missions in Lancashire the Roman Catholic Diocese of Liverpool 1850–2000* (Liverpool, 2005), p. 76; Rev. Charles Garrett, *Loving Counsels: Sermons and Addresses* (London, 1887), p. 122; Hughes, *Evan Roberts*, p. 11; Fred. James Powicke, *A History of the Cheshire County Union of Congregational Churches Prepared (to Commemorate Its Centenary, 1806–1906) at the Request of the Executive Committee* (Manchester, 1907), p. 251.

68　D. A. Gowland, *Methodist Secessions: The Origins of Free Methodism in Three Lancashire Towns: Manchester, Rochdale, Liverpool* (Manchester, 1979); H. D. Roberts, 'Nonconformity in Liverpool: Origins and History', in Pike, *Liverpool and Birkenhead*, pp. 76–7; A. L. M. Cook, *St. Andrew's Kirk, Rodney Street* (Liverpool, 1981); Sellars, 'Congregationalists and Presbyterians', p. 76.

69　Piper, *A Century of Service the Story of the Liverpool North End Domestic Mission Society's First Hundred Years 1859–1959*, pp. 40–3: letter of H. H. Hawkes to the editor of the *Post* and *Mercury*, 23 July 1909; Frank Neal, 'The Birkenhead Garibaldi Riots of 1862', *THSL&C*, 131 (1982), pp. 89–111; idem., 'Sectarian Violence in Victorian Liverpool', in S. Body and J. Carre (eds.), *Ville et Violence Dans le Monde Anglophone* (Clermont-Ferrand, 1989), pp. 43–61; Saho Matsumoto-Best, *Britain and the Papacy in the Age of Revolution 1846–1851* (Woodbridge, 2003); Brendan Keelan, *Sectarianism, Politics and Progress Merseyside 1800–1914* (Kindle self-publishing, 2020), pp. 29–79; Eric Taplin, review of Frank Neal, *Sectarian Violence: The Liverpool Experience, 1819–1914: An Aspect of Anglo-Irish History* (Manchester, 1988), *International Labor and Working Class History*, 37 (1990), p. 93; E. J. Feuchtwanger, *Democracy and Empire: Britain 1865–1914* (London, 1985), p. 24; Orchard, *Liverpool's Legion of Honour*, p. 621; Laura Kelly, 'The Irish, Politics and Sectarianism in Nineteenth-Century Liverpool', warwick.ac.uk>chm>migration; John Bostedt, 'More Than One Working Class: Protestant-Catholic Riots in Edward Liverpool', in John Belchem (ed.), *Popular Politics, Riot and Labour: Essays in Liverpool Labour History 1790–1940* (Liverpool, 1992), p. 178; Jenkins, 'Nationalism and Sectarian Violence', pp. 164–80; Matteo Tiratelli, 'Rioting and Time: Collective Violence in Manchester, Liverpool and Glasgow, 1800–1939', unpublished DPhil thesis, University of Manchester (2018); Dan Jackson, '"Friends of the Union": Liverpool, Ulster, and Home Rule, 1910–1914', *THSL&C*, 152 (2003), pp. 103–32.

70　Holt, *Walking Together*, p. 193; Lucie Nottingham, *Rathbone Brothers from Merchant to Bankers 1742–1992* (Oxford, 1992), p. 16; LRO, 289 Quaker Records, Box 7, A list of the members of the Hardshaw West Monthly Meeting in the Counties of Lancashire, Cheshire and Denbighshire, 1837–1860.

71 John Lansley, 'The Involvement of the Liverpool Business Elite in the Voluntary Sector', in J. C. Martín de la Cruz and R. Román Alcalá (eds.), *Las Cuidades Históricas Patrimonio y Sociabilidad* (Córdoba, 2000), pp. 499–500; Orchard, *Liverpool's Legion of Honour*, p. 181 (with reference to the shipowner Alfred Booth and his wife); LRO, DUR,1/4, Holt Family diaries (by Emma Holt, later Anne Holt), 7 January 1862.

72 Crosbie Smith, Ian Higginson and Phillip Wolstenholme, '"Avoiding Equally Extravagance and Parsimony": The Moral Economy of the Ocean Steamship', *Technology and Culture*, 44, 3 (2003), pp. 443–69; 'Orchard, *Liverpool's Legion of Honour*, pp. 465, 494, 543–4; Pike, *Liverpool and Birkenhead*, p. 155.

73 Orchard, *Liverpool's Legion of Honour*, pp. 542–5; Dutton, *Odyssey of an Edwardian Liberal*, p. 5. For a discussion of Positivism, see Eugene Thomas Long, *Twentieth-Century Western Philosophy of Religion 1900–2000* (Handbook of Contemporary Philosophy of Religion, vol. 1) (Dordrecht, 2002), specifically Chapter 6, 'Positivism and the Science of Religion', pp. 74–102. Auguste Compte (1798–1857) systematised his earlier work on Positivism as a secular religion—a 'Religion of Humanity'—with its own priests and calendar of saints.

74 Crosbie Smith, '"A Most Terrific Passage": Putting Faith into Atlantic Steam Navigation', in Robert Lee (ed.), *Commerce and Culture Nineteenth-Century Business Elites* (Farnham, 2011), p. 303.

75 Pike, *Liverpool and Birkenhead, Passim*.

76 Mark A. Smith, 'Religion', in Chris Williams (ed.), *A Companion to 19th-Century Britain* (Oxford, 2004), pp. 337–52; W. D. Rubinstein, 'British Businessmen as Wealth-Holders, 1870–1914: A Response', *BH*, 34, 2 (1992), p. 178; William C. Lubenow, *Liberal Intellectuals and Public Culture in Modern Britain, 1815–1914: Making Words Flesh* (Rochester, 2010), p. 193.

77 Orchard, *Liverpool's Legion of Honour*, names beginning N to Z; Wallace and Taylor, *Bulls and Bears*; Pike, *Liverpool and Birkenhead*. Ten out of the 42 merchants born in the 1850s were listed as 'religious', but only four and one respectively from those born in the two following decades from a cohort sample of 38 and 15.

78 Deacon's Court, *Jubilee Memorial of Canning Street Presbyterian Church Liverpool (1846–1896)* (Liverpool, 1896), p. 7; LRO, DUR 1/2, Holt Family—family diaries, George Holt Senior, 13 February, 28 December 1845, 26 January 1851, 29 January, 29 February 1852; DUR 1/5, Anne Holt, 2 January 1881 287 LMM, Central Hall, Renshaw Street; Anon., *The Story of Wavertree Congregational Chapel Formerly Trinity Chapel 1836–1986* (Liverpool, 1986); Black, *The Scots Churches in England*, p. 341; LRO, 920 DUR 1/6, Holt Family diary, (maintained by Robert D. Holt), 18 December 1892; Bebbington, *Victorian Nonconformity*, p. 7. For a general discussion of the decline in religious commitment, see Anthony Symondson (ed.), *The Victorian Crisis of Faith: Six Lectures* (London, 1970).

79 LRO, DUR 1/2 Holt Family—family diaries, George Holt Senior, 6 January, 25 March 1851; 286 PGB, 1/1/1, Princes Gate Baptist Chapel, Princes Boulevard, Minute Book 1881–94, 2 November 1882, p. 91; 285 WOO/2/1, Woolton Congregational Chapel, Church Book; 285 FUR, 4/2/1, Fairfield Presbyterian Church Elders' Districts 1880–1885. According to George Holt, the family of William Lapsell of Woolton had all been of the 'nonconformist faith', but the death of his only child had thrown a 'gloom over his views and prospects of life' and he had begun to frequent the 'established Church'.

80 Smith, *My Life-Work*, pp. 15, 76; Hugh Shimmin, *Publicity the True Cure of Social Evils: Liverpool Life: Its Pleasures, Practices, and Pastimes* (Liverpool, 1856), pp. 22–3; see also Randolph Cock, John Davies, Robert Lee, and Sari Mäenpää, Chapter 2 and Joseph Sharples and Adrian Jarvis, Chapter 9.

81 Smith, *My Life-Work*, p. 530; Bebbington, 'Nonconformity', pp. 634, 649, 652; P. J. Weller, *Democracy and Sectarianism a Political and Social History of Liverpool 1868–1939* (Cambridge, 1981), p. 227.

82 Simon Gunn, 'The "Failure" of the Victorian Middle Class: A Critique', in John Seed and Janet Wolff (eds.), *Culture of Capital: Art, Power and the Nineteenth-Century Middle Class* (Manchester, 1988), p. 31; *The Public Culture of the Victorian Middle Class*, p. 107; Smith, 'Urban Elites', p. 267; John Garrard, *Leadership and Power in Victorian Industrial Towns 1830–80* (Manchester, 1983), p. 58; Berghoff, 'Regional Variations in Provincial Business Biography', p. 68; E. P. Hennock, *Fit and Proper Persons Ideal and Reality in Nineteenth-Century Urban Government* (Studies in Urban History, 2) (London, 1973); Alan J. Kidd, 'Outcast Manchester: Voluntary Charity, Poor Relief and the

Casual Poor 1860–1905', in A. J. Kidd and K. W. Roberts (eds.), *City, Class and Culture: Studies of Social Policy and Cultural Production in Victorian Manchester* (Manchester, 1985), p. 58.

83 R. J. Morris, 'Structure, Culture and Society in British Towns', in Martin Daunton (ed.), *TCUHB, 3: 1840–1950* (Cambridge, 2000), p. 411; Robert Gray and Donna Loftus, 'Industrial Regulation, Urban Space and the Boundaries of the Workplace: Mid-Victorian Nottingham', *UH*, 26, 2 (1999), p. 218; Philip Harling, 'The Centrality of Locality: The Local State, Local Democracy, and Local Consciousness in Late-Victorian and Edwardian Britain', *Journal of Victorian Culture*, 9, 2 (2004), p. 217; George H. Pumphrey, *The Story of Liverpool's Public Services* (Liverpool, 1940); Linda J. Jones, 'Public Pursuit of Private Profit? Liberal Businessmen and Municipal Politics in Birmingham, 1865–1900', *BH*, 25, 3 (1983), pp. 240–59; Derek Fraser, *Power and Authority in the Victorian City* (Oxford, 1979); Johnston, *Clydeside Capital*, p. 120; Roy A. Church, *Economic and Social Change in a Midland Town: Victorian Nottingham 1815–1900* (London, 1966), pp. 181–2; John Garrard, 'The Middle Classes and 19th Century National and Local Politics', in John Garrard et al. (eds.), *The Middle Class in Politics* (Farnborough, 1978), pp. 37–44.

84 Simon Gunn, 'Class, Identity and the Urban: The Middle Class in England, c.1790–1950', *UH*, 31, 1 (2004), p. 32; James Moore and John Smith, 'Corruption and Urban Governance', in James Moore and John Smith (eds.), *Corruption in Urban Politics and Society, Britain 1780–1950* (Aldershot, 2007), p. 15; Richard H. Trainor, 'The "Decline" of British Urban Governance since 1850: A Reassessment', in R. J. Morris and Richard H. Trainor (eds.), *Urban Governance: Britain and beyond since 1750* (Aldershot, 2000), pp. 28–46.

85 Garrard, *Leadership and Power*, p. 4; Gray and Loftus, 'Industrial Regulation', p. 227; R. J. Morris, 'The Middle Class and British Towns and Cities in the Industrial Revolution 1780–1870', in D. Fraser and A. Sutcliffe (eds.), *The Pursuit of Urban History* (Leicester, 1983), pp. 286–306.

86 See, for example, Brian D. White, *A History of the Corporation of Liverpool 1835–1914* (Liverpool, 1951); Francois Vigier, *Change and Apathy: Liverpool and Manchester during the Industrial Revolution* (Cambridge, MA, 1970); Weller, *Democracy and Sectarianism*; Collins, *Politics and Elections*.

87 Margaret Simey (edited by David Bingham), *From Rhetoric to Reality a Study of the Work of F. G. D'Aeth, Social Administrator* (Liverpool, 2005), p. 23; Smith, 'Urban Elites', p. 260.

88 Michael Power, 'Creating a Port: Liverpool 1695–1715', *THSL&C*, 149 (2000), p. 65; Diana E. Ascott, Fiona Lewis and Michael Power, *Liverpool 1660–1750: People, Prosperity and Power* (Liverpool, 2006), p. 179; Sheryllynne Haggerty, *'Merely for Money'? Business Culture in the British Atlantic* (Liverpool, 2011), p. 26; Bennett, *The Voice of Liverpool Business*, p. 2; F. E. Sanderson, 'The Structure of Politics in Liverpool, 1780–1807', *THSL&C*, 127 (1977), pp. 70–2; Belchem and Hardy, 'Second Metropolis', p. 61; W. A. Gibson Martin, *A Century of Liverpool's Commerce* (Liverpool, 1950), p. 13.

89 James Aspinall, *Liverpool a Few Years Since by an Old Stager* (3rd ed., Liverpool, 1885), p. 46; John Haggerty and Sheryllynne Haggerty, 'The Life Cycle of a Metropolitan Business Network: Liverpool 1750–1810', *Explorations in Economic History*, 48, 2 (2011), p. 192; Jon Stobart, 'Culture versus Commerce: Societies and Spaces for Elites in Eighteenth-Century Liverpool', *Journal of Historical Geography*, 28, 4 (2002), p. 479; Lynn, 'Trade and Politics', pp. 107–8.

90 Collins, *Politics and Elections*, pp. 25–6, 71, 111; Picton, *Memorials of Liverpool Vol. 1-Historical*, p. 538; White, *A History of the Corporation*, p. 100.

91 John Davies, 'Political Satire: Nineteenth-Century Comic Histories of Liverpool', *THSL&C*, 157 (2008), pp. 93–112; William Shepherd, *The True and Wonderful History of Dick Liver* (Liverpool, 1824, 1832); *The Liverpool Review: A Magazine Devoted to Religious, Social, Industrial, Educational and Artistic Activities of the Diocese* (Liverpool, 1878–1883), vols. 1–6; John K. Walton and Alastair Wilcox, 'Introduction', in Walton and Wilcox (eds.), *Low Life and Moral Improvement in Mid-Victorian Britain: Liverpool through the Journalism of Hugh Shimmin* (Leicester, 1991), pp. 13–14; Lucy Kilfoyle, 'The Political Life of the "Porcupine": Provincial Power and the Satirical Press, 1860–1880', unpublished PhD, University of Liverpool (2018). Shimmin was briefly imprisoned for libel in 1870 when his accusations against the shipping companies could not be proved in court.

92 Michael J. Turner, 'Political Leadership and Parties 1846–1900', in Chris Williams (ed.), *A Companion to Nineteenth-Century Britain* (Oxford, 2004), p. 154.

93 Collins, *Politics and Elections*, p. 197; *The Builder*, 20 April 1884; Joseph Sharples, *Liverpool* (Pevsner Architectural Guides) (New Haven and London, 2004), p. 147; Orchard, *Liverpool's Legion of Honour*, pp. 60, 62.

94 Antonia Taddei, 'London Clubs in the Late Nineteenth Century', University of Oxford, Discussion Papers in Economic and Social History, 28 April 1999, p. 19; W. J. Fisher, 'Liberal Clubs and the Liberal Party', *Monthly Review*, 17 December 1904, pp. 127–36; Michael Braham, *Southport Liberal Association the First 100 Years* (Preston, 1985); *Kelly's Directory of Liverpool and Suburbs with Which Is Included Birkenhead and Neighbourhood, 1897* (London, 1897), pp. 65–6.

95 'Vindex' (Col. W. W. Biggs), *Some Reasons for the Conservatism of Liverpool: A Lecture* (Liverpool, c.1880); Jon Lawrence, 'Class and Gender in the Making of Urban Toryism, 1880–1914', *English Historical Review*, 108, 428 (1993), pp. 629–52; John Belchem, *Merseypride: Essays in Liverpool Exceptionalism* (Liverpool, 2000), p. 14; Waller, *Democracy and Sectarianism*, p. 161; A. B. Forwood, 'Democratic Toryism', *Contemporary Review*, 43 (1883), pp. 294–303; Orchard, Liverpool's Legion of Honour, p. 305; Stanley Salvidge, *Salvidge of Liverpool Behind the Political Scene* (London, 1934); Orchard, *Liverpool's Legion of Honour*, p. 618. For a more detailed discussion of the role of working men's clubs, see J. A. Garrard, 'Parties, Members and Voters after 1867: A Local Study', *Historical Journal*, 20 (1977), pp. 145–63. Salvidge was born at 54 Park Street, Birkenhead, in 1863 and later resided at 'Braxted', Hoylake.

96 D. George Boyce and Alan O'Day (eds.), *Gladstone and Ireland: Politics, Religion and Nationality in the Victorian Age* (Basingstoke and New York, 2010); Waller, *Democracy and Sectarianism*, pp. 73, 88, 93, 119; Mrs J. W. Alsop, *The Life of James W. Alsop* (Liverpool, 1926), pp. 49–55; William C. Lubenow, *Liberal Intellectuals and Political Culture in Modern Britain, 1815–1914: Making Words Flesh* (Woodbridge and Rochester, 2010), p. 193.

97 John Belchem, *Irish, Catholic and Scouse: The History of the Liverpool Irish, 1800–1939* (Liverpool, 2007), pp. xi, 17–18; Jenkins, 'Nationalism and Sectarian Violence', p. 165; Neal, *Sectarian Violence*, p. 219; B. O'Connell, 'The Irish National Party in Liverpool, 1873–1922', unpublished M.A. thesis, University of Liverpool (1971), Appendix.

98 Richard Rodger, '"There Is No Nobler Sphere Than to Take Part in Municipal Work": Public Administration in Historical Perspective', in Dieter Schott and M. Toyka-Seid (eds.), *Die Europäische Stadt und ihre Umwelt* (Darmstadt, 2008), pp. 169–92.

99 Belchem and Hardy, 'Second Metropolis', p. 65; Shimmin, *Pen-and-Ink Sketches*; White, *A History of the Corporation of Liverpool*, p. 88; John K. Walton, *Lancashire a Social History, 1558–1939* (Manchester, 1987), p. 228.

100 *Kelly's Directory of Liverpool and Suburbs*, pp. lxi–lxii; White, *A History of the Corporation of Liverpool*, p. 189; Garrard, *Leadership and Power*, p. 25; Orchard, *Liverpool's Legion of Honour*, p. 202, in reference to the iron and tinplate merchant Alan H. Bright.

101 J. Sandeman Allen, 'The Trade and Commerce of Liverpool', in Alfred Holt (ed.), *Merseyside: A Handbook to Liverpool and District Prepared on the Occasion of the Meeting of the British Association for the Advancement of Science in Liverpool, September 1923* (Liverpool, 1923), p. 181; Belchem, *Irish, Catholic and Scouse*, p. 16. Even in rural Cheshire, members of the upper class, including merchants and businessmen from Liverpool and Manchester who had acquired extensive estates, withdrew increasingly from local government in the early twentieth century, although it is unclear where this was a result of a greater demand for councillors with more relevant professional qualifications or because they were displayed by men (and women) whose social esteem had been gained through political work. See John Michael Lee, *Social Leaders and Public Persons: A Study of County Government in Cheshire since 1888* (Oxford, 1963), p. 234; James Hinton, *Women, Social Leadership and the Second World War Continuities of Class* (Oxford, 2002), p. 139.

102 For a discussion of the role of mayors and other civic leaders, see John Garrard (ed.), *Heads of the Local State: Mayors, Provosts and Burgomasters since 1800* (Aldershot, 2007).

103 Hennock, *Fit and Proper Persons*, pp. 299–300; Orchard, *Liverpool's Legion of Honour*, pp. 565–6; George Chandler, *An Illustrated History of Liverpool* (Liverpool, 1972), p. 113; Jon Stobart, 'Identity, Competition and Place in the Five Towns', *UH*, 30, 2 (2003), pp. 163–82.

104 Orchard, *Liverpool's Legion of Honour*, pp. 334–5, 438–9; County Borough of Birkenhead, *Birkenhead 1877–1974* (Birkenhead, 1974), p. 9; Elizabeth Davey, *Birkenhead: A History* (Chichester, 2009), p. 96; Kenneth Warren, *Steel, Ships and Men: Cammell Laird, 1824–1993* (Liverpool, 1998), pp. 90–108.

105 The list of Freemen included the merchants William Cliff (1891), William Rathbone M.P. (1891), Samuel Greg Rathbone (1894), Robert Durning Holt (1904), and Robert Gladstone (1911), together with the sugar refiner Henry Tate (1891), the businessman and banker John Brancker (1900), and the merchant and shipowner alderman Sir William Bower Forwood (1902).

106 John Garrard, 'Urban Elites, 1850–1914: The Rule and Decline of a New Squirearchy', *Albion*, 27 (1995), pp. 583–622; G. C. Baugh, 'Government Grants in Aid of the Rates in England and Wales, 1889–1990', *Historical Research*, 65 (1992), pp. 215–37; Simon Szreter, 'A Central Role for Local Government? The Example of Late Victorian Britain', *History & Policy, Policy Papers*, 2 May 2002.

107 James Aspinall, *Liverpool a Few Years Since by an Old Stager* (3rd ed., Liverpool, 1883), p. 113; Orchard, *Liverpool's Legion of Honour*, p. 202; Chapter 2, this volume. For a critical assessment of civic engagement after 1918, see Laura Balderstone, 'Semi-Detached Britain? Reviewing Suburban Engagement in Twentieth-Century Society', *UH*, 41, 1 (20124), pp. 141–60.

108 Sheila Marriner, *The Economic and Social Development of Merseyside* (London and Canberra, 1982), p. 93.

109 Orchard, *Liverpool's Legion of Honour*, p. 49; White, *A History of the Corporation of Liverpool*, p. 190; Collins, *Politics and Elections*, p. 233; Tony Lane, *Liverpool Gateway of Empire* (London, 1987), p. 43; Adrian Jarvis, 'The Port of Liverpool and the Shipowners', pp. 1–22; 'The Members of the Mersey Docks & Harbour Board and Their Way of Doing Business', *IJMH*, 6 (1994), pp. 122–39; Martin, *A Century of Liverpool Commerce*; Shimmin, *Pen-and-Ink Sketches*, p. 45. For a discussion of the role of trade associations, see Chapter 3. Despite the local importance of the drinks industry and the prominent role of brewers such as Cains (1858), Higsons (1780), Threlfalls (1849), and Walkers (c.1840), only in the latter case has there been detailed research. The Birkenhead Amalgamated Brewery Co. (1865) brought together two older firms, Aspinall's Anchor Brewery and Cook's Argyle Brewery. For an overview of the heritage legacy of the brewing industry, see Lynn Pearson, *Built to Brew: The History and Heritage of the Brewery* (Swindon, 2014).

110 For example, the successful cotton broker George Holt was a member of Liverpool Town Council for 21 years (1835–56) serving on the Library and Museum Committee and a chairman of the Water Committee, while the sugar and coffee merchant B. Vincent Hall was a councillor for the 'greater part of thirty years': Orchard, *Liverpool's Legion of Honour*, pp. 396–7, 347. See also Michael J. Turner, 'Political Leadership and Political Parties, 1846–1900', in Chris Williams (ed.), *A Companion to 19th-Century Britain* (Oxford, 2004), pp. 140–55.

111 Orchard, *Liverpool's Legion of Honour*, pp. 638, 408, 290, 369, 419, 271,363–4, 664–5; Pike, *Liverpool and Birkenhead*, pp. 103–283; Arthur C. Wardle, *Benjamin Bowring and His Descendents a Record of Mercantile Achievement* (London, 1938), p. 117.

112 Margaret Escott, 'Liverpool', in D. R. Fisher (ed.), *The History of Parliament: The House of Commons 1820–1932* (Cambridge, 2009); Michael Brock, *Great Reform Act* (London, 1973); Fabio Braggion and Lyndon Moore, 'The Economic Benefits of Political Connections in Late Victorian Britain', *Journal of Economic History*, 73, 1 (2013), pp. 142–76; D. W. Bebington, 'Unitarian Members of Parliament in the Nineteenth Century: A Catalogue', *Transactions of the Unitarian Historical Society*, 24, 3 (2009), pp. 153–75. Parliamentary electoral successes elsewhere reinforced the spatial fragmentation of the mercantile community which resulted from the acquisition of rural estates and county retreats: see the earlier discussion of this issue in this chapter.

113 Orchard, *Liverpool's Legion of Honour*; Coop and Taylor, *Bulls and Bears*; Pike, *Liverpool and Birkenhead*. The respective sample sizes were as follows: 169/613; 19/83 and 43/206.

114 Lees, *The Hurricane Port*, p. 91; Orchard, *Liverpool's Legion of Honour*, pp. 688–9; Smith, *My Life-Work*, p. 126; James Moore, 'The Art of Philanthropy: The Formation and Development of the Walker Art Gallery in Liverpool', *Museum and Society*, 2, 2 (2004), pp. 72–3. He became Mmayor of Liverpool in 1873, donated £20,000 for the erection of a civic art gallery, and was subsequently knighted. See Richard Foster and Julian Treuherz, 'Foreword', in Board of Trustees of the National Museums and Galleries on Merseyside (ed.), *The Walker Art Gallery* (London, 1990), p. 10.

115 Waller, *Democracy and Sectarianism*, p. 11; Tim Malcolm, *Anti-Booze Crusades in Victorian Liverpool* (Birkenhead, 2005), p. 45; Eliza A. Wood, *Memorials of James Wood, LL.D., J.P. of Grove House, Southport* (London, 1902), pp. 96–9; Alistair F. Mutch, 'Manchester and Liverpool Public Houses Compared, 1840–1914', *Manchester Region History Review*, 16 (2003), p. 26; White, *A History of the Corporation of Liverpool*, p. 108; Orchard, *Liverpool's Legion of Honour*, pp. 227, 449; Wardle, *Benjamin Bowring*, p. 173.

116 See Randolph Cock, John Davies, Robert Lee, and Sari Mäenpää, Chapter 2; Sir Ernest B. Royden, *Thomas Royden & Sons Shipbuilders Liverpool 1818–1893* (privately published, 1953), pp. 10–12. In the early 1850s there had been four principal shipyards on the Liverpool side of the Mersey: by 1900 there was only one.

117 Smith, *My Life-Work*, p. 113; Coop and Taylor, *Bulls and Bears*, p. 20; Orchard, *Liverpool's Legion of Honour*, p. 313; Malcolm Falkus, *The Blue Funnel Legend a History of the Ocean Steam Ship Company 1865–1973* (London, 1990), p. 19; Donald M. MacRaild, *Faith, Fraternity and Fighting: The Orange Order and Irish Migrants in Northern England, c.1850–1920* (Liverpool, 2005), pp. 3, 160; *The Tablet*, 16 April 1910, p. 22.

118 A. C. Howe, *Free Trade and Liberal England, 1846–1946* (Oxford, 1997); 'Free Trade and the Victorians', in A. Marrison (ed.), *Free Trade and Its Reception, 1815–1960* (London, 1998); John Belchem, 'The Church, the Throne and the People: Ships, Colonies and Commerce: Popular Toryism in Early Victorian Liverpool', *THSL&C*, 143 (1993), pp. 37, 48; J. W. Burrow, *Whigs and Liberals: Continuity and Change in English Political Thought* (Oxford, 1988), pp. 1–49; Anna Gambles, *Protection and Politics: Conservative Economic Discourse, 1815–1852* (Rochester, 1999), p. 9.

119 Birrell, *Some Early Recollections of Liverpool*, p. 15; MLP database; John Hussey, *Cruisers, Cotton and Confederates: Liverpool Waterfront in the Days of the Confederacy* (Birkenhead, 2009); Frank. J. Merli (ed.), *The Alabama, British Neutrality, and the American Civil War* (Bloomington, 2004); John Vaughan and K. Williams, *A Brief History of 19 Abercromby Square* (Liverpool, 1996); Wilbur Devereux Jones, *The Confederate Rams at Birkenhead: A Chapter in Anglo-American Relations* (Confederate Centennial Studies, 19) (Tuscaloosa, 1961). See also 'Liverpool's Abercromby Square and the Confederacy During the U.S. Civil War', https://ldhi.library.cofc.edu>exhibition>show, and Joseph Sharples, Chapter 8.

120 Peter Cain (ed.), *Free Trade and Protection* (Bristol, 1996); Orchard, *Liverpool's Legion of Honour*, p. 482.

121 G. R. Searle, *Entrepreneurial Politics in Mid-Victorian Britain* (Oxford, 1992); R. Brent, *Liberal Anglican Politics: Whiggery, Religion and Reform, 1830–1841* (Oxford, 1987); J. P. Parry, *Democracy and Religion: Gladstone and the Liberal Party, 1867–1875* (Cambridge, 1986).

122 LRO, 329 CON 1/1/2, Liverpool Constitutional Association minutes, 22 July 1878–18 October 1898, Jubilee of the Liverpool Constitutional Association 50th Annual Report, 1897–98 To which is added extracts of the Records of the Formation of Conservative and Constitutional Organisations in Liverpool (Liverpool, 1898); Annual Report for 1893–94 (Liverpool, 1894), pp. 2–3.

123 Grange Conservative Club, *Jubilee Souvenir, 1876–1926* (Birkenhead, 1926), p. 11; Orchard, *Liverpool's Legion of Honour*, pp. 289, 437, 440, 551–2; A. Cooke, *A Gift from the Churchills: The Primrose League, 1883–2004* (London, 2010); M. Pugh, *The Tories and the People, 1880–1935* (Oxford, 1985); Diana Elaine Sheets, 'British Conservatism and the Primrose League: The Changing Character of Popular Politics, 1885–1903', unpublished D.Phil., Columbia (1986), p. 3. Almost two thirds of the 30 vice-presidents and four of the five trustees of the Grange Conservative Club were drawn from the merchant community.

124 Orchard, *Liverpool's Legion of Honour*, pp. 200, 397, 459–60, 517.

125 Waller, *Democracy and Sectarianism*, pp. 91, 142; LRO, 920 DUR, 1/6, Holt Family Diary, (maintained by Robert D. Holt), 1 July 1891; DUR 1/7, Family diary kept by Robert D. Holt, 6 February 1901; Lawrence, 'Class and Gender', p. 636.

126 Anon., *Recollections of Old Liverpool by a Nonagenarian* (Liverpool, 1836), pp. 74–5; LRO, 920 DUR 1/2, Holt Family—family diaries, George Holt Senior, 30th March 1851; *Daily Post*, 28th September 1894; LRO, 920 MEL, 5, Melly Correspondence, 1857–59, 6th and 10th April 1859; 920 MEL, 23, George Melly MP Private Correspondence, vol. 17, 1872, 4524 (9 November 1872), 4579 (29 May 1872). Sir Arthur Bower Forwood (1836–98), together with his younger brother, William, had profited immensely from the turmoil of the American Civil War: he was elected a Conservative city councillor in 1871 and held the Ormskirk Parliamentary seat from 1885 until his death. He was a resolute champion of the Union, the Empire, the Monarchy, and the Church of England, and criticised Liverpool's merchants for their 'timidity'.

127 Dutton, *Odyssey of an Edward Liberal*, pp. xv, 5, 7, 19. Holt's continuing commitment to Unitarianism was evident in his presidency of the British and Foreign Unitarian Association in 1918 and his role as president of the International Congress of Free Christian and Other Religious Liberals (1921–36). He was created a baronet for his services to shipping in January 1935.

128 Berghoff, 'Regional Variations in Provincial Business Biography', p. 68; Jarvis, 'The Port of Liverpool and the Shipowners', p. 136; Orchard, *Liverpool's Legion of Honour*, pp. 199, 250, 257, 263, 330, 334, 356. For example, Thomas Cockbain, a merchant and the Chilean Consul in Liverpool, took no part in public affairs.

129   Orchard, *Liverpool's Legion of Honour*, pp. 198, 202, 421, 464, 533–4; Peter N. Davies, *The Trade Makers: Elder Dempster in West Africa, 1852–1972 1973–1989* (St. John's, Newfoundland, 2000), p. 54; Sheila Marriner, 'Rathbone's Trading Activities in the Middle of the Nineteenth Century', *THSL&C*, 108 (1959), p. 126; Aspinall, *Liverpool a Few Years Since*, p. 98; Arthur Behrend, *Portrait of a Family Firm Bahr, Behrend & Co. 1793–1945* (Liverpool, 1970), p. 39.

130   See Randolph Cock, John Davies, Robert Lee, and Sari Mäenpää, Chapter 2; Orchard, *Liverpool's Legion of Honour*, pp. 312, 404, 546; Harriet Anna Whiting, *Alfred Booth, Some Memories, Letters and Other Family Records* (Liverpool, 1917), pp. 113–14.

131   H. Berghoff and R. Müller, 'Tired Pioneers and Dynamic Newcomers? A Comparative Essay on English and German Entrepreneurial History, 1870–1914', *EcHR*, 47, 2 (1994), p. 282; Orchard, *Liverpool's Legion of Honour*, pp. 299, 411–15, 677; Wilton J. Ismay, *The Ismay Line: The White Star Line, and the Ismay Family Story* (Liverpool and London, 1961); Adam Kirkaldy, *History of British Shipping from the Beginning until WW1* (Bremen, 2009), p. 93; Lynn, 'Trade and Politics', pp. 99–120; *Our Shipping Highlights*, pp. 92, 122.

132   Shimmin, *Pen-and-Ink Sketches*, pp. 92, 100, 171; Orchard, *Liverpool's Legion of Honour*, p. 640; Smith, *My Life Work*, p. 135. Smith also dreaded the possibility that his election would lead to 'the breaking up of my home life'.

133   Shimmin, *Pen-and-Ink Sketches*, pp. 70, 108, 165; Orchard, *Liverpool's Legion of Honour*, pp. 329–30, 543–5, 579–80, 619–20, 723; LRO, DUR 1/2, Holt Family—family diaries, George Holt Senior, 11 November 1845; Wardle, *Benjamin Bowring*, pp. 171–4; Lynn, 'Trade and Politics', p. 105; Waller, *Democracy and Sectarianism*, p. 489.

134   Joseph Sharples, 'Secular Gothic Revival Architecture in Mid-Nineteenth-Century Liverpool', in Marios Costambeys, Andrew Harmer and Martin Heale (eds.), *The Making of the Middle Ages: Liverpool Essays* (Liverpool, 2007), pp. 206–34.

135   See Robert Lee, Chapter 1 and Graeme Milne, Chapter 4; MAL, D/LUA/1/1, Liverpool Underwriters' Association, Committee Minutes, 1802–09; Johann Jakob Sturz, *A Review, Financial, Statistical & Commercial, of the Empire of Brazil and Its Resources* (London, 1837), pp. 132–7; Marriner, *The Economic and Social Development of Merseyside*, p. 42; Thomas Baines, *Liverpool in 1859: The Port and Town of Liverpool and the Harbour, Docks and Commerce of the Mersey in 1859* (London, 1859), p. 122; *The Incorporated Chamber of Commerce of Liverpool, Fifty-Second Annual Report* (Liverpool, 1902), p. 199; W. O. Henderson, 'The American Chamber of Commerce for the Port of Liverpool, 1801–1908', *THSL&C*, 85 (1933), p. 49; Mersey Docks & Harbour Board, *The Port of Liverpool (Ninth Edition)* (Liverpool, 1935–6), p. 129; *Gore's Directory of Liverpool and Its Environs, Including the Cheshire Side* (Liverpool, 1896). In 1902 these included the Cotton Association, the Underwriters' Association, the Shipowners' Association, the West India Association, the Liverpool Steamship Owners' Association, the General Brokers' Association, the Corn Trade Association, the Timber Trade Association, the Provision Trade Association, the Salt Chamber of Commerce, the Liverpool Wool Brokers' Association, the Liverpool Stock Exchange, the Liverpool Shipping and Forward Agents' Association, the City of Liverpool and District Butchers' Association, and the Liverpool Jute Goods Association.

136   Margaret C. Levenstein, 'Mass Production Conquers the Pool: Firm Organization and the Nature of Competition in the Nineteenth Century', *JEH*, 55, 3 (1995), pp. 575–611; Jeffrey Fear, 'Cartels' and Luca Lanzalacco, 'Business Interest Associations', in Geoffrey Jones and Jonathan Zeitlin (eds.), *The Oxford Handbook of Business History* (Oxford, 2008), pp. 268–9 and pp. 293–315 respectively; W. Streeck et al., *Governing Interests: Business Associations Facing Internationalization* (London and New York, 2005).

137   Baines, *Liverpool in 1859*, p. 122; Leslie Bethell, *The Abolition of the Brazilian Slave Trade: Britain, Brazil and the Slave* (Cambridge, 1970), p. 364; *Report of the Special Committee of the Liverpool Steamship Owners' Association, November 20th, 1863 to Examine and Report Upon the Returns Recently Issued by the Mersey Docks and Harbour Board, Showing the Revenue Derived from Steamers and Sailing Vessels* (Liverpool, 1864); Milne, *Trade and Traders*, p. 204; L. H. Powell, *History of the Liverpool Steam Ship Owners' Association 1858–1958* (Liverpool, 1958), pp. 13–14; Henderson, 'The American Chamber of Commerce', pp. 2, 32, 34–5; William Otto Henderson, *The Lancashire Cotton Famine 1861–65* (Manchester, 1934), p. 29.

138   Thomas Ellison, *The Cotton Trade of Great Britain: Including a History of the Liverpool Cotton Market, and of the Cotton Brokers' Association* (London, 1886), p. 181; LRO 380 COT/1/1, Liverpool

Cotton Brokers' Association, Constitution, Laws and Usages, 1871–1881; Baines, *Liverpool in 1859*, pp. 126–7; *Bye-Laws of the Liverpool Corn Trade Association, Limited in Force on and after 1st June, 1911* (Liverpool, n.d.), pp. 6–7; James Taylor, *Boardroom Scandal: The Criminalization of Fraud in Nineteenth-Century Britain* (Oxford, 2013); see Graeme Milne, Chapters 3 and 4.

139 Rajiv Sethi and E. Somanathan, 'The Evolution of Social Norms in Common Property Resource Use', *American Economic Review*, 86, 4 (1996), pp. 766–88; Francesca Carnevali, 'Social Capital and Trade Associations in America, c.1860–1914: A Microhistory Approach', *EcHR*, 64, 3 (2011), p. 909.

140 Nigel Hall, 'The Cotton Brokers and the Development of the Liverpool Cotton Market c.1800 to 1914', unpublished D.Phil., University of Oxford (1999), p. 9; *Bye-Laws of the Liverpool Corn Trade Association*, Section B, Rules 2 and 3, Section H, pp. 6–7, 77–8; Orchard, *Liverpool's Legion of Honour*, pp. 407, 526. In the late nineteenth century, the governing bodies of trade associations had on average no more than 16 members.

141 *The Porcupine*, 13 October 1877, letter from 'A. M.'; Ellison, *The Cotton Trade*, pp. 277–8; Nigel Hall, 'The Business Interests of Liverpool's Cotton Brokers, c.1800–1914', *Northern History*, 41, 2, (2004), pp. 348–9; idem., 'The Governance of the Liverpool Raw Cotton Marker', *Northern History*, 53, 1 (2016), pp. 98–151; Allen, 'The Trade and Commerce of Liverpool', p. 183; Forwood, *Recollections*, p. 80; MAL D/SO/2/1/6, Liverpool Seamen's Orphan Institution, Report of the Year Ending 31st December 1889 (Liverpool, 1890), p. 24; Powell, *A Hundred Years On*, p. 22; P. L. Cottrell, 'The Steamship on the Mersey, 1815–80 Investment and Ownership', in P. L. Cottrell and D. H. Aldcroft (eds.), *Shipping Trade and Commerce Essays in Memory of Ralph Davis* (Leicester, 1981), p. 137; Baines, *Liverpool in 1859*, pp. 124–5, 128; Henderson, 'The American Chamber of Commerce', pp. 6, 10. For a discussion of the dispute between cotton brokers and import merchants, see Graeme Milne, Chapter 3.

142 Allen, 'The Trade and Commerce of Liverpool', p. 180: see also Graeme Milne, Chapter 3.

143 Bennett, *The Voice of Liverpool Business*, pp. 2, 103; 'Chronicle of Occurrences', *The British Almanac of the Society for the Diffusion of Useful Knowledge, for the Year of Our Lord, 1848* (London, 1848), pp. 251 (26 November 1846), 261 (22 and 30 November 1847). During this crisis period, for example, with mass starvation in Ireland and the imminent of collapse of speculative development in new railway companies, 'numerous meetings' were held in Liverpool and other provincial centres, including Manchester and Birmingham, involving merchants and delegates from Liverpool's Stock Exchange presented their case in London.

144 Baines, *Liverpool in 1859*, pp. 122–3; Belchem and Hardy, 'Second Metropolis', p. 61; Johnson, *Clydeside Capital*, pp. 75–6; Ewen A. Cameron, 'Glasgow's Going Round and Round: Some Recent Scottish Urban History', *UH*, 30, 2 (2003), p. 283.

145 Ronald Johnston, *Clydeside Capital, 1870–1920: A Social History of Employers* (East Lothian, 2002), pp. 200, 205; Philip Ollerenshaw and Peter Wardley, 'Economic Growth and the Business Community in Bristol since 1840', in Madge Dresser and Philip Ollerenshaw (eds.), *The Making of Modern Bristol* (Tiverton, 1996), p. 140; Arthur W. Silver, *Manchester Men and Indian Cotton, 1847–1872* (Manchester, 1966); Roland Smith, 'The Manchester Chamber of Commerce and the Increasing Foreign Competition to Lancashire Cotton Textiles, 1873–1896', *Bulletin of the John Rylands Library*, 38 (1956), p. 531; Eugene Ridings, 'Chambers of Commerce and Business Elites in Great Britain and Brazil in the Nineteenth Century: Some Comparisons', *Business History Review*, 75, 4 (2002), pp. 739–73; Orchard, *Liverpool's Legion of Honour*, p. 517; Anthony Webster, 'Liverpool's Asian Networks 1800–1914: Some Insights into a Provincial British Commercial Network', in Sheryllynne Haggerty, Anthony Webster and Nick White (eds.), *The Empire in One City: Liverpool's Inconvenient Imperial Past* (Manchester, 2008), pp. 35–54; E. H. H. Green, 'The Political Economy of Empire 1880–1914', in Andrew Porter (ed.), *The Oxford History of the British Empire vol. 3: The Nineteenth Century* (Oxford, 1999), p. 358; Martin, *A Century of Liverpool's Commerce*, pp. 26, 61.

146 'Report of the Proceedings at the 52nd Annual Meeting of the Liverpool Chamber of Commerce a Year's Progress', *The Incorporated Chamber of Commerce of Liverpool, Fifty-Second Annual Report* (Liverpool, 1902), p. 190; Forwood, *Recollections*, p. 80.

147 'Report of the Proceedings at the 52nd Annual Meeting', reply of Sir Edward Russell, p. 191; *The Chamber of Commerce of Liverpool (Incorporated) Forty-Second Annual Report* (Liverpool, 1892), List of Members. In 1891, for example, from a total of 750 members 236 (31.4 per cent) came from the same firm or family.

148 Baines, *Liverpool in 1859*, p. 123; *The Chamber of Commerce of Liverpool (Incorporated) Forty-Second Annual Report*; Pike, *Liverpool and Birkenhead*, p. 143; Braithwaite Poole, *The Commerce of Liverpool* (London and Liverpool, 1854); Ken McCarron, *Meat at Woodside the Birkenhead Livestock Trade 1878–1981* (Birkenhead, 1991); Johnston, *Clydeside Capital*, p. 79; J. Davies, 'The Liverpool Chamber of Commerce and the Burma-China Railway', *THSL&C*, 139 (1989), p. 130; Orchard, *Liverpool's Legion of Honour*, pp. 544, 546. In 1891, the following trade associations were formally represented by deputies: the Cotton Association, the Corn Trade Association, the General Brokers' Association, the Salt Chamber of Commerce, the Shipowners' Association, the Steam Ship Owners' Association, the Timber Trade Association, the West India Association, the Wool Brokers' Association, the Provision Trade Association, and the Underwriters' Association. Two deputies each were also selected by the Iron and General Metal Trades section, the East India and China Trade section, the African Trade section, and the Tobacco Trade section, while the Cotton Trade section only had the right to nominate a single deputy. See LRO 380 COM/26, Register of Members, including membership lists and directories of Industry (n.d.).

149 John Scott and Catherine Griff, *Directors of Industry: The British Corporate Network 1904–1976* (Cambridge, 1984); John Scott, 'Transformation in the British Economic Elite', *International Studies in Sociology and Social Anthropology*, 90 (2003), pp. 155–73; Mark Brayshay, Mark Cleary and John Selwood, 'Interlocking Directorships and Trans-National Linkages with the British Empire, 1900–1930', *Area*, 37, 2 (2005), pp. 209–22; 'Social Networks and the Transnational Reach of the Corporate Class in the Early-Twentieth Century', *Journal of Historical Geography*, 33, 1 (2007), pp. 144–67; Michael Unseem, *The Inner Circle: Large Corporations and the Rise of Business Political Activity in the U.S. and U.K.* (New York and Oxford, 1984); Bruce Cronin, 'National and Transnational Structures of the British Corporate Elite', in Georgina Murray and John Scott (eds.), *Financial Elites and Transnational Business: Who Rules the World* (Cheltenham, 2012), pp. 177–92.

150 Scott, 'Transformation in the British Economic Elite', p. 164; Gordon Boyce, 'Network Knowledge and Network Routines: Negotiating Activities between Shipowners and Shipbuilders', *BH*, 45, 2 (2003), p. 59.

151 Geoffrey Jones, *Merchants to Multinationals: British Trading Companies in the Nineteenth and Twentieth Centuries* (Oxford, 2000), pp. 24–5; Ron Harris, *Industrializing English Law: Entrepreneurship and Business Organization 1720–1844* (Cambridge, 2000), pp. 287–8; Mark Freeman, Robin Pearson and James Taylor, *Shareholder Democracies? Corporate Governance in Britain and Ireland before 1850* (Chicago, 2012). The adoption of a joint-stock form had been available to firms operating in specific sectors of the economy prior to 1844.

152 Pugh, *Absolute Integrity*, pp. 34, 50, 75.

153 See Randolph Cock, John Davies, Robert Lee, and Sari Mäenpää, Chapter 2 and Graeme Milne, Chapter 3; Josephine Maltby, 'UK Joint-Stock Companies Legislation 1844–1900: Accounting Publicity and "Mercantile Caution', *Accounting History*, 3, 1 (1998), pp. 9–32; James Taylor, 'Company Fraud in Victorian Britain: The Royal British Bank Scandal of 1856', *English Historical Review*, 122 (497) (2007), pp. 700–24; Cottrell, 'The Steamships on the Mersey', p. 141; Francis E. Hyde, *Liverpool and the Mersey the Development of a Port 1700–1970* (Newton Abbot, 1971), p. 64; Taylor, *Creating Capitalism*; Cubbin, *Harrisons of Liverpool a Chronicle of Ships and Men 1830–2002*, p. 52; Lynn, 'Trade and Politics in 19th Century Liverpool', pp. 112–13; Graeme G. Acheson and John D. Turner, 'The Death Blow to Unlimited Liability in Victorian Britain: The City of Glasgow Failure', *Explorations in Economic History*, 45, 3 (2008), pp. 235–53; Milne, *Trade and Traders*, p. 143; LRO, 614 INF 5/6, *The One Hundred and Forty-Fifth Report of the Liverpool Royal Infirmary*, p. 10. The cotton broker Samuel Smith never remembered 'a time of deeper depression than 1878–9' which resulted from the failure of the bank: see Smith, *My Life Work*, p. 119.

154 Scott, 'Transformation in the British Economic Elite', pp. 162–3; Bunting, 'Origins of the American Corporate Network', p. 136; Roy, 'Interlocking Directorates', p. 148.

155 Orchard, *Liverpool's Legion of Honour*, pp. 324, 417, 456, 463. Jackson was chairman of the Wirral Railway Co., but also a director of the Bettisfield Colliery Co. and the Mississippi and Dominion Steam Ship Co.

156 M. Collins and P. Hudson, 'Provincial Bank Lending: Yorkshire and Merseyside 1826–60', *Bulletin of Economic Research*, 31 (1979), pp. 69–79; Lucy Newton, 'Regional Bank-Industry Relations during the Mid-Nineteenth Century: Links between Bankers and Manufacturing in Sheffield, c.1850 to c.1885', *BH*, 38, 3, pp. 64–83.

157 Hall, 'The Business Interests of Liverpool's Cotton Brokers', p. 350; John Dodgson, 'The Historical Approach to Identifying Wider Economic Benefits from Major Urban Rail Investments: The Liverpool Overhead Railway: Lessons from the Past and for the Future', Transport Economists Group Seminar, 25 May 2011.

158 George Chandler, *Four Centuries of Banking as Illustrated by the Bankers, Customers and Staff Associated with the Constituent Banks of Martins Bank Limited* (London, 1964), vol. 1, pp. 238–40; Pugh, *Absolute Integrity: The Union Marine and General Insurance Co. Ltd 1863–1963* (Liverpool, 1963).

159 Pike, *Liverpool and Birkenhead*, pp. 126, 183.

160 Orchard, *Liverpool's Legion of Honour*, pp. 150, 158, 308 (the shipowner William Bower Forwood), 324, 418 (the timber merchant D. Jardine), 489, 564, 596 (the cotton broker George H. Robertson), 633 (the shipowner Samuel G. Sinclair), 634–5, 676; Thomas Diefenbach, *Hierarchy and Organisation: Toward a General Theory of Hierarchical Social Systems* (New York and Oxford, 2013); MLP database. Only five of the 23 shipowners were members of the Royal Liverpool Yacht Club, four were members of the Wellington Club, and one was a member of the Royal Liverpool Golf Club, while none of them were members of the Athenaeum. For a discussion of the role of these clubs, see Sari Mäenpää, Chapter 5.

161 Jarvis, *Liverpool*, pp. 2, 8, 13–19. For a wider discussion of merchant involvement in the slave trade, its relative profitability, and the effective management of risk, see David Richardson, 'Profitability in the Bristol-Liverpool Slave Trade', *Outre-Mers. Revue d'histoire* (1975), pp. 301–8; the contributions in David Richardson, Suzanne Schwarz and Anthony Tibbles (eds.), *Liverpool and Transatlantic Slavery* (Liverpool, 2007) by Kenneth Morgan, 'Liverpool's Dominance in the British Slave Trade' (pp. 14–42), David Pope, 'The Wealth and Social Aspirations of Liverpool's Slave Merchants of the Second Half of the Eighteenth Century' (pp. 164–226) and Jane Longmore, '"Cemented by the Blood of a Negro?" The Impact of the Slave Trade on Eighteenth Century Liverpool' (pp. 227–51); Sheryllynne Haggerty, 'Risk and Management in the Liverpool Slave Trade', *BH*, 51 (2009), pp. 817–34; idem., 'Risk, Networks and Privateering in Liverpool during the Seven Years War, 1756–1763', *IJMH*, 30, 1 (2018), pp. 30–51; Katie McDade, 'Liverpool Slave Merchant Entrepreneurial Networks, 1725–1807', *BH*, 53, 7 (2011), pp. 1092–109. For a more detailed discussion of merchant housing, see Joseph Sharples, Chapter 8.

162 Lawton, 'The Components of Demographic Change', Table 4.1, p. 98 and Figure 4.3, p. 104; Adrian Jarvis, *Liverpool Central Docks, 1793–1905: An Illustrated History* (Stroud, 1991); David Paul, *Liverpool Docks: A Short History* (Stroud, 2016); Thomas Baines, *History of the Commerce and Town of Liverpool and of the Rise of Manufacturing Industry in the Adjoining Counties* (London, 1852), pp. 829–40; see Randolph Cock, John Davies, Robert Lee, and Sari Mäenpää (Chapter 2), Joseph Sharples and Adrian Jarvis (Chapter 9), Robert Lee (Chapter 10); Belchem, 'Second Metropolis', p. 61. From the start of the nineteenth century until 1861, Liverpool's population growth rate was unprecedented, at 150.5 (1801–1831) and 151.2 (1831–1861) per cent respectively. For a discussion of port-hinterland and foreland connections, see Robert Lee, 'Port-Towns and Their Hinterlands (and Forelands): A Critical Review', in Robert Lee and Paul McNamara (eds.), *Port Cities and Their Hinterlands* (London, 2021), Chapter 1.

163 William Allingham (Patricius Walker), *Rambles by Patricius Walker* (London, 1873), p. 211; Albrecht Cordes and Margrit Schulte-Beerbühl (eds.), *Dealing with Economic Failure: Between Norm and Practice (15th to 21st centuries)* (Bern and Oxford, 2016); Jason Long, 'The Surprising Social Mobility of Victorian Britain', *European Review of Economic History*, 17, 1 (2013), pp. 1–23; see Cock, Davies, Lee, and Mäenpää, Chapter 2.

164 Andrea Caracausi and Christof Jeggle (eds.), *Commercial Networks and European Cities, 1400–1800* (London, 2014); Wheeler, *The Old Enemies*; Denis G. Paz (ed.), *Nineteenth-Century English Religious Traditions: Retrospect and Prospect* (Westport and London, 1995); *Popular Anti-Catholicism in Mid-Victorian England* (Stanford, 1992), pp. 197–224; Neal, 'The Birkenhead Garibaldi Riots', p. 89.

165 Lee, 'The Socio-Economic and Demographic Characteristics of Port-Cities', pp. 167–8; Alexander Damen, 'It's Not What You Know It's Who You Know: Political Connectedness and Political Engagement at the Local Level', *Journal of Society*, 51, 4 (2015), pp, 827–42; Marriner and Davies, 'Business and Society', Chapter 3.

166 P. Windolf, 'Elite Networks in Germany and Britain', *Sociology*, 32, 2 (1998), pp. 321–51; Andrew M. Pettigrew, 'On Studying Managerial Elites', *Strategic Management Journal*, 13 (Special Issue) (1992), pp. 163–82.

12 Associational Culture, Social Influence, and the Cultural Embeddedness of Merchant Networks

A Reassessment

Robert Lee

This chapter will re-examine the social embeddedness of merchant networks and the extent to which existing patterns of merchant involvement diminished or were replaced by other forms of interaction during the nineteenth century. In pursuing this agenda, the claim that members of the merchant community were heavily involved in philanthropic activities and charitable work, as an integral element in their daily lives, will be reassessed, while the disengagement of merchants from learned societies and a lack of interest in scientific and technological developments serve as indicators of their diminishing role within civic society. Active involvement in philanthropic undertakings and leadership roles in clubs and societies offered a range of networking opportunities well before company directorships created a further interlocking mechanism within sections of the merchant community. If voluntary societies were part of a 'class project' which provided the 'theatrical scaffolding' for the bourgeois drama of the nineteenth century, an active engagement in charitable work was recognised as part of a wider civilising mission and reflected the overriding need to establish a civic society based on the moral principles of the dominant middle class. Indeed, an emphasis on self-help predicated on a belief in the possibility of both material and spiritual improvement justified the establishment of a wide range of welfare societies intended to enable members of the working class to achieve this objective, while also seeking to defuse deep-rooted social problems which potentially threatened the existing fabric of society. In both cases, albeit for somewhat different reasons, it is generally assumed that the level of participation by members of the middle class was extensive. Private associations, often physically located at the heart of cities such as Liverpool, rapidly occupied a strategic position in bourgeois culture, while merchants and professional men were able to gain a disproportionate influence in the voluntary sector with relative ease, primarily because of their wealth and business experience. The usefulness of non-denominational private clubs and associations for members of the merchant community, whether for networking purposes or for supporting the long-term interests of individual family firms, has already been explored, but insufficient attention has been paid to the impact of suburbanisation on the articulation of associational culture. Indeed, in the case of the Wirral, population growth from the mid-nineteenth century, the relocation of Liverpool merchants to rural areas on the other side of the River Mersey, and the proliferation of alternative sites for social action and connectivity contributed to a fragmentation of business networking. A critical review of other aspects of networking within Merseyside's mercantile community, including activities that contributed to associational culture, social influence, and cultural embeddedness, suggests that current interpretations are insufficiently robust.

In order to analyse the contemporary significance of voluntary associations and charitable enterprises for business networking it is important to explore changes in both their transactional density and operational framework, as well as the actual extent of merchant involvement. All too often historians are inclined to accept at face value the contemporary claims made by

DOI: 10.4324/9781315597836-12

the honorary officers of (upper-) middle-class associations and societies, without exploring the context in which they operated, while the official self-image of Liverpool and its mercantile community is prioritised over a more rigorous analysis of the underlying reality with all its complexities and contradictions. This chapter will provide a more critical approach for evaluating the role of merchants in the formation of civic society. To achieve this objective, the following sections will analyse the networking framework of philanthropy and charitable work, the role of merchants as philanthropic benefactors, and the significance of associational culture, exemplified by the role of learned societies, for business purposes. In all three cases, the picture that emerges differs markedly from that of the embedded historiography.[1]

Philanthropy and Charitable Work

As far as charitable work was concerned, many contemporaries emphasised both the benevolence of the merchant community and the significant extent of welfare provision, while later commentators have accepted the view that wealth went hand in hand with deep social obligations, an attitude reinforced by religion and social ambition. If Liverpool's commercial success in the early nineteenth century provided the means, 'the hand and heart of benevolence was ever ready to impart aid to the distressed': 'numerous' provident societies were established; and the level of educational provision funded by philanthropy was seen as a 'cause for rejoicing'. Almost a century later, the lord mayor claimed that Liverpool did more for charity than any other city: 128 distinct charitable institutions were enumerated by the Charity Organization Society; the city was justly famous for its 'generosity'; and its citizens were more aware of the 'misery of the people' than elsewhere. A good deal of their philanthropic activities was 'pioneering', while an active involvement in educational initiatives at all levels reflected a firm belief in the role of education and culture as important civilising influences. Picton, however, had previously challenged the official view and argued that the city was 'poor in munificent foundations for charitable purposes', at least in comparison with London, but there were numerous societies and institutions for the relief of poverty, and the needs of 'ordinary citizens' were not overlooked. Moreover, Liverpool's approach to social welfare issues was 'essentially practical', in line with the precepts of its merchant community: its citizens provided significant support for the development of charitable institutions where the level of active participation had been 'outstanding'.[2]

Sometimes, Liverpool played a pioneering role in establishing specific types of charitable institutions, such as the School for the Blind (1790) and the Children's Hospital in Upper Hill Street (1851). The Liverpool Society for the Prevention of Cruelty to Children (1883) was the first of its type, although similar societies were soon established both locally (in Birkenhead and Bootle) and nationally. Its formation had been proposed by the cotton broker Samuel Smith who thought 'it spoke a great deal for the philanthropic and public spirit of this city that the idea of this Society had been taken up so promptly'. Indeed, the proliferation of charities in the nineteenth century was a direct result of a tradition of support from members of the merchant community. It was reported that some of the 'best men' in Liverpool took time off from their business activities to manage local charities, such as the Ladies' Charity (established in 1796) which was 'generally well and fashionably attended', and the Shipwreck and Humane Society (founded in 1839) included many 'noted names' amongst its subscribers, perhaps influenced by their religious commitment and the precepts of William Davis. Individual charities, such as the League of Welldoers with its Grand Matinee held at Olympia in November 1906, attracted widespread support, particularly from the Consular Corps, while philanthropy provided a mechanism for the wives and daughters of merchants to play an increasingly important role in the public domain.[3]

In fact, the level of financial support for charities was seldom, if ever, adequate to address the scale and severity of the welfare problems created by Liverpool's rapid development. Because of the prevalence of dock-related casual labour markets, high rates of in-migration, and urban overcrowding, the working class in ports such as Liverpool suffered from systemic poverty. The general irregularity of work and economic unpredictability, winter and seasonal 'slackness', and the cumulative health consequences of inadequate earnings and poor working conditions were critical factors in determining poverty levels. The situation in the late 1840s was particularly acute: the meetings of the Liverpool Health of Towns' Association constantly emphasised its 'great unhealthiness'; Dr. W. H. Duncan (appointed in 1847 as Liverpool's first Medical Officer of Health) provided trenchant criticism of the extent of overcrowding, particularly in cellar dwellings, which resulted in excessive rates of cholera mortality; while J. Hunter Robertson M.D. delivered a scathing indictment of the complicity of some of Birkenhead's improvement commissioners in constructing cottages and tenements that were unfit for human habitation. Indeed, the consequences were all too visible as Liverpool, like some other large cities, was 'abandoned in its congestion, filth and disease'. According to some American visitors, this resulted in countless lives being destroyed by 'coarseness', 'vulgarity', and 'hopelessness' as a direct result of the unparalleled extent of 'poverty and decrepitude'. The 'bodily health and mental condition' of patients from Liverpool admitted to the Rainhill Asylum, many of whom had been born in Ireland, were 'bad': they were often poorly nourished and emaciated, a clear indication of serious neglect and a diet with a low caloric intake. In 1885, Samuel Smith, then a Liberal M.P. for Liverpool (1882–85), published an article on 'Destitute Children' in *The Methodist Times* 'to waken public conscience' about the scale of 'an evil we observe every day'. The Christmas Appeals of the Liverpool Council of Social Service in 1911 on behalf of the Mercantile Marine Service Association was designed to raise funds for nearly 1,000 deserving applicants for the nautical charities who were 'without hope of being elected to vacancies on the list of recipients of pensions or homes'. But despite evidence of superficial public concern over the scale and consequences of deprivation and destitution, including the mayor's annual 'Treat for the Poor' held in the magnificent and imposing great hall of St. George's Hall (Figure 12.1) and mayoral involvement in the actual distribution of food for the poor, their underlying causes were not adequately addressed by the Tory city council. Philanthropic fund-raising events, such as the Fancy Dress Ball held in the same venue on 23 April 1864 in aid of St. Ann's Dispensary, undoubtedly raised revenue for good causes, but they were really for the enjoyment of their upper-middle-class participants. Nor did appeals to the Christian conscience of elite members of Liverpool's business community cut very much ice.[4]

The range and scale of the welfare problems facing Liverpool are all too evident in the reports of the charitable institutions. From a sample of 24 charities (for which subscription data are available) three examples, with a focus respectively on the reform of prostitutes, the care of orphans, and the prevention of cruelty to children, will serve to illustrate the persistent shortfall in institutional provision.[5] Following a public declaration in October 1809 advocating the establishment of a Society for the Reformation of Prostitutes, progress in realising its objectives was initially slow. Prostitution was already widespread in the port-city and some form of institutional protection was needed for those 'unfortunate and inconsiderate women who shall be desirous to return to the paths of virtue which they have forsaken'. But Liverpool acquired an unenviable reputation as the 'capital of prostitution' and the 'black spot for commercial sexuality' in Victorian England: in the early 1890s, the Female Penitentiary only catered on average for just over 40 inmates; and the opening of 'several new Institutions' of a similar character failed to address the underlying problems. Three orphan asylums were established from 1840 onwards, the Female Orphan Asylum (1840), the Asylum for Orphan Boys at 21 Hope Street (1852), and

THE MAYOR OF LIVERPOOL'S TREAT FOR THE POOR.

Figure 12.1 'The Mayor of Liverpool's Treat for the Poor', *The Illustrated London News*, 31 January 1874

the Infant Orphan Asylum (1858), but the level of provision failed to meet contemporary needs, despite the fact that the imposition of strict rules reduced the level of demand considerably (for example, orphans were only admitted if they had lost both parents, were legitimate, healthy, with no means of support, had been baptised in the Church of England, and, in the case of orphan boys had been born within seven miles of Liverpool Exchange). The 378 cases brought to the attention of the Liverpool Society for the Prevention of Cruelty to Children between the date of its foundation in April 1883 and the following October involved aggravated assault, neglect, exposure, vagrancy, and wanton abuse, although members were only too aware that this was simply an indicator of the true scale of 'cruel neglect'.[6]

Contrary to public claims, only a small proportion of the local population was willing to support charitable enterprises. According to Shimmin, there were few 'generous and energetic persons' who never failed in their Christian duty, while the bulk of the town's population was 'a solid, inert, almost insoluble mass, not warmed or melted by any impulse or any sunny ray of charity'. The number of subscribers failed to keep pace with the expansion of voluntary institutional provision, despite the fact that philanthropy was interpreted as evidence of adherence to 'high moral values', while many contemporaries, including those involved in municipal administration, utterly failed to realise the scale of 'social degradation'. In the early 1850s, 689 citizens contributed over half of all the money subscribed to Liverpool's existing charities, with 122 'gentlemen' carrying a disproportionate share, despite the fact that the role of many voluntary institutions, including the Liverpool Female Penitentiary, was visibly constrained by limited capacity, while it was admitted that 'many, very many, know little of the Female Orphan Asylum at all, and many who kindly subscribe have never inspected it'. But the situation was no different 20 years later, when an analysis of 38 leading charities reveals a combined subscription list of only 6,668 individuals with an average contribution of four guineas. There was a clear preference for supporting only one institution (52 per cent of the total number of subscribers), while 1,193 individuals accounted for considerably more than half of the subscriptions. By the end of the century, the total number of subscribers had risen to no more than 8,000 (from a total population of almost 900,000), but only 1,030 citizens contributed to the 106 charities on the list of the Central Relief and Charity Organisation Society. A few years later, its receipts for supporting the 306 charities on its list were insufficient and subscriptions were made to only a small number of organisations, including the Liverpool Dog's Home (one guinea). Based on Grisewood's calculations, roughly 15,000 inhabitants had property with a rateable value of £30 or more and were therefore able financially to support local charities, but nearly half of them 'never taste the luxury of doing good, in this form at least'. Many members of the mercantile community were noticeable by their absence and charitable institutions on Merseyside continued to depend on a very narrow operational base.[7]

If Liverpool's charities were 'very numerous and very excellent', the demands were 'very far indeed in excess of supply' and almost all consistently reported grave concerns over the inadequacy of subscription income. Of course, it might be argued that it was in the interest of honorary treasurers of charitable institutions to emphasise the need for additional support, but there can be no mistaking the seriousness of the underlying problem. The Committee of the Liverpool Seamen's Orphan Institution (1869) noted that a significant number of shipowners, although 'men of substance', had yet to become subscribers and that many persons 'known to be interested in shipping' were 'conspicuous by their absence': even by the early 1900s 'several shipping firms' failed to give anything at all. The lack of funds for the Liverpool Female Penitentiary was a 'constant source of anxiety'; St. Paul's Eye Hospital reported a 'deficiency of income' because it was 'so poorly supported'; and financial contributions to the Liverpool Infirmary for Children in 1895 were 'quite inadequate for the requirement', even though it was generally regarded as a 'Pet Charity'. Income from bequests was unreliable and unpredictable and the pool of potential subscribers remained relatively static over time. A rapid growth in demand during periods of economic crisis or continued depressions in shipping, as was the case in 1901–03, invariably coincided with a dramatic fall in revenue, while philanthropy was not a priority for the shareholders of limited companies as it had been for the senior partners of private firms.[8] The problem of systemic underfunding for many, if not all, of Liverpool charities and the unwillingness of some shipowners even to support welfare institutions for mariners and their dependents indicates that many members of the merchant community 'ignored their obligations to such charities' and were unwilling to 'loosen their purse strings'. The underlying cause was self-evident: the city's commerce and trade was simply regarded as 'a happy hunting ground, in which to make a fortune; then to carry it away to sunnier climes and spend it there', an attitude that led to a 'slackening of interest in the city' and 'a disregard of its squalor and ugliness'.[9]

However, the networking function of charitable activity was articulated not through membership and the payment of subscriptions, but through the willingness of merchants to contribute to the leadership and management of individual charities, even if some of their contemporaries failed to recognise any moral responsibility for the plight of those in need. In some cases, the extent of individual commitment was unquestionable. The Liverpool North End Domestic Mission Society (established in 1859) benefited considerably from the active commitment of some of the most prominent Unitarians, all of whom were merchants and shipowners. Richard P.

Rathbone held the post of president for 27 years (1860–77). Alfred Booth became its secretary and treasurer in 1861, posts which he was forced to relinquish three years later when he left for America, 'having business in New York which detained him indefinitely', but on his return in 1874 he resumed the role as treasurer and remained in office for 30 years. The shipowner James Beazley, as chairman of the executive committee, 'laboured' on behalf of the Liverpool Seamen's Orphan Institution, 'with equal cordiality, energy and dogged perseverance'; the general produce broker A. M. Jackson was an 'active member' and trustee of 'many educational and charitable institutions'; and the cotton broker James Lister was 'active' and 'exceedingly useful in assisting to manage various charities'. If the corn merchant Thomas A. Leigh, who was known for his 'deep interest in young women', was only a trustee of the Gordon Hall Institute, William Rathbone was chairman, patron, or trustee of 'numerous benevolent institutions'. The sack contractor William Oulton served on numerous committees, having shown 'an active share' in religious and philanthropic work 'from youth upward'.[10]

Seventy-nine of the merchants listed in Orchard's biographical compilation (or 12.8 per cent of the sample) held office in local charities (whether as chairman, honorary secretary, or honorary treasurer), although others may have played an important role as committee members. At the Liverpool Female Orphan Asylum in 1862 almost all the committee members came from the merchant community, whereas between 1872 and 1881 it supplied just over one third of the Hahnemann Hospital's committee.[11] On average, almost two thirds of the members of charity committees were merchants (Table 12.1), while their contribution to maritime charities was even greater, particularly as far as the management of both the Liverpool Sailor's Home and the Training Ship *Indefatigable* was concerned (94.4 per cent) (Table 12.2).

By the early 1890s, however, only 164 of the 613 most prominent members of the merchant community (26.7 per cent) are known to have been actively involved in local charities, although the second half of the nineteenth century had seen a significant proliferation of philanthropic enterprises in Liverpool.[12] Many merchants failed to contribute to charitable at work at all. Sir

Table 12.1 The extent of merchant committee representation on Liverpool charities

Charity	Date	Committee Total	Merchants	%
Southern & Toxteth Hospital	1853	31	18	48.6
Hahnemann Hospital	1872–81	34	12	35.2
"	1892–93	33	13	39.3
Liverpool Infirmary for Children	1862	16	13	81.2
"	1871	16	14	87.5
"	1880	15	13	86.6
"	1890–1901	15	12	80.0
"	1901–02	34	23	67.6
Salisbury House School	1861–81	47	33	70.2
Liverpool Female Orphan Asylum	1851	14	9	64.2
"	1862	17	15	88.2
"	1872	18	14	77.7
"	1882	15	8	53.3
LSPCfromC	1884	40	28	70.0
Total		345	225	65.5
Average per charity		24.6	16.0	

Note: LSPCfromC—Liverpool Society for the Protection of Children from Cruelty

Sources: MLP database; Liverpool Record Office, annual reports of the individual charities

Table 12.2 Merchant representation on the committees of Liverpool's maritime charities, 1869–1912 (in per cent)

Charity	Date	Committee	Merchants	%
Training Ship *Indefatigable*	1902	18	17	94.4
LSOI Executive	1869	11	9	81.8
"	1912	11	9	81.1
" General Committee	1869	29	24	82.7
"	1881	51	41	80.3
"	1892	39	28	71.7
"	1902	45	37	82.2
"	1912	45	39	86.6
Seamen and Boatmen's Friend Society	1909	10	3	33.3
Liverpool Seamen's Friend Society	1911	56	34	60.7
Liverpool Sailor's Home	1912	18	17	94.4
Total		333	258	77.4
Average		30.2	23.4	

Note: LSOI—Liverpool Seamen's Orphan Institution

Sources: MLP database; annual reports of the individual maritime charities held at the Maritime Archives and Library (Merseyside Maritime Museum)

Percy Edward Bates, one of the most prominent local shipowners, was simply 'not benevolent' and his name was not on any charitable list; the sugar refiner J. H. Higson was not known for any church or charitable work; the two brothers Rowland E. L. and John Naylor, although partners in the wealthy banking firm of Leyland & Bullins, lived 'retired lives', 'not mixing in political or charitable work'; and the stock broker Henry Heywood Noble, despite an excellent education, had 'no evident interest in charitable institutions'. In other cases, individual merchants were simply 'too busy' to accept a seat on a committee. According to Orchard, many men who were eminently able in commerce, like the timber merchant and auctioneer Peter Owen, gave all their attention to their business interests and deliberately avoided involvement in other activities. The merchant, shipowner, and shipbroker Walter Glynn was destined to stand in 'that small group of Liverpool merchants who are known all over the world as chief in the city' (provided he lived to an old age), but apart from acting as chairman of the Much Woolton Local Board and 'probably useful in many other ways', he was not directly involved in charitable work. Far from being isolated exceptions, just over one fifth of Liverpool's merchant elite had no tangible involvement in public work of this nature, despite the contemporary social and cultural significance attached to charitable giving. Moreover, the situation prior to the outbreak of the First World War was no better. Only 11 of the 83 members and ring traders of Liverpool's Cotton Exchange (or 13.2 per cent) were involved in charitable activities and of the 171 stock and share brokers included in Pike's volume, 73 (or 42.6 per cent) had no known involvement with local charities.[13]

In assessing the wider significance of philanthropic activity for business networking, two points need to be emphasised. Firstly, insufficient attention has been paid to the way in which local charities operated and their leading figures interacted. Despite their business skills and wealth, only a small proportion of the merchant community was actively involved in managing charitable institutions on a regular basis and the way business was conducted affected both the nature and extent of networking. The average committee size varied considerably according to the type of charity, but executive committees (where they were created, as was the case with the Liverpool Seamen's Orphan Institution) were generally small, despite the considerable range

SEAMENS' ORPHAN INSTITUTION AT LIVERPOOL

Figure 12.2 The Seamen's Orphanage, Liverpool opened by the Duke of Edinburgh, *The Graphic*,
6 January 1872

and scale of their tasks (Figure 12.2). Committee members were often charged with a wide range of responsibilities relating to financial and personnel management, overseeing building projects, securing subscriptions and legacies, and determining future strategy. In the case of the Liverpool Sailor's Home, for example, they were enjoined in 1852 to pay their own 'medical man' to ensure there was adequate cover for sick residents from a 'Professional gentleman'; a special sub-committee was authorised to draw checks upon the savings bank 'to the extent of £2,000'; and they were involved in assessing applications for posts in the charity, including that of superintendent. A three-fold increase in the number of boarders eventually meant that the building by the early 1870s had reached its 'utmost capacity', while the construction of new docks in the north end of Liverpool justified the erection of a new branch that could cater for 140 seamen and 10 officers. Inevitably, this led to a significant increase in the duties of the committee members (Figure 12.3). The honorary post of president of a charity did not necessarily entail 'much active services', although it often involved considerable expenditure. But this was not invariably the case: during his presidency of the Liverpool Seamen's Friend Society, the shipowner John Japp threw himself into work 'with all the strength of his ardent nature'. By contrast, the duties of elected officers were extensive. A chairman was expected to ensure 'wise, energetic, and admirable management'; an honorary secretary was tasked with maintaining the subscription list, general correspondence, and the production of the annual report; while an honorary treasurer's obligations were particularly onerous given the precarious financial position of many charities, the frequency of business correspondence, the possibility of an embezzlement of funds, and the risk of bogus collections.[14]

THE ILLUSTRATED LONDON NEWS, DEC. 9, 1876.—564

Figure 12.3 'New Branch Sailors' Home, Liverpool', *The Illustrated London News*, 9 December 1876, p. 564

The operational dynamics of charitable committees, however, were sometimes complex. They were *de facto*, self-perpetuating bodies, with attendance and membership affected by work pressures, temporary absences from Liverpool, residential relocation, ill-health, and retirement from business. Some charities, such as the Liverpool Female Penitentiary, had a residency requirement that stipulated that committee members and trustees had to live within a ten-mile radius of Liverpool. This inevitably led to a reduction in membership as a result of suburbanisation and out-migration: for example, Henry Tate's relocation to London meant that he could no longer participate in the committee work of the Hahnemann Hospital. Committees normally met on a monthly or fortnightly basis and had a low quorum requirement ranging from three (St. Paul's Eye Hospital and the Hahnemann Hospital) to five (the Liverpool Infirmary for Children). But attendance rates were frequently poor either as a result of 'unavoidable absences' or because members were 'much engaged during the week' and some meetings were inquorate. In 1883, the shipowner T. H. Ismay was prevented from attending the AGM and some of the committee meetings of the Liverpool Seamen's Orphan Institution because of engagements in London and the process of establishing days which were convenient for all members of the executive committee in the early 1900s was problematic, particularly when the treasurer, the shipowner E. A. Beazley, was away in London on Thursdays and Fridays ('on alternate days') and others were absent for extended periods of time. Effective networking and the prosecution of a charity's interests were compromised by the absence of committee members: attendance rates at the Board of Economy of the Liverpool Royal Infirmary fluctuated between 37.6 per cent (1882) and 42.3 per cent (1902); while the Management Committee of the Liverpool Sailors' Home had a membership of ten, but the average attendance between 1888 and 1895 was less than five and occasionally, as in April 1889, only one member was present.[15]

It was not uncommon for committees to be structurally imbalanced. Attendance by a small core of 'senior' members, many of whom served for extended periods of time as part of a well-established clique, was relatively stable, particularly in the case of some of the maritime charities, but overall there was a high turnover rate that reflected the underlying extent of transience within the merchant community. In the case of the Hahnemann Hospital, 12 of the 32 committee members served continuously throughout the period between 1873 and 1881, but six were only involved for a single year: the Liverpool Infirmary for Children's committee had a lower persistence rate with just 6 of the 31 elected members, including the honorary secretary and treasurer, serving without a break between 1902 and 1912. Liverpool may well have been 'proud to claim as her own, men who are ever ready and willing to assist at the call of charity', but only a few members of the merchant community were able or sufficiently committed to devote themselves to committee work for an extended period of time. Joseph Hubback, a successful corn merchant and mayor of Liverpool (1869–70), served as chairman of the Liverpool Infirmary for Children for a decade (from 1861 to 1870–1); the shipowner and merchant Henry Stokes was on the committee for the Liverpool Sailors Home for 37 years and acted as chairman on several occasions (1888, 1889, 1896–98); while the hide and leather merchant John Christopher Gale served 'for many years' as honorary treasurer to the Home for Incurables. Major charities attracted considerable support from individual members of the merchant community and benefited from their business expertise for many years. James Beazley, a leading shipowner, was invited to take over the chairmanship of the Executive Committee of the Liverpool Seamen's Orphan Institution on its foundation in 1868 and remained in post until 1887, having secured the construction of the orphanage through 'unwearied zeal and organising power' and devoted 'his time and energy to its interests': his son James H. Beazley was elected chairman in 1902, but he was regarded by Orchard as less active in charities than his father. The West India merchant Hamilton B. Gilmour was chairman of the Liverpool Royal Infirmary between 1879 and 1896–97, and the shipowner Ralph Brocklebank fulfilled the same role for 14 years (1898–99 to 1912), having previously been elected honorary treasurer in 1879. But local charities quite often depended on the 'same names', and an extended period of service was the exception, not the norm. From a networking perspective there were obvious benefits in overlapping interests, as was the case with the Liverpool Sailors' Home in the early twentieth century when 30 per cent of its committee members were also involved in managing the interests of the Liverpool Seamen's Orphan Institution, but active involvement in more than one charity was rare.[16]

The implicit benefits of charitable engagement for networking purposes within the business community were occasionally undermined by conflict and hostility. Firstly, decision-making within committees was seldom a seamless process and tensions existed between an established core of members and relative newcomers. The Liverpool Seamen's Orphan Institution had been established to assist children 'of all denominations', although religious instruction and prayers were to be provided in accordance with the precepts of the Church of England. Religious practices in the orphanage, however, were not always sufficiently robust for 'protestors or protestants', as was the case in 1878 when a formal reassurance had to be given that there would be no deviation from the 'lines which were laid down in the beginning'. In 1885, there was a public complaint by 'one of the most bigoted, political of men in Liverpool' about the orphanage and the work of the executive committee which was 'nothing more or less than an attack . . . upon the Church of England'; and in 1903 a dispute over the attendance of the chairman's wife at the ladies visitors committee led to the resignation of the shipowner R. G. Allan. An active involvement in local charities, far from fostering effective networking within an elite group of the merchant community, had the potential to be divisive and confrontational with potentially negative consequences for the prosecution of business interests.[17]

Secondly, the significance of charitable activity for business networking continued to be mediated through religion as a great deal of charity was delivered along strictly confessional lines. Charitable giving remained, in part, a competitive undertaking and was not necessarily a unifying, conciliatory force. As in other port-cities and urban centres, many charities were associated with specific congregations and by the 1890s most churches maintained an 'endless cluster of societies' often with a well-defined charitable function. When new charities were established as a result of private endowments, their terms of reference were set out by the donors, as was the case with the Turner Memorial Home of Rest for Chronic Sufferers (1884), and even when a conscious attempt was made to preserve a non-sectarian and non-political character, religion and ethnicity continued to influence the nature of charitable giving. The Strangers' Friend Society (1796) had been established by Methodists to assist 'miserable beings' in need, irrespective of their faith, but their own poor continued to be relieved from other sources; the Welsh Charity School (1804) provided instruction and clothing for poor children of Welsh parents (provided they had been born in or near to Liverpool); and the Caledonian Free School (1808) offered elementary education to the children of Scotch parents 'in indigent circumstances'. The situation later in the nineteenth century was no different, despite the creation of new charities designed to operate on non-denominational lines. Sectarianism remained deeply entrenched in Liverpool society in a manner that was apparently 'unique to England'. The main religious issue was not the clash between Dissent and the Establishment, but the conflict between Protestants and Roman Catholics. As a result, efforts to develop charitable institutions free of religious restrictions seldom succeeded. The Orange Order was particularly strong in the city with the largest known Orange procession (with almost 8,000 participants) taking place on 12 July 1876. Catholics, like most other confessional groups, had developed their own charitable infrastructure and claimed that support for Irish Roman Catholics was far more effective than anything provided by Protestants for their co-religionists. At the same time, the children taken in by all three orphan asylums were required to have been baptised in the Church of England and were to be educated 'in the principles of the Established Church'. In such a context, it was an uphill struggle to provide non-confessional charitable institutions. The founders of the North End Domestic Society (1859) had hoped support would not depend 'exclusively' on members of any one sect, but in reality almost all of the subscriptions came from Unitarians; and many attempts to develop a non-denominational charitable framework failed because of the persistence of sectarianism.[18]

It is difficult to reconstruct the overall pattern of charitable giving amongst members of the merchant community, although many ministers and priests, including Charles Garrett whose 'extraordinary influence' was founded on 'active philanthropy', exhorted all men to be 'zealous for good works'. However, denominational preferences persisted. Henry Jump, a Roman Catholic corn merchant, who lived 'a blameless life' characterised by a strong commitment to charitable work, was chairman of the annual Catholic Ball and 'truly the father of the poor', while the sugar broker, Edward P. Parry, who was 'the most devoted lay helper' to the Bishop of Liverpool, only supported Church of England charities, including the Church Temperance Society. John Riley, a general merchant who specialised in toys and fancy goods, was a director of the Liverpool Guardian Society, but devoted much of his time to the Wesleyan Schools in Vine Street, while the 'affections and activities' of the iron merchant Samuel Stitt were chiefly evident in 'religious and benevolent objects, mostly in connection with Presbyterianism'.[19]

Although the list of charitable institutions is not comprehensive, it provides an indication of the range of institutions supported by individual merchants. Out of a total of 164 merchants, 54 (32.9 per cent) were only involved with sectarian charities; a further 22 (13.4 per cent) were associated with both sectarian and non-denominational institutions; while 83 (50.6 per cent) had a broader commitment to charitable work not tied to a particular religion. To this extent, an involvement in charitable activity was just as likely to generate face-to-face meetings with a narrow circle of co-religionists as with a wider group of local merchants, while the continued importance of sectarian charities would have strengthened trust relations but only within a clearly defined denominational framework. Shared agency and mutual experience, as developed through active involvement in philanthropy and charitable giving, continued to be based to a significant degree on confessional affiliation, rather than providing a basis for more effective networking across the merchant community. Historians have emphasised the significant involvement by businessmen in the management of the voluntary sector, but even in the case of denominational charities only a minority of Liverpool's merchants were actively engaged.

Entrepreneurial Philanthropy: Merseyside Merchants as Benefactors

The priority of many Liverpool merchants and members of the business community was the accumulation of wealth, and their overriding commitment to this objective precluded, almost by necessity, the allocation of time to the active support of charitable enterprises. Despite the increasing recognition of the importance of philanthropy as a means of addressing deep-seated welfare issues and its cultural and social endorsement by the middle class, only a minority of the port-city's elite merchants (as listed in Orchard's volume) was actively involved in managing public charities. For others, an annual subscription to a well-known charity was merely 'outward social varnish'. Indeed, subscribers could have their names recorded in annual reports as patrons of life-members in return for a single payment of £50 and £10 respectively (as was the case with the Liverpool Society for the Prevention of Cruelty to Children), even if they failed to take a close interest in its later development.[20]

If day-to-day pressures of managing an important Liverpool business precluded any regular commitment to local charities, particularly as a committee member or an honorary officer, the opportunity of becoming a major benefactor for either civic or charitable objectives offered a means of securing peer approval, prestige, an extended networking circle, and social power, even if the ostensible motive was presented as religious, caritative, or an act of municipal benevolence. Many historians have argued that the nineteenth century was 'a great philanthropic age', when private benefactors played a critical role in supporting the provision of hospitals, institutional welfare for 'the deserving poor', educational facilities, particularly at the secondary and tertiary levels, and public amenities, including art galleries, museums, urban parks, and drinking fountains. In 1851, the cotton merchant George Holt expressed his vigorous opposition to the use of public (council) money for charitable purposes, an ideology that was shared to varying degrees by both Tories and Liberals, as well as by members of local ratepayers' associations. The persistence of such an attitude until the late nineteenth century required, by necessity, private benefactors and philanthropists to provide the funding necessary to ameliorate the social problems generated by low pay, poverty, poor housing, and ill health, but also to take forward capital expenditure needed to improve civic facilities and sustain Liverpool's international profile.[21]

Recent research on 'philanthrocapitalism', 'star philanthropy', or 'celanthropy' has highlighted the apparent similarity between the current emphasis on the role of individual benefactors and private enterprise in addressing social problems and the contribution made by prominent reformers in the second half of the nineteenth century, including figures such as George Peabody (1795–1869) 'the founder of modern philanthropy', Dr. Thomas Barnardo (1845–1905) an extraordinary 'social entrepreneur', and Octavia Hill (1838–1912) a 'moving force' behind the development of social housing. But the motives behind major philanthropic gestures are more difficult to entangle. George Peabody, it is alleged, was 'thrifty, even miserly with his employees and relatives'; Dr. Barnardo may have become 'world famous' in working for the victims of British industrialisation, but from a modern perspective the policy from 1870 onwards of 'shipping out' young orphans to Canada and more distant destinations in the British Empire was highly questionable; while Octavia Hill remained critical of 'kindly, but unrigorous philanthropy' and was a committed opponent of municipal socialism, subsidised housing, and government intervention, whether local or central, in housing provision. Apart from the problem of disentangling the motives of major benefactors, or social entrepreneurs, other issues have been seldom addressed. Little is known in detail about how financiers like Peabody acquired their extensive wealth or the proportion that he allocated for charitable purposes. Barnardo's business model was questionable and his charitable enterprises were dogged by debt; the way he ran his empire became an object of litigation initiated by the Charity Organisation Society; and Catholics resented his constant advocacy of Protestantism because of its negative impact on children in his care from Catholic families. Despite her important role in raising awareness about the scale and consequences of inadequate working-class housing, Octavia Hill's charitable enterprises could only ever benefit a small minority of London's residents and her opposition to local government involvement arguably led to a delay in the adoption of major rehousing schemes.[22]

Today, there is an increasing tendency to view the contribution of wealthy private benefactors as a solution to the systemic problems of state welfare systems that have been systematically underfunded and subject to severe austerity. According to Sandbrook, by the end of the Victorian era 'wealth came hand in hand with deep social obligations' at a time when the absence of adequate welfare support placed a very high value on philanthropic generosity. Even if there was growing concern over how charity could be secured and its value guaranteed, it has been suggested that this period signified an increased commitment to humanitarian reforms and the impact of philanthropy in reforming power inequalities. Certainly, entrepreneurial benefactors appear to have played a significant role in alleviating some of Liverpool's social problems. According to a report on the Grand Fancy Dress Ball, held in St. George's Hall Tuesday 14 February 1860 to raise funds for a number of charities, including the Royal Infirmary, the North and South Hospitals and Dispensaries, and the National Life Boat Institution, the port's 'merchant princes' and tradesmen had become 'proverbial for their noble charities and self-sacrificing works'. It was admitted that in a large commercial town such as Liverpool 'there must always be a vast amount of suffering which never meets the public eye', but because of the contribution of benefactors and philanthropists the needs of 'innumerable cases' could be met, at least in part. In order to examine the financial commitment to social welfare provision by merchants and other members of Merseyside's business community, the following section will focus on three issues: the role of the sugar refiner Sir Henry Tate (1819–1899) and the brewer Sir Andrew Barclay Walker (1824–1893) as major charitable and civic benefactors; the extent to which elite members of the merchant community fulfilled their much heralded role in providing financial support for worthy causes; and the significance of private benefactions in the development of University College Liverpool.[23]

Private Benefactors

(i) Sir Henry Tate, Bart

The career of Sir Henry Tate is well known, even if the absence of archives from the second half of the nineteenth century precludes a rigorous analysis of the operation of his business enterprise. He was one of many immigrants to Liverpool (in his case from Chorley in Lancashire); having been apprenticed to one of his older brothers who had become a Liverpool grocer, he set up his own business in 1849 and opened a second store at 42–44 Hamilton Street in 1851 in Birkenhead; by 1855 he had six shops on Merseyside and two years later he was involved in the wholesale trade. The turning point in his business career occurred in 1859 with a diversification into sugar refining in partnership with John Wright with a refinery in Manesty Lane. By the end of the nineteenth century, Henry Tate & Sons had become the foremost sugar refiners in Britain.[24]

He had also received countless accolades as 'one of the greatest benefactors of mankind', with the Tate Gallery in London (originally the National Gallery of British Art) regarded justifiably as 'his lasting memorial'. The list of his benefactions was certainly impressive: his initial offer of £80,000 towards the costs of building the National Gallery of British Art at Millbank (which was opened in 1897), together with a gift of 65 paintings and 3 sculptures (valued at £75,000), was supplemented by a further payment for an extension (1898–9) consisting of nine further rooms and a sculpture hall. The total cost of the building was £105,000 (excluding the extension), but Tate's original offer had already led *Punch* (22 March 1890) to crown 'the Potent Tate' 'the King of the National Picture Donors'. His support for what quickly became known as the Tate Gallery dwarfed all previous benefactions (although other donations were made anonymously). From a combined total of £115,662 endowments (excluding the Tate), £62,500 (54 per cent) was in support of higher education; £41,063 (35.5 per cent) was allocated to health projects; and £8,600 (7.4 per cent) for secondary and general education, including £5,000 for the Tate Institute in Silverstown, £2,000 for scholarships at Liverpool Institute and the funding of three public libraries for the inhabitants of South London in Balham, South Lambeth and Brixton. He was also a supporter of the National Thrift Society. Although London became the focal point for most of his charitable expenditure, he made substantial contributions to Liverpool setting aside, in 1885, £22,000 for the construction of the homeopathic Hahnemann Hospital (followed by further donations of over £5,000), £8,000 for the Liverpool Royal Infirmary, and a total of £45,500 for University College, Liverpool. He was not only the donor of 'the great picture gallery', but in the year before his death promised £500 towards the purchase of the old Lambeth Baths as a site for a polytechnic. When Sir Henry died in 1899, the public tributes were full of praise for 'A national benefactor' and 'One of the munificent merchant princes whose names take an honourable place in the national record', but he was an exceptionally wealthy businessman. At the time of his offer to fund the creation of the National Gallery of British Art, he also acquired a £150,000 shareholding in the development of railways in Argentina which generated a solid yield over a sustained time period. By the mid-1890s, the value of his share portfolio in five companies in Argentina and Uruguay amounted to £113,910.[25]

Tate's wealth was accumulated when the sugar refining industry was facing considerable difficulties, largely, but not entirely, due to the increasing competition of beet sugar from continental Europe. French refined sugar flooded the British market; some sugar loaf producers were faced with 'extinction'; between 1880 and 1882 a considerable number of companies failed; while a new wave of bankruptcies was reported in the late 1880s. In the 1890s, two Liverpool firms, Macfie and Jager, built new refineries (at Goole and Leith respectively) and those firms that diversified into the production of industrial sugar proved to be more resilient. Crosfield

& Barrow (Liverpool), however, suffered a 'spcctacular' bankruptcy and production was only continued intermittently until the end of the century. The reasons for Tate's success in a difficult trading market were two-fold. Firstly, there was a willingness to adopt new technologies by acquiring patents taken out by French, German, and Belgian scientists, including the method of purifying sugar developed by Bovin and Loiseau (a process which had been introduced at the new Love Lane Factory in Liverpool by the mid-1870s), the Langen cube-making process (acquired in 1875), and Gustav Adant's method of producing superior quality sugar cubes (1892). Secondly, the company pursued a successful strategy of brand marketing supported by targeted advice on how to make the best recipes with the firm's sugar products, while the publicity surrounding his numerous benefactions must have had a positive impact on its sales and turnover. When Henry Tate & Sons finally went public in 1903, with almost all the shares bought by family members, its overall share value was £799,330.[26]

There can be little doubt that Henry Tate was convinced of the benefits which would arise from his benefactions. By making such a generous donation to the building of a national gallery, 'justice would be done to British Art' and 'gratification' would be 'bestowed on this and future generations', even if its founding was far from straightforward. However, he has been accused, with some cause, of founding a gallery 'that added new connotations to his name other than that of a sugar magnate who acquired companies and associated wealth through slavery'. If not directly implicated in the slave trade, the indentured labourers who cut the cane destined for Tate's refineries in Liverpool and London were undoubtedly subjected to wage slavery and harsh working conditions. Indeed, the competitiveness of sugar cane was dependent on the ability of producers to keep wage costs low. The abolition of slavery on the British sugar plantations of the West Indies and Central America in 1833 led to extensive compensation for the owners of estates and their slaves, but almost no provision was made for the future needs of those who were legally freed from slavery. Land allocation to encourage the emergence of an independent peasantry was inadequate, while the cultural and economic legacy of slavery condemned future generations to a lifetime of unrelenting labour. The available evidence suggests that the 'freed' men and women of the sugar plantations suffered a reduction in living standards, restricted educational progress, and a lower level of life expectancy. The first indentured labourers (whether recruited in India, China, Spain, or Portugal) arrived in the late 1830s and after a transitional period they formed the backbone of the plantation workforce, as estate owners sought to limit their reliance on jobbing gangs of ex-slaves and to replicate a compliant workforce bonded to work in the fields for a specified period of time. According to Craton, the use of indentured labour was little better than 'a new system of slavery'. A system of exploitation, developed under slavery and reconfigured using indentured labourers, continued to reap huge profits for sugar refiners which were used subsequently by some of them to support philanthropic causes in Britain. It is inconceivable that Henry Tate did not know of the working conditions on sugar plantations when he made the decision in 1859 to become a partner with John Wright. Indeed, a few years later he was instrumental in establishing the Richmond Cavendish Co. to manufacture 'Cavendish' and 'Negrohead' Virginian tobacco which had been prohibited in Britain up until 1868. Previously, supplies of these types of tobacco had been 'thrown into the hands of the slaveholders of New Orleans and Richmond', in the latter case employing approximately 22,000 slaves. After liquidating a deficit from the company's first year of operation in 1865, under Tate's chairmanship it achieved a net profit of £3,194 14s 1d in 1866 and the foundations had been laid for 'a lucrative and prosperous business.'[27]

Like many of the other subscribers to the Homoeopathic Dispensary, including Colonel Charles Grayson who had experienced 'benefits for many years', Henry Tate was a firm believer in homeopathy's curative powers. The Liverpool Homoeopathic Dispensary (LHD) had been founded in 1841 in premises at 41 Frederick Street. By 1860, it was located in a new build-ing, partly designed by the architect Peter Ellis (1805–1884), the costs of which were met by subscriptions (including £20 from Tate), but its geographical coverage was extended by the establishment in 1866 of a Northern Dispensary intended to meet the needs of the growing number of dockworkers employed at the North Docks. Liverpool was at the forefront in provid-ing homoeopathic medication. Dr. John James Drysdale M.D., who became the dispensary's leading physician, was the lead editor of *The British Journal of Homoeopathic Medicine* (first published in 1842); he played a major role in establishing the British Homeopathic Association (whose first president in 1847 was the 8th Duke of Beaufort); and in 1857 he was elected presi-dent of the Homoeopathic Medico Chirurgical Society of Liverpool. The rising popularity of homeopathy was fuelled by three factors: its endorsement by members of the Royal Family and leading members of the aristocracy; an increasing rejection of aggressive therapies prescribed by trained physicians (including bleeding, catomel, purgatives and strong opiates); and evidence which suggested that its outcomes were as good as, if not better than, those of professional medicine. Just over 30 years after its opening the Liverpool Dispensary had treated 175,567 patients: in 1872, 11,512 new patients were seen, and 4,193 visits had been carried out to 1,212 homes. It was a free medical charity whereby access to homeopathic treatment did not require a formal process of application and validation which applied in the case of all voluntary hospitals (although recommendations from subscribers did entitle patients 'precedence in order of attend-ance') and many of its patients were discharged 'very much improved'.[28]

Both as a reflection of Tate's personal preference for homoeopathic medicine and as a major contribution to the welfare of Liverpool's poorer classes, his decision in 1885 to donate £22,000 for the construction of a new hospital (the Hahnemann Hospital) made eminent sense (Figure 12.4).

Figure 12.4 The Hahnemann Homeopathic Hospital, Liverpool (late-nineteenth century photograph)

The site was chosen because of its height (invariably interpreted by Victorians as essential for health), it was designed by two eminent architects, Francis Usher Holme (1844–1913) and his uncle George Holme (1822–1915), and included many innovative features, such as hydraulic lifts and an advanced heating and ventilation system. Tate's association with the LHD went back many years. He served on its committee at a time when almost 30 per cent of its members came from the merchant and business community and was elected chairman for three consecutive years (1878–80), a post he was only forced to relinquish in 1881 because engagements elsewhere, primarily in London, 'prevented me from going to Liverpool'. His formal apologies to the annual general meeting contained two important points. Firstly, in hoping that a 'good chairman' could quickly be found, he set out the qualities that were needed to fulfil this role, namely a man 'who has some time at his disposal, to enable him to take a personal interest in the affairs and conduct of the two important Dispensaries'. Secondly, he offered an assurance that he would always take 'a warm interest' in their work and a commitment to contribute funds 'if any extension is thought necessary'. In fact, Tate's financial contribution to the LHD was considerable: each year he donated £25, in addition to paying his subscription of one guinea. For some time, its committee had expressed its hope that Liverpool would possess 'a Hospital for the Homoeopathic Treatment of Diseases', but even in 1882 the cotton broker Alexander Eccles remained sanguine 'that, at present, funds could be raised for the erection of a homoeopathic hospital' to rival the level of provision in London (1850) and Birmingham (1859). It was only as a result of Tate's 'munificent' benefaction that this objective was finally realised. He became president of the LHD, an office which he retained until his death, while his second wife, Ann, became its lady patroness and president of its committee of lady visitors. After the opening of the Hahnemann Hospital, the Tate family maintained its financial support: in 1892 nine members of the family contributed a total of £247 1s, while in 1896 Henry Tate donated £5,000 to the creation of an Endowment Fund.[29]

However, in pursuing a cause which reflected his personal commitment to homoeopathic medicine, Tate ignored the cumulative impact of improvements in medical science and the reality of maintaining in-patient care within a hospital context. In terms of patient outcome, homoeopathy could rival 'traditional' medicine in the mid-nineteenth century at a time when physicians had no real understanding of disease causation and continued to rely on a belief in the primary role of miasmas whereby 'noxious particles' rose from 'vitiated air', rolling slowly 'to corrupt the better portions of town' and giving rise to a 'moral pestilence'. Not surprisingly, this was also a time of open warfare between orthodox medicine and homoeopathy. By the 1880s, however, the development of bacteriology, improved surgical techniques, and a move away from aggressive treatments had gradually tipped the scales in favour of established medicine. In 1882, the number of attendances at the two dispensaries was 72,193: by the start of the 1890s it had fallen to 63,156 (a reduction of over 14 per cent), a trend that continued into the next century. According to Nicholls, homoeopathy had originally represented a powerful intellectual and economic challenge to the 'regular profession', but even as early as the 1870s there were signs of decline and the discipline was 'all but moribund' by the early twentieth century. Although the pace of change should not be exaggerated, there is little doubt that contemporary observers were fully aware of the trend. The situation in Liverpool was compounded by financial problems. A deficit of £236 4s in 1896 prompted a suggestion that 'patients should be led to feel that the privileges they get were worth paying for', but by 1900 it had risen to £328 10s. There was a pressing need for new subscribers, although this was a problem faced by many voluntary hospitals as well, while the costs of supporting over 400 hospital in-patients represented a drain on resources. The beneficence of Henry Tate and his family in supporting the LHD cannot be doubted, specifically in the case of his financial support for the design, construction, and fitting out of the Hahnemann Hospital. Counterfactually, however, it demonstrates an inherent problem with the role of private benefactors who often pursued an agenda that failed to reflect the needs of contemporary society. Undoubtedly, homoeopathy offered valuable (and free) support for many of Liverpool's poorest residents, particularly in the city's north end, but by the time it was opened the popularity of homoeopathic remedies was already beginning to wane.[30]

Surprisingly little is known about Tate and biographical evidence is limited in its coverage. There was, we are told, a 'humility about the man'; his 'family's life was always private', just like Tate himself; under the influence of his second wife he was 'attracted to the Congregational Church', but his life remained influenced by his Unitarian upbringing. At the same time, there is evidence that Tate enjoyed grand balls and official receptions, but also saw it as his duty to attend the funerals of other prominent members of the mercantile community. He was a member of the organising committee for the Grand Fancy Dress Ball in St. George's Hall in March 1864; attended a banquet in the town hall in June 1866 in honour of His Royal Highness the Duke of Edinburgh; and was an invited guest at the farewell dinner for Lieutenant-Colonel Trimble in January 1875 having served for some years as the commandant of the 15th Liverpool Artillery Volunteers. He served for three years as a councillor for the Lime Street ward (1863–66), having been elected unopposed. If Tate was not equipped for the 'hurly-burly of political life', he was nevertheless active in support of the Liberal cause: he attended meetings to secure the election of John Rogers in the Great George ward; was elected to the council's watch committee (in November 1865); and was a subscriber to the funds raised for W. E. Gladstone's 'substantial' testimonial. He had a 'kind and genial temperament', but he was still 'a self-made man' who had 'worked himself up the social ladder by years of honest, careful, and shrewd attention to business' in the 'best style of the successful tradesman'. In a ward of shopkeepers, he knew the importance of avoiding 'the infliction of new rates' and would resist 'reckless and ill-digested and costly schemes of so-called improvement' and was 'by habit and business an economist in the administration of local government'. Moreover, he had already 'amassed very considerable property' even before he became a successful sugar refiner, partly as a result of his chairmanship of the Liverpool Land Company. By the time of its first general meeting in 1863, it had already acquired three fields in Breck Road which were to be laid out for houses at an annual rental of £18–20: 13 years later with Tate still as chairman the company registered a net profit of £21,448 8s 5d, which justified the payment of a 15 per cent dividend and an allocation of £1,000 to the directors for their services. He may have always been 'in the van of progress', but his sugar refineries were a cause of serious air pollution. Tate was summoned before the Liverpool Police Court on a number of occasions and was found guilty of infringing the Smoke Nuisances Act: he was fined 20s for the 'discharge of an undue quantity of smoke' in May 1862; 20s and costs for emitting a 'dense volume of smoke' in June 1863; and 40s and costs following the emission of large quantities of smoke from 'one of their chimneys' in May 1875. Fires were also a problem: in 1874, while attempting to extinguish 'a conflagration in the sugar house of Henry Tate and Sons of Manesty Lane', a young officer in the Liverpool police force, Alexander Burgess, lost his life and an appeal was launched to provide aid for his father 'who had been deprived of all assistance from his son'.[31]

According to Jones, there was 'nothing haphazard about his giving', because he sought to maximise the welfare benefits of his numerous benefactions. But personal preference also played a major role. His interest in art may well have been stimulated by his first wife, Jane, who was a member of the Liverpool Society of Fine Arts and won a £5 prize for her painting in its competition in October 1858 which attracted interest from 'a large number of subscribers', while his family's continuing support for the LHD was simply an expression of Tate's belief in the efficacy of homoeopathic remedies. When he received the Honorary Freedom of the City of Liverpool in June 1891, he was praised for his 'eminent services' and 'many acts of munificence' and his funding of the Tate Gallery in London was justifiably rewarded with a baronetcy which he was finally persuaded to accept. However, his extensive wealth was built on the wage slavery of the sugar (and tobacco) plantations of the Caribbean (and elsewhere), where every life was 'edged with a casual finality' even when there was a primary reliance on imported indentured labour. At the same time, the decision to fund the establishment of the Hahnemann Hospital in Liverpool coincided with the start of a significant decline in the popularity of homoeopathic medicine in the face of constant criticism from the medical establishment and a visible improvement in patient outcomes in institutional medicine as physicians began to assimilate new theories of disease causation. Like many other artistic, educational and medical institutions which accepted funding from benefactors whose wealth rested on the profitability of slavery or the systemic exploitation of indentured labour, the main recipients of Tate's benefactions (whether in Liverpool or London) have been forced to reassess the wider implications of his legacy.[32]

(ii) Sir Andrew Barclay Walker, Bart

Some elements of the press regarded Henry Tate as a 'sugar boiler' because of his apparent poor taste in pictures, while Andrew Barclay Walker was derided by some of those opposed to the persistent dominance of Toryism in Liverpool as 'The Barman Knight'. But whereas Tate's critics showed no interest in the harsh realities of wage slavery on the sugar plantations which were the source of his wealth, Walker's indictment, articulated in a series of pamphlets on Liverpool Conservatives who were 'utterly void of all political knowledge or precepts', rested entirely on how he had accumulated a fortune as a brewer and owner of countless public houses.[33] Walker's family background is well known. He was born at Auchinflower, Ayrshire in 1824, the second son of Peter Walker (1795–1879) of the Fort Brewery, Ayr, and his wife, Mary (who died in 1846). After completing his education at Ayr Academy and Liverpool Institute, he became a partner in his father's business. The family had migrated to Liverpool where his father established a small brewery in Ray Street, near St. Paul's Square, and by 1846 three further breweries were operating in Warrington. The firm's regional profile was strengthened by the opening in 1877 of a brewery in Burton-upon-Trent (A. B. Walker & Sons) which specialised in high-quality bitter ales; in 1879, following the death of his father, Walker became the sole proprietor of the Warrington breweries; and the firm became a limited liability company in 1890 (Peter Walker & Son, Warrington & Burton Ltd.), with Walker as its first chairman. He was described in *Vanity Fair* as 'a good-looking, courtly gentleman' and 'a good Tory' (Figure 12.5).[34]

The provision of art galleries in the provincial towns and cities of Britain during the nineteenth century was a drawn-out process and, despite a general recognition of their important role in the formation and consolidation of urban culture, metropolitan institutions have attracted the most attention. As Moore has demonstrated, the role of local authorities varied considerably. In some cases, the failure of private benefactors to fund art galleries led to public intervention, while Manchester Corporation assumed responsibility for private institutions that were failing. The Museums Act of 1845 permitted municipal boroughs (with populations of over 10,000) to levy a 1/2d rate for the establishment of museums, some of which offered picture gallery space, and this was reinforced by the Public Libraries and Museums Acts of 1850 and 1855. But the pace of progress was held back by the overriding commitment to restrict public expenditure, an objective which was held, to varying degrees, by Liberals and Tories alike. As was the case with other improvements to the civic realm, particularly public parks, permissive legislation reinforced a dependency on private philanthropy and wealthy benefactors. As Woodson-Boulton

Figure 12.5 'Sir Andrew Barclay Walker', *Vanity Fair*, 'Men of the Day', No. 471 (1890)

has emphasised, even when the permitted rate was raised to 1d in the pound in 1855, local authorities were unable to take forward capital-intensive development projects; private initiative was a precondition for establishing local art galleries; and public funding was restricted to covering administrative and maintenance costs. Almost invariably, support for the provision of art museums was dependent on 'the synergy of multiple actors', who often had competing, if not contradictory, views about the aesthetic and moral purpose of art.[35]

The origins of what became the Walker Art Gallery, arguably the largest municipal art gallery in England, are well known. In 1819 a small group of subscribers to the Liverpool Royal Institution purchased 37 pictures from the collection of William Roscoe who was forced to sell them because of the bankruptcy three years earlier of Roscoe, Clark & Roscoe, a bank in which William Roscoe was the senior partner. The intention was to prevent the collection's dispersal and to use them to facilitate 'the advancement of the FINE ARTS in the Town of Liverpool'.

But it was not until 1843 that a purpose-built art gallery was erected to display the collection. Exhibitions of contemporary paintings had been held intermittently in Liverpool since 1774 and from 1810, under the aegis of the Liverpool Academy, this became an annual event. The Liverpool Society for the Fine Arts was established in 1858: it organised annual exhibitions and built up a permanent collection with works from exhibitors. However, the Pre-Raphaelite dispute of the mid-nineteenth century effectively destroyed the Liverpool Academy: its last annual exhibition was held in 1867 and its demise 'threatened Liverpool's position as a major regional art centre'. The response of the city council to the need for a public gallery as a focal point for art exhibitions was muted, even if it was understood that it would strengthen Liverpool's reputation as a centre for cultural excellence and satisfy the demands of an association of citizens formed in 1850 with the intention of promoting the creation of an art gallery, library, and museum. These objectives were enshrined in an Act of Parliament (1852). But, as was the case with H. P. Horner's innovative plans of 1850 for creating 'a belt of garden or parkland' surrounding the town centre when the corporation's response was characterised by *The Porcupine* as 'passive and measly', the development of an institutional infrastructure for the arts was delayed by cost considerations and ultimately remained dependent on private benefactors.[36]

The offer in 1853 of £6,000 by (Sir) William Brown (1784–1864), a highly successful merchant and banker who had been born in the USA, towards the construction of 'a suitable library for Liverpool' ultimately led to the opening to the public of the William Brown Library and Museum in October 1861. He undoubtedly possessed to an exceptional degree 'the genius of the merchant', but according to Orchard the gift of the building was only given 'under pressure, after much judicious handling' and 'grudgingly' at a time when 'a possible baronetcy loomed before him': by the end of the century his gift of up to £40,000 was no longer seen as an example of 'exceptional self-sacrifice': after all he was reputed to have been a millionaire 'thrice over' when he died. More importantly, its success delayed even further progress with the creation of a suitable civic art gallery. It provided space for displaying some of the art treasures, including medieval manuscripts, ivories, and enamels, donated in 1867 (and valued at £80,000) by Joseph Mayer, a jeweller, goldsmith, and antiquarian, which had previously been housed in his own private museum in Colquitt Street, opened in 1852.[37]

The political context which led to Andrew Barclay Walker's offer to fund a new art gallery, as envisaged in the early 1850s, has been discussed in detail by James Moore. What is immediately clear is the extent of active opposition by members of the temperance movement, which at that time was 'increasing in strength', and by other political opponents. By the early 1830 there were probably around 127 temperance societies in England located predominantly in the northern manufacturing districts, but the passing of the Beer Act of 1830 led to the opening of many more outlets selling alcohol and rising public concern over the moral and social ramifications of excess beer consumption. If Preston was the 'Jerusalem of the teetotalism', Liverpool, because of the nature and human consequences of its port economy, quickly became a focal point for temperance mobilisation. The origins of the temperance movement can be traced back to 1829, but the first recorded temperance meeting was held in October 1834 when it condemned the 'great national evil' of 'excessive use of intoxicating liquor, principally by the lower-class': by the early 1850s there were at least 32 temperance and Rechabite societies active in Liverpool and Birkenhead. From 1835 the local temperance societies held an annual festival, generally in July as a counter attraction to race week and its 'usual dissipation', although in May 1856 a Grand Temperance Exhibition and Festival was held on an 'encampment' in Birkenhead (on a large field adjoining 'Claughton Park'), with substantial wooden buildings (one with a glass roof) and a range of exhibitions, non-alcoholic refreshment stalls, and provision for archery. During the following years, the strength of the movement increased significantly, despite numerous internal divisions, whether class- or religion-based. It published a wide range of both local and national periodicals, targeting younger members of the temperance movement, as well as medical practitioners, and reinforced the moral argument for teetotalism as a 'natural' condition that benefited both the individual and the state.[38]

There was some concern over the way Major Walker, described as an alderman and wine and spirit merchant, was elected mayor in November 1873 following the jubilation of the 'grog interest' at the outcome of the municipal elections, but the chairman of the Library, Museum, and Arts Committee gratefully acknowledged 'his noble and munificent offer of a gallery of art' and it was J. A. Picton, the leader of the Liberal Party, who proposed that it should be called 'The Walker Gallery of Art'. His subsequent nomination as mayor in November 1876, with the standard allowance of £2,700, was only possible because precedent was put aside, while his knighthood in the following year was acknowledged by the political elite as a recognition of his 'princely liberalism' and his desire 'to elevate the taste and advance the moral condition of the people'. Such views were not universally held. Details of temperance society membership were seldom included in the contemporary biographies compiled by either Orchard or Pike, but occasionally there is evidence of a deep commitment to the cause. The merchant and shipowner William Benjamin Bowring became president of the United Kingdom Temperance Alliance and contested (unsuccessfully) the Abercromby Division parliamentary seat on a platform that included a direct veto over the liquor trade, while the iron merchant William Sprotson Caine, who was elected to Parliament in 1884–85, was a Baptist and an 'amateur' preacher for whom temperance was 'the first love of his life'. David Munro Drysdale, a highly successful timber and stave merchant, had been an abstainer since 1866; the shipowner Francis Henderson was a Presbyterian and 'a total abstainer'; and the timber merchant John Herbert Roberts M.P. acquired extensive tracts of land, including Parliament Fields which they subdivided into plots and either sold or leased for building purposes 'always stipulating that no public house shall be erected'. Even if both Liverpool and Birkenhead were 'not very God-fearing localities', the strength of religious commitment by certain members of the mercantile community remained considerable. A dislike, even hatred, of the drink trade with all its consequences for the people of Merseyside was embedded in virtually all non-conformist denominations, whether Baptist, Congregationalist, Methodist, Quaker, Unitarian, or Welsh Methodist. The Church of England Temperance Society played an increasingly important role in mobilising public opinion. By the early 1890s there were 128 adult branches (from a total of 203 parishes), together with 149 juvenile and 20 women's branches. Unlike the local Tory Party which had close links with the drinks trade, many middle-class supporters of the Liberal Party were strong supporters of the Temperance Movement.[39]

Opposition to Walker's gift of a new art gallery took on a more tangible form on the day of its official opening, when he was presented with an ornate casket including the design of the building, which had been manufactured by Elkington & Co. of Birmingham (by the 1860s one of the world's leading makers of silverware). Activists from local temperance societies condemned his links with the drinks trade and his use of philanthropy as a blatant means of self-promotion, but they were also annoyed at the plans for a testimonial subscription to mark his 'generosity' with major employers pressurising their workers to contribute. A demonstration at the opening ceremony involved the presentation of an alternative casket, with the new gallery represented as a reward for iniquity with its walls bearing testimony to the damage inflicted by Walker's business (472 brothels 'known to police', 23,556 drunkards, and 2,318 licensed 'drunkeries'), but all this was deemed acceptable by the gallery's benefactor if it resulted in the offer of a baronetcy. However, this only served to inflame public criticism at how his knighthood had been bought, even if there was nothing strictly illegal about this practice. But criticism from the local press continued, particularly by the *Liberal Review*, while many of the leading clergymen were highly critical of the drinks industry. As early as 1865 Rev. John Jones had attempted to establish a clear link between drunkenness and premature death. Hugh Stowell Brown, the minister at the Baptist Myrtle Street Church, viewed strong drink as 'the disgrace, the curse' which threatened to be 'the ruin of the country'; the Baptist minister Charles Garrett (1823–1886), who was a teetotaller and Rechabite, condemned 'strong drink' as 'the chief material enemy of our children' which had 'slain' tens of thousands at a rate of six persons every hour, both 'directly, and indirectly'; while Rev. Canon Richard Hobson (born in 1834) had been a devoted temperance reformer for 'many years'. By the early 1890s criticism of Walker had not abated: according to the Rev. Robert Veitch, Walker's business success was 'the undoing of the city', as his business as a brewer 'was manifestly the cause of more poverty, crime and moral degradation than all other influences put together'. Faced with such determined opposition and trenchant but 'respectable' criticism of his brewing activities and his underlying motives in gifting the new art gallery to the people of Liverpool, it is not surprising that Walker's attempt to recast his public image as a benefactor and philanthropist failed: his new role as a patron of the arts 'simply brought his lifelong association with the brewing industry into focus'. Moreover, Walker never enjoyed a reputation as a connoisseur of fine art, unlike other leading members of Liverpool society. The flax and hemp broker John Albert Bencke had 'fine specimens of the modern Continental schools', the banker George Rae had 'the largest collection of the late D. G. Rossetti in England', while the cotton merchant Theodor von Sobbe possessed some fine paintings' including Sir Frederic Leighton's *Rubinella*. If George W. Moss ('not in active business') had 'a famous collection of water colours', the shipowner James Harrison was regarded as 'an excellent judge of modern painting' and the commission merchant and cotton broker Francis Charles Anthony Minoprio was 'a cultured and intelligent critic of painting'. Walker had no such record as a well-known art collector or a judge of fine art, while the fact that he had almost nothing to do with the management of the new gallery reinforced popular belief that his benefaction served primarily political ends and, more importantly, his overriding desire for a knighthood.[40]

Indeed, the case against Walker was a commanding one. Firstly, by the mid-nineteenth century Liverpool had a reputation as 'the most drunken, the most criminal, the most pauper-oppressed, and the most death-stricken town in England'. But such a wide-ranging indictment of alcohol abuse needs to be viewed with some caution. In 1873 there was no direct correlation between the number of licensed premises and the number of arrests for drunkenness (per 1,000 population): Norwich had the highest density of public houses, but the lowest ratio of arrests; Liverpool had the highest frequency of arrests for drunkenness, but six other northern towns (Huddersfield, Bradford, Hull, Halifax, Leeds, and Blackburn) had a higher proportion of licensed premises to population. Despite increased social capital investment in better sewerage, water supply, and improvements in housing and public health facilities, especially after the 1860s, overall mortality remained consistently above the national average. Even at the end of the century there was a substantial geographical variation by district in crude mortality rates (per 1,000) between Sefton Park (10.7) with its upper-middle-class residents and Exchange (36.5) which provided accommodation for working-class men dependent on dock labour. If alcohol dependency led to an increased death rate from liver cirrhosis, this has yet to receive serious attention and fatalities associated with drunken brawls were probably statistically insignificant, although offences such as 'drunk and stabbing' or 'drunk and assaulting' rose from 14,114 in 1866 to 22,031 ten years later. In fact, high rates of infant and child mortality were the main determinants of Liverpool's overall death rate during this period: large cities had persistently high excess child mortality, primarily as a result of population density, while the increase in infant mortality which was particularly noticeable in the 1890s has been linked with a number of factors, including infant feeding practices and the virulence of measles (normally correlated with population density). Although demographic data for this period are relatively robust (apart from a possible under-registration of infant deaths), statistics on drunkenness and crime are less reliable as they reflected variations in the effectiveness of local policing and different political strategies designed to combat the consequences of excessive alcohol consumption. However, the indirect impact of the drink problem on women and children cannot be disputed. Licensed premises were implicated directly in supporting prostitution, especially in 'Sailortown', while drunkenness in many cases led to a neglect of family responsibilities. The Liverpool Society for the Prevention of Cruelty to Children was established in 1883 specifically to confront problems of malnutrition, poor hygiene (as a result of neglect), as well as violence and beatings. Many women, whether wives, prostitutes, or casual acquaintances, were victims of rape and physical assault by intoxicated men. To this extent, the drink trade was a direct cause of a great deal of human suffering, as advocates of the Temperance Movement insisted.[41]

Walker's commercial success as a brewer reinforced his culpability for the social and family consequences of drunkenness. According to Orchard, he 'never was poor', but was essentially the 'architect of his own prosperity'; he was a 'consummate organizer', a 'shrewd judge of men', and a highly successful 'bargain-maker'. During the 1830s and 1840s there had been a rapid increase in the number of beer houses (which did not require annual approval by local magistrates), but Liverpool still had many more pubs with full licenses than Manchester. Between 1861 and 1866 a group of local magistrates with close links to the brewing industry and the Tory Party agitated for 'free licensing' and the abandonment of the neighbourhood test, with the merchant Robertson Gladstone claiming that the supply of public houses should be determined solely by demand. Over 400 beer houses were converted into fully licensed premises. It was not until 1869 that the remaining beer houses were brought under legal control and their licences subject to annual renewal. By 1876, according to the Head Constable, Major John James Greig, Liverpool had 1,919 public houses and 334 beer houses. Walker's firm profited from these developments, but his increasing control of the drinks trade both on Merseyside and in wider regional context was reinforced by organisational innovations designed to maximise profitability. From the 1850s he appointed salaried managers for the public houses he controlled (rather than depending on licensees); adopted a policy of extending pubs into nearby premises (in the face of legal challenges); and understood the need to improve their retail design which led to the construction of some architecturally impressive buildings. According to Mutch, he was a 'significant innovator in managerial practice', while seeking to increase productivity by taking out patents for improved brewery apparatus.[42]

Even in the 1830s the drinks trade in Liverpool was already dominated by common brewers: by 1880 there were only two licensed victuallers (brewing ale on their own premises for sale to customers), with no one licensed to sell beer in an independent capacity. This trend reflected the growing control of the drinks trade by a select group of breweries, including the firm owned by Andrew Barclay Walker, which bought up 'small men' who were not endowed with his 'splendid commercial talents'. Some of his critics believed that his breweries were probably responsible for 10 per cent of Liverpool's public houses, but this was almost certainly an underestimate. The number of common brewers fell by almost 70 per cent between 1850 and 1900 (from 88 to 28) and of the 581 public houses owned in 1891 by the four largest companies (Peter Walker & Son, Robert Cain, Rowland Bent, and Threlfalls), Walker's brewing empire controlled 241 or approximately a quarter of all the city's licensed premises. Some small-scale brewers continued to survive. For example, T. May Smith, the manager of Linley's Kensington Brewery (and the Conservative chairman of the Walton Divisional Council), was also a wine and spirit merchant on his own account and a proprietor of six licensed premises, but the profitability of

Walker's management model only served to strengthen the company's dominance of the local market. Walker may well have enjoyed his role as Liverpool's mayor, which involved, during his first term of office, attending a grand ball at London's Mansion House in honour of the Duke of Edinburgh and his bride with the municipal state carriage having been forwarded in advance 'in order that Liverpool be properly presented', but neither events of national significance nor his apparent generosity in funding a new art gallery could disguise the questionable source of his wealth. To this extent, he was directly responsible for a significant proportion of the suffering caused by alcohol addiction and drunkenness in Liverpool (and elsewhere) over a 50-year period, whose victims included the old woman 'with grey hair in the gutter', the deserted wife, and the young girl 'with the first sad eyes of a ruined life'. A satirical print from c.1877, 'A Fresco for the Walker Art Gallery' (after Harry Furniss), highlighted the unavoidable link between the brewing trade and its social consequences. Presided over by the figure of Death, men in a public house are seen toasting their contributions to the new art gallery: but the cost to both them and their families was considerable. They became involved in fights, cast themselves into Liverpool's docks, and were condemned to the gallows: their wives and children were forced to seek relief in the workhouse crying 'Curse the Drink'.[43]

The Myth of the Entrepreneurial Benefactor

It is often claimed that the roots of 'entrepreneurial philanthropy' can be traced back to the second half of the nineteenth century and that benefactors, like Walker and Tate, by displaying an 'interested disinterest', used charitable acts to legitimate their social status and to strengthen the competitive advantage of their firms in line with wider strategic considerations. Both benefactors endowed new art galleries (one national, the other local) and supported other charitable objectives in Liverpool; they were rewarded with knighthoods and became Freemen of the City of Liverpool (in 1889 and 1891 respectively). They were also part of the established trend of out-migration from Merseyside, with Walker becoming a 'County gentleman' on his estate at Osmaston Manor in Derbyshire (purchased for £250,0000) and Tate taking up residence at his mansion at Park Hill, Streatham. It became his permanent home between 1880 and his death, 'an oasis of peace and tranquillity in a county house setting' unrivalled in South London, with the extensive gardens redesigned by Robert Marnock. But Tate's legacies were tainted by the dependency of his sugar-refining business on the persistence of slave wages on Caribbean plantations, while Walker's attempt to disguise the damaging effects of his success as a brewer only served to focus greater public attention on the human impact of alcohol dependency. Unfortunately, historians who utilise case studies from the past to justify a greater role for private benefactors in achieving contemporary objectives, whether in relation to the arts, education, or medicine, seldom analyse the context in which charitable bequests were made, their underlying motives, or the proportion of total wealth which was allocated for this purpose. Both Walker and Tate were immensely wealthy: Walker was reputed to be 'richest man among us', while Tate's sugar-refining business became one of the largest in Europe.[44]

Estimating the net wealth of major benefactors at death is not straightforward. It was only after 1858 that all wills were proved by the state with the details of grants of probate listed in the *National Probate Calendar*, but these only covered effects that were personal property of the deceased or unsettled assets. Most, if not all, prominent members of Liverpool's mercantile community utilised the available opportunities for inheritance planning to reduce tax liability to probate duty (levied on the net value of the personal estate), succession duty (payable from 1853), and legacy duty (paid at differential rates on all legacies in personalty according to the relationship of each legatee to the deceased). To achieve this objective, they disposed of landed property and businesses to family members or by sale to third parties, created complex trusts for surviving wives, children, and other relatives, settled life policies on their wives, and in some cases allocated funds for charitable purposes as a means of reducing tax liability.[45]

Nevertheless, the available probate data offer some indication of the deceased's wealth. On their deaths in 1893 and 1899, Walker left £2,876,781 18s 10d and Tate £1,263,565 5s 5d (or £321.4m and £143.3m, respectively, in 2019 prices using the RPI-based purchasing power calculator). Clearly, the total value of their assets prior to making inheritance provisions and drawing up a final will would have been substantially higher. Walker died leaving 'much freehold property'. He had purchased Osmaston Hall and its Derbyshire estate in 1884 for £250,000, but the market value of Gateacre Grange, his family home on the outskirts of Liverpool since the late 1860s, is unknown. In addition, he owned the Belle Vue Estates and adjoining property at Little Woolton (left to his eldest son, Peter Carlaw Walker) and the Knoll, a hunting lodge at Barton-under-Needwood in Staffordshire (inherited by John Reid Walker). Walker also left £100,000 in his will for his brother Arthur, and the value of his steam yacht, the *Cuhona*, on which he entertained members of the Royal Family, including the Prince of Wales, must have been considerable. His business interests continued to be profitable, as he 'pushed steadily on his work of acquisition', whether through the purchase of additional breweries (in Burton-on-Trent) and an Irish distillery, or as a result of extensive investment in coalmining in South Wales.[46]

In comparison, the value of his known benefactions was modest, although estimating total life-time donations is not straightforward, simply because accurate data are difficult to obtain. His funding of the new art gallery in Liverpool amounted to £20,000 with an additional £11,500 for the 1882 extension, although in 1874 any enlargement was regarded as 'scarcely probable' given that the eight rooms in the upper floor offered up to 1,000 lineal feet of hanging space. Other authors have suggested, incorrectly, that he contributed either £25,000 or in excess of £50,000 to the original building and £11,750 for the extension. Claims that he contributed 'other large sums to charities, art and literature in Liverpool throughout his life' cannot be substantiated. However, he did provide over £20,000 in 1886 for the construction of what became the Walker Engineering Laboratories at University College, Liverpool (with its main laboratory, drawing hall, and wood-working department); at Gateacre he donated a village green to the Little Woolton Board of Health and funded the construction of a new school which meant that the existing building could be used as an institute, library, and reading room; and he contributed £1,000 in 1890 to the construction of a new hospital in Derby (the Derbyshire Royal Infirmary), when the old General Infirmary (from 1810) was condemned as hazardous following a major disease outbreak. According to Orchard, Walker had 'given away' approximately 5 per cent of his wealth: even if his benefactions totalled £75,000 (rather than the known or estimated donations of £57,500) this would only have represented 2.6 per cent of his probate wealth. At a time when many brewery owners were keen to refurbish their image in the face of the Temperance Movement and increasing public criticism of the drinks trade, it is unlikely that Walker made any significant benefactions anonymously.[47]

An outline of Sir Henry Tate's benefactions has already been provided (see previous), but once again there are problems in locating and assessing the value of all his individual donations. Some authors believe, mistakenly, that he contributed £500,000 to the construction of what became the Tate Gallery, rather than a combined total (cash, painting, and sculptures, including the cost of the extension) of £180,000. University College, Liverpool, was the second most important beneficiary, with Tate donating a total of £45,500 between 1883 and 1896, followed by the Liverpool Homoeopathic Dispensary and the Hahnemann Hospital (£28,062), including an annual donation of £25 and a subscription of one guinea from approximately 1860 until the year of his death. Further benefactions (£17,000) were made in support of higher educa-tion, specifically the Unitarian Church's Mansfield College in Oxford and Manchester College (£17,000) and £3,500 for Bedford College for Women. Financial support was provided to the Liverpool Institute (£2,000 for scholarships) and approximately £16,000 for three free librar-ies in South London, together with £500 towards the purchase of land for what was intended to become Lambeth Polytechnic. In addition to his support for the practice of homoeopathic medicine, a donation of £8,000 was made to the Liverpool Royal Infirmary and £5,000 towards the Queen Victoria's Jubilee Trust intended for the Queen's Institute of District Nurses, to which Lady Tate contributed a further £1,000 in memory of her late husband; the Tate Institute in Silvertown received £5,000 to establish a non-sectarian, apolitical meeting place for working people, including employees from the nearby sugar refinery. In Tate's case it is reasonable to assume that further donations were made anonymously. The total of known benefactions was £295,662, but the final amount was probably higher.[48]

As in the case of Walker, it is difficult to estimate accurately Tate's overall wealth at the time of his death. Unlike his heir, (Sir) William Henry Tate (1842–1921) who acquired a coun-try estate at Bodrhyddan, Rhuddlan, Flintshire, Henry Tate did not seek the status of a county gentleman, perhaps because his extensive residence at Park Hill, Streatham offered facilities that more than met his and his wife's needs. In 1891, he employed 15 staff (who, in turn, had 14 dependents), including a footman, a groom, and a coachman (accommodated at Park Hill Stables), a head gardener (at Gardener's Cottage), three under-gardeners (at the Under Garden-ers' Cottage), and a cowman (in the Cowman's House). His effects at death, after a long illness, had a probate value of £1,264,215 5s 5d (£143.4m in 2019 prices), although, again, the official figure excluded property or previous disbursements to family members and friends, as well as the market value of one of the most successful sugar-refining empires in Europe, if not the world. Nevertheless, Tate emerges as an archetypal entrepreneurial benefactor whose life-time donations amounted to approximately 23 per cent of his probate wealth.

Even if the relative extent of their charitable donations differed markedly, Tate and Walker had something in common: they were both members of the elite Wellington Club in Liverpool. Probate evidence of deceased members between 1860 and 1918 provides some evidence of shifts in relative wealth by occupation, but also highlights the extent to which the upper eche-lons of the mercantile community were more than able to act as entrepreneurial benefactors. The average level of probate wealth (in 2019 prices) rose steadily during the last three decades of the nineteenth century, reaching a peak of £26.9m in the 1890s, but the following decade witnessed

Table 12.3 Median probate wealth of members of the Wellington Club by occupation, 1860–1918 (in 2019 prices)

Occupation	Sample Size	Median Wealth (£m)
general merchant	41	41.4
raw material merchant	44	40.8
general broker	9	35.6
manufacturer	10	34.6
fuel merchant	3	22.1
foodstuffs merchant	13	17.7
shipowner	19	15.5
finance	5	4.3

Sources: The Wellington Club membership records; probate data

a marked decline to £10.9m with a slight increase to £14.1m between 1910 and 1919. Given its prominent status and its primary function as a social venue for the rich, the Wellington Club had strict membership criteria and to this extent the sample was self-selecting, but there were noticeable differences in median wealth by occupation (Table 12.9): with general merchants, raw material merchants, general brokers, and manufacturers all registering assets of over £30m at death, whereas the small sample from the world of finance had only £4.3m, perhaps reflecting the increasing transfer of financial business to London.[49]

Orchard regarded Andrew Barclay Walker as a man who 'had not rendered any public service or manifested any talent except that of amassing wealth', whereas Henry Tate was 'kind-hearted' and 'always willing to help a distressed acquaintance'. But how representative were these two case studies of the willingness of fellow members of the Wellington Club to authorise entrepreneurial benefactions, for personal or publicity reasons? Detailed information on charitable giving is only recorded in 37 cases and a majority (20) had no profile as major donors for deserving causes or civic improvements. Given the nature and intended dissemination of the biographical source material, significant benefactions would almost certainly have been recorded, but the evidence confirms the unwillingness of many wealthy members of the mercantile community to use some of their wealth to support good causes. The chairman of the General Brokers' Association, George R. Cox, listed as 'one of the very wealthy gentlemen' in Liverpool, was not involved in supporting charitable work; the timber and stave merchant Peter Owen, whose business enjoyed a worldwide reputation, 'like many other gentlemen eminently able in commerce' deliberately avoided being involved in other directions; while the shipowner Edward Percy Bates was 'a businessman to the core' and 'benevolence has nothing to do with vast schemes for amassing wealth'. The 'very wealthy coal proprietor John Grant Morris had done nothing in recent years 'to arrest attention'; Robertson Gladstone, the 'greatest member of one our great local families', was 'mainly engaged, like all his race, in taking care of his own interests'; while in the case of the shipowner James Jenkinson Bibby it was simply noted that he lived in Shropshire. Indeed, of those who were known to contribute financially to charitable causes, substantial donations were seldom mentioned: Thomas Sutton Timmis J.P., who was prominent in Widnes public affairs, had made a gift of £2,500 to establish six free scholarships at Farnworth Grammar School for boys educated at public elementary schools in Widnes; and Hans Gaspard Schintz (1837–1912) who was 'addicted to charity' set aside £20,000 (together with his wife) for local charities, especially the Liverpool Home for Incurables. However, they were exceptions: the majority, irrespective of their extensive wealth, were not known as major benefactors.[50]

Further evidence of the weak response to charitable and civic need on the part of Liverpool's multi-millionaires can be found in their published obituaries. From a total of 402 listed in the MLD, only 122 (30.3 per cent) had been involved in charities in various capacities, but a mere 20 (4.9 per cent) are known to have left substantial financial bequests. However, there were notable exceptions. Adam Cliff (1781–1851) was an extensive slave holder and plantation owner, but his son, William, who took over the family firm, proved to be a highly successful merchant and shipowner and a major benefactor. He founded the Home for Aged Seamen in Liscard at a cost of approximately £30,000, which was opened in 1882 by H.R.H. the Duke of Edinburgh. In order to meet the needs of aged mariners and their wives 13 cottages were built in the gardens, some of which were named after donors who contributed £500 each, including 'Chaddock' and 'Forward' (two prominent Liverpool shipowners). One of the cottages was named after Cliff himself (Figure 12.6). In addition, he established three homes for homeless children and in 1883 donated £100 to the Liverpool Society for the Prevention of Cruelty to Children. At his death 1891 he left an estate of £319,091 18s 5d (£35.1m in 2019 prices). The motive

Figure 12.6 'Cliff House', Mariners' Park, Wallasey (pre-1914 postcard)

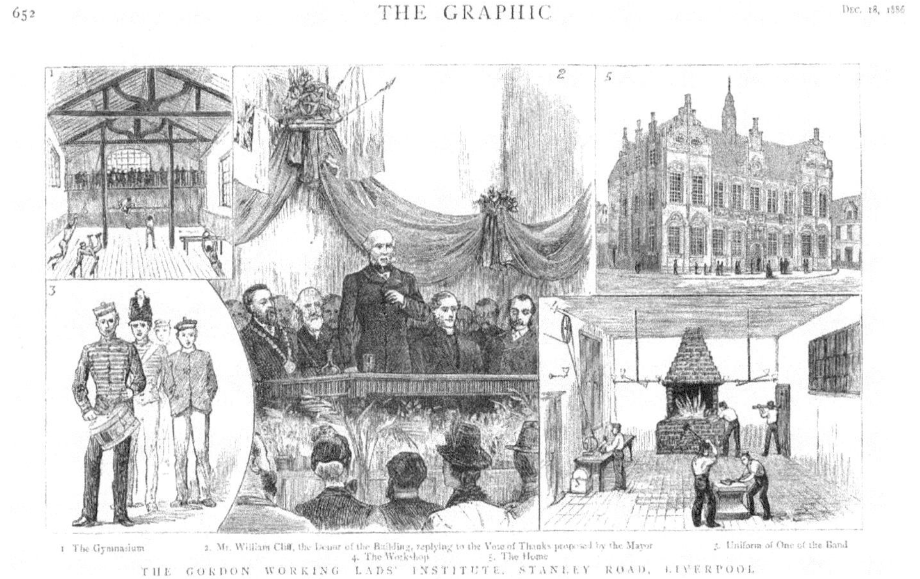

Figure 12.7 'The Gordon Working Lads' Institute, Stanley Road, Liverpool', *The Graphic*, 18 December 1886, p. 652

behind his main benefaction was a personal one as the Home for Aged Seamen was established in memory of his daughter Rosa Webster, who died in April 1879 at the age of 24, while the Gordon Working-Class Lads' Institute in Kirkdale was erected in 1886 at a cost of £50,000 as a memorial to his eldest son who had died at the age of eleven in 1853 (Figure 12.7). Other benefactions by Liverpool merchants were also intended as memorials to deceased family members. The Florence Institute for Boys was opened in 1890 by Sir Bernard Hall, a landowner and West India merchant, alderman (for St. Paul's Ward), and former mayor of Liverpool (1879–80), as 'an acceptable place of recreation and instruction for the poor and working boys' in the Dingle, Toxteth, in memory of his daughter Florence who had died at the age of 22 on a visit to Paris to further her education. When the formal announcement of his 'noble gift' was made, Hall and his family were in Cannes, in the south of France. He died in 1890 leaving an estate of £533,552 16s, before the official unveiling of a medallion to his 'guardian angel' could take place. The event was attended by Thomas Holder on behalf of the trustees and as a former colleague on the city council who 'always found him a most kind, warm-hearted, and generous friend': he only wished that there were 'more such men in Liverpool'. Finally, the Andrew Gibson Memorial Home for Seaman's Widows, which was opened in 1906 at a cost of £25–30,000 (specifically for the widows of shipmasters and officers), was donated by his son Andrew Junior of Andrew Gibson & Co., a wealthy shipowner, in memory of his father.[51]

In other cases, sector-specific benefactions were made to address persistent deficiencies in welfare provision, specifically in the case of the shipping industry. The shipowner Thomas Henry Ismay donated £20,000 in 1887 for the establishment of the Liverpool Seamen's Pension Fund in order to provide an annual pension of £20 for deserving seamen sailing from Liverpool, irrespective of rank, who were past work. The failure to include any provision for the widows of sailors whose lives had been lost 'while they were on active duty' was rectified by the creation by his wife of the Margaret Ismay Widows Fund. Both funds were administered by the Mercantile Marine Services Association 'with conspicuous success and with practically no expense to the funds'. The Ismay family, together with the White Star Line, contributed £52,000 towards the two funds. But the limitations of private (and company) benefactions were evident in the small number of pensioners who could be supported: on average around 120 former seafarers (the majority masters and officers) benefited from the scheme each year, while only 74 women had been supported since the addition of the separate fund for widows who might be left 'destitute'. In response to the *Titanic* disaster on 14 April 1912, his son, J. Bruce Ismay, the chairman and managing director of the White Star Line and president of the International Mercantile Marine Company, immediately made available £10,000 (supplemented by a further £1,000 from his American-born wife) for the sufferers from the 'terrible disaster'. In 1919, following the huge death toll of merchant seamen during the First World War he set aside £25,000 to establish the National Mercantile Marine Fund to support the widows and children of sailors with a specific preference for those whose home port had been Liverpool. But, again, the level of provision, though welcome, did not address the underlying problems faced by seafarers and their families, whether in peacetime or war. In 1917, an estimate of Ismay's financial affairs valued his assets at £831,692 19s 6d (£46.9m in 2019 prices) excluding property and furniture at Sandheys, the family home in Mossley Hill, Liverpool, 15 Hill Street in Mayfair, London, and 'Costello', (a lodge in Casla, Co. Galway where he could enjoy angling) valued collectively at £40,347 19s. Mrs. Ismay's estate, which was valued separately on the basis of their original marriage settlement, amounted to £29,254 6s, with a further £45,706 of inherited assets in the USA from the Delaplaine and Schieffelin estates.[52]

Other prominent members of the mercantile community made significant bequests in their wills, even if their role as benefactors had been more circumscribed during their lifetimes. Alexander Elder (1834–1915) was the co-founder with John Dempster (1837–1914) of Elder Dempster & Co. Ltd. During the 1850s both became employees of the shipbuilder W. and H. Laird in Birkenhead, the former as the superintendent engineer for the African Steam Ship Co., established by Macgregor Laird, the latter as a junior clerk. The formation of the British and African

Steam Navigation Co. in 1866 by Dempster and Elder laid the basis of what was to become one of Britain's most successful shipping companies, specialising in the West African trade, but with the directors also acting as general merchants, steam-packet agents, and insurance brokers. The company operated out of Glasgow and Liverpool, but most of its business by the early twentieth century was dealt with at African House, 6 Water Street, Liverpool. When Alexander Elder died in 1915, he left a net estate of £308,873 7s 8d (£24.9m in 2019 prices), of which £206,000 (£16.3m), or two thirds of his gross assets, was set aside for a wide range of charitable purposes in both port-cities. Glasgow charities were the main beneficiaries, including a benefaction of £100,000 for the purchase of land and the erection of an infirmary or hospital in the neighbourhood of Govan 'for poor persons when sick or injured' in memory of his late parents and it was to be called the David Elder Infirmary. By comparison, only £14,500 was donated to Liverpool charities, with six hospitals (the Royal Southern, the Royal Infirmary, the David Lewis Northern Hospital, the Liverpool Maternity Hospital and Ladies Charity, the Liverpool Blue Coat Hospital, and the Southport Convalescence Hospital and Sea Bathing Infirmary) receiving a total of £9,500. A further sum of £500 was donated to the Liverpool School of Tropical Medicine; £2,000 was allocated to the Liverpool Seamen's Orphan Institution; while other charities which supported the welfare needs of merchant seafarers and their dependents were also recipients under the terms of Elder's will. Such a level of entrepreneurial benefaction was unusual for this period, although Mary Elder (who had been born in Northwich in 1843) predeceased her husband; the marriage was childless; and all his half-sisters and half-brothers, together with his brothers, John, the ship designer and engineer, and David Junior, had already died in 1869 and 1873 respectively. There were no other surviving relatives to whom he could have bequeathed his considerable fortune.[53]

Even when a few leading members of Merseyside's business community made significant benefactions for charitable or civic purposes, the level of commitment in relation to their wealth was generally disappointing. From a sample of entrepreneurial benefactors (Table 12.4), the brewer Sir Andrew Barclay Walker, despite his apparent munificence, devoted only 1.6 per cent of his immense wealth to local causes, whereas Sir Henry Tate gave away 23.6 per cent from his probate effects which were £178m lower than those of Walker. The case of Alexander Elder, the co-founder of the Elder Dempster Co., indicates that 'munificent' benefactions were indeed possible, although there were no surviving dependents or relatives who might otherwise have received legacies. The same was true as far as the timber merchant Roger Lyon Jones was concerned. Apart from legacies (free of legacy duty) totalling around £40,000 to distant relatives, including the granddaughter of his late half-brother, James Lyon, £100 for each of his godchildren, bequests to a few friends, and an annuity of £90 each year for his 'faithful' butler, Richard Jones, all the residue of his estate was to be distributed to Liverpool charities. These included all the major hospitals (£20–25,000), three orphan asylums (£10,000 each), and the Ladies' Work Society (Bold Street), the Society for the Relief of Sick and Distressed Needlewomen, and the Establishment for Needlewomen in Great Orford-street (£500 each). Although Jones was 'well known in the higher circles of society', he had retired from local political life, representing the South Toxteth ward for the Conservatives in 1850 and had retreated into 'private life'. Again, like Elder, there were no surviving family relatives. Several points need to be emphasised. Half of the entrepreneurs devoted between 1.6 and 5.4 per cent of their probate assets to charitable causes; two of the main benefactors, Sir Henry Tate and Alexander Elder, allocated only a small proportion of their wealth to Merseyside initiatives; substantial benefactions were often linked with the memorialisation of deceased children or relatives; and the apparent generosity of Bruce Ismay was compromised by the contributions of the White Star Line to the Liverpool Seamen's Fund (the value of which is unknown) and the fact that the funds made available in the

Table 12.4 Entrepreneurial benefactions as a proportion of total probate wealth (in 2019 prices)

Name	Occupation	Date of Death	Probate (£m)	Benefactions	%
John Laird	shipbuilder	1874	18.7	544,100	2.9
Roger Lyon Jones	timber merchant	1875	33.2	20,880,000	62.8
Bernard Hall	West India merchant	1890	59.1	1,330,000	2.2
William Cliff	shipowner	1891	35.1	4,221,000	12.0
A. B. Walker	brewer	1893	287.6	5,177,000	1.6
Henry Tate	sugar refiner (Liverpool)	1899	143.4	33,867,800 9,080,000	6.3
T. W. Cookson	oil merchant	1905	17.3	440,100	2.5
Alexander Elder	shipowner (Liverpool)	1914	29.8	19,920,000 1,402,000	66.8 4.7
J. Bruce Ismay	shipowner	(1917)/1937	49.2	7,922,000	16.1
A. Gibson	shipowner	1933	50.0	2,709,000	5.4
Total			723.4	53.3 (£)	7.3

Notes:
1. The value of benefactions, where possible, has been calculated according to the year in which they were made.
2. The assets of J. Bruce Ismay are taken from the papers relating to his will, not from probate data at the time of his death in 1937.
3. The total benefactions reflect charitable endowments relating primarily to Merseyside. The inclusion of total gifts (particularly in the case of Henry Tate and Alexander Elder) inevitably generated a higher overall figure (approximately £193.2m, or 26.7 per cent of the total probate valuation). This again highlights the extent to which successful Liverpool merchants and shipowners made significant bequests elsewhere.

Additional details: John Laird made two important benefactions, the Birkenhead Borough Hospital (1863) and the Laird School of Art (1871); Thomas Worthington Cookson's Bankhall Girls' Institute in Stanley Road was built in 1889. It was described by R. D. Holt, who chaired the annual meeting of the institute in 1894 as 'a small organisation': see 'The Bankhall Girls' Institute', *LM*, 27 October 1894. Nor should the role of other benefactors be neglected, including the wool merchant Christopher Rawdon (1780–1858) who set up with his brother James a fund to support Unitarian charities, specifically for educational purposes. The Rawdon Trust, which subsequently became known as the Anfield Delph Trust administered by the city council, funded the establishment of the Rawdon Reading Room in Breck Road in 1905: see David Harrison, *Christopher Rawdon: The Last Philanthropist* (Bury St. Edmunds, 2016).

Sources: MLP database; newspaper reports; MMMMAL, B/AW 3/1, 2–24, Valuation of the Estate of Alexander Elder; DX/504/6/1–12, Papers regarding the will of J. Bruce Ismay (1912–17); Giles, *Building a Better Society*, pp. 41–48

immediate aftermath of the sinking of the *Titanic* were a necessary response to the scale of the disaster and the public criticism that he was subject to for escaping from the stricken vessel. Historians who emphasise the willingness of leading entrepreneurs in the pre-1914 period to make major benefactions, whether in support of health and social welfare objectives or to improve the cultural life of major cities, such as Liverpool, seldom place them in context. With very few exceptions, the scale of benefactions in relation to their known assets at death was extremely modest: the available data suggests that a re-assessment of the model of the entrepreneurial benefactor is long overdue because it fails to provide any support for those who advocate a return to the 'Victorian tradition of philanthropy' as a means of reducing state welfare expenditure.[54]

The case studies also reveal the underlying attitudes that motivated entrepreneurial benefactions. Some of the initiatives were deliberately aimed at young teenagers deemed to be in a 'difficult age' when their 'passions' were strongest; they were 'unwelcome amongst boys, and scouted by men'; and prowled about the streets 'getting initiated into the arts of vice and crime'. Indeed, it was suggested that 'Their life is mere vegetation', a perilous state which could only be improved by privately funded initiatives which offered a combination of mental culture, organised recreation, and 'healthful and elevating amusements'. They were intended to be Christian, but 'unsectarian' in their approach, but with an emphasis on inculcating military discipline. For example, at the Gordon Boys' Memorial Institute (1886) founded by a donation of the merchant and ship-owner William Cliff as a memorial to his eldest son while the Institute was equipped with a gymnasium and a workshop, a 'Cliff military brigade' was established for military drill. Although there was some understanding of the underlying factors which led teenagers into difficulties, including the 'innumerable precarious employments of a large city', there was no commitment to addressing them and the condescending approach of benefactors and their supporters was matched by an expectation that institutional provision would result in an increase in deference. More importantly, the establishment of separate facilities for young boys and girls was prompted by self-interest, because 'the proletariat may strangle us unless we teach it the same values which have elevated the other classes of society'. Moreover, entrepreneurial benefactors seldom made provision for the running costs of their charitable institutions. The future maintenance of the Gordon Working Lads' Institute depended on the ability of the committee to generate at least £250 annually through subscriptions (although Samuel Smith M.P. donated £400): a year later £2,200 was still needed to complete an endowment fund of £5,000, despite a donation of £20 by Queen Victoria. A similar problem was evident in the case of John Laird's benefactions. Admittedly the 1860s and early 1870s were not an easy time for shipbuilders: the 13 Merseyside yards registered a record output in 1864, while the completion of *HMS Agincourt* in the following year (built at a cost of almost £500,000) allowed Laird Brothers to maintain the firm's momentum. By 1867, however, its output was only 1,538 tons, the lowest figure since 1849. But John Laird was a very wealthy entrepreneur, yet he deliberately limited the scope of his benefactions. His initial donation to what was to be Birkenhead Borough Hospital (designed by Walter Scott) was not to exceed £3,000, but after necessary alterations to the original plans his final commitment was 'not less than £5,000'. The committee of the Birkenhead Hospital and Dispensary, of which Laird was a member, had previously encountered difficulties in increasing its building fund and the money for maintaining a larger purpose-built hospital was deemed to be insufficient. However, there was a degree of self-interest in Laird's benefaction: shipbuilding yards were notorious for their poor working conditions, with high accident and fatality rates, and it was always the intention that serious cases would be dealt with by staff at the new hospital. Again, in the case of what became the Laird School of Art, Laird made no provision for its future maintenance: he was 'happy' to continue to subscribe £2–3 annually, but expected the committee to find 50 gentlemen in Birkenhead willing to pay £1 each, or 100 who were expected to contribute 10s each year. Not surprisingly, Laird and other family members spearheaded attempts to inculcate workers with 'self-help principles' and alerted the middle class to the 'evils' of haphazard charity'. Because of the unwillingness of entrepreneurs to contribute to endowment funds to maintain their charitable institutions, their future was not assured: a few years after its opening, the Bankhall Girls' Institute was in deficit, with only a single response (£5 from the Lord Bishop of Liverpool) to a previous appeal, despite the fact that most of the work was carried out by ladies 'who devoted their time and energies' in 'a truly philanthropic nature'. There were only two exceptions. Henry Tate committed £5,000 towards the endowment fund of the Hahnemann Hospital and the will of Roger Lyon Jones deliberately specified that the bequests to at least 52 charities were to be 'invested or permanently secured for their benefit', fully recognising the difficulties managers encountered 'to keep up and sustain annual income'.[55]

A Missed Opportunity: The Extent of Merchant Funding in the Development of University College, Liverpool

A great deal has been written about the development of civic universities in the latter decades of the nineteenth century. Unlike most higher educational institutions in continental Europe which were supported financially by the state or church authorities from an early date, the foundation of provincial universities in England and Wales was a drawn-out process: between 1850 and the death of Edward VII seven universities (Birmingham, Manchester, Liverpool, Sheffield, Leeds, Nottingham, and Bristol) were established: in most cases they incorporated earlier discipline-specific schools and colleges; and it was not until the early twentieth century that they finally gained their royal charters. In the absence of any central government funding (until 1889 when a treasury grant of £15,000 was shared between the different institutions), all the provincial universities were heavily dependent on fee income and 'creative benefactors' who contributed a disproportionate share of development funding, as was the case at Owens College, Manchester, where they provided 45 per cent of revenue in 1890. In all cases, according to Anderson, 'it was local business and professional men who took the initiative and superintended development', with the result that university colleges had a consciously middle-class character which represented the 'independent bourgeois culture of the North'.[56]

However, the role of major benefactors remains disputed. If the 'sacredness' of endowments were accepted by many Tories, it was criticised by some Liberals as an obstacle to a fully competitive market economy and despite the promise of an enhanced status, both locally and nationally, the contribution of major benefactors was 'patchy'. In the case of Nottingham University, it was an anonymous donation in 1877 of £10,000 which provided the impetus for later developments, while private benefactors played a critical role in establishing the academic profile of higher education institutions in London in the late nineteenth century. The centenary history of the University of Liverpool (University College, Liverpool) fulfils its expected function: even if it lacks an analytical framework, it develops and maintains a sound narrative. Inevitably, it commemorates and memorialises the contributions made by local businessmen and eminent members of the mercantile community, including the merchant, politician, and philanthropist William Rathbone (1819–1902), the shipowner George Holt ('a major benefactor of the College'; 'the most princely of the early benefactors'), and the sugar refiner Henry Tate, who contributed a 'munificent' £5,000. Indeed, the lay members of the University Council in 1903, in its first year of operation, included many who had already given 'outstanding service', such as Robert Gladstone (treasurer), Sir John Brunner, Dr. E. K. Muspratt (president), and John Rankin, the 'most generous and unfailing of benefactors'. Both the 15th Earl of Derby and his son, Frederick Arthur, had been 'generous' in their interest and support'. Whenever other financial needs arose, they were supplied by 'private munificence'.[57]

Such praise is well merited, but it fails to acknowledge the operational constraints which delayed the development of University College as a result of the reluctance of many elite members of Liverpool's mercantile community to support its objectives. It was claimed that the college enjoyed 'the enthusiastic support of a large and influential body of citizens', but its scale was 'exceedingly modest'; the accommodation 'inadequate'; and the staffing level minimal. For two years following the appointment of a professor of mathematics in 1882–3, the college's first principal, Gerald Henry Rendall, had to supplement the stipend out of his own salary because at least a third of the required endowment was still lacking. The original resolution at a town hall meeting to establish a science college had been passed in May 1871: at the time of a further meeting in 1878 less than £110,000 had been raised from benefactors (of which £70,000 was intended for seven professorships); even in 1884 University College was still 'in a rudimentary state'.[58]

As David Burns has demonstrated, a small group of prominent Unitarians, drawn mostly from the congregation of the Rev. Charles Beard (1827–1888) at the Chapel in Renshaw Street, played a leading role in realising the aspirations for a University College and in providing a significant proportion of the required funding. Regarded in some quarters as the 'Aristocracy of Dissent', their impact was 'profound'. A significant number of the college's chairs were endowed by prominent Unitarian families, such as the Rathbones, the Holts, and the Gaskells, either individually or collectively. They were particularly prominent in ensuring the college had an increasing range of professorships in relevant disciplines, with shipowners, industrial chemists, and sugar refiners to the fore. Moreover, five chairs, namely in Greek (1881), English literature (1881), Latin (1884), ancient history (1884), and mathematics (1884), were established with the support of 'the Citizens of Liverpool', among whom were leading Unitarians (Table 12.5). In fact, between 1881 and 1919, 12 chairs were created without an endowment, supported out of general funds and often for limited periods of time. A few were established in recognition of the scholarship of existing members of staff, such as the chair in Celtic for Kuno Meyer in 1908 (discontinued on the outbreak of the First World War) and Sir James George Frazer, the only holder of the unendowed chair in social anthropology (1907–1922). But other chairs which lacked an endowment were in highly relevant disciplines, including medicine (1882), obstetrics and gynaecology (1884), public health (1897), comparative pathology (1906), cytology (1907), veterinary medicine (1904), tropical sanitation (1912), and regional surgery (1913).[59]

In all probability the leading role of Unitarian merchants and businessmen in founding and supporting University College in a city still dominated by sectarian tensions simply reduced the supply of potential benefactors. William Rathbone accepted that the idea of creating a University College had been taken forward under the aegis of two consecutive 'Conservative Mayors' (the shipowners A. B. Forwood and Thomas Bland Royden), 'but it would never do to let us "Radicals and Infidels", as they chose to call us, have the credit for raising all the money'. According to Burns, Rathbone together with Rev. Charles Beard and James Campbell Brown (the chairman of the Royal Infirmary School of Medicine since 1877) were the 'practical founding fathers' of University College: they were all Unitarians, as were those leading members of Liverpool's business and mercantile communities who were its major benefactors. In the case of 26 of the named chairs where the denominational (or political) background of the benefactors can be established with some certainty, irrespective of whether they had been endowed individually or in conjunction with fellow merchants and co-religionists, 15 (57.6 per cent) were supported by Unitarians, five by members of the Church of England and the Tory Party, three by Presbyterians, two by the aristocracy (the Earls of Sefton), and one by Queen Victoria (with a contribution from the mayor of Liverpool). The shipowner, George Holt, contributed over £40,000 (for named chairs, research scholarships, and capital expenditure on infrastructure); both the alkali manufacturer (Sir) John Brunner and the shipowner John Rankin provided financial support for three chairs; and the timber merchant, David Jardine, funded (with others) two professorships. With few exceptions, major funding support from leading Tory families was very limited and Church of England adherents were infuriated by the explicit exclusion of a theology faculty which led evangelical clergy to denounce it as 'a godless scheme' and 'a godless institution', while simultaneously plans to establish a bishopric in Liverpool and to build a suitable cathedral further reduced the level of support for University College.[60]

According to Muir, the first holder of the Andrew Geddes and John Rankin Chair of Modern History (1906–1913), 'most of the great merchants of Liverpool were interested only in two things—money-making and good living'. Despite an emphasis on the college's importance in promoting civic pride and its role as an educational institution 'of the city', merchants who had taken degrees in Oxford and Cambridge simply 'laughed at the idea of turning a trading town into a seat of a university'. Only when 'academic drift' away from some of the original principles that underpinned their early development in favour of the Oxbridge model was local support more forthcoming. If the development of University College was held back by 'poverty', other higher education institutions in provincial England and Wales were more successful in

Table 12.5 University College, Liverpool (Liverpool University): endowment of chairs, 1880–1919

Year	Chair	Named	Benefactor(s)	Background
1881	English Literature	King Alfred	William, Samuel, and Philip Rathbone	Shipowners, general merchants, insurance brokers
1881	Natural History (Zoology)	Derby	15th Earl of Derby	Aristocrat
1881	Inorganic Chemistry	Grant	Mrs. Grant (of Rock Ferry) and Sir John T. Brunner	Not known; alkali manufacturer, M.P.
1881	Greek	Gladstone	Col. A. H. Brown, William Crosfield, and James Barrow	Sugar refiners
1881	Philosophy	(unnamed)	Balfour, Williamson & Co., David Jardine, John Rew, Samuel Smith, and Scottish trading houses of Liverpool	Wood broker and merchant; cotton broker; cotton broker, M.P.
1881	Physics	Lyon Jones	Trustees of the Roger Lyon Jones Trust	Timber merchant (deceased)
1882	Pure Mathematics	(unnamed)	W. P. Sinclair; citizens and shipowners of Liverpool	Shipowner
1884	History	Robert Gladstone	Robert Gladstone	East India merchant, director of Ogilvy, Gillanders & Co.
1884	History	William Rathbone	Hugh Rathbone	Grain merchant, Ross T. Smyth & Co., son-in-law of late William Rathbone
1886	Engineering	Thomas Harrison	Thomas Harrison	Shipowner
1894	Law	Victoria Chair	HM Queen Victoria, Earl of Sefton, Sir William B. Bowring, legal profession	Queen, aristocracy, shipowner and merchant, lawyers
1894	Botany	Holbrook Gaskell	Holbrook Gaskell and other Liverpool citizens	Industrial chemist
1894	Pathology	George Holt	George Holt	Shipowner
1894	Anatomy	Derby	Rt. Hon. Frederick Arthur, 16th Earl of Derby	Aristocrat
1902	Physiology	George Holt	George Holt and William Johnston	Shipowner; timber merchant
1902	Biochemistry	William Johnston	William Johnston	Timber merchant
1902	Tropical Medicine	Alfred Jones	Sir Alfred Jones and others	Shipowner
1903	Electro-technics	David Jardine	David Jardine	Wood-broker and merchant, senior in Farnworth & Jardine, director of Cunard & Co., board member, Royal Insurance, chairman, Finance Committee, Mersey Docks and Harbour Board
1903	Physical Chemistry	Brunner	Rt. Hon. Sir John Brunner	Alkali manufacturer, M.P.
1903	Common Law	(not named)	Members of the legal profession and others	Lawyers
1904	English and Philology	Baines	F. C. Baines	Executors acting for Thomas Baines (deceased), son and son-in-law of E. K. Muspratt
1905	French	James Barrow	Mrs. James Barrow (widow)	In memory of her late husband, sugar refiner (Barrow & Co.) director of Royal Insurance Co., Overhead Railway Co. and Sea Insurance Co.

1906	Classical Archaeology	Charles W. Jones	Mrs. George Holt, Alfred Booth, and C. W. Jones	Widow of shipowner; shipowners
1906	Modern History	Andrew Geddes and John Rankin	Miss Elizabeth Geddes, Southport	In memory of her father, a successful shipowner
1906	Archaeology (Methods and Practice)	John Rankin	John Rankin	Merchant and shipowner, Rankin, Gilmour & Co., local M.P., J.P.
1906	Egyptology	Brunner	John T. Brunner	Alkali manufacturer, M.P.
1907	Archaeology	Charles W. Jones	Sydney Jones	Shipowner, Holt & Co., son.
1908	Civil Engineering	John William Hughes	John William Hughes	Shipowner, T. and J. Harrison
1908	Russian	Bowes	John Lord Bowes; Rankin, Gilmour & Co.	Wool-broker; merchants and shipowners
1908	Spanish	Gilmour	Captain George Gilmour (of Birkenhead)	General merchant (Mexico), retired Captain, 21st Fusiliers
1909	Naval Architecture	Alexander Elder	Alexander Elder	Co-founder, Elder Dempster Line
1912	Civic Design	Lever	William Hesketh Lever, First Lord Leverhulme	Soap manufacturer (Port Sunlight)
1913	Parasitology	Walter Myers	Committee of the School of Tropical Medicine	
1915	Organic Chemistry	Heath Harrison	Heath Harrison	Shipowner
1916	Geology	George Herdman	Professor W. A. Herdman and Mrs. Herdman	University professor: in memory of their son, George Andrew Herdman, killed in action in 1916
1917	Geography	John Rankin	John Rankin	Merchant and shipowner
1918	Commerce	Chaddock	Mrs. A. W. Chaddock	Widow of shipowner
1919	English Literature	Andrew Cecil Bradley	John Rankin and others (partial endowment only)	Merchant and shipowner
1919	Oceanography		Professor William Abbott Herdman & Mrs. Herdman	Academic

Notes on chair designation:

Law (1894): initially this was an unendowed chair between 1892 and 1894.

Anatomy (1894): a lectureship was attached to the Liverpool Royal Infirmary, School of Medicine prior to 1881; it was endowed in 1894.

Pathology (1894): a chair had been established in 1884, but it was not until a decade later than it was endowed by George Holt.

Modern History (1906): Miss Elizabeth Geddes endowed a lectureship in modern history in 1900: with her consent this was used as a part endowment of the chair, the balance provided by John Rankin.

Geology (1916): William Abbott Herdman (1858–1924) held the Derby chair of zoology from 1881 to 1919, after which he became the professor of oceanography, a chair which he also endowed.

Sources: MLP database; *The University of Liverpool 1903–1953 A Jubilee Book* (Liverpool, 1953), pp. 49–63; *University of Liverpool Calendar: Session 2007–2008* (Liverpool, 2007), pp. 453–90; David Peter Burns, 'British Decline, commercial influence and the provision of technical education on Merseyside between 1870 and 1914', unpublished Ph.D. thesis, School of History, University of Liverpool (2006), specifically Chapters 3, 5, and 8.

attracting substantial benefactions in their constant search for donors. Owens College in Manchester had been founded in 1846 following a legacy of £96,942 from John Owens, a wealthy merchant and industrialist, and a committed Congregationalist who had never married. It was opened three years later as an explicitly non-sectarian educational institution and by 1873 the number of day and evening students had risen to 327 and 513 respectively. John Rylands, Manchester's 'wealthiest merchant', and his widow, Enriqueta Augustina Rylands (who had been born in Cuba in 1842), played an even more important role in consolidating the reputation of what had become Victoria College. Both Rylands and his second wife were Congregationalists 'of a profound philanthropic disposition'; the final cost of completing the John Rylands Library was £244,086; and her will made provision for charitable bequests of £448,000 (from a total estate of £3,448,692) for religious and educational purposes. University College, Liverpool, was never able to call upon comparable benefactions. Indeed, other civic universities, whether in Birmingham or Bristol, had greater success in recruiting major benefactors.[61]

The relative lack of major benefactors was also evident in relation to capital projects. For some time after its foundation, staff and students were confronted by inadequate accommodation until the demolition of most of the Lunatic Asylum on Brownlow Hill, which had been acquired at the 'modest' cost of £19,000 provided by the tobacco manufacturer Thomas Cope. The finalising of the transaction was overtaken by events with the council transferring the building and its grounds to the new college free of charge, following the inclusion of this measure in the Liverpool Improvement Act of 1882. But the upgrading of the site was a slow process: proper equipment was not available; some teaching took place in a 'tumble down old dwelling house in Brownlow Hill', in the 1890s architectural work was spread over three sites, which included a set of corrugated iron sheds in the college precinct; while it was fully understood by the council and senate that independent status would require additional staff together with suitable buildings and modern equipment.[62]

The evidence indicates that capital projects were less popular with benefactors than the endowment of a named chair (Table 12.6). The twelve projects taken forward with either individual or collective funding between the inauguration of University College and the outbreak of the First World War involved donations of approximately £296,000; they were almost invariably more expensive than endowing a professorship which required a relatively standard benefaction of £10,000 throughout this period (despite a cumulative loss in value of 5 per cent by 1914); and, unlike buildings which needed to be upgraded or replaced over time, a named chair offered the possibility of permanent memorialisation. Some of these figures need to be treated with caution, because they were part of a broader package and the delay in realising building projects could be considerable. For example, Lever's donation in 1910 of £60,000 (part of the proceeds from a successful libel action against *The Daily Mail* and other newspapers) included provision for 'work' in civic design and tropical medicine, as well the creation of a chair in Russian, but a new building for civic design was not to be completed until the interwar period. By contrast, the endowment of 36 new chairs during the same period involved raising £362,000 from benefactors, including £12,000 from the shipowner Alexander Elder whose gift in 1912 led to the creation of the UK's third chair in naval architecture.

Private benefactors also played an important role in endowing fellowships, scholarships, studentships, and prizes. The donations varied widely from an annual sum (often £100) for a fixed time period to significant bequests intended to generate enough interest to maintain a fellowship in perpetuity. In 1888, Henry Tate 'set apart' £2,000 for the creation of the Charles Beard Foundation, in memory of Rev. Charles Beard who had been one of the college's founders, with scholarships and fellowships intended for the advancement of 'Art Studies', particularly in history. Other benefactors included well-known Unitarian families, such as the Holts,

Table 12.6 University College/Liverpool University: private benefactions for capital developments, 1882–1910 (in £)

Year	Development	Value £	Name	Benefactor(s)
1882	New chemistry building	13,000	(not designated)	George Holt (shipowner), Henry Tate (sugar refiner), and others
1886	Engineering laboratory	23,000	Walker	Sir Andrew Barclay Walker (brewer)
1887	Victoria Building (library)	20,000	Tate	Henry Tate (sugar refiner)
1896	Chemistry laboratory	c.15,000	Gossage Laboratory	F. C. Gossage (son, soap-maker)
1896	Metallurgy laboratory	c.15,000	Metallurgical Laboratory	John T. Brunner, E. K. Muspratt (alkali manufacturers), Lever Bros. (soap manufacturers)
1894 (1898)	Physiology and Pathology laboratories (Schools of Physiology and Pathology)	c.30,000	Thompson-Yates Laboratories	Rev. Samuel Ashton Thompson-Yates (grandson and beneficiary of the West India merchant and Unitarian, Joseph Brooks Yates)
1898 (1904)	Physics laboratory	25,000	Oliver Lodge Laboratory	Mrs. George Holt and others (£10,000) (shipowners)
1901	Botanical laboratories	13,000	Hartley Botanical Laboratories	William P. Hartley (jam manufacturer)
1902 (1903)	Bio-chemistry laboratory	25,000	William Johnston Bio-Chemistry Laboratory (and chair)	William Johnston (timber merchant)
1903 (1906)	Physical chemistry	17,000	Muspratt Building	E. K. Muspratt (alkali manufacturer)
1903 (1906)	Mechanical engineering laboratory	40,000	Harrison Hughes Mechanical Engineering Laboratories	J. W. Hughes, Heath Harrison, and Fenwick Harrison (shipowners)
1910	Tropical Medicine Building	60,000	Tropical Medicine	William Hesketh Lever (soap manufacturer, Port Sunlight)

Notes:

Victoria Building (1887): a public appeal was launched in 1887 (the year of Queen Victoria's Jubilee) for £35,000 to build a new administrative, teaching, and research centre for the college. Five months later only £7,625 had been raised, including 1,000 guineas from T. W. Oakshott, the mayor, and £1,000 from Henry Tate.

Botanical laboratories (1901): Hartley had already contributed £4,300 for the clock and bells in the tower of the Victoria Building and funded in 1911 the acquisition of a complete wireless station.

Bio-chemistry laboratories (1903): Johnston's benefaction also included funding to establish the first chair of biochemistry in the UK.

Sources: Thomas Kelly, *For Advancement of Learning The University of Liverpool 1881–1981* (Liverpool, 1981); David Peter Burns, 'British Decline, commercial influence and the provision of technical education on Merseyside between 1870 and 1914', unpublished Ph.D. thesis, School of History, University of Liverpool (2006); 'Opening of the Johnston Laboratories for Medical Research in the University College, Liverpool', *Nature*, 68 (1903), pp. 44–5; R.A. Morton, 'Biochemistry at Liverpool—1902–1971', *Medical History*, 16,4 (1972), pp. 310–20; Emma Wilson, 'Biochemistry, the early years at Liverpool', *Trends in Biochemical Sciences*, 27, 12 (2002), pp. 639–40; G.A. Pitt, 'Liverpool: the early years of biochemistry', *Biochemical Society Transactions*, 31, 1 (2003), pp. 16–9; 'Opening of the Thompson-Yates Laboratories at University College Liverpool', *Nature*, 58 (1898), pp. 575–6; 'The Rev. S.A. Thompson-Yates', *Charity Organisation Review*, 14, 84 (1903), pp. 326–8; 'Hartley Botanical Laboratories of University College, Liverpool', *Nature*, 61 (1900), pp. 454–5; Michael Sanderson, *The University and British Industry: 1850–1970* (Routledge Library Editions: Higher Education) (London, 2018).

the Rathbones, Frederick Herbert Gossage, and William Johnston, who were already involved in supporting the college in different ways. The range of donors, in terms of their wealth and occupation, varied considerably. On the one hand, the Oceanic Steam Navigation Co. Ltd. ('commonly known as the White Star Line') donated £2,000 in 1895 to establish in perpetuity the Sir Edward Harland Memorial Scholarship in memory of one of the UK's most eminent marine engineers and naval architects (Harland & Wolff), who had also been M.P. for Belfast: on the other hand, a committee of workmen employed at the Walker Engineering Laboratory organised an industrial exhibition in 1900 which raised £1,300 to endow a Liverpool Working-men's Scholarship (£35 annually for three years), which carried with it a Free Studentship of the University, open to the sons of Liverpool workingmen wishing to study engineering. Other awards were the result of donations by members of staff (particularly by lecturers in the faculty of medicine). But the expansion of the college (University) was not matched by an increased willingness to endow fellowship and scholarships: eight were established in the 1880s, ten in the 1890s, and eight in the first decade of the twentieth century, despite the claim that the achievement of independence generated new pride in the university.[63]

In contrast to the slow response of central government to the need to sustain the growth of provincial university colleges in terms of both teaching and research, local authorities were more proactive, but only to a limited degree. Apart from the initial transfer of the Lunatic Asylum and its surrounding land to University College, financial support from Liverpool Council was minimal, almost certainly because of the assumption that the future developments would be sustained by endowments and donations. Even when the council's medical officer of health, E. W. Hope, was appointed to the new chair of public health in 1897, it remained unendowed. But increasing collaboration in delivering technical instruction and teacher training, in line with Liverpool's needs created additional revenue streams for the college and widespread interest at the start of the twentieth century in pursuing independent university status led to an annual grant from the council of £10,000. By 1905–06, local authority support, including money provided by the Technical Instruction Fund, accounted for over one quarter of the university's income, while in 1899 Wallasey Urban District Council established two scholarships (one male, one female) for students who had attended either a public or private school in the local authority for at least two years prior to the examination.[64]

Between the mid-1890s and the outbreak of the First World War, total revenue rose substantially (Table 12.7), primarily as a result of an increase in treasury grants in aid, as well as support from other government sources and local authorities (specifically Liverpool Council). Income from endowments and donations, which accounted for 35 per cent of total revenue in the mid-1890s, was still important in 1913–14, but its significance had diminished. Income from this source, by definition, was unstable. Indeed, research undertaken by Burns drawing on the University Council's Gift Books (1901–14) has highlighted the marginal role of limited companies in supporting educational improvements and the overwhelming predominance of small-scale donations (£1–£10), particularly in the early years of the century and in 1910. By 1914, Manchester had a far higher endowment level, but among the civic universities of northern England, Liverpool was in second place.[65]

However, despite the importance of endowment income, whether for the creation of new chairs or for capital projects, the level of involvement by members of the mercantile and business community was disappointing. Some of the benefactors, such as Sir Henry Tate and Sir Andrew Barclay Walker, had accumulated their wealth by questionable means, either by exploiting the labour conditions on the post-emancipation plantations of the Caribbean, or the alcohol dependency of Liverpool workers and their families, whose livelihoods were undermined by the continued absence of secure employment in an economy dominated by shipping and trade.

Table 12.7 University College/Liverpool University: sources of income, 1894–1914 (in per cent)

Income Source	1894–95	1900–01	1905–06	1913–14
Treasury grants, other government sources	9	12	42	32
Local authorities	12	5	19	15
Technical Instruction Fund	10	7	8	4
Fees	34	50	24	25
Endowments and donations	35	26	9	24
Total income (£)	17,000	25,000	61,000	84,000

Source: David Peter Burns, 'British Decline, commercial influence and the provision of technical education on Merseyside between 1870 and 1914', unpublished Ph.D. thesis, School of History, University of Liverpool (2006), Chapter 8.

Walker may well have argued that his endowment of new engineering laboratories was for 'the benefit of the citizens of Liverpool' and a suitable way of celebrating the Queen's Jubilee, but the generosity of 'this great drink seller' inevitably became the object of intense criticism as the college welcomed a substantial gift 'from the hands of the terrible drink trade' of which Walker was the figurehead. Other benefactors had a questionable background, at least from a contemporary perspective. The Rev. Samuel Ashton Thompson-Yates whose benefaction funded the construction of physiology and pathology laboratories (1894–98) came from a 'notable mercantile and shipping family', but his grandfather, Joseph Brooks Yates, had been a West India merchant until his death and involved, implicitly, in the profits of the slave plantations. As has been noted, a high proportion of the 'merchant princes' who supported University College (and the University of Liverpool) financially, were Unitarians, but the extent of involvement by members of other denominations, whether Church of England or Roman Catholic, was minimal or non-existent. Their motives varied: self-interest in resourcing research facilities of direct relevance to their business enterprises (particularly on the part of chemical manufacturers and shipowners); a desire to memorialise either themselves or deceased family members (including parents, husbands, and sons who had lost their lives prematurely); a need to rehabilitate the image of their main sources of wealth, whether the drinks trade or sugar-refining; a deep commitment to philanthropy and the provision of improved educational facilities (as was the case with many of the Unitarian benefactors); a sense of civic pride; or even social advancement. Moreover, almost all the known benefactors were very wealthy men. This was true in the case of Walker and Tate, but Thompson-Yates, on his death, left an estate valued at £233,652 12s 4d (£25.2m in 2019 prices). Sir John Brunner M.P., chairman of Brunner Mond & Co., had endowed three chairs, but left £906,000 (£41.9m), having already made generous settlements to his five married daughters and transferred all his investments to his sons. Sir William Pickles Hartley, the jam manufacturer, had purchased a 40-acre site at Aintree in 1886 for a new factory and a model village. In January 1877 he had vowed to give a specific proportion of his income to charitable and religious causes. He became the largest benefactor to Primitive Methodism and donated funding to build the college's botanical laboratories which subsequently carried his name. When he died in 1922 his estate amounted to £1m (£50.9m in 2019 prices).[66]

It would be a difficult task to calculate the combined wealth of Liverpool's mercantile and business community, but some of the benefactors to the College and University were immensely wealthy plutocrats. In most cases they supported a range of charitable objectives, but their commitment to the development of higher education in Liverpool, although well received, represented a very small proportion of their total wealth (as registered for probate purposes). The number of major benefactors was relatively small, with many elite figures, particularly from the

Tory Party and the Church of England, prominent by their absence. The establishment of University College in 1882 was a turning point in creating a research and teaching framework that would meet the challenges facing Merseyside and its hinterlands at a time when other European countries with state-funded higher education provision (such as Imperial Germany) had already established an international reputation in applied science and other disciplines. By comparison, Liverpool University did not become an independent institution until 1903; nine of the scientific and engineering laboratories built as a result of private benefactions were only established after the mid-1890s; and accommodation for research and teaching prior to that date had been inadequate. It was not uncommon for newly endowed professorships (including those held by H. S. Hele-Shaw and Oliver Lodge) to be filled despite the absence of appropriate facilities. When Orchard started work on his compilation of 'numerous memoirs of living (and departed) worthies', he estimated that Liverpool had 2,000 notables 'worthy of attention', of whom 298 were senior partners in firms that were 'the most prominent and honoured in the eyes of the mercantile community' (excluding limited liability companies). They accounted for just under half of the 606 'most notable firms', including cotton brokers and merchants. In the absence of accurate data, it can only be assumed that a significant proportion of them were extremely wealthy and more than capable of contributing to the development of higher education in Liverpool. The fact that this task was left to a small number of donors is itself an indictment of the port-city's merchant and business class. The failure to respond, both collectively and individually, to the appeals for support by the college and university authorities meant that Liverpool was unable to seize an opportunity to compete more effectively with Manchester and to reduce what became a systemic gap in terms of research excellence and student numbers.[67]

Associational Culture and the Role of Learned Societies

According to Chandler, the establishment of clubs in nineteenth-century Liverpool helped to develop 'a new esprit de corps' within the merchant community. Clubs, particularly those which offered an extended range of social activities, served as focal points for 'constant interaction' and by fostering regular proximity reinforced networking within the commercial elite. Within this context, associations, clubs, and societies played an increasingly important role in sustaining reputation and trust.[68] Certainly, contemporaries were all too ready to emphasise their proliferation and the extensive involvement of local merchants. By 1851, it was asserted that Liverpool had more 'temples dedicated to the improvement of mankind' than any other city in the country. It had 'so many active Societies' for the advancement of science, literature, and the arts; learned societies were 'extremely various' in terms of their composition and purpose; and in many instances, as was the case with the Historic Society of Lancashire and Cheshire, they were supported by 'many of the more active and thoughtful members' of the merchant community.[69]

An earlier chapter, by analysing a sample of cross-sectional clubs and associations covering cultural, social, and sporting activities, confirmed their importance for facilitating contacts within the business community, establishing the reputation of newcomers, and ensuring the survival of individual family firms. But any assessment of their role in extending the 'radius of trust' or in strengthening business networks is complicated by the increasing density and complexity of associational culture in the second half of the nineteenth century, the limited survival of records from many local clubs and societies, and the extent of involvement by members of Liverpool's merchant community in regional and national associations. Nor is it feasible at this stage to utilise cluster analysis to explore the significance of associational membership in facilitating closeness centrality, as Haggerty and Haggerty have demonstrated in an important study of Liverpool's merchants in the second half of the eighteenth century based on a relatively limited number of merchant actors and a small sample of political, cultural, and social institutions. To explore this theme in greater detail and to test the normative assumptions which underpin a great deal of recent research in this field, the analysis will focus on the role of learned societies in order to assess the changing extent of merchant participation and their importance for networking.[70]

Recent research on Liverpool has identified different phases in the foundation of learned societies which reflected cultural, economic, and political factors. Apparently, mid-eighteenth-century merchants were concerned only with money-making, membership of clubs which offered opportunities for drinking, dining, and sharing the latest gossip, as well as theatrical productions and music concerts. This was followed by an increasing emphasis on the need for 'intellectual self-improvement', 'the amenities of civilized life', and a 'detailed cultural aesthetic' which firmly located an interest in art and science in the social calendar. Increasing economic success necessitated the acquisition of a different socio-cultural identity, primarily to draw a veil, if possible, over Liverpool's extensive involvement in the slave trade and to deflect criticism that it had been 'the metropolis of slavery'. An associational framework was needed to bridge political divisions, foster business and professional networking, specifically among the merchant community, and promote 'common fellowship' within the middle classes. The Royal Institution (1814), envisaged as a 'cultural institution' and formally opened in 1817, became the operational base for most learned societies: it was designed to 'mould a new generation of Liverpool scholar-businessmen' and the founding of six learned societies between 1836 and 1849 is evidence of its success (although two of them, the Natural History Society and the Liverpool Statistical Society, only survived for a few years). Even if membership varied, from men of national scientific or artistic standing to those who were committed amateurs, underpinning this expansion was a belief in a commonality of purpose: 'the companionship of men of similar tastes and habits' whose 'thirst for knowledge' had been satisfied at the same fountain with an interest in literary or scientific inquiry based on 'the common ground of friendship'. It has been argued that the role of learned societies from the 1840s onwards was undermined by 'a rising tide of public enterprise', reinforced by a greater emphasis on the need to reinforce individual (rather than associational) status, yet, surprisingly, a further 22 societies were created from 1848 onward (Table 12.8). How sustainable is such a view? Did they fulfil their objectives and provide a basis for intellectual self-improvement as well as business networking? If elite merchants were prominent in the foundation of learned societies in the early decades of the nineteenth century, was this level of involvement sustained in subsequent decades as more specialist, science-based societies were established? What proportion of the merchant community was involved in the learned societies and to what extent was membership a reflection of professional interests or a personal, subjective decision? At a time of high rates of population mobility, how stable was society membership and were networking opportunities compromised by factors such as out-migration, business conditions, or the health costs of urban life? Did the gradual acceptance of women members affect the networking function of learned societies?[71]

Today, a learned society is viewed as a body which pursues the scholarly study of a specific field or discipline, but this criterion is difficult to apply in the nineteenth century, particularly if a society never produced its own *Proceedings* or *Transactions*. At a national level learned societies played an important role in shaping scientific knowledge and practice: in Liverpool 'a plethora' of learned societies helped to promote the arts, literature, science, and technology while underpinning the development of a 'detailed cultural aesthetic of the middle classes', although Rev. Abraham Hume's roll of provincial learned societies included only two from Liverpool, namely the Literary and Philosophical Society and the Polytechnic Society. Certainly,

Table 12.8 Merchant involvement in learned societies in Liverpool and Birkenhead (founded between 1804 and 1906 and including regional associations for Lancashire and Cheshire)

Society	Founded	c.1850–1879 Merchants	%	c.1880–1910 Merchants	%
LSEASTC	1804–14	no data			
L&PS	1812	33	23.9	30	20.5
RI	1814	128	36.5		
PS	1825	103	53.1	133	40.0
NHS	1836–44	21	27.2 (1)		
PolyS	1838	22	12.6		
LSS	1838–40	no data			
A&AS	1848	0	0.0	0	0.0
HSL&C	1848	33	18.0	28	25.9
LCA	1849	0	0.0	0	
NHMS	1853–68				
LPS	1853	6	20.6		
BL&SS	1857	48	40.3		
LGS	1859	12	20.6	3	5.4
LNFC	1860			3	10.3 (2)
LASA	1862				
LAPA	1863	2 (3)	12.5	4	5.6 (4)
MS	1868			22	9.6
LES	1875			0	0.0
L&CES	1877			5	12.5
BSLS	1878			17	14.4
RSL&C	1878			1	
LGA	1880				
LAS	1881			2	4.6 (5)
LSSA	1881			2	2.0
LBS	1886			7	13.7
LPS	1889			5	5.3
LGeogS	1891			158	38.9
LBS	1906			5	3.0
Merchants: total/ average/median		408/34/21		425/22/5	

(1) data from 1839 only
(2) data extracted from lists of new members in 1887 and 1900 respectively, in the absence of complete membership lists
(3) honorary officers and council members (1853–56)
(4) data from a list of Merseyside exhibitors to the Northern Photographic Exhibition promoted and organised by the Association
(5) new members elected in 1887

* excluding professional societies

Abbreviations: LSEASTC (Liverpool Society for the Encouragement of Arts, Science, Trade, and Commerce [formed from the Liverpool Association of Science and Arts]); L&PS (Literary and Philosophical Society); RI (The Royal Institution); PS (Philomathic Society); NHS (Natural History Society); PolyS (Polytechnic Society); A&AS (Architecture and Archaeological Society); HSL&C (Historic Society of Lancashire and Cheshire); LCA (Liverpool Chemists' Association); NH&MS (Natural History and Microscopical Society); Liverpool Photographic Society (LPS); BL&SS (Birkenhead Literary and Scientific Society); LGS (Liverpool Geological Society); LNFC (Liverpool Naturalists' Field Club); LASA (Liverpool Association of Science and Arts); LAPA (Liverpool Amateur Photographic Association); MS (Microscopical Society); LES (Liverpool Engineers' Society); L&CES (Lancashire and Cheshire Entomological Society); BSLS (Birkenhead Shakspere Literary Society); RSL&C (Record Society of Lancashire and Cheshire); LGA (Liverpool Geology Association); SCI (Society of Chemical Industry); LAS (Liverpool Astronomical Society); LSSA (Liverpool Science Students' Association); LBS (Liverpool Biology Society); LPS (Liverpool Physical Society); LGeogS (Liverpool Geographical Society); LBS (Liverpool Botanical Society)

Notes:

The following societies have not been included in the analysis because they served professional interests: the Incorporated Society of Liverpool Accountants (1871) and the Liverpool Chemists' Association (1885). Although the Society of Chemical Industry held its first meeting in Liverpool in 1881, it quickly became a national organisation based at the office of the Chemical Society in London: the Liverpool Section's meetings were regularly reported in *The Journal of the Society of Chemical Industry*. See D. W. Broad, *Centennial History of the Liverpool Section Society of Chemical Industries 1881–1981* (London, 1981). Data on other societies which only existed for a short time, including the Liverpool Statistical Society (1838–40) and the Liverpool Association for the Promotion of Social Science (1859), are not available.

Information on the years of the membership lists from which the data was extracted can be found in the following references.

Sources: Proceedings of the Literary and Philosophical Society of Liverpool during the Thirty-eighth and Thirty-ninth Sessions, 1849 to 1851, No. IV (Liverpool, 1851), Members, 1850–51, pp. 2–7; *Proceedings of the Literary and Philosophical Society of Liverpool During the Eighty-Ninth Session, 1899–1900, No. LIV* (London and Liverpool, 1900), pp. vi–xiii; *Proceedings of the Liverpool Philomathic Society During Its Seventy-Seventh Session, 1901–02*, Vol. XLVII (Liverpool, 1902), pp. cvii–cxvii; University of Liverpool, Special Collections, LRI, Proprietors of the Liverpool Royal Institution, February 1879; *Proceedings of the Liverpool Philomathic Society During Its Thirty-First Session, 1855–56, Vol. 1* (Liverpool, 1856), pp. 9–11; LRO, 060 LIT 7/1, Natural History Society, Names of Members 1841; 680 POL 2/1, Council Minutes, Liverpool Polytechnic Society, 1839 to 1873, list of members, 1860; *Transactions of the Historic Society of Lancashire and Cheshire, Session 1848–9* (Liverpool, 1849), pp. vii–xiii; *Transactions of the Historic Society of Lancashire and Cheshire For The Year 1902—Vol. LIV, New Series—Vol. XVIII* (Liverpool, 1904), pp. xiii–xxiii' Birkenhead Reference Library, BC IV 280, *The Laws and Annual Reports of the Birkenhead Literary and Scientific Society from its formation in 1857 to the end of the year 1900* (Birkenhead 1900), List of members, 1868–69, pp. 6–8; *Abstract of the Proceedings of the Liverpool Geological Society, Session The Twelfth, 1870–71* (Liverpool, 1871), pp. 76–78; R. W. Brotham and J. H. Milton (eds.), *Proceedings of the Liverpool Geological Society, Sessions XLVI–L, 1904–1909, Vol. X* (Liverpool, 1909), pp. xi–xii; LRO, 570 NAT/1, Liverpool Naturalists' Field Club, Register of Members, c.1900; The Liverpool Amateur Photographic Association in conjunction with The Manchester Amateur Photographic Association and The Leeds Camera Club, Northern *Photographic Exhibition, Walker Art Gallery, 22 March–13 April 1907* (Liverpool, 1907); *Eighteenth Annual Report of the Liverpool Microscopical Society, Abstract of Proceedings and List of Members, January 1887* (Liverpool, 1887), Session XIX, 1887; LRO, 620 ENG/7/1, Liverpool Engineers' Society, Dates of Election and Introduction of Members, 1892–1927, Session XXVII, 1900–01; *Fourteenth Annual Report of The Lancashire and Cheshire Entomological Society*, Session 1890 (Liverpool, 1891), p. 4; *Birkenhead Shakspere Literary Society, Report of the 2nd Session, 1879–80* (Birkenhead, 1880), pp. 8–11; LRO, LAS/1/1, Minute Book of the Liverpool Astronomical Society, 7th Series, 1887–88; *Liverpool Science Students' Association Annual Report and Proceedings, Session 1889–90* (Liverpool, 1890), pp. 29–31; *Proceedings of and Transactions of the Liverpool Biological Society, Vol. XVII, 1902–03* (Liverpool, 1903), pp. xx–xxiii; Liverpool Physical Society, *Report of the Council for the 1st Session, 1889–90* (Liverpool 1890), List of Members, September 1890, pp. 10–12; *The Second Annual Report of the Council of the Liverpool Geographical Society For Year Ending December 31st, 1893* (Liverpool, 1894), pp. 15–21.

the original societies set out a wide intellectual agenda. The Literary and Philosophical Society fostered a range of interests 'over a wide field of Science and Literature', while some of its published papers confirmed a 'high level of philological curiosity' amongst the town's intelligentsia. The Philomathic Society had an all-embracing agenda based on the 'attainment of knowledge by discussion', while Hume, as the president of the Historic Society, welcomed the existence of numerous associations 'for acquiring and diffusing knowledge', regarded a 'diversity of subject' as 'a manifest advantage' and emphasised the important role of the society in a modern town, such as Liverpool, because 'it reminds us constantly of what is ancient'. The Lancashire and Cheshire Antiquarian Society also had an extensive disciplinary focus embracing 'History, Architecture, Manners, Customs, Arts and Traditions'. By contrast, the Polytechnic Society was established in 1838 'to promote the knowledge of science in the factory, as well as out of it'. According to James Taylor, its president in 1872, that objective remained valid, given that scientific progress was still dependent, at least to some extent, on the workshop and the factory 'frequently becomes the birth-place of much that is of scientific character'. Perhaps, not surprisingly, most of the science-based learned societies created in the second half of the nineteenth century had a sharply defined focus, whether relating to the 'cultivation and advancement of Microscopy', the 'practical study of Natural and Physical Science', the reading and discussing of 'original communications on engineering subjects' or the 'promotion, advancement and study of Physical Science'.[72]

However, some of the 'learned' societies catered primarily for professional practitioners, whether lawyers, architects, chemists, physicians, or photographers, although in certain cases they gradually accepted members from the wider public with a common interest in their subject. In fact, law and medicine developed an organisational framework at a relatively early date, but deliberately excluded non-practitioners and their formal institutions were not classified as learned societies even if they were concerned with disseminating specialist knowledge. A Liverpool Law Library Society was established in 1827 with a membership fee of 15 guineas; from 1834 onwards it was known as the Liverpool Law Society; and its overriding professional function was made explicit on its incorporation in 1869, with a commitment to protect 'the character, status and interest of the Attorneys and Solicitors practising in Liverpool or within 20 miles thereof'. Although the Manchester Law Association (1809–15) was criticised for prioritising social events, the proliferation of provincial law societies in the late eighteenth and early nineteenth centuries was evidence not only of self-interest, but also a recognition of the need for institutional consolidation at a time of increasing industrial development. The growth of commerce and trade generated a significant demand for legal services connected with the freighting of ships, salvage, and commercial disputes, while attorneys-at-law played an increasing role in early capital markets in Lancashire, specifically in Liverpool, but associational structures, including the Metropolitan and Provincial Law Societies Association, were always intended to reinforce professional interests.[73]

The foundation of the Liverpool Architectural and Archaeological Society (1848) followed precedents elsewhere in the country: the deliberate inclusion of archaeology served as a 'signifier of erudition and knowledge'; its meetings covered wider issues relating to sanitary and welfare reform; but it was not intended for 'gentlemen connoisseurs'. The idea of establishing a society was taken up at a meeting at the 'hospitable table' of the oil merchant and land developer William Jackson M.P. which was held at the Manor House, Claughton, early in 1848. A meeting of local architects was convened by circular for the first of March when it was decided that an architectural society should be founded 'to consist of all the gentlemen practising the profession of Architecture in Liverpool and Birkenhead'. In 1876, when it became the Liverpool Architectural Society, it was controlled by 'men active in their profession', whose main concern was the provision of better educational facilities for architectural students. The Liverpool Chemists' Association (1849) was intended to promote the 'advancement of Chemistry and Pharmacy', but also to protect 'the Trade Interests' of its members, while right from its inception in 1853 there were tensions between amateur and professional members of the Liverpool Photographic Society. An exclusionary policy was evident in the case of the Liverpool Engineering Society (1875–76): ordinary membership was restricted to 'engineers of any branch of the profession' and student membership was limited to young men under the age of 21 'in course of training to become Engineers': only in 1889 was a new category of associate member created for men 'who, by their connection with science or the arts, are qualified to concur with Engineers in the advancement of professional knowledge', but almost all the new members were practising engineers recruited from Liverpool's hinterland. The shipowner Alfred Holt M.I.C.E. was an early member and became its president in 1881, but he was an exception; very few representatives of the mercantile community had an appropriate qualification in civil engineering, and only a handful of papers were presented on the commercial or financial aspects of the shipping industry. Indeed, by 1900 there was a much higher proportion of full members with proper engineering qualifications which reinforced the society's professional focus. The members of the

Liverpool Section of the Society of Chemical Industry (1879) were almost entirely consulting or analytical chemists.[74]

It is generally assumed that learned societies, particularly those that were primarily town-based, provided a basis for 'cultural assertion' by the middle class. They played a key role in the construction of social identity and helped to strengthen relational cohesion within the urban elite. But there has been no detailed analysis of their actual operation in Liverpool, or any attempt to assess the extent to which they facilitated high-trust linkages within the business community. Table 12.8 lists 29 learned societies from Liverpool and Birkenhead covering the period between 1804 and 1906. Membership data was derived from their annual reports, where available, for two sub-periods (1850–1879 and 1880–1909) in order to reflect compositional changes over time. Initially, Liverpool's learned societies represented wider intellectual interests rather than a focus on mercantile and industrial pursuits, even though it has been claimed that science and technology were 'at a discount in the culture of commerce'. Merchants were actively involved in their establishment: they accounted for 56 of the initial names on the Literary and Philosophical Society's roll (1812); all six founding members of the Liverpool Philomathic Society (1825) and just under 13 per cent of the early members of the Liverpool Polytechnic Society (1838). However, this level of commitment was not maintained. Their involvement in the Royal Institution diminished: by the 1860s just four of the 21 elected members of court were involved in trade and by 1879 only 128 of the 350 proprietors were merchants, although shares were often retained by individual families over two or three generations. Despite the overriding importance of commerce and trade to Merseyside's economy, only the Philomathic Society and the Birkenhead Literary and Scientific Society recorded a level of merchant participation of 40 per cent or more between 1850 and 1879 and the former was the only society to retain that position prior to 1910.[75]

The participation of merchants in other learned societies for which membership data are available was limited. The Polytechnic Society was established in February 1839 as a forum for discussing and examining 'new inventions of improvements in the arts.' In the early 1850s, it still enjoyed a reputation 'as a valuable test by which to try the merits of any practical invention' and it was proud of the fact that 'gentlemen residing at a distance from Liverpool' attended its meetings to present their 'discoveries'. But by 1860 only 22 merchants were members, although some of the presentations dealt with highly relevant issues, including patents designed to improve the performance of ships. If scientific inventions failed to attract widespread interest among Liverpool's merchant community, this was equally the case in relation to the diffusion of 'useful' historical knowledge. Despite a strategy of bringing 'non-scientific subjects into greater prominence', the initial interest on the part of local merchants in the Historic Society of Lancashire and Cheshire (founded in 1848) was disappointing: of the 183 individual, non-institutional members who fulfilled the residence requirement, only 33 (18 per cent) were drawn from commerce and trade. The severity of the economic crisis in the late 1840s explains the initial low level of interest and by the early 1860s 76 local merchants were listed as members, but it never gained the same popularity within the merchant community as the Philomathic Society. A similar lack of engagement was evident in the case of the Geological Society, despite the undoubted success of the London Society in promoting wider interest by the wealthier middle class in what was represented as a strictly empirical science. At its first session in January 1860 great emphasis was placed on the benefits which would accrue 'to the community at large from the existence of such an association'. Initial reports of its activities highlighted its 'successful scientific career' reinforced by a wide range of discussion papers, an annual excursion from 1861 onwards, and active involvement in local issues, including the geological arrangement of fossils in Liverpool's New Museum. But only 12 merchants became members and the level of support from the business community remained limited. In fact, the late nineteenth century witnessed a progressive disengagement by merchants from learned societies, even in the case of the Philomathic Society, while they were conspicuous by their absence from most of the new learned societies established from the 1860s onwards, particularly those with a scientific focus, such as the Liverpool Astronomical Society and the Liverpool Physical Society.[76]

A proposal for establishing an amateur society for coordinating 'astronomic observations' was made in 1880 by Rev. T. E. Espin, rector of Wallasey, and the initial response was positive. It was predicated on the assumption that the study of science would be facilitated if 'amateurs' could meet and compare their observations. By 1888, the society had 641 members, including Arthur Mee (the editor of the *Children's Encyclopedia*) and enjoyed a national reputation. Its president and chairman were accomplished professionals (Fellows of the Royal Astronomical Society); satisfactory attendance at astronomy classes was rewarded with certificates of competence; and it was financially self-supporting. It attracted support from a broad spectrum of the population: the 42 new members accepted in October 1887 included a baker, a carter, a cashier, a police officer, a warehouseman, and an analytical and consulting chemist. Apart from a tobacco broker and a tea dealer, there were no other members of the merchant community.[77]

The Liverpool Physical Society was founded in February 1889 when Professor Oliver Lodge, DSc., LL.D., FRS gave his first presidential address. It was intended to be a 'working society of members', willing to study seriously 'the enormous groups of phenomena' associated with physical science. Again, the initial response was encouraging, with 86 members recruited (but only 78 subscriptions received). Lodge was the chief driving force behind the new society and the principal organiser of its activities. He was fortunate to be able to draw on the support of relatives and prominent friends from the merchant community, including Eva and S. Heywood Melly, George Holt (and three family members, including his niece, Jane Brandreth Holt who became the first woman to obtain a first class honours degree in experimental physics at the University of London). But merchants accounted for just over 5 per cent of the membership and were outnumbered by academics from related disciplines, teachers from local public schools (such as Merchant Taylors), and corresponding members classified as 'gentlemen of leisure'. With a few notable exceptions, the society failed to attract many women members, although they included Mrs. R. F. Steele, of 31 Prince's Avenue, 'apparently of foreign origin' who was not accompanied by her husband. Already in its second year of operation, the society's meetings began to attract fewer people: it was taken over by University College staff and became a research unit 'by accident'.[78]

It could be argued that these two cases were atypical: one required night-time observations of the sky; the other was overtly academic and never likely to recruit large numbers of members from the merchant community. But they were representative of a general trend, since science, despite its increasingly crucial role in contemporary society, failed to attract widespread support. The object of the Liverpool Biological Society (1888) was 'the advancement of Biological Science', but an annual membership fee of one guinea suggests that the intention was to develop a strong middle-class profile, with active participation from senior academic staff at University College, local medical practitioners, and members of other eminent societies. The work of the Liverpool Marine Biology Committee had already been supported directly by the shipowners George Holt and Sir James Poole, both of whom offered to lend a steam-tug for dredging expeditions, while the Liverpool Salvage Association had made available 'the services of one or other of their steamers on several occasions'. It is not surprising, therefore, that 13 merchants, including the shipowner Charles W. Jones were among the society's original members. By 1902–03, Alfred Holt and his son were members, but only five additional representatives of the mercantile community supported the society. Even where there was an overlapping commercial interest between the society's research agenda and maritime concerns, it failed to attract a wider audience primarily because of its academic agenda.[79]

In the 1830s, merchants accounted for more than a quarter of the membership of the Natural History Society. But there was little, if any, support for formal engagement with its successor bodies (even if their objects were slightly different). The 1860 membership list of the Liverpool Naturalists' Field Club included only three merchants, as well as George Wynne (the editor of the *Liverpool Mercury*) and his wife, although subsequently the cotton trader Arthur Kilpin Bulley (1861–1942), a pioneering plantsman and the creator of what became Ness Gardens on the Wirral, became a member of the General Committee and the salt merchant William Henry Holt, of 11 Ashville Road, Birkenhead, served as its President (1892–1906). Support from the mercantile community for the Liverpool Botanical Society (founded in 1906) was virtually non-existent. Out of a total membership of 163 (in its second session, excluding non-Merseyside residents) only 5 were from the commercial community, including a P&O clerk, a fruit merchant, and a branch manager of the Lancashire and Yorkshire Bank. Again, the emphasis on the encouragement and promotion of 'original work and research' might have deterred active participation by men involved in commerce and trade who, in any case, probably had little interest in 'the results of the recent Fungus foray' held on 27 October at Raby Mere.[80]

The available data confirm this trend (see Table 12.8) and place in doubt the central role that learned societies are assumed to have played in business networking. By using the decennial totals of Merseyside merchants derived from the MLP database (averaged over the two sub-periods, 1850–1879 and 1880–1909), their overall participation level can be estimated. If an allowance is made for dual or multiple membership, approximately 225 and 387 merchants, respectively, were listed as members, or 9.3 and 9.7 per cent of the total registered during a period when the size of the mercantile community almost doubled. Moreover, total learned society membership for the latter period was inflated by the widespread support by the merchant community for the Geographical Society (1891), fuelled by the justifiable criticism of Liverpool's slow response to what was perceived as a national cause. The driver behind its formation was the need to 'render assistance' to the commercial interests of the city, the community and the country, based on a link between improved geographical knowledge, Liverpool's future prosperity as 'the first seaport of the world', and imperial objectives. In 1893, its 158 members from the world of trade and commerce represented almost 40 per cent of the total. If they are excluded from the analysis, then the overall participation rate was no higher than 5.2 per cent. The initial level of support highlights what the merchant community was capable of: it also reveals a declining commitment to learned societies in general. Average membership fell from 34 to 17; median membership collapsed from 21 to 5; and 9 learned societies between 1880 and 1909 had 5 or fewer members who were merchants.[81]

Evidence from collective biographies reinforces this picture. As has been noted, their value as a source is partly dependent on the depth and range of information collated by their authors or provided by those who agreed to submit material. In comparison with political office-holding, national recognition, or even club membership, the registration of involvement in learned societies may not have been a priority. Nevertheless, of the 386 entries in Orchard's *Liverpool Legion of Honour* relating to merchants and traders, only 26 cited membership of a learned society, of whom 16 were involved with the Philomathic Society where a number of them served as president or were 'brilliant' or 'esteemed' members. But they represented barely 7 per cent of all the entries from those involved in the mercantile community. In some cases, merchants were involved with national organisations with no mention of any local affiliations, while other entries simply report that they either 'read many papers before local societies' or were 'much liked' by their members. Coop and Taylor's list of the 83 members and ring traders of the Cotton

Exchange is similarly disappointing. Only in very few cases was there a reference to learned society membership: Lieut.-Col. Arthur G. Haywood took a 'great interest' in the Liverpool Amateur Photographic Association; W. H. Lloyd was an 'old member' of the Philomathic Society; and Richard Steel, J.P., 'a man of wide culture', had been a member for 42 and 30 years respectively of the Philomathic Society and the Literary and Philosophical Society and was duly elected their President in 1881 and 1883. The low level of involvement in learned societies by leading representatives from Liverpool's world of commerce and trade emphasises the extent to which they were no longer deemed to be indispensable for the city's intellectual improvement and that intellectual associations had ceased to play a key role in business networking.[82]

Various explanations can be put forward to account for the disengagement of the mercantile community from learned societies. Firstly, it was indicative of a growing divide between literary and scientific cultures. This is not the place to reprise the 'Two Cultures' debate of the late 1950s and early 1960s, but its origins can be found in the mid-nineteenth century when science and technology as key elements in the industrial revolution began to threaten traditional high culture, as represented by the classics, literature, and art. Evidence of a widening disciplinary divide was already evident in the mid-nineteenth century: in 1855, Michael Faraday was scathing in his condemnation of traditional classical education and its failure to teach 'even the simplest principles of chemistry or mechanics'; while W. E. Gladstone, despite his national political profile and his reputation as a distinguished classical and Biblical scholar 'refused to have anything to do with science'. Indeed, in learned societies in conservative, commercial cities, such as Bristol and Newcastle, attempts to include more science-based presentations provoked opposition from members with contrary views about institutional priorities.[83]

By and large, those learned societies established in the early decades of the nineteenth century sought to capture new members from a relatively small, but growing pool of potential candidates by adopting objects which embraced both the arts and sciences. The Literary and Philosophical Society covered a 'wide field of Science and Literature' with three designated sub-categories by the early 1850s for Literature and the Fine Arts (A); Nature, Philosophy, and Science (B); and Natural History, including Geology and Ethics (C). The remit of the Philomathic Society was extensive, provided the debates contributed to the 'attainment of knowledge', while the Polytechnic Society focussed on 'new inventions or improvements in the arts'. The Historic Society laid down initially eleven fields of inquiry, but a few years later a sectional framework was adopted which included archaeology (historic documents, antiquities, church registers, and military antiquities), general literature (genealogy and biographies, costumes, customs and traditions, and topographical description), architecture (architecture and the fine arts), Science (natural history), and Miscellaneous (trade, commerce and inventions, and Parliamentary Papers). This was designed to appeal to a wide audience of potential members, but trade and commerce, previously treated as a separate sub-category, were now downgraded with no formal representation on Council. The establishment of the Birkenhead Literary and Scientific Society (1857), at a time when the township had only just recovered from the severe economic depression of the late 1840s, was conceived of in a similar fashion: it was not intended to compete with the three debating societies which already existed, but was envisaged as a 'general town society' open to all parties irrespective of their religious denomination and focussing equally on literature and science. This was very much in line with the Enlightenment assumption, itself based on the Renaissance universalist spirit, that art and science had a great deal in common, with no sharp boundaries. They existed on a continuum defined by 'the purity of reason', with a substantial overlap between the two extremes, and because they both reflected aspects of the divine there could be no question of subordination. It is salutary to note, however, that by the 1870s the retention of such an enlightened, interdisciplinary approach had become difficult to maintain: in 1878–79, confronted with a proposal to wind up the Historic Society, its secretary, C. T. Gatty, was forced to announce a return to its original mission, namely to concentrate on 'strictly historical and archaeological lines'.[84]

Secondly, the move away from general learned societies and the fragmentation of disciplines within the sciences had a wider significance as they heralded a change in the way they operated. Traditionally, members of learned societies were expected to make useful contributions to proceedings by reading a paper, contributing to debates, and by making donations in kind (books and journals for a library and lithographs and artefacts for a museum) or cash (beyond the payment of annual subscriptions and entrance fees, if applicable). Even if the Philomathic Society were 'simply a Debating Society', by the 1830s the conduct of members was characterised by apathy with very few voting on either side of the issues being debated: it was only in 1855 that papers on literary and general subjects could be substituted for ordinary debates 'on certain occasions'. Many learned societies found it difficult to persuade members to offer papers for public discussion or to compete for prizes. The Committee of the Liverpool Polytechnic Society felt it necessary in 1846 to prepare a list of 'desirable and suitable subjects' 'to ensure a regular supply of Papers', but no paper was available for the meeting held on 16 March and a further plea had to be issued to members. The situation in the early 1870s was no different: the majority of the papers presented in 1872 were given 'by persons outside the society' because the Honorary Secretary encountered difficulty 'in traducing the members themselves to assist in promoting the interest of the Society'. Indeed, the Literary and Philosophical Society had to take even stronger measures in the mid-1850s, threatening a fine of one shilling if members failed to 'file one or more questions for the consideration of the Committee' at the first meeting every month, although it was recognised that such a measure was 'not at all calculated to win recruits'.[85]

Questions of commitment and personal sacrifice in the service of learned societies were not all that common before the mid-nineteenth century and it was recognised that some members, including merchants, did not have time to participate fully in meetings and other events. But the science-based societies established after the 1850s required a different level of involvement which almost certainly precluded regular participation by men still active in business and trade. There was a new emphasis on field work, the collection and registration of samples, whether of fossils, plants, or butterflies, and the formal reporting of results. The Liverpool Astronomical Society expected members to communicate results of their observations 'no matter how trivial they might appear', because amateurs were capable of 'work of great value' and should not be discouraged. The Committee of the Liverpool Science Students' Association in the late 1880s was frequently forced to urge upon its members 'the desirability and importance of individual investigation and research', while the members of the Lancashire and Cheshire Entomological Society were invited 'to bring captures and objects of interest for exhibition', a practice which added 'much to our enjoyment and instruction'. Even if societies were intended for enthusiastic amateurs, they were organised increasingly on a semi-professional basis. For example, in 1889 the Liverpool Microscopical Society appointed 'referees in several departments' to promote 'greater activity' among its members'.[86]

This expectation of increased participation in the scientific work of individual societies was reinforced by the growing popularity of excursions and field meetings. As a result of local field work, the Natural History Society collated sufficient data to publish a study of Liverpool's flora: other societies set aside one day (during spring) 'in a period of favourable weather' to visit 'some place within an attainable distance of the society's centre' for a 'most agreeable' excursion. In 1845, the Literary and Philosophical Society organised an outing to 'the sub-marine forest' at Leasowe on the Wirral when 'interest and enjoyment were sustained throughout the day'. By the late nineteenth century many of the societies offered eight or nine excursions each year (weather permitting). In some cases they catered for 'various tastes and for all grades of members' (whether beginners, advanced workers, or specialists), despite an admission that this was a 'somewhat difficult task', and outings were planned to locations which were 'easy of access by boat or train', so that 'Young Collectors' could exploit the 'great facilities' on offer. There can be little doubt that these regular events were enjoyed by members and that they fostered a spirit of camaraderie, particularly when they ended, as was the case in September 1878 with a group of approximately 30 members from the Liverpool Amateur Photographic Society, with tea at Hawarden Castle, the seat of William E. Gladstone (who had recently ended his first term as Prime Minister). The first excursion of the Liverpool Science Students' Association to Shotwick in May 1889 gave everyone an 'exhilarating feeling of buoyancy and intense enjoyment which lovers of nature cannot fail to experience', while members of the Liverpool Microscopical Society regarded Knowsley Park, Bromborough, Eastham, and Hooton (on the Wirral) as their 'happy hunting grounds' which provided clear evidence of the proliferation of foreign species as a result of Merseyside's substantial sea traffic. Given the popularity of excursions and field meetings, the range of destinations was expanded to include more distant locations such as Betwys-y-Coed, Thornton Le Moors and Plemstall, and Hawkstone, Shropshire (the seat of Lord Hill), utilising the benefits of an integrated railway network and improved transport connections. But there was a continuing emphasis on contributing to scientific development and historical research. Fieldwork was important in extending local natural knowledge: it promoted networking, mediated social differences, and promoted collective voluntarism in the pursuit of science. The Liverpool Students' Scientific Association, for example, laid out a programme in 1881 which involved 'systematic practical scientific work' for each of the session's outings. However, the expectation that members would undertake, albeit in an amateur fashion, a continuing programme of research, together with active involvement in fieldwork activities, would have been difficult, if not impossible, to deliver by merchant members of the new science-based societies, if only because of time constraints and business pressures. The problem was compounded by the increasing popularity of weekend and overseas excursions (for example, the Lancashire and Cheshire Antiquarian Society organised a nine-day visit to Holland in 1906). From this perspective, their mode of operation was less compatible with the daily demands of trade and commerce: this may have acted as a barrier to membership, but, equally, the mercantile community as a whole was probably less interested in science-based disciplines in contrast to more traditional learned societies which covered a wider range of topics.[87]

Thirdly, the slow, but perceptible, increase in female participation in some learned societies began to address the traditional gender imbalance in a manner which might have deterred male membership. The early learned societies were exclusively male preserves and their members were very proud indeed of their privileged status. The Literary and Philosophical Society remained wedded to its principles: it was not until 1883 that the first woman member was elected and then with the proviso that lady members would only be entitled to attend 'less academic' lectures. The Liverpool Philomathic Society was opposed to admitting women members throughout the nineteenth century. Both in 1863 and 1874 the presence of ladies was not deemed to be 'conducive to the Society's interests', while the President's address in 1900 was firmly anti-feminist: the Society was seen as 'a bulwark against the flood of feminine invasion of men's privileges and prerogatives', a stance which met with widespread approval from its male membership. Neither the Natural History Society, the Liverpool Statistical Society, nor the Polytechnic Society allowed female members, as Liverpool men continued to claim their innate superiority in appreciating and understanding the arts and sciences in a middle-class society dominated by the belief in the existence of separate, gender-specific spheres. Despite its attempt to increase membership, the Historic Society was noticeably reticent at recruiting women. The meeting in 1864 to celebrate the tercentenary of Shakespeare's birth was 'remarkably successful' and was attended by ladies and gentlemen, but they were not members of the society and it was not until the end of the 1860s that the first woman (Miss Legh, of the Limes, Hale) was elected a member followed by Miss Farrington of Worden Hall, Preston, in January 1871. Occasionally women were permitted to participate in the Literary and Philosophical Society's proceedings, but only as a special concession at the last meeting of a session.[88]

Despite gaps in the membership data, most learned societies were resolute in turning their backs on admitting women. It was only in the 1880s that this position began to change, but women were hardly visible and were marginal participants in society activities. Seven of the learned societies had admitted women members by the start of the twentieth century but progress was often slow. When some societies moved away from an all-male membership, only one woman was elected, as was the case with the Liverpool Amateur Photographic Association (for which 'women were eligible'), the Liverpool Biological Society, and the Lancashire and Cheshire Entomological Society. The Naturalist's Field Club, however, right from its inception in 1860, had no restrictions on the election of female members. Approximately 400 men and women joined the Club in the first few months following its foundation: by the early 1880s, out of a total membership of 472 (including members resident outside of Merseyside and honorary members) 137 (29 per cent) were female; and in 1900 over one third of the newly elected members were women (Table 12.9). Although there was a strong element of family clustering (for example, Auguste Cros was listed with three daughters), a surprising number were 'independent' women with no other male relative listed as a member. By the mid-1890s, Miss E. M. Wood served on the General Committee as the Societies' botanical referee and, together with her mother and 20 other women, she contributed in 1902 to the publication of *The Flora of the Liverpool District*. Female members enjoyed considerable success in winning excursion prizes, a competition that was open to both ladies and gentlemen. But it was only after the turn of the century that there was any significant improvement in the level of female participation, particularly in the more specialised scientific learned societies.[89]

Orchard, in his compilation of biographical information on the 'best people' in Liverpool, was dismissive of the participation of women in learned societies and claimed that 'of purely intellectual centres, open alike to ladies and gentlemen, there are none of commanding importance'. Inevitably, there was continued opposition to female membership: admission would interfere seriously with the pursuit of scientific objects; fashion styles would make their participation on excursions problematic (by wearing flimsy shoes, 'precious hats', and voluminous skirts); and 'secretly no one regarded their presence as much more than decorative'. However,

Table 12.9 Female membership of learned societies on Merseyside, 1880–1909 (by decade, in per cent)

Society	Date founded	1880s women/ total members	%	1890s women/total members	%	1900s women/total members	%
L&PS	1812			5/51[+]	9.8	18	12.3
LNFC	1860		29.0			(new members)	33.3
MS	1868			9	3.9		
L&CES	1877			1/150	2.5	6/40	15.0
LGeoS	1880					2	3.6
LBS	1886			1		3/56	5.3
LBS	1906					95/183	50.8

+ new members elected in 1894.

Note: For source references for the various societies and associations, see Table 12.8.

the records of the specialist, science-oriented societies established in the post-1860 period demonstrate the ability of female members to contribute significantly to scientific development. Indeed, in 1896, when Liverpool hosted the annual (peripatetic) meeting of the British Association for the Advancement of Science, reports from some of the disciplines which had a high proportion of female members, including the Naturalists' Field Club, were included in the official handbook. Increasingly, women played a visible role at such meetings, not simply as 'part of the social circuitry surrounding the civic engagement with science', but as amateur botanists or entomologists who were contributing to scientific knowledge. Academic recognition, in turn, validated their presence within science-based learned societies. If merchants were noticeable by their absence from the membership lists of these societies, by the early twentieth century women were playing an increasingly important role.[90]

Fourthly, in terms of business networking, it is difficult to estimate the practical utility for merchants and traders of their participation in learned societies, particularly if this involved excursions and field meetings. The programme of the Philomathic Society continued to offer discussion papers on themes which would have been of interest to members from the merchant community. Its 1902–03 session, for example, included papers discussing whether municipal trading would be advantageous for the community; the threat to the pre-eminence of Great Britain's mercantile marine from countries aided by official bounties; and the risks posed by the increasing wealth of the United States to Britain's commercial prosperity. But in the absence of nominative attendance lists, it is difficult to know which merchants were present at individual meetings. It was claimed that the Philomathic was ideal for members 'fond of intellectual excitements after business', and the increase in total membership in the latter decades of the nineteenth century suggests that it enjoyed substantial popularity (Table 12.10). But this is not confirmed by average attendance data. Whereas approximately one third of the society's members attended regular meetings in the mid-nineteenth century, in the 1901–02 session average attendance was no more than 14.5 per cent. Moreover, this was indicative of a general trend. Its popularity was adversely affected by economic crises (as in 1872–73) and from the early 1880s onwards there was a continuous decline in its appeal. In the 1890s and early 1900s, fewer than 8 per cent of its membership attended individual meetings, which undermines the case that they served as a basis for interactive activity and relational cohesion. The society's annual dinners, however, remained important events, particularly for members who belonged to Liverpool's elite (whether commercial or professional), with a string of eminent speakers, including Lord Carrington (1900), Winston Churchill (1901), the Earl of Halsbury (1902), George Wyndham MP (1903), and Giles Gilbert Scott (1904).[91]

Table 12.10 The Liverpool Philomathic Society: attendance data, 1847–48 to 1901–02

Years	Average Membership	Average Attendance	%	Smallest Attendance	%	Largest Attendance	%
1847–48	51	19	37.2	11	21.5	27	52.9
1852–53	87	29	33.3	19	21.8	49	56.3
1862–63	222	51	22.9	35	15.7	74	33.3
1872–73	199	33	16.5	16	8.0	45	22.6
1882–83	349	60	17.9	45	12.8	180	51.5
1892–93	319	54	16.9	24	7.5	90	28.2
1901–02	330	48	4.5	26	7.8	61	18.4

Source: Proceedings of the Liverpool Philomathic Society for the various years

The two volumes of the Literary and Philosophical Society's Centenary Roll provide another means of assessing the involvement of members in its proceedings. In 1854–55, almost 70 per cent of those elected went on to deliver papers or other contributions: 40 years later only 6 of the 51 new members (11.7 per cent) went on to play a similar role prior to 1912. Even in the mid-nineteenth century, however, some notable members did not make a meaningful contribution to the society's deliberations. Of the 1854–55 cohort, the colliery owner and railway entrepreneur Charles Grey Mott, although active in politics and an energetic member of the Birkenhead Literary and Scientific Society, 'did not at any time contribute a paper to the Society'; the merchant George Melly (from a well-established Liverpool merchant family) failed to deliver either a paper or a communication, as was the case with the provision merchant John Jones of 55 Rodney Street; while the merchant Francis Prange never offered to read a paper, despite being elected president of the Liverpool Chamber of Commerce in 1872. Some members were 'frequent attenders', but they tended to be from the ecclesiastical, legal, and medical professions. The active participation rate of members elected in 1894 was noticeably inferior to the earlier cohort, but at least some of them contributed to the centenary fund, including the alkali manufacturer Roscoe Brunner and Robert Kirkwood Mackenzie, MD, 'Physician in Private to His Highness the Maharajah of Baroda' (£5).[92]

Data from the Historic Society provides further evidence of the limited networking role that membership of a learned society provided. It succeeded in recruiting (and retaining) important establishment figures and 'some exalted personages': in 1892 the Bishop of Chester was its president, with dukes and earls among its vice-presidents. But almost one fifth (17.5 per cent) of the original members were Anglican ministers including its first secretary, the Reverend Abraham Hume, who remained in post until 1857 and was subsequently elected president (1869–74). Such a high level of participation by representatives of the Established Church was never to be matched again, but the presence of 43 ministers may have deterred membership applications from merchants and traders of other faiths, particularly in Liverpool and Merseyside.[93]

It could be argued that growing cooperation between learned societies offered enhanced opportunities for networking, whether for academic, business, or social reasons. From the 1860s onwards sub-committees of various councils were set up to take forward important new plans, such as William Brown's offer in 1861 to endow a 'special Museum', while the organisation of special events, including the Shakespeare Tercentenary in 1864, involved delegates from a number of societies. In the same year, there was a literary gathering of all the learned societies in the town hall to hear a presentation by Charles Mosely. Cooperation between the learned societies was even more important when national organisations decided to hold their annual meetings in Liverpool, including the five visits to Merseyside of the British Association for the Advancement of Science (Liverpool, 1837, 1854, 1870, 1896; Southport, 1903), the two meetings of the National Association for the Promotion of Social Science (1858, 1876) and the Congress of the Royal Institute of Public Health (1903). They all required a great deal of preparation: senior figures from learned societies were involved directly in local executive committees and publications sub-committees, and undoubtedly suffered from 'intense anxiety' in the days prior to the opening event in the hope that all the efforts of local management would fulfil the 'scale and wants' of the 'august assembly' and 'the wealth and intelligence of the town which it is about to honour its presence'.[94]

At a practical level, moreover, steps were taken to encourage 'some degree of cooperation' between learned societies by promoting reciprocal invitations to lectures, allowing members or honorary officers of other societies to attend 'public' (but not business) meetings, organising joint excursions or even amalgamating with like-minded institutions to reinforce their scientific work, as was the case when the Geology Society merged with the Geology Association whose members had worked as a separate organisation since 1880 and had always been 'of the most friendly character'. Indeed, from 1872 onward formal meetings of delegated society officers were held at the Royal Institution, initially with the intention to 'obtain first class Lectures upon any subject', but subsequently the Association of Officers of Learned Societies organised an annual soirée, usually held in St. George's Hall, where they collectively presented their scientific work to the wider public, as well as *Conversazione* for members from 'kindred societies'. These events were well attended, but largely by members of the learned societies involved, although they reinforced the spirit of cooperation and collaboration. Indeed, some of the society reports reflect a real sense of friendship and mutual respect among members, but this was based to a large extent on a shared passion for the discipline (and its allied subjects). Given the virtual absence of merchants and other members of Liverpool's commercial community from science-based societies, it is unlikely that collaborative ventures with other learned societies had any impact on business networking.[95]

Membership of learned societies, however, was inherently unstable. Historians, when assessing their contribution to networking, tend to see election to membership as an access point for enjoying programme activities, as well as ancillary business and social benefits. But in the mid-nineteenth century, at a time of high levels of both in- and out-migration, with mortality rates inflated by epidemic diseases, such as cholera and typhus, a considerable loss of members was inevitable. The presence of institutional and life members, irrespective of whether they continued to participate in the society's activities, was offset by a significant turnover in membership. By 1860–61, 74 (18.1 per cent) of the Historic Society's original members were still subscribers, but by the end of that decade only 35 remained. In 1880–81, only 27 (13 per cent) of those elected during the 1860s were still members. The retention rate for members resident on Merseyside was significantly lower than that of non-residents, primarily as a result of out-migration, but also as a result of the cumulative cost of urban living in terms of higher morbidity and mortality rates. All too often the Council struck out the names of those who 'ceased to feel an interest in its operation'; the Honorary Treasurer always had to deal with the issue of unpaid subscriptions; and the annual reports contain references to the premature death of members. In 1900, the loss of Richard Bennett, 'a remarkable man', was noted, a member of council of 'great commercial capacity', who was self-made and self-taught, but had been 'cut off in the prime of life', while James I. Thornely had been 'carried off by typhoid fever in his 35th year'. To this extent, the networking opportunities which membership of learned societies provided were constrained by the harsh reality of daily life in the nineteenth century, even for those who enjoyed a relatively privileged status. Moreover, membership did not necessarily provide a suitable framework for networking beyond the collective pursuit of a learned society's objects.[96]

Like other civic associations, including charitable bodies, learned societies have been seen traditionally as a key element in cultural assertion in the nineteenth century. They were units of activity based on a local, urban community; they fostered interconnections between elite residents and institutions; and their promotion of both arts- and science-based disciplines contributed to the expansion of the knowledge economy and the intellectual standing of their town or city in what was often a competitive national context. From a business perspective, because members were recruited from a well-defined and relatively homogenous socio-economic subset, they delivered high-trust linkages by encouraging networking and bonding between groups of key actors within the local economy. Similar claims have been made in relation to Liverpool's learned societies. Earlier research emphasised their importance in contributing to a new public profile of the port-city, where commerce and culture were developed in tandem to enhance its national and international profile. Particularly in the first half of the nineteenth century, merchants played a key role in transforming its intellectual profile, while membership of learned societies offered tangible benefits in terms of social status and opportunities for business networking. Indeed, election to membership in a learned society was proof itself of integration within an institutional framework wherein networking was viewed as an expected outcome.

However, the evidence from the second half of the nineteenth century places in doubt many of these assumptions. Undoubtedly, Liverpool, together with Birkenhead, were well endowed with learned societies and their number grew considerably between 1853 and 1906. But the various attempts in the 1850s and 1860s to create a more viable institutional framework by securing a merger of a group of learned societies failed and the subsequent proliferation of smaller, science-based societies contributed to a further fragmentation of the intellectual landscape. Despite the persistence of a real or perceived hierarchy, there was a trend towards growing cooperation between most of the learned societies. However, this could not disguise a clear disparity in terms of total membership and annual income. Some of the societies founded in the second half of the nineteenth century, including the Microscopical Society, the Birkenhead Shakspere Literary Society, the Liverpool Science Students' Association, the Geographical Society, and the Botany Society, all managed to recruit a reasonably-sized membership and science-based disciplines often adopted lower membership fees to widen their appeal. But the involvement of merchants was modest, while some learned societies were dissolved or forced to merge with like-minded bodies because of financial difficulties. What stands out is the relatively limited level of merchant participation in learned societies even before 1850 (with the notable exception of the Philomathic Society) and the lack of involvement in science-based societies established in subsequent decades. Technological change, whether in transport services, communications, or office management, was of increasing importance to Liverpool's mercantile community, but interest in disciplines such as biology, physics, or botany was limited, while exclusion from professional bodies, such as the Chemists' Association or the Engineering Society, made little sense for merchants interested in how their trading world would be moulded by the future performance of export-oriented industries in Liverpool's immediate hinterlands or the need for improvements in the port-city's dock and transport infrastructure.

Conclusion

As far as merchant involvement in philanthropy and charitable work was concerned, which was often hailed as a hallmark of middle-class commitment to counter the worst excesses of a laissez-faire economic system, the traditional interpretation has often been a positive one. Even if some merchants were unconcerned about the persistence of widespread poverty or were firm adherents to the concept of 'self-help', Liverpool, like other towns and cities, witnessed during his period an 'upsurge of charitable effort', motivated primarily by humanistic and religious reasons. Some families, like the Rathbones and the jam manufacturer (Sir) William Pickles Hartley, set aside a specified proportion of their annual income for philanthropic purposes; others left behind substantial legacies for a wide range of local charities. However, the MLP database, together with archival data, provided an opportunity to test the existing hypothesis and to assess the significance of charitable activities for business networking. Clearly, several merchants considered it their duty to support charitable work and to invest considerable time in attempting to ameliorate the port-city's chronic social problems. But they were very much a minority: the funding of most local charities was inadequate, and the level of annual subscriptions fell markedly during periodic crises which frequently caused a rapid increase in the demand for relief and support. More importantly, the proportion of prominent merchants who were actively involved in managing charities in the 1890s was only 26.7 per cent while over one fifth were not involved at all in charitable work. Even if some charities benefited from the presence over time of a core group of experienced committee members and honorary officers, overall turnover was high, while the net-working benefits from collaborative work on behalf of those who were destitute, ill, needy, and poor were undermined by the prioritisation of business pressures and internal disputes. Indeed, a great deal of charitable provision continued to be provided along sectarian lines, thereby reinforcing the underlying fragmentation within the mercantile community.

A similar outcome is evident in relation to the philanthropy of the merchant class. Because of the wealth generated by commerce and trade, it has always been taken for granted that Liverpool's civic infrastructure, including those institutions which provided healthcare, education, social welfare, and cultural enrichment for most of the nineteenth century, were the result of private benefactions and merchant munificence. Again, a closer analysis of the available data casts a different light on the philanthropy of leading members of the mercantile community. As Giles noted, a great deal of 'good work' was achieved through the funding provided by both individuals and collective subscribers to civic and religious projects, but the following points need to be emphasised. Firstly, as two case studies illustrate, the motives behind benefactions did not necessarily reflect charitable or humanistic ideals, but self-interest. The raw sugar which was imported from the Caribbean (and elsewhere) for use in (Sir) Henry Tate's sugar-refining plants, in particular at Manesty Lane and Love Lane, came from plantations which used indentured labour within a management system that for many decades remained embedded in slavery, while (Sir) Andrew Barclay Walker had made his fortune as a successful brewer and was decried by contemporaries for the way in which the drinks trade had caused so much individual and family suffering and aggravated the social problems which confronted Liverpool and its hinterlands. Without doubt, their benefactions were well received by the city council (the Walker Art Gallery, 1877) and University College, Liverpool (the Walker Engineering Laboratories; the Henry Tate Library, and the western block of the new Victoria Building, 1887–92). But in both cases, the 'munificent' funding served ulterior purposes: it improved the public image of the benefactors, almost certainly helped to increase sales of their products, and led to upward social mobility with the award of knighthoods. Secondly, the relative 'munificence' of individual benefactors must be assessed in relation to their overall wealth as registered by probate. With few exceptions, when there were no family claimants to an estate, entrepreneurial benefactors were extremely parsimonious in setting aside funds for charities or other worthy causes when measured against their immense wealth. Thirdly, when the opportunity finally occurred in 1881 to take forward a long-cherished objective, namely the formal establishment of University College, Liverpool, the response from prominent members of the mercantile community, with the notable exception of a small group of Unitarians, was muted and the endowment gap with Victoria College, Manchester (University of Manchester) has never been bridged.[97]

Finally, there was a marked reduction in civic involvement by members of the mercantile community from the mid-nineteenth century onwards. Despite a general acceptance of the importance of voluntary associations for the consolidation of middle-class culture, the integration of civil society and the establishment of high-trust linkages, the initial dominance of leading merchants in the establishment and management of learned societies was gradually eroded. This trend was evident in the case of societies created in the early decades of the nineteenth century, but it was particularly pronounced in science-based associations. The growth of discipline-based specialisation was part of a wider process, but it accentuated the degree of fragmentation within Merseyside's merchant community. Moreover, changes in the way science-oriented learned societies operated, with an increasing emphasis on experimental work and field trips and their greater willingness to admit female members (albeit very gradually), made them less attractive to prospective members from commerce and trade because of time constraints or their lack of interest in scientific development. Although learned societies offered a forum for networking beyond the narrow boundaries of business interests, whether as a fruit merchant or insurance broker, the older societies retained high membership fees; it was not uncommon for honorary secretaries to encounter difficulties in putting together a season's programme; and some societies operated under very tight financial margins. Ironically, the foundation of University College, Liverpool, led to the gradual undermining of their role (particularly those that were science-based), as academics with better access to research facilities began to play a dominant role in their intellectual management and the role of 'amateurs' became circumscribed.

Notes

1 See Chapters 6 (Sari Mäenpää) and 10 (Robert Lee).
2 David Cannadine, 'Fred Freeman Annual Lecture on Philanthropy', University of Liverpool, 12 November 2013, p. 5; Henry Smithers, *Liverpool Its Commerce, Statistics and Institutions with a History of the Cotton Trade* (Liverpool, 1825), pp. 233–4; F. G. D'Aeth, 'Liverpool and Her Philanthropy', in Alfred Holt (ed.), *Merseyside a Handbook to Liverpool and District Prepared on the Occasion of the Meeting of the British Association for the Advancement of Science in Liverpool, September 1923* (Liverpool, 1923), pp. 162, 165; Margaret Simey (edited by David Bingham), *From Rhetoric to Reality a Study of the Work of F.G. D'Aeth, Social Administrator* (Liverpool, 2005), pp. 5, 23, 49; Alan Brack, *All They Need Is Love* (Neston, 1983), p. 42; Picton, *Memorials of Liverpool*, vol. 2, p. 211; Thomas H. Bickerton, *A Medical History of Liverpool from the Earliest Days to the Year 1920* (Liverpool, 1936). The 128 charities were divided into six groups: medical, penitentiary, homes for the aged, pension, and miscellaneous. See 'Liverpool Charities', in William Farrer and J. Brownhill (eds.), *A History of the County of Lancaster*, vol. 4 (London, 1911), pp. 55–7.
3 Michael W. Royden, *Pioneers and Perseverance a History of the Royal School for the Blind, Liverpool 1791–1991 a Biennial Celebration* (Birkenhead, 1991); Monica Flegel, *Conceptualizing Cruelty to Children in Nineteenth-Century England Literature, Representation and the NSPCC* (Farnham, 2009), pp. 19, 39; LRO, CRU 13/1, Liverpool Society for the Prevention of Cruelty to Children Instituted April 1833, p. 6; Henry Lacey (publ.), *Pictorial Liverpool: Its Annals; Commerce; Shipping; Institutions; Public Buildings; Sights; Excursions; etc., etc. a New and Complete Handbook for Resident, Visitor, and Tourist* (2nd edn, Liverpool, 1844), p. 212; Jeffery Sydney, *The Liverpool Shipwreck and Humane Society 1839–1939* (Liverpool, 1939), p. 23; William Davis, *Hints to Philanthropists or a Collective View of Practical Means for Improving the Conditions of the Poor and Labouring Classes of Society* (Bath, 1821); LRO, 364 LWD/27, The League of Welldoers, press cuttings and correspondence, 1905–1917; F. K. Prochaska, *Women and Philanthropy in Nineteenth-Century England* (Oxford, 1980); Mary Clare Martin, 'Women and Philanthropy in Walthamstow and Leyton, 1740–1870', *London Journal*, 19 (1994), pp. 119–50.
4 Lee, 'The Socio-Economic and Demographic Characteristics of Port Cities', pp. 164–7; Iain Cooper Taylor, 'Black Spot on the Mersey: A Study of Environment and Society in the Eighteenth and Nineteenth Century', unpublished PhD, University of Liverpool (1976); 'Meeting of the Inhabitants of Liverpool: Health of Towns' Association', *Liverpool Mercury*, 25 April 1845, p. 6; John Sutherland (ed.), *The Liverpool Health of Towns' Advocate; Published under the Sanction of the Committee of the Liverpool Health of Towns' Association* (London, 1846–1847); W. M. Frazer, *Duncan of Liverpool Being an Account of the Work of Dr W. H. Duncan Medical Officer of Health of Liverpool 1847–1863* (Preston, 1997); J. Hunter Robertson, *The Present Sanatory Condition of Birkenhead* (Birkenhead, 1847); Paul Laxton, 'Fighting for Public Health: Dr. Duncan and His Adversaries, 1847–63', in Sally Sheard and Helen Power (eds.), *Body and City: Histories of Urban Public Health* (Aldershot, 2000), pp. 59–88; Humphreys, *Sin, Organized Charity and the Poor Law in Victorian England*, p. 67; 'The Greater Liverpool of Today: Story of the Great Harbour of the Mersey—Trade, Traffic, Shipping, Industries and Growth of Great Britain's Chief Entrepôt', *American European News*, II (May–June 1895), p. 64; George N. Kates (ed.), *Willa Cather in Europe* (Lincoln, NM, 1988); David Seed, *American Travellers in Liverpool* (Liverpool, 2008), p. 289; Catherine Cox, Hilary Marland and Sarah York, 'Emaciated, Exhausted and Excited: The Bodies and Minds of the Irish in Nineteenth-Century Lancashire Asylums', *Journal of Social History*, 46, 2 (2012), pp. 500–24; Peter Greaves, 'Regional Differences in the Mid-Victorian Diet and Their Impact on Health', (The Royal Society of Medical Journals) pen, *JRSM Open*, 1 March 2018; *Liverpool Mercury*, 29 April 1885; 'Distribution of Food to Poor by the Mayor

of Liverpool', *Illustrated London News*, 1886; The Joseph Sharples, *Liverpool* (Pevsner Architectural Guides) (New Haven and London, 2004), pp. 49–58; LRO, COU. 1/1, Liverpool Council of Social Service, Local Newscuttings, 1909–1913, Christmas Appeal, 16 December 1911; '*The Poor Rich Man and the Rich Poor Man', Sketches of Life and Character in Liverpool etc. by the late W. W. C, 1870–75* (no publisher, c.1880).

5 The sample consists of eight charities each from the welfare, medical, and maritime sectors. By the late 1880s, the following charitable institutions provided support for destitute or homeless children: the Girls' Preventive Home (Peel Street), the Training Home for Girls (North Hill Street), the Seamen's Orphanage (Newsham Park), the Catholic Girls' Orphanage (Falkner Street), the Boys' Home (Great George's Square), the Newsboys' Home (Everton), the Midnight Mission, the Children's Home (Edgeworth, near Bolton), the Infants' Hospital (Nile Street), and the Sheltering Home for Destitute Children (Byrom Street).

6 LRO 364 FEM 1, folios 2, 10–24; 364 FEM 2, *The Eighty-Second Annual Report of the Liverpool Female Penitentiary from January to December, 1892* (Liverpool, 1893), p. 6; Philip Howell, David Beckingham and Francesca Moore, 'Managed Zones for Sex Workers in Liverpool: Contemporary Proposals, Victorian Parallels', *Transactions of the Institute of British Geographers*, 33, 2 (2008), pp. 233–50, specifically p. 236; Marcy Kay Wilson, '"Dear Little Living Arguments": Orphans and Other Poor, Baltimore and Liverpool, 1840–1910', unpublished PhD, University of Maryland (2009), p. 102; LRO, 362 Salisbury House School; LRO,179, CRU, 13/1, Liverpool Society for the Prevention of Cruelty to Children, First Report, 1883–84, pp. 6, 14; For a useful overview of charitable provision, see Colum Giles, *Building a Better Society Liverpool's Historic Institutional Buildings* (Swindon, 2008).

7 Hugh Shimmin, 'Liverpool's Hour of Misery', *Porcupine*, 6, 19 January 1867, pp. 493–4; LRO, 362 SAL 4/1/1 (2), Female Orphan Asylum, *Report of the Liverpool Female Orphan Asylum, 28th February 1853* (Liverpool, 1853), p. 7; William Grisewood, 'The Poor of Liverpool: Notes on Their Condition, Based on an Inquiry Made by the Liverpool Central Relief and Charity Organisation Society', in idem., *Poor of Liverpool—Elberfeld System—Sundry Pamphlets* (Liverpool, 1899), pp. 25–6; The Liverpool Central Relief and Charity Organisation Society, Report, No. 136 (Liverpool, 1908); Lane, *Liverpool Gateway of Empire*, p. 81; Forwood, *Recollections*, p. 206; A. Hume, 'Analysis of the Subscribers to the Various Liverpool Charities', *THSL&C*, 7 (1854–55), pp. 22–7. Grisewood was the secretary to the Liverpool Central Aid and Charity Organization Society, honorary secretary and treasurer of the Home for Epileptics, Maghull (established in 1888), a national campaigner for improved care for the 'feeble-minded', and an admirer of the Elberfeld System of poor relief in Germany: see W. Grisewood and A. F. Hanewinkel, *Jubilee Celebrations of the Elberfeld Poor Law* (Liverpool, 1903); Kathryn Burtinshaw and John Burt, *Lunatics, Imbeciles and Idiots: A History of Insanity in Nineteenth-Century Britain and Ireland* (Barnsley, 2017), Chapter 14.

8 MAL, D/SO/2/1/1, RLSOI for the Year Ending 31st December 1869 (Liverpool, 1870), p. 8; 2/1/2, *Report of the Liverpool Orphan Seamen's Institution for the year ending 31st December 1876* (Liverpool, 1877), p. 25; 2/1/8, RLSOI for the Year Ending 31st December 1901 (Liverpool, 1902), p. 26; LRO, FEM 6 and 7, *93rd Annual Report of the Liverpool Female Penitentiary January-December 1903* (Liverpool, 1904), p. 4; 614 PAU/7/2, *St Paul's Eye Hospital Twentieth Annual Report, 1892* (Liverpool, 1893), p. 11; CHI/1/2/16, *48th Annual Report of the Liverpool Infirmary for Children, 1895* (Liverpool, 1896), pp. 5–6; Sir William B. Forwood, *Reminiscences of a Liverpool Shipowner 1850–1920* (Liverpool, 1920), p. 17.

9 LRO, 614 INF 5/6, *The One hundred and Forty-fifth Report of the Liverpool Royal Infirmary for the year 1893* (Liverpool, 1894), p. 10; MAL, D/SO/2/1/4, RLSOI for the Year Ending 31st December 1887 (Liverpool, 1888), p. 27.

10 Piper, *A Century of Service*, pp. 44–5; Orchard, *Liverpool's Legion of Honour*, pp. 259, 415, 451, 458, 533, 582; T. W. M. Lund, *The Ideal Citizen: An Appreciation of Philip Rathbone* (Liverpool, 1896), pp. 7–8. I am grateful to Joseph Sharples for bring this source to my attention.

11 Clifford Brewer, *A Brief History of the Liverpool Hahnemann (Homoeopathic) Hospital 1887–1972* (Liverpool, 1972).

12 'Liverpool: Charities', in Victorian County History, *A History of the County of Lancashire* (London, 1911), vol. 4, pp. 55–7. In the first half of the nineteenth century, 12 new charities (whether educational, medical, or welfare) were established, in contrast to 31 between 1850 and 1899. The list only covered major philanthropic institutions in Liverpool: it understates their overall development during this period and does not include similar institutions elsewhere on Merseyside.

13 Orchard, *Liverpool's Legion of Honour*, pp. 152, 156, 332, 388, 518, 523, 533–4; MAL, D/SO/1/1/6, Committee Minute Book, Liverpool Seaman's Orphan Institution, 17 June 1912, letter of 'regret' from J. Robertson; Coop and Taylor, *Bulls and Bears*; Pike, *Contemporary Biographies*. One hundred thirty-one merchants (or 21.3 per cent of Orchard's sample) failed to demonstrate any public involvement of this nature, although there may have been an element of under-reporting. It should be noted that Edward Percy Bates, the son of Sir Percy Edward Bates, who had been born in 1845 was only to be met 'in connection with polo and every kind of fashionable amusement'.

14 MAL/LH/3/2/1, Liverpool Sailor's Home, General Committee, Minutes, 9 March 1852; 1 October 1852; 22 December 1852; P/CC/SF/1/3, Liverpool Seamen's Friend Society, 90th Report of the Liverpool Seamen's Friend Society, 1 January–31 December 1911, p. 7; D/SO/2/1/3, RLSOI for the Year Ending 31st December 1882 (Liverpool, 1883), p. 24; LRO, 614 CHI/1/2/4, Liverpool Infirmary for Children, Report for Year 1862 (Liverpool, 1863), p. 10; MAL, D/SO/4/2/3, Liverpool Seamen's Orphan Institution, Treasurer's Letter Books, J. Poole, E. Beazley, 8 November 1895–6 May 1913; A. L. M. Cock, *Liverpool's Northern Hospital 1834–1978* (Liverpool, 1981), p. 40; LRO, M364/14/53, League of Welldoers, bogus collections, 20 November 1906.

15 LRO, FEM 2, The Eighty-Second Annual Report of the Liverpool Female Penitentiary from January to December, 1892 (Liverpool, 1893), Special General Meeting, p. 2; MAL, D/SO/2/1/3, RLSOI for the Year Ending 31st December 1883 (Liverpool 1884), p. 24; LRO, 920 DUR 1/2, George Holt, 16 June 1846; MAL, DSO/6/6/5, List of Executive Committee members and times convenient for meetings, c.1908; LRO, 614 INF 2/12, Board of Economy of Liverpool Royal Infirmary, 1 July 1880–24 December 1895; INF 2/13, Liverpool Royal Infirmary Board of Economy, 9 January 1896–12 December 1907; MAL, D/LH/3/3/3, Liverpool Sailors' Home, Management Committee, minutes of Sub-Committee, 3 October 1876–31 December 1895, Attendance of Committee at Sailors Home 1888–1895.

16 LRO 614 INF 5/10, Report of the Liverpool Royal Infirmary, 1902 (Liverpool, 1903), pp. 7, 71–2; *"In Memoriam" or, Funeral Records of Liverpool Celebrities, Containing many Interesting Reminiscences of Local Men* (Liverpool, 1876), Introduction; MAL, P/CC/LH/1/2/1, Liverpool Sailors' Home, 68th Annual Report for the year 1911 (Liverpool 1912), p. 8; LRO, 614 PRI/9/4, Home for Incurables, Thirty-Seventh Annual Report, 1906 (Liverpool, 1907), p. 18; MAL, D/SO/2/1/1, RLSOI for the Year Ending 31st December 1873 (Liverpool, 1874), p. 14; D/SO/2/1/4, Liverpool Seamen's Orphan Institution, Annual Report for the year ending 31st December 1887 (Liverpool, 1888), p. 24; Orchard, *Liverpool's Legion of Honour*, p. 159; D/SO/2/1/6, Liverpool Seamen's Orphan Institution, Annual Report for the year ending 31st December 1905 (Liverpool, 1906), p. 34; D/LH/3/2/3, Liverpool Sailor's Home, Committee Book, 1912; Grisewood, *The Poor of Liverpool*, p. 25. In 1898, 52 per cent of the subscribers to 83 leading charities only supported one institution.

17 D/SO/5/17–20, letter from Hugh Shimmin, 1878, who felt 'something akin to contempt for those who while professing Christian principles, do dishonour to the great cause for which the Saviour died' by criticising the management of the charity without submitting their concerns to the committee; D/SO/5/1/2/25, letter from A. Balfour, 18 March 1878; D/SO/5/1, 34, letter of James Beazley to Balfour, 16 March 1885; D/SO/7/1/45, events leading to the resignation of Chairman R.G. Allan and his wife, 1903.

18 Moore, 'The Art of philanthropy', p. 68; Martin Gorsky, *Patterns of Philanthropy: Charity and Society in Nineteenth-Century Bristol* (Woodbridge, 1999), p. 149; Morris, 'Clubs, Societies and Associations', p. 420; LRO, 362 Turner Memorial Home of Rest, Dingle; Jan Alexander MacGregor, 'In Search of Ethnicity: Jewish and Celtic Identities in Liverpool and Glasgow 1850–1900', unpublished MPhil thesis, University of Liverpool (2003), p. 69; Smithers, *Liverpool Its Commerce, Statistics and Institutions*, p. 244; John Belchem, 'The Immigrant Alternative: Ethnic and Sectarian Mutuality among the Liverpool Irish during the Nineteenth Century', in O. Ashton, R. Fyson and S. Roberts (eds.), *The Duty of Discontent: Essays for Dorothy Thompson* (London, 1995), pp. 231–50; Patricia Runaghan, *Father Nugent's Liverpool 1849–1905* (Birkenhead, 2003); R. B. Walker, 'Religious Changes in Liverpool in the Nineteenth Century', *The Journal of Ecclesiastical History*, 19, 2 (1968), pp. 195–211; Frank Neal, *Sectarian Violence: The Liverpool Experience, 1819–1914* (Manchester, 1998); LRO, 362 SAL 4/1/1 (2), Report of the Liverpool Female Orphan Asylum, 24th February 1851 (Liverpool, 1851), p. 10; C. A. Piper, *A Century of Service: The Story of the Liverpool North End Domestic Mission Society's First Hundred Years 1859–1959* (Liverpool, 1959), p. 8.

19 Garrett, *Loving Counsels*, p. 125; Orchard, *Liverpool's Legion of Honour*, pp. 428, 538, 593, 656. Garrett started his ministry in Liverpool in 1849 and died in 1900, a few months after having stood down as the president of the Wesleyan Conference. He led the Liverpool Mission and was instrumental in

founding the British Workmen House Ltd., which established over 80 'cocoa' houses throughout Liver-pool. See Rev. Marshall Randles, 'The Late Rev. Charles Garrett', *The Wesleyan-Methodist Magazine*, 123 (December 1900), pp. 925–7; Roger Standing, 'Charles Garrett and the Birth of the Wesleyan Central Mission Movement', *Wesley and Methodist Studies*, 6 (2014), pp. 89–123.

20 Orchard, *Liverpool's Legion of Honour*, p. 727.

21 Gertrude Himmelfarb, 'The Age of Philanthropy', *Wilson Quarterly*, 21, 2 (1997), pp. 48–56; LRO, 920 DUR 1/2, Holt Family, family diaries, 11 November 1844–31 December 1854, 14 June 1846.

22 Jo Littler, 'The New Victorians? Celebrity Charity and the Demise of the Welfare State', *Celebrity Studies*, 6, 4 (2015), pp. 471–85; June Rose, *For the Sake of the Children: Inside Dr. Barnardo's, 120 Years of Caring for Children* (London, 1987); Felix C. Robb, 'George Peabody (1795–1869)', *Peabody Journal of Education*, 70, 1 (The Legacy of George Peabody: Special Bicentenary) (1994), pp. 17–32; Franklin Parker, *George Peabody: A Biography* (Nashville, 1995); Christine Wagg and James McHugh, *Homes for London: The George Peabody Story* (London, 2017); Anthony S. Wohl, 'Octavia Hill and the Homes of the London Poor' *The Journal of British Studies*, 10, 2 (1971), pp. 105–31; Gillian Darley, *Octavia Hill: A Life* (London, 1990); Charlotte Gray, 'Dr. Thomas Barnardo's Orphans Were Shipping 500 km to Save Body and Soul', *CMA Journal*, 121 (6 October 1979), pp. 981–7; Marjorie Kohli, *The Golden Bridge: Young Immigrants to Canada, 1833–1939* (Toronto, 2003); Jacqueline Banerjee, 'Dr. Barnardo and His Work for Children', *The Victorian Web* (www.victorianweb.org.history.orphanages.barnardo's); Jane Garnett, 'At Home in the Metropolis: Gender and the Ideal of Service', in Elizabeth Baigent and Ben Cowell (eds.), *'Nobler Imaginings and Mightier Struggles': Octavia Hill, Social Activism, and the Remaking of British Society* (Institute of Historical Research) (London, 2016), p. 243. Between 1882 and the end of the 1920s, Barnardo's sent almost 27,000 children to Canada. For some orphans assisted emigration offered new opportunities, but many were subject to abuse and ill treatment. For an overview of this issue, see Marjorie Harper and Stephen Constantine, *Migration and Empire* (Oxford History of the British Empire, Companion Series) (Oxford, 2010).

23 Matthew Bishop and Michael Green, *Philanthrocapitalism: How the Rich Can Save the World and Why We Should Let Them* (New York, 2008); Dominic Sandrook, 'Why Don't Britain's Rich Give to Charity Like Wealthy Americans', *Mail Online*, 20 December 2010; Robert H. Bremner, *Giving: Charity and Philanthropy in History* (New Jersey, 1994), p. 121; Keith A. Francis, 'Fundraising Theology? Anglican Charity Sermons and Nineteenth-Century Social Causes', in Marilyn D. Button and Jessica A. Sheetz-Nquyen (eds.), *Victorians and the Case for Charity: Essays on Responses to English Poverty by the State, the Church and the Liberals* (North Carolina, 2004), pp. 94–120; Daniel Siegel, *Charity and Condescension: Victorian Literature and the Dilemma of Philanthropy* (Series in Victorian Studies, vol. 1) (Athens, Ohio University Press, 2012); 'Grand Fancy Dress Ball', *LM*, 15 February 1860, p. 4.

24 For more detailed information on Tate's business operations, see Tom Jones, *Henry Tate, 1819–199: A Biographical Sketch* (London, 1960); J. A. Watson, *A Hundred Years of Sugar Refining: The Story of Love Lane Refinery 1872–1972* (Liverpool, 1973); Antony Hughill, *Sugar and All That: A History of Tate and Lyle* (London, 1978); Phillipe Chalmin, *The Making of a Sugar Giant: Tate and Lyle, 1859–1989* (trans. by Erica Long-Michalke) (Chur, 1990).

25 Roger Munting, 'Tate, Sir Henry, First Baronet', https://doi.org/10.1093/ref:odnb/26984; Frances Spalding, *The Tate A History* (London, 1998), pp. 12–13; *South London Press*, 18 June 1898, 13 January 1900; *Evening Star*, 6 December 1899; *The Lambeth Field Club*, 16 July 1904; Hughill, *Sugar and All That*, p. 44; Colin M. Lewis, *British Railways in Argentina, 1857–1914: A Case Study of Foreign Investment* (London, 1983), p. 218; Charles Jones, 'Who Invested in Argentina and Uruguay?', *Business Archives*, 48, NS, 4, 4 (1982), p. 11. The early 1890s would have been a promising time to invest in Argentine railway companies because stock prices were lower than before the Baring Crisis (1890) and London had an active secondary market in the shares of the main railway companies. Two photographs of British-built locomotives in Argentina from c.1894 are included in an excellent volume by M. H. J. Finch, *South American Steam* (Truro, 1974), p. 24. Tate may well have sold some of his original shares by the mid-1890s. I am grateful to my friends and former colleagues Rory Miller and Henry Finch for this information.

26 Calmin, *The Making of a Sugar Giant*, pp. 55–6; Munting, 'Tate, Sir Henry'.

27 Amy Woodson-Boulton, 'The Art of Compromise the Founding of the National Gallery of British Art, 1890–1892', *Museum and Society*, 2, 3 (2003), pp. 147–69; Michael Craton, 'The Transition from Slavery to Free Wage Labour in the Caribbean, 1780–1890: A Survey with Particular Reference to Recent Scholarship', *Slavery & Abolition*, 13, 2 (1992), p. 45; H. Tinker, *A New System of Slavery,*

the Export of Indian Labour Overseas, 1833–1920 (London, 1974); S. A. Singh, 'Historiography of Indians in the Caribbean', *Journal of Caribbean History* (2015); Pieter C. Emmer, '"A Spirit of Independence" or Lack of Education for the Market? Freedman and Asian Indentured Labourers in the Post-Emancipation Caribbean', in Howard Temperly (ed.), *After Slavery: Emancipation and Its Discontents* (London, 2000), pp. 150–68; R. W. Beachey, *British and West Indian Sugar Industry in the 19th Century* (Oxford, 1957); Belinda Coate, *Poverty and the Sugar Industry* (Oxfam Public Affairs Unit) (Oxford, 1987); 'The Richmond Cavendish Co. Ltd.', *LM*, 1 January 1867; 'The Richmond Cavendish Company, Annual General Meeting', 1 March 1870. On the other hand, the evidence for direct link between refined sugar consumption and diabetes did not begin to emerge until after 1906, with case studies of wealthy Bengali residents in Calcutta and from other countries. See R. Charles (later Sir Richard Havelock Charles), 'Diabetes in the Tropics', *British Medical Journal*, 19 (1907), pp. 1051–64; Richard J. Johnson, Laura Sánchez-Lozada, Peter Andrew and Michael A. Lanaspa, 'Perspective: A Historical and Scientific Perspective of Sugar and Its Relation with Obesity and Diabetes', *Advances in Nutrition*, 8, 3 (2017), pp. 412–22. For the long-term legacy of Caribbean (Barbadian) slavery, see Andrea Stuart, *Sugar in the Blood: A Family's Story of Slavery and Empire* (London, 2012). Given the widespread dissemination of pro-emancipation publicity in America and its reporting in Britain, it would have been surprising if Tate did not know of the extent to which the sale of slaves and the breaking up of families was almost entirely driven by profit motives. See Michael Tadman, *Speculators and Slaves: Masters, Traders, and Slaves in the Old South* (Madison, 1989), pp. 133–78, which remains an important work in this field.

28 'Homoeopathic Dispensary', *Liverpool Mercury*, 27 January 1873, p. 3; Clifford Brewer, *A Brief History of the Liverpool Hahnemann (Homoeopathic) Hospital, 1887–1987* (Liverpool, 1987); Robert Ainsworth and Graham Jones, *In the Footsteps of Peter Ellis: Architect of Oriel Chambers and 16 Cook Street* (Liverpool History Society) (Liverpool, 2013), pp. 189–92, 200–2; Sue Young Histories the Liverpool Homeopathic Hospital, 25 November 2009 (www.sueyounghistories.com.2009-11-25); Anna Bosanquet and Maria Lorentzon, 'Patients at the London Homoeopathic Hospital, 1889–1923', *British Homoeopathic Journal*, 86 (1997), p. 166; 'Homoeopathic Dispensary', *Liverpool Mercury*, 27 January 1873, p. 3; Bernard Leary, 'Homoeopathic Prescribing in the Late 19th Century', *Journal of the History of Medicine*, 83, 4 (1994), p. 243; LRO, HAH, 8/2/1, *Report of The Liverpool Homoeopathic Dispensary Instigated for the Gratuitous Relief of the Sick Poor from December 31st, 1871 to December 31st, 1872* (Liverpool, 1872).

29 LRO, HAH, 8/2/1, *Fortieth Annual Report of the Liverpool Homoeopathic Dispensary Instituted for the Gratuitous Relief of the Sick Poor, 1881* (Liverpool, 1882), 26 January 1882 (letter from Henry Tate, London, 25 January); HAH, 8/2/2, *Fiftieth Annual Report of the Liverpool Hahnemann Hospital and Homoeopathic Dispensaries, 1891* (Liverpool, 1892), p. 45. For further details on F. &G. Holme, see Martin Greaney, *Liverpool: A Landscape History* (Liverpool, 2013).

30 Leary, 'Cholera and Homoeopathy', p. 191 for the classic description of the moral implications of miasmas in Charles Dickens, *Dombey and Son* (London, 1970), vol. 2, p. 255; Philip A. Nicholls, *Homeopathy and the Medical Profession* (London and New York, 1988); Irvine Loudon, 'A Brief History of Homeopath', *Journal of the Royal Society of Medicine*, 99, 12 (2006), pp. 607–10; The statistical data was extracted from the relevant annual reports of the LHD and the Hahnemann Hospital.

31 Jones, *Henry Tate*, p. 28; Munting, 'Tate, Sir Henry'; *LM*, 'Liverpool Police Court the Smoke Nuisance', 29 May 1862, p. 5; 'Liverpool Police Court', 11 June 1863, p. 5; 'Municipal Elections', 13 October 1863; 'The Municipal Elections for 1863', 21 October 1863; 'Grand Fancy Dress Ball', 2 March 1864, pp. 5–6; 'Meeting of the Friends of Mr. John Rogers', 21 October 1864; 'South Lancashire Election Meeting of the Liberal Electors at the Amphitheatre', 12 July 1865; 'Town Council', 10 November 1865; 'Banquet at the Town Hall', 28 January 1868, p. 3; 'Testimonial to the Right Hon. W. E. Gladstone, M.P.', 15 March 1869, p. 3; 'Administrative Changes: An Appeal to the Benevolent', 19 February 1874; 'Funeral of the Late Mr. J. H. Macrae', 10 April 1874, p. 3; 'Farewell Dinner to Lt.-Colonel Trimble', 14 January 1875, p. 7; 'Liverpool Police Court, Smoke Cases', 4 February 1875, p. 8; 'Local News, Liverpool Land Company, 13th Annual General Meeting', 19 March 1875.

32 *LM*, 'The Liverpool Society of Fine Arts', 30 October 1858; Jones, *Henry Tate*, p. 32; Jessica Moody, 'The Memory of Slavery in Liverpool in Public Discourse from the Nineteenth Century to the Present Day', unpublished PhD, University of York (2014); Esi Edugyan, *Washington Black* (London, 2018), pp. 414–4. See the case studies in Katie Donnington, Ryan Hanley and Jessica Moody (eds.), *Britain's History and Memory of Transatlantic Slavery: Local Nuisances of a 'National Sin'* (Studies in International Slavery, 11) (Liverpool, 2016); Jessica Moody, *The Persistence of Memory: Remembering*

Slavery in Liverpool, 'Slaving Capital of the World' (Studies in International Slavery, 18) (Liverpool, 2020); Lucy Ball, 'Memory, Myth and Forgetting: The British Transatlantic Slave Trade', unpublished DPhil thesis, University of Portsmouth, 2013.

33 Spalding, *The Tate*, pp. 13–14; *LM*, 'Letters to the Editors', 2 March 1880, p. 3.

34 C. W. Sutton (revised by Fiona Wood), 'Walker, Sir Andrew Barclay, First Baronet (1824–1893)', https://doi.org/10.1093/ref.odnb/28468.

35 Giles Waterfield, *The People's Galleries: Art Museums and Exhibitions in Britain, 1800–1914* (Yale, 2015); Amy Woodson-Boulton, *Transformative Beauty: Art Museums in Industrial Britain* (Stanford, 2012); 'Victorian Museums and Victorian Society', *History Compass*, 6, 1 (2008), pp. 109–46; 'A Window onto Nature: Visual Language, Aesthetic Ideology, and the Art of Social Transformation', in Amy Woodson-Boulton and Minsoo King (eds.), *Visions of the Industrial Age, 1830–1914: Modernity and the Anxiety of Representation* (Aldershot, 2008), pp. 139–61; Christopher Whitehead, *The Public Art Museum in Nineteenth-Century-Britain: The Development of the National Gallery* (Perspectives on Collecting, 1) (Aldershot, 2005); Jesús-Pedro Lorente, 'Galleries of Modern Art in Nineteenth-Century Paris and London: Their Location and Urban Influence', *UH*, 22, 2 (1995), pp. 187–204.

36 Edward Morris, 'The Formation of the Gallery of Art in the Liverpool Royal Institution, 1816–1819', *THSL&C*, 142 (1992), p. 88; James Moore, 'The Art of philanthropy? The Formation and Development of the Walker Art Gallery in Liverpool', *Museum and Society*, 2, 2 (2004), p. 70; Katy Layton-Jones and Robert Lee, *Places of Health and Amusement: Liverpool's Historic Parks and Gardens* (Swindon, 2008), p. 25.

37 'Sir William Brown, of Liverpool', *The Sydney Morning Herald*, 25 May 1869, p. 3; Orchard, *Liverpool's Legion of Honour*, pp. 212–13; Robert Veitch, 'Civic Patriotism; or, Studies in Liverpool Citizen Life', IV.—Sir William Brown', in R. A. Armstrong, C. F. Aked and Robert Veitch (eds.), *The Liverpool Pulpit*, 4 (1895), pp. 29–31. In 1856, Brown offered to double his original offer if a further sum was given by others. Unsurprisingly, there was no response: he covered the whole cost of the development (£40,000), with the corporation contributing £25,000, largely by acquiring the site for the new library and museum. Brown was the founder of the banking house Brown, Shipley, and Co.; his business 'continued to prosper mightily' at one stage controlling one sixth of all Anglo-American trade, including raw cotton imports, and, by implication, his wealth was based to a large extent on the exploitation of slave labour. Although one of the port-city's 'greatest merchants' with a 'handsome income', he conducted deals in his private office and did not 'frequent the Flags'.

38 Moore, 'The Art of Philanthropy?', pp. 70–2; *The Walker Art Gallery* (with a Foreword by David Fleming and Julian Treuherz) (London, 1994), p. 10; Annemarie McAllister, 'Temperance Periodicals', in A. King, A. Easley and J. Morton (eds.), *Routledge Handbook to Nineteenth-Century British Periodicals and Newspapers* (London, 2016), pp. 342–54; 'On the Temperance Movement', www.branchcollective.org.>ps_articles=annemarieMcAllister; Joseph Livesey, *The Life and Teachings of Joseph Livesey, Comprising His Autobiography with an Introductory Review . . . by John Pearce* (London, 1885), p. 66; 'Temperance Meeting', *LM*, 17 October 1834, p. 8; 'Temperance Festival, *LM*, 21 July 1837, p. 8; 'Grand Temperance Industrial Exhibition and Festival', *LM*, 12 May 1856, p. 3. For an overview of the temperance movement, see Lilian Lewis Shiman, *Crusade against Drink in Victorian England* (London, 1988); Brian Harrison, *Drink and the Victorians: The Temperance Question in England 1815 to 1872* (Keele, 1994); Thora Hands, *Drinking in Victorian and Edwardian Britain: Beyond the Spectre of the Drunkard* (Basingstoke, 2018) (e-book). For Liverpool, see P. T. Winskill and Joseph Thomas, *A History of the Temperance Movement in Liverpool and District from Its Introduction in 1829 Down to the Year 1887* (Liverpool, 1887); R. B. Rose, 'John Finch, 1784–1857 a Liverpool Disciple of Robert Owen', *THSL&C*, 139 (1957), pp.159–184. By the early 1890s, the 203 parishes of the Liverpool Church of England diocese had a total of 297 temperance branches: for adults (128), juveniles (149), and for women (20). See James Clifford Dunn, 'A Force to Be Reckoned with? The Temperance Movement and the "Drink Question"', MPhil, University of Central Lancashire (1999), p. 20.

39 'The Municipal Election', *LM*, 26 September 1873, p. 6; 'Summary', *LM*, 11 November 1873, p. 6; 'Local News', *LM*, 1 December 1873, p. 6; 'Liverpool Town Council', *LM*, 10 November 1876; 'Knighthood of the Mayor', *LM*, 6 November 1877, p. 6; Orchard, *Liverpool's Legion of Honour*, pp. 67, 194–5, 223–7, 281–3, 368–9; Peter Turner Winskill, *Temperance Standard Bearers of the Nineteenth Century: A Biographical and Statistical Temperance Dictionary*, (Manchester and Liverpool, 1898), vol. 2, p. 47; James Clifford Dunn, 'A Force to Be Reckoned with? The Temperance Movement and the "Drink Question", 1895–1933', unpublished MPhil, University of Central Lancashire (1999),

p. 20. Some Roman Catholics were also active in the Temperance Movement, including John H. Holmes, a lithographic printer, who was one of the founders of the Liverpool Catholic Teetotal Crusade and Speaker's Guild.

40 'The Walker Fine-Art Gallery, Liverpool', *The Illustrated London News*, 8 September 1877, pp. 17–18; Moore, 'The Art of Philanthropy?', p. 74; Orchard, *Liverpool's Legion of Honour*, pp. 171, 357, 503, 512, 576, 690, 687; Wayne Clarke, *A Ready Man: Hugh Stowell Brown: Preacher, Activist, Friend of the Poor* (Watford, 2019); Rev. John Jones, *The Slain in Liverpool during 1864 by Drink Including Social, Medical and Criminal Statistic of Drunkenness* (Liverpool, 1865); *Hugh Stowell Brown, A Memorial Volume Edited by His Son-in-Law W. S. Caine M.P.* (London, 1888); Garrett, *Loving Counsels*, pp. 167, 256; Winskill, *Temperance Standard Bearers of the Nineteenth Century*, p. 43; Veitch, 'Civic Patriotism', vol. 4 (1895), pp. 5–8.

41 *The Times*, 28 August 1866; *First Report from the Select Committee of the House of Lords on Intemperance Together with the Minutes of Evidence and An Appendix* (London, 1877), pp. 334–5, Appendix C, Papers handed in by Mr. (William) Rathbone, 27 February 1877, in reply to Question 264; Naomi Williams and Graham Mooney, 'Infant Mortality in an "Age of Great Cities": London and the English Provincial Cities Compared, c.1840–1910', *Continuity and Change*, 9, 2 (1994), pp. 185–212; Simon Szreter and M. Woolcock, 'Health by Association? Social Capital, Social Theory, and the Political Economy of Public Health', *International Journal of Epidemiology*, 33 (2004), pp. 750–67; I. Gregory, 'Different Places, Different Stories: Infant Mortality Decline in England and Wales, 1851–1911', *Annals of the Association of American Geographers*, 98, 4 (2008), pp. 733–94; Hannatiis Jaddla and Alice Read, 'The Geography of Early Childhood Mortality in England and Wales, 1881–1911', *Demographic Research*, 37, 5 Article 58 (12 December 2017), pp. 1861–90; David Beckingham, 'Gender, Space, and Drunkenness: Liverpool's Licensed Premises, 1860–1914', *Annals of the Association of American Geographers*, 102, 3 (2012), p. 653. The data supplied by Rathbone related to 20 towns north of Birmingham with a population of 50,000 or more for the year ending 29 September 1873. For a wider discussion of 'sailortown', see Robert Lee, 'The Seafarers' Urban World: A Critical Review', *IJMH*, 25, 1 (2013), pp. 23–64; Graeme Milne, *People, Place and Power on the Nineteenth-Century Waterfront: Sailortown* (Basingstoke, 2016).

42 Orchard, *Liverpool's Legion of Honour*, pp. 689–92; Alistair Mutch, 'Manchester and Liverpool Public Houses Compared, 1840–1914', *Manchester Region History Review* (2003), pp. 22–9; 'Magistrates and Public House Managers, 1840–1914: Another Case of Liverpool Exceptionalism?', *Northern History*, 40 (2003), pp. 325–42; 'Public Houses as Multiple Retailing: Peter Walker & Son 1846–1914', *Business History*, 48 (2006), pp. 1–19; 'The Design of Liverpool Pubs in the Nineteenth Century', *Journal of the Brewery History Society*, 127 (2008), pp. 1–26; 'Brewing in the North West 1840–1914: Sowing the Seeds of Service Sector Management?', *Manchester Region History Review*, 21 (2010), pp. 69–86; *The Walker Art Gallery*, p. 10; 'Latest and Telegraphic News Local Patents, *LM*, 26 February 1876, p. 7.

43 Veitch, 'Civic Patriotism', p. 6; Terence R. Gourvish and Richard G. Wilson, *The British Brewing Industry 1830–1980* (Cambridge, 1994), pp. 70–1; Mutch, 'Brewing in the North West', pp. 8–9; Orchard, *Liverpool's Legion of Honour*, p. 644; Veitch, 'Civic Patriotism', p. 8; Walter Besant and James Rice, *The Seamy Side* (London, 1881), Chapter 5, 'The Journal of a Deserted Wife'; Giles Waterfield, *The People's Galleries: Art Museums and Exhibitions in Britain 1800–1914* (New Haven and London, 2016), p. 259.

44 Charles Harvey, Mairi Maclean and Roy Suddaby, 'Historical Perspectives on Entrepreneurship and Philanthropy', *Business History Review*, 93, 3, 1 (2019), pp. 446, 469; Alice Shepherd and Steven Toms, 'Entrepreneurship Strategy, and Business Philanthropy: Cotton Textiles in the British Industrial Revolution', *Business History Review*, 93, 3 (2019), pp. 503–27; Brian Bloice and Daphne Marchant, *'Park Hill', Streatham* (London, 2004) (published by the Streatham Society).

45 Rothery, 'The Wealth of the English Landed Gentry', pp. 253–4; Thompson, 'Life after Death', p. 42; S. A. J. Keibeck, 'From Probate Inventories to Households: Correcting the Probate Record for Wealth Bias', Working Paper, Cambridge University, 1/2016. For example, prior to the marriage of the broker Robert Hinshaw to Elizabeth Stockley (widow) in October 1877, £15,000 of consolidated stock in the London and North Western Railway (with a value of £22,000) was put in a trust which would continue after his death with beneficial interest to his widow. See LRO 920 MD 76, Marriage settlement, 20 October 1877; Indenture (Legacy and Succession Duty Office, Somerset House, London 3 May 1898.

46 Murch, 'Reflexivity', p. 20; *Liverpool Daily Post*, 28 February 1893; Graeme Milne, 'North of England Shipowners and Their Business Connections', in Lewis R. Fischer and Even Lange (eds.),

International Merchant Shipping in the Nineteenth and Twentieth Centuries: The Comparative Dimension (Research in Maritime History, No. 37) (St. John's, Newfoundland, 2008), p. 157. Originally, Osmaston Manor had 70 rooms, together with a bake house, a wash house, and a brewing house. It had a subterranean railway and hot air central heating and came with 3,500 acres including parkland which had been laid out with advice from Joseph Paxton. The annual rent roll yielded £6,000. The Grange at Gateacre contained 21 bedrooms, several drawing rooms, a library, a music room, a billiards room, and a smoking room. See Beryl Plant and Mike Chitty, *Gateacre and Belle Vue* (Stroud, 2012). The principal rooms of Walker's steam yacht were designed by (Sir) Ernest George and Harold Ainsworth Peto, with the ceilings painted by G. F. Malins: they deliberately ignored any maritime connotations and treated them just like a high-quality domestic interior. It had an extensive library, which offered lighter reading for guests, including a new edition of the book by Walter Besant and James Rice, *The Seamy Side: A Story* (London, 1881), the front cover suitably inscribed 'S. Yacht Cuhona'. See Joanna Banham (ed.), *Encylopedia of Interior Design*, vols. 1–2, A-Z (London and New York, 1997), p. 485. Walker was regarded as a 'good yachtsman': together with his son, Andrew, he owned several yachts, including the large racing yacht *Ailsa*: he also presented the Barclay-Walker Challenge Cup to the North Shannon Yacht Club for half-deckers, colleens, and half-raters.

47 Orchard, *Liverpool's Legion of Honour*, p. 691; 'The Walker Art Gallery, Liverpool', *Graphic*, 8 August 1874, p. 8; Waterfield, *The People's Galleries*, p. 259; Edward Morris, *Public Art Collections in North West England: A History and Guide* (Liverpool, 2001), pp. 88–9; *The Walker Art Gallery*, pp. 10–11; C. W. Sutton, 'Walker, Sir Andrew Barclay'; The University of Liverpool, A Description of the Harrison-Hughes Engineering Laboratories Opened on Saturday, May 18, 1912 by the Right Honourable The Viscount Haldane of Cloan also A Brief Description of The Walker Engineering Laboratories (Liverpool, 1912); V. M. Leveaux, *The History of the Derbyshire General Infirmary, 1810–1894* (Cromford, 1999); Paul Elliott, 'The Derbyshire General Infirmary and the Derby Philosophers: The Application of Industrial Architecture and Technology to Medical Institutions in Early-Nineteenth Century England', *Medical History*, 46, 1 (2002), pp. 65–92.

48 Bruce Ingham, *Henry Tate* (London, 2015); Munting, 'Tate'. The major donations to University College, Liverpool included £5,000 as a contribution to additional income (1883); £3,000 for fellowships and scholarships in memory of his friend, Rev. Charles Beard (1888); £20,000 for a new library (subsequently known as the Tate Library) with further grants of £5,500 (1890) and £5,000 (1896) for providing standard works and to update its stock; £1,000 for the creation of technical science scholarships (1890); and £5,000 for the establishment of a University Training College and Hostel to enable 'alert' elementary schoolmasters to benefit from access to university education. For further details, see Jones, *Henry Tate*, pp. 28–30; *The University of Liverpool Calendar 1905* (Liverpool, 1905), pp. 373–4, 387–8.

49 See Sari Mäenpää, Chapter 6.

50 Orchard, *Liverpool's Legion of Honour*, pp. 152–5, 250, 534–5, 662–3, 690–1.

51 MLP Database; 'The Florence Boys' Institute: A Noble Gift', *LM*, 12 December 1888, p. 6. Part of Bernard Hall's fortune was derived from the slave trade if only indirectly, since his wife (Mary Ann Titley) had been born in Kingston, Jamaica, the daughter of the merchant William Titley, who was the awardee in the case of nine claims in Kingston, St. Elizabeth, St. Ann, and St. Thomas-in-the-Vale, either in his own name or as a trustee and guardian. See 'William Titley', *Legacies of British Slave-Ownership Database*, www.depts-live.ucl.ac.uk/lbs/person/view/16930 [accessed 29th September 2020]. The Gordon Working-Class Lads' Institute was named to commemorate in perpetuity Major-General Charles Gordon who had been killed at the battle of Khartoum in 1885. Another example of a benefaction designed to memorialise family members was the Gregson Memorial Institute and Museum, commissioned by Isabella Gregson and designed by A. P. Fry in 1895 in memory of her parents and other relatives, possibly including her grandfather Matthew Gregson (1749–1824), a highly successful upholsterer and property speculator, who played an important role in Liverpool's cultural development in the early nineteenth century. See Giles, *Building a Better Society*, pp. 46–7.

52 MMMMAL, DX/504/4/1/1, 2/2–5, Correspondence and newscuttings concerning J. Bruce Ismay and the Earl of Derby, regarding the Liverpool Seamen's Pension Fund by the Mercantile Marine (widows) Fund and the Titanic Relief Fund, 11 May 1912; Newscuttings, *Courier*, 29 April and 9 May 1912; DX/504/6/1–12, Papers regarding the will of J. Bruce Ismay (1912–17); Alan Scarth, *Titanic and Liverpool* (Liverpool, 2009), p. 195; F. Wilson, *How to Survive the Titanic, or, the Sinking of J. Bruce Ismay* (2011). After some discussion, a separate Titanic Fund was set up in Liverpool, once it was agreed that it 'must command a greater support than that given to a sectional charity', but there were

fears on the part of the Liverpool Trades and Labour Council that money subscribed for those who had suffered from the disaster 'would not only be boarded up, but fenced off from them'. Dawpool, Thurstaston, 'a fine and acknowledged masterpiece' according to *Country Life*, had been designed and built by Richard Norman Shaw (1882–86) at a reputed cost of £50,000, the estate with its 390 acres having been acquired by Thomas Henry Ismay in 1877. It was intended to be a 'pleasure building', but never fulfilled the original expectations. The family of J. Bruce Ismay moved out in 1907 because it was 'surplus to requirements' and it was eventually demolished in 1927.

53 MMMMAL, B/AW/3–1, 2–24, Valuation of Estate of Alexander Elder, died 25 January 1915, aged 81; Crosbie Smith, 'Witnessing Power: John Elder and the Making of the Marine Compound Engine, 1850–1858', *Technology and Culture*, 55, 1 (2014), pp. 76–106. For an overview of the history and development of Elder Dempster & Co., the study by Peter N. Davies, *The Trade Makers: Elder Dempster in West Africa, 1852–1972, 1973–1989* (St. John's, Newfoundland, 2000) remains indispensable.

54 John Nickson, 'Britain Needs to Return to the Victorian Tradition of Philanthropy', *The Financial Times*, 7 July 2013. The Victorian emphasis on memorialisation, whether of monarchs, writers, military engagements, or pets, has been well researched: see, for example, Tom Smith, '"A Grand Work of Noble Conception": The Victoria Memorial and Imperial London', in Felix Driver and David Gilbert (eds.), *Imperial Cities Landscape, Display and Identity* (Manchester), Chapter 2; Christopher A. Whatley, 'Robert Burns: Memorialisation and the "Heart-beating" of Victorian Scotland', in Murray Pittock (ed.), *Robert Burns in Global Culture* (Langham, Maryland, 2011), pp. 204–28; Mary Connelly and Peter Donaldson, 'South African War (1899–1902) Memorials in Britain: A Case Study of Memorialization in London and Kent', *War and Society*, 29, 1 (2010), pp. 20–46; Teres Maguire, 'Animal Angst: Victorians Memorialize Their Pets', in Deborah Denenholz Morse and Martin A. Danahay (eds.), *Victorian Animal Dreams: Representation of Animals in Victorian Literature and Culture (Nineteenth Century)* (Aldershot, 2007), pp. 15–34.

55 'The Florence Boys' Institute: A Noble Gift', *LM*, 12 December 1888, p. 6; 'The Gordon Institute', *LM*, 29 July 1885, p. 6; 'Gordon Institute to the Editors of the Liverpool Mercury', *LM*, 29 August 1885, p. 7; 'Gordon Working Lads' Institute', *LM*, 1 June 1886, p. 6 (First Annual Meeting); Prochaska, 'Philanthropy', pp. 357–95; Warren, *Steel, Ships and Men*, pp. 91–3; 'Shipbuilding on the Mersey', *The Cardiff Times*, 28 November 1862, p. 3; 'Liberal Offer by Mr. John Laird', *LM*, 20 December 1861, p. 7; 'Birkenhead Borough Hospital', *LM*, 23 November 1863, p. 3; 'Birkenhead Government School of Art', *LM*, 3 February 1863, p. 6; 'Birkenhead School (Government) of Arts', *LM*, 16 February 1870, p. 6; Kevin Moore, *The Mersey Ship Repairers: Life and Work in a Port Industry* (Liverpool, 1988), p. 68; Robert Humphreys, *Sin, Organized Charity and the Poor Law in Victorian England* (Basingstoke, 1995), p. 77; 'The Bankhall Girls' Trust', *LM*, 27 October 1894; 'Local News Death of an Ex-Town Councillor', *LM*, 4 January 1875, p. 3; 'The Late Mr. Roger Lyons Jones' Bequests to Local Charities', *LM*, 19 January 1875; 'Distribution of the Lyon Jones Estate', *LM*, 1 January 1876, p. 1. Walter Scott was a prominent architect in Birkenhead who had previously been the town's borough surveyor. He designed many of the mansions and semi-villas in Clifton Park and Birkenhead Park.

56 P. Riddle, 'Political Authority and University Formation in Europe, 1200–1800', *Sociological Perspectives*, 36, 1 (1993), pp. 45–62; Michael Sanderson, 'The English Civic Universities and the "Industrial Spirit", 1870–1914', *Historical Research*, 61 (1988), pp. 90–104; *The Universities and British Industrialisation, 1850–1970* (London, 1972); Leonard Schwarz, 'Professions, Elites and Universities in England, 1870–1970', *The Historical Journal*, 47, 4 (2004), pp. 941–62; P. Vallance, 'The Historical Roots and Development of the Civic University', in J. Goddard, E. Hazelcorn, L. Kempton and P. Vallance (eds.), *The Civic University: The Leadership and Policy Challenges* (Cheltenham, 2016), pp. 16–33; Charles Grant Robertson, 'The Provincial Universities', *The Sociological Review*, 31, 3 (1939), pp. 248–59; H. Stuart Jones, 'The English Civic Universities: Endowments and the Commemoration of Benefactors', in Jill Peters and Laurence Goldman (eds.), *Dethroning Historical Reputations: Universities, Museums and the Commemorization of Benefactors* (London, 2018), pp. 25–34; R. D. Anderson, *Universities and Elites in Britain since 1800* (Studies in Economic and Social History) (Basingstoke, 1992), pp. 18, 37–8.

57 Jones, 'The English Civic Universities', p. 26; Robert Anderson, 'University Fees in Historical Perspective', *History & Policy*, Policy Papers, 8 February 2016; Jill Pellow, 'A Metropolitan University Fit for Empire: The Role of Private Benefactions in the Early History of the London School of Economics and Political Science and Imperial College of Science and Technology, 1885–89', *History of Universities*, 26, 1 (2012), pp. 202–45; Thomas Kelly, *For Advancement of Learning the University of Liverpool 1881–1981* (Liverpool, 1981), Chapters 1–4, in particular, pp. 47, 63; 'Liverpool: The

University', in William Farrer and J. Brownbill (eds.), *A History of the County of Lancaster*, vol. 4 (London, 1911), pp. 53–4; *The University of Liverpool 1903–1953: A Jubilee Book* (Liverpool, 1953), pp. 7, 10.

58 Kelly, *For Advancement of Learning*, pp. 55–65.

59 David Peter Burns, 'British Decline, Commercial influence and the Provision of Technical Education on Merseyside between 1870 and 1914', unpublished PhD thesis, School of History, University of Liverpool (2006), in particular chapter 5; Alexander Gordon, 'Beard, Charles', in Sidney Lee (ed.), *Dictionary of National Biography* (1st supplement) (London, 1901); Ian Sellars, 'Liverpool Nonconformity (1786–1914)', PhD, University of Keele (1969), Chapter 9, in particular p. 248. It was only in 1884 that the Liverpool Royal Infirmary School of Medicine became part of University College: in some cases lectureships provided teaching cover for medical disciplines; exceptionally, as was the case with the lectureship in surgery, it was converted into an unendowed chair. For the role of George Holt, in supporting the research of Oliver Lodge, in endowing two chairs (physiology and pathology) and research studentships, and in providing funds for the George Holt building, see Stella V. F. Butler, 'Centers and Peripheries: The Development of British Physiology, 1870–1914', *Journal of the History of Biology*, 21, 3 (1988), pp. 77–96. I am grateful for the information that David Burns kindly made available.

60 Sellars, 'Liverpool Nonconformity', p. 248; Burns, 'British Decline', Chapter 8; William Rathbone VI, A sketch of family history during four generations, compiled from old letters and papers, and rough notes written by William Rathbone VI: for the use of his children (privately published, 1894); Sally M. Horrocks, 'Industrial Chemistry and Its Changing Patrons at the University of Liverpool, 1926–1951', *Technology and Culture*, 48, 1 (2007), pp. 43–4.

61 Ramsay Muir, *A History of Liverpool* (2nd ed., London, 1907), pp. 333; *The University of Liverpool: Its Present State* (Liverpool, 1907); Anderson, 'University Fees'; Sarah V. Barnes, 'England's Civic Universities and the Triumph of the Oxbridge Ideal', *History of Education Quarterly*, 36, 3 (1996), pp. 271–305; 'The Owens College, Manchester', *Nature*, 8 (1873), pp. 506–9; D. A. Farnie, 'John Rylands of Manchester', *Bulletin of the John Rylands University Library of Manchester*, 75 (1993), pp. 3–103; 'Enriqueta Augustina Rylands, 1843–1908, Founder of the John Rylands Library', *Bulletin of the John Rylands University Library of Manchester*, 71, 2 (1989), pp. 3–38; Jones, 'The English Civic Universities', p. 29. Officially, the John Rylands Library, one of the finest charity libraries in Britain, only became part of the University of Manchester in 1972.

62 Kelly, *For Advancement of Learning*, pp. 49–51, 70, 81, 127.

63 *The University of Liverpool Calendar 1905*, pp. 382–421; William Maguire, *Belfast: A History* (Towns and Cities Histories) (Lancaster, 2009), pp. 73–4, 106–7, 143, 150, 152; Michael Sanderson, *The University and British Industry: 1850–1970* (Routledge Library Editions: Higher Education) (London, 2018).

64 'Liverpool: The University', pp. 53–4; *The University of Liverpool Calendar*, p. 400.

65 Burns, 'British Decline', Chapter 5; Kelly, *For Advancement of Learning*, p. 139.

66 Burns, 'British Decline', Chapter 8; Stephen E. Koss, *Sir John Brunner: Radical Plutocrat 1842–1919* (Cambridge, 1970); Arthur S. Peake, *The Life of Sir William Hartley* (London, 1926); David M. Young, *Change and Decay: Primitive Methodism from Late Victorian Times till World War I* (History of Primitive Methodism, vol. 2) (Stoke-on-Trent, 2017). Hartley, like Tate, sometimes preferred to donate part of any sums requested in the expectation that others would be encouraged to contribute. It has even been argued that merchants in the eighteenth century were more motivated by social recognition than by profits: see the contributions in Pierre Gervais, Yannick Lemarchand, and Dominique Margairaz (eds.), *Merchants and Profits in the Age of Commerce, 1680–1830* (London, 2015). National celebratory events, such as Queen Victoria's Diamond Jubilee, were sometimes contested at a local level: see Elizabeth Hammerton and David Cannadine, 'Conflict and Consensus on a Ceremonial Occasion: The Diamond Jubilee in Cambridge in 1897', *The Historical Journal*, 24, 1 (1981), pp. 111–46.

67 Between 1840 and 1870 the major centres for biochemical research were the German medical faculties, although there was a clear trend to transfer them to philosophical (science) faculties, although there was considerable disparity between the German states in their overall expenditure on higher education and technology. R. E. Kohler, *From Medical Chemistry to Biochemistry* (Monographs on the History of Science) (Cambridge, 1982), p. 399; Robert Lee, '"Relative Backwardness" and Long-Run Development: Economic, Demographic and Social Change, 1780–1870', in John Breuilly (ed.), *Nineteenth-Century Germany: Politics, Culture, and Society 1780–1918* (2nd ed., London, 2020), p. 69; Orchard, *Liverpool's Legion of Honour*, pp. xviii, xxi, 79–96. For an overview of the provision of science and

technology at Liverpool, see G. W. Roderick and M. D. Stephens, 'The Development of Science and Technology in a Civic University: Liverpool "1881–1914"', *The Irish Journal of Education*, 9, 2 (1975), pp. 77–96; June Jones, 'Science, Utility and the Second City of Empire: The Sciences and Especially the Medical Sciences at Liverpool University 1881–1921', PhD, University of Manchester (1989).

68 Chandler, *Liverpool*, p. 456; Milne, 'Maritime Liverpool', p. 297.

69 J. Hudson, *The History of Adult Education* (London, 1851), p. 96; Stobart, 'Culture versus Commerce', p. 481; C. T. Gatty, 'Advertisement', *THSL&C, 35th Session, vol. 7, 1878–79* (Liverpool, 1879), p. iii; J. T. Danson, 'On the Uses of Learned Societies: And in Particular of the Historic Society', *THSL&C*, 11, 1958–59 (Liverpool, 1859), p. 233; John Towne Danson, *Economic and Statistical Studies, 1840–1890* (London, 1906), p. 30.

70 See Sari Mäenpää, Chapter 6; Jon Stobart, 'Information, Trust and Reputation', *Scandinavian Journal of History*, 30, 3 (2005), p. 301; Orchard, *Liverpool's Legion of Honour*, p. 653; Haggerty and Haggerty, 'The Life Cycle of a Metropolitan Business Network'. At least one of the seven Liverpool members of the Eighty Club in 1895, the tea merchant John Davies of Rough Grange, Gateacre, was from the merchant community: see the Eighty Club, *Report for 1894* (London, 1895), List of members, pp. 17–34.

71 Arline Wilson, 'The Cultural Identity of Liverpool, 1790–1850: The Early Learned Societies', *THSLCH*, 141, 1997 (Liverpool, 1998), pp. 55–80; '"The Florence of the North"? The Civic Culture of Liverpool in the Early Nineteenth Century', in Alan Kidd and David Nicholls (eds.), *Gender, Civic Culture and Consumerism: Middle-Class Identity in Britain 1800–1940* (Manchester, 1999), pp. 34–46; *William Roscoe: Commerce and Culture* (Liverpool, 2008), pp. 28–9; Rev. A. Hume, *The Learned Societies and Printing Clubs of the United Kingdom* (London, 1853), pp. 12–13. As far as limiting Liverpool's public culpability in the slave trade was concerned, John Towne Danson, in a paper presented to the British Association in 1856 based on 'well-arranged facts', demonstrated that England (and particularly Liverpool) continued to rely almost entirely on slave-grown cotton. See Professor E. C. K. Gonner, 'Introduction', in John Towne Danson (eds.), *Economic and Statistical Studies, 1840–1890* (London, 1896), p. 55.

72 See Louise Miskell, *Meeting Places: Scientific Congresses and Urban Identity in Victorian Britain* (Farnham, 2013); Derek Orange, 'Science in Early Nineteenth-Century York: The Yorkshire Philosophical Society and the British Association', in Charles Feinstein (ed.), *York, 1831–1981: 150 Years of Scientific Endeavour and Social Change* (York, 1981), pp. 1–29; Belchem, *Merseyside*, p. 11; Alan Kidd and David Nicholls, 'Introduction: History, Culture and the Middle Classes', in Kidd and Nichols, *Gender, Civic Culture and Consumerism*, p. 7; Rev. A. Hume LL.D, 'The Inaugural Address', *THSL&C*, Session 1, No. 1, 1848–49 (Liverpool, 1849), p. 3; *The Learned Societies and Printing Clubs of the United Kingdom* (London, 1853), pp. xvi–xvii; W. S. F. Pickering, 'Abraham Hume (1814–1884): A Forgotten Pioneer in Religious Sociology', *Archives de sociologies des religions*, 33 (1972), pp. 33–48; 'The Lancashire and Cheshire Antiquarian Society, Rules, *Preamble*', *TL&CAS, vol. 1, 1883* (Manchester 1884), p. 5; *PL&PS of Liverpool, 1844–45, Session XXXIV* (Liverpool, 1845), p. i; Andrew Wawn, *The Vikings and the Victorians: Inventing the Old North in 19th-Century Britain* (Cambridge, 2000), p. 354; *Journal of the Liverpool Polytechnic Society*, Thirty-Fifth Session, Ninth Meeting, 23 December 1872, President's Closing Address, Liverpool, 1874, p. 102; 'Presidential Address to the Liverpool Physical Society by Professor Oliver Lodge', Proceedings of the Liverpool Physical Society, vol. 1 for 3 Sessions, 1889–92, Liverpool, 1892, p. 2.

73 Tony Twemlow, 'Liverpool Law Society', in Noel Fagan, Graeme Bryson and Charles Elston (eds.), *A Century of Liverpool Lawyers* (Liverpool, 2002), pp. 9–11. For research on the development of the legal professions, specifically in the North West, see Vivienne Rose Parrott, 'Pettyfogging to Respectability a History of the Development of the Profession of Solicitors in the Manchester Area 1800–1914', unpublished PhD, University of Salford (1992), pp. 27–8, 48–51; Peter Howell Williams, *A Gentleman's Calling: The Liverpool Attorney-at-Law* (Liverpool, 1980); B. L. Anderson, 'The Attorney and the Early Capital Market in Lancashire', in F. Crouzet (ed.), *Capital Formation in the Industrial Revolution* (London, 1972), pp. 223–55; Philip Aylett, 'A Profession in the Market Place: The Distribution of Attorneys in England and Wales 1730–1800', *Law and History Review*, 5, 1 (1987) pp. 4, 7, 14; H. Kirk, *Portrait of a Profession* (London, 1976). See also; Brian Abel-Smith and R. Stevens, *Lawyers & the Courts: A Sociological Study of the English Legal System 1750–1965* (London, 1967). Apart from the Liverpool Medical Institution (founded in 1837 on the site used as a medical library since 1779), a number of medical societies had been established, including the Liverpool Medical and Pathological

Society (1838), while the 1830s saw the publication of several medical journals, some of which failed to attract sufficient support.

74 F. J. M., 'The Development of the Liverpool Architectural Society over the last One Hundred Years', *Journal of the Royal Institute of British Architects* (June 1948); Miles Broughton, 'Charles (Reed) Verelst and the Liverpool Archaeological and Architectural Society', unpublished ms (n.d.); Christopher Crouch, *Design Culture in Liverpool 1880–1914 the Origins of the Liverpool School of Architecture* (Liverpool, 2002), p. 75; LRO, CHE 1/1, Liverpool Chemists' Association, Council Minutes, 21 July 1887, 12 July 1895; The Liverpool Chemists' Association, Railway and Canal Traffic Act 1888, May 1889; J. H. Hirst, *The First Hundred Years* (Liverpool, 1949); John Hannay (ed.), *Encyclopedia of Nineteenth-Century Photography* (London, 2007), vol. 1, p. 1304; Adrian Jarvis, 'G. F. Lyster and the Role of the Dock Engineer 1861–1897', *Mariner's Mirror*, 78, 2 (1992), pp. 177–99; LRO 620 1/1, LES, Minutes of General Meetings, 1885–96, 14 April 1889; ENG 7/1, LES, Dates of Election and Introduction of Members, 1892–1927, Session XXVII, 21 November, 5 December 1900, 16 January 1901; ENG 6/1, LES, Candidates' Proposal Forms, Session XXIX–XXX, 1902–3, No. 1, (1); Adrian Jarvis, 'British Provincial Institutions and the Maritime Industries, 1857–1939', in David J. Starkey and Hugh Murphy (eds.), *Beyond Shipping and Shipbuilding: Britain's Ancillary Maritime Interests in the Twentieth Century* (Hull, 2007), pp. 12–14; Alfred Holt, 'Review of the Progress of Steam Shipping during the Last Quarter of a Century', *Minutes of Proceedings of the Institution of Civil Engineers*, vol. 51 (1877–78), pp. 2–11.

75 Morris, 'Class, Societies and Associations', p. 410; Wilson, '"The Florence of the North?"', p. 19; LUSP&A, LRI, 1/1/1, List of subscribers and proprietors, 1814–1879; LRI, 1.1.4, List of proprietors, shares transferred and members of the general committee, 1861–1867.

76 Belchem, *Merseyside*, p. 11; LRO, 680 POL 2/1, Council Minutes, Liverpool Polytechnic Society, A, 1839 to 1873, 4 February 1839, Annual Meeting, 13 January 1862, exhibited model by J. Scott Collins of an 'Apparatus for Reefing and Furling the Sails of Ships'; 'Liverpool Polytechnic Society', *Liverpool Mercury*, 22 February 1839; 24 January 1851; Rev. A. Hume, 'The Inaugural Address', *PHSL&C*, Series 1, no. 1, 1848–49 (Liverpool, 1849), pp. vii–xiii, 3–11; *THSL&C*, New Series, vol. 3, Session 1862–63 (Liverpool, 1863), pp. vii–xix; Ralph O'Connor, 'Facts and fancies: The Geological Society of London and the Wider Public, 1807–1837', in Geological Society of London, *Special Publications*, 317 (2009), pp. 331–40; Henry Duckworth, President, 'Inauguration Address', Session First, 10 January 1860 and Honorary Secretary's Report, Session Fifth, 1863–64, in *Abstract of the Proceedings of the Liverpool Geological Association for the First Ten Sessions* (Liverpool, 1870), p. 3 and 1 respectively; William Hewitt, *Liverpool Geological Society: A Retrospect of Fifty Year's Existence and Work* (Liverpool, 1910).

77 LRO, 520 LAS/1/1, Minute Book of the Liverpool Astronomical Society, sessions 2 (1882–83), 7 (1887–88) and 8 (1888–89); A. Anderson, 'The History of Liverpool Astronomical Society', in *Year Book of Astronomy* (1965).

78 *Proceedings of the Liverpool Physical Society*, vol. 1 for 3 Sessions, 1889–92 (Liverpool, 1892), inaugural meeting, 16th February 1889; Report of the Committee for the First Session, 1889–90, List of Members September, 1890; Peter Rowlands, *Oliver Lodge and the Liverpool Physical Society* (Liverpool Historical Studies, no. 4) (Liverpool, 1990), p. 49.

79 *Proceedings of the Liverpool Biological Society*, vol. 2, Session 1887–8 (Liverpool, 1888), pp. 105–16; 95–104; *PLBS*, vol. 3, Session 1888–9 (Liverpool, 1889), pp. 226–9; *Proceedings and Transactions of the Liverpool Biological Society*, vol. 4, Session 1889–90 (Liverpool, 1890); *PTLBS*, vol. 17, Session 1902–03 (Liverpool, 1903), pp. xx–xxiii. A presentation during the second session 1887–88 by Isaac L. Thompson, FLS, FRMS of 'Notes on a visit to Madeira and the Canary Island' might have appealed to merchants, but this may not have been the case in relation to Alice Heath's 'Notes on a Tract of Modified Ectodermin Crania anomala and Lingula anatina'.

80 LRO, 570 NAT/1, *LNFC, Register of Members* (Liverpool, 1860); C. Theodore Green (ed.), *The Flora of the Liverpool District* (Liverpool, 1902), p. vi; *Proceedings of the Liverpool Botanical Society First and Second Sessions from April 1906 to 31st December 1906 and for the Year Ending 31st December 1907* (Liverpool, 1908), pp. 5–7, 57–60.

81 Its influence was short-lived: by the Edwardian era membership levels were falling; in 1903, 17 prominent members died who had 'invariably evinced great interest; after the death in 1909 of its chairman Sir Alfred Lews Jones, staff from Elder Dempster & Co., together with other merchants, ceased to attend, because of the society's failure to deliver commercial utility, as originally promised. Despite some high-profile lectures, most were illustrated travelogues, such Paul Lange's (an insurance broker

and member of the society) 'well thought out' presentation of an account of a holiday in Iceland covering the manners and customs of the Icelanders. Not surprisingly, there was an emphasis on exploration,
both in the Arctic and Antarctic, but very few of the contributions offered new insights into commercial
or economic geography and little information on foreign competition or how to exploit new resources.

82 Orchard, *Liverpool's Legion of Honour*, pp. 593–4, 603, 636, 664; Coop and Taylor, *Bulls and Bears*,
   nos. 44, 56 and 71.

83 Lisa Jardine, 'C. P. Snow's Two Cultures Revisited the 2009 C. P. Snow Lecture: Given in Christ's
   College, 14 October 2009', *Christ's College Magazine*, 235 (Cambridge, 2010), pp. 49–56; Stefan
   Collini (ed.), *F. R. Leavis, Two Cultures? The Significance of C.P. Snow* (Cambridge, 2013); Frank A.
   J. L. James, 'Introduction: Some Significance of the Two Cultures Debate', *Interdisciplinary Science
   Reviews*, 41, 2–3 (2016), pp. 107–17; James O. Young, 'Inquiry in the Arts and Science', *Philosophy*,
   71, 276 (1996), pp. 255–6; Richard Tames, *Economy and Society in 19th Century Britain* (London
   and New York, 2015), p. 119; Michael Neve, 'Science in a Commercial City: Bristol 1820–60', in
   Ian Inkster and Jack Morrell (eds.), *Metropolis and Province: Science in British Culture, 1780–1850*
   (London, 1983), pp. 179–204; Rosemary Sweet, *The English Town, 1680–1840: Government, Society
   and Culture* (2nd edn, London and New York, 2014), pp. 250–1.

84 *PLPS of Liverpool for 1844–45*, Session xxxiv (Liverpool, 1845), p. i; *PLPS*, 55th session, 1855–56
   (Liverpool, 1856), p. 15; Henry Ardene Ormerod, *The Liverpool Royal Institution: A Record and a
   Retrospect* (Liverpool, 1953); *The Stranger in Liverpool with Plates of the Principal Buildings and
   a New and Correct Map of the Town* 12th edn, Liverpool, 1841), p. 153; 'The Liverpool Philomathic
   Society', *PLPS During the Thirty-First Session, 1855–56* (Liverpool, 1856), vol. 1, p. 3; 'Liverpool
   Polytechnic Society First Public Meeting, Tuesday Evening', *Liverpool Mercury*, 22 February 1839; R.
   Sydney Marsden, *History of The Birkenhead Literary and Scientific Society 1857–1907* (Birkenhead,
   1907), p. 2; Eric Shatzberg, 'From Art to Applied Sciences', *Isis*, 103, 3 (2012), pp. 557–8; *HS&LC,
   Proceedings and Papers, Session II, 1849–50* (Liverpool, 1851), pp. v–vii and *Session III, 1850–51*
   (Liverpool, 1851), Reverend A. Hume, 'Concluding Address', pp. 130–6; *THSL&C*, XXXI (1878–9),
   advertisement, cited by Michael E Rose, 'Clio, Culture and The City: Historical Societies in Their
   Nineteenth-Century Urban Context', *THSL&C*, 147 (1997), p. 151.

85 *Proceedings of the LPS during Its Thirty-First Session, 1855–56* (Liverpool, 1856), vol. 1, pp. 3–6;
   LSSA, Annual Report and Proceedings, Session 1886–67 (Liverpool, 1887), p. 7; LRO, 680PoL 2/1,
   Council Minutes, Liverpool Polytechnic Society from 1839 to 1873, 15 January, 17 December 1846
   (Report of Council to Annual Meeting): according to the Council, 'if it be their desire to maintain the
   Society in a flourishing and useful condition, the members must combine to impart that interest and
   utility to its future meetings, which alone can render these meetings attractive'; *Journal of the Liverpool Polytechnic Society, 35th Session, 1872, Annual Report* (Liverpool, 1872), p. 2; *Proceedings of
   the LPS of Liverpool during the Fifty-Fifth Session, 1855–56* (Liverpool, 1856), pp. 11–12.

86 LR0, 520 LAS/1/1, Minute Book of the Liverpool Astronomical Society, 9th October 1882, second
   series; LSSA, *Annual Report and Proceedings, Session 1888–89* (Liverpool 1889), p. 9; *Fourteenth
   Annual Report of the Lancashire and Cheshire Entomological Society, Session 1890* (Liverpool, 1891),
   p. 7; *Transactions of the LMS, Twentieth Annual Report, January 1889* (Liverpool, 1889), p. 5.

87 Hume, *The Learned Societies*, p. 33; T. B. Hall and W. Armistead, *A Flora of Liverpool by T. B. Hall*
   (London, 1838); Wood, *The History of the Liverpool Amateur Photographic Association*, 21 September 1878: this was a joint excursion with the Manchester Photographic Society (founded in 1855)
   with approximately 30 members and at least 22 cameras; they were received by Gladstone in person. The excursion to Betwys-y-Coed took place as early as June 1864. *LSSA Ninth Annual Report
   and Proceedings, Session 1889–90* (Liverpool, 1890), p. 9; *Twenty-Sixth Annual Report of the LMS
   for 1894* (Liverpool,1895), p. iv; *THSL&C, New Series vol. X for the Session 1869–70* (Liverpool,
   1870), p. 295; *THSL&C, for the Year 1900* (Liverpool, 1902), vol. 52, p. 254; *TL&CAS*, vol. 24, 1906
   (Manchester, 1907), p. 186; Steve McWilliams, 'Field Naturalists and the Role of the Lancashire and
   Cheshire Entomological Society in Promoting Entomology', *Journal of the Lancashire and Cheshire
   Entomology Society*, 129 (2005), pp. 3–6; Charles W. J. Withers and Diarmid A. Finnegan, 'Natu-
   ral History Societies, Fieldwork and Local Knowledge in Nineteenth-Century Scotland: Towards a
   Historical Geography of Civic Science', *Cultural Geographies*, 10 (2003), pp. 334–53; Diarmid A.
   Finnegan, *Natural History Societies and Civic Culture in Victorian Scotland* (Science and Culture in
   the Nineteenth Century, No. 9) (London and New York, 2009; 2nd ed. 2016), pp. 6–7.

88 Wilson, '"The Florence of the North"', p. 39; 'The Cultural Identity of Liverpool', pp. 73–5; 'President's Address', *PL&PS, Session 1899–1900* (Liverpool, 1900), p. xxix; *THSL&C, New Series, Vol.*

iv, *Sixteenth Session, 1863–64* (Liverpool, 1864), p. 228; 'List of Members: Session XXII, 1869–70', *THSL&C, New Series, Vol. xi, Session 1870–71* (Liverpool, 1871), p. xiii; *PL&PS*, 1872–73, 13th meeting, 21st April 1873. The marketing strategy for raising the profile of the Historic Society and recruiting more members was laid down by the Rev. A. Hume in 1869: it was 'the only one of public foundation' having been established at a 'Town's meeting'; it was unique in prioritising the 'investigation of the District' as part of its proceedings and distinguishing between residents and non-residents; it covered 'the whole range of inquiry'; it had operated successfully on a sectional basis since 1854 and proactively sought papers, rather than 'receiving from meeting to meeting such as come voluntarily or coincidently'. See Rev. A. Hume, 'Address to the Members of the Historic Society of Lancashire and Cheshire', *THSL&C, Vol. x, New Series, Session 1869–70* (Liverpool, 1870), p. 6.

89 *PLNFC, For the Year 1882–1883* (Liverpool, 1883), pp. 77, 89–98; David Elliston Allen, *The Naturalist in Britain: A Social History* (London, 1976), p. 164; Green (ed.), *The Flora of the Liverpool District*, p. vii; Cynthia Burek and Thomas A. Hose, 'The Role of Local Societies in Early Modern Geotourism: A Case Study of the Chester Society of Natural Science and the Woolhope Naturalists' Field Club', in Thomas Hose (ed.), *Appreciating Physical Landscape: Three Hundred Years of Geotourism* (Geological Society, Special Publication 417) (London, 2015); Cythia V. Burek and M. Kölbl-Ebert, 'The Historical Problems of Travel for Women Undertaking Geological Fieldwork', in C. V. Burek and B. Higgs (eds.), *The Role of Women in the History of Geotourism* (Geological Society, Special Publication, 281) (London, 2007), pp. 115–22. Not all sister societies admitted women: even in 1918 the Woolhope Naturalists' Field Club regarded their presence as damaging to its intellectual interests.

90 Orchard, *Liverpool's Legion of Honour*, p. 53; David E. Allen, *The Naturalist in Britain: A Social History* (London, 1976), p. 167; W. A. Herdman, 'Preface, British Association, Liverpool, 1896', in idem (ed.), *Handbook to Liverpool and the Neighbourhood, Prepared by Various Authors for the Publication Sub-Committee* (Liverpool, 1896), pp. iii–iv; Rebekah Wright and Charles W. J. Withers, 'Science and Sociability: Women as Audience at the British Association for the Advancement of Science, 1831–1901', *Isis*, 99, 1 (2008), pp. 1–27; Charles Withers, 'Scales of the Geographies of Civic Science: Practice and Experience in the Meetings of the British Association for the Advancement of Science in Britain and Ireland, c.1845–1900', in David N. Livingstone and Charles W. J. Withers (eds.), *Geographies of Nineteenth-Century Science* (Chicago and London, 2011), p. 113. The National Association for the Promotion of Social Science (1857) had a similar impact when it held its 1858 meeting in Liverpool, by accepting women as full members from its inception and allowing them to present papers so that it became 'a matter of course'. See Kathleen E. McCone, 'The National Association for the Promotion of Social Science and the Advancement of Victorian Women', *Atlantis*, 8, 1 (1982), pp. 46, 58. Liverpool regularly hosted such meetings whether convened by the British Association for the Advancement of Science, the National Association for the Promotion of Social Science, or the National Association for the Advancement of Art and its Application to Industry (1888). The cumulative impact of these national events on Liverpool's learned societies has still to be examined in detail.

91 *PLPS, 77th Session, 1901–02* (Liverpool, 1902), meetings held on 6th November 1901 and 20th November 1901; UoLSC&A, LPS 3/2, Seating plans, ticket applications, with note of payment, menu cards and toast lists for the Liverpool Philomathic Society dinners (2 Nov. 1899–23 March 1926.

92 LRO, 060 LIT 3/1, Literary and Philosophical Society of Liverpool Centenary Roll 1812 to 1912, vol. 1 (to 800) (Liverpool, 1912), new members admitted in 1854, 1855; LRO 060 LIT Literary and Philosophical Society of Liverpool Centenary Roll 1812 to 1912, vol. 2 (Liverpool, 1912), new members elected in 1894. Although based on a small sample of 43 members elected in 1854–55 and 51 in 1894, the data provides a good indication of the trend in participation rates over time. Prange's involvement in the L&PS was limited because 'his large fortune rapidly shrank' as the opening of the Suez Canal in 1869 and an influx of Indian and Chinese products affected his firm's 'very extensive business'.

93 Orchard, *Liverpool's Legion of Honour*, p. 56. It is worth noting that Anglican ministers played a disproportional role in other learned societies: for example, Rev. E. N. Hoare became a member of the L&PS in 1894: he was subsequently elected vice-president in 1898 and president in 1899.

94 The British Association's meeting in Liverpool in 1837 acted as a catalyst for the formation of a local Statistical Society which by January the following year had 85 members, largely drawn from Liverpool's commercial and manufacturing sectors with a strong representation by Liberals and Unitarians. See 'Provincial Statistical Societies in the United Kingdom', *Journal of the Statistical Society of London*, 1, 1 (London, 1938), pp. 48–50; Christopher O'Brien, 'The Origins and Originator of Early Statistical Societies: A Comparison of Liverpool and Manchester', *Journal of the Royal Statistical Society, Series A (Statistics in Society)*, 174, 1 (January 2011), pp. 52–61; W. N. Tayler, Report of the Second

Annual Meeting of the National Association for the Promotion of Social Science, held at Liverpool, in October, 1858 (London, 1859); 'The National Association for the Promotion of Social Science', *LM*, 18 September 1858; E. W. Hope (ed.), *City of Liverpool: Handbook Compiled for the Congress of the Royal Institute of Public Health, 1903* (Liverpool, 1903). For material on the BAAS and its provincial impact, see Jack Morrell and Arnold Thackray, *Gentlemen of Science: Early Years of the British Association for the Advancement of Science* (Oxford, 1981); R. M. Macleod, J. R. Friday and C. Gregor, *The Corresponding Societies of the British Association for the Advancement of Science, 1833–1929* (London, 1975); Charles Withers, Rebekah Higgitt and Diarmid Finnegan, 'Historical Geographies Provincial Science: Themes in the Setting and Reception of the British Association for the Advancement of Science in Britain and Ireland, 1831–c.1939', *British Journal of the History of Science*, 41, 3 (2008), pp. 385–415. Some of the Liverpool societies, such as the Microscopic Society, were in any case on the list of the association's corresponding societies.

95 LRO, POL 2/1, Council Minutes of the Liverpool Polytechnic Society, A 1839 to 1873, 8 December 1862, and the first meeting of the Association of Officers of the Learned Societies, 26 March 1872; *PL&PS of Liverpool for the Forth-Third Session 1853–54*, No. 8 (Liverpool, 1854), Second Meeting, 1853; LRO, 506 SCI, Minute Book of the Liverpool Science Students' Association, 16 July 1884; William Hewitt, 'President's Address, Liverpool Geological Society', in J. H. Milton (ed.), *Proceedings of the LGS, Sessions LI–LIV, 1910–1913* (Liverpool, 1914), vol. 11, pp. 79–83; *Forty-First Annual Report of the Liverpool Microscopical Society, January 1910* (Liverpool, 1910), p. 4.

96 *THSL&C for the Year 1900*, vol. 52, New Series XVI (Liverpool, 1902), pp. 253–4. Bennett had found time, 'in the intervals of business', to complete a comparative history of corn milling in all ages, while Thornely had been an expert on local monumental brasses. Reports of the premature death of honorary officers and members of learned societies were not uncommon: Paul Lange (born in Berlin in 1847) had a successful career in insurance; he pursued photography 'as a relaxation' and was president of LAPA twice (1890–91 and 1899); and he contributed original photographs of relatively unexplored areas of Norway to a travel book written by E. J. Goodman, *New Ground in Norway Ringerike-Telemarken-Saetersdalen* (London, 1896). He died suddenly in 1903 on a holiday trip to his native city. See *The Amateur Photographer*, 28th May 1903. These were systemic problems faced by all learned societies, almost irrespective of their provincial location. For example, the Leeds Philosophical and Literary Society had to cope with the frequent loss of older members, the problem of securing adequate funding which 'often furnished a theme of lamentation', the occasional failure to recruit new members, and competition from other societies offering 'very liberal rates of membership', 'equally accessible to all'. See E. Kitson Clark, *The History of Life of the Leeds Philosophical and Literary Society* (Leeds, 1924), pp. 37, 45, 46.

97 Giles, *Building a Better Society*, pp. 2, 7, 11. In the case of Tate, however, he had twice declined the honour of a baronetcy, but this was finally accepted in 1898 on the completion of the Tate Gallery, London, after pressure from Lord Salisbury who intimated that a refusal would be interpreted as a direct snub to the Royal Family.

13 Postscript

Robert Lee

In setting out the objectives of the Mercantile Liverpool Project attention was focussed on three issues. Firstly, the creation of a robust analytical framework was essential to enable the research team to move beyond the limitations of the existing historiography of the merchant community. This has always been based on elite groups, whether defined by religious affiliation (such as the Unitarians) or by occupation, including, for example, steamship owners and cotton merchants. All too often our understanding of the changing role of merchants has been dependent on the selective availability of largely institutional archival material which reflects the disproportionate contribution of elite merchants to associational culture, civic development, commerce and trade, philanthropy, politics, religion, and social welfare. Those who were less successful, whose businesses collapsed as a result of bankruptcy, or who simply failed to establish a tenable niche in the competitive commercial life of the city have largely, if not entirely, been ignored. Historians and social scientists who have analysed the merchant communities of other port-cities have all too often shown a similar, if understandable, preference for basing their research on a small number of leading families.

By contrast, the design, creation, and completion of the Mercantile Liverpool database provided for the first time a means of analysing Liverpool's business community in a comprehensive and systemic manner. Inevitably, it would have been helpful if additional material had been available on merchants whose commercial operations were small-scale, particularly in the coal trade which included some highly successful large-scale operators and a plethora of traders who catered essentially for local needs. But recreating their business networks in the absence of accounts and correspondence would not have been straightforward, while the lack of personal papers and information on associational membership, whether church- or trade-based, would have restricted any analysis of their social embeddedness at a local level.

Other issues would have benefited from a more detailed analysis, including the impact of the choice of schooling on the socialisation of merchants' children (primarily their sons, but gradually some of their daughters), the networking frameworks offered by Freemasonry and the Volunteer Movement, and the relationship between merchants and the professional classes. As might be expected, a great deal has been written on the history of individual schools, but almost always on a chronological and institutional basis.[1] As yet, no attention has been paid to the wider, societal role of Merseyside schools during the nineteenth century, specifically those that catered for the children of merchants, except, to some extent, on the Wirral.[2] But archival evidence highlights the potential relevance of schools for business networking: a day school, such as the Liverpool Institute, promoted intergenerational continuity by drawing from the families of those who were 'old boys of the evening classes' from the 1840s and 1850s; George Holt, from whom the school premises were rented, had 'some business connection' to other members of the Board, including the shipowner James Aiken and

DOI: 10.4324/9781315597836-13

William Blain Senior (one of the original trustees); while established figures, such as James Bryce M.P., gave an address at an annual prize meeting on the subject of 'Education of Men of Business'. School involvement enabled governors and trustees to exercise patronage by recommending new pupils; to endow scholarships and prizes; or to participate in school-based societies (such as the Mental Improvement Society of the Liverpool Mechanics Institute intended to stimulate the discussion of literary, scientific, commercial, and historical issues), while admission registers provide evidence of the extent to which some sons of merchants were destined to follow in their fathers' footsteps. Indeed, little is known of the role of formal schooling or other informal activities in providing a basis for friendship amongst children from the mercantile community which might have influenced business networking in later years. Public occasions, such as the Children's Fancy Dress Ball held in Liverpool in January 1877, reflected an increasingly popular and prestigious type of event which catered almost exclusively for elite families. The children of both sexes were often dressed in historic costumes (whether as seventeenth-century cavaliers or 'Britannia' with her trident and shield), but it is impossible to assess whether these events helped to mould longer term friendships, while data on more informal, family-based occasions is limited.[3]

Equally, business historians have paid little, if any, attention to the role played by the Volunteer Movement in providing a further networking framework for Merseyside merchants and traders. At a time when regular troops were stationed throughout the Empire, tensions between Britain and France following the Orsini affair prompted Jonathan Peel, the Secretary of State for War, to authorise the formation of volunteer rifle corps as well as artillery corps in coastal towns with defence requirements. The overall response was impressive: not surprisingly Oxford and Cambridge registered the highest estimated recruitment rate (14 per 1,000 population), but they were followed by Edinburgh and Liverpool (9) and then by Glasgow and Manchester (8). In Liverpool, the first meeting of the committee elected to coordinate the town's response to the national call for volunteers was held on 24 May 1859 in the Council Chamber of the Town Hall. The need was for young men 'who could arm and clothe themselves', although J. P. Heywood declared that he would be 'very willing to subscribe, and liberally' so that those who would benefit from financial assistance would be able to do so. In fact, there was considerable variation in the social and class composition of the different units: the 66th Lancs. (Liverpool Borough Guard) R.V.C, raised by Joseph Mayer, consisted largely of skilled craftsmen and specialist retailers; the 80th Lancs. (Liverpool Press Guard) drew its manpower from the staff of three local newspapers (the *Albion*, *Mercury*, and the *Weekly Chronicle*); while the 15th Lancs. (Mersey Iron Works) was entirely dominated by the employees of the large-scale factory after which the corps was known.

Whereas the volunteer movement during the Revolutionary and Napoleonic Wars has been the object of recent academic research, the 1859 Volunteer Movement has been relatively ignored. Apart from Beckett's study of the Rifle Volunteer Movement and county- and city-based surveys of specific units, coverage remains limited. The level of support from Liverpool and Birkenhead was impressive: advertisements from gun manufacturers and military bootmakers were placed in the local press and an anonymous correspondent to the *Liverpool Mercury* even suggested that members of the nobility and the aristocracy with an annual income of more than £2,000 should be subject to a special tax (if they did not come forward voluntarily) to pay for the cost of equipment for 'many fine, respectable, spirited young fellows' who otherwise would be unable to enlist. The public response to what was deemed to be a national crisis was accompanied by inspections of the newly formed volunteer corps by the Queen; the taking of formal oaths, as in the case of Liverpool Press Guard (80th Lancashire Rifle Volunteers) on 2 March 1861 in St. George's Hall; the presentation of silver bugles to specific units; dedicated religious services for the volunteers at St. Nicholas' Church; and a volunteer camp on Crosby Sands. The significance of the Volunteer Movement for business networking was obvious: it was understood that all officers should be young merchants, the sons of merchants (specifically from the cotton trade), or of gentlemen; and the evidence from Birkenhead and the Wirral confirms how voluntary military service helped to strengthen cohesion within the local mercantile community and reinforced traditional class roles. It may well be that there was an increasing dependency on tradesmen, instead of merchants, with a decline in the representation of men deemed to be of 'professional' standing, but, equally, there can be little doubt that some leading merchants, including the cotton broker George Melly took their military role extremely seriously. Indeed, the ship builder William Laird was the only representative from Merseyside who was invited to serve on the War Office Rules Committee in 1859, which was drawn from men who were already playing a prominent role in the movement, although the 5th Cheshire Artillery Volunteer Corps (Laird's Iron Works) founded in 1860 was disbanded nine years later.[4] However, there was no opportunity to explore this theme in depth or to analyse the changing composition of individual corps in terms of the occupation background of their officers and NCOs, but the high officer turnover, the decline in recruitment rates in later years, as well as the amalgamation and disbanding of some Liverpool and South Lancashire units suggest limitations in networking opportunities.

In setting out the operational framework of the MLP database, the reasons for excluding members of the professional classes, particularly solicitors and other lawyers, as well as accountants, have already been explained, despite the fact that the Incorporated Society of Liverpool Accountants was the first professional body to be established in Britain in 1870. Equally, an analysis of the role of Freemasonry in facilitating business networking was limited by funding constraints, since only The Merchants' Lodge (founded in 1780) registered a merchant membership of over 25 per cent, the cut-off point for including nominal information from this type of source in the database. Both topics deserved closer attention. Freemasonry was part of an expanding global network; it was part of the development of clubs, societies, and fraternities; and, in many cases, membership in the brotherhood helped Masons to make contact and find employment by utilising strong networking systems, a benefit that was invaluable at a time of high levels of mobility. But there is a lack of statistical data and insufficient case studies of Merseyside Masons and their lodges. Moreover, the increasing complexity of commercial transactions with the expansion of futures trading practices, increased levels of capitalisation, and legislative changes affecting business operations, bankruptcy, and auditing reinforced the need for sound legal advice. However, there have been very few studies of legal firms on Merseyside and their relationship to the mercantile community, despite the fact that some of the lawyers also followed successful political careers, while the increasing rationalisation of solicitor practices has led to the loss of considerable archival material. Despite their potential relevance for exploring specific aspects of business networking, both topics were beyond the reach of our project.[5]

Nor was there an opportunity to explore the wider cultural environment of Liverpool and the Wirral, in terms of the growing range of opportunities for public interaction or the gender-specific construction of urban space. Insufficient research has been undertaken on the development of retailing in Liverpool and Birkenhead, or the gender-specific networking encouraged by the increased provision of consumer-oriented goods and services aimed specifically at the middle class. Apart from formal occasions in the Town Hall and St. George's Hall, whether for raising funds for local charities, welcoming important visitors to the city (such as the Sultan of Zanzibar in July 1875, the Shah of Persia in July 1889, and Price Fushimi of Japan in June 1907), or special musical and theatrical performances, nominative data on those who attended major cultural events are seldom, if ever, available. Over time, facilities for large-scale cultural events increased markedly, including theatres and concert and variety halls, particularly in the 1860s, the late nineteenth century, and the immediate pre-1914 period when there were approximately 50 establishments. They ranged from a theatre established in the Zoological Gardens shortly after its opening in 1832 which offered 'Vaudeville fares' until the gardens were closed, to the 'new concert hall' for the Liverpool Philharmonic Society (founded in 1840) capable of seating 2,100 and an orchestra of 250 which signified the importance of music, at least for the upper middle class. Other venues fell victim to street improvements, relocation, or fire (including the Liverpool Colosseum Music Hall which burned down in October 1874 with the loss of 37 lives). Unfortunately, data on audience numbers or their social composition is limited; most studies focus on the programmes on offer (and the actors and musicians who performed); and few researchers have placed their work within a theoretical context by examining the changing role of cultural establishments in facilitating social networking, even in the case of concert halls and theatres which catered for the upper middle class, or promoting the increasing popularity and assimilation of 'exotic' cultures.[6]

Too little is known of the cultural history of nineteenth-century Merseyside to assess its significance for informal networking or its contribution to the creation of 'spaces of sociability'. This is particularly the case in relation to informal activities, such as shopping, which sometimes had a broader social function. In the early nineteenth century, Lord Street, one of Liverpool's major thoroughfares, had various retailers, specialising, for example, in china, glass, and carpets, but contemporary prints reveal only a moderate level of activity. The development of a retailing infrastructure reflected the growing wealth of the mercantile community. St. John's Market (designed by John Foster Jn.) was opened in 1822 as one of the first fully enclosed and roofed market halls, with 5 shopping avenues, 136 stone-trimmed Classical arches and window bays, supported by 116 interior cast-iron pillars. Bold Street, after it ceased to be the site of a rope-walk around 1780, became predominantly residential. In the early 1830s former residences were converted into retail premises and 1838 witnessed the out-migration of its last merchant, Thomas Tobin. After this it became the most fashionable shopping street in Liverpool and was almost totally given over to shops, including Bright's and Woolwright's 'whose establishments glisten with attractions for the fair which Aladdin's palace could not boast of'. From the mid-nineteenth century large-scale and increasingly ornate department stores dominated the retail sector. In 1832, the American brothers William and James Reddecliffe Jeffrey established Compton House in Church Street, arguably the first purpose-built department store in Britain; in 1853 the brothers George Henry and Henry Boswell Lee founded what quickly became a very fashionable establishment (George Henry Lee); and a Welsh immigrant, Owen Owen, started a draper's store in London Road in 1868 which became the basis of a national chain. Their success was underpinned by a recognition of the importance of price and quality competition, technological innovation, advertising, and the need to ensure customer satisfaction (for example, by providing 'store walkers' to escort shoppers to individual departments). Inevitably, this led to the gradual marginalisation of small, owner-occupied shops which tended to stock a limited range of goods. But exclusive fashion stores in Bold Street, as well as J. Collinson & Son (Liverpool's 'smartest shoemaker'), together with high quality milliners (such as De Moysey in Ranelagh Street) continued to maintain their market share. The wider significance of these structural changes in Liverpool's retail industry, particularly in terms of the social framework of shopping habits by families from the Merseyside's merchant community, has still to be explored.[7]

If Bold Street was intended to rival London's Bond Street, it has yet to attract detailed analysis. Other metropolitan shopping centres, including Regent Street, have been studied in depth,

VIEW OF LEWIS'S GOOD HOUSE OF BUSINESS IN RANELAGH-STREET, LIVERPOOL, WHERE THE PUBLIC ARE PROVIDED WITH THE VERY BEST ARTICLES, ALL AT FAIR PRICES.

Figure 13.1 'View of Lewis's Good House of Business in Ranelagh Street, Liverpool, Where The Public
Are Provided With The Very Best Articles, All At Fair Prices', *Illustrated London News*,
3 February 1883

while different types of nineteenth-century shops have been discussed from an architectural perspective. But little is known about the role of shopping in terms of social interaction and networking, although selective diary evidence and contemporary literature provide an insight into the problems created by an overwhelming choice of goods presented to the prospective purchaser in a situation where it became 'impossible to choose'. If some shoppers were 'fussy', not all shopkeepers were 'inspired', adapting their manner and language 'either respectful or familiar, as may best suit the rank or the taste of his customer'.[8] What is clear, however, is the wealth produced by trade and commerce in Liverpool and the extent to which some of this was spent locally on conspicuous consumption and by ordering more specialist and fashionable items from further afield, such as Paris and Milan. Bold Street, so it was claimed, offered the finest goods money could buy, with shopkeepers stocking the very latest fashions, for example in bustles and crinolines. Dressmakers and weavers could he engaged separately for creating unique designs for important balls in the Town Hall; exquisite (sometimes historical) fancy dresses were often a requirement for the wives of upper-middle-class merchants; and the immense wardrobe assembled by Mrs. Tinne (1886–1966), in terms of its range and immense cost, is a good illustration of the social importance of dressing well. But too little is known about shopping as a type of informal networking, particularly (although not exclusively) for women. Servants could easily be sent out to purchase standard items (particularly groceries), which could also be delivered on account. On some occasions, the mistress of the household may have been accompanied by a servant, not to offer comments on the suitability of ribbons or silks, but to carry them safely home once a purchase had been made. Networking within this context was also age-dependent: whereas the finest shopping streets were sometimes thronged with numerous, relatively young, 'promenading parties', contemporary pictures of shop interiors suggest that more elderly women preferred to make critical choices themselves, rather than in the company of 'competitive' friends. Indeed, the most exclusive shops offered a bespoke, made-to-measure dress-making service and some had a reputation for catering for the 'carriage trade', namely the local gentry and the mercantile elite. Shopping, in such a context, did not necessarily offer extensive opportunities for social networking.[9]

Nor has sexual orientation as a possible factor influencing business networking ever been taken into consideration although there was an increasing tendency between the mid-nineteenth century and 1914 for the sons of Liverpool merchants to be educated at public schools before progressing to either Oxford or Cambridge. The so-called 'secret sin' was 'learned' initially at both private and public schools and often affected later relationships. Recent research has indicated that the Victorians had a more lenient attitude to homosexuality than earlier authors had posited, although the extent to which it was tolerated within the Merseyside's merchant community or constituted a basis for networking remains unknown.[10]

Despite these omissions, the database offers a unique opportunity to analyse Liverpool's business community in detail and to move beyond a static description of elite groups using a diachronic model as a basis for in-depth analysis. Indeed, one outcome of the project was a recognition that historians researching the dynamics of mercantile communities, business networking, and gender roles would benefit from widening their analytical framework and by exploring specific themes in greater depth. The contributors to the Mercantile Liverpool Project were drawn from a number of research areas, including architectural, business, economic, gender, maritime, and social history, as well as from computer science, in particular database management. It was only on this basis that we were able to analyse and explore the inevitable complexities involved in the articulation of networks of influence and power.

In contrast to earlier studies of Liverpool's mercantile community, a multi-disciplinary approach was adopted in order to embrace a wide range of networking activities, some of which inevitably overlapped, whether they were embedded in the worlds of business, politics, religion, gender, or social interaction. Despite its status as a world port, Liverpool's business community has never been analysed in detail. Nor has the role of networks of trust, however constituted, been explored systematically as a means of reducing commercial risk. Each of the book's main sections covers issues that are central to our understanding of the changing dynamics of business networking. Inevitably, a primary focus of research was on business practices and business structures and how Merseyside's trading environment adapted both to external factors, including technological innovation, improved communication systems, the deepening and widening of hinterland and foreland markets, and transport infrastructure developments, and internal operational and organisational pressures, whether in relation to the role of trade associations, an increased dependency on credit-protection agencies, and other measures designed to maintain Liverpool's reputation as an international centre of trade and commerce.[11] But business success was reinforced visually by urban redevelopment, the construction of speculative office blocks which sought to imitate the grand urban buildings of the Italian Renaissance, the location of specific trades in separate, well-defined zones, and architectural design innovations which reflected the daily operational needs of the city's expanding business centre, including the importance of supporting business networking.[12]

Of equal importance was the need to focus on the interaction between social networks based on shared values and business culture and the role of families and households in supporting business activity, including overlapping networks created by the charitable and philanthropic contributions of the wives and daughters of merchants. Equally relevant was the extent to which the architectural designs and the interior decoration of their residences reflected the self-image, aspirations, and social esteem of members of the merchant community.[13] Buildings, as well as their decorative styles and the landscaping of gardens, helped to construct individual identity and the external perception of social standing. They were a means of reinforcing existing class divisions which enabled successful merchants to enjoy domestic lifestyles that mirrored (or exceeded) those of contemporaries of equivalent or superior social status. Even if the late nineteenth century witnessed an increasing criticism of the clutter associated with more traditional Victorian drawing rooms, interior designs were chosen to represent commercial success; the home was intended to represent cultural values; and most purchasing decisions conveyed a wider meaning.[14]

Although it was a longer-term process, the scale, geographical distribution, and social implications of extensive suburbanisation had a perceptible impact on the articulation of networking by merchants and their families, particularly in the second half of the nineteenth century, while out-migration offered new opportunities for residential development, the design of housing more in keeping with contemporary requirements, and the spatial replication of social exclusivity. Out-migration to the Wirral, however, had wider implications as the township of Birkenhead (envisaged by contemporaries as 'the city of the future'), together with Wallasey and other existing settlements, were separate local authorities. They had their own municipal powers and responsibilities which offered opportunities for exercising political power and influence or acquired them in the course of the period under consideration. Too often Liverpool historians have ignored events which took place on the other side of the River Mersey, even if the process of urbanisation in Birkenhead and Wallasey had wider implications for business networking. By analysing the development of a separate and, perhaps, competitive frameworks of associations, charitable institutions, and clubs on the Wirral the issue of core-periphery relations can be explored in detail. This, in turn, provided a means of assessing whether the process of suburbanisation process beyond the boundaries of Liverpool ultimately contributed to a fragmentation of its existing business culture, as merchants, whether resident on the Wirral or South Lancashire increasingly prioritised 'local' associational activities.[15]

Even with the wealth of material generated from the MLP database, deconstructing the networks of Liverpool merchants was not a straightforward task. Several points deserve emphasis. Firstly, elements within the overall networking framework underwent considerable change over time. On the one hand, their spatial scope was extended by communication and transport improvements; the consolidation of Liverpool's regional role which affected its relationship with its immediate hinterlands; and changes to company law and the growth in joint-stock companies led to interlocking directorates which enabled prominent merchants to benefit even more from networking opportunities. Conversely, institutional changes, specifically the increase in sector-specific trade associations, led to a concentration on networking within clearly defined areas, while the Chamber of Commerce after its formal reconstitution in 1874 as a company limited by guarantee operated through trade sections and committees. Far from representing the port-city's trading interests at all levels, it was dominated by steamship owners and well-established firms and was criticised for being insufficiently dynamic and too inward looking.

A similar process of specialisation can be found in respect to cultural networks, irrespective of whether they were based on charitable enterprises or scientific interests. However, regular networking opportunities were often limited to committee members and honorary officers, some of whom served for extensive periods of time with an undiminished commitment to a charity's objects. Suburbanisation led to the establishment of new charities, particularly in the north end of the city, but the overall level of participation by members of the mercantile community was disappointing; very few merchants were directly involved in more than one charity; and the overall level of funding was generally inadequate in relation to the city's needs. The trend towards the creation of specialist learned societies from the 1850s onwards had a similar effect, with very few merchants showing any interest in modern science, despite its potential relevance for the future of their businesses.

In both cases, institutional and cultural specialisation exacerbated divisions within the mercantile community, at a time when deeply embedded religious differences and party-political divisions had already led to a marked degree of fragmentation amongst merchants and traders, as well as within Liverpool's population in general. Set against a background of a gradual decline in church attendance, some nonconformist merchants, including Unitarians, continued to demonstrate a 'crusading spirit', with religious convictions that were also visible among those who belonged to the Church of England. Other merchants may well have been indifferent to the competitive evangelism of different denominations or regarded religion as essentially a private matter, but the repercussions of sectarianism were still pervasive, particularly in structuring the delivery of charity and social welfare where networking was conducted primarily on a denominational basis. Moreover, religious divisions were replicated in local politics, with evidence of increasing antagonism and hostility between the main parties in the years before the outbreak of the First World War. At the same time, shipowners, merchants, and brewers who had dominated local politics in the mid-nineteenth century were no longer in control of the levers of power, as local government was increasingly abandoned to 'inferior men'.

Other variables influenced networking among merchants and traders. Wealth disparity was marked, particularly on an occupation-specific level, and was all too evident even among the plutocracy (including members of the Wellington Club). In contrast to those who profited from the business opportunities of the port-city, some suffered commercial failure, bankruptcy, and downward social mobility. Moreover, the wealth disparity between the lives of many cotton traders, for example, and those who simply passed by the new Cotton Exchange on their way to work was all too visible (Figures 13.2a and 13.2b). Out-migration from the urban core, led to a weakening of traditional ties, as those who settled on the Wirral or South Lancashire developed their own networks closer to home, while the acquisition of county residences with a suitable acreage of land reinforced the spatial fragmentation of both business and social networks. Indeed, Liverpool's population was still highly transient: many merchant families changed their residence fairly frequently, whether within a local district or over greater distances well beyond the boundaries of the port-city; while other reasons, including both premature death and old age, accounted for the disappearance from the 'scene' of well-known families.

The MLP database offers an unrivalled insight into the composition and activities of the mercantile community of Liverpool and Merseyside. Even if funding limitations and the selective survival of archival material, because of neglect, fires, and wartime destruction, made it impossible to achieve a comprehensive reconstruction of the business and social lives of merchants, the project's methodology represents a major advance in comparison with the analytical limitations of a great deal of the existing historiography. Previous studies have focussed almost exclusively on merchants who have been prominent in Liverpool's 'directing class' who have been credited with 'abounding, exuberant, extraordinary, tenacious vitality', and who clearly possessed the qualities endorsed by contemporary guidebooks on how to do business including the importance of diligence, the need for a 'directing faculty', and

Figures 13.2a The Liverpool Cotton Exchange designed by Matear & Simon, 1905–06: the grand trading floor with its highly polished columns made of Larvikite rock, opened in 1906 (contemporary photograph)

'wisdom applied to practice'.[16] Even if a minority of merchants possessed some of these talents, they were deployed primarily for commercial rather than civic purposes, such as benevolent work. By analysing the mercantile community, as a whole, rather than focussing on an elite group, the limitations of existing interpretations have become all too apparent. The extent of charitable engagement with Liverpool's systemic social problems, including destitution and poverty, casual labour and unemployment, poor and insanitary housing conditions, and an unacceptable class-specific differential in average life-expectancy, was weak and inadequate. But, with notable exceptions, the financial support by merchants most registered charitable enterprises was poor; suburbanisation, selective out-migration and the acquisition of 'country' residences led to a re-direction of charitable giving; and probate data confirm the very limited extent of endowments for good causes, particularly on the part of the merchant plutocracy as a whole.

The project also highlighted the need to analyse the operation of merchant networks within a wider framework that incorporates a range of variables which determined the nature and extent of actor interaction, whether in a business, religious, political, cultural, or spatial context. Without such a multi-variable and interdisciplinary framework, it will be impossible to assess the robustness of the dominant assumptions of network theory or to re-examine the embedded

Figures 13.2b The real world: workers in Old Hall Street outside Liverpool's new Cotton Exchange
(photograph, c. 1910) (Cavendish Archive)

myths surrounding the role of merchants and businessmen in the period between 1850 and 1914,
whether on Merseyside or in other major ports and cities.

Notes

1 See, for example, David Wainwright, *Liverpool Gentlemen a History of Liverpool College, an Inde-*
pendent Day School from 1840 (London, 1960); Herbert J. Tiffen, *A History of the Liverpool Institute*
Schools 1825 to 1835 (Liverpool, 1935); Kathleen A. Goodacre, *A History of St. Edmund's College,*
Liverpool Remembered with Affection (Ormskirk, 1991); J. Brophy, *The Story of St. Margaret's Boys'*
School (Liverpool, 1976); Pat Heery and Bill Bewley, *The History of St. Francis Xavier's College, Liv-*
erpool, Liverpool, c.1840–1902 (London, 2002); Maurice Whitehead, 'The contribution of the Society
of Jesus to secondary education in Liverpool: The history of the development of St. Francis Zavier's
College, c.1840–1902', unpublished PhD, University of Hull (1984); LRO, 373 INS 12/19; Alfred
Holt, 'The Early Days of Blackburne House School,' An Address Delivered at The Liverpool Institute,
29th February, 1924.
2 See Robert Lee, Chapter 10.

3   LRO, 373, INS 12/18, 'Some Institute Recollections' by Diogenese, a very "Old Boy" (reprinted from the Liverpool Institute Schools Magazine, for private circulation (Christmas, 1900); 373 INS 33/2/1 Members who have recommended pupils; 373 Col 1/1/1/1/3/1, Admission Register, Liverpool Collegiate (High), 1906–10; 373 INS 12/16, Mental Improvement Society of the Liverpool Mechanics Institution, *Address Delivered to the Mental Improvement Society of the Liverpool Mechanics Institution, at the Opening of the Session 1845 By W. B. Hodgson, Principal of the Institution, and Ex-Officio President of the Society* (Liverpool, 1845); INS 12/17/2, Liverpool Institution Scholarships and Prizes attached to the several schools, with the date of foundation, the conditions under which each is given, and the funds from which it is derived; 'Children's Fancy Dress Ball at Liverpool', *The Graphic*, 20 January 1877, p. 53. The Mansion House, London, hosted a series of fancy-dress balls for children and juveniles, including a ball to celebrate *Twelfth Night* in 1859. They were almost certainly part of the social calendar, not only in London but also in the principal provincial towns, such as Liverpool.

4   Austin Gee, *The British Volunteer Movement, 1794–1814* (Oxford, 2003); Alan Forrest and Karen Hag (eds.), *Soldiers, Citizens and Civilians: Experiences and Perceptions of the Revolutionary and Napoleonic Wars, 1790–1810* (Basingstoke, 2009); Ian F. W. Beckett, *Riflemen Form a Study of the Rifle Volunteer Movement 1859–1908* (2nd edn, Barnsley, 2007), pp. 24, 58–74, 295–7, 312; Stephen Bull, *Volunteer! The Lancashire Rifle Volunteers, 1859–1885* (Lancashire, 1993); Peter Duckers, *Soldiers of Shropshire* (Stroud, 2000); Derek Harrison, *A History of the Shropshire Artillery Volunteer Corps, 23rd July 1860–1st April 1908* (London, 2015); Tim Anderson and Derek Driscoll BSM, *The Bristol Gunners: The History of the Gloucestershire Volunteer Artillery, 1859–2014* (London, 2013); An admirer of the Volunteers, 'Rifle Volunteers', *Liverpool Mercury*, Correspondence, 13 July 1859, p. 4. For examples of local firms exploiting the new market for military equipment, see the advertisements by Joseph Bentley & Son, Gun Manufacturer, 6 Castle Street and Blakey Brothers Military Bootmaker—*Liverpool Mercury*, 'Advertisements and Notices', 17 June 1859, 30 June 1859; 'Swearing in of the Lancashire Engineer Volunteers in St. George's Hall', *The Illustrated London News*, 5 January 1861, p. 5; 'Liverpool Press Guard (80th Lancashire Rifle Volunteers) Taking the Oaths in St. George's Hall', *The Illustrated London News*, 2 March 1861, p. 203; LRO, 252 CAM, Edward A. Pitcairn Campbell, 'A Sermon Preached before the Liverpool Press Guard or 80th Lancashire Rifle Volunteers on Sunday, 26 October 1862 at St. Nicholas' Church (printed for the members of the 80th LRV); Robert Lee, Chapter 10. The extensive diaries and correspondence of Captain George Melly provide an invaluable insight into how the Volunteer Movement operated: see LRO. 920 MEL, Melly family papers; 825 MEL, *A Week at the North Fort by a Gunner of the Fourth Brigade, Lancashire Artillery Volunteers* (Liverpool, 1863); 741.91 WOO, George Melly: Testimonial from 4th Brigade, Liverpool Artillery Volunteers; view of silver vase presented December 1863. Melly regarded the movement as 'a vast power for good in purifying and strengthening our social system': see R. B. Rose, 'Liverpool Volunteers of 1859', *Liverpool Libraries, Museum and Arts Committee Bulletin*, 6, 1 (1956); 'The Volunteers of 1859', *Journal of the Society of Army Historical Research*, 37, 151 (1959), p. 108.

5   See Randolph Cock, John Davies, Robert Lee, and Sari Mäenpää, Chapter 2; Sir Harold Howitt (ed.), *The History of the Institute of Chartered Accountants in England and Wales 1880–1965 and Its Founder Accounting Bodies 1870–1880* (London, 1966); Liverpool Society of Chartered Accountants, *Chartered 150: A Commemoration Issue of Chartered ONE to Celebrate the Sesquicentenary of the Liverpool Society of Chartered Accountants* (Liverpool, 2020), pp. 8–14; John Macnab, R. N. R., *History of the Merchants' Lodge of Freemasons No. 241 Liverpool—1780–1907* (Liverpool, 1907); (Wor. Br.) J. Cater-Giles (comp. and ed.), *To Celebrate the Centenary of the Liverpool Masonic Hall Hope Street, Liverpool, October 8th, 1858 to October 8th, 1958* (Liverpool, 1958); Roger Burt, 'Freemasonry and Business Networking during the Victorian Period', *EcHR*, 56, 4 (2003), pp. 657–88; *Miners, Mariners & Masons: The Global Network of Victorian Freemasonry* (Exeter, 2020); Peter Clark, *British Clubs and Societies 1580–1800: The Origins of an Associative World* (Oxford, 2000); Jessica Harland-Jacobs, *Builders of Empire: Freemasonry and British Imperialism, 1717–1927* (Chapel Hill, 2007); David Harrison, *Christopher Rawdon the Lost Philanthropist* (Liverpool, 2016); Graeme Milne, Chapter 4, above; Noel Fagan, Graeme Bryson and Charles Elston, *A Century of Liverpool Lawyers* (Liverpool, 2002); Charles Eyre Pascoe, *A Practical Handbook to the Principle Professions: Compiled from Authentic Sources and Based on the Most Recent Regulations Concerning Admission to the Navy, Army and Civil Service (Home and India), the Legal and Medical Professions* (London, 1978); John F. Bulley and John William Willis Burt, *A Manual of the Law and Practice of Bankruptcy, An Amended* (London, 1870). Among Merseyside lawyers who followed successful political careers

were Edward Ewart Whitley, senior partner of Whitley, Maddock, Hampson, and Castle (M.P. for Liverpool and Everton, 1880–1892) and F. E. Smith of Birkenhead who quickly established a reputation as a formidable advocate, was elected M.P. for the Walton division (1903–18) having cultivated the Tory 'boss' of Liverpool's Conservative Party, and in 1918/19 was created Baron Birkenhead.

6 Colin Pooley, 'Living in Liverpool: The Modern City', in John Belchem (ed.), *Liverpool 800: Culture Character & History* (Liverpool, 2006), p. 239. Earlier work by economic historians focussed on the changing market share of different retail units (co-operative societies, department stores, and multiples, but it proved difficult to collate statistical data. Any attempt to quantify the impact of retailing developments on the social networking patterns of customers, whether on a class-specific or occupational basis, would be even more challenging. Liverpool witnessed the opening of three further department stores in the years before the outbreak of the First World War: Blacklers, 1908; Woolworths, 1909; and T.J. Hughes, 1912, but only Lewis's has been analysed in any depth. See James B. Jefferys, *Retail Trading in Britain 1850–1950* (Cambridge, 1954); F. G. Pennance and B. S. Yamey, 'Competition in the Retail Grocery Trade 1850–1939', *Economica*, 22, 88 (1955), pp. 303–17; Asa Briggs,

7 Ian Mitchell, *Tradition and Innovation in English Retailing, 1700 to 1850: Narratives of Consumption* (London, 2014), Chapter 8, 'Civic Pride: Market Halls'; J. A. Picton, *Memorials of Liverpool Historical and Topographical including a History of the Dock Estate, vol. 2: Topographical* (London, 1873), pp. 265–7; Alison Adburgam, 'Shopping for Clothes in the 19th Century', *Costume*, 1, 2 (June, 1965), pp. 3–10. For the development of department stores, see Cock, Davies, Lee, and Mäenpää, Chapter 2. A similar process was visible in Birkenhead, when a new public marker 'of a high standard' was erected in 1834 (at accost of £3,150): according to the *Liverpool Mercury* (17 September 1835), the 'substantial, as well as delicate profusion with which the stalls were supplied, spoke well for the gastronomic capacities of the good people of Birkenhead'. A far grander market formally approved in 1843 had 3 arcades, 42 shops, and 80 stalls, extensive vaults, and decorative fountains. It cost approximately £32,000.

8 Hermione Hobhouse, *A History of Regent Street* (London, 1975); Kathryn A. Morrison, *English Shops and Shopping: An Architectural History* (New Haven and London, 2004).

9 Anthea Jarvis, *High Society: Display of Formal Dress for Fashionable People* (Liverpool, 1980); *Liverpool Fashion: Its Makers and Wearers* (Liverpool, 1981); Anthea Jarvis and Patricia Raine, *Fancy Dress* (Princes Risborough, 1984); Pauline Rushton, *Mrs Tinne's Wardrobe: A Liverpool Lady's Clothes* 1900–1940 (Liverpool, 2006). For an insight into these issues, I am grateful for the advice of Kicki Eriksson-Lee; for a discussion of wealth-holding within the mercantile community, see Cock, Davies, Lee, and Mäenpää, Chapter 2, and Robert Lee, Chapter 12.

10 On cultural (theatrical and musical) events, see R. J. Broadbent, *The Annals of the Liverpool Stage from the Earliest Time to the Present Time Together with Some Account of the Theatre and Music Halls in Bootle and Birkenhead* (Liverpool, 1901), pp. 255–6; Ros Merkin, *Liverpool Playhouse: A Theatre and Its City* (Liverpool, 2011); *Liverpool's Royal Court: A Brave Adventure* (Liverpool, 2019); Arthur Lloyd, 'Liverpool Theatres and Halls Past and Present', www.arthurlloyd.co.uk 2001–2021; Alexandra Appleton, 'In Search of an Identity: The Changing Fortunes of Liverpool's Theatre Royal, 1772–1855', unpublished PhD, Royal Holloway, University of London (2015); 'Dramatic and Proud: Images of a Complex Maritime Society at Liverpool's Theatre Royal, 1772–1800', in Wolfgang Klooss (ed.), *Writing Coast and Sea*, LKU, Literatur in Wissenschaft, 44, 2/3 (2011); William Ignatius Argent, *Half a Century of Music in Liverpool* (Liverpool, 1889); Bertram B. Benas, 'Merseyside Orchestras: An Introduction to the History of Local Instrumental Music', *THSL&C*, 95 (1943), pp. 95–117; Stephen Gent, '"The Liverpool Phil": A Brief History of the Royal Liverpool Philharmonic Orchestra: Part 1', *Liverpool History Journal*, 14 (2015); Glynn Williams, 'Opera in 19th Century Liverpool', *Liverpool History Journal*, 15 (2016); Elaine Chalus, 'Spaces of Sociability in Fashionable Society: Brighton and Nice, c.1825–35', in Elaine Chalus and Marjo Kaartinen (eds.), *Gendering Spaces in European Towns, 1500–1914* (Abingdon, 2019), pp. 75–95. On homosexuality in general, see Jeffrey Weeks, *Coming Out: Homosexual Politics in Britain from the Nineteenth Century to the Present* (London, 1977); Sebastian Buckle, *The Way Out: A History of Homosexuality in Modern Britain* (New York, 2015); Jeff Evans, 'The Victorians' Surprisingly Lenient Attitude towards Gay Men', *History Extra*, 7 April 2015.

11 See Graeme Milne, Chapters 3 and 4.

12 See Joseph Sharples, Chapter 5.

13 See the contributions of Sari Mäenpää (Chapter 6), Robert Lee and Sari Mäenpää (Chapter 7), and Joseph Sharples (Chapter 8).

14 See Chapters 7 (Robert Lee and Sari Mäenpää) and 8 (Joseph Sharples); Deborah Cohen, *Household Gods: The British and Their Household Possessions* (New Hampshire, 2006); Nick Hayes, '"Calculating Class": Housing, Lifestyle and Status in the Provincial English City, 1900–1950', *UH*, 36, 1 (2009), pp. 123–4; Anne Massey, 'Modern History and Interior Design', in Graeme Brooks and Lois Weinthal (eds.), *The Handbook of Interior Architecture and Design* (London, 2013), pp. 15–27, in particular p. 16; Kathryn Rachel Ferry, 'Clutter and the Clash of Middle-Class Tastes in the Domestic Interior', *Open Cultural Studies*, 1 (2017), pp. 113–24.

15 See the contributions by Adrian Jarvis and Joseph Sharples (Chapter 9) and Robert Lee (Chapter 10).

16 Margaret Simey, *Charitable Effort in Liverpool in the Nineteenth Century* (Liverpool, 1951), pp. 86–7, 91; Robert Humphreys, *Sin, Organized Charity and the Poor Law in Victorian England* (Basingstoke, 1995), p. 68; R. Samuel, *How to Do Business a Pocket Manual of Practical Affairs and Guide to Success in Life* (New York, c.1857), pp. 18–19.

Index

Note: Page numbers in *italics* indicates figures, page numbers in **bold** indicate tables, and those with "n" indicate footnotes on the corresponding pages.

A. B. Walker & Sons 411
Adam, Robert 215
Adams, J. B. 336
Adant, Gustav 407
advertisements 14, 28–9, 35, 126, 220, 279, 302, 467, 469
Afalo, F. G. 339
Africa 5–7, 10, 53, **61**, 76, 363–64, 365, 368, 422–23; *see also* South Africa; West Africa
African House 423
agents/agencies 26, 28, 31, 63, 78, 173, 327; *see also* brokers/brokerage; age distribution of male agents on Merseyside **12**; database of 12; emigrant 50, 247; female 11–12; listed in directories 33–4, 56; monitoring of 96–101; political affiliation and 359; steam-packet agents 423; in suburbanisation process 250
Aikin, Edmund 222
Aikin, James 187
Aikin, Mrs. 187, 188
Ainslie, P. B. 240
Alfred Holt & Company 362
Allan, Alexander 26
Allan, Bryce 26, 343
Allan, Margaret 191
Allan, R. G. 191, 402
Allan Brothers & Co. 26, 85
Allerton 61, 221, 222, 229, 230, 237, 240, 250, 253, 263, 334
Allerton Hall 227, 331
Allerton Priory 223, 245
Allingham, Walter 50, 247, 373
American Civil War 14, 76, 84, 92, 105, 169, 328, 360
Anderson, B. L. 75
Anderson, R. D. 426
Anderson, Rev. T. D. 116–17
André, Edouard 245
Andrew Gibson & Co. 422

Anglicanism 347, 351, 352
Anthony, William Hollis 335
antisemitism 347, 348
Antony Gibbs & Son 96–9
Antwerp 5
apple imports 77
apprenticeships 12, 82, 85, 178, 216, 366
arbitration 80, 105, 278, 366
architecture; *see also* offices: dining rooms, galleries, libraries, and billiard rooms 222–28, *224*, *226*, *227*, *228*; exterior 14, 110; Grecian 113; interior 125, 213–14, 216, 218, 222, *344*, 472; Liverpool's eighteenth century 210, 211, 213–15; of merchant's home 174, 215–30; towers and suburban gardens 229–30
aristocracy 146, 168, 222, 262–63, 285, 334–35, 339, 341, 426–27
Armour, Matthew Wilson 229
Armstrong, Joseph 345
Arnold, Mathew 175
art 9, 15, 124–25, 183–84, 225–26, 309–10, 406–7, 410–15, 417–18, 430, 435, 442
Arthur, Frederick 426
Ashton, Nicholas 215, 240
Asia *59*, 61, 367, 372
Aspinall, Clarke 306
Aspinall, H. K. 341
Aspinall, James 245, 271
Aspinall family 303–4
assimilation: acculturation 469; integration 329; naturalisation 61–2
associations; *see also* Chambers of Commerce; clubs; learned societies; regulation: Africa Association 365; America Association 366, 367; Brazilian Association 365, 366, 367; Brokers Association 6, 366, 420; East India and China Association 10; Incorporated Society of Liverpool Accountants 468;

Joint West Africa Committee 88; Ladies' Liberal Association 182; Ladies Sanitary Association 182, 187; Liverpool and London Steamship Protection Association 365; Liverpool Corn Trade Association 84, 345, 366; Liverpool Cotton Association 84–5, 105, 367; Liverpool Cotton Brokers' Association 84; Liverpool Ladies Association 187; Liverpool Philomathic Society 7, 32, 149, 151, 305, 439, 444, **446**; Liverpool Provision Trades Association 84; Liverpool Sailing Shipowners' Mutual Protection and Indemnity Association 365; Liverpool Salvage Association 440; Liverpool Shipowners' Freight, Demurrage and Defence Association 365; Liverpool Shipping and Forwarding Agents' Association 365; Liverpool Steamship Owners Association 30, 52; Liverpool Underwriters Association 6, 87; Manchester and Liverpool Agricultural Society 294, 298; Shipowners Association 367, 368–69; South African Merchants Committee 86; Steamship Owners' Association 366, 367; trading standards and 5, 84; West India Association 6–7; Wirral Agricultural Society 275
Atherton, James 239, 279
Atherton, Olivia 188
Atkin, George 289, 290, 296, 303, 309
Atkin, John 296
Atkin, P. W. 301
Atkin & Co. 296
Atkinson, Joseph 253
auctions, decline of 78–9
Audubon, John James 214, 238, 240
Australia *59*, **61**, 94, 302
Avison, Thomas 114, 131, 230

Bager, Johan Peter 3
Bagshaw, Margaret 11–12
Bahr, Behrend, & Ross 363
Bahr, George 363
Bailey, Sir Joseph 116, 132, 134
Bailey's Liverpool Directory 215
Baker, William 211
Balfour, Alexander 146, 173, 277, 343
Ball, George H. 275
balls 144–45, 153, 155, 169, 223, 252, 308–9, 334, 410, 417
Bamford, Arthur J. J. 331
banking 7–8, 56–7, 97–9, 334, 370; *see also* banks
Bank of England 81, 93, 113, 116, 121, 129, 132
Bank of Liverpool 51, 98, 135, 171, 254, 362, 369, 371

bankruptcy 2, 4, 42, 65, 84, 98, 101–2, 103, 105, 157, 171–72, 212, 216, 220, 296, 327–28, 343, 373, 406–7, 466, 468, 473
banks 2, 14, 57, 80–1, 93, 96–8, 100, 369, 370–71; *see also* bills of exchange; securities; Adelphi 121; Bank of Liverpool 51, 98, 135, 171, 254, 362, 369, 371; Bank of Nigeria 371; Barned's Bank 93; British & American Mortgage Co. 94; Brown Shipley 95, 97; Liverpool & Manchester District Bank 97; Liverpool Union Bank 80, 102; Mercantile & exchange 121, 135; National & Provincial Bank of England 93; North & South Wales Bank 80, 93, 95, 98, 100; North-Western 121
Banner, Harmood 114, 131, 334
Baptists 304, 342, 346, 347, 349, 414–15
Barber, William 275
Barings 80, 94, 97, 99–100
Barnardo, Dr. Thomas 405
Barrow, James 223, 371, **428**
Barry, Charles 126–27
Bates, Edward 10, 331–32
Bates, Edward Percy 10, 335, 420
Bates, Sir Edward 52–3, 358
Bates, Sir Percy Edward 398–99
Baylee, Rev. Dr Joseph 346, 348
Bayliffe, Edward 350
Beard, Rev. Charles 426–27, 430
Beausire, Joseph 253
Beazley, E. A. 401
Beazley, James 305–6, 307, 398, 402
Beazley, James H. 306, 402
Belcher, Michael 221, 228
Bellis, Walter J. 176
Bellis & Meek 169
Bencke, John Albert 64, 415
Bennett, Richard 448
Bennison, Jonathan 240
Benson, Moses 213, 331
Benson, Richard 176
Benson, Robert 169
Benson, Sarah (nee Rathbone) 169, 188
Bent, Rowland 416
Berlin Produce Exchange 104
Bibby, Arthur 335
Bibby, Frank 10, 124
Bibby, James 169, 176
Bibby, James Jenkinson 52, 245, 246, 337, 420
Bibby, J. Hartley 51
Bibby, John 170, 225
Bibby, Margaret (nee Pye) 169
Bibby, Mary (nee Pye) 169
Bibby family 8
Bibby Line 8, 245
Bickersteth, Herbert 345
Biggs, William 180

Bigland, Amos 170
Bigland, Ann 170
Bigland, Sarah 170
Bigland, Sons & Jeffreys 92
Bigland family 304
bills of exchange 80; *see also* banks; relationship
 to futures trading and 80
Billson, Alfred 125, 301
Bingham, William 304
Birdseye, C. F. 105
Birkenhead 4, *4*, 11–12, **12**, 15, 43, 47, 50, 56,
 65, 77, 146, 177, 188–89, 228, 271, **273**,
 273–76, 278–82, 285–93, 302–4
Birkenhead Borough Hospital *186*, 187, **286**, 303
Birkenhead Hotel 146
Birkenhead Institute 289, 294, 302
Birkenhead Land and Building Co. 279
Birkenhead Literary and Scientific Society **183**,
 183–84, 282, **286**, 298, 301
Birkenhead Park 4, 15, 152–53, 241–42, *243*, 260,
 261, 278–79, *279*, 280, 287, *298*
Birkenhead Railway 247, 259
Birkenhead Ruskin Society 285, **286**, 294, 301
Birkenhead School *288*, 288–89, 294, 301
Birkenhead Society 281
Birkenhead Society of Friends 290–91, 297, 304
Birkenhead Young Men's Christian Association
 291, 297
Birkenhead Young Women's Christian
 Association 291
Bisbrown, Cuthbert 238
Blackler's 55
Blackwell, George 173
Blackwell, Jane 173
Blain, William Senior 467
Bland, James 222, 226, 245
Blessig, Phillip 180
Blessing, Braun & Co. 61
Blundell, H. B. H. 129, 133
Blundell, William 244
Blundellsands 47, 65, 175, 219, 229, 244, 258
Boer War 362
Bolton 100
Booth, Alfred 179, 182, 187, 225, 363, 398
Booth, Anna 8, 170; *see also* Holt, Anna (nee
 Booth)
Booth, Charles 170, 178, 309
Booth, Lydia 187
Booth, Thomas 215, 218, 241, 247
Bootle 12, 29, 43, 56, 170, 253, 256, 276, 338,
 343–44, 394
Boston 98, 104
Boult, James 125
Bourgeoise, Jules 125
Bower, William 173
Bowes, James Lord 125, 184, 225
Bowring, Benjamin 364

Bowring, Charles Clement 170
Bowring, Charles Tricks 229, 357
Bowring, Violet Camilla (nee Ball) 170
Bowring, William Benjamin 360, 414
Boyle, J. F. 337
Bradshaw, Harold Chalton 214
Bramley-Moore, John 219, 358
Brancker, Charles H. 51
Brancker, John 309, 363
Brancker, John Barnes 365
Brandon, Thomas 92
Brassey, Lord 280
Brassey, Thomas 280, 301, 302
Braun, Francis C. 64, 229
brewing/breweries 338, 359, 411, 415–17, 418
Bridge, George 276
Bridson, Edward 184
Bridson, John 184
Bright, Allan H. 182
Bright, Edith 182
Bright, Heywood 51
Bright, Hugh 362
Bristol 3, 105, **216**, 426, 430, 442
Britton, John 240, 247
Broadbent, Emily 180
Broadbent, Margaret 180
Broadbent, Mary 180
Broadbent, Robert 180
Brockelbank, T. & R. 100
Brocklebank, Ralph 92, 176, 337, 402
Brocklebank, Sir Thomas 53, 277, 334, 336
Brocklebank & Co. 100
Brocklehurst, Henry 371
Brocklehurst, Robert 226
brokers/brokerage 2, 5–7, 28, 33–4, 37, 64, 82–5;
 see also agents; associations; seller brokers
 vs buyer brokers 27, 79–80
Brown, Dr. Campbell 145
Brown, George A. 175
Brown, George Henry 180, 345
Brown, Hugh Stowell 415
Brown, James Campbell 427
Brown, Sir William 254, 413
Brown, Stewart H. 59
Brown, William 60, 116–17, 119–20, 127, 134,
 135, 223, 447
Brunner, Mond & Co. 433
Brunner, Roscoe 447
Brunner, Sir John 246, 426, 427, 433
Bryce, James 467
Bryson, James A. 304
Bulley, Arthur Kilpin 275, 360, 441
Bulley, Samuel M. 309
Bulloch, Jessie 169
Burns, David 426–27
Burns, John 86
Burrell, Edward 278

Busch, Edward P. 64
Busch, Gustav 64
Bushell, Christopher 280, 365
business culture 2, 10–11; *see also* reputation;
    cohesion 5–7, 9–10, 182–91; establishing
    reliability 2, 77–81, 94; establishing
    trustworthiness 10, 39, 92–3, 94;
    homogeneity 5–6; obligation 2, 7, 14–15,
    141–42; reputation and 1, 10–11, 13–14,
    76, 92–101; social capital 1–3, 141, 144,
    167, 170, 324–25, 366; trust 1–2, 7, 10–11,
    92–4, 96–8
business cycles *see* trade
Butler, Josephine 187

Cain, Robert 416
Caine, William Sprotson 294, 359, 414
Calder, Miss 190
Calder, Mrs 190
Callender, Andrew 293, 304
Callender, Miss M. 293
Calvinism 290, 342, 343, 346–49
Canada 60, 304, 330, 405
canals 14, 15, 244; Manchester Ship Canal 14
capital; *see also* networks: reputation and 96–101;
    responsible capital 98; for social capital
    (*see* business culture)
Caribbean *see* West Indies
Caroe, W. D. 128
Carrington, Lord 446
cartelisation *see* cartels
cartels 36, 81
Case, Anna 214
Case, Thomas 214
Catholicism *see* Roman Catholicism
Cavendish, Spencer *see* Hartington, Lord (Spencer
    Cavendish)
Chadwick, John 210–11
Chambers of Commerce: American 6, 366–67;
    Central and Associated Chambers of
    Agriculture 104; Liverpool 5–6, 88, 122,
    126, 353, 357, 367–68, **368**, 372–73,
    375, 447, 473; London 88, 122, 126;
    Manchester 88, 104; New Orleans and
    Mobile 366; New York 105; Oriel 126
Chandler, Alfred 1n1
Chapple, Frederick 220, 225
charity *see* philanthropy
Charles Page & Co. 327
chemical manufacture 220, 221, 225, 244, 359,
    433
Cheshire 32, 43, 49, 65, 148, 149, 152, **152**,
    154–55, 179, 183, 215, 245–46, 271, 284,
    287, 298, 331–32, 434
Childwall 53, 229, 237
cholera epidemic (1849) 275, 395, 448
Cholmondeley, Thomas 341

Chorley 249, 406
churches 12, 29, 128, 168, 169, 248, 271, **284**,
    286, 290, 293–94, **295**, 296–97, 303–4,
    342–47, 351–52, 403; *see also* religion
Churchill, Winston 446
Church of England 150–51, 185, 290–91, 300,
    342, 346–47, 348–49, 402–3, 427, 433–34
Civil War (US) *see* American Civil War
Clark, Walter C. 225
class 141; of brokers 82; clubs and 144–53;
    commercial 11; directing 17; family
    members/domestic staff relationships
    and 176–78; hierarchies 109; high 64;
    identity, women and 182–91; merchant
    11–12, 65–6, 119; middle 1–2, 16–17,
    28, 46, 141, 144, 165–66; social 176–77;
    suburbanisation and 270–71
Clay, Henry 214
Clayton, Charles 281
Clayton, Mrs. 213
Clayton, Sarah 213, 215
clerks 76, 98, 110; *see also* clerkships; Census
    Office 31; female commercial 11–12;
    trading on own account and 84–5
clerkships 12; *see also* education
Clibborn, Frederic 290
Clibborn, Henrietta 290
Clibborn family 304
Cliff, Adam 420
Cliff, William 425
Cliff House 420–21, *421*
Clifton Park 241, 278
Clover, G. R. 228
Clover Clayton 281
clubs; *see also* associations; learned societies:
    Aigburth Bowling Club 297; Bebington
    Bowling Club 276, **286**, 287, **295**, 297,
    302, 303; Birkenhead Model Yacht Club
    281; Birkenhead Park Cricket Club 276;
    Birkenhead Park Rugby Club 287, 298,
    301; Birkenhead Photographic Association
    291; Canning Club 183; Claughton
    Bowling Club 276, 285, **286**, 287, 294,
    295, 301; Claughton Model Yacht Club
    281; Conservative Club House 354, *354*;
    Cricket 277, 297; fees and 149, 154–55,
    159; Grange Conservative Club 281, 285,
    286, **295**, 361; Hilbre Island Club 192;
    Hoylake and West Kirby Parliamentary
    Debating Society 183, 282, **283**;
    intersections of class, politics, religion
    and 1–2, 9–10; Junior Conservative
    Club 305, 354; Junior Reform Club 305,
    354; Liverpool Conservative Club 305;
    Liverpool Harriers 276; Liverpool Junior
    Conservative Club 305, 354; Mosslake
    Fields Cricket Club 276; New Brighton

Cricket and Bowling Club 276; New
Brighton Football Club 287; overlapping
memberships and 297; Prenton Golf Club
277; Primrose League **283**, 284, 300, 361;
Reform Club 156, 305, 354, 361; Royal
Cork Yacht Club 153; Royal Liverpool
Golf Club 32, 146, *147*, 149, 152–55,
157, 158, 285, 287, **287**; Royal Mersey
Yacht Club 9, 32, 63, 146, *147*, 152–57,
285, **287**; Royal Rock Beagle Hunt 276,
287, 338–39; Royal Rock Ferry Palatine
Bowling Club 297; Royal Thames Yacht
Club 153; Southern Club 360; St Andrews
Golf Club 153; Wallasey Cricket Club
276; Wallasey Yacht Club 296; Wellington
Club 32, 51, **51–2**, 52, 53, 144–45,
145, 149, 151, 153–55, 183, 192, 305,
308–9, 335–36, **419**, 419–20, 473; Wirral
Footpaths and Open Spaces Preservations
Society 281, 285, **286**, 297; Wirral
Harriers 276; Wirral Ramblers Association
285; Young Men's Christian Association
(YMCA) 291; YZ Club 32, 145, 151, 153
clusters/clustering 11, 83, 129, 241, 290–91, 312,
365, 445
coal 4, 31, 36, *38*, 38–9, 58–9, 77, 173, 326, 368
Cockerell, C. R. 116, 121, 122, 132, 134
coffee 4, 146
coffee houses 110, 144
collaboration *see* cooperation
Colling, J. K. 134, 226
Colquitt, John 211, *212*
Colton, W. R. 125
commerce raiding *see* privateering
Commercial Bank 116, 121, 132
committees *see* associations
commodities *see* apple imports; coal; coffee;
copper; corn; cotton; grain; grape imports;
hemp; hides; livestock trade; meat; salt;
spirits; tallow; tea; tobacco; wine
communication 9, 28, 77–81; *see also* networks;
long-distance 96
communication technology; *see also* newspapers:
British & Irish Telephone & Electric
Works 94; business practices and 2, 9,
13–14, 79–80, 130, 330; circulars 9, 28;
mail 77–8; print 2, 27–30, 78; productivity
and 78; reliability of 78; telegraph 2, 78,
329; telephone 2, 78, 329
commuting 56, 152–53, 240, 250–51, 255–63
competition 10, 28, 81, 85–6, 117, 127–28, 255,
259, 261, 347, 352–53, 365–66, 406–7
compting houses *see* counting houses
Compton House 55, 469
Coney, John 345
conference system 86
Congregationalism 346

Connolly, Lawrence 355
consumption (consumerism) 55, 77, 413, 416, 471;
see also shopping
contract enforcement 104–5; *see also* associations;
courts; regulation; Liverpool Cotton
Contract 105
Cooke, Isaac Bancroft 301
Cookson, E. H. 222
Cookson, Henry 228
co-operation 141, 142, 166
Cope, Thomas 430
copper 38, 97
corn 4, 31, 37, 82, 85, 104, 130
Cornelius & Bourgeoise 125
Corn Exchange 42, 84, 113, 133, 357; *see also*
exchange
Corn Laws 104, 360
Corn Trade Association 366
corporations 110–12, 238, 248, 252, 257; *see also*
government
Corrie, Edgar 219
costs *see* information; transaction costs
Cotterell, Harry 371
cotton 3–5, 30, 37; brokers 9, 42, 51, **52**, 53, 58;
milling 103n76; raw 4, 56, **56**, 58; spinners
78, 99, 104, 114
Cotton Exchange: Liverpool 10, 42, 103–4,
276, **343**, 345, 358, 360, 399; Matear &
Simon's 126; New York 104
councils 9, 130, 148, 155, 280–81, 352–65;
Common Council 6–7, 112; Wellington
Club 51
counting houses 112, 211, 213, 223; *see also*
offices
countryside 51, 239–40, 270, 331
courts 100, 101–2, 105, 122, 247; *see also* contract
enforcement
Cox, George R. 420
credit: credibility/creditability 197; creditors
49, 65, 94, 101–3, 105, 172, 197;
creditworthiness 82, 99, 155; reliability
and 94, 99–100, 105, 220, 325
credit protection agencies 472
Cressington Park 65, 241, 255, 258
crisis 98, 397, 439; American Civil War 84;
economic, late 1840s 327–28; of 1825 57;
financial, of 1907 105; housing market
278; network-based communications and
324–25; periods 14
Crompton, Albert 223, 244, 350
Crook, John Taylor 173
Cropper, Anne 175
Cropper, James 169, 176, 182, 192, 332, 336, 344
Cropper, John 175, 345
Cropper, J. W. 191
Cropper, Margaret 182
Crosby 31, 43, 47, 262

Crosfield, William 344, 363, **428**
Crosfield & Barrow 406–7
Culshaw, William 114, 116, 218, 229
Culshaw & Sumners 118, 119, *119, 123–24, 128,*
        131–36, 245
culture *see* business culture
Cunard, William 8; *see also* shipping companies
Customs 2, 113, 367, 437

Dale, Robert Norris 363
Dalton, John 214, 240
Danson, Francis Chatillon 306
Darwin, Charles 351
data linking 25–6, 29–30; *see also* fuzzy matching
Davenport, George 335
Davies, Peter 18, 374
Davis, William 394
Dawson, Pudsey 215
D. & C. MacIver 280
Dear, John Arnitt 358
de Beer Baruchson, Arnold 118, 119
decision-making 7, 87, 88, 402; *see also* Rational
        Choice Theory
Defoe, Daniel 210
de Larrinaga, Ramon 60, 63
Dempster, John 253, 422–23
Denman, Charlotte (nee Hope) 171
Denman, George 171
de Olano, Jose Antonio 63
department stores 55, 469; *see also* shopping
depression 3–4, 328, 397, 442; *see also* Great
        Depression
diaspora 324, 355
Dicksee, Lawrence 96
directories *see* trade directories
directorships 9, 11, 13, 16, 94, 325, 369–72,
        370, 393; *see also* joint stock companies;
        partnerships; shareholders
disease 307, 395, 409, 411, 418, 448
diversification 2, 3, 11, 13, 279, 324, 365–72;
        see also specialisation
Dixon, Joshua 237–38
Dobell, George Curzon 335
docks: Liverpool 3–4, 40–1, 76, 114, 237–38, 254,
        259, *262*, 400, 417; *see also* Old Dock
        (Liverpool); wet docks
Dod, Joseph 309
domestic life *see* spheres, public and private
domestic staff *see* servants
Douglas, John 246
Douglas, Peter 255
Dovey, Henry 173
Dovey, Mary 173
Dowie, J. Muir 146, 277
Dowie, Kenneth McKenzie 170
Doyle, J. Francis 122
Draco, Emmanuel Pantoleon 53

Drinkwater, James 172
Drinkwater, Sir George 331
drunkenness 145, 415–17
Drysdale, David Munro 414
Drysdale, Donald Munro 345
Drysdale, Dr John James 408
Duarte, Ricardo T. 183
Dun, R. G. 99
Dunbar, Sir George 111, 215
Duncan, David 275
Duncan, Dr W. H. 275, 395
Duncombe, William Ernest 341
Durning: family 239
duties *see* taxes

Earle, Arthur 169, 176
Earle, Thomas 239–40, 250, 331; *see also* T. & W.
        Earle
Earle, William 177, 331; *see also* T. & W. Earle
Earle family 151, 258
Earl of Bessborough 341
Earl of Derby 285, 426
Earl of Halsbury 446
Easton, Thomas 361
Eccles, Alexander 357, 361, 409
Eddowes, Stanton 280
Edge Hill 258, 259, 344
Edina 43
education: apprenticeships 12, 82, 85, 178, 216,
        366; clerkships 12; schools 8, 12, 31,
        263–64, 271, 276, **284**, **286**, 287–89,
        293–94, **295**, 301–3, 311, 420, 426,
        431, 471
Edwards, E. E. 51
Egerton, Sir Philip 341
Egypt 328
Elder, Alexander 53, 422–23, **424**, **429**, 430
Elder David 423
Elder David Junior 423
Elder John 253n85, 426
Elder Mary 423
electrification 152, 259–61, 309; *see also* offices
Elliot, John 303
Ellis, Peter 125–26, 135, 136, 408
Ellison, J. F. 301
Ellison, Thomas 114, 117, 131
emigration *see* migration
Enfield, William 239
Espin, Rev. T. E. 440
ethnicity *see* networks
Europe 5, 60–2, **61**, **62**, 104, 270, 360, 372, 417,
        419, 426–27
Evans, Edward 363
Evans, James 250
Evans, Sons & Co. 363
Everard, William 215
Everton 56, 111, 214, 221, 239–40, 247, 279, 354

Ewart, J. C. 119, 132

Exchange, New and Old 1, 13–14, 78–9, 84, 104, 109, 112, 129, 277–78, 282, 369; rebuilding 111–12, 114, 129

Exchange Building 42, *117*, 126, 135; *see also* Corn Exchange; Town Hall

Exchange Flags 42, 83, 112, 118, 129

exports *see* trade

exurbanisation 46; *see also* suburbanisation

face-to-face contact 13, 42, 301, 310, 312, 324, 372, 404

factionalism 353

failure: bankruptcy 2, 53, 65, 101–5, 219–22, 473; classification 11; entrepreneurial 2, 7; solvency 94

Falkner, E. D. 44, 248

family/family firm 157–59; *see also* networks; nepotism 157–58; succession 14, 97–8, 145–46, 157–58, 166, 182, 195

Farnworth, John 364

Farrer, William 119, 121, 134

fashion 16, 210, 218–19, 304, 445–46, 469, 471

femininity 444–45

Fiennes, Celia 210

Finlay, Henry 168

Finlay, Mary Jane 168

firms; *see also* succession: commercial 7–10; individual 11–13; longevity of 25, 39–42; social networks and 1–3, 14–15; steamship 37–8, *38*; suburbanisation and 15–16

Fish, Edward Duncombe 346

fishing 338

Fletcher, Potter 211

Fletcher, Thomas 216, 244

Forbes, Edward 211

Forman, John T. 146, 277

Formby Gas Co. 371

Forney, John W. 210

Forwood, Arthur, MP 86

Forwood, Arthur Bower (A. B.) 354, 361, 365, 427

Forwood, Ernest Harrison 170

Forwood, Isabell (nee Muspratt) 170

Forwood, William B. 173, 179, 222, 229, 257

Forwood family 151

Foster, John Junior 114, 469

Foster, John Senior 112, 215–17

Foster & Griffin 114

Fox, Charles H. 281

Fox & Barret 126

foxhunting 338–41; *see also* hunting

Frame, James 168

Francis, Ellen 12

fraud 4, 101–5, 353, 366

Frazer, Sir James George 427

Frederick Huth & Co. 57

Freemasons 32

free trade 104, 359–60

Friend, Edward 297

Frodsham, Ellison 172

Frodsham, Harriett 172–73

Furnival, William 253

futures trading 13, 78–80, 103–5, 468; *see also* bills of exchange; speculation

fuzzy matching 27, 30; *see also* data linking

Gage, Michael Alexander 131, 219, 238–39

Gair, Henry W. 363

Gale, John Christopher 402; *see also* John Gale & Co.

Gale, Mrs 188

Galloway, Robert 309

Galway, James 360

Gamble, David 221

Gardener, Joseph 258

gardens 111, 211, 213, 215–16, 219, 229–30, 242, 247, 249–50, 332–34, 472

Gardner, R. C. 245

Garrett, Rev. Charles 348, 403, 415

Gascoigne family 239

Gascoyne, Bamber 229

Gaskell, Holbrook 225, **428**

Gatty, C. T. 443

Geddes, Andrew 427, **429**

Gee, W. H. 245

geography *see* Merseyside; space

George Holt & Co. 115–16

Germany 62, 143, 179, 329, 342, 363; *see also* Hamburg

Gibbons, John 248

gift-giving 177, 179, 198, 341, 367, 415, 420

Gildart family 214

Gilfillan, Archibald 173

Gilfillan, Margaret 173

Gilmour, Hamilton B. 371, 402

Ginsbury, Christian D. 145

Gladstone, Henry Neville 337

Gladstone, John 215, 219, 332, 363

Gladstone, Maud 337

Gladstone, Robert 332, 339, 364, 426, **428**

Gladstone, Robertson 125, 331, 416, 420

Gladstone, Thomas Steuart 332

Gladstone, William Ewart 84, 87, 175, 337, 364, 410, 442, 444

globalisation 13, 75–7

Glynn, Walter 399

golf/golfing 56, 144, 146–48, *147*, 152–55, 157, 276–77, 285, **287**, 339

Gore's Directory 12, 25–30, 111, 263

Gossage, Frederick Herbert 432

Gossage, William 52

Gostenhofer, Charles (C. T.) 293, 300, 356

Gostenhofer, Miss 293

government: admiralty 86–7; Colonial Office 88; High Sheriffs 174–75, 336, 337, 373; Justices of the Peace 337, 350; Mersey Docks & Harbour Board 9, 252, 351, 357, 362–63, 366; subsidies 85, 86–7; Town Hall 3, 110, 112, 114, 129, 467, 468; troop transport 86–7
Graham, Duncan 337
Graham, John 343
Graham, Rowe & Co. 337
grain: corn 4, 31, 37, 82, 85, 104, 130; wheat 60, 77, 104
Grain Transport and Storage Co. 371
Granovetter, Mark 1
grape imports 77
Graves, Samuel R. 10, 170, 254
Graves bros 51
Grayson & Ould 128
Great Depression (1873-1896) 12, 41, 48, 52, 273, 327–28
Greece 59, 342
Gregson, Isabella 188
Gregson, Matthew 215
Greig, Major John James 416
Grellier, William 121, 122, 133
Guion, Stephen Barker 60
Gunn, Simon 141, 281

Hadwen, Isaac 218
Hall, Charlton Robert 344–45
Hall, Sir Bernard 422, **424**
Halle, Charles 223
Hamburg 5, 62; *see also* Germany
Hamilton, Jackson & Co. 280
Harford, Austin 355
Hargraves, James 113
Harland, Sir Edward 432
Harland & Wolff 432
Harrison, Frederick James 8, 335
Harrison, James 246, 278, 335, 415, **429**
Harrison, Thomas Fenwick 246, 335, **428**
Harrison, Walter A. 195
Harrison family 57, 329–30
Hartington, Lord (Spencer Cavendish) 87
Hartley, Jesse 251
Hartley, Sir William Pickles **431**, 433, 449
Hawthorne, Nathaniel 62, 219, 227, 229, 241, 264, 275
Hawthorne, Sophia 223
Haywood, Arthur G. 442
Haywood, Francis 227
Hazlehurst, Mrs 217–18, 229
Hazlehurst, Thomas 217, 229
health 46, 97, 158, 176, 239, 271, 274–77, 395–96
Heap, William 300
Heaton family 304

Hele-Shaw, H. S. 434
Hemelryk, P. E. J. 358
hemp 4, 35, 415
Henderson, Francis 357, 414
Henderson, Gilbert 212–13, 214
Henderson, W. R. 253
Henry Pooley & Son 359
Henry Tate & Sons 406, 407, 410
Herdman, William 109, *110*
Heswall 65, 274, 277
Heywood, Arthur 98, 211, 214
Heywood, Benjamin 211
Heywood, Benjamin Arthur 222
Heywood, John Pemberton 230, 245–46, 264, 467
Heywood, Pemberton 343
hides, tanning 5
Higgin, Susan 188
Higgins, Alan 333
Higgins, William 135, 228
Higson, J. H. 399
Higson, John 246
Hill, Octavia 405
Hind, Miss 191
Hind family 303–4
Hinshaw, Robert 171
Hinson, George Canning 173
Hirsch, Rev. David Jacoby 348
Hobson, Rev. Canon Richard 415
Hodgson, Adam 240, 333
Hodgson, David 364
Hodgson, Thomas 211
Holder, Thomas 422
holiday homes 244–47
Holland *see* Netherlands
Holme, A. F. 363
Holme, Francis Usher 409
Holme, George 409
Holme, James 364
Holmes, J. G. 284
Holt, Alfred 8, 125, 170, 230, 245, 350, 362, 438, 440–41; *see also* Alfred Holt & Co.
Holt, Anna (née Booth) 8, 170, 178
Holt, Anne 170, 171, 172, 174, 177, 179, 182, 189, 195, 351
Holt, Emma 58–9, 174, 177–78, 182, 195, 248
Holt, Frances 189
Holt, George 8, 51, 53, 58, 83, 115–16, 119, 131, 132, 166, 171, 174–75, 177, 182, 192, 195, 197, 225, 226, 230, 244, 248, 260, 275, 309, 327, 351, 361, 365, 404, 426, 427, **428**, **429**, **431**, 440, 466
Holt, Jane Brandreth 440
Holt, John 83, 86
Holt, Lawrencina 182–83
Holt, Mrs (Philip) 188
Holt, Philip 170, 195, 350

Holt, Richard 335, 350, 358, 360, 362
Holt, Robert 182, 361
Holt, Robert Durning 175, 195, 197, 223, 229,
    331, 335
Holt, William 170, 195, 223, 225
Holt, William Henry 441
Holt family 57, 65, 166, 170–71, 174–76, 178–79,
    189, 192, 223, 244–45, 248, 258, 329, 330,
    360, 427, 431; *see also* Melly, Cecily
    (nee Holt)
homeopathy, orthodox medicine and 407–8
honesty 2, 42, 76, 169, 328–29; *see also* business
    culture
Hope, E. W. 432
Hope, John 215
Hope, Samuel 278
Hornblower, Lewis 118, 244, 245
Hornby, George G. 334
Hornby, Hugh Frederick 227
Hornby, Thomas 252
Horner, H. P. 413
Horsfall, George Henry 245, 331
Horsfall, T. B. 245
Horsfall, Thomas 331
Horsfall family 10, 245, 331
Horwood, Richard 213
hospitals 185–87, 271, **286**, 291–94, **295**, **308**,
    408–9, 423; *see also* philanthropy
Houghton, John 214
Hoult, Joseph 364
Housden, James 297
household *see* spheres, public and private
houses, terraced 15, 212–13, 216, 218–21,
    241, 248
Houston, R. P. 331
Hoylake 47, 146–48, 183, 260, 270, 273–77,
    281–92, 300–302, 312–13
Hubback, J. H. 366
Hubback, Joseph 94–5, 402
Huggins, Samuel 129, 222
Hughes, Hugh Price 346
Hughes, T. J. 55
Hull 105, 415
Hume, Rev. Abraham 148, 435, 437, 447
hunting 273, 335, 338–41
Hutchinson, Edward 357
Hutchinson, Samuel Mason 305
Hyslop, Maxwell 169, 218

identity 8, 25, 60, 151, 154, 213, 280, 293; class
    174–78, 182–83, 237; confessional 325,
    327; denominational 351–52, 364; local
    associational 304–10; occupational
    166–67; shared 297–98; socio-cultural
    435, 439; urban 281–82
immigration *see* migration

Imperial Tobacco Company 83
imports *see* trade
India 53, 338, 367; Buildings, construction
    of 115–17, 122, 131; East, trade 10,
    35–6, 332; global economic instability
    and 327–29; indentured labourers 407;
    steamship companies 86–7; West, trade
    5–7, 357, 360
individualism 81, 85–6
industrialisation 46, 237, 405
industrialists 53, 146, 430
industry 52, 238–40; brewing 359, 415, 416;
    chemical 438–39; cotton 99–100, 328–29;
    drinks 355, 415; marine insurance 87–8;
    railway 258; retail 469–71; shipowning 30;
    shipping 76–7, 81–8, 422; sugar refining
    406–7; textile 60, 77
infant mortality 275, 415–16
information 1–10; *see also* communication
    technology; networks; census 30–1;
    costs 9, 96, 99–100, 143; information
    asymmetries 2, 76–7; information costs
    96, 143; Mercantile Liverpool Project
    Database and 11–13, 25–6; monitoring
    systems 96–101; networks 142–43;
    reputation and 93–5, 99; systems 2, 13,
    142; from trade directories 26–30; women
    and 178–79
infrastructure 3, 13, 47–9, 76–7, 88, 178, 248–50,
    274, **283**, 283–84, 288–89, 305, 309,
    311–12, 403, 427, 449–50
Inman, Ernest 296
Inman, William 223, 296–97, 306
in-migration *see* migration
innovation 76–7, 122, 416, 469, 472; *see also*
    communication technology; English
    Electric Light Co. 94; futures trading
    78–81; London & Provincial Street
    Lighting Co. 94
insolvency *see* failure
institutions 2–3, 6–7, 12–13, 57, 80–1, 83–4,
    98, 121, 143–46, 148–49, 185–89, 271,
    290–92, 294, 305–6, 353–54, 357,
    394–400, 403–4, 411, 425–26, 435, 450
insurance 2, 7, 52, **56**, 80, 86–7, 110, 126, 131–36,
    353, 356, 369–71; Liverpool, London &
    Globe Insurance 94, 371; marine 7, 87
intermarriage *see* marriage; networks
intermediaries *see* agents
investment 6–7, 52, 170–73, 256, 271, 273,
    278–80, 327, 331, 334, 418; *see also*
    capital; credit
Ireland 84, 95, 97, 143, **287**, 329, 331, 342,
    345, 349
Irish Nationalism 59, 151, 330, 348, 352–56,
    361, 374

iron 4, 36, 40, 77, 119, 122, 124, 126, 213, 242, 248, 275, 276, 294, 297, 300–301, 304, 331, 359, 368, 403, 414
Irvine, James 297
Isaac, J. R. 247
Islam 342
Ismay, James H. 176
Ismay, J. Bruce 57, 171, 174, 422, 423–24, **424**
Ismay, Margaret 188, 222, 245
Ismay, Mrs (James H.) 188, 422
Ismay, Thomas Henry 8, 53, 65, 85–6, 168, 172, 222, 223, 226, 245, 246–47, 249, 306, 307, 364, 401, 422; *see also* shipping companies

Jackson, A. M. 398
Jackson, John 84–5
Jackson, Thomas Hughes 146, 275, 339, 370
Jackson, William 278, 280, 438
Jager 406
Jamaica *see* West Indies
James Finlay & Co. 364
Japp, John 400
Jardine, David 427, **428**
Jeffery, J. R. 221
Jenkins, Johnson 303
Jennings, Thomas 357
John Gale & Co. 327
Johnson, John Owens 333
Johnston, Robert Sutherland 173
Johnston, William **428**, **431**, 432
joint stock companies 10, 13, 27, 88; *see also* directorships; partnerships; shareholders; creditability and 197; interlocking directorships and 369–72, **370**, 473; limited liability and 121, 369; management and finance of 101; morality and 83, 93–4, 95, 369; reputation and 96
Jolly & Gaskell 92
Jones, Alfred 88, **428**
Jones, Charles W. **429**, 440
Jones, Geoffrey 369n151
Jones, Henry 279–80
Jones, John 447
Jones, Owen 333
Jones, Rev. John 218, 415
Jones, Rev. Joshua 350
Jones, Richard 423
Jones, Robert 35
Jones, Roger Lyon 423, **424**, 425, **428**
Jones, Sir Alfred Lewis 250, 296, 363, 367
Joynson, Thomas 119, 133
J. R. Gorst & Co. 252
Judaism: antisemitism and 347–48; Sephardi 347
Jump, Henry 403
Just, William 328

Karck, Ella 187
Kellock, Charles Walford 339
Kellock, William Walter 339
Kemp, Edward 197, 332–34
Kennedy, David 351
Kensington 240, 247, 255, 336
Kent, Richard 213
Kern, Hans 168, 343
Keswick spirituality 347; *see also* religion
Kind, John 61
King, Colonel V. A. 276, 294, 296
kinship *see* networks
Kirby, Edmund 228, 263
Kleinworts 97
Knott, James 85
Knotty Ash 187, 237, 255
Kurtz, A. G. 220, 223, 225, 230, 244, 247, 248
Kurtz, Mrs 334

ladies *see* women
Laird, Egerton 296, 303
Laird, E. K. 303
Laird, J. M. 303
Laird, John Senior 280, 281, 294, 298, *299*, 300, 303, 356, 358, 361, **424**, 425
Laird, Macgregor 166, 177, 328, 422
Laird, William 278, 356, 468; *see also* W. & H. Laird Co.
Laird family 275, 293, 294–95, 302, 303
Lake District 49, 176, 332
Lamport, Charles 176
Lamport & Holt 53, 195
Lancashire 65, 148–49, 245–46, **287**, 333, 336, **436**; *see also* textiles; relationship to Liverpool 31–2, 76–7, **152**, 152–55
landed society *see* aristocracy
landownership 278, 337
Langley, Charles 309
Langton, Charles 334
Langton, Mrs 191
Langton, William 254
Langton family 151
l'Anson, Edward 121
Lapell, William 172, 195
Latin America *see* South America
lawyers 129, 148, 213, 238, **428**, 438, 468
Lazarus, J. G. 348
Lea, John 359
learned societies 65, 142, 144, 155–56, 393–94; *see also* associations; clubs; Amateur Musical Union 184, 309; Amicable Book Society 144, 183; Birkenhead Choral Union 291; Birkenhead Dramatic Society 293; Birkenhead Fair Trial and Relief Committee 281; Birkenhead Literary and Scientific Society 183, 281–82, 298, 301, 304; Birkenhead Literary Society 282;

Birkenhead Ruskin Society **183**, 184, 285, 294, 301; Birkenhead Shakspere Literary Society **183**, 184, 449; Botany Society 449; British Association for the Advancement of Science 446, 447; Canning Debating Society 281; Claughton and Cleveland Club 281; collaboration between 447–49; Deeside Literary and Debating Society 282, **283**, 284; Eclectic Society for the Furtherance of Literature, Philosophy, Science and Art 281; fees and 154–55, 159, **433**, 443, 449; French Literary Society 184; Geographical Society (1891) 441; Geology Association 447–48; Geology Society 447–48; Grange Road Literary Society 281; Hamilton Debating Society 281; Historic Society for Lancashire and Cheshire 32, 148; Historic Society of New York 153; Hoylake and West Kirby Parliamentary Debating Society 281, 282, **283**; Italian Literary Society **183**, 184, 310; Lancashire and Cheshire Antiquarian Society 437, 444; Lancashire and Cheshire Entomological Society 443, 445; Liscard Orchestral Society 281; Liverpool Amateur Photographic Society 444; Liverpool Architectural and Archaeological Society (1848) 438; Liverpool Astronomical Society 440, 443; Liverpool Athenaeum 31, 148, *148*; Liverpool Biological Society (1888) 440; Liverpool Botanical Society 441; Liverpool Chemists' Association (1849) 438; Liverpool Engineering Society 438; Liverpool Institute Debating Society 297; Liverpool Law Library Society 438; Liverpool Library 144, **183**, 183–84, 309; Liverpool Literary and Philosophical Society 149, 155, 435, **436**, 437, 439, 442–44, 445, 447; Liverpool Lyceum 110–11, 183, 305, 309; Liverpool Marine Biology Committee 440; Liverpool Philomathic Society 7, 32, 149, 151, 305, 439, 444, **446**; Liverpool Photographic Society 438; Liverpool Physical Society 440; Liverpool Royal Institution (1814) 222, 412; Liverpool Sacred Harmonic Society 183, **183**; Liverpool Science Students' Association; Liverpool Students' Scientific Association 443–44, 449; Liverpool Section of the Society of Chemical Industry (1879) 439; Liverpool Statistical Society 435, 444; Manchester Law Association 438; Mental Improvement Society of the Liverpool Mechanics Institute 467; merchant involvement and **436**, 449–51; Metropolitan and Provincial Law Societies Association 438; Museum of Japanese Art **183**, 184, 225, 310; National Association for the Promotion of Social Science 447; Natural History Society 435, 441, 443, 444; Naturalist's Field Club 445; networks and 434–51; New Brighton Amateur Operatic Society 281; Newcastle Literary and Philosophical Society 153; overlapping memberships and 182–91; Oxton Quoit Club 293; Philalethians 183; Polytechnic Society 305, 435, **436**, 437, 439, 442, 443, 444; Rock Ferry Athenaeum Debating Society 282; Rock Ferry Horticultural Society 281; Royal Astronomical Society 440; Royal Institute of Public Health 447; Seacombe Parliamentary and Debating Society 282; Seacombe St. Paul's Literary and Debating Society 281; Southport Literary and Philosophical Society 153; St Cecilia Choral Society 281; Trinity Presbyterian Church Literary Society 281; turnover and 448, 450; Union News Room 111; West Kirby Choral Society **283**, 284; West Kirby Christian Institute **283**, 291, 297, 301; West Kirby Literary Society **183**, 184, 199, 282, **283**, 284, 285, 294, 302–3; Wirral Footpaths and Open Spaces Preservation Society 281, 285, 297; Wirral Philharmonic Society 294, 298; women and 445–46

Leather, Joseph 220–21
Ledward, John Arthur 301
Lee, George Henry 55, 469
Legge, H. J. 301
Leicester, Peter 215
Leigh, John Shaw 239
Leigh, Joseph 245
Leigh, Thomas Allan 345, 350, 398
Leighton, Frederic 225, 415
Leslie, Mary 222
letters of recommendation *see* recommendations
Lever, William Hesketh **429**, **431**
Lewis's 55
Leyland *see* shipping companies
Leyland, Charles 334
Leyland, Christopher J. 336
Leyland, Frederick 53, 94, 228, 337
Leyland, Frederick Richards 124–25, 225, 246
Leyland, Thomas 334
Leyland & Bullins 399
libraries 144, 226–28, 305
limited liability 16, 36–7, 40, 83, 93, 301, 325, 369, 371; *see also* joint stock companies
Link, J. W. 100
Lister, James 398
literary societies 184

Littledale, Harold 195, 334
Littledale, Thomas 9, 173, 364; *see also* T. & J.
    Littledale & Co.
Liverpool, London & Globe Insurance 94, 371
Liverpool Electric Supply Co. 371
Liverpool Legal and General Insurance Co. 362
Liverpool Life and Fire Insurance Co. 369
Liverpool & London Insurance Co. 116, 118, 119,
    121, 134
Liverpool School of Maritime History 7, 8
Liverpool School of Tropical Medicine 423
Liverpool Stock Exchange 121
livestock trade 368
Livingstone, Joseph Gibbons 361
Lloyd, W. H. 442
Lockerby, William 248
Locket, Richard R. 222, 223, 226
Lockhart, William P. 275, 350
Lodge, Oliver **431**, 434, 440
Londini, Dr. 310
London 49, 65, 77–8, 87, 100, 104, 121–22, **152**,
    152–53, 176, 210, 246–47, 278–79, **287**,
    297, 303, 354, 394, 401–2, 407
Long Depression *see* Great Depression
Loudon, John Claudius 332–33
Lowe, William 97
Lugar, Robert 240
Lund, Rev. T. W. M. 245
Lyon, James 423

Macfie 406
MacGregor, Alexander 218
MacIver, Charles 277, 280, 343; *see also* D. & C.
    MacIver
MacIver, David 281, 300, 306, 360, 361, 364;
    see also D. & C. MacIver
MacIver, Harold 10
MacIver, Henry 328
MacIver family 57, 65, 94
Mackenzie, Robert Kirkwood 447
Mackmurdo, A. H 244
mail *see* communication technology
management 9–10, 75, 93, 96, 275–76, 290,
    293, 335, 415; of charities 397–404;
    of churches 344–45; competence of
    a widow 167–70; domestic 165–67,
    175–78; household 195–99; of joint-stock
    companies 101–2; of late nineteenth-
    century Liverpool firms **39–40**, 39–42,
    41; women in medical institutions and
    186–91
Manchester 31, 51, 77, 88, 99–100, 105, 106, **152**,
    156, 178, 216, **216**, 229, 237–38, 255, 304,
    426, 430–32
Manchester Ship Canal 14
Manufacturing 17, 35, 75, 141, 289, 309, 357,
    370–71; British, nineteenth century 75–7;

cotton 103–5; tobacco 3; in trade
    directories 29–30
marine insurance *see* insurance
Marquis, John 293
Marquis, May 293
Marquis, Robert 303
Marquis of Anglesey 285
Marquis of Hertford 168
marriage 10, 60, 62, 82, 143, 145, 166–72, 174,
    180–82, 197–98, 324, 326; *see also*
    networks
Marriner, Sheila 7, 18, 75, 374
Marshall, Alfred 75
masculinity 159–60, 196
Mason & Ryder 181
Mather, John Phillips 343
Matheson, Thomas 304, 350
Mathews, John 303
Mawson, Thomas 337
Maxwell, Maxwell Hyslop 169, 218
Mayer, Joseph 413, 467
McGilchrist, Charles R. B. 345
McGregor, Messrs 116
McQuie, Ellen (nee Broadribb) 169
McQuie, James B. 169
McQuie, Peter Robinson 166, 169, 173, 175, 195
Meade, King & Robinson 92
Meagher, Thomas 99
Mears, Henry 276
meat 80, 94; frozen meat 77; meat trade 5, 42, 368
medical charities: Andrew Gibson Memorial
    Home for Seaman's Widows 422;
    Asylum for Orphan Boys (1852) 395;
    Bankhall Girls' Institute 425; Birkenhead
    and Wirral Children's Hospital 306;
    Birkenhead Borough Road Mission 306;
    Birkenhead Dispensary (1828) 291;
    Birkenhead Ladies' Charity and Lying-
    in-Hospital (1845) 291; Blackpool Street
    Mission 306; Bluecoat Hospital 306; Blue
    Coat School 246; Caledonian Free School
    (1808) 403; Charitable Society, The
    185; Charity Organization Society 394;
    Children's Hospital in Upper Hill Street
    (1851) 394; Church Temperance Society
    403; Convalescent Home for Children
    (1881) 275; David Elder Infirmary, The
    423; David Lewis Northern Hospital, The
    423; Establishment for Needlewomen
    423; Gordon Boys' Memorial Institute
    (1886) 425; Gordon Hall Institute 398;
    Gordon Working Lads' Institute *421*, 425;
    Heswall Children's Hospital 291; Home
    for Aged Seamen 420, *421*; Hospital for
    Decayed Seamen (f. 1751) 144; Hostel
    of Hope (1909) 187; Hoylake Benevolent
    Tontine Society 283; Infant Orphan

Asylum (1858) 396; Ladies' Branch
Society (1817) 187; Ladies Knitting
Guild 186; Ladies' Work Society 423;
Laird School of Art, The 425; Lancashire
Female Refuge (1823) 189; League of
Welldoers, The 394; Leasowe Open Air
Hospital for Sick Children (1914) 187;
Liverpool Blue Coat Hospital and the
Southport Convalescence Hospital 423;
Liverpool Council of Education 306;
Liverpool County Hospital for Chronic
Diseases of Children 291; Liverpool
Dog's Home 397; Liverpool Dorcas and
Spinning Society (1817) 187; Liverpool
Guardian Society 403; Liverpool Health
of Towns' Association 395; Liverpool
Hebrew Philanthropic Society 347;
Liverpool Magdalen Institution 185;
Liverpool Maternity Hospital and Ladies
Charity, The 423; Liverpool Open Air
Hospital for Children 275; Liverpool
Self-Help Society for Girls 187; National
Life Boat Institution 405; National
Mercantile Marine Fund 422; National
Thrift Society 406; National Vigilance
Society 187; North End Domestic Society
(1859) 403; North West Seamen and
Boatmen's Finance Society 307; Royal
Southern, The 423; Saint Paul's Eye and
Ear Hospital (1871) 186; School for the
Blind (1790) 394; School for the Deaf and
Dumb (1825) 189; Sea Bathing Infirmary
423; Seacombe Cottage Hospital and
Dispensary for Children (1869) 291;
Shaftesbury Boys' Club 306; Society for
the Prevention of Cruelty to Animals,
The 340; Society for the Reformation of
Prostitutes 395; Society for the Relief
of Sick and Distressed Needlewomen
423; Southern and Toxteth Hospital
(1842) 186; Strangers' Friend Society,
The (1796) 403; Traveller's Aid Society
187–88; Turner Memorial Home of
Rest for Chronic Sufferers (1884) 403;
Welsh Charity School (1804) 403; West
Kirby Benevolent Fund 283; West Kirby
Convalescent Home for Children 306
medical institutions *see* philanthropy
medicine 408, 417, 427, **428**–**29**, 438;
    homoeopathic 408–11, 419; traditional
    409; tropical 430; veterinary 254, 427
Mediterranean, Liverpool trade with 52, 60, 76–7,
    245
Mee, Arthur 440
Meek, John 169
Melly, André 175–76
Melly, Andrew 178

Melly, Cecily (nee Holt) 170
Melly, Charles P. 174, 189, 192
Melly, Eva 440
Melly, Florence 189
Melly, George 83, 87, 166, 170, 173, 177, 191,
    218, 335, 341, 347, 362, 447, 468
Melly, Hugh M. 170
Melly, S. Heywood 440
Melly family 192
Members of Parliament 358
men: fathers 159, 181, 192, 195, 467; husbands
    15, 165, 170, 172–74, 179, 184, 190, 192,
    198; sons 34, 154, 157–59, 166–68, 181,
    195, 289, 329, 338–40, 375, 432–33,
    466–68
Mercantile Marine Service Association 395, 422
merchant community; *see also* business culture;
    competition: business organisation types
    in 36–9; communications and 77–81;
    concentration of 75–7; development of
    Liverpool's 5–10; firms and associations
    81–8; lifespans of firms in 39–42;
    Liverpool's dock infrastructure and 3–5;
    Mercantile Liverpool Project 10–18; size
    of 32–6; turnover in 2, 9, 40, 55–6, 117,
    329, 402, 449–50; wealth of 50–9
merchants; *see also* merchant community:
    monitoring 96–101; nationality and birth
    country of 59–64; structures of 93–5
Merchants' Lodge 32, 468
Merrifield, Ziegler & Co. 310
Mersey Dock and Harbour Board (MD&HB) *see*
    government
Mersey Forge Co. 51, 369, 371
Merseyside: Birkenhead 4, *4*, 11–12, **12**, 15, 43,
    47, 50, 56, 65, 77, 146, 177, 188–89, 228,
    271, **273**, 273–76, 278–82, 285–93, 302–4;
    Bootle 12, 29, 43, 56, 170, 253, 256,
    276, 338, 343–44, 394; Liverpool 1–18,
    25–66, 109–30, 141–60, 270–313, 324–75;
    Wallasey 11, 12, **12**, 56, 261, 270, **273**,
    273–77, 287, 291–93, 297–98, 311, 472;
    Wirral 270–313
Methodism: Calvinistic 290, 342, 343, 346,
    348–49; Primitive 342, 346, 433;
    Wesleyan 290, 342, 344–46, 347, 349
Meyer, Arnold 211–12
Meyer, Kuno 427
migration 42, 49, 76, 96; *see also* suburbanisation;
    emigration (out-migration) 16, 17, 44, 49,
    65, 199, 270–71, 273–75, 325, 330–37,
    373, 417, 448, 469, 472–73; family 169;
    immigration (in-migration) 55, 61, 64,
    271, 329–30, 342, 347, 372–73, 395;
    internal 65
military 51, 146, 167–68, 349, 362, 424–25,
    467–68; *see also* Volunteer Movement

Minoprio, Charles 225
Minoprio, Francis Charles Anthony 415
Minoprio, William Henry 173
Minshall, William 59
Mocatta, Maurice 280, 281, 361
Moffat, Isabel 169
Montefiore, Claude J. G. 348
Montgomery, Robert 176
Moore, James 413
Morris, John Grant 59, 223, 245, 246, 365, 420
Moscow Gas Works 97
Mosely, Charles 447
Moss, George W. 415
Moss, William 237–38
Mossley Hill 29, 46, 64, 197, 221, 230, 237, 240–41, 248, 263, 344, 422
Mott, Charles Grey 278, 280, 301, 447
Muspratt, Dr E. K. 223, 361, 426, **428**, **431**
Muspratt, Isabel 170
Muspratt, James 223, 227
Muspratt family 53
Mussabini, Pierre 53
Myers, Messrs 121, 133

Nash, John 114, 229
National Protestant Electoral Federation 355
Naylor, Dorothy 334
Naylor, Jeremiah Todd 240
Naylor, John 245, 333, 334, 399
Naylor, R. C. 119, 134, 226
Naylor, Rowland E. L. 399
Neilson, Robert 170
neologianism 347; *see also* religion
nepotism 157–58
Nesfield, Eden 245
Netherlands 125, 218
network analysis 17, 142–43, 165, 198–99, 324–27
networks; *see also* clusters; network analysis: business 1–3, 6–8, 14–15, 142–43, 154–59, 166–67, 324–26, 352–72; capital and 1–3, 8–9, 167–70; commercial success and 10–11, 18, 324, 329–31, 335, 337–38, 372–75; cultural 12, 473–76; definitions 1, 324–25; ethnic 1, 2–3, 7, 17, 324–25, 327, 372–74; family 143, 167, 170, 178, 182–91, 198; friendships 1, 15, 159, 178, 193, 195, 199, 284; and information 1–2, 8–9, 142–43; kinship 75, 141–43, 158–59; learned societies and 143–44, 393–94, 434–49; marriage 10, 60, 62, 142–43, 167–70; philanthropy and 15, 394–451; political 142–43, 324–75; religious 142–43; social 14–15, 143–44, 178–79; social embeddedness and 197, 393–451; strong and weak ties 1, 7, 144, 325; women and 170–73, 178–79

Neumann, C. W. 229
New Ferry 47, 65, 177, 251, 282, 287, 304, 338
newspapers: advertisements and 14, 28–29, 35, 126, 220, 279, 302, 467, 469; *Albion* 116, 467; *Baily's Hunting Directory* 340; *Baily's Magazine of Sports and Pastimes* 340; *Birkenhead and Cheshire Advertiser, The* 279; *Builder, The* 116–17, 118, 126–27; *Commercial List* 99; *County Gentleman, The* 340; *Daily Post* 100, 275, 362; *Fairplay* 93–4; *Field, The* 340; libel and 100, 430; *Liberal Review* 125, 229, 241, 252, 415; *Liverpool Mercury* 340; *Liverpool Review* 93, 102, 353; *Liverpool Review of Politics, The* 353; *Methodist Times, The* 346, 395; *New Sporting Magazine, The* (1831) 340; *Porcupine, The* 81, 82, 102, 118, 122, 124, 154, 220, 230, 244, 413; *Punch* 406; *Shipping World* 95; *Society, Literature and Art* 353; *Sporting Pictorial* 340; *Sportsman, The* 340; *Weekly Chronicle* 467; *Wide World Magazine* 100
New York relationship to Liverpool 60, 80–1, 122
Nicholas Waterhouse & Sons 121
Nickels, Walter L. 306
Noble, Henry Heywood 399
nonconformity 345–46, 347, 350, 365, 374
North America 60–2, 76, 80, 84
North East England 77
Norway 55, 245, 338, 342

obligations 2, 7, 14–15, 141–42; *see also* business culture
offices; *see also* counting houses: construction, capital and profitability of 115–17; lighting and 125–26; merchants as property developers and 119–21; office buildings near the Liverpool Exchange **131–36**; style and symbolic significance of office blocks 126–29, *127–28*; supply of office accommodation and 118; Victorian office blocks and 121–25, *123–24*
oil 4, 33, 37, 225, 331, 368; *see also* palm oil; petroleum 5, 85
Old Dock (Liverpool) 110–11, 210–16, 238
Oldham 100
Orange Order 349, 355, 403
Orchard, B. Guinness (B. G.) 32, 66, 81, **82**, 99, 119–20, 145, 223, 241–42, 245–46, 326, 328, 330–32, 334, 339, 351, 359, 363, 369–70, **370**, 398, 399, 402, 404, 413–14, 416, 418, 420, 434, 441, 445–46
Oulton, William 398
out-migration *see* migration
Owen, Owen 55, 469
Owen, Peter 192, 334, 363, 399, 420
Owens, Alastair 158n80

Owens, John 430
Oxton 29, 253, 273, 274–76, 280, 285, 288–91,
    293, 297–98, 301, 302, 310, 311, 343

Pacific Loan and Discount Co. 371
palm oil 5, 278, 328, 331; *see also* oil
Panizzi, Antonio 227
Pardoe, James 211
Parker, Alfred T. 332
Parker, S. Sandbach 335
parks 15, 46, 56, 229, 242–43, 244, 263–64, 349,
    404, 411; public 229–30, 244, 263–64,
    411; residential 46; urban 15, 56, 404
Parks, Bruce and Mungo 271
Parr, Edward 237
Parr, Thomas 213, 245
Parry, Edward Penbury 345, 348, 403
partnerships 2, 11, 13, 26, 29, 32–42, *35–38*, **39–**
    40, **41**, 64, 82–3, 83, 92, 94, 98, 167, 169,
    172, 176, 195, 197, 329, 363, 364, 369,
    406; *see also* directorships; joint stock
    companies; shareholders; sole traders;
    father and son 34, *35*; kinship, friendship
    and 141–60; longevity of **39–40**, 39–42,
    41; marriage 167, 174; rise of 37–8, *37–8*;
    selection of partners and 169
passenger lines *see* shipping companies
path dependency 325
Paton, Alfred Vaughan 301
Patterson, John 350, 364
Paul, Edward 363, 366
Paxton, Joseph 242, 278, *279*, 322, 332
Peabody, George 405
Pearson, Charles 345
Peel, Jonathan 467
Pemberton, J. A. 281
Peters, Ralph 128–29, 135, **135**
Peter Walker & Son 411, 416
petroleum *see* oil
philanthropy: Birkenhead Borough Hospital *186*,
    187, **286**, 292, **295**, 296, 303, 306, 425;
    entrepreneurial philanthropy 404–34;
    Female Orphan Asylum 186–91, 307, 395,
    397, 398, **398**; Florence Institute for Boys
    306, 422; Home for Incurables 187–91,
    271, **308**, 402, 420; Hoylake Cottage
    Hospital (1906) **286**, 292, **295**; Ladies'
    Benevolent Society (1810) 185, 187;
    Ladies' Charity (1796) 185, 394; levels
    of charitability/attendance and 307–8;
    Liverpool Children's Association 187,
    275; Liverpool Female Orphan Asylum,
    The (1840) 186–91, 307, 395, 397, 398,
    398; Liverpool Female Penitentiary (1809)
    185, 187, 190, 191, 271, 308, **308**, 395,
    397, 401; Liverpool Hahnemann Hospital
    190, 307, 398, **398**, 401, 402, 406, 408–11,

418, 425; Liverpool Homoeopathic
    Dispensary 186, 407–8, 418–19;
    Liverpool House of Help (1890) 187,
    189, 191, 308, **308**; Liverpool Infirmary
    for Children 188–91, 307, 397, **398**,
    401, 402; Liverpool Institute 288, 289,
    297, 350, 406, 411, 419, 466; Liverpool
    Ladies' Sanitary Association 182, 187;
    Liverpool North End Domestic Mission
    Society (1859) 349, 397; Liverpool Rescue
    Society and House of Help 189, 191,
    308, **308**; Liverpool Royal Infirmary (f.
    1749) 186, 188–89, **308**, 401–2, 405, 406,
    419, 423; Liverpool Sailors' Home 307,
    308, 398, **399**, 400, *401*, 402; Liverpool
    Seamen's Orphan Institution 186, 188,
    306, 307, 397, 398, 399, 401–2, 423;
    Liverpool Seamen's Pension Fund 306,
    422; Liverpool Shipwreck and Humane
    Society (1839) 306, 394; Liverpool
    Society for the Prevention of Cruelty to
    Children 186, 305, 307, 394, 395–96, 404,
    416, 420; Margaret Ismay Widows Fund,
    The 306, 422; networks and 15, 394–451,
    472; Princes Park Hospital 187, 189,
    190, 307; religion and 403–4, 414, 427;
    Salisbury House School 307, **398**; Seamen
    and Boatmen's Friend Society 186, **399**;
    Tate Institute 406, 419; Training Ship
    Indefatigable 307, 398, 399; Wallasey
    Cottage Hospital **286**, 292, **295**; Wallasey
    Dispensary 291, 300; Wirral Hospital and
    Dispensary for Sick Children 187–91, *292*,
    292–93, 301–3; women and 182–91
Phoenix Fire Co. 128
Picton, Sir James (J. A.) 145
Pilkington, A. J. 361
Pim, Joseph 278
policing/constabulary 99, 349, 410, 416
politics: business and 324–75; Conservative Party
    and 354–55, 357–62, 364–65; corruption
    and 324, 353, 358, 409; Liberal Party
    and 193, 354–55, 359–61, 364–65, 374,
    414; local 10, 17, 281, 325, 326, 352–53,
    357, 363–65, 423, 473; national 442;
    philanthropy and 353, 357, 362, 373;
    political fragmentation 237, 374; Tory
    Party and 357, 359, 362, 364, 374, 414,
    416, 427, 434
pollution 196, 257, 410
Poole, Sir James 440
population growth 237, 260, 261, 273, **273**, 287,
    290, 330, 372, 393
Portugal 347, 407
post *see* communication technology
Potter, T. O. 285
Potter, William 296, 343

Potts, R. B. 297
poverty 129, 149, 275, 328–29, 395, 404, 415,
    427, 449, 475
Prange, Francis 447
Prenton 56, 273, 274, 277
Presbyterians 151, 345–47, 349, 351, 427;
    Egremont Presbyterian Church 300,
    345; Seacombe Presbyterian Church of
    England 290–91, 297; Trinity Presbyterian
    Church 188, 281, **286**, 290–91, 293,
    294, **295**, 297, 302, 304, 345; United
    Presbyterian Church 290; Welsh
    Presbyterian 342
Preston, Robert 360
Preston, William 245
Preston & Fawcett Engineering Co. 360
Price, Francis R. 278
Price, William 100
Primrose League 284, 300, 361
Prince's Dock 114
print *see* communication technology
Prioleau, Charles Kuhn 219, 228, 360
Prior, Edith 59
Prior, Julius Alexander 59
privateering 6, 372
Procter, Charles J. 301
productivity 76, 78, 230, 328, 406, 416; *see also*
    communication technology; relationship to
    technology 442
professionals 151, 187, 251, 440
property: developers 119–21; landed 49, 52, 61,
    65, 325, 331–32; rural 176, 337; suburban
    17–18; women's right to own 171, 197
protectionism 85, 328, 360
Protestantism 347, 349, 350, 360, 405
P. Schilizzi, & Co. 60
Pye, John 169
Pye family *see* Bibby, Margaret (nee Pye); Bibby,
    Mary (nee Pye)
Pyne, C. 114
Pyne, G. 114

Quakers 169–70, 173, 178, 344, 350, 414;
    Birkenhead Society of Friends 188–89,
    290–91, 297, 304; Liverpool Friends
    Institute 346; Society of Quakers 364
Queen Insurance Co. 121, **134**, 370

Radcliffe, Sir David 371
Rae, George 415
Raffles, William Winter 172, 220
railway mania (1848) 3, 278, 343
railways: Demerara Railway Co. 371; Lancashire
    and Yorkshire Railway (L&YR) 171,
    258–59; Liverpool Overhead Railway
    261, 371; L&MR 259; London and North
    West Railway Co. (LNWR) 171, 248, 250;

Mersey Railway 152–53, 259–60, 261,
    309; Northern Railway Line 152; Wirral
    Railway Company 152
Ralli, Michael A. 64
Ralli, Pandia A. 223
Ralli Bros 94
Ramsay, David 343
Ranger, Morris 103, 104, 220
Rankin, Gilmour & Co. 335, **429**
Rankin, John 225, 336, 426, 427, **429**
Rankin, Robert 53
Rankin, Sir James 353
Rathbone, Benson 225, 230
Rathbone, Eleanor 189
Rathbone, Hugh **428**
Rathbone, Mrs (Benson) 188
Rathbone, Philip Henry 192, *193*, 225, **428**
Rathbone, Richard 214, 240, 397–98
Rathbone, Samuel Greg 364, **428**
Rathbone, Sarah (Benson) 169
Rathbone, William 87, 189, 240, 358, 363, 398,
    426, 427, **428**
Rathbone, William, IV 169, 350
Rathbone, William, V 350
Rathbone, William, VI 95
Rathbone Bros & Co. 7, 98, 364
Rathbone family 8, 53, 75, 87, 95, 178, 189, 192,
    241, 329, 427, 432, 449
rational choice theory 325
Ravenscroft, Mrs S. 191
raw materials 4, *33*, 51, 56, 58, 76–77
Rayner, Joseph 227
Rayner, Lloyd 223–24
Rea, Daniel Key 345
reading *see* libraries; literary societies
reciprocity *see* obligations
recommendations 10, 58, 82, 155–56, 332, 369,
    408
reference agencies 96, 99, 106; *see also* business
    culture; reputation; British Mercantile
    Agency 99; Stubbs Mercantile Offices 99
regulation 87–8, 94, 105, 144, 153, 156–57, 159,
    186, 366; self-regulation 88, 105
Reid, John 343
Reilly, Charles 214, 241
reliability *see* business culture
religion 5, 8, 16, 17, 18, 63, 75, 151, 169, 182,
    192, 308, 324–25, 342, 345, 352, 364,
    365, 374, 394, 403–4, 414, 427, 466,
    472, 473; *see also* Church of England;
    networks; Presbyterians; Quakers;
    Unitarian; Wesleyans; denominational
    exclusivity/cohesion and 346–48,
    350–51; missionaries and 348; religious
    antagonism/prejudice and 349
Rendal, Lord 337
Rendall, Gerald Henry 426

Rensburg, Henry 223
renting 48, 64, 244, 291
reputation 92–106; *see also* business culture;
    recommendations; reference agencies;
    character books 97–9; community 94–8,
    101–2; heritage 92–3, 95; individual
    93–5; international 434; national 215, 440;
    respectability 7, 13, 15, 95, 153, 165, 182,
    198, 210, 219, 222; social life and 142,
    223; women and 174, 175, 198
reputation brokers 14
Richmond Cavendish Co., The 407
Riley, John 403
risk: of failure 2, 39, 40, 42, 363; high-risk
    activities 6, 324, 372; of over-supply 118;
    risk-minimisation strategies 79, 160; risk-
    taking and risk-spreading 27, 30, 40, 142;
    social risk 156; to third parties 79
ritualism 347; *see also* religion
Robert Jones & Sons 35
Roberts, John 337
Roberts, W. J. 227
Robertson, G. H. F. 337
Robertson, J. Hunter, M.D. 395
Robertson, Thomas Stanley 332
Robinson, Colonel H. J. 335
Rogers, Fletcher 42
Rogers, John 410
Roman Catholicism 342, 349, 374
Roscoe, Clark & Roscoe 412
Roscoe, William 112, 215, 227, 247, 412
Rose, Mary 158
Rossetti, D. G. 225
Rotterdam 5
Rowe, George 211
rowing 339
Rowlinson, Mrs. 218
Rowlinson, Richard 114, 218
Royal Bank Chambers 121
Royal Insurance Co. Ltd 52, 121, **133**, 370, 371
Royden, Sir Thomas 52, 307
Royden, Thomas Bland 427
rural *see* countryside
Rutherford, William 362
Rutter, George W. 36
Ryder, John 181
Rylands, Enriqueta Augustina 430
Rylands, John 430
Ryle, J. C. 347

salt 4, 240, 367, 368, 441
Salvidge, Archibald 354, 362
Samuelson, Edward 364–65
Sand, Thomas 228
Sandbach, Parker, and Company 169
Sandbach, Tinne & Co. 335
Sandys, Colonel T. M. 349

San Francisco 99
satire 353
Scandinavia 63, 143
Schintz, Hans Gaspard 53, 332, 338, 420
Schintz, Miss 191
Schintz, Susan Dora Cecilia 338
Schintz & Co. 332
schools *see* education
Schröder, J. H. 57
Schwabe, Gustavus Christian 64, 228, 246, 334
Scotland 153, 245, 304, 329, 331, 332, 339, 342,
    349, 351, 355, relationship to Liverpool
Scott, George Gilbert 221
Scott, Giles Gilbert 446
Scott, Walter 64, 228, 425
Seacombe 47, 64, 65, 250, *251*, 273, 275, 279–82,
    300, 310, 343
Seacombe Cottage Hospital and Dispensary for
    Children 291–92, 294
Seacombe Parliamentary 282
Seacombe Presbyterian Church of England
    290–91, 297
Sea Insurance Co. 51
sectarianism 141, 347, 352, 355, 365, 374, 403,
    473; *see also* religion
securities 80, 98, 100, 366; *see also* banks
Seel, Thomas 114, 211, 213, 214
Sefton Park 29, 46, 56, 59, 64, 170, 219, 221, 229,
    241, 242, 245, 247–48, 263, 346, 415
Sephardi Jews *see* Judaism
Sephton, Mrs 188
Servais, Julius 184
servants 15, 25, 53–61, 64–5, 70–1, 73, 151, 167,
    174, 176–79, 181, 186, 195–96, 199,
    203–4, 207, 209, 213, 218, 221, 223, 229,
    233, 240, 244, 250–51, 263, 266–68, 276,
    290, 343, 471
Seyd & Co. 99
Seymour, Lady Margaret 168
Shand, Francis 357
shareholders 83, 93, 95, 101, 112, 171, 263, 276,
    279, 287, 288–89, 293–94, 298, 301, 309–
    10, 367, 370, 397; *see also* directorships;
    joint stock companies; partnerships
shares 30, 37, 52, 98, 112–13, 117, 159, 171, 172,
    289, 301, 309, 407, 439
Shaw, George 151
Shaw, Richard Norman 128, 246
Shepherd, William 353
Sherriff, James 239
Shimmin, Hugh 264, 353, 355, 396
Shipley, Joseph 229
shipping; *see also* shipping companies: shipowners
    2, 9–10, 12, 20, 30, 50, 52–3, 56, 60, 67,
    76, 78, 81, 85–8, 93–4, 122, 151–52, 191,
    276–77, 294, 307–108, 312, 329–30, 332,
    343, 355–56, 359–60, 363, 367–68, 370,

372, 375, 378, 392, 397, 399, 420, 424, 427–30, 433, 440, 473; steamboats 109; steamships 13, 36, 37, 77–8; tonnage 5, 41, 57

shipping companies; *see also* associations: Allan Bros 26, 85; Bibby Line 8; Black Star Line 60; Blue Funnel 7, 8; British & African Steam Navigation Co. 83, 423; British and Eastern Shipping Company 339; Collins Line 36; Cunard 7, 42, 86, 94, 116, 350; Cunard Line 36; Elder Dempster 7, 85, 363, 422, 423; Frederick Leyland & Co. 53, 94, 228, 337; Harrisons 7, 57, 329, 330; Inman Line 30, 85; International Navigation Co. 85; Liverpool and North Wales Steamship Co. 8; Liverpool & Mediterranean Screw Steam Shipping Co. 52; Liverpool & Philadelphia Steam Ship Co. 296; Nord Deutscher Lloyd 42; Oceanic Steam Navigation Co. 223, 364, 432; Ocean Steamship Co. 83, 87, 171, 223, 350; Pacific Steam Navigation Co. 86, 328; Peninsular & Oriental Steam Navigation Co. 119; West India & Pacific Steam Navigation Co. 86; White Star Line 76, 172, 228, 302, 364, 422, 423, 432; Yeoward & Co. 8

Shone, J. A. 297

shooting 276, 335, 337–41; grouse-shooting 176, 338–41

shopping 55, 253, 256, 469–71; *see also* department stores

Silliman, Benjamin 240

Sincalir, Samuel G. 335

Sing, Roger Percy 306

Sir Ernest George & Peto 226

slavery; *see also* slave trade: indentured labourers 407, 411, 450; legacy of 407; wage slavery 407, 411

slave trade 3, 6, 50–1, 93, 143, 144, 278–79, 327, 331, 353, 366, 407, 435

Smart, Samuel 173

Smith, Adam 325, 332

Smith, Charles W. 104

Smith, Elisha 371

Smith, James 332, 357

Smith, John 297

Smith, Mary 178

Smith, Philip 345

Smith, Samuel 297, 345, 346, 351, 352, 359, 394, 395, 425

Smith, T. May 416

Soane, John 114, 214

soap manufacture 52, 363

social capital *see* business culture

Social Network Analysis *see* network analysis

Social Network Analysis: see network analysis

social visiting 170, 198

societies *see* associations; clubs

sole traders 33, 37–42, **39–40**, **41**, 167; *see also* partnerships

South Africa 53, 86, 362

South Africa Conciliation League 362

South America 5, 53, 61, 253, 328, 337, 371

Southern and Toxteth Hospital 186, **398**

Southport 47, 153, 257–59, 262, 305, 331, 354, 423, 447

South Wales 77, 116, 418

space; *see also* suburbanisation; urbanisation: circulation 15, 122, 223; civic 310; gendered 249; lettable 121; office 112; Open Spaces Preservation Society 281, 285, 297; parks 15, 46, 56, 229, 242, 244, 263–64, 404, 411; public 185; urban 17, 42, 468; warehouse 112, 115

Spain 63, 125, 347, 407

Sparling, John 240

specialisation 2, 5, 6, 9, 13, 17, 25, 33–6, 64, 130, 176, 329, 450, 473; *see also* diversification

speculation 79, 80, 98, 100, 104, 172, 221, 241, 278–79, 327–28, 373; *see also* futures trading

Spence, James 360

spheres, public and private 15, 144, 157, 165

spinsters 171, 172, 180, 182, 187, 189, 198; *see also* widows; women

spirits 4, 61, 146, 172, 195, 212, 218, 245, 278, 280, 333, 344, 357, 365, 414, 416

sport 226, 274–77, 287, 310, 339, 340

sports clubs *see* clubs

Springmann, Emil 64

Stahlknecht, J. F. 310

Stahlknecht, Theodor 184

Standard Marine Insurance Co. 371

Staniforth, Thomas 331

Staniforth family 175

steam *see* shipping

Steel, Richard 442

Steele, Mrs R. F. 440

Steenstrand, William 103

Steers, Thomas 211

Stitt, James **132**, 158

Stitt, John J. 158

Stitt, Samuel 119, **136**, 158, 275, 297, 300, 301, 302, 304, 345, 351, 403

Stitt Brothers 158

Stock, James Henry 338

Stock, John 119, **135**

Stock Exchange 42, 84, 105, 121

Stockley, Elizabeth 171

stocks *see* shares

Stokes, Henry 402

Stolterfoht, J. Nicholas 345

Stowe, Harriet Beecher 175

Stripe, H. E. 124
suburbanisation; *see also* Wirral: business culture
    and 15–16; determinants of 237–38; early
    twentieth century and the fragmentation
    of the suburban hinterland 263–64;
    horseback and carriages and 250–55, *251*;
    horse-drawn public transport and electric
    tramcars 255–63, *256–57, 260, 261, 262*;
    networks of influence and power 16–17;
    railways and 248–50, *249*; rural retreats
    and 196–97
suburbs of Liverpool and Merseyside 168, 311–12
succession 14, 97–8 145–146, 157–58, 166, 182,
    195, 216, 246, 417; *see also* nepotism
sugar 3, 4, 52, 116, 190, 331–32, 344–45, 348,
    365, 403, 411; competition between cane
    and beet 406; cubes 407; purifying 407;
    refining/refiners/refineries 3, 30, 52, 223,
    303, 309, 328, 335, 344, 359, 361, 371,
    399, 405–7, 410, 417, 419, 426–27, **428**,
    433, 450
Summerson 121
Swainson, John 228
Swan, James 239
Sweden 55, 63, 329, 342
Swedenborgian New Church 342, 347
Syria 59

Taine, Hippolyte 229
tallow 4
tanning *see* hides
Tappenbeck, Augustus 64
Tapscott, William 101
Tate, Ann (second wife to Sir Henry) 409, 410
Tate, Henry Junior 190
Tate, Jane (first wife to Sir Henry) 410
Tate, Miss 190
Tate, Sir Henry 52, 190, 309, 328, 401, 405, 406–
    11, 418–20, 423, **424**, 425, 426, 431, 432,
    450; *see also* Henry Tate & Sons
Tate, Sir William Henry 419
Tate Gallery 406, 411, 418
Taunton, George Edwin 53, 335
taverns 144
taxes: income 51; inheritance 417–18; land tax
    assessments 119; reform 360; salt tax 367;
    tea duties 367; window tax 51, 216
Tayleur, Charles 246
Taylor, Edmund 281, 358, 361
Taylor, Edward 297
Taylor, Joseph 280
tea 4, 55, 173, 174, 296, 304, 367, 440, 444
telecommunications *see* communication
    technology
telegraph *see* communication technology
telephone *see* communication technology
temperance movement 359, 413–14, 416, 418

tennis 339
textiles 35, 57, 60, 106, 371; Lancashire 77
Theosophical Society 342
Thomas, W. Aubrey 122
Thompson, Henry 220, 303
Thompson, Samuel 220
Thompson, Samuel Henry 220
Thompson-Yates, Rev. Samuel Ashton **431**, 433
Thomson, Lt. Colonel 254
Thornely, James I. 448
Threlfalls 416
timber 4, 5, 31, 36, 60, 98, 122, 125, 126, 192,
    222, 226, 227, 238, 327, 329, 330, **330**,
    333–36, 345, 363, 364, 399, 414, 420, 423,
    427, **428**
Timmis, Thomas Sutton 52, 230, 420
tin 371
Tinley, Agnes Sarah 179
Tinne, J. A. 92
Tinne, John Ernest 169, 371
T. & J Brocklebank Ltd 53
T. & J. Littledale & Co. 364
tobacco 3, 4, 35, 83, 211, 218, 275, 303, 364, 407,
    411, 430, 440; *see also* Imperial Tobacco
    Company; Richmond Cavendish Co., The
Tobin, James 10
Tobin, James A. 296
Tobin, Sir John 278–79, 331
Tobin, Thomas 469
Tobin family 10, 331, 365
Todd, Jeremiah 195, 240
Tosh, John 165, 192
Town Hall 3, 110, 112, 114, 129, 225, 252,
    410, 426, 447, 467, 468, 471; *see also*
    Exchange
Toxteth 46, 64, 170, 186, 189, 247, 255, 371, 422,
    423
Toxteth Park 221, 239, *239*, 240, 372
trade: cycles 41, 329; emigrant trade 5, 60, 101,
    357; exports 4, 9, 40, 60, 170, 328, 449;
    imports 3, 4–5, 59, 77, 97, 170, 328;
    international 2, 3, 5, 60, 77, 143, 330,
    372; slave trade 3, 6, 50–1, 93, 143, 144,
    278–79, 327, 331, 353, 366, 407, 435; sole
    traders 33, 37–42, **39–40**, **41**, 167
trade associations *see* associations
trade directories: *Bailey's Liverpool Directory*
    215; Gore's Directory 12, 25–30, 111, 263;
    Kelly's Directory 354
trading community *see* merchant community
trading standards *see* associations
transaction costs 1, 2, 14, 142, 166, 310, 312, 327
transport; *see also* canals; railway; shipping:
    brougham 250, 252; coach and carriage
    250–55, *251*; electrification and 152,
    259–61, 309; ferry 47, 65, 148, 249–51,
    260–61, 271, 273, 287, 311; horse-drawn

public transport and electric tramcars
255–63, *256–57*, *260*, *261*, *262*; motor
cars 263; omnibus 109, 255–56; railways
248–50, *249*
trust 10, 92–106; *see also* business culture
trustworthiness *see* business culture; credit
Turks 59, 62, 330
Turner, Edward 195
Turner, Edward Wrake 166, 173, 345
Turner, John H. 244
Turner, Mrs (Charles) 188
T. & W. Earle 211
Twigge, John 334
typhus epidemic (1847) 275
Tyrer, James 364
Tyres, Henry 75

Ulster, relationship to Liverpool 100, 350
uncertainty 39, 96, 98, 143, 169, 221, 327, 369
Union Marine Insurance Co. 362, 371
Unitarians 8, 143, 151, 166, 174–75, 192, 343,
345–47, 350–52, 374, 397–98, 403,
426–27, 433, 450, 466, 473; *see also*
networks; Charles Melly's Ragged Schools
189; Liverpool Domestic Mission 189,
347; Training School for Nurses 189;
Unitarian Institute (1889) 189
United Grain Elevator Ltd. 371
university 241, 254, 264, 426, 427, 432, 434
University College, Liverpool 406, 418, 425–34,
428–29, **431**, **433**, 450–51
urbanisation 55, 472; *see also* countryside; urban
culture 14, 411

values *see* business culture
Vance, Stitt & Co. 158
Veitch, Rev. Robert 415
Verelst, Charles 333
Villa Allerton 245
visiting 78, 130, 166, 174, 175, 178–79, 240;
female visiting 186, 199; gardens 230;
Ladies Visiting Committee 188–90; social
170, 198
Volunteer Movement 17, 65–6, 149, 271, 297, 300,
362, 466, 467–68
von Heyder, Theodor 61
von Keyserlingk: Baroness 168; General 168
von Sobbe, Theodor 415

Wade, John Merrett 303
Wales 169, 214, 275, 329, 342, 343, 418, 426;
North 49, 245, 249, 331, 332, 339; South
77, 116, 418
Walker, Arthur 418
Walker, John Reid 418
Walker, Patricius *see* Allingham, Walter
Walker, Peter 411; *see also* Peter Walker & Son

Walker, Peter Carlaw 418
Walker, Sir Andrew Barclay 52, 225, 226, 230,
245, 336, 337, 338, 365, 405, 411–17, *412*,
420, 423, **424**, **431**, 432, 450; *see also* A.
B. Walker & Sons
Walker Art Gallery 225, 412, 417, 450
Wall, George 284, 301
Wallace, James 212, 213, 215
Walmsley, John Banks 229
Ward, Margaret 11
warehouses 14, 44, 76, 109, 111–17, 126, 130,
210, 211, 213, 214; fireproofing and
14, 109
Warren, George 335
Waterhouse, Alfred 223–24, 245
Waterloo 47, 229, 242, 244, 259
Wavertree 168, 239, 256, 343, 351
W. & D. Busby 254
wealth: amassing 420; club membership and 153–55;
dining rooms, galleries, libraries, and billiard
rooms as symbols of 222–28, *224*, *226*, *227*,
228; disparity 473; of merchant community
50–59; probate **51–2**, 52, 53, 419, **419**, **424**;
reputation and 155–57
Weightman, William 245
Weld & Co. 104–5
Wesleyans 346–47, 349, 352; Liverpool Wesleyan
Mission (1876) 189, 344, 345
West Africa 76, 83, 85–6, 88, 222, 278–79,
331–32, 371, 423
West Indies 92, 331, 364, 365, 371, 407; Jamaica
214
West Kirby 56, 65, 152, 183, 260, 270, **273**,
273–75, 282–83, **283**, 284, 285, 289, 291,
297, 300, 302, 305, 309–12
West Kirby Benevolent Fund 283
West Kirby Choral Society 284
West Kirby Christian Institute 291, 297, 301
West Kirby Convalescent Home for Children 306
West Kirby District Council 280
West Kirby Literary 184, 199, 282, 284, 285, **286**,
294, **295**, 302
West Kirby Parliamentary Debating Society
281, 282
wet docks 372
Whalley, Thomas 92
wheat 60, 77, 104
Whetton, Thomas 215
Whishaw, Constance 187
Whistler, J. M. 225, 246
Whitaker, Whitehead & Co. 103–4
Whiting, Joshua 280
W. & H. Laird Co. 422
widows 171–73, 197, 306, 422; *see also* spinsters;
women
Wilckens, Henry 212
Wild, Joseph Henry 276

William Gossage & Sons 52
Williams, Eva 310
Williamson, Balfour 253, **428**
Williamson, Frederick Augustus 336
Williamson, John 280, 306
Williamson, Stephen 358
Williamson, William 239
Willink, Daniel 218
Willmer, Arthur Washington 176
Wilson, Hartley 345
Wilson, Henry Threlfall 172, 195, 302
Wilson, John 345, 364
Wilson, William 129
wine 4, 61, 146, 172, 195, 212, 218, 245, 278, 280,
        333, 344, 357, 365, 414, 416
Winmore & Co. 125, 219–20
Wirral 270–313; associational infrastructure
        of Hoylake and West Kirby **283**;
        associational involvement of Wirral
        merchants by category **295**; average rates
        of population growth in **273**; Birkenhead
        School *289*; business priorities and
        the level of merchant associational
        involvement 302–4; creation of new
        networks of associational culture on
        285–93; 1844 Plan of New Park *279*;
        factors behind merchant relocation 274–
        77; 'The Greys' Trooping the Colours,
        Birkenhead Park *298*; Heswall Golf Club
        277; introduction 271; Liverpool and,
        local associational identity and traditional
        allegiances 304–10; localism and
        associational involvement on **286**; map of
        272; Mariners' Park, Wallasey *307*; Mr.
        John Laird MP *299*; New Church at Upton
        296; pleasure, profit, and politics 277–81;
        residential location and the network
        embeddedness of Wirral merchants
        293–302; St. Aidan's Theological College,
        Birkenhead *300*; spatial distribution
        of members of the RLGC and the
        RMYC **287**; spatial pattern of local
        involvement in associational culture on
        284; subscribers to Liverpool charities
        308; suburbanisation, locality, and
        associational framework 281–85; timing
        and scale of suburban development on
        271–74; Wirral Hospital and Dispensary
        for Sick Children *292*
Wirral Waterworks Co. 371
Wise, Pastor George 349
women wives; *see also* networks; spinsters;
        widows; daughters 9, 15, 55, 61, 145, 157,
        165–71, 173, 176, 182, 184, 187, 190, 197,
        199, 293, 309, 338, 394, 433, 455, 466,
        472; Ladies' Committee 185, 199; wives
        9, 15, 55, 145, 165–77, 184, 187, 190, 192,
        197–99, 256, 293, 334, 394, 416–18, 420,
        471, 472
Wood, Henry J. 306
Wood, James 359
Wood, James Marke 225
Wood, John 110, 215
Wood, John Marke 51
Wood, Miss E. M. 445
Woodhouse, Sam 333
Woolworth's 55
World War I 2, 5, 10, 17, 34, 37, 38, 41, 47, 50, 64,
        187, 263, 270, 271, 273, 325, 326,
        341, 349, 352, 372, 399, 422, 427, 430,
        432, 473
Wright, Catherine 189
Wright, John 406, 407
Wyatt, James 112, 215
Wyatt, T. H. 117, 126, **135**
Wyndham, George 446
Wynne, George 441
Wynne, Robert 250

Yates, Jane Ellen 188
Yates, Joseph Brooks 433
Yates, Richard Vaughan 230, 243

Ziegler, John Hastings 347

Milton Keynes UK
Ingram Content Group UK Ltd.
UKHW050651140224
437806UK00004B/12